A BRIEF

FOR THE

TRIAL OF CRIMINAL CASES.

BY
AUSTIN ABBOTT,

Assisted by WILLIAM C. BEECHER,
Late Assistant District Attorney
of the City of New York.

To determine the policy of counsel, neither principles nor precedents alone suffice. In the conflict of precedents, a knowledge of sound principles is of paramount importance, but to apply a principle safely, attention to the technical significance of the precedents is essential.

SECOND AND ENLARGED EDITION BY THE PUBLISHERS' EDITORIAL STAFF.

Fred B. Rothman & Co.
Littleton, Colorado
1994

Library of Congress Cataloging-in-Publication Data

Abbott, Austin, 1831-1896.
A brief for the trial of criminal cases / by Austin Abbott. -- 2nd and enl. ed. / by the publisher's editorial staff.
p. cm.
Originally published: Rochester, N.Y. : Lawyers' Co-operative Pub. Co., 1902.
Includes index.
ISBN 0-8377-1911-9
1. Criminal procedure--United States. I. Beecher, William Constantine, 1849- . II. Lawyers Co-operative Publishing Company. III. Title.
KF9619.A72 1994
345.73'05--dc20
[347.3055] 94-19791
CIP

Printed in United States of America

The paper used in this publication meets the minimum requirements of American National Standard for Information Sciences—Permanence of Paper for Printed Library Materials, ANSI Z39.48-1984.

A BRIEF

FOR THE

TRIAL OF CRIMINAL CASES.

BY

AUSTIN ABBOTT,

Assisted by WILLIAM C. BEECHER,

Late Assistant District Attorney
of the City of New York.

To determine the policy of counsel, neither principles nor precedents alone suffice. In the conflict of precedents, a knowledge of sound principles is of paramount importance, but to apply a principle safely, attention to the technical significance of the precedents is essential.

SECOND AND ENLARGED EDITION BY THE PUBLISHERS' EDITORIAL STAFF.

THE LAWYERS' CO-OPERATIVE PUBLISHING COMPANY,
ROCHESTER, N. Y.
1902.

PREFACE TO THE FIRST EDITION.

This volume, prepared in consequence of many requests from members of the profession, is the second in a series of practical manuals for the aid of the practitioner, the preparation of which has grown out of my custom of making careful briefs in preparation for trial in all cases in which I have been concerned. In using selections from these briefs as the nucleus of such a work, I have of course pruned out everything ephemeral, and have modified whatever, on careful consideration of the subject in a broad light, I could feel might be unreliable as a general guide, and have extended the topics systematically, so that scarcely anything of my original briefs can be recognized, but I have adhered to the form of a trial brief as being the best for assistance in everyday practice.

The line which I laid out to pursue in the preparation of this volume, like that of the similar Brief for Jury Trial in Civil Cases, lies along that constantly debated border ground between familiar general principles on the one hand and the ever-varying phases of application by which those principles are incessantly tested and molded anew.

On the one hand, I have used but little space to state the commonplaces of the law, however much space they may deservedly fill in the treatises. On the other, I have not taken space to give rulings on very peculiar and unusual points,—much less to quote in detail comments on either class of questions. My aim has been to present those debatable questions which are now most constantly mooted at the trial,—to carry the exposition of each into sufficient detail to meet all ordinary aspects of the subject, and upon such questions to furnish counsel with the materials for discussion and discrimination, arranged in that concise analytic form which we all find the most convenient as an aid to the memory in dealing with questions which may unexpectedly arise in court; a form equally advantageous also as an aid in making that thorough preparation for trial that is becoming more and more essential.

In order that I might not err through lack of actual experience in any special class of cases, I enlisted at the outset the assistance of William C. Beecher, Esq., whose experience in prosecution, both as Assistant District Attorney in New York County, and thereafter as active counsel for the New York Society for the Suppression of Vice, and in defense in a long succession of causes since his term as Assistant District Attorney expired, has peculiarly qualified him to aid me in the most practical and useful manner; also the assistance of Morris Cooper, Esq. (author of a work on Referees), whose experience, both in defense and in authorship, has enabled him, in carrying out my preparations in detail, to analyze in a very intelligent manner a very large number of selected authorities. I am also indebted for valuable assistance, in extended research on various special subjects, to Messrs. Sumner B. Stiles, J. Hope Caldwell, Charles J. Osborn, and Frederick H. Cooke.

These pages, however, present only a fraction of the authorities that have been analyzed and compared. I have sifted out of the inexhaustible mine of reported adjudications those which have appeared to me convenient and suitable authorities in the various jurisdictions, and fit to be cited in court if necessary, in support of a rule of practical importance at the present day; the value of the result here, as in the Trial Brief for Civil Cases and in Trial Evidence, depends much upon thus getting rid of the encumbrance of that which is obsolete, or for various reasons unworthy to control, leaving in compact form a concise indication of useful authorities. I have sought to give the varying rules in different jurisdictions, so that each practitioner may have a brief adapted to the rulings of his home tribunal.

My hope is that what is here set down may prove useful, not only in preparation for trial, but more especially in enabling Bench and Bar, engaged in trial, to come at once to the debatable point raised by an offer or objection; to deal with the question at once in the situation in which the existing state of the authorities present it; to appreciate more readily the reason and consequences of the rule; to see it quickly in the varied light in which varied applications of the law present it, and thus to avoid or shorten profitless discussion on what is settled, and facilitate those necessary and noble controversies of the forum on the adequacy and completeness of which the safe administration of criminal justice must always depend.

AUSTIN ABBOTT.

NEW YORK, JANUARY, 1889.

PREFACE TO THE SECOND EDITION.

The Brief for the Trial of Criminal Cases, published by Austin Abbott in 1889, has had extensive use and has been greatly appreciated by the profession. After thirteen years the demand for a new edition which would bring the book down to date has resulted in the present enlargement of the original work. The present volume, though at a casual glance it does not appear so, is in reality about twice the size of the former when the quantity of its contents is considered, and it contains also about twice as many cited authorities. Nearly one hundred entirely new sections have been added. Most of the chapters show considerable additions,—especially those on Pleas to the Indictment, Postponement, Selection of Jurors, Reception of Evidence, Rules of Evidence, and Instructing the Jury, while some of the chapters contain more than twice as much as they did in the first edition. Those most enlarged include the chapters on Counsel, Presence and Custody of Accused, Arraignment, Demurrer to Indictment, Removal of Cause, Change of Venue, Right to a Speedy Trial, Separate Trial, Supervision of Jury, and Documents for Jury. This enlarged work is submitted to the profession in the belief that it will be found to be a very valuable aid in the trial of criminal causes.

TABLE OF CONTENTS

X. Books.

XI. Character.

XII. Confessions.

XIII. Consciousness of guilt.

XIV. Convicts as witnesses.

BRIEF

— FOR —

Trial of Criminal Cases.

I.—COUNSEL.

1. For the accused; a constitutional right.

One criminally accused has a constitutional right to have the assistance of his counsel.[1]

[1]In the English criminal jurisprudence, for some unaccountable reason, the right to be assisted by counsel in all cases was not a feature of trial by jury,—at least not until the reign of William IV. See *Wilson* v. *State,* 3 Heisk. 232, where the English rule is discussed at some length.

And it undoubtedly was to abolish this disgraceful feature in criminal trials by jury that the right to have the assistance of counsel was made a part of the organic law of almost every state in the Union.

And the 6th Amendment of the Federal Constitution provides that in the United States courts "the accused shall enjoy the right to have the assistance of counsel for his defense." And the provisions of this amendment apply to courts of the territories of the United States. *Thompson* v. *Utah,* 170 U. S. 343, 42 L. ed. 1061, 18 Sup. Ct. Rep. 620.

In New York the Constitution (art. 1, § 6) provides that "in any trial and any court the party accused shall be allowed to appear and to defend in person and with counsel, as in civil actions." This provision is enacted also in the Code of Criminal Procedure (§ 8, subd. 2). The right is not waived or suspended by his taking the stand as a witness in his own behalf. *People* v. *Brown,* 72 N. Y. 571, 28 Am. Rep. 183.

Under the Constitution and laws a lawyer who is accused of crime is equally entitled, with other persons, in every stage of his trial, "to appear and defend in person and with counsel." The rights of individuals in this respect are not to be gauged by their profession or occupation. *People* v. *Napthaly,* 105 Cal. 641, 39 Pac. 29.

In *State* v. *Adams,* 20 Kan. 311, Brewer, J., in discussing section 10 of the Bill of Rights of that state, providing, among other privileges which the accused did not have at common law, that "the accused shall be allowed to appear and defend in person or by counsel," said that the language used implied a permission or privilege, rather than an absolute right,—that is, that the accused might have, etc., if he wished, and if he did not so wish, he might forego.

And when the court asked the accused if he wished counsel, offering to appoint such counsel, which he declined, and none were appointed, there can be said to be no violation of this constitutional right. *Stokes* v. *State,* 73 Ga. 816; *State* v. *Moore,* 121 Mo. 514, 26 S. W. 345, holding that it is no part of the court's duty to force counsel upon an unwilling defendant.

In *Barton* v. *State,* 34 Tex. Crim. Rep. 613, 31 S. W. 671, the defendant after conviction filed an affidavit stating that he had had no counsel until his cause was called for trial, when counsel was assigned to him; that the trial proceeded without any preparation therefor; and that since his conviction counsel had been employed for him. But as he had failed to object to the counsel assigned or to proceeding with the trial, and did not even state that any further preparation was necessary before going to trial, it was held that he was not entitled to a new trial.

Absence of counsel for the accused when the case was regularly called for trial was no reason for not proceeding with the trial, where the accused expressed his readiness and consent thereto, after a fruitless search for counsel, who left the courtroom before the case was called, but left no word with any person. *State* v. *Williams,* 45 La. Ann. 936, 12 So. 932.

But a new trial will be granted where the defendant's affidavit and that of his physician show that he was unable to attend the trial, and that he had employed counsel, who was absent without his knowledge. *Payne* v. *Com.* 16 Ky. L. Rep. 839, 30 S. W. 416.

The right conferred by the Georgia Constitution was held, in *Keaton* v. *State,* 7 Ga. 190, to be infringed by an instruction expressing surprise by the court that acquittal was attempted under the evidence, although reversal of the conviction was refused on the ground that, taken altogether, the charge was not so erroneous as to require it.

A statute imposing an occupation tax upon lawyers does not violate Tex. Const. art. 1, § 10, giving to an accused the right to be heard by himself or counsel or both. *Ex parte Williams,* 31 Tex. Crim. Rep. 262, 21 L. R. A. 783, 20 S. W. 580.

In Massachusetts there is no constitutional provision guarantying counsel to an accused, and no statutory provision in respect to counsel, except in the case of an indictment for capital crime. And in *McDonald* v. *Com.* 173 Mass. 322, 53 N. E. 874,—a prosecution for forgery,—it was held that the provisions of the 6th Amendment to the Federal Constitution, referred to above, do not apply to criminal proceedings in state courts.

As to the effect of unreasonable limitation of the time of argument, see *post,* Division XLI.

2. — a continuing right.

The right of the accused to have counsel, and, for this purpose, a reasonable time to send for him,[1] and opportunity for the interview,[2] attaches from the time he is brought before a magistrate for examination,[3] and continues through all the stages of the prosecution.[4]

[1]In *People* v. *Restell,* 3 Hill, 289, it was held that a deposition of a witness taken before a magistrate on the examination of the accused without his counsel being present, after he had requested and sent for one, could not be read against him because a reasonable time had not been allowed for the counsel's attendance.

In obedience to this constitutional guaranty, statutes in some of the states provide in effect that the committing magistrate must inform the accused of his right to the aid of counsel in every stage of the proceedings, and must before the examination allow him a reasonable time to send for his counsel, and upon request must require a peace officer to take the message to such counsel in the town or city. See, for example, N. Y. Code Crim. Proc. §§ 188, 189; Cal. Code Crim. Proc. §§ 858, 859.

And refusal by the committing magistrate to postpone the examination in order to allow the accused time to procure counsel is a violation of both the Constitution and the statute; and an examination held under such circumstances is in no sense a legal one,—and this irrespective of whether the accused be in prison or admitted to bail. *People* v. *Napthaly,* 105 Cal. 641, 39 Pac. 29. This case holds, too, that the fact that the accused asked for a postponement of the examination to procure counsel was evidence of his knowledge of his right to counsel, and obviated the necessity of his being informed thereof by the magistrate.

In *People* v. *Elliott,* 80 Cal. 296, 22 Pac. 207, the court said that it did not think that the objection that the committing magistrate had not given the defendant time to procure counsel, and that none was furnished him by the court at the preliminary hearing, was sufficient ground for setting aside the information; and it held that, even conceding that it was, certainly the information was not to be set aside where the defendant was informed, when first brought before the magistrate, of his right to counsel at all stages of the proceedings, and it appeared that the examination was postponed nine days with his consent, and there was nothing in the record to show that he expressed any desire to have counsel appointed.

[2]In *People ex rel. Burgess* v. *Risley*, 1 N. Y. Crim. Rep. 492, it was held that this constitutional provision confers upon the accused every privilege which will make the presence of counsel upon the trial a valuable right, and must include a private interview with him prior to the trial, and even before indictment. Mandamus to compel the sheriff to allow an interview with counsel was granted.

The constitutional right of an accused "to defend himself, and to have the attendance of counsel," guaranteed by La. Const. art. 8, is invaded where the accused is, within three days after his indictment for murder, placed on trial without opportunity to previously consult counsel assigned him, who has been engaged in the trial of other cases. *State* v. *Pool*, 50 La. Ann. 449, 23 So. 503.

[3]*People* v. *Restell*, 3 Hill, 289; N. Y. Code Crim. Proc. §§ 188, 189.

[4]*People ex rel. Burgess* v. *Risley*, 1 N. Y. Crim. Rep. 492.

In *People* v. *Palmer*, 43 Hun, 397, refusal of the court to allow the prisoner with his counsel to accompany the jury when viewing the scene of the crime, under N. Y. Code Crim. Proc. § 411, was held to be a violation of his right to counsel. [Learned, P. J.] Compare *post*, Division XXXIX.

3. — remedy for refusal.

If the right is refused, the court under whose process the accused is held should be applied to for an order directing the right to be allowed;[1] or, if necessary, application should be made to the supreme court[2] for a mandamus to the jailer.[3]

[1]In *People ex rel. Callan* v. *Walsh*, N. Y. Supreme Ct. 1887, Lawrence, J., on denying an application which was not sustained on the merits, added: "Apart from that, I see no reason why the judge of the general sessions, if he has assigned counsel for a prisoner, and that counsel is denied an opportunity for consultation with his client, cannot direct that such consultation be allowed. . . . The judges of the court in which the prisoner has been arraigned and may be tried and convicted are the proper authorities to decide whether those prisoners are denied any rights which the law guarantees to them." N. Y. Daily Reg. Jan. 18, 1887.

[2]Under N. Y. Code Civ. Proc. § 241, a judge of a superior city court has the same power.

[3]See *People ex rel. Burgess* v. *Risley*, 1 N. Y. Crim. Rep. 492.

4. — assignment by the court.

By express statute in most of the states,[1] and also in the courts of the United States,[2] the right to the assistance of counsel is secured to the accused by provisions making it the duty[3] of the court to assign counsel, when requested,[4] to defend accused persons who are themselves unable to employ counsel.[5]

The duty of the court to assign counsel to a prisoner who has none carries with it the further power and duty to allow whatever is necessary and proper to enable the assigned counsel to discharge his duty.[6]

But the court need not assign any particular person selected by the accused.[7]

[1] The constitutionality of a statute authorizing the appointment of counsel to defend persons accused of crime who shall be unable to employ counsel was said to be unquestioned, in *Mobile Commissioners' Ct.* v. *Turner*, 45 Ala. 199.

[2] U. S. Rev. Stat. § 1034, provides that "every person who is indicted of treason or other capital crime shall be allowed to make his full defense by counsel learned in the law; and the court before which he is tried, or some judge thereof, shall immediately, upon his request, assign to him such counsel, not exceeding two, as he may desire, and they shall have free access to him at all seasonable hours."

[3] In the absence of any express statute on the subject, it would probably not be asserted that the assignment of counsel to a prisoner who has none is a duty of the court,—certainly not where the assignment would be against the consent of the prisoner. *State* v. *Moore,* 121 Mo. 514, 26 S. W. 345.

On the other hand, there are cases expressly recognizing and upholding the power of the court to so assign counsel, although there is no statute authorizing it. *Vise* v. *Hamilton County,* 19 Ill. 78; *State* v. *Dill,* 9 Houst. (Del.) 495, 18 Atl. 763 (*dictum*).

In *People* v. *Goldenson,* 76 Cal. 328, 19 Pac. 161, it was insisted that the judge had no authority to appoint counsel because the prisoner had already employed counsel of his own choice, and because he neither desired, nor was he unable, to employ another; that it is only when the prisoner desires counsel and is unable to employ one that the judge has authority to appoint. The prisoner, who, it is claimed, was insane at the time of the offense and at the time of the trial, had just unsuccessfully applied for a continuance because of his counsel's absence. But the court, in holding the appointment of counsel by the trial judge proper, argued that it was not a question whether the prisoner desired counsel and was able to employ one, but the question was who should represent him; that whatever might be the right of counsel where there was no question of insanity, the trial judge was certainly acting only in accordance with every principle of law, justice, and humanity in appointing counsel under the circumstances of this case.

In Texas the court is required to appoint counsel for the accused, under Code Crim. Proc. art. 511, only when the punishment may be capital. *Austin* v. *State* (Tex. Crim. App.) 51 S. W. 249. In all other cases the appointment of counsel is a matter resting in the discretion of the trial judge. *Pennington* v. *State*, 13 Tex. App. 44.

A conviction is not affected by the fact that the court in appointing counsel to defend the accused limited the appointment to that court and to the trial term. *Ryan* v. *State*, 83 Wis. 486, 53 N. W. 836.

Nor will a conviction be disturbed on the ground that the accused followed the prosecuting attorney's advice before trial to the effect that the state could not make out a case, and that he need not employ counsel, where the prosecuting attorney denies any recollection of such advice, and had nothing to do with the prosecution of the case, and the defendant does not show that he had any defense that was not set up, or that there were any witnesses who would have testified for him. *Williams* v. *State* (Tex. Crim. App.) 48 S. W. 515.

That an accused cannot complain that no counsel was assigned him, where he did not make request therefor, see *State* v. *De Serrant*, 33 La. Ann. 979; *State* v. *Perry*, 48 La. Ann. 651, 19 So. 684; *State* v. *Whitesides*, 49 La. Ann. 352, 21 So. 540; *State* v. *Raney*, 63 N. J. L. 363, 43 Atl. 677.

A conviction will not be disturbed because the record shows that the defendant did not have counsel, unless it appears that he was denied the right to be so represented. The appellate court cannot presume that the trial court denied the right, or failed, if he was unable to employ counsel, to assign counsel for him. *Barnes* v. *Com.* 92 Va. 794, 23 S. E. 784; *Cathcart* v. *Com.* 37 Pa. 108; *Brown* v. *State*, 12 Ark. 623.

The fact that the court appointed counsel to defend an accused, before an indictment was found against him, and at the same time set a day for the trial, does not entitle him to a new trial, where the day set for the trial was subsequent to the finding of the indictment, and the accused sent a message to the court requesting that counsel be appointed for him. *Charlon* v. *State*, 106 Ga. 400, 32 S. E. 347.

The fact that the parents of an adult defendant accused of crime possess means with which they could employ counsel does not justify the trial judge in holding that the defendant is not a poor person within the meaning of the Indiana statute. *Hendryx* v. *State*, 130 Ind. 265, 29 N. E. 1131. And the erroneous refusal of the judge to assign counsel in this case was held not to have been cured by the fact that an attorney volunteered to, and did, defend, but against the prisoner's objections.

But where the examination of the accused in open court discloses that he is not a pauper, but, on the contrary, possesses means ample to employ counsel, it is not error to refuse to appoint counsel for him. *Cross* v. *State*, 132 Ind. 65, 31 N. E. 473.

See further, as to this right, cases in note to *Gore* v. *State* (Ark.) 5 L. R. A. 832.

[6]In *People* v. *Willett*, 1 How. Pr. N. S. 196, 3 N. Y. Crim. Rep. 324, this rule was given as the reason for granting a motion on behalf of a prisoner convicted of murder, that a copy of a stenographer's notes of the trial be furnished at the county's expense, to enable a bill of exceptions to be prepared.

[7]In *Burton* v. *State*, 75 Ind. 477, it was held that refusal to be governed by request in the selection was not error unless there was in the particular circumstances an abuse of discretion.

A defendant in a criminal case cannot, by refusing to be represented by counsel appointed by the court, or by anyone other than the counsel selected by himself, coerce the court to appoint the latter to defend him at the public expense. He may have whatever counsel he chooses to retain, and he may refuse to accept the services of any counsel not wanted by him; but, to be defended at the public expense, he must accept the services of any reputable attorney the court may in its discretion see fit to appoint. *Baker* v. *State*, 86 Wis. 474, 56 N. W. 1089.

In *People* v. *Murray*, 52 Mich. 28, 17 N. W. 843, it was said to be customary to allow the defendant to choose for himself; but it was also held that where counsel assigned acts without objection upon the part of the defendant, and without complaint that he does not fairly represent his client, the appellate court will not interfere.

5. — additional counsel.

It is not an abuse of discretion for the court, after the jury is partially selected, to refuse the application of one accused of murder to have another attorney joined as additional counsel, where the latter is a relative of the judge, and his appointment would disqualify the judge, and would result in a discharge of the jurors selected and a continuance of the trial.[1]

[1]*People* v. *Gregory*, 120 Cal. 16, 52 Pac. 41.

6. — number of counsel.

The number of counsel required to secure to an accused unable to pay for their services a fair and impartial trial is within the discretion of the trial court.[1]

[1]*Keyes* v. *State*, 122 Ind. 527, 23 N. E. 1097.

7. — to prosecute appeal.

Refusal to appoint counsel to prosecute an appeal from a conviction, on the ground that defendant was without means to employ counsel, will not be considered on appeal, where the defendant was represented by counsel at the trial.[1]

[1]*State* v. *Cross*, 95 Iowa, 629, 64 N. W. 614, where the court said that the

purpose of the statute in permitting the appointment of an attorney for the defendant in a criminal case is to enable him to have the assistance of an attorney in making his defense, to prevent a failure of justice. "If the defense has already been made, there is neither reason nor authority for the appointment."

And under the Iowa Code (§§ 5313, 5314), providing for the appointment of counsel for an accused who appears for arraignment without counsel, and that the counsel appointed may at his option follow the case into the supreme court, a trial court cannot appoint counsel to prosecute an appeal to the supreme court and to retry the case if a new trial be granted, where the request for his appointment is made after conviction on the second trial. *State* v. *Cater*, 109 Iowa, 69, 80 N. W. 222.

8. — compensation.

As to whether, in the absence of statute, counsel assigned to defend persons accused of crime have any claim against the county for their fees and disbursements, the decisions are conflicting.[1]

[1]See *Howard County Comrs.* v. *Pollard*, 153 Ind. 371, 55 N. E. 87 (*dictum*); *Webb* v. *Baird*, 6 Ind. 13; *Hall* v. *Washington County*, 2 G. Greene, 473; *Dane County* v. *Smith*, 13 Wis. 585, 80 Am. Dec. 754, establishing the liability for fees.

But by the weight of authority there is no liability for fees. *Case* v. *Shawnee County Comrs.* 4 Kan. 511; *Lamont* v. *Solano County*, 49 Cal. 159; *Elam* v. *Johnson*, 48 Ga. 348; *Kelley* v. *Andrew County*, 43 Mo. 338; *Johnston* v. *Lewis & Clarke County*, 2 Mont. 159; *Wright* v. *State*, 3 Heisk. 256; *State* v. *Simmons*, 43 La. Ann. 991, 10 So. 382; *Arkansas County* v. *Freeman*, 31 Ark. 266; *Rowe* v. *Yuba County*, 17 Cal. 61; *Vise* v. *Hamilton County*, 19 Ill. 78; *Bacon* v. *Wayne County*, 1 Mich. 461 (now regulated by statute); *Wayne County* v. *Waller*, 90 Pa. 99, 35 Am. Rep. 636; *People ex rel. Brown* v. *Onondaga County Supers.* 3 How. Pr. N. S. 1, 4 N. Y. Crim. Rep. 102; *Dismukes* v. *Noxubee County Supers.* 58 Miss. 612, 38 Am. Rep. 339; *People ex rel. Ransom* v. *Niagara County Supers.* 78 N. Y. 622.

Nor for necessary disbursements. *Wayne County* v. *Waller*, 90 Pa. 99, 35 Am. Rep. 636.

In some of the states this is regulated by statute. Thus, in Michigan: 3 Comp. Laws (12018) § 1. See *Withey* v. *Osceola Circuit Judge*, 108 Mich. 168, 65 N. W. 668, and *People* v. *Hanifan*, 99 Mich. 516, 59 N. W. 611, construing this statute.

In Alabama a statute passed in 1868 authorized the appointment in certain counties of counsel to defend poor prisoners, fixing the compensation of such counsel at one half of that allowed by law to solicitors. And in *Mobile Commissioners' Ct.* v. *Turner*, 45 Ala. 199, it was held that counsel so appointed were entitled to the compensation provided by that statute, whether the prosecution resulted in an acquittal or a conviction; that the amount in cases of conviction was to be governed by the solicitor's fee allowed in case of such a conviction; and that where the prosecution resulted in acquittal, dismissal, or *nolle prosequi*, the compensation was governed by the grade of the offense charged, on which there might have been a conviction.

In Nevada a statute allows counsel appointed by the court "such fee as the court may fix, not to exceed $50," and provides that he cannot be compelled to follow a case to another county or into the supreme court, but that if he does so he may recover an enlarged compensation, to be graduated on a scale corresponding to the prices allowed. And in *Washoe County* v. *Humboldt County*, 14 Nev. 123, it was held that counsel so appointed is entitled to a fee not exceeding $50 for defending the case in the county where the prisoner was indicted; and if the cause is transferred to another county, and counsel voluntarily follows the case and defends the prisoner there, he is entitled to an additional compensation not to exceed $50; and that if the case is thereafter followed to the supreme court, counsel would be entitled to a further compensation not to exceed $50.

In Ohio a statute (1 S. & C. Stat. 1894) provides "that it shall not be lawful for the county auditor of any county in this state to audit or allow any account, bill, or claim hereafter presented by any attorney or counselor at law for services performed under the provisions of the 14th section of the act entitled 'An Act Directing the Mode of Proceeding in Criminal Cases,' until said account, bill, or claim shall have been examined and allowed by the county commissioners of the proper county, and the amount so allowed for such services certified by said county commissioners." Previous to that statute a practice had prevailed by which courts allowed and certified, and the county auditor paid, fees to counsel assigned to prisoners; and in *Geauga County Comrs.* v. *Ranney*, 13 Ohio St. 388, it was held to be the intention of the legislature by this statute to place the county commissioners in the position before assumed by the courts, of allowing such a fee as might be deemed proper, and that no appeal from the county commissioners would lie to the court of common pleas by counsel who were dissatisfied with an award made by such county commissioners.

Where two or more persons are jointly indicted for a capital offense, and by order of court are tried jointly, and on application therefor the court assigns different counsel for each, the judge presiding has authority under the Maine statute to allow not exceeding $150 in all for the services of counsel for any one trial, including services upon appeal or upon exceptions before the lower court. *Anonymous*, 76 Me. 207.

N. Y. Code Crim. Proc. § 308, fixing the compensation to be allowed counsel in capital cases, applies to the trial and appellate courts separately, and not collectively. *People* v. *Ferraro*, 162 N. Y. 545, 57 N. E. 167, Overruling in effect *People ex rel. Czaki* v. *Coler*, 44 App. Div. 183, 60 N. Y. Supp. 556.

9. In aid of prosecution; private counsel.

With the consent of the court private counsel may be allowed to assist the prosecution.[1]

[1] *Macfarland's Trial*, 8 Abb. Pr. N. S. 57, Citing 1 Bishop, Crim. Proc. § 998;

United States v. *Hanway,* 2 Wall. Jr. 139, Fed. Cas. No. 15,299; *Rounds* v. *State,* 57 Wis. 45, 14 N. W. 865; *State* v. *Orrick,* 106 Mo. 111, 17 S. W. 176, 329.

So held of assistant counsel employed by the prosecuting witness or relatives and friends. *State* v. *Shreves,* 81 Iowa, 615, 47 N. W. 899 (holding that such practice is not forbidden by act of 21st Gen. Assem. chap. 73, § 4); *State* v. *Rue,* 72 Minn. 296, 75 N. W. 235; *People* v. *Calton,* 5 Utah, 451, 16 Pac. 902; *People* v. *Tidwell,* 4 Utah, 506, 12 Pac. 61; *Bennyfield* v. *Com.* 13 Ky. L. Rep. 446, 17 S. W. 271.

Even though he is complainant's attorney in a civil action against the accused. *State* v. *Shinner,* 76 Iowa, 147, 40 N. W. 144.

And a conviction will not be disturbed on appeal because the prosecuting attorney and the acting prosecuting attorney did not participate in the prosecution,—especially where they were ill. *Taylor* v. *State* (Tex. Crim. App.) 42 S. W. 285.

And in *People* v. *Foote,* 93 Mich. 38, 52 N. W. 1036, it was held to be discretionary with the court to permit the business associate of the prosecuting officer, who had attended a prosecution for the People in the justice's court, but who was not employed by any private party, and had no interest in the matter, to assist.

In Louisiana the district attorney may employ counsel to assist him, and the closing argument may be made by such counsel, instead of by the district attorney. *State* v. *Mack,* 45 La. Ann. 1155, 14 So. 141.

And the accused cannot complain that a former district attorney assists. *State* v. *Reed,* 49 La. Ann. 704, 21 So. 732.

The Nebraska statute allowing the appointment of an attorney to perform the duties of a county attorney in case of the latter's disability was held in *Korth* v. *State,* 46 Neb. 631, 65 N. W. 792, not to be in conflict with the Nebraska Bill of Rights, § 10, requiring the legislature to provide by law for holding persons to answer for criminal offenses on information of a public prosecutor.

10. — appointing counsel to assist prosecution.

It is within the discretion of the court to direct the employment of counsel to assist the prosecution on a trial for felony.[1]

[1] *Shular* v. *State,* 105 Ind. 289, 55 Am. Rep. 211, 4 N. E. 870 (Citing *Wood* v. *State,* 92 Ind. 269; *Siebert* v. *State,* 95 Ind. 471; *Tull* v. *State ex rel. Glessner,* 99 Ind. 238; *Bradshaw* v. *State,* 17 Neb. 147, 22 N. W. 361; *State* v. *Montgomery,* 65 Iowa, 483, 22 N. W. 639); *Hall* v. *State,* 132 Ind. 317, 31 N. E. 536; *Com.* v. *Eisenhower,* 181 Pa. 470, 37 Atl. 521.

S. P., *Com.* v. *Scott,* 123 Mass. 222, 25 Am. Rep. 81 (saying that this may be done in a criminal case, if the interests of public justice seem to require, and the counsel acts without assurance or expectation of compensation from any private person).

And the court may appoint as such counsel an attorney employed by persons interested in securing a vigorous and effective prosecution. *Keyes* v. *State,* 122 Ind. 527, 23 N. E. 1097.

11. Amicus curiæ.

The refusal of the court to allow private counsel to act in aid of the prosecution does not preclude such counsel from offering suggestions as *amicus curiæ.*[1]

[1]*People* v. *Gibbs,* 70 Mich. 425, 38 N. W. 257.

II.—INTERPRETER.

1. Power of court.

The court has inherent power, in the absence of statute,[1] to resort to the aid of an expert to interpret language other than English, whether vocal or symbolic, when used on the trial, if foreign either to the accused, or the court, or a juror, or a witness whose testimony may depend upon it.[2]

[1]In *Schall* v. *Eisner,* 58 Ga. 190, it was held that a code provision allowing evidence to be given through an interpreter merely re-enacts what has always been the law.

[2]*State* v. *Hamilton,* 42 La. Ann. 1204, 8 So. 304; *Horn* v. *State,* 98 Ala. 23, 13 So. 329; *Territory* v. *Thomason,* 4 N. M. 154, 13 Pac. 223 (holding that if part of the jury not understanding English cannot communicate with the others, the court can permit a sworn interpreter to aid their communication with each other in deliberation). See also cases in note to *Com.* v. *Vose* (Mass.) 17 L. R. A. 813.

In *Skaggs* v. *State,* 108 Ind. 53, 8 N. E. 695, it was held that, under the statute (Ind. Rev. Stat. 1881, § 495) providing that interpreters may be sworn to interpret truly whenever necessary, a person having even an imperfect knowledge of the sign language might be sworn to interpret a deaf and dumb witness; and the court might thus employ two persons at once.

And a witness who has an imperfect knowledge of the English language may be allowed to give his testimony through an interpreter, even after he has given some testimony in English. *State* v. *Severson,* 78 Iowa, 653, 43 N. W. 533.

2. Oath.

An interpreter, unless he be a sworn officer acting under statute authority, should be sworn in the cause.[1]

[1]This results from the nature of his function when called in aid of the court without statute authority. See *Form of Oath of an Interpreter,* in 2 Abb. New Pr. 700.

3. Function of interpreter.

In the absence of statute, the function of the interpreter is that of an expert witness, though called, it may be, by the court.[1]

[1]A person is not incompetent to act as interpreter before the grand jury because he is also a witness. *People* v. *Ramirez,* 56 Cal. 533, 38 Am. Rep. 73.

The fact that the interpreter is assisted by one or more persons present, unsworn, and uses their knowledge to assist his own judgment in case of doubt, giving his own interpretation finally to the court, is not ground for new trial. *United States* v. *Gibert,* 2 Sumn. 19, Fed. Cas. No. 15,204.

4. Rebuttal.

The accuracy of the interpretation of the sworn interpreter may be impeached, and is ultimately to be determined by the jury.[1]

[1]*Skaggs* v. *State,* 108 Ind. 53, 8 N. E. 695 (*dictum*), Citing *United States* v. *Gibert,* 2 Sumn. 19, Fed. Cas. No. 15,204; *Schnier* v. *People,* 23 Ill. 17. See also cases in note to *Com.* v. *Vose* (Mass.) 17 L. R. A. 813.

III.—CONTEMPT.

1. Inherent power of court.

The court has inherent power, even without the aid of statute, to punish contempt committed in the immediate view and presence of the court, or so near thereto as to obstruct the administration of justice, as well as the misbehavior of its officers in official transactions, and disobedience or resistance by any person of a lawful command of the court.[1]

[1] *Ex parte Terry,* 128 U. S. 289, 32 L. ed. 405, 9 Supp. Ct. Rep. 77, Affirming 36 Fed. 419 (violence in presence of the court, and resistance to officers; form of commitment sustained, 128 U. S. 297, 32 L. ed. 406, 9 Sup. Ct. Rep. 77). For similar cases, see *Ex parte Stice,* 70 Cal. 51, 11 Pac. 459; *Re Rea,* 14 Cox C. C. 139; *Re Percy,* 2 Daly, 530. And see cases cited in notes to *Baker* v. *State* (Ga.) 4 L. R. A. 128, and *State* v. *Kaiser* (Or.) 8 L. R. A. 584.

In *Hale* v. *State,* 55 Ohio St. 210, 36 L. R. A. 254, 45 N. E. 199, it was held that the legislature is without authority to abridge the power of a court created by the Constitution to punish contempts summarily, such power being inherent and necessary to the exercise of its judicial functions; and that the statute under consideration in that case (Rev. Stat. §§ 6906, 6907) would not be so construed as to impute to the legislature an intention to abridge such power. If the court obtains its powers from the Constitution, then its power to punish for contempt can be taken away only by constitutional provision. On the other hand, if the court is merely a creature of the legislature, it is not unreasonable to say that the power which created it, or which has the constitutional right to determine its jurisdiction, may restrict it in respect to the punishment for contempt. For authorities on this question, see note to *Hale* v. *State* (Ohio) 36 L. R. A. 254.

2. Acts and omissions in presence of court.

A contempt is committed where a witness contumaciously and unlawfully refuses to be sworn or affirmed,[1] or to answer a proper question on examination in court or before the grand inquest,[2] or fraudulently evades appearance when under recognizance,[3] or violates the order of exclusion,[4] or whenever the person accused is guilty of any wilful act which is calculated in its consequences to impede, embarrass, or obstruct the court in the administration of justice.[5]

[1]N. Y. Pen. Code, § 143, subd. 6.

[2]*People ex rel. Hackley* v. *Kelly,* 24 N. Y. 74. Refusal to answer question before the grand jury; form of commitment sustained. In this case it appeared by the record returned that, the relator and the grand jury being present in court, it was stated on the part of the jury that the relator had declined to answer the interrogatory, basing his refusal upon the constitutional provision (art. 1, § 6) against compelling a witness to give evidence against himself. It was held that, as the question thus came before the court, the relator had waived the formality of having the interrogatory repeated in the jury room, and the court was at liberty to act as it did upon that waiver; and that the refusal, in respect of its being a contempt, was committed "in the immediate view and presence of the court;" and that the court was, under the statute regulating the punishment of such contempts, authorized to act without further evidence. And see N. Y. Pen. Code, § 143, subd. 6.

See also, on this question, *People ex rel. Phelps* v. *Fancher,* 2 Hun, 226, 4 Thomp. & C. 467, Reversing 15 Abb. Pr. N. S. 38 (refusal to testify before grand jury); *People ex rel. Mitchell* v. *Sheriff,* 7 Abb. Pr. 96 (refusal of witness to produce document; form of commitment sustained); *Re Ellerbe,* 13 Fed. 530 (witness refusing to obey subpœna, and, departing from the district, arrested in another district).

As to whether or not an expert witness can be punished as for contempt for refusing to testify without receiving compensation other than ordinary witness fees, see *Dixon* v. *People,* 168 Ill. 179, 48 N. E. 108, S. C., with note, 39 L. R. A. 116; and authorities reviewed in note to *Flinn* v. *Prairie County* (Ark.) 27 L. R. A. 669.

[3]*Com.* v. *Carter,* 11 Pick. 277.

[4]*People* v. *Boscovitch,* 20 Cal. 436.

[5]*Cheadle* v. *State,* 110 Ind. 301, 11 N. E. 426. And see cases cited in notes to *Baker* v. *State* (Ga.) 4 L. R. A. 128, and *State* v. *Kaiser* (Or.) 8 L. R. A. 584.

Such as assaulting or threatening an adversary for instituting a suit, or a counselor for being retained, or a juror for rendering verdict, or a jailer for keeping one in safe custody. 1 Hawk. P. C. chap. 21, § 14; 3 Inst. 142.

Or arranging with a juror to convey intelligence by signals as to how the jury stood with regard to their verdict. *State* v. *Doty,* 32 N. J. L. 403, 90 Am. Dec. 671.

Or using contumelious words to or of the court in its presence and while the judge is in execution of his office. *State* v. *Johnson*, 2 Bay, 385.

And as to letters to the court or jury, see *Bergh's Case*, 16 Abb. Pr. N. S. 266. See also cases cited in note to *State* v. *Kaiser* (Or.) 8 L. R. A. 584.

For authorities as to whether or not allegations in applications for change of venue may be contempt of court, see *Thomas* v. *People*, 14 Colo. 254, 9 L. R. A. 569, 23 Pac. 326; *Mullin* v. *People*, 15 Colo. 437, 24 Pac. 880, S. C., with note, 9 L. R. A. 566.

The power of the court to exclude traffic from the street by a temporary barricade, when necessary to secure sufficient silence for the proceedings, was sustained in *Belvin* v. *Richmond*, 85 Va. 574, 1 L. R. A. 807, 8 S. E. 378, holding that an action by one injured by the barricade would not lie.

3. Newspaper publications.

A newspaper publication during the course of a trial, which reflects on the court, or assails the litigants, or seeks to intimidate the witnesses, or spreads before the jury an opinion on the merits of the controversy, or threatens them with public odium, or attempts to dictate the decision, or in any improper way endeavors to influence the determination,—is a contempt of court.[1]

[1] *People* v. *Durrant*, 116 Cal. 179, 48 Pac. 75; *Re Cheeseman*, 49 N. J. L. 115, 60 Am. Rep. 596, 6 Atl. 513; *State* v. *Frew*, 24 W. Va. 416, 49 Am. Rep. 257. And for other authorities on this question, see cases cited in note to *State* v. *Kaiser* (Or.) 8 L. R. A. 584.

But the publication must have reference to a pending suit or proceeding. *State* v. *Kaiser*, 20 Or. 50, 8 L. R. A. 584, 23 Pac. 964. And not to proceedings which are past and ended. *Cheadle* v. *State*, 110 Ind. 301, 11 N. E. 426.

In *State* v. *Tugwell*, 19 Wash. 238, 52 Pac. 1056, it is held that, under the inherent power vested in courts by the common law respecting the punishment of contempts, and under the authority of Ballinger's Code, § 5798, providing that "disorderly, contemptuous, or insolent behavior toward the judge while holding the court, tending to impair its authority, or to interrupt the due course of a trial or other judicial proceedings," shall be deemed a contempt of court, the publication in a newspaper, while a cause is pending on appeal before the supreme court, of an article reflecting on the integrity of the court or of one of the judges thereof, and which tends to embarrass and disturb the conclusion of the court in the determination of the cause pending before it, is such conduct as to warrant the court's proceeding against the offender by attachment for contempt. This case also holds in this connection that a cause on appeal to the supreme court remains pending, and within the jurisdiction of the court to make any modification of its decision, until the final judgment has been rendered and the remittitur issued thereon.

IV.—CHALLENGES TO THE GRAND JURY.

[The rule varies in different jurisdictions as to whether objections to the grand jury are to be presented by challenge, by plea in abatement (see *post,* Division XVIII.), or by motion to quash (see *post,* Division XIV.). And see *Gibbs* v. *State,* 45 N. J. L. 379, 46 Am. Rep. 782, and cases cited; note to *State ex rel. Dunn* v. *Noyes* (Wis.) 27 L. R. A. 776. As to qualifications of grand jurors generally, see note to *State* v. *Russell* (Iowa) 28 L. R. A. 195. As to the right of women to serve on the grand jury, see cases in note to *State ex rel. Crow* v. *Hostetter* (Mo.) 38 L. R. A. 214.]

1. Objections to the array.

At common law,[1] and by express statute in some of the states,[2] but not under the New York statute,[3] a person held on a criminal charge may interpose a challenge to the array of the grand jury, on grounds affecting the validity of the whole panel.

[1]*State* v. *Swayze* (N. J.) 2 Crim. L. Mag. 361 (*dictum,* in case of bias of sheriff); *State* v. *McNamara,* 3 Nev. 70; *Cody* v. *State,* 3 How. (Miss.) 27.

It is said in Thompson & Merriam on Juries, § 507, that there is no case showing any authentic instance of a challenge allowed to grand jurors, either individually or to the array, at common law; and it is asserted in § 519 that the right exists in the states of the Union only by force of statute law. See *People* v. *Lauder,* 82 Mich. 109, 46 N. W. 956.

[2]In California a challenge to the panel is allowed by the statute (Pen. Code, §§ 895, 896) on the ground (1) that the requisite number of ballots was not drawn from the jury box of the county; (2) that notice of the drawing of the grand jury was not given; or (3) that the drawing was not had in the presence of the officers designated by law.

And these are the only grounds of challenge to the panel which the statute recognizes; all others are excluded, apparently *ex industria*. *People* v. *Southwell*, 46 Cal. 141; *People* v. *Simmons*, 119 Cal. 1, 50 Pac. 844.

In Minnesota a challenge to the panel is allowed by statute (Gen. Stat. 1894, § 7189) for that (1) the requisite number of ballots was not drawn from the grand jury box of the county; (2) the drawing was not had in the presence of the officer designated by law; (3) the drawing was not had at least fifteen days before court. *State* v. *Russell*, 69 Minn. 503, 72 N. W. 832.

In Iowa the Code (§ 5241) authorizes challenges to the panel, before the jury is sworn, only for the reason that the grand jury was not selected, drawn, or summoned as prescribed by law. *State* v. *Russell*, 90 Iowa, 569, 28 L. R. A. 195, 58 N. W. 915. And one who has been held to abide its action cannot, by a motion to quash, challenge the grand jury after it is sworn. *State* v. *Pierce*, 90 Iowa, 506, 58 N. W. 891. And a challenge on the ground that the grand jury was not appointed, drawn, and summoned as prescribed by law is properly overruled where it was drawn and summoned in the manner provided by law at the time, although the law was subsequently changed before the finding of the indictment. *State* v. *Wiltsey*, 103 Iowa, 54, 72 N. W. 415.

In Montana the criminal practice act (Comp. Stat. div. 3, § 119) provides for challenges to the panel. *State* v. *King*, 9 Mont. 445, 24 Pac. 265.

In Texas, by statute (Pen. Code, arts. 377, 380), challenges to the array are the exclusive mode of objecting to the legality of the grand jury, and are allowed only on the grounds,(1) that the persons summoned are not the persons who were selected, and (2) that the officer summoning jurors by order of the court acted corruptly. *Kemp* v. *State*, 11 Tex. App. 174; *Hart* v. *State*, 15 Tex. App. 202, 49 Am. Rep. 188. But a defendant confined in jail, who desires to avail himself of this right under this statute to challenge the array of the grand jury, must request that he be brought into court for that purpose; and in the absence of such a request he cannot complain that he was not afforded an opportunity to exercise such right. *Webb* v. *State* (Tex. Crim. App.) 40 S. W. 989.

In Oregon the statute (Hill's Code, § 1234) denies the right of challenge either to the panel or to an individual grand juror, except when made by the court on the ground that the grand jurors are not qualified to act as such. *State* v. *Dale*, 8 Or. 229, applies the rule enacted by this statute, but says nothing about the statute itself.

Under the New York statute (Code Crim. Proc. § 238) no challenge is allowed to the panel or to the array of the grand jury. *People* v. *Hooghkerk*, 96 N. Y. 149; *Carpenter* v. *People*, 64 N. Y. 483. But the court may in its discretion at any time discharge the panel, and order another to be summoned, for one or more of four causes set out in the statute.

2. — verification.

A challenge to the array of grand jurors need not be verified.[1]

[1] *Cox* v. *People*, 80 N. Y. 500, Affirming 19 Hun, 430, holding it not within 2 N. Y. Rev. Stat. 731, § 1, which requires dilatory pleas to be proved by affidavit, etc.

3. — to individuals.

At common law,[1] and by statute in several of the states,[2] a person held to answer a criminal charge may challenge one or more individual grand jurors for any cause not affecting the whole panel.[3]

[1] *State* v. *Rockafellow*, 6 N. J. L. 332 (*dictum*, in case of statutory disqualification); *Kitrol* v. *State*, 9 Fla. 9 (now regulated by statute, § 2810); *Musick* v. *People*, 40 Ill. 268 (recognizing the right, but holding the expression of opinion that the prisoner was guilty not to be ground for such challenge); *People* v. *Jewett*, 3 Wend. 314 (*dictum*, in case of bias); *Com.* v. *Clark*, 2 Browne (Pa.) 323; *United States* v. *Richardson*, 28 Fed. 61 (*dictum*, in case of objection to method of drawing and summoning). For other authorities see *post*, Division XVIII.

In *McQuillen* v. *State*, 8 Smedes & M. 587, it is said that a prisoner who is in court, and against whom an indictment is about to be preferred, may undoubtedly challenge for cause; this is not questioned.

In West Virginia the grand jury cannot be challenged for favor, though it may be for cause; but the court has no power to test the qualifications of those on the list by questioning them as to whether they entertain or have expressed an opinion as to the guilt of a person whose case will be presented to them. *Eastham* v. *Holt*, 43 W. Va. 599, 27 S. E. 883, 31 S. E. 259.

[2] In New York the Code of Criminal Procedure (§§ 237 *et seq.*) enumerates the causes of challenge, and regulates the practice.

In Iowa one so held may challenge individual jurors for two causes only: (1) That the juror is prosecutor upon a charge against the defendant, and (2) that he has formed or expressed such an opinion on the merits as would disqualify him as a petit juror. *State* v. *Shelton*, 64 Iowa, 333, 20 N. W. 459 (holding evidence insufficient to show prejudice or disqualification by reason of opinion). But the fact that a brother of the prosecutor is a grand juror is not ground for challenge. *State* v. *Russell*, 90 Iowa, 569, 28 L. R. A. 195, 58 N. W. 915.

In California the Penal Code (§§ 894, 896) provides for challenges to individual jurors on the ground of minority, alienage, insanity, that the juror is prosecutor, that he is witness for the prosecution, duly subpœnaed, or that he is so biased or prejudiced that he cannot act impartially and without prejudice to the substantial rights of the challenger; although having formed or expressed an opinion upon the charge, founded upon public rumor, statements in public journals, or common notoriety, is not ground for challenge, if one make it satisfactorily appear to the court that he can still act fairly and impartially. *People*

v. *Gray*, 61 Cal. 164 (involving the ground last enumerated, and holding the challenge to have been properly disallowed).

In Michigan a person so held may challenge a grand juror upon the ground that he is prosecutor upon any charge against such person (3 Comp. Laws 1881, § 7). And it was said in *People* v. *Lauder*, 82 Mich. 109, 46 N. W. 956, to be "evident, as was held in *Thayer* v. *People*, 2 Dougl. (Mich.) 417, that this right of challenge allowed in these sections can only be exercised by a person shown to the court to be under prosecution, and whose case is about to be submitted to them."

In Arkansas the statute gives to a person held to answer a criminal charge the right to challenge a grand juror on the ground that he is a prosecutor upon any charge against such person, or that he is a witness for the prosecution. In *Hudspeth* v. *State*, 50 Ark. 534, 9 S. W. 1, this statute was held to apply only to persons held to answer criminal charges to be investigated and acted upon, and not to a person already indicted, but against whom a second indictment for the same offense is found by a grand jury impaneled after the discovery of the destruction of the first indictment, but not in his presence. In this case, upon discovery of the destruction of the first indictment, the defendant was brought into court and the charge submitted, in his presence, and in that of his counsel, to the grand jury for their action, and it was held that, as he did not then object to any of the jurors, he had waived the objection, and could not raise it by a subsequent motion to set aside the indictment.

In Texas, by statute (Pen. Code, arts. 377, 381), challenge to an individual grand juror is the exclusive mode of objecting to his qualifications, and is allowed only on the grounds (1) that the juror is not qualified, (2) that he is prosecutor on a charge against the accused, and (3) that he is related by consanguinity or affinity to some person held to bail or confined upon criminal charge. *Kemp* v. *State*, 11 Tex. App. 174.

In *Mershon* v. *State*, 51 Ind. 14, it was held that, if the defendant fails to challenge when he can do so, he should be regarded as having waived the right.

[c]*United States* v. *Richardson*, 28 Fed. 61. For conflict of authorities as to bias by expression of opinion, see *State* v. *Hamlin*, 47 Conn. 95, 36 Am. Rep. 54.

It seems that the objection that a juror in a United States court has been summoned oftener than once in two years, contrary to U. S. Rev. Stat. § 812, does not apply to a grand juror; but if it does, it can only be taken by challenge. It is not ground for attacking the indictment. *United States* v. *Reeves*, 3 Woods, 199, Fed. Cas. No. 16,139.

Challenge of an individual grand juror should be interposed before he is sworn. *State* v. *Hamlin*, 47 Conn. 95, 36 Am. Rep. 54.

4. — — mode of taking.

Objections to particular grand jurors, even though founded on the method of drawing and summoning, are not to be taken by challenge to the array.[1]

[1] *United States* v. *Richardson*, 28 Fed. 61. Gray, J., quotes and follows the statement of Bradley, J., in *United States* v. *Gale*, 109 U. S. 65, 67, 71, 27 L. ed. 857–859, 3 Sup. Ct. Rep. 1, in these words: "The defendants should either have moved to quash the indictment or have pleaded in abatement, if they had no opportunity or did not see fit to challenge the array. This, we think, is the true doctrine in cases where the objection does not go to the subversion of all the proceedings taken in impaneling and swearing the grand jury, but relates only to the qualification or disqualification of certain persons sworn upon the jury or excluded therefrom, or to mere irregularities in constituting the panel. There are cases, undoubtedly, which admit of a different consideration, and in which the objection to the grand jury may be taken at any time. These are where the whole proceeding of forming the panels is void, as where the jury is not a jury of the court or term in which the indictment is found, or has been selected by persons having no authority whatever to select them, or where they have not been sworn, or where some other fundamental requisite has not been complied with. *United States* v. *Gale*, 109 U. S. 65, 67, 71, 27 L. ed. 857–859, 3 Sup. Ct. Rep. 1."

5. — Federal courts.

A state statute is applicable to the organization of grand jurors in the Federal courts sitting within the state.[1]

[1] U. S. Rev. Stat. (2d ed.) § 800 (5 Stat. at L. 394). But with some margin for discretion. *United States* v. *Richardson*, 28 Fed. 61.

And no objection is available in these courts for any causes not specified in the state statute. *United States* v. *Tallman*, 10 Blatchf. 21, 28, Fed. Cas. No. 16,429, 12 Myer's Fed. Dec. § 1845, Citing and approving *United States* v. *Reed*, 2 Blatchf. 435, Fed. Cas. No. 16,134.

V.—PRESENCE AND CUSTODY OF THE ACCUSED.

1. Presence, when necessary.
2. Prisoner under civil process.
3. Officer—custody.
4. Manacling.

1. Presence, when necessary.

It is error to proceed with the trial in the absence of the defendant, when a felony is charged,[1] but not when the charge is a misdemeanor only.[2]

[1]*State* v. *Myrick,* 38 Kan. 238, 16 Pac. 330; *Dougherty* v. *Com.* 69 Pa. 286; *State* v. *Kelly,* 97 N. C. 404, 2 S. E. 185; *Adams* v. *State,* 28 Fla. 511, 10 So. 106; *Brown* v. *State,* 24 Ark. 620; *People* v. *Sprague,* 54 Cal. 92; *Coleman* v. *Com.* 90 Va. 635, 19 S. E. 161.

Thus, submitting the case to the jury, and sending them to their room, is part of the trial, and should not be done in the absence of the accused. *Allen* v. *Com.* 86 Ky. 642, 6 S. W. 645.

The rule requiring his presence is for the benefit of the accused, and to secure him the means of intelligent attention to the proceeding, that he may have a regular trial. It is not an arbitrary rule which must be carried out beyond those limits and against his own opposition. If he had a right to prevent his own trial by persisting in disturbances which stopped the proceedings, there would be no better resistance to a capital indictment than mere obstreperousness.

And the constitutional right of the person charged with a felony to be present during his trial is not violated by a statute permitting the trial to proceed in his absence, if he absents himself pending the trial. *Gore* v. *State,* 52 Ark. 285, 5 L. R. A. 832, 12 S. W. 564.

Nor will a conviction be reversed because of his absence for half a day during his trial, where he was present on a previous day, and afterward when a verdict was rendered, and his counsel made no application to have him brought into court. *State* v. *McGraw,* 35 S. C. 283, 14 S. E. 630.

Nor is it error to hear arguments in his absence, on motions and demurrers, before the commencement of the trial. *Miller* v. *State,* 29 Neb. 437, 45 N. W. 451.

Or to allow an amendment to the information in his absence, before trial. *State* v. *Beatty*, 45 Kan. 492, 25 Pac. 899.

And in *State* v. *Hasledahl*, 3 N. D. 36, 53 N. W. 430, it was held that a statute requiring the personal presence of one accused of a felony does not apply to the making of an order allowing the prosecuting officer to file a new information curing a technical defect.

Excluding from the courtroom a defendant jointly indicted and tried with another, while the latter was testifying, was held, in *Richards* v. *State*, 91 Tenn. 723, 20 S. W. 533, to be a violation of the right to be heard by himself and his counsel guaranteed by the Tennessee Constitution to every defendant in a criminal prosecution.

But it is held to be discretionary with the trial court to allow a defendant accused of murder to have a codefendant who is to be separately tried present ready for consultation, instead of calling him when needed. *State* v. *Weems*, 96 Iowa, 426, 65 N. W. 387.

In *McIver* v. *State* (Tex. Crim. App.) 37 S. W. 745, it was held that one indicted, apart from defendant, for burglary alleged to have been committed by the two acting together, might be brought into court and seated by the defendant for the purpose of identifying the two together. See also *State* v. *Hyde*, 22 Wash. 551, 61 Pac. 719, for a similar holding, where the two were jointly indicted.

And for other authorities on this question, see note to *Gore* v. *State* (Ark.) 5 L. R. A. 832.

[a]*State* v. *Baxter*, 41 Kan. 516, 21 Pac. 650; *Godfreidson* v. *People*, 88 Ill. 284; *Sharp* v. *Com.* 16 Ky. L. Rep. 840, 30 S. W. 414; *Canada* v. *Com.* 9 Dana, 304 (so holding when the defendant is under recognizance); *State* v. *Lucker*, 40 S. C. 549, 18 S. E. 797; *Shiflett* v. *Com.* 90 Va. 386, 18 S. E. 838. *Contra*, *Garman* v. *State*, 66 Miss. 196, 5 So. 385; *Slocovitch* v. *State*, 46 Ala. 227.

In Colorado the Criminal Code (§ 272) provides that the trial for criminal offenses shall be conducted according to the common law unless otherwise provided for; and in *Lawn* v. *People*, 11 Colo. 343, 18 Pac. 281, it was held error to try a defendant for a misdemeanor punishable by fine and imprisonment in jail, in the absence of himself and his attorney, notwithstanding that the case was an appeal from the justice of the peace, and that the bond was for the payment of the fine, and not for the defendant's appearance in the appellate court.

In *State* v. *Young*, 86 Iowa, 406, 53 N. W. 272, it is held error to permit the defendant's counsel in a misdemeanor case to withdraw after the case is called for trial, and to proceed with the trial in the defendant's absence, without anyone representing him, although a statute allows the trial to proceed in his absence if he appears by counsel.

Other authorities showing the rule as to the presence of the accused at the various steps of the trial will be found under the appropriate heads in the subsequent chapters.

2. Prisoner under civil process.

Under the New York statute, where a person who has been indicted for a criminal offense is held by a sheriff by virtue of a mandate in a civil action or special proceeding, the court in which the indictment is pending may make an order requiring the sheriff to bring him before the court; whereupon the court may make such disposition of the prisoner as to it seems proper.[1]

[1]N. Y. Code Civ. Proc. § 156, adding that "the sheriff's fees and expenses, in so doing, are a county charge of the county wherein the court is sitting." Mr. Throop's note is: "L. 1871, chap. 208, § 1 (9 Edm. 67), amended so as to require the sheriff to bring up the prisoner, by adding the last sentence for obvious reasons of justice, and by omitting the phrase 'upon the habeas corpus,' etc., not only because it is unnecessary, but also because, in many cases to which the section extends, a habeas corpus could not issue."

3. Officer—custody.

The accused may be taken into actual custody at the commencement of the trial, even though he may previously have been admitted to bail.[1]

[1]This rule is followed in all cases, whether of felony or misdemeanor, in the New York courts. The power of the court to order this in its discretion is recognized by Code Crim. Proc. § 422.

4. Manacling.

The accused cannot be manacled or shackled during his trial,[1] unless there be evident danger of escape or of his doing violence.[2]

Unnecessary manacling or shackling against the defendant's wish constitutes reversible error.[3]

The rule applies equally to the arraignment and subsequent stages of the trial.[4]

[1]4 Bl. Com. 322; 1 Chitty, Crim. Law, 531; *Rex* v. *Twenty-nine Regicides*, 5 How. St. Tr. 981, note; *Rex* v. *Cranburne*, 13 How. St. Tr. 222; *Rex* v. *Waite*, 1 Leach C. L. 36.

[2]*Lee* v. *State*, 51 Miss. 566; *Faire* v. *State*, 58 Ala 74; Wharton, Pl. & Pr. § 540*a;* Hale, Book II. p. 219; *Upstone* v. *People*, 109 Ill. 169 (accused was handcuffed on hearing of motion for new trial; held no error); *State* v. *Williams*, 18 Wash. 47, 50 Pac. 580, S. C., 39 L. R. A. 821, with note reviewing exhaustively the authorities on this question.

In *State* v. *Duncan*, 115 Mo. 288, 22 S. W. 699, it was held that the court has a right to permit an armed guard to keep watch during the trial over a prisoner charged with murder in the first degree.

[3]*State* v. *Smith*, 11 Or. 205, 8 Pac. 343; *State* v. *Kring*, 64 Mo. 591; *Peo-*

ple v. *Harrington,* 42 Cal. 165, 10 Am. Rep. 296. See also cases in note to *State* v. *Williams* (Wash.) 39 L. R. A. 821.

[4]Burns, Jus. P. Title, *Arraignment.*

The rights of a defendant charged with murder under Ariz. Pen. Code, ¶ 1106, providing that one charged with a public offense shall not, before conviction, be subjected to any more restraint than is necessary for his detention to answer the charge, are not violated by the fact that he is in shackles at the time of his arraignment, but not at the time of the trial, where he is a lawless and desperate character. *Parker* v. *Territory* (Ariz.) 52 Pac. 361.

VI.—ARRAIGNMENT.

1. Necessity for arraignment.
2. Waiver of arraignment.
3. Time for arraignment.
4. Record to show arraignment.
5. Joint arraignment.
6. Formalities.
7. Statutory substitution of true name.
8. Rearraignment.
9. Reinstatement after withdrawal of plea.

1. Necessity for arraignment.

Failure to arraign a defendant accused of a felony is fatal to a conviction.[1] But where the charge is for a misdemeanor only, it is usually held that arraignment of the accused is unnecessary.[2]

[1]*State* v. *Moore,* 30 S. C. 69, 8 S. E. 437; *Johnson* v. *People,* 22 Ill. 314; *People* v. *Bradner,* 107 N. Y. 1, 13 N. E. 87: *Grigg* v. *People.* 31 Mich. 471; *State* v. *Wilson,* 42 Kan. 587, 22 Pac. 622: *State* v. *Baker,* 57 Kan. 541, 46 Pac. 947; *State* v. *Hopper,* 142 Mo. 478, 44 S. W. 272; *Browning* v. *State,* 54 Neb. 203, 74 N. W. 631, and cases cited.

But the substantial rights of an accused are not so prejudiced as to require a new trial, by failure to arraign him in the probate court, when the cause is transferred by consent to the district court and duly tried there. *Jones* v. *Territory,* 5 Okla. 536, 49 Pac. 934.

[2]*Johns* v. *State,* 104 Ind. 557, 4 N. E. 153; *Johnson* v. *People,* 22 Ill. 314 (*dictum*); *State* v. *Moore,* 30 S. C. 69, 8 S. E. 437 (*dictum*); *Salfner* v. *State,* 84 Md. 299, 35 Atl. 885; *Lynch* v. *State,* 99 Tenn. 124, 41 S. W. 348. For other authorities on this question, see note to *Parkinson* v. *People* (Ill.) 10 L. R. A. 91.

2. Waiver of arraignment.

And some of the courts hold that an accused, even where the charge is for felony, may waive arraignment.[1]

[1]*State* v. *Robinson*, 36 La. Ann. 873; *State* v. *Glave*, 51 Kan. 330, 33 Pac. 8; *Kelly* v. *People*, 132 Ill. 363, 24 N. E. 56; *State* v. *Winstrand*, 37 Iowa. 111; *State* v. *Grate*, 68 Mo. 22; *Molihan* v. *State*, 30 Ind. 266; *Mitchell* v. *State*, 22 Ga. 211, 68 Am. Dec. 493; *People* v. *McHale*, 39 N. Y. S. R. 758, 15 N. Y. Supp. 496. See also *State* v. *Pierce*, 77 Iowa, 245, 42 N. W. 181, where the power of the accused to waive arraignment is recognized, but it is held that he must make known his wish to do so.

In *Goodin* v. *State*, 16 Ohio St. 344, it was held that the fact that the record showed waiver of arraignment of the defendant was not cause for reversal, because it also appeared that an arraignment was in fact had.

But it has been held that an attorney has no authority to waive arraignment of a defendant charged with a felony, in his absence. *State* v. *McMichael*, 50 La. Ann. 428, 23 So. 992, and cases cited.

3. Time for arraignment.

The arraignment of the accused must be the first step in the progress of the trial; it must precede the impaneling of the jury and the hearing of the evidence; and failure to so arraign the defendant is reversible error which is not cured by arraignment after the trial has begun.[1]

[1]*Parkinson* v. *People*, 135 Ill. 401, 10 L. R. A. 91, with note, 25 N. E. 764; *State* v. *Montgomery*, 63 Mo. 296; *People* v. *McHale*, 39 N. Y. S. R. 758, 15 N. Y. Supp. 496; *State* v. *Hughes*, 1 Ala. 655; *Dansby* v. *United States* (Ind. Terr.) 51 S. W. 1083.

In *Weaver* v. *State*, 83 Ind. 289, it was held error to impanel and swear the jury before arraignment; but it was further held that the court might of its own motion, on discovering, after the jury were sworn but before any evidence was given, that the defendant was not arraigned, cause him to be arraigned and the jury resworn, and then proceed with the trial. See also *Browning* v. *State*, 54 Neb. 203, 74 N. W. 631, and cases cited.

And in *Morris* v. *State*, 30 Tex. App. 95, 16 S. W. 757, it was held that a conviction would not be set aside on appeal because the record showed an arraignment after the jury was impaneled.

In *Disney* v. *Com.* 9 Ky. L. Rep. 413, 5 S. W. 360, the court said that arraignment of an accused might be deferred until the jurors were all selected; and it was held that the procedure outlined in *Weaver* v. *State*, 83 Ind. 289, *supra*, was proper.

4. Record to show arraignment.

In those courts in which the arraignment of the accused is regarded as indispensable it is also held that the record must affirmatively show the fact of arraignment.[1]

[1]*Grigg* v. *People,* 31 Mich. 471; *State* v. *Wilson,* 42 Kan. 587, 22 Pac. 622; *People* v. *Gaines,* 52 Cal. 480; *Warrace* v. *State,* 27 Fla. 362, 8 So. 748; *Hanson* v. *State,* 43 Ohio St. 376, 1 N. E. 136. *Contra, People* v. *Ah Hop,* 1 Idaho, 698. And in *State* v. *Winstrand,* 37 Iowa, 110, it was held that where the record is silent as to arraignment that fact will be presumed.

Where the case appears to have been tried on a plea of not guilty, failure of the record to show affirmatively the fact of arraignment is a mere irregularity, and not prejudicial. *State* v. *Bowman,* 78 Iowa, 519, 43 N. W. 302.

In South Dakota it is held that where a record shows the presence personally and by counsel of a defendant charged with a felony, his announcement of ready for trial, and a trial on the merits without objection, failure to show affirmatively the fact of arraignment is not ground for reversal. *State* v. *Reddington,* 7 S. D. 368, 64 N. W. 170.

In *People* v. *Eppinger,* 109 Cal 294, 41 Pac. 1037, it is held that an irregularity in the minutes of the court showing that the defendant was arraigned for forgery instead of uttering a fictitious check will be disregarded on appeal.

5. Joint arraignment.

When two or more are jointly indicted, they may be jointly arraigned; and it is not error to deny an application for separate arraignment.[1]

[1]Bishop, Crim. Proc. (3d ed.) § 729; *Whitehead* v. *Com.* 19 Gratt. 640.

6. Formalities.

In arraigning a prisoner it is not necessary that he be asked how he shall be tried;[1] nor need he hold up his hand; but any acknowledgment that he is the person called is sufficient.[2] Nor need the indictment be read, if a copy has been furnished pursuant to statute.[3]

In New York it is sufficient to state the charge, asking the prisoner if he plead guilty or not guilty, unless he demands that the indictment be read or a copy furnished to him, in which case his demand must be granted.[4]

[1]*United States* v. *Gibert,* 2 Sumn. 19, Fed. Cas. No. 15,204.

The formalities once attendant upon the arraignment of a prisoner are not now required, and it is sufficient if that which is done amounts in substance to an arraignment. *Parkinson* v. *People,* 135 Ill. 401, 25 N. E. 764, with note 10 L. R. A. 91.

A prisoner, when brought to the bar of the court to answer the accusation contained in the indictment, is "arraigned," within the meaning of the Virginia Code, providing that he may demand to be tried, in case of felony, in the circuit court, upon his "arraignment." *Stoneham* v. *Com.* 86 Va. 523, 10 S. E. 238.

[2]*People* v. *Frost,* 5 Park. Crim. Rep. 52; *State* v. *Weeden,* 133 Mo. 70, 34 S. W. 473.

[3]*Minich* v. *People,* 8 Colo. 440, 9 Pac. 4, holding as above, although it was shown that it was furnished him only a few minutes before he was called upon to plead, his counsel having stated without objection, "We have read the indictment, and know its contents."

And in *Ussery* v. *Territory* (Ariz.) 36 Pac. 35, it was held that the failure of the clerk to read the indictment to the jury as required by Ariz. Pen. Code, § 1643, is not reversible error, where the defendant fails to save any exception to such omission.

In *Com.* v. *Hill,* 14 Mass. 207, it was held that in the case of a deaf and dumb defendant the indictment might be read to him, on his arraignment, in sign language.

[4]Code Crim. Proc. § 309.

7. Statutory substitution of true name.

By statute in many of the states, if on the arraignment the accused allege another name to be his true name, the court must direct it to be entered on the minutes; and subsequent proceedings may be had against him under such name, referring also to the name by which he was indicted.[1]

[1]See, for example, N. Y. Code Crim. Proc. § 310; Nev. Comp. Laws, § 4202; Bates's (Ohio) Anno. Stat. § 7254; Sand. & H. (Ark.) Dig. § 2079 (allowing this on discovery of true name at any time before execution of sentence). And see *Phillips* v. *State,* 35 Ark. 384; *Lasure* v. *State,* 19 Ohio St. 43. As to misnomer and plea thereof, see *post,* Division XVIII. As to change of name pending indictment, see *post,* Division XVIII.

8. Rearraignment.

The accused having once been arraigned and pleaded, a rearraignment is not necessary upon a second trial;[1] nor, on change of venue, in the county whither the issue has been removed.[2] Otherwise after amendment of the information.[3]

[1]Bishop, Crim. Proc. (3d ed.) § 730; *Hayes* v. *State,* 58 Ga. 35; *Byrd* v. *State,* 1 How (Miss.) 247; *Poole* v. *People,* 24 Colo. 510, 52 Pac. 1025;

Reynolds v. *State,* 34 Fla. 175, 16 So. 78; *State* v. *Stewart,* 26 S C. 125, 1 S. E. 468.

But in *State* v. *Barnes,* 59 Mo. 154, rearraignment was held essential where, after commencing the trial as for murder in the first degree, the court directed it to proceed as for the second degree.

And one convicted of murder on arraignment and plea of guilty, and whose insanity at the time of the plea was subsequently made a ground for his motion for a new trial, was properly rearraigned where, on the case being again called for trial, he requested permission to enter a plea of not guilty. *Shaw* v. *State,* 32 Tex. Crim. Rep. 155, 22 S. W. 588. The court said that usually a rearraignment under the same indictment might be unnecessary, yet it would be difficult to see how it could or should operate as error; and that, under the facts of this case, the trial court acted with due prudence and caution in causing the second arraignment.

[a] *Davis* v. *State,* 39 Md. 355; *Vance* v. *Com.* 2 Va. Cas. 162.

But that the defendant was arraigned twice, once before and once after change of venue, does not constitute fatal error. *Meyers* v. *State,* 37 Tex. Crim. Rep. 208, 39 S. W. 111; *Gardner* v. *People,* 4 Ill. 83.

And a defendant not previously arraigned may be arraigned in the court to which the change of venue is granted. *State* v. *Renfrow,* 111 Mo. 589, 20 S. W. 299; *State* v. *Good,* 132 Mo. 114, 33 S. W. 790; *Hudley* v. *State,* 36 Ark. 237 (where it was said to be better, however, to require it before the venue was changed, but held that arraignment in the county to which the change was taken was not error of which the defendant could complain).

[a] *Com.* v. *Pistorius,* 12 Phila. 550; *People* v. *Moody,* 69 Cal. 184, 10 Pac. 392.

But the amendment of certain counts of an indictment, after a mistrial, without rearraignment of the defendant, is not cause for reversal, where the charges made do not affect the body, but are in the caption, of the particular counts, and all of such counts are eliminated upon the motion in arrest. *Gardes* v. *United States,* 30 C. C. A. 596, 58 U. S. App. 219, 87 Fed. 172. To similar effect, see *State* v. *Beatty,* 45 Kan. 492, 25 Pac. 899, where the defendant had waived arraignment on the original information, which was later amended in matter of form only.

9. Reinstatement after withdrawal of plea.

If defendant is duly arraigned and pleads "not guilty," but by leave of the court withdraws his plea for the purpose of moving to dismiss the indictment, and, after denial of the motion, proceeds to trial without rearraignment, the former arraignment will be considered as reinstated by such denial of the motion.[1]

[1] *People* v. *Bradner,* 107 N. Y. 1, 10, 13 N. E. 87, Affirming 44 Hun, 233. *Contra, State* v. *Hunter,* 43 La. Ann. 157, 8 So. 624.

VII.—STANDING MUTE.

1. Effect. | 2. Accused bound by the plea.

1. Effect.

If the accused will not plead or demur to the indictment in due course, the court must direct the clerk to enter a plea of not guilty; and the trial proceeds thereon as if the plea had been interposed by the accused.[1]

[1] U. S. Rev. Stat. § 1032 (providing that thereupon the cause shall be deemed at issue, and shall, without further form or ceremony, be tried by jury); *Re Smith*, 13 Fed. 25 (to the effect that this statute applies to informations and complaints); N. Y. Code Crim. Proc. § 342; Ind. Rev. Stat. § 1766; *United States* v. *Borger*, 19 Blatchf. 249, 7 Fed. 193; *Com.* v. *Place*, 153 Pa. 314, 26 Atl. 620; *Weaver* v. *State*, 83 Ind. 289; *Johns* v. *State*, 104 Ind. 557, 4 N. E. 153; *Com.* v. *Lannan*, 13 Allen, 563 (request to plead further after putting in invalid plea); *Com.* v. *Quirk*, 155 Mass. 296, 29 N. E. 514 (under Mass. Pub. Stat. chap. 213, § 37); *State* v. *Saunders*, 53 Mo. 234 (under 2 Wagner, Stat. 1095, § 5, to same effect as in text); *Gorman* v. *State*, 6 Tex. App. 112 (under similar statute); 1 Bishop, Crim. Proc. § 703*a;* Wharton, Crim. Pl. & Pr. § 417. See also cases in note to *Parkinson* v. *People* (Ill.) 10 L. R. A. 92.

2. Accused bound by the plea.

If the accused thus stands mute, he cannot afterwards object that he did not formally plead.[1]

[1] *People* v. *Osterhout*, 34 Hun, 260 (prisoner was present with his counsel but did not ask to plead); *Com.* v. *McKenna*, 125 Mass. 397; *Johns* v. *State*, 104 Ind. 557, 4 N. E. 153 (but the plea entered for him must appear in the record); *Hunt* v. *State*, 9 Tex. App. 570; *Gaiocchio* v. *State*, 9 Tex. App. 387; *Freeman* v. *State*, 6 Tex. App. 462; *State* v. *Saunders*, 53 Mo 234 (entry *nunc pro tunc*, to defeat motion in arrest, held error).

But his refusal to plead does not waive any objection to the jurisdiction of the court, or to the legal sufficiency of the case against him. *People*

v. *Gregory*, 30 Mich. 371 (conviction reversed because the offense was barred by limitation, and for want of jurisdiction of the trial court).

Where the defendant, although arraigned and offered an opportunity to plead, only does so through his counsel, and not in person, the matter stands as if he stood mute, and the court may then order his plea of not guilty to be entered, as the law requires to be done (Pen. Code, § 1029) when none is entered by the defendant in person. *People* v. *Bowman*, 81 Cal. 566, 22 Pac. 917.

VIII.—DISCHARGE ON MOTION.

1. For failure to indict.
2. For former jeopardy.
3. For delay of trial.

1. For failure to indict.

The accused may be discharged on motion, if the grand jury has been discharged from the term without having found an indictment against him,[1] unless the prosecution show good cause to the contrary.[2]

[1]*Bennett* v. *State*, 27 Tex. 701 (holding it error to deny such a motion).

In Nebraska, prosecutions may be either upon information or indictment; and one committed to jail by the examining magistrate in default of bail is not entitled to a discharge without showing that no indictment has been found, as well as that no information has been filed against him, under Neb. Crim. Code, § 389, providing for a discharge of such person if he is not "indicted" at the term of court at which he is held to answer. *State ex rel. Conroy* v. *Miller*, 43 Neb. 860, 62 N. W. 238.

An order withdrawing an information, with leave to file another, is not within the provisions of Wash. Code Crim. Proc. § 1372, requiring the reason of the court's action to be set forth in the order; but is within § 1315, providing that, when a mistake has been made in charging the proper offense, defendant shall not be discharged if there is good cause to detain him, but the court must recognize him to answer the offense shown. *State* v. *Hansen*, 10 Wash. 235, 38 Pac. 1023.

[2]N. Y. Code Crim. Proc. § 667. In New York, if the grand jury refuses to indict, it must return to the court the complaint, with an indorsement stating that it has been dismissed. The court may order it to be resubmitted. *Id.* § 667.

2. For former jeopardy.

If the accused has previously been in jeopardy, he may be discharged on a motion.[1]

[1] *State* v. *Washington*, 90 N. C. 664; *State* v. *Washington*, 89 N. C. 535, 45 Am. Rep. 700; *People* v. *Goodwin*, 18 Johns. 187, 9 Am. Dec. 203 (*dictum*); *Wright* v. *State*, 7 Ind. 324. Murder; jury rendered a verdict of guilty of an assault and battery, and that the prisoner be fined; and the action of the lower court in denying the prisoner's motion in arrest had been reversed. Held, on application for habeas corpus, that his remedy was by motion to discharge in the lower court. The verdict was a nullity, but a valid indictment still stood against him, to which a plea of former jeopardy would be good. S. P., *Ex parte Ruthven*, 17 Mo. 541 (denying habeas corpus).

In *People* v. *Jordan*, 63 Cal. 219, the prisoner was discharged on motion (whether made at time of second trial, or before, does not appear), where, after the court had intimated its intention of sustaining a demurrer to an indictment for a misdemeanor, the district attorney filed a new information for the same offense, but before a formal decision had been rendered on the demurrer. Practice not questioned.

In *Benedict* v. *State*, 44 Ohio St. 679, 11 N. E. 125, a motion to discharge for former jeopardy was made after the jury had been sworn on the second trial, upon an entry of the court journal, it appearing therefrom that the jury was discharged without stating any reason. The motion was entertained by the court, but the state was allowed to amend the record by inserting therein the reason for the discharge, taken from the judge's minutes; and the prisoner's motion for a discharge was thereupon overruled. Nothing was said as to the propriety of such a motion. As to what is former jeopardy, see *post*, Division XVIII.

3. For delay of trial.

If the right of the accused to a speedy trial is denied to his prejudice, he may be discharged on motion.[1]

[1] See authorities under *post*, Division XXI. As to *nolle prosequi*, and motion to dismiss in nature of *nolle prosequi*, see *post*, Division XXVII.

IX.—PRESENT MENTAL INCAPACITY.

1. Ground for suspending proceedings.
2. At what stage available.
3. Court may order inquiry.
4. Judge's decision.
5. Peremptory challenges.
6. Second inquiry.

1. Ground for suspending proceedings.

If, by reason of insanity,[1] idiocy,[2] drunkenness,[3] or other present infirmity, the accused is unable to plead or to defend himself, he cannot be tried upon a criminal charge during the continuance of the incapacity.

[1] *Freeman* v. *People*, 4 Denio, 9, 47 Am. Dec. 216 (the leading case); *People* v. *McElvaine*, 125 N. Y. 596, 26 N. E. 929; *Com.* v. *Braley*, 1 Mass. 103; *Jones* v. *State*, 13 Ala. 153; 1 Hale, P. C. 34.

"It is undoubtedly the law," said the court in *State* v. *Peacock*, 50 N. J. L. 34, 11 Atl. 270, "that a person who, by reason of insanity, is unable to comprehend his position, and of making his defense, cannot be placed upon trial for a crime. If the court, either before or during the progress of such a trial, either from observation or upon the suggestion of counsel, have facts brought to its attention which raises a doubt of the condition of defendant's mind in this respect, the question should be settled before another step is taken. The method of settling this preliminary question, where it is not the subject of statutory regulation, is within the discretion of the trial court. The court can itself enter upon the inquiry, or submit the question to another jury impaneled for that purpose."

A trial to inquire into the sanity of a person under indictment has nothing to do with the prisoner's mental condition at the time when he is alleged to have committed the crime, except in so far as that mental condition may aid the court in the determination of his present condition. *State* v. *O'Grady*, 5 Ohio S. & C. P. Dec. 654.

In some of the states and territories there are statutes regulating this question. Thus, in Oklahoma (Code Crim. Proc. § 5372, 5380). *Maass* v. *Phillips* (Okla.) 61 Pac. 1057. And compare the various codes and statutes.

In Georgia the Code (§§ 951–953) provides for special pleas of insanity, and the trial of the issues made thereon, in cases of mental derangement existing at the time of the trial; and in no case can this special defense be put in without an averment of the existence of this diseased condition of the mind at that time. The defense of insanity at the time of the offense with which the defendant is charged cannot be raised by such a special plea under this statute. *Danforth* v. *State*, 75 Ga. 614.

[2]*State* v. *Harris*, 53 N. C. (8 Jones L.) 136, 78 Am. Dec. 272; *Queen* v. *Berry*, L. R. 1 Q. B. Div. 447; *Rex* v. *Pritchard*, 7 Car. & P. 303; *Rex* v. *Dyson*, 7 Car. & P. 305 (cases of idiotic deaf mutes).

[3]*Taffe* v. *State*, 23 Ark. 34.

2. At what stage available.

Such an infirmity ought to be disclosed to the court upon arraignment, if it then exists;[1] but if at any stage of the trial a doubt arises as to the prisoner's mental competency, that question must be disposed of before proceeding further.[2]

[1]*Com.* v. *Taylor*, 16 Phila. 439 (where the court refused to accept a suggestion of present insanity after the jury had been sworn).

[2]*Guagando* v. *State*, 41 Tex. 626 (holding it error to refuse to receive a suggestion of present insanity after the jury had been sworn); *People* v. *Ah Ying*, 42 Cal. 18 (holding that, even without suggestion of insanity, the court should, of its own motion, suspend the trial until the question of sanity is settled); *Reg.* v. *Southey*, 4 Fost. & F. 864 (here the question of insanity was not raised until evidence upon the general issue had been received). *Contra*, holding that all of the issues, including that of the defendant's mental condition, may be tried together. *State* v. *Gould*, 40 Kan. 258, 19 Pac. 739.

3. Court may order inquiry.

The trial court may, of its own motion, decline to try the accused until the question of his present mental competency is settled.[1]

[1]*Rex* v. *Frith*, 22 How. St. Tr. 307; *Com.* v. *Braley*, 1 Mass. 103; *People* v. *Ah Ying*, 42 Cal. 18.

N. Y. Code Crim. Proc. §§ 658, 659, provides that if a defendant in confinement under indictment appears to be, at any time, before or after conviction, insane, the court in which the indictment is pending, unless defendant is under sentence of death, may appoint a commission to examine him as to his present sanity, and if found insane the trial or judgment must be suspended until he becomes sane. *People* v. *McElvaine*, 125 N. Y. 596, 26 N. E. 929. See also N. Y. Pen. Code, § 20.

For a discussion of the procedure see Ordronaux's Judicial Aspects of Insanity, and his articles in 2 Crim. L. Mag. 591, etc.

4. Judge's decision.

If the judge has no doubt of the prisoner's sanity he may refuse to direct a trial of the question.[1]

[1]*Webber* v. *Com.* 119 Pa. 223, 13 Atl. 427.

5. Peremptory challenges.

At common law peremptory challenges cannot be interposed on the trial of the collateral issue of present insanity. They are allowed only upon the trial of the main issue.[1]

[1]*Freeman* v. *People,* 4 Denio, 9, 22, 47 Am. Dec. 216.

6. Second inquiry.

The question of present insanity may be retried on arraigning a prisoner at a subsequent term, without vacating the former decision or ordering a new trial of it.[1]

[1]*People* v. *Farrel,* 31 Cal. 576.

A person indicted for a crime is not, as a matter of right, entitled to more than one trial, under Ga. Pen. Code, §§ 951, 953, upon a special plea of insanity at the time of trial, but it is within the sound discretion of the trial judge under the common law to allow a second investigation upon the question of insanity, by reason of a change of conditions since the first examination. *Flanagan* v. *State,* 103 Ga. 619, 30 S. E. 550.

X.—DEMAND FOR COPY OF INDICTMENT.

1. The right. 2. Time of service.

1. The right.

The right to a copy of the indictment is secured by statute in most of the states;[1] and it is error to force the accused to trial without furnishing him with a copy.[2] But such omission, or untimely service, or service of incorrect copy, is waived by asking for time in which to plead,[3] or pleading to the merits,[4] or by going to trial without objection.[5]

[1]In New York, "if the defendant demands it, the indictment must be read

or a copy thereof furnished to him before requiring him to plead." N. Y. Code Crim. Proc. § 307.

U. S. Rev. Stat. § 1033, provides that when a person is indicted for treason, a copy of the indictment, together with a list of witnesses and jurors, shall be delivered to him three entire days before trial; and if indicted for any other capital offense the same shall be delivered two entire days before trial.

In Texas a defendant on bail is entitled to a copy of the indictment only when he requests it, and cannot complain if it is furnished him as early as possible after it is requested (Code Crim. Proc. art. 506). *Abrigo* v. *State*, 29 Tex. App. 143, 15 S. W. 408.

But he is entitled to a copy of the indictment although an indictment had formerly been presented against him for the same offense, in which the name of a defendant included in the second bill was omitted. *Stokes* v. *State*, 35 Tex. Crim. Rep. 279, 33 S. W. 350.

In Nebraska the right of one charged with felony to a copy of the indictment or information and one day to prepare for trial, given by Crim. Code, § 436, is a substantial right, to deny which is error; and such right extends to an amendment inserting a material averment. *Zink* v. *State*, 34 Neb. 37, 51 N. W. 294.

In Alabama it is sufficient to serve a copy of the indictment and venire upon defendant in person, or upon counsel appearing for him, under Code, § 4449. *Johnson* v. *State*, 94 Ala. 35, 10 So. 667; *Henderson* v. *State*, 98 Ala. 35, 13 So. 146.

But in Louisiana the service must be made on the accused by delivering the same to him personally, under Rev. Stat. § 992, providing that every person who shall be indicted shall have a copy of the indictment and a list of the jury which is to pass on his trial "delivered to him" at least two days before his trial. *State* v. *Stewart*, 47 La. Ann. 410, 16 So. 945.

At common law the accused was not entitled to a copy of the indictment in cases of treason and felony, as a matter of right, but was in cases of misdemeanors. Foster, C. L. 228; Hawk. P. C. bk. 2, chap. 39, § 13; 1 East, Crim. Law, 112; 2 Hale, P. C. 236; *Vane's Case*, 1 Lev. 68; S. C., 1 Sid. 85; 1 Chitty, Crim. Law, 403, 404; S. P., *Fulwood's Case*, Cro. Car. 483.

Acknowledgment of service by accused in open court is conclusive. *Wesley* v. *State*, 52 Ala. 182.

Bain v. *State*, 70 Ala. 4; *Driskill* v. *State*, 45 Ala. 21 (so holding, although the demand was coupled with a request for a copy of the venire, to which he had no right. Conviction reversed); *Moses* v. *State*, 9 Baxt. 229; *Nokes* v. *State*, 6 Coldw. 297; *Logan* v. *United States*, 144 U. S. 263, 36 L. ed. 429, 12 Sup. Ct. Rep. 617 (that U. S. Rev. Stat. § 1033, *supra*, is mandatory); *Nutt* v. *State*, 63 Ala. 180 (here defendant was indicted for the murder of Luke Hodnett, but the paper served upon him described the slain as Luke Hadnett. Held, that the court erred in ruling defendant to trial. Conviction reversed); *McKinney* v. *People*, 7 Ill. 540, 43 Am. Dec. 65 (admitting the right of the accused to a copy on the first trial; but holding it was not incumbent on the prosecution to furnish it again at subsequent trials).

In *United States* v. *Bickford,* 4 Blatchf. 337, Fed. Cas. No. 14,591, it was held that in cases not capital the prisoner is not entitled to a copy of the indictment at the government's expense.

In *United States* v. *Williams,* 1 Cranch, C. C. 178, Fed. Cas. No 16,709, a prosecution for counterfeiting, the court ordered the defendants to be furnished with a copy of the indictment.

[3]*People* v. *Lightner,* 49 Cal. 226.

[4]*Record* v. *State,* 36 Tex. 521; *Wade* v. *State,* 50 Ala. 164; *Johnson* v. *State,* 43 Ark. 391; *United States* v. *Curtis,* 4 Mason, 232, Fed. Cas. No. 14,905; *Minich* v. *People,* 8 Colo. 440, 9 Pac. 4; *State* v. *Johnson,* Walk. (Miss.) 392; *Loper* v. *State,* 3 How. (Miss.) 429; *Ben* v. *State,* 22 Ala. 9, 58 Am. Dec. 234; *United States* v. *Cornell,* 2 Mason, 91, Fed. Cas. No. 14,868; *Kelly* v. *People,* 132 Ill. 363, 24 N. E. 56; *State* v. *Schmidt,* 137 Mo. 266, 38 S. W. 938.

If upon arraignment the day for trial is set by consent of prisoner's counsel, and the trial is subsequently adjourned, it is too late at the adjourned day to demand for the first time the service of a copy of the indictment and three days' delay. *State* v. *Briggs,* 27 S. C. 80, 2 S. E. 854.

In Illinois a minor accused of a crime may waive the right to a copy of the indictment and list of witnesses and jurors, as there is no difference between criminal proceedings against minors and those against adults. *Bartley* v. *People,* 156 Ill. 234, 40 N. E. 831.

[5]*Taylor* v. *State,* 11 Lea, 708; *Wright* v. *State,* 42 Ark. 94 (holding that unless the record shows that the copy was not furnished, the court will presume that it was furnished, or that it was waived by defendant); *Clarke* v. *State,* 78 Ala. 474, 56 Am. Rep. 45 (holding that when the record discloses an order for the service of a copy of the indictment, but is silent as to the service, the court, in absence of objection, will presume compliance); *Miller* v. *State,* 45 Ala. 24; *State* v. *Jackson* 12 La. Ann. 679; *State* v. *Schmidt,* 137 Mo. 266, 38 S. W. 938; *Lord* v. *State,* 18 N. H. 173; *Fouts* v. *State,* 8 Ohio St. 98; *State* v. *Russell,* 33 La. Ann. 135. *Contra, Robertson* v. *State,* 43 Ala. 325 (holding that tardy delivery, and to counsel instead of to accused, was error, notwithstanding defendant went to trial without objection).

2. Time of service.

A statute requiring service of a copy of indictment before trial refers to the trial before a jury, and not to the previous arraignment.[1]

[1]*United States* v. *Curtis,* 4 Mason, 232, Fed. Cas. No. 14,905 (so held on motion in arrest); *United States* v. *Neverson,* 1 Mackey, 152 (no error to overrule demand made on arraignment).

In Kansas a person accused of a capital crime has the right to insist on the delivery to him or his attorney of a certified copy of the information at least forty-eight hours before arraignment. *State* v. *Wilson,* 42 Kan. 587, 22 Pac. 622.

XI.—DEMURRER TO INDICTMENT.

[At common law a defect which is available on demurrer to the indictment is equally available on motion in arrest of judgment.]

1. Right to demur.
2. When.
3. Matters dependent on extrinsic evidence.
4. Limitations.
5. Several counts.
6. Leave to plead over—at common law.
7. — statutory rule.
8. Judgment sustaining demurrer.
9. Presence of the accused.

1. Right to demur.

On arraignment the accused has in all cases a right to interpose a demurrer to the indictment.[1]

[1] F. F. Heard, in 1 Crim. L. Mag. 452 (article on Interposing the Statute of Limitations by Demurrer). The practice is to file a written demurrer.

All obections to an indictment in Oklahoma, except that it does not state facts sufficient to constitute a public offense or to give the court jurisdiction, are waived by failure to challenge the sufficiency thereof by a motion to quash or by a demurrer. *Rhea* v. *United States,* 6 Okla. 249, 50 Pac. 992.

And failure to demur on grounds allowed by the California statute waives them as objections, and the defendant cannot move to arrest the judgment. *People* v. *Swenson,* 49 Cal. 388.

Except that defects in an information which are matters of substance, and not of form, are not waived by failing to demur, but are cause for arrest of judgment. *People* v. *Ross,* 103 Cal. 425, 37 Pac. 379.

2. When.

A demurrer to an indictment should be interposed before a plea has been entered;[1] but the court may, in its discretion, permit a plea to be withdrawn in order to entertain a demurrer.[2]

[1]Wharton, Crim. Pl. & Pr. 407b; *People* v. *Turner,* 39 Cal. 370; *State* v. *Boudreaux,* 14 La. Ann. 88 (to the effect that a demurrer must be interposed before the jury is sworn).

In Kentucky a demurrer to an indictment for duplicity cannot be made after plea to the indictment, as Crim. Code, § 157, provides that the defendant, upon his arraignment or upon the call of the indictment for trial, must either move to set it aside or plead thereto. *Moore* v. *Com.* 18 Ky. L. Rep. 129, 35 S. W. 283. Compare *Ellis* v. *Com.* 78 Ky. 130, where the court said there is no provision in the Kentucky Criminal Code (§ 165) which prohibits the filing of a demurrer after a plea of not guilty, or after the jury is sworn, and before the trial.

[2]*Reg.* v. *Purchase,* 1 Car. & M. 617. N. Y. Code Crim. Proc. § 322.

In several of the states it is provided by statute that "both the demurrer and the plea must be put in, either at the time of the arraignment or at such other time as may be allowed to the defendant for that purpose." See, for example, N. Y. Code Crim. Proc. § 322; Minn. Stat. § 7291; Cal. Code Crim. Proc. § 1003.

It is a common practice in New York to permit the prisoner to plead, with leave to withdraw the plea and demur.

3. Matters dependent on extrinsic evidence.

Objections not apparent on the face of the indictment are not ground of demurrer.[1]

[1]For instance, misnomer: *United States* v. *Howard,* 1 Sawy. 507, Fed. Cas. No. 15,402 (holding that misnomer must be objected to by plea).

So, an indictment is not demurrable for matter *dehors* the pleadings and the record. *Jackson* v. *State,* 64 Ga. 344.

Nor because the minutes of evidence returned by the grand jury have not been filed with the clerk as required by statute. *State* v. *Briggs,* 68 Iowa, 416, 27 N. W. 358.

A demurrer is not a proper method of attacking an indictment on the ground of the alleged disqualification of a grand juror; but the attack should be made by motion to quash, or special plea in abatement supported by evidence. *Cooper* v. *State,* 106 Ga. 119, 32 S. E. 23.

Demurrer to an indictment goes only to the sufficiency thereof, and not to questions affecting the regularity or legality of the organization of the grand jury; such questions must be raised by a motion under Okla. Stat. 1893, § 5110, as amended by Okla. Sess. Laws 1895, p. 196, to set aside the indictment; or if the facts were not known to the defendant or his counsel until after the jury was sworn for the trial of the cause, they may be presented upon a motion for a new trial. *Patswald* v. *United States,* 5 Okla. 351, 49 Pac. 57.

In California the Code of Criminal Procedure (§ 1004) allows the defendant to demur to the indictment or information upon certain grounds which must appear upon the face thereof. And the grounds enumerated in that section are the only grounds upon which a demurrer will lie. *People* v. *Schmidt,* 64 Cal. 260, 30 Pac. 816. Thus, objection to the indefiniteness as to time, of the expression "was and is," in the averment in an information charging the making and passing of a fictitious check with intent to defraud, that the purported payee "was and is" a fictitious person, must be taken by demurrer under the California Penal Code; and if not so taken is waived. *People* v. *Ellenwood,* 119 Cal. 166, 51 Pac. 553. But a defendant cannot, under this section, demur to an information on the ground that it is uncertain. *People* v. *Markham,* 64 Cal. 157, 30 Pac. 620. And the question of jurisdiction of the court over certain territory within which the offense with which the accused is charged was committed cannot be raised by demurrer or motion in arrest of judgment, but is a matter of defense. *People* v. *Fredericks,* 106 Cal. 554, 39 Pac. 944.

In Mississippi an indictment drawn under Code 1892, § 1209, for malicious mischief, is demurrable where it is clear that the defendants are indictable only under § 1315, for a wilful or malicious trespass on the property of another. *Barkley* v. *State* (Miss.) 23 So. 185.

So, also, an indictment is demurrable which charges that defendant unlawfully, feloniously, wilfully, and burglariously broke and entered a dwelling with the wilful, felonious, and burglarious intent to commit some crime to the jurors unknown. *State* v. *Buchanan,* 75 Miss. 349, 22 So. 875.

Under the Ohio Code of Criminal Procedure (§ 7251) an accused may demur when the facts stated in the indictment do not constitute an offense punishable by the laws of that state, or when the intent is not alleged, and proof thereof is necessary to make out the offense charged. *Davis* v. *State,* 32 Ohio St. 24.

In Texas the Code of Criminal Procedure (arts. 528, 529) provides what exceptions may be taken to indictments, dividing them into two classes, —exceptions which go to the substance and exceptions which go to the form; and the grounds enumerated therein are the only ones available. *West* v. *State,* 6 Tex. App. 485; *State* v. *Shwartz,* 25 Tex. 764.

In Kentucky the question of duplicity of an indictment can be raised only by a demurrer, and not by a motion to quash, under Crim. Code, art. 2, chap. 2, title 6, § 165. *Moore* v. *Com.* 18 Ky. L. Rep. 129, 35 S. W. 283.

4. Limitations.

The statute of limitations cannot be taken advantage of on demurrer.[1]

[1] *United States* v. *Cook,* 17 Wall. 168, 21 L. ed. 538; *State* v. *McIntire,* 58 Iowa, 572, 12 N. W. 593; *State* v. *Gill,* 33 Ark. 129. But see an able article combatting this view, by F. F. Heard, in 1 Crim. L. Mag. 452.

Contra, by express statute in Texas (Code Crim. Proc. art. 624), *Drummond* v. *State*, 4 Tex. App. 150.

5. Several counts.

A general demurrer to an indictment containing several counts cannot be sustained if any of the counts are good.[1]

[1] *Hendricks* v. *Com.* 75 Va. 934; *State* v. *Miles*, 89 Me. 142, 36 Atl. 70; *West* v. *State*, 70 Miss. 600, 12 So. 903.

If the demurrer is general, and goes, not to each count, but to the indictment as a whole, and there is one good count, the demurrer should not be sustained unless the indictment as a whole is bad. But where the demurrer is to each count, it should be sustained as to those counts which are bad; and where the verdict is general, the conviction must be reversed for error in overruling demurrers to some of the counts of the indictment, although the remaining counts are good. *Avirett* v. *State*, 76 Md. 510, 25 Atl. 676, 987. "If all the counts but one were bad," said the court, "and each was demurred to, the traverser was, as a matter of strict legal right, entitled, by the judgment of the court, to have the vicious counts eliminated before being compelled to plead not guilty. Forcing him, despite his demurrer, into a trial upon counts which were bad, and each one of which he had assailed, was a prejudicial error that no general verdict could cure, notwithstanding there was one good count in the indictment. It may well be that under an indictment containing several counts, all of which except one are bad, and each one of which has been demurred to, a general verdict of guilty might be rendered upon evidence adduced in support of the defective counts, while no evidence was offered under the good count; and thus a conviction would be secured upon the very counts which the court below improperly sustained as good. It is the absolute legal right of the accused not to be tried upon defective counts, the sufficiency of which he has separately challenged by demurrers; and it is no answer, after his demurrers have been wrongfully overruled and a general verdict of guilty on all the counts has been rendered, to say that he has not been injured by the erroneous judgment entered against him, because there is one good count in the indictment."

Error in overruling a demurrer to one of the counts of an information is not prejudicial, where the prosecuting attorney, at the close of the state's testimony, entered a *nolle prosequi* to such count, and the evidence offered in support of it was equally competent to establish the charge contained in the count upon which the conviction was had. *Bartley* v. *State*, 53 Neb. 310, 73 N. W. 744, 55 Neb. 294, 75 N. W. 832.

And overruling a demurrer to a count of an indictment for a felony is not prejudicial to defendant, where all the facts set up therein are alleged in another count which is substantially the same. *Pryor* v. *Com.* (Va.) 26 S. E. 864.

6. Leave to plead over—at common law.

At common law, as administered in the American courts, in a case of misdemeanor, judgment, on overruling a demurrer to an indictment, should be absolute against the defendant, unless the court, in its discretion, allows him to plead guilty.[1]

In a case of felony, the judgment should not be absolute, but the court should always allow defendant to withdraw the demurrer and plead over.[2]

[1] *Com.* v. *Fogg*, 6 Leigh, 638 (discretionary); *State* v. *Shaw*, 8 Humph. 32 (demurrer sustained in trial court; held untenable on appeal, and final judgment rendered against defendant); *People* v. *Taylor*, 3 Denio, 91 (demurrer sustained in trial court, but held untenable on appeal; judgment absolute rendered against defendant); *Wickwire* v. *State*, 19 Conn. 477; *State* v. *Merrill*, 37 Me. 329; *McCuen* v. *State*, 19 Ark. 630; *Com.* v. *Gloucester*, 110 Mass. 492 (upon overruling defendants' demurrer, it was not error to render final judgment against them, though the court might have permitted them to plead over).

[2] *State* v. *Wilkins*, 17 Vt. 151 (leave to plead granted by the appellate court); 1 Chitty, Crim. Law, 441; 1 Bishop, Crim. Proc. § 782.

Bishop says: "With us, in misdemeanor, the judgment against a defendant on his demurrer is final, unless he has leave to withdraw it or answer over. In felony it [the judgment] is in some of the states, and perhaps all, that he answer over. Not all our courts hold a demurrer to be an admission for purposes other than those of the demurrer itself." 1 Bishop, Crim. Proc. §§ 784 *et seq.*

As to leave to plead over, see also *post*, Division XVIII.

7. — statutory rule.

By statute, in the courts of the United States,[1] and in most of the states,[2] the right to plead over is secured in all cases on the overruling of a demurrer to an indictment.

[1] U. S. Rev. Stat. § 1026, providing that in every case where the demurrer is overruled the judgment shall be *respondeat ouster.*

[2] Thus, in New York the Code of Criminal Procedure (§ 330) provides that "if the demurrer be disallowed the court must permit the defendant, at his election, to plead; which he must do forthwith, or at such time as the court may allow. If he do not plead, judgment must be pronounced against him, if the crime charged is a misdemeanor; otherwise a plea of not guilty must be entered."

In Minnesota the statute (§ 7300) provides that if the demurrer is disallowed or the indictment amended the court shall permit the defendant, at his election, to plead, which he must do forthwith, or at such time as the court may allow. If he does not plead, judgment shall be pronounced against him. And where a case is remanded upon affirmance of an order overruling a demurrer, and the prisoner is brought before the court for sentence, the court has power to permit him to plead over. *State* v. *Abrisch,* 42 Minn. 202, 43 N. W. 1115.

In Iowa the defendant has the right to plead over; but if he fails so to do final judgment may be rendered against him on the demurrer, and, if necessary, a jury impaneled to inquire and ascertain the degree of the offense. Code, § 5332. And failure to enter such plea is a mere technical error or irregularity in no way affecting the substantial rights of the defendant, where the case is treated in every respect as though a plea had been entered. *State* v. *Greene,* 66 Iowa, 11, 23 N. W. 154.

In Ohio (Code Crim. Proc. § 7256), after demurrer is overruled, the accused may plead not guilty or in bar. And the trial court cannot proceed to final judgment without a plea of guilty or a finding by a jury. *Hirn* v. *State,* 1 Ohio St. 15.

In California there is a statute similar to the New York statute, except that the clause as to the court's entering a plea of not guilty is omitted. And in *People* v. *King,* 28 Cal. 265, it was held that the court may, upon the defendant's refusal to plead, lawfully, and indeed should, pronounce judgment upon him as upon a plea of guilty, and that the constitutional guaranty of trial by jury is not violated thereby. But it was also held that entering a plea of not guilty and proceeding to a trial by jury affords no ground for a reversal of a judgment of conviction. To the same effect, see *People* v. *Jocelyn,* 29 Cal. 562.

8. Judgment sustaining demurrer.

If a demurrer to the indictment is sustained, final judgment may be entered.[1]

[1]The New York Code of Criminal Procedure provides as follows: "§ 327. If the demurrer be allowed, the judgment is final upon the indictment demurred to, and is a bar to another prosecution for the same offense, unless the court, being of opinion that the objection on which the demurrer is allowed may be avoided in a new indictment, direct the case to be resubmitted to the same or another grand jury." And Minnesota and California have similar statutes. Cal. Code Crim. Proc. § 1008; Minn. Stat. § 7297. *People* v. *Jordan,* 63 Cal. 219, Citing and applying the California statute; *State* v. *Comfort,* 22 Minn. 271, Citing and applying the Minnesota statute.

And § 328 of the New York Code of Criminal Procedure provides that if the court does not direct the case to be resubmitted, the defendant, if in custody, must be discharged, or, if admitted to bail, his bail is exonerated, or, if he have deposited money instead of bail, the money must be refunded to him.

Note as to appeal.

In respect to the requisites and effect of an appeal by the prosecution from an order or judgment sustaining a demurrer to an indictment, see *People* v. *Wooster,* 16 Cal. 435, holding that failure to except to a ruling sustaining a demurrer to pleading constitutes a waiver of the right to appeal, and must be considered an acquiescence in the judgment; and *State* v. *Granville*, 45 Ohio St. 264, 12 N. E. 803, holding that the purpose of the bill of exceptions, by a prosecuting attorney, to the decision of a court, for which provision is made in Ohio Rev. Stat. § 7305, is not to obtain a reversal of the judgment of the court in the case in which the bill is taken, and a trial of the indictment there, but simply to determine the law to govern in a similar case.

9. Presence of the accused.

It is not essential that the accused be present at the time the court overrules his demurrer to an indictment for grand larceny, although a statute provides that defendant must be personally present at the trial if the prosecution is for a felony.[1]

[1] *State* v. *Woolsey*, 19 Utah, 486, 57 Pac. 426, and cases cited; *State* v. *Spotted Hawk*, 22 Mont. 33, 55 Pac. 1026.

XII.—INSPECTING MINUTES OF GRAND JURY.

1. Discretionary.
2. When to be asked.

1. Discretionary.

A motion to permit the accused or his counsel to examine the minutes of the grand jury, or to be furnished with a copy thereof, is within the power of the trial court,[1] but is addressed to its discretion.[2]

[1] *People* v. *Naughton*, 38 How. Pr. 430. Here the court, on denying the motion on the facts of the case, says that it is entirely within the power of the court to grant the motion; and such a motion should be granted if the accused cannot otherwise ascertain the specific nature of the charges.

[2] *Eighmy* v. *People*, 79 N. Y. 546. Here, when the trial upon an indictment for perjury came on, the accused, before a jury was impaneled, moved to order the district attorney to disclose what evidence was produced before the grand jury, with a view of moving to quash the indictment, on the ground that there was not sufficient evidence before the grand jury to sustain it. Held, no error to deny the motion; "it was a matter rest-

ing in the discretion of the court, and is not the subject of review upon this writ of error." This case was followed in *People* v. *Bellows*, 1 How. Pr. N. S. 149 (motion denied for want of sufficient grounds).

People v. *Jaehne*, 103 N. Y. 182, 8 N. E. 374, holds that the defendant, as a matter of right, is not entitled to be furnished with the evidence taken before the grand jury. Nor will he be permitted to inspect the minutes except for some special reason, such as to enable him to move to set aside the indictment; and where sufficient grounds have not been shown for the granting of the privilege, and if it also appears that thereby information might be given to other suspected persons not in custody, the motion will be denied. See also *United States* v. *Southmayd*, 6 Biss. 321, Fed. Cas. No. 16,361.

In *Cannon* v. *People*, 141 Ill. 270, 30 N. E. 1027, where it was held that a person indicted for murder is not entitled to a copy of the minutes of the testimony taken before the grand jury, the court said: "We have been referred to no authority sustaining the practice insisted upon. Indeed, the practice in this state has been uniformly the reverse. . . . There was no error in the refusal of the court in the respect indicated."

2. When to be asked.

A motion for leave to examine the minutes of the grand jury, or to have a copy, is not too late if made at any time before the actual trial.[1]

[1] *People* v. *Naughton*, 38 How. Pr. 430.

XIII.—DEMAND FOR LIST OF WITNESSES.

1. Witnesses examined by grand jury. 2. Prosecutor and other witnesses proposed to be called.

1. Witnesses examined by grand jury.

By statute in many of the states[1] the accused has a right to require that the names of the witnesses examined before the grand jury be furnished to him before trial.[2]

[1] N. Y. Code Crim. Proc. § 271, directs that the names of witnesses examined before the grand jury be indorsed on the indictment, but that, if omitted,

the court must, on application of defendant, direct the names of such witnesses, as they appear on the minutes of the grand jury, to be furnished him forthwith.

U. S. Rev. Stat. § 1033, provides that a list of the jury and witnesses to be produced on the trial, stating the place of abode of each juror and witness, together with the indictment, shall be delivered to a person indicted for treason, three days before trial, and for any other capital offense, two days before trial. Compare other codes and statutes on this question.

[2]*Com.* v. *Locke*, 14 Pick. 485 (holding it, in murder, a matter of right); *Com.* v. *Knapp*, 9 Pick. 496, 20 Am. Dec. 491.

Contra, in cases not capital. See following authorities: 1 Chitty, Crim. Law, 322 (where it is said that in "high treason the defendant is entitled to a copy of the names of the witnesses examined before the grand jury, by virtue of a particular statute [7 Anne, chap. 21, § 11], but the right extends to no inferior offenses, nor can the court grant it in their discretion"); *United States* v. *Shepard*, 1 Abb. (U. S.) 431, Fed. Cas. No. 16,273 (on motion to quash an indictment, held, that it was not required at common law that the names of witnesses for the prosecution should be indorsed on the indictment or information).

In *King* v. *State*, 5 How. (Miss.) 730, it was held not necessary for the grand jury to make return of the witnesses examined or the evidence taken before it.

But in *United States* v. *Southmayd*, 6 Biss. 321, Fed. Cas. No. 16,361, it was held that in all cases where there has been no preliminary examination the court in its discretion may order a list of witnesses before the grand jury to be furnished.

As to the right of the prosecution to call witnesses whose names were not furnished, see *post*, Division XXXVII.

2. Prosecutor and other witnesses proposed to be called.

In cases not capital the accused has no right, in the absence of statute,[1] to require the district attorney to furnish him with the names of the prosecutor and witnesses intended to be called upon the trial.[2]

[1]In Illinois every person charged with treason, murder, or other felonious crime shall be furnished, previous to his arraignment, with a list of witnesses. In all other cases he shall, at the request of himself or counsel, be furnished with such list (1 Starr & C. Anno. Stat. p. 1395, ¶ 604). *Kota* v. *People*, 136 Ill. 655, 27 N. E. 53.

In California the reading of the list of witnesses to defendant at the time of his arraignment, required by Cal. Pen. Code, § 988, applies only to an arraignment upon an indictment, and not upon an information. *People* v. *Neary*, 104 Cal. 373, 37 Pac. 943.

Felonies and misdemeanors are on the same footing, under the Georgia statute (Code, § 946); but the defendant is not entitled to the list except upon demand. *Bird* v. *State*, 50 Ga. 585.

[3]In *United States* v. *Butler*, 1 Hughes, 457, Fed. Cas. No. 14,700, upon trial of an indictment for conspiracy to prevent one from voting, defendants, after pleading not guilty, asked to be furnished with the names of the prosecutor and the witnesses. It was held (Chief Justice Waite, sitting with Circuit Judge Bond) that there was no practice justifying such a demand. The ruling is stated in the headnote thus: "The district attorney is not bound to furnish the defendants with the names of the prosecutor and witnesses in a criminal case not capital."

In *Bratt* v. *State* (Tex. Crim. App.) 41 S. W. 624, it was held that the refusal to require the state to disclose the names of all the private prosecutors on a trial for theft of cattle is not ground for reversal, where it does not appear that such information would have any bearing on the case.

XIV.—MOTIONS TO QUASH.

[The general policy of the courts now is to restrict motions to quash, both in respect to the grounds upon which they will be sustained and the time at which they must be made, to as narrow limits as is consistent with securing justice to the accused.]

1. When to be made.
2. Presence of the accused.
3. Irregularities of grand jury.
4. Evidence illegal or insufficient.
5. Formalities.
6. Several defendants.
7. One or more bad counts.
8. Uncertainty.
9. Duplicity.
10. Want of jurisdiction.
11. Pendency of another suit.
12. Extrinsic facts.
13. — how shown.
14. Granting discretionary.
15. Waiver by plea.

1. When to be made.

A motion to quash or set aside an indictment[1] upon a ground which would be fatal to a verdict may be made at any time.[2] But when made after plea the court may properly require the plea to be withdrawn before entertaining the motion.[3]

If made upon any other ground, it must be made before the plea is entered,[4] or after the plea has been by leave of court withdrawn.[5] It is in the discretion of the court to grant such leave at any time, with leave to renew the plea if the motion should be denied.[6]

[1]The reasons for the rules stated in the text are: (1) That the court should not spend time on a trial which clearly must be futile; (2) but, on the other hand, if accused takes issue on the indictment, the court should not on technical objection subsequently raised, nor in a doubtful case of even substantial objections, set aside the indictment and thus discharge the recognizance, and perhaps give the accused a pretext for claiming, when indicted again, that he has been once in jeopardy; and also, perhaps, let in the statute of limitations.

If the objection is such that a conviction might nevertheless stand, the motion should not usually be granted unless seasonably made.

And a formal defect in an indictment, curable by amendment, must be taken advantage of, if at all, before the jury is sworn; and it will not be held ground for affirming an erroneous judgment quashing the indictment. *Com.* v. *Williams*, 149 Pa. 54, 24 Atl. 158.

In *State* v. *Beach* (Ind.) 43 N. E. 949, after the close of the state's evidence the court, on the defendant's motion, instructed the jury to return a verdict of not guilty, to which the state excepted. On appeal the appellee urged the insufficiency of the indictment to support a verdict of guilty, and that it was therefore proper to order a verdict of not guilty; but the court held that the direction of the verdict of not guilty for the reason that the indictment or information does not state a public offense deprives the state of its rights, and frees the accused from liability of further prosecution of the offense charged; and that the question whether the indictment or information does state a public offense is to be presented by a motion to quash or a motion to arrest.

In *United States* v. *Gooding*, 12 Wheat. 460, 6 L. ed. 693, Mr. Justice Story said: "Undoubtedly, according to the regular course of practice, objections to the form and sufficiency of an indictment ought to be discussed upon a motion to quash the indictment, which may be granted or refused in the discretion of the court, or upon demurrer to the indictment, or upon a motion in arrest of judgment, which are matters of right. The defendant has no right to insist that such objections should be discussed or decided during the trial of the facts by the jury. It would be very inconvenient and embarrassing to allow a discussion of such topics during the progress of the cause before the jury, and introduce much confusion into the administration of public justice. But we think it is not wholly incompetent for the court to entertain such questions during the trial, in the exercise of a sound discretion. It should, however, be rarely done, and only under circumstances of an extraordinary nature. The circuit court, in the present case, did allow the introduction and discussion of these questions during the trial, and was divided upon the propriety of the practice. We can only certify that the court possessed the authority, but that it ought not to be exercised except on very urgent occasions." And it was held, accordingly, "that the objections taken to the form and sufficiency of the indictment by the defendant's counsel were not matters of right which the defendant might insist upon, and discuss, and require to be decided during the trial of the issue by the jury; and that the same should, according to the regular course of practice, have been discussed on a motion to quash the indictment, or on demurrer, or on motion in arrest of judgment; but that the court had, nevertheless, competent authority, in the exercise of a sound discretion, to permit such objections to be discussed and decided during the trial."

And in *People* v. *Smith*, 94 Mich. 644, 54 N. W. 487, it was held that the objection that the information was defective for not alleging when, why, or by whom the larceny charged was committed, cannot be taken on appeal, but is to be raised on a motion to quash, or a demurrer.

'Thus, such a motion based on the want of jurisdiction of the court below, though made for the first time in the appellate court, was entertained in *Justice* v. *State*, 17 Ind. 56, and a conviction for larceny reversed. Worden, J., said: "Where a party is charged with a felony, in a court not having jurisdiction over the subject-matter, the defect of jurisdiction can be taken advantage of on motion to quash in arrest of judgment and on appeal."

And a motion made during the trial, on the ground that there was no law in force to punish the alleged offense, has been allowed. *State* v. *Benthall*, 82 N. C. 664; *People* v. *Williams*, 1 Idaho, 85.

And this principle was conceded, also, by *Wilder* v. *State*, 47 Ga. 522, cited below.

But the objection to the sufficiency of the indictment or information cannot be raised by objecting to the introduction of any testimony in support of it. *United States* v. *Harmon*, 45 Fed. 414; *State* v. *Bodeckar*, 11 Wash. 417, 39 Pac. 645; *People* v. *Drennan*, 86 Mich. 445, 49 N. W. 215; *State* v. *Duncan*, 116 Mo. 288, 22 S. W. 699.

And in *State* v. *Barr*, 54 Kan. 230, 38 Pac. 289, it was held that the objection that the information was verified only upon information and belief could not be first raised by a plea in abatement filed just before the trial, but that it should be made by motion to quash the warrant before the recognizance for the appearance given. But in *State* v. *Kent*, 5 N. D. 516, *sub nom. State* v. *Pancoast*, 35 L. R. A. 518, 67 N. W. 1052, it was held that a motion to set aside an information for improper verification cannot be made after a plea of not guilty and one trial upon that plea; nor can the objection be raised by motion in arrest, since under the North Dakota statutes a motion in arrest reaches only defects available on demurrer.

But a defendant who, upon his arraignment, is given a day to plead or to answer the indictment, may, before otherwise pleading thereto, and in answer to the arraignment, move to set the indictment aside; and when such time is allowed him by the court the Oregon statute (Hill's Code, § 1315) requiring a motion to set aside the indictment to be made and heard at the arraignment, unless for good cause the court postpone the hearing to a future time, does not preclude him from making the motion at any time before so otherwise pleading. *State* v. *Pool*, 20 Or. 150, 25 Pac. 375.

*In *Mentor* v. *People*, 30 Mich. 91, it was held that the effect of entertaining a motion after plea is to withdraw the plea and preclude the accused from claiming afterwards that he has been put in jeopardy on the indictment.

In *State* v. *Reeves*, 97 Mo. 668, 10 S. W. 841, however, it was held that a motion to quash, although filed with the consent of the court after the plea of not guilty is entered but not withdrawn, does not have the effect of withdrawing that plea; but that a motion to quash is in order at any time down to the rendition of the verdict, and this without any withdrawal of the plea of not guilty,—Citing 1 Bishop, Crim. Proc. § 762.

Wilder v. *State*, 47 Ga. 522; *State* v. *McCarty*, 4 R. I. 82 (motion on the ground that complaint and warrant were not taken by the magistrate in the statutory form denied because first made in the appellate court); *State* v. *Jarvis*, 63 N. C. 556; *State* v. *Barnes*, 29 Me. 561; *State* v. *M'Gregor*, 41 N. H. 407 (motion on ground of misnomer or want of addition); *United States* v. *O'Brien*, 7 Int. Rev. Rec. 62, Fed. Cas. No. 15,909 (holding that where the motion is made after plea and witnesses sworn, it would only be allowed in cases entirely free from doubt); *Kerr* v. *State*, 36 Ohio St. 614 (holding that an objection to an improper presentment of the indictment under the Ohio statute cannot be raised after plea, where there is no motion to quash); *Bishop* v. *Com.* 22 Ky. L. Rep. 760, 58 S. W. 817 (objection that summoning a special grand jury of bystanders, upon discharging the entire grand jury, cannot be made on appeal for the first time).

Under the New York Code of Criminal Procedure (§§ 313, 315) the motion must be made in season to be heard at the time of arraignment; but the court may for good cause postpone the hearing.

In Minnesota an indictment can be attacked for defects in the organization of the grand jury, only at the time of the arraignment, unless the court for good cause shown allows the motion to be made at a subsequent time. *State* v. *Schumm*, 47 Minn. 373, 50 N. W. 362; *State* v. *Dick*, 47 Minn. 375, 50 N. W. 362.

Under the Alabama statute (see note 1, § 3, *infra*) a motion to quash comes too late when made after the continuance of the cause at each term at the instance of defendant, and at several other terms by the state, unless the defendant shows that he did not know the facts earlier, and he satisfactorily explains why he did not sooner ascertain them. *Moorer* v. *State*, 115 Ala. 119, 22 So. 592.

In Louisiana a motion to quash on the ground of the illegal organization of the grand jury is too late unless filed on the first day of the term; and it will be denied unless exceptional circumstances are stated, showing clearly that a compliance with the law in this respect is impracticable. *State* v. *Herbert*, 50 La. Ann. 401, 23 So. 300.

But in *State* v. *Strickland*, 41 La. Ann. 513, 6 So. 471, it was held that a motion to quash for the reason that the clerk of the court was not sworn as a member of the jury commission is seasonably made after arraignment, but before trial, where the record shows that the defect was not known to the accused or his counsel on the first day of the term or before arraignment.

And in *State* v. *Taylor*, 43 La. Ann. 1131, 10 So. 203, a motion to quash for irregularity in drawing the grand jury, made before arraignment and at the same time at which the indictment was found, was held seasonable.

But in *State* v. *Leftwich*, 46 La. Ann. 1194, 15 So. 411, it was held that if a motion to quash for irregularity in drawing the grand jury may be made after the first day of the term, it will be deemed too late when made several days after the indictment is found and ten days after the beginning of the term; especially when the accused is in custody awaiting the grand jury's action when the term begins, and all the facts on which the indictment is based are then known to his counsel.

[8]*State* v. *Jones*, 88 N. C. 671; *West* v. *State*, 48 Ind. 483 (adding, however, that it was discretionary to hear the motion without requiring withdrawal of plea); *Nicholls* v. *State*, 5 N. J. L. 539.

People v. *Villarino*, 66 Cal 228, 5 Pac. 154, holds that, even after the plea of not guilty, the defendant has the right, at any time before trial, to apply to the court for leave to withdraw his plea, for the purpose of moving to set aside the information.

[9]*Mentor* v. *People*, 30 Mich. 91.

In *State* v. *Collyer*, 17 Nev. 275, 30 Pac. 891, a trial for assault with intent to kill, the defendant moved for leave to withdraw a plea of not guilty, and to move to quash the indictment, because the persons who found it were not duly selected; but it was held on appeal, and sustaining the conviction, that the motion was made technically too late; but that in the exercise of a sound discretion the court might have entertained it, and should have done so if of opinion that there was merit in the application.

In *State* v. *Riffe*, 10 W. Va. 794, an application two years after plea but before trial, for leave to withdraw plea and to move to quash, was held to have been properly granted.

Larison v. *State*, 49 N. J. L. 256, 60 Am. Rep. 606, 9 Atl. 700, holds that, under the New Jersey statute, technical objections to the indictment must be raised by demurrer or by motion to quash before the jury are sworn.

That the defendant has a right to withdraw a plea and move, see *State* v. *Hale*, 44 Iowa, 96.

In *Morton* v. *People*, 47 Ill. 468, the defendant's plea of not guilty was afterwards by agreement withdrawn to allow him to move to quash with the stipulation that if his motion was overruled the trial should immediately proceed; and it was held that the effect of the stipulation was to reinstate the plea after the motion was overruled. See also *Hensche* v. *People*, 16 Mich. 46.

2. Presence of the accused.

It is not necessary that the accused be present in court at the time of the argument of the motion.[1]

[1] *People* v. *Vail*, 6 Abb. N. C. 206 (denying motion of district attorney to require accused to be present); *Epps* v. *State*, 102 Ind. 539, 1 N. E. 491 (holding absence not error, notwithstanding a statute requiring presence of the accused during "trial"); *Territory* v. *Gay*, 2 Dak. 125, 2 N. W. 477; *State* v. *Hardaway*, 50 La. Ann. 1345, 24 So. 320; *State* v. *Little Whirlwind*, 22 Mont. 425, 56 Pac. 820 (holding that a motion to quash is not a part of the trial at which the defendant's presence is necessary); *State* v. *Atkinson*, 40 S. C. 363, 18 S. E. 1021 (holding to the same effect as the *Little Whirlwind Case;* and also that the constitutional right of defendants, charged with murder, to be fully heard in their defense by themselves, or by their counsel, or by both, as they may elect, is not violated by sending them back to jail during the hearing of their motion to quash the indictment, where they in fact elected before pleading to be heard only by their counsel, by entering a demurrer and moving to quash the indictment through their counsel).

3. Irregularities of grand jury.

In the absence of statutory regulation to the contrary,[1] it is ground for quashing an indictment on motion that the grand jury was illegally constituted,[2] or that its proceedings were unlawful.[3]

But objections which are grounds for challenge only to the favor are not grounds for a motion to quash.[4]

[1] In Alabama the Code (§ 5269) denies the right of an accused to object to an indictment on any ground going to the formation of the grand jury, except that the jurors were not drawn in the presence of the officers designated by law; and a motion to quash based upon the alleged irregularity of the grand jury for other reasons will not be entertained. *Kitt* v. *State*, 117 Ala. 213, 23 So. 485.

In Louisiana the statute specifically provides that "no such defect or irregularity in the drawing thereof or the summoning of the jury shall be sufficient cause (to challenge the venire), if it shall not appear that some fraud has been practised, or some great wrong committed, that would work a great and irreparable injury;" and a motion to quash on a challenge to the general venire, based on alleged irregularities in the manner of drawing and summoning the jurors, is demurrable when it alleges neither fraud, wrong, nor injury. *State* v. *Simmons*, 43 La. Ann. 991, 10 So. 382.

In *State* v. *Bradley*, 32 La. Ann. 402, it is held that an indictment will not be quashed because the clerk of the court who acts as jury commissioner in drawing and summoning the grand jury never has been sworn. So held, also, in *Linnehan* v. *State*, 116 Ala. 471, 22 So. 662. See also *Com.* v. *Valsalka*, 181 Pa. 17, 37 Atl. 405.

In California the Penal Code provides that an indictment may be set aside on motion "when the defendant had not been held to answer before the finding of the indictment, on any ground which would have been good ground for challenge, either to the panel or to any individual grand juror." And in *People* v. *Simmons*, 119 Cal. 1, 50 Pac. 844, it was held that the defendant, not having been held to answer said charge, was in a position to avail himself of the privilege given by said provision; but it was also held that the objection to the juror in question (he not being a taxpayer) was not ground for an objection to the panel.

In Arkansas the statute (§ 2098) provides that "every person held to answer a criminal charge may object to the competency of any one summoned to serve as a grand juror, before he is sworn, on the ground that he is the prosecutor or complainant upon any charge against such person, or that he is a witness on the part of the prosecution;" and it is held that this section applies only to persons held to answer criminal charges which have not been previously investigated and acted upon by a grand jury, and not to a person already indicted. *Baker* v. *State*, 58 Ark. 513, 25 S. W. 603. But an indictment will not be held bad because the accused was not allowed to be present while the grand jury which returned it was being impaneled, and was not allowed to challenge grand jurors for cause, where it does not appear that any grand juror was a prosecutor or witness against him, or that he was prejudiced by such action. *Hamilton* v. *State*, 62 Ark. 543, 36 S. W. 1054.

[a] *State* v. *Lawrence*, 12 Or. 297, 7 Pac. 116 (statute for impaneling grand jury unconstitutional); *United States* v. *Gale*, 109 U. S. 65, 27 L. ed. 857, 3 Sup. Ct. Rep. 1 (*dictum*); *State* v. *Cole*, 17 Wis. 674; *Com.* v. *Jadwin* (Pa.) 1 Crim. L. Mag. 231 (where the indictment in a case which the grand jury could not originate did not come to them from the magistrate or district attorney); *United States* v. *Antz*, 4 Woods, 176 (absence of the legal venire facias under the United States courts); *People* v. *Strong*, 1 Abb. Pr. N. S. 244 (holding the general rule to be as above set out; yet, where the interference of the grand jury is necessary to prevent the statute of limitations from attaching, the indictment will not be quashed because of such illegal origin). Compare *People* v. *Petrea*, 92 N. Y. 128 (holding that some constitutional right of the defendant must be invaded. If the indictment is found by a grand jury of good and lawful men, selected and drawn under color of law, it is a good indictment within the sense of the Constitution, although the law under which the selection was made be void. Followed in *People* v. *Fitzpatrick*, 30 Hun, 493). And for an exhaustive collection of cases treating of the organization of the grand jury generally, see note to *State ex rel. Dunn* v. *Noyes* (Wis.) 2 L. R. A. 776. As to the qualifications of grand jurors generally, see note to *State* v. *Russell* (Iowa) 28 L. R. A. 195.

In Iowa a motion to set aside an indictment may be made under § 4337 of the Code, and must be sustained when the grand jury were not selected, drawn, summoned, impaneled, or sworn as prescribed by law. *State* v. *Russell*, 90 Iowa, 569, 28 L. R. A. 195, 58 N. W. 915.

[b] Thus, an indictment was quashed in *United States* v. *Kilpatrick*, 16 Fed.

765, because a witness was improperly permitted to discuss the case with the grand jury in its room.

And in Texas the presence of the assistant county attorney while the grand jury was discussing the propriety of finding the indictment, although not when it voted, is a violation of Tex. Code Crim. Proc. art. 394, and is ground for setting the indictment aside.

Otherwise in Iowa, unless it be shown that he was not required or permitted by law to be present. *State* v. *Fertig*, 98 Iowa, 139, 67 N. W. 87.

And in Arkansas, when he was not present when the grand jury was deliberating or voting, and nothing was said by him to influence its finding. *Bennett* v. *State*, 62 Ark. 516, 36 S. W. 947.

But the presence of the judge in the grand-jury room during its deliberations, and his urging and directing it to find the indictment, is ground under the Iowa statute for setting the indictment aside. *State* v. *Will*, 97 Iowa, 58, 65 N. W. 1010. As to the effect of improper influence or interference with the grand jury generally, see cases reviewed in note to *Clair* v. *State* (Neb.) 28 L. R. A. 367.

In *People* v. *Sellick*, 4 N. Y. Crim. Rep. 429, the indictment was set aside because it appeared that prior to the indictment a number of the grand jurors had interviewed a person outside of the grand-jury room concerning the charge, and because the communications were of such a character that the court conclusively presumed the grand jury to have been improperly influenced.

In New York, under the Code of Criminal Procedure (§§ 313–315), a motion to set aside the indictment on the ground that it was not found, indorsed, presented, filed, kept, and unshown before arrest, or because a person other than the judge or district attorney was present when it was considered, is matter of right in the court in which the defendant is arraigned; but the defendant is precluded from taking these objections if a motion to set aside be not seasonably made. And under §§ 272 and 313 an indictment may be set aside on motion if not presented as prescribed by the foreman, in the presence of the jury, to the court.

In *State* v. *McNinch*, 12 S. C. 89, the fact that the circuit solicitor went, upon request, into the jury room, after they had agreed, and instructed them how to write the finding, was held not sufficient ground for quashing the indictment.

And a constitutional requirement of "presentment or indictment by a grand jury" is violated by a statute providing that ten persons shall constitute the grand jury, and that eight of them may find an indictment. *State* v. *Hartley*, 22 Nev. 342, 28 L. R. A. 33, 40 Pac. 372. And that less than twelve jurors concurred in finding an indictment was held in *People* v. *Shattuck*, 6 Abb. N. C. 33, to be ground for quashing an indictment. S. P. N. Y. Code Crim. Proc. § 268.

But in *State* v. *Fowler*, 52 Iowa, 103, 2 N. W. 983, it was held that the fact that one grand juror was withdrawn while considering the indictment, and another substituted, and the witnesses already heard not re-examined, could not be considered on a motion to quash.

And in *People* v. *Simmons*, 119 Cal. 1, 50 Pac. 844, it was held that the absence of a qualified grand juror during the consideration of the charge, thus reducing the panel below the requisite statutory number, does not affect the validity of the indictment under Cal. Code Crim. Proc. § 192.

And in *United States* v. *Wilson*, 6 McLean, 604, Fed. Cas. No. 16,737, it was held that the motion would not be granted because the bill was found and returned by fourteen grand jurors, the others being absent though impaneled.

For an exhaustive collection of cases as to the number of grand jurors necessary or proper to act, see note to *State* v. *Belvel* (Iowa) 27 L. R. A. 846; and as to the number of grand jurors necessary to concur in finding an indictment, see note to *State* v. *Hartley* (Nev.) 28 L. R. A. 33.

In *Allen* v. *State*, 61 Miss. 627, it was held that the intoxication of a grand juror while considering the indictment could not be considered on a motion to quash.

And a demurrer is properly sustained to a motion to quash on the ground that the proceedings of the grand jury "were otherwise irregular and contrary to law." Such an objection is merely formal. *Baker* v. *State*, 58 Ark. 513, 25 S. W. 603. For a collection of cases as to unlawful proceedings by a grand jury, see note to *People* v. *Singer*, 18 Abb. N. C. 99.

[4]*People* v. *Jewett*, 3 Wend. 314 (holding that, notwithstanding the accused had no opportunity to object in season, the delay and embarrassment of justice forbids the objection after the grand jury is sworn. The ground of objection here was bias); *Rolland* v. *Com.* 82 Pa. 306, 22 Am. Rep. 758 (held, that it was no ground for quashing an indictment for burglary in breaking into a bank that two of the grand jurors by whom it was found were stockholders of the bank. The objection should have been raised by challenge).

In New York motions to quash, unless involving a constitutional right, can be made only for the causes enumerated in the Code of Civil Procedure. *People* v. *Petrea*, 92 N. Y. 128.

And an indictment for adultery will not be set aside in Iowa because a brother of defendant's husband was a member of the grand jury and took part in the proceedings. *State* v. *Russell*, 98 Iowa, 652, 68 N. W. 433.

And a plea in abatement, or a motion to quash an indictment on the ground that a member of the grand jury which found the indictment was related by affinity to the prosecutor within a prohibited degree, cannot be sustained, where the accused had an opportunity to raise the question by challenge before the finding of the indictment. *Lascelles* v. *State*, 90 Ga. 347, 16 S. E. 945.

4. Evidence illegal or insufficient.

It has been held by some courts,[1] but denied by others,[2] that an indictment will be quashed if it plainly appears to the court to have been found upon wholly incompetent or insufficient evidence. But if the grand jury acted upon legal testimony reaching the whole case, the court will not weigh its sufficiency.[3]

And an indictment will be quashed where the accused was required to testify before the grand jury concerning the charge under investigation,[4] unless he waived his privilege and testified voluntarily.[5]

[1]*United States* v. *Coolidge*, 2 Gall. 364, Fed. Cas. No. 14,858 (indictment quashed because found on the testimony of an unsworn witness); *People* v. *Restenblatt*, 1 Abb. Pr. 268 (indictment quashed because it clearly appeared to the court that there was no legal evidence before the grand jury to support the charge).

In *United States* v. *Farrington*, 5 Fed. 343, it was held that in extreme cases, when the court can see that the finding of the grand jury is based on utterly insufficient evidence or such palpably incompetent evidence as to indicate that the indictment resulted from prejudice or was found in wilful disregard of the rights of the accused, the indictment should be quashed.

In *People* v. *Brickner*, 8 N. Y. Crim. Rep. 217, 15 N. Y. Supp. 528, it was held that the court had inherent power to set aside an indictment, either of its own motion or upon the suggestion of an *amicus curiæ*, or upon motion, when the evidence before the grand jury was insufficient to support it; and that evidence of covert acts in furtherance of an alleged conspiracy was insufficient, in the absence of evidence of the existence of the conspiracy.

So, an indictment has been quashed because the prisoner's wife was without his consent called before the grand jury to testify against him concerning the matter which must have influenced the jury's decision. *People* v. *Briggs*, 60 How. Pr. 17; *People* v. *Moore*, 65 How. Pr. 177. See also cases reviewed in note to *Com.* v. *Hayden* (Mass.) 28 L. R. A. 322.

And in *People* v. *Sellick*, 4 N. Y. Crim. Rep. 329, an indictment for abortion was set aside because the grand jury, contrary to Code Civ. Proc. § 834, received the evidence of physicians who attended the woman in a professional capacity.

In *Hope* v. *People*, 83 N. Y. 418, 38 Am. Rep. 460, it was held that the insufficiency and incompetency of evidence on which an indictment was found could not be raised by plea; and there is *dicta* to the effect that it would not be ground for a motion to quash, as it was not shown that the incompetent evidence was the only evidence received, or that some fact material to the case of the prosecution was established thereby, or that the indictment was not based on other sufficient evidence.

That one of the grand jurors, however, was one of the witnesses upon whose testimony the indictment was found, does not invalidate the indictment. *Com.* v. *Hayden*, 163 Mass. 453, 28 L. R. A. 318, 40 N. E. 843. It was also held in this case that the motion to dismiss, by which alone the question above considered was raised, must also have been overruled, for the technical reason that neither of the facts alleged in it as avoiding the indictment appeared upon the record of the cause, and so could not be availed of by a motion to dismiss. For other cases as to an indictment on the knowledge of the grand jury, see note to *State* v. *Peterson* (Minn.) 28 L. R. A. 324.

In Alabama a statute providing for a punishment for seduction further provides that no indictment or conviction shall be had under this section on the uncorroborated testimony of the woman whose seduction is charged; and an indictment will be quashed where it is found upon such uncorroborated testimony. *Hart* v. *State,* 117 Ala. 183, 23 So. 43.

In Indiana a statute (Rev. Stat. 1881, § 5963) provides that a notary public has no authority to perform an official act until he has procured a seal, and that his official acts are void unless attested by his seal; and a motion to quash an information founded upon an affidavit taken by a notary to which the seal is not attached should be granted; and the addition of the seal pending a motion in arrest will not cure the defect. *Miller* v. *State,* 122 Ind. 355, 24 N. E. 156.

[a]*State* v. *Dayton,* 23 N. J. L. 49, 53 Am. Dec. 270 (holding that the fact that there was no legal or competent evidence before the grand jury affords no ground for a motion to quash an indictment. Criticising *United States* v. *Coolidge,* 2 Gall. 364, Fed. Cas. No. 14,858); *State* v. *Boyd,* 2 Hill L. 288, 27 Am. Dec. 376 (motion denied where the indictment was found on the testimony of the wife of the accused); *People* v. *Sebring,* 66 Mich. 705, 33 N. W. 809; *State* v. *Fowler,* 52 Iowa, 103, 2 N. W. 983; *People* v. *Hulbut,* 4 Denio, 133, 47 Am. Dec. 244 (statutory rule); *United States* v. *Brown,* 1 Sawy. 531, Fed. Cas. No. 14,671 (holding that only objections appearing on face of the indictment can be considered, and that affidavits that the indictment was founded upon the testimony of the accused cannot be received); *Dockery* v. *State,* 35 Tex. Crim. Rep. 487, 34 S. W. 281. See also *State* v. *Shreve,* 137 Mo. 1, 38 S. W. 548, to the effect that an indictment will not be quashed merely because an incompetent witness testified before the grand jury, where sufficient competent evidence was introduced. As to the competency of evidence generally, before the grand jury, see cases reviewed in note to *Com.* v. *Hayden* (Mass.) 28 L. R. A. 318.

The rule in Mississippi is that no inquiry can be entertained the object of which is to show that the indictment was found without the examination of any sworn witnesses; and that grand jurors are not competent witnesses to show upon what evidence an indictment was found; but where, as in *Hammond* v. *State,* 74 Miss. 214, 24 So. 149, such testimony is received without objection on the part of the state, it will be considered.

In Montana the grand jury is directed by the statute to conduct its investigation by means of legal evidence, to the best of its knowledge and information, and to reject illegal evidence whenever it becomes aware of it; but the indictment will not be annulled because of its failure to reject such evidence. *Territory* v. *Pendry,* 9 Mont. 67, 22 Pac. 760. And the court also held that refusal to allow a member of the jury to answer a question as to whether he knew what was legal evidence was proper.

[a]*People* v. *Strong,* 1 Abb. Pr. N. S. 244; *United States* v. *Reed,* 2 Blatchf.

235, Fed. Cas. No. 16, 134 (to the effect that the court will never inquire into the sufficiency of the evidence before the grand jury); *Stewart* v. *State*, 24 Ind. 142; *Agee* v. *State*, 117 Ala. 169, 23 So. 486; *State* v. *Chandler*, 45 La. Ann. 49, 12 So. 315; *Kingsbury* v. *State*, 37 Tex. Crim. Rep. 259, 39 S. W. 365. But see *People* v. *Clark*, 8 N. Y. Crim. Rep. 169, 14 N. Y. Supp. 642, where it is held that courts will entertain motions to set aside indictments for causes not distinctly authorized by the provisions of the New York Criminal Code.

For a review of the cases generally, as to the sufficiency of evidence before the grand jury to sustain an indictment, see note to *State* v. *Peterson* (Minn.) 28 L. R. A. 324.

[4] *United States* v. *Edgerton*, 80 Fed. 374; *Boone* v. *People*, 148 Ill. 440, 36 N. E. 99; *State* v. *Froiseth*, 16 Minn. 296, Gil. 260 (indictment quashed although it does not even appear that the defendant was in custody); *People* v. *Singer*, 18 Abb. N. C. 96 (to the same effect although it appeared that the necessary caution had been given to the defendant).

But that persons indicted appeared before the grand jury, and were interrogated as witnesses at a time when they were imprisoned in jail under capiases from the recorder's court, is not ground for quashing the indictment, where they were informed that they had the right to decline to answer any questions tending to incriminate them or render them liable to a criminal prosecution. *State* v. *Donelon*, 45 La. Ann. 744, 12 So. 922.

And that a person, in the investigation of another charge by the grand jury, may have been required to give evidence which would have been material on the particular charge for which he was indicted, is not ground for setting aside the indictment on the ground that he was required to testify against himself, unless it appears from the indorsement or entry of his name on the indictment as a witness that the grand jury found the bill in whole or in part on his evidence. *State* v. *Hawks*, 56 Minn. 129, 57 N. W. 455.

In Texas the fact that the accused was taken before the grand jury and required to testify to facts criminative of himself is not ground for quashing the indictment. *Mencheca* v. *State* (Tex. Crim. App.) 28 S. W. 203; *Spearman* v. *State*, 34 Tex. Crim. Rep. 279, 30 S. W. 229.

[5] *Mackin* v. *People*, 115 Ill. 312, 56 Am. Rep. 167, 3 N. E. 222, holding that an indictment cannot be objected to because it is founded on testimony given voluntarily by the accused before the grand jury while in consideration of another matter. The indictment was for perjured testimony given before the grand jury. See more fully on this question, cases reviewed in note to *Com.* v. *Hayden* (Minn.) 28 L. R. A. 318.

5. Formalities.

In some jurisdictions an indictment may be quashed because of its failure to comply with legal requirements as to its caption, form, indorsement, etc., or with some special statutory formality.[1]

[1] In New York, under the Code of Criminal Procedure (§§ 268, 313), an in-

dictment may be set aside on motion if not indorsed a "true bill" and the indorsement signed by the foreman of the grand jury. But other objections to the formal indictment as prescribed by §§ 275, 276, must be taken by demurrer. See § 323. See also *ante*, Division XI.

But an objection that the indictment was not so indorsed comes too late after plea. *State* v. *Cross*, 44 W. Va. 315, 29 S. E. 527.

In *Walker* v. *State*, 7 Tex. App. 52, an indictment was quashed because of failure to comply with the statutory requirements as to form.

But an indictment should not be quashed on matters of form which are amendable under the statutes. *Com.* v. *Morningstar*, 144 Pa. 103, 22 Atl. 867.

So, failure to state in the caption of the information the name of the court in which it is to be filed is a mere formal defect, and impairs no substantial rights of the accused. *State* v. *Brennan*, 2 S. D. 384, 50 N. W. 625.

And interlineations or erasures in an indictment, apparently made before the grand jury acted thereon, present no cause for its quashal. *Jones* v. *State*, 99 Ga. 46, 25 S. E. 617.

And the mere omission to state the defendant's name in the title of the indictment, as required by statute, is not fatal where he is named in the body thereof, as this is not a defect tending to prejudice his rights upon the merits in order to bring it within the statutes to that effect. *Dukes* v. *State*, 11 Ind. 557, 71 Am. Dec. 370.

So, also, omission by the grand jury to write the names of the witnesses at the foot of the indictment, as required by statute, upon whose evidence the indictment was found, is no ground for quashing. *State* v. *Johnson*, 33 Ark. 174; *Com.* v. *Williams*, 5 Gratt. 702; *Shelton* v. *Com.* 89 Va. 450, 16 S. E. 355.

In California the Penal Code (§ 943) directs that the names of witnesses before the grand jury be indorsed on the indictment, and § 995 makes an omission thereof ground for setting the indictment aside. In *People* v. *Breen*, 130 Cal. 72, 62 Pac. 408, defendant moved to set aside his indictment because "Mrs. Susie O." was a witness on the trial, while the name of "Mrs. E. O." was indorsed on the indictment. One of the grand jurors testified that Mrs. Susie O. was a witness before the grand jury; the husband of Mrs. E. O. testified that defendant referred to witness's wife as "Susie;" and a letter from Mrs. E. O. was in evidence, signed "Susie O." But it was held that Mrs. Susie O. and Mrs. E. O. were sufficiently identified as the same person to warrant a denial of the motion.

6. Several defendants.

An indictment against two or more defendants may be quashed as to some, and not as to all,[1] unless the objection on which the motion is based is common to all of the defendants.[2]

[1] *State* v. *Compton*, 13 W. Va. 852; Wharton, Crim. Pl. & Pr. § 389.

But in *Bishop* v. *Com.* 22 Ky. L. Rep. 760, 58 S. W. 817, it was held that an appellant could not avail himself of an objection to an indictment made by his codefendant.

[a]*People* v. *Eckford,* 7 Cow. 535, holding that where an indictment is quashed because it does not sufficiently charge a conspiracy, upon the application of one of several defendants, it should stand quashed as to all without need of another motion.

Wharton, Crim. Pl. & Pr. § 389, says that in conspiracy there can be no severance, and if the indictment is quashed as to some, it must be as to all.

The granting of a motion to dismiss an indictment against one of two defendants jointly indicted, because the indictment was found by a grand jury to which the charge had been submitted without the direction of the court, after a previous dismissal by a former grand jury, is equivalent to a severance of the trial, where the other defendant does not move to dismiss, but pleads to the indictment; and the indictment is not thereby dismissed *ipso facto* as to him. *Sutton* v. *Com.* 97 Ky. 308, 30 S. W. 661.

7. One or more bad counts.

If one of several counts is good, the entire indictment will not be quashed because the others are defective.[1]

[1]*Bryant* v. *State,* 106 Ind. 549, 7 N. E. 217; *Com.* v. *Hawkins,* 3 Gray, 463; *Dukes* v. *State,* 11 Ind. 557, 71 Am. Dec. 370; *State* v. *Woodward,* 21 Mo. 265 (holding that it was not error to quash one or more bad counts and allow the others to remain); *King* v. *State,* 10 Tex. 281 (to same effect); *State* v. *Jones,* 10 Humph. 41 (to same effect); *State* v. *Rector,* 11 Mo. 28 (holding that it was error to quash an indictment that had one good count); *State* v. *Staker,* 3 Ind. 570 (to same effect); *People* v. *Dowling,* 84 N. Y. 478; *Com.* v. *Lapham,* 156 Mass. 480, 31 N. E. 638.

And a motion directed to an indictment or information as a whole will be denied unless applicable to each count thereof. *Blodgett* v. *State,* 50 Neb. 121, 69 N. W. 751.

8. Uncertainty.

An indictment may be quashed[1] because it fails to allege with reasonable certainty any material fact necessary to constitute the alleged crime; or because the facts as alleged do not constitute a crime.[2] In most of the states, however, many of the formal averments required by the English common law are dispensed with.[3]

[1]The question whether or not an indictment states facts constituting a public offense should be presented by a motion to quash or a motion in arrest, and cannot be raised by a motion for direction of a verdict of not guilty. *State* v. *Beach,* 147 Ind. 74, 36 L. R. A. 179, 46 N. E. 145; Reversing on rehearing 43 N. E. 949. Nor can it be raised by objection

to evidence after the jury has been sworn. *State* v. *Ashe*, 44 Kan. 84, 24 Pac. 72.

In *Rankin* v. *Jauman* (Idaho) 36 Pac. 502, the court said that in a case where the information fails to state a cause of action, by reason of the facts not being sufficiently set forth, a demurrer should be interposed; for if the demurrer be sustained the party may amend, if he so desires, and can. In a case where the information could not be so amended as to state a cause of action, or the court could, under no circumstances, have jurisdiction, a motion to dismiss might be entertained. But it was held also in this case, on a motion to set aside the information grounded on the legal insufficiency of an information presented under Idaho Rev. Stat. 1887, § 7459, providing for the removal from office of one guilty of charging and collecting illegal fees for services, that the objections are sufficient if they are intelligibly presented in writing, irrespective of the name which is given to them.

An objection on the ground that the offense charged in an information differs from that named in the complaint should be made by plea in abatement, instead of by motion to quash. *Whitner* v. *State*, 46 Neb. 144, 64 N. W. 704.

Nor is it ground for setting aside a criminal information that it charges the accused with a different crime from that for which he was held to answer before the committing magistrate. *State* v. *Myers*, 8 Wash. 177, 35 Pac. 580, 756.

The objection that an indictment for subornation of perjury is bad because it does not charge that defendant "corruptly" did the act set forth is not available on motion to quash, the defect being merely formal, and one which should be assigned specifically, under Mass. Pub. Stat. chap. 214, § 25. *Com.* v. *Lane*, 157 Mass. 462, 32 N. E. 655.

In Mississippi objections to an indictment for defects appearing on its face can only be taken under the Code, § 1354, by demurrer, and not by motion to quash. *Gates* v. *State*, 1 Miss. 874, 16 So. 342.

'*State* v. *Beard*, 25 N. J. L. 384 (indictment for perjury quashed because it did not appear that the statement on which the perjury was assigned was material); *State* v. *Robinson*, 29 N. H. 275 (indictment set aside for insufficiency to state a statutory crime); *People* v. *Eckford*, 7 Cow. 535 (indictment for conspiracy quashed because the means agreed upon, as alleged, did not appear to be criminal); *Braddy* v. *State*, 102 Ga. 568, 27 S. E. 670 (indictment defective for not naming the day or month on which the crime was committed); *State* v. *Roach*, 3 N. C. (2 Hayw.) 352, 2 Am. Dec. 626 (quashing indictment for not stating the day on which the offense was committed); *Murphy* v. *State*, 106 Ind. 96, 55 Am. Rep. 722, 5 N. E. 767 (where the indictment charged the offense on an impossible day); *United States* v. *Crittenden*, Hempst. 61 (where the time was stated as "on or about"); *People* v. *Williams*, 1 Idaho, 85 (where the time that the alleged offense was committed was before the time when the statute making it a crime was enacted).

A motion made after plea should be denied unless the insufficiency of the indictment was of such a nature that no judgment could be rendered on it. *United States* v. *Bartow*, 10 Fed. 874; *Com.* v. *Eastman*, 1 Cush. 189, 48 Am. Dec. 596.

Objections of this nature, under the New York Criminal Code, must be taken by demurrer or motion to arrest judgment. See §§ 323, 331, 364.

In *Larison* v. *State*, 49 N. J. L. 256, 60 Am. Rep. 606, 9 Atl. 700, it was held that where an indictment insufficiently charged a statutory offense, objections of this nature, under N. J. Rev. Stat. 277, § 53, must be taken by demurrer or motion to quash before the jury is sworn.

Dukes v. *State*, 11 Ind. 557, 71 Am. Dec. 370 (holding that an indictment charging murder need not describe the weapon or the wound inflicted with the particularity required by the common law); *State* v. *Dayton*, 23 N. J. L. 49, 53 Am. Dec. 270 (holding that it is immaterial at the present time whether an indictment charging a statutory offense concludes, "against form of the statute" or "statutes").

An indictment for murder which charges the killing of "T. H." *alias* "T. J." is not defective or void for duplicity or uncertainty. Omitting the word "dictus" is immaterial. *Kennedy* v. *People*, 39 N. Y. 245, 5 Abb. Pr. N. S. 147.

9. Duplicity.

An indictment may be quashed because it charges two distinct offenses.[1]

[1] *State* v. *Wilson*, 121 N. C. 650, 28 S. E. 416; Wharton, Crim. Pl. & Pr. 8th ed. § 243; *Knopf* v. *State*, 84 Ind. 316 (two offenses in one count, in information for maintaining a nuisance). But whether or not an indictment will be quashed for the reason that different felonies are charged in different counts is much in the discretion of the court; for the reasons (1) that it is often difficult to determine from an inspection of the indictment whether such distinct and different felonies are so charged; (2) the prosecution may inform the court in advance that but one offense is charged, and that it will ask a conviction for that one only; (3) the court may compel the prosecution to elect upon which count it will proceed; and (4) the court may compel the prosecution to elect after the evidence may have developed the fact that the felonies are distinct and such as cannot be found in one indictment. *Glover* v. *State*, 109 Ind. 391, 10 N. E. 282.

By N. Y. Code Crim. Proc. § 323, this objection must be raised by demurrer. See *ante*, Division XI.

Where an arrest is made on an affidavit containing sufficient allegations to constitute a charge under one section of an ordinance, and some words found in another section describing another and different offense, proceedings will not be quashed on the ground that separate and distinct offenses are charged; but all words not necessary to describe the offense first charged will be stricken out as surplusage. *Brown* v. *Toledo*, 5 Ohio S. & C. P. Dec. 210.

10. Want of jurisdiction.

An indictment may be quashed for want of jurisdiction of the trial court.[1]

[1]*State* v. *Benthall*, 82 N. C. 664, holding it not error so to quash, even after plea of not guilty.

The want of jurisdiction of the court under N. Y. Code Crim. Proc. §§ 323, 331, may be raised by demurrer, or at the trial, under plea of not guilty, or by motion in arrest. But this rule cannot require a court to proceed where it has no jurisdiction, merely because such statutory objection is not made.

And in *People* v. *More*, 68 Cal. 500, 9 Pac. 461, it was held that upon information for manslaughter the objection that the offense was committed beyond the jurisdiction of the court cannot be availed of by motion to set aside the information, but may be under a plea of not guilty. As to plea to jurisdiction, see *post*, Division XVIII.

And a motion to quash an information on the ground that the court has no jurisdiction to try defendant because of a failure to comply with the law in his arrest and preliminary examination is waived unless made before plea or trial. *State* v. *Collins* (Idaho) 38 Pac. 38; *State* v. *Clark* (Idaho) 35 Pac. 710.

But an information should be quashed where defendant files an affidavit alleging positively that he has never had a preliminary examination on the charge preferred in the information as required by the Idaho statute, unless the prosecution refutes such affidavit by producing the depositions taken on the preliminary examination, or other competent proof that such examination was had or waived by defendant. *State* v. *Farris* (Idaho) 51 Pac. 772.

And an information filed by the state's attorney against one whose preliminary examination has been conducted by a justice of the peace, after the filing in due time of a proper affidavit for a transfer of the action to another justice, in violation of N. D. Rev. Codes, § 7953, is irregular and voidable, and should, under § 8082, be set aside on defendant's motion. *State* v. *Weltner*, 7 N. D. 522, 75 N. W. 779.

11. Pendency of another suit.

"If there be at any time pending against the same defendant two indictments for the same offense, or two indictments for the same matter, although charged as different offenses, the indictment first found shall be deemed to be superseded by such second indictment, and shall be quashed."[1]

[1]2 N. Y. Rev. Stat. 727, title IV. art. 2, chap. 2, § 42, expressly retained in the repealing act of 1886, chaps. 593, 829.

12. Extrinsic facts.

Upon a motion to quash, the allegations in the indictment will be presumed to be true,[1] and cannot be contradicted by proof of extraneous facts,[2] except upon the consent of all parties.[3]

[1]*People* v. *Vail*, 6 Abb. N. C. 206, 57 How. Pr. 81.

[2]*Com.* v. *Church*, 1 Pa. St. 109, 44 Am. Dec. 112 (holding that although the quashing of an indictment is discretionary, yet the discretion is limited by rules, and that it is error to quash for extrinsic facts); *Broward* v. *State*, 9 Fla. 422 (holding as above against a motion to quash an indictment for trespassing on public lands, on showing that the state had no title).

[3]Wharton, Am. Crim. Law, 7th ed. 520, after admitting the general rule, in a note to that section, says, "By consent, however, extraneous matters may be brought in." This is cited and approved in *People* v. *Clews*, 57 How. Pr. 245, 249, holding upon motion to quash that *ex parte* affidavits could not be received to contradict or explain allegations in the indictment affecting the jurisdiction of the court, without the consent of the district attorney, as both parties have a right to insist upon common-law proof upon all the main and important facts in the indictment. The doctrine laid down in Bishop, Crim. Proc. § 763, that the court may, in its discretion, go outside of the indictment and record, and try the whole question on affidavits, is expressly disapproved in this case.

In *United States* v. *Brown*, 1 Sawy. 531, Fed. Cas. No. 14,671, where the accused, in support of a motion to quash, offered an affidavit to the effect that some of them were compelled to appear before the grand jury and testify, Deady, J., says: "Neither the motion to set aside nor the motion to quash will lie where the objection does not appear or arise upon the face of the indictment, or perhaps the records of the court. This being so, the affidavits of the defendants impugning the conduct and judgment of the grand jury cannot be considered upon the hearing of this motion. If the contrary practice were established there would be no need of grand juries, and the court would necessarily assume the function of both indicting and trying criminals; for it is safe to presume that in most cases the defendant would object to being tried upon the indictment, and support such objection by his affidavit that he believed the grand jury acted upon incompetent or insufficient evidence. The wit of man could not devise a mode of indicting which would not be liable to this objection from the defendant."

In *Dixon* v. *State*, 74 Miss. 271, 20 So. 839, it was held that the court might, in the absence of objections, hear affidavits on a motion to quash an indictment.

But in *Com.* v. *Hayden*, 163 Mass. 453, 28 L. R. A. 318, 40 N. E. 846, it was held that a motion to dismiss an indictment could not be based on facts not appearing on the record.

13. — how shown.

Upon a motion to quash, the facts relied on which do not appear on the face of the indictment or of the record of the court must, unless limited,[1] be supported by affidavit or by the testimony of competent witnesses;[2] and for such a purpose the grand juror may be examined as to the proceedings of the grand jury, the only limitation being that it may not be shown how an individual grand juror voted or what was said by the grand jurors during the investigation.[3]

[1]*United States* v. *Tallman*, 10 Blatchf. 21, Fed. Cas. No. 16,429, holds that it is competent for the court to dispose of a motion to quash an indictment, founded on an agreed statement of facts, at the solicitation of the counsel for all the parties.

[2]*United States* v. *Coolidge*, 2 Gall. 363, Fed. Cas. No. 14,858 (holding that facts not appearing of record must be supported by affidavit); *People* v. *Petrea*, 1 N. Y. Crim. Rep. 198 (holding that, it being a mere motion, the practice requires affidavit. The prisoner may not simply offer to prove the facts, and except to the rejection of the offer. Learned, P. J., Affirmed in 92 N. Y. 128, but this point is not considered. Compare opinion of Deady, J., in note to last section).

The state's attorney may testify to statements of a witness before the grand jury within his knowledge, if it would be proper for the grand juror to testify to the same, as, under the Florida statutes, it is his duty, when required by the grand jury, to examine witnesses in its presence, and to give it advice upon legal matters. *Jenkins* v. *State*, 35 Fla. 737, 18 So. 182.

But evidence *aliunde* the return of the justice to show that no other testimony than that in the complaint, which was made upon information and belief, was taken by him before issuing a warrant, is inadmissible upon a motion to quash an information made after the jury has been impaneled to try the cause. *People* v. *Whipple*, 108 Mich. 587, 66 N. W. 490.

An affidavit on a motion to quash an indictment, made as to the best of affiant's knowledge and belief, affords no evidence in support of the motion. *Smith* v. *State* (Miss.) 18 So. 116.

[3]*People* v. *Shattuck*, 6 Abb. N. C. 33; *United States* v. *Farrington*, 5 Fed. 343 (to same effect); *Ex parte Sontag*, 64 Cal. 525, 2 Pac. 405 (holding, in proceedings for contempt, that a grand juror cannot be asked how he voted, although he may testify whether twelve concurred in the indictment).

A member of a grand jury may be required, when public justice demands, to testify to any fact otherwise competent, the disclosure of which would not violate Fla. Rev. Stat. § 2813, providing that a grand juror shall not be permitted to state in what manner he or any other one voted, or what opinion was expressed by any juror in relation to a question. The provisions of § 2814, as to the cases in which a grand juror may be required to testify, are not exclusive. *Jenkins* v. *State*, 35 Fla. 737, 18 So. 182.

The affidavit of a grand juror may be received to show that the judge of the court, at his own instance, in violation of Iowa Code, § 4337, subd. 4, visited the grand jury while in session, and directed it to indict for a certain crime a party subsequently indicted for such crime, although § 4284 requires the grand jury to keep secret its proceedings and the testimony given before it. *State* v. *Will*, 97 Iowa, 58, 65 N. W. 1010.

14. Granting discretionary.

It is discretionary with the court to deny a motion to quash,[1] especially when made after plea; and the motion will be granted only if it clearly appears that no judgment could be rendered on the indictment.[2] The denial of the motion cannot be reviewed on appeal.[3]

[1]A motion to quash an indictment is addressed to the discretion of the trial court. *State* v. *Watson*, 20 R. I. 354, 39 Atl. 193.

[2]*United States* v. *Pond*, 2 Curt. C. C. 265, Fed. Cas. No. 16,067 (holding that a defect pleadable in abatement, and cured by pleading over, is no ground for quashing an indictment, as the motion must be based on such defects as would make the judgment erroneous); *Com.* v. *Hawkins*, 3 Gray, 463 (holding that an indictment should not be quashed unless the court can see that it is so defective that it would not support a verdict. Motion made after pleading); *United States* v. *Stowell*, 2 Curt. C. C. 153, Fed. Cas. No. 16,409 (holding that the court in its discretion would quash an indictment when all the counts failed to state any offense); *Respublica* v. *Cleaver*, 4 Yates, 69 (holding that it is entirely discretionary); *People* v. *Walters*, 5 Park. Crim. Rep. 661 (holding that the defendant was not entitled to prevail on the motion, no matter how defective the indictment might be. Motion made after pleading).

In *Rex.* v. *Crookes*, 3 Burr, 1841 (selling by false weights, A. D. 1766), the King's Bench declared that it was not obliged to quash an indictment for defective averments therein, and for allegations which did not bring the offense within the jurisdiction of the court.

In *Rex* v. *Sutton*, 4 Burr. 2116, it was held that the court, not being bound, would not quash an indictment for nuisance, but would leave the defendant to demur.

In *State* v. *Dayton*, 23 N. J. L. 49, 53 Am. Dec. 270, it was held that in all cases it is a matter of discretion to quash an indictment, and such discretion will be exercised only in cases entirely free from doubt. See also *Proctor* v. *State*, 55 N. J. L. 472, 26 Atl. 804, where it was held that the discretion of a court to quash an indictment on motion will not be exercised except upon the clearest and plainest ground; but defendant will be left to a demurrer, motion in arrest, or writ of error.

Under N. C. Code, § 1741, providing that all exceptions to grand jurors on account of their disqualifications shall be taken before the grand jury is sworn and impaneled, by motion to quash the indictment, the prisoner has the right to make such motion up to the time when he is arraigned and enters his plea; and it is within the sound discretion of the judge to allow the motion after the plea is entered and until the jury is sworn and impaneled. *State* v. *Gardner*, 104 N. C. 739, 10 S. E. 146. But to deny a motion made after the plea, but before the impaneling of the jury, on the ground that it was not in apt time, is error.

[a]*People* v. *Petrea,* 1 N. Y. Crim. Rep. 201 (holding that the refusal of the court to grant a motion to set aside an indictment as prescribed by N. Y. Code Crim. Proc. § 313, cannot be reviewed on appeal. Learned, P. J., Affirmed in 92 N. Y. 128, this point not being considered); *Wood* v. *People,* 1 Hun, 381, 3 Thomp. & C. 506 (holding that an exception to the denial of a motion to quash could not be availed of on appeal because such motion is addressed to the discretion of the court, and is not subject to exception. And the case was still stronger against the plaintiff in error, as the motion was made after plea of not guilty. Reversed in 59 N. Y. 117, on other grounds); *People* v. *Davis,* 56 N. Y. 95 (holding that the accused, not having a legal right to have the sufficiency of an indictment determined on a motion to quash, the denial of the motion was not a proper subject of exception. The motion was made after the jury was sworn). In other jurisdictions there are cases to the contrary.

15. Waiver by plea.

A pending motion to quash is waived by pleading to the merits.[1]

[1]*Long* v. *People,* 102 Ill. 331; *State* v. *Johnson,* 89 Iowa, 1, 56 N. W. 404; *Carpenter* v. *State,* 62 Ark. 286, 36 S. W. 900.

Failure to raise the objection of improper verification of the complaint before plea to the merits waives any rights the defendant may have to object either to the original verification of the complaint before the committing magistrate, or to the verification of the information in the trial court. *State* v. *McCaffery,* 16 Mont. 33, 40 Pac. 63, and cases cited.

And a motion to dismiss a complaint charging defendant with a crime is properly refused where he has previously pleaded "Not guilty" to the charge, although another defendant is joined in the complaint, and the crime is one that only one person could commit. *State* v. *Smith,* 62 Minn. 540, 64 N. W. 1022.

XV.—REMOVAL OF CAUSE.

1. From one state court to another.
2. — common-law right of prosecution.
3. — effect of statutes.
4. From one Federal court to another.
5. From a state to a Federal court; Federal question causes.
6. — denial of civil rights.
7. — Federal officers.
8. — time when.
9. — effect of removal.
10. — alienage.

1. From one state court to another.

Under statutes allowing removal from one state court to another[1] "for cause shown,"[2] such good cause exists, not only when the obtaining of a fair and impartial trial requires the removal, but also whenever the situation and official standing of the accused, the widespread and clearly divided line of popular opinion, and the circumstances of the alleged crime, as well as the important legal questions which it presents, so magnify the importance of the cause as to justify its removal from the inferior to the superior tribunal for trial.[3]

[1]In Alabama a statute (Pamphlet Acts 1874–5, p. 235) required the circuit court to transfer to the county court indictments for misdemeanors which were still pending and untried at the adjournment of the circuit court, and in express terms declared that the transfer must be ordered, and the papers, with a certified copy of all docket entries and minutes of proceedings had therein, delivered to the county court before the jurisdiction of the circuit court ceased. And where such a transfer had not been ordered, nor the papers and proceedings certified as required, a plea to the jurisdiction of the circuit court for that the indictment had been continued before the adjournment of the last preceding term of court, and was still pending and untried at such adjournment, and was hence such a case as should be transferred to the county court under this statute, was held bad on demurrer in *Green* v. *State*, 59 Ala. 68.

In *Ex parte State*, 115 Ala. 133, 22 So. 556, under an act of the general assembly, conferring upon the county court exclusive jurisdiction of all misdemeanors committed in the county, certain indictments then pending in the circuit court were, by order of that court, transferred to the county court, where they remained on docket, and were regularly continued for several terms. The supreme court subsequently declared the statute unconstitutional, whereupon the judge of the county court ordered the indictment retransferred to the circuit court for trial. The indictments had been transmitted from the docket of the circuit court while they were pending in the county court, and it was objected that this fact worked a discontinuance of the causes; but this was held error, and the court further held that, upon the refusal of the circuit court to docket and reinstate the indictment, mandamus would lie to compel the judge of that court to do so.

In Georgia a statute enacted in 1872 (Acts 1871–2, p. 298, § 22) provided that all misdemeanors pending in the superior court of a county at the time of the establishment of a county court for that county should be transferred for trial to such county court. A subsequent statute (Acts 1878–9, p. 132, § 11) provides for the manner of trial in the county court of "such indictments or presentments as may be transferred" thereto by the superior court. And in *Dismuke* v. *State*, 105 Ga. 589, 31 S. E. 561, it is held that while the statute last cited does not expressly confer upon the superior courts authority to transfer misdemeanors to the county courts for trial, yet the existence of that power is clearly recognized, and the law is to be construed as giving them authority to transfer, in their discretion, all misdemeanor causes, without reference to the court in which such causes originated. But the judges of the superior courts have no authority to grant orders in vacation transferring such causes.

In Illinois a statute (Starr & C. [Ill.] Stat. p. 1189, ¶ 238) provides that indictments found by the grand jury of the circuit court for offenses cognizable in the county court may, in the discretion of the circuit court, be certified to the county court for process and trial. The subsequent sections prescribe the form of certificate to be indorsed upon the back of the indictment by the clerk of the circuit court, and that such indorsement shall be a sufficient record to authorize the trial of the defendant in the county court. And in *Fanning* v. *People*, 10 Ill. App. 70, it was held that the circuit court has under this statute the discretion either to retain the indictment or to certify it to the county court for process and trial, and that the exercise of this discretion does not depend upon the consent or nonconsent of the defendant; but after the circuit court has retained jurisdiction of the cause, taken bail from the defendant, overruled his motion for change of venue, had him arraigned and a plea of not guilty entered, it cannot then certify the cause to the county court without his consent.

The charter of Detroit, Michigan, requires certain indictments returned to the circuit court, to be forthwith certified to the recorder's court, and gives that court complete jurisdiction as if they had been presented in that court, with full power to take all further proceedings thereon; but where an indictment is so certified, and upon arraignment the defendant desires to put in pleas in abatement, which cannot be disposed of in a recorder's court, mandamus will lie to compel the recall of the indictments to the circuit court from the recorder's court on refusal of the circuit court to order a return of the record, and of the recorder's court to certify it back. *Lauder* v. *Reilley*, 79 Mich. 602, 44 N. W. 961. The court said that, inasmuch as the only purpose of sending indictments to the recorder's court is for trial, the better practice would be to have the prisoner arraigned and issue joined on the merits before the record is certified down, but that where this is not done the record certainly cannot be regarded as beyond recall when justice requires it.

And in *People* v. *Hurst*, 41 Mich. 328, 1 N. W. 1027, it was held that there was no error in transferring an indictment for perjury presented to the circuit court of Wayne county to the recorder's court of the city of Detroit. The court said that it knew of no rule prohibiting the transfer of suits from one court of original, to another court of concurrent, jurisdiction, unless at such a stage as to involve a conflict.

In New Jersey a statute (1 Gen. Stat. p. 367) expressly provides for removal of criminal causes from courts of oyer and terminer and quarter sessions into the supreme court by writs of certiorari, upon the application of either the prosecution or the defendant; and where the application is made by the state, the reason for the allowance of the writ need not appear, but they will be presumed to exist; but in the case of an application by the defendant there must be special cause shown for granting the writ. *State* v. *New Jersey Jockey Club*, 52 N. J. L. 493, 19 Atl. 976; *State* v. *Zabriskie*, 43 N. J. L. 369. These cases also hold that under this statute the right of application is in the prosecutor of the pleas of the county in which the indictment has been returned, and not in the attorney general.

And failure of the record of a cause which has been transferred from the oyer and terminer to the court of quarter sessions, to show that the indictment was "ordered" by the former to be "delivered" to the latter court, or to show that it was "filed and entered" in the latter court as the statute directs,—is fatal. *Cruiser* v. *State*, 18 N. J. L. 206.

And the return of the judges of oyer and terminer to a writ of certiroari by the supreme court, removing the indictment from the former to the latter court, should certify the record itself; and a return to which is annexed by a wafer a paper supposed to be the original indictment, and nothing more is wholly insufficient. The individual indictment presented by the grand jury never comes up with the certiorari, but the record only, which contains the whole proceeding against defendant, to any part of which he may except. *State* v. *Gibbons*, 4 N. J. L. 40; *State* v. *Dayton*, 4 N. J. L. 57.

After an indictment has been removed by certiorari from the oyer and terminer to the supreme court, and then sent down to the circuit court, where the defendant has had a verdict, the state cannot be permitted to show by a certificate of the clerk of the oyer and terminer, or even by the production of the original indictment, that the return made by the oyer and terminer is untrue. *State* v. *Jones*, 11 N. J. L. 289.

In *Sailer* v. *State*, 16 N. J. L. 357, the defendant applied for certiorari to remove into the supreme court indictments found against him in the general quarter sessions, to which the state objected because the defendant had not appeared or pleaded to the indictment; and the court held that no step could be taken by the defendant until he submitted himself to the jurisdiction of the court.

In North Carolina a statute (1 Code 83, §§ 1241, 1242) provides that in those counties in which inferior courts may be established those courts and the superior courts shall alike have power to try all causes coming within the limited jurisdiction of the inferior courts, whether returned to one or the other court; and directs that whenever any case shall be left untried in either court, and the party accused shall be confined in jail, it shall be the duty of the clerk of the court in which it may be pending to transfer it to the next court, of either kind, that may be held in the county, and that the court to which it is so transferred shall proceed to try it as if it had there originated; and, further, it provides "that in such cases the handing over of the papers by the clerk of one court to the clerk of the other, where the cause is to be tried, and the docketing of the cause in the same, with the receipt of the latter on the docket of the former, shall be deemed a sufficient transfer of the cause from one court to the other." And in *State* v. *Mott*, 86 N. C. 621, it was held that the provision as to the entry of the receipt of the one to the other is merely directory. In this case the same person was clerk of both courts, and all the papers in the cause were transferred by him to the superior court without the entry of a formal receipt therefor from himself as the clerk of that court upon the docket of the inferior court, but only a minute in the words "transferred to the superior court."

It was also held in this case that the fact that the defendant's coindictees had given bail for their appearance at the next term of the inferior court did not make it error to transfer this particular defendant's cause to the superior court. "The statute is a remedial one," said the court, "partially, as we have seen, for the benefit of the accused, and is therefore to be liberally interpreted; and we can conceive of no good reason why one defendant, so circumstanced as to be within the mischief, should be deprived of its benefit merely because his codefendants were more fortunate than himself in being able to escape confinement."

When an inferior court having original jurisdiction of a case transfers it improperly for trial or hearing to a higher court which can take cognizance of it only on appeal, an order in the nature of a procedendo that the case be sent back to the lower tribunal for trial is the proper procedure. *State* v. *Sykes*, 104 N. C. 700, 10 S. E. 158.

In Texas a statute (Code Crim. Proc. art. 435) provides that upon the filing of an indictment in the district court of each county, charging an offense of which that court has no jurisdiction, the judge thereof shall make an order transferring the indictment to such inferior court as may have jurisdiction, stating in the order the cause transferred and to what court transferred. And by article 437 it is the duty of the district clerk without delay to deliver the indictment in all cases transferred, together with all the papers relating to each case, to the proper tribunal, as directed in the order of transfer, and to accompany each case with a certified copy of all the proceedings taken therein in the district court. Substantial compliance with the Texas statute is all that is required. *Brannon* v. *State*, 23 Tex. App. 428, 5 S. W. 132. For other cases involving the application of this statute, see *Johnson* v. *State*, 28 Tex. App. 562, 13 S. W. 1005; *Lynn* v. *State*, 28 Tex. App. 515, 13 S. W. 867; *Walker* v. *State*, 7 Tex. App. 52; *McDonald* v. *State*, 7 Tex. App. 113; *Gaston* v. *State*, 11 Tex. App. 143; *Thompson* v. *State*, 2 Tex. App. 82; *Hawkins* v. *State*, 17 Tex. App. 593, 50 Am. Rep. 129; *Hasley* v. *State*, 14 Tex. App. 217; *Hildreth* v. *State*, 19 Tex. App. 195; *Hernandez* v. *State*, 19 Tex. App. 408; *Estes* v. *State*, 33 Tex. Crim. Rep. 561, 28 S. W. 469; *Tellison* v. *State*, 35 Tex. Crim. Rep. 388, 33 S. W. 1082; *Malloy* v. *State*, 35 Tex. Crim. Rep. 389, 33 S. W. 1082; *Moore* v. *State*, 36 Tex. Crim. Rep. 88, 35 S. W. 668; *Austin* v. *State*, 38 Tex. Crim. Rep. 8, 40 S. W. 724; *Schwartz* v. *State*, 38 Tex. Crim. Rep. 26, 40 S. W. 976; *Koenig* v. *State*, 33 Tex. Crim. Rep. 367, 26 S. W. 835; *Friedlander* v. *State*, 7 Tex. App. 204; *Coker* v. *State*, 7 Tex. App. 83; *Brumley* v. *State*, 11 Tex. App. 114.

And article 438 requires all causes transferred from the district court to be entered on the docket of the court to which they are transferred; but this statute does not require the filing of the indictment itself in the latter court, although it is said that this would be the better practice. *Short* v. *State* (Tex. Crim. App.) 29 S. W. 1073.

The Texas statute gives no power to the district court to transfer a felony, and such a transfer, being a mere nullity, does not devest the district court of jurisdiction; and it is not necessary for the county court to make an order sending the case back to the district court. *Fossett* v. *State*, 11 Tex. App. 40.

It makes no difference whether or not the district court had adjourned when the order for the transfer was made, so long as the record shows that the indictment was returned into open court by the grand jury. *Williams* v. *State*, 37 Tex. Crim. Rep. 238, 39 S. W. 664.

In *Chaffin* v. *State* (Tex. Crim. App.) 24 S. W. 411, it was held that there is no authority in law to transfer a cause from the county to the district court because of prejudice on the part of the county judge.

Another Texas statute (Acts 1895, p. 181) authorizes the judges of two designated judicial districts, in their discretion, to transfer causes from one of the courts to the other, but does not require a copy of the orders of transfer to accompany the transfer. *Cummings* v. *State*, 37 Tex. Crim. Rep. 436, 35 S. W. 979.

In Virginia a statute (Va. Code, § 4016) provides that the county courts, except where otherwise provided, shall have exclusive original jurisdiction for the trial of all presentments, indictments, and informations for offenses committed within their respective counties, and also of all presentments, indictments, and informations then pending in said courts, except that a person to be tried for any felony for which he may be punished with death may, upon his arraignment in the county court, demand to be tried in the circuit court having jurisdiction over the county for which said county court is held. Upon such demand the accused must be remanded for trial in the said circuit court, and all the material witnesses desired for the prosecution or defense recognized for their attendance at such trial. And when a person is remanded as aforesaid by a county court, the clerk thereof must certify and transmit to the clerk of the court in which such person is to be tried a transcript of the record of the proceedings in said county court in relation to the prosecution, and copies of the indictment and recognizances, and other papers connected with the case. Such transcripts and copies are to be used with the same effect as the originals.

And in *Drier* v. *Com.* 89 Va. 529, 16 S. E. 672, it was held that the defendant, upon his arraignment in the county court, need not be informed, either by the clerk or the court, of his right under this statute to be tried in the circuit court.

And it is not fatal to a judgment of conviction that the transcript of the record of an indictment certified from the county court to the circuit court under the Virginia statute, on the defendant's election to be tried in the latter court, shows that no *venire facias* for the summoning of a grand jury was ever issued. *Watson* v. *Com.* 87 Va. 608, 13 S. E. 22.

But where the copy of the record of an indictment transferred from the county to the circuit court on the defendant's election to be tried in the latter court is entirely without the requisite certificate of the clerk of the county court, the circuit court acquires no jurisdiction to try the defendant. *Mitchell* v. *Com.* 89 Va. 826, 17 S. E. 480.

And after an indictment has been transferred from the county to the circuit court under the Virginia statute, the latter court has no power to remand the case to the county court for any purpose,—not even on the motion of the prisoner himself; and such an order of remandment is a nullity. If the county court fails to certify any part of the record, the duty of the circuit court is to have the record certified up as the law directs. *Nicholas* v. *Com.* 91 Va. 741, 21 S. E. 364.

In *Howell* v. *Com.* 86 Va. 817, 11 S. E. 238, the defendant, upon arraignment in the county court, elected to be tried in the circuit court. Subsequently he was produced before that court, but the cause and copies of the indictments and proceedings in the county court had not been certified; whereupon the defendant moved the court to remand him to the county court for trial, which motion the court allowed. On his subsequent production before the county court he objected to trial in that court because he had elected to be tried in the circuit court, and the record and proceedings had never been certified to the circuit court as required by law. It was held that after the defendant's election to be tried in the circuit court the jurisdiction of the county court ceased, and that if the cause was not properly before the circuit court the proper course was to cause the record to be certified as the law directed; and the conviction before the county court was accordingly set aside, and the cause remanded to the circuit court for trial.

'N. Y. Code Crim. Proc. § 344, provides that a criminal action presented by indictment may, at any time before trial, on the application of the defendant, for good cause shown, be removed from the county or city court in which it is pending to the supreme court held in the same county.

'*People* v. *Sessions*, 10 Abb. N. C. 192, Followed in *People* v. *Squire*, 4 N. Y. Crim. Rep. 444, 1 N. Y. S. R. 534. Compare *People* v. *Rourke*, 11 Abb. N. C. 89, where it is held, upon an application to remove an indictment to oyer and terminer of the same county, that where there are no difficult legal questions to be passed upon, or they have already been passed upon by the court, an application of this kind will not be granted simply because local feeling endangers a fair trial.

In the *Squires Case* it was urged for the People, as against the defendant's application to remove the indictment from the general sessions into the oyer and terminer, that the former court was of equal jurisdiction in the trial of criminal matters with the latter court, and that the judge likely to preside at the time at which the indictment, if remaining in the sessions, would be moved for trial, was one whose learning, integrity, and ability fitted him to preside over the most important trials; but that court, quoting from the *Sessions Case* said that, in deciding upon such an application, it is impossible that the court or judge to whom it is addressed should regard the personnel of the magistrate who is to preside in the lower court. The tribunal or court which the laws of the state make the superior one must, in the administration of justice, be so regarded.

The novelty and gravity of the question of law involved in the trial of or on the demurrer to an indictment may constitute good cause under § 344. *People* v. *Clark*, 15 N. Y. Supp. 79. This was an indictment for violating the car-heating act (Laws N. Y. 1887, chap. 616, as amended by Laws 1888, chap. 189; Laws 1889, chap. 76; and Laws 1890, chap. 421).

But the high character and political prominence of individuals are not such circumstances as alone constitute good cause for removing the indictment from the court of general sessions to the court of oyer and terminer, on the application of the defendant, under § 344, *Ibid.*

Nor is public clamor, as affecting the probability of the defendant's having a fair trial in the court of sessions, good cause under § 344. "The influence," said the court in this case, "which is supposed to operate against a defendant, could not affect the judges of the court of sessions any more than judges of any other court; and if it is to be regarded as relating to jurors only, it would certainly affect these in the court of oyer and terminer quite as much as those in the court of sessions, for they are drawn from the same box, and are selected from the same body of citizens."

2. — common-law right of prosecution.

At common law it has always been competent for the counsel for the state to remove criminal actions from the oyer and terminer to a higher tribunal by certiorari.[1]

[1]*People* v. *Baker*, 3 Abb. Pr. 42, 3 Park. Crim. Rep. 181 (holding the New York Revised Statutes not to have limited this common-law right of the people); 1 Chitty, Crim. Law, 377 (saying that the acts of Parliament regulating the practice in certiorari in criminal cases "apply only to writs of certiorari on the part of the defendants, and therefore the Crown and a private prosecutor may still obtain them without affidavit or recognizance, unless expressly prohibited by particular statute"). And see *State* v. *Zabriskie*, 43 N. J. L. 369, where it was said that the authority of the officer representing the state in the prosecution of its criminal laws, to remove at any time into the court which in the state is the representative of the King's Bench a record of a criminal cause, has been repeatedly recognized in this country.

3. — effect of statutes.

Statutes as to removal do not, in the absence of express provision, limit the common-law right of the state to have the cause removed on its application.[1]

[1]*People* v. *Baker*, 3 Abb. Pr. 42, 3 Park. Crim. Rep. 181.

In *Com.* v. *Balph*, 111 Pa. 365, 3 Atl. 220, it was held that Pa. Const. art. 5, § 3, fixing the jurisdiction of the supreme court of that state, did not repeal the act of June 16, 1836, or the act of March 31, 1860, conferring upon that court the power to remove criminal causes into that court by certiorari, although it did operate to prevent their trying indictments in the nisi prius, but each judge still has the power to sit and try indictments in any county in the state. "Authorities are abundant," said the court, "that the judges of this court, by virtue of their offices, may act as judges of the oyer and terminer in the several counties; but there is no authority that one or more judges of this court, when holding a court of oyer and terminer in a county, can remove a case to or from that county, which could not be so removed by the same court when held by one or more judges of the court of common pleas. The jurisdiction and powers of the court of oyer and terminer are defined by the laws. A judge of this court may go into the county of Warren and preside over the court of oyer and terminer, and while he is there holding said court the judges of the common pleas shall not act as judges of the oyer and terminer. Had the petitioners requested that some of the judges of this court should hold a court of oyer and terminer in the county of Warren, it might be considered whether their aspersions of the able and upright president judge of the court of quarter sessions are cause for granting their request. Then it might be inquired, What power has the court of oyer and terminer over a case pending in the quarter sessions, held by a judge of the common pleas, and which may be lawfully tried in the quarter sessions?" To the same effect is *Quay's Petition*, 189 Pa. 517, 42 Atl. 199. And see *Com.* v. *Delamater*, 145 Pa. 210, 22 Atl. 1098; *Com.* v. *Smith*, 185 Pa. 553, 40 Atl. 73.

4. From one Federal court to another.

A Federal statute provides that whenever the district attorney deems it necessary any circuit court may, by order entered on its minutes, remit any indictment pending therein to the next session of the district court of the same district, where the offense charged is cognizable by the district court. And, in like manner, any district court may remit to the next session of the circuit court of the same district any indictment pending in the district court.[1]

And another Federal statute provides that any district court may, by order entered on its minutes, remit any indictment pending therein to the next session of the circuit court for the same district, when, in the opinion of such district court, difficult and important questions of law are involved in the case.[2]

[1]U. S. Rev. Stat. § 1037. And see cases cited in note to *Jewett* v. *United States* (C. C. App. 1st C.) 53 L. R. A. 568.

The offense of selling spirituous liquors to an Indian in violation of an act of Congress, declared by act of Congress to be cognizable in the district courts, is, by virtue of the judiciary act of 1789, cognizable in the circuit court also, and an indictment may, under the above statute, be remitted by the district court to the circuit court. *United States* v. *Holliday*, 3 Wall. 407, 18 L. ed. 182. The indictment in this case originated in the district court, and was remitted to the circuit court, from which it was certified to the supreme court on the question whether the offense charged was one of which the circuit court had original jurisdiction; for of course, under the statute, if that court did not have such jurisdiction, the removal was improper; but the question was answered in favor of the circuit court's jurisdiction.

And the circuit court has jurisdiction of an indictment for assaulting and obstructing an enrolling officer, which, after remission to the district court on motion of the district attorney, has subsequently upon his motion been remitted back by the district court into the circuit court. *United States* v. *Murphy*, 3 Wall. 649, 18 L. ed. 217. The court said that it saw no reason, either in the nature of the transaction or in the language of the statute, why a cause so brought into the district court should not be sent back under the proper circumstances; that, as the order could only be made on motion of the district attorney, or whenever, in the opinion of the district court, difficult and important questions of law were involved, there was no danger of collision between the courts on account of such orders; and that, as they tended to the despatch of business and to sound decisions on legal propositions, there was no reason for limiting the rule further than the language of the statute required.

[3]U. S. Rev. Stat. § 1038.

But the fact that there are questions of law involved which are new, and have not yet been passed upon in the Federal courts, does not necessarily clothe them with the qualities of "difficult" and "important." *United States* v. *O'Sullivan*, 9 N. Y. Legal Obs. 193, Fed. Cas. No. 15,973. In this case it was held also that this statute does not contemplate, nor would a district judge be justified in, remitting a cause to the circuit court because in his charge to the grand jury he had given a particular exposition of the crimes act, when it was not made to appear that his exposition was in conflict with that of any other court.

5. From a state to a Federal court; Federal question causes.

One prosecuted in a state court for an alleged offense against state laws has the right, before trial, to remove the cause from the state court to a Federal court, if it appears that a Federal question will be involved in the trial.[1]

[1]*Tennessee* v. *Davis*, 100 U. S. 257, 265–271, 25 L. ed. 648, 651–653 (holding as above in a case removed to the circuit court under U. S. Rev. Stat. § 643), Followed in *Strauder* v. *West Virginia*, 100 U. S. 313, 25 L. ed. 664, holding to the same effect in a case removed under U. S. Rev. Stat. § 641. Compare with *State* v. *Ziebold* (Kan.) 8 Crim. L. Mag. 617, holding that where it has been decided by the United States Supreme Court that no Federal question exists, the cause will not be certified to an inferior Federal court by the state court.

In the exercise of this power U. S. Rev. Stat. § 641, provides that, "when any civil suit or criminal prosecution is commenced in any state court, for any cause whatsoever, against any person who is denied or cannot enforce in the judicial tribunals of the state, or in the part of the state where such suit or prosecution is pending, any right secured to him by any law providing for the equal civil rights of citizens of the United States, or against any officer, civil or military, or other person, for any arrest or imprisonment or other trespasses or wrongs, made or committed by virtue of or under color of authority derived from any law providing for equal rights as aforesaid, or for refusing to do any act on the ground that it would be inconsistent with such law,—such suit or prosecution may, upon the petition of such defendant filed in said state court, at any time before the trial or final hearing of the cause, stating the facts and verified by oath, be removed for trial into the next circuit court to be held in the district where it is pending." The remainder of the section makes provision for the removal of papers, and § 642 provides for the issue of a writ of *habeas corpus cum causa* for the delivery of an imprisoned defendant into the custody of the United States courts.

See also, in this connection, U. S. Rev. Stat §§ 1977 *et seq.*, to the effect that the civil rights of all citizens shall be the same as those enjoyed by white citizens.

U. S. Rev. Stat. § 643, provides in substance that when any civil suit or criminal prosecution is commenced in a state court, against any officer appointed under or acting by authority of any revenue law of the United States now or hereafter enacted, or against any person acting under color of his office or of any such law, or is commenced against any person holding property or estate by title derived from any such officer, and affects the validity of any such revenue law, or is commenced against any officer of the United States, or other person, on account of an act done under the provisions of title 26, *The Electric Franchise,* or on account of any right, title, or authority claimed by such officer or other person, under any of the said provisions, the said suit or prosecution may, at any time before the trial or final hearing thereof, be removed for trial into the circuit court next to be held in the district where the same is pending, upon petition of said defendant to said circuit court.

The practice:—A certified petition must be presented to the state court showing that a Federal question is involved. See 1 Abbott New Pr. & Forms, 741 *et seq.* Then a writ of certiorari is granted for the removal of the record in the state court to the Federal court; if it appears that no Federal question is involved, a motion to remand will be granted by the Federal court.

In *Ex parte Anderson,* 3 Woods, 124, Fed. Cas. No. 349, the petition was dismissed because it did not sufficiently show that a Federal question was involved.

In *Virginia* v. *Rives,* 100 U. S. 313, 316, *sub nom. Ex parte Virginia,* 25 L. ed. 667, 668, Strong, J., said: "If the petition filed in the state court before trial, and duly verified by the oath of the defendants, exhibited a sufficient ground for a removal of the prosecutions into the circuit court of the United States, they were in legal effect thus removed, and the writ of habeas corpus was properly issued." See, further, authorities reviewed in note to *Jewett* v. *United States* (C. C. App. 1st C.) 53 L. R. A. 568.

6. — denial of civil rights.

The Federal statute providing for the removal of causes against persons deprived of their civil rights, to the United States circuit court, authorizes the removal of the case only before the trial;[1] and it will not, therefore, embrace a case in which the right may be denied by judicial action during trial, or by discrimination against the accused in the sentence or in the mode of executing the sentence.[2] The statute has reference only to a legislative denial of the civil rights, because in such a case only can the defendant affirm on oath before trial that his rights are denied.[3]

[1]U. S. Rev. Stat. § 641 (above cited).

[2]*Virginia* v. *Rives,* 100 U. S. 313, 319, *sub nom. Ex parte Virginia,* 25 L. ed. 667, 669, holding as above.

[3]*Virginia* v. *Rives,* 100 U. S. 313, *sub nom. Ex parte Virginia,* 25 L. ed. 667 (holding, upon the trial of a colored person for murder, that a removal could not be had because, under the selection by the state officer, both the grand and petit jury would be composed entirely of white persons, no such discrimination having been directed by state statute); *Texas* v. *Gaines,* 2 Woods, 342, Fed. Cas. No. 13,847 (holding it not enough to show that there was so much prejudice against the accused by reason of his color that a fair trial would be endangered); *Strauder* v. *West Virginia,* 100 U. S. 303, 25 L. ed. 664 (holding an indictment against a colored man for murder to have been rightly removed to the Federal courts, because the state statute permitted only white men to serve on the jury). Compare with *Neal* v. *Delaware,* 103 U. S. 370, 26 L. ed. 567 (holding that the adoption of the 15th Amendment of the Federal Constitution rendered inoperative a provision in the then existing Constitution of a state, whereby suffrage was limited to the white race, and therefore a statute confining the selection of jurors to electors would be enlarged so as to embrace all those who would be entitled to vote by the state Constitution as modified, and would furnish no ground for removal of a cause under § 641, U. S. Rev. Stat. Otherwise if the state had enacted since the 14th Amendment a statute in conflict therewith, or its courts had refused to recognize its provisions as the supreme law of the land), Followed in *Bush* v. *Kentucky,* 107 U. S. 110, 116, 27 L. ed 354, 356, 1 Sup. Ct. Rep. 625 (holding no ground for removal to be furnished when the highest state court had itself declared the discriminating statute as to jurors to be unconstitutional). See, more fully, note to *Jewett* v. *United States* (C. C. App. 1st C.) 53 L. R. A. 568.

7. — Federal officers.

The Federal statute providing for the removal of causes against its officers[1] extends to United States marshals while engaged in enforcing the revenue law,[2] but not to a board of canvassers of votes at a presidential election, appointed under a state statute.[3]

[1]U. S. Rev. Stat. § 643 (above cited). And see cases reviewed in note to *Jewett* v. *United States* (C. C. App. 1st C.) 53 L. R. A. 568.

[a]*Davis* v. *South Carolina,* 107 U. S. 597, 27 L. ed. 574, 2 Sup. Ct. Rep. 636.

[a]*Ex parte Anderson,* 3 Woods, 124, Fed. Cas. No. 349.

In *Davis* v. *South Carolina,* 107 U. S. 597, 600, 27 L. ed. 574, 575, 2 Sup. Ct. Rep. 636, Matthews, J., said: "The prosecution against Davis was removed into the circuit court in strict compliance with the statute. His petition set out the necessary facts showing that the homicide which was charged against him as a crime took place while he was in discharge of his official duty; it was verified and certified as required by law." Petition given in full in this case.

In *State* v. *Fletcher,* 22 Fed. 776, a deputy marshal who had been indicted for murder and held for trial in a state court, in his petition for a removal of the case to the United States court, denied that he committed the murder, and averred that the indictment was found against him for acts done by him, if done at all, as a deputy marshal, while in the performance of his duties at an election to choose a representative to Congress; and it was held that the petition did not state facts entitling him to removal. The reason assigned by the court was: "Nothing short of a positive averment that they did the act for which they stand indicted, and did it in the line of their duty as deputy marshals of the United States, or under color of their authority as such officers, will entitle them to a removal of the case from the state court to this court for trial."

8. — time when.

The prosecution is not deemed commenced for the purpose of removal, within the meaning of the statute in reference to Federal officers, until the finding of the indictment.[1]

[1]*Virginia* v. *Paul,* 148 U. S. 107, 37 L. ed. 386, 13 Sup. Ct. Rep. 536; *Georgia* v. *O'Grady,* 3 Woods, 496, Fed. Cas. No. 5,352; *Com.* v. *Artman,* 5 Phila. 304.

9. — effect of removal.

All further proceedings of the state court, after the removal of the cause to the United States circuit court, under U. S. Rev. Stat. §§ 641, 643, are absolutely void.[1]

[1]*Virginia* v. *Rives,* 100 U. S. 313; *sub nom. Ex parte Virginia,* 25 L. ed. 667 (holding as above under § 643); *Davis* v. *South Carolina,* 107 U. S. 597, 27 L. ed. 574, 2 Sup. Ct. Rep. 636 (holding, subsequent to removal, an action upon the defendant's recognizance in the state court, for nonappearance, to be *coram non judice*); *State* v. *Dunlap,* 65 N. C. 491, 6 Am. Rep. 746 (holding that, where it appears by affidavit of the accused under the act of Congress of April 9, 1886, he cannot have a fair trial by reason of prejudice against his race, the state court will proceed no further until certified of the action of the circuit court of the United States). See, further, cases cited in note to *Jewett* v. *United States* (C. C. App. 1st C.) 53 L. R. A. 568.

10. — alienage.

A criminal case cannot be removed from a state to a Federal court under the act of November 3, 1875, on account of citizenship or alienage.[1]

[1]*New Hampshire* v. *Grand Trunk R. Co.* 3 Fed. 887.

XVI.—CHANGE OF VENUE.

1. The right at common law.
2. — under statutes.
3. Joint defendants.
4. Time to apply for.
5. For what causes.
6. Clear case necessary.
7. Counter affidavits.

1. The right at common law.

At common law[1] a criminal court of general jurisdiction has power, where a fair and impartial trial cannot be had, to change the venue to an adjoining county.[2]

[1]For constitutional restrictions and their proper interpretation, see *Watt* v. *People*, 126 Ill. 9, 1 L. R. A. 403, 18 N. E. 340; *State* v. *Myers*, 21 Ohio L. J. 57, and an article on right of trial by jury, in 5 Crim. L. Mag. 771, 780.

[2]Chitty, Crim. Law, 201 (King's Bench); *Price* v. *State*, 8 Gill, 295.

The reasonableness of the rule is supported by Mr. Justice Miller, in 21 Am. Law Rev. 867; *People* v. *Baker*, 3 Abb. Pr. 42, 3 Park. Crim. Rep. 181 (holding that ordinarily an adjoining county will be selected, if it seems to be demanded by necessity which requires a change).

As to appointing and compensating attorneys at the expense of the original county, see *State ex rel. Allen County Comrs.* v. *Miller*, 107 Ind. 39, 7 N. E. 758.

In New York it is common practice for the district attorney of the county where the indictment was found to try the case, with the assistance, if desired, of the district attorney of the county where the trial is had.

The remitting of indictments from the United States circuit to the United States district court, and conversely, is provided for by U. S. Rev. Stat. §§ 1037–1039. See note to *Jewett* v. *United States* (C. C. App. 1st C.) 53 L. R. A. 568, where the authorities are reviewed.

2. — under statutes.

In most states this question is regulated by statute,[1] and the granting of the change is matter of right if the application therefor conforms to all the requirements of the statute.[2]

[1]See, for example, N. Y. Code Crim. Proc. §§ 343, 353, regulating the practice in detail. Compare the codes and statutes of other states on this question.

The provision of the California Constitution, that "the right of trial by jury shall be secured to all and remain inviolate," confers upon a prisoner the common-law right to have the jury selected from the county where the offense is supposed to have been committed; and Cal. Pen. Code, § 1033, providing for a change of venue, without defendant's consent, on application of the district attorney, if no jury can be obtained in the county where the action is pending, is therefore unconstitutional. *People* v. *Powell*, 87 Cal. 348, 25 Pac. 481, S. C., with note, 11 L. R. A. 75.

This case also holds that an application by the district attorney for change of venue because a fair and impartial jury cannot be obtained, without showing that no jury can be obtained, does not make a case for change under § 1033, although the application would be sufficient if made by the defendant.

In Missouri the procedure for a change of venue in a criminal case, on the ground of prejudice, prescribed by act 1895, repealing Mo. Rev. Stat. 1889, § 4156, does not conflict with Mo. Const. 1875, art. 2, §§ 22, 23. *State* v. *Dyer*, 139 Mo. 199, 40 S. W. 768. The court said that the right to a change of venue was purely statutory, the Constitution nowhere guaranteeing such a right; and that it was entirely competent for the legislature, in permitting a change of venue, to prescribe the mode of procedure for obtaining such change.

[2]*Hussey* v. *State*, 87 Ala. 121, 6 So. 420. See also other cases in § 5, *infra*.

An agreement by the prosecuting attorney, the attorney for defendant, and the defendant, to change the venue back to the original county, waives the requirement of an application by defendant for that purpose; and defendant cannot complain of the change. *State* v. *Taylor*, 132 Mo. 282, 33 S. W. 1145. "The right to a change of venue," said the court, "being a privilege accorded to the defendant alone, and not to the state, no valid reason appears to us why he may not stipulate for such a change, or waive it if he sees fit. It involves in no sense a waiver of any constitutional right. But in this case the defendant was not waiving any right. He was simply obtaining a privilege by a more speedy route than that accorded him by the statute. The waiver was by the prosecuting attorney of the petition and supporting affidavits. A defendant in a criminal case, in a matter in which his constitutional rights are not invaded, can no more be allowed to deal unfairly with the court and the state than a party in a civil case. Having made his election, and the court having awarded him a change of venue at his own request, he cannot now complain of the privilege granted him."

In Texas no authority is given by the statute to change the venue in a misdemeanor case. *Henderson* v. *State* (Tex. Crim. App.) 39 S. W. 116; *Halsell* v. *State*, 29 Tex. App. 22, 18 S. W. 418; *Johnson* v. *State*, 31 Tex. Crim. Rep. 456, 20 S. W. 985 (criminal libel).

So, in Colorado the defendant in a contempt proceeding has no right to a change of venue, or to demand a hearing before another judge. *Bloom* v. *People*, 23 Colo. 416, 48 Pac. 519.

3. Joint defendants.

One of two defendants jointly indicted has a right to apply for a change of venue as to himself separately.[1]

[1]*Shular* v. *State*, 105 Ind. 289, 55 Am. Rep. 211, 4 N. E. 870, Citing *State* v. *Carothers*, 1 G. Greene, 464; *State* v. *Martin*, 24 N. C. (2 Ired. L.) 101; *State* v. *Wetherford*, 25 Mo. 439; *Hunter* v. *People*, 2 Ill. 453; *John* v. *State*, 2 Ala. 290; 1 Bishop, Crim. Law, § 75; Wharton, Crim. Pl. & Pr. 8th ed. 602; *Brown* v. *State*, 18 Ohio St. 496; and holding that the effect of granting the order is to sever the defenses, leaving the defendant who does not apply for a change to be tried by the court where the indictment was found, and carrying the trial of the other defendant to the court to which the cause was ordered after his application.

4. Time to apply for.

Before the jury is completely selected the venue may be changed.[1] The application is too late after the full panel is selected.[2]

[1]*Price* v. *State*, 8 Gill, 295 (application after ten had been sworn not too late).

Otherwise under N. Y. Code Crim. Proc. § 353, which requires a certified copy of order of removal to be filed before a juror is sworn.

In *State* v. *Adams*, 81 Iowa, 593, 47 N. W. 770, the application was filed when the cause was called for trial upon the eleventh day of the term of court. After a delay of twenty-four hours to allow the state to file counter affidavits, the defendant asked for further time to file additional affidavits, which was refused and his application denied; and it was held that, as the record disclosed no reason for the delay in making his application, the ruling of the court was correct.

In Mississippi the statute (Code 1892, § 1415) requires applications for change of venue in capital cases to be made before a special venire shall be drawn, unless upon some ground occurring after such drawing. But an application after the first venire has been quashed, but before the second has been issued, is not too late. *Purvis* v. *State*, 71 Miss. 706, 14 So. 268.

In Alabama the statute (Code 1886, § 4485) requires the application to be made as early as practicable before the trial, but it may be made after conviction, on a new trial being granted. But an application made when the cause is first called regularly for trial, more than a month after arraignment and two months after indictment, without any excuse for its not having been made earlier, is too late. *Byers* v. *State*, 105 Ala. 31, 16 So. 716.

[2]*People* v. *Cotta*, 49 Cal. 166.

5. For what causes.

A change of venue may be had upon the application either of the prosecution[1] or the defense,[2] on the ground that a fair and impartial trial cannot be had in the county where the indictment was found;[3] but not for convenience of witnesses.[4]

[1] *People* v. *Baker*, 3 Abb. Pr. 42, 3 Park. Crim. Rep. 181, holding, also, that if a large number of witnesses for the accused are too poor to bear the expense of a journey to another county, an application on behalf of the People will be granted only upon condition that the district attorney shall make arrangement for payment.

A change of venue in case an impartial trial cannot be had in the county where the crime was committed is not confined to the accused by Ky. Const. art. 13, § 12, giving the accused a right to a speedy public trial by an impartial jury of the vicinage; but, under art. 2, § 8, providing for a general law on the subject, a change may be had on the application of the commonwealth. *Com.* v. *Davidson*, 91 Ky. 162, 15 S. W. 53.

[3] N. Y. Code Crim. Proc. § 344.

[4] Under this note a few selected cases are set out, sufficient to illustrate and support the rule stated in the text.

Thus, the excitement or prejudice existing against one indicted for murder, which will require the allowance of his application for a change of venue, must be such that because of it he cannot receive a fair and impartial trial in the county in which the venue is laid. *State* v. *Foster*, 91 Iowa, 164, 59 N. W. 8.

And it is error to deny a change of venue in a prosecution for rape, where the trial was had within a short time after the alleged commission of the offense came to the knowledge of the public, and there was great prejudice against the defendant, as evidenced by determined attempts to lynch him. *Thompson* v. *State*, 117 Ala. 67, 23 So. 676.

But the fact that the crime with which the accused is charged was one against public property does not necessarily prejudice him, and is not of itself ground for a change of venue. *State* v. *Rogers*, 54 Kan. 683, 39 Pac. 219.

And the fact that a mob assembled, intent on hanging the prisoner, but was prevented by the sheriff, does not necessarily entitle him to a change of venue, where a large number of the most prominent citizens of the county make affidavit that there is not such prejudice against him as will justify a reasonable apprehension that he cannot be fairly and impartially tried in the county. *Jamison* v. *People*, 145 Ill. 357, 34 N. E. 486.

Nor is a defendant charged with murder entitled to a change of venue on the ground of prejudice against him in the county, simply because the sheriff, under an apprehension that he might be mobbed, called for troops, and the governor responded, and troops were at court when the trial occurred. *Harrison* v. *State* (Tex. Crim. App.) 43 S. W. 1002.

So, newspaper comment unfavorable to the defendant is not sufficient ground for changing the venue in a criminal case. *State* v. *Smarr*, 121 N. C. 669, 28 S. E. 549.

A remark made in private by a trial judge, that a witness who had testified before him in a larceny case "was a grand scoundrel," does not show such prejudice as to require a transfer of the case to another court, under N. C. Acts 1885, chap. 63, § 16. *State* v. *Johnson*, 104 N. C. 780, 10 S. E. 257.

An order changing the venue in a criminal case is not conclusive of prejudice upon a subsequent application for a change by the same person in another cause, since by the time of the latter action the prejudice may have passed away. *Blain* v. *State*, 34 Tex. Crim. Rep. 448, 31 S. W. 368.

One arrested upon a charge of felony, and taken before the St. Louis court of criminal correction for preliminary examination, may have a change of venue upon an affidavit of prejudice of the judge, under Mo. Rev. Stat. 1889, § 4174, providing for a change on such affidavit in any criminal prosecution pending in a circuit or criminal court, and Mo. Crim. Code, § 4303, making the provisions of the Criminal Code concerning circuit courts applicable to the St. Louis court. *Ex parte Bedard*, 106 Mo. 616, 17 S. W. 693.

But the venue of a criminal action will not be changed on a second trial, on the ground of prejudice of the presiding judge, merely because he formed an opinion as to the guilt of defendant on the first trial. *State* v. *La Grange*, 90 Iowa, 64, 62 N. W. 664.

In Texas prejudice of a trial judge is not a statutory ground for a change of venue of a prosecution for murder. *Gaines* v. *State*, 38 Tex. Crim. Rep. 202, 42 S. W. 385, Citing *People* v. *Mahoney*, 18 Cal. 185; *People* v. *Williams*, 24 Cal. 31; *McCauley* v. *Weller*, 12 Cal. 500.

Under the Wisconsin statute, another judge may be substituted for one alleged to be prejudiced against the accused, instead of awarding a change of venue. *State* v. *Hirth*, 67 Wis. 368, 30 N. W. 353.

But the death of a judge on account of whose alleged prejudice an order was made changing the place of trial, which was subsequently vacated because the change was to the wrong county, renders the affidavit of his prejudice inoperative; and where no other valid order is made changing the place of trial his successor has jurisdiction to try the case. *Winn* v. *State*, 82 Wis. 571, 52 N. W. 775.

[4] *People* v. *Harris*, 4 Denio, 150.

By the practice both in England and in this country, the place of trial will not be changed for the convenience of witnesses or parties, but only where it clearly appears a fair and impartial trial cannot be had.

6. Clear case necessary.

It must be shown affirmatively and clearly that a fair and impartial trial cannot be had in the county where the indictment is pending.[1]

[1] *People* v. *Baker*, 3 Abb. Pr. 42, 3 Park. Crim. Rep. 181 (application of dis-

trict attorney granted as fulfilling this test); *People* v. *Squire*, 4 N. Y. Crim. Rep. 444, 1 N. Y. S. R. 534 (application of defendant granted); *People* v. *Sharp*, 5 N. Y. Crim. Rep. 155 (holding it insufficient to show general newspaper denunciations although they may have been widely read; as a juror is not disqualified under the New York Code by reason of having read newspaper accounts, if he can declare he believes his verdict would not be influenced by it; and no evidence of any public expression having been offered to show that the newspapers had unduly affected public opinion, the motion should be denied); *State* v. *Hildreth*, 31 N. C. (9 Ired. L.) 429, 51 Am. Dec. 364 (holding that it is the province of the trial court to determine the sufficiency of the cause assigned, and its discretion cannot be reviewed on error); *State* v. *Perigo*, 70 Iowa, 657, 28 N. W. 452 (refusal not to be interfered with on appeal, unless abuse of discretion be shown; citing cases); *Findley* v. *State*, 5 Blackf. 576, 36 Am. Dec. 557 (holding that refusal cannot be reviewed on error under the Indiana statute [Rev. Stat. 1838, p. 603], leaving it to the discretion of the court), Followed in *Sumner* v. *State*, 5 Blackf. 579, 36 Am. Dec. 561. See also *Masterson* v. *State*, 144 Ind. 240, 43 N. E. 138 (holding likewise under Ind. Rev. Stat. 1894, § 1840); *State* v. *St. Clair* (Idaho) 53 Pac. 1 (holding it discretionary under Idaho Rev. Stat. § 7770, and that the application is properly denied when supported only by defendant's affidavit); *State* v. *Helm*, 92 Iowa, 540, 61 N. W. 246 (holding that it is not an abuse of discretion to refuse a change of venue of a prosecution for murder, on the ground of alleged excitement and prejudice, where the showing for the change is not strong, and is fully rebutted by the counter affidavits).

An affidavit for a change of venue must state the facts and circumstances from which the conclusion is deduced that a fair and impartial trial cannot be had. *Territory* v. *Egan*, 3 Dak. 119, 13 N. W. 568.

And a mere expression of opinion on an application for a change of venue, that one accused of crime can or cannot have a fair and impartial trial, is worthless as evidence, unless supported by sufficient reasons testified to as facts. *Salm* v. *State*, 89 Ala. 56, 8 So. 66; *Jackson* v. *State*, 104 Ala. 1, 16 So. 523.

But a petition for a change of venue on the ground that the inhabitants of the county are so prejudiced against defendant that he cannot obtain a fair trial, signed and sworn to by defendant and supported by the affidavit of two witnesses, is not insufficient as a mere conclusion. *Jackson* v. *State*, 54 Ark. 243, 15 S. W. 607.

The venue of a trial for murder will not be changed simply because a number of witnesses testify to some prejudice against defendant in the county. *Harrison* v. *State* (Tex. Crim. App.) 43 S. W. 1002.

The fact that a jury free from exception can be impaneled is not conclusive, on a motion for a change of venue, that prejudice does not exist endangering a fair trial, and does not justify the court in refusing to receive other evidence offered in support of such motion. *State* v. *Flaherty*, 42 W. Va. 240, 24 S. E. 885.

In Kentucky the trial court has no discretion to deny defendant's application for a change of venue in a criminal case, if his application makes a prima facie case therefor, and the commonwealth does not avail itself of the opportunity given it by Ky. act April 1, 1880, to combat the prima facie case. *Draughan* v. *Com.* 20 Ky. L. Rep. 102, 45 S. W. 367; *Higgins* v. *Com.* 94 Ky. 54, 21 S. W. 231. But a refusal to change the venue of a trial for homicide is not an abuse of discretion, where the deceased was a stranger in the county, without friends or acquaintances, and defendant is a member of an influential and well-known family. *Leslie* v. *Com.* 19 Ky. L. Rep. 201, 42 S. W. 1095.

So, in Missouri a change of venue should be granted to defendant in a criminal trial, if he makes out a prima facie case, unless the prosecuting attorney avails himself of his privilege to rebut it, under Mo. Rev. Stat. 1889, § 4156. *State* v. *Goddard*, 146 Mo. 177, 48 S. W. 82, Citing *Higgins* v. *Com.* 94 Ky. 54, 21 S. W. 231; *Draughan* v. *Com.* 20 Ky. L. Rep. 102, 45 S. W. 368; *Ex parte Chase*, 43 Ala. 303; *Birdsong* v. *State*, 47 Ala. 74; *People* v. *Yoakum*, 53 Cal. 566. But it is discretionary unless all the provisions of the statute are complied with to secure it as of strict right. *State* v. *Turlington*, 102 Mo. 642, 15 S. W. 141. A prima facie case for the change of venue of a criminal action, however, is not made, under this statute, by the mere presentation of an application for such change, supported by the affidavit of a credible witness. *State* v. *Tatlow*, 136 Mo. 678, 38 S. W. 552. Nor by the affidavit of defendant alone, instead of by the affidavit of two or more credible, disinterested citizens of the county. *State* v. *Lanahan*, 144 Mo. 31, 45 S. W. 1090.

The provisions of S. D. Laws 1891, chap. 50, for a change of venue in a criminal case, because of prejudice of the presiding judge, are mandatory. *State* v. *Henning*, 3 S. D. 492, 54 N. W. 536.

7. Counter affidavits.

The admission of counter affidavits offered by the prosecution on an application for a change of venue does not violate the constitutional provision providing that in all criminal prosecutions the accused shall have the right to be confronted by witnesses.[1]

[1] *Hussey* v. *State*, 87 Ala. 121, 6 So. 420. "The supposed constitutional objection," said the court, "cannot be sustained to such counter affidavits when offered by the state. It is only in 'criminal prosecutions' that the right of the accused to be confronted by his witnesses is secured. This has reference only to the trial proper,—or those proceedings which follow between the commencement of the trial and the verdict of acquittal or conviction. It manifestly has never been supposed to extend to the preliminary proceedings in the grand-jury room, upon which the indictment is founded, or other collateral proceedings. It is akin to the right to be heard by counsel, to demand the nature and cause of the accusation, to have compulsory process for witnesses, to be exempt from giving evidence against oneself, and to have a speedy trial by an impartial jury; which are guaranties enumerated in the same clause of the

Constitution, and must be interpreted by the principle of *noscitur a sociis.* Const. 1875, art. 1, § 7. All these are rights secured during the trial of the defendant,—not on the investigation of issues collateral or preliminary to his prosecution."

XVII.—BILL OF PARTICULARS.

1. In what cases ordered.
2. When.
3. Discretionary.
4. Form.

1. In what cases ordered.

If the charge against the accused is so general or indefinite that he cannot properly declare his defense, the court should order the prosecuting officer to give him a bill of particulars.[1]

[1]*Com.* v. *Snelling,* 15 Pick. 321 (leading case); *People* v. *Bellows,* 2 N. Y. Crim. Rep. 12, 1 How. Pr. N. S. 149; *People* v. *Jaehne,* 4 N. Y. Crim. Rep. 161 (*dictum*); Wharton, Crim. Pl. & Pr. § 702; Bishop, Crim. Proc. § 643; *Williams* v. *Com.* 10 Pittsb. L. J. 101; *Com.* v. *Giles,* 1 Gray, 466; *United States* v. *Bennett,* 16 Blatchf. 338, Fed. Cas. No. 14,571 (holding in effect as above, where the indictment for mailing an obscene book did not set forth the passage relied on; but holding that as a bill of particulars had not been demanded, the accused could not urge, in arrest of judgment, that he was not sufficiently informed of the charge); *State* v. *Wooley,* 59 Vt. 357, 10 Atl. 85 (upon charge of violation of the excise law, held that, in cases of this kind, the accused is entitled to a specification of offenses); *Thalheim* v. *State,* 38 Fla. 169, 20 So. 938. And see *United States* v. *Ross,* Morris (Iowa) 164 (false pretenses).

In *Hamilton* v. *People,* 24 Colo. 301, 51 Pac. 425, it was held that a defendant charged with a conspiracy to commit burglary should demand a bill of particulars of the premises proposed to be burglarized, where they are not given, if he desires to know such facts. Otherwise he cannot object that the indictment does not name the owners of the houses to be burglarized, or does not definitely locate the premises.

But one present with his counsel at the hearing before a justice of the peace, and who there heard the testimony upon which he was committed to answer for the crime charged in the indictment, cannot demand a bill of particulars on the ground that the indictment does not set forth specifically the crime charged or the manner in which it was committed. *Com.* v. *Eagan,* 190 Pa. 10, 42 Atl. 374.

And in *Com.* v. *Buccieri,* 153 Pa. 535, 570, 26 Atl. 228, 245, it was held that a conviction of murder under an indictment in the general form prescribed by Pa. Crim. Code, 1860, would not be reversed for refusal to direct the furnishing of a bill of particulars, where defendant had not been surprised by unexpected proof.

2. When.

Application for a bill of particulars must be made before the case is opened to the jury.[1]

[1] *Com.* v. *Snelling,* 15 Pick. 321.

3. Discretionary.

It is discretionary with the court to refuse to order a bill of particulars; and the refusal cannot be reviewed on error or appeal, except on the ground of an abuse of discretion.[1]

[1] *Com.* v. *Wood,* 4 Gray, 11; *People* v. *McKinney,* 10 Mich. 54 (here, however, the court intimated that there might be cases where the refusal to order a bill of particulars might amount to so gross an abuse of discretion as to require the courts to recognize it as a ground for error); *State* v. *Miller,* 3 N. J. L. 381; *Lauer* v. *District of Columbia,* 11 App. D. C. 453, and cases cited; *Thalheim* v. *State,* 38 Fla. 169, 20 So. 938. S. P. *Volkavitch* v. *Com.* (Pa.) 11 Cent. Rep. 179, 12 Atl. 84.

4. Form.

The bill of particulars need not be drawn with technical nicety; it is sufficient if it affords to the accused fair notice of the proof intended to be given to establish the general charge.[1]

[1] *Com.* v. *Davis,* 11 Pick. 432 (holding, on appeal from conviction, that a bill of particulars is no part of the record, and need not be drawn with technical nicety. It is simply a notice of the proof intended to be given to establish the general charge); *State* v. *Bacon,* 41 Vt. 526, 98 Am. Dec. 616 (holding that it is discretionary with the trial court to say how specific a bill of particulars shall be); *State* v. *Hill,* 13 R. I. 314 (refusal to require a stricter specification of the places where an alleged nuisance was committed held discretionary, and not subject to exception); *State* v. *Wooley,* 59 Vt. 357, 10 Atl. 85 (holding sufficiency a matter of discretion, and overruling objection that it referred to some witnesses as unknown. Ross, J., says: "The state's attorney, after specifying the witnesses summoned, added, 'and there are various other witnesses unknown to the state's attorney at present.' It is the general form of charging the offense prescribed by the statute which gives the right to a specification. If the form of the indictment required as specific a statement of the offense as is required by the common-law rules of criminal pleading, no further specification of the offense would be legally required. Hence the respondent is not legally entitled to a more minute detail of statement of the facts necessary to constitute the of-

fense in the indictment and specification, when taken together, than he would be entitled to in an indictment at common law. In an indictment at common law a good sale, furnishing, or giving away could be charged as made to a person unknown to the grand jurors, and for that reason not named. In legal effect, this is the charge in this respect, by the specifications furnished. There was no legal error in allowing offenses to be proved by or to such other unknown and, for that reason, unnamed witnesses"); *State* v. *Jules*, 85 Md. 305, 36 Atl. 1027 (holding that a bill of particulars of false pretenses, intended to be given in evidence, and of the names of the witnesses, contemplated by Md. Code, art. 27, § 288, in the prosecutions for obtaining money under false pretenses, is not required to be drawn with the strictest adherence to technical rules of pleading).

But a reference to a paper filed in another court of inferior jurisdiction, in which are stated the details of the offense for which defendant is indicted, is not a proper furnishing of a bill of particulars, but such bill should be furnished and filed in the case pending and in the court to which the application is made. *Thalheim* v. *State*, 38 Fla. 169, 20 So.. 938.

XVIII.—PLEAS TO THE INDICTMENT.

I. PLEA TO THE JURISDICTION.

1. When proper.

At common law, if the court has not jurisdiction of an offense of the class charged, the accused may plead to the jurisdiction without answering as to the crime;[1] and, if the question of jurisdiction be determined against him, may afterward plead to the offense.[2] The court has power, and it is its duty, to sustain a valid objection to jurisdiction, at whatever stage it is substantiated.

[1]Wharton, Crim. Pl. & Prac. § 422; 2 Hale, P. C. 256.

A plea to the jurisdiction of the court is too late after pleading not guilty. *State* v. *Watson*, 20 R. I. 354, 39 Atl. 193.

A plea to the jurisdiction is properly overruled where it does not in fact challenge the jurisdiction of the court, but sets out matter which is plainly matter of defense to be shown at the trial upon the merits. *Salina* v. *Cooper*, 45 Kan. 12, 25 Pac. 233.

[2]2 Hale, P. C. 256. A formal plea to the jurisdiction is not common, because the objection is always available even in arrest of judgment or on error; but there are cases in which the right of the accused to have the

question of jurisdiction determined before he is required to submit to a trial of issues raised on the indictment is important.

A defendant who appears and pleads to an indictment waives the objection that the case has been improperly transferred to the trial court. He should have pleaded to the jurisdiction. *Webb* v. *State* (Tex. Crim. App.) 58 S. W. 82.

And a defendant in a criminal prosecution who, without objecting to the manner of his arrest or of his being brought before the court, pleads to the indictment or complaint, thereby waives all objection that he is not properly before it for the purpose of being tried; and the court has jurisdiction of the person. *State ex rel. Brown* v. *Fitzgerald,* 51 Minn. 534, 53 N. W. 799.

2. Acts without the territorial jurisdiction.

The objection that the particular offense with which the accused is charged, although not denied to be one of a class of which the court may take cognizance, was committed beyond the territorial jurisdiction of the court, is to be tried under a plea of not guilty.[1]

[1]*State* v. *Mitchell,* 83 N. C. 674; *Fitch* v. *Com.* 92 Va. 824, 24 S. E. 272. When specially pleaded at common law this was not termed a plea to the jurisdiction, but a "foreign plea." See also *ante,* Division XIV. § 10; *post,* Division XXXIX. § 49.

A plea to the jurisdiction by one indicted for taking oysters without a license within the waters of Chesapeake bay and not within the waters of any county is properly overruled, where although it states that defendant was a citizen of, and the oysters were taken out of the waters of, a certain county where he had a license, yet the description therein of the locality and county lines, while showing that the oysters may have been taken in such county, does not clearly and distinctly establish that the place where they were taken was in fact in such county. *Taylor* v. *State,* 79 Md. 130, 28 Atl. 815.

II. Misnomer.

For the Statutory Substitution of True Name, see *ante,* Division VI.

3. Common-law rule as to misnomer, etc.

At common law misnomer,[1] want of addition, and wrong addition should be taken advantage of by plea in abatement,[2] at the time of arraignment.[3]

[1]Whether in given or surname. *Washington* v. *State,* 68 Ala. 85 (George Washington, instead of George Washington Holmes).

[2]*Smith* v. *State,* 8 Ohio, 294; *Gabe* v. *State,* 6 Ark. 519; *Adams* v. *State,* 67

Ala. 89; *Com.* v. *Lewis*, 1 Met. 151 (description of A. B. as wife of C. D.); *State* v. *Brunell*, 29 Wis. 435; *United States* v. *Howard*, 1 Sawy. 507, Fed. Cas. No. 15,402. Misnomer is matter of abatement only. 1 Throop's Dig. (Mass.) 726 (313), Citing also *Turns* v. *Com.* 6 Met. 224; *Com.* v. *Dedham*, 16 Mass. 141 (misnomer not ground of arrest of judgment); S. P. *State* v. *Knowlton*, 70 Me. 200. See also *Com.* v. *Butler*, 1 Allen, 4; *Com.* v. *Darcey*, 12 Allen, 539; *Com.* v. *Fredericks*, 119 Mass. 199. Such an objection will not be entertained for the first time on appeal. *State* v. *Branham*, 13 S. C. 389.

In Indiana, and perhaps elsewhere, motion to quash has been sustained on this ground. *Burton* v. *State*, 75 Ind. 477; *Gardner* v. *State*, 4 Ind. 632 (this was on a complaint, not indictment).

[3]*State* v. *Jackson*, 82 N. C. 565; *State* v. *M'Gregor*, 41 N. H. 407; *Wilcox* v. *State*, 31 Tex. 586. See Paschal's Dig. § 2937.

But a plea in abatement because of a misnomer is too late when first made at the third term after defendant's arraignment, and after he has pleaded to the indictment and had the cause continued. *Grimes* v. *State*, 105 Ala. 86, 17 So. 184.

So, in *Henry* v. *State*, 38 Tex. Crim. Rep. 306, 42 S. W. 559, it is held that a suggestion by defendant that the name under which he is indicted is not his true name, and that the prosecution proceed against him in his real name, is properly refused when first made after defendant has pleaded not guilty under the name contained in the indictment, under Tex. Code Crim. Proc. 1895, art. 548, authorizing a motion, on defendant's arraignment, that the prosecution proceed against defendant in his true name as alleged by him.

4. Waiver.

To omit it at that stage, or to plead over, waives the defect.[1] And a plea taking the objection is waived by a demurrer.[2]

[1]*Kelley* v. *State*, 25 Ark. 392; *State* v. *Brunell*, 29 Wis. 435; *State* v. *Duestoe*, 1 Bay, 377; *Smith* v. *State*, 8 Ohio, 294; *Morningstar* v. *State*, 52 Ala. 405; Wharton, Crim. Pl. (8th ed.) § 426; *People* v. *Smith*, 1 Park Crim. Rep. 329. But compare *United States* v. *De Quilfeldt*, 5 Fed. 276, holding that where a married woman is described as single, and fails to plead the wrong addition in abatement, she is not, nevertheless, concluded by a plea of not guilty, but may prove the fact on the trial; information for counterfeiting.

[2]*Haley* v. *State*, 63 Ala. 89.

Even though he was ignorant at the time of arraignment, provided he was sufficiently identified. *State* v. *Burns*, 8 Nev. 251 (Thomas L. Bryne indicted as Thomas L. Burns). This, under Nev. Laws 1861, §§ 270–272, p. 464, providing that defendant is to declare his true name on the arraignment, and, if he gives a different name, that shall be entered on the minutes and subsequent proceedings.

5. Requisites of plea.

A plea of misnomer must disclose the right true name of the accused,[1] and must also deny that he was known or called by the name stated in the indictment.[2]

[1] *State* v. *Hughes,* 1 Swan, 261; *Rex* v. *Checkets,* 6 Maule & S. 88; *United States* v. *Howard,* 1 Sawy. 507, Fed. Cas. No. 15,402; *Barnesciotta* v. *People,* 10 Hun, 137, Affirmed in 69 N. Y. 612.

[2] *Wren* v. *State,* 70 Ala. 1 (holding a plea thus defective to be bad on demurrer. Nor can such negation be implied from the affirmation that the accused was known and called by the name averred to be his true and correct name); *United States* v. *Janes,* 74 Fed. 543; *Ruffin* v. *State,* 124 Ala. 91, 27 So. 307; *Henderson* v. *State,* 95 Ga. 326, 22 S. E. 537.

6. Demurrer to plea.

The state may demur to a plea of misnomer.[1]

[1] *Barnesciotta* v. *People,* 10 Hun, 137, Affirmed in 69 N. Y. 612; *Rex* v. *Clark,* 1 Dowl. & R. 43; *Pace* v. *State,* 69 Ala. 231, 44 Am. Rep. 513; *Waldron* v. *State,* 41 Fla. 265, 26 So. 701.

7. — how tried.

The issue of *idem sonans,* when arising on demurrer to the plea, is to be determined by the court.[1]

[1] *State* v. *Haverly,* 21 Mo. 498; *Sayres* v. *State,* 30 Ala. 15 (holding that the issue is generally triable by the court); *Lynes* v. *State,* 5 Port. (Ala.) 236, 30 Am. Dec. 557 (reversing judgment for error in court below in sustaining demurrer to plea, the defendant, whose real name was George Lyons, having been indicted as George Lines).

8. Replication.

A replication averring that the defendant is known as well by one name as the other is a full answer to the plea of misnomer.[1]

[1] *Washington* v. *State,* 68 Ala. 85.

9. — pleading over.

If misnomer is pleaded in abatement to an indictment for a misdemeanor, and the issue is found against the defendant, he is not entitled to plead over as matter of right.[1]

[1] *Com.* v. *Carr,* 114 Mass. 280, 19 Am. Rep. 345, adding *dictum* that it is otherwise if the plea in abatement is demurred to and overruled as mat-

ter of law; the rule in cases of misdemeanor being the same as in civil actions.

As to pleading over, compare *ante*, Division XI.

10. Change of name pending indictment.

If defendant's name is changed pending indictment, it is not necessary to change it in the indictment.[1]

[1]*Com.* v. *Phillipsburg*, 10 Mass. 78.

III. Objections to grand jury.

11. In what cases interposed by plea.

It has been held in most of the states that where a party has not had an opportunity to object to the composition of a grand jury, he may by plea in abatement, if interposed seasonably,[1] set up objections to the panel,[2] or to the want of statutory[3] qualifications of a juror, which in their nature would constitute a challenge for principal cause,[4]—such as alienage, etc.,—as distinguished from a challenge to the favor[5] arising from bias, interest, and the like, or to the legality of its proceedings.[6]

[1]See also *ante*, Divisions IV., XIV.; *infra*, §§ 22–46; and cases in notes to *State ex rel Dunn* v. *Noyes* (Wis.) 27 L. R. A. 776, and *State* v. *Russell* (Iowa) 28 L. R. A. 195.

Where a defendant has challenged the array of a grand jury, alleging facts in support thereof, he cannot afterward plead the same facts in abatement.

McClary v. *State*, 75 Ind. 260, holding such a plea demurrable.

A party charged with a crime may, when the grand jury is impaneled, be placed under such circumstances as will excuse him from availing himself of his statutory right to challenge or object to the grand jurors before they are sworn, and for that reason be permitted thereafter to exercise it by a plea in abatement. *Hauk* v. *State*, 148 Ind. 238, 46 N. E. 127, 47 N. E. 465. In this case the defendant averred that he was in jail at the time the grand jury was in session and when they returned the indictment, but did not aver either that he attempted in any way to avail himself of his right to challenge, or that he was prevented by any circumstances from doing so at the proper time; and it was held that his plea was properly overruled.

In *Crawford* v. *State*, 112 Ala. 1, 21 So. 214, it was recognized that cases might arise in which the objection allowed by statute as the ground for a plea in abatement was not known until after the defendant had pleaded to the merits, but the defendant should ask leave to withdraw his plea in order to file his plea in abatement.

But a plea in abatement alleging irregularities in drawing grand jurors, filed two weeks after court convened and five days after the indictment was returned, is too late, where it does not allege any reason for the delay. *Agnew* v. *United States*, 165 U. S. 36, 41 L. ed. 624, 17 Sup. Ct. Rep. 235.

State v. *Flemming*, 66 Me. 142, 22 Am. Rep. 552 (holding that it is a godd plea in abatement that the indictment was found by a grand jury summoned by *venire facias* not bearing the seal of the court); *Henning* v. *State*, 106 Ind. 386, 55 Am. Rep. 756, 6 N. E. 803 (holding that errors or irregularities in the selecting or impaneling of a grand jury are properly taken advantage of by plea in abatement, if the indictment and record entries show that it was returned into open court); *Tervin* v. *State*, 37 Fla. 396, 20 So. 551 (holding that the remedy for such an irregularity in the drawing or impaneling of the grand jury as would render the indictment illegal is by plea in abatement, and not by motion to quash). See also cases in notes to *State ex rel. Dunn* v. *Noyes* (Wis.) 27 L. R. A. 776, and *State* v. *Russell* (Iowa) 28 L. R. A. 195.

For cases of objection that the grand jury was improperly summoned, see *Jones* v. *State*, 18 Fla. 889; *Jones* v. *State*, 18 Neb. 401, 25 N. W. 527; *Wilburn* v. *State*, 21 Ark. 198; *State* v. *Greenwood*, 5 Port. (Ala.) 474.

For cases of irregular drawing of grand jurors, see *State* v. *Hughes*, 1 Ala. 655; *United States* v. *Rondeau*, 4 Woods, 185; *Avirett* v. *State*, 76 Md. 510, 25 Atl. 676, 987; *Bohannan* v. *State*, 15 Neb. 209, 18 N. W. 129; S. P. *Wallace* v. *State*, 2 Lea, 29.

In *Sage* v. *State*, 127 Ind. 15, 26 N. E. 667, it was held that an error or irregularity in calling or impaneling grand jurors is not ground for a judgment in abatement, where qualified jurors are secured.

In Alabama the only objection allowed by statute to be interposed by a plea in abatement is that the jurors were not drawn in the presence of the officers designated by law. And mere clerical errors of the clerk of the court in transcribing the names of grand jurors regularly drawn and summoned are not available. *Germolgez* v. *State*, 99 Ala. 216, 13 So. 517. Nor is the supplying of grand jurors to fill the places of those who fail to appear, without first making an order discharging them. *Ibid.* Nor is the fact that the jury commissioner drew more than twenty-five names, and from those names selected the persons composing the grand jury, without regard to the order in which the names were drawn. *Linehan* v. *State*, 113 Ala. 70, 21 So. 497.

In *Crawford* v. *State*, 112 Ala. 1, 21 So. 214, it was held that an oral plea alleging irregularity in the drawing of the grand jury need not be entertained.

In some jurisdictions, however, it is the rule that objections to the members of a grand jury, or to the array, cannot be raised by plea in abatement, but must be raised by challenge before indictment or by motion to quash. *Stanley* v. *United States*, 1 Okla. 336, 33 Pac. 1025; *Gilmore* v. *People*, 87 Ill. App. 128; *State* v. *Freeze*, 30 Mo. App. 347; *Gibbs* v. *State*, 45 N. J. L. 379, 46 Am. Rep. 782 (holding that it makes no difference in the application of this rule that the facts alleged in the plea constitute a challenge for principal cause, and not for favor only; plea based on malicious misconduct of sheriff in selecting jury and malice of jurors). An exception in case of lack of statute qualification seems to be admitted.

[5]The right to prove that a grand juror lacked a positive qualification prescribed by statute—such as that a grand juror was not a freeholder—should be allowed under a statute which does not prescribe the manner in which advantage is to be taken of such a defect. *State* v. *Rockafellow*, 6 N. J. L. 332.

To the contrary in the case of an alien grand juror. *Boyington* v. *State*, 2 Port. (Ala.) 100.

A plea in abatement to an indictment, on the ground that the accused had no opportunity to challenge the grand jury, is insufficient on demurrer when it fails to allege the existence of any of the statutory grounds of challenge. *State* v. *Williamson*, 106 Mo. 162, 17 S. W. 172.

[6]*United States* v. *Hammond*, 2 Woods, 197, Fed. Cas. No. 15,294, held as above, where the plea was based on U. S. Rev. Stat. § 820, which provides in effect that participation in rebellion against the United States shall constitute a cause for disqualification and challenge to a grand or petit juror.

In *State* v. *Davis*, 12 R. I. 492, 34 Am. Rep. 704, the plea was sustained upon the ground that a grand juror did not have the necessary statutory qualifications as to property.

In *Reich* v. *State*, 53 Ga. 73, 21 Am. Rep. 265, the plea that a grand juror was an alien was held good.

In *United States* v. *Richardson*, 28 Fed. 61, it was held that the objection that two of the grand jurors were not drawn and summoned as prescribed by law could be pleaded in abatement, even though the defendant was under recognizance to await the action of the grand jury, and had an opportunity to interpose the objection by challenge. The plea in this case was adjudged bad for other causes.

In *Adams* v. *State*, 28 Fla. 511, 10 So. 106, it is held that it is not a good plea in abatement that two members of the grand jury that found an indictment were not registered within the time prescribed by the general election law, where they were registered within that prescribed by another statute providing for the election of delegates to the constitutional convention held in 1885.

In *People* v. *Lauder*, 82 Mich. 109, 46 N. W. 956, it is held that one indicted by the grand jury cannot complain that a member was an attorney, and was at the time acting as special assistant prosecuting attorney for the sole purpose of prosecuting a case for contempt against a third person. This case also holds that the fact that after the twenty original grand jurors impaneled and sworn had organized and begun their deliberations, another name was drawn and a new juror sworn who subsequently acted as a grand juror, is not ground for sustaining a plea in abatement to the indictment. How. (Mich.) Stat. §§ 9496, 9497.

In *State* v. *Sharp*, 110 N. C. 604, 14 S. E. 504, it is held that an indictment will not be quashed in North Carolina because a son of the prosecutor was a member of the grand jury, took part in the discussion, and favored the finding of the indictment.

A plea in abatement to the effect that a member of the grand jury that found an indictment was not a qualified juror at the time his name was selected and placed in the jury box by the county commissioners, but which does not allege that the juror was disqualified at the time he was impaneled or performed service as such,—is bad. *Shiver* v. *State*, 41 Fla. 630, 27 So. 36.

And in *State* v. *Rife*, 18 R. I. 596, 30 Atl. 467, it was held that a plea in abatement to an indictment for disqualification of a grand juror is insufficient, where it negatives the existence of one only of the alternative facts upon which the particular qualification rests.

In *State* v. *Rickey*, 10 N. J. L. 83, the rule is conceded to be otherwise than as stated in the text, of a challenge for principal cause for the want of a leading qualification prescribed by the statute.

And in *Boyington* v. *State*, 2 Port. (Ala.) 100, the prisoner, who was arraigned for murder, filed pleas in abatement on the ground that one grand juror was an alien and another had expressed an opinion on guilt; and it was held no error to strike out the pleas, because such objections must be taken by challenge to the poll.

In *People* v. *Jewett*, 6 Wend. 386, S. C., on motion to quash, 3 Wend. 314, there is *dictum* to the effect that the objection that a grand juror had not the requisite legal qualifications cannot be raised by plea, but that it must be taken by challenge. The qualifications on which the plea was based were not statutory. This case is distinguished on this point in *United States* v. *Hammond*, 2 Woods, 197, Fed. Cas. No. 15,294.

For cases of alienage, see *State* v. *Cole*, 17 Wis. 674; *Com.* v. *Cherry*, 2 Va. Cas. 20.

For disqualification of grand jurors, see *State* v. *Chairs*, 9 Baxt. 196; *Epperson* v. *State*, 5 Lea, 291; *Kitrol* v. *State*, 9 Fla. 9; *Wills* v. *State*, 69 Ind. 286; *State* v. *Smith*, 80 N. C. 410; *State* v. *Middleton*, 5 Port. (Ala.) 484; *Stanley* v. *State*, 16 Tex. 557.

As to the objection that another indictment is pending as ground for a plea in abatement, see *Hardin* v. *State*, 22 Ind. 347.

United States v. *Williams*, 1 Dill. 485, Fed. Cas. No. 16,716, held that a plea in abatement that certain grand jurors were disqualified by statute on account of bias was bad; and distinguished cases where the plea was based on statutory disqualifications which would constitute a challenge for principal cause.

In *United States* v. *Reeves*, 3 Woods, 199, Fed. Cas. No. 16,139, it is held in effect that where a statute makes objections to a grand juror a ground of challenge merely, and not an absolute disqualification, such an objection cannot be raised by a plea in abatement.

And in *State* v. *Hamlin*, 47 Conn. 95, 36 Am. Rep. 54, it is held that an objection to a grand juror on account of his expression of an opinion cannot be pleaded in abatement, and it seems that, if taken at all, it must be by challenge before the jury is sworn. An objection that less than twelve concurred in finding the indictment is not maintainable by plea, because such a fact cannot be inquired into by the court.

So, in *State* v. *Easter*, 30 Ohio St. 542, 27 Am. Rep. 478, it is held that the objection of disqualification of a grand juror—as of an alleged interest in the prosecution—cannot be raised by plea in abatement, but must be made before indictment found, or before the grand jury is sworn.

In *Musick* v. *People*, 40 Ill. 268, it is held that objections to grand jurors on the ground of expression of opinion must be taken before the grand jurors take the oath. To the same effect, *United States* v. *White*, 5 Cranch C. C. 457, Fed. Cas. No. 16,679.

In *State* v. *Swayze* (N. J.) 2 Crim. L. Mag. 361, defendant pleaded in abatement, (1) bias of grand jurors who had entertained and expressed opinions; (2) malice on part of sheriff who selected and summoned them, in selecting several who were sworn to be inimical to defendant; and it was held that while these objections might have been interposed by challenge to the favor before the grand jurors were sworn they could not be pleaded in abatement. A demurrer was sustained. (*Note.*—It does not appear at what precise state of the case these pleas were put in, but presumably they were upon arraignment).

Pointer v. *State*, 89 Ind. 255. And see cases reviewed in note to *Clair* v. *State* (Neb.) 28 L R. A. 367.

So, an indictment should be quashed where an attorney for the prosecution procured himself to be summoned as a witness before the grand jury, and urged the finding of the indictment. *Welch* v. *State*, 68 Miss. 341, 8 So. 673.

And an indictment found by a grand jury is void where the stenographer, by express order of court, was present while the witnesses were being examined, and took stenographic notes of the testimony, although he retired before the jury commenced their deliberations. *State* v. *Bowman*, 90 Me. 363, 38 Atl. 331, Distinguishing *State* v. *Clough*, 49 Me. 573.

But the mere presence of a stenographer, not a member of the grand jury, in the grand-jury room, and while a case is under consideration, and the taking of notes by her for the use of the prosecution, are not sufficient to abate an indictment, unless it appears that the defendant was injured in his substantial rights thereby. *State* v. *Bates*, 148 Ind. 610, 48 N. E. 2, and cases cited.

Nor will an indictment be abated because the state's attorney, with the consent of the court and of the grand jury, took his stenographer with him into the grand-jury room, for the purpose of taking down the full testimony of the witnesses, when she was not present when the grand jury was deliberating or voting, and it was not shown that the defendant was prejudiced thereby. *State* v. *Brewster*, 70 Vt. 341, 42 L. R. A. 444, 40 Atl. 1037, and cases cited.

Nor because the prosecuting attorney went into the grand-jury room, examined witnesses, and talked in the presence of the grand jury about the testimony of such witnesses, and thus, as alleged, unlawfully conspired against the defendant to procure the grand jury to find the indictment. *State* v. *Baker*, 33 W. Va. 319, 10 S. E. 639.

A plea that one who was not an officer of the court or a member of the grand jury was allowed to remain in the jury room during the deliberations of the grand jury is properly rejected where it does not allege that the person stated was not a witness sworn and sent to the grand jury by the court, but it is inferentially alleged that he was a witness, it being stated that he examined other witnesses. *Lawrence* v. *Com.* 86 Va. 573, 10 S. E. 840.

Improper language used by a judge in his charge to the grand jury, immediately so explained and qualified as to create no prejudice, is not ground for a plea in abatement to the indictment. *State* v. *Turlington*, 102 Mo. 642, 15 S. W. 141.

One indicted by a grand jury has no such personal interest in a compliance by the foreman with Fla. Rev. Stat. § 2809, requiring the latter to return the list of all witnesses sworn before the grand jury during the term, as will cause noncompliance to affect his rights under the indictment, or make it a ground for abatement of the prosecution, or furnish him with any ground of exception after conviction. *Hathaway* v. *State*, 32 Fla. 56, 13 So. 592.

For the authorities on the number of jurors necessary to form a grand jury, see note to *State* v. *Belvel* (Iowa) 27 L. R. A. 846. And for the number of grand jurors necessary to concur in finding an indictment, see note to *State* v. *Hartley* (Nev.) 28 L. R. A. 33.

12. Waiver.

By pleading to the merits, defects in the organization of the grand jury are waived,[1] subject to the discretionary power of the court to allow the plea to be withdrawn.[2]

[1] *Carpenter* v. *State*, 62 Ark. 286, 36 S. W. 900; *State* v. *Brown*, 2 Marv. (Del.) 380, 36 Atl. 458; *Deitz* v. *State*, 123 Ind. 85, 23 N. E. 1086; *State* v. *Kouhns*, 103 Iowa, 720, 73 N. W. 353; *Territory* v. *Armijo*, 7 N. M. 571, 37 Pac. 1117; *State* v. *Ostrander*, 18 Iowa, 435 (objections to the regularity of the organization of the grand jury must be taken before a plea of not guilty); *State* v. *Martin*, 82 N. C. 672 (denying motion to quash, made after pleading not guilty). And see cases in notes to *State* v. *Russell* (Iowa) 28 L. R. A. 195, and *State ex rel. Dunn* v. *Noyes* (Wis.) 27 L. R. A. 776.

In *People* v. *Griffin*, 2 Barb. 427, such defects were held waived when not objected to until after the People's case was closed. See also *Brantley* v. *State*, 13 Smedes & M. 468; *People* v. *Robinson*, 2 Park. Crim. Rep. 235 (objection to grand jury); *State* v. *Washington*, 33 La. Ann. 896; *State* v. *Clifton*, 73 Mo. 430 (after verdict); *State* v. *Wilkinson*, 76 Me. 317 (objection that the foreman of the grand jury did not return into court a list of witnesses sworn before the grand jury, too late after verdict); *State* v. *Hughes*, 1 Ala. 655 (murder; objection held too late on motion in arrest); *Territory* v. *Romero*, 2 N. M. 474 (alienage of grand juror); *Green* v. *State*, 59 Md. 123, 43 Am. Rep. 542 (grand juror over age); *Johnson* v. *State*, 7 Tex. App. 210 (failure to show that indictment was by grand jury of proper county, and by them returned into the proper court); *State* v. *Smallwood*, 68 Mo. 192 (objection that indictment did not show that grand jury was impaneled and sworn, too late after verdict); *State* v. *Washington*, 33 La. Ann. 896 (objection held too late on motion for new trial); *State* v. *Ruthven*, 58 Iowa, 121, 12 N. W. 235 (here it was held that a defendant who was in court personally or by attorney when his case was submitted to the grand jury waived his right to object subsequently by not objecting to the panel then).

[2]In *State* v. *Collyer*, 17 Nev. 275, 30 Pac. 891, after pleading not guilty, upon trial for assault with intent to kill, defendant requested leave to withdraw his plea, and moved to quash on account of irregularities in the selection of the grand jury; and it was held that by pleading defendant had waived his right to object to the selection or impaneling of the jury. In the exercise, however, of a sound discretion, the application may be granted if meritorious and made before the trial actually commences.

13. Evidence.

The incompetency, irrelevancy, and insufficiency of evidence produced before the grand jury are not proper grounds for a plea to the indictment.[1]

[1]*Hope* v. *People*, 83 N. Y. 418, 38 Am. Rep. 460 (conceding apparently that a question of competency might be raised by proper motion to quash); *State* v. *Dayton*, 23 N. J. L. 49, 53 Am. Dec. 270 (conceding, however, that a motion to quash may in some cases be discretionary). And see cases in notes to *Com.* v. *Hayden* (Mass.) 28 L. R. A. 318, and *State* v. *Peterson* (Minn.) 28 L. R. A. 324. Compare *ante*, Division XIV.

And a plea in abatement which merely alleges that certain persons whose names were on the back of the indictment, and who testified before the grand jury, were not required to take the prescribed oath, is insufficient, as it does not show that the indictment might not have been found on the evidence of other witnesses whose names were not indorsed on the indictment, to whom a lawful oath was administered. *Timberlake* v. *State*, 100 Ga. 66, 27 S. E. 158.

So, a plea in abatement alleging that the required oath was not administered to a specified witness on his examination by the grand jury is insufficient without an allegation that the indictment was found true solely on the testimony of such witness. *Lennard* v. *State*, 104 Ga. 546, 30 S. E. 780.

One subpœnaed before the grand jury to give evidence, who did not refuse to answer any interrogatory, or claim his privilege not to give evidence criminating himself, thereby waived his privilege, and cannot sustain a plea in abatement to the indictment found against him, on the ground that he was compelled to appear and testify. *People* v. *Lauder*, 82 Mich. 109, 46 N. W. 956. This case also holds that a plea in abatement to an indictment, alleging that defendant, being ignorant that the indictment and charge against him were pending, was subpœnaed and appeared before the grand jury, and while under legal restraint was compelled to take his oath, and, without having the aid and advice of counsel, was compelled to and did testify to facts material and necessary to prove the truth of the charge against him and to sustain the indictment as a true bill; and that upon his testimony and that of certain other witnesses the indictment was found,—is bad for uncertainty and insufficiency.

14. Requisites of plea.

A plea in abatement, being regarded as a "dilatory" plea, is required to be accurate and precise, free from ambiguity, and certain to every point.[1]

And by rule of court in some jurisdictions it is required to be verified when consisting of matters of fact not apparent on the face of the record.[2]

[1] *Knight* v. *State* (Fla.) 28 So. 759; *Reeves* v. *State*, 29 Fla. 527, 10 So. 901; *Tervin* v. *State*, 37 Fla. 396, 20 So. 551; *Shepherd* v. *State*, 36 Fla. 374, 18 So. 773; *People* v. *Lauder*, 82 Mich. 109, 46 N. W. 956, and cases cited; *State* v. *Rife*, 18 R. I. 596, 30 Atl. 467.

It must not only answer fully what is necessary to be answered, but it must also anticipate and exclude all such supposable matters as would, if alleged on the opposite side, defeat the same. *State* v. *Rife*, 18 R. I. 596, 30 Atl. 467, and cases cited.

And a plea in abatement of an indictment, stating that the drawing of grand jurors tended to the defendant's injury and prejudice, without stating any grounds for such conclusion, is fatally defective. *Agnew* v. *United States*, 165 U. S. 36, 41 L. ed. 624, 17 Sup. Ct. Rep. 235.

[2] *State* v. *Allen*, 91 Me. 258, 39 Atl. 994, holding such rule of court to be merely an affirmance of the common-law doctrine in this respect.

IV. Former jeopardy.

15. Former jeopardy.

The provisions of the Codes of several states as to pleas contemplate only a plea of guilty or not guilty, or of former conviction or acquittal of the offense charged; and provide that all other matters of fact tending to establish a defense may be given in evidence under a plea of not guilty. It would seem, therefore, that by such Codes the fact of former jeopardy, where there has been no conviction or acquittal, should not be pleaded, but should rather be given in evidence under a plea of not guilty, as a matter tending to establish a defense.[1]

[1] *People* v. *Cage*, 48 Cal. 323, 17 Am. Rep. 436, holding as above under Cal. Penal Code, §§ 1016, 1020.

N. Y. Code Crim. Proc. §§ 332, 339, make similar provisions to those above stated.

16. Jeopardy, when incurred.

Under the usual constitutional provisions that the accused shall not twice be put in jeopardy for the same offense,[1] it has generally been held that such jeopardy has been incurred, and avails as a plea in bar of a subsequent trial for the same offense,[2] if the accused was put on trial upon a valid indictment,[3] and the jury were sworn,[4] unless such jury, without having rendered a verdict, were discharged for good cause,[5] or with the defendant's consent.[6]

[1]See, for example, N. Y. Const. art. 1, § 6, which provides that "no person shall be subject to be twice put in jeopardy for the same offense." And compare other constitutional provisions on this question.

The provisions of the United States Constitution, 5th Amendment, on this question, do not bind the states. *Fox* v. *Ohio*, 5 How. 410, 12 L ed. 213 (*dictum*); *United States* v. *Keen*, 1 McLean, 429, 437, Fed. Cas. No. 15,510 (*dictum*); *Jackson ex dem. Wood* v. *Wood*, 2 Cow. 819; *Livingston* v. *New York*, 8 Wend. 85, 100, 22 Am. Dec. 622; *Barker* v. *People*, 3 Cow. 686, 15 Am. Rep. 322; *State* v. *Shirer*, 20 S. C. 392. *Contra*, *State* v. *Moor*, Walk. (Miss.) 134, 12 Am. Dec. 541. Other cases are cited in Bishop, Crim. Law Mag. § 981, note 3; and in article in 27 Am. L. Reg. N. S. 548; same article in 20 Ohio L. J. 347, 348.

The validity of a plea of former jeopardy for an offense committed before an amendment of the Constitution, interposed on a trial after such amendment, will be governed by the provisions of the amended Constitution, where it is in favor of the accused, and such amended Constitution declares that the provisions of all laws inconsistent with such Constitution shall cease upon its adoption. *State* v. *Richardson*, 47 S. C. 166, 35 L. R. A. 238, 25 S. E. 220. This case also holds that withdrawing a case from the jury and dismissing the jury, merely because a witness is absent, amount to an acquittal, and that the prisoner cannot again be placed on trial.

In *State* v. *Hager*, 61 Kan. 504, 48 L. R. A. 254, 59 Pac. 1080, it is held that a hearing on a plea of former jeopardy is not such a hearing on a plea going to the innocence of the accused as will constitute in itself ground for a plea of former jeopardy, in case, on appeal, the first of such pleas should be decided against accused.

A person is not twice put in jeopardy for the same offense, merely because under statutory authority a more severe sentence is imposed upon conviction of a second offense. *Moore* v. *Missouri*, 159 U. S. 673, 40 L. ed. 301, 16 Sup. Ct. Rep. 179. See further, on this question, authorities reviewed in notes to *Re Miller* (Mich.) 34 L. R. A. 399, and *State ex rel. Garvey* v. *Whitaker* (La.) 35 L. R. A. 579.

So, in *Chenowith* v. *Com.* 11 Ky. L. Rep. 561, 12 S. W. 585, it was held that a Kentucky statute (Gen. Stat. chap. 29, art. 1, § 12) providing that every person convicted a second time of felony shall be confined in the penitentiary not less than double the time of the first conviction, does not violate the constitutional provision that no one for the same offense shall be twice put in jeopardy.

And a person is not twice put in jeopardy because he is subjected to an action for a penalty, as well as to a criminal prosecution for the same offense. *State ex rel. Beedle* v. *Schoonover*, 135 Ind. 526, 21 L. R. A. 767, 35 N. E. 119.

So, in *Memphis* v. *Smythe*, 104 Tenn. 702, 58 S. W. 215, a prosecution for violating a health ordinance, the defendant was fined by the recorder's court, but on appeal to the circuit court the cause was dismissed. On appeal by the city the defendant moved to dismiss on the ground that, it being in the nature of a criminal proceeding, he had been once in jeopardy; but it was held that the motion was not well taken, as a warrant for a fine or penalty imposed for violation of a town ordinance is civil in character, and in the nature of an action of debt.

It is no bar to a criminal prosecution that defendant was arrested three several times for the same offense, and was brought before a justice and discharged at the instance of the prosecuting attorney, such arrest being prior to the examination, and no testimony being taken. *Jambor* v. *State*, 75 Wis. 664, 44 N. W. 963.

Nor is the dismissal by a police court of previous charges of the same offense a bar to further prosecution against the accused under Cal. Pen. Code, §§ 999, 1387. *Patterson* v. *Police Judge's Ct.* 123 Cal. 453, 56 Pac. 105.

But in *Brown* v. *State*, 105 Ala. 117, 16 So. 929, it was held that one charged in the affidavit upon which a warrant was issued by a justice of the peace, with the larceny of several distinct articles, each of which offense would constitute petit larceny, and bound over by the justice to await the action of the grand jury, without taking final jurisdiction of any of the offenses charged, might interpose the plea of former jeopardy before the justice as a defense to all of several indictments for petit larceny found by the grand jury. "It was beyond the power and jurisdiction of the justice," said the court, "after trial had, to merge the several petit larcenies to make one grand larceny out of them, as he attempted to do, and bind the defendant over for that offense; and it was equally beyond his power to bind the defendant over to the grand jury to answer for any one or more of the several distinct misdemeanors with which he was charged in said affidavit and warrant, and of which the justice had jurisdiction to finally try and punish him."

And the defense of former jeopardy will not be available to a prisoner bound over by the county judge, under the Georgia statute, upon his trial in the superior court for a felony, although at the time the county judge stopped the trial in the county court the evidence for both sides was in, and the counsel had begun their argument to the jury. *Cunningham* v. *State*, 80 Ga. 4, 5 S. E. 251.

But under the special provisions governing the criminal court of Atlanta, a party placed on trial is in legal jeopardy, and may avail himself of such defense in a subsequent prosecution in the superior court for the same act, although the former court, it appearing that the offense was beyond its jurisdiction, stopped the trial and bound the defendant over to the next term of the superior court, since such action was beyond its power. *Bell* v. *State*, 103 Ga. 397, 30 S. E. 294.

One accused of a crime cannot be deprived of the plea of former jeopardy by the court's withholding judgment in the former case. *Emmons* v. *State*, 34 Tex. Crim. Rep. 98, 29 S. W. 474, 475.

•In *Parchman* v. *State*, 2 Tex. App. 228, 28 Am. Rep. 435, after the jury had been sworn on the trial of an indictment for theft, a *nolle prosequi* was entered at the instance of the district attorney, for misnomer of the owner of the property. But it was held, upon another indictment containing the true name of the owner, that the former trial could not be pleaded in bar, it not being the same offense. See authorities on same point cited under *infra*, §§ 23 *et seq.*

In *Hilands* v. *Com.* 114 Pa. 372, 6 Atl. 267, the court overruled the plea of former jeopardy to an indictment for involuntary manslaughter, when former indictment was for felonious homicide, the two offenses not being the same. See cases cited under *post*, Division XXVII.

By N. Y. Pen. Code, § 35, the jury may convict of the crime charged, or any lower degree; former jeopardy, therefore, could be pleaded to a second indictment charging a lower degree of the same crime as charged in a former trial. *Ibid.* § 36. See *infra*, § 27.

But a person who has been put in legal jeopardy of a conviction of an offense which is a necessary element in, and constitutes an essential part of, another offense, may plead such jeopardy as a bar to a subsequent prosecution for the latter offense, if founded upon the same act. *Bell* v. *State*, 103 Ga. 397, 30 S. E. 294.

•One is not put in jeopardy under a complaint which is dismissed on his own motion as insufficient, whether in fact it is sufficient or not, and such dismissal is not a bar to a prosecution for the same offense under another complaint. *Von Rueden* v. *State*, 96 Wis. 671, 71 N. W. 1048, Citing *People* v. *Casborus*, 13 Johns. 351; *Shepherd* v. *People*, 25 N. Y. 420; *Com.* v. *Gould*, 12 Gray, 173. See also *State* v. *Hays*, 78 Mo. 600; *State* v. *Smith*, 88 Iowa, 178, 55 N. W. 198; and *Pritchett* v. *State*, 2 Sneed, 285, 62 Am. Dec. 468, so hoding where the indictments had been quashed upon the former trial as insufficient upon motion of the defendants, and the jury discharged.

So, allowing an informal amendment on a motion to quash an indictment after the parties have announced ready, and a jury has been impaneled and sworn, and the indictment read, and defendant called upon to enter his plea, but before he has entered it, does not place him in jeopardy so as to prevent another trial. *Yerger* v. *State* (Tex. Crim. App.) 41 S. W. 621, Citing *Link* v. *State*, 3 Heisk. 252; *United States* v. *Riley*, 5 Blatchf. 204, Fed. Cas. No. 16,164.

And in *Brown* v. *State*, 109 Ga. 570, 34 S. E. 1031, it was held that the accused could not set up former jeopardy upon an accusation which was quashed on a demurrer filed by himself, though the judge, at the time the demurrer was submitted, overruled it, and allowed the case to proceed to the extent of introducing testimony, but afterwards recalled his original ruling, and adjudged that the demurrer was good and the accusation insufficient in law.

Nor can former jeopardy be pleaded where the dismissal was for variance between the indictment and the proof, when under no circumstances could a conviction have been sustained under the first indictment. *Williams* v. *State*, 42 Ark. 35.

And in *State* v. *Reiff*, 14 Wash. 664, 45 Pac. 318, it was held that the discharge by the court of defendant in an information for obtaining property by false impersonation, because of a variance between the proof and the information, was not a bar to a subsequent information, under 2 Hill's (Wash.) Pen. Code, § 234, based on the same transaction, charging him with obtaining the property under false pretenses.

Nor is one put in legal jeopardy by being placed on trial under an indictment which, during the trial, is discovered to be defective, and the prosecution permitted to dismiss the indictment. *Jackson* v. *State*, 37 Tex. Crim. Rep. 128, 38 S. W. 1002. Compare *Lee* v. *State*, 26 Ark. 260, 7 Am. Rep. 611, where it is held that jeopardy was incurred when, during the pendency of a former trial for the same offense, the indictment was quashed upon insufficient grounds at the suggestion of the district attorney; and *State* v. *Crutch*, Houst. Crim. Rep. (Del.) 204, where a *nolle prosequi* was entered after the jury were sworn, upon discovering the defect in the indictment. See also *Walton* v. *State*, 3 Sneed, 687.

And this is true whether the indictment at the trial was set aside at the prosecuting attorney's instance or *nolle prosequied*, as the legal effect on another case is the same. *State ex rel. Graves* v. *Primm*, 61 Mo. 166. See, on same point, authorities cited under *infra*, §§ 23 *et seq.*

In California a statute (Pen. Code, § 1008) provides that the allowance of a demurrer to an information or indictment is a bar to another prosecution for the same offense, unless the court, being of opinion that the objection on which the demurrer is allowed may be avoided by a new indictment or information, directs the case to be submitted to another grand jury, or directs a new information to be filed. Another statute (Pen. Code, § 1117) provides that if the jury is discharged because the facts as charged do not constitute an offense punishable by law, the court must order that the defendant, if in custody, be discharged, unless in its opinion a new indictment or information can be framed, upon which the defendant can be legally convicted, in which case it may direct the district attorney to file a new information, etc. And the district attorney may, under § 1117, without an order of court, file a new information against one who has been discharged because of a fatal defect in the first information. And § 1008 applies only when a demurrer to the new information has been interposed. *People* v. *Ammerman*, 118 Cal. 23, 50 Pac. 15. And in *Ex parte Williams*, 116 Cal. 512, 48 Pac. 499, it is held that a permissive order granting leave to the district attorney to file a new information is not equivalent to the mandatory order contemplated by § 1008.

State v. *Burket*, 2 Mill. Const. 155, 12 Am. Dec. 662, holding that if, after swearing part of the jury, it is found that the remainder cannot be procured, the prisoner is not so put on his trial as to be entitled to his discharge, because jeopardy is not incurred or the prisoner put on his trial unless he is before a court competent in every respect to try the offense with which he is charged. See cases in next note.

In *State* v. *Briggs*, 27 S. C. 80, 2 S. E. 854, it was held that an adjournment because the whole panel of jurors was exhausted without obtaining a jury was not a bar to a subsequent trial.

The discharge of the jury by the court in a criminal trial, upon its failure to agree, does not constitute a legal bar to a future trial. *Anderson* v. *State*, 86 Md. 479, 38 Atl. 937, and cases cited; *Com.* v. *Cody*, 165 Mass. 133, 42 N. E. 575; *People* v. *Schoeneth*, 44 Mich. 489, 7 N. W. 70; *United States* v. *Percz*, 9 Wheat. 579, with note to 6 L. ed. U. S. 165. See also cases reviewed in notes to *Re Lange*, 21 L. ed. U. S. 872, and *Com.* v. *Fitzpatrick* (Pa.) 1 L. R. A. 451.

And in *People* v. *Reagle*, 60 Barb. 527, discharge for misconduct of the jury in separating was held not to support a plea of jeopardy.

In *People* v. *Green*, 13 Wend. 55, it was held that discharging the jury for disagreement was wholly within the discretion of the trial court, and that it could not be pleaded in bar to a subsequent indictment for the same offense. To the same effect, *State* v. *Blackman*, 35 La. Ann. 483.

And a mistrial of an action against one indicted for arson, the jury disagreeing, and the subsequent return of a new indictment, either because the former was lost or erroneously stated the name of the owner of the destroyed property, do not sustain a plea of former jeopardy interposed upon a subsequent trial. *Thompson* v. *Com.* 15 Ky. L. Rep. 838, 25 S. W. 1059.

The discharge of a jury after one day's deliberation, because the court was satisfied that agreement was impossible, is not a bar to another trial, under the Colorado Constitution, which provides that "if the jury disagree, . . . the accused shall not be deemed to have been in jeopardy." *Re Allison*, 13 Colo. 525, 10 L. R. A. 790, 22 Pac. 820.

But in *Hooper* v. *State* (Tex. Crim. App.) 42 S. W. 398, it was held that a trial of a criminal action in which the jury were dismissed on their failure to agree, after they had been out only two and a half or three hours, put defendant in jeopardy so as to prevent a subsequent trial for the same offense. In this case the record showed no adjudications of the reasons for the discharge.

In *Whitten* v. *State*, 61 Miss. 717, it was held that the unnecessary discharge of the jury after only three and a half hours' deliberation, in a murder case, sustained a plea of former jeopardy.

In California the statute authorizes the discharge of the jury after the cause has been submitted to them, upon "the expiration of such time as the court may deem proper," if "it satisfactorily appears that there is no reasonable probability that the jury can agree." Pen. Code, § 1140. And this statute was held constitutional in *People* v. *James*, 97 Cal. 400, 32 Pac. 317. To the same effect is the Oregon statute. *State* v. *Shaffer*, 23 Or. 555, 32 Pac. 545.

In *People* v. *Cage*, 48 Cal. 323, 17 Am. Rep. 436, it was held that the discretion of the court in this regard must be exercised on some kind of evidence; that the jury should announce their inability to agree in the presence of the court; and that where they are discharged upon the court's receiving a communication from the sheriff in answer to an inquiry of the jury by the sheriff, to the effect that they cannot agree, the defendant may set up former jeopardy upon a subsequent trial for the same offense.

But in *People* v. *Greene*, 100 Cal. 140, 34 Pac. 630, it was held that the reasons upon which the court deems it proper to discharge the jury are not required to be placed on record; it is sufficient that it shows the jury were unable to agree. The judge is not bound to take as final the statement of the jury that they cannot agree upon a verdict, but when such a statement is made, the court below, familiar with the nature of the evidence, and probably the temperaments of the men who compose the jury, is better qualified to say whether there is a reasonable probability of an agreement than the appellate court; certainly the latter ought not to interfere with the ruling except in cases of clear abuse of discretion. In this case the jury returned into court after having deliberated six hours, and stated to the judge that they were unable to agree, and it was held that the dismissal of the jury was not sufficient to sustain a plea of former jeopardy in a subsequent trial.

And the failure of a jury to agree, and their consequent discharge, avoid the plea, on a subsequent trial, of once in jeopardy, although they were instructed to return a verdict of "not guilty" because there was no evidence of defendant's guilt, and, upon their return into court after deliberation, the foreman stated that they did not want to render a verdict, and wished to be discharged, giving his reason. *People* v. *James*, 97 Cal. 400, 32 Pac. 317.

The rule is stated thus in *State* v. *Reinhart*, 26 Or. 466, 38 Pac. 822: "When the jury, after having deliberated upon their verdict such a length of time as the trial court may deem reasonable, shall make known in open court, in the presence of the defendant, their inability to agree, and the court, having in view all the circumstances surrounding the case, and being satisfied with such report, causes a finding to that effect to be entered in the journal, and thereupon discharges the jury, the apparent jeopardy, which the record shows attached when the jury were impaneled, is annulled, and the defendant may again be put on trial for the same offense; and in such case the findings of the trial court are not subject to review by this court, and cannot be questioned on a plea of former jeopardy." The statute in Oregon is the same as that in California.

In Kansas the record must show a statutory reason or a lawful necessity for such discharge. And in *State* v. *Allen*, 59 Kan. 758, 54 Pac. 1060, it was held that such reason or necessity was not shown by the record entry reciting that "the jury not having agreed upon a verdict in the above-entitled cause, the jury is discharged from further consideration of this case."

But a record reciting that the jury "were absent some time considering of their verdict," and, upon being returned to the jury box, the foreman, in reply to an inquiry by the court, stated, in the presence of the remainder of the jury, and without dissent by any of them, that there was no probability of their agreeing upon a verdict, and the court thereupon discharged them, "because they were unable to agree upon a verdict,"—was held in *State* v. *Hager*, 61 Kan. 504, 48 L. R. A. 254, 59 Pac. 1080, not to show an arbitrary or unreasonable exercise of the court's authority in discharging the jury, but, on the contrary, to show facts from which a presumption of a correct exercise of judicial authority arose, and that it would not support a plea of former jeopardy when the defendant was again put upon trial. "The tribunal primarily intrusted with the duty of determining whether a jury has been kept together until there is no probability of their agreeing," said the court in this case, "is the trial court. The questions whether they have been so kept together and whether there is a probability of their agreeing are judicial questions. As such they cannot be arbitrarily or capriciously determined by the court. The court must be satisfied that the jury in all probability cannot agree to a verdict, before it should order their discharge. However, when it does become of that conviction, and enters it of record, the correctness of its view and the soundness of its conclusions are not subject to review, unless the record of its action discloses it to be in error. Unless the record discloses hastily formed conclusions, immature judgment, or capricious conduct, the action of the trial judge cannot be reviewed by this or any other court."

But neither the district court of a county to which a criminal action has been transferred by change of venue from another county of the same district, nor the judge of the district at chambers, has power to vacate or amend the journal entry of a judgment or order of the court of the county from which the removal was made, so as to show a legal discharge of the jury at a former trial had in such county, and thereby defeat the defendant's plea of former jeopardy, based upon the record as it stood when the change of venue was made. *State* v. *Start* (Kan.) 61 Pac. 394.

In Virginia the statute says: "In any criminal case the court may discharge the jury when it appears that they cannot agree in a verdict, or that there is a manifest necessity for such discharge." And in *Jones* v. *Com.* 86 Va. 740, 10 S. E. 1004, the discharge of a jury by the court, on failure to agree after having deliberated four hours, was held not to bar the further trial of the prisoner.

The ending of the regular term of the court is not an extreme necessity which will justify discharging the jury in a capital case before they have agreed upon a verdict, when the court has power to extend the time. *Com.* v. *Fitzpatrick*, 121 Pa. 109, 15 Atl. 466, with note to 1 L. R. A. 451.

In Mississippi a statute (Code 1880, § 2292) provides that "when the trial or hearing of any case, civil or criminal, has been commenced, and is in progress in any court, and the time for the expiration of the term as prescribed by law shall arrive, the court may proceed with such trial or hearing, and bring it to a conclusion in the same manner and with the same effect as if the stated term had not expired." And in *Whitten* v.

State, 61 Miss. 717, it was held that this statute is mandatory, and that some other necessity than the expiration of the term must justify the discharge of the jury. To the same effect is *Helm* v. *State*, 66 Miss. 537, 6 So. 322. Prior to this statute the rule was otherwise. *State* v. *Moor*, Walk. (Miss.) 134, 12 Am. Dec. 541.

Illness of the judge or a juror may be good cause for discharging the jury. *Mixon* v. *State*, 55 Ala. 129, 28 Am. Rep. 695 (illness of juror); *State* v. *Tatman*, 59 Iowa, 471, 13 N. W. 632 (illness of judge's wife compelling him to adjourn court).

Thus in Nebraska a statute (Code Crim. Proc. § 485) provides that in case a jury is discharged on account of sickness of a juror or other accident or calamity requiring their discharge, the court shall, upon directing the discharge, order the reasons therefor to be entered upon the journal, and such discharge shall be without prejudice to the prosecution. And in *Davis* v. *State*, 51 Neb. 301, 70 N. W. 984, it was held that insanity of a juror is an accident or calamity within such a statute.

And in *State* v. *Nelson*, 19 R. I. 467, 33 L. R. A. 559, 34 Atl. 990, it is held that the discharge of the jury after a criminal trial has progressed several days, against the objection of defendant, upon information by telephone to some officer in attendance on the court that one of the jurors is sick and unable to proceed with the trial, without further proof of the fact,—is a bar to a second trial under R. I. Const. art. 1, § 7, providing that no person shall, "after acquittal," be tried for the same offense.

In *United States* v. *Watson*, 3 Ben. 1, Fed. Cas. No. 16,651, it is held that a further trial cannot be had on indictment where it appears that the jury have never been sworn for the trial of such indictment, but were discharged because of the illness of the district attorney and the absence of his witness, it not appearing by the minutes that the illness occurred after the jury were sworn or that the assistant district attorney could not conduct the trial.

But in *People* v. *Ross*, 85 Cal. 383, 24 Pac. 789, it was held that the commencement of the trial and the discharge of the jury on account of the sickness of one of the jurors do not constitute jeopardy, and that evidence of such proceeding is inadmissible to support a plea of former jeopardy in a subsequent trial for the same offense.

So, in *Ellis* v. *State*, 25 Fla. 702, 6 So. 768, it was held that the discharge of a jury in a case of manifest necessity—such as the sudden sickness of a juror, and the like—will not exempt the prisoner from again being tried for the same offense.

And a plea of former jeopardy is not sustained by the fact that the former trial was suspended for several days to permit the trial of another cause by another judge, and that at the conculsion of that cause the jury was discharged because of the illness of the judge. *State* v. *Ulrich*, 110 Mo. 350, 19 S. W. 656.

Nor will the withdrawal and discharge of a juror in a criminal case, who becomes too ill to discharge his duties during the progress of the trial, after which a new juror is impaneled and the trial commenced *de novo* as authorized by Shannon's (Tenn.) Code, § 5840, authorize a plea of former jeopardy. *De Berry* v. *State*, 99 Tenn. 207, 42 S. W. 31.

In *Com.* v. *McCormick*, 130 Mass. 61, 39 Am. Rep. 423, discharge because one of the jurors was discovered to be a surety upon a recognizance in the cause entered by one of the defendants before trial was held not to sustain the plea.

By the discharge of a jury from giving any verdict, whenever in the opinion of the court there is a manifest necessity for the act, or the ends of public justice would otherwise be defeated,—such as the fact that a juror is disqualified because he was a member of the grand jury which returned the indictment,—and a trial by another jury, the defendant is not twice put in jeopardy within the meaning of U. S. Const. 5th Amend. *Thompson* v. *United States*, 155 U. S. 271, 39 L. ed. 146, 15 Sup. Ct. Rep. 73. To the same effect is *Roberts* v. *State*, 72 Miss. 728, 18 So. 481.

Whitmore v. *State*, 43 Ark. 271, holds that jeopardy was incurred when the court, of its own motion, after the jury had been sworn, it appearing that one of their number had been on the grand jury which found the indictment, withdrew him and substituted another in his stead, the jury then being resworn. To the same effect see *O'Brian* v. *Com.* 9 Bush. 333, 15 Am. Rep. 715.

Mitchell v. *State*, 42 Ohio St. 383, holds that a discharge for variance, with a view to another prosecution, sustains the plea.

But it is not sufficient cause for discharge that the prosecution is not prepared to go on with the case after the jury is sworn. *Klock* v. *People*, 2 Park. Crim. Rep. 676, Following *People* v. *Barrett*, 2 Cai. 304, 2 Am. Dec. 239. And see *Pizano* v. *State*, 20 Tex. App. 139, 54 Am. Rep. 511, where a plea of former jeopardy was upheld, the jury on the former trial having been discharged because the prosecution did not have the witnesses in court.

In *United States* v. *Riley*, 5 Blatchf. 204, Fed. Cas. No. 16, 164, it was held that it could not be objected that the defendant was twice put in jeopardy, where a jury which had been impaneled and sworn by inadvertence before the prisoner had been arraigned and had pleaded was discharged by the court and a new jury directed to be impaneled in the regular order. To the same effect see *State* v. *Bronkol*, 5 N. D. 507, 67 N. W. 680.

A party is not entitled to an acquittal where he has been put in jeopardy, and by his own motion, or with his consent, the jury before whom he stood has been discharged. *People* v. *Gardner*, 62 Mich. 307, 29 N. W. 19.

And *People* v. *Higgins*, 59 Cal. 357, holds that a discharge because of defendant's own acts does not sustain the plea.

Hilands v. *Com.* 111 Pa. 1, 56 Am. Rep. 235, 2 Atl. 70, holds it error not to sustain a plea of former jeopardy, where a former jury upon a trial of the same indictment had been dismissed without consent of the defendant, because the court believed an irregularity had been committed by its permitting such jury after it had been sworn to separate over night with defendant's consent.

An illegal discharge of a jury on Sunday, in case of their disagreement, is a bar to a further prosecution for the same offense; and the defendant cannot waive the right of the public that a jury shall not be discharged on Sunday in case of a disagreement. *Ex parte Tice*, 32 Or. 179, 49 Pac. 1038, and cases cited.

The fact that the prosecuting attorney desires to enter a *nolle prosequi* after the jury is sworn, if the indictment is valid, is no ground for a discharge of the jury. *Reynolds* v. *State*, 3 Ga. 53. See also *State* v. *Elden*, 41 Me. 165; *McCauley* v. *State*, 26 Ala. 135.

But compare with *Reg.* v. *Davison*, 8 Cox C. C. 360 (in misdemeanor, discretionary, and not a bar; former indictment); *Conway* v. *Regina*, 7 Ir. L. Rep. 149, 1 Cox C. C. 210 (unnecessary discharge of jury operates as acquittal); *Grant* v. *People*, 4 Park. Crim. Rep. 527, Distinguished, but not questioned, in *People* v. *Dohring*, 59 N. Y. 380, 17 Am. Rep. 349; *People* v. *Goldstein*, 32 Cal. 432. See cases cited under § 17, *infra*. As to the power to discharge jury, see also *post*, Division XXXI. § 125. Some authorities say "absolute necessity," instead of "for good cause."

Com. v. *Sholes*, 13 Allen, 554; *United States* v. *Watson*, 3 Ben. 1, Fed. Cas. No. 16,651 (*dictum*, that the sufficiency of the reason for discharging the jury is immaterial if the defendant consented). And see *United States* v. *Morris*, 1 Curt. C. C. 23, Fed. Cas. No. 15,815.

A plea of former jeopardy is not maintainable where at the previous trial the defendant expressly agreed that the jury might be discharged on condition that the case should be continued. *Arcia* v. *State*, 28 Tex. App. 198, 12 S. W. 599.

In *Tervin* v. *State*, 37 Fla. 396, 20 So. 551, it was held that jeopardy does not attach so as to preclude a further trial of the defendant for the same offense, upon a felony trial, where the plea discloses that the jury were discharged, though without the consent of the defendant, after a separation for the night, which they had procured by representing to the sheriff that they had agreed upon a verdict, and sealed the same in compliance with the permission granted them by the court with the consent of the accused, the purported verdict being in fact to the effect that they agreed to disagree. The plea in this case did not allege that discharge was without necessity, but rested upon the absence of the defendant's consent to such disagreement; and the court held that the consent of the defendant was not necessary to the proper discharge of the jury, if such discharge became otherwise necessary.

But in *Wright* v. *State*, 35 Tex. Crim. Rep. 158, 32 S. W. 701, it was held that discharge of a jury without the consent of defendant, after they have been out from 4 o'clock P. M. to 10 o'clock the following morning, on their statement that there is no possibility of their agreeing, is a bar to a subsequent prosecution for the same offense, under Tex. Code Crim. Proc. art. 701, authorizing the court in its discretion to discharge the jury where they have been "kept together for such time as to render it altogether improbable" that they can agree.

So, erroneously discharging the jury, under Iowa Code, §§ 5389, 5390, on the mistaken supposition that the evidence showed that the crime was committed in another county, and committing the prisoner to await a warrant therefrom, amounts to an acquittal, and he cannot be tried again. *State* v. *Spayde,* 110 Iowa, 726, 80 N. W. 1058.

Quashing an indictment does not prevent prosecuting by information for the same offense. *United States* v. *Nagle,* 17 Blatchf. 258, Fed. Cas. No. 15,852; N. Y. Code Crim. Proc. § 320.

But discharge of a juror by court outside the courtroom, after the evidence for the state is complete and in the absence of defendant, on a mere statement by the sheriff that the juror's wife is very sick, is a bar to a subsequent prosecution of defendant. *Upchurch* v. *State,* 36 Tex. Crim. Rep. 624, 38 S. W. 206, with note in 44 L. R. A. 694, reviewing fully the authorities on the question of former jeopardy by reason of the discharge of the jury in the prisoner's absence.

17. Effect of nolle prosequi.

A former prosecution, though terminated by a *nolle prosequi*[1] entered against the prisoner's objection, whether with or without the consent of the court, bars a subsequent prosecution[2] for the same offense, unless the *nolle prosequi* was entered before the jury was sworn.[3]

[1]As to the power of *nolle prosequi,* see *post,* Division XXVII.

[2]*State* v. *M'Kee,* 1 Bail. L. 651, 21 Am. Dec. 499 (*nolle prosequi* after summing up before the jury by defendant's counsel, and after the jury had been charged by the court); *Boswell* v. *State,* 111 Ind. 47, 11 N. E. 788 (*nolle prosequi* after plea of guilty); *Huff* v. *Com.* 19 Ky. L. Rep. 1064, 42 S. W. 907 (dismissal after jury sworn and state's evidence given); *Com.* v. *Smith,* 149 Mass. 9, 20 N. E. 161 (where the court *nolle prosequied* the case after hearing evidence of government); *State* v. *Richardson,* 47 S. C. 166, 35 L. R. A. 238, 25 S. E. 220 (*dictum*); *State* v. *Stebbins,* 29 Conn. 463, 79 Am. Dec. 223 (*dictum*); *United States* v. *Shoemaker,* 2 McLean, 114, Fed. Cas. No. 16,279 (after witnesses were sworn); *Mount* v. *State,* 14 Ohio, 295, 45 Am. Dec. 542 (after conviction); *Jones* v. *State,* 55 Ga. 625 (after the case had gone to the jury); *Grogan* v. *State,* 44 Ala. 9; *Williams* v. *Com.* 78 Ky. 93; *Reynolds* v. *State,* 3 Ga. 53; *Com.* v. *Tuck,* 20 Pick. 356; *Mount* v. *State,* 14 Ohio, 295, 45 Am. Dec. 542; *State* v. *Champeau,* 52 Vt. 313, 36 Am. Rep. 754 (basing this conclusion on the long and undisputed practice in the county courts); *Franklin* v. *State,* 85 Ga. 570, 11 S. E. 876 (*nolle prosequi* after plea of not guilty and jury were sworn).

Compare *People* v. *Pline,* 61 Mich. 247, 28 N. W. 83, to the effect that a *nolle prosequi* entered after a disagreement of the jury and consequent discharge for good cause does not bar a subsequent prosecution for the same offense.

[3]As to the rule in conspiracy, see *State* v. *Jackson,* 7 S. C. N. S. 283, 24 Am. Rep. 476, holding that where, upon a charge of conspiracy to defraud against two, a *nolle prosequi* is entered against one before verdict, judg-

ment cannot be rendered against the other, as the *nolle prosequi* leaves the indictment charging the accused with conspiring by himself.

Dismissal by the prosecuting officer as to a count upon which the defendant was put upon trial, and thus placed in jeopardy, operates as an acquittal of that count. *State* v. *Patterson,* 116 Mo. 505, 22 S. W. 696.

But if the defendant does not claim a verdict, but waives his right to insist upon it, and the prosecuting officer by the advice of the court enters a *nolle prosequi,* or a discontinuance of the prosecution, a subsequent trial for the same offense is not barred. *State* v. *Garvey,* 42 Conn. 232.

And a criminal prosecution continued nisi, in which the defendant was never tried, is no bar to a second prosecution. *Com.* v. *Galligan,* 156 Mass. 270, 30 N. E. 1142. The court said that a continuance nisi amounts to a discontinuance; that this, however, is not equivalent to an acquittal; that the defendant was never put upon trial in that prosecution, and the discontinuance which was the result of the continuance nisi was no more a bar to the new complaint than an entry of *nolle prosequi* before the commencement of the trial would be; and cited *Com.* v. *Tuck,* 20 Pick. 356; *Com.* v. *Scott,* 121 Mass. 33.

In Oregon the statute provides that a criminal action, after indictment, can only be dismissed by the court, either on its own motion or on the application of the district attorney, and in furtherance of justice, and that the reason of the dismissal must be set forth in the journal; but such a dismissal is not a bar to another prosecution for the same offense, if the crime charged be a felony. Hill's Code, §§ 1527, 1528, 1529. And in *State* v. *Reinhart,* 26 Or. 466, 38 Pac. 822, it was held that the dismissal of an indictment for felony before jeopardy attaches is not a bar to another prosecution for the same offense, although the reason for the dismissal is not set forth in the journal as required by this statute.

In *People* v. *Ny Sam Chung,* 94 Cal. 304, 29 Pac. 642, the defendants were put upon trial upon a charge of petit larceny by a court of competent jurisdiction, and upon the conclusion of the evidence, the court, believing that the evidence proved grand larceny, refused to render judgment, but dismissed the action of its own motion. Subsequently the defendants were put on trial for grand larceny in another court having jurisdiction of that offense, where they pleaded the action of the former court as former jeopardy. On appeal it was held that jeopardy had attached to them long before the court dismissed the action, and it could not deprive them of any benefit to be derived from that jeopardy by refusing to allow the case to go to judgment, even though it was aware that by reason of an error of law committed during the progress of the trial, or by reason of insufficiency of the evidence to support the charge, a mistrial would be the necessary result; and that if the evidence in the case proved a petit larceny the court should have found the defendants guilty; if the proof was lacking to establish such offense, it should have found the defendants not guilty.

'*State* v. *Ingram,* 16 Kan. 14; *O'Brien* v. *State,* 91 Ala. 25, 8 So. 560; *Jackson* v. *State,* 76 Ga. 551; *Dye* v. *State,* 130 Ind. 87, 29 N. E. 771; *Dilger* v. *Com.* 88 Ky. 551, 11 S. W. 651 (*dictum*); *People* v. *Kuhn,* 67 Mich. 463,

35 N. W. 88; *Ex parte Donaldson*, 44 Mo. 149; *State* v. *Blackwell*, 9 Ala. 79; *State* v. *Hornsby*, 8 Rob. (La.) 583, 41 Am. Dec. 314 (holding that where a former conviction has been set aside and a new trial granted, and the district attorney has thereupon entered a *nolle prosequi*, the accused may be tried upon a new indictment charging the offense of which he was convicted).

That an indictment on which a change of venue has been taken is then *nolle prosequied* does not bar the prosecution of another indictment for the same offense. *State* v. *McLeod*, 136 Mo. 109, 37 S. W. 828.

An order entered at the instance of the commonwealth's attorney, before trial, that one indicted for malicious cutting would be tried for a misdemeanor only, instead of a felony, after which the case was dismissed and referred again to the grand jury, which again returned an indictment for malicious cutting,—does not prevent the trial court from trying and convicting the prisoner on that charge, although the order was never set aside. *King* v. *Com.* 15 Ky. L. Rep. 247, 22 S. W. 750.

But a plea of former jeopardy in a prosecution for assault and battery should be sustained where it is shown thereunder that *nolle prosequi* was entered over defendant's objections in a former prosecution for the same assault, under an information which did not give the true name of the person assaulted, but described him by a name by which he was commonly known. *Elehash* v. *State*, 35 Tex. Crim. Rep. 599, 34 S. W. 928.

18. — as to one of several counts.

A prosecution terminated by a *nolle prosequi* entered as to one count is no bar to a prosecution under the remaining counts.[1]

[1]*Barnett* v. *State*, 54 Ala. 579; *Dealy* v. *United States*, 152 U. S. 539, 38 L. ed. 545, 14 Sup. Ct. Rep. 680; *State* v. *Taylor*, 84 N. C. 773. See also *State* v. *Whittier*, 21 Me. 341, 38 Am. Dec. 272, holding that a *nolle prosequi* may be entered as to one count, and not as to the others, where it is objected that an irregularity exists sufficient to warrant the setting aside of a verdict.

But *Hall* v. *People*, 43 Mich. 417, 5 N. W. 449, holds that where a prisoner has been once in jeopardy upon a count which was withdrawn by the judge at the trial, he cannot be afterward held upon it.

In *Com.* v. *Dunster*, 145 Mass. 101, 13 N. E. 350. however, this rule was recognized, and several cases were cited; but it was said that in all such cases the matter upon which the *nolle prosequi* operates is a distinct and independent charge, and, when entered, the *nolle prosequi* leaves an offense formally as well as substantially charged, being the same offense which was charged in the original complaint or indictment. And it was held that the prosecuting officer cannot, by means of a *nolle prosequi*, put the defendant upon trial for an offense differing from any offense with which he was formally charged in the complaint or indictment, and that where there is no distinct offense alleged upon which the *nolle prosequi* can operate, and yet leave an offense sufficiently charged upon which the defendant can be convicted, the entry of *nolle prosequi* bars further prosecution.

In *Murphy* v. *State,* 25 Neb. 807, 41 N. W. 792, the indictment charged the defendant with four separate violations of the liquor law of the state. He was placed upon trial under three counts in the indictment. Before entering upon the trial he filed his special plea in bar, alleging that upon arraignment he pleaded not guilty to each of the four counts thereof, when he was placed upon trial and the jury impaneled and sworn to try the issue thus joined; that the county attorney, over his objection and protest, then elected to proceed with the trial under but one of the counts; that upon said trial a verdict of not guilty was returned by the jury, when he was discharged by the court. It was held that the court erred in sustaining a general demurrer interposed by the prosecution to this plea.

19. — as to state's evidence.

A prosecution terminated by an agreement to turn state's evidence, or to plead guilty to another indictment, is no bar to a further prosecution for the same offense.[1]

[1] *State* v. *Lopez,* 19 Mo. 254, holding that if such agreement can be recognized anywhere it must be by the executive on an application for pardon, and with the executive it might have very great weight. See also *State* v. *Lyon,* 81 N. C. 600, 31 Am. Rep. 518. Compare *State* v. *Graham,* 41 N. J. L. 15, 32 Am. Rep. 174 (holding, upon the attorney general's application to the appellate court for instructions as to what course to pursue, that an accomplice who becomes state's evidence is entitled to judicial recommendation to the pardoning power; but that, inasmuch as there was no agreement with the accused not to prosecute, a *nolle prosequi* should not be entered, leaving the accused, if convicted, to executive clemency); *Whiskey Cases,* 99 U. S. 594, 25 L. ed. 399 (holding that where an accomplice, under an agreement with the district attorney that he should not be further prosecuted, testified fairly and fully against his associates, a *nolle prosequi* not having been entered, he may not plead such agreement in bar to further prosecution against him, or avail himself of it upon trial, but has merely an equitable title to executive clemency); and *United States* v. *Lee,* 4 McLean, 103, Fed. Cas. No. 15,588. See also *Com.* v. *Knapp,* 10 Pick. 493, 20 Am. Dec. 534.

A contrary doctrine has been followed in Texas. *Bowden* v. *State,* 1 Tex. App. 137 (*nolle prosequi* upon defendant's agreement to turn state's evidence; error to sustain demurrer of state to plea setting up this fact). See also *Hardin* v. *State,* 12 Tex. App. 186.

A plea of having turned state's evidence against accomplices, put in on a trial for burglary, and not denied by the state, should not be submitted to a jury, but belongs to the consideration of the court, which should enter a *nolle prosequi* or dismiss the case. *Camron* v. *State,* 32 Tex. Crim. Rep. 180, 22 S. W. 682. In this case the court said: "We do not think such a defense as we are here considering comes under the character of special pleas which are to be submitted and passed upon by a jury, as former acquittal or conviction or the constitutional plea of former jeopardy, . . . but rather belongs to those matters addressed solely to the consideration of the court, and for which a *nolle prosequi* should be entered, or the case dismissed; and where such a defense is set up, and not denied by the state, and it appears that a valid contract was made by the proper officers representing the state, and the contract has been carried out by the defendant in good faith, the court should dismiss the cause, setting up in the judgment the reasons therefor. . . . While it is true that any such contract should be made with the district or county attorney with the consent of the court, . . . yet we think, where the court sees the contract was made and the defendant acted in perfect good faith, it should be recognized by the court."

20. Requisites of plea.

The plea must show that there was in fact a jeopardy for the same offense, and aver the facts.[1]

[1]*Lyman* v. *State*, 47 Ala. 686; *McCauley* v. *State*, 26 Ala. 135; *Atkins* v. *State*, 16 Ark. 568; *Wilson* v. *State*, 16 Ark. 601; *Bird* v. *State*, 53 Ga. 602 (former indictment *nolle prosequied*, with defendant's consent). Compare *People* v. *Jones*, 48 Mich. 554, 12 N. W. 848 (allegation of discharge of jury sufficient though absence of necessity was not alleged). As to plea of pendency of former indictment, see § 47, *infra*.

A plea of former acquittal resulting from a discharge of the jury, in the absence of defendant, after it had had the case under consideration some twelve hours, is insufficient where it fails to set out by exhibit the judgment of mistrial and discharge of the jury. *Wheelock* v. *State* (Tex. Crim. App.) 38 S. W. 182.

But *Woodward* v. *State* (Tex. Crim. App.) 58 S. W. 135, holds that a plea of former jeopardy, based on a mistrial in the same court, is not defective because it does not set out the indictment, verdict, and judgment in full, since the court must take judicial notice thereof.

21. Verdict set aside on application of accused.

The plea of once in jeopardy is not sustained by proof of a former trial of the same indictment, resulting in a verdict of guilty, which has been set aside at the instance of defendant.[1]

[1]*Com.* v. *Arnold*, 83 Ky. 1, 6 Crim. L. Mag. 61, with note collating cases pro and con; *State* v. *Blaisdell*, 59 N. H. 328 (perjury; verdict set aside on motion for misconduct of jury), Following *State* v. *Prescott*, 7 N. H. 287; *Taylor* v. *State*, 110 Ga. 150, 35 S. E. 161; *State* v. *Bowman*, 94 Iowa, 228, 62 N. W. 759 (verdict set aside for lack of competent evidence).

As to the rule where the verdict is as to one of several counts or for a lesser degree, see *infra*, §§ 27, 39.

Where final judgment is reversed on account of an erroneous sentence, and the case remanded, under Mass. Pub. Stat. chap. 187, § 13, for a proper sentence, after the prisoner has served a part of his time under the original sentence, the resentence does not put him twice in jeopardy, within the meaning of the Constitution. *Com.* v. *Murphy*, 174 Mass. 369, 54 N. E. 860, with note in 48 L. R. A. 393, Affirmed in 177 U. S. 155, 44 L. ed. 711, 20 Sup. Ct. Rep. 639.

So held also in *McDonald* v. *State*, 79 Wis. 651, 48 N. W. 863, of the Wisconsin statute (Wis. Rev. Stat. § 2412) requiring the resentence of prisoners upon reversal of a judgment against them for an error in the sentence.

V. Former acquittal or former conviction.

[These pleas are essentially distinct in matter of fact, and therefore of allegation; but the same rules of procedure apply to each. They are founded upon the well-established principle that the accused shall not be twice tried for the same offense.

In *Simco* v. *State*, 9 Tex. App. 338, the court attempted to draw a distinction between the two pleas, holding that "former acquittal" is available where the transaction was the same, and the two indictments were susceptible of, and must be sustained by, the same proof, while "former conviction" requires only that the transaction or fact should be the same; but this rule does not seem to have been followed.]

22. The objection to be raised by plea.

The objection of a former acquittal or former conviction must be taken by plea;[1] and an improper refusal to accept such plea is error.[2]

[1]*State* v. *Barnes*, 32 Me. 530; *Pitner* v. *State*, 44 Tex. 578 (habeas corpus not a proper remedy); *Brill* v. *State*, 1 Tex. App. 152 (same effect); *Ex parte Clements*, 50 Ala. 459 (nor will mandamus be awarded); *Burton* v. *State*, 115 Ala. 1, 22 So. 585; *Guenther* v. *People*, 22 Colo. 121, 43 Pac. 499; *Ball* v. *State*, 67 Miss. 358, 7 So. 353. And see *Rickles* v. *State*, 68 Ala. 538 (holding record of former conviction or acquittal not admissible under plea of not guilty). Compare *State* v. *Martin*, 30 Wis. 216, 11 Am. Rep. 567, holding that after reversal on the second trial no new plea need be interposed, especially if defendant had not been rearraigned.

N. Y. Code Crim. Proc. § 332, recognizes this plea, and provides that it may be pleaded either with or without the plea of not guilty.

In *Mann* v. *State*, 23 Fla. 610, 3 So. 207, the defendant moved in arrest of a judgment of conviction for murder upon the grounds (1) that there had been a former trial upon an indictment which had been *nolle prose-*

quied, and a second indictment and trial thereunder resulting in the conviction appealed from; and (2) that the jury in the first trial had found a verdict of guilty, with recommendation to mercy, while the jury in the second trial found a verdict of guilty, without such recommendation. It was held that the motion was properly overruled because, so far as the pleadings and records up to the time of the motion showed, the second trial was entirely new; but the court said that even if the question had been properly presented it would not have availed; that the motion did not present the case of a person on trial for a higher offense and convicted of a lower grade of that offense. The recommendation to mercy did not change the nature or grade of the crime, but only the manner of punishment.

Some of the courts hold that such a plea is necessary where the verdict has been in another court, or in the same court upon another indictment, because the plea would be necessary to present extraneous matters from another record; but that where the verdict has been in the same court upon the same indictment no plea is necessary, because the court will take judicial notice, or, more correctly speaking, will look through the entire record of the case. *State* v. *Cross*, 44 W. Va. 315, 29 S. E. 527.

People v. *Bennett*, 114 Cal. 56, 45 Pac. 1013, was a case in which the defendant was twice tried in the same court upon the same indictment; and it was there ruled that, in order to avail himself of the plea of once in jeopardy, the defendant must plead it specially; but that he could not raise the question upon his motion for a new trial. But upon an application for a writ of habeas corpus by the same defendant (reported in 84 Fed. 324), the Federal court held that no such plea or evidence is necessary, because the court itself is bound to take judicial notice of every step shown by its own record to have been taken in the prosecution of the case before it,—notice not only of the petitioner's arraignment, and of his plea upon such arraignment, but also of the verdict rendered upon the former trial of the same case, and entered upon the record of the court as a perpetual memorial of its rendition; and, having judicial knowledge of such facts, the court is bound to know that, under the Constitution, it no longer has jurisdiction to retry the petitioner for the offense of which he had been acquitted by such former verdict. But it was also held that a writ of habeas corpus is not available to the defendant in such case; that his remedy is by writ of error to the United States Supreme Court.

In *State* v. *Fry*, 98 Tenn. 323, 39 S. W. 231, it was held that acquittal of one of several offenses embraced in an indictment, resulting by implication from a verdict of guilty upon a former trial as to the other offenses charged, is available on a subsequent retrial, without a formal plea, as it fully appears from the record.

And in *Johnson* v. *State*, 27 Fla. 245, 9 So. 208, it was held that, upon the second trial of a person whose conviction of a lesser offense under an indictment charging a higher has been reversed at his instance, it is unnecessary to specially plead acquittal of the higher grade; but he may be tried upon the same indictment for the offense of which he was convicted, with directions to the jury to confine their inquiries to that grade and those lower which may be legally included.

In *Mixon* v. *State*, 35 Tex. Crim. Rep. 458, 34 S. W. 290, it was held to be "immaterial whether the plea setting up this defense [of former acquittal] was in proper form or not. The former acquittal having been in the same court, it was competent for the court to take cognizance of such acquittal, under a plea of not guilty, notwithstanding a new indictment was found in said case, and the defendant put upon trial upon such new indictment."

[2]*State* v. *Johnson*, 11 Nev. 273 (statutory); *Com.* v. *Robinson*, 126 Mass. 259, 30 Am. Rep. 674.

23. Test.

Unless the facts proved upon the trial under the first indictment would warrant a conviction under the second indictment, an acquittal upon the first indictment is no bar to the second.[1]

[1]*Rex* v. *Vandercomb*, 2 Leach C. L. 708; *Foster* v. *State*, 39 Ala. 229; *Com.* v. *Bakeman*, 105 Mass. 53; *State* v. *Ingalls*, 98 Iowa, 728, 68 N. W. 445; *Turner* v. *Com.* 19 Ky. L. Rep. 1161, 42 S. W. 1129; *State* v. *English*, 14 Mont. 399, 36 Pac. 815; *Winn* v. *State*, 82 Wis. 571, 52 N. W. 775.

Or, as it is stated by some of the courts, the plea of *autrefois acquit* is good where the evidence necessary to support the second indictment would have been sufficient to secure a legal conviction upon the first. *Davis* v. *People*, 22 Colo, 1, 43 Pac. 122; *State* v. *Waterman*, 87 Iowa, 255, 54 N. W. 359; *State* v. *Williams*, 45 La. Ann. 936, 12 So. 932.

In *Dill* v. *People*, 19 Colo. 469, 36 Pac. 229, the rule for determining whether or not a plea of *autrefois acquit* is sufficient in law is stated thus: Was the matter set out in second indictment admissible as evidence under the first, and could a conviction have been properly maintained upon such evidence? If yes, then the plea is sufficient; otherwise it is not.

In *State* v. *Brownrigg*, 87 Me. 500, 33 Atl. 11, the test was held to be, not what facts were offered in evidence in the trial upon the first indictment. but, from the record, what facts might have been proved under that indictment, and whether the same facts, if proved under the second indictment, would warrant a conviction.

24. Same act being several offenses of same degree.

When several offenses of the same kind and degree are committed at the same time by the same act, a conviction or acquittal of one bars a prosecution for the others.[1]

[1]Thus, a conviction or acquittal under either of two informations charging identical assault of the same person—one charging an intent to kill, the other to rob—is a bar to a trial under the other. *State* v. *Chinault*, 55 Kan. 326, 40 Pac. 662.

And a plea of former acquittal on a charge of forcible trespass bars a prosecution for forcible entry and detainer which the prosecuting officer admits was the same transaction. *State* v. *Lawson*, 123 N. C. 740, 31 S. E. 667.

And an acquittal under an indictment charging defendant with carrying on his person "brass knuckles" bars a subsequent prosecution for carrying on his person knuckles made of a hard substance other than brass. *Morrison* v. *State*, 38 Tex. Crim. Rep. 392, 43 S. W. 113.

And a prosecution for breach of the peace by shooting and firing off pistols and other firearms in the streets bars a prosecution for wilfully and maliciously injuring the courthouse by shooting through the windows, predicated upon the same acts. *Reddy* v. *Com.* 97 Ky. 784, 31 S. W. 730. "The commonwealth," said the court, "by giving different names to the same thing done, or by prosecuting under different statutes, cannot multiply offenses out of one and the same thing done by the accused."

So, too, a conviction for rudely displaying a pistol, and firing the same at and near a church, is a bar to a prosecution based on the same transaction, for firing into the church. *Landrum* v. *State*, 37 Tex. Crim. Rep. 666, 40 S. W. 737.

The mere fact that in a former indictment for larceny the description of the things alleged to have been stolen was such that the same evidence which would warrant a conviction upon that indictment might also be sufficient to warrant a conviction of the offenses charged in the present indictment does not, of itself, raise a presumption that the former offense was the same, so as to support a plea of former acquittal, without further evidence of their identity. However it might be in a case where the former descriptions of the articles and the averments of the time and place of the offense so far corresponded as to appear on the face of the indictment to relate to the same larceny subsequently charged, the defendant must go further, and prove the identity of the offenses, in a case where in both indictments the amount of property charged to have been stolen and the time of the alleged larceny differ from the averments of the former indictments. *Com.* v. *Fredericks*, 155 Mass. 455, 29 N. E. 622.

In *Quitzow* v. *State*, 1 Tex. App. 47, 28 Am. Rep. 396, the theft of several articles at one time and by one act was held to constitute but one offense; and acquittal or conviction of the theft of one article is a bar to the prosecution for theft of the other. To the same effect, *Wilson* v. *State*, 45 Tex. 76, 23 Am. Rep. 602. And *Hudson* v. *State*, 9 Tex. App. 151, 35 Am. Rep. 732, holds to the same effect, even when the articles belonged to different persons. But see *contra*, as to this last point, *Wright* v. *State*, 17 Tex. App. 152.

A prosecution upon a charge laid at a date anterior to a former indictment is barred by a conviction or acquittal upon such former indictment, where the offense charged is a continuing one. *People* v. *Cox*, 107 Mich. 435, 65 N. W. 283. So holding of the offense of continuous keeping of house of illfame resorted to for purposes of prostitution, in violation of 3 How. (Mich.) Anno. Stat. § 9286. But a conviction of selling liquors on a specified day without having paid the annual tax is not a bar to a subsequent prosecution for selling liquors on a previous day in the same year without having paid such tax, under 3 How. (Mich.) Stat. § 2283*d*1, providing that each violation of the act shall constitute a separate and complete offense. *People* v. *Gault,* 104 Mich. 575, 62 N. W. 724.

So, a conviction under an indictment for keeping a common nuisance on May 1, and on divers other days between such day and the finding of the indictment, October 31, is a bar to a second indictment at the following April term, charging defendant with keeping a common nuisance October 17, and on divers other days between that day and the finding of such indictment. *State* v. *Brownrigg,* 87 Me. 500, 33 Atl. 11.

And an acquittal under a complaint for unlawfully exposing intoxicating liquors for sale on a certain day, "and on divers times and days between that day and November 21, 1892," is a bar, by virtue of Mass. Pub. Stat. chap. 200, § 6, to a second complaint for the same offense on November 20, 1892, notwithstanding the former complaint was received and sworn to November 20, and on the former trial all evidence against the defendant concerning November 20 was excluded at his request. *Com.* v. *Goulet,* 160 Mass. 276, 35 N. E. 780. See also *Com.* v. *Robinson,* 126 Mass. 259, 30 Am. Rep. 674, holding an acquittal for illegally selling intoxicating liquors from January 1 to May 28 to be a bar to a complaint for like offenses from January 1 to August 1 of the same year.

But under N. Y. Stat. (Laws 1857, chap. 628) each sale constitutes a separate offense; and an acquittal on a charge of selling liquor after a certain date is no bar to an indictment for sales made prior to that date. *People* v. *Sinell,* 131 N. Y. 571, 30 N. E. 47.

And a plea of former acquittal of keeping a liquor nuisance is no defense to acts committed after the return of the former indictment. *State* v. *Ingraham,* 96 Iowa, 278, 65 N. W. 152.

And a conviction for keeping an unlicensed dramshop on a given day is no bar to a prosecution for keeping it on a subsequent day, under an ordinance providing that each day it is kept shall constitute a separate offense, where the proof to support both charges is not the same; and it is immaterial that both days are included within the period for which one license should be issued. *Eureka Springs* v. *O'Neal,* 56 Ark. 350, 19 S. W. 969.

A complaint charging one with having, on a designated day and on divers days thereafter, up to and including another designated day, unlawfully conducted, opened, and carried on a certain gambling game known as faro, does not charge a continuous offense, such that a conviction thereon would be a defense to an indictment charging him with conducting such game on a designated day intermediate between the other two. *People* v. *Sullivan,* 9 Utah, 195, 33 Pac. 701.

An acquittal under an indictment charging defendant with uttering a forged instrument, with the fraudulent intent to procure goods, wares, and merchandise from a specified person, is a bar to a subsequent prosecution under an indictment charging defendant with the offense of obtaining the same property by false pretenses. *Huff* v. *Com.* 19 Ky. L. Rep. 1064, 42 S. W. 907.

In *State* v. *Egglesht*, 41 Iowa, 574, 20 Am. Rep. 612, it was held that a conviction for uttering one of four forged checks, drawn on different parties, but delivered to a teller of a bank at the same time, barred a subsequent prosecution for the issuing of the others, as the whole transaction constituted but one offense.

But an acquittal under an information for uttering and publishing a forged note, charging that the names of specified persons were forged by defendant, is not a bar to a subsequent prosecution for forgery, as the allegation in the former information that defendant forged such names is simply descriptive. *Beyerline* v. *State*, 147 Ind. 125, 45 N. E. 772.

25. — being different offenses.

When the same act of the accused constitutes two or more offenses, the lesser of which is necessarily involved in the greater, and when the facts necessary to convict on a second prosecution would necessarily have convicted on the first, then the first prosecution to final judgment is a bar to the second.[1]

But when the same act constitutes two or more distinct offenses, the lesser of which is not necessarily involved in the greater, and the facts necessary to convict on a second prosecution would not necessarily have convicted on the first, then the first prosecution will not bar the second, although the offenses were both committed at the same time and by the same act.[2]

[1]*State* v. *Gleason*, 56 Iowa, 203, 9 N. W. 126 (that conviction of simple larceny bars prosecution for same act as larceny from the person); *Dinkey* v. *Com.* 17 Pa. 126, 55 Am. Dec. 542 (acquittal for seduction bars indictment for fornication); *State* v. *Colgate*, 31 Kan. 511, 47 Am. Rep. 507, 3 Pac. 346 (an acquittal of arson of a building is a bar to a subsequent prosecution for arson of the books of account); *State* v. *Cooper*, 13 N. J. L. 361, 25 Am. Dec. 490 (holding that conviction of arson may be pleaded in bar to an indictment for murder arising from the unintentional killing of a person while in commission of the same arson). And see *Triplett* v. *Com.* 84 Ky. 193, 1 S. W. 84; *Bryant* v. *State*, 72 Ind. 400; *Com.* v. *Bass* (Pa.) 8 Crim. L. Mag. 218; *United States* v. *Lancaster*, 2 McLean, 431, Fed. Cas. No. 15,556; *Ex parte Rogers*, 10 Tex. App. 655, 38 Am. Rep. 654; *Smith* v. *State*, 85 Ind. 553; *State* v. *Wiles*, 26 Minn. 381, 4 N. W. 615.

Thus, a conviction of robbery under an indictment alleging it to have been committed by assault, by violence, or by putting in fear of life or bodily injury, is a bar to a subsequent prosecution for assault with intent to murder, for the same offense. *Wilcox* v. *State*, 6 Lea, 571, 40 Am. Rep. 53; *Moore* v. *State*, 33 Tex. Crim. Rep. 166, 25 S. W. 1120. The court in the last case, quoting from the *Wilcox Case* said that the "assault or violence in the robbery case being an essential element or ingredient of the offense, and constituting an important and material part of that offense, as it does in the offense of assault with intent to commit murder, and having been once punished in the robbery case, as a material part thereof, it cannot be again punished, as it would be if the judgment below were allowed to stand."

And a conviction of assault with intent to murder bars a subsequent prosecution for robbery based on the same transaction. *Herera* v. *State*, 35 Tex. Crim. Rep. 607, 34 S. W. 943.

And a conviction of aggravated assault, after discharge by a magistrate on a charge of assault with intent to kill, is a bar to a subsequent indictment for assault with intent to kill. *State* v. *Smith*, 53 Ark. 24, 13 S. W. 391. See also *Moore* v. *State*, 71 Ala. 307 (that conviction of assault and battery is a bar to an indictment for assault with intent to murder).

In California the Penal Code (§ 1159) provides that the "jury may find the defendant guilty of any offense the commission of which is necessarily included in that with which he is charged, or of an attempt to commit the offense." And one who has been convicted of assault, upon an information charging him with assault with intent to kill, cannot thereafter be prosecuted for mayhem committed during the same assault, without violating the constitutional provision protecting him against being twice convicted of the same offense, as under the charge of mayhem he might again be convicted of assault. *People* v. *Defoor*, 100 Cal. 150, 34 Pac. 642.

A finding by the jury of grand larceny under an indictment charging both burglary and larceny, but which is defective as an indictment for larceny, is a bar to a subsequent trial for burglary, but not to a subsequent indictment for the larceny. *Bowen* v. *State*, 106 Ala. 178, 17 So. 335.

In *State* v. *DeGraffenreid*, 9 Baxt. 287, a conviction of burglary with intent to commit larceny was held to bar an indictment for the larceny.

And in *Roberts* v. *State*, 14 Ga. 8, 58 Am. Dec. 529, a conviction for burglary was held to bar an indictment for a robbery.

And in *State* v. *St. Clair*, 42 La. Ann. 755, 7 So. 713, it is held that a verdict of guilty of larceny, on a joint indictment for burglary and larceny, in a single count, is legal and valid, and constitutes a bar to a new trial, where the court sends the jury out again on the ground that their finding is not responsive, and, on their failure to agree, discharges them.

But *Loakman* v. *State*, 32 Tex. Crim. Rep. 563, 25 S. W. 22, holds that a previous conviction of theft committed at the time of a burglary is not a bar to a prosecution for the burglary. This case also overrules previous Texas cases to the contrary. To the same effect, *State* v. *Ingalls*, 98 Iowa, 728, 68 N. W. 445.

In Michigan the Constitution provides that no person, after acquittal upon the merits, shall be tried for the same offense. And a conviction of burglary on an information charging that defendant broke and entered with intent to steal will not bar a prosecution for larceny committed at the same time. *People* v. *Parrow*, 80 Mich. 567, 45 N. W. 514.

So, in Minnesota, a statute (Pen. Code, § 393) provides that any person who enters a building under such circumstances as to constitute burglary, and commits any crime therein, is punishable therefor, as well as for the burglary, and may be prosecuted for each crime separately. And *State* v. *Hackett*, 47 Minn. 425, 50 N. W. 472, holds that an acquittal for burglary does not bar a prosecution for larceny involving the same act.

An acquittal under an indictment charging the setting fire to a building "of" a person named, who in fact was in possession thereof, is a bar to a subsequent indictment for arson charging the burning of the same building, which is alleged to have belonged to a person other than the person named in the former indictment, but to have been used by the latter. *State* v. *Copeland*, 46 S. C. 13, 23 S. E. 980.

To the effect that a plea of former conviction or acquittal cannot be sustained when the offenses are different, though committed by the same act, see *State* v. *Ross*, 4 Lea, 442; *State* v. *Martin*, 76 Mo. 337; *People* v. *Helbing*, 61 Cal. 620; *State* v. *Stewart* (Or.) 3 West Coast Rep. 229; *Howard* v. *State*, 8 Tex. App. 447; *Potter* v. *State*, 9 Tex. App. 55; *Teat* v. *State*, 53 Miss. 439, 24 Am. Rep. 708.

A plea of *autrefois acquit* showing on its face that the offense for which the prisoner was formerly tried is separate and distinct from that for which he stands indicted is demurrable. *State* v. *Evans*, 33 W. Va. 417, 10 S. E. 792. In this case the plea showed that the killing was the result of a separate act in each case, committed under degrees of provocation not necessarily identical, accompanied by apprehensions not necessarily the same. In fine, every element to constitute two separate offenses appeared on the face of the plea to exist in this case, and therefore the demurrer was properly sustained. See also, as holding likewise, *State* v. *Robinson*, 12 Wash. 491, 41 Pac. 884; *Winn* v. *State*, 82 Wis. 571, 52 N. W. 775; *Ashton* v. *State*, 31 Tex. Crim. Rep. 482, 21 S. W. 48; *People* v. *Ochotski*, 115 Mich. 601, 73 N. W. 889. In *State* v. *Nash*, 86 N. C. 651, 41 Am. Rep. 472, where a person fired two shots in quick succession into a crowd, wounding two, it was held that an acquittal for an assault on one was no bar to an indictment for assault on the other. The court in this case cited and approved *People* v. *Warren*, 1 Park. Crim. Rep. 338, holding that an acquittal on a charge of attempting to poison A was no bar to an indictment for an attempt to poison B, although both crimes were committed on the same occasion and by the same act of preparation. To the same effect, *People* v. *Majors*, 65 Cal. 138, 52 Am. Rep. 295, 3 Pac. 597. And see *Jones* v. *State*, 61 Ark. 88, 32 S. W. 81, holding that the fact that the act of the accused in killing the person of the murder of whom he has been convicted was so closely connected in point of time with the act of killing another as to render it impossible to separate the evidence relating to each of them does not necessarily make the killing of the two one act or one offense, so as to render the conviction a bar to a prosecution for the murder of the other. But *Clem* v. *State*, 42 Ind. 420, 13 Am. Rep. 369, holds that when two persons are killed by the same act, a conviction of the killing of one may be pleaded in bar to an indictment for killing the other.

In *State* v. *Elder*, 65 Ind. 282, 32 Am. Rep. 69, it is held that an acquittal for murder of an unborn child by an attempt to produce a miscarriage is no bar to an indictment for an attempt to produce a miscarriage.

So, robbing different individual passengers on a stage, at the same time and in rapid succession, constitutes a distinct offense for each individual; and a conviction for robbing one is no bar to a prosecution for robbing others. *Re Allison*, 13 Colo. 525, 10 L. R. A. 790, 22 Pac. 820.

So held also in *Keeton* v. *Com.* 92 Ky. 522, 18 S. W. 359, of a robbery simultaneously committed by the accused upon two persons, although he drew a pistol on each at the same time, and the property was simultaneously delivered to him by both. In this case the defendant insisted that the act of robbery, if committed, was but one offense; and, the pistol having been pointed at both persons robbed at the same time, and the property of each surrendered at the same time, the verdict and judgment in the one case was properly pleaded in bar to the other. But the court rejected this view of the law, saying that if the defendant was guilty, it was robbery from the person of each of the owners of this property; as much so as if he had gone to the one and taken from him his property, and then to the other; and that the fact that the pistol was drawn on each at the same time, and the property delivered at once, did not make the offense a unit.

Nor is an acquittal of the theft of a horse a bar to a subsequent prosecution for the theft of another horse taken at the same time. *Wright* v. *State*, 37 Tex. Crim. Rep. 627, 40 S. W. 491.

And an acquittal of stealing a steer is not a bar to another prosecution for stealing a cow, on the ground that both thefts were a part of the same transaction, where the steer was stolen from one herd and driven away, and left at some distance, and half an hour afterwards defendant stole the cow from another herd half a mile distant from the place where he stole the steer. *State* v. *English*, 14 Mont. 399, 36 Pac. 815. The taking of the two animals was at different times, and at different places, under different circumstances, and from different owners. Each was in itself an absolute, complete, and independent offense.

The acquittal of the principal in the commission of a felony is not a bar to a prosecution against an accessory before the fact under a joint information against the two. *State* v. *Bogue*, 52 Kan. 79, 34 Pac. 410. It was otherwise at common law; but the statutes enacted by the various states have had the effect to do away with those subtile distinctions of the common law between principals in the first and second degrees and accessories before the fact, and to permit the trial of participants in the crime independently of each other, so that each shall suffer punishment for his own guilt, without being dependent upon the result of the prosecutions against others. Of course, if the crime be committed through the instrumentality of another, the acts of such instrument, essential to establish the guilt of the person on trial, must be shown. The statute does not in any manner enlarge or diminish the essential elements of criminality. It merely does away with a somewhat arbitrary nomenclature which has come down from English jurisprudence, and has been found to be a serious stumbling block in the administration of criminal justice.

In *State* v. *Buzzell,* 58 N. H. 257, 42 Am. Rep. 586, it was held that acquittal as principal in a murder was no bar to an indictment as accessory before the fact. But compare *Davis* v. *People,* 22 Colo. 1, 43 Pac. 122, where it was held that acquittal of a person charged as a principal in an indictment for larceny, but tried thereunder as an accessory before the fact on the theory that he was not present when the larceny was committed, but devised the transaction and advised and encouraged his codefendant to commit the crime,—was a bar to a subsequent prosecution for conspiring to commit the larceny. But this case also holds that the conviction or acquittal of a defendant indicted and tried as a principal, for larceny, is not a bar to a subsequent prosecution for conspiracy to commit such larceny, as by Colo. Sess. Laws 1891, p. 125, § 2, a conspiracy to commit a felony is made a felony, and the doctrine of merger therefore does not apply.

Nor does a trial for compelling a woman to be defiled against her will, under Iowa Code, § 3862, bar a subsequent indictment for a conspiracy in accomplishing such defilement. *State* v. *Brown,* 95 Iowa, 381, 64 N. W. 277. The offenses are entirely separate and distinct, although those involved in this and the former case grew out of the same transaction. The indictment in the former case charged the compelling of the defilement,—an offense which could have been committed without the aid of a conspiracy. The indictment in this case charges the crime of conspiracy,—an offense which could have been committed even though its object had not been accomplished. The crime is completed when the conspiracy is formed.

An acquittal of an officer of an insolvent bank upon a charge of receiving money on deposit from one particular person is not, under the Missouri statute, a bar to a prosecution for receiving money thereafter on deposit from another individual at a different time, as they are separate and distinct offenses. *State* v. *Burlingame,* 146 Mo. 207, 48 S. W. 72. The plea in this case was based upon the fact that defendant had, upon two separate occasions, prior to the finding of this indictment, been indicted, tried, and acquitted upon a similar charge of receiving money on deposit in said bank while the same was in a failing condition, and that, inasmuch as the crime of receiving money on deposit under circumstances such as are found in this case was a continuing offense, his having been previously tried and acquitted worked a complete defense to any further prosecution. But the court said: "It is true that the offense charged in those indictments, and the one in this case, have some of the same constituent elements; that is, it is the same bank and banker, the same condition of insolvency, and the same knowledge of insolvency; but neither one of them nor all of them constitute a crime; but, when in addition thereto, with knowledge of such facts, a president or other officer of a bank receives money on deposit, then he is guilty of larceny under the statute. The receiving of money on deposit by an officer of an insolvent bank, or one in failing circumstances, from one particular person or firm, is not, we think, a continuous offense, and is not a bar to a prosecution for receiving money thereafter on deposit from another and different individual, at a different time, but are separate and distinct offenses. The one has no interest in common with the other, and the proof to this extent must of necessity be entirely different. It could with the same propriety be said that an officer who receives illegal fees from different persons at different times is guilty of but one offense,—a doctrine that no lawyer would approve. The offense was not, we think, a continuing one, but each receipt of moneys on deposit under the circumstances prohibited by statute was a separate and distinct offense."

And an acquittal of a county treasurer under an indictment for larceny of public money by converting to his own use a specified amount is not a bar to a subsequent prosecution for refusal subsequently to turn over to his successor a larger specified amount, unless it is shown that the failure to turn it over was due to the same identical act involved in the former prosecution. *State* v. *Howe,* 27 Or. 138, 44 Pac. 672.

An acquittal for rape does not bar a prosecution for incest based on the same transaction. *Stewart* v. *State,* 35 Tex. Crim. Rep. 174, 32 S. W. 766.

Nor is a trial for adultery a bar to a subsequent prosecution for seduction under promise to marry, based upon the same act. *Smith* v. *Com.* 17 Ky. L. Rep. 541, 32 S. W. 137.

Nor does an acquittal on a charge of rape bar a conviction for adultery committed with the same female at a different time; but it does bar prosecution for adultery arising out of the same transaction. *State* v. *Shedrick,* 69 Vt. 428, 38 Atl. 75.

26. — misdemeanor.

A conviction for a misdemeanor will not bar a prosecution for felony, although the act which constitutes the misdemeanor is also involved in the felony.[1]

[1]*State* v. *Hattabough,* 66 Ind. 223, 35 Am. Rep. 339, note, holding that a prosecution for assault and battery was no bar to a prosecution for assault and battery with intent to commit murder; Citing *People* v. *Saunders,* 4 Park. Crim. Rep. 196, to the effect that a former conviction of assault on the prosecutrix was not a bar to an indictment for rape committed while engaged in the same assault. And see *Taylor* v. *State,* 36 Ark. 84; *Southworth* v. *State,* 42 Ark. 270; *State* v. *Martin,* 76 Mo. 337 (under statute). Compare with *State* v. *Nichols,* 38 Ark. 550; *State* v. *Gleason,* 56 Iowa, 203, 9 N. W. 126.

And a prosecution for assault with a deadly weapon, with intent to inflict bodily harm, is not barred by a former conviction of displaying a deadly weapon in a rude, angry, and insolent manner. *Territory* v. *Stocker,* 9 Mont. 6, 22 Pac. 496.

But a former conviction or acquittal for a simple assault, before a justice of the peace, is a complete defense on a subsequent trial for affray, in the North Carolina superior court, where in the latter court the defendant is shown not to have used any deadly weapon, and not to have inflicted any serious injury, although the other party to the affray did so. *State* v. *Albertson,* 113 N. C. 633, 18 S. E. 321.

And a defendant tried for fornication cannot be lawfully subjected to a prosecution for rape based on the same act, pending the deliberations of the jury in the fornication case; and a verdict in that case constitutes a bar to the prosecution for rape. *Com.* v. *Arner,* 149 Pa. 35, 24 Atl. 83.

So, also, a conviction before a justice of the peace on an information charging only a common assault, of one who is plainly guilty of a felonious assault, is a bar to a prosecution for the latter offense, unless collusion is shown. *State* v. *Hatcher,* 136 Mo. 641, 38 S. W. 719.

27. Implied acquittal of other degrees or counts.

Conviction of a lower degree or of one of several offenses is an implied acquittal of all higher degrees and other offenses charged in the indictment.[1]

[1]*People* v. *Cignarale,* 110 N. Y. 23, 17 N. W. 135, citing cases, and holding the rule to be the same in homicide as in minor offenses. And for cases involving and applying this doctrine, see *People* v. *McDonald,* 49 Hun, 67, 1 N. Y. Supp. 703; *State* v. *Patterson,* 116 Mo. 505, 22 S. W. 696; *Roland* v. *People,* 23 Colo. 283, 47 Pac. 269; *State* v. *Cross,* 44 W. Va. 315, 29 S. E. 527.

But a verdict of "guilty of arson," against one charged in one count of an indictment with burning a barn, and in the other with burning a dwelling house as part of the same transaction, cannot be set up as an acquittal of the offense of burning the barn, as the burning of either a barn or a dwelling house is arson. *State* v. *Fry,* 98 Tenn. 323, 39 S. W. 231.

And a verdict of manslaughter in the first degree, which the court refuses to receive because there are no degrees of manslaughter, does not amount to an acquittal of the higher offense of murder, so as to prevent the jury, after retiring again, from rendering a verdict of murder in the first degree. *Grant* v. *State,* 33 Fla. 291, 23 L. R. A. 723, 14 So. 757.

And that a person convicted of murder and recommended to mercy, upon a *nolle prosequi* and second trial for the same offense is again convicted without such recommendation, does not violate the rule which prohibits a trial for a higher grade of the offense than that found on conviction in a former trial. *Mann* v. *State,* 23 Fla. 610, 3 So. 207.

28. Subsequent aggravation.

If, after a prosecution for an offense, a new fact supervenes for which the defendant is responsible, and which changes the character of the offense, and, together with the previous facts, constitutes a new and distinct crime, an acquittal or conviction of the first offense is no bar to an indictment for the other distinct crime.[1]

[1]*State* v. *Littlefield,* 70 Me. 452, 35 Am. Rep. 335, holding a former convic-

tion of an assault and battery no bar to an indictment for manslaughter, where the injuries resulted in death after the former conviction. And see *Achterberg* v. *State*, 8 Tex. App. 463.

29. Jurisdiction of court.

If it appear that the offense of which the defendant was formerly acquitted or convicted was against another jurisdiction,[1] or if the court in which the conviction or acquittal was had, had no jurisdiction[2] of the offense, or was improperly constituted,[3] the plea of former acquittal or conviction cannot be sustained.

[1]*United States* v. *Cashiel*, 1 Hughes, 552, Fed. Cas. No. 14,744 (holding that an acquittal by a court-martial is no bar to an indictment in a court of law); *Smith* v. *State*, 67 Miss. 116, 7 So. 208 (holding that a former acquittal before a justice of the peace will not protect the defendant where it does not appear that the offense charged was committed within the territorial limits of the justice); *Territory* v. *Coleman*, 1 Or. 191 (holding that former conviction of an act under a Federal statute cannot be pleaded in bar of prosecution for such act under territorial statute).

And that a conviction in the United States circuit court, of an offense of which that court had no jurisdiction, does not bar a prosecution for the same offense in the state court, see *Blyew* v. *Com.* 91 Ky. 200, 15 S. W. 356.

N. Y. Code Crim. Proc. § 139, provides that "when an act charged as a crime is within the jurisdiction of another state, territory, or country, as well as within the jurisdiction of this state, a conviction or acquittal thereof in the former is a bar to the prosecution or indictment therefor in this state."

As to the effect of a conviction or acquittal under a city ordinance as a bar to a prosecution for the same act under a state statute, and *vice versa*, see *Greenwood* v. *State*, 6 Baxt. 567, 32 Am. Rep. 539; *McRea* v. *Americus*, 59 Ga. 168, 27 Am. Rep. 390; *Robbins* v. *People*, 95 Ill. 175; *Richardson* v. *State*, 35 Ark. 367, 19 S. W. 1052; *Van Buren* v. *Wells*, 53 Ark. 368, 14 S. W. 38; *Powell* v. *State*, 89 Ala. 172, 8 So. 109; *McInerney* v. *Denver*, 17 Colo. 302, 29 Pac. 516; *State* v. *Flint*, 63 Conn. 248, 28 Atl. 28; *Theisen* v. *McDavid*, 34 Fla. 440, 26 L. R. A. 234, 16 So. 321; *People* v. *Furman*, 85 Mich. 110, 48 N. W. 169; *Turner* v. *State* (Tex. Crim. App.) 44 S. W. 1132; *State* v. *Harris*, 50 Minn. 128, 52 N. W. 387, 531; *Ex parte Freeland*, 38 Tex. Crim. Rep. 321, 42 S. W. 295.

[2]*Campbell* v. *People*, 109 Ill. 565, 50 Am. Rep. 621. Demurrer to plea was sustained because it appeared on the face of the plea that the court on the former trial had no jurisdiction of the offense. And see *Nicholson* v. *State*, 72 Ala. 176.

A trial in a court having jurisdiction of an offense is not barred by a prior conviction in a court having no jurisdiction. *State* v. *Phillips*, 104 N. C. 786, 10 S. E. 463; *Alford* v. *State*, 25 Fla. 852, 6 So. 857; *People* v. *Hamburg*, 84 Cal. 468, 24 Pac. 298.

Nor does the trial of one and his incarceration in execution of the judgment place him in jeopardy, where the court was without jurisdiction to try him at the term at which he was tried. *Re McClaskey,* 2 Okla. 568, 37 Pac. 854. A trial and conviction by the court at a time when the court has lost jurisdiction of the case, as where the judge does not appear on the first day of the term, and there is no law providing for its adjournment until he does appear,—is void, and the judgment a nullity, and cannot be made ground of a plea of former jeopardy.

The state may defeat a plea of former conviction by showing that the court in which the defendant was convicted had no jurisdiction, without alleging that fact in its replication, as the rules in civil cases have no application to criminal procedure, and Iowa Code, § 4349, expressly provides that no replication or further pleading is necessary to a plea of former adjudication. *State* v. *Jamison,* 104 Iowa, 343, 73 N. W. 831.

[a]*Johnson* v. *State,* 63 Ga. 386 (incapacity of judge to preside in the circuit where trial was had); *State* v. *Cross,* 44 W. Va. 315, 29 S. E. 527.

So a trial for and conviction of larceny in the New York court of sessions, one of the two justices of the peace in which is related to defendant within the sixth degree, and so incapable of acting as a member of the court during the trial, under N. Y. Code Civ. Proc. § 46, applying to all trials, civil and criminal, are not a bar to a subsequent trial. *People* v. *Connor,* 142 N. Y. 130, 36 N. E. 807.

30. Sufficiency of indictment on former trial.

Neither conviction nor acquittal on a void indictment can be pleaded in bar to a subsequent indictment for the same offense.[1]

[1]*People* v. *Casborus,* 13 Johns. 351 (arrest of judgment of conviction is no bar to a second indictment, as the effect of arresting judgment is the same as quashing the indictment, and it must be presumed that the indictment was bad); *Grisham* v. *State,* 19 Tex. App. 504; *Davis* v. *State,* 37 Tex. Crim. Rep. 359, 38 S. W. 616, 39 S. W. 937; *Timon* v. *State,* 34 Tex. Crim. Rep. 363, 30 S. W. 808; *State* v. *Watson,* 20 R. I. 354, 39 Atl. 193; *State* v. *Lee,* 114 N. C. 844, 19 S. E. 375; *State* v. *Meekins,* 41 La. Ann. 543, 6 So. 822; *State* v. *Foster,* 8 La. Ann. 290, 58 Am. Dec. 678; *Dinkey* v. *Com.* 17 Pa. 126, 55 Am. Dec. 542. And see, S. P., *United States* v. *Bicksler,* 1 Mackey, 341; *People* v. *Campbell,* 59 Cal. 243, 43 Am. Rep. 257; *State* v. *Priebnow,* 16 Neb. 131, 19 N. W. 628; *People* v. *Barrett,* 1 Johns. 67; *State* v. *Owen,* 78 Mo. 367; *State* v. *Jenkins,* 20 S. C. 351; *State* v. *Sherburne,* 58 N. H. 535; *Weston* v. *State,* 63 Ala. 155; *State* v. *Gill,* 33 Ark. 129.

N. Y. Code Crim. Proc. §§ 340, 341, provides that when an indictment is dismissed upon an objection to its form or substance, without a judgment of acquittal, it is not deemed an acquittal of the same offense. When, however, the defendant is acquitted on the merits, he is deemed acquitted of the same offense, notwithstanding a defect in form or substance in the indictment on which he was acquitted.

And by § 327 it is provided that if a demurrer to an indictment be allowed the judgment is final and a bar to another prosecution for the same offense, unless the court, being of opinion that the objection on which the demurrer is allowed may be avoided in a new indictment, directs the case to be resubmitted to the same or another grand jury. See to the same effect Cal. Pen. Code, § 1008; *People* v. *Jordan*, 63 Cal. 219.

It makes no difference that the second information was filed before the judgment on demurrer. When the judgment on demurrer was rendered, there being no direction for a new information or resubmission, it became and was a bar to another prosecution for the same offense. *Ibid.*

But irregularity, if any, on the part of the district attorney in procuring an indictment for the offense, instead of filing a new information, after the court has sustained a demurrer to the information and directed a new information to be filed as provided by Cal. Pen. Code, § 1008, is not available on a plea of former acquittal or a motion in arrest of judgment. *People* v. *Whelan*, 117 Cal. 559, 49 Pac. 583.

So, under the Iowa statute one whose demurrer to an indictment on the ground that it contained matter which was a legal defense to its prosecution was sustained by the district court, and his discharge directed, may interpose a plea of former acquittal to a subsequent indictment setting out a little more fully the facts charged in the first, where a resubmission of the cause was not ordered and although the ruling of the district court was reversed on appeal. *State* v. *Fields*, 106 Iowa, 406, 76 N. W. 802.

In Texas the statute (Code Crim. Proc. art. 525) provides that the only special pleas which can be heard for a defendant are (1) that he has been before legally convicted in a court of competent jurisdiction, after having been tried upon the merits for the same offense; (2) that he has been before acquitted by a jury of the accusation against him, in a court of competent jurisdiction,—whether the acquittal was regular or irregular. And it was held in *Mixon* v. *State*, 35 Tex. Crim. Rep. 458, 34 S. W. 290, that a conviction of manslaughter on an insufficient indictment is a bar to a prosecution for murder in the first or second degree on a new and sufficient indictment for the same offense.

In Arkansas, by statute (Mansf. Dig. § 2176) jeopardy attaches after verdict and judgment thereon whether the indictment is sufficient in form or substance or not. But jeopardy will not attach, on the bringing in of a verdict of acquittal or conviction on an insufficient indictment, until a judgment has been entered thereon. *Harp* v. *State*, 59 Ark. 113, 26 S. W. 714.

In Oregon a statute (Hill's Anno. Laws, § 1338) provides that an acquittal on the merits is a bar, notwithstanding a defect in form or substance in the indictment. And an acquittal by the direction of the court, after the testimony of the state is concluded, on the ground that the indictment is fatally defective, will not support a plea of former jeopardy. *State* v. *Littschke*, 27 Or. 189, 40 Pac. 167.

31. Irregularity in drawing grand jury.

A mere irregularity in drawing the grand jury which found the former indictment, though such as to be cause for reversal or arrest of the former judgment, does not render the indictment void so as to defeat the plea.[1]

[1]*Kohlheimer* v. *State*, 39 Miss. 548, 77 Am. Dec. 689.

As to irregularities of grand jury, see also *ante*, Divisions IV. and XIV.

32. Acquittal for variance.

A plea of former acquittal is not sustainable where the acquittal was on the ground of a variance on the first trial between the indictment and the proof.[1]

[1]*Canter* v. *People*, 1 Abb. App. Dec. 305; N. Y. Code Crim. Proc. § 340. But see notes to § 16, *supra*.

An acquittal under an indictment for burglary in breaking into the house of one person is no bar to a similar indictment, based on the same crime, for breaking into the house of another person. *State* v. *Brown*, 33 S. C. 151, 11 S. E. 641.

And an acquittal, under the direction of the court, of stealing money, on the ground that the evidence will not support such a charge, is not a bar to a subsequent action for swindling with regard to the same money. *Lewis* v. *State* (Tex. Crim. App.) 24 S. W. 906.

Nor does an acquittal under an indictment charging defendant with false swearing before a justice of the peace bar a prosecution for false swearing in regard to the same matter before the county judge. *Turner* v. *Com.* 19 Ky. L. Rep. 1161, 42 S. W. 1129.

In Montana a statute (Crim. Prac. act, § 223) provides that the formal acquittal for variance between indictment and proof, or on objection to the form or substance of the indictment, shall not be an acquittal of the same offense. And an acquittal on the ground of variance between "Maze," the name of defendant, and "Moys," the name given in the indictment, is insufficient to bar a further prosecution. *State* v. *Sullivan*, 9 Mont. 490, 24 Pac. 23.

In *Gaskins* v. *Com.* 97 Ky. 494, 30 S. W. 1017, it is held that, under the Kentucky statute (Ky. Crim. Code, § 178) which provides that the dismissal of an indictment for variance between the indictment and proof shall not bar another prosecution for the same offense, a verdict under a peremptory instruction, finding defendant not guilty as charged in the indictment, which charges him with murder, is a bar to a subsequent prosecution for assisting, counseling, and advising another to commit the murder.

33. Judgment by fraud.

A conviction or acquittal procured by fraud or collusion cannot be pleaded to a subsequent prosecution for the same offense.[1]

[1]*State* v. *Green*, 16 Iowa, 239; *State* v. *Simpson*, 28 Minn. 66, 41 Am. Rep.

269, 9 N. W. 78; *McFarland* v. *State*, 68 Wis. 400, 60 Am. Rep. 867, 32 N. W. 226; *Halloran* v. *State*, 80 Ind. 586; *State* v. *Colvin*, 11 Humph. 599, 54 Am. Dec. 58; *Warriner* v. *State*, 3 Tex. App. 104, 30 Am. Rep. 124; *Watkins* v. *State*, 68 Ind. 427, 34 Am. Rep. 273; *Moore* v. *State*, 71 Ala. 307; *State* v. *Smith*, 57 Kan. 673, 47 Pac. 541, and cases cited.

But *Shideler* v. *State*, 129 Ind. 523, 528, 16 L. R. A. 225, 28 N. E. 537, 29 N. E. 36, holds that where the prosecution is in fact regularly commenced by the prosecuting attorney, and is thereafter carried to final judgment, the state being represented throughout by its sworn officer, who, however, pending the prosecution, is corrupted and paid to secure acquittal instead of conviction, a judgment of acquittal so procured is not void, and is a complete bar to a second prosecution for the same offense, since, if treated as void, there will remain a valid pending prosecution, and, if not void, it cannot be collaterally attacked.

34. Informal verdict.

When a verdict of guilty is set aside by the court, because not in proper form to sustain a conviction, and a new trial is granted, the defendant is not regarded as having been in legal jeopardy, and cannot plead this as a former acquittal.[1]

[1]*Kendall* v. *State*, 65 Ala. 492; S. P., *Robinson* v. *State*, 23 Tex. App. 315, 4 S. W. 904.

35. Verdict without judgment.

The plea of former acquittal or conviction may be sustained where there has been a verdict, although no judgment has been entered thereon,[1] or a void judgment has been entered in which the defendant has acquiesced,[2] unless it appears that the former proceedings on which the plea is based have not yet been concluded.[3]

[1]*Shepherd* v. *People*, 25 N. Y. 406, 420; *Mount* v. *State*, 14 Ohio, 295, 45 Am. Dec. 542; *State* v. *Norvell*, 2 Yerg. 24, 24 Am. Dec. 458. *Contra*, *State* v. *Priebnow*, 16 Neg. 131, 19 N. W. 628 (statutory). And see N. Y. Code Crim. Proc. § 334, subd. 4, providing that in statutory form of plea there shall be an allegation of judgment.

[2]*People* v. *Cramer*, 5 Park. Crim. Rep. 171; *McGinnis* v. *State*, 9 Humph. 43, 49 Am. Dec. 697 (conviction under an unconstitutional statute acquiesced in by defendant); *Com.* v. *Loud*, 3 Met. 328, 37 Am. Dec. 139; *Kelly* v. *People*, 115 Ill. 583, 56 Am. Rep. 184, 4 N. E. 644.

[3]*United States* v. *Martin*, 28 Fed. 812, holding that pendency of a motion to arrest judgment will defeat such plea.

36. Verdict under void instruction.

Where a defendant has been acquitted by the jury under instruction from the court to acquit, he has been once in jeopardy, and cannot be retried, though the court had no power to so instruct the jury to acquit, but was only authorized to advise them.[1]

[1]*People* v. *Horn,* 70 Cal. 17, 11 Pac. 470.

37. Withdrawal of part of charge during trial.

If a plea of former conviction or acquittal relates only to a charge obviously inserted in the present indictment as matter of aggravation of another charge therein, the prosecution may defeat the plea by withdrawing the incidental charge to which it relates.[1]

[1]*State* v. *Struble,* 71 Iowa, 11, 32 N. W. 1 (withdrawal of charge of assault with intent to kill from an indictment for burglary).

38. Former void trial.

A former trial which was void because had without a jury, against the objection of the state, will not sustain a plea of a former acquittal or conviction.[1]

[1]*State* v. *Mead,* 4 Blackf. 309, 30 Am. Dec. 661.

39. Effect of getting reversal, etc.

A previous verdict of conviction which has been set aside[1] or reversed,[2] or judgment on which has been arrested,[3] at defendant's instance, is not available to sustain a plea of former conviction or former jeopardy as to the offense established by the conviction.

But if the verdict expressly or by implication acquitted the defendant of another count or offense or a higher degree of the same offense,[4] and the conviction has been set aside or reversed, or judgment thereon arrested at the instance of the accused, he may upon a subsequent trial plead the former acquittal,[5] but not the former conviction.[6] Otherwise under the New York statute by which a reversal revives the indictment as to all its parts, and it stands as if there had been no trial.[7]

[1]*Kendall* v. *State,* 65 Ala. 492 (verdict of guilty set aside on defendant's motion, because not in the form required by statute); *Gibson* v. *State,* 26 Fla. 109, 7 So. 376; *Hudson* v. *People,* 29 Ill. App. 454; *Com.* v. *Brown,* 167 Mass. 144, 45 N. E. 1; *State* v. *Thompson,* 10 Mont. 549, 27 Pac. 349; *People* v. *Murray,* 89 Mich. 276, 14 L. R. A. 809, 50 N. W. 995 (verdict set aside because defendant was denied a public trial).

In *People* v. *Cignarale,* 110 N. Y. 23, 17 N. E. 135, a judgment entered on a plea of guilty of murder in the second degree, set aside and plea withdrawn by leave of court, was held to be no bar to a subsequent conviction of murder in the first degree. By obtaining an order for a new trial, the accused waived the claim that he could not be again tried, and the withdrawal of the plea of guilty of the lesser degree waived the acquittal of higher degree implied in the acceptance of that plea.

A plea of former jeopardy by a prosecution resulting in defendant's conviction of the theft of a mule at the same time with a theft of a second mule for stealing which defendant is on trial is properly overruled, where a motion for a new trial was pending in the former case at the time said plea was set up, which was subsequently granted, and no request was made by defendant for postponement of the second trial until the former case had been disposed of. *Maines* v. *State*, 37 Tex. Crim. Rep. 617, 40 S. W. 490.

•*Simco* v. *State*, 9 Tex. App. 338; *State* v. *Thurston*, 3 Heisk. 67 (plea of former conviction reversed, and indictment dismissed as bad on demurrer); *McGinn* v. *State*, 46 Neb. 427, 30 L. R. A. 450, 65 N. W. 46; *Carpenter* v. *State*, 62 Ark. 286, 36 S. W. 900; *People* v. *Tucker*, 117 Cal. 229, 49 Pac. 134; *Lovett* v. *State*, 33 Fla. 389, 14 So. 837; *State* v. *Reddington*, 8 S. D. 315, 66 N. W. 464.

In *State* v. *Wyse*, 33 S. C. 582, 12 S. E. 556, it was held that the provisions of S. C. Const. art. 1, § 18, that "no person, after having been once acquitted by a jury, shall again, for the same offense, be put in jeopardy of his life or liberty," supersedes the common law, and repeals it whenever the two are inconsistent with each other; and a person whose conviction has been reversed on appeal cannot avail himself of the objection that a new trial is subjecting him a second time to jeopardy.

•Where there has been a trial for an offense, and a verdict of guilty, and on motion of the defendant the court arrests the judgment, the defendant has not been in the jeopardy which forbids a second trial, whether upon the same indictment or upon a new one. *Bedee* v. *People*, 73 Ill. 320.

Sustaining a motion in arrest of judgment operates as an acquittal, under Cal. Pen. Code, § 1188, only where no evidence has been given sufficient to charge defendant with any offense. It is not necessary that the evidence should be sufficient to convict. *People* v. *Eppinger*, 109 Cal. 294, 41 Pac. 1037.

•If the conviction was on confession or plea of guilty, a withdrawal of the plea will extinguish the implied acquittal. *People* v. *Cignarale*, 110 N. Y. 23, 17 N. E. 135.

•Where an accused was tried upon an indictment that in a single count charged the highest degree of an offense, and that included lower degrees of the same crime, or one that in several counts charged such highest degree and the lower degrees, and he was convicted of one of such lower grades of the offense, on a new trial, obtained at his request, he cannot again be tried for, or convicted of, any higher grade of crime than that of which he was at first convicted. *Johnson* v. *State*, 27 Fla. 245, 9 So. 208.

In *People* v. *Dowling*, 84 N. Y. 478, 483, Folger, Ch. J., says: "New trials are granted in criminal cases . . . on the ground that by asking for a correction of errors made on the first trial he [the accused] does waive his constitutional protection and does himself ask for a new trial, though it bring him twice in jeopardy. But that waiver, unless it be expressly of the benefit of the verdict of acquittal, goes no further than the accused himself extends it. . . . He is not to be supposed to ask correction or reversal of so much of it [the judgment] as acquitted him of offense. . . . As to that, the plea of *autrefois acquit* can be upheld, though the plea of *autrefois convict* cannot be upheld as to the offense of which the verdict was guilty." Motion to strike out count of which the accused was formerly acquitted denied; error, new trial as to that count. Followed in *Sullivan* v. *People*, 27 Hun, 35. This was before the New York Code of Criminal Procedure went into effect.

Thus, a verdict finding one guilty of simple abduction is a bar to further prosecution upon a charge of kidnapping and of felonious abduction, under the Texas statutes. *Mason* v. *State*, 29 Tex. App. 24, 14 S. W. 71.

And where a person is indicted for selling several kinds of mortgaged personal property, a conviction of removing only one of such kinds is an acquittal as to the others, so as to be pleadable in bar of another prosecution as to the latter. *Foster* v. *State*, 88 Ala. 182, 7 So. 185.

The provision of Cal. Pen. Code, § 1180, that the granting of a new trial places the parties in the same position as if no trial had been had, does not, where an accused charged with two or more offenses in an indictment is acquitted of one and convicted of the other, place him, upon the granting of a new trial, in the same position, as to the offense of which he is acquitted, as if no trial had been had, and subject him again to trial for such offense, since such effect would render the statute unconstitutional. *People* v. *Gordon*, 99 Cal. 227, 33 Pac. 901, so holding of a conviction of an assault with a deadly weapon, under a charge of assault with intent to commit murder; reversed on appeal.

A verdict of guilty on one of several counts, in a criminal prosecution before a justice of the peace, is, where nothing is said as to the other counts, equivalent to a verdict of not guilty as to the counts not mentioned; and, on appeal to the district court by the defendant, he can be there tried only for the offense charged in the count on which he was convicted in the justice's court. *State* v. *Wood*, 49 Kan. 711, 31 Pac. 786; *State* v. *Severson*, 79 Iowa, 750, 45 N. W. 305.

In *Bell* v. *State*, 48 Ala. 684, 17 Am. Rep. 40, it was held that where the accused has been tried on an indictment charging burglary and larceny, and convicted of the former, he cannot be retried for larceny, though the conviction has been reversed on error.

But one convicted on one trial, of the offense of housebreaking with intent to commit larceny, and on a second trial of grand larceny, under an indictment charging in one count both offenses, which are of equal degree, is rightly put on trial on the whole indictment upon obtaining a second new trial, under Va. Code 1887, § 4040, providing that if a new trial is granted the accused he shall not be tried for any "higher offense" than that of which he was convicted on the last trial. *Benton* v. *Com.* 91 Va. 782, 21 S. E. 495.

The cases in which this question most usually arises are homicide cases where the defendant, charged with murder in the first degree, is convicted of some lower degree of homicide, and, upon a new trial obtained at his instance on motion or after an appeal, he seeks to confine the prosecution to the degree of homicide of which he was first convicted. The authorities differ on this question. In many of the states it is held that when, on an indictment for murder, the accused is found guilty of a lower degree of homicide, it is virtually an acquittal of the higher degrees of homicide; and that, if the verdict is set aside, and a new trial granted, at the instance of the accused, he cannot on such trial be convicted of homicide higher than that of which he was first convicted; that the only effect of setting aside the verdict for the lesser crime is to leave that issue open for another trial, and also to leave undetermined the further question of whether the accused has committed any criminal homicide of a grade less than that of which he was convicted. The case of *State* v. *Belden*, 33 Wis. 121, 14 Am. Rep. 748, is a leading case holding thus. See also *State* v. *Murphy*, 13 Wash. 229, 43 Pac. 44; *Re Bennett*, 84 Fed. 324, and cases cited; *State* v. *Steeves*, 29 Or. 85, 43 Pac. 947; *Nutt* v. *State*, 63 Ala. 180; *State* v. *Martin*, 30 Wis. 216, 11 Am. Rep. 567; *Johnson* v. *State*, 29 Ark. 31, 21 Am. Rep. 154; *Sipple* v. *People*, 10 Ill. App. 144; *State* v. *Bruffey*, 11 Mo. App. 79, 75 Mo. 389.

But in other states the courts hold to the contrary. They say that the necessary result of reversing the judgment and granting a new trial is to set aside the whole verdict, and that having been done at the instance of the accused, it can operate neither as an acquittal nor a bar to the further prosecution of any part of the crime charged; that, the verdict being set aside, it leaves at issue and undetermined the question of the homicide, and also the question of whether the accused committed it, if one was committed; that, on the retrial on a plea of not guilty, the legal presumption of innocence prevails, and the state is bound to prove every essential fact; that the only effect, therefore, that can be given to the part of the verdict that acquitted the accused of murder in the first degree, after the rest of it has been set aside is to regard it as finding the quality of an act, the existence of which is undetermined, which would be a verdict to the effect that if the accused committed the homicide, it was not such a killing as made it murder in the first degree, which would be untenable, as there can be no legal determination of the character of the malice of the accused in respect to a homicide that he is not found to have committed, or rather, of which, under his plea, he is presumed to be innocent. A verdict of murder in the second degree is only an implied acquittal of murder in the first degree; and, if the verdict from which the inference is drawn is set aside, nothing remains to sustain the inference, the verdict and its incidents fall together, and the indictment is left to stand, as to the crime of which the accused was convicted, as though there had been no trial. *State* v. *Behimer*, 20 Ohio St. 572, 14 Am. Rep. 752, note; *State* v. *Bradley*, 67 Vt. 465, 32 Atl. 238, and cases cited; *State* v. *Hornsby*, 8 Rob. (La.) 583, 41 Am. Dec. 314; *Waller* v. *State*, 104 Ga. 505, 30 S. E. 835; *State* v. *Kessler*, 15 Utah, 142, 49 Pac. 293, and cases cited; *Ball* v. *United States*, 163 U. S. 662, 41 L. ed. 300, 16 Sup. Ct. Rep. 1192; *State* v. *Billings*, 140 Mo.

193, 41 S. W. 778; *Com.* v. *Arnold,* 83 Ky. 1; *Bohanan* v. *State,* 18 Neb. 57, 53 Am. Rep. 791, 24 N. W. 390; *State* v. *Miller,* 35 Kan. 328, 10 Pac. 865; *People* v. *Keefer,* 65 Cal. 232, 3 Pac. 818 (in effect overruling *People* v. *Gilmore,* 4 Cal. 376, 60 Am. Dec. 620, which held that, notwithstanding Cal. Crim. Code, § 439, provides that the granting of a new trial places the parties in the same position as if no trial had been had, the defendant might, upon new trial after a reversal of conviction of manslaughter upon an indictment for murder, plead former acquittal as to murder; but might be retried for manslaughter); *State* v. *McCord,* 8 Kan. 232, 12 Am. Rep. 469.

[6] *State* v. *Stephens,* 13 S. C. 285; *Sutcliffe* v. *State,* 18 Ohio, 469, 51 Am. Dec. 459; authorities before cited. See *post,* Division XLVIII.

[7] The rule has been changed by N. Y. Pen. Code, § 36, and N. Y. Code Crim. Proc. §§ 464, 544 *et seq.*, under which, by procuring reversal of a conviction for a lesser degree, or for one of several offenses, the indictment stands as if there had been no trial, and the accused may be tried again precisely as if there had been no conviction. *People* v. *Palmer,* 109 N. Y. 413, 17 N. E. 213, Affirming 43 Hun, 397.

40. Civil judgment not pleadable.

Recovery of damages, in a civil action, for the acts charged in an indictment, is not a bar to a criminal prosecution therefor.[1]

[1] *United States* v. *Buntin,* 10 Fed. 730, S. P., *Com.* v. *Somerville,* 1 Va. Cas. 164, 5 Am. Dec. 514.

In *State ex rel. Scobey* v. *Stevens,* 103 Ind. 55, 53 Am. Rep. 482, 2 N. E. 214, it was held that a statute making an act a crime, and also permitting a civil action for the same offense, with punitive damages, is not unconstitutional as putting the defendant twice in jeopardy.

So, in *State ex rel. Duensing* v. *Roby,* 142 Ind. 168, 33 L. R. A. 213, 41 N. E. 145, it was held that a suit for an injunction against the violation of a statute, and punishment for contempt of such an injunction, in addition to a criminal prosecution for the illegal act, did not violate the constitutional provision against putting a person twice in jeopardy for the same offense.

So, the removal of excise commissioners from office under the consolidation act, § 109 (N. Y. Laws 1882), is not such a "punishment" for a neglect of duty as would bar an indictment under N. Y. Pen. Code, § 117, making such neglect a misdemeanor. *People* v. *Meakim,* 133 N. Y. 214, 30 N. E. 828. This case also holds that the award of a peremptory mandamus and imposition of a fine, under N. Y. Code Civ. Proc, § 2090, against excise commissioners for neglect of duty, is no bar to an indictment under N. Y. Pen. Code, § 117, making such neglect a misdemeanor.

41. Requisites of plea of former jeopardy, acquittal, or conviction.

The plea must allege that the two offenses are identical,[1] and should set out the previous indictment,[2] and the proceedings thereunder.[3]

[1] *McQuoid* v. *People*, 8 Ill. 76; *Evans* v. *State*, 54 Ark. 227, 15 S. W. 360; *King* v. *State*, 43 Tex. 351; *State* v. *Wister*, 62 Mo. 592; *State* v. *Horneman*, 16 Kan. 452; *Quitzow* v. *State*, 1 Tex. App. 47, 28 Am. Rep. 396 (plea showing former trial and conviction; error to sustain demurrer thereto); *Newberry* v. *State*, 26 Fla. 334, 8 So. 445.

Pleas of former acquittal and former conviction are pleas in bar, and are viewed with liberality, and are not required to be so certain as an indictment; but they must aver facts essential to the defense sought to be presented thereby. *State* v. *Cross*, 44 W. Va. 315, 29 S. E. 527.

But a statement by defendant in a plea of former acquittal, that he is willing to verify the same, is a sufficient verification. *Guenther* v. *People*, 22 Colo. 121, 43 Pac. 999.

In California, by statute (Pen. Code, § 1017), if the defendant plead a former conviction or acquittal, the form is as follows: "The defendant pleads that he has already been convicted (or acquitted) of the offense charged by the judgment of the court of ——— (naming it), rendered at ——— (naming the place), on the — day of ———." If he plead once in jeopardy, the form is as follows: "The defendant pleads that he has been once in jeopardy for the offense charged (specifying the time, place, and court)." And pleas as follows: "First, defendant pleads not guilty of the offense charged; second, a former acquittal; third, once in jeopardy,"—are insufficient. *People* v. *O'Leary*, 77 Cal. 30, 22 Pac. 24. "The object of these forms is plain," said the court. "The People should be informed of the circumstances as to time, place, and court. None of these circumstances are named in the plea actually entered upon the minutes of the court below; and we cannot resort to the written document, which, it is claimed, was filed at the time the plea was entered, in aid of the plea actually entered."

[2] *Crocker* v. *State*, 47 Ga. 568; *Smith* v. *State*, 52 Ala. 407; *Rex* v. *Taylor*, 5 Dowl. & R. 422, 3 Barn. & C. 502; *Henry* v. *State*, 33 Ala. 389; *Grisham* v. *State*, 19 Tex. App. 504; *Wilson* v. *State*, 68 Ga. 827.

Pleas of former conviction or acquittal must state the offense involved in the former trial, its identity with that involved in the second prosecution, and the identity of the person of the accused with the person before tried, and must vouch the record of the former trial; *i. e.*, must contain the expression, after alleging the proceedings on the former trial to show the essentials of such pleading, "as by the record thereof fully appears," or an equivalent expression. *State* v. *Cross*, 44 W. Va. 315, 29 S. E. 527.

[3] *Campbell* v. *People*, 109 Ill. 565, 50 Am. Rep. 621; *Cross* v. *State*, 117 Ala. 73, 23 So. 784; *Davis* v. *State*, 51 Neb. 301, 70 N. W. 984; *Wheelock* v. *State* (Tex. Crim. App.) 38 S. W. 182; *Williams* v. *State*, 13 Tex. App. 285; *Wortham* v. *Com.* 5 Rand. (Va.) 669.

A plea of former acquittal is prima facie sufficient if it shows that a jury was impaneled, and that the prosecution went into proofs by witnesses until it rested its case, because this entitles defendant to a verdict; and if there was a necessary discharge of the jury, preventing verdict, it should be set up by replication. *People* v. *Jones*, 48 Mich. 554, 12 N. W. 848; *Page* v. *Com.* 27 Gratt. 954 (holding that a plea tendered as of former acquittal, but showing conviction, is demurrable).

The New York statute prescribes the form. Code Crim. Proc. § 334, subd. 4.

And a plea of *autrefois convict* must verify the alleged conviction by the record. *Evans* v. *State*, 54 Ark. 227, 15 S. W. 360.

A plea alleging that defendant was on a specified day tried and acquitted of the identical offense alleged in the information, to which are attached pleadings in which the offense charged is the same as to dates, parties, and offense, and a judgment showing an acquittal,—is a sufficient plea of former acquittal. *McCullough* v. *State* (Tex. Crim. App.) 34 S. W. 753.

And a plea of former acquittal reciting that copies of the verdict, judgment, and indictment are attached as exhibits, is not objectionable for lacking verification by the record, where although they are not marked as exhibits to, or designated as part of, the plea, the record on appeal does in fact contain the indictment, verdict, and judgment. *Harp* v. *State*, 59 Ark. 113, 26 S. W. 714. The court said that the presumption was that they were brought into the transcript just as they were offered, whether as attached to the plea or produced for the inspection of the court; that if the defendant had not designated them as exhibits, the clerk could not do so; but, at any rate, they were a part of the record, which was proof convincing that they were considered by the court in some form in passing upon the demurrer; otherwise the clerk was guilty of officiousness or inadvertence.

42. Time of pleading.

The plea should be filed at the time of arraignment, but if the conviction or acquittal is not perfected until after arraignment, the plea should be afterwards allowed.[1]

[1]*Pearce* v. *Com.* 5 Ky. L. Rep. 407. Here an indictment was pending against the defendant, and he was being prosecuted on another indictment in the same court for the same offense; in the latter case, a verdict of guilty having been rendered and judgment entered thereon after the trial in this case had been commenced; and it was held that he was entitled to file the plea.

In *State* v. *Watson*, 20 R. I. 354, 39 Atl. 193, it was said that the rules of criminal pleading require that a plea to the jurisdiction, like a demurrer, plea in abatement, plea in bar, or any other special plea whatever, shall precede the plea of not guilty. If the special plea is determined against the defendant, the practice is to then allow him to plead over.

In *Davis* v. *State*, 51 Neb. 315, 70 N. W. 984, it was held that a plea in bar will not lie while there is of record a plea of not guilty, unless the latter plea be withdrawn; and that it seems to be a matter left by the law to the sound discretion of the trial court, whether he will permit a prisoner to withdraw a plea of not guilty and file a plea in bar. The court said, however, that it had no doubt that if a prisoner, after a plea of not guilty, should tender a lawful and proper plea in bar, stating facts which had occurred or come to his knowledge since the entry of his plea of not guilty, and which facts, if true, would entitle him to a discharge, then it would be the duty of the court to permit the prisoner to withdraw his plea of not guilty, and file the plea in bar.

The court may properly refuse to allow defendant to file a plea of former conviction pending the trial of an issue under a plea of not guilty, under Ga. Pen. Code, § 950, providing that if the prisoner, on being arraigned, shall demur to the indictment, or plead to the jurisdiction of the court, or in abatement, or any special plea in bar, the demurrer or plea shall be made in writing, and if such demurrer or plea is decided against him, he may, nevertheless, plead, and rely on the general issue of not guilty. *Hall* v. *State*, 103 Ga. 403, 29 S. E. 915.

And the plea of former acquittal cannot be interposed in bar after a verdict of guilty. *Barton* v. *State* (Tex. Crim. App.) 43 S. W. 987.

43. When presented with a plea of not guilty.

If a plea of former acquittal or former conviction is interposed with a plea of not guilty, the plea of not guilty should not be tried until the other plea has been disposed of;[1] submitting both is reversible error.[2] In cases of misdemeanor, however, going to trial without objection waives the irregularity;[3] and if both pleas should be submitted, the jury should pass on the special plea.[4]

[1] *Lee* v. *State*, 26 Ark. 260, 7 Am. Rep. 611; *Com.* v. *Crawley*, 12 Va. L. J. 489.

Plea of former acquittal is special plea in bar of matter wholly independent of general plea of not guilty, and does not properly or legally displace it, but when it is overruled the general plea remains with the issue formed by it for trial. *Tandy* v. *State*, 94 Wis. 498, 69 N. W. 160.

[2] *Foster* v. *State*, 39 Ala. 229; *Henry* v. *State*, 33 Ala. 389; *Com.* v. *Merrill*, 8 Allen, 545 (held error to submit pleas of former conviction and not guilty together); *Com.* v. *Bakeman*, 105 Mass. 53; *Com.* v. *Demuth*, 12 Serg. & R. 389; *Rex* v. *Roche*, 1 Leach C. L. 134. And see *State* v. *Respass*, 85 N. C. 534. *Contra*, *Pritchford* v. *State*, 2 Tex. App. 69; *Davis* v. *State*, 42 Tex. 494 (holding that it is proper to submit the two pleas together, yet a failure of the jury to pass upon each plea is error); *Solliday* v. *Com.* 28 Pa. 13 (failure of the jury to pass upon each of the pleas of former conviction and not guilty, error).

[3] *Faulk* v. *State*, 52 Ala. 415; *Dominick* v. *State*, 40 Ala. 680, 91 Am. Dec. 496.

[4] *Deaton* v. *State*, 44 Tex. 446, under Paschal's Dig. art. 3091.

44. Substituting special plea for not guilty.

It is discretionary with the court to permit a plea of not guilty to be withdrawn, and a plea of former acquittal or conviction to be substituted.[1]

[1] *Phillips* v. *People*, 55 Ill. 429; *State* v. *Salge*, 2 Nev. 321; *United States* v. *Harmison*, 3 Sawy. 556, Fed. Cas. No. 15,308; *People* v. *Allen*, 43 N. Y. 28 (defect in organizing grand jury).

It may be matter of right to the accused. See § 46, *infra*.

45. How determined.

The issue raised by a plea of former acquittal or conviction is for the jury,[1] under proper instructions of the court;[2] but if the plea shows on its face a different offense, or is wholly insufficient, it need not be submitted to the jury.[3]

[1] N. Y. Code Crim. Proc. §§ 354, 355;; *Fenton* v. *State*, 33 Tex. Crim. Rep. 633, 28 S. W. 537; *Grant* v. *People*, 4 Park. Crim. Rep. 527; *Com.* v. *Bosworth*, 113 Mass. 200 (failure to submit to the jury, held error); *Troy* v. *State*, 10 Tex. App. 319; *Quitzow* v. *State*, 1 Tex. App. 47, 28 Am. Rep. 396; *Grisham* v. *State*, 19 Tex. App. 504 (holding that if the plea is sufficient to admit of and is supported by any evidence at the trial, it is the duty of the court to submit the issue to the jury). As to the evidence to prove such pleas, see *post*, Division XXXIX.

[2] *Wilson* v. *State*, 45 Tex. 76, 23 Am. Rep. 602; *Martha* v. *State*, 26 Ala. 72 (holding that upon the trial of this issue the court may declare to the jury the legal effect of the record set up in bar, and, when it is a fact, may charge the jury that the plea is not sustained by the proof).

In *State* v. *Jamison*, 104 Iowa, 343, 73 N. W. 831, it is held that when, under the law, or for want of evidence, the plea is not sustained, the court may so charge the jury.

In *State* v. *Robinson*, 12 Wash. 491, 41 Pac. 884, where the court instructed the jury to disregard all evidence relating to the question of former acquittal, it was held that as the ruling of the court in so doing was founded upon the theory that the undisputed facts showed that appellant had never been acquitted of the crime with which he was charged in the information upon which he was on trial, this instruction was clearly erroneous, if any proof had been introduced which tended in any degree to show that the appellant had been acquitted of the crime so charged; but that if there was no such proof, defendant had no right to complain of the ruling of the court in denying his motion for a discharge, or in not giving him a separate trial upon the issues raised upon the plea of former acquittal.

[3] *Hite* v. *State*, 9 Yerg. 357; *Simco* v. *State*, 9 Tex. App. 338; *State* v. *Meekins*, 41 La. Ann. 543, 6 So. 822.

Where the offenses charged in different indictments are so diverse as not to admit of proof that they are the same, the court may decide the issue without submitting it to the jury. *Epps* v. *State,* 38 Tex. Crim. Rep. 284, 42 S. W. 552, and cases cited; *Wright* v. *State,* 37 Tex. Crim. Rep. 627, 40 S. W. 491.

It is further held in Texas that there is a distinction between a conviction and an acquittal. In case of conviction it is held that the state can carve but once; and, where the offense is separable,—that is, when different articles are stolen at the same time belonging to different persons,—the state can combine all the articles stolen at the same time in the same indictment, or it can carve out such as it pleases, and embody in the same indictment; but a conviction will bar a subsequent prosecution for theft of any of said articles which were taken at the same time. The same principle, however, does not apply in case of acquittal; that is, if different articles are stolen at the same time and place, constituting one transaction, but they belong to different persons, if there are different indictments charging the possession and ownership in different persons, an acquittal under one indictment for theft from one person will not bar a prosecution for theft of different property, or even the same property, from another person; that is, *autrefois acquit* is available only in cases where the transaction is the same, and the two indictments are susceptible of and must be sustained by the same proof. *Autrefois convict* only requires that the transaction, or the facts constituting it, be the same.

46. Pleading over.

If defendant's plea of former acquittal or former conviction be found against him, he should be allowed to plead the general issue.[1]

[1] *Barge* v. *Com.* 3 Penr. & W. 262, 23 Am. Dec. 81; *McFarland* v. *State,* 68 Wis. 400, 60 Am. Rep. 867, 32 N. W. 227 (holding it error for the court to pronounce a judgment of conviction after the jury has found against the defendant under a plea of former conviction or acquittal, without a trial of the issue under a plea of not guilty); *Fulkner* v. *State,* 3 Heisk. 33 (under a statute to that effect); *Com.* v. *Goddard,* 13 Mass. 455; *Hirn* v. *State,* 1 Ohio St. 15 (holding that on overruling any special plea defendant must be allowed to plead over).

But *contra, Crippen* v. *State,* 3 Heisk. 25 (discretionary to refuse to permit the accused to plead not guilty after the issue upon a plea of former conviction has been found against him).

VI. Pending of another prosecution.

47. Another indictment pending.

The pendency of a previous indictment is not matter for a plea in abatement.[1]

[1] *Eldridge* v. *State,* 27 Fla. 162, 9 So. 448; *Com.* v. *Brown,* 167 Mass. 144, 45 N. E. 1; *Bonner* v. *State,* 29 Tex. App. 223, 15 S. W. 821; *People* v. *Fisher,* 14 Wend. 9, 28 Am. Dec. 501; *Smith* v. *Com.* 104 Pa. 339 (cases of two indictments in same count); *Bell* v. *State,* 115 Ala. 87, 22 So.

453; *State* v. *Keena*, 64 Conn. 212, 29 Atl. 470; *Kalloch* v. *San Francisco City & County Super. Ct.* 56 Cal. 229. And see *State* v. *Andrew*, 76 Mo. 101; *Mackin* v. *People* (Ill.) 8 Crim. L. Mag. 692, 8 N. E. 178 (indictment in state court and another in United States court); *United States* v. *Neverson*, 1 Mackey, 152 (holding that, even if the former indictment has been pleaded to, it is no bar to an arraignment on a second indictment); *State* v. *Eaton*, 75 Mo. 586; *Cack* v. *State* (Tex.) 2 Week. Jur. 283.

48. — qui tam prosecution.

Where the whole or part of a penalty goes to the informer, he who first brings a *qui tam* action, or commences a prosecution by indictment or information, acquires the right to the penalty; and that prosecution, until it is determined, excludes all others.[1]

[1] 1 Throop's (Mass.) Dig. 728 (351, 352), Citing *Com.* v. *Churchill*, 5 Mass. 174; *Com.* v. *Cheney*, 6 Mass. 347; *Com.* v. *Drew*, 3 Cush. 279.

The pendency of such an action at the time when an indictment for the same offense is returned must be pleaded and proved like a plea of *autrefois acquit* or *autrefois convict*, and will defeat the indictment. *Com.* v. *Howard*, 13 Mass. 221; *Com.* v. *Murphy*, 2 Gray, 510.

VII. Pardon.

49. How set up.

An executive pardon in force when the defendant is arraigned must be specially pleaded.[1] If issued after arraignment it may be brought to the notice of the court on motion at any stage of the trial, whenever received;[2] otherwise it will be waived.[3]

[1] Bacon, Abr., Pardon, G. 2; 4 Bl. Com. 394.

Otherwise of a general legislative pardon without exceptions; for this the court must judicially notice.

[2] *Com.* v. *Lockwood*, 109 Mass. 323, 12 Am. Rep. 699; *Com.* v. *Mash*, 7 Met. 472; *State* v. *Woolery*, 29 Mo. 300; *Duncan* v. *Com.* 4 Serg. & R. 449; 4 Bl. Com. 369; Wharton, Crim. Pl. & Pr. § 526.

[3] *United States* v. *Wilson*, 7 Pet. 150, 8 L. ed. 640.

The constitutional abolition of attainder and corruption of blood supersedes the old doctrine that a pardon for one offense might be pleaded in bar of any other felony committed before the pardon. Note to *Crenshaw* v. *State* (Tenn.) 17 Am. Dec. 794.

VIII. Not guilty.

50. Leave to withdraw.

It is in the discretion of the court to allow a plea of not guilty to be withdrawn for the purpose of substituting a different plea,[1] or for the purpose of a motion.[2]

[1] 1 Chitty, Crim. Law, 436; *Rex* v. *Knighty*, Holt, 398; *State* v. *Salge*, 2 Nev. 321 (discretionary, except to plead something occurring since last motion, and then matter of right); *Phillips* v. *People*, 55 Ill. 429; *People* v. *Allen*, 43 N. Y. 28; *Hubbard* v. *State*, 72 Ala. 164; *Savage* v. *State*, 18 Fla. 909; *People* v. *Lewis*, 64 Cal. 401, 1 Pac. 490; *People* v. *Shem Ah Fook*, 64 Cal. 380, 1 Pac. 347.

[2] *Taylor* v. *Com.* 42 Phila. Legal. Int. 193; *People* v. *Lee*, 17 Cal. 76.

IX. Nolo contendere.

[The object of this plea is to submit, if the punishment be imposed, but without conceding guilt as matter of fact by a plea of guilty that would admit the facts alleged, and might be used in evidence against the defendant in another proceeding.]

51. Not of right.

The plea of *nolo contendere* cannot be put in without leave of court. It is discretionary with the court to receive such a plea, and usually it is allowed, if at all, only in inferior misdemeanors.[1]

[1] Bishop, Crim. Proc. § 802; 1 Chitty, Crim. Law, 431; *Com.* v. *Horton*, 9 Pick. 206.

52. Subsequent proceedings.

The effect of a plea of *nolo contendere* upon all subsequent proceedings on the indictment is the same as that of a plea of guilty.[1]

[1] *United States* v. *Hartwell*, 3 Cliff. 221, Fed. Cas. No. 15,318.

A plea of *nolo contendere*, though not technically a plea of guilty, justifies the court in imposing sentence. *Com.* v. *Holstine*, 132 Pa. 357, 19 Atl. 273.

X. Guilty.

53. How interposed.

A plea of guilty can be put in only by the defendant himself, in open court,[1] except upon indictment against a corporation, in which case it may be put in by counsel.[2]

[1] N. Y. Code Crim. Proc. § 3335; *Saunders* v. *State*, 10 Tex. App. 336 (so holding, under the Texas Code. It may be made orally, but must be entered on the record); *People* v. *McCrory*, 41 Cal. 458 (plea of guilty

of murder in the second degree orally made in open court, in defendant's presence and hearing, by his counsel, afterwards withdrawn by leave of court).

The accused should be examined as to whether the plea is voluntarily submitted if it is so required by statute.

As to whether the statute requiring examination has been sufficiently complied with, see *People* v. *Ferguson*, 48 Mich. 41, 11 N. W. 777; *Clark* v. *People*, 44 Mich. 308, 6 N. W. 682; *People* v. *Lewis*, 51 Mich. 172, 16 N. W. 326; *Frosh* v. *State*, 11 Tex. App. 280.

The Ohio Statute (Rev. Stat. § 7316) providing that if the offense charged be murder, and the accused be convicted by confession in open court, the court shall examine the witnesses, and determine the degree of the crime, and pronounce sentence accordingly,—was held constitutional in *Craig* v. *State*, 49 Ohio St. 415, 16 L. R. A. 358, 30 N. E. 1120.

A plea of guilty will not be accepted until defendant has had opportunity to consult counsel where, upon inquiry, it appears that the acts done do not constitute the offense charged. *United States* v. *Safford*, 66 Fed. 942.

One of several defendants charged with the same offense, who has contributed towards a fund to employ counsel to defend them, by whom a plea of guilty is interposed as to all the defendants but one, as to the indictment against whom a test case is made, cannot, after waiting a year, during which judgment is suspended on the decision of the test case against him, repudiate the plea of guilty on the ground that it was unauthorized. *Territory* v. *Cook*, 7 N. M. 248, 33 Pac. 1022.

[2]N. Y. Code Crim. Proc. § 335.

54. Not to be conditional.

A plea of guilty, expressed to be upon a condition, should be disregarded; and if the defendant refuses to plead further, the court should direct a plea of not guilty to be entered.[1]

[1]*State* v. *Kring*, 11 Mo. App. 92.

But a plea of guilty to a good part of the indictment, upon the prosecution's withdrawing or striking out other parts, will sustain sentence. *State* v. *Buck*, 59 Iowa, 382, 13 N. W. 342 (indictment for forging a promissory note and uttering the same; the latter count withdrawn); *Ferrell* v. *State*, 2 Lea, 25 (indictment for assault and battery with intent to kill; the intent to kill stricken out).

55. Withdrawal.

Another plea cannot be submitted for the plea of not guilty, without leave of court.[1] But the court, in its discretion, at any time before judgment, may permit a plea of guilty to be withdrawn, and a plea of not guilty to be substituted.[2] The refusal to grant such leave is reviewable on error.[3]

[1]Throop's (Mass.) Dig. 729 (363); Citing *Com.* v. *Blake*, 12 Allen, 188 and

Com. v. *Lannan*, 13 Allen, 563; and holding that the rule is the same upon appeal to the supreme court after conviction in a police court.

In *State* v. *Shanley*, 38 W. Va. 516, 18 S. E. 734, it was held that a plea of guilty upon an indictment for selling liquor without a license might be entered without formally and expressly withdrawing a plea of not guilty previously entered.

[5] N. Y. Crim. Code, § 337.

The motion will be denied if the plea has been deliberately put in. *United States* v. *Bayaud*, 23 Fed. 721 (expectation of being able to compromise with the government for violation of the revenue law not sufficient). And see *Mastronada* v. *State*, 60 Miss. 86; *People* v. *Lepper*, 51 Mich. 196, 16 N. W. 377; *Reg.* v. *Sell*, 9 Car. & P. 346 (motion denied after judgment pronounced); *State* v. *Cotton*, 24 N. H. 143 (motion denied after motion in arrest of judgment); *Com.* v. *Hagarman*, 10 Allen, 401. See also authorities cited below.

In *State* v. *Shanley*, 38 W. Va. 516, 18 S. E. 734, it was held that the court may permit the plea of guilty to be withdrawn and another plea to be entered in its place, in the exercise of a sound discretion, if justice and a fair trial on the merits require it; but it must be in time, and the reason for it must be made to appear clearly and distinctly.

In Michigan, by statute (How. Stat. § 9558), in all cases of appeal from a criminal conviction on a plea of guilty, it is the right of the accused to withdraw his plea of guilty, and have the case retried upon the merits; and the court is required to ascertain whether a plea of guilty, in case the accused chooses to stand upon such plea, is voluntary or not. And the statute applies to appealed cases begun on a warrant, as well as to cases on information or indictment. *People* v. *Richmond*, 57 Mich. 399, 24 N. W. 124.

[6] *People* v. *Joyce*, 4 N. Y. Crim. Rep. 341 (discretion reviewable under New York Criminal Code); *Gardner* v. *People*, 106 Ill. 76 (holding upon an indictment for murder, where it appeared that the accused was wholly ignorant of our language and institutions, and was without understanding sufficient to act intelligently, that it was the duty of the court to permit him to withdraw his plea of guilty, especially when put in without advice of counsel); *People* v. *Scott*, 59 Cal. 341 (holding it error to refuse to grant the motion, where there was evidence sufficient to raise a doubt as to the sanity of defendant at the time he pleaded guilty); *State* v. *Stephens*, 71 Mo. 535 (holding it error to refuse to permit the plea to be withdrawn by the accused, when given under the mistaken idea that thereby the lowest sentence allowed by law would be passed upon him); *State* v. *Kraft*, 10 Iowa, 330 (held error for the court to refuse to permit withdrawal under a statute providing that "the court may permit the plea of guilty to be withdrawn"). See also *State* v. *Oehlshlager*, 38 Iowa, 297; Davis v. *State*, 20 Ga. 674 (holding that if the defendant pleads guilty to one of several indictments, mistaking it for another, he should be permitted to correct it during the trial; and it is error to reject the evidence showing the fact).

But the refusal of leave will not be disturbed on appeal, unless it be glaringly unjust. *State* v. *Delahoussaye,* 37 La. Ann. 551; *Conover* v. *State,* 86 Ind. 99.

It was not an abuse of discretion requiring reversal, for a trial court to refuse to permit an accused to withdraw his plea of guilty on the ground that the prosecuting attorney induced him to enter it under the belief that he would merely be fined and not imprisoned, where no such definite promise was shown to have been made, and the only basis for such supposition was an interview between the county attorney and third parties, who understood and told defendant that he would only be fined. *State* v. *Yates,* 52 Kan. 566, 35 Pac. 209.

56. Effect of plea.

The plea of guilty, unless withdrawn,[1] has the same effect in respect to the subsequent proceedings thereon against the accused as a verdict of guilty;[2] and if it is unqualified, he may be sentenced to any degree of punishment imposed by law for the offense alleged in the indictment.[3]

But judgment cannot be rendered against him upon his pleading guilty of a crime not charged in the indictment.[4]

[1] *People* v. *Cignarale,* 110 N. Y. 32, 17 N. E. 135.

[2] *People ex rel. Evans* v. *McEwan,* 2 N. Y. Crim. Rep. 313.

[3] *Territory* v. *Miller* (Dak.) 8 Crim. L. Mag. 286 (so held notwithstanding the statute prescribed, in cases of murder, the punishment of death or imprisonment for life, at the discretion of the jury); *People* v. *Delany,* 49 Cal. 395 (holding that the plea admitted an allegation that the offense was a second offense). But see, *contra, Garvey* v. *People,* 6 Colo. 559, 45 Am. Rep. 531, holding that, after the plea of guilty to an indictment for murder, the accused may be punished only for the lowest degree of homicide.

In *People* v. *Morris,* 80 Mich. 634, 8 L. R. A. 685, 45 N. W. 591, it was held that a plea of guilty to an information charging larceny, under a general statute, in one count, and horse stealing in another, applied to both counts, and authorized sentence for horse stealing.

But a plea of guilty on an accusation merely charging generally a violation of a penal ordinance of a city prohibiting under the same penalty each of several distinct and separate acts, some of which are within the corporate power to punish, while others are not, without specifying any act, cannot be applied to the one class of acts rather than to the other; and no punishment can be inflicted in the proceeding. *Collins* v. *Hall,* 92 Ga. 411, 17 S. E. 622.

[4] *State* v. *Queen,* 91 N. C. 659, so holding where one indicted for burglary with intent to commit murder pleaded "guilty of larceny."

57. — admits only the facts.

The plea of guilty, though an acknowledgment of the facts charged, does not admit that such facts constitute an offense.[1]

[1] *Crow* v. *State*, 6 Tex. 334 (indictment for betting; conviction reversed because no legal offense was charged); *Fletcher* v. *State*, 12 Ark. 169 (indictment for disturbing congregation; conviction reversed because no legal offense was charged).

Thus the allegation in an indictment for embezzlement under Neb. Crim. Code, § 124, that the defendant was charged with the collection, safe-keeping, transfer, and disbursement of the public money, as contemplated by that section, is an allegation of law, and is not admitted by the plea of guilty. *Moore* v. *State*, 53 Neb. 831, 74 N. W. 319.

And a plea of guilty to a charge of violating a city ordinance is only an admission that defendant committed the acts charged, and is immaterial where the ordinance is invalid. *Grossman* v. *Oakland*, 30 Or. 478, 36 L. R. A. 593, 41 Pac. 5.

XI. Joinder of pleas.

58. Not guilty and special matter in bar.

At common law a plea of the general issue to the whole indictment cannot be accompanied by a plea of special matter in bar. But a plea of not guilty as to part of the indictment may be accompanied by a plea of special matter in bar of the rest of the indictment.[1]

[1] *Nauer* v. *Thomas*, 13 Allen, 572, 580.

59. Several pleas in bar.

At common law several pleas in bar, interposing separate grounds of defense, are bad on demurrer.[1]

[1] *Nauer* v. *Thomas*, 13 Allen, 572, 580.

60. Several defenses in one plea.

At common law a special plea in bar is bad, which sets up several distinct matters, either of which would be a defense.[1]

[1] *Nauer* v. *Thomas*, 13 Allen, 572, 579.

Such pleas are now generally disused.

61. Several pleas in abatement.

Two or more pleas in abatement not repugnant to one another are allowable, both in cases of misdemeanor and felony.[1]

[1] *United States* v. *Richardson*, 28 Fed. 61, and cases cited.

XII. Motion to strike out.

62. Idle plea.

A plea may be struck out on motion, on the ground that the issue presented is already conclusively determined by the record, and therefore the plea is idle.[1]

[1]*People* v. *Harding*, 53 Mich. 48, 51 Am. Rep. 95, 18 N. W. 555, 53 Mich. 481, 19 N. W. 155.

In Iowa a statute (Iowa Code, § 4359) authorizes only the pleas of guilty, not guilty, and of former conviction or acquittal; and in *State* v. *Caywood*, 96 Iowa, 367, 65 N. W. 385, it was held that a special plea filed in trial for perjury, in addition to one of former acquittal, setting out in detail what defendant claimed was an issue at the former trial, and averring that the same thing in substance was in issue in the case at bar, of which matters he had been acquitted in the former trial,—was properly stricken out.

XIX.—DEMURRER TO PLEA.

1. The right to demur.
2. Whole case.
3. Effect.
4. Uncertainty.
5. Prayer.
6. Indictment may be attacked.

1. The right to demur.

The prosecution has a right to demur to any plea for insufficiency.[1]

[1]*State* v. *Priebnow*, 16 Neb. 131, 19 N. W. 628 (demurrer to plea of former acquittal); *Rex* v. *Cooke*, 2 Barn. & C. 618 (motion to quash a plea in abatement to an indictment for conspiracy denied, because demurrer was the proper remedy); Bishop, Crim. Proc. § 793 (where he says: "The proper course for the prosecuting officer, where the plea is bad, is to demur to it"); *Buzzard* v. *State*, 20 Ark. 106 (sustaining demurrer to plea to an indictment for gambling); *Marshall* v. *State*, 6 Neb. 120, 29 Am. Rep. 363 (sustaining demurrer for insufficiency of plea of former conviction); *State* v. *Havely*, 21 Mo. 498 (a court may say, as a matter of law, upon demurrer to a plea in abatement to an indictment, that "Owens D. Havely" and "Owen D. Haverly" are *idem sonans*); *McQuoid* v. *People*, 8 Ill. 76 (sustaining demurrer to plea of previous acquittal because it failed to state the identity of the two offenses).

Although a plea of *autrefois acquit* which on its face shows that it is not the same offense of which the prisoner was before acquitted is demurrable, advantage may be taken of it upon a replication of *nul tiel* record, and the issue may be tried by the court. *Hite* v. *State*, 9 Yerg. 198.

The prosecuting attorney may interpose a demurrer to a plea in bar offered under Neb. Crim. Code, § 449, by a prisoner indicted for a felony, and have the judgment of the court whether the facts stated in such plea are sufficient, if true, to prevent the trial of the prisoner for the crime charged. *Arnold* v. *State*, 38 Neb. 752, 57 N. W. 378.

So, a plea in bar of an indictment or information may be demurred to when it is insufficient in form, or it appears from its face that the facts alleged are not in law a bar to the prosecution; but otherwise issue should be joined by replication. *Smith* v. *State*, 42 Neb. 356, 60 N. W. 585.

And it is error to proceed to trial and judgment on the issues of fact, without disposing of questions of law raised by a demurrer to a plea. *Ditch* v. *People*, 31 Ill. App. 368.

In Kentucky by statute (Crim. Code, § 179) a plea of former acquittal is considered as controverted by denial, and no demurrer or reply is required. *Com.* v. *Rose*, 21 Ky. L. Rep. 1281, 54 S. W. 863.

2. Whole case.

A plea, to be good as a bar to the whole indictment, must meet the whole case. If it does not, it is bad on demurrer.[1]

[1] *Moore* v. *Mississippi*, 21 Wall. 636, 22 L. ed. 653 (indictment with five counts for selling lottery tickets and two for keeping a gaming table. Plea not answering the latter held demurrable).

And plea of conviction for murder of a specified person, in bar to a prosecution for assault with intent to murder another person, is demurrable where such plea does not contain the indictment, conviction, and judgment of the court. *Washington* v. *State*, 35 Tex. Crim. Rep. 156, 32 S. W. 694.

But the falsity of a plea of former acquittal is not a ground of demurrer. *McCullough* v. *State* (Tex. Crim. App.) 34 S. W. 753.

3. Effect.

Demurrer to a plea admits facts alleged therein, but denies their legal sufficiency to entitle defendant to acquittal.[1]

[1] *Roberts* v. *State*, 14 Ga. 8, 58 Am. Dec. 528 (holding that a demurrer to a plea of former conviction admits that the charge relates to the same transaction, but does not admit that the charge is the same in each case); *Smith* v. *State*, 42 Neb. 356, 60 N. W. 585.

In *State* v. *Ackerman*, 64 N. J. L. 99, 45 Atl. 27, after a plea of *autrefois acquit*, the requisites of the statute having been well pleaded,—that is, that the defendant has been lawfully acquitted of the same offense charged in the indictment,—if a demurrer by the state be interposed to such plea, then the plea stands admitted, and the judgment by the court must be in favor of the defendant,—that he be discharged of the premises contained in the indictment, and that he go without day.

4. Uncertainty.

A plea in abatement must be certain to every intent, and it must stand or fall on its own allegations.[1]

[1] *State* v. *Emery*, 59 Vt. 84, 7 Atl. 129 (failure to specify the indictment pleaded to, in a plea in abatement, to the legality of the grand jury; also failure to allege wherein the illegality consisted); *United States* v. *Hammond*, 2 Woods, 197, Fed. Cas. No. 15,294 (holding that a plea that one of the grand jurors is disqualified under U. S. Rev. Stat., for engaging in insurrection and rebellion, without setting forth the time and place, lacks precision, and is bad on demurrer).

5. Prayer.

A plea in abatement is bad on demurrer if it prays a dismissal and discharge, which is the prayer of a plea in bar.[1]

[1] *United States* v. *Hammond*, 2 Woods, 197, Fed. Cas. No. 15,294.

6. Indictment may be attacked.

On demurrer to plea, judgment is to be given against the party committing the first fault in pleading.[1]

[1] *United States* v. *Lawrence*, 13 Blatchf. 295, Fed. Cas. No. 15,573.

Note on the remedy to review decision sustaining demurrer to plea.

If a plea is overruled on demurrer, and the defendant merely excepts and pleads over, he will be deemed to have waived the objection. The way to review such a decision is to cause an order to be entered on the decision, and review that order by appeal or writ of error. *People* v. *Reagle*, 60 Barb. 527, 543, holding that the question was not brought up by a record containing an exception to the ruling as if it had been a ruling on the trial. Compare N. Y. Code Crim. Proc. § 326, 485, subd. 2, 517.

XX.—THE RIGHT TO TRIAL BY JURY.

1. Constitutional right inviolable.
2. Minor offenses.
3. Appeal triable by jury not enough.

1. Constitutional right inviolable.

In criminal cases a trial by jury is a constitutional right[1] which the accused cannot be deprived of by law,[2] nor in capital cases even voluntarily waive,[3] unless expressly permitted to do so by statute.[4]

But he may waive the qualifications or the legal manner of selection of jurors.[5]

[1]U. S. Const. 6th Amend. provides that "in all criminal prosecutions the accused shall enjoy the right to a . . . trial by an impartial jury of the state and district wherein the crime shall have been committed," etc. This applies only in the United States courts. *Twitchell* v. *Pennsylvania,* 7 Wall. 321, 19 L. ed. 223; *State* v. *Bates,* 14 Utah, 293, 43 L. R. A. 33, 47 Pac. 78; *Lee* v. *Tillotson,* 24 Wend. 337; *State* v. *Whitaker,* 114 N. C. 818, 19 S. E. 376. Other cases are cited in articles in 27 Am. L. Reg. N. S. 548; and 20 Ohio L. J. 347, 348.

N. Y. Const. art. 1, § 2, provides that "the trial by jury in all cases in which it has been heretofore used shall remain inviolate forever, but a jury trial may be waived by the parties in all civil cases, in the manner prescribed by law."

N. Y. Code Crim. Proc. § 355, provides that "an issue of fact must be tried by a jury of the county in which the indictment was found, unless the action be removed."

Defendant in a criminal case is entitled to trial by a jury in attendance at a term of court regularly designated; and he may challenge a panel summoned at a term not fixed in accordance with the statute; and a judgment of conviction based upon the verdict of a jury so summoned will be reversed. *State* v. *Bristol,* 21 Mont. 578, 55 Pac. 107.

The class of minor offenses which were triable without a jury at the adoption of a constitution which guaranteed the right of trial by jury in criminal prosecutions could not be subsequently extended by statute to include an offense which had always been triable by jury and was indictable at common law,—such as the offense of keeping a bawdy house. *Miller* v. *Iowa,* 88 Va. 618, 629, 15 L. R. A. 441, 444, 14 S. E. 161, 342, 979.

The constitutional right of trial by jury does not extend to the determination of the term of imprisonment by the jury. *People ex rel. Bradley* v. *Illinois State Reformatory,* 148 Ill. 413, 23 L. R. A. 139, 36 N. E. 76.

[2]*People ex rel. Killeen* v. *Baird,* 11 Hun, 289 (holding that, under the New York Constitution, a person accused of selling liquor in violation of law is entitled to a jury trial, and the legislature cannot deprive him of this right), Following *Wynehamer* v. *People,* 13 N. Y. 378 (see note on this case in Abbott, Cases Criticised, 867); and *Hill* v. *People,* 20 N. Y. 363, holding to same effect.

But the constitutional right of an accused person to trial by jury is not violated by taking away from the jury the right to fix his punishment. *Miller* v. *State,* 149 Ind. 607, 40 L. R. A. 109, 49 N. E. 894.

Nor by a statute (Ill. act June 26, 1895, § 1) providing that every adult convicted of felony or other crime punishable by imprisonment in the penitentiary, except treason or murder, shall be sentenced thereto, but that the court shall not "fix the limit or duration of the sentence." *George* v. *People,* 167 Ill. 447, 47 N. E. 741.

Nor by a statute providing for the determination by the court of the degree of crime, upon a plea of guilty of murder. *State* v. *Almy*, 67 N. H. 274, 22 L. R. A. 744, 28 Atl. 372.

Nor by a statute authorizing the accused to waive the right of trial by jury, and to elect to be tried by the judge. *State* v. *Robinson*, 43 La. Ann. 383, 8 So. 937.

Nor by a statute (Tenn. Laws 1895, chap. 67) providing that the proof of certain things enumerated shall be prima facie evidence of fraudulent intent in procuring accommodations at a hotel, inn, or boarding house, which is made a misdemeanor. *State* v. *Yardley*, 95 Tenn. 546, 34 L. R. A. 656, 32 S. W. 481.

Nor by a statute making the failure, suspension, or involuntary liquidation of a banker within thirty days of the receiving of a deposit prima facie evidence of his intent to defraud. *Meadowcroft* v. *People*, 163 Ill. 56, 35 L. R. A. 176, 45 N. E. 303, 991.

Nor by a statute making the mere possession of prohibited articles, even without knowing what they are, an offense. *Ford* v. *State*, 85 Md. 465, 41 L. R. A. 551, 37 Atl. 172.

Nor by a statute providing that a jury in a criminal case shall be selected from a special list made from the general list by a jury commissioner. *People* v. *Dunn*, 157 N. Y. 528, 43 L. R. A. 247, 52 N. E. 572.

Nor by a statute (N. H. Pub. Stat. chap. 209, § 7) enacting that the court shall direct the number of jurors to be summoned, and from what towns. *State* v. *Moore*, 69 N. H. 102, 40 Atl. 702.

Nor by a statute (Cal. Pen. Code, § 1121) authorizing the court in its discretion to permit the separation of the jury. *People* v. *Chaves*, 122 Cal. 134, 54 Pac. 596.

[a]*Cancemi* v. *People*, 18 N. Y. 136. Upon a trial for murder, where one of the jurors withdrew during the trial, with the consent of the accused, held, that the further proceedings of the court were without jurisdiction, and that the substantial constitution of legal tribunals and the fundamental mode of their proceedings were not within the power of the parties to alter by consent. Error; judgment reversed. Leading case. See also note on this case in Abbott, Cases Criticised, 131; and cases reviewed in notes to *King* v. *State* (Tenn.) 3 L. R. A. 211, and *Gore* v. *State* (Ark.) 5 L. R. A. 832.

The following authorities hold to the same effect: *State* v. *Carman*, 63 Iowa, 130, 50 Am. Rep. 741, 18 N. W. 691 (under Iowa Code Crim. Proc. § 4350); *State* v. *Douglass*, 96 Iowa, 308, 65 N. W. 151 (refusing to distinguish between felonies and misdemeanors in this respect); *Territory* v. *Ah Wah*, 4 Mont. 149, 47 Am. Rep. 341, 1 Pac. 732 (murder). And see *Neales* v. *State*, 10 Mo. 498; *Wilson* v. *State*, 16 Ark. 601; *People* v. *O'Neil*, 48 Cal. 257; *State* v. *Mansfield*, 41 Mo. 470; *State* v. *Holt*, 90 N. C. 749, 47 Am. Rep. 544 (holding, where a jury had been waived, that the judgment of conviction was not only irregular, but absolutely void).

In *Arnold* v. *State*, 38 Neb. 752, 57 N. W. 378, it was held that the issues raised by a plea in bar under Neb. Crim. Code, § 449, and the prosecution's reply thereto, must, where the plea is good, be tried by a jury;

and that it is beyond the power of the prosecuting officer and the accused by agreement to provide for any other mode of trial.

In Minnesota a person accused in a municipal court of an offense within the jurisdiction of justices of the peace may waive the right of trial by jury and consent to a trial by the court, since the Constitution (art. 1, § 6) provides only that the accused shall enjoy the right to a speedy and public trial by jury, and not that all crimes shall be tried by jury. *State* v. *Woodling*, 53 Minn. 142, 54 N. W. 1068; *State* v. *Bannock*, 53 Minn. 419, 55 N. W. 558.

In Illinois it has been held that a prisoner convicted, without a jury, of a felony (obtaining money by means of a confidence game), should be released upon habeas corpus. *People* v. *Lyons*, 5 Crim. L. Mag. 674, with note collecting authorities. Compare *Kelly* v. *People*, 115 Ill. 583, 56 Am. Rep. 184, 4 N. E. 644, where it was held that a conviction was not absolutely void because the accused waived a trial by jury, but erroneous merely, and could not therefore be attacked collaterally. In *People* v. *Lyons*, 5 Crim. L. Mag. 670, it was held that the accused might expressly, though not impliedly, waive a trial by jury. But in *Morgan* v. *People*, 136 Ill. 161, 26 N. E. 651, it was held that the consent of defendant in an indictment for a felony (in that case assault, with intent to murder), who pleads not guilty, cannot confer jurisdiction upon the judge to try the case without a jury,—Citing and following *Harris* v. *People*, 128 Ill. 585, 21 N. E. 563.

In Michigan a person accused of an offense triable in a justice's court cannot be deprived of his right to elect to be tried without a jury, under How. (Mich.) Stat. § 7097, providing that if no jury be demanded the court shall try the issue and that if the accused shall not have waived his right to trial by jury, a jury shall be summoned. *People* v. *State*, 94 Mich. 437, 54 N. W. 171. The court, quoting from *Ward* v. *People*, 30 Mich. 116, said that "the law secures to him the right of being tried in either way, as he may prefer; and . . . he may sometimes prefer to be tried by the court without a jury."

In misdemeanors the accused may, by consent, be tried by less than twelve jurors. *Com.* v. *Dailey*, 12 Cush. 80; *State* v. *Borowsky*, 11 Nev. 119; *Murphy* v. *Com.* 1 Met. (Ky.) 365 (limiting the principle to cases punishable by fine only); *State* v. *Van Matre*, 49 Mo. 268 (holding that it must appear that defendant consented). See also *State* v. *Kaufman*, 51 Iowa, 578, 33 Am. Rep. 148, 2 N. W. 275, holding that, with the consent of the trial judge, the accused could consent to be tried by eleven jurors, even in a felony.

In *Bullard* v. *State*, 38 Tex. 504, 19 Am. Rep. 30, under a statute providing for trial by twelve jurors it was held error to try the accused by a jury of thirteen.

In *Re Staff*, 63 Wis. 285, 53 Am. Rep. 285, holding that the accused may effectually waive a trial by jury, if expressly permitted to do so by statute, notwithstanding the Constitution. And see *Mayo* v. *Com.* 11 Va. L. J. 88, holding that he may not do so in absence of statute. Compare *People* v. *Cook*, 45 Hun, 34; *State* v. *Worden*, 46 Conn. 349, 33 Am. Rep. 27; S. C., 1 Crim. L. Mag. 178, with note collating authorities and similar statutes (holding a statute giving the accused a right to elect to be tried without a jury to be constitutional); *People ex rel. Sammous* v. *Wandell*, 21 Hun, 515 (infant may waive in petit larceny); *People* v. *Cook*, 45 Hun, 34 (tacit waiver).

In Georgia the right of trial by jury may be waived in misdemeanor cases, under Ga. Code, § 10, providing that a person may waive or renounce what the law has established in his favor, when he does not thereby injure others or affect the public interest. *Logan* v. *State*, 86 Ga. 266, 12 S. E. 406.

The right to trial by jury in a court of special sessions, upon demand therefor, before any testimony has been taken, is not lost by an election, upon arraignment, to be tried without a jury, and a waiver of the right to a jury trial, under N. Y. Code Crim. Proc. § 702, providing that the accused may demand a trial by jury before the court hears any testimony. *People* v. *Molinet*, 13 Misc. 301, 34 N. Y. Supp. 1114.

Cancemi v. *People*, 18 N. Y. 136, admits that the accused may waive the want of qualifications of a juror. Cited on this point in *Pierson* v. *People*, 79 N. Y. 424, 430, 35 Am. Rep. 524, holding that an irregular drawing of jurors may be waived. See, as to grounds of challenge and waiver of them, *post*, Division XXXI.

Statutes exist in various states providing for juries of less than twelve in certain inferior criminal courts. As to the constitutionality of verdict by less than all the jurors, see cases in note to *Jacksonville, T. & K. W. R. Co.* v. *Adams* (Fla.) 24 L. R. A. 272.

In New York state, in courts of special sessions outside of the city and county of New York and the city of Albany, if no jury be demanded the accused is tried by the court; if a jury be demanded, one consisting of six jurors is awarded. Code Crim. Proc. §§ 701–710; *People* v. *Hulett*, 39 N. Y. S. R. 646, 15 N. Y. Supp. 630. In the other criminal courts of the state, if a jury is demandable of right, it consists, as at common law, of twelve men. N. Y. Code Crim. Proc. § 387.

2. Minor offenses.

The constitutional right to a trial by jury extends only to capital cases, felonies, and infamous crimes, as at common law, and to cases of such nature as those for which trial by jury was provided by statute before the Constitution, and not to other minor offenses.[1]

[1] N. Y. Const. art. 1, § 2 (above); *People ex rel. Booth* v. *Fisher*, 20 Barb. 652 (holding that the right to a trial by jury, as provided by the New York Constitution, extends only to infamous crimes indictable at common law, and not to misdemeanors); *State* v. *Conlin*, 27 Vt. 319; *State, Ward, Prosecutor*, v. *New Brunswick Street & Sewer Comrs.* (holding as above), 49 N. J. L. 552, 10 Atl. 109 (holding that where the Constitution provides that "the right of trial by jury shall remain inviolate," the meaning of the language is that where the right to a jury existed before the Constitution, it cannot be taken away by the legislature; but where there was not such right previously, it was not extended to such

cases); *Wynehamer* v. *People*, 13 N. Y. 378, 425, 426 (holding that where a misdemeanor created by statute was triable by jury before the adoption of the Constitution, similar statutory offenses created since the Constitution must also be tried by jury. Violation of excise law), Followed in *People ex rel. Killeen* v. *Baird*, 11 Hun, 289; S. P., *Hill* v. *People*, 20 N. Y. 363, 18 How. Pr. 289 (intoxication in a public place). And for other cases holding that the right does not extend to the trial of the offense charged, see *Wong* v. *Astoria*, 13 Or. 538, 11 Pac. 295 (violations of city ordinances); *Manderscheid* v. *Plymouth County District Ct.* 69 Iowa, 240, 28 N. W. 551 (contempt of court); *People* v. *Van Houten*, 13 Misc. 603, 35 N. Y. Supp. 186 (violation of village ordinance); *Cooper* v. *People ex rel. Wyatt*, 13 Colo. 337, 6 L. R. A. 430, 22 Pac. 790 (contempt of court); *Re Deaton*, 105 N. C. 59, 11 S. E. 244 (contempt of court); *Bassette* v. *State*, 51 N. J. L. 502, 18 Atl. 354 (prosecuting under New Jersey disorderly act); *State* v. *Griggs*, 34 W. Va. 78, 11 S. E. 740 (betting on an election); *Com.* v. *Waldman*, 140 Pa. 89, 11 L. R. A. 563, 21 Atl. 248 (violation of Sunday law); *Davis* v. *State*, 92 Tenn. 634, 23 S. W. 59 (proceedings for disbarment of attorney); *Burke* v. *Territory*, 2 Okla. 499, 37 Pac. 829 (contempt proceedings); *State* v. *Markuson*, 5 N. D. 147, 64 N. W. 934; S. C., 7 N. D. 155, 73 N. W. 82 (contempt proceedings).

In expressly providing for trial by jury the constitutions of the various states use phrases of different degrees of definiteness of description. These phrases may be divided into three classes: (1) It is laid down that the right "shall remain inviolate," implying that it shall be continued as it was known and used before; (2) it is provided the right "shall be inviolate;" and (3) others provide more explicitly and expressly that it "shall be as heretofore used." The interpretation has been uniformly given to the operative clauses of the Constitution, in whichever of the three modes pointed out they may be expressed, that the right is to be confined to those classes of cases only in which it was used at the time of the adoption of the Constitution, unless it is expressly restricted or extended to others. *Stilwell* v. *Kellogg*, 14 Wis. 462; *Koppikus* v. *State Capitol Comrs.* 16 Cal. 248; *Whitehurst* v. *Coleen*, 53 Ill. 247; *Ross* v. *Irving*, 14 Ill. 171; *Whallon* v. *Bancroft*, 4 Minn. 109, Gil. 70; *Lake Erie, W. & St. L. R. Co.* v. *Heath*, 9 Ind. 558; *Byers* v. *Com.* 42 Pa. 89; *Howe* v. *Plainfield*, 37 N. J. L. 145; Proffatt, Trial by Jury, 127, § 87. And see other cases reviewed in note to *Grand Rapids & I. R. Co.* v. *Sparrow* (C. C. W. D. Mich.) 1 L. R. A. 480.

The constitutional provision securing to citizens the right of trial by jury in criminal cases does not mean that there should be a trial by jury in all cases which may arise. It does not apply to proceedings on a presentment or complaint before a justice of the peace. *Goddard* v. *State*, 12 Conn. 454. Nor to an application for appeal from inferior courts. *Weed's Appeal*, 35 Conn. 455. Nor to summary convictions of rogues and vagabonds. *Byers* v. *Com.* 42 Pa. 89; *Haines* v. *Levin*, 51 Pa. 412. See further, on this question, note to *Anderson* v. *O'Donnell* (S. C.) 1 L. R. A. 633.

In *State* v. *Whitaker*, 114 N. C. 818, 19 S. E. 376, it is held that a city ordinance is not unconstitutional because it fails to provide for a jury trial on a prosecution for an alleged violation thereof, as N. C. Const. art. 1, § 13, authorizes the legislature to vest the trial of petit misdemeanors in inferior courts, without a jury, if the right of appeal is preserved.

3. Appeal triable by jury not enough.

The fact that the accused, after being compelled to submit to trial without jury, has a right to appeal to a court where he will have a jury trial, does not justify forcing him to trial without jury in the inferior court.[1]

[1] *Callan* v. *Wilson*, 127 U. S. 540, 555, 32 L. ed. 223, 228, 8 Sup. Ct. Rep. 1301 (the only exception recognized by the opinion is that class of minor offenses where jury trial is not of right); *State* v. *Gerry*, 68 N. H. 495, 38 L. R. A. 228, 38 Atl. 272; *Danner* v. *State*, 89 Md. 220, 42 Atl. 965; *Reeves* v. *State*, 96 Ala. 33, 11 So. 296; *Miller* v. *Com.* 88 Va. 618, 629, 15 L. R. A. 441, 444, 14 S. E. 161, 342, 979. *Contra*, *Wong* v. *Astoria*, 13 Or. 538, 11 Pac. 295 (holding that it is not a deprivation of the right to a trial by jury that the party is not able to obtain it in the inferior court, if provision is made whereby it can be secured upon an appeal by a reasonably simple procedure. The charge was of keeping a bawdy house, which, it seems, is not one of which jury trial is of right); *Jones* v. *Robbins*, 8 Gray, 329, 341.

In *Collier* v. *Territory*, 2 Okla. 444, 37 Pac. 819, it is held that a statute providing that a criminal case of which the justice's court has jurisdiction may be tried before a jury of six men, and giving the right of appeal to the district court, where the accused may be tried by a jury of twelve men,—is not unconstitutional.

XXI.—RIGHT TO A SPEEDY TRIAL.

1. The right of the accused.
2. Remedy for denial.

1. The right of the accused.

By the constitutions and statutes of most of the states the accused is guaranteed a speedy trial.[1]

[1] U. S. Const. 6th Amend. applies only to the United States courts. See *ante*, Division XX. § 1, note 1; N. Y. Code Crim. Proc. § 8.

This right as guaranteed by the California Constitution implies a reasonable time for the state to provide courts and juries and to procure witnesses, but imposes a special duty upon the state with reference to such cases; and if the duty is not performed, the prosecution should be dismissed. *People* v. *Buckley*, 116 Cal. 146, 47 Pac. 1009.

2. Remedy for denial.

The right to a speedy trial may be enforced by motion to discharge, motion to dismiss, or habeas corpus, when it appears that the delay of the prosecution is oppressive and without good cause;[1] but such right cannot be claimed if there be good cause arising from necessary regulations of procedure, or to give the prosecution reasonable time to prepare for trial, or if the delay originate from the accused himself.[2]

[1]*State* v. *Thompson*, 32 Minn. 144, 19 N. W. 730 (holding that an indictment should be dismissed on motion where it appears that three terms of the court had intervened between that at which the indictment was found and that at which the arraignment was made, no good cause having been shown); *United States* v. *Fox*, 3 Mont. 512 (holding that if, by reason of the laches of the prosecution in preparing for trial, the trial is delayed beyond the period when there is a term at which the trial might be had, the accused is entitled to discharge on habeas corpus); *Com.* v. *Prophet*, 1 Browne (Pa.) 135 (a prisoner accused of larceny was on motion discharged because he was, against the statute, confined in prison more than two sessions after his commitment); *Green* v. *Com.* 1 Rob. (Va.) 731 (a prisoner confined upon an indictment, not brought to trial within statutory limitation, discharged on habeas corpus).

So, an indictment should be dismissed where the state neglects for seven months, and during three terms of the court after it is found, to arraign the defendant, or call for her appearance, or forfeit her bail. *State* v. *Radoicich*, 66 Minn. 294, 69 N. W. 25.

And the court is not deprived of jurisdiction to discharge a defendant for failure to bring him to trial before the expiration of the statutory period, because the case has been continued, and the continuance has not been set aside. *State* v. *Wear*, 145 Mo. 162, 46 S. W. 1099.

Nor does the offer of a prosecuting attorney to enter a *nolle prosequi*, and its refusal by the court, deprive the court of jurisdiction to discharge the defendant. *Ibid.;* holding also that the prosecuting attorney, by asking for a continuance after his offer to enter a *nolle prosequi* and its refusal by the court, recognizes and acknowledges the continued pendency of the cause in the trial court, and is estopped to assert that such offer and refusal deprive the court of jurisdiction to discharge the defendant.

But the fact that an accused was not brought to trial before the end of the third term after the finding of the indictment, and that the delay was not on his application or for want of time to try the case, will not entitle him to his discharge, where the last continuance was by the court of its own motion, and was not caused by any laches on the part of the state. *State* v. *Marshall*, 115 Mo. 383, 22 S. W. 452.

A term at which there was a trial resulting in a disagreement is not to be included in determining whether or not a subsequent trial is within the limit fixed by the Illinois statute. *Gillespie* v. *People*, 176 Ill. 238, 52 N. E. 250. Compare *Davis* v. *State*, 51 Neb. 301, 70 N. W. 984, where it is held that a defendant is brought to trial, within the meaning of the Nebraska statute, where a trial is had, although it results in a disagreement and discharge of the jury. And see *State* v. *Enke*, 85 Iowa, 35, 51 N. W. 1146, where it is held that a person indicted at one term, in September, put on trial at the next term, in November, when the jury disagrees, and the case, with all others undisposed of, is continued to the next term, in January, at which time he is brought to trial, is not entitled to dismissal of the prosecution because of unreasonable delay, under Iowa Code, § 4614, although the record does not show the cause for the continuance. And in *State* v. *Bulling*, 105 Mo. 204, 15 S. W. 367, 16 S. W. 830, it was held that a trial *coram non judice*, and void because the judge who held it was disqualified, was a trial within the meaning of the Missouri statute.

The term at which defendant was committed, and at which the indictment was returned, is not to be included in determining the limit fixed by the statutes within which a defendant must be brought to trial. *Gillespie* v. *People*, 176 Ill. 238, 52 N. E. 250; *Hammond* v. *State*, 39 Neb. 252, 58 N. W. 92; *Whitner* v. *State*, 46 Neb. 144, 64 N. W. 704; *Kibler* v. *Com.* 94 Va. 804, 26 S. E. 858. See also *Davis* v. *Com.* 89 Va. 132, 15 S. E. 388, holding that the statute is satisfied by trial at the fourth term held after indictment.

Nixon v. *State*, 2 Smedes & M. 497, 41 Am. Dec. 601, holding, upon a writ of habeas corpus, that by a speedy trial is intended a trial conducted according to fixed rules and regulations and proceedings of law, free from vexatious, capricious, and oppressive delays manufactured by ministers of justice. Denial of writ where the delay originated from the accused himself, affirmed. And see *People* v. *Shufelt*, 61 Mich. 237, 28 N. W. 79, holding that twenty-one days' delay of the trial of a respondent, out on his own recognizance, was no violation of his right to a speedy trial.

As to motion to discharge, see *ante*, Division VIII.

In Missouri a defendant is not entitled to his discharge under Rev. Stat. 1889, § 4222, unless it appears that the case has been continued over two entire terms at the instance of the court or of the state. *State* v. *Billings*, 140 Mo. 193, 41 S. W. 778.

So, an accused is not entitled to be discharged because not brought to trial within the statutory period, where the delay was due to continuances and a change of venue granted and awarded on the application of the accused, and not to any fault on the part of the state. *State* v. *Steen*, 115 Mo. 474, 22 S. W. 461.

And a delay in the trial by the consent of all the parties will be deemed to have "happened on the application" of all the parties to the proceeding, within the meaning of the Illinois statute (1 Starr & C. Anno. Stat. 1896, chap. 38, ¶ 623, § 18), providing that a person committed for a criminal offense, and not admitted to bail, or tried at a term of the court commencing within four months of the date of commitment, "shall be set at liberty by the court, unless the delay shall happen on the application of the prisoner." *Healy* v. *People*, 177 Ill. 306, 52 N. E. 426.

But the benefit of the guaranty of the California Constitution of a speedy trial cannot be denied because of the absence of witnesses for the state, where no diligence to procure their attendance is shown. *People* v. *Buckley*, 116 Cal. 146, 47 Pac. 1009.

Nor does a postponement of one day on the application of defendant entirely deprive him of the guaranty. *Ibid.*

The right to a discharge for failure to bring the indictment to trial, given one accused of crime within the statutes fixing the limit within which the trial must be had, is confined to those persons in actual confinement. *State* v. *Williams*, 35 S. C. 160, 14 S. E. 309. See also *Gillespie* v. *People*, 176 Ill. 238, 52 N. E. 250 (holding that the Illinois statute does not apply to a defendant who was not committed for the offense for which he was put upon trial, but pleaded guilty to another felony, and has been in the state penitentiary ever since, except when brought into court for trial for the offense in question); *Meadowcroft* v. *People*, 163 Ill. 56, 35 L. R. A. 176, 45 N. E. 303 (holding that defendants were not entitled to discharge where they were out on bail, and never appeared in court until the term at which they were tried); *Hammond* v. *State*, 39 Neb. 252, 58 N. W. 92 (so holding of one who had never been committed to jail or otherwise detained in custody); *Ex parte Trester*, 53 Neb. 148, 73 N. W. 545 (holding that one admitted to bail after a preliminary examination on a criminal charge, who becomes a fugitive, is not, after his return or apprehension, entitled to a discharge, under Neb. Crim. Code, §§ 389, 391, because no information was filed at the term at which he was recognized to appear, and while he was a fugitive).

Nor does such a statute apply where a new trial has been granted the defendant,—at least until after the expiration of sixty days from making the order setting aside the trial. *Re Murphy*, 7 Wash. 257, 34 Pac. 834.

Or where he has appealed from a conviction and had his case sent back for a second trial. *People* v. *Lundin*, 120 Cal. 308, 52 Pac. 807.

XXII.—RIGHT TO A PUBLIC TRIAL.

1. Exclusion of inconvenient numbers. 2. Exclusion on account of public morality.

1. Exclusion of inconvenient numbers.

The requirement of public trial[1] is fairly met if, without partiality or favoritism, a reasonable number of the public is admitted, notwithstanding that many whose presence would be of no service to the accused, and who would only be drawn thither by idle curiosity, are excluded altogether.[2]

[1]See U. S. Const. 6th Amend. (applicable only in United States courts. See *ante*, Division XX. § 1, note 1); N. Y. Code Crim. Proc. § 8, subd. 1.

[2]*People* v. *Kerrigan*, 73 Cal. 222, 14 Pac. 849; *State* v. *Brooks*, 92 Mo. 542, 5 S. W. 257, 330.

The trial court should not permit the courtroom to become so crowded, on a trial for murder, as to impede the progress of the trial by rendering it difficult for the jurors to enter or leave the box, or by preventing the free movement of counsel and witnesses; or permit the bystanders to come into such close contact with the jury that the latter can hear the remarks of the former as to the guilt or innocence of the accused. *Myers* v. *State*, 97 Ga. 76, 25 S. E. 252.

And a conviction of murder will not be disturbed because people were admitted to the courtroom during the trial, by ticket, on the ground that it was impossible for any friend of defendant to be present, where it is not shown that any friend of his was excluded. *Jackson* v. *Com.* 100 Ky. 268, 38 S. W. 1091, Denying rehearing of 100 Ky. 239, 38 S. W. 422.

And sending the jury out of the courtroom while counsel are arguing and reading authorities to the court upon requests to charge is not a violation of Wash. Const. art. 1, § 22, providing that defendants in criminal prosecutions shall have a speedy public trial by an impartial jury. *State* v. *Coella*, 3 Wash. 99, 28 Pac. 28.

But the constitutional right to a "public trial" was violated by an order of the court to a police officer stationed at the door of the courtroom, to "see that the room is not overcrowded, but that all respectable citizens be admitted, and have an opportunity to get in whenever they shall apply," where it is shown that citizens and taxpayers were excluded by such officer while the seats provided for spectators were not all occupied. *People* v. *Murray*, 89 Mich. 276, 50 N. W. 995, S. C. with note in 14 L. R. A. 809.

And the fact that the people might have obtained admission to a courtroom by a private entrance through the clerk's office is no answer to the charge that the constitutional right to a public trial was denied by an order of the court in pursuance of which they were refused admittance at the public entrance. *Ibid.*

So an *ex parte* order made at chambers, that the sheriff take the accused to another parish to be present at the examination of a witness for the state physically unable to attend the trial, as well as the use on the trial of the deposition so taken, is a violation of La. Const. art. 8, guaranteeing a public trial. *State* v. *Chambers*, 44 La. Ann. 603, 10 So. 886.

2. Exclusion on account of public morality.

The exclusion by the court of all persons other than those interested in the case, where, from the character of the charge and nature of the evidence, public morality would be injuriously affected, does not violate the right to a public trial.[1]

[1]Cooley, Const. Lim. 312; *People* v. *Swafford*, 65 Cal. 223, 3 Pac. 809 (abduction for purposes of prostitution. Held, also, that, in the absence of anything to show the contrary, exclusion will be presumed to have been with the defendant's consent); *Grimmett* v. *State*, 22 Tex. App. 36, 2 S. W. 631 (exclusion of the general public during trial for rape held proper). But *People* v. *Hartman*, 103 Cal. 242, 37 Pac. 153, holds that an order excluding from the courtroom, during the trial of a rape case, all persons except the court officers and the defendant, violates the defendant's right to a public trial.

XXIII.—SETTING DOWN FOR TRIAL.

1. Absence of accused.

The absence of the accused at the time when his case is assigned for trial is not error.[1]

[1]*State* v. *Clark*, 32 La. Ann. 558. *Contra*, *Hames* v. *State*, 113 Ala. 674, 21 So. 341. Compare *Smith* v. *State*, 98 Ala. 55, 13 So. 508, where it is held that the clerk of the city court of Montgomery is authorized under Ala. Acts 1872–73, p. 261, and by the general provision of Ala. Code 1886, § 4447, to set down the day for the trial of one indicted for larceny, without an order of the court, and without the prisoner's being present, either in person or by counsel.

2. Advancing cause out of order.

It is error to advance a cause over a large number of others on the docket, where it is likely to surprise the defendant and force him to trial unprepared;[1] but where defendant is in jail, the term of court very short, and jail cases by rule of court are entitled to a preference, it is not error.[2]

[1]*Thomas* v. *State*, 36 Tex. 315. Compare *Stevens* v. *State* (Tex. Crim. App.) 49 S. W. 105, where it is held that the court has power to take up a

case out of its order on the docket, in the absence of some special reason for not doing so.

[2]*Wright* v. *State,* 10 Tex. App. 476. Term only one week.

By N. Y. Code Crim. Proc. § 357, the defendant is entitled to at least two days after plea to prepare for his trial, if he requests it.

3. Order of trials.

Where separate trials are granted to two or more defendants jointly indicted, the order of their trials rests in the discretion of the prosecuting officer,[1] subject to the direction of the court.[2]

[1]*Shay* v. *Com.* 36 Pa. 305 (separate trials granted to joint defendants indicted for murder; order of trial is discretionary with prosecuting officer); *Reg.* v. *Bennett,* and *Reg.* v. *Bond,* 10 Cox C. C. 331; *Patterson* v. *People,* 46 Barb. 625.

[2]*People* v. *McIntyre,* 1 Park. Crim. Rep. 371, Affirmed as *McIntyre* v. *People,* 9 N. Y. 38.

4. Trials at irregular term.

Submitting to a trial, without objection, at an irregular term, is a waiver of the irregularity.[1]

[1]*Smurr* v. *State,* 105 Ind. 125, 4 N. E. 445.

XXIV.—POSTPONEMENT OR CONTINUANCE.

[Applications for postponements, or, as they are frequently called, continuances, are to be made when the case is reached or called for trial. Under the title ADJOURNMENTS, *post,* Division XXXIV., will be found the rules regulating the putting off of trials after they have been commenced. Applications for postponements are, when asked by the accused, always to be made upon affidavits. When requested by the state, it is in the discretion of the court to require affidavits or not. See *Turner* v. *State,* 25 Ga. 146.

The motion is addressed primarily to the discretion of the trial court; and therefore the points here given, especially in reference to the absence of witnesses, are not so much rules of law as indications of the practice, and of the considerations usually applied on an appeal or motion for new trial founded on a denial of such an application. It will be seen that the refusal to grant a continuance does under some circumstances constitute error. In such cases, to render the objection available, the nature and grounds of the application must appear in the record.]

1. When to be asked.

At common law application for continuance before submitting to arraignment is premature.[1]

But under statutes requiring arraignment and trial to be promptly had unless good cause for continuance is shown, or entitling the accused to apply for a change of venue, it is error to refuse an application on cause, merely because made before arraignment, or to impose a waiver of the right to ask a change of venue as a condition of granting the continuance.[2]

But a continuance asked when the venire is ordered is properly refused, because it is not then known whether the witnesses will or will not be absent at the time about to be set for the trial.[3]

Nor will a continuance be granted after verdict for newly discovered evidence, unless it appears that the application was not made for delay, and that the accused and his counsel were ignorant of such evidence before verdict.[4]

[1]*Anderson* v. *Com.* 83 Va. 326, 2 S. E. 281.

[2]*Ibid.*

[3]*Story* v. *State,* 68 Miss. 609, 10 So. 47.

[4]*Farmer* v. *State,* 95 Ga. 498, 20 S. E. 494.

2. Presence of the accused.

A criminal prosecution may properly be continued in the absence of the accused, before his arraignment.[1]

[1]*Kibler* v. *Com.* 94 Va. 804, 26 S. E. 858. Compare *Benton* v. *Com.* 91 Va. 782, 21 S. E. 495, where the accused assigned as error the objection that the record did not show that the prisoner was personally present in court when his case was continued to a later day of that term of the court. But the court said that if it were conceded, which it did not, that it was necessary that one indicted for a felony should be personally present in court when a motion was made by his counsel for a continuance of the case, and that the record should show this, the record in that case, if it did not expressly affirm the fact of the personal presence in court of the accused when his case was continued, did clearly negative the claim that he was not present; and it overruled the assignment of error.

And in *State* v. *Duncan,* 7 Wash. 336, 35 Pac. 117, it was held that to grant a continuance without the personal presence of the accused does not violate the Washington Constitution (art. 1, § 22), providing that in criminal prosecutions the accused shall have a right to appear and defend in person and by counsel, since that provision has reference to matters connected with the trial, and not to anything preliminary thereto.

3. Pendency of another action.

Another indictment[1] or a civil action[2] pending against the accused is not ground for a postponement.

[1]*Loeffner* v. *State,* 10 Ohio St. 598.

[2]*Eighmy* v. *People,* 79 N. Y. 546; *Com.* v. *Bliss,* 1 Mass. 32; *Com.* v. *Elliott,* 2 Mass. 372.

And a prosecution against county commissioners for misdemeanor in office will not be continued simply to allow the determination of an appeal from the report of the county auditors surcharging them with the amount alleged in the indictment to have been fraudulently obtained by them. *Com.* v. *Hurd,* 177 Pa. 481, 35 Atl. 682.

4. Public excitement.

Public excitement operating to the prejudice of the accused may constitute good ground for a postponement;[1] but only under very aggravated circumstances is this cause alone sufficient.[2]

[1]*Bishop* v. *State*, 9 Ga. 121; *Reg.* v. *Bolam*, 2 Moody & R. 192. See also *State* v. *Wells*, 61 Iowa, 629, 47 Am. Rep. 822, 17 N. W. 90; *State* v. *Poe*, 8 Lea, 647.

But that public excitement or prejudice is not ground for a postponement, although it may be for change of venue, see *Jones* v. *State*, 37 Tex. Crim. Rep. 433, 35 S. W. 975; *Laughlin* v. *Com.* 18 Ky. L. Rep. 640, 37 S. W. 590.

Nor is the publication of newspaper articles prejudicing the public ground for postponement of the trial, the remedy being change of place of the trial. *State* v. *Hawkins*, 18 Or. 476, 23 Pac. 475, 477. "If the newspaper articles," said the court, "had been of so serious and inflammatory a character as to actually cause so deep a prejudice in the public mind as to preclude a fair and impartial trial in the county, the proper motion was not for a postponement, but for a change of the place of trial."

In *State* v. *Abshire*, 47 La. Ann. 542, 17 So. 141, it was held that the allowance *vel non* of a continuance in a criminal case, on the ground that a fair and impartial trial cannot be had at the time set for trial, owing to the public excitement being so great against him as to intimidate and swerve a jury,—is within the sound and judicial discretion of the judge under the particular circumstances. The court said, further, that "the existence of popular excitement against the accused is not a sufficient cause for the postponement of a trial, unless it be sufficient 'to intimidate and swerve the jury.' "

So, in *King* v. *State*, 91 Tenn. 617, 20 S. W. 169, the court held a continuance on the ground of too great excitement to be in the sound discretion of the court since the passage of Mill. & V. (Tenn.) Code, § 6038,—especially where one continuance on the ground has been granted.

But in *Ballard* v. *State*, 31 Fla. 266, 12 So. 865, it was held that a motion for a continuance made on the ground of great public excitement putting the accused in danger of violence and necessitating guards for his protection, which is prejudicial to him, and giving just and reasonable cause for apprehending that a fair jury cannot be obtained, is properly refused where the motion is not supported by any evidence to corroborate the affidavit of the accused, and there is no attempt to show that he was prevented from getting corroborative evidence. To similar effect, see *Stevens* v. *State*, 93 Ga. 307, 20 S. E. 331.

And the refusal of an application for a continuance in a murder trial, based mainly on averments that there are such excitement and passion in the community as to prevent a fair trial, will not be held an abuse of discretion, although a continuance might properly be granted because of the brief time for preparation afforded defendant, where no application for a change of venue on account of public prejudice is made, and there is no trouble in securing jurors who have not formed opinions on the merits of the case. *State* v. *Asbell,* 57 Kan. 398, 46 Pac. 770.

[3]*Thomas* v. *State,* 27 Ga. 287; *Woolfolk* v. *State,* 85 Ga. 69, 11 S. E. 814; *Cox* v. *State,* 64 Ga. 374, 37 Am. Rep. 76; *Beavers* v. *State,* 58 Ind. 530. And see *Maddox* v. *State,* 32 Ga. 581, 79 Am. Dec. 307; and *Joyce* v. *Com.* 78 Va. 287.

5. Opportunity to prepare.

Insufficient time or opportunity to prepare for defense may constitute a ground for postponement which it will be error to refuse;[1] but this has usually been held discretionary.[2] The state, however, it seems, is always entitled to a postponement.[3]

[1]*State* v. *Dakin,* 52 Iowa, 395, 3 N. W. 411; *State* v. *Lewis,* 74 Mo. 222 (continuance granted in order to allow a new counsel to prepare for trial, where the prisoner had been betrayed by his counsel); *State* v. *Nash,* 7 Iowa, 347 (allowed for the purpose of taking material testimony); *Metts* v. *State,* 29 Ga. 271.

N. Y. Code Crim. Proc. § 357, provides that after plea the defendant is entitled to at least two days to prepare for his trial, if he requires it.

Counsel appointed by the court to defend a person accused of a felony should be allowed a reasonable time for the preparation of the defense. *Hunt* v. *State,* 102 Ga. 569, 27 S. E. 670; *Claxon* v. *Com.* 17 Ky. L. Rep. 284, 30 S. W. 998.

Especially where he would otherwise be obliged to neglect the business of paying clients. *North* v. *People,* 139 Ill. 81, 28 N. E. 966.

So, a continuance in a murder case, applied for, with proper showing, at the term in which the indictment was found, on the ground that a material witness was absent, and on the further ground that the counsel who had been employed to conduct the case in all respects except as to the making of one address had, on the night before, withdrawn, leaving only the associate counsel, who was unprepared to go on with the trial,—should have been granted, or further time given for the preparation of the defense. *Jackson* v. *State,* 88 Ga. 784, 15 S. E. 677.

And a person indicted for murder, at a distance from his home, is entitled to a continuance of a trial called within twelve days after he is indicted, during which time he has been in jail, to procure the attendance of counsel in whom he has confidence, and who, by reason of his duties as a United States officer, is unable to attend until the second day after the case is called. *Bates* v. *Com.* 13 Ky. L. Rep. 132, 16 S. W. 528.

Failure to notify defendant, charged with a crime, of the calling of a special term at which he is to be tried, as required by the Missouri statute, does not deprive the court of jurisdiction, although it may afford defendant good ground for a continuance. *State* v. *Kavanaugh,* 133 Mo. 452, 33 S. W. 33, Affirmed in Banc in 34 S. W. 842.

[3]*State* v. *Wilson,* 33 La. Ann. 261; *State* v. *Poe,* 8 Lea, 647; *People* v. *Fuller,* 2 Park. Crim. Rep. 16; *Revel* v. *State,* 26 Ga. 275 (recent finding of in-

dictment no ground for continuance); *Craft* v. *Com.* 24 Gratt. 602 (failure to furnish accused with a list of petit jurors, until the day of trial, not sufficient); *Dunn* v. *People,* 109 Ill. 635 (no error to deny the motion where it was shown that the accused's counsel was too much occupied to prepare for trial); *Reg.* v. *Gordon,* Car. & M. 410 (application by defendant for postponement because arrested while on his way to counsel to deliver him his brief held insufficient, no collusion with prosecutor being shown).

And an application is properly refused where the defendant has had ample time in which to prepare for trial, but has failed to do so through his own neglect. *Hamilton* v. *State,* 62 Ark. 543, 36 S. W. 1054; *Hayden* v. *Com.* 20 Ky. L. Rep. 274, 45 S. W. 886; *People* v. *Ward,* 105 Cal. 335, 38 Pac. 945 (especially where the application is not supported by affidavit or other written evidence).

Or where he fails to disclose by a plain and consistent statement facts preventing the preparation for trial. *Conrad* v. *State,* 144 Ind. 290, 43 N. E. 221.

And the trial court may properly refuse a continuance upon defendant's claim that by reason of his poverty he has not been able to retain counsel for his defense, and that those appointed for him on the day before the application have not had time to prepare his defense, where he has had ample time to apply to the court for the appointment of counsel, and was represented by counsel when arraigned. *State* v. *Inks,* 135 Mo. 678, 37 S. W. 942.

In *Ballard* v. *State,* 31 Fla. 266, 12 So. 865, the application was held to have been properly refused because the affidavit showed no effort at preparing the defense nor any obstruction thereof, no refusal to the prisoner of an opportunity to see and confer with his counsel nor any delay in procuring counsel, and no reason why the time was not sufficient for preparing his defense, and consulting satisfactorily with counsel, and properly informing them of the facts of the case.

And a refusal was upheld in *Com.* v. *Bezek,* 168 Pa. 603, 32 Atl. 109, where the defendant contended that his counsel was assigned only on the Friday before the Monday on which the case was called, and that he was unable to speak English, and it was impossible to procure an interpreter or prepare a defense.

[a]*Com.* v. *Carter,* 11 Pick. 277. Prosecution entitled to continuance where necessary witness had departed at instigation of prisoner's friends, though without connivance of the prisoner.

6. Absence of counsel.

Absence of the attorney or counsel of the accused is a ground not favored, and does not of itself give a right to a postponement,[1]—especially if a prior postponement has been had.[2]

But absence of counsel[3] because of illness, particularly sudden illness, rendering it impracticable to secure other counsel in time, might present a case in which it would be error to refuse a postponement.[4]

And absence of the prosecuting attorney because of illness is sufficient cause for an adjournment in a justice's court.[5]

[3]*Wright* v. *State,* 18 Ga. 383; *Roberts* v. *People,* 9 Colo. 458, 13 Pac. 631 (holding that the judge cannot be required to postpone the business of his court to suit the convenience of the attorney for the accused, who may desire to attend other courts,—especially where, upon the calling of the case, the defendant appears with new counsel and manifests a readiness to proceed); *Van Horn* v. *State,* 5 Wyo. 501, 40 Pac. 964 (absence of counsel in adjoining county attending court not sufficient).

Thus, absence of one of the prisoner's counsel is not sufficient, where he is ably and faithfully represented by other competent counsel. *State* v. *Sullivan,* 43 Kan. 563, 23 Pac. 645; *State* v. *Frost,* 103 Tenn. 685, 54 S. W. 986; *State* v. *Parker,* 106 Mo. 217, 17 S. W. 180 (especially where most of the questions of law have been settled on a previous appeal, and the trial does not take place until eight days after the application).

So held, also, of the absence of leading counsel. *Walker* v. *State,* 13 Tex. App. 618; *Long* v. *People,* 135 Ill. 435, 10 L. R. A. 48, 25 N. E. 851; *Mixon* v. *State,* 36 Tex. Crim. Rep. 66, 35 S. W. 394. Especially where it does not appear that the counsel absent is leading counsel. *Marshall* v. *State,* 94 Ga. 589, 20 S. E. 432.

And the denial of an application for a continuance upon the ground that one of the defendant's attorneys was ill does not constitute reversible error, where it appears that he fully discharged his duty on the trial. *Hayden* v. *Com.* 20 Ky. L. Rep. 274, 45 S. W. 886. And that there was no lack of counsel to conduct the defense skillfully and zealously. *Hourigan* v. *Com.* 94 Ky. 520, 23 S. W. 355.

[4]*State* v. *Dubois,* 24 La. Ann. 309.

It is no abuse of discretion to refuse a continuance on account of the illness and absence of leading counsel, where there has been a previous continuance on the same ground, and notice given a month before the trial, by the presiding judge, to both the leading and associate counsel, that another continuance for that cause will not be granted, and there is no statement on oath, as required by Ga. Code, § 3525, that the application is not made for delay. *Burnett* v. *State,* 87 Ga. 622, 13 S. E. 552.

So, it is within the discretion of a criminal court to refuse to pass a case for the second time because defendant's counsel are engaged in a civil court, where it has adopted a rule that no case shall be passed, continued, or postponed by reason of the engagment of counsel in any other court. *Feinberg* v. *People,* 174 Ill. 609, 51 N. E. 798.

[5]Thus, the unexpected absence, on the morning of the trial, of the local counsel for defendant charged with murder, without any notice to defendant, is ground for a continuance. *Leslie* v. *Com.* 19 Ky. L. Rep. 1201, 42 S. W. 1095.

And one indicted for murder, who has engaged in his defense a firm of attorneys, relying on its senior member to conduct the defense in person, who absents himself from the term of court for the first two and a half days of the term, under the honest belief that the case of his client will not be reached during that time, of which facts the trial judge is fully aware,—should not be compelled to go to trial on the beginning of the third day of the term, with counsel appointed by the court, where a postponement until the afternoon is requested, under the Georgia Bill of Rights, entitling every person charged with an offense to the "privilege and benefit of counsel." *Delk* v. *State*, 100 Ga. 61, 27 S. E. 152.

[4] *Bagwell* v. *State*, 56 Ga. 406 (third continuance); *People* v. *Logan*, 4 Cal. 188; *Daugherty* v. *State*, 33 Tex. Crim. Rep. 173, 26 S. W. 60.

[5] *People* v. *Shufelt*, 61 Mich. 237, 28 N. W. 79.

7. Absence of the accused.

Absence of the accused is good ground for postponement in all felonies;[1] but it is not ground for postponement in misdemeanors, if he appear by counsel,[2] except, perhaps, where the offense can be punished by imprisonment.[3]

[1] *Brown* v. *State*, 24 Ark. 620; *State* v. *Cross*, 27 Mo. 332; *People* v. *Perkins*, 1 Wend. 91; *Andrews* v. *State*, 2 Sneed, 550; *People* v. *Kohler*, 5 Cal. 72; *Jackson* v. *Com.* 19 Gratt. 656; *Prine* v. *Com.* 18 Pa. 103; *Shapoonmash* v. *United States*, 1 Wash. Terr. 188; *Graham* v. *State*, 40 Ala. 659; *State* v. *Bertin*, 24 La. Ann. 46; *State* v. *Dooly*, 64 Mo. 146; *State* v. *Allen*, 64 Mo. 67; *Clark* v. *State*, 4 Humph. 254; *Burley* v. *State*, 1 Neb. 385; *Dunn* v. *Com.* 6 Pa. 384; *Sneed* v. *State*, 5 Ark. 431, 41 Am. Dec. 102; *Sweeden* v. *State*, 19 Ark. 205; N. Y. Code Crim. Proc. § 465.

A motion to continue a murder trial upon the ground that the accused is physically unable to go to trial is addressed to the discretion of the trial court, where the testimony of medical experts on that question is conflicting. *McDaniel* v. *State*, 103 Ga. 268, 30 S. E. 29.

And an application for a continuance on the ground of the sickness and disability of defendant is properly refused where the good faith of the application is challenged by the prosecution, and two committees of physicians are appointed to examine into his condition, one of which takes charge of him for several days, and upon a hearing it is found that he is able to be placed on trial, and is in a suitable condition physically to be present. *State* v. *Rogers*, 56 Kan. 362, 43 Pac. 256.

A quarantine for five days, for fear of smallpox, is not sufficient ground for further postponement of a murder trial. *State* v. *Thompson*, 132 Mo. 301, 34 S. W. 31.

[2] *Steele* v. *Com.* 3 Dana, 84; *Sweeden* v. *State*, 19 Ark. 205; *Sawyer* v. *Joiner*, 16 Vt. 497; *United States* v. *Leckie*, 1 Sprague, 227, Fed. Cas. No. 15,583; N. Y. Code Crim. Proc. § 356. *Contra*, *Slocovitch* v. *State*, 46 Ala. 227.

[3] *Ex parte Tracy*, 25 Vt. 93; *People* v. *Charles*, 1 Edm. Sel. Cas. 264.

This exception is not recognized by the New York statute above cited.

8. Absence of witness or evidence; general rule.

The absence of witnesses[1] whose testimony is material and probably true,[2] and would be likely to have an effect upon another trial, and whom the applicant has exercised due diligence to procure, and expects to have present at the time to which postponement is asked, might present a case in which it would be error to refuse the postponement asked.[3]

Illness of a witness subpœnaed is good ground for a postponement.[4]

But a postponement to procure the testimony of witnesses who are beyond the jurisdiction of the court will not be granted, where, although having had adequate opportunity, the applicant has used no diligence to procure their deposition.[5]

[1]The rule is here stated with reference to witnesses, but it applies with equal force to documentary evidence.

[2]*Burnly* v. *State* (Tex. App.) 14 S. W. 1008.

But where the testimony of the absent witness is not probably true in the light of the record, refusal to postpone is not error. *Martinez* v. *State* (Tex. Crim. Rep.) 57 S. W. 829.

[3]*Burnly* v. *State* (Tex. App.) 14 S. W. 1008; *Embry* v. *Com.* 11 Ky. L. Rep. 515, 12 S. W. 383; *State* v. *Lund,* 49 Kan. 580, 31 Pac. 146; *Ryder* v. *State,* 100 Ga. 528, 38 L. R. A. 721, 28 S. E. 246; *North* v. *People,* 139 Ill. 81, 28 N. E. 966; *Claxon* v. *Com.* 17 Ky. L. Rep. 284, 30 S. W. 998; *State* v. *Maddox,* 117 Mo. 667, 23 S. W. 771; *State* v. *Metcalf,* 17 Mont. 417, 43 Pac. 182; *Rucker* v. *State* (Tex. Crim. App.) 40 S. W. 991; *Phillips* v. *Com.* 90 Va. 401, 18 S. E. 841. And see cases *infra,* § 26.

Thus, the denial of a continuance for absent witnesses whose evidence might have changed the result, where their absence was due to a mistake of the clerk in directing the subpœnas to the sheriff of the wrong county, and where the failure to have them or their affidavits in court on application for a new trial was excused by the lack of power of the prisoner to obtain them,—will require a reversal of his conviction. *Hill* v. *State* (Miss.) 17 So. 375.

And the failure of attorneys for a defendant in a capital case, after a continuance until the next term has been denied, to repeat the application, should not prevent the court from continuing the case on its own motion, where, on application for continuance to a later day in the term, strong proof has been presented that depositions have been taken which if true, establish the prisoner's innocence, and have been mailed, but through some delay have not arrived on the day finally set for trial. *State* v. *Foster,* 79 Iowa, 726, 45 N. W. 385.

In *Clark* v. *State* (Tex. Crim. App.) 33 S. W. 224, it is held that the first application for continuance on the ground of absent witnesses should be granted, although other witnesses were present at the same time and place as to which the testimony of the absent witnesses is sought.

People v. *Foote,* 93 Mich. 38, 52 N. W. 1036, holds that it is within the discretion of the court in a criminal case to refuse a delay for the purpose of procuring witnesses.

[4]*Lofton* v. *State*, 14 Ind. 1; *Jenks* v. *State*, 39 Ind. 1; *Phillips* v. *State*, 35 Tex. Crim. Rep. 480, 34 S. W. 272.

In *People* v. *Logan*, 123 Cal. 414, 56 Pac. 56, however, it was held that a continuance on the ground of sickness and inability of a witness to attend trial, not made until after the jury were impaneled, was properly refused, where it appeared that the witness would probably be unable for a period of two months to testify at the trial.

[5]*State* v. *McCoy*, 111 Mo. 517, 20 S. W. 240; *Haile* v. *State* (Tex. Crim. App.) 43 S. W. 999; *State* v. *Farrington*, 90 Iowa, 673, 57 N. W. 606; *State* v. *Lewis*, 56 Kan. 374, 43 Pac. 265; *People* v. *Ah Lee Doon*, 97 Cal. 171, 31 Pac. 933.

And due diligence by defendant in a criminal trial requires that he procure the deposition of a witness who was sick at a former trial, and is old and infirm, so that there is no reasonable expectation of procuring her attendance at any time; and he will not be allowed a postponement on the second trial, in order to procure her testimony. *Brittain* v. *State* (Tex. Crim. App.) 40 S. W. 297.

Nor will postponement be granted because the testimony of a witness, which was to be taken by a deposition, has not arrived, for the alleged reason that she is ill in bed, where there is nothing to show that she is so ill that the testimony could not be taken in her room, while there has been great negligence in forwarding the interrogatories. *DeAlberts* v. *State*, 34 Tex. Crim. Rep. 508, 31 S. W. 391.

And refusal to postpone, to procure the attendance or evidence of a witness out of the state, in behalf of defendant, is not an abuse of discretion, where he was not brought to trial until the term after the indictment was found, and the solicitor was given no opportunity to consent to or refuse an examination of the witness by commission. *State* v. *Murphy*, 48 S. C. 1, 25 S. E. 43.

In North Dakota, under Rev. Codes 1895, §§ 8385–8398, prescribing the method of obtaining the deposition of nonresident witnesses, an application for a postponement to take the testimony of such witnesses cannot be granted except in connection with an application for a commission. *State* v. *Murphy*, 9 N. D. 175, 82 N. W. 738.

9. — diligence; burden of proof.

On an application on behalf of the accused, the burden is on him to show diligence; not on the prosecution to show the want of it.[1]

[1]*Walker* v. *State*, 13 Tex. App. 618.

10. —— before indictment.

Diligence is not obligatory before indictment found, even though the accused be in custody.[1]

[1]*State* v. *Wood*, 68 Mo. 444. Compare *United States* v. *Moore*, Wall. Sr. 23,

Fed. Cas. No. 15,805, holding that if the accused could have availed himself of compulsory process before indictment, his omission to do so, while not such negligence as to deprive him of the right to a postponement, will yet justify the court in imposing terms.

11. — — confinement of the accused.

The fact that the accused was in jail does not excuse the omission to take the testimony of a foreign witness by deposition, if the law allowed depositions.[1]

[1]*McDermott* v. *State,* 89 Ind. 189.

12. — — unanticipated evidence.

The defendant in a criminal case is required to anticipate the case of the prosecution, and prepare, as far as possible, his evidence to meet it.[1] But diligence in respect to testimony needed to meet circumstantial evidence which is not involved in the body of the offense, but only tends indirectly to prove guilt, is not obligatory, except from the time the defense learns of the intention of the prosecution to adduce such evidence.[2]

[1]And if any part of the evidence is temporarily beyond the jurisdiction of the state, and defendant shows all that the statute requires for a continuance, no discretion of the court, or misjudgment or misapprehension of the facts stated, can deprive him of such continuance. *Pettit* v. *State,* 135 Ind. 393, 34 N. E. 1118.

So, one who claims to be surprised by evidence should ask to withdraw his announcement of ready, and to continue the cause; and he should set out the facts expected to be proved. *Loveless* v. *State* (Tex. Crim. App.) 44 S. W. 508.

It is well established that the state may, upon the trial, call other witnesses, provided the defendant be furnished with the names of such witnesses in time to prepare his defense. If, when notice of new witnesses is given, the defendant desires further time to enable him to meet the evidence of such witnesses, he must interpose a timely application to the court to secure such time; and, in case such application is denied, and a review of such ruling is sought in the appellate court, the motion, with the affidavits filed in support thereof, must be made a part of the record by a bill of exceptions. *Askew* v. *People,* 23 Colo. 446, 48 Pac. 524. In this case neither the motion nor the affidavits were so preserved.

But the overruling of a motion by defendant in a criminal prosecution, for a continuance because of the misspelling of the names of witnesses for the state as indorsed upon the indictment, is not sufficient to base error upon, in the absence of a showing that defendant was surprised and misled. *State* v. *Everitt,* 14 Wash. 574, 45 Pac. 150.

[2]*Kennedy* v. *State,* 81 Ind. 379.

13. —— prosecution not expected to be ready.

A mistaken belief that the prosecution would not be ready for trial so soon is not ground for continuance.[1]

[1]*State* v. *Smith*, 60 Iowa, 755, 15 N. W. 593.

14. —— time to enforce process.

If due service of the proper process for the attendance of a witness who is within the jurisdiction is shown, and the witness is absent, and no reason is shown why the process should not be executed, the accused is entitled to time necessary to bring him into court, at least before the end of the trial.[1]

[1]*State* v. *Roark*, 23 Kan. 147.

In *Massie* v. *State*, 30 Tex. App. 64, 16 S. W. 770, it was held that, in order to entitle defendant to a continuance to procure the attendance of witnesses who disobeyed a subpœna served upon them at a previous term of the court, he must resort to an attachment at once to enforce their attendance, and not merely procure the issuance of a new subpœna.

15. —— effort to procure.

To establish the use of due diligence to compel the attendance of a witness who has been within the jurisdiction, the accused must show either—

1. That the proper process[1] to compel his attendance was seasonably[2] and duly issued[3] and served, or, if not served, delivered to the proper officer[4] or a competent person for service, and what has been done therewith;[5] and, if delivered to an officer, whether any return has been made,[6] and if so, what.[7]

Or, 2. That sufficient time has not been allowed him to do so.

[1]A postponement for the absence of a witness will be refused for want of sufficient diligence, where no process has been issued for such witness. *Gerstenkorn* v. *State*, 38 Tex. Crim. Rep. 621, 44 S. W. 503.

And diligence to procure the attendance before the second trial of witnesses for whom process was issued for the first trial, but who were not present thereat, requires that defendant applying for a continuance on the ground of their absence shall have issued new process for the witnesses. *Brittain* v. *State* (Tex. Crim. App.) 40 S. W. 297.

And a statement in an affidavit for a continuance in a criminal trial, that defendant issued a subpœna to the sheriffs of certain counties, commanding each to summon a witness, does not show that he caused the proper officer to issue a proper subpœna to each of the sheriffs, commanding him to summon the witness to appear in the court in which the trial was had, to testify in the cause on his behalf. *Ransbottom* v. *State*, 144 Ind. 250, 43 N. E. 218.

In Texas an applicant for postponement because of the absence of witnesses must, in addition to having had them subpœnaed, have asked for an attachment against them, before he can show such diligence as will entitle him to a postponement. *Blain* v. *State*, 34 Tex. Crim. Rep. 448, 31 S. W. 368; *Chaplin* v. *State*, 7 Tex. App. 87. And an application for continuance for absent witnesses should state whether process issued for them was subpœna or attachment, and should also state how it was issued and forwarded. *Dove* v. *State*, 36 Tex. Crim. Rep. 105, 35 S. W. 648. And the motion is properly denied where the attachment was not issued to the county where the witness was supposed to reside. *Guagando* v. *State*, 41 Tex. 626.

The failure of an accused to ask for an additional process to procure the attendance of a witness, for eleven days intervening between the return of a prior process "Not found" and the date of trial, is a lack of diligence justifying refusal of a continuance. *Evans* v. *State* (Tex. Crim. App.) 31 S. W. 648.

[a]*State* v. *Burns*, 54 Mo. 274 (no error to refuse continuance where it is shown that the subpœnas were issued only two days before the cause was set for trial, and the witnesses were not found); *Henderson* v. *State*, 22 Tex. 593 (issue after the commencement of the term, and seven days before the trial, returned following day, "Not served," held not to be a sufficient excuse); *Gaston* v. *State*, 11 Tex. App. 143 (acceptance of service of subpœna by a witness 11 miles distant from the place of trial, on the morning of the trial, is no sufficient ground for continuance). See also *Roussell* v. *Com.* 28 Gratt. 930; *Dingman* v. *State*, 48 Wis. 485, 4 N. W. 668 (issue of subpœna a few days before the trial, witness having before service left the state, held insufficient).

And a postponement for an absent witness is properly refused for lack of diligence where the subpœna served on him was returned nine days before the trial, and no further process was asked, notwithstanding his absence from court. *Longacre* v. *State* (Tex. Crim. App.) 41 S. W. 629.

Or where no subpœna for him was issued until the day before that set for the trial, and the one asking for his continuance knew ten days earlier that he would be required as a witness. *State* v. *Thompson*, 132 Mo. 301, 34 S. W. 31.

Or where he caused a subpœna to be issued for such witness nearly six months after the indictment was found, and, upon its return unserved, did nothing further for nearly five months. *Tanner* v. *State* (Tex. Crim. App.) 44 S. W. 489.

Or where the witness is a resident of another county, and the attachment was not issued to that county until twenty days after the prosecution had commenced and about twenty-two days before the trial was had, and no reason is shown why it was not sued out earlier, and no effort is shown to have the writ returned on the day when it was made returnable. *Christian* v. *State* (Tex. Crim. App.) 39 S. W. 682.

Or where the one applying therefor made no effort to secure the attendance of the witness, who has no fixed place of abode, or to keep advised of his wanderings, until a few days before the trial. *State* v. *Craemer,* 12 Wash. 217, 40 Pac. 944.

Nor is sufficient diligence shown by an application stating that the witness had left his home some time during a specified week, and defendant knew that he had not been served with subpœna four days before the end of the same week. *Longacre* v. *State* (Tex. Crim. App.) 41 S. W. 629.

And failure to seek process for witness until ten days prior to the trial is such want of diligence as will defeat an application for continuance because of his absence, where the witness failed to attend the preceding term of the court in obedience to process previously served upon him. *Myers* v. *State* (Tex. Crim. App.) 33 S. W. 865.

But sufficient diligence is shown by the fact that the accused did not learn of the presence of the witness at the scene of the crime until Saturday, and did not know what his testimony would be until the next day, and on the following Monday procured an attachment for him. *Phipps* v. *State,* 34 Tex. Crim. Rep. 560, 31 S. W. 397.

And to the effect that postponement was properly refused for lack of showing of sufficient diligence, see *Kidd* v. *State,* 101 Ga. 528, 28 S. E. 990; *Conrad* v. *State,* 144 Ind. 290, 43 N. E. 221; *State* v. *McClain,* 49 Kan. 730, 31 Pac. 790; *State* v. *Thompson,* 141 Mo. 408, 42 S. W. 949; *Teague* v. *State* (Tex. Crim. App.) 31 S. W. 401; *State* v. *Hutchinson,* 14 Wash. 580, 45 Pac. 156.

Thomas v. *State,* 61 Miss. 60 (holding that absence of a material witness is no ground for a continuance, even in a capital case, if compulsory process might have been but was not obtained); *People* v. *Lampson,* 70 Cal. 204, 11 Pac. 593 (continuance refused where the affidavit failed to show the issuing of a proper subpœna, and it did not appear that the sheriff was informed where the witness resided); *Wall* v. *State,* 18 Tex. 682, 70 Am. Dec. 302 (affidavit defective where it fails to show that a subpœna was asked for); *Williams* v. *State,* 10 Tex. App. 114 (holding that issue by the proper authorities must be shown).

Cantu v. *State,* 1 Tex. App. 402 (affidavit insufficient because it did not show when the subpœna was delivered, or to what officer). See also *Buie* v. *State,* 1 Tex. App. 452 (where the affidavit did not show subpœna to have been given to the proper officer, or what was done with it); *Murray* v. *State,* 1 Tex. App. 417 (service and return by proper officer not shown); and *Cooper* v. *State,* 7 Tex. App. 194; *Skipworth* v. *State,* 8 Tex. App. 135 (holding that delivery to sheriff of wrong county not enough).

And an application to postpone for an absent witness is properly refused where the affidavit does not show when the subpœna was issued or served on the witness, and no attachment is asked for such witness. *State* v. *White,* 126 Mo. 591, 29 S. W. 591.

The application, where it shows issuance of subpœna ten days before the trial, should show when the return thereon was made into court, and whether it was served or not. *Bain* v. *State* (Tex. Crim. App.) 33 S. W. 966.

And postponement is properly refused where it appears simply that a subpœna was left at the house of the witness, but the time of its issuance is not shown. *Masterson* v. *State* (Tex. Crim. App.) 34 S. W. 279.

But in *Ransbottom* v. *State*, 144 Ind. 250, 43 N. E. 218, it is held that in Indiana an affidavit for a continuance on the ground of the absence of a witness is not required to show that the sheriff in serving the subpœna left the same at the residence of the witness, the latter not being found.

[5]*Burton* v. *State*, 9 Tex. App. 605 (holding that if sent to another county the mode of transmission should be shown); *Hailes* v. *State*, 10 Tex. App. 490 (promise of one sheriff to forward to another not enough); *People* v. *Lampson*, 70 Cal. 204, 11 Pac. 593 (sheriff not informed where witness resided); *Grant* v. *State*, 2 Tex. App. 163. See also *Walton* v. *Com.* 32 Gratt. 855; *Hewitt* v. *Com.* 17 Gratt. 627; *State* v. *Walker*, 69 Mo. 274 (holding it error to deny continuance where it is shown that the witness was subpœnaed and has secreted himself to avoid attachment).

[6]*Cooper* v. *State*, 7 Tex. App. 194. The presumption that the officer has done his duty does not avail.

[7]A return not executed for want of fees held not fatal to the application. *Walton* v. *Com.*, 32 Gratt. 855.

A prisoner's poverty has been taken into consideration to mitigate an apparent want of diligence in applying for a postponement. *Reg.* v. *Langhurst*, 10 Cox C. C. 353, 4 Fost. & F. 969.

16. — — witness whom the magistrate admonished to attend or the prosecution subpoenaed.

The mere fact that a witness examined before a magistrate was admonished by him to attend,[1] or that a witness was subpœnaed by the prosecution[2] does not give the accused a right to expect his attendance, without process on the part of the accused, and to demand a postponement because of his absence.

[1]*Rainwater* v. *Com.*, 5 Ky. L. Rep. 103.

[2]*State* v. *Hayden*, 45 Iowa, 11.

A defendant who relies upon process for an absent witness, issued by the prosecution, as ground for a postponement, must show that such adversary used due diligence to procure the attendance of the witness. *Mixon* v. *State*, 36 Tex. Crim. Rep. 66, 35 S. W. 394.

17. — promise to attend.

But the absence of a witness whom the applicant omitted to subpœna is good ground for a postponement, if the witness promised to attend, and the applicant in good faith relied thereupon,[1] or the applicant had a right to expect his attendance, as in the case of a witness bound over to attend.[2]

[1]*People* v. *Brown*, 46 Cal. 102. Reliance upon the promise of a nonresident witness to attend.

But where defendant failed to subpœna the absent witness for the alleged reason that he was informed the witness would be present at the trial, the absence of the witness is not ground for continuance. *State* v. *Barker*, 43 Kan. 262, 23 Pac. 575.

[2]In considering the question of diligence on a motion by the accused to postpone on account of the absence of a witness, the fact that the commonwealth had such witness recognized should have the same effect as if he had been recognized at the instance of the accused. *Saylor* v. *Com.*, 97 Ky. 184, 30 S. W. 390.

But *State* v. *Luke*, 104 Mo. 563, 16 S. W. 242, holds that the fact that defendant supposed the absent witness had been recognized by the state to be present at the trial does not excuse his failure to exercise proper diligence to enforce his attendance.

18. —— reluctant witness.

An application, otherwise regular, should not be denied merely because of the improbability that an absent witness whose testimony is desired will voluntarily expose himself to arrest.[1]

And a party who is surprised by the unauthorized withdrawal of his witnesses after the commencement of the trial is entitled to a postponement.[2]

[1]*State* v. *Farr*, 33 Iowa, 553.

And where the statements of the accused, as well as of the sheriff, and all the circumstances attending the sudden departure of a witness, tend to show that the accused was interested in having him present, and that his absence was to avoid imprisonment for nonpayment of a fine imposed for his nonattendance, a continuance should be granted, where his testimony is important to the accused, and tends to corroborate his statement as to the manner in which the killing occurred. *Costigan* v. *Com.*, 11 Ky. L. Rep. 617, 12 S. W. 629.

[2]*Price* v. *People*, 131 Ill. 223, 23 N. E. 639.

19. —— witness convicted.

The fact that the desired witness has been convicted of crime, and has appealed, is not ground for postponement in expectation of reversal of the conviction on appeal, even where such witness was jointly indicted with the accused, and severance was allowed to enable the one now on trial to avail himself of the testimony of the other.[1]

And a postponement will not be granted for the testimony of an ex-convict who is not shown to have been pardoned, where it is not probable that he would testify as alleged in the motion for continuance, or that his testimony would be true if he should so testify.[2]

[1] *Slawson* v. *State*, 7 Tex. App. 63; *Krebs* v. *State*, 8 Tex. App. 1.

[2] *King* v. *State*, 34 Tex. Crim. Rep. 228, 29 S. W. 1086.

And a postponement of a trial for larceny at the request of the state's attorney, against the objection of defendant, for the purpose of obtaining the testimony of a convicted felon whose term of imprisonment does not expire until the next term of court, is improper under Va. Code 1887, § 4016, providing that one accused of a felony shall, unless good cause be shown for a continuance, be arraigned and tried at the same term at which the indictment is found. *Benton* v. *Com.*, 90 Va. 328, 18 S. E. 282.

20. — ability to procure the evidence.

Facts should be shown sustaining a reasonable expectation of securing the desired evidence[1] within a reasonable time.[2]

If this be shown, it is not an objection to the application that the witness is beyond the jurisdiction.[3]

[1] *Polin* v. *State*, 14 Neb. 540, 16 N. W. 898; *Strickland* v. *State*, 13 Tex. App. 364; *State* v. *O'Neil*, 13 Or. 183, 9 Pac. 284 (a statement that the defendant is confident that he can procure the attendance of the witnesses is not enough).

And a postponement will be refused where the application fails to state facts and show reasonable grounds for believing that the attendance or testimony of the witnesses will be procured at the next term of court, as required by Iowa Code, § 2750. *State* v. *Farrington*, 90 Iowa, 673, 57 N. W. 606.

[2] *People* v. *Lewis*, 64 Cal. 401, 1 Pac. 490.

[3] *White* v. *Com.*, 80 Ky. 480; *People* v. *Vermilyea*, 7 Cow. 369 (here it was shown that the witness promised to come); *Contra* (holding that the absence of a foreign witness does not constitute a ground for postponement which it will be error to refuse), *State* v. *Williams*, 69 Mo. 110; *Gladden* v. *State*, 13 Fla. 623; *Com.* v. *Millard*, 1 Mass. 6; *Rex* v. *D'Eon*, 1 W. Bl. 510, 3 Burr. 1513 (no diligence shown or probability that witness would attend or would be material if present); *Harris* v. *State*, 8 Tex. App. 90; (absence of fugitive witness in parts unknown not ground for third continuance).

21. — — inability to get other evidence.

Inability to procure the desired evidence from any other source must be shown.[1] But this rule, according to some authorities, should not be applied unless the applicant has already had a postponement or continuance.[2]

[1] *Dunn* v. *People*, 109 Ill. 635; *Smith* v. *State*, 58 Miss. 867; *State* v. *Simms*, 68 Mo. 305; *People* v. *Garns*, 2 Utah, 260; *Wall* v. *State*, 18 Tex. 682, 70 Am. Dec. 302; *State* v. *Carter*, 51 La. Ann. 442, 25 So. 385; *Craft* v. *State* (Tex. Crim. App.) 31 S. W. 367.

The court cannot consider the fact that the defendant at a previous term applied for a continuance to obtain the evidence of other witnesses who, it was alleged, would testify to the facts sought to be proved by the witness in question, and that in such application defendant swore that he could not prove the same facts by any other witness whose testimony could be as readily procured. *Pettit* v. *State*, 135 Ind. 393, 34 N. E. 1118.

And that the affidavit under Ind. Rev. Stat. 1894, § 1850, which requires a statement that defendant is unable to procure facts by any other witness whose testimony can be as readily procured, discloses that the facts proposed to be proved are within the personal knowledge of the defendant, is not a cause for the refusal of the continuance. *Ransbottom* v. *State*, 144 Ind. 250, 43 N. E. 218.

[2] *Pinckord* v. *State*, 13 Tex. App. 468; *Land* v. *State*, 34 Tex. Crim. Rep. 330, 30 S. W. 788.

22. —— incompetent evidence.

The motion should be denied if the desired evidence is legally inadmissible.[1]

[1] *Krebs* v. *State*, 8 Tex. App. 1; *Faulkner* v. *Territory*, 6 N. M. 464, 30 Pac. 905; *Delk* v. *State*, 99 Ga. 667, 26 S. E. 752; *Smith* v. *Com.*, 13 Ky. L. Rep. 612, 17 S. W. 868; *State* v. *Hollier*, 49 La. Ann. 371, 21 So. 633; *Moore* v. *State* (Tex. Crim. App.) 33 S. W. 980; *Myers* v. *Com.*, 90 Va. 705, 19 S. E. 881; *Carthaus* v. *State*, 78 Wis. 560, 47 N. W. 629; *Hamilton* v. *State*, 62 Ark. 543, 36 S. W. 1054; *State* v. *McDonough*, 104 Iowa, 6, 73 N. W. 357.

But on motion for a new trial, in error, and on appeal, the evidence will be deemed to have been admissible if in the course of the trial it became admissible and its absence was prejudicial. *Wooldridge* v. *State*, 13 Tex. App. 443, S. P., *State* v. *Rigsby*, 6 Lea, 554.

23. —— cumulative evidence or evidence as to character.

Refusal to postpone for the sake of obtaining cumulative evidence,[1] or evidence as to the good character of the accused,[2] is not error.

[1] *Nelms* v. *State*, 58 Miss. 362; *Varnadoe* v. *State*, 67 Ga. 768; *Trabune* v. *Com.*, 13 Ky. L. Rep. 343, 17 S. W. 186; *Wells* v. *State* (Miss.) 18 So. 117; *McKinney* v. *State*, 3 Wyo. 719, 16 L. R. A. 710, 30 Pac. 293; *Maxey* v. *State*, 66 Ark. 523, 52 S. W. 2; *Contra*, *Bostick* v. *State*, 10

Tex. App. 705. And compare *Burnly* v. *State* (Tex. App.) 14 S. W. 1008, to the effect that because absent evidence is cumulative is no ground for refusing a first application to postpone,—especially where such testimony would tell strongly in defendant's favor, and the evidence is conflicting, and all due diligence has been used to have the testimony on the trial. *Porter* v. *State* (Tex. Crim. App.) 32 S. W. 692.

But the general rule that a trial will not be postponed for the purpose of obtaining cumulative evidence does not apply where the only evidence at hand is that of an interested party,—especially where he is the accused under indictment for murder. *People* v. *Ah Lee Doon,* 97 Cal. 171, 31 Pac. 933.

[3]*Steele* v. *People,* 45 Ill. 152; *McNealy* v. *State,* 17 Fla. 198; *Ballard* v. *State,* 31 Fla. 266, 12 So. 865.

An application to postpone on the ground of absent witnesses living in another county than that of defendant's residence, by whom he states that he expects to prove a "good reputation" in the community where he lives, is properly refused, where there is no statement that the witnesses ever knew him in their own county or his, and no diligence to procure their attendance has been used. *Whitaker* v. *State* (Tex. Crim. App.) 31 S. W. 518.

24. Contents of affidavit as to absent witness or document.

An affidavit to support an application to postpone on account of the absence of evidence[1] must show (I.) the materiality of the desired evidence;[2] (II.) facts showing due diligence already exercised in the endeavor to procure it;[3] and (III.) assurance of the probable presence of the evidence at the time proposed.[4]

An application founded upon an affidavit conforming to these requisites[5] ought to be granted, unless it appears that the absence is collusive or procured by the applicant, or that the affidavit is false or made for the purpose of delay.[6]

[1]This rule is generally stated (for it usually so occurs) as relating to witnesses, but it applies to documents also.

And it is prejudicial error to deny an application by defendant for leave to prepare and present a statement setting forth the testimony of witnesses whose depositions were suppressed during the trial because they did not appear to be correctly transcribed by the stenographer, in order that the state may admit the same to be their testimony, and, in the event of its refusal so to admit, for the postponement of the case a sufficient time to have the depositions returned to the stenographer and properly transcribed, where the imperfection of the depositions was not due to defendant's fault. *State* v. *Brown,* 55 Kan. 766, 42 Pac. 363.

A postponement of a trial is properly refused where the affidavit therefor does not assert that there are any absent witnesses, and the motion seems to be based on the suggestion that counsel wants time, and that it is not customary to try such an indictment so soon after it is found. *People* v. *Shea,* 147 N. Y. 78, 41 N. E. 505.

So also where the witnesses alleged to be absent are present and testify at the trial. *State* v. *Pierce,* 136 Mo. 34, 37 S. W. 815.

[s]*Hyde* v. *State,* 16 Tex. 445, 67 Am. Dec. 632; *Moody* v. *People,* 20 Ill. 315; *Steele* v. *People,* 45 Ill. 152; *Rex* v. *D'Eon,* 3 Burr. 1513, 1 W. Bl. 510; *People* v. *Vermilyea,* 7 Cow. 369; *State* v. *Painter,* 40 Iowa, 298 (holding it error to deny the motion on application by the People, where the affidavit showed the materiality of the evidence); *State* v. *Files,* 3 Brev. 304, 1 Treadway Const. 234; *Strauss* v. *State,* 58 Miss. 53; *People* v. *Anderson,* 53 Mich. 60, 18 N. W. 561; *State* v. *Bennett,* 52 Iowa, 724, 2 N. W. 1103; *Polin* v. *State,* 14 Neb. 540, 16 N. W. 898; *State* v. *Celestin,* 48 La. Ann. 272, 19 So. 119.

And in some jurisdictions the affidavit must also aver that defendant believes that the facts he expects to prove by the absent witnesses are true. *State* v. *Dusenberry,* 112 Mo. 277, 20 S. W. 461 (required by Mo. Rev. Stat. 1889, § 4181); *Price* v. *State,* 57 Ark. 165, 20 S. W. 1091.

[s]*Hyde* v. *State,* 16 Tex. 445, 67 Am. Dec. 632; *State* v. *Lange,* 59 Mo. 418; *State* v. *Hagan,* 22 Kan. 490; *Pullen* v. *State,* 11 Tex. App. 89; *Wray* v. *People,* 78 Ill. 212; *State* v. *Smith,* 8 Rich. L. 460; *Mackey* v. *Com.,* 80 Ky. 345; *Blige* v. *State,* 20 Fla. 742, 51 Am. Rep. 628; *McDermott* v. *State,* 89 Ind. 187; *State* v. *Lewis,* 74 Mo. 222 (where, in consequence of being betrayed by his attorney defendant's material witnesses were absent when the case was called for trial; held error to refuse a postponement); *Moody* v. *Com.,* 19 Ky. L. Rep. 1198, 43 S. W. 209; *Cannon* v. *State,* 75 Miss. 364, 22 So. 827; *Faulkner* v. *Territory,* 6 N. M. 464, 30 Pac. 905.

It is insufficient to urge that diligence has been used, without showing the facts. *Smith* v. *Com.,* 13 Ky. L. Rep. 612, 17 S. W. 868; *Ransbottom* v. *State,* 144 Ind. 250, 43 N. E. 218; *Tanner* v. *State* (Tex. Crim. App.) 44 S. W. 489.

And an affidavit is insufficient where it does not disclose how the affiant learned what the witness's testimony would be, or show why he was not subpœnaed while within the jurisdiction, and there is a strong inference that other witnesses could prove the same facts. *State* v. *Hawkins,* 18 Or. 476, 23 Pac. 475, 477.

And an affidavit averring that witnesses were not served because they could not be found does not sufficiently show due diligence. Whether they could be found or not was a matter depending on the diligence exercised by the defendant, and the law imposes the duty upon him to show his acts done, if any, in trying to find the witnesses, so that the court, looking at them, may determine whether they amounted to legal diligence. *Territory* v. *Anderson,* 4 N. M. 213, 13 Pac. 21.

And allegations that the absent witnesses are somewhere within the state, and that their whereabouts cannot be ascertained by defendant, are so contradictory that they may be disregarded. *State* v. *Wilson,* 9 Wash. 218, 37 Pac. 424.

But an omission to state that a subpœna was issued in ample time, and returned, is immaterial if such facts are shown by the exhibition of the subpœna itself and the officer's return thereon, and by calling the court's attention to it. *Vogt* v. *Com.*, 92 Ky. 68, 17 S. W. 213.

[4]*Hyde* v. *State*, 16 Tex. 445, 67 Am. Dec. 632; *State* v. *Hagan*, 22 Kan. 490; *People* v. *Francis*, 38 Cal. 183; *Harris* v. *State*, 8 Tex. App. 90; *State* v. *Robinson*, 29 La. Ann. 364; *People* v. *Lewis*, 64 Cal. 401, 1 Pac. 490; *People* v. *Ah Yute*, 53 Cal. 613; *Dacey* v. *People*, 116 Ill. 555, 6 N. E. 165; *Polin* v. *State*, 14 Neb. 540, 16 N. W. 898; *State* v. *Gray*, 19 Nev. 212, 8 Pac. 456; *Faulkner* v. *Territory*, 6 N. M. 464, 30 Pac. 905; *Hamilton* v. *State*, 62 Ark. 543, 36 S. W. 1054; *State* v. *Alred*, 117 Mo. 471, 22 S. W. 363.

The affidavit for a postponement to procure a nonresident witness should state not only a bona fide belief that he can be procured, but also the grounds of such belief. *State* v. *Harrison*, 36 W. Va. 729, 18 L. R. A. 224, 15 S. E. 982.

[5]*Shirwin* v. *People*, 69 Ill. 55; *Skaro* v. *State*, 43 Tex. 88; *People* v. *McCrory*, 41 Cal. 458; *Dutton* v. *State*, 5 Ind. 533; *State* v. *Moultrie*, 33 La. Ann. 1146; *People* v. *Lee* (Cal.) 8 Pac. 685; *Territory* v. *Davis* (Ariz.) 10 Pac. 359; *State* v. *Burwell*, 34 Kan. 312, 8 Pac. 470; *Austine* v. *People*, 110 Ill. 248; *Welch* v. *Com.*, 90 Va. 318, 18 S. E. 273; *Elliott* v. *State*, 34 Neb. 48, 51 N. W. 315; *English* v. *State* (Tex. App.) 16 S. W. 306.

[6]*Porter* v. *State*, 3 Lea, 496.

In some jurisdictions the affidavit must show the applicant's good faith by alleging that the witnesses are not absent by his procurement or consent, and that the application is not for delay. *Crews* v. *People*, 120 Ill. 317, 11 N. E. 404; *White* v. *State*, 9 Tex. App. 41; *State* v. *Bradley*, 90 Mo. 160, 2 S. W. 284; *Bryant* v. *State*, 34 Fla 291, 16 So. 177; *Bresnan* v. *State* (Tex. Crim. App.) 43 S. W. 111. And in *State* v. *Belvel*, 89 Iowa, 405, 27 L. R. A. 846, 56 N. W. 545, it is held that a postponement asked because of the absence of certain witnesses is properly refused where unjustifiable attempts have been made by the one applying therefor to prevent the attendance of one of such witnesses, and it appears that the application is not made in good faith, or that due diligence has not been used.

25. — materiality; disclosure of evidence.

To establish materiality, the affidavit must state what is expected to be proved by the absent witness or document.[1]

But, according to some authorities, this rule should not be applied unless the applicant has already had a postponement or continuance.[2]

[1]*People* v. *Wilson*, 3 Park. Crim. Rep. 199; *Wiggins* v. *State*, 101 Ga. 502, 29 S. E. 26; *Long* v. *People*, 135 Ill. 435, 10 L. R. A. 48, 25 N. E. 851; *Smith* v. *State*, 132 Ind. 145, 31 N. E. 807; *State* v. *Osborne*, 96 Iowa, 281, 65 N. W. 159; *People* v. *Burwell*, 106 Mich. 27, 63 N. W. 986; *State* v. *Strattman*, 100 Mo. 540, 13 S. W. 814; *Dixon* v. *State*, 46 Neb. 298,

64 N. W. 961; *Faulkner* v. *Territory*, 6 N. M. 464, 30 Pac. 905; *Leach* v. *State*, 99 Tenn. 584, 42 S. W. 195; *Dove* v. *State*, 36 Tex. Crim. Rep. 105, 35 S. W. 648; *State* v. *Wilson*, 9 Wash. 218, 37 Pac. 424.

And an affidavit to postpone, to procure records of insane asylums in which defendant has been incarcerated, must show the competency of such records. *Faulkner* v. *Territory*, 6 N. M. 464, 30 Pac. 905.

[2] *State* v. *Maguire*, 69 Mo. 197.

26. — form of allegations.

The affidavit must state facts, and not mere legal conclusions,[1] and the description of the expected testimony must not be indefinite or evasive.[2]

[1] *State* v. *McCoy*, 29 La. Ann. 593; *State* v. *Good*, 132 Mo. 114, 33 S. W. 790; *Faulkner* v. *Territory*, 6 N. M. 464, 30 Pac. 905.

Where the affidavits are so contradictory and unreasonable as to make it manifest that applicant has no good grounds for further postponement, and no defense to the charge, the postponement will be denied. *Haywood* v. *Com.*, 11 Ky. L. Rep. 355, 12 S. W. 131.

It is within the discretion of the trial court to allow an amendment to an affidavit for a continuance. *Com.* v. *Hourigan*, 89 Ky. 305, 12 S. W. 550; *State* v. *Good*, 132 Mo. 114, 33 S. W. 790; *State* v. *Hilsabeck*, 132 Mo. 348, 34 S. W. 38.

But the accused is entitled, where the state admits that the witness will swear to the facts stated in his affidavit for a continuance, without objecting to the materiality of the evidence, to amend his affidavit on the trial, by showing its materiality, upon the objection being then raised for the first time. *McNeally* v. *State*, 5 Wyo. 59, 36 Pac. 824.

[2] *Williams* v. *State*, 10 Tex. App. 114; *Campbell* v. *State* (Tex. Crim. App.) 28 S. W. 808.

27. — — source of information.

Allegations on information and belief, if not accompanied by the affidavit of the informant, must state his name and residence, and indicate sufficient reason for not presenting his affidavit.[1]

[1] *Comstock* v. *State*, 14 Neb. 205, 15 N. W. 355; S. P., *Labbaite* v. *State*, 6 Tex. App. 257.

And the statement in an affidavit for the postponement of a trial on the ground of the absence of a witness who is without the state, that he will return to the jurisdiction within such reasonable time as to prevent an unusual delay in the trial of the cause, not giving the source of the affiant's information or reasons for his belief,—is insufficient. *People* v. *Leyshon*, 108 Cal. 440, 41 Pac. 480.

28. —— what witnesses.

Names of the desired witnesses and their residence must be stated, or the fact that they are unknown.[1]

[1] *State* v. *Underwood,* 76 Mo. 630; *Colton* v. *State,* 7 Tex. App. 50; *State* v. *Inks,* 135 Mo. 678, 37 S. W. 942.

And an application to postpone to procure the testimony of unknown witnesses is properly refused where it is unreasonable to suppose that defendant will ever be able to ascertain the names of such witnesses,—especially where their testimony would not be material. *Henderson* v. *State* (Tex. Crim. App.) 39 S. W. 116.

29. Presumptions.

Nothing is to be supplied by presumption in aid of the facts stated in support of an application for a postponement. The presumption is that the applicant will state the facts as strongly as he can.[1]

[1] *Cantu* v. *State,* 1 Tex. App. 402.

30. Repeated continuances.

After repeated continuances the court may examine the moving affidavits more strictly than upon a first application,[1] and it may not be error to refuse a second continuance asked on the same ground as before,[2] especially if the witnesses have gone beyond the jurisdiction of the court.[3]

[1] *State* v. *Maguire,* 69 Mo. 197.

[2] A third application to postpone for the absence of witnesses is properly refused where defendant might by proper diligence have learned of their contemplated absence in time to take their depositions. *State* v. *Tatlow,* 136 Mo. 678, 38 S. W. 552.

So also where such witnesses have not been summoned, and the motion is not supported by affidavit of the materiality of the evidence. *Schonberger* v. *Com.,* 86 Va. 489, 10 S. E. 713.

And a conviction will not be reversed for the trial court's refusal to grant a postponement because the accused's attorney was engaged in another court, where there had been repeated adjournments, and the court offered to assign other counsel. *State* v. *Hedgepeth,* 125 Mo. 14, 28 S. W. 160.

[3] *Johnson* v. *State,* 58 Ga. 491. Compare with *State* v. *Walker,* 69 Mo. 274, holding that, notwithstanding five continuances had been granted, it was error to refuse a continuance, the witnesses having secreted themselves to avoid service of an attachment.

31. Suspicious circumstances.

If there are suspicious circumstances attending the application, the court will require the applicant to be more minute in stating the facts than would otherwise be necessary,[1] and a denial of the motion, with an offer to take the testimony of an absent witness at his residence, is justifiable.[2]

[1] *People* v. *Vermilyea*, 7 Cow. 369.

[2] *Webster* v. *People*, 92 N. Y. 422; S. C., 1 N. Y. Crim. Rep. 190.

32. Court must not be influenced by personal knowledge.

The judge should not be influenced by personal knowledge of want of integrity on the part of the person making the application.[1]

[1] *Fox* v. *State*, 9 Ga. 373. Compare with *State* v. *Lindsey*, 14 La. Ann. 42; and *Poole* v. *State*, 18 Ga. 567 (where the action of the court in despatching a messenger to satisfy itself concerning the alleged absence of material witness was sustained).

33. Opposing postponement by counter affidavits.

The court may, in its discretion, receive counter affidavits to show that a witness has not been subpœnaed, or is inaccessible or absent without leave;[1] or to show want of diligence, or the improbability of obtaining the testimony at all, or at the time to which it is proposed to postpone the trial;[2] or to negative the statement that the accused could not prepare his defense while imprisoned, or that access by counsel was denied him.[3]

But evidence to disprove the facts which the applicant desires postponement to enable him to prove is inadmissible,[4] unless by way of showing bad faith in the application.

[1] *Horn* v. *State*, 62 Ga. 362; *People* v. *Cleveland*, 49 Cal. 577.

On an application for a postponement based on the alleged absence of witnesses, counter affidavits are properly allowed to be filed contradicting the averments of the affidavits in support of the application, other than those as to the testimony of the witnesses. *State* v. *Murdy*, 81 Iowa, 603, 47 N. Y. 867. In this case the grounds set up were illness of counsel and absence of witnesses; and the counter affidavits filed tended to show that the alleged sickness of the attorneys for defendant did not exist; that one of them was not in fact employed until about the time the cause should have been ready for trial, if then; and that the witnesses who, it was claimed, were sick and unable to attend court, were in fact in good health, or in such condition of health that they could readily attend court without danger of injury. None of the counter affidavits sought to contradict the averments of the affidavits as to what the testimony of the witnesses would be.

But refusal to strike out counter affidavits in resistance to an application for a postponement is not erroneous, although a part of such affidavits is objectionable, where no attempt is made to designate the objectionable part. *State* v. *Belvel,* 89 Iowa, 405, 27 L. R. A. 846, 56 N. W. 545. The counter affidavits in this case showed in regard to one of the absent witnesses that defendant not only did not in good faith attempt to secure her attendance, but that, by himself and his attorney, he made extraordinary and unjustifiable attempts to prevent it, after she had been required to appear by the state. And the hearing also showed facts which justified the court in concluding that the application for a postponement was not made in good faith, and that defendant had not used due diligence to procure the testimony which he claimed to need. And it was held that there was no error in the refusal to postpone.

In some jurisdictions the affidavit of the accused for a continuance is, for the purposes of the motion, taken as true; and no counter affidavit or evidence *aliunde* can be received, pro or con. *State* v. *Abshire,* 47 La. Ann. 542, 17 So. 141; *Price* v. *People,* 131 Ill. 223, 23 N. E. 639. The case last cited holds, however, that an error in permitting the filing of counter affidavits is not prejudicial where the postponement afforded the accused reasonable time to prepare his defense and secure the attendance of his witnesses.

[2] *Hyde* v. *State,* 16 Tex. 445, 67 Am. Dec. 630; *Rex* v. *D'Eon,* 1 W. Bl. 510, 3 Burr. 1513.

[3] *Stewart* v. *State,* 58 Ga. 577.

[4] *Hair* v. *State,* 16 Neb. 604, 21 N. W. 464, 14 Neb. 503, 16 N. W. 829; *Williams* v. *State,* 6 Neb. 334; *State* v. *Dakin,* 52 Iowa, 395, 3 N. W. 411; *Horn* v. *State,* 62 Ga. 362. But see, *contra, State* v. *Mann,* 83 Mo. 589.

In *State* v. *Good,* 132 Mo. 114, 33 S. W. 790, it is held that the truth of the allegations of affidavits upon which an application for postponement is based, as to what the testimony of the absent witnesses would be, cannot be controverted by counter affidavits, except where fraud or imposition is suggested, or where there is good reason to believe the object is delay.

But in *State* v. *Hilsabeck,* 132 Mo. 348, 34 S. W. 38, it was held that a counter affidavit made by a witness for whose absence a postponement was asked might be received to controvert the truth of the allegations in the application therefor.

So held in *Wilkins* v. *State,* 35 Tex. Crim. Rep. 525, 34 S. W. 627, of affidavits of witnesses for whose absence defendant had asked a postponement alleging that they knew nothing of the matters which defendant proposed to prove by them.

A complete showing for a postponement for the absence of a witness should not be disregarded, and the postponement refused, merely because it appears by a counter showing that the witness had in effect stated to another that she knew nothing about the case, and had not communicated to her husband any knowledge as to the facts involved. *Kennedy* v. *State,* 101 Ga. 559, 28 S. E. 979.

But the right of the opposite party to file objections to an application for a postponement, under N. M. Comp. Laws 1884, § 2052, does not extend to a denial of allegations of fact, but only to questioning its legal sufficiency. *Territory* v. *Kinney*, 3 N. M. 656, 9 Pac. 599.

34. — by admitting the desired facts.

Where the applicant discloses what facts he intends to prove by the absent evidence, it is a sufficient answer to the application for the adverse counsel to admit the truth of those facts.[1] But the admission must be unqualified.[2]

It is not enough to admit that the desired witness would swear to such a fact.[3]

[1] *Browning* v. *State*, 33 Miss. 47; *State* v. *St. Clair* (Idaho) 53 Pac. 1; *State* v. *Wiltsey*, 103 Iowa, 54, 72 N. W. 415; *State* v. *Stickney*, 53 Kan. 308, 36 Pac. 714; *Smith* v. *Com.*, 19 Ky. L. Rep. 1073, 42 S. W. 1138; *State* v. *Gibbs*, 10 Mont. 213, 10 L. R. A. 749, 25 Pac. 289; *Catron* v. *State*, 52 Neb. 389, 72 N. W. 354; *Strauss* v. *State*, 58 Miss. 53; *Pannell* v. *State*, 29 Ga. 681. And see cases cited in note to *State* v. *Gibbs* (Mont.) 10 L. R. A. 749; *Contra*, *Goodman* v. *State*, Meigs, 195 (prisoner not to be deprived of right to have witnesses personally present); *State* v. *Berkley*, 92 Mo. 41, 4 S. W. 24 (holding that therefore a statute forbidding postponement if the prosecution admits the facts set out in the affidavit of continuance is unconstitutional). See also dissenting opinion of Sherwood, J., in *State* v. *Jennings*, 81 Mo. 185, 51 Am. Rep. 236, and authorities cited; *State* v. *Jewell*, 90 Mo. 467, 3 S. W. 77; *People* v. *Savant*, 112 Mich. 297, 70 N. W. 576 (where it is held that it is not necessary to admit that the proposed testimony is true).

The constitutional right of the accused to meet the witnesses face to face, and to have "process to compel their attendance," if a reasonable time for that purpose has already elapsed, is not violated by a denial of a postponement on an admission by the prosecuting attorney that an absent witness would testify as alleged in the defendant's affidavit for a postponement, without requiring an admission of the facts which such testimony would prove if true (*Hoyt* v. *People*, 144 Ill. 588, 30 N. E. 315; S. C., with note, 16 L. R. A. 239); nor by a statute permitting the denial of postponement for absent witnesses for the defendant, provided the prosecuting attorney will admit that the witnesses if present would testify as alleged in the affidavits (*Akins* v. *Com.*, 98 Ky. 539, 32 L. R. A. 108, 33 S. W. 948; *State* v. *Hutchinson*, 14 Wash. 580, 45 Pac. 156; *Keating* v. *People*, 160 Ill. 480, 43 N. E. 724).

As to the use of the admission as evidence, see *post*, Division XXXIX.

[2] *People* v. *Brown*, 54 Cal. 243; *People* v. *Vermilyea*, 7 Cow. 369; *State* v. *McLane*, 15 Nev. 345 (holding that an admission "that if the witness [named] were present, he would testify to the facts set forth in the affidavit, and that such facts are true," is not equivalent to the necessary unqualified admission that the facts are true).

[3] *Van Meter* v. *People*, 60 Ill. 168; *Miller* v. *State*, 9 Ind. 340; *Wassels* v. *State*, 26 Ind. 30; *Powers* v. *State*, 80 Ind. 77; *People* v. *Diaz*, 6 Cal.

248; *Statham* v. *State*, 42 Ark. 273; *Hyde* v. *State*, 16 Tex. 445, 67 Am. Dec. 632 (*dictum*); *State* v. *Baker*, 13 Lea, 326; *Contra*, *State* v. *Hatfield*, 72 Mo. 518.

35. — — withdrawing admission on witness appearing.

If, after making the admission, to avoid a postponement, the absent witness appears, it is not error to permit the state to withdraw such admission, and refuse the postponement.[1]

[1] *Betts* v. *State*, 66 Ga. 508.

36. — — sending for the witness.

The announcement by the court that it is ready to send for the absent witness cannot deprive the accused of a right to a postponement.[1]

But if the absent witness is actually sent for and brought in, or appears personally in court, the application may be denied.[2]

[1] *Worthy* v. *State*, 44 Ga. 449.

[2] *Betts* v. *State*, 66 Ga. 508; *McDermott* v. *State*, 89 Ind. 187.

37. Extent discretionary.

The length of time allowed by a postponement is discretionary.[1]

[1] *Ferguson's Case*, 3 Gratt, 594, 46 Am. Dec. 196.

38. Effect; jointly indicted defendants.

Where defendants are jointly indicted, a postponement granted to one operates as a postponement to the others, in the absence of a severance.[1]

[1] *Krebs* v. *State*, 3 Tex. App. 348; *Thompson* v. *State*, 9 Tex. App. 301; *Contra*, *White* v. *State*, 31 Ind. 262.

Otherwise of a change of venue. See *ante*, Division XVI., § 2.

39. Remedy for refusal.

In New York and several other states an exception does not lie to the refusal of an application for postponement or continuance.[1]

In those jurisdictions where it does lie, an appellate court will not interfere, except in cases of very clear abuse or substantial prejudice to the applicant.[2]

[1] *Webster* v. *People*, 92 N. Y. 422; S. C., 1 N. Y. Crim. Rep. 190; *Eighmy* v. *People*, 79 N. Y. 546; *People* v. *Horton*, 4 Park. Crim. 222; *People* v. *Colt*, 3 Hill, 432; *Baxter* v. *People*, 8 Ill. 368; *State* v. *Pike*, 20 N. H. 344; *State* v. *Nicholson*, 14 La. Ann. 798; *Com.* v. *Donovan*, 99 Mass. 425, 96 Am. Dec. 765; *Com.* v. *Drake*, 124 Mass. 21.

[4] *Detro* v. *State*, 4 Ind. 200; *Hoover* v. *State*, 48 Neb. 184, 66 N. W. 1117; *Betts* v. *State*, 66 Ga. 508; *McDaniel* v. *State*, 8 Smedes & M. 401; *Freleigh* v. *State*, 8 Mo. 606; *Hamilton* v. *State*, 62 Ark. 543, 36 S. W. 1054, and cases cited; *Green* v. *State*, 13 Mo. 382; *Bates* v. *Com.*, 13 Ky. L. Rep. 132, 16 S. W. 528 (holding that refusal to postpone is, under Ky. Code, § 280, subject to exception. "If it were not so," said the court, "then the accused would be deprived of a fair trial. If, for instance, a material witness for him be absent, and due diligence has been exercised to procure his attendance, it would be a reversible error to compel the defendant to try without having the benefit of the testimony. We do not, of course, mean that the trial court has no discretion in the matter of continuances. It is, however, a legal one; and, if it be so exercised as to deprive the accused, when not in fault, of a fair trial, justice requires that he should not be remediless"); *Ogle* v. *State*, 33 Miss. 383; *Jenkins* v. *State*, 30 Tex. 444; *Holt* v. *State*, 11 Ohio St. 691; *Ballard* v. *State*, 31 Fla. 266, 12 So. 865. See also *Sims* v. *State*, 21 Tex. App. 649, 1 S. W. 465 (new trial granted where it was developed on the trial that the evidence upon which the accused based his motion for continuance, which was denied, would have been material); *Territory* v. *Davis* (Ariz.) 10 Pac. 359 (holding it not to have been a just use of discretion of the court to refuse a continuance, where it appeared on the second trial for murder that material witnesses since the first trial had left the territory without the defendant's consent or knowledge, and the trial court had informed the counsel that the case would not be called again that term, and one of the leading counsel had fallen sick since the first trial).

And for cases generally where it has been held erroneous to refuse continuance, see authorities before cited in this Division.

And it may be stated that matters of continuance rest largely within the discretion of the trial court, and that, unless it be made to appear that such discretion has been unwisely exercised, the reviewing court will not interfere. *State* v. *Cochran*, 147 Mo. 504, 49 S. W. 558. The presumption is in favor of the ruling of the court; and in order to convict it of error it devolves upon the party complaining to show that the application for the continuance was improperly overruled, and that his rights have been prejudiced by reason thereof.

XXV.—SEPARATE TRIALS.

1. Discretionary.
2. When to be asked.
3. Opposition by codefendant.
4. Effect of granting.

1. Discretionary.

In the absence of statute,[1] it is discretionary with the trial judge to grant[2] or to refuse[3] a separate trial to persons jointly indicted, upon motion of either the accused or the prosecution.[4]

[1] In many of the states the common-law rule is changed by statute giving

the right to a separate trial in felonies, leaving it discretionary in misdemeanors. Thus, N. Y. Code Crim. Proc. § 391, provides that "when two or more defendants are jointly indicted for a felony, any defendant requiring it must be tried separately. In other cases, defendants jointly indicted may be tried separately or jointly, in the discretion of the court."

A statute giving separate trial under a joint indictment does not apply to a joint information. *Lawrence* v. *State*, 10 Ind. 453.

A Colorado statute (Sess. Laws 1891, p. 132, § 1) provides that one of two or more defendants jointly indicted for a felony shall be tried separately if there is material and admissible evidence against a codefendant, not relating to the latter's reputation, which would be inadmissible against the former if tried alone; and these provisions are positive and unequivocal; and when a case as therein contemplated is presented, it is the duty of the court to grant a severance as matter of right. *Davis* v. *People*, 22 Colo. 1, 43 Pac. 122, and cases cited, holding the statute applicable to cases of conspiracy, as statements of a conspirator after the consummation of the conspiracy are not admissible against a coconspirator. "It is clear," said the court, "that the legislature by the enactment intended to change the common-law rule that existed prior thereto, which left the granting of separate trials to defendants jointly indicted to the discretion of the court."

In Minnesota the common-law rule is so far modified by statute that the defendant is entitled to a severance as matter of right, if he require it; but the court may also so direct upon application of the state. *State* v. *Thaden*, 43 Minn. 325, 45 N. W. 614 (*dictum*). This case also holds that where one of several defendants jointly indicted moves separately for a trial, and a jury is sworn without objection by such defendant, the failure to enter a formal order for a separate trial is not prejudicial error or ground for a new trial.

In Texas defendants jointly indicted and prosecuted have not only the right to sever, but they have the right by agreement to indicate and fix the order in which they are to be tried. Tex. Code Crim. Proc. arts. 669, 670. Such severance is a matter of right. And an agreement between several persons jointly indicted, that all but one of them shall be first tried, which is signed only by the one whose trial is postponed, is not binding upon the others, so as to deprive them of their right to a severance and to indicate the order of trial. *Teiman* v. *State*, 28 Tex. App. 144, 12 S. W. 742, Citing *Willey* v. *State*, 22 Tex. App. 408, 3 S. W. 570.

And upon failure to agree as to which shall be first put on trial, the court may, under this statute, order the trial, in the first instance, of one whose case was first called for trial. *Chumley* v. *State*, 32 Tex. Crim. Rep. 255, 26 S. W. 406.

Another Texas statute (Code Crim. Proc. art. 707 [art. 669*a*]) permits either of two or more defendants prosecuted by separate indictments for offenses growing out of the same transaction, to procure the trial of the other defendant first, upon the former's affidavit that the evidence of the latter is immaterial to the defense of the former, and that there is not sufficient evidence to secure the latter's conviction. And the state cannot deprive defendant of this statutory right by its agreement not to prosecute the latter if he will testify truly on the trial of the former, or of others indicted for offenses arising out of the same transaction. *Price* v. *State* (Tex. Crim. App.) 40 S. W. 596.

And it is error to deny a motion for a severance, by one of two persons separately indicted for the same offense, and that the other be first tried, made on affidavits showing that the evidence is not sufficient to convict the other party, whose testimony is material to defendant, and who accompanies defendant's motion with a petition praying that a postponement previously granted him on the ground of absence of witnesses be set aside, and stating that he is ready to go to trial, and that all the state's witnesses are present. *Davis* v. *State,* 33 Tex. Crim. Rep. 344, 26 S. W. 410.

But an application for a severance is properly refused where the granting of it would operate as a postponement. *Bryant* v. *State* (Tex. Crim. App.) 50 S. W. 950.

State v. *Yancey,* 3 Brev. 306, 1 Treadway Const. 241; *Com.* v. *Hughes,* 11 Phila. 430; *Com.* v. *James,* 99 Mass. 438 (holding that the motion should be granted in a capital cause, if the commonwealth intends to prove the confession of one, and it may prejudice the other); *Roesel* v. *State,* 62 N. J. L. 216, 41 Atl. 408.

So held also under some of the statutes. *Metz* v. *State,* 46 Neb. 547, 65 N. W. 190; *People* v. *Fuhrmann,* 103 Mich. 593, 61 N. W. 865.

People v. *Howell,* 4 Johns. 296 (under statute respecting forgery. There was then no right of peremptory challenge); *United States* v. *Marchant,* 12 Wheat. 480, 6 L. ed. 700 (does not interfere with peremptory challenge); *Roberson* v. *State,* 40 Fla. 509, 24 So. 474; *Com.* v. *Bingham,* 158 Mass. 169, 33 N. E. 341; *State* v. *Mitchell,* 49 S. C. 410, 27 S. E. 424, and cases cited; *Com.* v. *Place,* 153 Pa. 314, 26 Atl. 620; *State* v. *Fournier,* 68 Vt. 262, 35 Atl. 178; *Com.* v. *Thompson,* 108 Mass. 461 (holding that no exception lies to a refusal to allow a separate trial); *Com.* v. *Robinson,* 1 Gray, 555; *Wall* v. *State,* 51 Miss. 396, 24 Am. Rep. 640; *Com.* v. *Lewis,* 25 Gratt. 938; *Jones* v. *Com.,* 31 Gratt. 830; *State* v. *Doolittle,* 58 N. H. 92; *People* v. *Alviso,* 55 Cal. 230; *State* v. *Meaker,* 54 Vt. 112; *Thompson* v. *State,* 25 Ala. 41; *State* v. *Wise,* 7 Rich. L. 412; *State* v. *McGrew,* 13 Rich. L. 316; *State* v. *Conley,* 39 Me. 78; *Maton* v. *People,* 15 Ill. 536 (does not affect right to peremptory challenge).

In *Emery* v. *State,* 101 Wis. 627, 78 N. W. 145, the court said: "Where persons are so circumstanced as to be properly triable together for a criminal offense, separate trials are not demandable as of right, except it be shown that a joint trial will so clearly be seriously prejudicial to one of the parties as to require a separate trial as to him to prevent injustice. The refusing or granting of such a motion is wholly within the discretion of the trial court, and its exercise, as in other cases of the exercise of discretionary power, cannot be successfully questioned except for a plain abuse of it. That was the rule at common law, and though it has been changed in many jurisdictions by statute, it has not been changed in this state."

But in *State* v. *Desroche*, 47 La. Ann. 651, 17 So. 209, it was held that an application for severance by two persons indicted for a crime should be granted, if seasonably asked, where the defenses are antagonistic, and the confessions of each incriminating the other are designed to be used in evidence. Compare *State* v. *Gournel*, 43 La. Ann. 197, 9 So. 436, holding that whether a severance shall be granted to one jointly indicted with others is in the discretion of the trial court.

Upon a joint indictment against several defendants, the court may direct the trial to proceed against one, on the application of the state. *State* v. *Thaden*, 43 Minn. 325, 45 N. W. 614. To same effect, *Com.* v. *Seeley*, 167 Mass. 163, 45 N. E. 91; *Roesel* v. *State*, 62 N. J. L. 216, 41 Atl. 408.

Prisoners jointly indicted may be tried separately against their objection. *United States* v. *Marchant*, 12 Wheat. 480, 6 L. ed. 700 (*dictum;* citing English common-law authority).

2. When to be asked.

The motion for a separate trial must be made before the jury is impaneled, or it will be deemed waived,[1] except where separate trial is a matter of right.[2]

[1]*McJunkins* v. *State*, 10 Ind. 140 (misdemeanor).

In Washington a defendant jointly indicted with another for a crime may avail himself of the right to a separate trial conferred by 2 Hill's Code, § 1313, at the time the cause is assigned for trial. A severance of trial afterwards is in the discretion of the court until the jury is sworn to try the cause, subsequent to which time a separate trial cannot be granted. *State* v. *Mason*, 19 Wash. 94, 52 Pac. 525.

And in Oklahoma, although persons jointly indicted for a felony have a right under Okla. Stat. 1893, chap. 68, art. 10, § 8, to a separate trial on requesting the same, such request must be made before the commencement of the trial; and the impaneling of the jury is the commencement for such purpose. *Nichols* v. *Territory*, 3 Okla. 622, 41 Pac. 108.

In Alabama a rule of court adopted June 21, 1889, provides that "where two or more persons charged with a capital offense are jointly indicted, either of them is entitled to demand a severance; but such right shall be considered as waived unless claimed at or before the time of arraignment, or, at latest, when the court at any term sets a day for the trial of the case, and makes an order to summon a special venire. In other than capital offenses, a severance may be demanded at any time before the case regularly goes to the jury." 86 Ala. 8, 6 So. 4. And a demand by defendants jointly indicted for a capital offense, for a severance of trial, made after they have been arraigned and have pleaded to the indictment, and after a day has been set for the trial, and after an order for the summoning of a special venire for trial of the cause,—is properly denied. *Givens* v. *State*, 109 Ala. 39, 19 So. 974.

And a motion to be allowed to withdraw their pleas, and to move for a severance as between themselves, by a portion of defendants jointly indicted, whose previous motion for a severance and that they be tried together, but separate from the other defendants, was granted, is properly overruled. *Malachi* v. *State,* 89 Ala. 134, 8 So. 104.

[2]*Babcock* v. *People,* 15 Hun, 347, 353 (holding the statutory right to a separate trial available, even on motion made after the jury are sworn); S. P., *State* v. *McLane,* 15 Nev. 345 (murder).

3. Opposition by codefendant.

An application for a separate trial is not to be denied because a codefendant opposes it.[1]

[1]*Armsby* v. *People,* 2 Thomp. & C. 157, Affirmed as *Kelley* v. *People,* 55 N. Y. 565, 14 Am. Rep. 342.

4. Effect of granting.

If application for separate trial is granted after witnesses or jury have been sworn, they must be resworn.[1]

[1]*Babcock* v. *People,* 15 Hun, 347.

XXVI.—COMPULSORY PROCESS FOR DEFENDANT'S WITNESSES.

1. The constitutional and statutory right.

The Constitution of the United States,[1] and constitutions[2] or statutes[3] of several states, secure to the accused the right to compulsory process for obtaining witnesses in his behalf.[4]

An application may be made during the trial.[5]

[1]U. S. Const. 6th Amend.

The constitutional provision that in criminal prosecutions the accused shall have compulsory process for obtaining witnesses in his favor is violated by Ariz. Pen. Code, § 775, providing that whoever, in another state or country, steals the property of another, and brings it into the territory of Arizona, may be convicted and punished as if the larceny had been committed within the territory, as the witnesses in such foreign country would not be amenable to the process of the courts of this territory. *Territory* v. *Hefley* (Ariz.) 33 Pac. 618.

[2]Poor's Am. Const., for collection of state constitutions. The Texas statute is applied in *Neyland* v. *State,* 13 Tex. App. 536.

[3]There is no constitutional provision in New York, but N. Y. Code Crim.

Proc. § 611, provides that "the clerk of a court at which an indictment is to be tried must at all times, upon the application of the defendant, and without charge, issue as many blank subpœnas, under the seal of the court and subscribed by him as clerk, for witnesses within the state, as may be required by the defendant." Section 612 gives the form of the subpœna. Section 613 provides for a *subpœna duces tecum*. The subpœna may be served by any person. Sections 636–657 provide a system of examining witnesses out of the state by commission on defendant's behalf, in trials on indictments.

[4]At common law a person accused of a capital crime was denied compulsory process for his witnesses; and when they voluntarily appeared in his behalf, he was not permitted to examine them under oath. *United States* v. *Reid*, 12 How. 361, 13 L. ed. 1023, and authorities cited. And see cases collected in note to *Gore* v. *State* (Ark.) 5 L. R. A. 833.

[5]*Edmondson* v. *State*, 43 Tex. 230.

2. Expenses.

This provision has been interpreted simply to mean that the accused shall not be debarred the right of issuing subpœnas for his witnesses, as in civil cases,[1] and not to entitle him, on application, to a decree of the court for an allowance to secure their attendance.[2]

[1]*State* v. *Hornsby*, 8 Rob. (La.) 554, 41 Am. Dec. 305, 310, holding, also, that when the court has a limited territorial jurisdiction, the right of the accused to compulsory process does not extend beyond such jurisdiction; and if his witness be without the territorial limit he must procure the testimony by commission.

[2]*Com.* v. *Lindsey*, 2 Chest. Co. Rep. 268. Here a pauper prisoner charged with murder applied to the court to decree an allowance to secure the attendance of witnesses. And it was held, denying the application, that there is no power, either statutory or common law, authorizing such a request; that the court will order process, and, in a case of this kind, compel the officers to serve the same, on the ground that they hold their office *cum onere*, and must render a service of this kind gratuitously.

3. Service.

The court may direct an officer to serve such process for a pauper defendant.[1]

[1]*Com.* v. *Lindsey*, 2 Chest. Co. Rep. 268.

XXVII.—NOLLE PROSEQUI.

1. Discretion of the prosecuting officer.
2. Right of the accused to object.
3. Power of the court.
4. Setting aside.

1. Discretion of the prosecuting officer.

At common law, and by statute in some of the states, before the jury is sworn, the state has a right to enter a *nolle prosequi* on the motion of its prosecuting attorney.[1]

In New York *nolle prosequi* is in form superseded by motion to quash.[2]

[1]*State* v. *Ingram,* 16 Kan. 14; *Ex parte Donaldson,* 44 Mo. 149; *State ex rel. Graves* v. *Primm,* 61 Mo. 166; *Com.* v. *Uhrig,* 167 Mass. 420, 45 N. E. 1047; *State* v. *Blackwell,* 9 Ala. 79; *State* v. *Champeau,* 52 Vt. 313, 36 Am. Rep. 754; *State* v. *Thompson,* 10 N. C. (3 Hawks) 613. See fully on this question, authorities reviewed in note to *State ex rel. Butler* v. *Moise* (La.) 35 L. R. A. 701.

The power rests not in the court, but in the prosecution. The attorney general can order it. The district attorney can procure the leave of court, or enter it, unless the court disallow it. The court cannot order it of its own motion. See *Moulton* v. *Beecher,* 1 Abb. N. C. 219, 220.

As to power of the United States district attorney to enter *nolle prosequi,* see *United States* v. *Stowell,* 2 Curt. C. C. 153, Fed. Cas. No. 16,409; *United States* v. *Watson,* 7 Blatchf. 60, Fed. Cas. No. 16,652; *United States* v. *Corrie,* 23 Monthly Law Rep. 145, Fed. Cas. No. 14,869; *United States* v. *Ingersoll,* Crabbe, 135, Fed. Cas. No. 15,440; and U. S. Rev. Stat. § 3230, requiring written permission of the Secretary of the Treasury and the Attorney General, in distillery-fraud cases.

Whether the prosecuting officer should assert an opinion different from the court, see 37 Alb. L. J. 163.

The district attorney in Louisiana may at his discretion dismiss the prosecution prior to verdict, subject to the prisoner's right to insist on the trial after the jury has been impaneled and the charge read; but he has no authority to dismiss without the consent of the court, after verdict and refusal to grant a motion for a new trial. *State ex rel. Bier* v. *Klock,* 48 La. Ann. 140, 18 So. 942.

In Texas, under Code Crim. Proc. arts. 38, 593, the prosecuting officer may, with the consent of the court, and for reasons filed and incorporated in the judgment of the court, *nol. pros.* and dismiss the prosecution. *Camron* v. *State,* 32 Tex. Crim. Rep. 180, 22 S. W. 682.

In Georgia a statute (Pen. Code, § 957) provides that "after an examination of the case in open court, and before it has been submitted to the jury, the solicitor general may enter a *nolle prosequi* with the consent of the court. After the case has been submitted to the jury, a *nolle prosequi* shall not be entered except by the consent of the defendant." And the provision of the statute forbidding the entering of a *nolle prosequi* without the consent of the accused, "after the case has been submitted to the jury," refers to a submission at the trial in which the motion to enter the *nolle prosequi* is made. The solicitor general may be allowed to enter a *nolle prosequi* over the objection of the accused, on the second trial, after the reversal of a conviction, on the ground that it was not supported by the evidence. *Lewis* v. *State,* 101 Ga. 532, 28 S. E. 970. "The object of § 957," said the court, "is to prevent entries of *nolle prosequi* by the solicitor general without the sanction and approval of the judge, who presumably will not allow such entries to be made except for good reason; and an examination in open court is required in order that the judge may have proper and lawful information upon which to base his action."

[2]N. Y. Code Crim. Proc. § 671. "The court may, either of its own motion or upon the application of the district attorney, and in furtherance of justice, order an action, after indictment, to be dismissed."

"Sec. 673. An order for the dismissal of the action, as provided in this chapter, is a bar to another prosecution for the same offense, if it be a misdemeanor; but it is not a bar if the offense charged is a felony."

Under a New York statute making it lawful for the district attorney to enter a *nolle prosequi* without leave of the court, it was held discretionary to refuse permission, and that this discretion was not reviewable. *Linsday* v. *People*, 63 N. Y. 143.

2. Right of the accused to object.

After the jury is sworn, the defendant acquires the right to have the cause disposed of by its verdict; and if, without cause or the defendant's consent, a *nolle prosequi* is entered and the jury discharged, this amounts to an acquittal, which the defendant may set up as a defense to a subsequent prosecution for the same offense.[1]

[1]*State* v. *Smith*, 49 N. H. 155, 6 Am. Rep. 480 (*dictum*, as above, in a case where complainant sought leave to prosecute the accused in order to recover a part of the fine, a *nolle prosequi* having been entered with defendant's consent. Motion denied); *Mount* v. *State*, 14 Ohio, 295, 45 Am. Dec. 542 (holding that a *nolle prosequi* entered after verdict and before sentence, without consent of defendant, amounts to an acquittal); *State* v. *M'Kee*, 1 Bail. L. 651, 21 Am. Dec. 499 (holding that a jury can be discharged for the following causes only, in order that the accused may be tried the second time: (1) Consent of prisoner; (2) illness of juror, court, or prisoner; (3) absence of one of the jurymen; (4) inability to agree on a verdict. Hence, that where *nolle prosequi* was entered, and jury discharged for another cause, the accused could not be retried); *United States* v. *Shoemaker*, 2 McLean, 114, Fed. Cas. No. 16,279; *Reynolds* v. *State*, 3 Ga. 53; *Grogan* v. *State*, 44 Ala. 9; *Barnett* v. *State*, 54 Ala. 579 (*nolle prosequi* entered to one of the counts; an acquittal as to such count); *State* v. *Taylor*, 84 N. C. 773 (as to one count); *Jones* v. *State*, 55 Ga. 625; *State* v. *Smith*, 67 Me. 328 (if, however, the indictment is insufficient, *nol. pros.* thereon will not amount to an acquittal). See also *Com.* v. *Tuck*, 20 Pick. 356; *Walton* v. *State*, 3 Sneed, 687; *Joy* v. *State*, 14 Ind. 139; *State* v. *Crutch*, Houst. Crim. Rep. (Del.) 204; *Contra*, *United States* v. *Watson*, 7 Blatchf. 60, Fed. Cas. No. 16,652 (holding that the court must enter a *nolle prosequi* on motion of the district attorney, as a matter of right, when moved before verdict. It does not appear when the motion was made in this case).

3. Power of the court.

In the absence of statute, the trial court has no power to enter a *nolle prosequi* to an indictment, except on motion of the prosecuting officer.[1]

[1] *People* v. *Bennett,* 49 N. Y. 137; *People* v. *McLeod,* 1 Hill, 377, 25 Wend. 483, 37 Am. Dec. 328. And see cases cited in note to *State ex rel. Butler* v. *Moise* (La.) 35 L. R. A. 708.

4. Setting aside.

Leave to enter a *nolle prosequi,* if improvidently granted, may be set aside on motion, provided that thereby no rights of the accused are impaired.[1]

Presence of the accused is not essential on such motion.[2]

[1] *State* v. *Nutting,* 39 Me. 359; *State* v. *Phelan,* 9 Baxt. 241 (where the *nolle prosequi* was entered by mistake at one term, and the mistake rectified at the following term).

[2] *State* v. *Phelan,* 9 Baxt. 241.

XXVIII.—DEMAND OF COPY OF PANEL OF THE TRIAL JURY.

Statutory right.

Under statutes usual in the various states,[1] securing to the accused, either upon or without demand, a copy of the list of trial jurors, if defendant does not claim the right before trial,[2] or allows the trial to proceed without objection,[3] he waives the right. He may waive it in open court, even in a capital case.[4] But if the objection is seasonably made, a failure to comply with the statute is error.[5]

[1] At common law there is no such right. Thompson & M. Juries, § 108; 1 Chitty, Crim. Law, 516; Hawk. P. C. Book 2, chap. 41, § 22; *Reg.* v. *Dowling,* 3 Cox C. C. 509; *United States* v. *Williams,* 1 Cranch, C. C. 178, Fed. Cas. No. 16,709; *Benton* v. *State,* 30 Ark. 328; *Wright* v. *State,* 35 Ark. 639.

Under the New York statute, the list of the jurors must be filed by the officer with the clerk of the court before the opening of the term, and the county clerk or sheriff must furnish a copy of the list of trial jurors, drawn to attend a term, to any person applying therefor and paying the fees. N. Y. Code Civ. Proc. §§ 1048, 1049.

[2]*State* v. *Russell,* 33 La. Ann. 135; *State* v. *Waters,* 1 Mo. App. 7 (agreeing on the jury; a waiver); *Wright* v. *State,* 35 Ark. 639.

[3]*Patterson* v. *State,* 48 N. J. L. 381, 4 Atl. 449, holding that the omission to furnish the list, to avail on error, must appear in the record. To the contrary as to the record. See *Lacy* v. *State,* 45 Ala. 80. See also *Bugg* v. *State,* 47 Ala. 50.

[4]*State* v. *Price,* 6 La. Ann. 691; *State* v. *Jackson,* 12 La. Ann. 679.

[5]*Bain* v. *State,* 70 Ala. 4 (murder); *Robertson* v. *State,* 43 Ala. 325 (murder; insufficient service, and a service on counsel, instead of on defendant, fatal); *State* v. *Aaron,* 4 N. J. L. 231, 7 Am. Dec. 592, 594, 599 (holding that if tales be awarded, in a case where the defendant is by statute entitled to a list of jurors two days before trial, he must have a list of talesmen for that length of time, unless his right be explicitly waived). The court expressed some doubt whether going to trial without objection may not waive the right to object.

Under the Alabama statute (Ala. Code 1886, § 4449) requiring service upon counsel one day before the day set for trial, copies of the venire and indictment found by defendant's counsel the day before the trial on his table, where they had been left by his partner not connected with the case, to whom they had been given for the counsel, were properly served. *Reese* v. *State,* 90 Ala. 624, 8 So. 818.

The Illinois statute requiring a list of the jurors to be furnished a prisoner before his arraignment is sufficiently complied with by furnishing a list of those drawn for the first two weeks of the term, although the trial is had before those drawn for the second two weeks, and such jurors are recalled at a time subsequent to such two weeks, after having been excused until that time; but a list of such jurors should be furnished the prisoner upon his request. *North* v. *People,* 139 Ill. 81, 28 N. E. 966.

And the list of jurors to be furnished to the accused on his request, under Fla. Rev. Stat. § 2901, is a list of those who have been summoned, and not merely of those drawn. *Collins* v. *State,* 31 Fla. 574, 12 So. 906.

The Colorado statute (Gen. Stat. 1883, § 953) provides that, previous to the arraignment of a prisoner for murder or other felonious crime, he shall be furnished with a copy in writing of a list of the jurors and witnesses; but a defendant who is furnished with a list of the witnesses and jurors before arraignment is not entitled to same upon retrial. *Helier* v. *People,* 2 Colo. App. 459, 31 Pac. 773.

The provision of the Texas statute (Code Crim. Proc. art. 617) that no defendant in a capital case shall be brought to trial until he has had one day's service of a copy of the veniremen summoned to try the case, unless he waives the right or is on bail,—is mandatory. *Jones* v. *State,* 33 Tex. Crim. Rep. 617, 28 S. W. 464.

But he is not entitled to service of a list of talesmen summoned. *Dow* v. *State,* 31 Tex. Crim. Rep. 278, 20 S. W. 583.

XXIX.—SELECTING THE JURORS FROM THE PANEL RETURNED.

1. Presence of the accused.
2. Waiver of objection by proceeding.
3. Power of court to correct error.
4. Absence of some of panel.

1. Presence of the accused.

The rule that the accused should be present during his trial[1] applies to the selection of jurors,[2] but not to the putting of the names in the box to be drawn from.[3]

[1]See *ante,* Division V.

[2]See *Matthews* v. *State,* 9 Lea, 128, 42 Am. Rep. 667. Here, while two jurors were selected, the prisoner, without objection, remained in the dock about 30 feet from the judge and where he could see and hear all that was done, and no objection was made. Held, that he was, in fact and law, present.

In *Fowler* v. *State,* 58 N. J. L. 423, 34 Atl. 682, it is held that the presence of the parties when the judge selects the jury list is not required by the New Jersey statute providing for struck juries.

[3]*Bearden* v. *State,* 44 Ark. 331.

2. Waiver of objection by proceeding.

Mere informalities and irregularities in selecting out of the panel returned the names of jurors to be called in the cause in hand must be objected to when they occur.[1] Proceeding with the trial without objection is a waiver.[2]

[1]*Hasselmeyer* v. *State,* 1 Tex. App. 690; *Moon* v. *State,* 68 Ga. 687 (panel not containing the statutory number; also a name incorrectly written); *State* v. *Simmons,* 51 N. C. (6 Jones L.) 309 (initials instead of full given name written on the slips for drawing).

[2]*State* v. *Ward,* 9 N. C. (2 Hawks) 443; *State* v. *Rigg,* 10 Nev. 284; *Clifton* v. *State,* 53 Ga. 241 (juror failing to answer on final call of full jury, and his place therefore filled with another).

The selection of talesmen and issuance of special venires are governed by local law and practice. See the following cases, citing and applying such local law and practice: *Ezell* v. *State,* 102 Ala. 101, 15 So. 810; *Linehan* v. *State,* 113 Ala. 70, 21 So. 497; *People* v. *Sehorn,* 116

Cal. 503, 48 Pac. 495; *Housh* v. *People*, 24 Colo. 262, 50 Pac. 1036; *Nesbit* v. *People*, 19 Colo. 441, 36 Pac. 221; *Lambright* v. *State*, 34 Fla. 564, 16 So. 582; *Simmons* v. *Cunningham* (Idaho) 39 Pac. 1109; *Healy* v. *People*, 177 Ill. 306, 52 N. E. 426; *State* v. *Rockwell*, 82 Iowa, 429, 48 N. W. 721; *State* v. *Geary*, 58 Kan. 502, 49 Pac. 596; *Laughlin* v. *Com.* 18 Ky. L. Rep. 640, 37 S. W. 590; *Roberts* v. *Com.* 94 Ky. 499, 22 S. W. 845; *State* v. *Nash*, 46 La. Ann. 194, 14 So. 607; *People* v. *Summers*, 115 Mich. 537, 73 N. W. 818; *People* v. *Considine*, 105 Mich. 149, 63 N. W. 196; *Matthews* v. *State* (1898) 1 Miss. Dec. No. 17, p. 148; *State* v. *Weeden*, 133 Mo. 70, 34 S. W. 473; *Barney* v. *State*, 49 Neb. 515, 68 N. W. 636; *Davis* v. *State*, 51 Neb. 301, 70 N. W. 984; *Johnson* v. *State*, 59 N. J. L. 535, 38 L. R. A. 373, 37 Atl. 949; *State* v. *Moore*, 120 N. C. 565, 26 S. E. 629; *State* v. *McDowell*, 123 N. C. 764, 31 S. E. 839; *State* v. *Smarr*, 121 N. C. 669, 28 S. E. 549; *State* v. *Stanton*, 118 N. C. 1182, 24 S. E. 536; *Chandler* v. *Colcord*, 1 Okla. 260, 32 Pac. 330; *Com.* v. *Weber*, 167 Pa. 153, 31 Atl. 481; *Adams* v. *State*, 35 Tex. Crim. Rep. 285, 33 S. W. 354; *Franklin* v. *State*, 34 Tex. Crim. Rep. 625, 31 S. W. 643; *Deon* v. *State*, 37 Tex. Crim. Rep. 506, 40 S. W. 266; *Wyatt* v. *State*, 38 Tex. Crim. Rep. 256, 42 S. W. 598; *State* v. *Cushing*, 17 Wash. 544, 50 Pac. 512; *State* v. *Bokien*, 14 Wash. 403, 44 Pac. 889.

3. Power of court to correct error.

In order to secure a legal and orderly selection, the trial court is vested with a summary power to correct palpable mistakes.[1]

[1]*Smith* v. *State*, 61 Miss. 754 (where the court ordered the box to be purged of fraudulent names, and the drawing to proceed. Murder; conviction affirmed).

4. Absence of some of panel.

The selection of the jury from the panel drawn to serve need not be delayed because some of the persons drawn are not present when the case is called for trial, but their places may be filled by others.[1]

[1]*United States* v. *Byrne*, 19 Blatchf. 259. Benedict, J., says: "We are not aware of any principle requiring us to hold that, upon a trial like the present, the fact that a juror's name is drawn out of the jury box in due course of the lot gives the defendant the legal right to have such person sworn as one of the jury." But see *infra*, Division XXXI. § 1.

Shelton v. *State*, 73 Ala. 5 (refusal to send for the absentees not error); *United States* v. *Bowen*, 3 MacArth. 64 (not error to call talesmen when the entire panel is not yet present); S. P., *Patterson* v. *State*, 48 N. J. L. 381, 4 Atl. 449; *Clifton* v. *State*, 53 Ga. 241.

XXX.—CHALLENGE TO THE ARRAY OR ENTIRE PANEL.

1. Modern rule.
2. Defects in venire or return.
3. Challenging.
4. Trying the challenge.

1. Modern rule.

Objections to individual jurors will not sustain a challenge to the array, in the absence of intentional unfairness on the part of the summoning officer.[1]

Under the New York statute a challenge to the panel can be founded only on a material departure, to the prejudice of the defendant, from the forms prescribed by the statute, in respect to the drawing and return of the jury, or on the intentional omission of the sheriff to summon one or more of the jurors drawn.[2]

It must appear that the accused is prejudiced thereby.[3] Merely formal irregularities are disregarded.[4]

[1]*Mitchell* v. *State,* 43 Tex. 512, 517; *Gray* v. *State,* 55 Ala. 86; *Hall* v. *State,* 40 Ala. 698. And see *infra,* note 4.

Thus the fact that two of the persons constituting a venire in a criminal case have served as jurors within twelve months last past is not a ground for quashing the venire. *Jones* v. *State,* 104 Ala. 30, 16 So. 135. So held also of a venire in which are included the names of persons who served upon the jury that passed upon issues submitted to them in the case of one jointly indicted with defendants. *Woodley* v. *State,* 103 Ala. 23, 15 So. 820. And of a venire containing the names of jurors who heard and tried a case against a party charged with an offense of the same character as that charged against the accused. *Anderson* v. *State,* 34 Tex. Crim. Rep. 96, 29 S. W. 384. See also *Staley* v. *State* (Tex. Crim. App.) 29 S. W. 272; *Schnell* v. *State,* 92 Ga. 459, 17 S. E. 966 (where the venire contained the names of jurors who had just served as a jury for the trial of another person indicted for a like offense growing out of the transaction involved in the pending indictment, and who rendered a verdict of guilty, and the evidence and witnesses were the same as in the present case).

Nor is the fact that some names on the jury panel were not on the last assessment roll of the county, as the law provides they should be. *People* v. *Searcey,* 121 Cal. 1, 41 L. R. A. 157, 53 Pac. 359.

Nor that one of the persons drawn to serve thereon is a nonresident of the county or of the state. *Johnson* v. *State,* 115 Ala. 690, 22 So. 1000.

And a challenge to a special venire cannot be sustained on the ground that persons whose names were put into the box were exempt from jury duty, as the exemption is a personal privilege, not a disqualification. *State* v. *Merriman*, 34 S. C. 16, 12 S. E. 619; Affirmed in 34 S. C. 576, 13 S. E. 328, 898. Compare *State* v. *Clark*, 121 Mo. 500, 26 S. W. 562, holding that a challenge which, although in form to the array, is based upon objections to the individual jurors of a panel, on the ground that they are over the legal age, is merely a challenge to the polls, and the accused cannot thereafter challenge the array.

[a]N. Y. Code Crim. Proc. § 362.

And a defendant is not prejudiced within the meaning of this section by the fact that the sheriff mailed the notices to the jurors, instead of serving them personally or leaving the notices at their residences, as required by N. Y. Code Civ. Proc. § 1048, where all of the jurors drawn who were qualified to sit personally appeared in court at the time appointed. *People* v. *Burgess*, 153 N. Y. 561, 47 N. E. 889, Rehearing denied in 154 N. Y. 760, 49 N. E. 1101.

[a]*Ferris* v. *People*, 35 N. Y. 125, 48 Barb. 17.

[a]*People* v. *Kiernan*, 101 N. Y. 618, 4 N. E. 130, 4 N. Y. Crim. Rep. 88; Affirming 3 N. Y. Crim. Rep. 247. See also *Scott* v. *State*, 29 Tex. App. 217, 15 S. W. 814, where it is held that the ruling of the trial court in refusing to quash the special venire for descrepancies between it and the copy served on defendant will not be disturbed where the record does not show any error more serious than mere irregularities not prejudicial to him.

Note on challenges to the array and the grounds thereof.

At common law the selecting and summoning of jurors was intrusted to the sheriff, and a challenge to the array was either principal or to the favor.

Under modern statutes in most of the United States the selection of jurors, under very diversified practice, is confided to officers or boards under various names, whose province is usually to make a list of all persons within certain limits who are qualified to be jurors. For the New York statutes see, on qualifications of jurors, Code Civ. Proc. §§ 1027–1082; and on formation of the same, §§ 1163–1180. On trial jurors in New York county, §§ 1079, 1125, 1174; on trial jurors in Kings county, §§ 1126–1162.

From this list the jurors for any term of court are drawn by lot by certain designated officers, and with prescribed formalities. The jurors so drawn are summoned by the sheriff or other executive officer. The change in the mode of selecting and summoning jurors has rendered obsolete many challenges to the array founded on the partiality of the sheriff; but his duty of summoning the jurors still connects him with the panel sufficiently to allow certain common-law challenges to the array.

As where the sheriff is interested in the case. *People* v. *Tweed*, 50 How. Pr. 280.

Or if he is prosecutor of an indictment. *King* v. *Sheppard*, 1 Leach C. L. 101.

Irregularities in the mode of selecting the list of jurors as specified in statutes are held not to be good ground of challenge to the array, such statutes being considered directory. *Forsythe* v. *State*, 6 Ohio, 19; *Thomas* v. *People*, 39 Mich. 309; *Johnson* v. *State*, 59 N. J. L. 271, 35 Atl. 787, 59 N. J. L. 535, 38 L. R. A. 373, 37 Atl. 949; *People* v. *Durrant*, 116 Cal. 179, 48 Pac. 75.

Under Cal. Pen. Code, § 1064, the only ground of challenge to the panel of a jury summoned by special venire is the bias of the officer who summoned them. *People* v. *Wallace*, 101 Cal. 281, 35 Pac. 862.

And failure of the court to appoint a person of African descent a member of the jury commissioners, or failure to include one or more of that class of citizens in the list from which grand and petit jurors are to be drawn, is not cause for setting aside the panel of petit jurors selected to try a person of that class for a felony, as the selection of one of that class, either as a commissioner or as one of the panel, is not required by the Kentucky statutes. *Smith* v. *Com.* 17 Ky. L. Rep. 1162, 33 S. W. 825.

The mere fact that persons qualified to be jurors are not upon the jury list, or that persons disqualified are, will not sustain a challenge to the array. *People* v. *Tweed*, 50 How. Pr. 280; *Dolan* v. *People*, 64 N. Y. 485; *State* v. *Green*, 43 La. Ann. 402, 9 So. 42; *State* v. *Foster*, 32 La. Ann. 34; *Foust* v. *Com.* 33 Pa. 338.

So of misnomer. *Jewell* v. *Com.* 22 Pa. 94; *Com.* v. *Walsh*, 124 Mass. 32; *Woodsides* v. *State*, 2 How. (Miss.) 655; *Brinkley* v. *State*, 54 Ga. 371; *State* v. *Neagle*, 65 Me. 468; *Bell* v. *State*, 115 Ala. 87, 22 So. 453.

And of the absence of the acting judge within a statute making him chairman of the board for selecting jurors, and providing that no meeting could be had or business transacted in his absence, where he was always present when the board met, and then, after directing that the list be prepared, went in to the courtroom and held court, while the other members prepared the lists, but always returned before the work was completed, and approved and signed the lists. *State* v. *Goodrich*, 67 Minn. 176, 69 N. W. 815.

An appellate court will not reverse the action of the trial court in overruling a challenge to the array of jurors in a criminal case, based upon a failure to comply with some of the regulations of the statute relating to the selection of juries, in the absence of any suggestion of fraud or injury to the substantial rights of the appellant. *Huntley* v. *Territory*, 7 Okla. 60, 54 Pac. 314.

Otherwise if the admission or exclusion of qualified persons is fraudulent or caused by prejudice. *People* v. *Tweed*, 50 How. Pr. 264; *Dolan* v. *People*, 64 N. Y. 485.

Or if a party was injured by the irregularity. *State* v. *Neagle*, 65 Me. 468.

And a venire is properly quashed and a special venire facias directed, as provided by Miss. Code, § 2386, where it is shown to the court that the board of supervisors has, through ignorance or obstinacy, disregarded the mandate of § 2358, in preparing the jury list from which the jury box is to be made, since there is, in contemplation of law, no jury box, and it would be useless for the court to draw a second venire facias from the same box whose illegality has caused the quashal of the first. *Purvis* v. *State*, 71 Miss. 706, 14 So. 268.

The courts have held that a list of jurors valid on its face is conclusive as to its regularity. *Gardiner* v. *People*, 6 Park. Crim. Rep. 157, 198; *State* v. *Allen*, 1 Ala. 442.

Statutes directing lists to be made out at certain times are merely directory, and if the jurors are individually qualified, the parties are not affected by a failure to make the list at a specified time. *Gardiner* v. *People*, 6 Park. Crim. Rep. 198; *State* v. *Massey*, 2 Hill L. 379; *Rafe* v. *State*, 20 Ga. 60; *Perry* v. *State*, 9 Wis. 19; *State* v. *Petrie*, 25 La. Ann. 386.

Or by the fact that no list was returned from one town. *Thomas* v. *People*, 39 Mich. 309; *State* v. *Frazier*, 54 Kan. 719, 39 Pac. 819.

Or that a mistake was made in the list of one city in a county. *Com.* v. *Walsh*, 124 Mass. 32.

So of an immaterial irregularity in the time for recording the list of jurors. *State* v. *Gut*, Gil. 315, 13 Minn. 341.

But otherwise if the list is not recorded at all, for the recording is required to enable parties to investigate. *Mitchell* v. *Likens*, 3 Blackf. 258; *Mitchell* v. *Denbo*, 3 Blackf. 259.

The form of the certificate of selection held to be material. *Carter* v. *State*, 56 Ga. 463; *Brinkley* v. *State*, 54 Ga. 371; *Gardiner* v. *People*, 6 Park. Crim. Rep. 157, 198; *State* v. *Clarkson*, 3 Ala. 378.

Also not marking the certificate "filed." *Brinkley* v. *State*, 54 Ga. 371.

Or the failure of commissioners to sign and certify the jury list. *Coker* v. *State*, 7 Tex. App. 83.

The acts of *de facto* jury commission, if regular, are deemed valid. *State* v. *McJunkin*, 7 S. C. N. S. 21; *Carpenter* v. *People*, 64 N. Y. 483; *Dolan* v. *People*, 64 N. Y. 485; *State* v. *Ferray*, 22 La. Ann. 423; *Cox* v. *State*, 64 Ga. 374, 37 Am. Rep. 76; *Wilcox* v. *Smith*, 5 Wend. 231, 21 Am. Dec. 213.

If, however, the selection is made by one officer, when the law imposes the duty upon another, a challenge to the array will be sustained. *People* v. *Labadie*, 66 Mich. 702, 33 N. W. 806, and cases cited; *Elkins* v. *State*, 1 Tex. App. 539; *Shackleford* v. *State*, 2 Tex. App. 385.

And the power of selecting cannot be delegated to another. *State* v. *Newhouse*, 29 La. Ann. 824.

The statutes prescribing the mode of drawing the panel are directory, and informalities or irregularities in carrying out their provisions are not material unless the party is prejudiced. *Rafe* v. *State*, 20 Ga. 64; *State* v. *Williams*, 3 Stew. (Ala.) 454; *Friery* v. *People*, 2 Abb. App. Dec. 215, 230, 2 Keyes, 424, 54 Barb. 319; *Ferris* v. *People*, 35 N. Y. 125, 48 Barb. 17; *State* v. *Guidry*, 28 La. Ann. 630; *Wilhelm* v. *People*, 72 Ill. 468; *Dotson* v. *State*, 62 Ala. 141, 34 Am. Rep. 2; *Rolland* v. *Com.* 82 Pac. 306, 22 Am. Rep. 758; *State* v. *Taylor*, 44 La. Ann. 783, 11 So. 132; *Gardiner* v. *People*, 6 Park. Crim. Rep. 192; *People* v. *Rogers*,

13 Abb. Pr. N. S. 370; *People* v. *Ah Chung*, 54 Cal. 398; *Dolan* v. *People*, 64 N. Y. 485.

And a challenge to the array on the ground that only four jurors were properly drawn is not available, as such a challenge must be for a cause that affects all the jurors alike. *State* v. *Hogan*, 67 Conn. 581, 35 Atl. 508.

But where the provisions of such statutes are violated in essential particulars, the rule is otherwise,—as when jurors were selected from the list, and not drawn by lot. *Jones* v. *State*, 3 Blackf. 37.

Or where the officer failed to draw from a class or list specified by law. *State* v. *Jenkins*, 32 Kan. 477, 4 Pac. 809.

Or where the officer rejected names drawn as not being qualified. *Anonymous*, 1 Browne (Pa.) 121.

Or where less than the number required by law were drawn. *Baker* v. *The Milwaukee*, 14 Iowa, 214. See also *Hunter* v. *State*, 34 Tex. Crim. Rep. 599, 31 S. W. 674, where the venire was for a less number than specified in the order of the court, and the statute (Tex. Crim. Code, art. 608) requires the order to specify the number to be summoned, and the clerk to issue the writ in accordance therewith.

Or where names were placed on the panel without being drawn. *McCloskey* v. *People*, 5 Park. Crim. Rep. 308.

Or where names were drawn from a box so that they were exposed to sight before being drawn. *Pringle* v. *Huse*, 1 Cow. 432.

Or where officer drew names for panels for two courts at one time, and arbitrarily divided them. *Gardner* v. *Turner*, 9 Johns. 260.

In many states challenges to the array for informalities in drawing jurors are controlled by statutes. Drawing is a ministerial act, and may be performed by a deputy duly appointed. *State* v. *Gay*, 25 La. Ann. 472; *People* v. *Fuller*, 2 Park. Crim. Rep. 16.

The time of drawing is not considered material. *Wilson* v. *State Bank*, 3 La. Ann. 196; *State* v. *Pitts*, 58 Mo. 556.

But where statutes require the drawing to be made a certain number of days prior to the sitting of a court, the time is material. *Powell* v. *People*, 5 Hun, 169; *Crane* v. *Dygert*, 4 Wend. 675; but *contra*, *State* v. *Pitts*, 58 Mo. 556.

This, however, must yield to necessity, as where the time had expired for which the petit jurors had been summoned, before the business of the term was completed, and a new jury was drawn in the mode required by the statute, and summoned, except that they were not summoned twenty days before court. Held no error to overrule a challenge to the array on this ground. *Rockford Ins. Co.* v. *Nelson*, 75 Ill. 548.

And see *Fanning* v. *People*, 10 Ill. App. 70. In this case a provision of the statute provided for the issue of a venire when the jury had not been summoned.

It seems that the requirements of the statute specifying the number of jurors in a panel must be strictly obeyed. *Gladden* v. *State*, 13 Fla. 623; *Donaldson* v. *Com.* 95 Pa. 21.

But *contra, Bales* v. *State,* 63 Ala. 30, under a statute expressly declaring that the provisions as to the securing of a jury should be directory.

A *venire facias* in a criminal case will not be quashed because the jurors were drawn from an old box, and not the legal box, under Miss. Code 1892, § 2387, which denies a challenge to the array in a criminal case for any cause except in case of a special *venire facias. Campbell* v. *State* (Miss.) 17 So. 441.

An objection which goes merely to the mode of service of a venire constitutes no ground of challenge to the panel, where the sheriff did not intentionally omit to summon any juror drawn, and all such jurors were in attendance. *People* v. *M'Kay,* 122 Cal. 628, 55 Pac. 594.

And the failure of the sheriff to find and summon three of the jurors whose names appear on a special venire drawn for the trial of a murder case is not a ground for quashing the venire. *Daughdrill* v. *State,* 113 Ala. 7, 21 So. 378.

And jurors summoned by the coroner are not disqualified because they have been summoned on the regular panel by the sheriff, to whom objection has been made, no objection having been made as to the fitness or competency of the jurors. *State* v. *Wiley,* 109 Mo. 439, 19 S. W. 197.

But the act of the sheriff in corruptly or wilfully summoning special jurors known to be prejudiced against defendant cannot be reached by a motion for a continuance at the trial, but the proper remedy is by a challenge to the array under Tex. Code Crim. Proc. 1879, art. 624. *Bateman* v. *State* (Tex. Crim. App.) 44 S. W. 290.

2. Defects in venire or return.

Informalities or defects in the venire or other process directing the officer to summon the jurors,[1] or in his return,[2] furnish no ground for challenge to the array.

[1]*State* v. *Cole,* 9 Humph. 627; *White* v. *Com.* 6 Binn. 179, 6 Am. Dec. 443; *State* v. *Alderson,* 10 Yerg. 523; *Fields* v. *State,* 52 Ala. 348; *Louw* v. *Davis,* 13 Johns. 227; *Poindexter* v. *Com.* 33 Gratt. 766.

The misnomer of one juror is no ground of challenge to the entire panel. *Bill* v. *State,* 29 Ala. 34. See also *supra,* note 4 of preceding section.

When a panel of qualified jurors has been secured and is in attendance, the failure to issue a venire, or the fact that the venire is defective, is of no consequence. *Maher* v. *State,* 1 Port. (Ala.) 265, 26 Am. Dec. 379; *Bird* v. *State,* 14 Ga. 43; *State* v. *Crosby,* Harp. L. 90; *Trembly* v. *State,* 20 Kan. 116; *Mackey* v. *People,* 2 Colo. 13; *State* v. *Marshall,* 36 Mo. 400. And a venire has been held unnecessary under statute. *State* v. *Harris,* 30 La. Ann. 90; *Samuels* v. *State,* 3 Mo. 68. Even where statutes required a venire as at common law. *Bird* v. *State,* 14 Ga. 43; *State* v. *Crosby,* Harp. L. 90.

But in *United States* v. *Reed,* 2 Blatchf. 435, Fed. Cas. No. 16,134, Nelson, J., was "inclined to think" that the want of a venire where the law required one was a cause of challenge to the array.

That the Christian names of jurors on a venire are indicted by the initial letters only is not a cause for quashing the venire. *Cole* v. *State*, 105 Ala. 76, 16 So. 762, holding also that the erasure from a venire of the names of jurors, by drawing a line through them, and the use of ditto marks to indicate the occupation of jurors, constitute technical objections which will not require quashing the venire.

[2]*People* v. *Jones*, 24 Mich. 215; *Rolland* v. *Com.* 82 Pa. 306, 322, 22 Am. Rep. 758; *State* v. *Stokely*, 16 Minn. 282, Gil. 249; *Fellows's Case*, 5 Me. 333; *Com.* v. *Green*, 1 Ashm. (Pa.) 289; *Davis* v. *State*, 25 Ohio St. 369; *State* v. *Cut*, 13 Minn. 341, Gil. 315.

And failure of an officer who has summoned a jury by virtue of a special venire, to make a return of his doings thereon until after the commencement of the trial, is not a sufficient reason for quashing the venire. *State* v. *Payne*, 6 Wash. 563, 34 Pac. 317.

3. Challenging.

At common law a challenge to the panel must be in writing, and interposed before a juror is sworn.[1]

This is the rule in New York, where the statute also requires that the facts constituting the ground of challenge be distinctly specified.[2]

If the challenge is not made before the jury is sworn,[3] or if the accused subsequently withdraws his challenge,[4] or insists that the trial proceed,[5] he thereby waives the same.

[1]Chitty, Crim. Law, 546; *State* v. *Taylor*, 134 Mo. 109, 35 S. W. 92, and cases cited.

And in Texas a defendant who wishes to challenge to the array on the ground that certain talesmen were summoned by an officer prejudiced against him must, under Code Crim. Proc. art. 626, make a motion in writing setting forth distinctly the grounds of his challenge, and support the same by his own affidavit, or that of some credible person. *Perry* v. *State* (Tex. Crim. App.) 34 S. W. 618.

[2]N. Y. Code Crim. Proc. § 363.

[3]*New York* v. *Mason*, 4 E. D. Smith, 142, 1 Abb. Pr. 344; *McDermott* v. *Hoffman*, 70 Pa. 31.

And a challenge to an array of jurors cannot be made after making challenges to the polls. *State* v. *Taylor*, 134 Mo. 109, 35 S. W. 92.

But a motion to quash the regular venire of jurors is in time, although made after the state's solicitor has announced ready for trial on defendant's plea of not guilty, if made before defendant has announced or been called upon to announce whether he is ready for trial. *Peters* v. *State*, 100 Ala. 10, 14 So. 896.

And a challenge to the array because the sheriff who summoned them was disqualified because of interest is in time if made before the state announces her challenges to the polls, although it might have been made earlier, where the sheriff has not made the return of the venire showing that the jury had been summoned by him before the trial. *State* v. *Powers*, 136 Mo. 194, 37 S. W. 936.

In Louisiana a motion to set aside a venire must be filed on the first day of the term subsequent to the presentation of the indictment (*State* v. *Pruett*, 49 La. Ann. 283, 21 So. 842), unless defendant shows that he could not have learned of the facts upon which the motion was based until a subsequent date (*State* v. *Labauve*, 46 La. Ann. 548, 15 So. 172).

[4]*Pierson* v. *People*, 79 N. Y. 424, 35 Am. Rep. 524, 18 Hun, 239.

[5]*Cox* v. *People*, 80 N. Y. 500. After verdict it is certainly too late. *State* v. *Williams*, 3 Stew. (Ala.) 454; *State* v. *Perry*, 44 N. C. (Busbee L.) 330; *State* v. *Massey*, 2 Hill L. 379; *Lyles* v. *Com.* 88 Va. 396, 13 S. E. 802.

4. Trying the challenge.

At common law the mode of trying a challenge to the array was left to the discretion of the trial judge. In New York,[1] and in probably a majority, if not all, of the states, the judge tries the challenge.[2]

[1]N. Y. Code Crim. Proc. § 366.

[2]And one challenging the array of jurors must stand ready to prove his challenge by proof of the illegality of the panel; and the better practice is to make the proof by affidavits, although it may be made by oral evidence. *Borrelli* v. *People*, 164 Ill. 549, 45 N. E. 1024.

XXXI.—SELECTION OF JURORS.

I. Challenges for cause or to the favor.
  1. The right to challenge.
  2. What law applies.
  3. Presence of the accused.
  4. When to challenge.
  5. Order in which to challenge.
  6. Interrogating proposed juror.
  7. — after juror sworn.
  8. What questions allowable.
  9. — limiting the inquiry.
  10. Adducing other evidence.
  11. Waiver.
  12. Withdrawing.

II. Grounds of challenge.
  13. Acquaintance, see *infra*, §§ 24, 49.
  14. Adverse party in civil action.
  15. Affinity.
  16. — how constituted.
  17. — termination.
  18. — burden of showing.
  19. Age.
  20. Alienage.
  21. Animosity, see *infra*, § 84.
  22. Association, see *infra*, §§ 62, 63.
  23. Attendance at examination.
  24. Attorney's relation to juror.
  25. Bet pending.
  26. Business relations with co-defendant.
  27. Challenge on a previous occasion.

I. Challenges for cause or to the favor.

[In the practice now established challenges other than peremptory, that is, challenges for any assignable cause, are either (1) for lack of statutory qualifications to serve as a juror at all, such as age, residence, property, etc., or (2) for actual or presumable bias in the particular cause to be tried. These latter questions of bias (which were formerly divided as "for principal cause" and "to the favor") now form two classes as follows: (1) Actual bias as a question of fact in the particular case, and to be shown by evidence of prejudice (formerly ground for what was called challenge to the favor). Where this is a pure question of fact, the determination of the court, or, of triers if they are employed, has the same final character as in the case of other questions of fact; (2) implied bias or bias conclusively presumed by the law from the relation out of which a concealed bias commonly arises, such as consanguinity, affinity, pecuniary or other legal interest, dependence in tenure or service, etc. (formerly ground for what was called challenge for principal cause). In such cases, the relation being established, the juror is disqualified, irrespective of whether he may not in fact be impartial.

Under these rules the common-law distinction of challenges for principal cause and challenges to the favor is no longer an adequate guide. Both grounds are now tried together in the same way; and the practical distinction is whether the circumstances shown are facts which, as matter of law, disqualify, or are merely evidence upon which it is matter of judicial judgment or discretion for the court to infer that the juror should be rejected as biased.

The New York statute enumerates several causes for challenge for implied bias, as matter of law, mostly identical with the chief grounds for challenge for principal cause on the ground of bias at common law, and makes all other grounds which suggest bias mere questions of fact, turning on whether, under the circumstances, actual bias is shown.

It results that some of the authorities below cited are chiefly valuable, not as showing that the relation mentioned is now, as matter of law, a disqualification, but rather as showing the line which the courts have pursued on motions for new trial, or on appeal, or on error, in reviewing the discretion of the trial court on the question whether the facts were evidence of actual bias.

The challenge, if review is desired, must be entered in the record; but the practice now is to allow each party to examine a juror when he is called, the prosecution examining first, and either party to interpose a challenge on such ground as he deems established by the result of the examination.]

1. The right to challenge.

The right to challenge jurors for a cause assigned, as distinguished from peremptory challenge, is a common-law right which cannot be taken away except by express statute.[1]

[1]*Barrett* v. *Long*, 3 H. L. Cas. 395, 415 (civil case).

In *People* v. *Ah Lee Doon*, 97 Cal. 171, 31 Pac. 933, counsel for the defendant called in question the constitutionality of a California statute taking away the challenge for implied bias on the ground that the juror has formed or expressed an unqualified opinion as to the guilt of the accused, their contention being that one of the essential constituents of the right of trial by jury secured by the Constitution is the right of a person accused of a crime to be tried by jurors who have never formed or expressed an unqualified opinion of his guilt, whether founded on newspaper reports or common rumor, or upon grounds more reliable; but the court ruled against their contention, stating that there was nothing to warrant them in pronouncing unconstitutional a statute which had been in unquestioned operation nearly eighteen years.

In California the Code provides that "before a juror is called the defendant must be informed by the court, or under its direction, that if he intends to challenge an individual juror he must do so when the juror appears, and before he is sworn." Pen. Code, § 1066. But a conviction will not be reversed for failure of the court to so inform defendant of his right to challenge jurors, where he was represented by counsel, since it will not be assumed that counsel was incompetent. *People* v. *Ellsworth*, 92 Cal. 594, 28 Pac. 604. Nor where it clearly appears that the defendant was not prejudiced thereby. *People* v. *O'Brien*, 88 Cal. 483, 26 Pac. 362. Otherwise as to one who appears without counsel, and is not informed of his right to challenge an individual juror. *People* v. *Moore*, 103 Cal. 508, 37 Pac. 510.

2. What law applies.

In the United States courts the state law as to disqualification, although applicable, is not exclusive of all other grounds; but the court may and should entertain any other objections to jurors which unfit them for duty.[1]

[1]*United States* v. *Benson*, 31 Fed. 896, Cited in *United States* v. *Jones*, 69 Fed. 973.

3. Presence of the accused.

The impaneling and examination of the jury is a part of the trial, within the rule requiring that in felonies the accused must be present at the trial.[1]

[1]*Hopt* v. *Utah*, 110 U. S. 574, 28 L. ed. 262, 4 Sup. Ct. Rep. 202 (holding that the trial of challenges for actual bias out of the presence of the accused was error, though no objection was made and no exception taken), Approved and followed in *State* v. *Smith*, 90 Mo. 37, 59 Am. Rep. 4, 1 S. W. 753 (holding that prejudice need not be shown, and that the error is not cured by offering to re-examine the jurors).

As to the general rule see *ante*, Divisions V. and XXIX.

The fact of sickness of an absent juror, which is one ground under the statute for discharging the jury, cannot be determined, on trial for a felony, in the absence of defendant from the courtroom. *State* v. *Smith*, 44 Kan. 75, 8 L. R. A. 774, 24 Pac. 84.

Nor may the court excuse special veniremen in the absence of the defendant. *Clay* v. *State*, 40 Tex. Crim. Rep. 593, 51 S. W. 370.

But the accused need not be present when a juror on the trial of his case is being examined for insanity. The court may examine any person acquainted with the mental condition of a juror in the presence or absence of the accused. *Smith* v. *State* (N. J. 1879) 2 N. J. L. J. 269.

And the excusing by the court, in the absence of defendant from the courtroom, of two jurors who had been sworn to answer questions, is no cause for reversal in the Kentucky court of appeals, in a criminal case, since the latter court could not review the trial court's action in excusing the jurors, and therefore defendant was not prejudiced by the fact that they were excused during his absence. *Hayden* v. *Com.* 20 Ky. L. Rep. 274, 45 S. W. 886.

4. When to challenge.

A challenge to an individual juror must be taken when he appears and before he is sworn.[1]

[1]Common law; and generally prevalent. See *Schnell* v. *State*, 92 Ga. 459, 17 S. E. 966 (so holding, unless the cause of challenge is not known until afterward); *Reg.* v. *Kerr*, 3 Legal News, 299; *State* v. *Dumphey*, 4 Minn. 438, Gil. 340; *Poindexter* v. *Com.* 33 Gratt. 766; *Ward* v. *State*, 1 Humph. 253.

And this is the rule as embodied in N. Y. Code Crim. Proc. § 371. But it must always be considered in connection with the qualifying rule of discretion of the court to set aside a juror for cause. After the juror is sworn, the right of a party to challenge ceases, but not the power of the court. See § 124.

In *People* v. *Dolan*, 51 Mich. 610, 17 N. W. 78, a jury had been impaneled during the temporary absence of the prosecuting attorney from the courtroom; it was sworn, and on his return he demanded the right to challenge a juror, which the court allowed against the defendant's objection. Held error.

Sustaining an objection to a juror after a verdict in a criminal case is in the discretion of the court, under Va. Code, § 3155. *Hodges* v. *Com.* 89 Va. 265, 15 S. E. 513.

The right of the state's attorney to challenge a juror, under the South Carolina practice, which has the force of law, continues until the prisoner has spoken. *State* v. *Haines*, 36 S. C. 504, 15 S. E. 555.

And the court may for cause permit a juror to be challenged by the state in a criminal trial, after he is sworn, and before the jury is completed, under Cal. Pen. Code, § 1068. *People* v. *Owens*, 123 Cal. 482, 56 Pac. 251.

5. Order in which to challenge.

In the absence of statutory regulation or a general rule of court, it rests in the discretion of the court to determine the order in which the right to challenge shall be exercised.[1]

[1]*Patterson* v. *State*, 48 N. J. L. 381, 4 Atl. 449, Citing *Com.* v. *Piper*, 120 Mass. 185; *State* v. *Pike*, 49 N. H. 406, 6 Am. Rep. 533; *Ossipee Hosiery & Woolen Mfg. Co.* v. *Canney*, 54 N. H. 295; *Schufflin* v. *State*, 20 Ohio St. 233 (it does not appear whether the question arose on challenge for cause or peremptory challenge). Compare *United States* v. *Brady* (*Star Route Case*) (D. C.) 3 Crim. L. Mag. 69.

A juror challenged on one side, and found indifferent, may still be challenged by the other side. Hirsh, Juries, § 446, Citing Co. Litt. 158*a;* Bacon, Abr. Juries, E. 16; 1 Chitty, Crim. Law, 545.

By N. Y. Code Crim. Proc. § 385, "challenges to an individual juror must be taken first by the People, and then by the defendant." This statute makes the order matter of right, and it is error after the box is filled to refuse to require the prosecution to exercise its right to challenge peremptorily any given juror, if at all, before the defense does so. *People* v. *McQuade*, 110 N. Y. 284, 1 L. R. A. 273, 18 N. E. 156, 21 Abb. N. C. 417. The clause formerly contained in this section, excepting peremptory challenges from its operation, was repealed in 1882.

By N. Y. Code Crim. Proc. § 386, "challenges of either party must be taken—(1) to the panel; (2) to an individual juror, for a general disqualification; (3) to an individual juror, for implied bias; (4) to an individual juror, for actual bias; (5) peremptory." In practice, challenges to the panel or array are too late after challenges to individuals, and challenges for any cause are available after general examination of the proposed juror; but either may, in the discretion of the court, be allowed out of this order; at least if no objection be made.

Under the Idaho statute the district attorney is properly permitted to exhaust his challenge for cause to each juror before passing such juror to the defense. *State* v. *Gorden* (Idaho) 48 Pac. 1061.

But under Ky. Crim. Code, § 215, requiring each party to exhaust his challenges to each juror before the other begins, a defendant cannot, after the panel is filled, challenge a juror who was accepted by the commonwealth, and not challenged by the defense. *Wiggins* v. *Com.* 20 Ky. L. Rep. 908, 47 S. W. 1073.

6. Interrogating proposed juror.

It is proper to allow a proposed juror to be interrogated by either party before any formal challenge has been interposed.[1]

[1]*State* v. *Lautenschlager*, 22 Minn. 514; *Johnson* v. *State*, 11 Lea, 47; *Donovan* v. *People*, 139 Ill. 412, 28 N. E. 964; N. Y. Code Crim. Proc. § 383; *Carnal* v. *People*, 1 Park. Crim. Rep. 272 (approving the somewhat general practice of settling questions to be put by the judge to each juror).

The oath to a juror challenged and sworn for examination need not specify the ground of challenge, unless this be required by counsel at the time. *Foster's Case*, 13 Abb. Pr. N. S. 372, note.

But it is proper for the trial court, in a criminal case, after it has put the usual questions to the jurors on defendant's motion, to decline to allow defendant's counsel to proceed with a general examination, in the absence of any showing of why the jurors should be questioned further. *Com.* v. *Thompson*, 159 Mass. 56, 33 N. E. 1111.

And the court may properly refuse to permit a juror to be interrogated by counsel for the purpose of eliciting information so that the right of peremptory challenge may be intelligently used, where no challenge has been interposed, and it is not proposed to put the juror under oath. *Clifford* v. *State*, 61 N. J. L. 217, 39 Atl. 721.

And that a juror was rejected without giving a prisoner opportunity to cross-examine him is no ground for appeal, where there is nothing to show that he sought to exercise the right. *People* v. *Wood*, 131 N. Y. 617, 30 N. E. 243.

Nor is a defendant on trial for the illegal sale of liquor entitled to put to each juror separately a general question as to his views in regard to the morality of liquor dealing, where the court has already put the inquiry to the panel as a whole. *State* v. *Munch*, 57 Mo. App. 207.

A defendant whose plea of former trial and conviction is tried and found against him before a trial upon the general issue is not entitled to examine the jurors before proceeding to the trial of the general issue, to ascertain if any member has any bias formed from the evidence and proceedings upon the special plea, as he is entitled to but one trial, which must be one continuous proceeding. *People* v. *Connor*, 142 N. Y. 130, 36 N. E. 807.

In *Shaw* v. *State*, 32 Tex. Crim. Rep. 155, 22 S. W. 588, the defendant insisted upon his right in person to interrogate the venireman as to his qualifications as a juror, which the court refused to permit, insisting that he must ask through his counsel, and should not ask the questions in person. To this the defendant excepted, but it was held that the discretion of the court was not abused, nor the rights of defendant infringed, in refusing him permission to interrogate the juror under the circumstances set forth in the bill of exceptions as qualified by the court. The discretion was not exercised until the defendant resorted to irrelevant and impertinent questions.

In *Jones* v. *State*, 35 Fla. 289, 17 So. 284, it was ruled upon the authority of *Pinder* v. *State*, 27 Fla. 370, 8 So. 837, that while the better practice is to permit examination of veniremen upon their *voir dire* by the counsel in the case, still there is nothing in the statute to prohibit the court from exclusively burdening itself with the entirety of such examination, if it sees proper to do so. The court refused counsel permission to examine a juror upon his *voir dire*.

In Alabama the statute lays down the rule for ascertaining the qualifications of jurors and the cause of challenge, and neither party has a right to interrogate a juror before he is challenged. *Hornsby* v. *State*, 94 Ala. 55, 10 So. 522. The question sought to be put to the juror in this case was whether he was willing to accord to a negro as fair a trial as he would to a white person.

In Connecticut the accused is not entitled, as matter of strict right, to examine each juror under oath; but the practice is controlled largely by the discretion of the trial court. *State* v. *Lee*, 69 Conn. 186, 37 Atl. 75. Refusal to permit such examination was upheld in this case.

In Georgia, when the challenge to the poll is made, it is the duty of the court to put the juror upon his *voir dire*, and to ask him such questions as will test his fairness and impartiality. He may ask him, or cause him to be asked by counsel, the statutory questions prescribed for use in the trial of felonies, or such other questions as will test his impartiality between the state and the accused. *Wells* v. *State*, 102 Ga. 658, 29 S.

E. 442. And upon a trial for a misdemeanor there is no right to examine a juror upon his *voir dire* without first challenging him and assigning a cause of challenge. *Schnell* v. *State*, 92 Ga. 459, 17 S. E. 966.

In *Story* v. *State*, 68 Miss. 609, 10 So. 47, it was held that there was nothing prejudicial to the defendant in the rule announced by the presiding judge for the examination of jurors. That rule was that the judge would undertake the examination of jurors upon their *voir dire* touching their competency, permitting and inviting counsel to suggest any questions they desired to be asked, but not permitting them directly to interrogate the jurors upon the subject of their competency; and after each juror had been found competent by the judge, he was then to be examined by counsel directly, with a view to peremptory challenge, but for no other purpose. "The rule thus announced," said the court, "is to be commended rather than reprehended, for its operation is to prevent an unnecessary consumption of the time of the court, assures full and impartial examination of jurors, and violates no right of one charged with crime. Under its operation an impartial jury, against no member of which is objection taken, was secured to the accused, without his having exhausted the peremptory challenges allowed him by law."

7. — after juror sworn.

It is in the discretion of the court, even after a juror has been sworn, to allow him to be further interrogated,[1] and if cause of disqualification be shown, a challenge for cause may be interposed and sustained.[2]

[1]*People* v. *Damon*, 13 Wend. 351. See also *Dilworth* v. *Com.* 12 Gratt. 689, 65 Am. Dec. 264, where it is held that it may be done at any time before verdict rendered, and at request of the commonwealth, for like cause, at any time when the discharge of the jury without the consent of the prisoner would not result in the discharge of the latter.

But *Vaughan* v. *State*, 58 Ark. 353, 24 S. W. 885, holds that failure to object to a juror precludes objection to a re-examination of him after his acceptance.

And in *State* v. *Donelon*, 45 La. Ann. 744, 12 So. 922, it was held that after a juror had been interrogated and cross-interrogated on his *voir dire* as to his qualifications, and had been adjudged competent by the trial judge, defendant's counsel had no right to reopen the question of competency, and investigate it anew.

[2]*People* v. *Damon*, 13 Wend. 351; *McGuire* v. *State*, 37 Miss. 369 (no error to sustain a challenge by the state to a juror, for cause, after he had been sworn, no testimony having yet been introduced).

In *People* v. *Durrant*, 116 Cal. 179, 48 Pac. 75, it was held that the trial court has power under Cal. Pen. Code, § 1068, so providing, on the impaneling of the jury in a criminal cause, and before the completion of the panel, to permit the re-examination of a juror who has been accepted, and to excuse such juror on his being peremptorily challenged.

As to power to set aside without challenge, see *infra*, § 126.

8. What questions allowable.

Upon the trial of a challenge for cause, the proposed juror may be asked any pertinent question tending to establish the challenge,[1] and not tending to disgrace him.[2]

[1]*Reynolds* v. *United States,* 98 U. S. 145, 25 L. ed. 244; *Johnson* v. *State,* 11 Lea, 47.

Thus, the prosecuting officer may ask jurors, on a murder trial, if they have conscientious scruples against capital punishment. *State* v. *Clark,* 32 La. Ann. 558; *State* v. *Dooley,* 89 Iowa, 584, 57 N. W. 414 (the question not precluded by Iowa Code, § 4407); *State* v. *Foster,* 91 Iowa, 164, 59 N. W. 8; *Jones* v. *Com.* 14 Ky. L. Rep. 223, 19 S. W. 844; *State* v. *Garrington,* 11 S. D. 178, 76 N. W. 326.

And it is error to refuse to allow questions tending to show that the juror is a member of a committee the members of which have agreed to indemnify each other for any prosecution that defendant may institute against them for false imprisonment. *Fleming* v. *State,* 11 Ind. 234.

So, one on trial for murder is entitled to ask jurors if they have formed an opinion that he is guilty, and believe at the time that he is guilty, and ought to be hung. *Randle* v. *State,* 34 Tex. Crim. Rep. 43, 28 S. W. 953. And one on trial for keeping a house of assignation, in exercising her right to challenge peremptorily, may, where she admits keeping the house specified at the time charged, ask a juror, in order to show actual bias, if he has heard any statement as to the character of the house from which he has formed an opinion of its character. *State* v. *Bresland,* 59 Minn. 281, 61 N. W. 450. Compare *Epps* v. *State,* 102 Ind. 539, 1 N. E. 491, where it was held not error to refuse to allow the question, "When you have an opinion on any subject, does it take much evidence to remove it?" And in *People* v. *Ah Lee Doon,* 97 Cal. 171, 31 Pac. 933, it was held to be within the sound discretion of the trial court to permit leading questions to be put to jurors challenged for actual bias because of their having formed and expressed an opinion based upon common rumor, and having a low opinion of the value of Chinese testimony.

Again, on the trial of an accomplice, defendant may ask the juror if he has formed an opinion as to the guilt of the principal offender. *Arnold* v. *State,* 9 Tex. App. 435; *State* v. *Steeves,* 29 Or. 85, 43 Pac. 947. But *Peddy* v. *State,* 31 Tex. Crim. Rep. 547, 21 S. W. 542, holds that it is not error on a murder trial to refuse to permit defendant's counsel to ask the jurors whether from hearsay or otherwise they have formed a conclusion as to the guilt or innocence of a coconspirator who has been previously tried and convicted, and is claimed by the state to have been the instigator of the conspiracy, where there is direct testimony that defendant was present at the homicide, as well as many circumstances in evidence corroborative of such testimony.

But questions as to what the jurors would or would not decide in a supposed state of the evidence, or as to what credibility they would give to certain evidence if adduced, are not allowable upon their examination on *voir dire*. *Com.* v. *Van Horn*, 4 Lack. L. News, 63; *Jenkins* v. *State*, 31 Fla. 196, 12 So. 677; *State* v. *Everitt*, 14 Wash. 574, 45 Pac. 150; *State* v. *Holedger*, 15 Wash. 443, 46 Pac. 652. So held also of the question whether the neglect or refusal of defendant to testify in his own behalf would create any presumption against him in the juror's mind. *Com.* v. *Wireback*, 190 Pa. 138, 42 Atl. 542. But in *People* v. *Keefer*, 97 Mich. 15, 56 N. W. 105, a trial for violation of the Michigan local-option law, it was held that defendant should be allowed to ask the jurors in which way they would give a verdict on the charge of engaging in the saloon business, if the evidence was equally balanced.

Nor is it proper to ask a juror on a trial for murder if he would find a man guilty on circumstantial evidence. *Lambright* v. *State*, 34 Fla. 564, 16 So. 582. And questions asked proposed jurors, as to whether they "understand the meaning of a circumstantial-evidence case," and as to whether a case hypothetically stated depends upon circumstantial evidence, are properly excluded. *Roberson* v. *State*, 40 Fla. 509, 24 So. 474.

Nor is it proper to ask a juror on his *voir dire* whether he would give the defendant the benefit of every reasonable doubt, if the court should fail or neglect to instruct him so to do. *Brown* v. *State*, 40 Fla. 459, 25 So. 63. And a question to a juror on his *voir dire* is improper, which seeks to learn if he would return a verdict in favor of defendant should a reasonable doubt remain regarding his guilt after hearing the testimony and instructions. *State* v. *Bokien*, 14 Wash. 403, 44 Pac. 889. And in *State* v. *Hinton*, 49 La. Ann. 1354, 22 So. 617, it was held that the court might properly exclude a question to a juror on a murder trial on his *voir dire*, whether he would acquit the defendant if from the evidence he had a reasonable doubt whether he acted in self-defense, where the juror had already answered affirmatively a question as to whether he would give the defendant the benefit of the doubt if he had a reasonable doubt as to his guilt.

Again, hypothetical questions calling for the juror's opinion on the race problem and his belief in the superiority of the white race, and that negroes ought to be tried by white jurors, are irrelevant; and the answers thereto cannot affect his qualifications, if he has no prejudice against defendant personally. *State* v. *Casey*, 44 La. Ann. 969, 11 So. 583. But in *Pinder* v. *State*, 27 Fla. 370, 8 So. 837, a trial of a negro, it was held error to exclude a question to the jurors on their *voir dire* as to whether they could give defendant as fair and impartial a trial as they could give a white man upon the same evidence.

Mechanics' & F. Bank v. *Smith*, 19 Johns. 115; *Ryder* v. *State*, 100 Ga. 528, 38 L. R. A. 721, 28 S. E. 246.

Or, as Blackstone says, "with regard to such causes of challenge as are not to his dishonor or discredit . . . to his disgrace or disadvantage." 3 Bl. Com. 364.

Or, as expressed in *People* v. *Fuller*, 2 Park. Crim. Rep. 16, such questions as do not "impeach his character or motives." S. P., *State* v. *Mann*, 83 Mo. 589.

9. — limiting the inquiry.

The court has power to control the extent of the inquiry, and confine it to questions going directly to facts[1] bearing on the disqualification suggested by the challenge under consideration.[2]

[1]*Pennsylvania Co.* v. *Rudel,* 100 Ill. 608 (civil case, holding it not error to exclude the question, "State briefly your idea of the duties of a juror," even when the avowed object is to test the mental capacity). And see *Epps* v. *State,* 102 Ind. 539, 1 N. E. 491, *supra,* § 8, note 1.

In *Com.* v. *Gee,* 6 Cush. 174, after the questions prescribed by statute had been put, the counsel for the defendants insisted upon the right to have other questions put to the jurors, for the purpose of furnishing ground for their exclusion from the panel, and they further insisted that they had the right personally to interrogate the jurors for this purpose. But the court ruled that the whole matter relative to the examination of jurors, beyond the provisions of the statute, is one that must be left to the sound judgment and judicial discretion of the presiding judge. This applies not only to the propounding of further questions to the jurors, but also to the manner of putting them. The counsel of a party has no right personally to interrogate the jurors with a view of showing their bias or prejudice by facts drawn out by a cross-examination or something very like it. The orderly conducting of trials will be better promoted by adhering as a general rule to the usual practice of interrogating the jurors by questions propounded by the court or by its order. See also *Com.* v. *Warner,* 173 Mass. 541, 54 N. E. 353. And the court may, in the exercise of this discretion, refuse to ask a juror, in a prosecution for unlawfully selling liquors, as to whether he has any prejudice against such sales that would prevent him from giving the same weight to the seller's testimony as he would give any other witness. *Com.* v. *Poisson,* 157 Mass. 510, 32 N. E. 906.

And in *State* v. *Chapman,* 1 S. D. 414, 10 L. R. A. 432, 47 N. W. 411, it is held that the extent to which a party should be allowed to go on the examination of a person called as a juror is not, and cannot be, governed by any fixed rules. Much rests in the discretion of the court as to what questions may or may not be answered; but in practice very great latitude is and generally ought to be indulged. To the same effect, *Nealon* v. *People,* 39 Ill. App. 481.

The examination of jurors on their *voir dire* in criminal trials need not be confined to the questions formulated in McClellan's (Fla.) Dig. § 10, p. 446, but may be varied and elaborated as the circumstances seem to require, to obtain a fair and impartial trial. *Pinder* v. *State,* 27 Fla. 370, 8 So. 837. To the same effect, *State* v. *Nance,* 25 S. C. 168.

A conviction will not be reversed because counsel for defendant were required to change a question asked one of the jurors so that it would not suggest that such juror would have a "desire" to give his verdict one way or the other if the evidence were even, and was required to ask the juror whether he would have a desire to give his verdict one way or the other, or which way he would find in such case. *People* v. *Caldwell,* 107 Mich. 374, 65 N. W. 213.

But granting defendants but ten minutes for the examination of the list of jurors summoned on a special venire will not justify a reversal, where it does not appear that defendants were prejudiced by failure to give a longer time. *Carthaus* v. *State*, 78 Wis. 560, 47 N. W. 629.

[2]*Stagner* v. *State*, 9 Tex. App. 440, adding that the juror is not to be examined like a witness under cross-examination.

10. Adducing other evidence.

After a proposed juror has been challenged, other witnesses may be called and examined by either party.[1]

[1]*People* v. *Fuller*, 2 Park. Crim. Rep. 16; N. Y. Code Crim. Proc. § 384. Compare *State* v. *Linde*, 54 Iowa, 139, 6 N. W. 168, holding it not error to deny defendant's motion to introduce oral evidence to prove grounds of challenge.

And the court need not ask each juror on his *voir dire* if he has any interest in the conviction or acquittal of defendant, or has made any promise or given any assurance that he would acquit or convict him, under Ala. Code, § 4332, providing that such cause for challenge need not be proved by the oath of the juror, but may be established "by other testimony only." *Bridges* v. *State*, 110 Ala. 15, 20 So. 348.

So, the district attorney may properly obtain information from the clerk of the court as to the fairness and responsibility of the jurors, where he is a stranger in the parish. *State* v. *Griffin*, 48 La. Ann. 1409, 20 So. 905.

11. Waiver.

A party having a right to challenge may decline to do so, and the adverse party cannot insist that the right be exercised.[1]

[1]*Murphy* v. *State*, 37 Ala. 142 (murder). In this case a statute provided that it should be a good challenge for cause by the state in all capital trials that a juror had a fixed opinion against capital punishment. But it was held that the accused could not compel the state to challenge the juror if the state was willing to waive the right.

In *Black* v. *State*, 9 Tex. App. 328, the trial court sustained a challenge by the state to a juror because he was related to the prosecutor. Held error, this challenge being available only to the accused.

So, defendant in a criminal trial may waive his right under the Illinois statute of having four jurors tendered as a panel, and upon waiving that right after two panels of four jurors each have been accepted and sworn, it is within the discretion of the court to call one or three jurors, and require the parties to pass upon them. *Kirkham* v. *People*, 170 Ill. 9, 48 N. E. 465.

But the court may set aside without challenge. See *infra*, § 126.

12. Withdrawing.

A challenge for cause to an individual juror, which has been sustained, cannot be withdrawn.[1]

[1]*State* v. *Allen*, 46 Conn. 531; *Isaac* v. *State*, 2 Head, 458; *State* v. *Lautenschlager*, 22 Minn. 514; *Biddle* v. *State*, 67 Md. 304, 10 Atl. 794. Compare *Pierson* v. *People*, 79 N. Y. 424, 35 Am. Rep. 524, Affirming 18 Hun, 239, where it was held that a challenge to the array could be withdrawn after it was sustained, and that withdrawing it waived the irregularity on which it was founded.

II. Grounds of challenge.

13. Acquaintance.

See *infra*, §§ 24. 49.

14. Adverse party in civil action.

That the proposed juror is a party adverse to the defendant in a civil action is a ground of challenge for implied bias, and an absolute disqualification, as matter of law, if the action implies malice or displeasure.[1]

If not, it is not necessarily, as matter of law, a disqualification at common law, but the question is whether he is actually biased.[2]

[1]*Pringle* v. *Huse*, 1 Cow. 438, note.

[2]*Ibid.*

But N. Y. Code Crim. Proc. § 376, subd. 1, and § 377, subd. 3, disregard the distinction, and make it a disqualification, as matter of law, in all cases.

In North Carolina a statute provides that a juror who has a suit pending and at issue in the court in which the accused is being tried is incompetent. *State* v. *Parish*, 104 N. C. 679, 10 S. E. 457. But a prosecuting witness is not a "party to an action," within the provisions of the statute. "The state and the defendant are the only parties to a criminal action by indictment. Indeed, the disqualification attaches only to a party to a suit pending and at an issue, and it is doubted if it apply at all to a defendant, even in a criminal action." *State* v. *Brady*, 107 N. C. 822, 12 S. E. 325.

15. Affinity.

Affinity within the ninth degree to the person alleged to be injured by the crime charged, or on whose complaint the prosecution was instituted, or to the defendant, is, as matter of law, a disqualification.[1]

[1]See authorities cited under *infra*, §

16. — how constituted.

The affinity must consist of a direct marriage tie between one of such persons and the other, or the blood relations of the other. Affinity by reason of the marriage of a relation of one to a relation of the other raises only a question whether there is bias as matter of fact.[1]

[1]Thus, on an indictment for murder, a proposed juror who stated that the sons of his wife by a former husband were second cousins to the deceased, and that his wife was still living, was held to be competent, in *Moses* v. *State,* 11 Humph. 232.

So, there is no relationship between the prosecutor and a juror whose granduncle married the grandmother of the prosecutor, so as to disqualify the juror, where he is not a descendant of such marriage. *McDuffie* v. *State,* 90 Ga. 786, 17 S. E. 105.

And that a juror's brother married the prisoner's sister does not render him incompetent to sit upon the trial, since marriage does not relate any of the husband's kindred to those of the wife. *Burns* v. *State,* 89 Ga. 527, 15 S. E. 748.

And that a relative of the prosecutor married a relative of another person does not make the latter related to the prosecutor, either by consanguinity or affinity, so as to disqualify him to act as juror. *Keener* v. *State,* 97 Ga. 388, 24 S. E. 28.

Nor is a juror whose second cousin married a first cousin of the prisoner incompetent in North Carolina by reason of consanguinity or affinity. *State* v. *Fuller,* 114 N. C. 885, 19 S. E. 797.

Nor is a juror in a criminal case in Montana disqualified because he is a brother-in-law of the district attorney, who is prosecuting,—especially where his examination upon his *voir dire* does not at all tend to show any bias, either implied or actual. *State* v. *Cadotte,* 17 Mont. 315, 42 Pac. 857.

17. — termination.

The affinity must be one subsisting at the time. The death of one of the parties to the marriage through which it is traced, without leaving issue of such marriage surviving, terminates the affinity.[1]

[1]Bishop, Crim. Proc. § 901; Proffatt, Trial by Jury, § 174; *State* v. *Shaw,* 25 N. C. (3 Ired. L.) 532 (holding competent a proposed juror who was cousin to the prisoner's former wife, who was dead, leaving no offspring); *Cain* v. *Ingham,* 7 Cow. 478 (civil case, holding proposed talesman competent where his father had married the defendant's brother's widow, the father being dead at the time of the trial); *Miller* v. *State,* 97 Ga. 653, 25 S. E. 366 (holding that a juror is not incompetent because of the relationship of his deceased wife to the accused, unless such wife left issue).

18. — burden of showing.

Affinity once being shown by the party challenging, it is for the other party to show that it has been terminated by death; and if that fact is not shown, the challenge should be sustained.[1]

[1] *Jaques* v. *Com.* 10 Gratt. 690.

19. Age.

At common law and under the New York statute a proposed juror is disqualified if less than twenty-one or more than sixty years of age; and this disqualification is ground of challenge, as matter of law.[1]

[1] N. Y. Code Civ. Proc. §§ 1027, 1126; N. Y. Code Crim. Proc. § 375, subd. 2 But in the city and county of New York the limit is seventy years. N. Y. Code Civ. Proc. § 1079. See Ala. Code, § 4300; Ga. Code, § 4681.

Contra, under the statutes of some of the states. *Brown* v. *State*, 40 Fla. 459, 25 So. 63 (Fla. Rev. Stat. § 1150); *State* v. *York*, 7 Kan. App. 291, 53 Pac. 838 (Kan. Gen. Stat. 1897, chap. 94, § 17); *People* v. *Rawn*, 90 Mich. 377, 51 N. W. 522. And under the Maine statute (chap. 106, § 2) providing that the board of municipal officers, "at least once in every three years shall prepare a list of jurors, under the age of seventy years, qualified to serve as jurors," it is held that this does not disqualify a person over that age, but merely gives him an exemption. *State* v. *Day*, 79 Me. 120, 8 Atl. 544. Compare *United States* v. *Angney*, 6 Mackey, 66 (holding the juror's fraudulent concealment of his lack of this qualification ground for new trial); *Burroughs* v. *State*, 33 Ga. 43 (holding it a sufficient ground for a new trial where the fact of the juror's disqualification on account of age was unknown to the accused until after the trial). *Contra*, *Williams* v. *State*, 37 Miss. 407. See also *Munroe* v. *Brigham*, 19 Pick. 368 (denying motion to set aside verdict on this ground, because the Massachusetts statute exempts persons over sixty-five years of age, but does not disqualify them); *Moore* v. *Cass*, 10 Kan. 288; *Murphy* v. *People*, 37 Ill. 447.

20. Alienage.

Alienage is an absolute disqualification.[1]

[1] Hirsh, Juries, § 436; *People* v. *Barker*, 60 Mich. 277, 27 N. W. 539 (holding it not improper for the court, upon discovering an alien upon the panel after it has been sworn, but before further proceedings are had, to discharge him, and direct another juror to be drawn in his stead, giving permission meantime to the defendant to challenge the other eleven jurors, either peremptorily or for cause); *Borst* v. *Beecker*, 6 Johns. 332 (civil case holding it error to overrule challenge). And in *People* v. *Spiegel*, 75 Hun, 161, 26 N. Y. Supp. 1041, it was held that a person of foreign nationality may be properly rejected as a juror, on the ground

of general incompetency, where it is apparent that he does not comprehend all the questions put to him. See also *infra*, § 49.

But see *State* v. *Quarrel*, 2 Bay, 150, 1 Am. Dec. 637, holding that, if the accused allows the alien to be sworn without objection, the alienage is not ground for a new trial.

And *Brown* v. *People*, 20 Colo. 161, 36 Pac. 1040, holds that the verdict on a trial for an offense which is not capital is not *per se* vitiated because one of the jurors is an alien. And *Territory* v. *Baker*, 4 N. M. 236, 13 Pac. 30; and *Territory* v. *Anderson*, 4 N. M. 213, 13 Pac. 21, hold that the fact that an alien sat on a jury without objection is not ground for reversal. See also *Rex* v. *Sutton*, 8 Barn. & C. 417 (conspiracy); *Chase* v. *People*, 40 Ill. 352; *State* v. *Vogel*, 22 Wis. 471 (holding that exception after verdict is insufficient except in a capital case). In *Schumaker* v. *State*, 5 Wis. 324, a murder trial, it was held error to deny a motion for a new trial for alienage of a juror, it appearing that such alienage was unknown till after the verdict. See also *Hill* v. *People*, 16 Mich. 351; *Johr* v. *People*, 26 Mich. 427 (holding the rule to be otherwise in a civil case).

In *Territory* v. *Hart*, 7 Mont. 489, 17 Pac. 718, it was held not error to allow naturalization to be perfected when the alienage was discovered in the course of the trial.

21. Animosity.

See *infra*, § 84.

22. Association.

See *infra*, §§ 62, 63.

23. Attendance at examination.

The mere fact of having heard part of the evidence before the committing magistrate, and formed some opinion upon it, does not, as matter of law, necessarily disqualify.[1]

[1] *Monroe* v. *State*, 23 Tex. 210, 76 Am. Dec. 58. Compare notes to *infra*, §§ 72 and 74.

24. Attorney's relation to juror.

Casual acquaintance with,[1] or unfriendly feeling toward,[2] an attorney engaged in the cause, is not, as matter of law, necessarily a disqualification.[3]

[1] *People* v. *McQuade*, 110 N. Y. 284, 1 L. R. A. 273, 18 N. E. 156; S. C., with note in 21 Abb. N. C. 417, holding it error, as matter of law, to sustain a challenge founded on the fact that the proposed juror once incidentally consulted the attorney on a matter not connected with the cause.

[2] *Hutchinson* v. *State*, 19 Neb. 262, 27 N. W. 113.

[2]A juror who lodges as a paying boarder in the house of an attorney during court week, up to the call of a criminal case in which the attorney is counsel for the prosecution, is not for that reason alone absolutely disqualified to sit as a juror in that case. *Statham* v. *State*, 84 Ga. 17, 10 S. E. 493.

As to client of attorney, see *infra*, § 31.

25. Bet pending.

The fact that the proposed juror has a bet, however trivial, depending on the result of the trial, is, at common law, a disqualification.[1]

[1]*Cluverius* v. *Com.* 81 Va. 787 (holding that the act of the court in standing the juror aside, even after he had been sworn, was proper, the commonwealth being ignorant of the fact of the wager at the time he was accepted), Citing with approval *Seaton* v. *Swem*, 58 Iowa, 41, 11 N. W. 726; *Essex* v. *McPherson*, 64 Ill. 349 (granting a new trial when it appeared after trial that one of the jurors had made a bet of a necktie that the result would be in favor of the defendant; civil case).

Under the New York statute (Code Crim. Proc. §§ 376, 377), it only raises the question whether the juror is actually biased.

26. Business relations with codefendant.

That a juror had had business relations with a codefendant of the prisoner (who severed in his defense), and that he supposed himself to entertain a feeling of "bias at the outset," has been held to be a good cause for challenge.[1]

[1]*Minich* v. *People*, 8 Colo. 440, 9 Pac. 4.

Under the New York statute it only raises the question whether he is actually biased.

27. Challenge on a previous occasion.

The fact that a juror was challenged peremptorily on a previous trial of the same cause,[1] or that he was so challenged on the trial of another person concerned in the same crime,[2] is not necessarily, as matter of law, a disqualification.

[1]*Wilson* v. *State*, 3 Tex. App. 63; *Com.* v. *Hailstock*, 2 Gratt. 564; *State* v. *Henley*, R. M. Charlt. (Ga.) 505; *Robertson* v. *State*, 4 Lea, 425; *Easterwood* v. *State*, 34 Tex. Crim. App. 400, 31 S. W. 294.

[2]*Cargen* v. *People*, 39 Mich. 549.

The fact that certain persons have shown themselves to be incompetent to serve as jurors in one case is not evidence that they are incompetent to serve in another. *State* v. *Fairlamb*, 121 Mo. 137, 25 S. W. 895.

28. Character.

Under the New York statute, bad character is a ground for challenge.[1]

[1]N. Y. Code Civ. Proc. § 1027, subd. 5, providing, as to the state at large other than New York and Kings counties, that the juror must be of "fair character, of approved integrity." In New York and Kings counties the provision is that he must be "of sound mind and good character."

N. Y. Code Civ. Proc. § 1079, subd. 5, § 1126, subd. 5.

N. Y. Code Crim. Proc. § 375, subd. 2.

In practice the question is rarely if ever raised, except by proof of conviction.

29. Citizenship and residence.

A juror is disqualified if not a male citizen of the United States and a resident of the county.[1]

[1]See N. Y. Code Civ. Proc. § 1079, for the city and county of New York; § 1126, for Kings county; § 1027, as to the rest of the state; made applicable in criminal cases by N. Y. Code Crim. Proc. § 375, subd. 2.

As to who is deemed a resident, see *United States* v. *Nardello*, 4 Mackey, 503; *United States* v. *Cross*, 9 Mackey, 365 (holding that a resident of the district is qualified to sit as a juror therein although he is a citizen of one of the states).

As to who is deemed a resident of the city and county of New York within the statute, see N. Y. Code Civ. Proc. § 1080.

Under such a statute in California (Pen. Code, § 1170), which makes no provision for an exception to the disallowance of a general challenge for cause to an individual juror, it is held that no exception lies to a refusal to sustain a challenge for nonresidence. *People* v. *Fong Ah Sing*, 70 Cal. 8, 11 Pac. 323.

As to citizenship in municipality, in penal prosecution, see *infra*, § 83.

And one who has not paid his poll tax, the payment of which is made by the Constitution an essential qualification of an elector and to registration, is disqualified to serve as a juror, where jurors must, under the Constitution, be qualified electors, although if he had paid the tax he could not have registered, because the necessary legislation has not been had. *Nail* v. *State*, 70 Miss. 32, 11 So. 793.

But an elector is qualified to be a juror under Mich. Laws 1893, No. 204, § 5, although he is not a full citizen. *People* v. *Considine*, 105 Mich. 149, 63 N. W. 196.

So, one is qualified to sit as a trial juror, under the Texas statutes, if the intention to become a citizen has been declared in due form, and the other conditions of age and residence exist. *Abrigo* v. *State*, 29 Tex. App. 143, 15 S. W. 408.

So, also, one residing in a county is a competent juror under Mo. Rev. Stat.

§ 6060, providing that every juror must be a male citizen of the state, although he does not possess the necessary qualifications of a voter. *State* v. *Fairlamb*, 121 Mo. 137, 25 S. W. 895.

But a juror who is clearly shown by his previous examination to be absolutely disqualified because he is not the head of a family may be discharged, when challenged, without further evidence, although, to be technically correct under N. M. Comp. Laws 1865, 502, the challenge should be interposed first, and the evidence introduced afterwards. *Territory* v. *Lopez*, 3 N. M. 156, 2 Pac. 364.

And that a juror is a registered voter does not render him competent under Miss. Const. § 264, declaring that no person shall be a grand or petit juror unless a qualified voter and able to read and write; and § 244, providing that every voter shall be able to read any section of the Constitution, notwithstanding Code 1892, § 2354, in prescribing who are competent jurors, makes a duly registered voter the equivalent of a qualified elector, since one may be duly registered, and not qualified as an elector. *Mabry* v. *State*, 71 Miss. 716, 14 So. 267.

A constitutional provision the operation of which depends upon future legislation, making registration one of the qualifications of an elector, and that no one but an elector shall be qualified to serve as a juror, is suspended until such legislation is had and the opportunity to register has been afforded. *Nail* v. *State*, 70 Miss. 32, 11 So. 793.

An Alabama statute (Ala. Crim. Code, § 4331, subd. 1) declares it a good ground of challenge to a juror that he has not been a resident "householder or freeholder" of the county for the last preceding year. And a juror is properly set aside where he is neither a householder nor a freeholder in the county, and has not been during the preceding year. *Williams* v. *State*, 109 Ala. 64, 19 So. 530. But a challenge on the ground that the juror is a nonresident of the county is properly overruled where he has claimed the county as his residence, and voted there for ten years, although from ignorance of the location of the county line he does not know whether he lives in that or the adjoining county. *Amos* v. *State*, 96 Ala. 120, 11 So. 424. And § 4331 is not repealed for Montgomery county by Ala. Sess. Acts 1887, p. 190, § 3, declaring that the jury list for such county shall be selected from the male residents, and expressly repealing for such county § 4299, requiring the sheriff to obtain biennially a list of all the resident householders and freeholders, from which the jurors must be selected. *Parker* v. *State*, 102 Ala. 128, 15 So. 819, Overruling *Ezell* v. *State*, 102 Ala. 101, 15 So. 810.

One did not lose his residence so as to be disqualified to act as juror, by removing from the state for a year and a half, returning two weeks before he acted as juror, where he went on account of his health, without any intention of making his permanent residence in the other state, did not vote in the latter state, and left a portion of his household goods in the place from which he removed, intending to return as soon as his health would permit. *State* v. *Burke*, 107 Iowa, 659, 78 N. W. 677.

And that a juror who is an elector of the county had, a few days before he was summoned, removed to another township of the county, does not deprive him of his qualifications as an elector, so as to make him incompetent as a juror. *People* v. *Wright*, 89 Mich. 70, 50 N. W. 792.

But a juror was properly excused where he had been absent from the state for two years with intent to change his domicil, and had returned only a short time before he was summoned, and such return was not shown to have been with an intention of remaining. *State* v. *Taylor*, 134 Mo. 109, 35 S. W. 92.

Whether a juror is a resident citizen of the county is a question of fact for the trial court. *Leslie* v. *State* (Tex. Crim. App.) 49 S. W. 73.

In Washington, notwithstanding the subsequent passage of a statute making women qualified electors, they cannot serve as jurors, grand or petit, under Wash. Code, § 2078, providing that "all qualified electors shall be competent to serve as petit jurors, and all qualified electors and householders shall be competent to serve as grand jurors." *Harland* v. *Territory*, 3 Wash. Terr. 131, 13 Pac. 453. See, further, note to *State* v. *Russell* (Iowa) 28 L. R. A. 204.

30. Civil rights.

See *infra*, § 32.

31. Client of attorney for people or defendant.

That the juror is a client of the attorney or counsel for the People or for the defendant is a disqualification.[1]

[1]This under the New York statute is classed as "implied bias;" and if the existence of the fact is ascertained, disqualification follows as matter of law. N. Y. Code Crim. Proc. § 376, subd. 1, § 377, subd. 2.

But in *Reg.* v. *Geach*, 9 Car. & P. 499, it was held to be no cause of challenge on behalf of the Crown that the juror was a client of the accused, —an attorney,—and that the juror had visited him as a friend since he had been in prison.

In *Block* v. *State*, 100 Ind. 357, it was held that a deputy of the prosecuting attorney, though not a lawyer, was incompetent notwithstanding the statute, after enumerating the challenges for cause, provided that they were the only challenges for cause that would be allowed, and this was not one of them.

As to attorney's relation to juror, see *supra*, § 24.

32. Combination against civil rights.

Complicity with any combination or conspiracy set forth in the title *Civil Rights* and the title *Crimes*, of the United States Revised Statutes, is a disqualification in any prosecution based upon or arising under those titles.[1]

[1]U. S. Rev. Stat. § 822.

33. Complainant, etc., in former criminal prosecution.

That the proposed juror has complained against or been accused by the defendant, in a criminal prosecution, is a disqualification as matter of law.[1]

[1]N. Y. Code Crim. Proc. § 376, subd. 1, § 377, subd. 3.

But see *State* v. *Brady*, 107 N. C. 822, 12 S. E. 325, where it is held that a prosecuting witness in another criminal action is not disqualified as a juror. He is not a party to an action within the meaning of the North Carolina statute.

34. Complicity in like offense.

Complicity of the proposed juror in a like offense to that charged is, as matter of law, a disqualification;[1] and such complicity may be inferred from his refusal to answer respecting it on the ground that answering would tend to criminate him.[2]

[1]*Reynolds* v. *United States*, 98 U. S. 145, 25 L. ed. 244, Affirming 1 Utah, 319.

[2]Thus, on an indictment for polygamy the juror's declining to answer whether he is living in polygamy, on the ground that it would tend to criminate him, is a sufficient admission to exclude him. *Ibid.*

35. Consanguinity.

Consanguinity within the ninth degree to the person alleged to be injured by the crime charged, or on whose complaint the prosecution was instituted, or to the defendant, is, as matter of law, a disqualification. This is the common-law rule, and generally prevalent.[1]

[1]3 Bl. Com. 363; Hirsh, Juries, § 313; Thornton, Juries, § 100; Maxwell, Crim. Proc. p. 584; *O'Connor* v. *State*, 9 Fla. 215.

This, under the New York statute, is classed as "implied bias;" and if the existence of the fact is ascertained, disqualification follows, as matter of law. N. Y. Code Crim. Proc. § 376, subd. 1, § 377, subd. 1. *People* v. *Clark*, 62 Hun, 84, 16 N. Y. Supp. 473, 695, holding that as third cousins are in the eighth degree of relationship to each other, a juror who is a third cousin to complainant may be challenged for implied bias. In civil cases the disqualification extends only to the sixth degree.

Substantially the same provision is to be found in Indiana, except that the limit is the fifth degree. Ind. Rev. Stat. 1881, § 240.

State v. *Perry*, 44 N. C. (Busbee L.) 330, sustained a challenge where the great grandmother of a juror was the sister of the grandmother of the accused.

And *Brown* v. *State*, 28 Ga. 439, holds it ground for new trial where a juror is related to the prosecutor as cousin.

Compare *People* v. *Waller*, 70 Mich. 237, 38 N. W. 261, where it is held that the fact that a juror is an own cousin of the prosecuting attorney, within the second degree of consanguinity, does not avoid the judgment.

The degree is ascertained by ascending from the juror to the common ancestor, and descending to the party, counting a degree for each person in both lines, including the juror and party, and excluding the common ancestor. See N. Y. Code Civ. Proc. § 46.

As to affinity, see *supra*, §§ 15–18.

The term "within," in the Tennessee statute disqualifying a juror in a criminal case who is related within the sixth degree to the prosecutor, includes relatives of the sixth degree. *Hamilton* v. *State*, 101 Tenn. 417, 47 S. W. 695.

And jurors related within the prohibited degree to stockholders of a corporation whose books were destroyed are incompetent to sit on the trial of an indictment for mutilating and destroying the books of the corporation with intent to defraud and injure it, although the corporation is not the formal prosecutor. *McElhannon* v. *State*, 99 Ga. 672, 26 S. E. 501.

A motion to set aside the acceptance of a juror by a defendant charged with murder, and to allow his challenge, either for cause or peremptorily, because of the juror's relationship to the deceased, should be allowed, although the panel has been completed and the jury specially sworn, where the juror on his *voir dire* swore he was not related to the deceased, and in impaneling the jury two challenges for cause were sustained because of the relationship of jurors to the defendant. *Garner* v. *State*, 76 Miss. 515, 25 So. 363.

36. Conscientious scruples.

See *infra*, §§ 93, 100.

37. Conspiracy.

See *supra*, §§ 32, 34.

38. Conversation with witness.

The mere fact of having conversed with a witness about the case does not, as matter of law, necessarily disqualify.[1]

[1] *Thomson* v. *People*, 24 Ill. 60, 76 Am. Dec. 733. Compare *Armistead* v. *Com.* 11 Leigh, 657, 37 Am. Dec. 633 (where an opinion formed upon information so received was held to disqualify); *United States Rolling-Stock Co.* v. *Weir*, 96 Ala. 396, 11 So. 436 (to the effect that a juror with whom a party has conversed as to the merits of the case is properly excused); *Trotter* v. *State*, 37 Tex. Crim. Rep. 468, 36 S. W. 278 (holding that a juror who says he has formed an opinion from talking to the witnesses in the case is properly excused, although he states that such opinion would not influence him in finding a verdict).

39. Convict.

A conviction for felony is a disqualification as matter of law.[1]

[1]*Pringle* v. *Huse*, 1 Cow. 438, note; N. Y. Code Crim. Proc. § 375 (classifying it as a general cause for challenge); *State* v. *Powers*, 10 Or. 145, 45 Am. Rep. 138 (*dictum* that conviction of a crime involving moral turpitude is a disqualification; but holding that the objection is too late after verdict, it being merely a ground for challenge). Compare *Boggs* v. *State*, 45 Ala. 30, 6 Am. Rep. 689, holding that conviction of assault, and actual imprisonment in the county jail, at the time of being drawn as a juror, is no disqualification and would not sustain a challenge, the court intimating that the proper remedy would be to excuse him at his own instance, or that of either party, on the ground of "physical inability to sit."

In *Jackson* v. *State*, 94 Ala. 85, 10 So. 509, it was held to be not error for the trial court, upon being informed that one of the persons from whom a jury is to be selected has been convicted of a felony, and has not been pardoned, to decline to exclude him unless he is challenged for that cause, where the defendant thereupon challenges him for cause, and the court sustains the challenge, his exclusion not being charged to defendant as one of his peremptory challenges.

But a pardon by the governor will remove the disqualification of a person as a juror, although granted after his sentence has been served out. *Easterwood* v. *State*, 34 Tex. Crim. Rep. 400, 31 S. W. 294.

40. Coroner's jury.

See *infra*, § 64.

41. Corporator.

See *infra*, §§ 62, 83.

42. Counsel.

See *supra*, § 24.

43. Disloyalty.

Avowed present disloyalty to the government is a sufficient cause for the discharge of a juror, irrespective of his refusal to take a test oath prescribed by the Constitution of the state; and where such disloyalty appears, it will be presumed, in the absence of evidence to the contrary, that his discharge was for such disloyalty, instead of for refusal to take the oath.[1]

[1]*Klinger* v. *Missouri*, 13 Wall. 257, 20 L. ed. 635.

44. Employee.

See *infra*, § 66.

45. Exemption a personal privilege.

A right to exemption from jury duty is not a cause of challenge,[1] but merely a personal privilege, which may be waived.[2]

[1]*State* v. *Forshner*, 43 N. H. 89, 80 Am. Dec. 132; *People* v. *Lange*, 90 Mich. 454, 51 N. W. 534; *State* v. *Toland*, 36 S. C. 515, 15 S. E. 599; *State* v. *Morningstar*, 23 La. Ann. 8; *Glassinger* v. *State*, 24 Ohio St. 206; *People* v. *Owens*, 123 Cal. 482, 56 Pac. 251; *Burns* v. *State*, 12 Tex. App. 269; *Green* v. *State*, 59 Md. 123, 43 Am. Rep. 542.

If a person exempt from jury duty desires to claim the privilege, he must insist upon his exemption before he is selected and accepted by the accused. *Powell* v. *State*, 48 Ala. 154.

It may, however, be error to excuse one not exempt. See *People* v. *McQuade*, 110 N. Y. 284, 1 L. R. A. 273, 18 N. E. 156, 21 Abb. N. C. 417.

And the discharge of a juror over objection of a party, upon his statement that he is an active member of a company of cadets and has attended drills regularly, is error, in the absence of evidence that such company is a part of the state troops, which under the Alabama statute are exempt from jury duty, as the court cannot take judicial notice of that fact. *Simon* v. *State*, 108 Ala. 27, 18 So. 731.

[2]As a general rule, unless the statute expressly provides otherwise, an exempt person may, when called, waive the privilege, and be sworn as a juror, unless otherwise subject to challenge. *State* v. *Day*, 79 Me. 120, 8 Atl. 544, holding that a person more than seventy years of age is not disqualified, although the statute directs that only names of persons under that age shall be placed in the jury box. See note on exemption in 22 Am. L. Rev. p. 464.

Previous service as a juror is, however, not merely a ground for exemption, but also, within certain limits, is ground for challenge, and therefore not within the above rule. See *infra*, §§ 101–104.

The certificate of exemption from jury duty issued to a member of the state troops, under a statute which declares that such certificate shall prove such exemption in any court, is not the exclusive means of proof of the exemption; but the examination of the person on his *voir dire* is sufficient unless controverted. *King* v. *State*, 90 Ala. 612, 8 So. 856.

In *Henderson* v. *State*, 98 Ala. 35, 13 So. 146, it is held that, upon the drawing of the name of a juror who is over age, the sheriff may properly announce the fact, and proceed to draw other names until the venire is exhausted; and such action constitutes no ground of objection on the ground that the name of the incompetent juror is served upon defendant.

46. Family.

See *infra*, § 66.

47. Felon.

See *supra*, § 39.

48. Freemason.

See *infra,* § 6?

49. Friendship.

Intimate acquaintance with a party does not necessarily, as matter of law, disqualify.[1]

[1] *Moore* v. *Cass,* 10 Kan. 288 (civil case).

It raises a question of actual bias. *Thorn's Case,* 4 N. Y. City Hall Rec. 81; note to *Greenfield* v. *People,* 6 Abb. N. C. 13.

But in *Com.* v. *Mosier,* 135 Pa. 221, 19 Atl. 943, it was held that a juror who had conversed with the defendant, and had exchanged cigars and drinks with him might be excluded for favor.

50. Grand juror.

See *infra,* § 65.

51. Guardian or ward.

Bearing to the defendant the relation of guardian or ward is a disqualification as matter of law.[1]

[1] This is the common-law rule. Under the New York statute it is classed as "implied bias;" and if the existence of the facts is ascertained, disqualification follows as matter of law. N. Y. Code Crim. Proc. § 376, subd. 1, § 377, subd. 1.

52. Ignorance of language.

Ignorance of the language in which the proceedings are held is a disqualification as matter of law,[1] even without any statutory provision to this effect.[2]

[1] Proffatt, Trial by Jury, § 118; Maxwell, Crim. Proc. 578; *State* v. *Push,* 23 La. Ann. 14; *Etheridge* v. *State,* 8 Tex. App. 133; *McCampbell* v. *State,* 9 Tex. App. 124, 35 Am. Rep. 726 (holding that a juror who does not understand or speak English cannot be forced upon a prisoner. The Texas statute is silent on this point). And see *Yanez* v. *State,* 6 Tex. App. 429, 32 Am. Rep. 591, holding that the objection is waived if not taken at the trial, especially if it does not appear that the defendant did not know of the disqualification of the juror at the time he was accepted. *Contra, Re Allison,* 13 Colo. 525, 10 L. R. A. 790, 22 Pac. 820.

A statute disqualifying persons from serving as jurors in criminal cases in a certain city, because of their inability to read and write the English language, does not violate Mo. Const. art. 2, § 28, which simply guarantees the right of trial by jury, without undertaking to prescribe the qualifications of jurors. *State* v. *Welsor,* 117 Mo. 570, 21 S. W. 443.

But the court cannot establish an arbitrary standard. *Campbell* v. *State*, 48 Ga. 353; *Lyles* v. *State*, 41 Tex. 172, 19 Am. Rep. 38 (*dictum*, to the effect that this rule should not exclude one who understands what is said, but speaks the language imperfectly).

In *People* v. *Davis* (Cal.) 36 Pac. 96, it is held that a person drawn as a juror, who testifies that he can read and speak the English language pretty well, and can write some, but not much, is not necessarily disqualified by the fact that he states that he cannot always understand what is said to him; but it is for the trial court in such case to determine whether he is sufficiently qualified to comprehend all that may be said during the trial in his hearing.

In New York and Kings counties a trial juror must be able to read and write the English language understandingly. N. Y. Code Civ. Proc. § 1079, subd. 5, and § 1126, subd. 5; N. Y. Code Crim. Proc. § 375, subd. 2. But no such provision is made for the state at large. N. Y. Code Civ. Proc. § 1027, subd. 5, prescribing merely that the juror shall be "well informed."

[a]Classed by the New York statute among "general" causes. N. Y. Code Crim. Proc. § 374, subd. 2.

In *Lyles* v. *State*, 41 Tex. 177, 19 Am. Rep. 38, it was held that, in the absence of any such statute, to overrule the objection raised by the defendant before the jury were sworn, that nine of their number did not understand the English language, was a violation of § 16, art. 1, Bill of Rights of the Constitution, which provides that "no person shall be deprived of life, liberty, property, etc., except by due course of the law of the land."

So, in *State* v. *Start*, 60 Kan. 256, 56 Pac. 15, it was held that the difficulty of securing a jury because so many of the residents of the county were foreigners who did not understand the English language was no excuse for allowing a disqualified person to sit on the jury, as under Kan. Crim. Code, § 205, if competent jurors cannot be found in the county, the cause may be removed to another county.

53. Illiteracy.

A statute allowing challenge to a juror on the ground that he "cannot read and write" means an inability to read and write the English language.[1]

[1]*Wright* v. *State*, 12 Tex. App. 163, holding, on appeal from a conviction of horse stealing, that it was error to overrule a challenge to a juror who could not read and write English, though the juror could read and write German.

And it is not necessary that he should be a scholar, it being sufficient if he can understand the witnesses and the argument of counsel. *State* v. *Casey*, 44 La. Ann. 969, 11 So. 583, holding further that the juror's intelligence is a matter for the trial judge's determination, in his sound discretion.

And inability of a juror to readily define the words "prejudice" and "bias" does not render him incompetent to sit on a trial for murder. *State* v. *Duestrow*, 137 Mo. 44, 38 S. W. 554, Motion to transfer to court in banc denied in 137 Mo. 91, 39 S. W. 266.

54. Infant.

See *supra*, § 19.

55. Intelligence of juror.

See *infra*, § 67.

56. Know-nothing.

See *infra*, § 63.

57. Landlord or tenant.

Bearing to the defendant the relation of landlord or tenant is, both at common law[1] and by statute,[2] a disqualification as matter of law.

[1] *Hathaway* v. *Helmer*, 25 Barb. 29. Civil case; reversing judgment for error in overruling defendant's challenge to a juror who was tenant of the plaintiff. It is stated in this case that this has always been regarded as a principal cause of challenge, Citing Graham, Pr. 2d. ed. 304.

[2] Cowen's Trial, 2d ed. 889; *Harrisburg Bank* v. *Forster*, 8 Watts, 304 (sustaining challenge to juror who was a tenant of a stockholder of the defendant bank). See also *Pipher* v. *Lodge*, 16 Serg. & R. 214 (tenant as a "cropper" from year to year disqualified, independent of the question whether or not the landlord may distrain); N. Y. Code Crim. Proc. § 376, subd. 1, § 377, subd. 2.

But see *Cummings* v. *Gann*, 52 Pa. 484, holding that a principal challenge to a juror *propter affectum* is not supported by evidence that the juror lodges at his own expense temporarily with the defendant, who is an innkeeper.

58. Language.

See *supra*, § 52.

59. Marriage.

See *supra*, §§ 15–18, 85.

60. Mason.

See *infra*, § 62.

61. Master or servant.

Bearing to the accused the relation of master or servant is a good cause for challenge.[1]

And an employer is incompetent to sit as a juror upon the trial for the murder of his employee.[2]

[1]This is, at common law, challenge for principal cause.

Under the New York statute it is classed as "implied bias;" and if the existence of the fact is ascertained, disqualification follows as matter of law. N. Y. Code Crim. Proc. § 376, subd. 1, § 377, subd. 2.

[2]*State* v. *Coella*, 3 Wash. 99, 28 Pac. 28.

62. Membership of same society.

Membership in the same society or organization with the accused, even though it be incorporated, does not, as matter of law, necessarily disqualify, but only raises a question whether actual bias exists.[1]

[1]*People* v. *Bodine*, 1 Denio, 281, 305; *Purple* v. *Horton*, 13 Wend. 9, 27 Am. Dec. 167 (opinion by Savage, J. Civil action for slander; held that a Freemason is not disqualified, as matter of principal cause, from sitting as a juror, where another Mason is a party, even though they be of the same degree. Blackstone's statement, that being of the same society or corporation is enough to exclude, is not, as a general rule, sound, in the present state of society). In the same case a challenge on the same ground was submitted to triers, who heard the oath which is taken by all Masons to aid each other, etc., and they held the juror indifferent. Held, no error.

In the Morgan trials, on an indictment for conspiracy to kidnap (one of the trials reported as *People* v. *Mather*, 4 Wend. 229, 21 Am. Dec. 122), a juror was challenged for principal cause, on the ground that he was a member of the society of Freemasons and of the degree of Royal Arch; and reliance was placed on the rule in Blackstone. The court held that "society" meant such as are recognized by law. Counsel offered to prove that the society of which the juror and defendant were both members was incorporated. After argument the court overruled the objection. But the triers, after proof of Freemasonry, rejected the juror. See also Edwards, Juryman's Guide, 95.

In Burr's Trial, vol. 1, p. 370, the chief justice said that if a juryman were to declare that the attempt to achieve the dismemberment of the union (a political society or body politic of which both the jurors and the defendant were members, and which was the prosecutor) was treason, it would not be a complete objection or disqualification.

Compare *Lewis* v. *Few*, Anthon N. P. 102, where, in a civil action for libel in publishing an address adopted at a political meeting, a person present and acting at such meeting was found incompetent.

63. — of society to prosecute crime.

Membership in an organization the object of which is to prosecute criminals, or persons charged with a particular kind of crime, but which is under no legal obligation to do so, does not, as matter of law, necessarily disqualify.[1]

But it is error to refuse to allow the accused to interrogate a proposed juror as to whether he belongs to such an association.[2]

[1] *Boyle* v. *People*, 4 Colo. 176, 34 Am. Rep. 76 (reviewing all the cases on the subject); *State* v. *Estlinbaum*, 47 Kan. 291, 27 Pac. 996; *State* v. *Flack*, 48 Kan. 146, 29 Pac. 571; *State* v. *Hoxsie*, 15 R. I. 1, 29 Atl. 97, 22 Atl. 1059; *Com.* v. *O'Neil*, 6 Gray, 343; *Musick* v. *People*, 40 Ill. 268; Hirsh, Juries, p. 134. See also *United States* v. *Borger*, 19 Blatchf. 249, 7 Fed. 193 (holding that a juror was not disqualified because he was prejudiced against the crime committed. So held even though he had contributed to a society engaged in the suppression of such crimes, but not within a year, nor was he a member; and where he stated that he could nevertheless render an impartial verdict); *State* v. *Wilson*, 8 Iowa, 407 (holding that the fact that a proposed juror upon the trial of an indictment for horse stealing was a member of an "association or organized company for the prosecution of persons generally arrested for horse stealing" did not necessarily disqualify him. These decisions are in the line of the weight of authority.

But there are decisions *contra*. See *Com.* v. *Eagan*, 4 Gray, 18 (contributing said to disqualify); *Rex* v. *Dolby*, 1 Car. & K. 238.

And the rule is clearly different where the prosecution was set on foot by the society. *State* v. *Moore*, 48 La. Ann. 380, 19 So. 285; *Com.* v. *Moore*, 143 Mass. 136, 58 Am. Rep. 128, 9 N. E. 25 (holding that a member of the "Law and Order Lodge," a society formed for the enforcement of the laws against the sale of intoxicating liquors, is not a competent juror to try a complaint for the illegal sale of such liquors, originated by an agent of the lodge appointed by it to make the complaint, because in so doing he in effect was acting as agent of the proposed juror). And the court distinguished *Com.* v. *O'Neil*, 6 Gray, 343, as decided on the ground of want of pecuniary interest, the question involved here not arising.

Compare also N. Y. Code Crim. Proc. § 377, subd. 3.

And a member of a posse that expends three days in a search for one accused of murder, the search extending to another parish, and being participated in by members of the coroner's jury,—is not a competent juror upon the trial. *State* v. *Defee*, 47 La. Ann. 193, 16 So. 734; *State* v. *Duncan*, 47 La. Ann. 1025, 17 So. 482.

[2] *State* v. *Mann*, 83 Mo. 589; *Fleming* v. *State*, 11 Ind. 234 (arson; in support of a challenge for cause, held error to refuse to allow the juror to answer these questions put to him by the defendant: "Were you not one of the Milford committee at the time that Fleming was arrested? and did you not counsel and direct that he should be kept in custody without

a warrant for some ten days? and was there not an agreement between the members of that committee to indemnify each other against any prosecution that Fleming might institute against them for said imprisonment? and do you consider his conviction in this case as necessary to your and your associates' protection from such prosecution?"); S. P., *Pierson* v. *State*, 11 Ind. 341 (exactly the same state of facts).

A juror who was a member of a secret organization bound by oath to oppose foreigners (*i. e.*, Know-nothings) would be incompetent if a foreigner were on trial. *People* v. *Reyes*, 5 Cal. 347.

64. — of coroner's jury.

Having served on a coroner's jury which inquired into the death of a person whose death is the subject of the indictment is a disqualification as matter of law.[1]

[1]This, under the New York statute, is classed as "implied bias," and if the existence of the facts is ascertained, disqualification follows as matter of law. N. Y. Code Crim. Proc. § 376, subd. 1, § 377, subd. 4; Cal. Pen. Code, § 107 (declaring such a juror incompetent). But see *O'Connor* v. *State*, 9 Fla. 215, holding that the trial court did not err in overruling a challenge to a juror who had presided as coroner on the inquest of the deceased, who heard all the evidence then before him, and who did not form or express any opinion as to guilt of the accused.

65. — of grand jury.

Having served on the grand jury which found the indictment is a disqualification as matter of law.[1]

[1]Hirsh, Juries, § 375; Thornton, Juries, § 96; Maxwell, Crim. Proc. p. 578; *Roy* v. *Percival*, Sid. 243; *Williams* v. *State*, 109 Ala. 64, 19 So. 530; *Rice* v. *State*, 16 Ind. 298 (assault; holding that it was error to deny motion for new trial on the ground that one of the jury was a member of the grand jury which found the indictment, it appearing that this fact was unknown to the defendant or his counsel until after verdict, the juror having testified on his *voir dire* that he had formed no opinion on the defendant's guilt or innocence; and that the defendant was not negligent in not further interrogating the juror). *Contra: Bristow* v. *Com.* 15 Gratt. 634 (denying motion for new trial); *Dilworth* v. *Com.* 12 Gratt. 689 (holding that the objection may be raised after such juror is sworn, and before evidence is introduced, if defendant is guitly of no laches in making the discovery); *Birdsong* v. *People*, 47 Ala. 68; *Greenwood* v. *State*, 34 Tex. 334; *Whitmore* v. *State*, 43 Ark. 271; *Stewart* v. *State*, 15 Ohio St. 155. But see *Rafe* v. *State*, 20 Ga. 60, holding that the mere fact that a person's name is on the grand jury list is not sufficient to exclude him from the petit jury.

In *Rogers* v. *Lamb*, 3 Blackf. 155, it was held that, in an action for malicious prosecution for causing the plaintiff to be indicted, etc., he may challenge any of the jurors who were on the grand jury that found the indictment.

This objection, under the New York statute, is classed as "implied bias," and if the existence of the fact is ascertained, disqualification follows as matter of law. N. Y. Code Crim. Proc. § 376, subd. 1, § 377, subd. 4.

But that one of the jurors who tries an indictment was on a grand jury which presented a bill charging defendant with a similar offense, but not the same one, does not disqualify him. *Johnson* v. *State*, 34 Tex. Crim. Rep. 115, 29 S. W. 473.

Nor is a juror incompetent because, at the time, he is a member of the grand jury, which has taken a recess to meet in the future, where the information against defendant was found by another grand jury. *People* v. *Ebanks*, 117 Cal. 652, 40 L. R. A. 269, 49 Pac. 1049.

And a defendant convicted of murder cannot complain that one of the trial jurors served on the grand jury which found the indictment, where such fact is merely a cause for challenge, under Tex. Code Crim. Proc. 1895, art. 673, subd. 7, although the juror stated on his *voir dire* that he had neither formed nor expressed an opinion as to the guilt or innocence of the defendant, but thereafter recalled the fact of his grand-jury service, and privately informed the court, who told him that it did not matter, —since the defendant is chargeable with lack of diligence for not interrogating the juror as to all the statutory grounds of challenge. *Self* v. *State*, 39 Tex. Crim. Rep. 455, 47 S. W. 26.

66. — of family or employee.

Being a member of the family of the defendant, or the person alleged to be injured by the offense charged, or on whose complaint the prosecution was instituted, or in his employment on wages, is a good cause for challenge.[1]

[1]This, under the New York statute, is classed as "implied bias," and if the existence of the facts is ascertained, disqualification follows as matter of law. N. Y. Code Crim. Proc. § 376, subd. 1, § 377, subd. 2.

67. Mental incapacity.

Mental capacity is a necessary qualification.

But there is no absolute right to put general questions to a proposed juror, irrelevant to the cause, for the purpose of testing his mental capacity. The examination in such respects is completely in the discretion of the court.[1]

[1]In New York and Kings counties a trial juror must be "intelligent and of sound mind." N. Y. Code Civ. Proc. § 1079, subd. 5, and § 1126, subd. 5. See N. Y. Code Crim. Proc. § 375, subd. 2.

In the state at large the provision is that he must be "of sound judgment and well informed." N. Y. Code Civ. Proc. § 1027, subd. 5.

And whether jurors are so intelligent as to meet the requirement of N. Y. Code Civ. Proc. § 1079, is in the sound discretion of the trial judge. *People* v. *McLaughlin*, 2 App. Div. 419, 37 N. Y. Supp. 1005.

68. Minor.

See *supra,* § 19.

69. Odd Fellows.

See *supra,* § 62.

70. Opinion on issue to be tried—general rule.

The fact that the proposed juror has formed and expressed, or has formed without having expressed,[1] an opinion as to the issue to be tried, is, as matter of law, a disqualification,[2] unless it appears that he can find an impartial verdict on the evidence without being influenced by the opinion.[3]

[1]*Armistead* v. *Com.* 11 Leigh, 657, 37 Am. Dec. 633.

This doctrine questioned in Grinnell's Points of Law in *Guiteau Case* (1881), Citing *Callender's Case*, Wharton St. Tr. 696.

[2]The common-law rule stops here. The qualification by the ensuing clause is introduced by the recent statutes.

[3]*Reynolds* v. *United States*, 98 U. S. 145, 25 L. ed. 244; Affirming 1 Utah, 319. Held not error to accept a juror who swore that he "believed" he had formed an opinion which he had never expressed, but which he did not think would influence his verdict. Waite, Ch. J., said: "The theory of the law is that a juror who has formed an opinion cannot be impartial. Every opinion which he may entertain need not necessarily have that effect. In these days of newspaper enterprise and universal education, every case of public interest is, almost as a matter of necessity, brought to the attention of all the intelligent people. . . . It is clear, therefore, that . . . the court will practically be called upon to determine whether the nature and strength of the opinion formed are such as in law necessarily to raise the presumption of partiality."

In *State* v. *Meaker*, 54 Vt. 112, Ross, J., in delivering the opinion of the court, says the opinion, to disqualify, "must be an abiding bias of the mind, based upon substantial facts in the case, in the existence of which he believes. Such is the result of our decisions, and of the great majority of the decisions of the courts of last resort in other jurisdictions." Followed in *State* v. *Meyer*, 58 Vt. 457, 3 Atl. 195.

"At common law," said Daniels, J., in *Pender* v. *People*, 18 Hun, 560, "a person who had formed or expressed an opinion as to the guilt or innocence of the accused was rendered incompetent by that circumstance merely, even though he might, in the exercise of his intelligence and judgment, be able to lay that opinion entirely out of view, and to hear and determine the case according to the evidence given in the progress of the trial."

The rule stated in the text is now generally prevalent throughout the country.

Alabama.—*Bales* v. *State*, 63 Ala. 30.

Arkansas.—*Dolan* v. *State*, 40 Ark. 454; *Hardin* v. *State*, 66 Ark. 53, 48 S. W. 904.

California.—*People* v. *Cochran*, 61 Cal. 548; *People* v. *Miller*, 125 Cal. 44, 57 Pac. 770.

Connecticut.—*State* v. *Smith*, 49 Conn. 376; *State* v. *Wilson*, 38 Conn. 127.

Florida.—*O'Connor* v. *State*, 9 Fla. 215; *Olive* v. *State*, 34 Fla. 203, 15 So. 925.

Georgia.—*Meyers* v. *State*, 97 Ga. 76, 25 S. E. 252.

Illinois.—*Spies* v. *Illinois*, 123 U. S. 131, *sub nom. Ex parte Spies*, 31 L. ed. 80, 8 Sup. Ct. Rep. 21; *Coughlin* v. *People*, 144 Ill. 140, 19 L. R. A. 57, 33 N. E. 1 (holding that a statute providing that a juror shall not be disqualified for having formed and expressed an opinion based on newspaper accounts, if the court is satisfied from his statement on oath that he can render a fair and impartial verdict, does not violate the constitutional guaranty of an impartial jury).

Indiana.—*Noe* v. *State*, 92 Ind. 92; *Stout* v. *State*, 90 Ind. 1. An Indiana statute provides that if the opinion is founded on reading newspaper statements, rumors, or hearsay, and not upon conversations with witnesses of the transaction, or "reading reports of their testimony," he may be allowed to serve as a juror, in the discretion of the court. And a person who has formed an opinion as to the guilt or innocence of a person charged with murder from reading in a newspaper an affidavit of an eyewitness to the facts of the murder, is disqualified to serve as a juror at the trial, even though he states on oath that he feels able to render an impartial verdict. *Woods* v. *State*, 134 Ind. 35, 33 N. E. 901. But the court properly exercises its discretion in overruling challenges for cause to jurors in a criminal case, where their examination clearly shows that they are capable of acting impartially, although they have formed an opinion based on reading accounts in the newspapers and talking with persons other than witnesses. *Hauk* v. *State*, 148 Ind. 238, 46 N. E. 127, Rehearing denied in 148 Ind. 264, 47 N. E. 465.

Iowa.—*State* v. *Bruce*, 48 Iowa, 530; *State* v. *Ormiston*, 66 Iowa, 143, 23 N. W. 370; *State* v. *Young*, 104 Iowa, 730, 74 N. W. 693.

Kansas.—*State* v. *Spaulding*, 24 Kan. 1; *State* v. *Treadwell*, 54 Kan. 507, 38 Pac. 799.

Louisiana.—*State* v. *Desmouchet*, 32 La. Ann. 1241; *State* v. *Birdwell*, 36 La. Ann. 859; *State* v. *Williams*, 49 La. Ann. 1148, 22 So. 759, and cases cited. But if a juror declares that he has a fixed opinion, his statement that such opinion will yield to contrary evidence will not qualify him. *State* v. *Ricks*, 32 La. Ann. 1098.

Maryland.—*Waters* v. *State*, 51 Md. 430.

Michigan.—*People* v. *O'Neill*, 107 Mich. 556, 65 N. W. 540.

Mississippi.—*Green* v. *State*, 72 Miss. 522, 17 So. 381, to the effect that the constitutional right of trial by an "impartial jury" does not prevent the legislature from providing that a mere opinion as to guilt or innocence shall not disqualify a person who has no bias of feeling or prejudice, and who makes oath that he is impartial.

Missouri.—*State* v. *Walton*, 74 Mo. 270; *State* v. *Barton*, 71 Mo. 289; *State* v. *Brown*, 71 Mo. 454; *State* v. *Hunt*, 141 Mo. 626, 43 S. W. 389.

Montana.—*State* v. *Sheerin*, 12 Mont. 539, 31 Pac. 543. But a juror who has formed a fixed opinion as to the guilt of the principal is incompetent to sit on the trial of an accessory before the fact. *State* v. *Gleim*, 17 Mont. 17, 31 L. R. A. 294, 41 Pac. 998.

Nebraska.—*Murphy* v. *State*, 15 Neb. 383, 19 N. W. 489; *Ward* v. *State*, 58 Neb. 719, 79 N. W. 725. But if the juror's opinion is so fixed that he cannot presume the accused to be innocent, he is subject to challenge, notwithstanding that he believes he can render an impartial verdict on the evidence. *Olive* v. *State*, 11 Neb. 1, 7 N. W. 444.

New Jersey.—*Wilson* v. *State*, 60 N. J. L. 171, 37 Atl. 954, 38 Atl. 428.

New York.—See *infra*, § 75.

North Carolina.—*State* v. *DeGraff*, 113 N. C. 689, 18 S. E. 507.

Ohio.—*McHugh* v. *State*, 42 Ohio St. 154.

But if the juror clearly shows himself incompetent on his *voir dire*, his declaration that he will render an impartial verdict will not make him competent. *Palmer* v. *State*, 13 Ohio L. J. 469.

Oklahoma.—*Huntley* v. *Terry*, 7 Okla. 60, 54 Pac. 314. But the court may sustain a challenge to a juror on the ground that he has formed an opinion based upon rumors and newspaper reports, although he answers that he will render a fair and impartial verdict. *Bradford* v. *Territory ex rel. Woods*, 2 Okla. 228, 37 Pac. 1061.

Oregon.—*State* v. *Kelly*, 28 Or. 225, 42 Pac. 217.

Pennsylvania.—*Com.* v. *Moss*, 6 Kulp, 31. But a juror is disqualified from sitting on a trial for murder, by having signed a petition reciting familiarity with the facts shown on a former trial, and requesting the court to accept a plea of not guilty of murder in the second degree as fully satisfying the requirements of justice. *Com.* v. *Cleary*, 148 Pa. 26, 23 Atl. 1110.

South Carolina.—*State* v. *Dodson*, 16 S. C. 453; *State* v. *Summers*, 36 S. C. 479, 15 S. E. 369. But though a juror states that he can find a verdict according to the law and the evidence, he is properly rejected where he swears that he served on a jury which convicted one jointly indicted with defendant; that in that case he discredited some of the witnesses, and would do likewise if they were examined in the present case, as he is not indifferent between the parties. *State* v. *James*, 34 S. C. 49, 12 S. E. 657, 34 S. C. 579, 13 S. E. 325, 899.

Tennessee.—*Conatser* v. *State*, 12 Lea, 436; *Woods* v. *State*, 99 Tenn. 182, 41 S. W. 811.

Texas.—*Post* v. *State*, 10 Tex. App. 579; *Hamlin* v. *State*, 39 Tex. Crim. Rep. 579, 47 S. W. 656. But a juror who, as deputy sheriff, has formed an opinion as to the guilt of the defendant from conversations with the sheriff, other deputies, and witnesses in the case, is incompetent. *Keaton* v. *State,* 40 Tex. Crim. Rep. 139, 49 S. W. 90.

Utah.—*People* v. *O'Loughlin,* 3 Utah, 133, 1 Pac. 653.

Vermont.—*State* v. *Meeker,* 54 Vt. 112; *State* v. *Meyer,* 58 Vt. 457, 3 Atl. 195.

Virginia.—*Poindexter* v. *Com.* 33 Gratt. 766; *Lyles* v. *Com.* 88 Va. 396, 13 S. E. 802.

Washington.—*State* v. *Carey,* 15 Wash. 549, 46 Pac. 1050.

Wisconsin.—*Baker* v. *State,* 88 Wis. 140, 59 N. W. 570.

United States.—*Hopt* v. *Utah,* 120 U. S. 430, 30 L. ed. 708, 7 Sup. Ct. Rep. 614; *Reynolds* v. *United States,* 98 U. S. 145, 25 L. ed. 244 (quoted in the beginning of this note); *Thiede* v. *Utah,* 159 U. S. 510, 40 L. ed. 237, 16 Sup. Ct. Rep. 62.

These statutes are constitutional. *Spies* v. *Illinois,* 123 U. S. 131, *sub nom. Ex parte Spies,* 31 L. ed. 80, 8 Sup. Ct. Rep. 21.

71. — as to corpus delicti.

Belief that the act charged was committed, without belief in the guilt of the accused, does not disqualify.[1] But belief that the accused committed the act, if no further explanation is given, does disqualify.[2]

[1]*State* v. *Thompson,* 9 Iowa, 188, 74 Am. Dec. 342 (homicide; juror who had formed opinion as to fact of the killing of the deceased by the defendant, but not as to the guilt of the defendant, competent); *State* v. *Sorter,* 52 Kan. 531, 34 Pac. 1036; *People* v. *Buddensieck,* 103 N. Y. 487, 57 Am. Rep. 766, 9 N. E. 44, Affirming 4 N. Y. Crim. Rep. 230 (manslaughter by negligence in erecting building which fell; juror having preconceived opinion that somebody had been guilty of negligence, not thereby disqualified); *State* v. *Willis,* 71 Conn. 293, 41 Atl. 820; Hirsh, Juries, § 352, and cases there cited; Maxwell, Crim. Proc. pp. 578–583. Compare *State* v. *Bryan,* 40 Iowa, 379.

So, a juror is not disqualified to sit on the trial of defendant charged with poisoning his wife, because he testifies that he has an impression that the wife died from the effect of poisoning, where he also testifies that he has no impression as to the guilt or innocence of the defendant, and has no such fixed opinion of the death from poisoning that he could not give defendant a fair and impartial trial. *People* v. *Foglesong,* 116 Mich. 556, 74 N. W. 730.

Nor is a juror disqualified, under the Missouri statute, to sit upon the trial of defendant charged with disseminating a newspaper devoted mainly to the publication of immoral conduct, in violation of Mo. Laws 1891, p. 125, because he has formed an opinion upon public talk that the paper should be suppressed, where he states that he could give an impartial verdict if selected as a juror, and would not permit the opinion formed on rumor to bias him. *State* v. *Van Wye,* 136 Mo. 227, 37 S. W. 938.

[2]*State* v. *Brown,* 15 Kan. 400.

So, upon a trial for violation of the Michigan local-option law, a juror who states that he supposes and understands that defendant is running a certain saloon, and that he sells intoxicating liquors there, should be excluded. *People* v. *Keefer*, 97 Mich. 15, 56 N. W. 105.

72. — hypothetical opinion.

A hypothetical opinion or impression, conditioned on the supposition that what has been heard or read of the case is true, does not, as matter of law, necessarily disqualify.[1]

[1]This principle for interpreting the common-law rule was generally argued, even before the statutory modification of that rule.

The rule as stated in the text finds support in the following cases: *Spence* v. *State*, 15 Lea, 539; *Leach* v. *People*, 53 Ill. 317, Citing *Smith* v. *Eames*, 4 Ill. 76, a leading case; S. C., with note, 36 Am. Dec. 521; *Daughdrill* v. *State*, 113 Ala. 7, 21 So. 378; *State* v. *Bronstine*, 147 Mo. 520, 49 S. W. 512; *Osiander* v. *Com.* 3 Leigh, 780, 24 Am. Dec. 693; *Bolln* v. *State*, 51 Neb. 581, 71 N. W. 444; *Hall* v. *Com.* 89 Va. 171, 15 S. E. 517 (holding that hypothetical opinion not previously expressed does not disqualify, if juror can decide according to the evidence without being influenced by it). See also *State* v. *Collins*, 70 N. C. 241, 16 Am. Rep. 771; Proffatt, Trial by Jury, § 184; Hirsh, Juries, §§ 345, 355, 356; Thornton, Juries, § 97; *People* v. *Crowley*, 102 N. Y. 234, 6 N. E. 384, Affirming 4 N. Y. Crim. Rep. 26; *Bohanan* v. *State*, 18 Neb. 57. 53 Am. Rep. 791, 24 N. W. 390 (opinion formed on reading newspaper reports not necessarily a disqualification).

The decision in *Greenfield* v. *People*, 74 N. Y. 277, S. C., with note, 6 Abb. N. C. 1, that opinion of guilt derived from reading published reports of the sworn testimony on a former trial was necessarily a disqualification, is still followed in New York, although with this exception later decisions on the present statute no longer put any particular stress upon the source of the opinion. With this exception the clear weight of authority now is to treat the juror as qualified if he swears, and the court also is satisfied, that he can render an impartial verdict on the evidence.

In *People* v. *Casey*, 96 N. Y. 115, a trial for murder, it was held error to overrule the challenge, unless juror so declared.

It is not error to overrule challenges to jurors who declare that they can do so. *People* v. *Cornetti*, 92 N. Y. 85; *People* v. *Dewey*, 20 N. Y. Week. Dig. 555; *People* v. *Welch*, 17 N. Y. Week. Dig. 28; *People* v. *Otto*, 101 N. Y. 690; *People* v. *Crowley*, 102 N. Y. 234; *People* v. *Buddensieck*, 103 N. Y. 487, 57 Am. Rep. 766, Affirming 4 N. Y. Crim. Rep. 230.

But in *People* v. *McQuade*, 21 Abb. N. C. 417, 421, the rule in the *Greenfield Case*, 74 N. Y. 277, was approved at general term.

73. — that requires evidence to remove.

The fact that the opinion is such as would require evidence to remove necessarily disqualifies,[1] unless it appears that should the proposed juror be accepted he could discard his opinion and render an impartial verdict upon the evidence, without being influenced by the opinion. In that case it does not disqualify.[2]

[1]*People* v. *Shufelt*, 61 Mich. 237, 28 N. W. 79; *People* v. *Fultz*, 109 Cal. 258, 41 Pac. 1040; *McGuire* v. *State*, 76 Miss. 504, 25 So. 495; *State* v. *Moody*, 18 Wash. 165, 51 Pac. 356; Proffatt, Trial by Jury, §§ 185, 186.

The reason is that the very object of the challenge for cause is to prevent the accused from being burdened with the added labor of overcoming a bias in the minds of jurors, in order to render them impartial.

[2]*People ex rel. Phelps* v. *New York County Oyer & Terminer Ct.* 83 N. Y. 436; *People* v. *Genet*, 19 Hun, 91; *Wilson* v. *People*, 94 Ill. 305 (holding juror competent who testified that, although he had formed such an opinion as would take evidence to remove, "he would be governed by the evidence in the case, and could give the defendant a fair and impartial trial according to the law and the evidence"); *People* v. *Scott*, 123 Cal. 434, 56 Pac. 102; *English* v. *State*, 31 Fla. 340, 356, 12 So. 689; *Smith* v. *Com.* 100 Ky. 133, 37 S. W. 586; *State* v. *Frier*, 45 La. Ann. 1434, 14 So. 296; *Green* v. *State*, 72 Miss. 522, 17 So. 381; *State* v. *Brown*, 28 Or. 147, 41 Pac. 1042; *Com.* v. *Crossmire*, 156 Pa. 304, 27 Atl. 40; *Suit* v. *State*, 30 Tex. App. 319, 17 S. W. 458; *Bryant* v. *State*, 7 Wyo. 311, 51 Pac. 879, 56 Pac. 596.

In *State* v. *Sawtelle*, 66 N. H. 488, 32 Atl. 831, it was held that the statement of a juror that he had so strong an opinion as to the guilt or innocence of the accused as to require evidence to change it did not necessarily render him incompetent, where he also stated that if he tried the case as a juror he would do his duty according to the explanation with reference to deciding the case upon the evidence that the court had given; but that the question of his competency was one of fact to be determined at the trial term, and the possibility or probability of obtaining jurors who had not formed an opinion was properly considered in determining that question.

On the other hand, there are cases holding to the contrary: *Vance* v. *State*, 56 Ark. 402, 19 S. W. 1066; *State* v. *Snodgrass*, 52 Kan. 174, 34 Pac. 750; *State* v. *Lattin*, 19 Wash. 57, 52 Pac. 314.

74. — founded on sworn evidence.

The fact that the opinion was founded on sworn evidence regularly taken against the accused does not, as matter of law, necessarily disqualify.[1]

[1]*Weston* v. *Com.* 111 Pa. 251, 2 Atl. 191 (holding jurors competent notwithstanding opinions formed on reading sworn testimony); *Com.* v. *Roddy*, 184 Pa. 274, 39 Atl. 211 (where the juror heard part of evidence on former trial); *Monroe* v. *State*, 23 Tex. 210, 76 Am. Dec. 58 (juror heard part of evidence before examining magistrate; nevertheless competent); *State* v. *Shelton*, 64 Iowa, 333, 20 N. W. 459 (opinion based on

reading in newspaper the evidence taken before the coroner does not necessarily disqualify); *Jones* v. *State*, 120 Ala. 303, 25 So. 204 (where the juror heard the evidence on the trial of one jointly indicted with the defendant on trial); *State* v. *Philpot*, 97 Iowa, 365, 66 N. W. 730 (to the same effect); *State* v. *Scott*, 1 Kan. App. 748, 42 Pac. 264 (where juror heard the evidence upon a preliminary plea in bar). *Contra*, in New York, *Greenfield* v. *People*, 74 N. Y. 277, 6 Abb. N. C. 1, with note; Reiterated in *People* v. *Hickman*, 113 Cal. 80, 45 Pac. 175; *Mabry* v. *State*, 71 Miss. 716, 14 So. 267.

So, in *State* v. *Taylor*, 134 Mo. 100, 35 S. W. 92, it was held that a person is not disqualified as a juror by hearing or reading part of the evidence taken at a former trial. So held also in *State* v. *Duestrow*, 137 Mo. 44, 91, 38 S. W. 554, 39 S. W. 266.

But *State* v. *Foley*, 144 Mo. 600, 46 S. W. 733, holds that persons who have listened for a day to the sworn testimony of the witnesses on a trial for murder, and who have conversed with a witness, and formed their opinion as to defendant's guilt from knowledge thus acquired and the reports of a newspaper giving substantially all the evidence on the trial,—are incompetent to act as jurors on a second trial, under Mo. Rev. Stat. 1889, § 4197, making it a good cause of challenge to a juror that he has formed or delivered an opinion on the issue or any material fact, unless it appears that such opinion is founded only on rumor and newspaper reports.

And *State* v. *Shackelford*, 148 Mo. 493, 50 S. W. 105, holds that where the accused seeks to disqualify a juror by reason of his having read a copy of the evidence before the coroner he must make it appear that he read the evidence itself, not some garbled statement of it, nor a mere editorial or reportorial comment thereon.

Shannon v. *State*, 34 Tex. Crim. Rep. 5, 28 S. W. 540, holds that a juror is absolutely disqualified, regardless of his ability to render an impartial judgment, where he has formed an opinion as to the guilt or innocence of the accused from the evidence in a companion case, and not from the reading of newspaper accounts or other sources mentioned in Wilson's Tex. Crim. Stat. § 2281 (Tex. Acts 1885, p. 90), allowing him to serve if, in spite of an opinion based on such source, he can render an impartial judgment. And *Drye* v. *State*, 40 Tex. Crim. Rep. 125, 49 S. W. 83, holds that a juror who has formed an opinion from hearing the facts of the case testified to on the trial of another cause by the state's witness, mainly relied on, in the pending prosecution, is incompetent.

75. — New York statute.

"The previous expression or formation of an opinion or impression in reference to the guilt or innocence of the defendant, or a present opinion or impression in reference thereto, is not a sufficient ground of challenge for actual bias, to any person otherwise legally qualified, if he declare on oath that he believes that such opinion or impression will not influence his verdict, and that he can render an impartial verdict according to the evidence, and the court is satisfied that he does not entertain such a present opinion or impression as would influence his verdict."[1]

[1]N. Y. Code Crim. Proc. § 376, subd. 2, last half. The statutes in other states, though in varying language, are to the same general effect. For decisions under this New York statute, see *People* v. *McGonegal*, 136 N. Y. 62, 32 N. E. 616; *People* v. *Wilmarth*, 156 N. Y. 566, 51 N. E. 277; Affirming 29 App. Div. 612, 51 N. Y. Supp. 688; *People* v. *Flaherty*, 27 App. Div. 535, 50 N. Y. Supp. 574.

For decisions under a prior New York statute (Laws 1872, chap. 475) holding that the formation of an opinion does not disqualify if the juror can render an impartial verdict on the evidence, see *Thomas* v. *People*, 67 N. Y. 218; Distinguished in 6 Abb. N. C. 11; *Phelps* v. *People*, 72 N. Y. 334; *Manke* v. *People*, 17 Hun, 410; *Pender* v. *People*, 18 Hun, 560; *Balbo* v. *People*, 80 N. Y. 484; *Abbott* v. *People*, 86 N. Y. 460; *Cox* v. *People*, 80 N. Y. 500; Affirming 19 Hun, 430.

After discussing the act of 1872 as to challenges to jurors in criminal cases, Mr. Merriam, in his paper on disqualification of jurors (Points of Law on Guiteau's Case, Boston; Little, Brown & Co. 1881), says: "The effect of the statute seems to be this: Under the law prior to the statute, a juror who avowed that he had formed or expressed a positive opinion as to the guilt or innocence of an accused person was by such avowal rendered incompetent. The law would not listen to any further statement, however confidently made, that notwithstanding such opinion he could give the accused a fair trial. Under the statute this supplementary statement may be made, and if the truth of it is made out to the satisfaction of the court, the juror is no longer subject to a principal challenge upon this score. The statute, then, is based upon the presumption that the juror can shut out from his consideration during the trial all previously formed opinions touching the case. It does not permit him to demand evidence to overcome his bias or preconceived opinions. In short, the juror must, under the statute, as at common law, "stand indifferent as he stands unsworn."

For a statute to a similar effect as the New York statute, see Horn. Ind. Stat. § 1793. Substantially the same provision is to be found in Illinois. 1 Starr & C. Anno. Stat. p. 2391, ¶ 14.

76. — right to interrogate further.

The statement of a proposed juror that he can try the case fairly, on the evidence, in spite of his preconceived opinion or impression, is not conclusive, but he may be further interrogated, and whether he is biased is a question of fact on the whole evidence.[1]

[1]*Balbo* v. *People*, 80 N. Y. 484, 19 Hun, 424; *People* v. *Reynolds*, 16 Cal. 129.

And a juror qualifies himself as such when he states that he could go into the jury box and leave his opinion behind him, and base his verdict solely upon the law and the evidence; and an additional question whether he would enter upon his duties presuming the prisoner innocent is unnecessary. *Com.* v. *Van Horn,* 188 Pa. 143, 41 Atl. 469.

77. — disclaimer of impartiality disqualifies; assertion of it raises question for court.

If the proposed juror testifies unqualifiedly that his opinion would influence his verdict, this is conclusive, and he must be rejected. If he does not, he still must be rejected if the court, on the whole examination, is not satisfied that he is impartial.[1]

[1]*Stagner* v. *State,* 9 Tex. App. 440.

Balbo v. *People,* 80 N. Y. 484, Affirming 19 Hun, 424, and *Cox* v. *People,* 80 N. Y. 500, Affirming 19 Hun, 430, hold that if a juror, on being challenged for principal cause, discloses on his examination that he has a fixed and definite opinion in the case on the merits, and nothing further is shown, then the rule of law which existed prior to the statute of 1872, chap. 427, applies, and the court is bound, as matter of law, to reject him as incompetent. But if, in addition, he states upon oath that he believes he can render an impartial verdict on the evidence, and that such previously formed opinion will not bias or influence him as a juror, the question of his competency is then to be determined by the court as a question of fact. In determining the question, the declaration of the juror is to be considered, but it is not controlling.

And a juror who on his examination states that he has formed an opinion based on what he has been told by parties directly interested in the case is not competent under Cal. Pen. Code, § 1076, making competent a juror who has formed an opinion founded on public rumor, statements in public journals, or common notoriety, if it appears to the court, on his declaration under oath, that he can and will act impartially and fairly upon the matters submitted,—especially where he makes no such declaration. *People* v. *Wells,* 100 Cal. 227, 34 Pac. 718.

Nor is a juror competent who has formed and expressed a positive opinion of the guilt of a prisoner and of certain specific and material facts, although it is based solely on newspaper accounts, even if he declares that he can render a fair and impartial verdict upon the evidence alone,—especially where this declaration is elicited by argumentative and persuasive examination by the court. *Coughlin* v. *People,* 144 Ill. 140, 19 L. R. A. 57, 33 N. E. 1.

So, a proposed juror who persists, until threatened by the court with contempt proceedings, in saying that he would require the accused to prove his innocence, and finally says reluctantly that he can try the defendant according to the law and the evidence,—is subject to challenge for cause. *State* v. *Fourchy,* 51 La. Ann. 228, 25 So. 109.

A juror is not the final judge of whether or not he can render a verdict in accordance with the evidence produced in court notwithstanding his preconceived opinion against defendant, but it must appear judicially from the attending conditions that he stands indifferent between the commonwealth and the prisoner, and can reach a conclusion uninfluenced by such opinion. *Com.* v. *House*, 3 Pa. Super. Ct. 304.

78. — juror's confidence in his own impartiality.

It is not essential that the proposed juror declares that he *knows* he would not be influenced by a previous or present opinion or impression. It is enough that he *believes* he would not be, and that he believes that he could render an impartial verdict.[1]

[1]*People* v. *Willett*, 36 Hun, 501; *State* v. *Wilson*, 38 Conn. 126.

So held of a juror who "thinks he could" disregard it and render a verdict upon the evidence, unless his manner discredits his ability or intention to do so. *Com.* v. *Eagan*, 190 Pa. 10, 42 Atl. 374.

Even although he does not use the word "believe." *People* v. *Martell*, 138 N. Y. 595, 33 N. E. 838.

Otherwise of a juror who states that he thinks that he could lay his opinion aside and decide the case according to the evidence, but that he has a fear on his mind in that respect. *State* v. *Ramsey*, 50 La. Ann. 1339, 24 So. 302.

79. — time.

The inquiry for the trial court is not confined to a preconceived opinion. It includes the question whether the juror now, at the time of being examined, has a disqualifying impression or opinion.[1]

[1]*Grissom* v. *State*, 8 Tex. App. 386.

80. — what the opinion is, not competent.

It is not error to refuse to compel a proposed juror who acknowledges he has an opinion to disclose whether it is of the guilt or innocence of the accused.[1]

[1]*Stagner* v. *State*, 9 Tex. App. 440, holding also that it is not proper to allow the counsel for the accused to ask if he can go into the jury box believing the accused is innocent until proved guilty. This would not secure impartiality, but the contrary. It is enough if he can presume him innocent till proved guilty.

A juror cannot be asked specifically whether he believes the prisoner guilty or innocent, because such an examination would have a tendency to create an impression, either for or against the prisoner, on the others. *State* v. *Bennett*, 14 La. Ann. 661. Murder; holding it no error to refuse to allow the juror to answer this question: "Have you or not formed or expressed the opinion, from what you have heard of the case, that the defendant is guilty?"

One examined as to his competency to sit as a juror cannot be asked what would be his opinion as to the guilt of the defendant, although the law presumed him to be innocent until he was proved to be guilty. *Com.* v. *Van Horn,* 188 Pa. 143, 41 Atl. 469.

And a juror who has stated that he has impressions as to the merits of the case cannot be asked whether they are favorable to the accused. *White* v. *Territory,* 1 Wash. 279, 24 Pac. 447.

81. — opinion on particular defense.

It is improper to ask a juror if he has formed an opinion on a particular line of defense which may be set up, as, for instance, insanity.[1]

[1]*State* v. *Arnold,* 12 Iowa, 479. The counsel for the prisoner propounded this question to a juror: "If the defense in this case should be the insanity of the defendant, have you formed or expressed an opinion upon the subject?" Held, that the question was open to this objection, that it stated only a supposed defense for the purpose of showing actual bias. Wright, J., said in this case: "Suppose that the jurors state that they have, then if the inquiry is pertinent or proper, they should be excluded. And though the defense should not be made on the trial, the defendant has had the advantage of an improper challenge."

82. Party in civil action.

See *supra,* § 14.

83. Pecuniary interest.

If the pecuniary interest of the juror be merely as a member of the town or county to whose treasury a fine is to be paid,[1] or if the juror is simply a citizen or taxpayer of a county to which the offense on trial has brought pecuniary damage, he is not *per se* disqualified.[2]

Bail of a defendant who is not in custody are disqualified.[3]

[1]Hirsh, Juries, § 412.

[2]*Phillips* v. *State,* 29 Ga. 105.

But otherwise where the juror has an individual claim to a fine or forfeiture which a conviction would produce. Hirsh, Juries, § 412; *Carr* v. *State,* 104 Ala. 4, 16 So. 150.

One who is indebted to the party is not absolutely disqualified, but the indebtedness is a circumstance to be considered on the question of bias. *People* v. *Bodine,* 1 Denio, 281, 306.

In *Springer* v. *State,* 34 Ga. 379, a verdict of guilty was set aside because it appeared that, during the progress of the trial, one of the prosecuting counsel kept the horse of a juror over night, in his stable, free of charge.

Com. v. *Brown,* 150 Mass. 334, 23 N. E. 98, sustained the constitutionality of a statute providing that mere inhabitancy of a town or county shall not disqualify a juror on a trial for unlawfully obtaining money from the treasury of the town or county.

So, the fact that one is a resident and taxpayer of a school district does not disqualify him as a juror in a prosecution for obtaining money by false pretenses by means of a sale of an invalid order of such district, the charge being that the purchaser of the order, and not the school district, was defrauded. *State* v. *McDonald*, 59 Kan. 241, 52 Pac. 453.

And one is not disqualified to sit as a juror on the trial of a city treasurer for making profit out of the public money intrusted to him, or for using it for a purpose not authorized by law, because he is a resident and taxpayer in the city, and has paid money to the city treasurer, with the conversion of which defendant is charged. *State* v. *Krug*, 12 Wash. 288, 41 Pac. 126.

[a]In *Anderson* v. *State*, 63 Ga. 675, the court held that when the accused is at large on bail at the time of trial, his bail is not a competent juror to try him, if objected to by the state. Bleckley, J., says: "Suppose the prisoner had concluded to leave the court and the country after the jury had retired, and this juror, his bail, had been of the panel charged with his case, and by any chance he had heard that his principal was gone, there would have been an improper motive to return a verdict of not guilty. Perhaps the bare risk of such a contingency would weigh upon a juror's mind, so as to incline him more to acquittal than conviction. Bail has his principal in friendly custody. While such custody continues, the bail is not a fit person to sit in judgment on his guilt or innocence."

84. Personal hostility.

It is a good ground of challenge that a juror has evinced feelings of hostility to a party.[1]

[1]*Brittain* v. *Allen*, 13 N. C. (2 Dev. L.) 120 (granting new trial for error in overruling defendant's challenge, although the hostility had no connection with the action to be tried); *Coleman's Case*, 2 N. Y. City Hall Rec. 89 (holding it proper to ask a juror whether he holds hostile feelings against the prosecutor by reason of a transaction touching the prosecutor's official duties).

So, a juror on a trial for murder may be examined as to whether he could return a verdict based wholly on the evidence and instructions, if it should appear that the wife of the defendant and the deceased were unduly intimate, and, on his stating that he doubts his ability to do so, may properly be excused. *Jones* v. *People*, 23 Colo. 276, 47 Pac. 275.

But prejudice of a juror against the attorney for the accused is not ground for a challenge for actual bias under the Idaho statute. *State* v. *Gorden* (Idaho) 48 Pac. 1061.

And the mere fact that a juror on a trial for murder may have known that defendant had already killed one man in another state, and was then wanted in a different state for killing another, does not in itself show that he had any bias or prejudice against defendant, or had ever formed or expressed any opinion as to his guilt or innocence of the crime for which he was on trial. *Kelly* v. *State,* 39 Fla. 122, 22 So. 303.

85. Physical incapacity.

The rule as to physical capacity of a trial juror, in New York, is that he must be "in the possession of his natural faculties, and not infirm or decrepit."[1]

A juror whose eyesight is so defective that he is unable to distinguish one from another of the faces of the witnesses, or to see the face of the defendant, and who cannot see the expressions of the witnesses, or observe their deportment or demeanor,—is incompetent to sit.[2]

The court has power to excuse a man from the jury in a criminal trial because he cannot hear, under the Ohio statute providing that any petit juror may be challenged for any cause that may render him at the time an unsuitable juror.[3]

[1] N. Y. Code Civ. Proc. §§ 1029, subd. 4, 1079, subd. 4, 1126, subd. 4; N. Y. Code Crim. Proc. § 375, subd. 2. See also *supra,* § 67.

[2] *Rhodes* v. *State,* 128 Ind. 189, 27 N. E. 866.

[3] *Ickes* v. *State,* 16 Ohio C. C. 31, 8 Ohio C. D. 442.

86. Prejudice against kind of evidence.

If counsel indicate an intention to adduce evidence of a particular kind,—such as circumstantial evidence[1] or the testimony of accomplices,[2] etc.,—a prejudice against such evidence may be shown; and its existence is presumptively a disqualification,[3] unless it be also shown that it would not prevent the juror from giving the testimony its lawful weight.[4]

[1] *State* v. *Leabo,* 89 Mo. 247, 1 S. W. 288, holding it not error to exclude those who declared that they would not convict of murder on circumstantial evidence alone. To the same effect, *Griffin* v. *State,* 90 Ala. 596, 8 So. 670; *Olive* v. *State,* 34 Fla. 203, 15 So. 925; *Holland* v. *State,* 39 Fla. 178, 22 So. 298; *State* v. *Frier,* 45 La. Ann. 1434, 14 So. 296; *State* v. *Young,* 119 Mo. 495, 24 S. W. 1038; *Little* v. *State,* 39 Tex. Crim. Rep. 654, 47 S. W. 984. See also *Cluverius* v. *Com.* 81 Va. 787; *Gates* v. *People,* 14 Ill. 433.

[2] *People* v. *O'Neil,* 109 N. Y. 251, 16 N. E. 68, holding it not error to allow the prosecution, after stating that they intended to examine as witnesses accomplices of the defendant who had turned state's evidence, to ask each juror whether he had such a prejudice against persons so testifying as would prevent his giving their testimony its legal weight.

[3] *Stoots* v. *State,* 108 Ind. 415, 9 N. E. 380. Prosecution for selling liquor

on Sunday; counsel for defense asked whether, if the accused were a witness in his own behalf, the proposed juror "would allow less weight and credit to his evidence than you would if he were not engaged in the business of selling liquor?" Held, error to overrule the challenge on his answering, "I think I should." Conviction therefore reversed. The court, per Niblack, J., said: "So far as we are advised it has never been held that a person called to serve as a juror, who admits that his prejudices against a business recognized as lawful are so fixed that he might not, and probably would not, give to the testimony of a party engaged in it as much weight and credit as he would if the party were employed in some other business, is a competent juror to try a cause involving the business against which such prejudices are admitted to exist. On the contrary, the fair inference from the drift of the authorities bearing on the general subject is that a person so moved by his prejudices is at least prima facie incompetent as a juror to try such a cause,"—Citing *Robinson* v. *Randall,* 82 Ill. 521; *Whitehall* v. *Meaux,* 8 Ill. App. 182; *Chandler* v. *Ruebelt,* 83 Ind. 139; *Shields* v. *State,* 95 Ind. 299; *Mima Queen* v. *Hepburn,* 7 Cranch, 290, 3 L. ed. 348; *People* v. *Allen,* 43 N.Y. 28; *Chicago & A. R. Co.* v. *Adler,* 56 Ill. 344; *Sam* v. *State,* 13 Smedes & M. 189; *Curry* v. *State,* 4 Neb. 545; *Block* v. *State,* 100 Ind. 357. See also *infra,* § 87.

[4]Practically conceded in *Stoots* v. *State,* 108 Ind. 415, 9 N. E. 380. Citing *Shields* v. *State,* 95 Ind. 299; *Butler* v. *State,* 97 Ind. 378; *People* v. *Carpenter,* 102 N. Y. 238, 6 N. E. 584.

The test is to inquire whether the preconceived disposition of an opinion that such evidence is in itself unworthy of credit, or an opinion that it should be specially scrutinized; whether it is an opinion for rejection or an opinion for caution; whether it is an opinion that, on general principles and as a rule, the testimony of an informer should go for nothing, or an opinion that concedes that it is one proper means of ascertaining the truth, so that when presented with corroboration it is the duty of the jury to act upon it as upon other evidence,—candidly and with an unprejudiced desire to ascertain the truth.

In a cause depending upon the testimony of persons of a particular religious faith (as Roman Catholic), a juror cannot be asked whether he is of opinion that a witness professing that faith is not to be believed on his oath. *Com.* v. *Buzzell,* 16 Pick. 153 (indictment for burning a Roman Catholic convent), sustained in *People* v. *Carpenter,* 38 Hun, 490, 493, which was affirmed in 102 N. Y. 238, 6 N. E. 584. And see *People* v. *Car Soy,* 57 Cal. 102.

87. — against business.

Prejudice against the business in which the accused is engaged, even though the offense charged relates to that business, is not, as matter of law, necessarily a disqualification.[1]

[1]*Kroer* v. *People,* 78 Ill. 294. Prosecution for selling liquor on Sunday; not error to overrule challenge to one who said on direct examination

that he had a prejudice against persons engaged in the business of saloon keeping, but on cross-examination said that his prejudice was against the traffic, and not the persons engaged in it. Sheldon, J., said: "The juror's feeling of aversion was only to the traffic in intoxicating liquors. Defendant was not entitled to have a jury of such persons as entertained the contrary feeling. He might as well have insisted upon having a jury composed of persons holding lax notions upon the subject of the observance of the Sabbath day. It did not appear that the juror had formed an opinion of the guilt of the defendant, or that he entertained a prejudice against him." See also *Thiede* v. *Utah*, 159 U. S. 510, 46 L. ed. 237, 16 Sup. Ct. Rep. 62; *Arnold* v. *State*, 38 Tex. Crim. Rep. 1, 40 S. W. 735; *Stoots* v. *People*, 108 Ind. 415, 9 N. E. 380 (*dictum*), Citing *Chandler* v. *Ruebelt*, 83 Ind. 139; *Shields* v. *State*, 95 Ind. 299; *Robinson* v. *Randall*, 82 Ill. 521; *Whitehall* v. *Meaux*, 8 Ill. App. 182; *United States* v. *Borger*, 19 Blatchf. 249, 7 Fed. 193; *United States* v. *Noelke*, 17 Blatchf. 554, 1 Fed. 426; *State* v. *Nelson*, 58 Iowa, 208, 12 N. W. 253; *Elliott* v. *State*, 73 Ind. 10; Thornton, Juries, § 94.

But in *Swigart* v. *State*, 67 Ind. 287, it was held that a juror who declared on his *voir dire* that he considered a licensed dealer was not engaged in a legitimate business, and could not be a moral man, was not a competent juror on the trial of a licensed dealer for an alleged violation of the liquor laws. See also *Winnesheik Ins. Co.* v. *Schueller*, 60 Ill. 465. Civil case, holding it error to overrule challenge by a defendant insurance company, the juror stating that he had a prejudice against such companies generally, founded on the fact that he could not comprehend their proceedings. Compare *Pemberton* v. *State*, 11 Ind. App. 297, 38 N. E. 1096, where it is held that the statement of a juror, in answer to a question by the accused's counsel, that he does not believe a man engaged in the sale of intoxicating liquor under a license is a moral man, does not render him incompetent in a prosecution for selling liquor to a minor.

In *People* v. *Keefer*, 97 Mich. 15, 56 N. W. 105, it was held that upon a trial for an offense against the Michigan local-option law a juror is not disqualified who states that he voted for such law, or that he is in favor of it and its enforcement, or that he is opposed to the saloon business, or has conscientious scruples against it and believes in prohibition. But in *People* v. *Wheeler*, 96 Mich. 1, 55 N. W. 371, a prosecution for keeping open a saloon on Sunday, it was held that a juror whose *voir dire* examination showed that he was prejudiced against the business of selling liquor, whether legal or not, and against persons engaged in such business, and that he was not sure that such prejudice would be removed by anything special in the case on trial,—was incompetent and should be rejected on a challenge for cause.

The fact that the juror was formerly a member of the police force, and had an unfavorable opinion of those accused of crime, would not disqualify. *People* v. *Reynolds*, 16 Cal. 128.

88. — against character of prisoner.

Belief that the character of the accused is bad does not, as matter of law, necessarily disqualify.[1]

[1] *People* v. *Allen*, 43 N. Y. 28; *Monroe* v. *State*, 23 Tex. 210, 76 Am. Dec. 58. Such belief is ground for challenge, and raises a question of fact only. It was formerly classed as a ground of challenge to the favor.

So, an unfavorable opinion of the character of the accused, without hostility or unfriendliness to him, will not disqualify. *Helm* v. *State*, 67 Miss. 562, 7 So. 487.

But a challenge for cause should be sustained in a criminal case where the juror has stated on his *voir dire* that he is part owner of a paper which has frequently denounced the defendant, and has read and approved of the editorials therein pronouncing the defendant guilty of the charge, although he states that to the best of his knowledge and belief he could render a verdict in accordance with the evidence produced in court. *Com.* v. *House*, 3 Pa. Super. Ct. 304.

89. — against class, race, etc.

The fact that the juror has some prejudice against the race to which the prisoner belongs does not necessarily, as matter of law, disqualify.[1]

[1] *Balbo* v. *People*, 80 N. Y. 484, Affirming 19 Hun, 424. Murder; juror on trial of an Italian said the Italians were a race he was "not particularly fond of and did not think much of, judging from those we have here;" held competent.

A prejudice against socialists, communists, and anarchists is nothing more than a prejudice against crime, which would not force a jury to prejudge an innocent and honest man, and would not, therefore, disqualify a juror in the trial of an indictment for a conspiracy of an anarchic nature. *Spies* v. *People*, 122 Ill. 1, 12 N. E. 865, 17 N. E. 898.

In *People* v. *Car Soy*, 57 Cal. 102, reversing conviction for robbery, it was held that it was proper for the defense to ask a juror if he would take the word of a Chinaman, if called as a witness, as soon as he would that of a white man, and that its exclusion was error.

In *People* v. *Mahoney*, 73 Hun, 601, 26 N. Y. Supp. 257, an action requiring the testimony of an informer, it was held that a juror who testified that his prejudice against an informer was so strong that it would take evidence to remove it, and who spoke very hesitatingly as to whether he would believe one if corroborated by other witnesses, was properly rejected.

So, in *Stricklin* v. *State* (Miss.) 13 So. 898, on the trial of a white man for the murder of a negro, it was held that jurors who stated that they were of opinion that an insult given by a negro would fully justify a white man in killing him, or that different rules should be applied in the trial of a white man for killing a negro from those which should control under other conditions,—were properly excluded.

90. — if relevant to issue.

Where the imputed motive for the alleged offense involves prejudice arising out of distinction of class, religious faith, or race, prejudice for or against either is a proper subject of challenge.[1]

[1]*People* v. *Christie*, 2 Park. Crim. Rep. 579, 2 Abb. Pr. 256. Indictment for riot arising out of prejudice between Roman Catholics and others. Defendants were members of a society of Hibernians and Catholics. Held competent to ask a juror, "Have you any bias or prejudice against Roman Catholics?" and that it was error to allow him to refuse to answer because answering would tend to disgrace him. The court said: The right to an impartial jury "is not to be sacrificed to the fear or apprehension of wounding the feelings of others. . . . There is neither dishonor nor disgrace attached to the fact that a man has formed an opinion upon any subject which agitates public consideration." And see *Com.* v. *Buzzell*, 16 Pick. 153, under *supra*, § 86.

91. — against defense.

A prejudice against a particular defense intended in the case, such as insanity, does not disqualify, if it is found to be an abstract opinion as to the propriety or impropriety of such defense in cases which have previously come to the juror's knowledge.[1] Otherwise of an opinion that such matter does not constitute a defense.[2]

[1]*People* v. *Carpenter*, 102 N. Y. 239, 6 N. E. 584, holding a juror competent who otherwise satisfied the test as to ability to render an impartial verdict on the evidence, although he said, "If the defense of insanity was interposed, I would have a prejudice against it," etc., explaining, however, that it was only against misuse of the defense that he was prejudiced, and not against a person who was insane. See *Butler* v. *State*, 97 Ind. 378, holding that a juror is not necessarily disqualified because he expresses an opinion that the defense of insanity should be carefully scrutinized, and also expresses himself as strongly opposed to feigned defenses of that character, but states further that he is not prejudiced against genuine defenses of that character.

And the fact that a juror states on his *voir dire* that he is prejudiced against the bogus plea of insanity will not disqualify him, where he also states that he has no prejudice against the accused and could give him an impartial trial, and, if his plea of insanity should be established to his reasonable satisfaction, he would find him not guilty. *State* v. *Welsor*, 117 Mo. 570, 21 S. W. 443.

So the overruling of a challenge to a juror because of his nonbelief in the defense of insanity is not error in a murder trial, where no defense of insanity is contemplated or interposed. *People* v. *Collins*, 105 Cal. 504, 39 Pac. 16.

[2]The danger of this rule, which the court should, by the exercise of discretion, guard against, is well stated in *People* v. *Carpenter*, 38 Hun, 490,

494, where the court said, among other things, that there is manifestly no power in a court to prevent counsel who has caused jurors to be discarded on account of their bias against a particular defense from abandoning that defense as soon as he has secured twelve men to his liking.

92. — against the offense.

An antipathy or prejudice against offenses such as that charged is not ground of challenge.[1]

[1]*Parker* v. *State*, 34 Ga. 262; *State* v. *Nicholls*, 50 La. Ann. 699, 23 So. 980; *People* v. *McGonegal*, 136 N. Y. 62, 32 N. E. 616; *Elliott* v. *State*, 73 Ind. 10; *United States* v. *Noelke*, 17 Blatchf. 554, 1 Fed. 426 (a prosecution for using the mail to promote lotteries holding that it is no objection to the competency of a juror that he is in favor of enforcing the laws against lotteries, and it is therefore no error to exclude a question to a juror to that effect).

So, a juror is not incompetent to serve on a trial for murder committed with a pistol, who states on his examination that he entertains a prejudice against a person in possession of a pistol, unless he has permission, and that the evidence would have to be stronger in his behalf than as though the pistol were not spoken of, where he further states that his verdict would not be influenced thereby in the least. *People* v. *Hughson*, 154 N. Y. 153, 47 N. E. 1092.

Nor is a juror incompetent on a trial for unlawfully keeping intoxicating liquors for sale as a beverage, merely because he is a prohibitionist in sentiment, and strongly opposed to the unlawful traffic in intoxicating liquor, where he has no bias or prejudice for or against defendant personally, and states that he will decide the case impartially on the law and evidence. *State* v. *Tomlinson*, 7 N. D. 294, 74 N. W. 995.

And a statement in reference to a murder committed by lying in wait, that any man who would waylay and shoot another ought to be hung, does not render the one making it incompetent to serve as a juror on a trial for the murder. *Leach* v. *State*, 99 Tenn. 584, 42 S. W. 195.

And jurors in a murder trial are not obnoxious to challenge for cause because they have formed opinions from hearsay, or have a prejudice against wife murderers, or state that defendant would have to prove that he was innocent before they would acquit him, which statement they subsequently retract and say that they did not intend to answer it that way, where they state that they could try the defendant fairly and impartially according to the testimony, and give him the full benefit of any reasonable doubt. *Deon* v. *State*, 37 Tex. Crim. Rep. 506, 40 S. W. 266.

93. — against the law.

Conscientious scruples against the law creating the offense,[1] or against the infliction of the punishment prescribed[2] are, as matter of law, a disqualification. So also of habitual practices or an avowal of opinions in defiance of the law relating to the offense charged.[3]

[1]*United States* v. *Reynolds*, 1 Utah, 226, Boreman, J. (a juror who has conscientious scruples against indicting a person for polygamy is disqualified from serving as a juror to try an indictment for such offense); *Com.* v. *Austin*, 7 Gray, 51 (holding that if a juror holds such an opinion of the unconstitutionality of the statute on which the prosecution is founded—illegal sale of intoxicating liquor—that he cannot convict, whatever the evidence may be, he is incompetent).

[2]See *infra*, § 100.

But in *State* v. *Vogan*, 56 Kan. 61, 42 Pac. 352, it is held that failure to excuse a juror upon challenge for cause by defendant under Kan. Code Crim. Proc. § 201, providing that no person who believes the punishment fixed by the law is too severe for the offense shall be sworn as a juror,—is not reversible error.

[3]*People* v. *Jones*, 1 Edm. Sel. Cas. 112. In this case Edmonds, J., said: "Would it be a discreet performance of that duty [the duty of the court to secure an unbiased jury] to have a Mormon, with his belief in many wives, serve as a juror on a trial for bigamy? To have one who believes in taking life for only a verbal insult sit as a juror in the case of a homicide growing out of offensive language? Such a line of action would be a mockery of justice." Compare *Dorr's Trial*, R. I. Supreme Ct. of 1844 (treason against the state), where the court refused to allow jurors to be asked if they voted for Dorr, and if they believed he was governor at the time in question.

94. Previous service.

See *infra*, §§ 101–104.

95. Property qualification.

A juror, although possessing the property qualification at the time when his name was put upon the list, may be challenged if he lacks it at the time of challenge.[1]

[1]*Armsby* v. *People*, 2 Thomp. & C. 158, Affirmed as *Kelley* v. *People*, 55 N. Y. 565, 14 Am. Rep. 342; *Aaron* v. *State*, 37 Ala. 106; *Com.* v. *Carter*, 2 Va. Cas. 319.

The requirement of the New York statute is that in order to be qualified to serve in the state generally, the person must be "assessed for personal property belonging to him in his own right to the amount of $250; or the owner of a freehold estate in real property situated in the county belonging to him, in his own right, of the value of $150; or the husband of a woman who is the owner of a like freehold estate belonging to her in her own right." N. Y. Code Civ. Proc. § 1027, subd. 3.

In the city and county of New York, he must be "the owner, in his own right, of real or personal property of the value of $250; or the husband of a woman who is the owner, in her own right, of real or personal property of that value." N. Y. Code Civ. Proc. § 1079, subd. 3.

In Kings county, he must be "the owner, in his own right, of real property of the value of $150, or of personal property of the value of $250; or the husband of a woman who is the owner, in her own right, of real or personal property of that value." N. Y. Code Civ. Proc. § 1126, subd. 3.

These clauses are extended to criminal cases by N. Y. Code Crim. Proc. § 375, subd. 2.

In the state at large (New York and Kings counties excepted) it is further provided: "But a person who was assessed on the last assessment roll of the town, for land in his possession, held under a contract for the purchase thereof, upon which improvements owned by him have been made to the value of $150, is qualified to serve as a trial juror, although he does not possess either of the qualifications specified in subdivision 3d [property qualification] of the last section, if he is qualified in every other respect." N. Y. Code Civ. Proc. § 1028.

As to meaning of "freehold estate" and "freeholder," compare 1 Abb. New Pr. 467; *State* v. *Mills*, 91 N. C. 581.

In California an assessment of property to two persons is an assessment against each, for the purposes of Cal. Code Civ. Proc. §§ 198, 199, and Pen. Code, § 1072, providing that a person, to be competent as a juror, must be assessed on the last assessment roll of the county or city and county, on property belonging to him. *People* v. *Owens*, 123 Cal. 482, 56 Pac. 251.

In Florida disqualification for jury service by nonpayment of a party's "last assessed capitation tax," within Fla. Laws 1891, chap. 4015, § 1, does not attach to a person until after the time has elapsed within which he is allowed by the revenue laws voluntarily to pay such tax without coercion. *Collins* v. *State*, 31 Fla. 574, 12 So. 906.

In North Carolina a juror is not incompetent under the statute requiring the selection, as jurors, of persons who have paid tax for the preceding year, by the fact that he has not paid his tax for the fiscal year ending previous to the last revision of the jury list, the tax list for which did not go into the sheriff's hands until after such revision. *State* v. *Davis*, 109 N. C. 780, 14 S. E. 55. See also *State* v. *Hargrave*, 100 N. C. 484, 6 S. E. 185.

Nor is it essential to the qualifications of a tales juror summoned for the trial of a case at the April term, 1894, who has paid his taxes for 1892, that he should have paid his taxes for 1893, under N. C. Code, § 1772, as amended by N. C. act 1889, chap. 559, requiring the county commissioners, on the 1st Monday of September, 1892, and every four years thereafter, to select from the tax returns of the preceding year the names of such persons only as had paid taxes for the preceding year. *State* v. *Sherman*, 115 N. C. 773, 20 S. E. 711.

In Michigan one whose name does not appear on any assessment roll in the county, and who is not a taxpayer therein, is incompetent to serve as a juror, under How. (Mich.) Ann. Stat. §§ 7554, 7555. *People* v. *Thacker*, 108 Mich. 652, 66 N. W. 562.

But in Kansas the failure of the assessor to place on the assessment roll the name of a person assessed for taxes does not disqualify the latter as a juror in the Kansas district court. *State* v. *Lowe*, 56 Kan. 594, 44 Pac. 20. And the mere showing that persons called as jurors did not pay taxes on personal property in the preceding year is insufficient to disqualify them as jurors under Kan. Gen. Stat. 1889, ¶¶ 3567, 3601, requiring the jury commissioners to select jurors from those on the assessment rolls for the preceding year, especially where it does not appear that they were not upon the assessment rolls made in the listing of personal property, or that they did not pay taxes on real estate. *State* v. *Reed*, 53 Kan. 767, 37 Pac. 174.

The provision of Wash. Laws 1895, p. 139, as to the qualifications of a juror, that he be a householder, applies to a juror summoned on an open venire to complete the panel in a criminal case after the regular panel has been exhausted. *State* v. *Lattin*, 19 Wash. 57, 52 Pac. 314.

The mere occupancy of a rented room and boarding in a private house does not constitute the occupant a householder, so as to qualify him to serve as a juror. *Lane* v. *State*, 29 Tex. App. 310, 15 S. W. 827.

So held of a venireman who occupies a room in his father's house by his permission, or a room furnished for him at his employer's house. *Maines* v. *State*, 35 Tex. Crim. Rep. 109, 31 S. W. 667.

96. Prosecutor in former case.

See *supra*, § 33.

97. Relationship.

See *supra*, §§ 15–18, 35.

98. Religious prejudice.

See *supra*, §§ 89, 93.

99. Residence.

See *supra*, § 29.

100. Scruples against death penalty.

Conscientious scruples against capital punishment, in trials of offenses punishable with death, disqualify.[1]

[1]Alabama.—*Stalls* v. *State*, 28 Ala. 25; *Griffin* v. *State*, 90 Ala. 596, 8 So. 670.

Arkansas.—*Jones* v. *State*, 58 Ark. 390, 24 S. W. 1073.

California.—*People* v. *Tanner*, 2 Cal. 257; *People* v. *Ah Chung*, 54 Cal. 398.

Colorado.—*Jones* v. *People*, 6 Colo. 452, 45 Am. Dec. 526.

Florida.—*Metzger* v. *State*, 18 Fla. 481.

Georgia.—*Williams* v. *State*, 3 Ga. 453; *Bell* v. *State*, 91 Ga. 15, 16 S. E. 207.

Indiana.—*Jones* v. *State*, 2 Blackf. 475; *Greenley* v. *State*, 60 Ind. 141; *Driskill* v. *State*, 7 Ind. 338; *Gross* v. *State*, 2 Ind. 329; *Davidson* v. *State*, 135 Ind. 254, 34 N. E. 972.

Iowa.—*Contra, State* v. *Lee*, 91 Iowa, 499, 60 N. W. 119.

Louisiana.—*State* v. *Nolan*, 13 La. Ann. 276; *State* v. *Stewart*, 45 La. Ann. 1164, 14 So. 143. But that a juror in a prosecution for murder has conscientious scruples against the infliction of the death penalty is not cause for challenge by the defendant, although the court may stand the juror aside on the motion of the prosecutrix or upon the juror's own request. *State* v. *Compagnet*, 48 La. Ann. 1470, 21 So. 46.

Massachusetts.—Rev. Stat. chap. 137, § 6; Gen. Stat. chap. 172, § 5.

Missouri.—*State* v. *David*, 131 Mo. 380, 33 S. W. 28.

Nebraska.—*Bradshaw* v. *State*, 17 Neb. 147, 22 N. W. 361; *Johnson* v. *State*, 34 Neb. 257, 51 N. W. 835.

Nevada.—*State* v. *Vaughan*, 23 Nev. 103, 43 Pac. 193.

New Hampshire.—*State* v. *Howard*, 17 N. H. 171.

New York.—*People* v. *Wood*, 131 N. Y. 617, 30 N. E. 243.

Ohio.—*State* v. *Town*, Wright (Ohio) 75; *Martin* v. *State*, 16 Ohio, 364.

Pennsylvania.—*Com.* v. *Valsalka*, 181 Pa. 17, 37 Atl. 405.

South Carolina.—*State* v. *Carter*, 49 S. C. 265, 27 S. E. 106.

Texas.—*Clanton* v. *State*, 13 Tex. App. 139; *Hyde* v. *State*, 16 Tex. 445, 67 Am. Dec. 630; *Sawyer* v. *State*, 39 Tex. Crim. Rep. 557, 47 S. W. 650.

Utah.—*State* v. *Kessler*, 15 Utah, 142, 49 Pac. 293.

U. S. Courts.—*United States* v. *Wilson*, Baldw. 78, Fed. Cas. No. 16,730.

Virginia.—*Clore's Case*, 8 Gratt. 606; *Cluverius* v. *Com.* 81 Va. 787; Hirsh, Juries, pp. 131–133.

Persons with conscientious scruples against the death penalty held incompetent jurors in capital cases, notwithstanding that the statute permitted the jury, in their discretion, to fix the punishment at imprisonment for life. *Spain* v. *State*, 59 Miss. 19.

In some cases it has been held that if a juror, disclosing that he has conscientious scruples against capital punishment, thinks that notwithstanding this he can render an impartial verdict on the evidence, he is competent. *Williams* v. *State*, 32 Miss. 389, 66 Am. Dec. 615; *People* v. *Stewart*, 7 Cal. 140; *People* v. *Wilson*, 3 Park. Crim. Rep. 199; *Stratton* v. *People*, 5 Colo. 276.

But this distinction is open to criticism. Thompson & M. Juries, § 202, says: "This conclusion may be strongly questioned. One conscientiously scrupulous of taking human life by process of law ought not, although willing, to be placed in such a position that, to observe his oath as a juror, he may be called upon to violate his conscience, or, on the other hand, to follow the dictates of his conscience, he may violate his oath. A juror ought not to be permitted to serve having, in one breath, affirmed and disaffirmed his competency."

Where the entertaining of a prejudice against capital punishment is only made a challenge for cause by the state, the accused cannot complain if the state forbears to exercise the right of challenge. *Murphy* v. *State*, 37 Ala. 142.

By the New York statute, if the crime charged be punishable with death, the entertaining of such conscientious opinions as would preclude the juror's finding the defendant guilty is a disqualification, in which case he should neither be permitted nor compelled to serve as a juror.

This is classed as "implied bias," and if the existence of the facts is ascertained, disqualification follows as matter of law. N. Y. Code Crim. Proc. § 376, subd. 1, § 377, subd. 8; Ind. Rev. Stat. (1881), § 1793; Thornton, Juries, § 99; Maxwell, Crim. Proc. p. 583.

For a prior statute substantially like the present, except that it applied to persons of religious denominations, see 3 N. Y. Rev. Stat. 6th ed. 1029, § 17.

And see *Walter* v. *People*, 32 N. Y. 147; *People* v. *Damon*, 13 Wend. 351; *Lowenberg* v. *People*, 5 Park. Crim. Rep. 414; *Williams* v. *State*, 3 Ga. 453 (holding that it makes no difference whether the existence of such scruples is disclosed by the answer to a question put to the juror upon his examination on his *voir dire*, or whether he volunteers the statement).

But see *People* v. *Stewart*, 7 Cal. 140. That a juror is "opposed to capital punishment on principle" does not imply that he has a conscientious opinion which would preclude him from finding a prisoner guilty in a capital case, because this is not equivalent to saying that he has conscientious scruples against capital punishment.

And *O'Brien* v. *People*, 36 N. Y. 277, 3 Abb. Pr. N. S. 368, holds that the statement of a juror that he has conscientious scruples as to finding a verdict in a case involving life and death, renders him incompetent, although he further states that he is not opposed to the policy of the law inflicting capital punishment. Distinguished in 6 Abb. N. C. 8.

Com. v. *Webster*, 5 Cush. 295, 52 Am. Dec. 711, holds that one who is opposed to capital punishment, and fears that his opinion may influence others of the jury, is, notwithstanding, competent to be sworn as a juror, if he believes he can give an unbiased verdict.

101. Service previously in same court.

By statute in several jurisdictions, previous service within two years in the same court is ground of challenge.[1]

[1]For instances, see *Smith* v. *State*, 102 Tenn. 721, 52 S. W. 182; *People* v. *Thacker*, 108 Mich. 652, 66 N. W. 562.

U. S. Rev. Stat. § 812, provides as follows: "No person shall be summoned as a juror in any circuit or district court more than once in two years, and it shall be sufficient cause of challenge to any juror called to be sworn in any cause that he has been summoned and attended said court as a juror at any term of said court held within two years prior to the time of such challenge." *United States* v. *Nardello*, 4 Mackey, 503. This statute does not apply in the District of Columbia, where the limit of time is one year.

North Carolina Code 1883, § 1733, provides "that it shall be a disqualification and ground of challenge to any tales juror that such juror has acted in the same court as grand, petit, or tales juror within two years next preceding such term of the court."

Such a statute applies only to talesmen. *State* v. *Whitfield*, 92 N. C. 831.

The Indiana statute (Acts 1883, p. 44) expressly provides that such service within one year shall be a sufficient cause for challenge. "The object of this statute is something more than to relieve men from the burden of sitting on juries oftener than once a year. It is to preserve the purity of the jury box and avert the evils arising from an overwillingness often exhibited to serve in the capacity of a juror,—to avoid the services of 'professional jurymen.'" Thornton, Juries, § 89.

In Kansas, that a juror served as such in a court of record during the year next preceding the trial does not disqualify him under Gen. Stat. 1889, chap. 54, § 3, unless he actually sat in the trial of a case. *State* v. *Lowe*, 56 Kan. 594, 44 Pac. 20.

In Illinois a person who has previously served as juror at the same term may be selected to fill a vacancy in the list of jurors summoned for a subsequent portion of the term. *North* v. *People*, 139 Ill. 81, 28 N. E. 966.

In New Jersey a struck juror is not a petit juror, within the meaning of the jury act, § 6, which makes service as a petit juror within three previous stated terms of the court a ground of challenge. *Moschell* v. *State*, 53 N. J. L. 498, 22 Atl. 50.

Grand jurors are not within Hill's (Or.) Code, § 947, providing that it shall be sufficient cause of challenge to any juror called "to be sworn in any cause" that he has been summoned as a juror at any time within a year prior thereto. *State* v. *Brown*, 28 Or. 147, 41 Pac. 1042.

In Florida the statute that "no person shall be drawn to serve on a grand or petit jury more than once during the same year" does not create a disqualification, but simply provides an exemption from jury duty. *Blount* v. *State*, 30 Fla. 287, 11 So. 547; *Lambright* v. *State*, 34 Fla. 564, 16 So. 582.

In Texas the provision of Rev. Stat. art. 3010, subd. 5, disqualifying a juror who has served within a specified time, does not apply to criminal trials. *Hunter* v. *State*, 30 Tex. App. 314, 17 S. W. 414.

102. — in civil trial based on same act.

Having served as a juror in a civil action brought against the defendant for the act now charged as a crime is a disqualification.[1]

[1]Thornton, Juries, § 102; Maxwell, Crim. Proc. p. 585.

This, under the New York statute, is classed as "implied bias," and if the existence of the facts is ascertained, disqualification follows as matter of law. N. Y. Code Crim. Proc. § 376, subd. 1, § 377, subd. 7.

103. — on former trial of same defendant.

Having been one of a jury formerly sworn to try the same indictment, and whose verdict was set aside, or which was discharged without a verdict, after the cause was submitted to it, is a disqualification.[1]

Having served as a juror in another cause against the same defendant,[2] unless involving the same facts,[3] is not a disqualification.

[1]Thornton, Juries, § 101.

This, under the New York statute, is classed as "implied bias," and if the existence of the facts is ascertained, disqualification follows as matter of law. N. Y. Code Crim. Proc. § 376, subd. 1, § 377, subd. 6.

[2]*Buck* v. *Com.* 42 Phila. Legal Int. 353; *Patterson* v. *State,* 48 N. J. L. 381, 4 Atl. 449 (sustaining the state's challenge to juror on the ground that he has served as a juror in another case of the state against the same defendant is reversible error); *Com.* v. *Hill,* 4 Allen, 591; *State* v. *Maloney,* 118 Mo. 112, 23 S. W. 1084.

[3]*Baker* v. *Harris,* 60 N. C. (1 Winst. L.) 277; *Dunn* v. *State,* 7 Tex. App. 600.

But *Patterson* v. *State,* 48 N. J. L. 381, 4 Atl. 449(holds that the fact that a juror had served in another case of the state against the same defendant at the same term, and that he had formed an opinion in that case, is not sufficient to sustain a challenge by the state. And *Stephens* v. *State,* 53 N. J. L. 245, 21 Atl. 1038, holds that a juror who sat in a previous trial of defendant for one of a series of embezzlements closely connected with each other cannot sit, if challenged, on a pending trial of another of such series.

Although where two cases are similar against the same defendant, yet involve different facts to be proved by different evidence, a juror who has served in the one case is competent also to serve in the other. *Com.* v. *Hill,* 4 Allen, 591 (first indictment for keeping a nuisance down to a certain time; second indictment for keeping the same nuisance after that time); *Arnold* v. *State,* 38 Tex. Crim. Rep. 1, 40 S. W. 734. Compare *Gilmore* v. *State,* 37 Tex. Crim. Rep. 81, 38 S. W. 787, where it is held that a challenge in a prosecution for violating the local-option law, on the ground that they served as jurors on a former prosecution for selling liquor to the same person, and believed defendant was guilty on the sworn testimony of the purchaser in such prior case, should be sustained, although they say they have no such opinion of defendant's guilt or innocence as will influence them in finding a verdict.

In *Garthwaite* v. *Tatum,* 21 Ark. 336, 76 Am. Dec. 402, a civil case, it was held that where a jury had rendered a verdict in one case and were called as jurors in another case brought by another plaintiff against the same defendant, in which the issues were the same, and the evidence would be the same as in the case already passed upon, the law presumed them to be under a disqualification. See also *Algier* v. *The Marie,* 14 Cal. 167 (civil case).

In *Curtis* v. *State,* 118 Ala. 125, 24 So. 111, it was held that jurors were properly excused where they had served upon the jury which had previously tried the same defendant in a similar case, and the right to exclude them was not affected by the fact that they were members of jury No. 1 of the regular juries for the week, and were in the box at the time the parties announced that they were ready for trial.

104. — on trial of another for same crime.

Having served on a trial jury which has tried another person for the crime charged in the indictment does not at common law disqualify.[1]

Otherwise under the New York statute.[2]

[1] 1 Chitty, Crim. Law, p. 543 (where he says: "It will be no ground of challenge that one of the panel had been on a former jury, which convicted others upon the same indictment, because every man must be tried upon the evidence of his own guilt, without reference to that of his associates;" 2 Hawk. P. C. § 29, p. 43; Proffatt, Trial by Jury, § 190; *State* v. *Anderson,* 5 Harr. (Del.) 493; *State* v. *Sheeley,* 15 Iowa, 404 (illegal voting; holds that the fact that a juror served on a trial jury which convicted another defendant of an offense similar to the one charged in the indictment is not good cause of challenge); *People* v. *Williams,* 118 Mich. 692, 77 N. W. 248.

But *Wickard* v. *State,* 109 Ala. 45, 19 So. 491, holds that one who has acted as juror on a trial for playing and betting at cards or dice at a given place is incompetent to act as a juror on the trial of another person at the same term of court, for playing and betting at the same game.

And *People* v. *Troy,* 96 Mich. 530, 56 N. W. 102, holds that it is error to permit a jury who sat on a trial for assault with intent to do great bodily harm, to sit in another case in which the facts are equally identical, and must have been called forth in the former trial.

And *Obenchain* v. *State,* 35 Tex. Crim. Rep. 490, 34 S. W. 278, holds that one who acted as juror on trial of another person for playing the same game of cards for which defendant is on trial is disqualified to act as a juror, although he states that he does not think he will be influenced by the opinion formed in the other trial.

[2] In *United States* v. *Wilson,* Baldw. 78, 84, Fed. Cas. No. 16,730, it was held that where there are separate trials on a joint indictment, one who was a juror on the trial of one, and found a verdict of guilty, is not, by that fact alone, incompetent as a juror on the trial of the other; but the fact is good ground for submitting the question of such juror's indifference to triers.

This, under the New York statute, is classed as "implied bias;" and if the existence of the facts is ascertained, disqualification follows as matter of law. N. Y. Code Crim. Proc. § 376, subd. 1, § 377, subd. 5.

105. Society.

See *supra,* § 62.

106. Subpoenaed as witness.

The mere fact that one called as a juror has been subpœnaed as a witness in the cause does not alone disqualify.[1]

[1]This device has been resorted to in some cases, and proved successful; but it ought not to be allowed in any case. A subpœna does not necessarily, as a matter of law, disqualify. *Queen* v. *Farrant,* L. R. 20 Q. B. Div. 58, holding that a magistrate was not disqualified to sit at the hearing of a complaint for assault by the fact that he had been subpœnaed by the prosecution, in consequence of his having, as surgeon, professionally attended the assaulted person. *Contra, Com.* v. *Jolliffe,* 7 Watts, 585.

And it is a disqualification under the Indiana statute. Ind. Rev. Stat. (1881) § 1793.

It is not a disqualification in civil cases. *Rankin* v. *Nelson,* 27 N. Y. Week. Dig. 348, 10 N. Y. S. R. 337.

In Alabama, by express statute, a juror is obnoxious to a challenge for cause by the state, where he has been summoned as a witness in the case both by the prosecution and the defendant. *Baldwin* v. *State,* 11 Ala. 111, 20 So. 528. But the court should not on its own motion order a juror to stand aside because he has been summoned as a witness for defendant. *Bell* v. *State,* 115 Ala. 87, 22 So. 453.

In North Carolina a challenge to a juror called as a talesman, on the ground of favor, is properly sustained where it is shown that he is attending the court in the expectation of being called upon as a witness for the adverse party, whether he is under subpœna or not, and notwithstanding he has no knowledge of the more material facts bearing upon the issue, and expects to testify only as to the character of the defendant. *State* v. *Barber,* 113 N. C. 711, 18 S. E. 515.

In Texas a juror summoned on special venire is not disqualified to sit as such because he has been summoned as a witness, where he does not testify to any material fact, under Code Crim. Proc. art. 636, subd. 6, providing that a witness in the case may be challenged for cause. *Seals* v. *State,* 35 Tex. Crim. Rep. 138, 32 S. W. 545. Nor are jurors incompetent because they were witnesses on the question of a change of venue. *Hardin* v. *State,* 40 Tex. Crim. Rep. 208, 49 S. W. 607.

107. Sympathy for accused.

If the proposed juror's examination shows that he can give an impartial verdict on the evidence, the fact that he avows sympathy for the prisoner, and desires to be excused from a position that he thinks inconsistent, does not require the court to excuse him or set him aside.[1]

[1] *Com.* v. *Webster,* 5 Cush. 295, 298, 52 Am. Dec. 711. *Contra, Giebel* v. *State,* 28 Tex. App. 151, 12 S. W. 591.

State v. *Punshon,* 133 Mo. 44, 34 S. W. 25, holds that a juror who states that he has formed an opinion as to defendant's guilt or innocence from newspaper reports, and that he is in sympathy with defendant, and cannot render a fair and impartial verdict, is properly refused.

108. Taxpayer.

See *supra,* § 83.

109. Tenant.

See *supra,* § 57.

110. Wager.

See *supra,* § 25.

111. Ward.

See *supra,* § 51.

112. Witness.

See *supra,* § 106.

III. Peremptory challenges.

113. Number.

At common law the accused, in cases of treason and felony, has a right to challenge peremptorily to the number of thirty-five.[1] In misdemeanors peremptory challenges are not allowed.[2]

This right cannot be taken away except by express statute.[3]

Under modern statutes the number of peremptory challenges varies with the law of the jurisdiction.[4]

To allow the prosecution more than its number of peremptory challenges,[5] or to refuse the full number to the accused,[6] is reversible error.

[1] Originally the state could challenge peremptorily to an unlimited extent, but by Stat. 33 Edw. I. chap. 4, the power of the state to challenge peremptorily at all was abrogated. A rule of practice then arose, which still exists in jurisdictions where the state does not challenge peremptorily, of allowing the state the privilege of setting aside jurors when called, without assigning cause, until the panel is exhausted, when, if the full number of jurors still remains, the jurors set aside are not called, but if the number remaining is insufficient to form a trial jury, the state assigns cause for rejecting the excepted jurors.

The practice is called "standing jurors aside without assigning present cause," and has been recognized in the United States courts, in *United States* v. *Wilson,* Baldw. 81, Fed. Cas. No. 16,730; *United States* v. *Douglass,* 2 Blatchf. 207, Fed. Cas. No. 14,989; *United States* v. *Shackleford,* 18 How. 588, 15 L. ed. 495; and in *Wormeley* v. *Com.* 10 Gratt. 658; *Smith* v. *Com.* 100 Pa. 324; *State* v. *Coleman,* 20 S. C. 441. And *Com.* v. *O'Brien,* 140 Pa. 555, 21 Atl. 385, holds that the right of the commonwealth to stand aside a juror applies to misdemeanors, as well as felonies, and to jurors brought into court on a special venire, as well as the regular panel.

Reading's Case, 7 How. St. Tr. 259; *Oates's Case,* 10 How. St. Tr. 1079; *United States* v. *Devlin,* 6 Blatchf. 71, Fed. Cas. No. 14,953; *Freeman* v. *People,* 4 Denio, 9, 47 Am. Dec. 216.

As to common-law right of challenge, see § 1, *supra.*

In Florida the provision of the statute that the accused in a capital case shall be entitled to but ten peremptory challenges is new matter which, to be of force, must be sustained by a valid enactment, since the statute in force at the time of the revision allowed twenty such challenges, and the right to the whole number has not been taken away otherwise than by the revision. *Mathis* v. *State,* 31 Fla. 291, 12 So. 681.

For the United States courts the statute is: "When the offense charged is treason or a capital offense, the defendant shall be entitled to twenty and the United States to five peremptory challenges. On the trial of any other felony, the defendant shall be entitled to ten and the United States to three peremptory challenges; and in all other cases, civil and criminal, each party shall be entitled to three peremptory challenges; and in all cases where there are several defendants or several plaintiffs, the parties on each side shall be deemed a single party for the purposes of all challenges under this section." U. S. Rev. Stat. § 819. "At the trial in summary cases, if by the jury, the United States and the accused shall each be entitled to three peremptory challenges." *Id.* § 4303. Peremptory challenges by the accused in excess of the number allowed by law must be disregarded. *Id.* § 1031.

The New York statute is as follows: "Peremptory challenges must be taken in number as follows: 1. If the crime charged be punishable with death, thirty. 2. If punishable with imprisonment for life, or for a term of ten years or more, twenty. [*People* v. *Keating,* 61 Hun, 260, 16 N. Y. Supp. 748.] In all other cases, five." Code Crim. Proc. § 373. Each party, counting all of several defendants as one, is entitled to this number.

In California one accused of rape is entitled to only ten peremptory challenges of jurors, under Cal. Pen. Code, § 1070. *People* v. *Fultz,* 109 Cal. 258, 41 Pac. 1040. Notwithstanding § 671 gives the court authority to sentence defendant to imprisonment for life upon conviction. *People* v. *Logan,* 123 Cal. 414, 56 Pac. 56.

In Delaware six challenges will be allowed the defendant in a proceeding to determine the father of a bastard, as it is a quasi-criminal proceeding, and dealt with by the courts as a criminal proceeding. *Vail* v. *State,* 1 Penn. (Del.) 8, 39 Atl. 451.

In Massachusetts defendant in an indictment for an offense not punishable with death or imprisonment for life is entitled to but two peremptory challenges under Pub. Stat. chap. 170, § 36. *Com.* v. *Uhrig,* 167 Mass. 420, 45 N. E. 1047.

In Missouri an accused, although indicted for murder in the first degree, if prosecuted only for murder in the second degree, which is punishable by imprisonment for not less than ten years, is entitled to only twelve, and not to twenty, peremptory challenges, under Rev. Stat. 1889, § 4200, giving twenty if the crime charged is punishable with death or imprisonment, and twelve if punishable by imprisonment for not less than the specified number of years. *State* v. *Talmage,* 107 Mo. 543, 17 S. W. 990.

N. J. Laws 1878, p. 284, allowing six peremptory challenges in certain cases, does not apply to struck juries. *Moschell* v. *State,* 53 N. J. L. 498, 22 Atl. 50.

And a defendant who, at the time nine jurors have been selected and two are excused for illness, has exhausted nine of his twenty-five peremptory challenges, is not, where the remaining seven are retained and others called to fill the panel, confined to eleven peremptory challenges, under Cal. Pen. Code, § 1123, providing that upon discharge of a juror for illness a new juror may be sworn and the trial begin anew, or the jury be discharged and a ney jury impaneled. *People* v. *Wong Ark,* 96 Cal. 125, 30 Pac. 1115.

The allowance to the state by Vt. Stat. 1896, No. 33, § 1, of the same number of peremptory challenges in a criminal case as are allowed to the defendant, does not impair its constitutional right to a common-law jury of twelve men. *State* v. *Noakes,* 70 Vt. 247, 40 Atl. 249.

[5]*Savage* v. *State,* 18 Fla. 909; *Schoeffler* v. *State,* 3 Wis. 823.

[6]*People* v. *O'Neil,* 61 Cal. 435; *People* v. *Harris,* 61 Cal. 136; *United States* v. *Dunn,* 3 Mackey, 151.

The right of the accused to a certain number of peremptory challenges cannot be abridged in any way, except with his own unqualified consent.

Thus, an information charging assault with intent to murder being brought to trial, defendant claimed the statutory allowance of thirty peremptory challenges. Thereupon the prosecuting officer elected to try defendant for simple assault only, in which case defendant was entitled to only five peremptory challenges. Held error. *People* v. *Comstock,* 55 Mich. 405, 21 N. W. 384.

Nor can the number of peremptory challenges be restricted by requiring the accused to take or waive them in an arbitrary or unreasonable order. *Schumaker* v. *State,* 5 Wis. 324, holding that it was error to require the accused to take or waive four challenges at a time.

But a refusal to allow the full number of peremptory challenges is not prejudicial error unless the party complaining desires to challenge a juror after exhausting the challenges allowed. *Snow* v. *Starr,* 75 Tex. 411, 12 S. W. 673.

And a conviction will not be disturbed on the ground that defendant was compelled to take a brother of a deputy sheriff as a juror because he had been misled by the clerk as to his number of challenges, as it was his duty to keep account of the number of challenges himself. *Miller* v. *State,* 36 Tex. Crim. Rep. 47, 35 S. W. 391.

114. Several counts.

Trying the accused on more than one count does not entitle him to more than one set of peremptory challenges.[1]

[1] *United States* v. *Groesbeck,* 4 Utah, 487, 11 Pac. 542.

115. Several joint defendants.

In the absence of statute clearly indicating the contrary,[1] defendants jointly indicted are each entitled to their full number of separate peremptory challenges,[2] but the prosecution is only entitled to one set, no matter how many persons are on trial.[3]

[1] The New York statute (Code Crim. Proc. § 360) is to the contrary, and provides that several defendants tried together cannot sever in challenging, but must join.

Under a statute allowing "each party" a certain number of peremptory challenges, two or more defendants jointly indicted and tried must unite in their challenges. "Party" does not mean "person." *State* v. *Cady,* 80 Me. 413, 14 Atl. 940. See also *Hamlin* v. *State,* 67 Md. 333, 10 Atl. 214, 301, placing the same construction upon a statute allowing "each party" to strike four names from a list of twenty drawn from the panel. Bryan, J., dissented. The court says: "The question is a new one in this court; but wherever it has arisen in the courts of other states upon similar statutes the construction we have adopted has been uniformly applied,"—Citing *State* v. *Reed,* 47 N. H. 466; *Snodgrass* v. *Hunt,* 15 Ind. 274; *Stone* v. *Segur,* 11 Allen, 568. And the court intimates that the contrary is the interpretation to be put upon the statute as to peremptory challenges, which gives the right to "the accused," and as to challenges for cause, which gives it to "any person." And see *Stone* v. *Segur,* 11 Allen, 568, 570, the leading civil case, intimating that under the words, "the defendant in a criminal cause," each of several defendants would be entitled to the full number of peremptory challenges.

In Kentucky the statute (Crim. Code, § 198) provides that when several defendants are tried together the challenge of any one defendant shall be considered the challenge of all. And a defendant is properly charged with peremptory challenges made by a codefendant whose trial is commenced with his, although a separate trial is subsequently granted. *Glass* v. *Com.* 16 Ky. L. Rep. 108, 26 S. W. 811.

In Alabama a statute (Ala. Acts 1888–89, pp. 77–79) allows twenty-one peremptory challenges on trial for capital offenses, and provides that on a trial of two or more defendants each is entitled to one half of the challenges allowed, and this statute is complied with by allowing eleven peremptory challenges to one of two joint defendants and ten to the other. *Gibson* v. *State*, 89 Ala. 121, 8 So. 98; *Malachi* v. *State*, 89 Ala. 134, 8 So. 104. But two defendants on trial for murder are not each entitled to twenty-one peremptory challenges on the ground that it is impossible for such provision to be exactly executed. *Gregg* v. *State*, 106 Ala. 44, 17 So. 321.

In Georgia it is the duty of the judge, where two or more persons are jointly tried for a felony, and each insists on having the full number of peremptory challenges to which he would be entitled if tried alone, to determine at once the total number of such challenges which will be allowed on a request by defendants when the first juror is called, under Pen. Code, § 274, giving every person indicted for such offense the right peremptorily to challenge twenty jurors. *Cumming* v. *State*, 99 Ga. 662, 27 S. E. 177.

The defendants collectively, and not separately, are entitled to but three peremptory challenges, when a jury has been struck for the trial of an indictment against two or more defendants for a crime not within the New Jersey criminal procedure act, § 71, permitting twenty peremptory challenges. *Moschell* v. *State*, 53 N. J. L. 498, 22 Atl. 50.

**United States* v. *Marchant*, 12 Wheat. 480, 6 L. ed. 700 (a leading case); *State* v. *Stoughton*, 51 Vt. 362; *State* v. *Durein*, 29 Kan. 688; *State* v. *Doolittle*, 58 N. H. 92.

In *People* v. *Welmer*, 110 Mich. 248, 68 N. W. 141, it is held that though those jointly charged with a misdemeanor must be tried together under How. (Mich.) Ann. Stat. § 9573, each defendant is entitled to the same number of peremptory challenges he would have had if separately tried.

**Savage* v. *State*, 18 Fla. 909; *Schoeffler* v. *State*, 3 Wis. 823; *State* v. *Earle*, 24 La. Ann. 38, 13 Am. Rep. 109, holding that although where two or more persons are indicted and tried jointly each defendant has the full number of peremptory challenges as if tried alone, yet the state is entitled to no more peremptory challenges than when the trial is against one alone, under a statute providing that "in all criminal prosecutions wherein defendant is allowed peremptory challenges the state shall be allowed to challenge without cause any number not exceeding six" (La. Rev. Stat. 1870, § 998).

But under the Illinois statute allowing the prosecution "a peremptory challenge of the same number of jurors that the accused is entitled to" (Ill. Rev. Stat. chap. 38, § 432), if there are several defendants, each entitled to the statutory number, the prosecution is entitled to as many peremptory challenges as the accused is, in the aggregate. *Spies* v. *People*, 122 Ill. 1, 12 N. E. 865, 17 N. E. 898, Approving *Loggins* v. *State*, 12 Tex. App. 65.

So, in Vermont the state is entitled to twelve peremptory challenges in a criminal case, under Stat. 1896, No. 33, § 1, allowing the state in criminal prosecutions the same number of peremptory challenges as are allowed to the defendant, where two defendants are jointly tried, each being entitled to six peremptory challenges. *State* v. *Noakes*, 70 Vt. 247, 40 Atl. 249; *State* v. *Marsh*, 70 Vt. 288, 40 Atl. 836.

In Georgia the state is entitled to half of the whole number of peremptory challenges allowed to both of the defendants, under Code, § 4643, where neither of two persons tried jointly for a capital offense waives his peremptory challenges. *Butler* v. *State*, 92 Ga. 601, 19 S. E. 51.

116. Interrogation before peremptory challenge.

Either party may interrogate a proposed juror for the purpose of determining whether to challenge him peremptorily.[1]

[1]*State* v. *Mann*, 83 Mo. 589 (reversing conviction for refusal); *Lavin* v. *People*, 69 Ill. 303 (to same effect); *Donovan* v. *People*, 139 Ill. 412, 28 N. E. 964. See also *supra*, § 6.

A proposed juror can be interrogated as to matter not ground for challenge for cause, to enable counsel to decide whether to challenge peremptorily. Opinion of Davis, P. J., in *People* v. *Carpenter*, 38 Hun, 490, 499, Affirmed on other grounds in 102 N. Y. 238, 6 N. E. 584. See also *Com.* v. *Knapp*, 9 Pick. 496, 20 Am. Dec. 491. And see, in a civil case, *Chicago & A. R. Co.* v. *Butolf*, 66 Ill. 347.

But *Clifford* v. *State*, 61 N. J. L. 217, 39 Atl. 721, holds that the trial court may properly refuse to permit a juror to be interrogated by counsel for the purpose of eliciting information, so that the right of peremptory challenge may be intelligently used, where no challenge has been interposed, and it is not proposed to put the juror under oath. Affirming 60 N. J. L. 287, 37 Atl. 1101, and Citing *King* v. *State*, 5 How. (Miss.) 730; *Bales* v. *State*, 63 Ala. 30; *State* v. *Creasman*, 32 N. C. (10 Ired. L.) 395.

117. When peremptory challenge to be interposed.

At common law a peremptory challenge may be interposed at any time before the juror is sworn.[1]

After a juror is sworn the court has power in its discretion to refuse to permit even the accused to interpose a peremptory challenge.[2]

[1]*People* v. *Damon*, 13 Wend. 351.

The reason of the rule is that the accused is entitled to the benefit of whatever means of judgment even the appearance or the demeanor may afford, up to the time of the juror being sworn.

The rule above stated is the one that generally prevails. *People* v. *Montgomery*, 53 Cal. 576; *Hooker* v. *State*, 4 Ohio, 348; *Murray* v. *State*, 48 Ala. 675; *People* v. *Carrier*, 46 Mich. 442, 9 N. W. 487; *People* v. *Carpenter*, 36 Hun, 315 (holding that even if the defense expresses itself satisfied with the juror, the right to challenge him peremptorily, unless expressly waived, is not lost until the juror is actually sworn).

But see *McMilan* v. *State*, 3 Tex. L. J. 202 (holding that it is not error to refuse to permit defendant to peremptorily challenge a juror already accepted by him); *State* v. *Pritchard*, 8 Wash. L. Rep. 632 (holding that a defendant has the right to interpose a peremptory challenge at any time before the juror is sworn to try the case, notwithstanding he is informed by the court that if he passes his challenge when the juror is called and examined upon his *voir dire,* he will be considered as having accepted all the jurors then in the box); *State* v. *Pike,* 49 N. H. 399, 6 Am. Rep. 533 (holding it not error to allow the prosecution to challenge peremptorily after a juror has been examined on oath and defendant's attorney has expressed himself content).

In the absence of statute, however, it is generally held to be purely in the discretion of the court to regulate the time and order of the challenges.

Compare *Com.* v. *Webster,* 5 Cush. 295, 52 Am. Dec. 711, where, without giving any reason, Shaw, Ch. J., and associates, held that defendant must exercise his right of peremptory challenge, if at all, before examining a juror as for bias, etc., with *Com.* v. *Knapp,* 9 Pick. 496, 20 Am. Dec. 491, where it was held that the accused might peremptorily challenge a juror after the examination as to bias had failed to show any cause for challenge.

It is said in some of the cases that a peremptory challenge may be allowed after the juror has been sworn; but the true rule we deem to be that the judge may, on cause shown to him, which need not be publicly stated (*Tweed's Case,* 13 Abb. Pr. N. S. 371, note, Davis, P. J.), set aside a juror. S. P. N. Y. Code Crim. Proc. § 371.

This is not a peremptory challenge, for the characteristic of peremptory challenge, namely, that no cause need be assigned, is wanting. *Ochs* v. *People,* 124 Ill. 399, 16 N. E. 662.

[3]*People* v. *Carpenter,* 102 N. Y. 239, 6 N. E. 584.

A peremptory challenge interposed after acceptance of the jury, and after they are sworn to try the cause, based upon facts communicated by a juror after that time, is not available unless a motion is made to set aside the submission of the cause to the jury. *Kurtz* v. *State,* 145 Ind. 119, 42 N. E. 1102.

But *People* v. *Bemmerly,* 87 Cal. 117, 25 Pac. 266, holds that a juror may be peremptorily challenged after he has been sworn, good reasons being shown therefor.

And *People* v. *Hughes,* 46 N. Y. S. R. 413, 19 N. Y. Supp. 550, holds that the court may, in its sound discretion, permit the People peremptorily to challenge a juror who was sworn while the jury was being selected, where counsel have learned facts inducing the challenge since he was sworn, without compelling them to disclose such facts.

In North Carolina the court has no power, under Code, § 1200, providing that in capital cases the state shall have four peremptory challenges, if such challenges are made before the juror is tendered to the prisoner, to allow the state peremptorily to challenge a juror after he has been passed by the state, tendered to, and accepted by the prisoner, although the juror has asked to be excused upon the ground that he is an intimate friend of the prisoner and connected with him by marriage, but not so as to disqualify him. *State* v. *Fuller,* 114 N. C. 885, 19 S. E. 797.

118. — by prosecution.

Unless otherwise provided by statute,[1] the accused has a right to require the prosecution to exercise its right of peremptory challenge as to any individual juror, before the accused is required to do so, either expressly or by proceeding in a manner indicating that he has elected not to do so.[2]

[1] *Spigener* v. *State*, 62 Ala. 383 (holding that, in the absence of any statute defining the practice, it is error to compel the accused to take his peremptory challenges before the state is called upon to do so); *State* v. *Degonia*, 69 Mo. 485 (holding that the state must announce its peremptory challenges before the accused can be compelled to do so).

[2] The rule is the same under N. Y. Code Crim. Proc. § 385, providing that "challenges to an individual juror must be taken first by the People and then by the defendant." *People* v. *McQuade*, 110 N. Y. 284, 1 L. R. A. 273, 18 N. E. 156, with note to 21 Abb. N. C. 417.

But the prosecution in a criminal case may reserve its peremptory challenge until after the challenges on both sides for actual bias have been disposed of, but must exercise it before it is known whether the juror is satisfactory to the defendant, and before he is sworn. *People* v. *McGonegal*, 136 N. Y. 62, 32 N. E. 616.

But this statute does not prevent the People from peremptorily challenging a juror after he has been challenged for bias and examined by defendant. *People* v. *McGonegal*, 42 N. Y. S. R. 307, 17 N. Y. Supp. 147.

For cases contrary to the rule stated in the text, see *Turpin* v. *State*, 55 Md. 462, holding that the order in which peremptory challenges shall be taken is discretionary with the trial court. And see *Com.* v. *Knapp*, 9 Pick. 496, 20 Am. Dec. 491, Overruled, or at least a contrary direction given, in *Com.* v. *Rogers*, 7 Met. 500, 41 Am. Dec. 458; *Com.* v. *Webster*, 5 Cush. 295, 52 Am. Dec. 711. But see *Com.* v. *McElhaney*, 111 Mass. 439.

In Arkansas a statute (Sand. & H. Dig. §§ 2210–2213) provides that the challenges to the juror shall first be made by the state and then by the defendant, and the state must exhaust her challenges to each particular juror before such juror is passed to the defendant for challenge or acceptance; and allowing the state to interpose peremptory challenges to jurors who have been accepted by the state and defendant constitutes reversible error, where the defendant exhausted his peremptory challenges before the jury was secured. *Williams* v. *State*, 63 Ark. 527, 39 S. W. 709.

In South Carolina the state can exercise its right of peremptory challenge at any time before the prisoner has spoken, even after the juryman has been presented to him. *State* v. *Corley*, 43 S. C. 127, 20 S. E. 989.

In North Dakota the court, after having improperly denied a challenge for cause interposed by the state, and after the juror has been peremptorily challenged, may sustain the challenge for cause and excuse the juror and allow the state the full number of peremptory challenges to which it is entitled by law, without deduction of the challenge interposed to such juror. *State* v. *Kent,* 5 N. D. 516, *sub nom. State* v. *Pancoast,* 35 L. R. A. 518, 67 N. W. 1052.

In Maryland the statutory right of peremptory challenge may be exercised by the state after calling and examining a juror on his *voir dire* and turning him over to the counsel for the prisoner, by whom he is accepted without further examination. *Rogers* v. *State,* 89 Md. 424, 43 Atl. 922.

In California permitting the prosecution peremptorily to challenge a juror passed by it, but not sworn, after the defense has meantime exercised four peremptory challenges to other jurors, is not prejudicial error. *People* v. *Dolan,* 96 Cal. 315, 31 Pac. 107.

119. — by the defense.

The right of the defense in cases of felony to challenge peremptorily exists up to the time the juror in question lays hold of the book, or otherwise complies with the direction of the court, to be sworn, and cannot be taken away by the court nor restricted to an earlier time.[1]

Unless otherwise required by the statute or the court, the accused has a right to reserve all peremptory challenges until the number of twelve is full, if the jurors are yet unsworn, and until after objections or challenges for cause have been disposed of.[2]

[1] *People* v. *Carpenter,* 36 Hun, 315. Davis, P. J., says: "At common law the right of peremptory challenge in cases of felony exists until the juror is actually sworn. *Morris's Case,* 4 How. St. Tr. 1250; Archbold, Crim. Pr. & Pl. 510; *Reg.* v. *Sullivan,* 8 Ad. & El. 831; *Reg.* v. *Wardle,* Car. & M. 647; *Lindsley* v. *People,* 6 Park. Crim. Rep. 233. Under the Constitution of the state of New York this became a part of the common law of the state, subject to such alterations and provisions as the legislature of the state shall, from time to time, make concerning the same (first Constitution, § 35), and each of the subsequent and amended constitutions has continued such adoption. The established provisions of the common law are preserved by the Code of Criminal Procedure by §§ 369 and 371, the first of which enacts that 'before a juror is called, the defendant must be informed by the court, or under its direction, that if he intends to challenge an individual juror he must do so when the juror appears and before he is sworn.' The second (§ 371) enacts that 'a challenge must be taken when the juror appears and before he is sworn, but the court may, in its discretion, set aside a juror at any time before evidence is given in the action.' These sections establish a rule for the benefit of the accused which not only defines his rights as to the time when his challenge may be made, but secures them to him by force of statutory law. Under that rule he may challenge a person who appears as a juror at any time before he is sworn, and it is not in the power of a court to deprive him of that right."

[2] *People* v. *Bodine,* 1 Denio, 281, 310.

So, in Kentucky, under Crim. Code Prac. § 215, providing that the challenges to the jury shall first be made by the commonwealth and then by defendant, and that each party must exhaust his challenge to each juror before the other begins, defendant cannot be required to exercise his right of peremptory challenge until twelve qualified jurors have been selected and accepted or challenged by the commonwealth. *Smith* v. *Com.* 20 Ky. L. Rep. 1848, 50 S. W. 241; *Shelby* v. *Com.* 91 Ky. 563, 16 S. W. 461.

And in Mississippi, under Code 1892, § 1423, providing that all peremptory challenges of the state shall be made before the juror is presented to the prisoner, and in all cases the accused shall have presented to him a full panel before being called upon to make his peremptory challenges, the defendant cannot be required to challenge individual jurors called to fill a panel from which jurors have been excused upon defendant's peremptory challenge, but the panel must be filled before he can be required to peremptorily challenge any of the new jurors. *Gibson* v. *State,* 70 Miss. 554, 12 So. 582; *State* v. *Mitchel* (Miss.) 12 So. 710.

But in Idaho the defendant, who, under the provisions of Rev. Stat. § 7830, has twice as many peremptory challenges as the state, must, after the state has made its first challenge, make two challenges before the state is again called upon to make its next peremptory challenge. *State* v. *Browne* (Idaho) 44 Pac. 552.

So, in Montana the defendant is properly required to exhaust two challenges to each challenge by the state, under Pen. Code, §§ 2044, 2045, entitling defendant to ten peremptory challenges and the state to five, and § 2057, providing that such challenges must be taken in the manner provided in Code Civ. Proc. § 1059, which provides that each party is entitled to four peremptory challenges, and that if no peremptory challenges are taken until the panel is full they must be taken by the parties "alternately." *State* v. *Sloan,* 22 Mont. 293, 56 Pac. 364.

And in Washington the legislature in making the law relating to the selection of jurors in civil actions applicable to criminal cases, by Code Proc. § 1297, overlooked the fact that an accused has twelve peremptory challenges while the prosecution has only six, and an accused is properly required to exercise two peremptory challenges to one by the state, and not to challenge one to the state's one, as provided by § 348, until the peremptory challenges are all exhausted. *State* v. *Eddon,* 8 Wash. 292, 36 Pac. 139.

A waiver by an accused of a peremptory challenge after a direction by the court to avail himself of all his remaining challenges, before requiring the state to exhaust its last challenge, constitutes a waiver of all his other challenges, in the absence of a statute prescribing the order of taking them, where the court tells him in advance that it will have that effect. *Gravely* v. *State,* 45 Neb. 878, 64 N. W. 452.

120. Cutting off delay by oath after examination.

The court may in its discretion require each party to present his peremptory challenge to any juror before he is sworn in as a juror, and may direct that each, unless so challenged, be sworn as soon as he has been found impartial, and may refuse to allow peremptory challenge afterward.[1]

[1]*People* v. *Carpenter*, 102 N. Y. 239, 6 N. E. 584, Affirming 36 Hun, 315, 16 Abb. N. C. 128, holding that the discretionary power of the court in this respect is not abridged by the New York statute (Code Crim. Proc. § 371) which provides that "a challenge must be taken when the juror appears, and before he is sworn; but the court may, in its discretion, for good cause, set aside a juror at any time before evidence is given in the action." The court says: "It is not claimed that any case was made calling for the exercise by the court of the discretion thus provided for, and the validity of this exception must depend upon the question as to whether there is any rule of practice which requires the court to postpone the swearing of the jury until the drawing of the panel is wholly completed. We have been referred to no authority to that effect, and the language of the provision quoted seems to imply that each juror is to be sworn as he is called and accepted by the parties. In *People* v. *Damon*, 13 Wend. 351, Judge Savage, in a capital case, says: 'The regular practice is to challenge jurors as they come to the book to be sworn, and before they are sworn; but I apprehend this is matter of practice, and may be departed from in the discretion of the court.' This is believed to be the general practice in the courts of this state, and such also seems to be the rule in the English courts (*Reg.* v. *Frost*, 9 Car. & P. 129), and also in the courts of many of the sister states (*Epps* v. *State*, 19 Ga. 102; *McFadden* v. *Com.* 23 Pa. 17, 62 Am. Dec. 308; *Rash* v. *State*, 61 Ala. 89; *State* v. *Potter*, 18 Conn. 166). The statute being silent as to the time when the jury shall be sworn, we think it was within the discretion of the trial court to determine the practice, and that no impairment of the prisoner's legal rights is made after he has been allowed a fair opportunity to interpose a peremptory challenge to a proposed juror, that he is foreclosed as to the further exercise of the right by the administration of the oath to the juror at any time after he has been examined and accepted."

121. Second oath.

If the jurors have been sworn severally, subsequently swearing them as a body does not restore the right to interpose a peremptory challenge before such second oath.[1]

[1]*People* v. *Carpenter*, 38 Hun, 490. And see decision above quoted.

122. Withdrawing.

That the court has discretionary power to allow the prosecution to withdraw a peremptory challenge in order to interpose a challenge for cause, see[1]

[1]*Savage* v. *State*, 18 Fla. 909. Compare *People* v. *McQuade*, 110 N. Y. 284, 1 L. R. A. 273, 18 N. E. 156, with note, 21 Abb. N. C. 417.

IV. General power of the court.

123. Error to excuse one not exempt.

An exception lies to the excusing of persons claiming to be exempt, when a legal ground of exemption is not shown.[1]

[1]Thus, where a statute exempted from jury duty members of incorporated fire companies, and upon a murder trial the judge excused several persons from jury duty, against the objection of the accused, upon the mere statement that they were firemen; held error. The further fact should have been shown that they were members of an incorporated fire company. *Phillips* v. *State*, 68 Ala. 469. See also *People* v. *McQuade*, 110 N. Y. 284, 1 L. R. A. 273, 18 N. E. 156, with note to 21 Abb. N. C. 417. *Contra*, see cases cited in note to *People* v. *McQuade*, 21 Abb. N. C. 417.

But the court may, in the exercise of a sound discretion, excuse a juror at his own request, as a favor to him before he is accepted as one of the panel. *State* v. *Barber*, 113 N. C. 711, 18 S. E. 515.

So, a juror may be excused, in the absence of defendant's counsel, because his business will suffer if he is compelled to serve as such, where such reason seems sufficient to the trial judge. *People* v. *Thacker*, 108 Mich. 652, 66 N. W. 562.

124. Court may set aside jurors.

The court may of its own motion, in the exercise of a sound discretion, set aside an incompetent juror at any time before evidence is given.[1]

[1]*Jefferson* v. *State*, 52 Miss. 767; *Douthitt* v. *State*, 144 Ind. 397, 42 N. E. 907; *Lewis* v. *State*, 9 Smedes & M. 115; *People* v. *Arceo*, 32 Cal. 40 (even against defendant's objection); *People* v. *Wilson*, 3 Park. Crim. Rep. 199; *People* v. *Barker*, 60 Mich. 277, 27 N. W. 539; *State* v. *Murphy*, 48 S. C. 1, 25 S. E. 43; *United States* v. *Cornell*, 2 Mason, 91, Fed. Cas. No. 14,868; *State* v. *Hill*, 46 La. Ann. 736, 15 So. 145; *United States* v. *Reed*, 2 Blatchf. 435, Fed. Cas. No. 16,134; *State* v. *Bauerle* 145 Mo. 1, 46 S. W. 609; *State* v. *Miller*, 29 Kan. 43; *Savage* v. *State*, 18 Fla. 909; *Taylor* v. *State*, 11 Lea, 708.

In *State* v. *Ring*, 29 Minn. 78, 11 N. W. 233, Dickinson, J., says: "It is the duty of the court to supervise, and within proper limits to control, the trial of causes before it to the end that justice may be administered in reality, as well as in form. The parties before the court might desire, from different motives, to accept an incompetent juror,—one entirely unacquainted with our language,—but the court is not required to yield its assent to such a proceeding, or take part in such a trial."

But in *Van Blaricum* v. *People*, 16 Ill. 364, 63 Am. Dec. 316, trial for larceny, it was held error to set aside four unchallenged jurymen because they had expressed an opinion, Caton, J., saying: "If the parties chose to have their cause tried by a prejudiced juror, it was not for the court to refuse them the right."

And the court should not on its own motion order a juror to stand aside because he has been summoned as a witness for defendant, under Ala. Code, § 4331, making it a cause of challenge of a juror by a party that the juror is a witness for the other party. *Bell* v. *State*, 115 Ala. 25, 22 So. 526.

So, if a juror is physically incapacitated the court may discharge him at any time before evidence has been given. *Ozburn* v. *State*, 87 Ga. 173, 13 S. E. 247; *Goodall* v. *State* (Tex. Crim. App.) 47 S. W. 359; *Hanvey* v. *State*, 68 Ga. 612; *Webb* v. *State*, 100 Ala. 47, 14 So. 865; *Hamilton* v. *State*, 62 Ark 543, 36 S. W. 1054; *People* v. *Van Horn*, 119 Cal. 323, 51 Pac. 538; *Silsby* v. *Foote*, 14 How. 218, 14 L. ed. 394; *State* v. *Moncla*, 39 La. Ann. 868, 2 S. E. 814; *Catron* v. *State*, 52 Neb. 389, 72 N. W. 354. *Contra*, *Ellison* v. *State*, 12 Tex. App. 557, where the court held that, if sickness or other cause rendered it impracticable to proceed with the jury as impaneled, the jury should be discharged and another organized.

125. Misconduct during selection of jury.

As to the power of the court to deal with the misconduct of a juror during the selection of a jury, see[1]

[1]*People* v. *Barker*, 60 Mich. 277, 27 N. W. 539 (juror discharged for gambling, etc.); *Com.* v. *McBride*, Pittsb. L. J. (1884), 482 (embracery); *People ex rel. Minsell* v. *New York County Oyer & Terminer Ct.* 36 Hun, 277, Affirmed in 101 N. Y. 245, 54 Am. Rep. 691, 4 N. E. 259 (as to foundation and limits of power to punish for contempt). See also *post*, Division XXXII.

126. Substituting a new juror and recommencing trial.

If by reason of any cause intervening before verdict the court is satisfied that a juror is unable to discharge his duties as such, it has power to discharge him, even after evidence has been heard, and to substitute another qualified juror, and commence the trial anew.[1]

[1]*State* v. *Davis*, 31 W. Va. 390, 7 S. E. 24; *Dilworth* v. *Com.* 12 Gratt. 689, 65 Am. Dec. 264 (holding that, it being first discovered after the jury was sworn that one of them had been a member of the grand jury, a challenge should be allowed).

In misdemeanors the accused may consent to go on before the remaining jurors, for he may waive his constitutional right. *State* v. *Sackett*, 39 Minn. 69, 38 N. W. 773. Compare notes, *supra*, § 124.

In North Dakota, on the discharge of a juror for sickness, and the drawing of another juror, under Dak. Comp. Laws, § 7401, which authorizes such drawing, or the discharge of the entire jury and the impaneling of another, only such peremptory challenges are allowed as have not been already exhausted in procuring the other eleven jurors. *State* v. *Hazledahl*, 2 N. D. 521, 16 L. R. A. 150, 52 N. W. 315.

But in *Simmons* v. *State*, 88 Ga. 272, 14 S. E. 613, it was held that the constitution of the jury on a trial for a felony could not, after all the evidence of the state had been heard, be changed against the objection of the prisoner and his insistence that a mistrial be declared, by discharging one of its members because he was one of the grand jury that found the indictment, and substituting a fresh juror in his place, and proceeding with the trial. But upon the death of the mother of a juror during the trial of a capital case, the court may inform the juror of the fact, and discharge him from further service, and declare a mistrial, whether or not the accused consents thereto. *Stocks* v. *State*, 91 Ga. 831, 18 S. E. 847.

So, in *People* v. *Buchanan*, 25 N. Y. Supp. 481, it was held that a jury should be discharged and a new jury impaneled, under N. Y. Code Crim. Proc. § 416, providing therefor if, before the conclusion of the trial, a juror becomes sick so as to be unable to perform his duty, only after investigation by the court, and its determination that the illness is of such a character as to render the juror unable to perform his duty.

And in *State* v. *Vaughan*, 23 Nev. 103, 43 Pac. 193, it was held that the whole jury should be discharged or defendant allowed to challenge them over again, where one of the jurors was excused for sufficient cause after the trial had been commenced and witnesses examined, instead of substituting a new juror in place of the one excused.

XXXII.—SWEARING THE JURY.

1. Presence of the accused.

In felony it is error to swear the jury in the absence of the accused.[1]

[1]*Dunn* v. *Com.* 6 Pa. 384; *Dougherty* v. *Com.* 69 Pa. 286; *Younger* v. *State*, 2 W. Va. 579.

2. Necessity of swearing for each case.

The jury must be sworn for the particular case to be tried.[1] If a separate trial is granted to one of two defendants after the jury and witnesses are sworn, the jury and witnesses must be resworn.[2]

[1]In *Barney* v. *People*, 22 Ill. 160, the court, without declaring it error, very severely condemned the practice of swearing the whole panel, at the commencement of the term, for all causes which may be submitted to it.

[2]*Babcock* v. *People*, 15 Hun, 347.

In *People* v. *Everhardt*, 104 N. Y. 591, 11 N. E. 62, Affirming 5 N. Y. Crim. Rep. 91, it is held that where defendant was indicted by several fictitious or alias names, and his true name is discovered during the trial, although thereafter the oath to the jurors and witnesses may be administered by omitting from it such fictitious names, their repetition is not illegal or prejudicial to the defendant.

3. Manner of swearing.

Whether the jurors shall be sworn as they are individually accepted, or in groups, or all together, is a matter of local procedure. It is discretionary with the court, unless regulated by statute.[1]

[1]*People* v. *Carpenter*, 38 Hun, 490, Affirmed in 102 N. Y. 238, 6 N. E. 584 (holding it no error to swear each juror as soon as accepted); *O'Connor* v. *State*, 9 Fla. 215 (holding that the trial court could delay the swearing until the entire jury had been selected). The same ruling was made in *Roberts* v. *State*, 65 Ga. 430 (deeming it discretionary), and *People* v. *Reynolds*, 16 Cal. 128 (holding that the trial court might adopt either mode in its discretion). *Contra, Lamb* v. *State*, 36 Wis. 424 (reversing a conviction of murder by holding it essential to swear the jury in a body).

In *O'Connor* v. *State*, 9 Fla. 215, it was held no error to swear the jury in groups of three.

And in *State* v. *Anderson*, 4 Nev. 265, it was held no error to swear eight jurors who had been accepted.

4. Form of oath.

When no form is prescribed by statute, a substantial compliance with the common law is deemed good.[1]

If the statute of the jurisdiction prescribes the form of oath, it should be strictly followed.[2]

[1]1 Chitty, Crim. Law, 551; 2 Hale, P. C. 293.

At common law the oath administered to the jury was the following: "You shall well and truly try, and true deliverance make between our sovereign lord the King and the prisoners at the bar, whom you shall have in charge, and a true verdict give according to your evidence. So help you God." In *State* v. *Angelo*, 18 Nev. 425, 4 Pac. 1080, the following oath was held sufficient: "To well and truly try this cause, and a true verdict render, according to the law and the evidence." *Fitzhugh* v. *State*, 13 Lea, 258, holds an oath, "well and truly try the issues joined," to be sufficient. And in *Minich* v. *People*, 8 Colo. 440, 9 Pac. 4, the following was held good: "Well and truly try the issues joined, and a true delivery make between the people of the state of Colorado and Si. Minich [the defendant], and a true verdict render according to the law and the evidence."

[2]*State* v. *Rollins*, 22 N. H. 528.

The entire failure to administer the oath prescribed by Ga. Pen. Code, § 970, to the jury in a criminal case, either literally or substantially, cannot be waived by defendant or by his counsel, either expressly or by silence. *Slaughter* v. *State*, 100 Ga. 323, 28 S. E. 159, Distinguishing *Smith* v. *State*, 63 Ga. 168; *State* v. *Robinson*, 36 La. Ann. 873; *State* v. *Baldwin*, 36 Kan. 1, 12 Pac. 318; *State* v. *Ice*, 34 W. Va. 244, 12 S. E. 695; *Vezain* v. *People*, 40 Ill. 397; *Lancaster* v. *State*, 91 Tenn. 267, 18 S. W. 177; *Hardenburgh* v. *Crary*, 15 How. Pr. 307; *People ex rel. Wands* v. *Albany Common Pleas*, 6 Wend. 548; *Dolan* v. *State*, 122 Ind. 141, 23 N. E. 761,—and Citing *Barney* v. *People*, 22 Ill. 160; *Stephens* v. *State*, 33 Tex. Crim. Rep. 101, 25 S. W. 286; *Hunnel* v. *State*, 86 Ind. 431.

In *Young* v. *Com.* 19 Ky. L. Rep. 929, 42 S. W. 1141, however, an oath to the jury requiring them to truly try the case and a true verdict render is held to be a substantial compliance with Ky. Crim. Code, § 217, providing that the jury shall be sworn substantially well and truly to try the "issue," and a true verdict render in the case.

Nor can a defendant after conviction of felony complain that the jury was sworn "a true verdict to render according to the evidence," instead of a "true verdict to render according to the law and the evidence," when the record clearly shows that the verdict was given, not upon the evidence alone, but by applying the law to the evidence. *State* v. *Musgrave*, 43 W. Va. 672, 28 S. E. 813.

In Texas the court should allow veniremen, if they so desire, to affirm, instead of swear, before testing their qualifications, under Tex. Rev. Stat. art. 3270, providing that the word "swear" or "sworn," unless a different meaning is apparent from the context, includes "affirm." *Riddles* v. *State* (Tex. Crim. App.) 46 S. W. 1058.

XXXIII.—SUPERVISION OF THE JURY.

1. Admonition to jury.
2. Oath of officer in charge.
3. Separation.
4. Objecting to irregularities, etc., during the trial.

1. Admonition to jury.

The court should, at each adjournment, admonish the jury "that it is their duty not to converse among themselves on any subject connected with the trial, or to form or express any opinion thereon, until the cause is finally submitted to them."[1]

[1] N. Y. Code Crim. Proc. § 415. If inadvertently omitted, counsel should request this to be done, if desired; for the omission without objection is

not ground for new trial. *People* v. *Draper*, 28 Hun, 1; *McCreary* v. *Com.* 29 Pa. 323; *Crocker* v. *Hoffman*, 48 Ind. 207.

In *State* v. *Cucuel*, 31 N. J. L. 249, it was held that the accused, as a matter of right, could not demand that the jurors be restricted in their communications beyond the subject of the trial, all restrictions beyond this limit being a matter of discretion.

An instruction at the beginning of the term that the jurors shall not talk with any person about any case that is to be tried, or listen to any conversation of others in regard thereto, is entirely proper. *People* v. *Taylor*, 93 Mich. 338, 53 N. W. 777.

In *People* v. *Thompson*, 84 Cal. 598, 24 Pac. 384, it was held that the court should strictly comply with Cal. Pen. Code, § 1122, as to admonishing the jury on their separations during the course of the trial.

But *State* v. *Bussey*, 58 Kan. 679, 50 Pac. 891, holds that the statutory admonition need not be given at each adjournment, where the jury are kept together during the whole trial under the charge of a sworn officer.

In *Barnes* v. *Com.* 92 Va. 794, 23 S. E. 784, a conviction in a capital case was reversed where the record fails to show that upon the adjournment of the court from one day to another the jury were committed to the custody of the proper officer, with instructions not to speak to them himself, nor to allow anyone else to speak to them touching the trial of the case.

2. Oath of officer in charge.

Either party is entitled to require that the officer[1] in whose custody the jury is placed, even though a sworn officer,[2] be specially sworn not to suffer any person to speak to, or to communicate with, the jurors concerning the case,[3] and not to do so himself.

[1]Sheriff not disqualified because also complainant and a witness on the trial, if not a private prosecutor. *People* v. *Coughlin*, 65 Mich. 704, 32 N. W. 905; *Reed* v. *Com.* 98 Va. 817, 36 S. E. 399; *State* v. *Rosencrans*, 9 N. D. 163, 82 N. W. 422. Compare *People* v. *Fellows*, 122 Cal. 233, 54 Pac. 830, where it is held that a sheriff who is disqualified on account of bias from summoning jurors is not a proper person to be intrusted with the care of a jury when they retire to deliberate.

Appointing a material witness for prosecution as bailiff to take charge of the jury after the charge by the judge is ground for new trial. *State* v. *Snyder*, 20 Kan. 306.

In Florida a bailiff to take charge of the jury is properly appointed by the sheriff, instead of by the judge, who by statute is authorized to appoint such bailiff only when the sheriff fails to attend in person or by deputy. *Nicholson* v. *State*, 38 Fla. 99, 20 So. 818.

In California an elisor may properly be appointed to take charge of the jury during a trial for murder, where the sheriff is disqualified and the coroner is physically unable to perform his duty. *People* v. *Ebanks*, 117 Cal. 652, 40 L. R. A. 269, 49 Pac. 1049.

The provision of the Texas statute requiring each juror upon their separation to be accompanied by a court officer cannot be waived by the defendant in a felony case. *English* v. *State*, 28 Tex. App. 500, 13 S. W. 775; *McCampbell* v. *State*, 37 Tex. Crim. Rep. 607, 40 S. W. 496.

[5]*Maynard* v. *State*, 9 Baxt. 225; *State* v. *McCormick*, 57 Kan. 440, 46 Pac. 777; N. Y. Code Crim. Proc. § 414; *People* v. *Montgomery*, 13 Abb. Pr. N. S. 207. *Contra*, *Johnson* v. *State*, 8 Baxt. 450.

It is not necessary that the sheriff and his deputies be sworn to keep the jury together, etc., as required by law, at each recess or adjournment during the progress of a trial for a felony. *State* v. *Ice*, 34 W. Va. 244, 12 S. E. 695.

[6]N. Y. Code Crim. Proc. § 414; *McKinney* v. *People*, 7 Ill. 540, 43 Am. Dec. 65; *Jackson* v. *People*, 36 Ill. App. 88 (to the effect that the oath required by the Illinois statute cannot be dispensed with, even in misdemeanors, except by agreement noted upon the minutes of the court); *Nicholson* v. *State*, 38 Fla. 99, 20 So. 818 (special oath necessary although it may be administered by the clerk in the judge's absence, and during a recess of the court).

Administering the statutory oath to the officer and admonishing the jury in the absence of defendant is not ground for reversal of the conviction, where, being on bail, he left the courtroom without the knowledge of the court, but was brought in as soon as his absence was noticed, and, before the jury left the box, was informed of what had been done, and made no objection. *Lee* v. *State*, 56 Ark. 4, 19 S. W. 16.

In *Reed* v. *Com.* 98 Va. 817, 36 S. E. 399, it was held that a conviction would not be reversed because the record, which showed that the jury on adjournment from day to day were placed in the custody of the proper officer, did not show that the usual oath was administered to him. To the same effect, under the Missouri statute, see *State* v. *Stubblefield*, 157 Mo. 360, 58 S. W. 337.

In Kansas the statute provides that after hearing the charge the jury may retire under the charge of an officer sworn to keep them together in some private or convenient place, without food, except such as the court shall order, and not to permit any person to speak or communicate with them, nor to do so himself, unless by order of the court, or to ask them whether they have agreed on their verdict, and return them into court or when ordered by the court, and that the officer shall not communicate the state of their deliberations to any person. In *State* v. *Lashell*, 9 Kan. App. 887, Appx. 61 Pac. 678, a prosecution for a violation of the prohibitory liquor law, the bailiff having charge of the jury took the following oath: "You do solemnly swear that you will take this jury in charge, and keep them together in some convenient place until they have agreed upon their verdict or are discharged by the court, unless otherwise directed by the court; that you will not suffer any communication to be made to them or make any yourself, except to ask them if they have agreed upon their verdict; and that you will not, before their verdict is rendered, communicate to any person the state of their deliberations on the verdict agreed upon." It was held that this oath was not sufficient, since it did not follow substantially the language of the statute; that it could not be cured by a showing that the bailiff did all that a proper oath would have required him to do; and that therefore defendant's conviction was invalid.

In *Buxton* v. *State*, 89 Tenn. 216, 14 S. W. 480, an oath by an officer in charge of the jury, swearing him to keep them together, separate and apart from all other persons, and not to talk with them about the cause, or allow others to do so, until he returned them into court,—was held to be insufficient, as he should have been sworn to keep them separate and apart from all persons, and not allow them to communicate with any person, or any person to communicate with them, and not to communicate with them himself about the trial, further than to ask them if they had agreed.

3. Separation.

In the discretion of the court, the jury may be permitted to separate in the intervals of the trial, until the case is finally committed to them,[1] but not thereafter until they have returned their verdict.[2]

In some jurisdictions no separation at any time is allowable in capital cases.

[1]N. Y. Code Crim. Proc. § 414 (providing that "the jurors sworn to try an indictment may, at any time before the submission of the cause to the jury, in the discretion of the court, be permitted to separate, or be kept in charge of proper officers"); *Johnson* v. *State*, 32 Ark. 309; *Walker* v. *State*, 40 Tex. Crim. Rep. 544, 51 S. W. 234; *People* v. *Callaghan*, 4 Utah, 49, 6 Pac. 49; *State* v. *M'Kee*, 1 Bail. L. 651, 21 Am. Dec. 499; *State* v. *Anderson*, 2 Bail. L. 565; *People* v. *Tarm Poi*, 86 Cal. 225, 24 Pac. 998; *Tervin* v. *State*, 37 Fla. 396, 20 So. 551; *Territory* v. *Chenowith*, 3 N. M. 318, 5 Pac. 532; *State* v. *Gray*, 100 Mo. 523, 13 S. W. 806; *Kennon* v. *Territory*, 5 Okla. 685, 50 Pac. 172; *State* v. *Durham*, 72 N. C. 447 (rape; not reversible error to permit a juror to attend as a witness in another trial under direction and supervision of the court); *State* v. *Olberman*, 33 Or. 556, 55 Pac. 866; *Davis* v. *State*, 15 Ohio, 72, 45 Am. Dec. 559; *McCreary* v. *Com.* 29 Pa. 323 (burglary; allowing jury to separate may be error in a capital felony, but in cases of less magnitude it is proper); *Frances* v. *State*, 6 Fla. 306 (discretionary in any case not capital). Compare *State* v. *Brown*, 2 Marv. (Del.) 380, 36 Atl. 458, where it is held that the jury in a prosecution for murder in the second degree ought not to separate during the trial.

That the court in a capital case allowed a juror taken ill during the trial to consult a physician in charge of a sworn officer, and to remain apart from the other jurors in charge of a sworn constable for over a day, upon the physician's reporting him too ill to come out, was not the misconduct contemplated by N. Y. Code Crim. Proc. § 465, and did not require reversal of a conviction, in the absence of anything to show that the juror was ever out of the charge of the officer, or had any communication with any person not connected with the trial. *People* v. *Hoch*, 150 N. Y. 291, 44 N. E. 976.

But a conviction will be reversed where it appears uncontradicted that there was a separation of the jury, and that one of them during the separation discussed the different phases of the case with the prisoners in the jail, and had a conversation with reference to the legal status of the codefendant indicted for the same offense, and heard that he had been sentenced for the crime. *Burris* v. *State*, 37 Tex. Crim. Rep. 587, 40 S. W. 284.

And the separation of the jury and mingling of its members with a promiscuous crowd of people, upon being taken from the courthouse because it was on fire, after they had retired for deliberation,—was ground for reversal. *State* v. *Church*, 7 S. D. 289, 64 N. W. 152.

In Iowa a statute (Code, § 4434) provides that "jurors sworn to try an indictment may, at any time before the final submission of the cause to them, in the discretion of the court, be permitted to separate, except where one of the parties objects thereto, or be kept together in charge of proper officers;" and to permit a jury to separate over objection of the defendant, on an adjournment of the trial because of the illness of one of the jurors, is reversible error. *State* v. *Garrity*, 98 Iowa, 101, 67 N. W. 92.

The request that the jury be kept together during the trial should be made to the court, although if originally made to the judge, and afterwards ruled upon by him in court as if made in court, it will be deemed to have been made in court, and its refusal is error. *State* v. *Smith*, 107 Iowa, 480, 78 N. W. 224.

So, in Washington a statute (Code Proc. § 1311) provides that jurors in criminal cases shall not be allowed to separate except by consent of the defendant and the prosecuting attorney, and a conviction will be reversed for error in permitting the jury to separate during the trial without the defendants' consent. *State* v. *Tommy*, 19 Wash. 270, 53 Pac. 157, where the court refers to (Wash.) Anno. Statutes & Codes, § 359; Ballinger's Anno. Codes & Statutes, § 4999, as providing specially that the jury in a criminal case may separate at any time before the submission of the cause to them, under proper admonition by the court.

In *State* v. *Holedger*, 15 Wash. 443, 46 Pac. 652, it is held that although it is improper for the court to ask counsel for the accused, in the hearing of the jury, if they have any objection to the separation of the jury, such action will not require a reversal, in the absence of any showing that the accused is prejudiced thereby.

'N. Y. Code Crim. Proc. § 421 (providing that if, after hearing the charge, the jury do not agree without retiring, one or more officers must be sworn to keep them together in some private and convenient place, etc.); *United States* v. *Swan*, 7 N. M. 306, 34 Pac. 533; *State* v. *Populus*, 12 La. Ann. 710 (holding that in all criminal cases, capital and otherwise, no separation of the jury, after they have received the charge of the court, can be allowed, and such separation will vitiate the verdict); *Smith* v. *State*, 40 Fla. 203, 23 So. 854; *State* v. *McCormick*, 84 Me. 566, 24 Atl. 938; *State* v. *Parrant*, 16 Minn. 178, Gil. 157 (error to permit separation after charge; Citing Minn. Gen. Stat. chap. 114, § 13). *Contra, State* v. *Babcock*, 1 Conn. 401 (murder; immemorial usage in Connecticut to allow separation); *Kennon* v. *Territory*, 5 Okla. 685, 50 Pac. 172; Del. Sess. Laws 1895, § 31, p. 201. Compare *Com.* v. *Heden*, 162 Mass. 521, 39 N. E. 181 (holding that permission to separate after agreeing upon their verdict may be given through the officer in charge, instead of directly by the judge in open court); *Com.* v. *McCauley*, 156 Mass. 49, 30 N. E. 76 (holding that the separation of one juror from the others after a verdict has been agreed upon, but before it is rendered, is no ground for reversal, when it appears that the appellant has not been prejudiced, and he has been afforded the opportunity of offering evidence of such prejudice).

In *McFalls* v. *State*, 66 Ark. 16, 48 S. W. 492, it was held that a conviction would not be reversed because one of the jurors, with the officer in charge of the jury, retired about ten steps from where the jury were locked up, and remained away for about five minutes, during which time, in response to a question from the officer, he stated that he thought the jury would get through in two or three hours, to which the officer replied, "If you do, I will get the judge to come over, and then we may get some rest to-night."

In Iowa separation of the jury in a criminal case, even for a misdemeanor, under a mistaken belief that they are authorized to render a sealed verdict, is misconduct requiring a reversal, although they reconvene within two hours, and render the same verdict in open court. *State* v. *Fertig*, 84 Iowa, 79, 50 N. W. 545. The court, in holding the Iowa statutes regulating the supervision of the jury during their deliberation on their verdict to be mandatory, said: "That they must be so regarded is quite apparent from the fact that by § 4434 the jury may, at any time before the final submission of the cause to them, in the discretion of the court, be permitted to separate. This provision plainly implies that no separation is permissible after the cause is submitted to the jury, unless by consent."

The Washington statute referred to *supra*, in note 1, does not apply to a separation after submission of the case to the jury; and a sealed verdict in a capital case being unauthorized by law in that state, a separation of the jury during the night, after signing, sealing, and delivering their verdict to the foreman, is ground for setting aside the conviction. *State* v. *Mason*, 19 Wash. 94, 52 Pac. 525. And the point is not waived by consent of defendant's counsel to a sealed verdict. *Anderson* v. *State*, 2 Wash. 183, 26 Pac. 267.

In *State* v. *Hodges*, 45 Kan. 389, 26 Pac. 676; and *State* v. *Emmons*, 45 Kan. 397, 26 Pac. 679, it was held that no material error was committed by allowing the jury in a criminal case, by direction given in the presence of counsel and defendant without objection, to inclose in a sealed envelope a verdict agreed upon during the night and a recess of the court, and to separate until the opening of the court in the morning, and then upon the opening of the verdict to declare it to be their verdict. And that the trial court might permit the jury to separate to procure dinner after final submission of a criminal case, under Kan. Crim. Code, § 274, authorizing a new trial when a jury has been separated "without leave of the court," after retiring to deliberate on their verdict, although

§ 237 requires the jury to retire under the charge of an officer sworn to keep them together in some private or convenient place, without food, except such as the court shall order, and not permit any person to communicate with them. *State* v. *McNeil*, 59 Kan. 599, 53 Pac. 876; Distinguishing *Madden* v. *State*, 1 Kan. 340.

4. Objecting to irregularities, etc., during the trial.

If during the trial the judge learns facts satisfying him of the disqualification of a juror by having been tampered with, or by his relations to the accused, the judge may in his discretion discharge the jury; and this is no bar to a new trial.[1]

But it is error to communicate such incriminating charges to the juror in the absence of the accused,[2] and proceed thereafter to a verdict.

[1]*People* v. *Reagle*, 60 Barb. 527. *Dictum*, that the court is judge of the necessity of a discharge, which may be for a disagreement, sickness of a juror, judge, or prisoner, or for any other proper reason; and holding, in affirming an order denying a motion in arrest of judgment, that an illegal discharge for disagreement, in the absence of associate judges, is equivalent to an unauthorized separation of the jury, and no bar to a new trial.

By N. Y. Code Crim. Proc. § 429, "whenever the jury is discharged without a verdict, the reason for the discharge must be entered on the minutes."

[2]*People ex rel. Flaherty* v. *Neilson*, 22 Hun, 1. Held reversible error for the judge to ask a juror out of court, and in presence of counsel, but in the absence of the accused, to read an anonymous letter, and state whether he knows its handwriting, which charges him with having played cards with sons of the accused, but of which there is no evidence. The court said "the tendency is to dominate the juror's free will, and to terrify him into a verdict for the People."

If the facts, not having occurred in open court, do not appear on the record, they may be inserted in the case and exceptions for appeal. *People* v. *Kelly*, 94 N. Y. 526, 2 N. Y. Crim. Rep. 15.

XXXIV.—ADJOURNMENTS.

[Adjournments, or suspensions of the trial after it has been commenced, are distinguished from continuances or postponements applied for before the trial is begun, which are treated in *supra*, Division XXIV. As to admonishing jury, see *supra,* Division XXXIII.]

1. Indefinite postponement. 2. Proceeding with another cause.

1. Indefinite postponement.

Even after arraignment and plea and selection of part of the jury, it is discretionary with the trial court to permit an indefinite postponement of the cause.[1]

[1]*People* v. *Ferris,* 48 Barb. 17.

2. Proceeding with another cause.

The court has power to proceed with another cause during a proper adjournment of a trial previously commenced.[1]

[1]*Jones* v. *State,* 8 Tex. App. 648.

XXXV.—THE OPENING.

1. Prosecution has the right.
2. Scope of the opening.
3. Remedy for improper opening.
4. Defendant's opening.

1. Prosecution has the right.

In a criminal case the prosecution always has the right and the duty of opening the case and offering evidence in support of the indictment,[1] irrespective of the nature of the defense.[2]

[1]N. Y. Code Crim. Proc. § 388, subd. 1.

And it is not error for an attorney other than the regular attorney for the commonwealth to state to the jury the nature of the charge on a trial for murder. *Roberts* v. *Com,* 94 Ky. 499, 22 S. W. 845.

[2]*Loeffner* v. *State,* 10 Ohio St. 598 (holding that upon the defense of insanity, the right to open and close rests with the prosecution); *State* v. *Felter,* 32 Iowa, 49 (holding that this is so, even where the killing is not controverted. A well-considered case. Conviction affirmed. Opinion by Cole, J., 1871). See *State* v. *Schnelle,* 24 W. Va. 767, holding that the accused is not entitled to open or close to the jury.

2. Scope of the opening.

The prosecuting attorney has a right to state in his opening what facts the prosecution intends to prove;[1] but not those of which he cannot offer competent evidence.[2]

His opening may be restricted accordingly by the court, and argument excluded.[3]

[1]*State* v. *Banks,* 10 Mo. App. 111; *State* v. *Sheets,* 89 N. C. 543.

Thus, a prosecuting attorney, in opening the case, may state to the jury that the defendant made forcible resistance to the officers when making his arrest, when he expects to offer evidence to prove the fact. *People* v. *Chalmers,* 5 Utah, 201, 14 Pac. 131, 5 Utah, 274, 15 Pac. 2.

And a statement by the prosecuting attorney in the opening of a case, that he expects to prove certain things, which he afterwards fails to do, is not reversible error, if it was made with a well-founded belief in its accuracy. *State* v. *Crafton,* 89 Iowa, 109, 56 N. W. 257. To the same effect, *People* v. *Gleason,* 127 Cal. 323, 59 Pac. 592.

It is immaterial whether or not the district attorney fully states all the evidence and facts in his opening statement to the jury. *People* v. *Ellsworth,* 92 Cal. 594, 28 Pac. 604.

It is not error for the trial court in a criminal case to ask the district attorney in his opening to define to the jury the crime charged, if he defines it correctly, or correctly to instruct the jury at the commencement of the trial as to their rights and the fundamental rights of the accused. *Ryan* v. *State,* 83 Wis. 486, 53 N. W. 836.

[2]*People* v. *Hettick,* 1 Wheeler C. C. 399.

In *O'Brien* v. *Com.* 89 Ky. 354, 12 S. W. 471, it was held that a Kentucky statute (Crim. Code, § 220) providing that the attorney for the commonwealth may state to the jury the nature of the charge against the defendant, and the law and evidence upon which he relies in support of it, is not to be construed to authorize him to read to the jury writings which he subsequently intends to offer as evidence.

[3]*People* v. *Bezy,* 67 Cal. 223, 7 Pac. 643.

3. Remedy for improper opening.

The counsel for the accused has a right to interpose and object to impropriety of the prosecuting counsel in the opening, and, if the court allows him to proceed therein, to take an exception to the ruling, and to request an instruction to the jury to correct the effect of such impropriety.[1]

[1]*Walsh* v. *People,* 88 N. Y. 458, holding that an exception to the act of impropriety, instead of to the ruling, will not avail.

The purpose of the opening address is to inform the jury as to the nature of the case in hand, and while deliberate misstatements of fact calculated to prejudice the accused, and not corrected by the court, would be ground for reversal, the rule is different where facts are honestly stated with the expectation of proving them, which, through some unforeseen circumstance, counsel fails to do.

Thus, while questions as to the reversal of a conviction in a criminal prosecution, for improper statements by the prosecuting attorney, usually arise out of the closing arguments of counsel, the rule is the same at whatever stage of the case the improper language is used. *People* v. *Lee Chuck*, 78 Cal. 329, 20 Pac. 719.

And an opening address in a criminal case, made by the district attorney against objection, containing not only a statement of the evidence which it was expected would be introduced, but also a full and exhaustive argument of the case, much of which was based upon a state of facts which did not appear in the evidence,—furnished ground for reversal of a judgment of conviction. *State* v. *Williams*, 63 Iowa, 140, 18 N. W. 682.

Statements of the district attorney in opening, however, are not ground for a new trial because they remain unproved, when they are neither scandalous nor unreasonable. *Com.* v. *Mudgett*, 4 Pa. Dist. R. 739.

And a judgment of conviction in a criminal case will not be reversed because of improper statements made by counsel for the state as to what he expected to prove during the course of the trial, where the court, when objection was made, though it refused to interfere, cautioned the jury that they must not regard such statements as evidence, and should only consider what was actually proved by the evidence in the case. *Thalheim* v. *State*, 38 Fla. 169, 20 So. 938; *Sterling* v. *State*, 89 Ga. 807, 15 S. E. 743; *State* v. *Haverly* (Idaho) 42 Pac. 506; *Reynolds* v. *State*, 147 Ind. 3, 46 N. E. 31; *Baker* v. *State*, 69 Wis. 32, 33 N. W. 52. See also cases reviewed in note to *People* v. *Fielding* (N. Y.) 46 L. R. A. 657.

4. Defendant's opening.

A motion to allow the defendant in a criminal action to make his opening statement after the testimony for the prosecution is in is addressed to the discretion of the court, and a refusal to grant it is not error where no inquiry is shown to have resulted.[1]

And counsel for defendant is properly restricted from stating in his opening address matters which would be inadmissible in evidence.[2]

[1] *Cannon* v. *People*, 141 Ill. 270, 30 N. E. 1027.

And a refusal to permit counsel to make the opening statement for defendant, immediately after the prosecuting attorney had made his opening statement, without waiting until the state had offered its evidence in chief, as provided by Mo. Rev. Stat. 1889, § 4208,—is not error calling for a reversal. *State* v. *Jackson*, 105 Mo. 196, 15 S. W. 333, 16 S. W. 829.

[2] *Meyer* v. *State* (Tex. Crim. App.) 41 S. W. 632.

On a trial for crime the judge should say nothing to the defendant, when about to make a statement of his defense, which could in any manner be likely to affect his credit with the jury. *Newberry* v. *State,* 26 Fla. 334, 8 So. 445; *Perry* v. *State,* 102 Ga. 365, 30 S. E. 903.

XXXVI.—COMPELLING PROSECUTION TO ELECT.

1. Several counts on same transaction. 2. — on separate transactions.

1. Several counts on same transaction.

If the indictment contains several counts setting forth the same offense committed in a different manner or by different means,[1] or if the facts alleged in each of the several counts constitute different grades of the same crime,[2] calling for different punishments, or constitute different crimes, but relate to and form part of the same transaction,[3] it is discretionary with the court whether to compel the prosecution to elect upon which count to rely, and it is not error to refuse.[4]

[1]*Corley* v. *State,* 50 Ark. 305, 7 S. W. 255 (*dictum*).

Where there are several counts in an indictment drawn to meet the different phases of the facts that will probably be proven, the judge will neither quash nor require an election. *State* v. *Parish,* 104 N. C. 679, 10 S. E. 457; *State* v. *Phillips,* 104 N. C. 786, 10 S. E. 463.

Nor should the state be required to elect as between several counts of an information charging the same offense in different ways. *Bartley* v. *State,* 53 Neb. 310, 73 N. W. 744, 55 Neb. 294, 75 N. W. 832.

So held upon the trial of an indictment for murder, both counts of which charge the same offense, but allege that it was committed with different instruments. *State* v. *Lanahan,* 144 Mo. 31, 45 S. W. 1090.

And the district attorney cannot be compelled to elect under which count of an indictment for robbery charging in separate counts the commission of the offense while armed with a dangerous weapon, by the aid of an accomplice, and by assault and the infliction of grievous bodily harm, he intends to submit the case. *People* v. *Moore,* 26 Misc. 168, 56 N. Y. Supp. 802.

So, on a trial for seduction under promise of marriage, it is not error to refuse to compel election, where the counts all charge but one and the same offense, with such variations as are prudentially fitted to meet variations in proof. *Armstrong* v. *People,* 70 N. Y. 38. To same effect in grand larceny. *People* v. *Dimick,* 41 Hun, 616.

And in *State* v. *Norton,* 28 S. C. 572, 6 S. E. 820, where one count charged that A, with aid of B, murdered deceased by shooting, and another that B, with aid of A, did it by cutting, it was held not to be error to refuse to compel election.

In *People* v. *Willson*, 109 N. Y. 345, 16 N. E. 540, it was held no error to refuse to compel election, where "all the counts charged murder in the first degree, the only variance being as to the means used to effect death, and the manner in which it was accomplished." The court said: "This mode of pleading in an indictment is expressly allowed by the Code of Criminal Procedure, §§ 278, 279 [which see below]; and even before the Code it was held to be discretionary,"—Citing *Armstrong* v. *People*, 70 N. Y. 38; *Hawker* v. *People*, 75 N. Y. 487.

So, the state should not be required to elect between two counts in an indictment for carrying a pistol as a weapon, one of which charges that the pistol was not such as is used in the army or navy of the United States, and the other that it was such a pistol, where the indictment states that the offenses in the two counts are one and the same,—especially where the latter count is invalid for failure to allege that the pistol was carried as a weapon. *State* v. *Bailey*, 62 Ark. 489, 36 S. W. 690.

Nor is it error to refuse to require the state to elect between the two counts of an information,—one under the Kansas crimes act, § 38, and the other under § 42 of the same act, concerning assaulting or stabbing another with intent to kill, maim, or disfigure,—as the provisions are so similar and the evidence to sustain them so nearly alike that defendant could not be prejudiced. *State* v. *Douglas*, 53 Kan. 669, 37 Pac. 172.

[a]Thus, in *Hawker* v. *People*, 75 N. Y. 487, a trial for abortion, it was held not to be error to refuse to compel election between a count under the 1st and a count under the 3d sections of the statute, although different means were alleged and the different grades of offense involved different punishment, since both counts related to the same transaction. To the same effect is *Moore* v. *State*, 37 Tex. Crim. Rep. 552, 40 S. W. 287.

Nor is the prosecution to be required to elect between two counts, the one charging murder and the other manslaughter, so long as the evidence shows that they relate to the same transaction. *Kelly* v. *People*, 17 Colo. 130, 29 Pac. 805.

[a]*Looney* v. *People*, 81 Ill. App. 370; *State* v. *Schmidt*, 137 Mo. 266, 38 S. W. 938; *State* v. *Sawtelle*, 66 N. H. 488, 32 Atl. 831; *State* v. *Robbins*, 123 N. C. 730, 31 S. E. 669; *State* v. *Spencer*, 15 Utah, 149, 49 Pac. 302, and cases cited; *Hanscom* v. *State*, 93 Wis. 273, 67 N. W. 419; *Goodhue* v. *People*, 94 Ill. 37 (*dictum*); see note 1 in next section. Compare *Com.* v. *McCluskey*, 123 Mass. 401 (an indictment in two counts, each charging that defendant kept and maintained a certain tenement [a different one in each case] for the illegal sale and illegal keeping of intoxicating liquors, and the court refused to order a separate trial on each count).

Thus, on a trial for rape and assault with intent to commit it, it is not error to refuse to compel election. *Roberts* v. *People*, 11 Colo. 213, 17 Pac. 637.

And *Reed* v. *State*, 147 Ind. 41, 46 N E. 135, holds that a motion to require the state to elect upon which count of an indictment charging in different counts burglary and larceny, as permitted by Ind. Rev. Stat. 1894, § 1817, the trial shall proceed,—is properly denied.

And the prosecution need not elect between different specific acts of pretending to tell fortunes proved against the defendant, as the offense is a continuing one. *People* v. *Elmer,* 109 Mich. 493, 67 N. W. 550.

Nor between two counts in an indictment for falsely and fraudulently altering a county warrant, which are based upon the same transaction, and are the same in all respects, except as to the person or body corporate that was intended to be defrauded. *Darby* v. *State,* 41 Fla. 274, 26 So. 315.

Nor between the counts of an indictment charging larceny of a sheep and the alteration of the brand upon such sheep, as the offenses are of the same general nature, and may properly be joined in different counts of the same indictment, to meet the different phases of the evidence. *Howard* v. *State,* 108 Ala. 571, 18 So. 813.

Nor upon which count it will seek a conviction, under an indictment for aggravated assault charging in separate counts two grounds of aggravation, to wit, the use of a deadly weapon, and causing serious bodily injury. *Timon* v. *State,* 34 Tex. Crim. Rep. 363, 30 S. W. 808.

[4]The rule as enacted in N. Y. Code Crim. Proc. § 278, is thus expressed: "The indictment must charge but one crime, and in one form, except as in the next section provided."

Ibid, § 279: "The crime may be charged in separate counts to have been committed in a different manner, or by different means; and where the acts complained of may constitute different crimes, such crimes may be charged in separate counts."

And for other cases than those cited *supra,* instancing the proper refusal to compel an election, see *Gantling* v. *State,* 40 Fla. 237, 23 So. 857; *Orr* v. *State,* 107 Ala. 35, 18 So. 142; *Ellis* v. *State,* 105 Ala. 72, 17 So. 119; *Murray* v. *State,* 25 Fla. 528, 6 So. 498; *Sanders* v. *State,* 88 Ga. 254, 14 S. E. 570.

2. — on separate transactions.

If several counts respectively allege facts constituting separate and distinct felonies not forming parts of one and the same transaction, the accused has a legal right to require the prosecution to elect between them.[1]

In the absence of statute, this right may be exercised by motion at the trial, whenever the grounds for it become apparent, even if it be not till the close of the evidence.[2]

Under the New York statute the right can be exercised only by demurrer. If no objection is made till the trial, the question is discretionary.[3]

[1]*Goodhue* v. *People,* 94 Ill. 37. Where the indictment charged substantially the same act of embezzlement in three counts, but the proof tended to

show three separate and distinct acts of embezzlement committed at different times, it was held to be reversible error to overrule defendant's motion, at the close of the evidence, to compel the prosecution to elect "as to which act of embezzlement they would claim a conviction." The court said: "If two or more offenses form a part of one transaction, and are such in nature that a defendant may be guilty of both, the prosecution will not, as a general rule, be put to an election, but may proceed under one indictment for the several offenses, though they be felonies. . . . In misdemeanors the prosecution may, in the discretion of the court trying the case, be required to confine the evidence to one offense, or, where evidence is given of two or more offenses, may be required to elect one charge to be submitted to the jury; but in cases of felony it is the right of the accused, if he demand it, that he be not put upon trial at the same time for more than one offense, except in cases where the several offenses are respectively parts of the same transaction." And for other instances in which it was held that the prosecution was to be put to an election, see *Nuckols* v. *State*, 109 Ala. 2, 19 So. 504 (election between several acts of gaming); *West* v. *People*, 137 Ill. 189, 27 N. E. 34, 34 N. E. 254; *State* v. *Lund*, 49 Kan. 208, 30 Pac. 518; *State* v. *Gaunts*, 60 Kan. 660, 57 Pac. 503; *People* v. *Rohrer*, 100 Mich. 126, 58 N. W. 661; *State* v. *Farmer*, 104 N. C. 887, 10 S. E. 563; *State* v. *Bouknight*, 55 S. C. 353, 33 S. E. 451; *State* v. *Boughner*, 7 S. D. 103, 63 N. W. 542; *State* v. *Plant*, 67 Vt. 454, 32 Atl. 237.

There are cases, however, which hold that it is in the discretion of the trial court whether the prosecuting attorney shall be compelled to elect upon which count he will proceed, where separate and distinct offenses are joined in the same information. *Martin* v. *State*, 79 Wis. 165, 48 N. W. 119; *State* v. *Hodges*, 45 Kan. 389, 26 Pac. 676; *State* v. *Emmons*, 45 Kan. 397, 26 Pac. 679.

And that the court may in its discretion refuse to compel the district attorney to elect, at the close of the evidence for the state, upon which count or counts of an indictment in four counts he will proceed. *Com.* v. *Smith*, 162 Mass. 508, 39 N. E. 111.

But the prosecution should not be required to elect between different offenses committed by defendant, before evidence of the different offenses has been admitted. *State* v. *Acheson*, 91 Me. 240, 39 Atl. 570.

And refusal to require the state to elect between two counts of an information charging defendant with different offenses is not prejudicial to the substantial rights of defendant, where a *nolle prosequi* is entered as the other count. *State* v. *Bussey*, 58 Kan. 679, 50 Pac. 891.

[8]See cases in note 1, *supra*.

In *State* v. *White*, 70 Vt. 225, 39 Atl. 1085, however, it is held to be wholly within the discretion of the Vermont county court to determine at what stage of the prosecution of a trial of defendant it will compel the state to elect upon which of two or more offenses which the evidence tends to show it will rely for the conviction. To the same effect is *Schintz* v. *People*, 178 Ill. 320, 52 N. E. 903.

And *State* v. *Hurd*, 101 Iowa, 391, 70 N. W. 613, holds that the court may, in the exercise of a sound discretion, delay putting the prosecution upon its election as to which of the several acts shown by the evidence it will rely upon for a conviction, until the close of its evidence. See also *Korth* v. *State,* 46 Neb. 631, 65 N. W. 792.

But *State* v. *Gomes,* 9 Kan. App. 63, 57 Pac. 262, holds that it is error for the court to refuse to require the state to elect at the conclusion of its evidence upon what particular act it will rely for conviction.

In Mississippi a motion by defendant to compel the state to elect upon which of two counts in the indictment it will proceed is too late when made after plea, and after all the evidence is in. *Cannon* v. *State,* 75 Miss. 364, 22 So. 827.

[8] *People* v. *McCarthy,* 110 N. Y. 309, 18 N. E. 128. Manslaughter; a count in the first and one in the second degree. In this case the court said: "Separate counts were proper under certain circumstances (Code Crim. Proc. § 279), and if more than one crime was charged except as permitted by that section, the proper and only remedy was by demurrer. Code Crim. Proc. §§ 324, 331. Nor had the defendant any legal right to the instruction asked for. Such an application is an appeal to the discretion of the judge, founded upon the supposition that the accusation extends to more than one charge, and might therefore embarrass the defendant in meeting it (*Reg.* v. *Trueman,* 8 Car. & P. 727; *Hawker* v. *People,* 75 N. Y. 487); and a denial of the application cannot be successfully assigned as error."

XXXVII.—PRESENCE AND OATH OF WITNESSES.

1. Right to be confronted with witnesses.
2. — to enforce attendance of adversary's witness.
3. Requiring prosecution to call the witnesses of the transaction.
4. Statute requiring names of witnesses heard by grand juries.
5. — as to rebutting witnesses.
6. — presence of the witnesses named.
7. — omitting to call them.
8. — right of the accused.
9. Swearing witness—presence of accused.
10. — oath.
11. Exclusion of witnesses.
12. Effect of disobedience.

1. Right to be confronted with witnesses.

The right to be confronted with the adverse witnesses, which is secured to the accused,[1] is mutual; and the prosecution may claim that the testimony of witnesses for the accused can be taken only in open court,[2] subject only to the same exceptions as qualify the right of the accused in case of testimony taken in a former proceeding from a witness who is since deceased or insane,[3] and in the case of testimony taken on deposition by consent.[4]

[1]In United States courts, secured by the Constitution of the United States. *People* v. *Penhollow,* 42 Hun, 103, and cases cited. But in New York, secured by the Bill of Rights. 1 N. Y. Rev. Stat. 7th ed. chap. 4, § 14, p. 270. And in many states by the state constitutions. And see cases reviewed in note to *Gore* v. *State* (Ark.) 5 L. R. A. 833.

The going on with a cross-examination, by prisoner's counsel, during a temporary absence of the prisoner, is not fatal. *People* v. *Bragle,* 88 N. Y. 585, 42 Am. Rep. 269, Affirming 10 Abb. N. C. 300.

One accused of crime is not confronted with the witness against him, within the meaning of the Utah Constitution (art. 1, § 12) when he is compelled to sit 24 feet from the witness, so that he cannot hear her testimony or see her face, although the witness stated that she was afraid to tell because she was afraid of the defendant, and would not testify until he was removed from immediately facing her. *State* v. *Mannion,* 19 Utah, 505, 45 L. R. A. 638, 57 Pac. 542; Citing *Hopt* v. *Utah,* 110 U. S. 574, 28 L. ed. 262, 4 Sup. Ct. Rep. 202; *State* v. *Myrick,* 38 Kan. 238, 16 Pac. 330; *State* v. *Thomas,* 64 N. C. 74; *Brown* v. *State,* 38 Tex. 483; *Lewis* v. *United States,* 146 U. S. 370, 36 L. ed. 1011, 13 Sup. Ct. Rep. 136.

But the right of the accused to be confronted by the witnesses does not extend to the preliminary proceedings before the grand jury, or to other collateral proceedings. *Hussey* v. *State,* 87 Ala. 121, 6 So. 420.

So, this right does not make a report of physicians as to the mental and physical condition of an accused person inadmissible, on application for continuance. *Lipscomb* v. *State,* 76 Miss. 223, 25 So. 158.

[2]*United States* v. *Angell,* 11 Fed. 34.

A statement that the contrary principle was sanctioned in Virginia, in *Ryan* v. *Com.* 80 Va. 385, is commented on in 10 Va. L. J. 70; and corrected in 10 Va. L. J. 255.

[3]The constitutional guaranty of the right of defendant to be confronted with his accusers is not violated by the admission of the testimony of a witness for the state on a former trial, pursuant to a stipulation to that effect between the People and the defendant. *Gillespie* v. *People,* 176 Ill. 238, 52 N. E. 250; *Sage* v. *State,* 127 Ind. 15, 26 N. E. 667; *State* v. *Cushing,* 17 Wash. 544, 50 Pac. 512, Disapproving *Cline* v. *State,* 36 Tex. Crim. Rep. 320, 36 S. W. 1099, 37 S. W. 722, and Citing *State* v. *Elliott,* 90 Mo. 350, 2 S. W. 411; *Mattox* v. *United States,* 156 U. S. 237, 39 L. ed. 409, 15 Sup. Ct. Rep. 337; *State* v. *Johnson,* 12 Nev. 121; *State* v. *Wilson,* 24 Kan. 189, 36 Am. Rep. 257. See more fully as to using former testimony, *post,* Division XXXIX.

[4]*People* v. *Murray,* 52 Mich. 288, 17 N. W. 843. Written stipulation by counsel for the prisoner and for the state, for the admission of depositions in evidence, is valid, for it waives the right to be confronted with the witnesses.

So, one accused of murder waives the right to be confronted with a witness on the trial by consenting in open court to take her deposition and cross-examining her when the deposition is taken. *State* v. *Bowker*, 26 Or. 309, 38 Pac. 124.

2. — to enforce attendance of adversary's witness.

If a witness subpœnaed and examined on the part of the government absents himself during the trial, and the accused wishes to examine him, the subpœna may be called for by the accused, and process issued to bring him in.[1]

[1]*Com.* v. *Buzzell*, 16 Pick. 153, so holding in a capital case. It does not appear whether the accused wanted the witness for strict cross-examination, or to call as his own witness. Compare *supra*, § 16, Division XXIV.

3. Requiring prosecution to call the witnesses of the transaction.

If it appears by the evidence adduced by the prosecution that there are other witnesses of the transaction which the prosecution has not called, the court may, before putting the accused upon his defense, direct the prosecution to call them.[1]

[1]Wharton, Crim. Ev. § 448; and Crim. Pl. & Pr. § 565. In *Hurd* v. *People*, 25 Mich. 405, 415, Christiancy, Ch. J., said: "The prosecution can never, in a criminal case, properly claim a conviction upon evidence which expressly or by implication shows but a part of the *res gestæ* or whole transaction, if it appear that the evidence of the rest of the transaction is attainable. . . . And, according to the well-established rules of the English courts, all the witnesses present at the transaction should be called by the prosecution before the prisoner is put to his defense, if such witnesses be present, or clearly attainable. See *Maher* v. *People*, 10 Mich. 212, 81 Am. Dec. 781. The English rule goes so far as to require the prosecutor to produce all present at the transaction, though they may be the near relatives of the prisoner. See *Chapman's Case*, 8 Car. & P. 558; *Orchard's Case*, 8 Car. & P. 559, note. . . . Doubtless, where the number present has been very great, the production of a part of them might be dispensed with, after so many had been sworn as to lead to the inference that the rest would be merely cumulative, and where there is no ground to suspect an intent to conceal a part of the transaction. Whether the rule should be enforced in all cases, when those not called are near relatives of the prisoner, or some other special cause for not calling exists, we need not here determine." Approved in *Territory* v. *Hanna*, 5 Mont. 246, 5 Pac. 252, Reversing conviction. To the same effect, article in 12 Va. L. J. 425. S. P., *Donaldson* v. *Com.* 11 Pittsb. L. J. 278. *Contra*, Craig, J., in a dissenting opinion in *Lamb* v. *People*, 96 Ill. 73, 91, says the English cases cited (in *Hurd* v. *People*, 25 Mich. 416) do not sustain the position, nor do they establish any definite rule,—Citing to the contrary *Rex* v. *Simmonds*, 1 Car. & P. 84; *Rex* v. *Bodle*, 6 Car. & P. 186; *Reg.* v. *Cassidy*, 1 Fost. & F. 79.

In *State* v. *Middleham*, 62 Iowa, 150, 17 N. W. 446, holding it not error to refuse the application, the case of *Maher* v. *People*, 10 Mich. 212, 81 Am. Dec. 781, is said not to sustain the position, but only to amount to a *dictum* that when it appears that a fact has been designedly omitted by the prosecution from the series constituting the *res gestæ* or entire transaction, the court ought to require the prosecutor to show the transaction as a whole; thus not requiring the production of all the witnesses present, but simply proof of the whole transaction. See also *State* v. *Dillon*, 74 Iowa, 653, 38 N. W. 525. Compare *Reg.* v. *Ritson*, 50 L. T. N. S. 727.

In *Com.* v. *Haskell*, 140 Mass. 128, 2 N. E. 773, the court, in overruling an exception to refusal to instruct the jury that it was the duty of the prosecution rather than of the defense to call a certain witness whose absence had been commented on by the district attorney, said, "There is no law which required the government, rather than the defendant, to hold or call him as a witness."

And in *Robinson* v. *State* (Tex. Crim. App.) 57 S. W. 811, it was held no error to refuse to require the state in a prosecution for manslaughter to put on the stand all the witnesses of the homicide.

4. Statute requiring names of witnesses heard by grand juries.

Under statutes directing that the names of the witnesses upon whose testimony an indictment is found be indorsed thereon, and furnished to the accused before trial,[1] it is usually held discretionary to permit witnesses for the prosecution in chief to be sworn, whose names were not so indorsed or furnished;[2] and also those indorsed with some misnomer, if properly identified at the trial.[3]

[1]Not required in United States court in cases not capital. *United States* v. *Butler*, 1 Hughes, 457, Fed. Cas. No. 14,700.

[2]*Gardner* v. *People*, 4 Ill. 83; *Gates* v. *People*, 14 Ill. 433; *Scott* v. *People*, 63 Ill. 508; *State* v. *McClintock*, 8 Iowa, 203; *People* v. *Bobney*, 19 Cal. 426; *Keener* v. *State*, 18 Ga. 194, 63 Am. Dec. 269; *Hill* v. *People*, 26 Mich. 496.

So held upon a showing by the prosecuting attorney that he was not apprised that the person called was a material witness before the trial commenced, nor until the very time of calling him. *State* v. *Loehr*, 93 Mo. 103, 5 S. W. 696.

And *State* v. *Tate*, 156 Mo. 119, 56 S. W. 1099, holds that the fact that a witness's name was not indorsed upon the indictment is not sufficient ground for excluding his testimony.

[3]*State* v. *Stanley*, 33 Iowa, 526. *Contra*, *Smith* v. *State*, 4 G. Greene, 189.

But in *State* v. *Abrahams*, 6 Iowa, 119, 71 Am. Dec. 399, it was held that a witness who had not been before the grand jury was not to be excluded because his name was not indorsed.

Andrews v. *People*, 117 Ill. 195, 7 N. E. 265, holds that where the foreman of the grand jury fails to indorse the names of the witnesses on the back of the indictment pursuant to statute, it is fatal to the indictment. But the names of five witnesses having been indorsed, the recital, "For other witnesses see Off. Palmer," was held harmless.

The omission so to indorse, where witness testified without objection, was held insufficient as ground for new trial, in *Ray* v. *State*, 1 G. Greene, 316, 48 Am. Dec. 379.

Nor is such omission ground for quashing indictment. *Com.* v. *Williams*, 5 Gratt. 702.

Under the Michigan and Nebraska statutes a person charged with a crime upon information has a right to have the names of the witnesses against him indorsed on the information before trial. *People* v. *O'Hare*, 2 Mich. N. P. 170, holding that after the trial has actually commenced, the court has no power to order that the names of additional witnesses known before the trial shall be indorsed upon the information. See *Stevens* v. *State*, 19 Neb. 647, 28 N. W. 304; *Parks* v. *State*, 20 Neb. 515, 31 N. W. 5, holding it error for the court to permit a witness whose name was not indorsed upon the information to be sworn by the state, although the name was omitted from mere inadvertence; adding that in cases where new witnesses become known to counsel or are ascertained to be necessary after the information has been filed with such witnesses indorsed thereon as were known to him at the time of filing, it is only necessary, in order to have the names of the additional witnesses indorsed, that he should make such a showing of facts as will bring to the knowledge of the court that the prosecutor has acted in good faith, and that the additional witnesses are necessary for the due presentation of the case.

In *State* v. *Dowd*, 39 Kan. 412, 18 Pac. 483, the objection was met by allowing names to be indorsed at the trial.

5. — as to rebutting witnesses.

Such a statutory requirement does not preclude the prosecution from calling rebutting witnesses who were not named,[1] or witnesses on a collateral question first raised by the evidence of the accused, such as the question of good character.[2]

[1] *State* v. *Gillick*, 10 Iowa, 98; *State* v. *Ruthven*, 58 Iowa, 121, 12 N. W. 235. *Contra*, under Mich. Comp. Laws, § 11934. *People* v. *Casey*, 124 Mich. 279, 82 N. W. 883.

[2] *State* v. *Huckins*, 23 Neb. 309, 36 N. W. 527.

6. — presence of the witnesses named.

It is the duty of the prosecuting officer to have in court the witnesses whose names are thus furnished.[1]

[1] *Reg.* v. *Cassidy*, 1 Fost. & F. 79; *Reg.* v. *Woodhead*, 2 Car. & K. 520 (*dictum;* the point ruled being that he was not bound to call them).

7. — omitting to call them

The prosecution is not bound to call all the witnesses whose names are indorsed on the indictment.[1]

[1]*State* v. *Cain*, 20 W. Va. 679 (reviewing authorities, and holding it unnecessary, even as to a witness bound over to appear); *Bressler* v. *People*, 117 Ill. 422, 8 N. E. 62 (holding also that one so omitted by the prosecution, if called by defendant, becomes the defendant's witness); *Reg.* v. *Woodhead*, 2 Car. & K. 520; *Reg.* v. *Edwards*, 3 Cox C. C. 82 (saying, however, that while the judge has the power to interfere, he will only exercise it in extreme cases); *Territory* v. *Thomason*, 4 N. M. 154, 13 Pac. 223 (holding, on an indictment for murder, that where the prosecuting attorney has fully and fairly developed the facts by witnesses called by him before resting his case, there is no error in the court's not requiring him to call all the witnesses to conversations with the defendant who were known and present); *Reg.* v. *Cassidy*, 1 Fost. & F. 79; *State* v. *Baxter*, 82 N. C. 602.

In *People* v. *Henshaw*, 52 Mich. 564, 18 N. W. 360, it was so held of cases other than homicide, and of witnesses not claimed to be able to testify to the *corpus delicti*. And in *Wellar* v. *People*, 30 Mich. 23 (homicide), it was held error to refuse to require the prosecution to call an eyewitness whose name was indorsed. To the same effect as last case, *Territory* v. *Hanna*, 5 Mont. 248, 5 Pac. 252. But *People* v. *Hughes*, 116 Mich. 80, 74 N. W. 309, holds that the prosecution does all that is required when it calls eyewitnesses, swears them for the People, and then tenders them to the accused for cross-examination.

8. — right of the accused.

Where the prosecution declines, on request, to call a witness whose name is indorsed, it is in the discretion of the judge whether he shall be called for the prisoner's counsel to examine him, before the prisoner is called on for his defense. If allowed, the examination will assume the form of a cross-examination, but the prisoner's counsel cannot call witnesses to contradict him.[1]

[1]*Rex* v. *Bodle*, 6 Car. & P. 186 (murder).

9. Swearing witness—presence of accused.

In felonies[1] it is error to proceed to the swearing of witnesses in the absence of the accused.[2]

[1]See the general rule as shown in *ante*, Division V.

[2]*Bearden* v. *State*, 44 Ark. 331.

10. — oath.

A witness sworn before a separate trial is ordered should be resworn after such order.[1]

[1]*Babcock* v. *People*, 15 Hun, 347.

As to form of oath and the rights of the parties as to it, see 1 Abb. New Pr. 230.

11. Exclusion of witnesses.

In the absence of statute, it is in the discretion of the court, but not a matter of right to either party, to direct that any or all of the witnesses be excluded from the courtroom during the taking of evidence.[1]

[1]Greenl. Ev. § 432; 1 Bishop, Crim. Proc. §§ 1188 *et seq.;* 2 Wharton, Crim. Pl. & Pr. § 569.

Greenleaf states the rule thus: "If the judge deems it essential to the discovery of truth that the witnesses should be examined out of the hearing of each other, he will so order it. This order, upon the motion or suggestion of either party, is rarely withheld; but by the weight of authority the party does not seem entitled to it as a matter of right.

Cobb, Ch. J., in *Binfield* v. *State*, 15 Neb. 484, 19 N. W. 607, adds: "In this, also, agree all of the cases which I have been able to find, except in the cases where the matter is regulated by express statute."

And for other cases sustaining the rule as thus stated, see *State* v. *Fitzsimmons*, 30 Mo. 236; *Benaway* v. *Conyne*, 3 Chand. (Wis.) 214; *Errissman* v. *Errissman*, 25 Ill. 136; *Carson* v. *State*, 80 Ga. 170, 5 S. E. 295; *Riley* v. *State*, 88 Ala. 193, 7 So. 149; *Vance* v. *State*, 56 Ark. 402, 19 S. W. 1066; *Zoldoske* v. *State*, 82 Wis. 580, 52 N. W. 778; *Com.* v. *Follansbee*, 155 Mass. 274, 29 N. E. 471; *People* v. *Considine*, 105 Mich. 149, 63 N. W. 196.

In *Com.* v. *Hersey*, 2 Allen, 173, a trial for murder (in banc, Bigelow, Ch. J., presiding), the court, in making such an order, excepted to those subpœnaed merely as experts, and refused to direct the officer in charge to prohibit reading the newspaper accounts of the evidence.

It was not an abuse of discretion to exclude a witness from the courtroom under a rule theretofore made, after he had testified, and was not to be again put on the stand, as announced after the witnesses were put under the rule. *Com.* v. *Phillips*, 12 Ky. L. Rep. 410, 14 S. W. 378.

12. Effect of disobedience.

If a witness disobeys the order excluding him from the courtroom, he may be excluded from testifying, if the party calling him connived at his disobedience;[1] otherwise not.[2]

[1]1 Bishop, Crim. Proc. § 1191; *State ex rel. Steigerwald* v. *Thomas*, 111 Ind. 515, 13 N. E. 35.

So, the court may properly refuse to allow a witness to testify for defendant, who has remained seated by him in the courtroom during the whole trial, after the court has ordered the exclusion of all the witnesses from the courtroom. *State* v. *Gesell*, 124 Mo. 531, 27 S. W. 1101.

1 Bishop, Crim. Proc. § 1191; *Parker* v. *State*, 67 Md. 329, 10 Atl. 219 (holding it error in a capital case); *State* v. *Falk*, 46 Kan. 498, 26 Pac. 1023; *Friedman* v. *Myers*, 39 N. Y. S. R. 192, 14 N. Y. Supp. 142. And *State* v. *Moore*, 156 Mo. 204, 56 S. W. 883, holds it to be discretionary with the court whether to permit a witness to testify, though he has heard part of the testimony of other witnesses.

So, where, during a trial for murder, a witness who has been "put under the rule" enters the courtroom and hears defendant's statement, it is not error to allow the witness to testify in rebuttal. *Bone* v. *State*, 68 Ga. 105, 12 S. E. 205.

In *Webb* v. *State*, 100 Ala. 47, 14 So. 865, it was held to be within the discretion of the trial court to permit a sheriff to be summoned as a witness as to defendant's having escaped from jail while confined under an indictment for murder, although the sheriff was not put under the rule with other witnesses.

XXXVIII.—RECEPTION OF EVIDENCE.

I. Order of proof.
- 1. Each side in turn must exhaust his case.
- 2. Right of rebuttal.
- 3. Anticipatory rebuttal.
- 4. Recalling for further examination or cross-examination.
- 5. — for reiteration.
- 6. Witness not called in chief, though requested.
- 7. Receiving conditionally on promise to connect.
- 8. Precluding offer by conceding fact.
- 9. Reopening.
- 10. Adjourning to enable evidence to be had.

II. Use of indictment and plea.
- 11. Reading the indictment.
- 12. Duplicity.
- 13. Proof confined by particulars.
- 14. Inconsistent allegations.
- 15. Omission of plea—coverture.
- 16. Overruled plea.

III. Offers and objections.
- 17. Offer without putting question.
- 18. Good faith of offer.
- 19. Calling for disclosure—before swearing witness.
- 20. — before putting question.
- 21. Opening the door for oneself.
- 22. — for the adversary.
- 23. Joint defendants.
- 24. Remoteness.
- 25. Consent of accused to admit.

IV. Examination of witnesses.
- 26. Examination to test competency.
- 27. Control of court over examination generally.
- 28. — over extent of examination.
- 29. Examination by the court.
- 30. Limiting number of witnesses.
- 31. Privilege of witnesses.
- 32. — when protected from effect of disclosure.
- 33. — question for court.

I. Order of proof.

1. Each side in turn must exhaust his case.

As a general rule, he who has the opening ought to introduce all his evidence to make out his side of the issue, except that which merely serves to answer the adversary's case; then the evidence of the adversary is heard; and finally the party who had the opening may introduce rebutting evidence which merely serves to answer or qualify his adversary's case.[1]

Rebutting evidence, within this rule, means, not all evidence whatever which contradicts the defendant's witnesses and corroborates the state's, but evidence in denial of some affirmative case or fact which the defendant has attempted to prove.[2] Neither side ought to be permitted to give evidence by piecemeal. But this rule does not prevent any party who has closed his case from supporting it further by the cross-examination of his adversary's witnesses,[3] nor from using parts of documents which the adversary has put in for the purpose of using other parts against him.[4]

And the judge has discretionary power to receive evidence in chief during the rebuttal,[5] even on the part of the prosecution.[6] This discretionary power is more fully exercised in behalf of the defendant in criminal than in civil cases.

[1] *Rex* v. *Stimpson*, 2 Car. & P. 415, where a witness offered by the prosecution was not allowed to testify to the principal fact charged, after the defendant's testimony had been put in.

The Iowa Code of Civil Procedure (§ 2779), prescribing the order of presenting evidence, states the rule thus: The party having the burden must first produce his, then the other party his, and it is then said that "the parties then will be confined to rebutting evidence unless the court for good reasons, in furtherance of justice, permit them to offer evidence in their original case." And in *State* v. *Yetzer*, 97 Iowa, 423, 66 N. W. 737, holds that the same rules obtain in criminal cases, so far as applicable, citing Iowa Code, § 4556.

In *Ridgely* v. *State*, 75 Md. 510, 23 Atl. 1099, the court states the rule thus: It is for the state to prove the allegation of the indictment on which it relies, and to produce all its evidence upon the issue on trial; and then the traversers are entitled to put in all their evidence. In reply the state, according to the settled rule, is restrained "to such new points and questions as may be first opened by the defendant's evidence,"—Citing 1 Greenl. Ev. 12th ed. 467*a*.

The Nebraska statute, stating the rule substantially as stated in the text, was held in *Argabright* v. *State*, 56 Neb. 363, 76 N. W. 876, not to be imperative, and not to prevent the defendant in a proper case from impeaching a witness called by the state in rebuttal.

In Texas a statute authorizes the court to allow testimony to be introduced at any time before the arguments are concluded, if it appears necessary to a due administration of justice. And for cases in which evidence was so admitted or refused under the application of this statute, see *Lourence* v. *State*, 31 Tex. Crim. Rep. 601, 21 S. W. 766; *Rogers* v. *State*, 40 Tex. Crim. Rep. 355, 50 S. W. 338; *Garza* v. *State* (Tex. Crim. App.) 49 S. W. 103; *Toler* v. *State* (Tex. Crim. App.) 56 S. W. 917; *Griffey* v. *State* (Tex. Crim. App.) 56 S. W. 335; *Hamilton* v. *State* (Tex. Crim. App.) 58 S. W. 93.

In *State* v. *Robbins*, 109 Iowa, 650, 80 N. W. 1061, the defendant asked, but was refused, the right to open and close the case to the jury. The theory of counsel seemed to be that because the defense of insanity had to be established by a preponderance of evidence, the affirmative of the whole case was with the defendant; but the court held this not to be so, saying that the burden in such a case, as in every other criminal trial, was upon the state to establish the commission of the offense by the defendant; that the plea of insanity did not amount to a confession that the act was done by the defendant, and did not relieve the state from the necessity of proving every fact essential to make out the crime; and concluded by holding that the burden was upon the state in the first instance, and that it had the right to open and close the case.

In *Brabston* v. *State*, 68 Miss. 208, 8 So. 326, it was held that the defendant was entitled to introduce testimony in rebuttal or explanation of evidence first brought out by the prosecution after the close of the defense.

[8] *O'Connell* v. *People*, 87 N. Y. 377, 41 Am. Rep. 379; *Smith* v. *State*, 92 Ala. 30, 9 So. 408; *Ridgely* v. *State*, 75 Md. 510, 23 Atl. 1099; *Com.* v. *Goodnow*, 154 Mass. 487, 28 N. E. 677; *Stephens* v. *Com.* 20 Ky. L. Rep. 544, 47 S. W. 229; *State* v. *Reick*, 43 Kan. 635, 23 Pac. 1076; *State* v. *Case*, 96 Iowa, 264, 65 N. W. 149; *Lillard* v. *State*, 151 Ind. 322, 50 N. E. 383;

People v. *Mitchell,* 94 Cal. 550, 29 Pac. 1106; *State* v. *Nelson,* 101 Mo. 464, 14 S. W. 712; *Kastner* v. *State,* 58 Neb. 767, 79 N. W. 713; *State* v. *Webb,* 18 Utah, 441, 56 Pac. 159; *State* v. *Marsh,* 70 Vt. 288, 40 Atl. 836; *Reed* v. *Com.* 98 Va. 817, 36 S. E. 399; *State* v. *Klein,* 19 Wash. 368, 53 Pac. 364.

But it is fatal error to permit the prosecution to prove its principal case under the head of corroborating evidence. *People* v. *Hillhouse,* 80 Mich. 580, 45 N. W. 484.

[3]*Com.* v. *Eastman,* 1 Cush. 189, 48 Am. Dec. 596. *Contra,* see *dictum* in *Campbell* v. *State,* 38 Ark. 498, where, however, it was held allowable in the discretion of the court.

[4]See *post,* Division XXXIX. § 198.

[5]*State* v. *Alford,* 31 Conn. 40; *State* v. *Fox,* 25 N. J. L. 566; *State* v. *Harrington,* 9 Nev. 91; *State* v. *Haynes,* 71 N. C. 79; *Collins* v. *People,* 98 Ill. 584, 38 Am. Rep. 105; *Com.* v. *Wilson,* 186 Pa. 1, 40 Atl. 283; *Wilkinson* v. *State,* 106 Ala. 23, 17 So. 458. Compare *Jackson* v. *State,* 64 Ga. 344, where it is held that the court may in its discretion refuse to allow defendant to put in evidence in chief after the prosecution has closed rebuttal, unless an excuse for holding the witness back is shown.

[6]*People* v. *Teixeira,* 123 Cal. 297, 55 Pac. 988; *Cooper* v. *State,* 103 Ga. 63, 29 S. E. 439; *State* v. *Bruce,* 48 Iowa, 530, 30 Am. Rep. 403; *State* v. *Yetzer,* 97 Iowa, 423, 66 N. W. 737; *Leighton* v. *People,* 88 N. Y. 117; *State* v. *King,* 84 N. C. 737; *State* v. *Curran,* 51 Iowa, 118, 49 N. W. 1006; *Magee* v. *State* (Tex. Crim. App.) 43 S. W. 98, 512; *King* v. *State,* 74 Miss. 576, 21 So. 235; *People* v. *Lewis,* 124 Cal. 551, 45 L. R. A. 783, 57 Pac. 470; *State* v. *Buchler,* 103 Mo. 203, 15 S. W. 331; *Ream* v. *State,* 52 Neb. 727, 73 N. W. 227; *Com.* v. *Weber,* 167 Pa. 153, 31 Atl. 481.

In *Moore* v. *State,* 96 Tenn. 209, 33 S. W. 1046, the court said: "While orderly procedure would suggest that the state should put its whole case in evidence in chief, and receive only its rebuttal testimony to meet the case of the prisoner, yet there is no fixed or inflexible rule which would require the trial judge to reject testimony in rebuttal which more properly should have been presented in the opening of the case. This is a matter resting in the sound discretion of the court below, and unless the case should disclose an abuse of that discretion, it would not be interfered with by this court."

In *Com.* v. *Carey,* 2 Brews. (Pa.) 404, evidence of threats by the accused against the deceased was received after the defendant's evidence had been closed, upon the district attorney's stating under oath that he first heard of it after the prosecution had closed.

In *Com.* v. *Brown,* 130 Mass. 279, on a joint trial of two, after the prosecution had rested, one of them testified on his own behalf, and the court allowed his testimony to be introduced against the other.

In Kentucky the Code (§ 220) requires the commonwealth to offer its evidence in chief at the beginning of the trial; and it is error to permit the commonwealth, after the defendant has closed his testimony, to introduce in chief a witness who has been regularly subpœnaed by the commonwealth, and has told the prosecuting attorney before the trial what he could prove, and has been in the courtroom during the trial, no good cause being shown for the introduction of his testimony out of its regular order. *Oldham* v. *Com.* 22 Ky. L. Rep. 520, 58 S. W. 418. To the same effect is *Williams* v. *Com.* 90 Ky. 596, 14 S. W. 595.

2. Right of rebuttal.

The rule that a party has a right to give evidence in rebuttal which tends to meet the affirmative case, if any, sought to be established by his adversary, applies notwithstanding such evidence incidentally tends also to corroborate the party's case in chief.[1]

But evidence merely in corroboration of the prosecuting witness is not proper rebutting evidence, although he was the sole witness for the state, and the only evidence for the accused assailed his reputation for truth and veracity, and the avowed purpose of such evidence in corroboration is to sustain the character of the prosecuting witness in that regard.[2]

[1] *State* v. *Lawrence*, 70 Vt. 524, 41 Atl. 1027; *Milrainey* v. *State*, 33 Tex. Crim. Rep. 577, 28 S. W. 537; *State* v. *Jacobs*, 28 S. C. 29, 4 S. E. 799; *People* v. *Kindra*, 102 Mich. 147, 60 N. W. 458; *Reynolds* v. *State*, 147 Ind. 3, 46 N. E. 31; *White* v. *State*, 100 Ga. 659, 28 S. E. 423.

The prosecuting attorney is not bound to know or anticipate the particular lines or special grounds of defense which will be set up, but he is authorized to await their development on the trial, and then to disprove them if he can; and the fact that in the counter attack matters may be adduced which have a tendency incidentally to strengthen the state's case does not render the testimony any the less rebuttal. *State* v. *Fourchy*, 51 La. Ann. 228, 25 So. 109.

So, in *State* v. *Magoon*, 50 Vt. 333, the court says that the rule that each party must in turn exhaust his case has never "been pushed to the extreme of rejecting, in the close, testimony which legitimately tended to weaken the effect of the testimony adduced by the respondent, because it also tended to strengthen and [fully] confirm the testimony introdued in the opening by the prosecution." Thus, if the prisoner gives evidence tending to rebut the legal presumption that every man is sane, the prosecutor may produce answering testimony. *O'Connell* v. *People*, 87 N. Y. 377, 41 Am. Rep. 379 (*dictum*), Followed in *Casey* v. *People*, 87 N. Y. 158, which was reversed on another ground in 96 N. Y. 115.

[2] *State* v. *Parish*, 22 Iowa, 284.

3. Anticipatory rebuttal.

The prosecution may be allowed, as a part of its case in chief, to give evidence to rebut matter which the defense avows its intention to rely upon.[1]

[1] Thus, *Com.* v. *Grose*, 99 Mass. 423, holds that the prosecution may prove

the admissions of the defendant containing an excuse for the act charged, and then show the falsity of the excuse.

And in *Levy* v. *People*, 80 N. Y. 327, a trial of an accessory in which the record of the conviction of the principals had been given in evidence, it was held proper to receive testimony as part of the state's case tending to show the commission of the crime by the principals, because the record of the conviction was only prima facie proof of their guilt, which presumption might be controverted by the defendant, and the latter's proofs rebutted by evidence *aliunde* the record.

But in *Hellyer* v. *People*, 186 Ill. 550, 58 N. E. 245,—a murder trial in which the defense was that the deceased, who was struck by a railroad train and killed, was not killed by the defendant,—it was held error to permit the prosecution in its evidence in chief to ask a witness if a railroad train of specified weight and speed could strike and kill the deceased without producing greater injuries than those found on the body, because such a question anticipated the defense.

4. Recalling for further examination or cross-examination.

The fact that a witness has been examined or cross-examined to some extent, and the party calling him has rested his case, does not preclude allowing the witness to be recalled for further examination or cross-examination.[1]

[1]*State* v. *Clyburn*, 16 S. C. 375 (holding it no error to suspend the taking of evidence for the defense and allow the prosecution to recall a witness to prove a single fact); *People* v. *Parton*, 49 Cal. 632 (*dictum*, that it would be error to refuse to allow the defense to further cross-examine a witness for the prosecution—in this case the prosecutrix—merely because the prosecution has rested; but holding that if the request be denied and the defendant subsequently calls the witness as his own, and the cross-examination shows that he was not injured, the error may be disregarded).

This seems to be very generally held a matter of discretion with the trial judge, as instanced by the following cases: *Brown* v. *State*, 72 Md. 468, 20 Atl. 186; *State* v. *Soper*, 148 Mo. 217, 49 S. W. 107; *State* v. *Fredericks*, 136 Mo. 51, 37 S. W. 832; *State* v. *Groves*, 119 N. C. 822, 25 S. E. 819; *State* v. *Robinson*, 32 Or. 43, 48 Pac. 357; *State* v. *Johnson*, 89 Iowa, 1, 56 N. W. 404.

5. — for reiteration.

It is improper for witnesses who have testified for the state to be reintroduced to contradict the evidence for the defendant, by repeating their testimony already delivered.[1] But on a controversy as to what the testimony of a witness was, the witness may be recalled for the purpose of settling such controversy.[2]

[1]*Dillard* v. *State*, 58 Miss. 368, where it is held, however, that as the prac-

tice in receiving evidence is largely discretionary, such repetition is not reversible error, if injustice has not been done.

[3]See, for instance, *Snodgrass* v. *Com.* 87 Va. 679, 17 S. E. 238; *Lafferty* v. *State* (Tex. Crim. App.) 35 S. W. 374; *Hayes* v. *State*, 36 Tex. Crim. Rep. 146, 35 S. W. 983 (after the cause had been submitted to them, and they had once retired); and *Benfield* v. *State*, 62 Ark. 365.

Compare *Wilson* v. *State*, 37 Tex. Crim. Rep. 373, 35 S. W. 390, 38 S. W. 624, 39 S. W. 373, where it was held that the witness need not be recalled at the request of the defendant's counsel, in order to settle such a controversy, under the Texas statute leaving it with the jury to make such a request.

And where a dispute arises after the close of the argument, as to whether the offense was proved to have been committed in a certain county or not, the judge may in his discretion allow the witnesses to be recalled for the purpose of settling the dispute. *Wiggins* v. *State*, 80 Ga. 468, 5 S. E. 503.

6. Witness not called in chief, though requested.

Noncompliance with the request of the accused that the prosecution call a specified witness before the accused be put to his defense does not preclude the prosecution from calling such witness in rebuttal.[1]

[1]*United States* v. *Bennett*, 17 Blatchf. 357, Fed. Cas. No. 14,572. In this case the court said: "Whether the evidence of McGuire [the witness] was necessary to make out a case for the prosecution belonged to the district attorney to determine for himself. . . . What the defendant would testify to could not be foreseen, and when the defendant's testimony compelled the production of evidence in rebuttal, the right of the prosecution to present such evidence by the testimony of any witness able to testify to the facts is not open to question."

7. Receiving conditionally on promise to connect.

If evidence apparently incompetent only because its relevancy is not apparent, or because it is not the best evidence, is offered, the court may receive it conditionally, if counsel gives assurance that he will supply the necessary foundation afterward.[1]

[1]*McCarney* v. *People*, 83 N. Y. 408, 415, 38 Am. Rep. 456 (grand larceny; Folger, J., says: "That a court may base its action upon the avowals and declared purposes of counsel is shown by *Dunn* v. *People*, 29 N. Y. 523. It seems to us that it would too much hamper the trial courts in their proceedings if they were much restricted in the exercise of a discretion in the order in which proof should be received. There must be a discretion rested in them, in such case, for the convenience and dispatch of business, and often for a proper understanding and appreciation of the testimony"); *United States* v. *Flowery*, 1 Sprague, 109, Fed.

Cas. No. 15,122 (fitting out a vessel to engage in the slave trade; evidence that the same vessel on a former voyage carried a cargo of slaves admitted on promise of district attorney to show that the accused had knowledge of such former voyage); *State* v. *Magoon*, 50 Vt. 333 (where the court says: "The order in which testimony shall be admitted is one of practice, rather than of strict right, and may, in the discretion of the court, be varied to meet the exigencies of a given case, without error being predicable thereon, unless it is manifest that the variance has operated to surprise or in some way work a legal disadvantage to the excepting party"); *McMurphey* v. *Harvey*, 58 Vt. 549, 4 Atl. 864 (prosecution for bastardy; Taft, J., applying this rule, says: "This salutary rule has always prevailed in this state"); *People* v. *Brotherton*, 47 Cal. 388 (forgery; on the trial of two jointly indicted, the court below allowed the declarations and acts of one, made and done in the absence of the other, to be given in evidence before the conspiracy; held no error, as sufficient proof of the conspiracy was afterwards given. It is a mere matter of convenience); *Dillin* v. *People*, 8 Mich. 357 (murder; evidence that defendant's father and counsel tampered with a witness admitted on promise to connect defendant therewith afterward); *Heard* v. *State*, 9 Tex. App. 1 (forgery; receiving proof of handwriting before proof of forgery disregarded); *Contra*, *People* v. *Millard*, 53 Mich. 63, 18 N. W. 562 (holding it error not only to refuse to strike it out on failure to connect, but error to receive it on promise to connect); *State* v. *Thomas*, 99 Mo. 235, 12 S. W. 643. See also *Rushing* v. *State*, 25 Tex. App. 607, 8 S. W. 807.

In *Zell* v. *Com.* 94 Pa. 258, the court disapproves the practice.

In *People* v. *Millard*, 53 Mich. 63, 18 N. W. 562, the court, per Campbell, J., says: "In a criminal case the prosecution should be allowed no such latitude. The mischief is effected when the testimony comes in, and gives color to all the subsequent views of the jury, so that they look suspiciously upon all that is said or done by the respondent which is open to any consideration of motive." The objection here was to evidence personal to the accused before proof of *corpus delicti*.

For other illustrations, see *post*, Division XXXIX., subdivs. XII., XV., and XVIII.

8. Precluding offer by conceding fact.

A party cannot, by admitting a fact, prevent the other party from proving it by legitimate evidence.[1]

[1]*Com.* v. *Costello*, 120 Mass. 369. Admission by the defendant held not to preclude the prosecution from proving the fact admitted. See also *Com.* v. *Miller*, 3 Cush. 243; *Com.* v. *McCarthy*, 119 Mass. 354; *Com.* v. *Williams*, 105 Mass. 62. For the same point in civil cases, see Civil Trial Brief, chap. IX. § 11.

9. Reopening.

Even after both parties have rested, the admission or exclusion of further evidence is in the discretion of the judge.[1] But an exception may be taken by the accused, available if the ruling be an abuse of discretion.[2] On reopening the case the court may prescribe the extent and limits thereof.[3]

[1]*State* v. *Bussey*, 58 Kan. 679, 50 Pac. 891; *Johnson* v. *State*, 85 Ga. 561, 11 S. E. 844; *State* v. *Baker*, 36 Mo. App. 58; *Schonberger* v. *Com.* 86 Va. 489, 10 S. E. 713; *State* v. *Isenhart*, 32 Or. 170, 52 Pac. 569; *State* v. *Laycock*, 141 Mo. 274, 42 S. W. 723; *State* v. *Martin*, 89 Me. 117, 35 Atl. 1023.

So, even though the further testimony be the re-examination of the witness who has once been examined. *People* v. *Rector*, 19 Wend. 569.

But in *State* v. *Dugan*, 4 Ohio Dec. Reprint, 93, the state's request to call a witness to rebut proof of an alibi made after the closing argument had begun was refused.

In Texas the trial court may in its discretion permit evidence to be introduced after the argument has commenced. *Leslie* v. *State* (Tex. Crim. App.) 49 S. W. 73. And see *supra*, § 1. But the case cannot be reopened to allow evidence to be introduced by the state, after the arguments have been closed, and the judge has read his charge to the jury. *Williams* v. *State*, 35 Tex. Crim. Rep. 183, 32 S. W. 893.

[2]See cases cited in preceding note, for the recognition of this rule.

[3]*State* v. *Harris*, 63 N. C. 1.

In civil cases it is also held that after the taking of further evidence has been commenced a party has a right to complete it, but not to go beyond the limits prescribed.

10. Adjourning to enable evidence to be had.

It is discretionary to permit an adjournment to allow further testimony to be introduced, even after one side has partially[1] or entirely concluded,[2] or after both sides have finished.[3] But an exception may be taken by the accused, available if the ruling be an abuse of discretion.

[1]*Johnson* v. *State*, 32 Ark. 309; *Winn* v. *State*, 43 Ark. 151; *State* v. *Manuel*, 64 N. C. 601.

Defendant in a criminal action should be allowed to withdraw his announcement of ready, and continue the cause, where depositions of certain witnesses on the question of alibi are suppressed in the midst of the trial, without previous notice to defendant to which he is entitled under Tex. Rev. Stat. 1895, art. 2289, made applicable to criminal trials by Tex. Code Crim. Proc. 1895, art. 803. *Blake* v. *State*, 38 Tex. Crim. Rep. 377, 43 S. W. 107.

[2]*United States* v. *Noelke*, 17 Blatchf. 554, 1 Fed. 426.

[3]*Hill* v. *State*, 37 Ark. 395; *Taylor* v. *Com.* 77 Va. 692.

II. Use of indictment and plea.

11. Reading the indictment.

It is error to allow the indictment to be read to the jury in the course of the evidence, without instructing them that it is not evidence, and for what purpose they may properly consider it.[1]

[1]*State* v. *Hart,* 66 Mo. 208; *Mace* v. *Com.* 5 Ky. L. Rep. & J. 695.

And *Wallace* v. *State* (Tex. Crim. App.) 49 S. W. 395, holds that the slanderous language charged in an information should not be read by the prosecuting attorney to a witness for the state, during his examination.

12. Duplicity.

If the indictment contains several counts, even such that the court might require the prosecution to elect between them, the accused has not a right to require evidence offered under one to be excluded because evidence under the other has been received.[1]

[1]*People* v. *Dunn,* 90 N. Y. 104. The remedy is demurrer, or motion to compel election.

13. Proof confined by particulars.

A party who has given a bill of particulars must be restricted in his proof upon the trial to the items specified in the bill.[1]

[1]*Williams* v. *Com.* 10 Pittsb. L. J. 101; *Com.* v. *Giles,* 1 Gray, 466 (holding it error to receive other items. Merrick, J., says when it [a bill of particulars] is once made, it concludes the right of all parties who are to be affected by it, and he who has furnished a bill of particulars under it must be confined to the particulars he has specified as closely and effectually as if they constituted essential allegations in a special declaration); *State* v. *Rowe,* 43 Vt. 265. *Contra,* see *State* v. *Hill,* 13 R. I. 314 (specification of locality); *Reg.* v. *Esdaile,* 1 Fost. & F. 213 (a case where no particulars were furnished).

14. Inconsistent allegations.

Allegations in one count of an indictment cannot be used as evidence to disprove the allegations in another count.[1]

[1]*Edmonds* v. *State,* 34 Ark. 720.

15. Omission of plea—coverture.

If a woman indicted as *sole* pleads without setting up her coverture, this is prima facie evidence on the trial that she is unmarried,[1] but is not conclusive.[2]

[1]Where a woman is indicted as a *feme sole,* and pleads to the indictment,

this is prima facie evidence that she is unmarried. *Seiler* v. *People,* 77 N. Y. 411.

[2]*United States* v. *De Quilfeldt,* 5 Fed. 276.

16. Overruled plea.

A plea which has been held invalid, and superseded by the plea on which the accused is tried, cannot be read in evidence against him.[1]

And a plea which is invalid, and which has been overruled as such, cannot be read in evidence on behalf of the accused, merely because the district attorney refused to reply to it.[2]

[1]*Com.* v. *Lannan,* 13 Allen, 563, 569. So held where the plea was drawn and signed by his counsel. The court decided the question on the analogy afforded by the Massachusetts statute as to civil cases, by the rule as to demurrer, and the rule as to confessions being inadmissible if made under hope of advantage.

So held, also, of a withdrawn plea of guilty, for which a plea of not guilty is substituted with the court's permission. *People* v. *Ryan,* 82 Cal. 617, 23 Pac. 121.

[2]*Com.* v. *Lannan,* 13 Allen, 563.

III. Offers and objections.

17. Offer without putting question.

An offer of oral evidence may be refused if the witness is not present in court,[1] and circumstances indicate that the offer is not made in good faith.[2]

[1]*Robinson* v. *State,* 1 Lea, 673.

[2]*Scotland County* v. *Hill,* 112 U. S. 183, 186, 28 L. ed. 692, 693, 5 Sup. Ct. Rep. 93 (civil case).

18. Good faith of offer.

If the good faith of an offer of evidence is doubted, the court may test it by requiring some attempt to make the proof, before ruling on the offer.[1]

[1]*Peacock* v. *State,* 50 N. J. L. 653, 14 Atl. 893 (holding that where a defendant in a criminal prosecution was present at the trial during the introduction of the evidence against him, and then absented himself, evidence that his absence was the result of his insanity was competent and of right admissible; and the ruling of the trial court that his insanity could not be shown, but that acts and conversation of the defendant might be proved to show that he was in an excited condition, was injuriously

erroneous, because if good faith had been doubted the court might thus have tested it.

19. Calling for disclosure—before swearing witness.

The court may, as a condition of allowing a witness to be sworn or examined, require counsel, if able to do so, to state the substance of what he proposes to prove by him.[1]

[1]*People* v. *White*, 14 Wend. 111.

In *State* v. *Small*, 26 Kan. 209 (embezzlement), it was held not error for the court to refuse to listen to the statements of the accused's counsel as to evidence proposed to be offered by him, when the character of his questions showed the evidence to be inadmissible.

In civil cases it is well settled that if no request for disclosure be made, it is error to refuse to allow a witness to be sworn, if he is competent to testify to something, although he may be incompetent as to other things.

20. — before putting question.

If a question calls for evidence which may or may not be relevant or material, the adverse party may require that counsel state the substance of what he proposes to prove;[1] and if he refuse to do so, the question may be excluded.[2] But this rule does not apply to strict cross-examination, because a party cannot in such a case state in advance what the witness will say.[3]

[1]*Wood* v. *State*, 92 Ind. 269; *State* v. *West*, 45 La. Ann. 14, 12 So. 7; *Berneker* v. *State*, 40 Neb. 810, 59 N. W. 372; *Boykin* v. *State*, 40 Fla. 484, 24 So. 141; *Bailey* v. *State* (Tex. Crim. App.) 38 S. W. 992.

[2]For some other cases of a proper rejection of the question because of the absence of such disclosure, see *Deatly* v. *Com.* 16 Ky. L. Rep. 895, 31 S. W. 722; *Baker* v. *State*, 30 Fla. 41, 11 So. 492; *State* v. *Hermann*, 117 Mo. 629, 23 S. W. 1071; *State* v. *Yokum*, 11 S. D. 544, 79 N. W. 835; *People* v. *Shaw*, 111 Cal. 171, 43 Pac. 593.

But the court may accept the statement of counsel as to what he will show, and upon the faith thereof temporarily refuse to strike out the evidence, or admit evidence offered. *People* v. *McLean*, 84 Cal. 480, 24 Pac. 32.

[3]*Batten* v. *State*, 80 Ind. 394; *Wood* v. *State*, 92 Ind. 269.

It is error to refuse a party permission to state what he expects to elicit by questions on cross-examination which are in proper form, if the inquiry be pertinent. *Barnes* v. *State*, 37 Tex. Crim. Rep. 320, 39 S. W. 684.

21. Opening the door for oneself.

The fact that a party has called out part of a conversation without objection from his adversary does not alone entitle him to call out the residue, if what has already been proven does not appear to be relevant.[1]

[1]*People* v. *White,* 14 Wend. 111.

For authorities in civil cases, see Civil Trial Brief, chaps. IX., XV.

22. — for the adversary.

Neither party has the right to give immaterial evidence merely because his adversary has previously given immaterial evidence on the same question without objection.[1]

[1]*People* v. *Dowling,* 84 N. Y. 478 (holding it not error to exclude the prisoner's explanation of the possession of stolen goods shown by the evidence, but not within the scope of the charge in the indictment); *Coleman* v. *People,* 55 N. Y. 81 (holding that evidence that the accused has committed another offense than that charged is not rendered competent by the fact that he has, without objection, adduced evidence tending to show that he is not guilty of such other offense). *Contra, State* v. *Withan,* 72 Me. 531.

In *Ford* v. *State,* 71 Ala. 385, it was held that the party who first gave the immaterial evidence could not complain that the other was allowed to meet it. See also *Winslow* v. *State,* 92 Ala. 78, 9 So. 728, where it is held that the admission of incompetent evidence to rebut other incompetent evidence is not error.

The rule is that it is discretionary, unless the first evidence was given against objection and exception.

So, on a trial for murder, the accused cannot complain of the admission of evidence showing the details of a former difficulty between himself and the deceased, where he cross-examined the state's witnesses as to such details, and also introduced one witness to prove the same facts. *Mealer* v. *State,* 32 Tex. Crim. Rep. 102, 22 S. W. 142.

For further authorities, see Civil Trial Brief, chap. IX.

23. Joint defendants.

Where several are tried together, evidence competent for[1] or against[2] either is admissible, although incompetent and prejudicial as against another.

[1]*Com.* v. *Robinson,* 1 Gray, 555.

[2]*Brandt* v. *Com.* 94 Pa. 290.

In *Owens* v. *State,* 94 Ala. 97, 10 So. 669, it is held that one defendant is not entitled to have excluded in its entirety evidence which is admissible against his codefendant, his remedy being to ask instructions limiting its effect so as to confine its influence to the latter.

24. Remoteness.

Relevant evidence offered on behalf of the accused should never be excluded merely on the ground of remoteness.[1]

[1] *State* v. *O'Neil*, 13 Or. 183, 9 Pac. 284, 286, and cases cited.

25. Consent of accused to admit.

The consent of the accused, upon the trial, in open court, that evidence otherwise incompetent be received against him, renders the evidence admissible.[1]

[1] *Bebee* v. *People*, 5 Hill, 32; *People* v. *Ah Ton*, 53 Cal. 741. And see *State* v. *Haddon*, 49 S. C. 308, 27 S. E. 194, to the effect that it is not error to permit an answer to a question to which objection was made but withdrawn.

So, a mutual stipulation of counsel, though made on behalf of the accused by counsel assigned by the court, not chosen by himself, to admit depositions on both sides, followed by the receiving of the depositions on the trial without objection,—is a waiver of the constitutional right to be confronted with the witnesses. *People* v. *Murray*, 52 Mich. 288, 17 N. W. 843. Opinion by Cooley, Ch. J.; Sherwood, J., dissented. Cooley, Ch. J., said: "When the court has made no ruling, we can have nothing to review. This court cannot relieve a party from a criminal conviction because of his own voluntary action on the trial." Sherwood, J., dissented in an elaborate opinion, saying: "It does not appear that the respondent either signed the written stipulation or knew its contents, or himself admitted in open court that he was willing that the testimony should be read when it was presented to the jury, unless his silence shall be made to speak against him. And while I have no doubt that under certain circumstances, by his own express agreement or that of his chosen attorney, he may make a binding stipulation to waive even his constitutional right to have the testimony of witnesses against him given in open court upon the stand, still I do not think that such agreement, or the authority of the attorney designated by the court to make the same (as in this case), can be implied from his silence or his failure to object to the deposition when offered before the jury."

And an objection to documents offered in evidence is waived by failing to ask for a ruling thereon, which was reserved at the time the offer was made. *State* v. *Cavanaugh*, 98 Iowa, 688, 68 N. W. 452.

IV. Examination of witnesses.

26. Examination to test competency.

The former practice requiring objection to the competency of a witness to be taken by either examining him on his *voir dire*, or by calling other witnesses to establish the fact on which the objection rested,[1] has been modified so that, while the objection should, if known, be made before the witness has testified in chief, a party may permit the witness to be sworn in chief, and raise the objection to his competency at any time during his examination,[2] subject to the qualification that the objection be made as soon as the incompetency is discovered.[3]

Before a witness can be permitted to testify as an expert, his competency must be established by a preliminary examination,[4] and the court may, in its discretion, allow a preliminary examination in respect of his qualification before permitting him to testify.[5]

[1]This question is fully developed, and the supporting authorities cited with reference to both civil and criminal trials, in Civil Trial Brief, chap. VII.

[2]*Fisher* v. *Willard*, 13 Mass. 379.

[3]*State* v. *Crab*, 121 Mo. 554, 26 S. W. 548; *Donelson* v. *Taylor*, 8 Pick. 389.

[4]*Polk* v. *State*, 36 Ark. 117; *State* v. *Secrest*, 80 N. C. 450; *Koons* v. *State*, 36 Ohio St. 195.

Other witnesses may be called to testify as to his competency. *Mendum* v. *Com.* 6 Rand. (Va.) 704; *State* v. *Maynes*, 61 Iowa, 119, 15 N. W. 864. But not after the witness has been permitted to testify. *Tullis* v. *Kidd*, 12 Ala. 648; *Brabo* v. *Martin*, 5 La. 275. *Contra*, *Thompson* v. *Ish*, 99 Mo. 160, 12 S. W. 510; *Mason* v. *Phelps*, 48 Mich. 126, 11 N. W. 413, 837. *Laros* v. *Com.* 84 Pa. 200, holds that one expert may testify to the skill of another who has already testified, where his knowledge of such skill is derived from personal observation.

A witness cannot be asked whether he has sufficient skill and experience to give an opinion, but he should be required to state facts from which the court may determine his competency. *Eggart* v. *State*, 40 Fla. 527, 25 So. 144.

[5]*Sarle* v. *Arnold*, 7 R. I. 582; *Re Gorkow*, 20 Wash. 563, 56 Pac. 385. And see Civil Trial Brief, chap. VII.

27. Control of court over examination generally.

The trial court, in the exercise of its control of the examination of witnesses,[1] may permit testimony to be given in narrative,[2] or may require the investigation to proceed by questions and answers.[3] It should protect a witness from insults, insinuations, and attacks of counsel,[4] and should see that unnecessary, indecent questions be not asked,[5] and that some indulgence be granted to a witness who is overcome with emotion.[6] It may properly see that the witness is given a fair opportunity to answer questions asked him, and in so doing to make any appropriate explanation of his testimony,[7] and may stop his examination for a time, where it seems calculated rather to confuse the witness than to elicit the truth.[8]

[1]"The manner of examining a witness is entirely within the discretion of the court before whom the witness is produced, and that discretion must be governed in a great measure by a knowledge of the character of the witness and from his demeanor during his examination." *Brown* v. *Burrus*, 8 Mo. 26.

[2]*Northern P. R. Co.* v. *Charless*, 2 C. C. A. 380, 7 U. S. App. 359, 51 Fed. 562.

[3]*Clark* v. *Field*, 42 Mich. 342, 4 N. W. 19.

[4]*State* v. *Taylor*, 118 Mo. 153, 24 S. W. 449; *People* v. *Durrant*, 116 Cal. 179, 48 Pac. 75.

It is alike the duty of the court to protect a witness unduly dealt by, and to abstain from interference when an examination is properly conducted. *Carney* v. *State*, 79 Ala. 14.

[5]Vulgar words should never be required of a witness when the truth can be conveyed with equal clearness and accuracy in becoming language. *State* v. *Laxton*, 78 N. C. 564. And the court should not permit a young child to be asked indecent questions; although, if a competent witness, there is no impropriety in asking him as to the social intimacy of parties. *People* v. *White*, 53 Mich. 537, 19 N. W. 174.

[6]*State* v. *Laxton*, 78 N. C. 564. And the court may, when it sees that the witness is embarrassed or hesitates while testifying, caution him not to become excited, and to think over what he is going to say. *Kearney* v. *State*, 101 Ga. 803, 29 S. E. 127.

[7]*Smalls* v. *State*, 102 Ga. 31, 29 S. E. 153.

The court may properly interpose to prevent unreasonable interruption by counsel, and permit witness to complete an unfinished sentence.

[8]*Weldon* v. *Third Ave. R. Co.* 3 App. Div. 370, 38 N. Y. Supp. 206.

So, it is proper for the court to remind the witness that he is under oath, where his answers show that he is disposed to equivocate, and even to testify falsely. *State* v. *Cleary*, 97 Iowa, 413, 66 N. W. 724.

Nor does the court abuse its authority in directing an unwilling witness to stand aside for ten minutes to collect his thoughts or in calling him an unwilling witness. *State* v. *Gillett*, 92 Iowa, 527, 61 N. W. 169.

28. — over extent of examination.

The court may refuse to allow questions to be repeated which have been fully answered,[1] or to permit further examination upon matters which have been already covered,[2] and may arrest an examination which is needlessly protracted.[3]

[1]*Plew* v. *State* (Tex. Crim. App.) 35 S. W. 366; *Buck* v. *Maddock*, 167 Ill. 219, 47 N. E. 208.

[3]*Pigg* v. *State*, 145 Ind. 560, 43 N. E. 309; *State* v. *Brown*, 100 Iowa, 50, 69 N. W. 277; *People* v. *Harrison*, 93 Mich. 594, 53 N. W. 725.

[4]*State* v. *Miller*, 93 Mo. 263, 6 S. W. 57; *State* v. *Southern*, 48 La. Ann. 628, 19 So. 668.

29. Examination by the court.

The judge may in his discretion interpose of his own motion to call out legal evidence by interrogating a witness under examination,[1] or to exclude illegal evidence offered by either party, though without objection by the other;[2] or to call a witness who should be called by the prosecution.[3] But it is error in so doing to express opinions prejudicial to the accused.[4]

[1]*Hill* v. *State*, 5 Lea, 725; *Colee* v. *State*, 75 Ind. 511; *Lycan* v. *People*, 107 Ill. 423 (*dictum*, that he may recall a witness or direct a person to be called as a witness); *People* v. *Bowers* (Cal.) 18 Pac. 660 (holding that the judge may ask leading questions); *State* v. *Nickens*, 122 Mo. 607, 27 S. W. 339; *State* v. *Hargroves*, 104 Tenn. 112, 56 S. W. 857.

The trial court has power to propound pertinent and properly framed questions to a witness; but the instances are rare, and the conditions exceptional in a high degree, which will justify it in entering upon and conducting an extended examination of the witness; and the exercise of a sound discretion will seldom deem such action necessary or advisable. *Dunn* v. *People*, 172 Ill. 582, 50 N. E. 137.

Especially where the witnesses are reluctant or evasive. *State* v. *Spiers*, 103 Iowa, 711, 73 N. W. 343; *Lockhart* v. *State*, 92 Ind. 452.

And *Hopperwood* v. *State*, 39 Tex. Crim. Rep. 15, 44 S. W. 841, holds that the court should not take charge of the examination of a witness unless the occasion clearly demands it; and when it does so the same rules should be applied as to the form of questions as apply to counsel in charge of a case.

In *Cobb* v. *State* (Miss.) 23 So. 1015, the court held that there was no impropriety in the interrogatories complained of, which had been addressed by the court to the defendant's witnesses, saying that the judge "is not a nonentity." It is his duty to see that the course of the trial is according to law, and to elicit the truth. He is not powerless to ask questions, and where the questions are proper it is his privilege, and may be even his duty to ask them.

The court should not privately confer with a witness, and then ask questions to elicit the facts as to which he has made inquiry. *Sparks* v. *State*, 59 Ala. 82.

Durrett v. *State*, 62 Ala. 434; *People* v. *Turcott*, 65 Cal. 126, 3 Pac. 461; *McClure* v. *Com.* 81 Ky. 448 (holding it the duty of the court to do so. The accused was a boy without counsel); *State* v. *May*, 142 Mo. 135, 43 S. W. 637.

So, it is proper for the court of its own motion to stop a witness who is about to state what another would have done, and instruct her to state merely what was done. *Simon* v. *State*, 108 Ala. 27, 18 So. 731.

[3]*State* v. *Cain*, 20 W. Va. 679.

[4]*Lycan* v. *People*, 107 Ill. 423; *Hubbard* v. *State*, 108 Ga. 786, 33 S. E. 814.

So it is error for the court to state in the presence of the jury that a witness refuses to answer the question asked, where the witness has merely stated that he has no recollection of the matter inquired about. *Manning* v. *State*, 37 Tex. Crim. Rep. 180, 39 S. W. 118.

30. Limiting number of witnesses.

A reasonable limitation of the number of witnesses to be called to testify to a particular fact is within the discretion of the trial court.[1]

[1]*State* v. *Beabout*, 100 Iowa, 155, 69 N. W. 429; *Com.* v. *Keller*, 191 Pa. 122, 43 Atl. 198; *State* v. *Carter*, 51 La. Ann. 422, 25 S. W. 385; *State* v. *Lamb*, 141 Mo. 298, 42 S. W. 827. And see Civil Trial Brief, chap. VII.

31. Privilege of witnesses.

It is the privilege of a witness to refuse to answer any question, where his answer will expose him to a criminal charge,[1] or will subject him to a penalty or forfeiture,[2] or will furnish an essential link in the chain of evidence establishing his liability.[3] But the privilege will not sustain him in his refusal to answer a question because his answer will expose him to a civil suit or liability,[4] nor because his answer will degrade or disgrace him, unless the evidence sought is immaterial to the issue.[5]

The privilege is personal to the witness,[6] unless the question is not pertinent,[7] but may be waived by him;[8] and a party cannot avail himself of the court's erroneous refusal to allow it.[9] A witness cannot claim his privilege as an excuse for his refusal to be sworn, but can only avail himself of it when an objectionable question is asked.[10]

The court may properly instruct the witness as to his privilege, when he appears in need of instruction, and it may even be his duty to do so.[11]

[1]*Burger* v. *State*, 83 Ala. 36, 3 So. 319; *Ex parte Clarke*, 103 Cal. 352, 37 Pac. 230; *Short* v. *State*, 4 Harr. (Del.) 568; *Ex parte Senior*, 37 Fla. 1, 32 L. R. A. 133, 19 So. 652; *Emery* v. *State*, 101 Wis. 627, 78 N. W. 145; *State* v. *Crittenden*, 38 La. Ann. 448; *State* v. *Talbott*, 73 Mo. 357; *Wallace* v. *State*, 41 Fla. 547, 26 So. 713; *Guy* v. *State*, 90 Md. 29, 44 Atl. 997.

It is not necessary that the witness claim his privilege, where the question is so framed that a responsive answer prima facie tends to criminate him. *Alston* v. *State*, 109 Ala. 51, 20 So. 81, and cases cited.

That a witness will be subjected to a criminal charge, however punishable, is clearly a sufficient ground for claiming the protection. See authorities reviewed in note to *Cooper* v. *State* (Ala.) 4 L. R. A. 766.

[2]*Com.* v. *Willard*, 22 Pick. 476.

[3]*Minters* v. *People*, 139 Ill. 363, 29 N. E. 45; *Stevens* v. *State*, 50 Kan. 712, 32 Pac. 350; *People* v. *Mather*, 4 Wend. 229, 21 Am. Dec. 122.

That a witness may refuse an answer to every incidental fact which might form the link in the chain of evidence establishing his liability to pain, penalty, or forfeiture, see note to *Rice* v. *Rice* (N. J. Eq.) 11 L. R. A. 591.

[4]*Com.* v. *Thurston*, 7 J. J. Marsh. 62; *Re Kip*, 1 Paige, 601. And see Civil Trial Brief, chap. VII.

[5]*Ex parte Rowe*, 7 Cal. 184; *State* v. *Pugsley*, 75 Iowa, 742, 38 N. W. 498; *Clementine* v. *State*, 14 Mo. 112; *Lohman* v. *People*, 1 N. Y. 385, 49 Am. Dec. 340; *Howel* v. *Com.* 5 Gratt. 664. *Contra*, *Taylor* v. *State*, 83 Ga. 647, 10 S. E. 442.

In Texas the irrelevancy of the question does not justify the refusal of the witness to answer. *Crockett* v. *State*, 40 Tex. Crim. Rep. 173, 49 S. W. 392.

[6]*Ex parte Senior*, 37 Fla. 1, 32 L. R. A. 133, 19 So. 652; *State* v. *Butler*, 47 S. C. 25, 24 S. E. 991; *Mitchell* v. *Com.* 12 Ky. L. Rep. 254, 14 S. W. 489; *State* v. *Wentworth*, 65 Me. 234, 20 Am. Rep. 688; *Com.* v. *Shaw*, 4 Cush. 594, 50 Am. Dec. 813; *State* v. *Foster*, 23 N. H. 348, 55 Am. Dec. 191; *Ingalls* v. *State*, 48 Wis. 647, 4 N. W. 785.

The privilege may be claimed by counsel where the witness is a party. *People* v. *Brown*, 72 N. Y. 571, 28 Am. Rep. 183. *Contra*, *State* v. *Kent*, 5 N. D. 516, *sub nom.* *State* v. *Pancoast*, 35 L. R. A. 518, 67 N. W. 1052.

In *Bolen* v. *People*, 184 Ill. 338, 56 N. E. 408, it was insisted that the court erred in refusing to inform the prosecuting witness that she need not answer questions put to her if such answers would incriminate her or add a link in the chain of evidence to convict her of any crime. But the court said: "A witness is not bound to answer questions which may form an essential link in the chain of evidence which will be sufficient to convict him of a crime. This right to refuse to answer questions which will criminate him is a privilege of which the witness may avail himself, or he may waive it. The right to claim the privilege is one resting with the witness alone, and his failure to claim his privilege cannot inure to the benefit of the defendant in a case, and is no ground for complaint by him. The right exists with the witness to inquire of the court the extent of his right to refuse, and when such inquiry is made by the witness, it is the duty of the court to inform him as to the extent of his rights and privilege; but it is not a matter which in any manner concerns the defendant or his counsel, and he has no right to assign error for the same."

[7]*Sharon* v. *Sharon*, 79 Cal. 633, 22 Pac. 26, 131; *South Bend* v. *Hardy*, 98 Ind. 583, 49 Am. Rep. 792.

[8]A witness who discloses part of the transaction with which he was crimin-

ally concerned, without claiming his privilege, must disclose the whole. *People* v. *Freshour*, 55 Cal. 375; *State* v. *Fay*, 43 Iowa, 651; *Com.* v. *Pratt*, 126 Mass. 462; *State* v. *Foster*, 23 N. H. 348, 55 Am. Dec. 191; *Foster* v. *People*, 18 Mich. 276; *Lockett* v. *State*, 63 Ala. 5; *Ex parte Senior*, 37 Fla. 1, 32 L. R. A. 133, 19 So. 652; *State* v. *Hall*, 20 Mo. App. 397.

A waiver must be knowingly and understandingly made, and no advantage be taken of the witness's ignorance. *United States* v. *Bell*, 81 Fed. 830; *Emery* v. *State*, 101 Wis. 627, 78 N. W. 145.

And a waiver is not binding upon the witness on a subsequent trial. *Emery* v. *State*, 101 Wis. 627, 78 N. W. 145.

And a disclosure made long before the trial cannot be relied upon as a waiver. *Samuel* v. *People*, 164 Ill. 379, 45 N. E. 728.

[9]*Samuel* v. *People*, 164 Ill. 379, 45 N. E. 728. *Dictum* to the contrary in *Com.* v. *Kimball*, 24 Pick. 366.

[10]*Ex parte Stice*, 70 Cal. 51, 11 Pac. 459; *Re Eckstein*, 148 Pa. 509, 24 Atl. 63. *Contra*, *Neale* v. *Coningham*, 1 Cranch. C. C. 76, Fed. Cas. No. 16,067.

[11]*Emery* v. *State*, 101 Wis. 627, 78 N. W. 145.

32. — when protected from effect of disclosure.

A witness cannot claim his privilege where the prosecution to which his answers will expose him is barred by the statute of limitations,[1] nor where he has been pardoned[2] or convicted[3] of the offense.[4] But neither a promise of the attorney general not to prosecute nor an equitable right to executive pardon[5] if a witness states fully and fairly all the truth will deprive him of his privilege.

Several courts of last resort have decided that no statute can deprive a witness of his constitutional privilege, unless it affords absolute immunity from the prosecution for the offense to which the incriminating question relates.[6] But there is equally high authority for the proposition that the privilege may be lawfully denied where the subsequent use of his testimony against the witness is prohibited.[7]

[1]*Calhoun* v. *Thompson*, 56 Ala. 166, 28 Am. Rep. 754; *Druggist Cases*, 85 Tenn. 449, 3 S. W. 490; *Floyd* v. *State*, 7 Tex. 215.

[2]*Brown* v. *Walker*, 161 U. S. 591, 40 L. ed. 819, 5 Inters. Com. Rep. 369, 16 Sup. Ct. Rep. 644.

[3]*Lothrop* v. *Roberts*, 16 Colo. 250, 27 Pac. 698.

[4]*Muller* v. *State*, 11 Lea, 18.

[5]*Ex parte Irvine*, 74 Fed. 954.

[6]*Counselman* v. *Hitchcock*, 142 U. S. 547, 35 L. ed. 1110, 3 Inters. Com. Rep. 816, 12 Sup. Ct. Rep. 195; *Emery's Case*, 107 Mass. 172, 9 Am. Rep. 22; *Cullen* v. *Com.* 24 Gratt. 624; *Ex parte Clarke*, 103 Cal. 352, 37 Pac. 230.

A statute affording such a complete immunity will deprive the witness of his privilege. *State* v. *Nowell*, 58 N. H. 314; *People* v. *Sharp*, 107 N. Y. 427, 14 N. E. 319; *Floyd* v. *State*, 7 Tex. 215; *Kendrick* v. *Com.* 78 Va. 493; *Ex parte Cohen*, 104 Cal. 524, 26 L. R. A. 423, 38 Pac. 364.

[7]*State* v. *Quarles*, 13 Ark. 307; *Re Buskett*, 106 Mo. 602, 14 L. R. A. 407, 17 S. W. 753.

For the effect of statutes prohibiting the use of testimony against the witness, see notes to *Re Buskett* (Mo.) 14 L. R. A. 407, and *United States* v. *James* (D. C. N. D. Ill.) 26 L. R. A. 418.

33. — question for court.

Whether any direct answer to the question can reasonably have a tendency to incriminate the witness is a question to be determined by the court, from all the circumstances of the case,[1] and the sworn statement of the witness that such will be the effect is not conclusive.[2] The danger to be apprehended must be real and appreciable,[3] but the privilege should be recognized and protected, where it is not clearly manifest that the answer called for can have no incriminating tendency.[4] The witness must be the judge of the effect of the particular answer which he must give,[5] and cannot be compelled to show how this effect is produced, since such a course would render his privilege valueless.[6]

[1]*Stevens* v. *State*, 50 Kan. 712, 32 Pac. 350; *Ex parte Irvine*, 74 Fed. 954; *Com.* v. *Bell*, 145 Pa. 374, 22 Atl. 641, 644; *Kirschner* v. *State*, 9 Wis. 140.

[2]*State* v. *Duffy*, 15 Iowa, 425.

The court should not, in such a case, compel the witness to testify, unless it clearly appears that he is mistaken. *Chamberlain* v. *Willson*, 12 Vt. 491, 36 Am. Dec. 356; *Temple* v. *Com.* 75 Va. 892.

[3]*State* v. *Thaden*, 43 Minn. 253, 45 N. W. 447.

[4]*People ex rel. Taylor* v. *Forbes*, 143 N. Y. 219, 38 N. E. 303; *Janvrin* v. *Scammon*, 29 N. H. 280.

[5]*Ward* v. *State*, 2 Mo. 120, 22 Am. Dec. 449; *Richman* v. *State*, 2 G. Greene, 532; *Kirschner* v. *State*, 9 Wis. 140; *Com.* v. *Braynard*, Thatcher C. C. 146; *Warner* v. *Lucas*, 10 Ohio, 336.

[6]*Ex parte Irvine*, 74 Fed. 954; *Merluzzi* v. *Gleeson*, 59 Md. 214; *People* v. *Mather*, 4 Wend. 229, 21 Am. Dec. 122; *Kirschner* v. *State*, 9 Wis. 140.

34. Expert's refusal to testify unless specially compensated.

It has been held that a physician or surgeon cannot be compelled to testify as an expert unless specially compensated.[1] But the weight of authority is to the effect that while he cannot be compelled to make any preliminary preparation without extra compensation, he cannot for that reason refuse to give such information as he already possesses.[2]

Webb v. *Page*, 1 Car. & K. 23; *Buchman* v. *State*, 59 Ind. 1, 26 Am. Rep. 75; *United States* v. *Howe*, 12 Cent. L. J. 193. *Dictum* to same effect in *People* v. *Montgomery*, 13 Abb. Pr. N. S. 207; *Re Roelker*, 1 Sprague, 276, Fed Cas. No. 11,995.

The effect of the decision in *Buchman* v. *State*, 59 Ind. 1, 26 Am. Rep. 75, has been nullified in Indiana by a legislative enactment evidently intended to meet this decision. See Horner's (Ind.) Stat. 1896, § 504.

And for an extended discussion of the compensation of expert witnesses, see note to *Flinn* v. *Prairie County* (Ark.) 27 L. R. A. 669. And as to the right of the state to require service of witnesses without compensation, see note to *Dixon* v. *People* (Ill.) 39 L. R. A. 116.

[2]*Ex parte Dement*, 53 Ala. 389, 25 Am. Rep. 611; *Flinn* v. *Prairie County*, 60 Ark. 204, 27 L. R. A. 669, 29 S. W. 459; *Dixon* v. *People*, 168 Ill. 179, 39 L. R. A. 116, 48 N. E. 108; *State* v. *Teipner*, 36 Minn. 535, 32 N. W. 678; *Summers* v. *State*, 5 Tex. App. 365, 32 Am. Rep. 573.

35. Questions generally.

Each question put to a witness need not be so comprehensive that the answer when taken alone shall be evidence of some issue in the cause. That the answer will be a link in the chain of proof is sufficient to render the question relevant.[1] The relevancy of preliminary questions need not be apparent when asked, where the answers lead up to or connect with testimony subsequently introduced.[2]

General questions touching a cause and the various issues involved are not objectionable,[3] unless asked in such a general way that no intelligent answer can be given.[4]

A compound question, only a part of which is proper, may rightfully be excluded as a whole;[5] and the court may, in its discretion, refuse to allow questions which are argumentative and apparently intended more to affect the jury by the form of the question than by the answer of the witness,[6] or which are so skilfully framed as to call out certain facts and exclude others connected with the same transaction.[7]

The admission of a proper question is not error because the witness misunderstands it or gives an improper answer,[8] and if no improper testimony is in fact given, the allowance of improper questions is immaterial.[9]

[1]*Atchison, T. & S. F. R. Co.* v. *Stanford*, 12 Kan. 354, 15 Am. Rep. 362; *Schuchardt* v. *Allen*, 1 Wall. 359, 17 L. ed. 642.

But to render a question, in itself apparently irrelevant, proper to be asked as a link in a chain of evidence, it must be accompanied with a proposal to follow it up at the proper time by proof of other facts which, if true, will make the question relevant. *Wyngert* v. *Norton*, 4 Mich. 286.

[2]*State* v. *Kent*, 5 N. D. 516, *sub nom. State* v. *Pancoast*, 35 L. R. A. 518, 67 N. W. 1052.

[3]*Mann* v. *State*, 23 Fla. 610, 3 So. 207.

[4]*Ferguson* v. *Moore*, 98 Tenn. 342, 39 S. W. 341.

[5]*George* v. *Norris*, 23 Ark. 121; *Wyman* v. *Gould*, 47 Me. 159; *Whiteford* v. *Burckmyer*, 1 Gill, 127, 39 Am. Dec. 640; *United States Sugar Ref. Co.* v. *Providence Steam & Gaspipe Co.* 10 C. C. A. 422, 18 U. S. App. 603, 62 Fed. 375.

[6]*State* v. *Leuth*, 5 Ohio C. C. 94.

[7]*Tyler* v. *Waddingham*, 58 Conn. 375, 8 L. R. A. 657, 20 Atl. 335.

[8]*Foster* v. *Dickerson*, 64 Vt. 233, 24 Atl. 253.

[9]*State* v. *Tippet*, 94 Iowa, 646, 63 N. W. 445; *State* v. *Merriman*, 34 S. C. 16, 12 S. E. 619; *Cochran* v. *United States*, 157 U. S. 286, 39 L. ed. 704, 15 Sup. Ct. Rep. 628.

36. — assuming facts not proved.

It is no objection to a question that it assumes facts as true which are not in dispute,[1] but a question which assumes the existence of a fact not shown by any evidence,[2] or which erroneously assumes a statement to have been made by the witness,[3] is properly excluded. After a witness has testified positively to a fact there is no reason why counsel should not formulate questions to be propounded to him on the theory that his testimony already given is true.[4]

[1]*Robinson* v. *Craver*, 88 Iowa, 381, 55 N. W. 492; *Willey* v. *Portsmouth*, 35 N. H. 303; *Hardcastle* v. *Heine*, 25 Misc. 146, 54 N. Y. Supp. 169; *Hays* v. *State* (Tex. Crim. App.) 20 S. W. 361.

[2]*Hine's Appeal*, 68 Conn. 551, 37 Atl. 384; *People* v. *Lange*, 90 Mich. 454, 51 N. W. 534; *Drake* v. *State*, 53 N. J. L. 23, 20 Atl. 747; *People* v. *Mather*, 4 Wend. 229, 21 Am. Dec. 122; *Klock* v. *State*, 60 Wis. 574, 19 N. W. 543.

A question which assumes a fact may be allowed when asked for the sole purpose of calling a witness's attention to the subject of his testimony. *Boothby* v. *Brown*, 40 Iowa, 104.

[3]*People* v. *Fong Ah Sing*, 70 Cal. 8, 11 Pac. 323; *People* v. *Brow*, 90 Hun, 509, 35 N. Y. Supp. 1009.

[4]*Barndt* v. *Frederick*, 78 Wis. 1, 11 L. R. A. 199, 47 N. W. 6.

37. — calling for expert opinions.

While some discretion as to the form of questions to be asked of an expert witness on direct examination[1] is confided to the trial judge,[2] any question being proper which will elicit an opinion as to the matter of skill or science in controversy, and at the same time exclude any opinion as to the effect of the evidence in establishing controverted facts,[3] such questions must be framed hypothetically unless the facts are admitted or undisputed, or the witness is personally acquainted with them.[4]

It is generally deemed improper to request an expert to give his opinion based upon his recollection of the testimony, without incorporating the testimony in the question,[5] especially if the evidence is conflicting.[6] But where the evidence is brief, clear, and uncontroverted, it is not improper to require the expert to give his opinion based on the assumption that such evidence is true.[7] And where a witness testifies to the particular facts on which the expert, who follows the witness while the facts are fresh in the minds of the jury, is to base his opinion, these facts need not be again stated in the question unless there is some doubt whether they are understood.[8]

[1]For cross-examination of experts, see *infra*, § 45.

[2]*Roraback* v. *Pennsylvania Co.* 58 Conn. 292, 20 Atl. 465.

[3]*Hunt* v. *Lowell Gaslight Co.* 8 Allen, 169, 85 Am. Dec. 697.

[4]*Craig* v. *Noblesville & S. C. Gravel Road Co.* 98 Ind. 109; *Chicago & A. R. Co.* v. *Glenny*, 175 Ill. 238, 51 N. E. 896; *State* v. *Maier*, 36 W. Va. 757, 15 S. E. 991.

When the facts are admitted or undisputed, the witness may be asked as to the conclusions to be drawn from them. *M'Naghten's Case*, 10 Clark & F. 200; *Coyle* v. *Com.* 104 Pa. 117; *Page* v. *State*, 61 Ala. 16; *State* v. *Klinger*, 46 Mo. 224.

The question need not be framed hypothetically where the witness is personally acquainted with the facts. *Brown* v. *Huffard*, 69 Mo. 305; *Bellefontaine & I. R. Co.* v. *Bailey*, 11 Ohio St. 333; *Mercer* v. *Vose*, 67 N. Y. 56; *Niendorff* v. *Manhattan R. Co.* 4 App. Div. 46, 38 N. Y. Supp. 690; *Boardman* v. *Woodman*, 47 N. H. 120. But the witness must state to the jury all the facts within his knowledge upon which his opinion is based. *Burns* v. *Barenfield*, 84 Ind. 43; *Dickinson* v. *Barber*, 9 Mass. 227, 6 Am. Dec. 58; *Hitchcock* v. *Burgett*, 38 Mich. 501; *People* v. *Strait*, 148 N. Y. 566, 42 N. E. 1045.

[5]The only safe rule in allowing an expert witness to give his opinion based upon testimony of others is to require the assumed facts upon which the opinion is desired to be stated hypothetically. *Craig* v. *Noblesville & S. C. Gravel Road Co.* 98 Ind. 109; *Stoddard* v. *Winchester*, 157 Mass. 567, 32 N. E. 948; *Reed* v. *State*, 62 Miss. 405; *Link* v. *Sheldon*, 136 N. Y. 1, 32 N. E. 696; *State* v. *Bowman*, 78 N. C. 509; *McMechen* v. *McMechen*, 17 W. Va. 683, 41 Am. Rep. 682; *Dexter* v. *Hall*, 15 Wall. 9, 21 L. ed. 73. *Contra, dictum*, in *Polk* v. *State*, 36 Ark. 117; *Howland* v. *Oakland Consol. Street R. Co.* 110 Cal. 513, 42 Pac. 983; *Jones* v. *Chicago, St. P. M. & O. R. Co.* 43 Minn. 279, 45 N. W. 444. But these, as well as the following cases, which seem to announce a contrary rule, are generally dis-

tinguishable on the ground that there was no conflict of evidence. *State* v. *Windsor*, 5 Harr. (Del.) 513; *Schneider* v. *Manning*, 121 Ill. 376, 12 N. E. 267; *Jerry* v. *Townshend*, 9 Md. 145; *Getchell* v. *Hill*, 21 Minn. 464; *Gilman* v. *Strafford*, 50 Vt. 723; *Wright* v. *Hardy*, 22 Wis. 348.

[6]An expert cannot be asked to give his opinion based upon conflicting testimony (*Gunter* v. *State*, 83 Ala. 96, 3 So. 600; *Pyle* v. *Pyle*, 158 Ill. 289, 41 N. E. 999; *Bishop* v. *Spining*, 38 Ind. 143; *Armendaiz* v. *Stillman*, 67 Tex. 458, 3 S. W. 678; *Allen* v. *Union P. R. Co.* 7 Utah, 239, 26 Pac. 297; *Livingston* v. *Com.* 14 Gratt. 592; *Luning* v. *State*, 2 Pinney, 215, 50 Am. Dec. 153); even though the question assumes the truth of the entire evidence (*Smith* v. *Hickenbottom*, 57 Iowa, 733, 11 N. W. 664; *Woodbury* v. *Obear*, 7 Gray, 467; *Kempsey* v. *McGinniss*, 21 Mich. 123; *Coyle* v. *Com.* 104 Pa. 117).

[7]*Atchison, T. & S. F. R. Co.* v. *Brassfield*, 51 Kan. 167, 32 Pac. 814; *Hunt* v. *Lowell Gaslight Co.* 8 Allen, 169, 85 Am. Dec. 697; *Yardley* v. *Cuthbertson*, 108 Pa. 395, 56 Am. Rep. 218, 1 Atl. 765; *State* v. *Hayden*, 51 Vt. 296; *Abbott* v. *Dwinnell*, 74 Wis. 514, 43 N. W. 496.

[8]*State* v. *Watson*, 81 Iowa, 380, 46 N. W. 868.

38. Hypothetical questions.

The facts assumed in a hypothetical question as the basis for an expert opinion must have some support in the evidence.[1] The question need not embrace all the facts in evidence,[2] though it must not exclude from the expert's consideration a material fact essential to an intelligent opinion.[3]

The question may be based upon the hypothesis of the truth of all the evidence, or upon a hypothesis specially framed on certain facts which the evidence tends to establish,[4] and, if within the probable or possible range of the evidence, is unobjectionable.[5] Whether or not the facts assumed are true or are established by the evidence is for the jury to determine,[6] and constitutes no available objection to the question.[7]

The question may be based in part upon the expert's personal examination and knowledge,[8] but the opinions of other expert witnesses should not be incorporated in it.[9]

While long hypothetical questions which ask the witness to usurp the functions of the jury, and involve many distinct facts and elements, are objectionable,[10] their length must necessarily depend upon the nature of the inquiry and the number of particulars which must be considered, and must rest largely in the discretion of the court.[11]

[1]*Bostic* v. *State*, 94 Ala. 45, 10 So. 602; *People* v. *Dunne*, 80 Cal. 34, 21 Pac. 1130; *State* v. *Scott*, 41 Minn. 365, 43 N. W. 62; *People* v. *Harris*, 136 N. Y. 423, 33 N. E. 65; *State* v. *Anderson*, 10 Or. 448.

Hypothetical questions are proper where they are directed to the effect of certain conditions, some of which, although not shown to exist in the particular case, are shown to be caused by the same general principles. *Kraatz* v. *Brush Electric Light Co.* 82 Mich. 457, 46 N. W. 787.

It is not reversible error to permit an expert witness to answer a hypothetical question assuming a fact unsupported by the evidence, where this fact is the only hypothesis of the question. *Hewitt* v. *Eisenbart,* 36 Neb. 794, 55 N. W. 252.

A hypothetical question cannot be based upon the assumption of the truth of extracts read by counsel from a medical treatise. *Re Mason,* 60 Hun, 46, 14 N. Y. Supp. 434.

[a]*People* v. *Durrant,* 116 Cal. 179, 48 Pac. 75; *Goodwin* v. *State,* 96 Ind. 550; *Coyle* v. *Com.* 104 Pa. 117.

The reason is that if, in the opinion of counsel, there is other evidence proper for the witness to consider, his attention may be called to it on cross-examination. *Davidson* v. *State,* 135 Ind. 254, 34 N. E. 972.

If there is no dispute as to the facts on which the witness is to base his opinion, it is proper to require that the question shall embrace them all. *Davis* v. *State,* 35 Ind. 496, 9 Am. Rep. 760. The question must fully and fairly reflect the facts (*Briggs* v. *Minneapolis Street R. Co.* 52 Minn. 36, 53 N. W. 1019; *Prentis* v. *Bates,* 88 Mich. 567, 50 N. W. 637; *Burgo* v. *State,* 26 Neb. 639, 42 N. W. 701; *Fisher* v. *Monroe,* 2 Misc. 326, 21 N. Y. Supp. 995), and the omission from the question of facts in evidence renders it improper, where by reason of such omission it manifestly fails to present the facts which it does include in their just and true relation (*Barber's Appeal,* 63 Conn. 393, 22 L. R. A. 90, 27 Atl. 973).

[b]*Senn* v. *Southern R. Co.* 108 Mo. 142, 18 S. W. 1007; *Vosburg* v. *Putney,* 80 Wis. 523, 14 L. R. A. 226, 50 N. W. 403; *Western Assur. Co.* v. *J. H. Mohlman Co.* 40 L. R. A. 561, 28 C. C. A. 157, 51 U. S. App. 577, 83 Fed. 811.

[c]*Gottlieb* v. *Hartman,* 3 Colo. 53; *Cole* v. *Fall Brook Coal Co.* 159 N. Y. 59, 53 N. E. 670.

In propounding hypothetical questions, counsel may assume any state of facts which there is evidence tending to prove. *People* v. *Hill,* 116 Cal. 562, 48 Pac. 711; *Jordan* v. *People,* 19 Colo. 417, 36 Pac. 218; *Barber's Appeal,* 63 Conn. 393, 22 L. R. A. 90, 27 Atl. 973; *Baker* v. *State,* 30 Fla. 41, 11 So. 492; *Louisville, N. A. & C. R. Co.* v. *Wood,* 113 Ind. 544, 14 N. E. 572, 16 N. E. 197; *Manatt* v. *Scott,* 106 Iowa, 203, 76 N. W. 717; *Peterson* v. *Chicago, M. & St. P. R. Co.* 38 Minn. 511, 39 N. W. 485; *Smith* v. *Chicago & A. R. Co.* 119 Mo. 246, 23 S. W. 784; *Omaha & R. Valley R. Co.* v. *Brady,* 39 Neb. 27, 57 N. W. 767; *Filer* v. *New York C. R. Co.* 49 N. Y. 42, 10 Am. Rep. 327; *Kerr* v. *Lunsford,* 31 W. Va. 659, 2 L. R. A. 688, 8 S. E. 493; *Tebo* v. *Augusta,* 90 Wis. 405, 63 N. W. 1045; *Sigafus* v. *Porter,* 28 C. C. A. 443, 51 U. S. App. 693, 84 Fed. 430.

It is sufficient if the facts hypothecated be proved by some witness, although not proved to a certainty, or with any degree of certainty. *Baxter* v. *Knox,* 19 Ky. L. Rep. 1973, 44 S. W. 972. But a party cannot, however, introduce contradictory evidence upon a given point, and base hypothetical questions upon the theory that some of the witnesses are correct and some mistaken. *Prentis* v. *Bates*, 88 Mich. 567, 50 N. W. 637.

[5]*Jackson* v. *Burnham*, 20 Colo. 532, 39 Pac. 577; *Powers* v. *Kansas City*, 56 Mo. App. 573; *Harnett* v. *Garvey*, 66 N. Y. 641.

[6]*Gottlieb* v. *Hartman*, 3 Colo. 53; *Louisville, N. A. & C. R. Co.* v. *Falvey*, 104 Ind. 409, 3 N. E. 389, 4 N. E. 908; *Grand Lodge, I. O. of M. A.* v. *Wieting*, 168 Ill. 408, 48 N. E. 59.

[7]*Deig* v. *Morehead*, 110 Ind. 451, 11 N. E. 458.

[8]*State* v. *Fournier*, 68 Vt. 262, 35 Atl. 178.

But a hypothetical case and personal examination cannot be joined in the same question, where the examination was, from the time it was made, little or no evidence of the point at issue. *State* v. *Welsor*, 117 Mo. 570, 21 S. W. 443.

[9]*Williams* v. *State*, 64 Md. 384, 1 Atl. 887.

[10]*People* v. *Brown*, 53 Mich. 531, 19 N. W. 172.

[11]*Forsyth* v. *Doolittle*, 120 U. S. 73, 30 L. ed. 586, 7 Sup. Ct. Rep. 408.

39. Leading questions.

A leading question is one which suggests to the witness the answer expected or desired.[1] That the question may be answered by "Yes" or "No" is not necessarily decisive of its character.[2] But it has been held that a question which embodies a material fact, and admits of a conclusive, affirmative, or negative answer, is open to that objection.[3] And it is sometimes said that a question which assumes the existence of facts material to the issue is leading.[4] A question which is suggestive of the answer is none the less leading because propounded in the alternative form.[5]

Introductory questions which are designed to lead the witness with the more expedition to the subject upon which he has desired to give his testimony are not objectionable;[6] nor are those objectionable which are necessarily leading in appearance because of the nature of the inquiry.[7]

Objections to questions as leading are addressed to the discretion of the trial court;[8] and the exercise of this discretion is not revisable on appeal[9] except for manifest abuse.[10]

The allowance of a leading question is not ground for reversal, where the facts embraced in it have been already,[11] or are subsequently, elicited by proper questions.[12]

[1]*Proper* v. *State*, 85 Wis. 626, 55 N. W. 1035.

A question which merely suggests the subject, and not the answer, is not leading. *Born* v. *Rosenow*, 84 Wis. 620, 54 N. W. 1089.

[2]A question is not objectionable as leading because it can be answered by

"Yes" or "No," unless it also suggests the desired answer. *Coogler* v. *Rhodes*, 38 Fla. 240, 21 So. 109; *Schlesinger* v. *Rogers*, 80 Ill. App. 420; *Woolheather* v. *Risley*, 38 Iowa, 486; *McKeown* v. *Harvey*, 40 Mich. 226; *Lott* v. *King*, 79 Tex. 292, 15 S. W. 231. But the question is leading when capable of eliciting by such an answer more than one simple proposition. *International & G. N. R. Co.* v. *Dalwigh*, 92 Tex. 655, 51 S. W. 500. And if the answer "Yes" or "No" will be conclusive, the question is objectionable as leading. *Nicholls* v. *Dowding*, 1 Starkie, 81; *Daly* v. *Melendy*, 32 Neb. 852, 49 N. W. 926.

[3]*Turney* v. *State*, 8 Smedes & M. 104, 47 Am. Dec. 74; *United States* v. *Angell*, 11 Fed. 34.

[4]*Klock* v. *State*, 60 Wis. 574, 19 N. W. 543.

[5]*State* v. *Johnson*, 29 La. Ann. 717; *People* v. *Mather*, 4 Wend. 229, 21 Am. Dec. 122.

[6]*State* v. *Walsh*, 44 La. Ann. 1122, 11 So. 811; *People* v. *Mather*, 4 Wend. 229, 21 Am. Dec. 122; *Hausenfluck* v. *Com.* 85 Va. 702, 8 S. E. 683.

[7]*Bullard* v. *Hascall*, 25 Mich. 132.

[8]*People* v. *Fong Ah Sing*, 70 Cal 8, 11 Pac. 323; *State* v. *Pugsley*, 75 Iowa, 742, 38 N. W. 498; *State* v. *Spidle*, 42 Kan. 441, 22 Pac. 620; *State* v. *Duestrow*, 137 Mo. 44, 38 S. W. 554, 39 S. W. 266; *State* v. *Chee Gong*, 17 Or. 635, 21 Pac. 882.

[9]*Krebs Mfg. Co.* v. *Brown*, 108 Ala. 508, 18 So. 659; *Stratford* v. *Sanford*, 9 Conn. 279; *Southern Exp. Co.* v. *Van Meter*, 17 Fla. 783, 35 Am. Rep. 107; *Parsons* v. *Huff*, 38 Me. 137; *York* v. *Pease*, 2 Gray, 282; *St. Louis & I. M. R. Co.* v. *Silver*, 56 Mo. 265; *Trenton Pass R. Co.* v. *Cooper*, 60 N. J. L. 219, 38 L. R. A. 637, 37 Atl. 730; *Ducker* v. *Whitson*, 112 N. C. 44, 16 S. E. 854; *Farmers' Mut. F. Ins. Co.* v. *Bair*, 87 Pa. 124; *Hopkinson* v. *Steel*, 12 Vt. 582.

The rule seems the same in New York. *Walker* v. *Dunspaugh*, 20 N. Y. 170; *Downs* v. *New York C. R. Co.* 47 N. Y. 83; *Brooker* v. *Filkins*, 9 Misc. 146, 29 N. Y. 68; *King* v. *Second Ave. R. Co.* 75 Hun, 17, 26 N. Y. Supp. 973. But the discretion is said to be revisable for abuse, in *Budlong* v. *Van Nostrand*, 24 Barb. 25; *Cope* v. *Sibley*, 12 Barb. 521; *Van Doren* v. *Jelliffe*, 1 Misc. 354, 26 N. Y. Supp. 636.

[10]*State* v. *Pugsley*, 75 Iowa, 742, 38 N. W. 498; *Turney* v. *State*, 8 Smedes & M. 104, 47 Am. Dec. 74.

[11]*People* v. *Fong Ah Sing*, 70 Cal. 8, 11 Pac. 323; *Hess* v. *Com.* 5 Ky. L. Rep. 590, 5 S. W. 751.

[12]*State* v. *Munson*, 7 Wash. 239, 34 Pac. 932.

40. — to one's own witness.

While leading questions to one's own witness are generally objectionable, the trial judge may in his discretion permit such questions to be put on direct or redirect examination to a witness whose answers have taken by surprise the party calling him,[1] or where the witness is hostile[2] or reluctant,[3] or so youthful,[4] ignorant,[5] or infirm[6] as to require his attention to be led, or where his memory has been exhausted without stating some particular which cannot be significantly pointed to by a general inquiry.[7]

By the weight of authority leading questions may be asked a witness who is called to impeach another witness by contradiction,[8] but there are decisions declaring that there is no reason for relaxing the general rule in favor of an impeaching witness.[9]

[1] *St. Clair* v. *United States*, 154 U. S. 134, 38 L. ed. 936, 14 Sup. Ct. Rep. 1002; *Babcock* v. *People*, 13 Colo. 515, 22 Pac. 817.

[2] *State* v. *Stevens*, 65 Conn. 93, 31 Atl. 496; *Navarro* v. *State*, 24 Tex. App. 378, 6 N. W. 542.

The witness cannot be deemed hostile merely because he states that he does not remember having made a certain statement, where he has not testified to anything prejudicial to, and has manifested no bias against, the party calling him, and the latter makes no further effort to refresh his memory. *Fisher* v. *Hart*, 149 Pa. 232, 24 Atl. 225.

[3] *State* v. *Duestrow*, 137 Mo. 44, 38 S. W. 554, 39 S. W. 266; *Robinson* v. *State* (Tex. Crim. App.) 49 S. W. 386; *Schuster* v. *State*, 80 Wis. 107, 49 N. W. 30.

[4] *Speckmann* v. *Kreig*, 79 Mo. App. 376; *Moody* v. *Rowell*, 17 Pick. 490, 28 Am. Dec. 317.

[5] *Rodriguez* v. *State*, 23 Tex. App. 503, 5 S. W. 255.

[6] *Belknap* v. *Stewart*, 38 Neb. 304, 56 N. W. 881; *Cheeney* v. *Arnold*, 18 Barb. 434.

[7] *Hartsfield* v. *State* (Tex. Crim. App.) 29 S. W. 777.

A witness may sometimes be asked leading questions which direct his attention to a particular item concerning which he has testified generally. *Graves* v. *Merchants & B. Ins. Co.* 82 Iowa, 637, 49 N. W. 65.

But *People* v. *Mather*, 4 Wend. 229, 21 Am. Dec. 122, holds that after a witness's memory as to a conversation has been exhausted he should not be asked a leading question directed to a particular portion of such conversation.

[8] *Rounds* v. *State*, 57 Wis. 45, 14 N. W. 865.

[9] *Wood* v. *State*, 31 Fla. 221, 12 So. 539; *Allen* v. *State*, 28 Ga. 396, 73 Am. Dec. 760.

41. Answers.

While it is desirable that a witness be positive in his testimony, it is sufficient if he testifies to the best of his knowledge and belief, where he is unable to state the facts positively;[1] and when required to narrate a previous conversation, he may give a general answer embodying its substance or purport, if he cannot recollect the precise words used.[2] So, when undertaking to state from memory the testimony given by another witness on a former hearing, he may give its substance, instead of the exact language,[3] but he cannot give his impression, unless it is made to appear that such impression is derived from his recollection,[4] and he cannot state the impression left on his mind by a conversation of which he cannot recall the substance.[5]

An answer is not necessarily objectionable as argumentative because the witness gives his reason for doing a particular thing, nor because it contains other than the statement of facts connected with the transaction in controversy.[6]

An answer must be responsive to the question,[7] and any irresponsive statement will be struck out, or the jury instructed to disregard it, upon a motion seasonably made.[8] A witness cannot be compelled to answer "Yes" or "No" to a question which is not so worded as to make such an answer appropriate.[9]

[1] *Rhode* v. *Louthain*, 8 Blackf. 413; *Fitschen* v. *Thomas*, 9 Mont. 52, 22 Pac. 450; *Swinney* v. *Booth*, 28 Tex. 113.

[2] *Seymour* v. *Harvey*, 11 Conn. 275; *Hope* v. *Machias Water Power & Mill Co.* 52 Me. 535; *Chambers* v. *Hill*, 34 Mich. 523; *Buchanan* v. *Atchison*, 39 Mo. 503; *Chaffee* v. *Cox*, 1 Hilt. 78.

[3] *State* v. *Jones*, 29 S. C. 201, 7 S. E. 296.

[4] *Clark* v. *Bigelow*, 16 Me. 246; *State* v. *Flanders*, 38 N. H. 324.

[5] *Crews* v. *Threadgill*, 35 Ala. 334; *Helm* v. *Cantrell*, 59 Ill. 525; *Wilder* v. *Peabody*, 21 Hun, 376.

But a witness who states that he cannot give the language used in a conversation may testify to the impression received and the idea formed therefrom. *State* v. *Donovan*, 61 Iowa, 278, 16 N. W. 130.

[6] *Burlington Gaslight Co.* v. *Greene*, 28 Iowa, 289.

[7] *Ryan* v. *People*, 79 N. Y. 593.

[8] See *infra*, § 54.

[9] *Quinn* v. *O'Keeffe*, 9 App. Div. 68, 41 N. Y. Supp. 116; *Vance* v. *Upson*, 66 Tex. 476, 1 S. W. 179.

42. Direct examination; adverse party.

The direct examination of a witness cannot properly be limited by the court to the question whether he agrees with or differs from the testimony of a prior witness with respect to a transaction at which he was present, even though the objecting party is allowed full privilege of cross-examination.[1] Nor can a witness be asked whether the facts stated in a particular paper are true. He should be interrogated as to those facts particularly.[2]

The court may refuse to permit a witness on his direct examination to detail the whole of a conversation to which he has referred.[3]

A party may aid the memory of his own witness by inquiring as to any circumstances tending to enable him to recollect more clearly or more certainly the fact sought to be proved.[4]

More than ordinary freedom is permitted in the direct examination of a witness who is hostile to the party calling him,[5] and this principle is recognized by those statutes which authorize one party to compel the other to testify in his behalf, such statutes generally providing that the examination may be conducted under the rule applicable to the cross-examination of other witnesses.[6]

[1] *Eames* v. *Eames,* 41 N. H. 177.

[2] *Richardson* v. *Golden,* 3 Wash. C. C. 109, Fed. Cas. No. 11,782.

[3] *Ayrault* v. *Chamberlain,* 33 Barb. 229.

[4] *O'Hagan* v. *Dillon,* 76 N. Y. 170; *State* v. *Jeandell,* 5 Harr. (Del.) 475.

[5] See *supra,* §§ 39, 40.

[6] *Childs* v. *Merrill,* 66 Vt. 302, 29 Atl. 532; *Re Brown,* 38 Minn. 112, 35 N. W. 726; *Pfefferkorn* v. *Seefield,* 66 Minn. 223, 68 N. W. 1072; *Coates Bros.* v. *Wilkes,* 92 N. C. 376.

43. Cross-examination; the right.

The right of cross-examination is deemed so essential that a party is not entitled to the benefit of the direct examination of a witness whom his adversary has had no opportunity to cross-examine;[1] otherwise where the party has failed to improve an opportunity for cross-examination when offered,[2] or has voluntarily deprived himself of the right.[3] A witness who on direct examination volunteers an uncalled-for statement which is allowed to go to the jury without objection may be cross-examined with reference thereto,[4] though if the statement is irrelevant such cross-examination is not a matter of right.[5]

The right to cross-examine is not affected because the testimony in chief was out of proper order to anticipate a defense,[6] or was unnecessary because of a statute permitting an affidavit to be filed in lieu thereof;[7] but there can be no cross-examination upon evidence which has been stricken out of the case.[8]

[1] A party is not entitled to the benefit of the direct examination of a witness who has died since he was examined in chief, and before the adverse party had an opportunity to avail himself of a cross-examination. *Kissam* v. *Forrest,* 25 Wend. 651. Or to complete an examination already begun. *Sperry* v. *Moore,* 42 Mich. 353, 4 N. W. 13. So held where the

witness became suddenly so severely ill as to render his cross-examination impossible. *People* v. *Cole,* 43 N. Y. 508, citing with approval *Kissam* v. *Forrest,* 25 Wend. 651, and declaring *Forrest* v. *Kissam,* 7 Hill, 463, to be "no authority." So, where the witness fails to appear for further cross-examination or refuses to answer a question pertinent and not privileged. *Burnett* v. *Phalon,* 11 Abb. Pr. 157.

[2]As where a witness who failed to appear for further cross-examination at the date fixed by the court was present in court between the time she was excused and the day fixed, and counsel and court were then reminded that she was actively engaged in seeking a position on an ocean vessel, and the propriety of then resuming her cross-examination was suggested and declined. *Townsend's Succession,* 40 La. Ann. 66, 3 So. 488. So, where the witness died during an adjournment taken before his cross-examination was completed, the circumstances attending the adjournment not being disclosed, and it not appearing that the party was deprived of the opportunity of then completing his cross-examination, if he had desired to do so. *Curtice* v. *West,* 50 Hun, 47, 2 N. Y. Supp. 507; Affirmed without opinion in 121 N. Y. 696, 24 N. E. 1099.

[3]A party who voluntarily deprived himself of his right to cross-examine a witness by consenting to the admission in evidence of the written showing of what the witness would prove cannot, after the trial has begun, complain that he was deprived of the right to cross-examine the witness. *Nelson* v. *Shelby Mfg. & Improv. Co.* 96 Ala. 515, 11 So. 695.

[4]*Apple* v. *Marion County Comrs.* 127 Ind. 553, 27 N. E. 166.

[5]*People* v. *French,* 95 Cal. 371, 30 Pac. 567.

[6]*Graham* v. *Larimer,* 83 Cal. 173, 23 Pac. 286.

[7]A party who takes the stand for the purpose of laying the foundation for the introduction of the record of a conveyance in place of the original, instead of filing an affidavit as permitted by statute, is subject to cross-examination to test the correctness and accuracy of his statement. *Jones* v. *State,* 35 Fla. 289, 17 So. 284; *Callison* v. *Smith,* 20 Kan. 36.

[8]*Jones* v. *State,* 35 Fla. 289, 17 So. 284.

44. — how far limited to direct.

By the English rule which is followed in several of the states a witness who has sworn and gives some evidence, however formal or unimportant, may be cross-examined in relation to all matters involved in the issues.[1] But a stricter rule, sometimes called by way of distinction the "American rule," obtains in the Federal and very many of the state courts. Under this rule the cross-examination of a witness is limited to an inquiry as to the facts and circumstances connected with the matters stated in his direct examination.[2] In the application of this rule much is left to the discretion of the trial court.[3]

A cross-examination always may include whatever tends to qualify or explain the direct testimony of a witness and to develop and unfold the whole transaction about which he has only been partially interrogated.[4] So, where one party introduces evidence of a part of a conversation, his adversary has a right to draw out all that was said in the conversation material to the case.[5]

[1] *Huntsville Belt Line & M. S. R. Co.* v. *Corpening,* 97 Ala. 681, 12 So. 295; *Dawson* v. *Callaway,* 18 Ga. 573; *News Pub. Co.* v. *Butler,* 95 Ga. 559, 22 S. E. 282; *King* v. *Atkins,* 33 La. Ann. 1057; *Beal* v. *Nichols,* 2 Gray, 262; *Ireland* v. *Cincinnati, W. & M. R. Co.* 79 Mich. 163, 44 N. W. 426; *Page* v. *Kankey,* 6 Mo. 433; *State* v. *Allen,* 107 N. C. 805, 11 S. E. 1016; *Kibler* v. *McIlwain,* 16 S. C. 551; *Rhine* v. *Blake,* 59 Tex. 240.

[2] *Braly* v. *Henry,* 77 Cal. 324, 19 Pac. 529; *Denver, T. & Ft. W. R. Co.* v. *Smock,* 23 Colo, 456, 48 Pac. 681; *Ashborn* v. *Waterbury,* 69 Conn. 217, 37 Atl. 498; *Woodbury* v. *District of Columbia,* 5 Mackey, 127; *Tischler* v. *Apple,* 30 Fla. 132, 11 So. 273; *Hartshorn* v. *Byrne,* 147 Ill. 418, 35 N. E. 622, Affirming 45 Ill. App. 250; *Cokely* v. *State,* 4 Iowa, 477; *Hunsinger* v. *Hofer,* 110 Ind. 390, 11 N. E. 463; *Atchison* v. *Rose,* 43 Kan. 605, 23 Pac. 561; *McCormick* v. *Gliem,* 13 Mont. 469, 34 Pac. 1016; *Atwood* v. *Marshall,* 52 Neb. 173, 71 N. W. 1064; *Buckley* v. *Buckley,* 14 Nev. 262; *Pearce* v. *Strickler,* 9 N. M. 467, 54 Pac. 748; *Neil* v. *Thorn,* 88 N. Y. 270; *People ex rel. Phelps* v. *New York County Court of Oyer & Terminer,* 83 N. Y. 436; *Rheinfeldt* v. *Dahlman,* 19 Misc. 162, 43 N. Y. Supp. 281. The early New York cases followed the English rule (*Varick* v. *Jackson ex dem. Eden,* 2 Wend. 166, 19 Am. Dec. 571; *Fulton Bank* v. *Stafford,* 2 Wend. 483), except in cases of inquest taken by default (*Hartness* v. *Boyd,* 5 Wend. 563; *Kerker* v. *Carter,* 1 Hill, 101; *State* v. *Kent,* 5 N. D. 516, *sub nom. State* v. *Pancoast,* 35 L. R. A. 518, 67 N. W. 1052; *Willis* v. *Lance,* 28 Or. 371, 43 Pac. 384, 487; *Fulton* v. *Central Bank,* 92 Pa. 112; *Rosum* v. *Hodges,* 1 S. D. 308, 9 L. R. A. 817, 47 N. W. 140; *People* v. *Thiede,* 11 Utah, 241, 39 Pac. 837; *Stiles* v. *Estabrook,* 66 Vt. 535, 29 Atl. 961; *Welcome* v. *Mitchell,* 81 Wis. 566, 51 N. W. 1080; *Philadelphia & T. R. Co.* v. *Stimpson,* 14 Pet. 448, 10 L. ed. 535).

[3] *Glenn* v. *Gleason,* 61 Iowa, 32, 15 N. W. 659; *Pennsylvania Co.* v. *Newmeyer,* 129 Ind. 401, 28 N. E. 860; *Neil* v. *Thorn,* 88 N. Y. 270; *Hardy* v. *Norton,* 66 Barb. 527; *Helser* v. *McGrath,* 52 Pa. 531; *Carroll* v. *Centralia Water Co.* 5 Wash. 613, 32 Pac. 609, 33 Pac. 431; *Stutz* v. *Chicago & N. W. R. Co.* 73 Wis. 147, 40 N. W. 653; *Davis* v. *Coblens,* 174 U. S. 719, 43 L. ed. 1147, 19 Sup. Ct. Rep. 832.

[4] *Wilson* v. *Wagar,* 26 Mich. 452; *Campau* v. *Dewey,* 9 Mich. 381, 419; *Haynes* v. *Ledyard,* 33 Mich. 319; *Ferguson* v. *Rutherford,* 7 Nev. 385; *Ah Doon* v. *Smith,* 25 Or. 89, 34 Pac. 1093; *Blake* v. *Powell,* 26 Kan. 320. And see, for instances, *Baird* v. *Daly,* 68 N. Y. 547; *Mayer* v. *People,* 80 N. Y. 364; *Graham* v. *Larimer,* 83 Cal. 173, 23 Pac. 286; *Olson* v. *Peterson,* 33 Neb. 358, 50 N. W. 155; *Day* v. *Donohue,* 62 N. J. L. 380, 41 Atl. 934; *Post Pub. Co.* v. *Hallam,* 8 C. C. A. 201, 16 U. S. App. 613, 59 Fed. 530; *Blough* v. *Parry,* 144 Ind. 463, 40 N. E. 70, 43 N. E.

560; *Pullen* v. *Pullen,* 41 N. J. Eq. 417, 5 Atl. 658; *Thomas* v. *Miller,* 151 Pa. 482, 25 Atl. 127.

[5]*Vogel* v. *Harris,* 112 Ind. 494, 14 N. E. 385; *Evans* v. *Mohr,* 42 Ill. App. 225; *Duttera* v. *Babylon,* 83 Md. 536, 35 Atl. 64; *State* v. *Kent,* 5 N. D. 516, *sub nom. State* v. *Pancoast,* 35 L. R. A. 518, 67 N. W. 1052; *Maxwell* v. *Bolles,* 28 Or. 1, 41 Pac. 661; *Gilmer* v. *Higley,* 110 U. S. 47, 28 L. ed. 62, 3 Sup. Ct. Rep. 471; *Eames* v. *Kaiser,* 142 U. S. 488, 35 L. ed. 1091, 12 Sup. Ct. Rep. 302.

[6]*Metzer* v. *State,* 39 Ind. 596; *United States* v. *Knowlton,* 3 Dak. 58, 13 N. W. 573; *Home Benefit Asso.* v. *Sargent,* 142 U. S. 691, 35 L. ed. 1160, 12 Sup. Ct. Rep. 332; *Watrous* v. *Cunningham,* 71 Cal. 30, 11 Pac. 811; *Patrick* v. *Crowe,* 15 Colo. 543, 25 Pac. 985; *Black* v. *Wabash, St. L. & P. R. Co.* 111 Ill. 351, 53 Am. Rep. 628.

But the admission of a part of the conversation does not warrant the introduction on cross-examination of other portions that do not tend to explain that already admitted, and that are objectionable on other grounds. *Hurlbut* v. *Boaz,* 4 Tex. Civ. App. 371, 23 S. W. 446.

45. — witnesses to opinions.

It is proper that opinion evidence be subjected to every legitimate test on cross-examination, in order that its value may be properly weighed;[1] and for this purpose the witness may be interrogated as to the grounds on which his opinion is based.[2]

Hypothetical questions may properly be asked of an expert witness on cross-examination,[3] especially to test his skill or knowledge;[4] and questions pertinent to the inquiry may be propounded for this purpose, although assuming facts for which there is no foundation in the evidence;[5] but the allowance of such questions rests in the sound discretion of the trial court.[6]

[1]A wide range should be given to the cross-examination of an expert witness, for the purpose of testing his knowledge of the subject-matter upon which he assumes to testify. *Hutchinson* v. *State,* 19 Neb. 262, 27 N. W. 113; *Birmingham Nat. Bank* v. *Bradley,* 108 Ala. 205, 19 So. 791; *Batten* v. *State,* 80 Ind. 394; *Clark* v. *State,* 12 Ohio, 483, 40 Am. Dec. 481; *Andre* v. *Hardin,* 32 Mich. 324; *Titus* v. *Gage,* 70 Vt. 14, 39 Atl. 246; *Chicago & A. R. Co.* v. *Redmond,* 171 Ill. 347, 49 N. E. 541; *Lewis* v. *Boston Gaslight Co.* 165 Mass. 411, 43 N. E. 178. For cases illustrative of the scope of cross-examination of expert witnesses on the question of insanity, see note to *Burt* v. *State* (Tex. Crim. App.) 39 L. R. A. 326. And for cross-examination of nonexperts on the question of insanity, see note to *Ryder* v. *State* (Ga.) 38 L. R. A. 743.

It is competent on cross-examination, for the purpose of testing his skill, to ask a medical witness the probable results of a personal injury. *Louisville, N. A. & C. R. Co.* v. *Lucas,* 119 Ind. 583, 6 L. R. A. 193, 21 N. E. 968; *State* v. *Reddick,* 7 Kan. 143. But a physician who has testified that an injury can probably be cured by a dangerous and intensely painful operation cannot be asked if he would submit to the operation himself if similarly afflicted. *Montgomery & E. R. Co.* v. *Mallette,* 92 Ala. 209, 9 So. 363.

A witness who has testified on direct examination, not only as to the facts in the case, but also as a medical expert, may be cross-examined, not only concerning the facts testified to in chief, but also to test his skill and knowledge as an expert. *Shields* v. *State,* 149 Ind. 395, 49 N. E. 351.

And a subscribing witness who has testified to the sanity of the testator may be cross-examined as to his qualification as an expert, where he testified upon direct examination that he was an experienced physician and surgeon, and attended the testator during his last illness. *Re Mullin,* 110 Cal. 252, 42 Pac. 645. But counsel cannot, on cross-examination, ask a witness who is not called or examined in chief as an expert, nor asked to give a professional opinion on the facts to which he testifies, questions permissible only in the case of an expert witness, unless he makes the witness his own. *Olmsted* v. *Gere,* 100 Pa. 127; *Verdelli* v. *Gray's Harbor Commercial Co.* 115 Cal. 517, 47 Pac. 364. And an expert whose direct testimony was confined to a contradiction of the theory of the experts of the adverse party cannot on cross-examination be asked a question which forms a part of the latter's affirmative case, and which cannot be justified as testing the competency of the witness. *Gridley* v. *Boggs,* 62 Cal. 190.

The value of the opinions of experts who have testified from comparison as to the genuineness of signatures may be tested by inquiring as to the genuineness of two signatures of a witness in the case, one admitted to be genuine, and the other claimed by him to have been written by another. *Johnston Harvester Co.* v. *Miller,* 72 Mich. 265, 40 N. W. 429.

But spurious signatures cannot be intermingled with the genuine, and a nonexpert witness be required on cross-examination to select the genuine. *Andrews* v. *Hayden,* 88 Ky. 455, 11 S. W. 428. Nor can the accuracy of an expert who has given his opinion upon the question whether a disputed and an admittedly genuine writing were written by the same person be tested by inquiring on cross-examination whether the disputed document and another writing of unknown authorship were in the same handwriting or written by the same person, as a collateral inquiry would thus be raised. *State* v. *Griswold,* 67 Conn. 290, 33 L. R. A. 227, 34 Atl. 1046. Otherwise where all the writings are claimed to have been written by the same person. *Thomas* v. *State,* 103 Ind. 419, 2 N. E. 808. And it has been held that the accuracy of the judgment of a handwriting expert cannot be tested on cross-examination by asking his opinion as to the genuineness of the handwriting on papers irrelevant to the issues. *Armstrong* v. *Thruston,* 11 Md. 148. Nor by requiring him to examine a number of slips containing unproved handwriting, and to state how many different kinds of handwriting he finds. *State* v. *Griswold,* 67 Conn. 290, 33 L. R. A. 227, 34 Atl. 1046.

A witness who answers a question on cross-examination as fully and specifically as he can with his present knowledge will not be compelled, for the purpose of further answers, to acquire further information, or increase his store of knowledge. *Celluloid Mfg. Co.* v. *Crane Chemical Co.* 14 N. J. L. J. 55.

[2]*Howes* v. *Colburn,* 165 Mass. 385, 43 N. E. 125; *Dresback* v. *State,* 38 Ohio St. 365; *Plummer* v. *Ossipee,* 59 N. H. 55; *Louisville, N. A. & C. R. Co.* v. *Falvey,* 104 Ind. 409, 3 N. E. 389, 4 N. E. 908.

[3]An expert witness who has been examined upon the theory of the party calling him may be cross-examined by taking his opinion based on any other set of facts assumed by the opposite party to have been proved, or upon a hypothetical case based upon the latter's theory. *Davis* v. *State,* 35 Ind. 496, 9 Am. Rep. 760; *Grubb* v. *State,* 117 Ind. 277, 20 N. E. 257, 725; *Conway* v. *State,* 118 Ind. 482, 21 N. E. 285; *People* v. *Lake,* 12 N. Y. 358; *Barney* v. *Fuller,* 39 N. Y. S. R. 926, 15 N. Y. Supp. 694, Affirmed in 133 N. Y. 605, 30 N. E. 1007.

[4]*People* v. *Sutton,* 73 Cal. 243, 15 Pac. 86.

[5]*Williams* v. *Great Northern R. Co.* 68 Minn. 55, 37 L. R. A. 199, 70 N. W. 860; *Dilleber* v. *Home L. Ins. Co.* 87 N. Y. 79; *Missouri, K. & T. R. Co.* v. *Johnson* (Tex. Civ. App.) 49 S. W. 265.

But it is improper on cross-examination erroneously to assume facts to have been proved, "especially when it is for the purpose of getting the opinion of an expert on a mere hypothesis, not to test his skill or accuracy, but to obtain evidence in support of the defense." *State* v. *Stokely,* 16 Minn. 282, Gil. 249. And generally hypothetical questions on cross-examination must be based on facts in evidence. *Smalley* v. *Appleton,* 75 Wis. 18, 43 N. W. 826; *People* v. *Dunne,* 80 Cal. 34, 21 Pac. 1130.

[6]*People* v. *Augsbury,* 97 N. Y. 501.

46. — to test credibility.

A witness may be interrogated on cross-examination with a view to test the extent of his knowledge, the accuracy of his recollection, and his habits of observation.[1] So his interest in the event of the suit, and his bias, prejudice, or hostility towards either of the parties, may be made the subject of inquiry for the purpose of testing the weight to be given to his testimony;[2] and he may be asked whether he has not made statements inconsistent with his testimony in chief, for the purpose of affecting credit,[3] or laying the foundation for his impeachment.[4]

The authorities are not harmonious upon the question whether counsel on cross-examination may ask questions relating to specific facts which tend to discredit the witness or to impeach his moral character, even though not relevant to the issues.[5] But even where such inquiries are not forbidden, their allowance or rejection rests in the sound discretion of the trial judge,[6] and he may exclude them on the objection of the party, where no claim of privilege is interposed.[7] And a witness cannot be cross-examined as to any fact which is collateral or irrelevant to the issue, merely for the purpose of contradicting him by other evidence, if he denies it.[8]

[7]*Davis* v. *California Powder Works,* 84 Cal. 617, 24 Pac. 387; *Sharp* v. *Hoffman,* 79 Cal. 404, 21 Pac. 846; *Hartford* v. *Champion,* 58 Conn. 268, 20 Atl. 471; *Schwartz* v. *Wood,* 51 N. Y. S. R. 4, 21 N. Y. Supp. 1053; *Derk* v. *Northern C. R. Co.* 164 Pa. 243, 30 Atl. 231; *Cunningham* v. *Austin & N. W. R. Co.* 88 Tex. 534, 31 S. W. 629; *Blankenship* v. *Chesapeake & O. R. Co.* 94 Va. 449, 27 S. E. 20.

Thus, a witness may be asked on cross-examination whether he understood a question propounded on his direct examination. *Pence* v. *Waugh,* 135 Ind. 143, 34 N. E. 860. And whether he has talked with others in reference to the facts of the case before going on the stand. *Boulden* v. *State,* 102 Ala. 78, 15 So. 341. And two witnesses who testify to facts observed by them while in company may be cross-examined as to concert of action between them, and as to how much the story of each or both has been changed or developed by conversation or otherwise. *State* v. *Hayward,* 62 Minn. 474, 65 N. W. 63. So, a witness may be asked whether he was not under the influence of intoxicating liquor at the time of the occurrence with reference to which he is testifying (*International & G. N. R. Co.* v. *Dyer,* 76 Tex. 156, 13 S. W. 377; *State* v. *Rhodes,* 44 S. C. 325, 21 S. E. 807, 22 S. E. 306), or whether he is not at the time of testifying under such influence. *Pool* v. *Pool,* 33 Ala. 145. But a witness cannot be asked whether or not she is addicted to the morphine habit, unless it is proposed to show that she was under its influence when the events happened about which she testifies or at the time of testifying, or it appears that her powers of recollection are impaired thereby. *State* v. *Gleim,* 17 Mont. 17, 31 L. R. A. 294, 41 Pac. 998. And the range which a cross-examination of this character may take is left to the sound discretion of the trial court. *A. G. Rhodes Furniture Co.* v. *Weeden,* 108 Ala. 252, 19 So. 318; *State* v. *Duffy,* 57 Conn. 525, 18 Atl. 791.

[8]*Alabama G. S. R. Co.* v. *Burgess,* 114 Ala. 587, 22 So. 169; *Long* v. *Booe,* 106 Ala. 570, 17 So. 716; *Gould* v. *Stafford,* 91 Cal. 146, 27 Pac. 543; *Hartman* v. *Rogers,* 69 Cal. 643, 11 Pac. 581; *Driggers* v. *State,* 38 Fla. 7, 20 So. 758; *Jacksonville, T. & K. W. R. Co.* v. *Wellman,* 26 Fla. 344, 7 So. 845; *Sage* v. *State,* 127 Ind. 15, 26 N. E. 667; *Harrington* v. *Hamburg,* 85 Iowa, 272, 52 N. W. 201; *Schloss* v. *Estey,* 114 Mich. 429, 72 N. W. 264; *Archer* v. *Helm,* 70 Miss. 874, 12 So. 702; *Cambeis* v. *Third Ave. R. Co.* 1 Misc. 158, 20 N. Y. Supp. 633; *Cady* v. *Bradshaw,* 116 N. Y. 188, 5 L. R. A. 557, 22 N. E. 371; *Wallach* v. *Kalccheim,* 25 Misc. 171, 54 N. Y. Supp. 148; *Hanson* v. *Red Rock Twp.* 7 S. D. 38, 63 N. W. 156; *Graham* v. *McReynolds,* 88 Tenn, 240, 12 S. W. 547; *Cox* v. *Missouri, K. & T. R. Co.* 20 Tex. Civ. App. 250, 48 S. W. 745; *Atkinson* v. *Reed* (Tex. Civ. App.) 49 S. W. 260; *Vermont Farm Mach. Co.* v. *Batchelder,* 68 Vt. 430, 35 Atl. 378; *Stossel* v. *Van De Vanter,* 16 Wash. 9, 47 Pac. 221; *Suit* v. *Bonnell,* 33 Wis. 180.

The prejudice must exist at the trial, or have arisen so recently that it may be assumed to continue down to that time (*Higham* v. *Gault,* 15 Hun, 383), and the interest must not be too remote (*Bevan* v. *Atlanta*

Nat. Bank, 142 Ill. 302, 31 N. E. 679), although the fact that the witness may have parted with his interest in the suit before the trial will not preclude the inquiry. *Trinity County Lumber Co.* v. *Denham*, 88 Tex. 203, 30 S. W. 856; *Klatt* v. *N. C. Foster Lumber Co.* 97 Wis. 641, 73 N. W. 563.

[3]*Freeman* v. *Hensley* (Cal.) 30 Pac. 792; *Lothrop* v. *Roberts*, 16 Colo. 250, 27 Pac. 698; *Chielinsky* v. *Hoopes & T. Co.* 1 Marv. (Del.) 273, 40 Atl. 1127; *Stanley* v. *Dunn*, 143 Ind. 495, 42 N. E. 908; *Robinson* v. *Craver*, 88 Iowa, 381, 55 N. W. 492; *Southern Kansas R. Co.* v. *Michaels*, 49 Kan. 388, 30 Pac. 408; *Watts* v. *Stevenson*, 165 Mass. 518, 43 N. E. 497; *Langworthy* v. *Green Twp.* 88 Mich. 207, 50 N. W. 130; *Lawlor* v. *Kemper*, 20 Mont. 13, 49 Pac. 398; *Beuerlien* v. *O'Leary*, 149 N. Y. 33, 43 N. E. 417; *Walley* v. *Deseret Nat. Bank*, 14 Utah, 305, 47 Pac. 147; *Stacy* v. *Milwaukee, L. S. & W. R. Co.* 72 Wis. 331, 39 N. W. 532.

A witness may be cross-examined as to his testimony on a former trial, inconsistent with his present testimony. *Brooks* v. *Rochester R. Co.* 156 N. Y. 244, 50 N. E. 945; *Waterman* v. *Chicago & A. R. Co.* 82 Wis. 613, 52 N. W. 247, 1136. And the record of his former testimony need not be produced. *Oderkirk* v. *Fargo*, 61 Hun, 418, 16 N. Y. Supp. 220. *Contra*, *People* v. *Ching Hing Chang*, 74 Cal. 389, 16 Pac. 201. If the inconsistent statements are in writing, they must be first produced and shown or read to the witness, or the nonproduction accounted for. *East Tennessee, V. & G. R. Co.* v. *Thompson*, 94 Ala. 636, 10 So. 280.

The extent of the interest or prejudice is as material as the main fact of its existence. *Blenkiron* v. *State*, 40 Neb. 11, 58 N. W. 587; *Stewart* v. *Kindel*, 15 Colo. 539, 25 Pac. 990; *State* v. *Collins*, 33 Kan. 77, 5 Pac. 368; *State* v. *Dee*, 14 Minn. 35, Gil. 27.

[4]*Hoye* v. *Chicago, M. & St. P. R. Co.* 46 Minn. 269, 48 N. W. 1117; *Hamilton* v. *Rich Hill Coal Min. Co.* 108 Mo. 364, 18 S. W. 977; *Vogt* v. *Baldwin*, 20 Mont. 322, 51 Pac. 157; *Krewson* v. *Purdon*, 13 Or. 563, 11 Pac. 281; *Missouri, K. & T. R. Co.* v. *Calnon*, 20 Tex. Civ. App. 697, 50 S. W. 422; *Walley* v. *Deseret Nat. Bank*, 14 Utah, 305, 47 Pac. 147; *Smith* v. *Watson*, 82 Va. 712, 1 S. E. 96; *Waterman* v. *Chicago & A. R. Co.* 82 Wis. 613, 52 N. W. 247, 1136.

And it is immaterial that counsel fails or has no intention to follow up the impeachment by the introduction of evidence to sustain the matters inquired into. *Texas Standard Oil Co.* v. *Hanlon*, 79 Tex. 678, 15 S. W. 703.

[5]The allowance of such questions seems to be favored in some jurisdictions as a proper mode of testing the credibility of the witness. *Wilbur* v. *Flood*, 16 Mich. 40, 93 Am. Dec. 203; *State* v. *Greenburg*, 59 Kan. 404, 53 Pac. 61; *Roberts* v. *Com.* 14 Ky. L. Rep. 219, 20 S. W. 267; *People* v. *Irving*, 95 N. Y. 541; *People ex rel. Phelps* v. *New York County Court of Oyer & Terminer*, 83 N. Y. 436; *Zanone* v. *State*, 97 Tenn. 101, 35 L. R. A. 556, 36 S. W. 711; *Muller* v. *St. Louis Hospital Asso.* 5 Mo. App. 390, Affirmed in 73 Mo. 243; *Carroll* v. *State*, 32 Tex. Crim. Rep. 431, 24 S. W. 100. So held, even under a statute providing that a witness cannot be impeached by evidence of wrongful acts. *Oxier* v. *United States*, 1 Ind. Terr. 85, 38 S. W. 331. But see *State* v. *Houx*, 109 Mo. 654, 19

S. W. 35 (holding that a witness cannot be cross-examined as to the immorality of his previous life, unless his answers tend directly to prove some issue); *Gulf, C. & S. F. R. Co.* v. *Johnson*, 83 Tex. 628, 19 S. W. 151 (holding that a witness cannot be asked whether he is a deserter from the United States Army). Under the guise of discrediting the witness, he cannot be questioned as to fraudulent transactions of the party calling him, collateral to the issue in which the witness participated. *Madden* v. *Koester*, 52 Iowa, 692, 3 N. W. 790.

The contrary rule is upheld in *Elliott* v. *Boyles*, 31 Pa. 67; *Holbrook* v. *Dow*, 12 Gray, 357; *Com.* v. *Schaffner*, 146 Mass. 512, 16 N. E. 280; *Crawford* v. *Christian*, 102 Wis. 51, 78 N. W. 406. But see *Prescott* v. *Ward*, 10 Allen, 203, in which it was held that so far as inquiries on cross-examination relating to matters entirely collateral and immaterial to the issue have a tendency to contradict the witness or disparage the character, it is discretionary in the court to allow or reject them. Such a course of examination is prohibited by statute in some states. *Anthony* v. *State* (Idaho) 55 Pac. 884; *Jones* v. *Duchow*, 87 Cal. 109, 23 Pac. 371, 25 Pac. 256.

It is generally permissible, and authorized by statute in some states, to interrogate a witness with respect to a prior conviction of crime, without producing the record of conviction. *State* v. *Martin*, 124 Mo. 514, 28 S. W. 12; *Handlin* v. *Law*, 34 Ill. App. 84; *State* v. *Merriman*, 34 S. C. 16, 12 S. E. 619; *McLaughlin* v. *Mencke*, 80 Md. 83, 30 Atl. 603; *State* v. *Adamson*, 43 Minn. 196, 45 N. W. 152; *Spiegel* v. *Hays*, 118 N. Y. 660, 22 N. E. 1105; *Perham* v. *Noel*, 20 App. Div. 516, 47 N. Y. Supp. 100; *Lights* v. *State*, 21 Tex. App. 308, 17 S. W. 428. *Contra*, *Clement* v. *Brooks*, 13 N. H. 92; *Com.* v. *Quin*, 5 Gray, 478; *Com.* v. *Sullivan*, 150 Mass. 315, 23 N. E. 47; *Buck* v. *Com.* 107 Pa. 486. In some states, evidence of this character is limited by statute to a conviction for a felony. *People* v. *Carolan*, 71 Cal. 195, 12 Pac. 52. Under such a statute a witness cannot be asked whether he was ever convicted of crime. *Hanners* v. *McClelland*, 74 Iowa, 318, 37 N. W. 389.

That an attorney may be asked on cross-examination whether he has been disbarred was held in *People* v. *Reavey*, 38 Hun, 418, and denied in *People* v. *Dorthy*, 20 App. Div. 308, 46 N. Y. Supp. 970. In affirming the latter case the court of appeals, without deciding the question, held that the witness cannot be required to answer or explain the charges on which the disbarment preceeding rested. *People* v. *Dorthy*, 156 N. Y. 237, 50 N. E. 800. A discharge or compulsory resignation from the police force was held in *Wroe* v. *State*, 20 Ohio St. 460, to be a proper subject of inquiry on cross-examination, but the opposite view was maintained in *Nolan* v. *Brooklyn City & N. R. Co.* 87 N. Y. 63, 41 Am. Rep. 345, in which it was held improper to ask a witness whether he had been expelled from the church to which he belonged. *People* v. *Dorthy*, 156 N. Y. 237, 50 N. E. 800.

It has been held that a witness may be asked whether he has ever been arrested or indicted. *Oxier* v. *United States*, 1 Ind. Terr. 85, 38 S. W. 331; *State* v. *Greenburg*, 59 Kan. 404, 53 Pac. 61; *Roberts* v. *Com.* 14 Ky. L. Rep. 219, 20 S. W. 267; *People* v. *Hite*, 8 Utah, 461, 33 Pac. 254;

Wroe v. *State*, 20 Ohio St. 460; *Linz* v. *Skinner*, 11 Tex. Civ. App. 512, 32 S. W. 915. But it would seem that such inquiry should be excluded, since the fact of indictment or arrest is not inconsistent with innocence. *State* v. *Brown*, 100 Iowa, 50, 69 N. W. 277; *McKesson* v. *Sherman*, 51 Wis. 303, 8 N. W. 200; *Van Bokkelen* v. *Berdell*, 130 N. Y. 141, 29 N. E. 254; *Smith* v. *Mulford*, 42 Hun, 347; *V. Loewer's Gambrinus Brewery Co.* v. *Bashman*, 45 N. Y. S. R. 48, 18 N. Y. Supp. 138. A witness cannot be asked if he has been sued for assault and battery for the purpose of discrediting him. *Yager* v. *Person*, 42 Hun, 400. Nor whether a suit for damages is pending against him because of false swearing in another case. *Pennsylvania Co.* v. *Bray*, 125 Ind. 229, 25 N. E. 439. Nor whether he has not pleaded the statute of limitations to certain specified claims. *Cecil* v. *Henderson*, 119 N. C. 422, 25 S. E. 1018. Nor can he be questioned with a view to showing that he is an habitual litigant. *Palmeri* v. *Manhattan R. Co.* 133 N. Y. 261, 16 L. R. A. 136, 30 N. E. 1001.

[6] *Bank of Cadiz* v. *Slemmons*, 34 Ohio St. 142, 32 Am. Rep. 364; *Bissell* v. *Starr*, 32 Mich. 297; *State* v. *May*, 33 S. C. 39, 11 S. E. 440; *Byrd* v. *Hudson*, 113 N. C. 203, 18 S. E. 209.

[7] *South Bend* v. *Hardy*, 98 Ind. 577, 49 Am. Rep. 792; *Third Great Western Turnp. Road Co.* v. *Loomis*, 32 N. Y. 127, 88 Am. Dec. 311; *People* v. *Braun*, 158 N. Y. 558, 53 N. E. 529; *State* v. *Bacon*, 13 Or. 143, 9 Pac. 393.

[8] *Eldridge* v. *State*, 27 Fla. 162, 9 So. 448; *Clinton* v. *State*, 33 Ohio St. 27; *Curran* v. *Percival*, 21 Neb. 434, 32 N. W. 213; *Com.* v. *Hourigan*, 89 Ky. 305, 12 S. W. 550; *Territory* v. *Campbell*, 9 Mont. 16, 22 Pac. 121; *State* v. *Grant*, 144 Mo. 56, 45 S. W. 1102; *People* v. *Van Tassel*, 156 N. Y. 561, 51 N. E. 274; *Moore* v. *Moore*, 73 Tex. 382, 11 S. W. 396.

But this rule does not limit the cross-examination, for the purpose of laying the foundation for impeachment, to the particular matters testified to by the witness on his direct examination, nor to such matters as bear directly and immediately upon the issue, where they are directly connected with the subject-matter of the examination in chief. *Seller* v. *Jenkins*, 97 Ind. 430.

The test as to whether a fact inquired of on cross-examination is collateral is whether the cross-examining party would be entitled to prove it as part of his own case, as tending to establish his plea. *Johnson* v. *State*, 22 Tex. App. 208, 2 S. W. 609; *Hildeburn* v. *Curran*, 65 Pa. 59.

47. Redirect examination.

A witness may be re-examined to rebut or neutralize any adverse inference which can be drawn from the evidence elicited on his cross-examination.[1] But the right to such re-examination extends only to such inquiries as tend to explain, modify, or rebut the facts or statements brought out in the cross-examination.[2] The court may, however, in its discretion, permit a witness to be re-examined with reference to subjects only brought out on either his cross-examination or his examination in chief.[3]

Where a subject is first introduced on cross-examination the party calling the witness may on his direct examination question him with reference thereto,[4] although the evidence would not have been competent on the examination in chief.[5]

[1] *State* v. *Glenn,* 95 N. C. 677.

[2] *State* v. *Ussery,* 118 N. C. 1177, 24 S. E. 414; *Schaser* v. *State,* 36 Wis. 429; *The Queen's Case,* 2 Brod. & B. 297.

[3] *Schlencker* v. *State,* 9 Neb. 241, 1 N. W. 857; *Donnelly* v. *State,* 26 N. J. L. 601.

[4] *Wadsworth* v. *Dunnan,* 117 Ala. 661, 23 So. 699; *Hamilton* v. *Miller,* 46 Kan. 486, 26 Pac. 1030; *Chicago, R. I. & P. R. Co.* v. *Griffith,* 44 Neb. 690, 62 N. W. 868; *Gray* v. *Cooper,* 65 N. C. 183; *Farmers' Bank* v. *Saling,* 33 Or. 394, 54 Pac. 190; *Chamberlin* v. *Fuller,* 59 Vt. 247, 9 Atl. 832; *Pullman's Palace Car Co.* v. *Harkins,* 5 C. C. A. 326, 17 U. S. App. 22, 55 Fed. 932.

An expert may be asked on redirect examination for the reasons of an opinion brought out on cross-examination. *Leslie* v. *Granite R. Co.* 172 Mass. 468, 52 N. E. 542. So, a witness may testify on redirect examination as to his reasons for his interest disclosed on cross-examination (*Postal Teleg. Cable Co.* v. *Hulsey,* 115 Ala. 193, 22 So. 854), and as to the reasons for his belief as expressed on cross-examination. *Pullen* v. *Pullen* (N. J.) 12 Atl. 138. The circumstances attending the conviction of a witness, which have been proved on his cross-examination, cannot be explained on a redirect examination (*Lamoureux* v. *New York, N. H. & H. R. Co.* 169 Mass. 338, 47 N. E. 1009), though the witness has a right to re-examination to show his innocence (*Sims* v. *Sims,* 75 N. Y. 466; *Wolkoff* v. *Tefft,* 27 Jones & S. 52, 12 N. Y. Supp. 464).

[5] *McElheny* v. *Pittsburgh, V. & C. R. Co.* 147 Pa. 1, 23 Atl. 392; *United States* v. *18 Barrels of High Wines,* 8 Blatchf. 475, Fed. Cas. No. 15,-033.

Cross-examination as to the irrelevant or incompetent matter does not bring it in issue so as to permit a redirect examination upon it. *Smith* v. *Dreer,* 3 Whart. 154; *Miller* v. *Illinois C. R. Co.* 89 Iowa, 567, 57 N. W. 418; *Roberts* v. *Boston,* 149 Mass. 346, 21 N. E. 668. *Contra, Dutcher* v. *Howard,* 15 Wash, 693, 47 Pac. 28. In *Sturgis* v. *Robbins,* 62 Me. 289, the allowance or rejection of relevant testimony on redirect examination under such circumstances was held discretionary with the trial court; and the admission of incompetent testimony on redirect examination was held immaterial, where substantially the same testimony was brought out on cross-examination.

48. Recross-examination.

An opportunity for further cross-examination should be extended where new matter has been elicited upon the redirect examination,[1] but it is proper for the court to restrict such recross-examination to the matters inquired into on the redirect.[2] And where nothing new has been brought out on redirect examination, a further cross-examination is not a right of counsel, and its allowance rests in the discretion of the court.[3]

[1] *Wood* v. *McGuire*, 17 Ga. 303.

[2] *State* v. *Southern*, 48 La. Ann. 628, 19 So. 668; *Thornton* v. *Thornton*, 39 Vt. 122.

[3] *State* v. *Hoppiss*, 27 N. C. (5 Ired. L.) 406; *Atlantic & D. R. Co.* v. *Reiger*, 95 Va. 418, 28 S. E. 590.

But the rejection of an offer to show on recross-examination an important fact omitted upon the cross-examination, the witness being still upon the stand, was an erroneous exercise of this discretion, which will not be sustained unless it is apparent that no injury resulted. *Knight* v. *Cunnington*, 6 Hun, 100.

49. Interpreters; deaf and dumb witnesses.

Where a witness cannot speak the English language, or speaks it very imperfectly, his testimony may properly be given through a sworn interpreter.[1] The accuracy of the interpreter's interpretation may be impeached,[2] and a witness who has testified through an interpreter may make corrections in his testimony as recorded, if he has been misinterpreted.[3]

Deaf mutes may give evidence either through an interpreter who can communicate with them by signs,[4] or by means of written questions and answers;[5] but the fact that they can read or write does not preclude the use of the former method.[6]

[1] *State* v. *Hamilton*, 42 La. Ann. 1204, 8 So. 304; *Chicago & A. R. Co.* v. *Shenk*, 131 Ill. 283, 23 N. E. 436; *State* v. *Severson*, 78 Iowa, 653, 43 N. W. 533; *Houpt* v. *Houpt*, Wright (Ohio) 156; *Norberg's Case*, 4 Mass. 81.

Under the California statute the granting or refusing of an application for an interpreter is vested in the discretion of the court. *People* v. *Young*, 108 Cal. 8, 41 Pac. 281.

A witness who wrote an agreement offered in evidence, which is in a foreign language, may translate it without being sworn as an interpreter. *Krewson* v. *Purdon*, 13 Or. 563, 11 Pac. 281. So, a witness may narrate in English the admissions of a party made in a foreign language. *Com.* v. *Kepper*, 114 Mass. 278. And a party is not bound to resort to an interpreter sworn as such to translate foreign words testified to by a witness, which he claims to have been incorrectly translated by the witness. *Thon* v. *Rochester R. Co.* 29 N. Y. Supp. 675.

Where the oath is administered to witnesses through an interpreter, it is not necessary that the clerk should repeat the oath to him as often as he is called upon to administer it to a witness. *Com.* v. *Jongras,* 181 Pa. 172, 37 Atl. 207.

As to the admissibility of evidence when given through an interpreter, see note to *Com.* v. *Vose* (Mass.) 17 L. R. A. 813.

[2]But the fact that an interpreter took counsel as to the correctness of the interpretation with other persons not sworn does not render the evidence incompetent, where the interpretation is given under oath. *United States* v. *Gibert,* 2 Sumn. 19 Fed. Cas. No. 15,204.

[3]*Erickson* v. *Milwaukee, L. S. & W. R. Co.* 93 Mich. 414, 53 N. W. 393.

[4]*Ruston's Case,* 1 Leach, C. L. 408; *Snyder* v. *Nations,* 5 Blackf. 295.

The interpreter need not be an expert if it is satisfactorily shown that he can correctly interpret the meaning of the communication required. *Skaggs* v. *State,* 108 Ind. 53, 8 N. E. 695; *State* v. *Weldon,* 39 S. C. 318, 24 L. R. A. 126, 17 S. E. 688.

A deaf and dumb person may be appointed as an additional interpreter to interpret between the deaf and dumb witness and the original interpreter, who can declare the testimony orally. *Skaggs* v. *State,* 108 Ind. 53, 8 N. E. 695.

[5]*Ritchey* v. *People,* 23 Colo. 314, 47 Pac. 272, 384.

[6]*State* v. *Howard,* 118 Mo. 127, 24 S. W. 41; *State* v. *De Wolf,* 8 Conn. 93, 20 Am. Dec. 90.

For extended discussion of deaf and dumb persons as witnesses, see note to *State* v. *Weldon* (S. C.) 24 L. R. A. 126.

50. Use of memoranda to refresh recollection.

A witness may refresh and assist his memory by the use of a memorandum made at or near the time to which it relates,[1] and may even be required to do so.[2] It does not seem to be necessary that the writing should be made by the witness himself, provided that, after inspecting it, he can speak to the facts from his own recollection,[3] or because of his confidence in the correctness of the memorandum.[4] But it cannot be so used where the witness neither recollects the facts nor remembers to have recognized the writing as true, since his testimony, so far as founded upon such a writing, is but hearsay.[5]

The writing need not be an original where the witness, after his memory has been refreshed thereby, can testify from his own recollection of the original facts,[6] and can state that the original was a correct statement of the facts, and that the writing used is a true copy.[7] Whether in such case the original must first be accounted for is not free from doubt,[8] but that the memorandum used is inadmissible in evidence is no objection to its use to refresh the memory.[9] Nor need the witness have an independent recollection of the facts, where he can state that at the time the memorandum was made he knew its contents, and knew them to be correct.[10]

Anything used in court to refresh the memory of a witness adverse counsel may see and cross-examine upon,[11] but memoranda which were consulted out of court need not be produced for inspection,[12] unless the witness testifies upon the faith of the papers which he has inspected, and not from his own memory refreshed or confirmed by the examination.[13] The manner in which such memoranda may be used must be left to some extent to the discretion of the court, and where they are voluminous, he may be permitted to refer to them, whenever necessary, and will not be required to examine them all before testifying.[14] Where the witness can neither read nor write, a memorandum signed with his mark cannot be read to him in the presence of the jury, but he must withdraw for that purpose.[15]

Surprise at unexpectedly adverse testimony has been held by the courts of last resort of several states to justify counsel in calling the attention of the witness to his previous testimony, deposition, or affidavit, for the purpose of refreshing his recollection,[16] but in other states such a course is not permitted,[17] and the doctrine has been vigorously assailed by the Supreme Court of the United States as an unwarranted violation of the general rule which restricts the right to refresh memory to contemporaneous memoranda or writing.[18] But where the witness has been examined as to what he stated in a deposition, he may unquestionably be permitted to refresh his recollection from the deposition.[19]

[1]*Woodruff* v. *State*, 61 Ark. 157, 32 S. W. 102; *Rohrig* v. *Pearson*, 15 Colo. 127, 24 Pac. 1083; *Adams* v. *Internal Improv. Fund*, 37 Fla. 266, 20 So. 266; *Brown* v. *Galesburg Pressed Brick & Tile Co.* 132 Ill. 648, 24 N. E. 522; *Sanders* v. *Wakefield*, 41 Kan. 11, 20 Pac. 518; *Atchison, T. & S. F. R. Co.* v. *Lawler*, 40 Neb. 356, 58 N. W. 968; *McCausland* v. *Ralston*, 12 Nev. 195, 28 Am. Rep. 781; *Wise* v. *Phœnix F. Ins. Co.* 101 N. Y. 637, 4 N. E. 634; *Friendly* v. *Lee*, 20 Or. 202, 25 Pac. 396; *Kahn* v. *Traders Ins. Co.* 4 Wyo. 419, 34 Pac. 1059; *Flint* v. *Kennedy*, 33 Fed. 820.

In California, by a Code provision, a witness may refresh his recollection by anything written under his direction, at the time when the fact occurred, or at any other time when the fact was fresh in his memory and he knew that the same was correctly stated in the writing. *McGowan* v. *McDonald*, 111 Cal. 57, 43 Pac. 418.

Refusal to permit a witness to refresh his recollection from memoranda is not erroneous where it is not shown by his testimony that his memory needs the aid of such writings to refresh it. *Hayden* v. *Hoxie*, 27 Ill. App. 533; *State* v. *Baldwin*, 36 Kan. 1, 12 Pac. 318; *Young* v. *Catlett*, 6 Duer, 437. Memoranda cannot be used unless made shortly after the time of the transaction, and while the facts must have been fresh in the memory. *Howell* v. *Carden,* 99 Ala. 100, 10 So. 640; Swartz v. *Chickering,* 58 Md. 291; *Schuyler Nat. Bank* v. *Bullong,* 24 Neb. 825, 40 N. W. 413; *Ballard* v. *Ballard,* 5 Rich. L. 495; *Bergman* v. *Shoudy,* 9 Wash. 331, 37 Pac. 453; *Maxwell* v. *Wilkinson,* 113 U. S. 656, *sub nom. Parsons* v. *Wilkinson,* 28 L. ed. 1037, 5 Sup. Ct. Rep. 691.

Where the original memorandum was made in time, it is immaterial when the copy was made, if it sufficiently appears to be a true copy. *Lawson* v. *Glass,* 6 Colo. 134.

A memorandum of items of work done on a building, prepared by the witness from an inspection of the premises, may be used to refresh recollection, although not made until long after the work was done. *Ahern* v. *Boyce,* 26 Mo. App. 558. And see *Johnston* v. *Farmers' F. Ins. Co.* 106 Mich. 96, 64 N. W. 5, in which a witness in an action on a policy of fire insurance was allowed to use a list of goods made by him from recollection a short time before the trial. It is no objection that the memorandum is written in characters which the witness alone can read. *State* v. *Cardoza,* 11 S. C. 195, 238.

[2] *Chapin* v. *Lapham,* 20 Pick. 467; *State* v. *Staton,* 114 N. C. 813, 19 S. E. 96.

[3] *State* v. *Lull,* 37 Me. 246; *Labaree* v. *Klosterman,* 33 Neb. 150, 49 N. W. 1102; *Huckins* v. *Peoples' Mut. F. Ins. Co.* 31 N. H. 238; *Huff* v. *Bennett,* 6 N. Y. 337; *State* v. *Finley,* 118 N. C. 1161, 24 S. E. 495; *Springs* v. *South Bound R. Co.* 46 S. C. 104, 24 S. E. 166; *Aldrich* v. *Griffith,* 66 Vt. 390, 29 Atl. 376; *Hill* v. *State,* 17 Wis. 675.

[4] *Bowden* v. *Spellman,* 59 Ark. 251, 27 S. W. 602; *Card* v. *Foot,* 56 Conn. 369, 15 Atl. 371; *Billingslea* v. *Smith,* 77 Md. 504, 26 Atl. 1077; *Coffin* v. *Vincent,* 12 Cush. 98; *Third Nat. Bank* v. *Owen,* 101 Mo. 558, 14 S. W. 632; *Crystal Ice Mfg. Co.* v. *San Antonio Brewing Asso.* 8 Tex. Civ. App. 1, 27 S. W. 210.

[5] *Orr* v. *Farmers' Alliance Warehouse & Commission Co.* 97 Ga. 241, 22 S. E. 937; *Chamberlain* v. *Sands,* 27 Me. 458; *Green* v. *Caulk,* 16 Md. 556; *Douglas* v. *Leighton,* 57 Minn. 81, 58 N. W. 827; *Fritz* v. *Burris,* 41 S. C. 149, 19 S. E. 304; *Steele* v. *Wisner,* 141 Pa. 63, 21 Atl. 527; *Tingley* v. *Fairhaven Land Co.* 9 Wash. 34, 36 Pac. 1098.

[6] *Lawson* v. *Glass,* 6 Colo. 134; *Finch* v. *Barclay,* 87 Ga. 393, 13 S. E. 566; *Bonnet* v. *Glattfeldt,* 120 Ill. 166, 11 N. E. 250; *Bullock* v. *Hunter,* 44 Md. 416; *Robinson* v. *Mulder,* 81 Mich. 75, 45 N. W. 505; *George* v. *Joy,* 19 N. H. 544; *Berry* v. *Jourdan,* 11 Rich. L. 67; *Flato* v. *Brod,* 37 Tex. 735; *Harrison* v. *Middleton,* 11 Gratt. 527; *Folsom* v. *Apple River Log-Driving Co.* 41 Wis. 602; *New York & C. Min. Syndicate & Co.* v. *Fraser,* 130 U. S. 611, 32 L. ed. 1031, 9 Sup. Ct. Rep. 665.

[7] *Calloway* v. *Varner,* 77 Ala. 541, 54 Am. Rep. 78; *People* v. *Munroe* (Cal.) 33 Pac. 776; *Chicago & A. R. Co.* v. *Adler,* 56 Ill. 344; *Anderson* v. *Imhoff,* 34 Neb. 335, 51 N. W. 854; *Mead* v. *McGraw,* 19 Ohio St. 57; *Houston & T. C. R. Co.* v. *Burke,* 55 Tex. 323, 40 Am. Rep. 808.

Where the notes of a reporter from which an article was written have been destroyed, he may be allowed to refer to and read the article as published, to refresh his memory, where it contains substantially the article written. *Hawes* v. *State*, 88 Ala. 37, 7 So. 302; *Com.* v. *Ford*, 130 Mass. 64, 39 Am. Rep. 426.

The correctness of a copy of a memorandum made by someone other than the witness must be proved before he will be allowed to refresh his memory from it. *Birmingham* v. *McPoland*, 96 Ala. 363, 11 So. 427. And a witness cannot refresh his memory from a memorandum made up at his dictation, by his attorney, from old letters, memoranda, and receipts. *Watson* v. *Miller*, 82 Tex. 279, 17 S. W. 1053.

[8]The weight of authority is to the effect that where a witness refers to a copy of a memorandum merely to refresh his recollection, the original need not be produced or accounted for. *Denver & R. G. R. Co.* v. *Wilson*, 4 Colo. App. 355, 36 Pac. 67; *Erie Preserving Co.* v. *Miller*, 52 Conn. 446, 52 Am. Rep. 607; *Com.* v. *Ford*, 130 Mass. 64, 39 Am. Rep. 426; *Harrison* v. *Middleton*, 11 Gratt. 527. *Contra*, *Jones* v. *Jones*, 94 N. C. 114; *Byrnes* v. *Pacific Exp. Co.* (Tex. App.) 15 S. W. 46. But his refusal to produce the original may be considered by the jury in weighing his testimony. *Chicago & A. R. Co.* v. *Adler*, 56 Ill. 344; *Davie* v. *Jones*, 68 Me. 393.

[9]*Morris* v. *Everly*, 19 Colo. 529, 36 Pac. 150; *Cameron* v. *Blackman*, 39 Mich. 108; *Mead* v. *White* (Pa.) 8 Atl. 913; *Birchall* v. *Bullough* [1896] 1 Q. B. 325, 65 L. J. Q. B. N. S. 252, 74 L. T. N. S. 27.

[10]*Acklen* v. *Hickman*, 63 Ala. 494, 35 Am. Rep. 54; *Burbank* v. *Dennis*, 101 Cal. 90, 35 Pac. 444; *Flynn* v. *Gardner*, 3 Ill. App. 253; *O'Brien* v. *Stambach*, 101 Iowa, 40, 69 N. W. 1133; *Wright* v. *Wright*, 58 Kan. 525, 50 Pac. 444; *Evans* v. *Murphy*, 87 Md. 498, 40 Atl. 109; *Costello* v. *Crowell*, 133 Mass. 352; *Stahl* v. *Duluth*, 71 Minn. 341, 74 N. W. 143; *Lipscomb* v. *Lyon*, 19 Neb. 511, 27 N. W. 731; *Abel* v. *Strimple*, 31 Mo. App. 86; *Bateman* v. *New York C. & H. R. R. Co.* 47 Hun, 429; *State* v. *Colwell*, 3 R. I. 132; *State* v. *Rawls*, 2 Nott & M'C. 332; *Davis* v. *Field*, 56 Vt. 426; *Harrison* v. *Middleton*, 11 Gratt. 527; *Schettler* v. *Jones*, 20 Wis. 412; *McClaskey* v. *Barr*, 45 Fed. 151. *Contra*, *Clark* v. *State*, 4 Ind. 156; *Redden* v. *Spruance*, 4 Harr. (Del.) 217; *Owings* v. *Shannon*, 1 A. K. Marsh, 188.

Otherwise where a paper was drawn up several weeks after the fact occurred, unless the witness can speak from his memory after being refreshed by it. *O'Neale* v. *Walton*, 1 Rich. L. 234.

[11]*Peck* v. *Lake*, 3 Lans. 136; *Atchison, T. & S. F. R. Co.* v. *Hays*, 8 Kan. App. 545, 54 Pac. 322; *Cortland Mfg. Co.* v. *Platt*, 83 Mich. 419, 47 N. W. 330; *Wernwag* v. *Chicago & A. R. Co.* 20 Mo. App. 473; *McKivitt* v. *Cone*, 30 Iowa, 455; *National Bank of Commerce* v. *First Nat. Bank*, 10 C. C. A. 87, 27 U. S. App. 88, 61 Fed. 809; *Chute* v. *State*, 19 Minn. 271, Gil. 230.

But he is not bound to introduce it in evidence. *Little* v. *Lichkoff*, 98 Ala. 321, 12 So. 429. And he may waive the right of inspection. *Adae* v. *Zangs*, 41 Iowa, 536; *Wernwag* v. *Chicago & A. R. Co.* 20 Mo. App. 473.

Where a witness consults a diary to refresh his memory with respect to a date, the entire book need not be exposed to inspection, but only such parts of it as he consults, or such as relate to the subject-matter of his testimony. *Com.* v. *Haley*, 13 Allen, 587. Otherwise, where the diary seems to have been prepared for the occasion, being kept for only a few days, but purporting to include the date in question. *Kouba* v. *Horacek*, 24 N. Y. S. R. 990, 6 N. Y. Supp. 250.

[12]*State* v. *Collins*, 15 S. C. 379, 40 Am. Rep. 697; *State* v. *Cheek*, 35 N. C. (13 Ired. L.) 114; *Wabash & E. Canal Co.* v. *Bledsoe*, 5 Ind. 133.

So held even under a statute providing that where a witness is allowed to refresh his memory the writing must be produced, and may be inspected by the adverse party, who may read it to the jury. *State* v. *Magers*, 36 Or. 38, 58 Pac. 892.

[13]*Hall* v. *Ray*, 18 N. H. 126.

[14]*Johnson* v. *Coles*, 21 Minn. 108; *Bullock* v. *Hunter*, 44 Md. 417.

[15]*Com.* v. *Fox*, 7 Gray, 585. In this case the witness was directed to withdraw with one counsel on each side, and have the paper read to her without comment.

[16]*Billingslea* v. *State*, 85 Ala. 323, 5 So. 137; *Stanley* v. *Stanley*, 112 Ind. 143, 13 N. E. 261; *State* v. *Miller*, 53 Iowa, 154, 4 N. W. 900; *State* v. *Sorter*, 52 Kan. 531, 34 Pac. 1036; *People* v. *Palmer*, 105 Mich. 568, 63 N. W. 656; *People* v. *Kelly*, 113 N. Y. 647, 21 N. E. 122; *George* v. *Triplett*, 5 N. D. 50, 63 N. W. 891; *Hurley* v. *State*, 46 Ohio St. 320, 4 L. R. A. 161, 21 N. E. 645.

The witness must, however, speak from his own recollection. *Howie* v. *Rea*, 75 N. C. 326.

[17]*Com.* v. *Phelps*, 11 Gray, 73; *Velott* v. *Lewis*, 102 Pa. 326.

[18]*Putnam* v. *United States*, 162 U. S. 687, 40 L. ed. 1118, 16 Sup. Ct. Rep. 923.

[19]*George* v. *Joy*, 19 N. H. 544.

V. Ruling on offers and objections.

[A statement of objection not indicating its ground is not sufficient to require exclusion, unless the objection be of such a nature that it could not be obviated, or it appears that the party making the offer could not have avoided the ground of objection had it been specifically stated. But it is not error to sustain such general objection if any sufficient ground for it exists, provided that there is no refusal of any request that the ground be specified.]

51. Questions, how tried.

Whether evidence is admissible or not is a question of law for the court; and questions of fact incidental to its determination are also for the court to determine for that purpose.[1]

[1]*Com.* v. *Morrell*, 99 Mass. 543 (evidence of loss to let in secondary evi-

dence); *Nicholson* v. *State*, 38 Md. 140 (voluntary character of confessions); *Com.* v. *Robinson*, 146 Mass. 571, 16 N. E. 452 (evidence of plan or common design to let in evidence of other murders); *State* v. *Spell*, 38 La. Ann. 20, and cases cited (threats); *People* v. *Smith*, 104 N. Y. 491, 58 Am. Rep. 537, 10 N. E. 873 (dying declarations); *Com.* v. *Sturtivant*, 117 Mass. 122, 19 Am. Rep. 401 (qualifications of expert); *Com.* v. *Coe*, 115 Mass. 481 (proof of standard of comparison of handwriting); *State* v. *Harris*, 45 La. Ann. 842, 13 So. 199 (threats); *Com.* v. *Sullivan*, 156 Mass. 229, 30 N. E. 1023 (sufficiency of notice to warrant introduction of secondary evidence); *State* v. *Miller*, 42 La. Ann. 1186, 8 So. 309 (confessions); *Com.* v. *Brewer*, 164 Mass. 577, 42 N. E. 92 (dying declarations); *State* v. *McKenzie*, 144 Mo. 40, 45 S. W. 1117 (voluntary character of confession); *People* v. *Kinney*, 124 Mich. 486, 83 N. W. 147 (qualification of nonexpert witness).

For further illustrations see *post*, Division XXXIX. §§ 12, 15, 18.

52. Hearing in presence of jury.

It is not error to hear the evidence[1] and argument[2] upon such a preliminary question in the hearing of the jury, if they are given to understand that the evidence is not for them.

But the court may, at its discretion, do so in the absence of the jury.[3]

[1] *People* v. *Smith*, 104 N. Y. 491, 58 Am. Rep. 537, 10 N. E. 873 (dying declarations; so held, even though in hearing the preliminary proof the judge allowed the proposed evidence, the competency of which was in question, to be given in full); *State* v. *Cain*, 20 W. Va. 679 (dying declarations; the court here laid some stress on the fact that the judge admonished the jury that the evidence was not for them); *State* v. *Shaffer*, 23 Or. 555, 32 Pac. 545; *State* v. *Murdy*, 81 Iowa, 603, 47 N. W. 867 (dying declarations); *Shepherd* v. *State*, 31 Neb. 389, 47 N. W. 1118 (voluntary character of confession); *Lefevre* v. *State*, 50 Ohio St. 584, 35 N. E. 523; *Austin* v. *Com.* 19 Ky. L. Rep. 474, 40 S. W. 905; *Sims* v. *State*, 36 Tex. Crim. Rep. 154, 36 S. W. 256.

[2] *State* v. *Wood*, 53 N. H. 484.

[3] *State* v. *Wood*, 53 N. H. 484; *Driggers* v. *State*, 38 Fla. 7, 20 So. 758; *State* v. *Row*, 81 Iowa, 138, 46 N. W. 872.

53. Cogency of preliminary proof.

When the competency of evidence depends upon the determination of an incidental fact by the court, such fact need not be established by a weight of evidence amounting to a demonstration. It is only necessary that there should be so much evidence as to make it proper to submit the whole testimony to the jury.[1]

[1] *Com.* v. *Robinson*, 146 Mass. 571, 16 N. E. 452.

VI. Striking out.

54. Right to strike out.

If illegal evidence has been received against objection, or upon a promise to render it competent, and the promise is not kept, the accused is entitled to have it struck out on motion.[1]

So also of the testimony of a witness for the prosecution whom the accused has had no opportunity to cross-examine.[2]

But a party calling out illegal testimony has no right to have it excluded on his own motion, and it is error to grant his motion to exclude it over his adversary's objection.[3]

[1] *Dillin* v. *People,* 8 Mich. 357; *Zell* v. *Com.* 94 Pa. 258. These cases hold that merely instructing the jury to disregard it does not cure the error. Compare *Hoyt* v. *Utah,* 120 U. S. 430, 30 L. ed. 708, 7 Sup. Ct. Rep. 614.

For other authorities on this question, see *supra,* § 7; and Civil Trial Brief, chapter XII., generally.

[2] *People* v. *Cole,* 43 N. Y. 508. And see *supra,* § 43.

[3] *Toliver* v. *State,* 94 Ala. 111, 10 So. 428.

55. — omission of objection.

The failure to object before an answer was made, if the grounds of objection were then apparent, precludes a subsequent motion to strike out the answer.[1]

[1] *People* v. *Chacon,* 102 N. Y. 669, 6 N. E. 303 (so holding even where the objection was that the witness was apparently proceeding to repeat an improper answer which had been already struck out. Counsel cannot lie by and speculate on the chances of first hearing what the witness will testify to, and then, when he finds the testimony unsatisfactory, move to strike it out); *State* v. *Wright,* 98 Iowa, 702, 68 N. W. 440; *Exon* v. *State* (Tex. Crim. App.) 33 S. W. 336; *Mabry* v. *State,* 71 Miss. 716, 14 So. 267; *Traylor* v. *State,* 100 Ala. 142, 14 So. 634; *People* v. *Nelson,* 85 Cal. 421, 24 Pac. 1006; *Goldman* v. *State,* 75 Md. 621, 23 Atl. 1097; *State* v. *Marcks,* 140 Mo. 656, 41 S. W. 973, 43 S. W. 1095.

I. ACCOMPLICE AS A WITNESS.

[The general principle is that accomplices are now competent for or against each other, unless jointly indicted; and even if jointly indicted, they are competent against each other if separately tried. But the courts have a discretion whether to allow one to be used against the other, because this may imply a promise of immunity. As to who is an accomplice, see *post*, Division XLII.]

1. Competency for the prosecution; discretion of court.

Accomplices, whether related as principal and accessory, or equally concerned in guilt, are, except on a joint trial of a joint indictment, competent witnesses for the prosecution.[1] But the court has power to refuse to allow the testimony of one who has not been finally convicted to be received against his accomplice, because of public policy, in view of the implied promise of immunity which results from receiving his testimony.[2]

[1]*People* v. *Whipple,* 9 Cow. 707; *State* v. *Stewart,* 142 Mo. 412, 44 S. W. 240; *State* v. *Riney,* 137 Mo. 102, 38 S. W. 718; *Brown* v. *State* (Fla.) 27 So. 869.

In *People* v. *Lohman,* 2 Barb. 216, the court says: "The law is well settled that a principal is a competent witness against an accessory. So also are accomplices against the copartners in crime." See also *People* v. *Costello,* 1 Denio, 83 (the rule is unquestioned, though the former idea, that the woman is an accomplice in an abortion practised on herself, is now abandoned); *Allison* v. *State,* 14 Tex. App. 402 (where it is held, under Tex. Code Crim. Proc. art. 730, to be no error to admit an accomplice as a witness for the state where the defendant was separately indicted and separately tried). And see authorities under *infra,* §§ 4–6.

It makes no difference that he is induced to testify by a promise of immunity; for the rule that a confession so induced is not competent applies only to confessions by the accused. *People* v. *O'Neil,* 48 Hun, 36.

The arrest of one on suspicion of complicity in a homicide is not ground for excluding his testimony in a prosecution for murder. Even though an accomplice he would still be competent, that fact going to the weight, and not to the competency, of his testimony. *State* v. *Reed,* 50 La. Ann. 990, 24 So. 131.

In Montana by express statute an accomplice is a competent witness for or against one jointly concerned in the commission of an offense; and he is not rendered incompetent because of any immunity offered him, nor is his testimony subject to rules governing admissions by a person on trial. *State* v. *Geddes,* 22 Mont. 68, 55 Pac. 919, Citing *Vaughan* v. *State,* 57 Ark. 1, 20 S. W. 588; *Black* v. *State,* 59 Wis. 471, 18 N. W. 457; *People* v. *O'Neil,* 48 Hun, 36.

In Indiana by express statute accomplices are competent witnesses where they consent to testify. The statute imposes no limitations and creates no exceptions. *Conway* v. *State,* 118 Ind. 482, 21 N. E. 285, and cases cited.

In Minnesota, prior to the amendment of 1868 to Gen. Stat. 1866, chap. 73, § 7, one defendant was not competent to become a witness for or against his codefendant until convicted, acquitted, or discharged. The amendment established a new rule; and, on a trial of one defendant under a joint indictment against two, his codefendant may offer himself as a witness, and give testimony in behalf of the state against the defendant on trial. *State* v. *Thaden,* 43 Minn. 325, 45 N. W. 614.

Under act of Congress March 16, 1878 (20 Stat. at L. 30, chap. 37), providing that in the trial of persons charged with criminal offenses in the courts of the United States "the person so charged shall, at his own request, but not otherwise, be a competent witness," one of two defendants jointly indicted and tried may, at his own request, be examined as a witness by the government. *Wolfson* v. *United States,* 41 C. C. A. 422, 101 Fed. 430, 102 Fed. 134. "This statute," said the court, "in terms, makes a defendant a competent witness. The statute does not say 'a competent witness for himself.' It does not say 'a competent witness for the government,' He is made simply, 'at his own request, but not otherwise,' a competent witness. It would clearly be improper for the government, while he was on trial, in the absence of a request on his part, to call him as a witness. The purpose of the law was to make defendants competent witnesses, but at the same time to preserve to them the right to remain silent without prejudice. When any defendant chooses to testify, the statute permits him to do so. It does not matter whether his testimony is for or against himself, or for or against his codefendant. The only limitation in the statute is that he shall not be made a witness except on his own request. Being sworn as a witness at his own request, he is amenable, generally, to the rules governing other witnesses. He could testify against or for his codefendant on trial with him, because the only reason why he could not do so at common law was that he was a party to the record, and interested in the case. In other words, the only common-law reason for his exclusion was that he was a defendant also on trial. The statute clearly removes that objection. The fact that two defendants were on trial does not prevent the statute applying. There is nothing in it to confine its operation to cases where but a single defendant is named in the indictment. At the time the statute was passed the law permitted two or more defendants to be jointly indicted. It was left in the discretion of the court to grant or refuse separate trials. *United States* v. *Marchant,* 12 Wheat. 480, 6 L. ed. 700. The Congress surely meant that this statute should be applied to cases where several defendants were indicted together, so as to make each of them a competent witness; otherwise it would have been left in the discretion of the court, where more than one were in the same indictment, to abrogate the statute by refusing a severance."

'*People* v. *Whipple,* 9 Cow. 707. On motion to examine principal against accessory on trial of accessory, after conviction of principal, but before judgment thereon, held that he was competent; but the court in its discretion should refuse to allow him to be used as a witness. Duer, Ch. J., says: "The principle deducible from the cases undoubtedly is that an accomplice, although a competent witness against the associates and partners of his guilt, is nevertheless only admissible from reasons of judicial necessity and policy, and in furtherance of the essential ends of public justice. And the question always addresses itself to the discretion of the court; not to their judgment as to the general competency of the witness, but to their sound legal discretion, whether, upon a full consideration of the facts and circumstances of the case, he shall be permitted to testify under an implied promise of pardon, which vests in him an equitable title thereto if he speaks the truth. . . . The motion now made, being thus addressed to our discretion, is to be regarded in the same light as if, instead of it, the public prosecutor had moved the court to suspend sentence upon Strang [witness], that he might be admitted as a witness against the prisoner. And it is so to be regarded, because his competency, after conviction, rests on the possibility of the judgment against him being arrested, and the present conviction set aside for irregularity or error. It is, moreover, to be considered as if Strang had already been admitted as a witness, had testified for the people on the present trial in the character of an accomplice, had told the whole truth to the satisfaction of the court, and by himself or his counsel now claimed of us to suspend the sentence of the law and recommend him for pardon."

2. — joint trial.

If jointly indicted it is discretionary with the court or district attorney to allow a *nolle prosequi* as to an accomplice,[1] or the court may direct his acquittal,[2] or, even after verdict, suspend sentence if necessary,[3] in order to enable the prosecution to call the accomplice as a witness.

This discretion is to be exercised in view of the fact that to use the accomplice as a witness for the state without previous acquittal impliedly promises him immunity from punishment.[4]

The power may be exercised at the trial, and without previous application or formal order.[5]

[1] *Linsday* v. *People,* 63 N. Y. 143 (held discretionary, and no error to grant the district attorney's application at the trial for leave to enter a *nol. pros.* as to one of the joint defendants, to render him competent against the other); *State* v. *Graham,* 41 N. J. L. 15, 32 Am. Rep. 174 (holding that the court may assent to the entering of a *nol. pros.* by the attorney general for the purpose of qualifying a joint defendant as a witness for the state); *Bolton* v. *State* (Tex. Crim. App.) 43 S. W. 984; *Love* v. *People,* 160 Ill. 501, 32 L. R. A. 139, 43 N. E. 710.

The authority or power on the part of the state to dismiss a case against a defendant and record his testimony against a codefendant, under Tex. Code Crim. Proc. 1895, art. 709, providing that the attorney representing the state may at any time under the rules provided in art. 37 dismiss a prosecution as to one or more defendants jointly indicted with others, and that the person so discharged may be introduced as a witness by either party, extends only to the particular case on trial, and not to any other distinct offense. *Ex parte Park,* 37 Tex. Crim. Rep. 590, 40 S. W. 300.

[2] *State* v. *Graham,* 41 N. J. L. 15, 32 Am. Rep. 174. *Dictum,* that the court may direct acquittal for the purpose, or accept a plea admitting guilt to such a degree as in the opinion of the court is requisite.

[3] *People* v. *Whipple,* 9 Cow. 707, 715 (*dictum*).

[4] *Linsday* v. *People,* 63 N. Y. 143, and *State* v. *Graham,* 41 N. J. L. 15, 32 Am. Rep. 174, cited *supra,* note 1. Compare, as to effect of refusal to testify, *United States* v. *Hinz,* 35 Fed. 272.

[1]*Linsday* v. *People*, 63 N. Y. 143 (cited *supra*, note 1), where the court says: "There is no practice in this state requiring a previous application or a formal order of the court to permit an accomplice to become a witness for the state."

3. — separate trials.

Persons jointly indicted are made competent against each other by directing separate trials, provided the court assents to receiving the testimony.[1]

[1]*Gilbert* v. *Com.* 21 Ky. L. Rep. 544, 51 S. W. 804; *Williams* v. *State* (Fla.) 27 So. 898; *People* v. *McCullough*, 81 Mich. 25, 45 N. W. 515; *Smith* v. *Com.* 90 Va. 759, 19 S. E. 843; *Edwards* v. *State*, 2 Wash. 291, 26 Pac. 258.

In *Wixson* v. *People*, 5 Park. Crim. Rep. 119, it is said they are competent against each other, with permission of the court, but not for each other though separately tried, while the indictment is pending against them. See also *Taylor* v. *People*, 12 Hun, 212. Following *Wixson* v. *People*, and disapproving *People* v. *Donnelly*, 1 Abb. Pr. 459.

In *State* v. *Barrows*, 76 Me. 401, 49 Am. Rep. 629, it is held, reviewing authorities, no error to admit one of two, jointly indicted, as a witness against his codefendant upon his separate trial, although the indictment against such witness is still pending and to it he has pleaded not guilty.

In *Carroll* v. *State*, 5 Neb. 31, it is held that a joint defendant is competent for the state on a separate trial, though not acquitted himself. Citing *Brown* v. *State*, 18 Ohio St. 509, to the same effect.

In *Noyes* v. *State*, 41 N. J. L. 418, it is held no error to admit codefendant as a witness for the state upon the separate trial of the defendant.

So also in *State* v. *Brien*, 32 N. J. L. 414, with a *dictum* that such codefendant would also be a competent witness for the defendant under the same circumstances.

In *Allen* v. *State*, 10 Ohio St. 287, it is held no error to admit a principal as a witness against his accessory and codefendant upon his separate trial, for it makes no difference whether an accomplice is indicted or not, as he is a competent witness, if not on trial at the same time with his codefendant.

4. Competency for each other.

Accomplices, whether related as principal and accessory, or equally concerned in guilt, are competent witnesses for each other, except when under a joint indictment.[1]

If tried under joint indictment, whether tried together or separately, neither is competent for the other.[2]

[1]*United States* v. *Hunter*, 1 Cranch C. C. 446, Fed. Cas. No. 15,425. It was here agreed to try separate indictments for joint assault at the same

time by the same jury; and it was held that the attorney for all the defendants could call and swear one as a witness for the others, as all were not jointly indicted.

In *McKenzie* v. *State*, 24 Ark. 636, the defendant called as a witness one who had been jointly indicted with him for the crime, but as to whom a *nolle prosequi* had been entered, and against whom a subsequent separate indictment was still pending; held reversible error to exclude him.

In *Lucre* v. *State*, 7 Baxt. 148, one indicted for stealing a horse from A was offered as a witness upon the separate trial of the defendant, separately indicted for stealing a horse from B which was stolen at the same time, and the evidence showed that the defendant and the witness had been found together in possession of the two horses. Held, reversible error to exclude such witness, as the indictments were separate, and not for the same offense; for accomplices are incompetent for each other only when jointly indicted, or at least when indicted for the same offense.

In *United States* v. *Hanway*, 2 Wall. Jr. 139, Fed. Cas. No. 15,299, on the trial of a defendant separately indicted for treason, it was held that one jointly indicted with defendant and others, in another indictment still pending, for the same offense, was a competent witness for the defendant.

Compare *Crutchfield* v. *State*, 7 Tex. App. 65 (holding under Tex. Code Crim. Proc. art. 731, no error to admit an accomplice as witness for defendant upon a separate trial and separate indictments); and *Jenkins* v. *State*, 30 Tex. App. 379, 17 S. W. 938 (holding that under art. 731 it was not error to exclude an accomplice who was being prosecuted under separate information). To the same effect, *Day* v. *State*, 27 Tex. App. 143, 11 S. W. 36, holding also, however, that the indictments must be for the same offense, and not merely for similar offenses, and that the burden is upon the state to show the incompetency of a witness by showing that the offense was the same.

[2] The reason is the common-law disqualification of a party to the record. See *Day* v. *State*, 27 Tex. App. 143, 11 S. W. 36, cited *supra*. *Contra*, *Jeffries* v. *Com.* 84 Ky. 237, 1 S. W. 442; *State* v. *Gigher*, 23 Iowa, 318; *McGinness* v. *State*, 4 Wyo. 115, 31 Pac. 978.

5. — joint indictment.

Persons jointly indicted are not made competent for each other until the charge against the one proposed as a witness has been disposed of.[1] Merely severing in trial is not, before verdict or *nolle prosequi*, enough to remove the disqualification.[2]

[1] *People* v. *Bill*, 10 Johns. 95 (holding that it is "a technical rule of evidence, and one well settled, that a party in the same suit or indictment cannot be a witness for his codefendant until he has been first acquitted or at least convicted. Whether the defendants be tried jointly or separately does not vary the rule"); *State* v. *Jones*, 51 Me. 125 (*dictum*, that "the general rule of law is that parties to the record in a criminal

case cannot be witnesses for each other. . . . There are, however, exceptions to the general rule. One is that if no evidence is given against one of several joint defendants the court may order his acquittal, and he may be used as a witness by them;" and holding it reversible error to exclude one joint defendant as a witness for the other after such joint defendant has voluntarily pleaded guilty; because the charge against him is then disposed of, and he is no longer a party to the issue to be tried).

[a]*People* v. *Bill*, 10 Johns. 95. Held no error to exclude one of two joint defendants offered as a witness for his codefendant on his separate trial.

People v. *Williams*, 19 Wend. 377; *McIntyre* v. *People*, 9 N. Y. 38; and *Com.* v. *Marsh*, 10 Pick. 57, all cite and follow *People* v. *Bill*, *supra*, on this point.

State v. *Dumphey*, 4 Minn. 438, Gil. 340, cites *Baker* v. *United States*, 1 Minn. 207, Gil. 181, and both follow *Com.* v. *Marsh*, *supra*, in holding it no error to exclude such a witness.

In *State* v. *Roberts*, 15 Mo. 28, it was held no error to exclude a codefendant as a witness for the defendant upon his separate trial,—Overruling *Garret* v. *State*, 6 Mo. 1, and holding that such a witness is incompetent unless acquitted or convicted.

Collier v. *State*, 20 Ark. 36, and *State* v. *Dunlop*, 65 N. C. 288, hold that an accessory jointly indicted with the defendant (principal) cannot be a witness for him on his separate trial. To same effect, *Warfield* v. *State*, 35 Tex. 736 (under Texas statute).

In *United States* v. *Reid*, 12 How. 361, 13 L. ed. 1023, it was held that § 34 of the judiciary act does not apply to trials for offenses against the United States; and that upon the separate trial, in a Federal court, of two persons jointly indicted for an offense against the United States, it is not error to exclude one offered as a witness for the other, notwithstanding such evidence would have been competent in the courts of the state where the trial was had, under a law of that state. *Contra*, *People* v. *Newberry*, 20 Cal. 439, and *Poteete* v. *State*, 9 Baxt. 261, 40 Am. Rep. 90 (both holding it error to exclude one joint defendant as a witness on the separate trial of the other); *State* v. *Brien*, 32 N. J. L. 414 (well-considered *dictum* that an accomplice would be competent on the separate trial of a codefendant even though jointly indicted; and held no error to allow such an accomplice to testify for the state); *Jones* v. *State*, 1 Ga. 610 (*dictum*, that joint defendants are competent witnesses for each other when tried separately).

And statutes have changed the rule in many jurisdictions. *Com.* v. *Brown*, 130 Mass. 279; *State* v. *Gigher*, 23 Iowa, 318; *State* v. *Stewart*, 51 Iowa, 312, 1 N. W. 646; *Marshall* v. *State*, 8 Ind. 498; *Hunt* v. *State*, 10 Ind. 69; *Lazier* v. *Com.* 10 Gratt. 708; *Marler* v. *State*, 67 Ala. 55, 42 Am. Rep. 95.

Where persons jointly indicted have been granted a severance, it is not error for the court to refuse to allow one against whom the indictment is pending to testify on behalf of the defense on the trial of his codefendant. *Brooks* v. *State* (Tex. Crim. App.) 56 S. W. 924.

6. — — how made competent.

The court has power, on the trial of a joint indictment, to submit the case to the jury as to one of the accused,[1] or direct an acquittal,[2] or allow a *nolle prosequi*[3] as to him, before completing the trial as to the other accused, in order to render the former competent as a witness for the latter.

But it is in the discretion of the court to refuse to do so.[4]

[1] In *People* v. *Vermilyea*, 7 Cow. 369, Savage, Ch. J., said: "The proper course was, if the testimony against Davis was slight, to have the jury pass on his case, and then introduce him as a witness on behalf of his codefendants."

[2] In *People* v. *Bill*, 10 Johns. 95, the court says: "The practice is, when nothing appears against one of the defendants, for the court to direct his immediate acquittal, so that the other defendant may use him as a witness." See also *State* v. *Roberts*, 15 Mo. 28. *Dictum* to same effect.

[3] *State* v. *Young*, 39 N. H. 283. *Dictum*, that nothing short of a *nolle prosequi* or acquittal, etc., will render a joint defendant competent for his codefendant; and holding a plea of *nolo contendere* insufficient.

[4] In *Com.* v. *Eastman*, 1 Cush. 189, 48 Am. Dec. 596, it is held discretionary whether to submit the case of one joint defendant to the jury to make him by acquittal competent for the others. The judge may refuse in his discretion, even if he thinks the weight of evidence is in favor of such defendant; for the defendants have no legal right to such submission if there is any evidence against such defendant.

In *Fitzgerald* v. *State*, 14 Mo. 413, it is held that on this principle it is no error to refuse to submit the case of one of the defendants to the jury so as to qualify him as a witness by his acquittal, even though the record shows that he was in the end acquitted when the case of both defendants was left to the jury.

7. Effect of plea or verdict.

A verdict of guilty[1] or a plea of guilty,[2] if accepted, removes the disqualification of an accomplice. A plea of *nolo contendere* does not.[3]

[1] *Wixson* v. *People*, 5 Park. Crim. Rep. 119 (*dictum*, that persons jointly indicted may be witnesses for each other if acquitted, "and even if convicted, unless it be for a crime which disqualifies, and then sentence must have followed the conviction"); *State* v. *Jones*, 51 Me. 125. See also *Com.* v. *Marsh*, 10 Pick. 57, 58 (*dictum*, that "after one of several defendants has been convicted by his own confession or otherwise, and the conviction does not make him incompetent," he may testify for or against the other defendants, for after conviction he is no longer a party to the issue); *Baker* v. *United States*, 1 Minn. 207, Gil. 181 (*dictum*, that a judgment against a joint defendant, or a discharge, would render him competent for his codefendant, and thus form an ex-

ception to the general rule); *State* v. *Stotts*, 26 Mo. 307 (holding it reversible error to exclude a joint defendant as witness for the defendant, where such joint defendant has been separately tried and convicted, and the only punishment was a fine, even though not paid).

State v. *Sullivan*, 20 R. I. 114, 37 Atl. 673, holds that a witness who has been convicted of the same crime as that for which defendant is on trial, and is serving a life sentence in the state prison therefor, is not incompetent by reason of such facts; but the weight of his testimony is for the jury.

[2]*Patterson* v. *Com.* 86 Ky. 313, 5 S. W. 387; *State* v. *Asbury*, 49 La. Ann. 1741, 23 So. 322; *State* v. *Savage*, 36 Or. 191, 60 Pac. 610, 61 Pac. 1128; *State* v. *Magone*, 32 Or. 206, 51 Pac. 452; *State* v. *Harrison*, 66 Vt. 523, 29 Atl. 807.

In *Com.* v. *Smith*, 12 Met. 238, one of two jointly indicted pleaded guilty, and it was held no error to admit him as a witness for the prosecution against the other. Shaw, Ch. J., said: "The reason [for exclusion] does not apply to one who, by conviction on his own confession, has ceased to be a party to the issue to be tried."

In *State* v. *Jones*, 51 Me. 125, it was held reversible error to exclude a codefendant offered as a witness for the defendant after a plea of guilty on the part of the codefendant. The court said: "After a party has been adjudged guilty or not guilty by a verdict, or has voluntarily admitted his guilt by plea, he has no longer any interest in the proceedings in court to determine the guilt or innocence of the others named in the indictment. 'He has ceased to be a party to the issue to be tried.'"

In *Henderson* v. *State*, 70 Ala. 23, 45 Am. Rep. 72, it was held no error to exclude a codefendant offered as a witness for the defendant where such codefendant had just pleaded guilty, but no judgment had been entered. The court held that nothing short of an order of severance, or an acquittal, or a *nolle prosequi* would qualify the accomplice. But *Woodley* v. *State*, 103 Ala. 23, 15 So. 820, holds that after the sentence has been pronounced he is a competent witness for the state.

[3]In *State* v. *Young*, 39 N. H. 283, it was held that a plea of *nole contendere* did not render one defendant upon the joint trial competent for the other. Nothing short of an acquittal, conviction, or a *nolle prosequi*, or a judgment against him upon his confession, would do so. See also *State* v. *Queen*, 65 N. C. 464. *Dictum*, that a "submission" of a codefendant would not suffice.

8. Consent of court.

The permission of the court, when required as a condition of receiving the testimony of an accomplice, need not be expressed by previous order, nor in any particular form.[1]

[1]*Linsday* v. *People*, 63 N. Y. 143.

9. — of witness.

The consent of the accomplice is not necessary to render him competent, although it may be to procuring the permission of the court, if permission be necessary. If the accomplice does not consent to testify when competent, he is compellable, by either side, subject, however, to the privilege of a witness to refuse to answer criminating questions.[1]

[1]The language of cases saying that the accomplice is competent, if called with his consent, is to be understood as referring to the waiver of privilege, or to a statutory provision requiring such consent, as, for example, in Indiana.

In South Dakota one jointly indicted with another for given offense may, if he so elects, become witness for the state against his codefendant, without having been first discharged from the information as required by Dak. Comp. Laws, §§ 7379, 7380, under § 7381, subsequently enacted, providing that in the trial of all indictments and other proceedings against persons charged with any crime the person charged shall at his own request be a competent witness. *State* v. *Smith,* 8 S. D. 547, 67 N. W. 619.

10. Extent of privilege.

Where there is a statute prohibiting testimony given under such circumstances from being used against the witness, so that he is fully protected, he cannot refuse to answer on the ground that the testimony would tend to criminate.[1]

[1]*Bedgood* v. *State,* 115 Ind. 275, 17 N. E. 621, 623.

11. Waiver of privilege.

If an accomplice voluntarily commences to testify as a witness, and being aware of his privilege gives testimony tending to criminate himself, he cannot afterward stop short of full disclosure, by claiming privilege.[1]

[1]*Com.* v. *Price,* 10 Gray, 472, 71 Am. Dec. 668 (where Metcalf, J., says: "He cannot be allowed to state such facts only as he pleases to state, and to withhold other facts,"—Cited and approved in *Ex parte Tittle,* 37 Tex. Crim. Rep. 590, 40 S. W. 598); *Foster* v. *People,* 18 Mich. 266.

12. Cross-examination of accomplice.

The defense is entitled to great latitude in the cross-examination of an accomplice for the purpose of testing the credit due to him as a witness.[1]

[1]*Marler* v. *State,* 67 Ala. 55, 42 Am. Rep. 95 (holding discretion not reversi-

ble unless manifestly abused); *State* v. *Geddes*, 22 Mont. 89, 55 Pac. 919; *State* v. *Kennedy*, 154 Mo. 268, 55 S. W. 293.

On a trial for stealing a horse, it is error to refuse to permit defendant to ask a self-confessed accomplice if the latter did not testify in the examining court that he (the accomplice) took the horse, such alleged statement being contradictory to his testimony on the trial. *Youree* v. *Territory* (Ariz.) 29 Pac. 894.

In Texas, notwithstanding Tex. Pen. Code, art. 91, providing that principals, accessories, or accomplices cannot be introduced as witnesses for one another, where an accomplice is placed on the stand by the state, and proof is made by him of an important fact happening at the time of the burglary, connecting defendant therewith, defendant may cross-examine him at the time, or recall him for that purpose. *Duffy* v. *State* (Tex. Crim. App.) 55 S. W. 176.

13. Right to prove agreement to testify.

If an accomplice testifies for the prosecution, the defense may prove the expectation of gain or immunity, whether founded upon any agreement with the prosecution or not, under which he testifies.[1]

[1]In *Tullis* v. *State*, 39 Ohio St. 200, it was held reversible error to strike out evidence elicited on cross-examination of an accomplice testifying for the prosecution against a codefendant on his separate trial, to the effect that the witness had been offered money and property by a third person if he would testify as he did for the state; and the court held that it was immaterial that the third person had no authority to make the offer on behalf of the prosecution.

In *Allen* v. *State*, 10 Ohio St. 287, it was held reversible error to exclude, on cross-examination of an accomplice testifying for the prosecution, the question: "If Allen is convicted, do you expect to be prosecuted?" the court said that the defense had a right to show that the witness "expected to be the gainer" by the conviction of the defendant, and that it was immaterial whether that expectation had come from his conversation with the prosecuting attorney "or from conversations with his own friends in whose information and representations he had implicit confidence." See also *People* v. *Langtree*, 64 Cal. 256, 30 Pac. 813; *United States* v. *Hinz*, 35 Fed. 272.

In *Brown* v. *State* (Tex. Crim. App.), 58 S. W. 131, it was held that defendant in a prosecution for theft was entitled to prove by one who had been jointly indicted with him, but as to whom the prosecution had been dismissed, that the district attorney had promised the witness that if he would go on the stand and swear the whole truth, he would dismiss the case against him, and not prosecute him, and that witness replied that he would only swear the truth; since it tended to show the innocence of the witness, and render him more credible before the jury.

II. Accounts and papers.

14. Compulsory production.

The private accounts and other documents of the accused seized by search warrant, or brought in by compulsion, are not evidence against him.[1]

[1] *Boyd* v. *United States,* 116 U. S. 616, 29 L. ed. 746, 6 Sup. Ct. Rep. 524, Reversing 24 Fed. 692, Cited and followed in *Ex parte Wilson,* 39 Tex. Crim. Rep. 630, 47 S. W. 996. But in *Trask* v. *People,* 151 Ill. 523, 38 N. E. 248, it is held that the fact that papers are unlawfully obtained by an officer from a party charged with a crime does not render them inadmissible against him.

Otherwise of ordinary articles. *Boyd* v. *United States,* 116 U. S. 616, 29 L. ed. 746, 6 Sup. Ct. Rep. 524, *supra; Chastang* v. *State,* 83 Ala. 29, 3 So. 304. And see *infra,* § 253.

State v. *Davis,* 108 Mo. 666, 18 S. W. 894, holds that a statute prohibiting druggists from selling liquors except on a physician's prescription, and requiring them to preserve all prescriptions, and to produce them in court or before any grand jury whenever required, and making their failure to do so a misdemeanor, does not violate Mo. Const. art. 2, § 23, providing that no person shall be compelled to testify against himself in a criminal case.

And *St. Joseph* v. *Levin,* 128 Mo. 588, 31 S. W. 101, holds that the constitutional provision that the people shall be secure from unreasonable searches and seizures is not violated by a regulation of pawnbrokers which requires them to keep a book describing all property received on deposit, and submit and exhibit it to the inspection of the mayor and police officers. This case also holds that a pawnbroker not charged with any crime cannot be protected against an ordinance requiring him to keep a book describing property received by him, and submit and exhibit it to the mayor and police officers, on the ground that it violates such constitutional provision, that no person "shall be compelled in any criminal case to be a witness against himself."

For an extensive review of the authorities on this question, see notes to *Cooper* v. *State* (Ala.) 4 L. R. A. 766; *O'Brien* v. *State* (Ind.) 9 L. R. A. 323; *Re Buskett* (Mo.) 14 L. R. A. 407; *United States* v. *James* (D. C. N. D. Ill.) 26 L. R. A. 418; and *Levy* v. *San Francisco Super. Ct.* (Cal.) 29 L. R. A. 811.

15. Statutory presumption from nonproduction.

The nonproduction by the accused of his private accounts and other documents is not an admission of the allegations which it is claimed they would prove; and a statute so declaring is unconstitutional.[1]

[1] *Boyd* v. *United States,* 116 U. S. 616, 29 L. ed. 746, 6 Sup. Ct. Rep. 524, *supra.*

III. Accused as a witness.

16. Accused as a witness; competency.

Under the present statutes of nearly all the states, and of the United States, the accused may in all cases testify as a witness in his own behalf; but his neglect or refusal to testify does not create any presumption against him. In the absence of such statute the accused is absolutely incompetent.[1]

[1]Alabama.—"On the trial of all indictments, complaints, or other criminal proceedings, the person on trial shall, at his own request, but not otherwise, be a competent witness; and his failure to make such request shall not create any presumption against him, nor be the subject of comment by counsel." Code, § 5297. This superseded a former act which allowed persons accused "to make a statement as to the facts in their own behalf, but not under oath." See statement as distinguished from testimony at the end of this note.

Arizona.—The rules for determining the competency of witnesses in civil actions are applicable also to criminal actions; and neither parties nor other persons who have an interest in the event of the suit are excluded. Pen. Code 1887, §§ 2036, 2037. "A defendant in a criminal action or proceeding cannot be compelled to be a witness against himself; but if he offer himself as a witness he may be cross-examined by the counsel for the territory, as to all matters about which he was examined in chief. His neglect or refusal to be a witness cannot in any manner prejudice him, nor be used against him on the trial or proceeding. *Id.* § 2040.

Arkansas.—"On the trial of all indictments, informations, complaints, and other proceedings against persons charged with the commission of crimes, offenses, and misdemeanors, the person so charged shall, at his own request, but not otherwise, be a competent witness, and his failure to make such requests shall not create any presumption against him." Sandels & H. Dig. § 2910.

California.—"A defendant in a criminal action or proceeding cannot be compelled to be a witness against himself; but if he offer himself as a witness he may be cross-examined by the counsel for the people as to all matters about which he was examined in chief. His neglect or refusal to be a witness cannot in any manner prejudice him, nor be used against him on the trial or proceeding." Code Crim. Proc. § 1323.

Colorado.—"In all criminal cases tried in any court of this state the accused, if he so desire, shall be sworn as a witness in the case, and the jury shall give his testimony such weight as they think it deserves; but in no case shall a neglect or refusal of the accused to testify be taken or considered any evidence of his guilt or innocence." 1 Mills's Anno. Stat. Crim. Code, chap. 36, § 1171.

Connecticut.—"Any person on trial for crime shall be a competent witness, and at his or her option may testify or refuse to testify upon such trial; and if such person has a husband or wife, he or she shall be a competent witness, but may elect or refuse to testify for or against the accused, except that a wife, when she has received personal violence from her husband, may upon his trial therefor be compelled to testify in the same manner as any other witness. The neglect or refusal of an accused party to testify shall not be commented upon to the court or jury." Gen. Stat. 1888, § 1623.

Delaware.—"Each and every person accused or who shall be accused of any felony, misdemeanor, or offense whatsoever, . . . shall, upon his or her trial before any tribunal established by the Constitution or laws of this state, have the right to testify in his or her own behalf, . . . provided, however, that a refusal or failure to testify shall not be construed or commented upon as an indication of guilt." Act of May 4, 1893, vol. 19, chap. 777, Laws 1893, p. 798.

District of Columbia.—See under "United States," below.

Florida.—"In all criminal prosecutions the accused may at his option be sworn as a witness in his own behalf, and shall in such case be subject to examination as other witnesses, but no accused shall be compelled to give testimony against himself, nor shall any prosecuting attorney be permitted before the court or jury to comment on the failure of the accused to testify in his own behalf." Acts 1895, chap. 4400 (No. 79). And the fact that a codefendant on a joint trial objects to his becoming a witness does not render him incompetent. *Williams* v. *State* (Fla.) 27 So. 898.

Georgia.—"No person who in any criminal proceeding is charged with the commission of any indictable offense, or any offense punishable on summary conviction, is competent or compellable to give evidence for or against himself [or herself]." Code 1896, § 1011. "In all criminal trials the prisoner shall have the right to make to the court and jury such statement in the case as he [or she] may deem proper in his [or her] defense. It shall not be under oath, and shall have such force only as the jury may think right to give it. They may believe it [such statement] in preference to the sworn testimony in the case. The prisoner shall not be compelled to answer any questions on cross-examination should he think proper to decline to answer." *Id.* § 1010. For cases see end of this note.

Idaho.—"A defendant in a criminal action or proceeding to which he is a party is not, without his consent, a competent witness for or against himself. His neglect or refusal to give such consent shall not in any manner prejudice him nor be used against him on the trial or proceeding." Rev. Stat. 1887, § 8143.

Illinois.—"No person shall be disqualified as a witness in any criminal case or proceeding by reason of his interest in the event of the same, as a party or otherwise, or by reason of his having been convicted of any crime; but such interest or conviction may be shown for the purpose of affecting his credibility; provided, however, that a defendant in any criminal case or proceeding shall only at his own request be deemed a competent witness, and his neglect to testify shall not create any presumption against him, nor shall the court permit any reference or comment to be made to or upon such neglect." 1 Starr & C. Anno. Stat. p. 1397, chap. 38, ¶ 609.

Indian Territory.—See under "United States," below.

Indiana.—"The following persons are competent witnesses: . . . 4th. The defendant to testify in his own behalf. But if the defendant does not testify, his failure to do so shall not be commented upon or referred to in the argument of the cause, nor commented upon, referred to, or in any manner considered by the jury trying the same; and it shall be the duty of the court, in such case, in its charge, to instruct the jury as to their duty under the provisions of this section." Horner's Anno. Stat. 1901, § 1798.

Iowa.—"Defendants in all criminal proceedings shall be competent witnesses in their own behalf, but cannot be called as witnesses by the state; and should a defendant not elect to become a witness, that fact shall not have any weight against him on the trial, nor shall the attorney or attorneys for the state during the trial refer to the fact that the defendant did not testify in his own behalf; and should they do so, such attorney or attorneys will be guilty of a misdemeanor, and defendant shall for that cause alone be entitled to a new trial." Code 1897, § 5484.

Kansas.—"No person shall be rendered incompetent to testify in criminal causes by reason of his being the person . . . on trial or examination; or by reason of being the husband or wife of the accused; but any such facts may be shown for the purpose of affecting his or her credibility; provided that no person on trial or examination, nor wife or husband of such person, shall be required to testify except as a witness on behalf of the person on trial or examination; and further provided that the neglect or refusal of the person on trial to testify, or of a wife to testify in behalf of her husband, shall not raise any presumption of guilt, nor shall that circumstance be referred to by any attorney prosecuting in the case, nor shall the same be considered by the court or jury before whom the trial takes place." Gen. Stat. 1899, § 5465. "If the accused shall not avail himself of his right to testify in any case, it shall not be construed to affect his innocence or guilt." *Id.* § 5466.

Kentucky.—"In all criminal and penal prosecutions now pending or hereafter instituted in any of the courts of this commonwealth, the defendant on trial, on his own request, shall be allowed to testify in his own behalf; but his failure to do so shall not be commented upon or be allowed to create any presumption against him or her." Act of May 1, 1886, Crim. Code 1899, p. 67, § 1. "The defendant requesting that he be allowed to testify shall not be allowed to testify in chief after any other witness has testified for the defense." *Id.* § 2. "If two or more persons are jointly indicted they may testify for each other unless a conspiracy is charged in the indictment and proved to the satisfaction of the court." *Id.* § 3. "If a conspiracy is charged in the indictment and proved to the satisfaction of the court, then each defendant named in the indictment may testify on his own behalf as above provided in §§ 1, 2 of this act." *Id.* § 4.

Louisiana.—"The competent witness in all criminal matters shall be a person of proper understanding; provided that the husband cannot be a witness for or against his wife, nor the wife for or against her husband, except in such cases as is now provided by law." Act 29, 1886, p. 39, Rev. Laws 1897, p. 276, § 1. "The circumstance of the witness being a party accused shall in no wise disqualify him from testifying, provided that no one shall be compelled to give evidence against himself; and provided that if the person accused avails himself of this privilege he shall be subject to all the rules that apply to other witnesses, and may be cross-examined as to all matters concerning which he gives his testimony; and provided further that his failure to testify shall not be construed for or against him; but all testimony shall be weighed and considered according to the general rules of evidence, and the trial judge shall so charge the jury." *Id.*, § 2.

Maine.—"In all criminal trials the accused shall, at his own request, but not otherwise, be a competent witness. He shall not be compelled to testify on cross-examination to facts that would convict, or furnish evidence to convict, him of any other crime than that for which he is on trial; and the fact that he does not testify in his own behalf shall not be taken as evidence of his guilt. The husband or wife of the accused is a competent witness." Rev. Stat. chap. 134, § 19. *State* v. *Witham*, 72 Me. 531, construing the second clause of the above act, holds that the statute refers only to independent crimes not relevant to the issue, but does not preclude or exclude evidence which charges or confesses extraneous circumstances the evidence of which from circumstances becomes relevant and material to the main question in issue.

Maryland.—"In the trial of all indictments, complaints, . . . the person so charged shall, at his own request, but not otherwise, be deemed a competent witness; but the neglect or refusal of any such person to testify shall not create any presumption against him." But the above shall not apply to any suit, action, bill, or other proceeding instituted in consequence of adultery. Pub. Gen. Laws, art. 35, § 3.

Massachusetts.—"In the trial of all indictments, complaints, and other proceedings against persons charged with the commission of crimes or offenses, a person so charged shall, at his own request, but not otherwise, be deemed a competent witness; and his neglect or refusal to testify shall not create any presumption against him." Pub. Stat. chap. 169, § 18, subd. 3. "The conviction of a witness of a crime may be shown to affect his credibility." *Id.*, § 19. And a person charged with crime who is defended by counsel has no right, without being sworn as a witness, to make a narrative statement to the jury. *Com.* v. *Burrough*, 162 Mass. 513, 39 N. E. 184; *Com.* v. *McConnell*, 162 Mass. 499, 39 N. E. 107.

Michigan.—"No person shall be disqualified as a witness in any criminal case or proceeding by reason of his interest in the event of the same as a party or otherwise, or by reason of his having been convicted of any crime; but such interest or conviction may be shown for the purpose of affecting his credibility; provided, however, that a defendant in any criminal case or proceeding shall only, at his own request, be deemed a competent witness, and his neglect to testify shall not create any presumption against him, nor shall the court permit any reference or comment to be made to or upon such neglect." Comp. Laws 1897, ¶ 10211.

Minnesota.—"On the trial of all indictments, . . . the person so charged shall, at his request, but not otherwise, be deemed a competent witness; nor shall the neglect or refusal to testify create any presumption against the defendant, nor shall such neglect be alluded to or commented upon by the prosecuting attorney or by the court." Stat. 1894, § 5658.

Mississippi.—"The accused shall be a competent witness for himself in any prosecution for crime against him; and the failure of the accused in any case to testify [in his own behalf] shall not operate to his prejudice, nor be commented on by counsel." Code, § 1741.

Missouri.—"No person shall be incompetent to testify as a witness in any criminal cause or prosecution by reason of being the person on trial or examination, or by reason of being the husband or wife of the accused; but any such facts may be shown for the purpose of affecting the credibility of such witness; provided that no person on trial or examination, nor wife or husband of such person, shall be required to testify, but any such person may, at the option of the defendant, testify in his behalf, or on behalf of a codefendant, and shall be liable to cross-examination as to any matter referred to in his examination in chief, and may be contradicted and impeached as any other witness in the case; provided that in no case shall husband or wife, when testifying under the provisions of this section for a defendant, be permitted to disclose confidential communications had or made between them in the relation of such husband and wife." Rev. Stat. 1899, § 2637.

Montana.—"A defendant in a criminal action or proceeding . . . may be sworn, and may testify in his own behalf, and the jury, in judging of his credibility and the weight to be given to his testimony, may take into consideration the fact that he is the defendant, and the nature and enormity of the crime of which he is accused. If the defendant does not claim the right to be sworn, or does not testify, it must not be used to his prejudice, and the attorney prosecuting must not comment to the court or jury on the same." Pen. Code, § 2442.

Nebraska.—"No person shall be disqualified as a witness in any criminal prosecution, by reason of his interest in the event of the same, as a party or otherwise, or by reason of his conviction of any crime, but such interest or conviction may be shown for the purpose of affecting his credibility. In the trial of all indictments, complaints, and other proceedings against persons charged with the commission of crimes or offenses, the person so charged shall, at his own request, but not otherwise, be deemed a competent witness; nor shall the neglect or refusal to testify create any presumption against him, nor shall any reference be made to, nor any comment upon, such neglect or refusal." Comp. Laws, § 7199.

Nevada.—"In the trial of all indictments, complaints, and other proceedings against persons charged with the commission of crimes or offenses, the person so charged shall, at his own request, but not otherwise, be deemed a competent witness; the credit to be given to his testimony being left solely to the jury, under the instructions of the court." Comp. Laws, § 4653. "Nothing herein contained shall be construed as compelling any such person to testify; and in all cases wherein the defendant to a criminal action declines to testify the court shall specially instruct the jury that no inference of guilt is to be drawn against him for that cause." *Id.*, § 4654.

New Hampshire.—"In the trial of indictments, . . . the person so charged shall at his own request, but not otherwise, be a competent witness." Pub. Stat. chap. 224, § 24. "Nothing herein contained shall be construed as compelling any such person to testify, nor shall any inference of his guilt result if he does not testify, nor shall the counsel for the prosecution comment thereon in case the respondent does not testify." *Id.* § 25.

New Jersey.—"Upon the trial of any indictment, allegation, or accusation of any person charged with crime, the person indicted or accused shall be admitted to testify as a witness upon such trial, if he shall offer himself as a witness therein in his own behalf." Gen. Stat. p. 1398, § 8. Section 1 provides that no such person offered as a witness, either in a civil or a criminal case, shall be excluded because of conviction for crime which may be shown on cross-examination to affect credibility; § 9 provides that a witness's interest or conviction of crime may be proved by examining him, and his answers may be contradicted.

New Mexico.—In the trial of all indictments, etc., "against persons charged with the commission of crimes, offenses, and misdemeanors, in the courts of this territory, the person so charged shall, at his own request, but not otherwise, be a competent witness; and his failure to make such request shall not create any presumption against him." Comp. Laws, § 3431.

New York.—"The defendant in all cases may testify as a witness in his own behalf, but his neglect or refusal to testify does not create any presumption against him." Code Crim. Proc. § 393.

North Carolina.—Same in language as Massachusetts statute, but adding: " . . . The husband or wife of the defendant in all criminal actions or proceedings shall be a competent witness for the defendant; but the failure of such witness to be examined shall not be used to the prejudice of the defense. But every such person examined as a witness shall be subjected to be cross-examined as other witnesses." Code 1883, § 1353, chap. 32.

North Dakota.—"In the trial of a criminal action or proceeding before any court or magistrate of this state, whether prosecuted by information, indictment, complaint, or otherwise, the defendant shall, at his own request, and not otherwise, be deemed a competent witness; but his neglect or refusal to testify shall not create or raise any presumption of guilt against him; nor shall such neglect or refusal be referred to by any attorney prosecuting the case, or considered by the court or jury before whom the trial takes place." Rev. Code, § 8191.

Ohio.—"No person shall be disqualified as a witness in any criminal prosecution by reason of his interest in the event of the same as a party or otherwise, or by reason of his conviction of any crime; and husband

and wife shall be competent witnesses to testify in behalf of each other in all criminal prosecutions; but such interest, conviction, or relationship may be shown for the purpose of affecting his or her credibility." Bates's Anno. Stat. § 7284.

Oklahoma.—"In the trial of all indictments, informations, complaints, and other proceedings against persons charged with the commission of a crime, offenses, and misdemeanors before any court or committing magistrate in this territory, the person charged shall, at his own request, but not otherwise, be a competent witness, and his failure to make such request shall not create any presumption against him, nor be mentioned on the trial; if commented upon by counsel it shall be ground for a new trial." Okla. Stat. § 5206.

Oregon.—In the trial of or examination upon all indictments, etc., "the person so charged or accused shall, at his own request, but not otherwise, be deemed a competent witness, the credit to be given to his testimony being left solely to the jury, under the instructions of the court; . . . provided his waiver of said right shall not create any presumption against him; that such defendant or accused, when offering his testimony as a witness in his own behalf, shall be deemed to have given to the prosecution a right to cross-examination upon all facts to which he has testified, tending to his conviction or acquittal." Hill's Anno. Laws, § 1365.

Pennsylvania.—"Except upon a preliminary hearing before a magistrate for the purpose of determining whether a person charged with a criminal offense triable in the court of oyer and terminer ought to be committed for trial, and except also upon a hearing under habeas corpus for the purpose of determining whether bail ought to be taken upon a commitment for murder in the first degree, or for the purpose of determining in any case how much bail ought to be required, or for the purpose of determining in any case whether a person committed for trial ought to be further held, and except also upon hearings before a grand jury, in none of which cases shall evidence for the defendant be heard, and except also, as is provided in § 2 of this act, all persons shall be fully competent witnesses in any criminal proceeding before any tribunal." 2 Pepper & L. Dig. title, *Witnesses*, § 1. Section 2 relates to conviction of perjury; to husband and wife; and to counsel and client. "Except defendants actually upon trial in a criminal court, any competent witness may be compelled to testify in any proceeding, civil or criminal; but he may not be compelled to answer any question which, in the opinion of the trial judge, would tend to criminate him; nor may the neglect or refusal of any defendant actually upon trial in a criminal court to offer himself as a witness be treated as creating any presumption against him, or be adversely referred to by court or counsel during the trial." *Id.*, § 22.

Rhode Island.—"No respondent in a criminal prosecution offering himself as a witness shall be excluded from testifying because he is such respondent; and neglect or refusal so to testify shall create no presumption, nor be used in argument against him." Gen. Laws, chap. 244, § 41. Section 42 admits husband and wife.

South Carolina.—"In the trial of all criminal cases the defendant shall be allowed to testify (if he desires to do so, and not otherwise) as to the facts and circumstances of the case." 2 Rev. Stat. Crim. § 63. "No person shall be required to answer any question tending to criminate himself; nor shall husband or wife be required to disclose any communication made to each other during their coverture; nor shall testimony given under the preceding section be afterwards used against the person testifying in any other criminal case, except upon an indictment for perjury founded on that testimony." *Id.*, § 64.

South Dakota.—"In the trial of all indictments, information, complaints, and other proceedings against persons charged with the commission of any crime, offenses, and misdemeanors before any court or committing magistrate in this state, the person charged shall, at his own request, but not otherwise, be a competent witness, and his failure to make such request shall not create any presumption against him." Anno. Stat. 1901, § 8650.

Tennessee.—"In the trial of all indictments, presentments, and other criminal proceedings, in any of the courts of this state, the party defendant thereto may, at his own request, but not otherwise, be a competent witness to testify therein." Code 1896, § 5600. "The failure of the party defendant to make such request, and to testify in his own behalf, shall not create any presumption against him. But the defendant desiring to testify shall do so before any other testimony for the defense is heard by the court trying the case." Id., § 5601. *Morgan* v. *State*, 86 Tenn. 472, 7 S. W. 456, construing the above act, contains a *dictum* that the last clause "is mandatory; and, unless pursued, the defendant will not be permitted to testify."

Texas.—"Any defendant in a criminal action shall be permitted to testify in his own behalf therein, but the failure of any defendant to so testify shall not be taken as a circumstance against him, nor shall the same be alluded to or commented on by counsel in the cause; provided that where there are two or more persons jointly charged or indicted, and a severance is had, the privilege of testifying shall be extended only to the person on trial." Rev. Stat. Code Crim. Proc. 1895, art. 770, p. 106.

Utah.—"If a defendant offers himself as a witness, he may be cross-examined by the counsel for the state the same as any other witness. His neglect or refusal to be a witness shall not in any manner prejudice him, nor be used against him on the trial or proceeding." Rev. Stat. 1898, § 5015.

Vermont.—In the trial of indictments, etc., "the person so charged shall, at his own request, and not otherwise, be deemed a competent witness, the credit to be given to his testimony being left solely to the jury, under the instructions of the court; but the refusal of such person to testify shall not be considered by the jury as evidence against him." Stat. 1894, § 1915.

Virginia.—"In any case of felony or misdemeanor, the accused may be sworn and examined in his own behalf, and be subject to cross-examination as any other witness; but his failure to testify shall create no presumption against him, nor be the subject of any comment before the court or jury by the prosecuting attorney." Code 1887, § 3897.

Washington.—"Any person accused of any crime in this state, by indictment, information, or otherwise, may, in the examination or trial of the cause, offer himself or herself as a witness in his or her own behalf, and shall be allowed to testify as other witnesses in such case, and when accused shall so testify, he or she shall be subject to all the rules of law relating to cross-examination of other witnesses; provided that nothing in this Code shall be construed to compel such accused persons to offer himself or herself as a witness in such case; and provided further that it shall be the duty of the court to instruct the jury that no inference of guilt shall arise against the accused if the accused shall fail or refuse to testify as a witness in his or her own behalf." Ballinger's Anno. Codes & Statutes, § 6941.

West Virginia.—In any trial or examination, etc., "for a felony or misdemeanor, the accused shall, at his or her own request (but not otherwise), be a competent witness on such trial and examination. The wife or husband of the accused shall also, at the request of the accused, but not otherwise, be a competent witness on such trial and examination. But a failure to make such request shall not create any presumption against him or her, nor shall any reference be made to nor comment upon such failure by any one during the progress of the trial in the hearing of the jury." Code 1891, chap. 152, § 19.

Wisconsin.—"In all criminal actions and proceedings the party charged shall, at his own request, but not otherwise, be a competent witness; but his refusal or omission to testify shall create no presumption against him, or any other party thereto." Sanborn & Berryman, Anno. Stat. § 4071. Section 4073 provides that convicted persons are competent, but such conviction may be proved by record or cross-examination to affect credibility.

Wyoming.—"The defendant in all criminal cases in all the courts in this state may be sworn and examined as a witness if he so elect, but shall not be required to testify in any case. If the defendant so elect, he may make a statement to the jury without being sworn, but the neglect or refusal to make such a statement shall not create any presumption against him, nor shall any reference be made to, nor shall any comment be made upon, such neglect or refusal." Rev. Stat. 1899, § 5346. See explanation as to such statement below.

United States Courts.—"In the trial of all indictments, informations, complaints, and other proceedings against persons charged with the commission of crimes, offenses, and misdemeanors in the United States courts, territorial courts, and courts-martial and courts of inquiry in any state or territory, including the District of Columbia, the person so charged shall, at his own request, but not otherwise, be a competent witness. And his failure to make such request shall not create any presumption against him." 1 U. S. Rev. Stat. Supp. p. 155 (20 Stat. at L. 30, p. 312, chap. 37), passed March 16, 1878.

"At his own request," in the statute, does not entitle him to request that he be called by the prosecution. *State* v. *Cohn*, 9 Nev. 179; *Com.* v. *Pratt*, 137 Mass. 98.

Statements as distinguished from testimony.—Under a statute (for example, see Georgia and Wyoming above) merely permitting the accused to make a statement to the jury, the accused is not a witness, and is not entitled to testify under oath (*People* v. *Thomas*, 9 Mich. 314, under a similar statute now repealed); nor is the statement to be confined by the limits applicable to testimony of a witness (*Coxwell* v. *State*, 66 Ga. 309); and if he makes a statement, the prosecution is not entitled to cross-examine him (*Chappell* v. *State*, 71 Ala. 322); even where the statute permits him to make a sworn statement (*Miller* v. *State*, 15 Fla. 577 [Florida statute now repealed. See *supra*]); and it has been held that in making an unsworn statement the accused cannot state his own motive, belief, or intention, unless he made them known at the time of the doing of the act as to which he is permitted to make a statement. See *Burke* v. *State*, 71 Ala. 377; and *Whezenant* v. *State*, 2 Ala. L. J. 189, cases arising under a statute now repealed.

An accused not sworn as a witness cannot, in making his statement to the jury, lay the foundation for introducing evidence in his favor that would otherwise be inadmissible,—such as incompetent or irrelevant uncommunicated threats by deceased. *Vaughn* v. *State*, 88 Ga. 731, 16 S. E. 64.

The accused having made one statement to the court and jury is not entitled, as a matter of right, to make a second statement, because the state after the first statement introduces evidence which strengthens the case against him. *Boston* v. *State*, 94 Ga. 590, 20 S. E. 98, 21 S. E. 603. See also *Sharp* v. *State*, 111 Ga. 176, 36 S. E. 633, holding that whether the accused should be allowed to make a second statement because the state has introduced additional evidence strengthening the case against him is a matter which is within the discretion of the trial court, and that refusal to permit it will not be interfered with, since the accused has no legal right to make more than one statement.

The presiding judge in a criminal case should not, while defendant is delivering his statement, or at its conclusion, propound a question to him seeking to elicit an answer touching the facts brought out by the evidence in the case. *Hackney* v. *State*, 101 Ga. 512, 28 S. E. 1007.

17. What law applicable in United States court.

The state statute is not applicable in a court of the United States.[1]

[1] *United States* v. *Hawthorne*, 1 Dill. 422, Fed. Cas. No. 15,332; *United States* v. *Black*, 1 Hask. 570, Fed. Cas. No. 14,602.

18. Accused competent although a convict.

The accused is now a competent witness in his own behalf, notwithstanding he may have been previously convicted of a felony; for the statutes giving him a right to testify are to be construed as superseding the common-law special disqualification of convicts to testify,[1] unless otherwise expressed.[2]

[1] *Morgan* v. *State*, 86 Tenn. 472, 7 S. W. 456 (assault with intent to commit murder in first degree. Upon defendant's offering himself as a witness the attorney general objected, and read a record of his conviction of larceny and judgment of infamy. Held error to sustain the objection. The court says: "The statute excepts no class or character of defendants, and the courts can except none") ; *Ransom* v. *State*, 49 Ark. 176, 4 S. W. 658. And see statutes set out *supra* in § 16.

[2] As in Pennsylvania, where the statute provides as follows: "In such criminal proceedings a person who has been convicted in a court of this commonwealth of perjury, which term is hereby declared to include subornation of perjury, shall not be a competent witness for any purpose, although his sentence may have been fully complied with, unless the judgment of conviction be judicially set aside or reversed, or unless the proceeding be one to punish or prevent injury or violence attempted, done, or threatened to his person or property, in which case he shall be competent to testify." See *supra*, § 16.

As to joint defendants testifying for each other, see *supra*, § 4.

19. Rights as a party.

The accused, by becoming a witness in his own behalf, loses no rights as a party;[1] but as a witness he waives, to the limited extent below stated, his privilege against criminating himself upon cross-examination.

[1] *People* v. *Brown*, 72 N. Y. 571, 573, 28 Am. Rep. 183; *Hanoff* v. *State*, 37 Ohio St. 178, 41 Am. Rep. 496 (*dictum*). See also two succeeding sections.

20. — to have aid of counsel on examination.

The accused testifying in his own behalf has a right to have his counsel interrogate him in the same manner as any other witness.[1]

[1] *Clark* v. *State*, 50 Ind. 514 (murder; error to stop interrogation, and direct the accused to give a general statement of the whole affair. Counsel should be allowed to interrogate as in case of other witnesses) ; *Fletcher* v. *State*, 49 Ind. 124, 19 Am. Rep. 673.

In *State* v. *House*, 55 Iowa, 466, 8 N. W. 307, the defendant's counsel withdrew from the case during the examination of the defendant himself as a witness, and upon the latter stating that owing to the condition of his counsel he was not properly represented and defended; whereupon the court appointed other counsel for him, who asked for a few days' adjournment in which to examine the evidence already introduced to prepare his defense, which request was denied. The court said that if it had appeared from the record that the counsel was intoxicated while engaged in the trial, and when he withdrew, and that the court refused an adjournment for a reasonable time to allow the new counsel to prepare his defense, the judgment would have been reversed; but that there was nothing in the record to show that counsel was intoxicated, or in any way incapacitated from properly discharging his duty to his client; that, on the contrary, the only imputation against him was by the defendant, and that not a direct charge, but a mere insinuation which the trial judge seemed to think was for the purpose of obtaining some advantage by a continuance. The court also said that what would have been its conclusion if the defendant's guilt had been doubtful need not be determined.

In *State* v. *Hendel* (Idaho) 35 Pac. 836, during the trial of one of the defendants who had been jointly indicted for murder, counsel for the defendant not on trial interposed and objected to the granting of a motion of the counsel for the defendant on trial on the ground that to do so would be to jeopardize his client by the destruction of evidence vital to his defense, for which error was assigned. But the court overruled the assignment saying that in its opinion it was the duty of counsel for the defendant not on trial, not only to be present at the trial of his coindictee, but vigilantly to watch and scrutinize the conduct of the trial to the end, that none of the legal rights of his client should be sacrificed or jeopardized in the interest of the other defendant.

21. — explanations of intent.

The counsel for the accused, in examining him as a witness in his own behalf, may call for his explanation of his conduct and language testified to either by himself[1] or by witnesses for the prosecution.[2]

[1]*People* v. *Quick*, 51 Mich. 547, 18 N. W. 375. Error to exclude the question, "Why did you do that?" See also *State* v. *Montgomery*, 65 Iowa, 483, 22 N. W. 641. And see *infra*, § 249.

[2]In *Donohue* v. *People*, 56 N. Y. 208, it was held that, in order to rebut testimony tending to show that defendant had written a letter to suborn witnesses, defendant (on trial for murder) was entitled to be examined as to the point that he held no communication for such purpose, in any way, as well as to writing letters; and that exclusion of such testimony was reversible error.

In *People* v. *Farrell*, 31 Cal. 576, it was held reversible error to exclude defendant's explanation of language of his given in evidence against him by the prosecution. To allow such explanation was the object of the statute.

In *Morrow* v. *State*, 48 Ind. 432, it was held error calling for reversal to exclude defendant's testimony explaining what he had said to a third person at a whispered conversation, which had been proved as a suspicious circumstance.

In *State* v. *Maynard*, 19 Nev. 284, 9 Pac. 514, it was held error to charge that acts are a safer foundation for conclusion than testimony to intent. See also *infra*, § 249; and Division XLII.

22. Court may interrogate.

When the accused testifies in his own behalf, the court may specially interrogate him to test the truth of his testimony.[1]

[1] *Gill* v. *People,* 3 Hun, 187, 5 Thomp. & C. 308, Affirmed in 60 N. Y. 643, without opinion.

Error cannot be predicated on the action of the judge in asking the defendant, when testifying as a witness in his own behalf, a question which was directly in line with the one just previously asked by his own counsel, and the answer to which was in effect the same. *Cline* v. *State,* 25 Ind. App. 331, 58 N. E. 210.

23. Cross-examination; within the limits of direct.

Under the settled rule that, by becoming a witness in his own behalf, the accused waives his right to refuse, on cross-examination, to answer questions as to matters upon which he was examined in chief, on the ground of tendency to criminate himself,[1] if he has testified generally as to what occurred within a specified period,[2] or as to his movements on a specified day,[3] he cannot on cross-examination refuse to answer as to all that occurred within that period, or all his conduct on that day.

If he denies his guilt, he may be cross-examined as to any matters which tend to establish guilt,[4] whether specifically interrogated as to them on direct or not.

[1] This rule obtains in all jurisdictions. See authorities under the succeeding sections. See also *Gill* v. *People,* 3 Hun, 187, 5 Thomp. & C. 308. In *Roddy* v. *Finnegan,* 43 Ind. 490, a civil case, it is held that a witness ordinarily may claim privilege as to anything that would incriminate him; but "where he is both party and witness for himself, he must be held on his cross-examination as waiving the privilege as to any matter about which he has given testimony in chief." Error to exclude such a question.

[2] *People* v. *Russell,* 46 Cal. 121.

So, the court may in its discretion permit the county attorney to cross-examine defendant charged with burglary, who takes the stand in his own behalf, at considerable length with reference to his various places of residence, his going under assumed names, and his whereabouts at particular times. *State* v. *Watson,* 102 Iowa, 651, 72 N. W. 283.

And the defendant in a murder trial, who undertook on direct examination to give an account in a general way of what occurred in a saloon from the time of his arrival until the homicide, may be asked on cross-examination with reference to scuffling or wrestling which took place between him and one of the other parties shortly before the homicide, athough he did not expressly refer to the occurrence in his direct examination. *State* v. *Weaver,* 35 Or. 415, 58 Pac. 109.

[3] *Boyle* v. *State,* 105 Ind. 469, 55 Am. Rep. 218, 5 N. E. 203.

[4]This follows from the principle of cross-examination, and seems to be conceded by most of the authorities that oppose the next rule. To this effect see also *Com.* v. *Burk,* 3 Lanc. L. Rev. 138. He may be asked what he thought or intended. *Territory* v. *Davis* (Ariz.; 1886) 10 West Coast Rep. 210.

24. — relevant to the issue, irrespective of limits of direct.

In those jurisdictions where cross-examination of the accused is not by the statute[1] expressly bounded by the examination in chief, the accused, by becoming a witness in his own behalf, so far waives his right to refuse to criminate himself that he cannot decline to answer questions relevant to the issue because tending to criminate him.[2]

Where the statute only gives the right to cross-examine as to the matters inquired of on direct, it is error to allow it to be carried further against objection.[3]

[1]See the statutes under *supra,* § 16. In *People* v. *O'Brien,* 66 Cal. 602, 6 Pac. 695, it was held reversible error to permit the accused to be cross-examined as to matters not testified to in his direct examination. Citing Cal. Pen. Code, § 1323. See further, *infra,* § 34.

[2]This is the rule applied in *People ex rel. Phelps* v. *New York County Ct. of Oyer & Terminer,* 83 N. Y. 436; *Rains* v. *State,* 88 Ala. 91, 7 So. 315; *Fitzpatrick* v. *United States,* 178 U. S. 304, 44 L. ed. 1078, 20 Sup. Ct. Rep. 944; *Frank* v. *State,* 94 Wis. 211, 68 N. W. 657; *Wallace* v. *State,* 41 Fla. 547, 26 So. 713; *State* v. *Larkins* (Idaho) 47 Pac. 945; *State* v. *Griswold,* 67 Conn. 290, 33 L. R. A. 227, 34 Atl. 1046; *Alexander* v. *State,* 40 Tex. Crim. Rep. 395, 49 S. W. 229, 50 S. W. 716; *State* v. *McGee,* 55 S. C. 247, 33 S. E. 353; *Guy* v. *State,* 90 Md. 29, 44 Atl. 997; *People* v. *Parmelee,* 112 Mich. 291, 70 N. W. 577; *Clarke* v. *State,* 78 Ala. 474, 56 Am. Rep. 45. See also *Com.* v. *Mullen,* 97 Mass. 545 (where it is held, on indictment for being a common seller of liquor, that by becoming a witness in his own behalf the defendant "waives his constitutional privilege of refusing to furnish evidence against himself, and may be interrogated as a general witness in the case." So laid down in holding that where a witness for the state had testified to sales of liquor seen through a glass door, and defendant testified that there was no glass in the door, he was properly compelled to answer whether there was not glass in the partition at the side of the door); *Com.* v. *Lannan,* 13 Allen, 563; *Com.* v. *Morgan,* 107 Mass. 199 (where the court held that on a trial for a criminal libel it was admissible, on cross-examination of the defendant, to ask him whether he was not the publisher of the newspaper in question, even though the question did tend to criminate him, as by taking the stand there was a waiver of his privilege, and [*per curiam*] "under our rule the cross-examination of a witness is not confined to the matters inquired of in chief"); *Com.* v. *Nichols,* 114

Mass. 285; S. C., with note 19 Am. Rep. 346 (where the court so held, and added in a *dictum:* "And a refusal to answer a question on the ground that it might criminate him is competent evidence against him when it would not be against an ordinary witness"); *State* v. *Ober*, 52 N. H. 459, 13 Am. Rep. 88 (on an indictment for keeping liquors, held that the conviction should be sustained, because the question asked on cross-examination was relevant to the issue, and when the defendant waived his privilege by becoming a witness, he subjected "himself to the peril of being examined as to any and every matter pertinent to the issue").

In *State* v. *Wentworth*, 65 Me. 234, 20 Am. Rep. 688, it was held no error on cross-examination of the accused, on trial for selling liquor, to ask him how many sales he had made himself personally, because by taking the stand he waived his privilege as to incriminating himself concerning the crime of which he was charged, and subjected "himself to the peril consequent upon a cross-examination as to all matters pertinent to the issue," whether inquired about in his direct examination or not.

In *Disque* v. *State*, 49 N. J. L. 249, 8 Atl. 281, it was held no error to allow the accused on trial for murder of his wife to be cross-examined as to his illtreatment of his wife prior to the time of killing, even though no questions on that subject had been asked him on the direct, for the question was relevant, and it is the general practice, both in civil and in criminal cases, to allow a testifying party to the record "to be cross-examined to the whole case," in the discretion of the court, even though it extends to pertinent fact not touched by the direct examination.

In *Spies* v. *People*, 122 Ill. 1, p. 235, 12 N. E. 865, 17 N. E. 898, the court says: "It is also objected that the cross-examination of those of the defendants who took the stand compelled them to give evidence against themselves. After a careful examination of the testimony of these defendants as set out in the record, we cannot see that they were cross-examined upon any subjects not connected with the direct examination. If a defendant offers himself as a witness to disprove a criminal charge, he cannot excuse himself from answering on the ground that by so doing he may incriminate himself. 'So far as concerns questions touching the merits, the defendant, by making himself a witness as to the offense, waives his privilege as to all matters connected with the offense. It has been ruled also that to affect his credibility he may be asked whether he had been concerned in other crimes, part of the same system.'" Citing Wharton, Crim. Ev. § 432. Judgment affirmed.

Contra, *Boyle* v. *State*, 105 Ind. 469, 55 Am. Rep. 218, 5 N. E. 203; Cooley, Const. Lim. 317, saying that he may stop where he pleases in the direct, and thus preserve his constitutional right to refuse to criminate himself by answering on cross-examination beyond that limit.

[a] *State* v. *Chamberlain*, 89 Mo. 129, 1 S. W. 145.

But where defendant in a criminal case testified that certain letters dated "St. Louis, Jan. 18," had reached his home after he left, it was proper to ask him on cross-examination when he left. *State* v. *Cunningham*, 154 Mo. 161, 55 S. W. 282.

And the defendant in a prosecution for seduction who has testified on direct examination that he continued to call on the prosecutrix once in three or four weeks for over two years, and until about the time of the alleged seduction, may be cross-examined as to why he discontinued his visits after that time. *State* v. *Eisenhour,* 132 Mo. 140, 33 S. W. 785.

So, defendant, charged with murder, who has testified on his direct examination that he was at work on the evening of the homicide, may properly be cross-examined as to the kind of work he was doing. *State* v. *McLaughlin,* 149 Mo. 19, 50 S. W. 315.

The fact that the court permitted an accused, testifying as a witness on his own behalf, to be cross-examined as to matters alleged not to have been inquired about upon his examination in chief, is not ground for reversal where the record does not show any abuse of the court's discretion in that regard. *State* v. *Moody,* 7 Wash. 395, 35 Pac. 132.

Nor will a conviction be reversed because the defendant was cross-examined as to matters with reference to which he had not testified on direct examination, where the testimony elicited did not tend to criminate him, nor his refusal to answer to prejudice him in the minds of the jurors. *State* v. *Moore,* 32 Or. 65, 48 Pac. 468.

And defendant in a murder trial, who undertook on his direct examination to account for the fact that he had a pistol in his possession at the time of the homicide, may be properly asked on cross-examination where he obtained it. *State* v. *Weaver,* 35 Or. 415, 58 Pac. 109.

25. Cross-examination affecting credit as a witness.

In those jurisdictions where cross-examination is not by the statute expressly bounded by the examination in chief,[1] the accused, by becoming a witness in his own behalf, subjects himself to cross-examination to impair his credit as a witness, to the same extent as any other witness.[2]

[1]See the statutes under *supra,* § 16.

As to the rule where the cross is thus limited by the direct, see *infra,* § 34.

[2]In such jurisdictions, therefore, it is in the discretion of the court to allow the cross-examination of the accused to be extended to matters immaterial to the issue, in order to affect his credibility. *McGuire* v. *People,* 3 Hun, 213, 5 Thomp. & C. 682, more fully, 48 How. Pr. 517; *Cowley* v. *People,* 8 Abb. N. C. 1, 34, less fully, 21 Hun, 415, Affirmed without noticing this point, in 83 N. Y. 464, 38 Am. Rep. 494; *McKeone* v. *People,* 6 Colo. 346; *Yanke* v. *State,* 51 Wis. 464, 8 N. W. 276; *State* v. *Huff,* 11 Nev. 17 (*dictum*).

26. — specific facts affecting credit; general rule.

The court in its discretion may allow the accused, when under cross-examination, to be asked as to specific facts which tend to discredit him, or to impeach his moral character as bearing on credibility.[1]

[1]Such is the general principle; but the courts are not agreed as to what facts do legitimately affect credibility. See cases under the next five sections, for illustrations.

In *People* v. *Casey*, 72 N. Y. 393, it was held not error to allow one on trial for assault to be asked as to previous altercations and assaults upon third persons in which he had been engaged.

In *State* v. *Huff*, 11 Nev. 17, the court, while approving the rule, yet held it reversible error to ask accused, on trial for murder, if he had not assaulted other persons, as it did not legitimately tend to discredit his veracity as a witness.

State v. *Gleim*, 17 Mont. 17, 31 L. R. A. 294, 41 Pac. 998, holds that cross-examination cannot extend to matters wholly remote from the question of guilt or innocence of the crime charged, so as to amount to a general assault upon his character.

And a defendant, charged with larceny, who admits, while testifying as a witness, that he has been disbarred from practising as an attorney, cannot be cross-examined as to the specific charges on which the disbarment proceedings were based. *People* v. *Dorthy*, 156 N. Y. 237, 50 N. E. 800, Affirming 20 App. Div. 308, 46 N. Y. Supp. 970.

27. — commission of an offense.

As tending to impair the credibility of the accused as a witness, the court in its discretion may allow him to be asked whether he has not committed a specified crime, if it be of a nature to impair his general credit as a witness, or tend to contradict testimony given by him.[1]

[1]*People* v. *Noelke*, 94 N. Y. 137, 46 Am. Rep. 128, Affirming 29 Hun, 461 (holding it not error to ask defendant on trial for offense against lottery laws, whether he had not previously been in the business of lottery tickets and lottery policies, since it was an inquiry as to the actual commission of crime to which an affirmative answer would tend to discredit the witness, besides being in this case pertinent to the issue); *People* v. *Irving*, 95 N. Y. 541 (assault; held no error to permit defendant to be asked, on cross-examination, if he had not committed an assault upon another person, as bearing upon his credibility, where he had given material testimony in conflict with that of the prosecution); *People* v. *Hooghkerk*, 96 N. Y. 149 (arson; held no error to allow cross-examination with reference to his connection with other fires, and with insurance on other property burned, as affecting his credibility); *People* v. *Eckert*, 2 N. Y. Crim. Rep. 470 (seduction; held proper to ask on cross-examination whether he had not had intercourse with another person; reversed on other grounds). See also, as supporting the text, *People* v. *Reavey*, 38 Hun, 418, reargument 39 Hun, 364 (larceny; allowable to ask the accused if he had not been suspended as an attorney for profes-

sional misconduct); *State* v. *Rozum*, 8 N. D. 548, 80 N. W. 477; *Borrego* v. *Territory*, 8 N. M. 446, 46 Pac. 349; *State* v. *Chingren*, 105 Iowa, 169, 74 N. W. 946; *Shears* v. *State*, 147 Ind. 51, 46 N. E. 331.

But in *People* v. *Iams*, 57 Cal. 115, a murder trial, it was held no error to exclude a question on cross-examination as to whether there had not been criminal intimacy between defendant and the wife of deceased, as the question was immaterial. Compare *People* v. *Phelan*, 123 Cal. 551, 56 Pac. 424, where it was held that questions asked of defendant charged with murder, on his cross-examination, containing an insinuation that he was himself a man of violent character, who required at times to be put under bonds, although highly improper, did not require a reversal.

In *Saffer* v. *United States*, 31 C. C. A. 1, 59 U. S. App. 311, 87 Fed. 329, it was held that a person accused of sending lascivious letters through the mails could not upon cross-examination be asked whether he did not occupy the same room with the addressee of the letter six months after the time of its mailing, if, from the state of the evidence, neither the question nor its answer would have any tendency to impeach his character for truth and veracity.

In a prosecution for rape it is error to compel defendant on cross-examination to answer questions concerning an attempt by him to debauch a child, which was not connected in the remotest degree with the crime for which he is being tried. *Anthony* v. *State* (Idaho) 55 Pac. 884.

And it is not competent to ask defendant in a criminal trial, on cross-examination, questions whose only possible object is to excite in the minds of the jury a suspicion that he has been guilty of other offenses than the one for which he is on trial. *Baker* v. *Com.* 20 Ky. L. Rep. 1778, 50 S. W. 54.

So, it is error to allow defendant in a prosecution for forgery to be interrogated as to other papers similar to that in question, unless it be first shown that such papers were forged, and the accused had culpable connection therewith. *State* v. *Lowry*, 42 W. Va. 205, 24 S. E. 561.

In *Downey* v. *State*, 115 Ala. 108, 22 So. 479, it was held that defendant, charged with betting at a game of cards at an outhouse where people resorted, could not be cross-examined as to whether he had followed the business of gambling for a livelihood for a long time.

And in Maine, by statute, cross-examination is not allowed as to any other crime than that on trial, but this statute is construed to relate only to independent crimes not relevant to the issue. See under Maine, *supra*, § 16. See also *State* v. *Carson*, 66 Me. 116, holding it reversible error to ask defendant on cross-examination whether he had assaulted other persons when drunk, the court applying the same rule to the defendant as to other witnesses,—that he could not be required to meet any evidence except that against his character for truth and veracity, and proof of having been convicted of an infamous crime.

28. — imprisonment.

For this purpose it is proper to allow him to be asked if he has ever been confined as a prisoner in a penitentiary or states prison,[1] or if he has been convicted of a felony,[2] but not whether he has been arrested[3] or indicted.[4]

[1]In *People* v. *Courtney*, 31 Hun, 199, Affirmed in 94 N. Y. 490, without passing upon this point, the rule is laid down that the defendant subjects himself to the same rules as other witnesses on cross-examination, and may be asked whether he has ever been confined as a prisoner in a penitentiary.

In *Com.* v. *Bonner*, 97 Mass. 587, it was held no error to ask the defendant (on trial for attempt to steal) "if he had been in the house of correction for any crime." Here the trial judge allowed the question for the purpose of showing that defendant had been convicted of a crime.

In *People* v. *Hovey*, 29 Hun, 382, Affirmed in 92 N. Y. 554, without noticing this point, 1 N. Y. Crim. Rep. 180, a murder trial, it was held no error to ask the accused how many times he had "been in prison," and "for what." The court said § 832 of the Code of Civil Procedure (see next note) "expressly authorizes such a line of examination."

In *Brown* v. *State*, 62 N. J. L. 666, 42 Atl. 811, it is held that defendant on a criminal trial may be asked on cross-examination whether he has been in any other prison and whether he has previously been convicted of crime.

[2]Since the abolition of the absolute common-law disqualification by conviction of felony, the fact of such conviction may, under the statutes of most of the states, be proved as bearing on credibility. The New York statute is as follows: N. Y. Code Civ. Proc. § 832. "The conviction may be proved for the purpose of affecting the weight of his testimony, either by the record or by his cross-examination, upon which he must answer any question relevant to that inquiry; and the party cross-examining him is not concluded by his answer to such a question." And see *People* v. *Johnson*, 57 Cal. 571 (to same effect, under California Penal Code); *People* v. *Sears*, 119 Cal. 267, 51 Pac. 325; *Clemmons* v. *State*, 39 Tex. Crim. Rep. 279, 45 S. W. 911; *Hyde* v. *Territory*, 8 Okla. 69, 56 Pac. 851.

In *Bartholomew* v. *People*, 104 Ill. 601, 44 Am. Rep. 97, it is held that it is the conviction, and not the punishment for the offense, that may be shown.

In *State* v. *Burton*, 2 Marv. (Del.) 446, 43 Atl. 254, however, it is held that defendant in a prosecution, under the Delaware statute, for pointing a pistol at another, cannot be asked on cross-examination, for the purpose of impairing his credibility, as to whether he has ever before been convicted of pointing a pistol at a man, since the offense, under the statute, is not necessarily an assault, and a conviction does not necessarily tend to disgrace or degrade the defendant.

[3]The reason is that no inference of guilt can be drawn from a mere arrest, much less an inference of guilt of an offense imputing inveracity. It is merely an accusation; and innocence is presumed. *People* v. *Brown*, 72 N. Y. 571, 28 Am. Rep. 183, Affirming 8 Hun, 562 (holding it error

to allow the question, "How many times have you been arrested?"); *People* v. *Crapo*, 76 N. Y. 288, 32 Am. Rep. 302 (burglary; held error to allow accused to be asked if he had been arrested on a charge of bigamy).

In *State* v. *Huff*, 11 Nev. 17, a murder trial, it was held to be error to allow him to be asked how many times he had been arrested for unlawfully beating men and women; it did not legitimately tend to discredit the defendant as a witness, for "it could be inferred that he was a violent-tempered man, perhaps a dangerous man, but not that he was a liar."

In *People* v. *Hamblin*, 68 Cal. 101, 8 Pac. 687, a murder trial, it was held error to compel the accused to answer whether he had not been arrested for shooting at people, and whether he did not know the unlawful nature of the business where he was doorkeeper. So held under California Code which restricts evidence for impeachment to that of general reputation for truth and veracity and conviction of a felony, and thus supercedes *People* v. *McCauley*, 45 Cal. 148, which seems to have held such a question proper. But in *Hanoff* v. *State*, 37 Ohio St. 178, 41 Am. Rep. 496, a murder trial, it was held to be no error to ask, in order to affect credibility, whether defendant had not been arrested for an assault; and that it was discretionary with the court to permit such questions, for abuse is guarded against by the witness's privilege and the power of the court to restrict cross-examination.

Where defendant on trial for murder had introduced a witness (his father) who testified that defendant had once been arrested and honorably acquitted on trial of a charge for shooting, held no error to allow defendant, on cross-examination, to be asked if he was arrested for the alleged shooting, since it was in reply to the direct; but the court did not pass upon its propriety in case there had been no direct testimony. *People* v. *Ogle*, 104 N. Y. 511, 11 N. E. 53.

So, too, in *State* v. *Bacon*, 13 Or. 143, 9 Pac. 393, it was held no error to permit a witness for the defendant to be asked on cross-examination "whether he and the defendant had not at one time been arrested on a charge of robbery," because it affected his credibility as tending to show his relations with the defendant; and that in general such questions were allowable in the exercise of a sound discretion by the court.

Vancleave v. *State*, 150 Ind. 273, 49 N. E. 1060, holds that the defendant on a trial for robbery may be cross-examined, for the purpose of affecting his credibility, as to a previous arrest and conviction of larceny, and as to a pending indictment for robbery of another person against him.

And *Cage* v. *State* (Tex. Crim. App.) 55 S. W. 63, holds that where defendant testifies in his own behalf, he cannot complain that he is asked on cross-examination how often he has been arrested, and for what, when his answer is beneficial to him.

And in *People* v. *Larsen*, 10 Utah, 143, 37 Pac. 258, it is held that requiring defendant on trial for an assault to state whether he has ever been arrested for a similar crime is not reversible error, where the question is objected to only on the ground that it is immaterial and irrelevant, and on cross-examination there is no claim that the question is privileged.

Ryan v. *People*, 79 N. Y. 594, Affirming 19 Hun, 188. *Dictum*, to the effect that evidence that a witness has been indicted is improper because it does not tend to discredit him. Followed in *Kober* v. *Miller*, 38 Hun, 184 (civil case).

In *Smith* v. *State*, 79 Ala. 21, it was held to be reversible error to allow a question as to whether the defendant had not been indicted for trespass, after warning,—Citing *Clarke* v. *State*, 78 Ala. 474, 56 Am. Rep. 45.

So, defendant on trial for keeping a disorderly house cannot be cross-examined as to an indictment against him for keeping a disorderly house at another place. *Roop* v. *State*, 58 N. J. L. 479, 34 Atl. 749.

And *Parker* v. *Com.* 21 Ky. L. Rep. 406, 51 S. W. 573, held that it was improper, on cross-examination of defendant charged with murder, to ask, "Have you ever been indicted for anything? Tell the jury . . . what all you have been indicted for," when the answers showed that the defendant had been indicted for carrying a pistol and shooting from ambush, although for the purpose of affecting the credibility of the witness, and notwithstanding the court instructed the jury not to consider these statements for any purpose against the defendant, except so far as they might affect his credibility as a witness. Compare *Eversole* v. *Com.* 17 Ky. L. Rep. 1259, 34 S. W. 231, however, which holds that a reference, on the cross-examination of defendant charged with murder, to indictments found against him in other cases, is not prejudicial where all evidence on that subject is subsequently excluded from the consideration of the jury.

So, one on trial for using the mails to defraud cannot be asked on cross-examination if his former partner is not under indictment for fraudulently using the mails, if no connection is shown between defendant and his former partner as to the matter for which he is being tried. *Tingle* v. *United States*, 30 C. C. A. 666, 58 U. S. App. 140, 87 Fed. 320.

And in *Vale* v. *People*, 161 Ill. 309, 43 N. E. 1091, it was held that compelling a woman accused of larceny, against her objection, to testify that her husband was tried for murder and acquitted the previous year, without evidence to connect her with the charge against her husband,—was reversible error.

But *People* v. *Clark*, 102 N. Y. 735, 8 N. E. 38, Affirming 38 Hun, 214, holds that where the accused testifies on his own behalf, it is within the discretion of the court to allow the prosecution, on cross-examination, to ask him if he has been accused or charged with anything disgraceful or criminal. See also *People* v. *Gale*, 50 Mich. 237, 15 N. W. 99, where it was held no error to ask defendant if he did not know, as a matter of fact, that a certain information to which he had pleaded was based on the complaint of a third person.

And in *Sebastian* v. *State* (Tex. Crim. App.) 53 S. W. 875, a criminal case, it was held competent to ask the accused, on cross-examination, and as touching his credibility, whether he had ever been indicted for any other offense, and what offenses. To the same effect, see *Mirando* v. *State* (Tex. Crim. App.) 50 S. W. 714; *Bolton* v. *State* (Tex. Crim. App.) 39 S. W. 672; *Ryan* v. *State*, 97 Tenn. 206, 36 S. W. 930 (holding also that, upon objection of his counsel that the best evidence should be offered, it is competent to offer the record of the indictments).

And in *State* v. *Mitchell*, 56 S. C. 524, 35 S. E. 210, a prosecution for violating the dispensary law, where the defendant had testified that he had sold no liquors since 1882, it was held not to be error to permit the state on cross-examination to ask him if he did not know that in 1883 and in 1884 he was indicted for such offense, and whether he did not pay a certain fine therefor in 1883.

In *Ogden* v. *People*, 134 Ill. 599, 25 N. E. 755, a prosecution for robbery, the defendant stated on cross-examination that he had once been indicted for an assault to kill, and convicted for an assault and battery. The question which elicited this information was objected to, and the court ruled that the witness might answer or not, as he desired. An affidavit submitted on the motion for a new trial showed that defendant's counsel misunderstood the ruling of the court, and told his client to answer the question. But the court held that the misapprehension of counsel could not be regarded as an error on the part of the court; stating also that it could hardly be supposed that the mere fact that the defendant had once been convicted of an assault and battery could have influenced the jury in the rendition of their verdict.

29. — as to acts of consciousness of guilt.

The accused may be asked on cross-examination whether he made any attempt to evade arrest.[1]

[1]*Ryan* v. *People*, 19 Hun, 188, Affirmed in 79 N. Y. 593; *Bagley* v. *Mason*, 69 Vt. 175, 37 Atl. 287.

In *State* v. *Kennon*, 45 La. Ann. 1192, 14 So. 187, it is held that prosecuting attorneys who seek to cross-examine an accused upon matters not legitimate in rebuttal, but which, it is claimed, may properly be asked by way of impeachment or attack upon the credibility of the witness,—as, for example, the defendant's flight,—should announce the object and purpose of their question, and offer to restrict the effect of the testimony.

30. — domestic relations; vagrancy.

As affecting credibility of the accused, who has testified on his own behalf, he may be asked questions tending to show that he has abandoned his home and become a vagrant.[1]

[1]*Yanke* v. *State*, 51 Wis. 464, 8 N. W. 276, a prosecution for assault with intent to kill. The testimony of the accused on material points was in direct conflict with that of the prosecuting witness, and also showed that he was a married man, and had not been with his wife for some weeks; and it was held to be no error to allow a question, on cross-examination, as to the length of time since he had lived with her, as the answer, tending to show that he had abandoned his home and had become a tramp, might have some bearing on his credibility.

31. Discretionary power of the court to exclude disparaging questions.

Where the accused is examined as a witness on his own behalf, the court may properly refuse to require him to answer a question tending to prove him guilty of a distinct offense, if the tendency appears to be to prejudice him with the jury directly upon the question of guilt of the offense for which he is on trial, rather than only indirectly, by impairing the credibility of his testimony.[1]

[1]In *People* v. *Brown,* 72 N. Y. 571, 28 Am. Rep. 183, an extreme case, a conviction was reversed on the ground that it was an error to allow such a question to be asked. Church, J., says: "I am of the opinion that the cross-examination of persons who are witnesses in their own behalf, when on trial for criminal offenses, should in general be limited to matters pertinent to the issue, or such as may be proved by other witnesses. I believe such a rule necessary to prevent a conviction for one offense by proof that the accused may have been guilty of others. Such a result can only be avoided practically by the observance of this rule." To the same effect, *Johnson* v. *State,* 8 Wyo. 494, 58 Pac. 761. See also note to *People* v. *Tice* (N. Y.) 15 L. R. A. 669.

In *Clarke* v. *State,* 78 Ala. 474, 56 Am. Rep. 45, a murder trial, it was held, approving the doctrine of *People* v. *Brown,* 72 N. Y. 571, 28 Am. Rep. 183, to be reversible error to ask on cross-examination: "Did you not belong to the Jesse James gang?" The court said that the only tests to which the defendant "subjects himself are cross-examination relating to any matter connected with the transaction or pertinent to the issue, and impeachments by assailing his general character or by proof of contradictory statements on other occasions. . . . The waiver of the constitutional immunity from compulsory self-examination should not be extended beyond facts which may be testified to by other witnesses or which may be relevant to the issue, or may tend to elucidate it. Within these limits the fullest cross-examination should be allowed; but its range into inquiries respecting past transactions and offenses separate and distinct is prohibited by the constitutional inhibition."

So, in *Buel* v. *State,* 104 Wis. 132, 80 N. W. 78, it was held that on the cross-examination of one accused of murder, where the evidence was all circumstantial, it was error to allow the state to ask questions which imputed to him the commission of various felonies, when such questions were not reasonably intended to affect his credibility, but were manifestly calculated to create prejudice in the minds of the jury.

32. Cross-examining as to previous inconsistent statements.

When the accused has testified as a witness on his own behalf, he may, within the same limits as any other witness, be cross-examined as to whether he has made previous statements inconsistent with his testimony, for the purpose of contradicting his testimony by proof of such statements.[1]

[1]*State* v. *Red,* 53 Iowa, 69, 4 N. W. 831; *State* v. *Abrams,* 11 Or. 169, 8 Pac. 327; *Com.* v. *Tolliver,* 119 Mass. 312; *Steele* v. *State,* 76 Miss. 387, 24 So. 910; *State* v. *Smith,* 57 Kan. 673, 47 Pac. 541; *State* v. *Helm,* 97 Iowa, 378, 66 Nev. 751; *State* v. *Bartmess,* 33 Or. 110, 54 Pac. 167.

And in *Kirby* v. *State,* 89 Ala. 63, 8 So. 110, where the defendant had on cross-examination denied having made a particular statement at a time and place named, imputing fault to himself in connection with the origin of the difficulty, it was held proper to further ask him if some other person did not, at the time and place named, make such statement in his presence and hearing, without objection or contradiction by him; and that upon his denial that such was the case, it was then proper for the prosecution to prove by another person, who was present at the time, that the statement was made at the time and place named, during a conversation in which the defendant participated.

But *Naugher* v. *State,* 116 Ala. 463, 23 So. 26, held that it was not competent for the state to impeach the testimony of defendant in a murder trial by asking him if he did not tell a witness that he had borrowed meat from the deceased, and, on his answering in the negative, introducing a witness to prove the contradictory statements, where there was no competent evidence of the fact of borrowing the meat, although such evidence would have been admissible as tending to rebut the effect of defendant's evidence as to the threats by deceased communicated to him.

And *Walton* v. *State* (Tex. Crim. App.) 55 S. W. 566, held that it was error to allow the prosecution to ask accused, on cross-examination, as to certain statements made by him while in the sheriff's custody, charged with theft, where he had not been cautioned that any statement he might make would be used against him, and, on his denial, to introduce evidence of such statements, since they were inadmissible either to contradict accused or as original testimony. See also *Morales* v. *State,* 36 Tex. Crim. Rep. 234, 36 S. W. 435, 846, holding that defendant cannot be examined as to confession made while in jail without having been warned, for the purpose of laying a predicate for his impeachment; and the state cannot be subsequently permitted to show that he made such a confession. Compare *Ford* v. *State,* 40 Tex. Crim. Rep. 280, 50 S. W. 350, holding that a memorandum of a statement voluntarily made by defendant charged with murder, after his arrest, and after he had been warned, might be used by the county attorney on the cross-examination of defendant.

33. —privileged communications.

The accused, when testifying in his own behalf, cannot be compelled to disclose privileged communications had between him and his attorney or counsel.[1]

[1]*Duttenhofer* v. *State,* 34 Ohio St. 91, 32 Am. Rep. 362 (disapproving the

Massachusetts case, below). And to the same effect, *Bigler* v. *Reyher*, 43 Ind. 112; N. Y. Code Civ. Proc. §§ 835, 836; *Alderman* v. *People*, 4 Mich. 414, 69 Am. Dec. 321 (*dictum*); *Hemenway* v. *Smith*, 28 Vt. 701; *Barker* v. *Kuhn*, 38 Iowa, 392 (holding that the enabling act should not be construed as opening the door which had been locked at common law); *State* v. *White*, 19 Kan. 445, 27 Am. Rep. 137 (held reversible error to compel the accused on cross-examination to disclose communications between himself and counsel in respect to which he did not testify on his direct examination. The court said: "The true view seems to be that communications which the lawyer is precluded from disclosing the client cannot be compelled to disclose"); *Herring* v. *State* (Tex. Crim. App.) 42 S. W. 301; *State* v. *James*, 34 S. C. 49, 12 S. E. 657, 34 S. C. 579, 13 S. E. 325, 899.

But where the defendant in a murder trial takes the stand on his own behalf, and voluntarily tells part of a confidential communication made to him by his wife, he may be compelled to disclose the remainder thereof. *State* v. *Turner*, 36 S. C. 534, 15 S. E. 602, 36 S. C. 608, 16 S. E. 687.

In *Com.* v. *Nichols*, 114 Mass. 285, 19 Am. Rep. 346, there is a *dictum* that "a party taking the stand as a witness in his own behalf may be cross-examined in relation to a communication between himself and his counsel as to which the latter would not be allowed to testify,"—Citing *Woburn* v. *Henshaw*, 101 Mass. 193, 3 Am. Rep. 333 (civil case).

34. Statutory limits of cross-examination.

In those jurisdictions where the statute allowing the accused to be a witness expressly provides for a cross-examination bounded by the limits of the direct,[1] it is implied that he can be cross-examined no further; and it is an error to allow him, against objection, to be cross-examined generally, either as to matters relevant to the issue[2] or as to his credibility,[3] even though in the same jurisdiction a different rule applies to other witnesses.[4]

[1] For the states in which the cross-examination of the accused is limited by the examination in chief by statute, see *supra*, § 16.

[2] *People* v. *McGungill*, 41 Cal. 431 (error to allow counsel for the prosecution to comment on defendant's refusal to be cross-examined as to the whole case, where he has testified in chief to only one point, *viz.*, denying an alleged conversation with a witness for the prosecution); *State* v. *Underwood*, 44 La. Ann. 852, 11 So. 277; *People* v. *Dole*, 122 Cal. 486, 55 Pac. 581, Reversing 51 Pac. 945; *State* v. *Grant*, 144 Mo. 56, 45 S. W. 1102.

[3] *State* v. *Saunders*, 14 Or. 300, 12 Pac. 441, holding that under the last clause of the Oregon statute it was reversible error to ask defendant on trial for murder whether he had killed another man in another state, and whether he was not a center shot, and whether he didn't always carry a pistol; for the statute intends to protect; even though conceding the general rule to be that such questions might be asked of other witnesses to affect their credibility.

In *State* v. *Lurch*, 12 Or. 99, 6 Pac. 408, a prosecution for forgery, it was held error to require defendant to write his name so as to compare it with the signature of the forged note, as it was a matter as to which he had not testified in chief.

In *State* v. *McLaughlin*, 76 Mo. 320, it was held that under the Missouri statute it was error to ask defendant as to other matters and crimes not testified to by him in chief. See also *State* v. *Chamberlain*, 89 Mo. 129, 1 S. W. 145, to the same effect. But in *State* v. *Owen*, 78 Mo. 367, under the same statute, it was held no error to ask the defendant: "Is this all you are willing to tell the jury about this case?" for, having been cross-examined at some length, it was merely equivalent to asking him: "Have you anything more to tell the jury?" And *State* v. *Sasseen*, 75 Mo. App. 197, holds that defendant in a criminal case, who has testified on direct examination that he has been a minister of the gospel for more than thirty years may be asked on cross-examination how many times he has pleaded guilty of larceny within that time, although ordinarily it is not permissible to uncover old crimes in order to discredit a witness or overthrow his moral character.

In *People* v. *Mullings*, 83 Cal. 138, 23 Pac. 229, it was held that a defendant in a criminal case who has offered himself as a witness in his own behalf, and has not testified in chief to any communications between his wife and himself, cannot, without his consent, be examined by the state as to any such communications.

See *State* v. *Saunders*, 14 Or. 300, 12 Pac. 441, and *State* v. *Porter*, 75 Mo. 171, holding that since the Missouri statute was passed, the same latitude is not allowed in cross-examination of the defendant as in the case of other witnesses.

In *People* v. *Louie Foo*, 112 Cal. 17, 44 Pac. 453, it was held that requiring defendant who had testified on his direct examination as to his whereabouts at the time of an assault with which he was charged, to testify on cross-examination whether he and his men had not made out some tickets on the night of the assault, and given them to some one so that he could swear he left clothes there that night,—was not prejudicial error, where he answered in the negative.

In some jurisdictions the statute expressly provides that the accused shall be subject to cross-examination as any other witness; that is to say, according to the rule governing cross-examination in that jurisdiction. See *supra*, § 16. And, in the absence of any such statutory provision, the courts lay down the same general rule. See, for example, cases cited, *supra*, § 24.

35. Aid of counsel.

Where the accused has testified in his own behalf, his counsel may, during cross-examination, interpose objection, not only to questions incompetent to other witnesses, but also to questions in violation of his privilege as a witness or right as a party.[1]

[1] *People* v. *Brown*, 72 N. Y. 571, 28 Am. Rep. 183, Affirming 8 Hun, 562.

The privilege here referred to was not on the ground that the question tended to criminate, but that, while calculated to degrade him, it had no direct bearing on any issue. The question was: "How many times have you been arrested?"

In *Hanoff* v. *State*, 37 Ohio St. 178, 41 Am. Rep. 496, there is *dictum* that "as a party his right to object to incompetent questions addressed to himself as a witness are the same as if they were addressed to any other witness." See also *supra*, § 19.

36. Recalling for further cross-examination.

The accused may be recalled for further cross-examination in the discretion of the court.[1]

[1]*State* v. *Horne*, 9 Kan. 119 (so holding, even for the purpose of laying the foundation for impeachment by contradicting him, if the cross-examination relates to the testimony he has given in his own behalf); *State* v. *Cohn*, 9 Nev. 179 (no error to permit recall for purpose of further cross-examination, where its effect is not to make the accused a witness for the state); *Thomas* v. *State*, 100 Ala. 53, 14 So. 621; *Anthony* v. *State* (Idaho) 55 Pac. 884; *Clay* v. *State*, 40 Tex. Crim. Rep. 493, 51 S. W. 370 (holding that this will not be deemed compelling him to give testimony against himself); *Com.* v. *Eisenhower*, 181 Pa. 470, 37 Atl. 521.

But he cannot be recalled as a witness for the state and compelled to testify in its favor. *State* v. *Lewis*, 56 Kan. 374, 43 Pac. 265.

37. — answer not relevant to merits.

The rule that the answer of a witness under cross-examination to a question not relevant[1] to the issue is conclusive on the party cross-examining, so that the falsity of the answer cannot be shown solely for the purpose of impairing the credibility of the witness by a mere contradiction, applies to the cross-examination of the accused when testifying on his own behalf.[2]

[1]One test or relevancy is whether the cross-examining party would be entitled to prove the fact as a part of his case. *Hildeburn* v. *Curran*, 65 Pa. 59, 63, where, laying down and applying this test, the court held it no error to exclude the evidence offered to contradict an answer to collateral matter. See also *George* v. *State*, 16 Neb. 318, 20 N. W. 311.

[2]*People* v. *Ware*, 29 Hun, 473, 1 N. Y. Crim. Rep. 166, Affirmed it seems in 92 N. Y. 653, without opinion, holding that, after asking the accused if he had not previously committed a similar crime, which he denied, it was error to allow the prosecution to prove that he had done so; *Marx* v. *People*, 63 Barb. 618; *Rosenweig* v. *People*, 63 Barb. 634, 6 Lans. 462; *George* v. *State*, 16 Neb. 318, 20 N. W. 311; *McKeone* v. *People*, 6 Colo. 346 (*dictum*).

38. — exceptions to the rule.

The rule preventing the contradiction of the accused as to an irrelevant matter drawn out on cross-examination does not preclude the prosecution from proving the falsity of his answers to questions on cross-examination affecting his credibility, where the matters inquired about, though not directly relevant to the issue, are in fact relevant[1] as tending to show an attempt to suborn a witness,[2] or to show intent,[3] of guilty knowledge,[4] or as discrediting or modifying the direct testimony of the accused.[5]

[1]In *People* v. *Eckert*, 2 N. Y. Crim. Rep. 470, 482, the accused, on trial for seduction under promise of marriage, denied on cross-examination that he had said that his father had untruthfully stated that he (the accused) "would rot in jail before he would marry the prosecutrix;" and it was held to be no error to admit proof in contradiction of such denial of the accused, as the evidence, though "somewhat remote," was relevant to the issue, as "it bore upon the question whether the defendant made to the prosecutrix a promise of marriage." But judgment was reversed on other grounds.

The proposition of the text also clearly follows from settled rules of evidence as applied to other witnesses.

In *Greenfield* v. *People*, 13 Hun, 242, 244, reversed on other grounds in 74 N. Y. 277, the court said: "A witness may be contradicted, not only as to his testimony in chief, but also as to matters drawn out on his cross-examination, material to the issue, especially where the contradictory statements tend to discredit, vary, modify, or explain the testimony given by him on his direct examination."

[2]In *Gulerette* v. *McKinley*, 27 Hun, 320, it was held no error to allow plaintiff to prove "that the defendant offered a witness a bribe to swear falsely against the plaintiff." And see *Morgan* v. *Frees*, 15 Barb. 352, to some effect.

[3]In *Weyman* v. *People*, 4 Hun, 511 (Affirmed, it seems, in 62 N. Y. 623, on the opinion below), Daniels, J., said: "The intent is the vital fact to be ascertained; and other acts, plainly within one common purpose or design, have been allowed as legal evidence of it. In treason, murder, robbery, arson, embezzlement, fraud, receiving stolen goods, . . . and other cases, such acts as proof of intent have been received, and no reason appears why larceny should not be included in the same principle;" and it was therefore held on trial for larceny to be no error to prove that the accused obtained money by fraudulent representations in the same way, and by similar means, in other cases about the same time. Hence, it is clear that if the accused should, upon cross-examination, deny that he was engaged in such other acts, it would be competent to contradict him, because the evidence in a proper case would be relevant to the issue of criminal intent.

[4]In *People* v. *Gibbs*, 93 N. Y. 470, 473, the court says: "Where guilty knowledge is an ingredient of the offense, evidence may be given of the

commission of other acts of a like character, where they are necessarily connected with that which is the subject of the prosecution, either by some connection of time or place, or as furnishing a clue to the motive on the part of the accused, as in the case of receiving stolen goods, knowing them to be such,"—Citing *Coleman* v. *People*, 58 N. Y. 555. Hence, if the accused should deny "other acts of a like character," on cross-examination, it would clearly be competent and relevant to contradict him.

[6]See *Greenfield* v. *People*, 13 Hun, 242, 244.

39. Impeaching by other witnesses.

If the accused has testified on his own behalf, he may be impeached like any other witness, by calling witnesses to show prior inconsistent statements or acts,[1] or to prove his bad character for veracity,[2] and, in several jurisdictions, to prove his general bad character,[3] but not by evidence of specific offenses.[4]

[1]*Com.* v. *Mason*, 116 Mass. 66 (no error to prove that the accused, on trial for sale of liquor, had sold liquor on a day subsequent to the time at which he testified he had sold out the business and thereafter had no connection with it); *Hicks* v. *State*, 99 Ala. 169, 13 So. 375; *McCoy* v. *State*, 46 Ark. 141; *People* v. *Gleason*, 122 Cal. 370, 55 Pac. 123; *Trusty* v. *Com.* 19 Ky. L. Rep. 706, 41 S. W. 766; *State* v. *Forsythe*, 99 Iowa, 1, 68 N. W. 446. See also Civil Trial Brief, chap. VIII.

In *Bailey* v. *State*, 40 Tex. Crim. Rep. 150, 49 S. W. 102, it was held that the defendant in a murder trial, who, in support of his theory of self-defense, testified circumstantially as to how the homicide occurred, could not be contradicted by proof that while under arrest, and without having been warned, he told the witness he had no recollection of the homicide.

[2]*Adams* v. *People*, 9 Hun, 89, where the court said that, under the New York statute, if the accused "became a witness, the truth of the evidence became a legitimate subject of inquiry. Its reliability might be attacked upon his cross-examination as to his character, as shown by his past life and conduct, or by introduction of witnesses to contradict any material evidence given by him. Besides these modes, the value of his testimony may be impeached by evidence of witnesses affecting his credit for veracity by reason of his general reputation. In respect to the evidence given by the accused, he may be treated as any other witness."

[3]*State* v. *Beal*, 68 Ind. 345, 34 Am. Rep. 263; *Morrison* v. *State*, 76 Ind. 335; *State* v. *Kirkpatrick*, 63 Iowa, 554, 19 N. W. 660; *State* v. *Clinton*, 67 Mo. 380, 29 Am. Rep. 506; *State* v. *Bulla*, 89 Mo. 595, 1 S. W. 764; *Peck* v. *State*, 86 Tenn. 259, 6 S. W. 389; *Mitchell* v. *State*, 94 Ala. 68, 10 So. 518; *Barton* v. *Com.* 17 Ky. L. Rep. 580, 32 S. W. 171, 396; *State* v. *Dyer*, 139 Mo. 199, 40 S. W. 768.

[4]*State* v. *Beaty*, 25 Mo. App. 214; *Stitz* v. *State*, 104 Ind. 359, 4 N. E. 145.

So, a defendant charged with having carnal knowledge of an unmarried female cannot be impeached as a witness by proof of specific acts of unchastity or immorality not connected with the crime charged, or of his having been arrested for such acts. *State* v. *Vandiver,* 149 Mo. 502, 50 S. W. 892.

And evidence of immoral connections, given to impeach the credibility of the defendant and of witnesses testifying in his behalf, is inadmissible when it consists of proof of particular facts which do not directly touch the question of their veracity. *Sweet* v. *Gilmore,* 52 S. C. 530, 30 S. E. 395.

40. — by proof of conviction of felony.

An accused testifying on his own behalf may be impeached like any other witness by proving that he has been convicted of a felony,[1] but not by proving a prior plea of guilty, without proof of conviction.[2]

[1] *People* v. *Satterlee,* 5 Hun, 167 (rape; no error to impeach by proof of record of conviction "for larceny, second offense, on plea of guilty"); *Combs* v. *State* (Tex. Crim. App.) 49 S. W. 585; *State* v. *Dyer,* 139 Mo. 199, 40 S. W. 768. See also N. Y. Pen. Code, § 714; *State* v. *McGuire,* 15 R. I. 23, 22 Atl. 1118, holding it no error to admit record of previous conviction of felony to impeach the credibility of the accused,—Citing R. I. Pub. Stat. chap. 214, § 38, which provides that "such conviction or sentence may be shown to affect his credibility." Similar statutory provisions exist in nearly all the states.

In *Ryan* v. *State,* 97 Tenn. 206, 36 S. W. 930, however, it was held that evidence, introduced by way of impeachment, that defendant in a criminal prosecution had been indicted for other offenses, should be withdrawn from the jury when it was developed by the record that defendant had been acquitted of some of the charges, and that the other indictments against him had been dismissed.

Bartholomew v. *People,* 104 Ill. 601, 44 Am. Rep. 97, holds that the offense must be an infamous one.

In *Prior* v. *State,* 99 Ala. 196, 13 So. 681, it was held that where the defendant on trial for the offense of carrying concealed weapons had testified for himself, the state could introduce a record of his prior conviction and sentence thereon of the offense of petit larceny, for the purpose solely of affecting his credibility as a witness.

But that fact must be proved by the record of the court where he was convicted, and not by oral testimony. *Thompson* v. *State,* 100 Ala. 70, 14 So. 878.

A defendant on a criminal trial, who testifies in his own behalf, cannot be impeached by showing that he has been arrested and tried for carrying concealed weapons and for discharging firearms, under Ky. Civ. Code, § 597, providing that a witness cannot be impeached by evidence of particular wrongful acts, except that it may be shown that he has been "convicted of felony." *Leslie* v. *Com.* 19 Ky. L. Rep. 1201, 42 S. W. 1095.

[2] *Com.* v. *Gorham,* 99 Mass. 420 (error to admit in evidence a former in-

dictment against the accused, upon the back of which the clerk of the court had indorsed, "The defendant pleads guilty," where it was shown that the defendant was not sentenced, and that the case for some reason was still pending and awaiting trial; for the Massachusetts statute allowing a conviction to be given in evidence to affect the credibility of the accused as a witness contemplates proof by a record of conviction, including judgment); *Marion* v. *State*, 16 Neb. 349, 20 N. W. 289 (plea of guilty, without judgment or sentence, not a conviction, within Neb. Civ. Code, § 338).

IV. Admissions.

41. Distinction between admission and confession.

Evidence of an admission or declaration of the accused, not amounting to a confession, is not to be excluded because drawn from him by threats or other inducements.[1]

Evidence of an admission of a fact not in itself involving criminal intent is not to be excluded for want of the preliminary proof required before receiving a confession, merely because it may, when connected with other facts, tend to establish guilt.[2]

[1] *McLain* v. *State*, 18 Neb. 154, 24 N. W. 720.

[2] In *People* v. *Parton*, 49 Cal. 632, a prosecution for rape, an admission of having taken improper liberties was held properly received as being an admission, and not a confession.

In *People* v. *Velarde*, 59 Cal. 457, a statement by accused seeking to account for his possession of stolen property was held competent.

In *State* v. *Red*, 53 Iowa, 69, 4 N. W. 831, a statement that certain articles in defendant's possession, and which he was seeking to conceal, were property of the person murdered, was held competent.

In *State* v. *Glynden*, 51 Iowa, 463, 1 N. W. 750, a statement of defendant that he was with deceased at or near the time and place of the murder was held competent.

In *People* v. *McCallam*, 3 N. Y. Crim. Rep. 189, Affirmed in 103 N. Y. 587, 9 N. E. 502, it is held that declarations made by one accused of a crime, denying any criminal act, not explaining suspicious circumstances for his own advantage,—are not confessions, and do not come within the provisions of § 395 of N. Y. Code Crim. Proc. providing that confessions made under the influence of fear, etc., are not admissible in evidence. Compare *People* v. *Mondon*, 38 Hun, 188, where, upon a trial for murder, it was held that the term "confession," as used in § 395, providing that "a confession of a defendant, whether in the course of judicial proceedings or to a private person, can be given in evidence against him, unless made under fear produced by threats," etc.,—is not to be restricted to admissions of guilt alone, but would include statements of the accused made before a coroner concerning his own conduct and relations with the deceased, while denying his guilt,—Reversed in 103 N.

Y. 211, 8 N. E. 496, 4 N. Y. Crim. Rep. 552, on the ground that the confessions were not voluntary.

In *Murphy* v. *People*, 63 N. Y. 590, Affirming 4 Hun, 102, 6 Thomp. & C. 369, it appeared that on the evening of a murder a mask was found near the scene. The accused, while conversing with the officer, who at the time had him under arrest, was asked by a third person, "Where did that mask come from?" He answered, "The children got that from the rag-a muffins," and immediately added, as if recollecting himself, "That mask had a black nose, and was torn down the face." The fact that a mask had been found had not been communicated to the prisoner when the conversation occurred. It was held admissible, for the purpose of connecting the prisoner with the mask.

Proof that statements were freely and voluntarily made is not necessary to render such statements admissible against the persons making them, where they were not confessions of guilt, and whatever inculpatory force they had arose, not from their intrinsic value, but from the comparison of them with other facts appearing in the case. *People* v. *Ashmead*, 118 Cal. 508, 50 Pac. 681.

And statements by an accused person not under oath, voluntarily made in answer to questions of a commissioner, not as a confession of guilt, but as explanations to avert suspicion from himself, are not inadmissible because the commissioner failed to inform him that he could have the aid of counsel, or to warn him that his statements might be used against him, or to advise him that he need not answer. *Wilson* v. *United States*, 162 U. S. 613, S. C., with note, 40 L. ed. 1090, 16 Sup. Ct. Rep. 895.

And an admission by defendant in a trial for murder by shooting, that a gun found in his house, with one barrel empty and one loaded and containing rags and paper similar to like articles found near the scene of the murder, was his gun, was held in *Hodge* v. *State*, 97 Ala. 37, 12 So. 164, to be admissible when shown to have been made without threats or the offer of any inducements.

In *Davis* v. *State* (Tex. Crim. App.) 24 S. W. 651, a remark of the defendant on trial for theft of hogs, made in the presence of the sheriff after the defendant had been warned that any statement he made could be used against him, and that he was not compelled to make any,—was held to be admissible in evidence against him.

So, a statement as to one's age, made while under arrest, and after being duly warned, may be used against the person making it, on a trial for an offense other than that for which he is under arrest, for the purpose of determining whether he was more than seventeen years old at the time of committing the offense for which he is on trial. *Henry* v. *State*, 38 Tex. Crim. Rep. 306, 42 S. W. 559.

42. Date of admission.

The time when an admission was made does not affect its competency as evidence, even though it was made years after the commission of the crime to which it relates, provided the time of the occurrence of the facts admitted is not too remote to render such facts admissible.[1]

[1]*Territory* v. *Dwenger*, 2 N. M. 73.

43. Statements by accused to the court.

Statements voluntarily made by the accused to the court, for the purpose of influencing its course in the cause, are competent to be proved before the jury, as evidence of the facts so stated, whenever they are relevant upon the trial.[1]

[1]In *State* v. *Fooks*, 65 Iowa, 196, 21 N. W. 559, a prosecution for obtaining money under false pretenses, it was held that requests made for the appointment of counsel upon the ground that defendant had no money to employ one were competent as an admission that he was a man without money or property.

In *Gonzales* v. *State*, 12 Tex. App. 657, a written admission made by the defendant to avoid a continuance, and not shown to have been made ignorantly or through mistake, nor obtained by improper means, was held not to be a confession, nor governed by the same rules as confessions; but was admissible.

44. — of fact which witness might prove.

An admission of the facts the adverse party proposes to prove by an absent witness is, upon the same trial, conclusive evidence against the party preventing postponement by making the admission, if it be given to the jury as a part of the evidence on the trial; otherwise it cannot be considered by them.[1]

[1]*Pannell* v. *State*, 29 Ga. 681; *Burchfield* v. *State*, 82 Ind. 580. See also *Dominges* v. *State*, 7 Smedes & M. 475, 45 Am. Dec. 315 (with note of change of the rule in Mississippi by statute); *Peterson* v. *State*, 63 Ala. 113 (*dictum;* and holding that if the admission be that the witnesses, if produced, would testify so and so, evidence that the facts were contrary to such testimony may be received).

45. — — what witness would testify.

An admission that a witness, if present, would testify to specified statements, does not conclude the party making it, either as to the competency or the credibility of the witness, nor as to the admissibility or the truth of the testimony.[1]

But evidence not going directly to the fact, but only to the question whether the witness named would have testified as stated, is not competent.[2]

A defendant who secures evidence in his own favor by an admission that an absent witness would so testify if present, which evidence is admitted over his objection that he is entitled to have the witness present, cannot complain that thereby his right to face his accusers has been violated.[3]

[1] *State* v. *Geddis,* 42 Iowa, 264; *Edmonds* v. *State,* 34 Ark. 720.

[2] *Peterson* v. *State,* 63 Ala. 113.

[3] *Ruiz* v. *Territory* (N. M.) 61 Pac. 126.

46. — — impeaching such witness.

If the fact desired to be proved was admitted, the party admitting it cannot impeach the absent witness.[1] If the admission were only that the witness would so testify, the witness, though absent, may be impeached.[2]

[1] *Powers* v. *State,* 80 Ind. 77; *Vinegar* v. *Com.* 19 Ky. L. Rep. 840, 42 S. W. 351.

The state, having admitted on the trial of a negro for a criminal offense that absent witnesses would testify to certain stated circumstances, cannot afterwards inquire and prove that the absent witnesses are negroes. *Fonville* v. *State,* 91 Ala. 39, 8 So. 688. The court said: "To inquire and prove that the absent witnesses were negroes certainly was irrelevant, unless the court judicially knew the color of the witnesses affected their credibility. If it was judicially known that, as a race, the witnesses were prima facie unworthy of belief, the question was both relevant and legal. We cannot judicially affirm of any race of people, of whatever color, as St. Paul did of the Cretians, that they were 'always liars.' Under the principle above declared, the objection to such a question, properly made and reserved, should be sustained."

[2] *State* v. *Swain,* 68 Mo. 605.

47. — producing the witness to contradict.

The concession of the prosecution that the witness would testify as stated in defendant's affidavit, or that the affidavit be read in evidence, does not preclude the prosecution from producing the witness himself to disprove the facts stated.[1]

[1] This rule, however, perhaps rests upon express statutes providing that when the admission is not of the fact, but of what the testimony would be, the proof of the testimony may be contradicted. *Edmonds* v. *State,* 34 Ark. 720; *State* v. *Mann,* 83 Mo. 589.

48. Admission on a former trial.

An admission made for the purposes of a previous trial, whether it be of the fact desired then to be proved[1] or of what would be the testimony of a witness then absent,[2] is inadmissible on a subsequent trial, although it is shown that the witness by whom the facts were to be proved has since died.

[1]*State* v. *Felter,* 32 Iowa, 49. See also *State* v. *Bryant,* 93 Mo. 273, 6 S. W. 102.

[2]*Powers* v. *State,* 87 Ind. 144, 151.

49. Admission by counsel.

A formal admission of a material fact,[1] made, either by the prosecuting officer or the counsel for the accused, in the course of the trial of the issues,[2] and for the purpose of influencing the course of the trial,[3] is conclusive respectively upon the state[4] and the accused, for the purposes of the trial.

The assumption of facts by counsel, however, merely for the purpose of argument,[5] or an informal statement of facts upon opening,[6] will not be construed as an admission of such facts.

[1]An admission of the law does not necessarily bind the client. *Mitchell* v. *Cotten,* 3 Fla. 134 (civil case).

Nor does an admission that a prima facie case exists. *Spaulding* v. *Hood,* 8 Cush. 602 (civil case).

[2]The fact that an admission of what an absent witness would prove is made before swearing the jury, even though made in their presence, is not enough. It should be presented as part of the evidence. *Lowrie* v. *Verner,* 3 Watts, 317 (civil case).

[3]Usually it must have been made for the purpose of dispensing with formal proof. *Bebee* v. *People,* 5 Hill, 32; *People* v. *Garcia,* 25 Cal. 531; *Com.* v. *Desmond,* 5 Gray, 80 (holding that where the counsel of a defendant in a criminal case argued that a witness for the prosecution was an accomplice and should have been corroborated, and the prosecuting attorney in his reply assumed and claimed that he was an accomplice, but had been corroborated, it was error for the court to instruct the jury in effect that if the jury were of opinion that the witness was not an accomplice, his testimony need not be corroborated, as the admission of the district attorney dispensed with the actual proof of the fact that the witness was an accomplice).

Compare with *Com.* v. *Elliot,* 110 Mass. 104; *Hackett* v. *State,* 13 Tex. App. 406 (where a written agreement to avoid a continuance was entered between the prosecuting officer and the defendant, to the effect that the latter might read in evidence the testimony of an absent witness as set forth in the application for continuance; and it was held that such an agreement did not preclude the state from introducing the absent witness upon the trial, if his presence could be had. Murder; judgment reversed on other grounds).

In a civil case an admission made even in the opening, not for the purpose of dispensing with proof by the adversary, but as an avowal of inability or disavowal of intention to prove, is enough. *Oscanyan* v. *Winchester Repeating Arms Co.* 103 U. S. 263, 26 L. ed. 541 (civil case).

[4]*People* v. *Tyler*, 36 Cal. 522; *Com.* v. *Desmond*, 5 Gray, 80.

[5]*Bebee* v. *People*, 5 Hill, 32 (here the prisoner's counsel had formally stipulated to admit testimony, otherwise incompetent, with the approbation of the court, which in a measure changed the course of trial, and suspended further efforts on the part of the prosecution to procure competent evidence of the fact; held that the defendant could not afterward retract and ask that the testimony should be excluded); *People* v. *Garcia*, 25 Cal. 531.

The court may relieve the party from an admission made by his attorney or counsel on the trial, if proper explanation be made. *Oscanyan* v. *Winchester Repeating Arms Co.* 103 U. S. 263, 26 L. ed. 541; S. P., *Behr* v. *Connecticut Mut. L. Ins. Co.* 2 Flipp. 692, 4 Fed. 357 (civil case).

But see *People* v. *Garcia*, 25 Cal. 531, where it was held not error to refuse to do so. Compare *Lewis* v. *Sumner*, 13 Met. 269.

Com. v. *Elliott*, 110 Mass. 104.

[6]*Flynn* v. *State*, 43 Ark. 289. In this case, upon a trial for murder, the counsel for the accused said something about the prisoner's planting himself on the right side of self-defense. It was insisted that this statement was a confession or admission of the shooting by the accused. It was held that it could not be so considered without determining what rights an attorney can waive for the accused on a trial for a felony; in any event the waiver or admission should be distinct and formal, and made for the purpose, in order to bind the accused. Judgment reversed.

50. — by prosecutor.

The complainant in the prosecution of an indictment, though the offense may have been committed against his property or person, is not a party to the proceedings in such a sense that his admissions and declarations are competent evidence in favor of the accused.[1]

[1]*Williams* v. *State*, 52 Ala. 412; *State* v. *Maitremme*, 14 La. Ann. 842 (holding that the admissions and declarations of the party injured by the criminal act, not forming a part of the *res gestæ*, are inadmissible in evidence except when received for the purpose of impeaching his attorney, or, in case of homicide, as dying declarations); *Com.* v. *Densmore*, 12 Allen, 535; *People* v. *McLaughlin*, 44 Cal. 435; *Belt* v. *State*, 103 Ga. 12, 29 S. E. 451; *Shields* v. *State*, 149 Ind. 395, 49 N. E. 351, and cases cited.

51. Admissions or confessions of third person in exoneration of the accused.

Evidence of declarations or confessions by a third person admitting that he committed the offense with which the prisoner is charged is inadmissible because hearsay.[1]

[1]*Greenfield* v. *People*, 85 N. Y. 75, 39 Am. Rep. 636, 641 (murder), Citing

Wharton, Crim. Ev. § 644; Wharton, Crim. Law, §§ 662, 684; 2 Best, Ev. §§ 559, 560, 563, 565, 578; *Lowry* v. *State*, 100 Ga. 574, 40 L. R. A. 95, 28 S. E. 419; *United States* v. *Mulholland*, 50 Fed. 413; *State* v. *Duncan*, 116 Mo. 288, 22 S. W. 699; *State* v. *West*, 45 La. Ann. 14, 12 So. 7; *State* v. *Pritchett*, 106 N. C. 667, 11 S. E. 357; *State* v. *Hack*, 118 Mo. 92, 23 S. W. 1089; *Horton* v. *State* (Tex. Crim. App.) 24 S. W. 28; *Davis* v. *Com.* 95 Ky. 19, 23 S. W. 585; *Welsh* v. *State*, 96 Ala. 92, 11 So. 450.

In *State* v. *Beaudet*, 53 Conn. 536, 55 Am. Rep. 155, 159, 4 Atl. 237, a prosecution for assault with intent to murder, it was held that although the accused might exculpate himself by showing that another was guilty, yet this rule went no further in favor of the accused than to allow him to show another's guilt by some appropriate evidence directly connecting that person with the *corpus delicti*. Therefore mere disconnected threats and declarations of third persons were inadmissible. If, however, they were part of the *res gestæ*, or if the threats were to commit a crime in a particular mode, and it was in fact so committed, perhaps they would be admissible,—Citing *State* v. *Davis*, 77 N. C. 483; *State* v. *Bishop*, 73 N. C. 44; *State* v. *May*, 15 N. C. (4 Dev. L.) 328; *State* v. *Duncan*, 28 N. C. (6 Ired. L.) 236; *State* v. *White*, 68 N. C. 158; *State* v. *Haynes*, 71 N. C. 79; *Crookham* v. *State*, 5 W. Va. 510; *Boothe* v. *State*, 4 Tex. App. 202; *Walker* v. *State*, 6 Tex. App. 576; Wharton, Crim. Ev. § 225; Wharton, Homicide, § 693; 2 Bishop, Crim. Proc. § 623; 1 Bishop, Crim. Proc. § 1248; *Com.* v. *Chabbock*, 1 Mass. 144; *Smith* v. *State*, 9 Ala. 990; *West* v. *State*, 76 Ala. 98; *Sharp* v. *State*, 6 Tex. App. 650; *Rhea* v. *State*, 10 Yerg. 258; *Greenfield* v. *People*, 85 N. Y. 75, 39 Am. Rep. 636; *State* v. *Johnson*, 30 La. Ann. 921; *Spar* v. *Coate*, 3 McCord L. 232; 2 Phillipps, Ev. 4th Am. ed. Cowen & Hill's Notes, 703, note.

Such evidence was also held inadmissible in *Daniel* v. *State*, 65 Ga. 199; *State* v. *Gee*, 92 N. C. 756; *Holt* v. *State*, 9 Tex. App. 571. See also Whart. Crim. Ev. § 225; *Sharp* v. *State*, 6 Tex. App. 650.

But where such third person testifies as a witness that he committed the offense at the instigation of the defendant, evidence of threats made by such accomplice against the deceased, showing motive personal to himself, is admissible as tending to show that the slayer acted from personal malice, without reference to the defendant. *Marler* v. *State*, 67 Ala. 55, 42 Am. Rep. 95.

52. Rebuttal.

Where the accused has testified in his own behalf, it is not error to allow the prosecution to prove, in contradiction of his testimony, declarations made by himself, although such as might have been offered as a part of the case in chief.[1]

[1]*Leighton* v. *People*, 10 Abb. N. C. 261, 12 N. Y. Week. Dig. 467, Affirmed in 88 N. Y. 117.

53. Admission contradicted by disproof of fact admitted.

Where a witness testifies to the defendant's admission to him of a matter of fact, evidence that the fact was not as so admitted is not competent merely to contradict the witness.[1]

[1]*Com.* v. *Parker,* 2 Cush. 212. See also *Collins* v. *Stephenson,* 8 Gray, 438.

V. Affidavits.

54. Affidavits used by the accused competent against him.

Statements material to the cause, whether as affecting the issue or contradicting a witness of the accused, contained in an affidavit made and used by the accused on a motion for a continuance or postponement, are competent evidence against him.[1]

[1]*Pledger* v. *State,* 77 Ga. 242, 3 S. E. 320; *Leslie* v. *State,* 35 Fla. 171, 17 So. 555; *Behler* v. *State,* 112 Ind. 140, 13 N. E. 272 (in this case the court says: "There is nothing giving to the statements in an affidavit for a continuance a privilege, nor is there anything which impresses upon them any compulsory or confidential features. The affidavit is a paper belonging to the files, public in its character, and freely executed"); *State* v. *Mayes,* 78 Mo. 307; *Com.* v. *Starr,* 4 Allen, 301 (holding the affidavit competent for the purpose of contradicting the testimony of the accused). Compare *Powers* v. *State,* 87 Ind. 144, where an admission by the prosecution of the truth of facts stated in an affidavit thus used on a former trial was held not to let in the affidavit on a second trial after the death of the witness.

An affidavit filed by the defendant in a prosecution for slander, in support of a motion for a continuance because of the absence of certain witnesses to prove actual sexual intercourse of the prosecutrix with another, is competent evidence against him, where, on the trial, after the state has rested, he admits the virtue of the prosecutrix, and attempts to justify the slander by swearing that he was simply repeating a rumor he had heard, and had requested the party to whom he had communicated the slanderous matter to say nothing about it. *State* v. *Mills,* 116 N. C. 1051, 21 S. E. 563.

That use does not admit truth of other statements, see *post,* Division XLII., § 20.

55. —— and falsity shown, if relevant.

Statements material to the issue contained in an affidavit made and used by the accused on a motion for continuance or postponement may be put in evidence for the purpose of proving their falsity, even though the accused has not testified as a witness, and his character has not been drawn in issue.[1]

[1]*State* v. *Bishop,* 98 N. C. 773, 4 S. E. 357. Here the court said: "The

affidavit was admissible as a statement or declaration of the defendant, voluntarily made, in regard to the crime with which he was charged, and the falsity of which it was competent for the state to show. Every act of the defendant in respect to the alleged crime, and every circumstance calculated to throw light upon it, and aid the jury in coming to a correct conclusion, is competent."

56. ——falsity cannot be shown if not relevant.

Statements not material to the issue cannot be read from such an affidavit for the purpose of proving their falsity, and thus showing the accused guilty of perjury, unless it may be in a case where it is rendered proper under the rules relative to evidence when character is drawn in issue, or in impeachment of the credibility of an accused who has testified in his own behalf.[1]

[1]*Farrell* v. *People,* 103 Ill. 17. Assault with intent to murder; insanity alone was relied on in defense, the assault and shooting not being controverted; held error to admit such an affidavit in which defendant denied the act alleged, and his guilt, it being wholly irrelevant to the issue of insanity, and the only object being to show his perjury. See also *Burris* v. *State,* 38 Ark. 221.

VI. Alibi.

[The controversies on this point turn on the underlying question whether it is in theory a distinct issue, or only in effect a special traverse of one element in the charge; namely, the element of presence at the time and place of the offense. In the former view, the burden is on the accused to establish it by a preponderance of evidence; and the accused cannot object to evidence of presence of rebuttal, although such evidence might have been relevant in chief. In the latter view, the burden does not shift to the defense, but the prosecution must prove presence when necessary to the truth of the charge, and prove it beyond a reasonable doubt; but, on the other hand, the jury may discredit even clear direct evidence of an *alibi,* by reason of their belief in circumstantial evidence of guilt. See, on this subject, *Ackerson* v. *People,* 124 Ill. 563, 16 N. E. 847, and cases cited in opinion and note; 22 Am. L. Rev. 297, and cases cited; *Watson* v. *Com.* 95 Pa. 418; *People* v. *Fong Ah Sing,* 64 Cal. 253, 28 Pac. 233; *State* v. *Reed,* 62 Iowa, 40, 17 N. W. 150, and cases cited. See also *post,* Division XLII., § 20.]

57. Declarations of accused.

Declarations as to where he had been, made by the accused on his return home shortly after the time in question, are not competent in his favor, as evidence of an *alibi*.[1]

[1]*State* v. *McCracken*, 66 Iowa, 569, 24 N. W. 43.

And in *State* v. *Bedard*, 65 Vt. 278, 26 Atl. 719, the details of conversations had by the prisoner during the period of an *alibi* which he sought to establish were held inadmissible in evidence, either as a part of the *res gestæ* or as proof of the time spent in the conversations.

So, on the trial of a complaint, under 2 How. (Mich.) Anno. Stat. § 9174, the testimony of the wife of an admitted accomplice, as to where her husband said he stayed on the night of the commission of the alleged offense, was purely hearsay, and erroneously admitted. *People* v. *O'Brien*, 60 Mich. 8, 26 N. W. 795.

According to *People* v. *Hare*, 57 Mich. 505, 24 N. W. 843, however, it is proper, for the purpose of proving an *alibi*, for counsel to examine their client as to conversations at a time and place inconsistent with guilt.

58. — contradicting.

An accused testifying on his own behalf to prove an *alibi* may be asked to describe what he saw at the place where he swears he was; and then may be contradicted by other evidence as to what was really to be seen there at that time.[1]

[1]*People* v. *Gibson*, 58 Mich. 368, 25 N. W. 316.

59. — by evidence of presence.

Whether the prosecution may rebut evidence of *alibi* by such evidence of the presence of the accused as might have been given as evidence in chief[1]—

[1]Compare:

Affirmative: *State* v. *Lewis*, 69 Mo. 92, holding that when evidence has been given on behalf of the prisoner to prove an *alibi*, the prosecution is entitled to offer rebutting evidence to prove his presence.

Negative: *Rex* v. *Hilditch*, 5 Car. & P. 299 (1832, Taunton, J.). The prosecution having closed, the defense put in evidence of an *alibi*. The prosecution then wished to call a witness in reply to prove that he saw all the prisoners near the place where the robbery was committed; held evidence in chief, and not in reply. Whatever is confirmation of the original case cannot be given in reply; only evidence going to cut down the case on the part of the defense, without being any confirmation of the case of the prosecution. The better opinion is that under the American practice it is in the discretion of the court to receive such evidence.

VII. Another offense.

60. General rule.

The cases in which offenses other than those charged in the indictment may be proved for the purpose of showing criminal intent or guilty knowledge are very few.[1]

When such evidence is offered, the question is whether it falls within a recognized exception to the general rule excluding evidence of an offense not charged in the indictment.[2]

[1] *People* v. *Corbin*, 56 N. Y. 363, 15 Am. Rep. 427, 429, holding that upon a charge of forgery evidence of the commission of other forgeries is not admissible for the purpose of showing a criminal intent. New trial granted. Compare *Bell* v. *State*, 57 Md. 108, allowing proof of other forgeries on the same bank to negative mistake, etc.

[2] *Coleman* v. *People*, 55 N. Y. 81; *Ryan* v. *State*, 60 N. J. L. 552, 38 Atl. 672.

61. —exceptions; fact common to both offenses.

Evidence tending to prove the accused guilty of an offense not charged in the indictment is not on that account incompetent, if it tends to prove any fact constituting an element in the offense that is charged in the indictment.[1]

For other exceptions, see *infra*, §§ 236–249, and §§ 618–623.

[1] *Weed* v. *People*, 56 N. Y. 628, Affirming 3 Thomp. & C. 50. Abortion; it having been shown that the accused had administered medicines to deceased which might produce miscarriage, and that a miscarriage was produced, whereby she died; held not error to admit a circular published by accused three years previously, tending to show that he was engaged in the business of consulting in reference to the procuring of abortions. The evidence had been held by the supreme court admissible as being corroborative.

To the same effect, citing numerous authorities, *People* v. *Sessions*, 58 Mich. 594, 26 N. W. 291, 295; *People* v. *Sanders*, 114 Cal. 216, 46 Pac. 153; *State* v. *Madigan*, 57 Minn. 430, 59 N. W. 490; *State* v. *Kelley*, 65 Vt. 531, 27 Atl. 203; *People* v. *Place*, 157 N. Y. 584, 52 N. E. 576; *State* v. *Fallon*, 2 N. D. 510, 52 N. W. 318, Citing *State* v. *Lapage*, 57 N. H. 245, 24 Am. Rep. 69.

"It is true, as a general rule, that on a prosecution for one crime it is not proper to prejudice the jury against the prisoner by showing him to have been guilty of another; but where the evidence is relevant and material on the question of the guilt of the prisoner of the crime for which he is upon trial, it cannot be excluded merely because it also proves him guilty of another crime." Rapallo, J., in *Hope* v. *People*, 83 N. Y. 418, 38 Am. Rep. 460. Robbery of the key to the street door of a bank; held not error to admit evidence that a burglary was committed on the bank on the same occasion, and that the gang who committed the burglary was the same that committed the robbery, such evidence, by connecting the accused with the burglary, tending to connect him also with the robbery. Also held that it was not error to admit evidence of the complicity of the prisoner in a previous concerting of a scheme to enter and rob the bank.

In *State* v. *Adams*, 20 Kan. 311, a prosecution for burglary and larceny, it was held that, there being testimony showing a conspiracy to commit a crime, evidence of acts done intermediate to the conspiracy and crime, in preparation of means for such crime, was properly admitted, although through some outside intervention the means so prepared were not actually used, but the crime was otherwise accomplished.

In *Kernan* v. *State*, 65 Md. 253, 4 Atl. 124, evidence of movements of the accused immediately previous to the offense was held not incompetent because involving proof of another crime. Compare *Com.* v. *Campbell*, 7 Allen, 541, 83 Am. Dec. 705.

In *State* v. *Kepper*, 65 Iowa, 745, 23 N. W. 304, evidence of a distinct crime was involved in proving the identity of the accused as the one who committed the crime charged in the indictment.

To make one criminal act evidence of another they must be connected as part of a general plan or design, or the connection may be shown by such circumstances of identification as necessarily prove that the person who committed one crime must have committed the other; but a mere isolated crime cannot be given in evidence. *Swan* v. *Com.* 104 Pa. 218. Here the accused was indicted with L. for burglary and larceny; held error to admit evidence of a subsequent felony, and goods found on the person of L., as against accused, as to whom no connection with the larceny had been shown.

In *McCartney* v. *State*, 3 Ind. 353, 56 Am. Dec. 510, 511, the fact that indictments were pending for such other offenses (uttering counterfeit notes) was held no objection to receiving the evidence of the offenses to show intent, etc. The same was held of other offenses for which the accused had been indicted and acquitted, but this can hardly be sustained.

In *Williams* v. *People*, 166 Ill. 132, 46 N. E. 749, a trial for assault with intent to commit larceny, it appeared that the defendants were following a show from place to place which daily attracted large crowds of people. They followed the show to Rock Island, where, as was usual, the streets were crowded with people. The defendants were there for the purpose and with the intent of stealing and picking pockets. What they did at Rock Island that day was in pursuance of a common object and purpose. Their acts and conduct were all connected. No evidence was offered for the purpose or with the view to prove the commission of another crime, but the court allowed the People to prove the conduct and acts of the plaintiff in error and the other defendants who were indicted with him, before and after the attempted robbery for which they were indicted, as tending to prove the issue involved.

In a prosecution for murder claimed to have been done accidentally, evidence of another killing by defendant, also claimed to have been done accidentally, is not admissible to show a system, unless the previous killing was done in the same manner as the latter killing, and some criminality attached to the former killing. *Barkman* v. *State* (Tex. Crim. App.) 52 S. W. 69.

VIII. Attempts.

62. Attempt at previous commission.

Evidence that the accused, at a time previous to the offense charged, but not too remote in point of time, attempted to commit the same offense, is competent as tending to show guilty intent.[1]

Otherwise of an attempt to commit the like offense against other persons or property.[2]

[1] *People* v. *O'Sullivan*, 104 N. Y. 481, 58 Am. Rep. 530, 10 N. E. 880 (rape).

So, in a prosecution for murder, evidence of an attempt by defendant to strike one other than the deceased just prior to the fatal affray, is admissible as *res gestæ*, where it is so inseparably connected with the homicide that the facts of one include those of the other. *State* v. *Fontenot*, 48 La. Ann. 305, 19 So. 111.

And evidence that a witness for defendant on trial for assault with intent to kill was one of those who attempted a robbery shortly before such assault, and shot an officer who tried to arrest them, is admissible, where there is evidence that an attempt to rob had been made by two persons answering the description of defendant and such witness, and that it was known to the officer assaulted by defendant, to show that they were together at the time and made such attempt, and that the officer was justified in arresting them, because he had a well-grounded belief that they were the parties making such attempt to rob. *State* v. *Foley*, 130 Mo. 482, 32 S. W. 973.

[2] *People* v. *O'Sullivan*, 104 N. Y. 481, 58 Am. Rep. 530, 10 N. E. 880, *supra*.

IX. Best and secondary.

[The rule that when the nonproduction of a written instrument is satisfactorily accounted for, secondary evidence of its existence and contents may be given, is applicable to criminal, as well as civil suits. *United States* v. *Reyburn*, 6 Pet. 352, 365, 8 L. ed. 424, 429 (indictment for cruising as a privateer under a foreign commission). The reason is that otherwise an offender would only have to destroy the document, and his escape from punishment would be sufficient.]

63. No best or secondary witnesses.

The distinction between primary and secondary evidence does not apply to witnesses;[1] but a subscribing witness must be produced or accounted for to prove the instrument, if its validity depends on its being attested by a subscribing witness;[2] otherwise his production is not necessary.[3]

[1] Thus, on the trial of an indictment for selling liquor to a minor, the lat-

ter's testimony as to his age was received, notwithstanding it was shown that his father and mother were both living. *State* v. *Cain,* 9 W. Va. 559.

The testimony of a person in regard to his own signature is not evidence of a grade superior to the testimony of a witness acquainted with the handwriting. *Lefferts* v. *State,* 49 N. J. L. 26, 6 Atl. 521. See also *Com.* v. *Pratt,* 137 Mass. 98; *Green* v. *Cawthorn,* 15 N. C. (4 Dev. L.) 410 (civil case); and Wharton, Crim. Ev. § 360.

An apparent exception to this rule is to be found on indictment for theft, if the law expressly requires the nonconsent of the owner to be shown. Here it is held that the best evidence of such nonconsent is the testimony of the owner himself, and it is error to admit secondary evidence of this fact without having first satisfactorily accounted for the absence of this best evidence. *Smith* v. *State,* 13 Tex. App. 507. See also *Hunter* v. *State,* 13 Tex. App. 16; *Stewart* v. *State,* 9 Tex. App. 321.

And where one person owns the property, and another person has the control, care, or management of it, the nonconsent of each must be proved (in larceny); and this proof should be made by the persons themselves, if they are obtainable; and if they are not to be had, their absence should be accounted for before the state can resort to circumstantial evidence. *Bowling* v. *State,* 13 Tex. App. 338, Following *Wilson* v. *State,* 12 Tex. App. 481. See also *Williamson* v. *State,* 13 Tex. App. 514.

But the court may require the prosecution to call certain witnesses in some cases. See *People* v. *Gordon,* 40 Mich. 716; and Division XXXVII., note.

[2]By statute. And for an exhaustive review of the authorities as to the necessity of calling subscribing witnesses to prove attested instruments, see note to *Garrett* v. *Hanshue* (Ohio) 35 L. R. A. 321.

[3]It was not so at common law.

64. Collateral facts.

The rule excluding secondary evidence does not apply to a collateral fact[1] not a part of the issue, and only incidentally involved.

[1]*Long* v. *State,* 10 Tex. App. 186. On indictment for counterfeiting it was proved that the accused had had access to certain convicts in the penitentiary; and the fact that their conviction was for counterfeiting was allowed to be proved by testimony of the officials of the penitentiary, it being a collateral fact, and the officials not having possession of the original record. See also *Klein* v. *Russell,* 19 Wall. 439, 464, 22 L. ed. 116, 124 (civil case).

So, a question to the mortgagee, in a prosecution under Ala. Code, § 3835, for removing mortgaged chattels with intent to defraud the mortgagee, as to whether he had not cut logs and timber from defendant's land, asked for the purpose of showing that there was no fraudulent intent because the mortgagor supposed the mortgage debt had been paid with such timber,—is not inadmissible on the ground that the timber contract was in writing, since, the question of intent arising collaterally, any legal evidence bearing thereon is admissible. *Cobb* v. *State,* 100 Ala. 19, 14 So. 362.

65. — on cross-examination.

The rule excluding secondary evidence does not apply to matter not relevant to the merits, but drawn out on cross-examination to test the temper and credibility of the witness,[1] except that if the contents of a document are sought to be used to discredit or contradict the witness, as containing his own statements contrary to his testimony, the original, not a copy, must be produced.[2]

[1] *Klein* v. *Russell,* 19 Wall. 439, 464, 22 L. ed. 116, 124 (civil case); *Kalk* v. *Fielding,* 50 Wis. 339, 7 N. W. 296 (civil case).

[2] *Newcomb* v. *Griswold,* 24 N. Y. 298 (civil case); *Pratt* v. *Norton,* 5 Thomp. & C. 8 (a certified copy assignment in bankruptcy; civil case). See also *Nash* v. *Hunt,* 116 Mass. 237, 248 (a copy pleading; civil case).

66. Condition of personal property.

Whenever evidence of the condition of an article of personal property is competent, its condition may be described by a witness without producing the article itself.[1]

[1] *Com.* v. *Pope,* 103 Mass. 440 (spots and stains on clothes of defendant); *Com.* v. *Welch,* 142 Mass. 473, 8 N. E. 342 (testimony of an officer that a tumbler which he seized under a search warrant contained intoxicating liquor), Following *Com.* v. *Pope,* 103 Mass. 440, *supra.*

67. Identity of personal property.

Oral evidence of the contents of a writing may be given without showing any reason for not producing it, where the evidence is offered merely for the purpose of identifying an article to which the writing was attached,[1] or as forming a part of the description of the place where the writing was found.[2]

[1] *Com.* v. *Hills,* 10 Cush. 530 (marks on goods stolen). See also *Com.* v. *Blood,* 11 Gray, 74; *Com.* v. *Morrell,* 99 Mass. 542 (writing upon a tag of a valise); *Com.* v. *Powers,* 116 Mass. 337 (United States Revenue stamp bearing a certain date upon a keg of whisky).

[2] *Com.* v. *Brown,* 124 Mass. 318, holding that parol evidence might be received to the effect that a written paper purporting to be a United States revenue license was hanging on the wall of an alleged barroom.

68. Forgery.

Forgery cannot be proved, even as a distinct offense from that charged, and for the purpose merely of showing criminal intent or guilty knowledge, without producing the paper alleged to have been forged, or accounting for its absence.[1]

[1]*State* v. *Breckenridge*, 67 Iowa, 204, 25 N. W. 130; *State* v. *Saunders*, 68 Iowa, 370, 27 N. W. 455.

69. Preliminary examination and confessions.

Where the proceedings at a coroner's inquest, or at the examination before a committing magistrate, are regular, and the record is such as to be admissible in evidence, parol proof is not admissible of statements made by a witness at the inquest or examination, in answer to questions put by or on behalf of the coroner or magistrate.[1]

[1]*Robinson* v. *State*, 87 Ind. 292 (coroner's inquest; not even to show that additional statements were made by the same person). See also *Cicero* v. *State*, 54 Ga. 156; *Wright* v. *State*, 50 Miss. 332; *State* v. *Branham*, 13 S. C. 389 (confessions to justice at a preliminary hearing).

But the rule is otherwise where the writing is not so authenticated as to render it competent evidence. *Guy* v. *State*, 9 Tex. App. 161 (confession of accused), Following *State* v. *Simien*, 30 La. Ann. 296; *Dunlap* v. *State*, 9 Tex. App. 179, 35 Am. Rep. 736 (applying the same principle to the testimony of a deceased witness).

But in *Crite* v. *Com.* (Va.) 12 Rep. 575, the testimony of a witness taken at the coroner's inquest was held inadmissible though it was shown that the witness had removed from the state, and efforts had been made by the prisoner to procure her voluntary attendance.

Where the examination of the prisoner was not reduced to writing it may be proved by parol. *King* v. *Huet*, 2 Leach, C. L. 821; *State* v. *Suggs*, 89 N. C. 527. See also *Brown* v. *State*, 71 Ind. 470. Testimony of witnesses before the coroner.

In England it is held that the magistrate's clerk must be called to prove that the examination was not taken down in writing. *Rex* v. *Packer*, 3 Russell, Crimes, 450.

The fact that the confession was reduced to writing by the magistrate's clerk does not render it inadmissible. *State* v. *Rover*, 13 Nev. 21.

An examination, though informal, may be used to refresh the memory of a witness who was present and took it down. *Rex* v. *Telicote*, 2 Starkie, 483; Wharton, Crim. Ev. 667, and cases there cited.

70. Court records.

The contents of court records cannot be proved[1] by parol, unless they have been lost after being returned into court.[2]

[1]*State* v. *Grayson*, 38 La. Ann. 788 (pendency of indictment in another court); *Heflin* v. *State*, 88 Ga. 151, 14 S. E. 112; *State* v. *Richardson*,

117 Mo. 586, 23 S. W. 769; *Com.* v. *Sullivan*, 161 Mass. 59, 36 N. E. 583; *Murphy* v. *State*, 108 Ala. 10, 18 So. 557.

So, parol testimony is inadmissible to show a requirement of bail by a justice, as it must be certified by the record. *Foat* v. *State*, 28 Tex. App. 527, 13 S. W. 867.

To exclude the testimony of a witness for having been convicted of felony, the record of such conviction must be produced. *Bratton* v. *State*, 34 Tex. Crim. Rep. 477, 31 S. W. 379. This case holds, however, that, for the purpose of impeaching a defendant who testifies that he has never been convicted of theft, the record of a former conviction is not necessary, but oral evidence of such fact may be given. To the same effect, see *McNeal* v. *State* (Tex. Crim. App.) 43 S. W. 792.

And parol evidence of the contents of a warrant of arrest is not admissible in a prosecution for aiding one detained under the warrant to escape, unless a foundation for secondary evidence is laid by accounting for the failure to produce the warrant or a certified copy of it. *Dubose* v. *State*, 115 Ala. 70, 22 So. 613.

Nor is oral evidence admissible to prove the finding and subsequent quashing of an indictment, such facts being provable only by the record. *State* v. *Daugherty*, 106 Mo. 182, 17 S. W. 303.

Parol evidence is admissible, however, under a plea of former acquittal, to establish or disprove the identity of the offense or of the person; but as to the form or substance of the indictment or exceptions thereto the record alone can be received as evidence. *State* v. *Hudkins*, 35 W. Va. 247, 13 S. E. 367.

But the docket of a justice of the peace who presided at a trial of an assault is not the best evidence to prove the identity of the justice with the assaulted party, so as to exclude the testimony of the justice to that fact. *Ex parte Ambrose*, 32 Tex. Crim. Rep. 468, 24 S. W. 291.

[a] *Com.* v. *Roark*, 8 Cush. 210 (criminal complaint and warrant). See also *Gordon* v. *State*, 46 N. J. L. 432; *State* v. *Whitney*, 38 La. Ann. 579 (admitting parol evidence of contents of indictment on trial); *People* v. *Coffman*, 59 Mich. 1, 26 N. W. 207 (admitting parol testimony to show that a preliminary hearing was had); *United States* v. *Walsh*, 22 Fed. 644 (holding that upon the trial of an indictment for perjury in swearing falsely in an application for naturalization, the clerk who made up the record would not be permitted to testify that it did not conform to the facts, in that it stated that the oath was made in court, whereas it was made before the clerk in his office). As to proving lost records, see note in *Goldman* v. *Kennedy*, 21 Abb. N. C. 367.

So, testimony of the magistrate before whom a former trial which is pleaded as former jeopardy took place is admissible to show the contents of the complaint, and that it was sworn to before him, on his testifying that he has made diligent search for the complaint, and it cannot be found. *Territory* v. *Stocker*, 9 Mont. 6, 22 Pac. 496.

And where the return of an examining magistrate fails to include the complaint and warrant referred to therein, on making sufficient proof of the loss of said missing papers it is competent for the People, in opposing a motion to quash, to make proof of their contents. *People* v. *Coffman*, 59 Mich. 1, 26 N. W. 207.

71. Recorded instrument.

An instrument recorded under a statute allowing record, but not making the record evidence equally with the original, cannot be proved by the record, nor by a certified copy of the record, without first laying a foundation for such secondary evidence.[1] Such record is, however, competent secondary evidence if the absence of the original is accounted for.[2]

[1] *State* v. *Penny*, 70 Iowa, 190, 30 N. W. 561. False pretenses in representation that there was no prior chattel mortgage on the property. The Iowa Code (§ 3702) makes duly certified copies evidence in all cases where the record could be admissible, but does not make the record admissible equally with the original.

[2] In *Com.* v. *Preece*, 140 Mass. 276, 5 N. E. 494 (arson), it was held that where a deed is not in the control of the government nor of the defendant, a registered copy is admissible to show ownership of the property destroyed.

72. Statute.

Original papers are not made merely secondary evidence by record pursuant to a statute requiring them to be filed or recorded.[1]

[1] *Chapman* v. *Gates*, 54 N. Y. 145 (county judge's order in highway proceedings; civil case); *Haddow* v. *Lundy*, 59 N. Y. 320 (surrogate's minutes; civil case).

73. Negativing existence of instrument that should be recorded.

For a decision that oral evidence of lack of license is not competent, if a license in such case must have been recorded, and the book is not produced, see—[1]

[1] *Hepler* v. *State*, 58 Wis. 46, 16 N. W. 42.

And that while the existence of a record can only be proved by its production, or the production of an unauthenticated copy thereof, its nonexistence may be proved by the testimony of one who is cognizant of such fact, see *Hornberger* v. *State*, 47 Neb. 40, 66 N. W. 23.

74. Oral admission of accused by fact provable only by writing.

Evidence of oral admissions by the accused is competent only when parol evidence of the fact sought to be shown by such admissions would be competent.[1]

[1] *Sherman* v. *People*, 13 Hun, 576, holding that the contents of a written in-

strument within the statute of frauds could not be shown by the verbal admissions of a party, without accounting for its absence.

Query, whether this rule applies where the statute is not in form a rule of evidence, but goes to the validity of the transaction, and the object of the offered admission is to prove the transaction irrespective of statutory validity.

75. Official character.

The official character of a public officer may be proved, when the question is not directly upon his right to the office, by proving his official acts, and by such other evidence as shows that he is an officer *de facto,* without producing his commission or any record of his appointment or election.[1]

[1]*Com.* v. *McCue,* 16 Gray, 226; *State* v. *Smith,* 38 La. Ann. 301; *Jacob* v. *United States,* 1 Brock. 520, Fed. Cas. No. 7,157.

So, evidence that one charged with perjury in making an affidavit as deputy sheriff was such deputy may be given without introducing his formal appointment as such, where he was acting as deputy. *Shely* v. *State,* 35 Tex. Crim. Rep. 190, 32 S. W. 901.

And the record of election and qualification of a county commissioner need not be introduced in evidence to show that he was such commissioner, on a trial for offering a bribe to him. *Rath* v. *State,* 35 Tex. Crim. Rep. 142, 33 S. W. 229.

And testimony of an officer that he was acting as such at the time of making an arrest is admissible, and it is not necessary to prove his official character by the record. *State* v. *Taylor,* 70 Vt. 1, 42 L. R. A. 673, 39 Atl. 447.

A sheriff may testify in a prosecution against his deputy for allowing the escape of a prisoner, that he gave the defendant written authority to act as deputy, as the Alabama statutes do not require the appointment to be in writing,—especially where he had previously made a personal demand on defendant for the paper, which was refused. *Pentecost* v. *State,* 107 Ala. 81, 18 So. 146.

76. Foundation for secondary.

There is no universal rule as to the necessary foundation for the introduction of secondary evidence; but the presiding judge must be reasonably satisfied that the document is lost, destroyed, or beyond the jurisdiction of the court. When no probable motive appears for withholding the document, less evidence is required than under suspicious circumstances.[1]

[1]Thus, where it appeared that diligent search was made for the missing papers by the witness and his two attorneys, in whose possession he had left them, and who had since removed to distant counties, his testimony was held sufficient proof of their loss to let in secondary evidence of

their contents, without the additional testimony of the attorneys. *Jernigan* v. *State*, 81 Ala. 58, 1 So. 72. See also *Haun* v. *State*, 13 Tex. App. 383, 44 Am. Rep. 706.

77. — how laid by prosecution.

A foundation for secondary evidence is not laid by the state by showing that the original document is not in the possession of the prosecuting witness, as he is not the party offering the evidence.[1]

[1]*State* v. *Penny*, 70 Iowa, 190, 30 N. W. 561.

78. — loss.

The person last known to have had possession of the document must be examined as a witness to prove the loss, unless inability to procure his testimony is shown.[1]

[1]*Kearney* v. *New York*, 92 N. Y. 617 (civil case).

79. — by negligence.

Upon an indictment for stealing bank notes, secondary evidence of their contents is admissible, if the best that can be produced, although the inability of the prosecution to produce them is the result of inexcusable negligence on the part of the bank officers.[1]

[1]*State* v. *Taunt*, 16 Minn. 109, Gil. 99.

80. — document beyond the jurisdiction.

The fact that a document is without the jurisdiction, and presumably not within the power of the party, is enough to let in secondary evidence without notice to produce.[1]

[1]*United States* v. *Reyburn*, 6 Pet. 352, 368, 8 L. ed. 424, 430. Foreign record of commission to privateer, being presumably such as the foreign government would refuse to allow copy of, in aid of indictment for acting under or promoting it. See also *People* v. *Howard*, 50 Mich. 241, 15 N. W. 101 (indictment for unlawful solicitation of insurance on behalf of a foreign company. Production of application unnecessary because in possession of company in the other state); *Bronson* v. *Tuthill*, 1 Abb. App. Dec. 206 (*dictum* in a civil case). But otherwise of the instrument on which the action is brought. *Shillito* v. *Robbins*, 7 Ohio L. J. 74, Citing *Van Alstyne* v. *National Commercial Bank*, 4 Abb. App. Dec. 449 (civil cases).

81. — document in possession of one criminated thereby.

It is a sufficient excuse for the nonproduction of a document to trace it to the possession of one interested in retaining it, and who, were he subpœnaed to produce it, could refuse to do so on the ground that it would tend to criminate him.[1]

[1]*United States* v. *Reyburn*, 6 Pet. 352, 366, 8 L. ed. 424, 429 (commission of privateer shown to have been in captain's possession, and he to be under indictment, and not found; held sufficient to let in secondary evidence of its character and contents against one on trial for issuing and delivering the commission); *State* v. *Kimbrough*, 13 N. C. (2 Dev. L.) 431 (secondary evidence of the contents of a written instrument in possession of the accused may be given by the prosecution, where the accused fails to produce such instrument after notice, notwithstanding the accused cannot be compelled to give evidence against himself by producing the paper. The admission of such evidence rests upon the principle that it is the best evidence in possession of the prosecution).

82. — existence of better evidence must clearly appear.

The party who objects that there is written evidence better than the oral evidence by which it is sought to establish a fact should make good his assertion by the writing itself, or by proof showing that it was once in existence.[1]

[1]*Allen* v. *State*, 8 Tex. App. 67. See also *Com.* v. *Goodwin*, 122 Mass. 19 (on indictment for threatening to accuse another of burning a building with intent to defraud an insurer, held not necessary to produce a written policy of insurance, if other evidence tending to show that the building was insured had been admitted without objection, and it did not necessarily appear therefrom that the insurance contract was in writing); *Burton* v. *Driggs*, 20 Wall. 125, 134, 22 L. ed. 299, 302 (civil case).

83. — notice to produce; necessity.

The prosecution need not give notice to produce where the indictment itself charges the accused with the possession of the writing,[1] or where the evidence traces it to his possession[2] or to that of an accomplice who could refuse to produce it on the ground of criminating tendency.[3]

[1]*State* v. *Mayberry*, 48 Me. 218 (holding that where the defendant is seasonably furnished with a copy of an indictment charging him with a fraudulent possession of a paper, secondary evidence of its contents may be received without giving him notice to produce); *People* v. *Holbrook*, 13 Johns. 90 (indictment for larceny of bank notes gives sufficient notice to produce them); *McGinnis* v. *State*, 24 Ind. 500 (to same effect); *Com.* v. *Messinger*, 1 Binn. 273, 2 Am. Dec. 441, 443, 446. But see *Rollins* v. *State*, 21 Tex. App. 148, 17 S. W. 466, where it was held error to permit the state to prove by parol the contents of an instrument alleged to have been forged, without notice to produce, although the indictment charged that it "is in the possession of the defendant, or is lost or destroyed, and access to the same cannot be had."

For leading civil cases, see *Howell* v. *Huyck*, 2 Abb. App. Dec. 423; *Lawson* v. *Bachman*, 81 N. Y. 616, Reversing 12 Jones & S. 396.

As to the necessity for averring possession in the indictment, see *State* v. *Parker*, 1 D. Chip. (Vt.) 298, 6 Am. Dec. 735.

[2]*State* v. *Gurnee*, 14 Kan. 121 (holding that secondary evidence of the contents of a written instrument may be introduced where it is shown that the original is in the possession of the accused, for he cannot be compelled to produce it as evidence against himself); *State* v. *McCauley*, 17 Wash. 88, 93, 49 Pac. 221, 51 Pac. 382.

[3]*United States* v. *Doebler*, Baldw. 519, Fed. Cas. No. 14,977, holding this rule applicable though the document be not alleged in the indictment.

84. — time of service.

The reasonableness of the length of notice rests in the discretion of the court. The fact that the defense announced its readiness for trial after being served with notice to produce precludes a subsequent objection that the notice was too short.[1]

[1]*State* v. *Davis*, 69 N. C. 313.

85. — sufficiency.

A notice to produce is to be deemed sufficient if it fairly apprise the party of the paper wanted, though it be informal and inaccurate in particulars.[1]

[1]*United States* v. *Duff*, 19 Batchf. 9, 6 Fed. 45. See also *Frank* v. *Manny*, 2 Daly, 92; and *Jones* v. *Parker*, 20 N. H. 31 (civil cases).

86. — secondary evidence of suppressed document.

Oral evidence to establish the contents of an instrument which the adverse party refuses to produce on notice is competent[1] although vague and indistinct.[2]

[1]*Com.* v. *Shurn*, 145 Mass. 150, 13 N. E. 395. Copy of receipt suppressed admitted.

And this principle applies although the document is suppressed, not by the party himself, but by someone acting in his interest. *Com.* v. *Snell*, 3 Mass. 82. Concealment of forged promissory note.

[2]*Benjamin* v. *Ellinger*, 80 Ky. 472 (civil case).

87. — of examination.

The proper way to supply evidence of the testimony of a witness taken before a coroner's inquest, and reduced to writing which has been since lost, is to introduce persons who were present at the inquest when the deposition was taken, and have them testify as to what was deposed.[1]

[1]*Reyes* v. *State,* 10 Tex. App. 1.

X. Books.

88. Books of science.

Statements made in books of inductive science, such as standard medical works, are not competent evidence for any purpose.[1]

Otherwise of books of exact science, such as Northampton tables and the like, if recognized by the court as such, or shown to be such by a qualified witness.[2]

[1]*Epps* v. *State,* 102 Ind. 539, 1 N. E. 491, 497; *State* v. *Baldwin,* 36 Kan. 3, 12 Pac. 318, 326; *Com.* v. *Wilson,* 1 Gray, 337; *Com.* v. *Sturtivant,* 117 Mass. 122, 19 Am. Rep. 401; *Com.* v. *Brown,* 121 Mass. 69; *People* v. *Millard,* 53 Mich. 63, 18 N. W. 562; *People* v. *Goldenson,* 76 Cal. 328, 19 Pac. 161. For earlier authorities see Civil Trial Brief, chap. XV., § 23; also *People* v. *Sessions,* 58 Mich. 594, 26 N. W. 291. *Contra, Bales* v. *State,* 63 Ala. 30; *State* v. *West,* Houst. Crim. Rep. (Del.) 371. See fully, on this question, authorities cited in note to *Union P. R. Co.* v. *Yates* (C. C. App. 8th C.) 40 L. R. A. 553.

Almanac admissible as refreshing memory in aid of judicial notice to show time of rising of sun. *People* v. *Chee Kee,* 61 Cal. 404.

[2]Abbott Trial Ev. 724; *Pinney* v. *Cahill* (Mich.) 22 Am. L. Reg. N. S. 105, note; *Ashworth* v. *Kittridge* (Mass.) 59 Am. Dec. 185, note. And for an exhaustive review of the authorities as to the use of both kinds of books mentioned in the text, see note to *Union P. R. Co.* v. *Yates* (C. C. App. 8th C.) 40 L. R. A. 553.

XI. Character.

[Character in these rules means reputation. The object for which the evidence of good character is received is to strengthen the presumption of innocence. Its admissibility, therefore, when offered by the accused, does not depend on character being already in issue, and the effect which may be given to it is as broad as that which may be given to the presumption of innocence. There are articles on evidence of character in criminal cases in 9 Crim. L. Mag. 443, and 12 Cent. L. J. 414. And see authorities reviewed in note to *State* v. *Hull* (R. I.) 20 L. R. A. 609.]

89. Prosecution cannot attack in first instance.

Whatever the crime charged, the prosecution cannot give evidence of the bad character of the accused, unless the accused has first adduced evidence of good character[1] as tending to support the presumption of innocence.[2]

If, however, the accused has testified as a witness, the prosecution may impeach him as a witness by evidence as to character, within the limits stated in a previous decision.[3]

[1]*State* v. *Lapage*, 57 N. H. 245, 289, 24 Am. Rep. 69 (murder); *State* v. *Thurtell*, 29 Kan. 148 (larceny); *People* v. *White*, 14 Wend. 111 (counterfeiting); *State* v. *Sibley* (Mo.) 31 S. W. 1033; *State* v. *Lodge*, 9 Houst. (Del.) 542, 33 Atl. 312. And see cases cited in note to *State* v. *Hull* (R. I.) 20 L. R. A. 609.

The state cannot put in issue the general character of a person on trial for crime, on the pretext of impeaching a witness by disproving the latter's statements, where defendant has not himself put such character in issue. *Carter* v. *State*, 36 Neb. 481, 54 N. W. 853.

[2]See *infra*, § 92.

[3]See *supra*, §§ 39, 40. And see Wharton, Crim. Ev. § 433.

In *McDonald* v. *Com.* 86 Ky. 10, 4 S. W. 687, it is held that notwithstanding the general rule that the prosecution cannot place the character of accused in issue until he shall have first attempted to establish his character by proof, yet when the accused testifies in his own behalf, he subjects himself to that character of examination that can be made of any other witness, and his inclination to tell the truth, or to swear falsely, may be shown by the prosecution in the usual mode of impeaching the general character of a witness for truth and veracity; and held not error to allow questions as to his character for veracity.

90. Competency for defense.

The accused may always adduce evidence of good character in respect to the trait involved in the charge on trial.[1]

He is not entitled to give evidence of general good character in other respects.[2]

[1]*Edgington* v. *United States*, 164 U. S. 361, 41 L. ed. 467, 17 Sup. Ct. Rep. 72 (prosecution for making false deposition; evidence of truth and veracity competent); *State* v. *Kinley*, 43 Iowa, 294 (perjury; error to exclude evidence of good character for truth); *State* v. *Cushing*, 14 Wash. 527, 45 Pac. 145 (murder; evidence of reputation for peace and quietude competent); *Lincecum* v. *State*, 29 Tex. App. 328, 15 S. W. 818 (rape; error to exclude evidence that defendant was a peaceable and law-abiding man); *State* v. *Hice*, 117 N. C. 782, 23 S. E. 357 (adultery and fornication; error to exclude evidence of good character); *State* v. *Snover*, 63 N. J. L. 382, 43 Atl. 1059 (rape; error to exclude evidence of reputation for "morality, virtue, and honesty in living"); *Hall* v. *State*, 132 Ind. 320, 31 N. E. 536 (murder by poisoning; error to exclude evidence of peace and quietude). And see cases cited in note to *State* v. *Hull* (R. I.) 20 L. R. A. 609.

[1]*Chung Sing* v. *United States* (Ariz.) 36 Pac. 205; *Hays* v. *State*, 110 Ala. 60, 20 So. 322 (larceny; evidence of truth and veracity not competent); *State* v. *Heacock*, 106 Iowa, 191, 76 N. W. 654; *People* v. *Cowgill*, 93 Cal. 596, 29 Pac. 228 (murder; evidence of truth, honesty, and integrity not competent); *People* v. *Josephs*, 7 Cal. 129 (rape; general good character not admissible); *Walker* v. *State*, 102 Ind. 502, 1 N. E. 856 (murder; general good character is not competent; character for peace and quietude is); *State* v. *Bloom*, 68 Ind. 54, 34 Am. Rep. 247, 248 (larceny; evidence restricted to character for honesty and integrity); *Kee* v. *State*, 28 Ark. 155; *Basye* v. *State*, 45 Neb. 261, 63 N. W. 811 (murder; honesty and integrity not competent; character as peaceable and quiet man is); *State* v. *Brooks*, 23 Mont. 154, 57 Pac. 1038 (murder; good character not provable by evidence that defendant had preached at divers times); *State* v. *O'Shea*, 59 Kan. 593, 53 Pac. 876 (assault with intent to kill; peace and quietude competent, but honesty and integrity not).

Testimony that defendant in a murder suit, who was in jail a short time after the killing, had during the time of his incarceration a good reputation as a peaceable and law-abiding man, is inadmissible upon his trial. *Hill* v. *State*, 37 Tex. Crim. Rep. 415, 35 S. W. 660. "We would presume," said the court, "that a man locked up in the jail . . . would be a law-abiding man. Good policy would dictate that he would be quiet and a submissive prisoner. In this place men do not generally make reputations as peaceable and law-abiding citizens. Their situations force them to be such." To the same effect, see *White* v. *State*, 111 Ala. 92, 21 So. 330; *Smalls* v. *State*, 102 Ga. 31, 29 S. E. 153.

91. — disposition not competent in excuse.

The accused cannot give evidence of his natural disposition as tending to excuse his act or mitigate his offense.[1]

[1]*Small* v. *Com.* 91 Pa. 304, 1 Crim. L. Mag. 331, 335, with note. See also *Fitzpatrick* v. *Com.* 81 Ky. 357; *Sindram* v. *People*, 88 N. Y. 196 (murder; evidence of passionate disposition not competent even to negative ability to exercise premeditation).

92. Competency of prosecution.

The general rule that if the accused has adduced evidence of good character, the prosecution may show bad character in respect to the trait involved,[1] applies only where the accused has distinctly manifested an election to put character in issue. It does not apply when the evidence adduced by the accused was not for the purpose of supporting the presumption of innocence, but indirect, and merely incidental to another purpose.[2]

[1]*Fuller* v. *State*, 117 Ala. 36, 23 So. 688; *State* v. *Foster*, 91 Iowa, 164, 59 N. W. 8.

It is competent for the state to ask questions in rebuttal, on the point of the defendant's good character, as broad as those propounded by respondent, to dispel any wrong impressions that might arise from answers to the latter. *State* v. *Wilkins,* 66 Vt. 1, 28 Atl. 323.

In *People* v. *Fair,* 43 Cal. 137, the trial of a woman for the murder of a man with whom she had been having unlawful intercourse, it was held that the fact that the defense had introduced evidence tending to show that her prospects had been injured by reason of her relations with deceased was not enough of itself to authorize the prosecution, against objection, to prove that her general character for chastity was bad.

93. — rebuttal confined to specific trait.

The rule does not allow evidence of general character, but only of character in respect to the trait involved in the charge.[1]

[1]*Johnson* v. *State,* 17 Tex. App. 565 (criminal assault; reversing judgment for error in allowing the prosecution to rebut by showing the defendant's reputation as a law-abiding man). Compare *State* v. *Williams,* 77 Mo. 310, as to allowing the state to prove his admissions of facts impeaching his character.

Evidence that the defendant charged with murder had a bad reputation for chastity in the community in which she lived, that she kept a house of prostitution, and had illegitimate children,—is inadmissible to enable the jury to determine the motive which actuated the deceased in catching hold of and stopping defendant in the road at the time of the homicide. *Thompson* v. *State,* 38 Tex. Crim. Rep. 335, 42 S. W. 974.

And the testimony of a deputy sheriff, "that he nearly always had a warrant for defendant's arrest," is inadmissible in rebuttal of evidence of the good character of defendant in a criminal action. *Murphy* v. *State,* 108 Ala. 10, 18 So. 557.

So, also, evidence that a defendant accused of miscegenation is "foolishly fond of women" is inadmissible upon the question of his general good character, or his character for chastity. *Cauley* v. *State,* 92 Ala. 71, 9 So. 456.

94. — disposition not competent on part of prosecution.

It is not competent for the prosecution to prove that the accused had a predisposition to the commission of such an offense as that charged. But his possession of the physical ability or other means for its commission may be proved.[1]

[1]*State* v. *Lapage,* 57 N. H. 245, 24 Am. Rep. 69. Murder; rape preceding a murder; new trial granted for this, among other errors. Compare *State* v. *Moelchen,* 53 Iowa, 310, 5 N. W. 186. Murder; holding it not error to allow questions put to show that the accused had been a soldier, and hence accustomed to scenes of blood and carnage, and so more prepared to take life.

95. Qualification of witness.

One who knows the character of the accused only from rumor is not competent.[1] So, a witness who has testified that he knows nothing of the reputation of defendant in the neighborhood in which he lives or is known is incompetent to testify as to his personal opinion of the character of the prisoner for peace and quiet.[2] And a witness stating that he is unacquainted with the general reputation of defendant on trial for threatening to take the life of another cannot give his opinion that defendant is a dangerous man.[3] And a witness may not testify to the general character of the defendant, upon information obtained by him after the commission of the offense with which he is charged.[4]

[1] *Haley* v. *State*, 63 Ala. 83, reversing conviction for error in receiving his testimony against the accused.

The testimony of a witness to the good character of the accused cannot be excluded merely because his only reason for so saying is that he never heard it discussed or questioned. *State* v. *Grate*, 68 Mo. 22 (murder; conviction reversed for error in excluding such evidence). The court says that frequently evidence of this negative character is the highest that can be obtained. See also *Lemons* v. *State*, 4 W. Va. 755, 6 Am. Rep. 293. A more fully considered case, where, however, the question arose on the character of a witness; conviction reversed for error in excluding such evidence.

[2] *Holmes* v. *State*, 88 Ala. 26, 7 So. 193.

[3] *Woods* v. *State*, 37 Tex. Crim. Rep. 459, 36 S. W. 96.

[4] *Buchanan* v. *State*, 120 Ala. 670, 25 So. 1024.

96. Limit of time.

Proof of character should be confined to a time prior to the publicity of the charge on trial.[1]

[1] *People* v. *McSweeney* (Cal.) 38 Pac. 743; *State* v. *Sprague*, 64 N. J. L. 419, 45 Atl. 788; *State* v. *King*, 9 S. D. 628, 70 N. W. 1046; *Lea* v. *State*, 94 Tenn. 495, 29 S. W. 900; *Graham* v. *State*, 29 Tex. App. 31, 13 S. W. 1013; *State* v. *Marks*, 16 Utah, 204, 51 Pac. 1089.

The reason is that otherwise the charge in question might be involved. But the rule is applied to restrict the evidence of good character offered by the accused, as well as that of bad character offered by the prosecution.

In *White* v. *Com.* 80 Ky. 480, a prosecution for larceny, evidence of character covering the period between the discovery of the perpetration of the offense and the time of the arrest was held inadmissible, and conviction reversed for error in receiving evidence of the defendant's character up to the time of the arrest.

In *State* v. *Kinley*, 43 Iowa. 294, it was held that accused could not give evidence of his character after indictment found.

In *State* v. *Forshner*, 43 N. H. 89, 80 Am. Dec. 132, a prosecution for rape, the prisoner offered evidence in regard to the character of the prosecutrix for chastity. It was held not error to require the witnesses to confine their testimony to what they knew of her character prior to the offense charged.

In *Com.* v. *Sacket*, 22 Pick. 394, however, it is held that if, on the trial of an indictment, the defendant introduces evidence of his good character prior to the commission of the crime charged, it is competent for the government to prove that subsequent to that time his character was bad.

The right to prove the good character of an accused was held, in *State* v. *Barr*, 11 Wash. 481, 29 L. R. A. 154, 39 Pac. 1080, to be properly confined to a few years previous to the crime, without allowing proof of his reputation long before, in boyhood days. "If a defendant puts in evidence as to good character," said the court, "it is competent for the prosecution to show bad character; and in order that this right of the prosecution may be made effective, it is necessary that the evidence on the part of the defendant should be confined to a time not too remote from the date of the commission of the crime. It would be impracticable for the prosecution in most cases to trace the life and habits of a defendant for more than a few years; and to allow him to go back to boyhood and put in proof which it would be out of the power of the prosecution to contradict, or in any manner rebut, however false it might be, would result in an advantage to the defendant which the rule in question never contemplated."

97. Actual disposition not competent.

The inquiry as to character must be confined to reputation. It is not competent to ask either the observation or the opinion of the witness, either as to the disposition of the accused or as to his conduct.[1]

[1] *Sawyer* v. *People*, 91 N. Y. 667, 1 N. Y. Crim. Rep. 249; *State* v. *Emery*, 59 Vt. 84, 7 Atl. 129. *Hirschman* v. *People*, 101 Ill. 568; *State* v. *Pearce*, 15 Nev. 188; *State* v. *King*, 78 Mo. 555. *Contra*, *State* v. *Sterrett*, 68 Iowa, 76, 25 N. W. 936.

98. Particular acts not competent.

It is not competent to show defendant's bad character by proof of specific acts.[1]

[1] *Bullock* v. *State* (N. J. L.) 47 Atl. 62; *Patterson* v. *State*, 41 Neb. 538, 59 N. W. 917; *State* v. *Welsor*, 117 Mo. 570, 21 S. W. 443; *State* v. *Donelon*, 45 La. Ann. 744, 12 So. 922; *Stalcup* v. *State*, 146 Ind. 270, 45 N. E. 334; *Nelson* v. *State*, 32 Fla. 244, 13 So. 361; *State* v. *Lapage*, 57 N. H. 245, 289, 24 Am. Rep. 69; *Com.* v. *O'Brien*, 119 Mass. 342, 20 Am. Rep. 325; *Hayward* v. *People*, 96 Ill. 492 (error to allow inquiry as to habits).

Evidence tending to show accused guilty of an independent crime not connected with or leading up to the one for which he is on trial is incompetent in rebuttal of evidence introduced by accused on his own behalf as to his good character, though accused has testified as a witness in his own behalf. *People* v. *Greenwall*, 108 N. Y. 296, 15 N. E. 404 (reversing conviction for error in admitting such evidence). The court says, citing authorities, "It is never proper, for the purpose of impeaching the character of a party or a witness, to call witnesses to prove specific acts of dishonesty, immorality, or crime. If the People desired to prove that the defendant's character was bad, the only course open to them was to call witnesses who were acquainted with his character. . . . But there was no foundation for calling witnesses to impeach the defendant's character. He had not, by any evidence on his part, really put his character in issue. All the evidence on the part of the People, as well as that on the part of the defense, tended to show that his character was bad."

As to proof of specific acts affecting character, drawn out on defendant's cross-examination, see *supra*, § 26.

On a trial for rape, evidence of a witness that he heard that defendant had killed a man some twelve years before the trial is inadmissible. *Brown* v. *State*, 72 Miss. 997, 17 So. 278.

In *Morgan* v. *State*, 88 Ala. 223, 6 So. 761, a prosecution for an assault with an intent to kill, it was held that the defendant, who had testified in his own behalf, and proved his good character for truth and veracity, without objection on the part of the state, could not object, on appeal, that the state in rebuttal was allowed to prove the acts or certain conduct of the defendant tending to show low and immoral associations.

99. — — explaining.

If evidence of particular facts has been admitted for the purpose of showing bad character of the accused, he has a right to adduce evidence in explanation of such facts.[1]

[1]*Olive* v. *State*, 11 Neb. 1, 7 N. W. 444. Murder; prosecution having, on cross-examination of witness, called for accused, brought out evidence of his having drawn a revolver on some one on a certain occasion; held error to refuse to allow accused to show by some witness the circumstances under which the revolver was used.

100. Explaining reports.

If a witness to good character admits that reports unfavorable to the accused were in circulation, the defense has a right to show what those reports were,—or at least their subject or nature, sufficiently to show whether they affected his character in the respect in which it is involved.[1]

[1]*Stape* v. *People*, 85 N. Y. 390. So held where the accused was a witness, and the object was to sustain his character for truth and veracity.

101. Doubt not necessary.

Evidence of good character is competent, irrespective of whether the case is left in doubt or not upon other proofs.[1]

[1] 1 Bishop, Crim. Proc. §§ 1115, 1116; *State* v. *Howell,* 100 Mo. 628, 14 S. W. 4.

Evidence of good character is admissible, not only in a case where doubt otherwise exists, but may be offered for the purpose of creating a doubt. *People* v. *Jassino,* 100 Mich. 537, 59 N. W. 230.

But evidence as to the previous good character of defendant charged with murder is inadmissible where his guilt is admitted. *People* v. *Miller,* 114 Cal. 10, 45 Pac. 986.

102. Cross-examination.

A witness who has testified to the good character of the accused may be asked on cross-examination if he has not heard of a specified charge against the accused.[1]

[1] *Ingraham* v. *State,* 67 Ala. 67. Murder; holding it not error to allow witness who has testified to the character of the accused for peace and quietude to be asked if he has not heard that accused has killed a man. See also *De Arman* v. *State,* 71 Ala. 351; *Rex* v. *Wood,* 5 Jur. 225, Cited in 1 Best, Ev. § 261.

XII. Confessions.

[The rule excluding confessions not voluntary does not apply to admissions not amounting to an acknowledgment of guilt (see §§ 41–53, 282–291, 627); nor to a statement of intent made before the commission of the offense (see §§ 173–184). Nor does it apply to witnesses generally, but only to confessions of the accused now on trial (see § 106).

The rule excluding confessions till after proof of *corpus delicti* (§§ 154–161) excludes many statements not excluded as confessions by reason of not being voluntary.]

103. Preliminary proof as to voluntary character.

When a confession by the accused is offered in evidence against him, the burden is on the prosecution to show that it was voluntary, before it can be received,[1] if objection be made.[2]

[1] For instances for application of this rule, see *Coffee* v. *State,* 25 Fla. 501, 6 So. 493; *Clayton* v. *State,* 31 Tex. Crim. Rep. 489, 21 S. W. 255; *Hite* v. *Com.* 96 Va. 489, 31 S. E. 895; *State* v. *Auguste,* 50 La. Ann. 488, 23 So. 612; *State* v. *Garvey,* 28 La. Ann. 925, 26 Am. Rep. 123 (man-

slaughter; holding it error to receive the confession against objection, without evidence of its voluntary character, even though it did not appear that improper influence was used); *Amos* v. *State*, 83 Ala. 1, 3 So. 749; *Nicholson* v. *State*, 38 Md. 140 (Bartol, Ch. J., saying that the law is well settled. Here it was held that it was so shown, and that the confession was properly received.

In *People* v. *Soto*, 49 Cal. 67, judgment was reversed, both for error in admitting the confession without such preliminary proof and for refusing to allow the defendant to show affirmatively that the confession was not voluntary. "When such a confession is offered in a criminal case it is incumbent on the prosecution to lay the foundation for its introduction by preliminary proof showing, prima facie, that it was freely and voluntarily made."

All confessions are prima facie involuntary, and in order to render them admissible it must be shown, prima facie, that they were voluntarily made, without the appliances of hope or fear, without extraneous inducement or pressure in either of those directions from other persons; and this is a condition precedent to their admissibility. Otherwise they are prima facie involuntary and illegal. *McAlpine* v. *State*, 117 Ala. 93, 23 So. 130.

Where, however, the facts and circumstances under which they were made affirmatively show that there were no improper influences proceeding from the person to whom they were made, or from any other person, or from the surrounding circumstances, the confessions are prima facie free and voluntary, and are admissible. *Washington* v. *State*, 106 Ala. 58, 17 So. 546; *People* v. *Kamaunu*, 110 Cal. 609, 42 Pac. 1090.

In *Rufer* v. *State*, 25 Ohio St. 464, McIlvaine, Ch. J., says: "There is no presumption of law, however, that such confessions are induced by improper representations made to the prisoner, but . . . they are presumed to be voluntary until the contrary is shown. Hence the burden of showing that such confessions were involuntary rests upon the accused." To similar effect, *Williams* v. *State*, 19 Tex. App. 276; *State* v. *Meyers*, 99 Mo. 107, 12 S. W. 516; *People* v. *Barker*, 60 Mich. 277, 27 N. W. 539.

In the absence of timely objection from the accused, the court will not exclude evidence of an alleged confession because preliminary proof was not offered on the part of the state to show that the confession was made freely and voluntarily, unless it appear from the evidence itself that the confession was obtained from the accused by means of promises or threats, or, in other words, that it was not voluntary. *Smith* v. *State*, 88 Ga. 627, 15 S. E. 675; *State* v. *Madison*, 47 La. Ann. 30, 16 So. 566; *State* v. *Davis*, 34 La. Ann. 351. In the case last cited no objection was made to the admissibility of the evidence, and no charge excluding it from the consideration of the jury was requested; and motion for new trial on the ground that the confession was allowed to go to the jury without the preliminary proof was denied.

"Confessions are not illegal evidence standing alone. They are received in criminal cases on the same principles as in civil. . . . It is the right of the prisoner to object to their coming in unless the circumstances under which they were made also come in; but if he or his counsel fail to object, and the confessions go to the jury without any special inquiry as to the circumstances, he is not entitled to a new trial." *Eberhart* v. *State,* 47 Ga. 598, 608, which rule was followed in *State* v. *Davis,* 34 La. Ann. 351, as "recognized by highly respectable authorities and which commends itself to the favorable consideration of the legal mind, both in reason and in law." There is no broader objection to proof of anything in the nature of confession, whether voluntary or not, before proof of *corpus delicti,* which see, *infra,* § 155.

That a mere general objection to the evidence, or that the question propounded calls for illegal and incompetent evidence, is sufficient for its exclusion in the absence of the proper predicate, see *McAlpine* v. *State,* 117 Ala. 93, 23 So. 130.

104. What are confessions within the rule as to voluntariness; gestures.

A confession made by gestures in response to inquiries, as well as one made by words, is inadmissible if the circumstances show that it was not voluntarily made.[1]

[1] *Nolen* v. *State,* 14 Tex. App. 474; S. C. with note, 46 Am. Rep. 247, 251. In this case the prisoner was taken to the scene of the murder, and asked what he had done with the body, and he pointed toward the spot where the body had been previously found. It was held that under the Texas statute, as he had not been cautioned, this was not voluntarily, within the rule; and that as no fact was discovered thereby, the pointing was merely equivalent to a verbal statement, and admitting evidence of it was error. Otherwise if the body had been discovered by this means; for then the rule that acts performed are admissible would apply,—Citing *Elizabeth* v. *State,* 27 Tex. 329.

105. — act or statement leading to discovery.

The right to prove the facts discovered makes it proper to prove the statement of the prisoner which led to the discovery, unless objection is made, in which case the confession, if involuntary, should be excluded. But it is still competent to prove that the fact was discovered in the place pointed out by the prisoner, and in consequence of his direction.[1]

[1] In *Duffy* v. *People,* 26 N. Y. 588, the prosecution asked for the facts discovered, telling the witness he need not state the words of the prisoner which led to their discovery. Selden, J., said: "The course pursued has usually been to admit proof of the words used by the prisoner with reference to the extraneous facts, and then to receive proof of the facts themselves (citing cases); but in *Com.* v. *Knapp,* 9 Pick. 511, 20 Am. Dec. 491, which was a case of murder, evidence was received of the finding of a weapon in consequence of the confessions of the prisoner, the confessions themselves being excluded. This course does not appear

to me to be objectionable unless the prisoner should choose to have so much of his statement as related to the facts discovered given in evidence in connection with the facts, which he would undoubtedly be entitled to." This case was an affirmance of 5 Park. Crim. Rep. 321, where Clerke, J., said: "Later authorities have established the rule that so much of the confession as relates strictly to the fact discovered by it may be given in evidence. For the reason of rejecting extorted confessions is the apprehension that the prisoner may have been induced by the promise of clemency to say what is false, but the fact discovered shows that so much of the confession as immediately relates to it is true."

In *Com.* v. *Knapp*, 9 Pick. 496, 511, 20 Am. Dec. 491, after the confessions had been ruled out, the witness was asked by the prosecution whether any place was pointed out by the prisoner where a weapon might be found. The counsel for the prisoner objected that he should not state any confession of the prisoner on the subject, but the court was clear that it was competent to prove that the weapon was found in the place pointed out by the prisoner and in consequence of his direction.

In *Done* v. *People*, 5 Park. Crim. Rep. 364, 390, objection was made to the admission of certain statements of accused which consisted in indicating a spot where search might be made for certain bills. It was held that whether or not these statements amounted to a confession, they being confirmed by witnesses who found the bills, in the place indicated, were properly admitted.

In *Rice* v. *State*, 3 Heisk. 215, a prosecution for receiving stolen goods, it was held that though a confession was improperly obtained, as by hope of reward or threat of punishment (here by both), yet if important facts were discovered by it, so much of it as discovered those facts was admissible. Hence it was held no error to admit evidence that the accused took the prosecutor to the place where the stolen property was found buried, although he claimed that a third person had given it to him,—Citing *Deathridge* v. *State*, 1 Sneed, 75; *Hudson* v. *State*, 9 Yerg. 408.

If information derived from a confession leads to a discovery of material facts which go to prove the commission of the crime alleged, so much of the confession as strictly relates to the facts discovered, and the facts themselves, are admissible in evidence, although the confession may not be shown to have been voluntary; for the reason that the discovery of the facts corroborates the truth of the confession to that extent. *Lowe* v. *State*, 88 Ala. 8, 7 So. 97.

Evidence of an independent fact connected with a criminal transaction, having evidentiary significance of its own, without reference to the means or method of discovery, even though discovered in consequence of a constrained confession of the prisoner, is admissible against him, unless the confession was obtained or the discovery made by the use of criminal violence; and where the independent fact is admissible, so much of the prisoner's acts and declarations as are necessary to account for the discovery are admissible to explain the manner of the discovery, but for this purpose only, and not as a confession. *Rusher* v. *State,* 94 Ga. 363, 21 S. E. 593.

A declaration to a sheriff, by one accused of murder, that he had pawned a watch taken from the murdered man, is admissible in connection with evidence identifying the watch, and proving that it was found, in pursuance of the statement of the accused, at the place described, no matter what promises were previously made to him. *State* v. *Willis,* 71 Conn. 293, 41 Atl. 820.

Confessions accompanied by a statement afterwards found to be true, of facts and circumstances tending to show guilt, and which lead to a discovery of the crime, are expressly excepted by Tex. Crim. Code Proc. art. 750, from the general rule that confessions made under arrest, and where the party was not cautioned, are inadmissible in evidence. *Sands* v. *State,* 30 Tex. App. 578, 18 S. W. 86.

But *State* v. *Garvey,* 28 La. Ann. 925, 26 Am. Rep. 123, 126, holds that the right to prove the act performed or fact discovered does not draw with it the right to prove the confession, if made under undue influence,—Citing 1 Phil. Ev. 411; Greenl. Ev. 231.

In *Williams* v. *Com.* 27 Gratt. 997 (larceny), the confession (which was excluded as involuntary) was to the effect that the money was lost at play. The gamblers, being sent for, paid part of it back, and the father of the defendant the balance, although denying that the defendant had lost any money with them. Held, it not being proved that the money paid by the gamblers was the identical money lost by the defendant, that what passed between the witness to whom the confession was made and the gamblers was inadmissible; that the influence which might produce a groundless confession might also produce groundless conduct. Conviction reversed.

The discovery, through a confession, of facts legally admissible in evidence, tending to show defendant guilty of the charge against him, does not render the confession itself admissible, where it was not voluntary and free from compulsion or inducement. *State* v. *Jones,* 46 La. Ann. 1395, 16 So. 369.

106. —incriminating another.

A statement by the accused which is not an admission of his own guilt, but tends to criminate a third person, is not within the rule of law that excludes confessions induced by promises and hopes of favor.[1]

[1]*State* v. *Carr,* 53 Vt. 37, 41 (murder).

107. —documents.

The inadmissibility of a confession wrongfully procured does not render inadmissible documents produced and delivered by the accused to those who received the confession, as a part of the same transaction.[1]

[1]*People* v. *Barker*, 60 Mich. 277, 27 N. W. 539.

It is well settled that facts discovered are competent, though discovered in consequence of a confession induced by threat or undue influence. *Duffy* v. *People*, 26 N. Y. 588.

108. — written and separate oral confession.

The fact that the accused made a written confession before a judge, so that oral evidence of the confession would be incompetent, does not render incompetent oral evidence of other confessions made at another time.[1]

[1]*State* v. *Wells*, 1 N. J. L. 424, 1 Am. Dec. 211, 215. Motion for new trial denied.

But a confession made orally to a sheriff, after a written statement has been made under a promise of immunity from prosecution, which has not been withdrawn, and which the accused relies upon, cannot be admitted in evidence against him. *Robinson* v. *People*, 159 Ill. 115, 42 N. E. 375.

109. — indirect evidence of consciousness of guilt.

An offer of a bribe by the accused to the officer, to permit him to escape, though made in the same conversation with a confession of the crime, is competent evidence by itself, independent of the confession.[1]

[1]*United States* v. *Barlow*, 1 Cranch C. C. 94, Fed. Cas. No. 14,521.

And an offer to compromise the crime of burglary and larceny, unaccepted by the prosecutor, may be proved by the state as an admission of guilt, or as disclosing possession of the property which is the subject of the burglary and larceny. *State* v. *Rodrigues*, 45 La. Ann. 1040, 13 So. 802.

And offers by one accused of burglary to restore the stolen property on condition that the prosecutor will make it easy for him are admissible as confessions. *State* v. *Jordan*, 87 Iowa, 86, 54 N. W. 63.

So, a proposition voluntarily made, without inducement or threat, by one under arrest, to a hotel keeper, who of his own motion he has summoned to him, to give up jewelry recently stolen from the latter's hotel, upon condition that he is released,—is such a voluntary confession as to the possession of stolen goods and as to knowledge of their theft as to be admissible in a subsequent trial of the prisoner for larceny thereof. *Leslie* v. *State*, 35 Fla. 184, 17 So. 559.

But confessions which one is induced to make by promises of assistance in avoiding arrest are involuntary and inadmissible. *Anderson* v. *State*, 104 Ala. 83, 16 So. 108.

110. — denial of guilt.

A declaration made by one accused of a crime, denying any criminal act, and explaining suspicious circumstances to his own advantage, is not a confession, and does not come within the rule that confessions must be voluntary to be admissible.[1]

[1] *State* v. *Novak*, 109 Iowa, 717, 79 N. W. 465; *People* v. *McCallam*, 3 N. Y. Crim. Rep. 189; *People* v. *Ammerman*, 118 Cal. 23, 50 Pac. 15; *State* v. *Cadotte*, 17 Mont. 315, 42 Pac. 857; *Taylor* v. *State*, 37 Neb. 788, 56 N. W. 623; *Mora* v. *People*, 19 Colo. 255, 35 Pac. 179, Citing and quoting from Abbott, Crim. Trial Brief, 1st ed. § 481.

Compare with *People* v. *Mondon*, 38 Hun, 188, where it was held that the term "confession" was not to be restricted to admissions of guilt alone, but would include statements made before a coroner, by one charged with murder, concerning his own conduct and relations with deceased, while denying his guilt.

111. Prima facie evidence of voluntariness.

In the absence of anything to indicate suspicion, evidence that no improper inducement was used by the persons to whom the confession was made, or who were present at the time, makes a prima facie case of voluntariness, without in the first instance proving that no one else previously presented any improper inducement, although it appears that the accused was previously in the custody of some one else.[1]

[1] *Hopt* v. *Utah*, 110 U. S. 574, and cases cited; same case with note, 28 L. ed. 262, 4 Sup. Ct. Rep. 202. To similar effect, see *Burton* v. *State*, 107 Ala. 109, 18 So. 284; *Holland* v. *State*, 39 Fla. 178, 22 So. 298.

The test of admissibility of the statements of one accused of the commission of a crime, whether made in the course of judicial proceedings or not, is whether they were voluntary, which fact can be determined by their nature and the circumstances under which made. *People* v. *Chapleau*, 121 N. Y. 266, 24 N. E. 469.

And according to *Snider* v. *State*, 56 Neb. 309, 76 N. W. 574, it is sufficient, in laying the foundation for a confession in a criminal case, to prove affirmatively all that occurred prior to and at the time of the confession, provided such affirmative proof excludes the hypothesis of inducements of hope or fear; and it is not necessary to expressly negative such inducements.

A statement made by an officer to one accused of murder, "that he need not talk at all if he did not want to, and that whatever he said could be used either for or against him," suggested neither a threat nor a promise of benefit, so as to render a confession made inadmissible. *Roesel* v. *State*, 62 N. J. L. 216, 41 Atl. 408.

And a confession apparently suggested by the prisoner himself, who signed it, and stated that it was correct after it was reduced to writing and read over and explained to him,—is admissible in evidence where the only testimony that it was not his free and voluntary act is that of the prisoner and his sister, who state that it was made by reason of threats and inducements held out by police officers, who, when examined as witnesses, distinctly contradict such testimony. *Rogers* v. *State*, 89 Md. 424, 43 Atl. 922.

State v. *Auguste*, 50 La. Ann. 488, 23 So. 612, holds that the rule with reference to the proof necessary to render a confession admissible is not that it shall be adequate to establish that it was voluntarily made, but it shall be sufficient to establish that it was voluntary. And the age, situation, and character of defendant, and the circumstances under which the confession was made, are to be considered in determining whether or not it was voluntary.

A confession or declaration tending to show guilt, made by an accused while under arrest, of his own volition, and without any threat, promise, or inducement held out to him by the officer or other person present,—is competent evidence on the trial of a criminal case. *State* v. *Davis* (Idaho) 53 Pac. 678.

112. Preliminary question to be tried by judge.

The preliminary question of the voluntary character of the alleged confession must, if objection be made, be determined by the court before the evidence can go to the jury. It is error to refuse to rule on the preliminary question, and allow the evidence to go to the jury as if the question were exclusively for them.[1]

[1]*Ellis* v. *State*, 65 Miss. 44, 3 So. 188, Overruling previous decision in *Gerrard* v. *State*, 50 Miss. 147; *Brown* v. *State*, 71 Ind. 470,—Citing Wharton, Crim. Ev. 8th ed., § 689; *State* v. *Elliott*, 45 Iowa, 486; *Willett* v. *People*, 27 Hun, 469 (so held where there was no conflict in the evidence on that question), Affirmed in 92 N. Y. 29, on other points; *Simmons* v. *State*, 61 Miss. 243 (stating the practice); *Nolen* v. *State*, 8 Tex. App. 585 (error to leave the admission to the jury, and attempt to control its effect by instructions). *People* v. *Kurtz*, 42 Hun, 335, rightly understood, sustains this rule, and concedes that either party is entitled to a ruling from the judge on the question of competency, before the evidence goes to the jury.

It is not inconsistent with this to hold that he may instruct them that if they believe the confession was not voluntary they may reject it, or they must regard the involuntary character of it in considering if it was true, and, unless true, reject it.

Hammond, J., after a careful examination of the authorities in *United States* v. *Stone*, 8 Fed. 232, says: "The elements entering into the preliminary inquiry by the judge, where he is called on to determine the competency of the evidence, are these: 1. Had the person to whom, or in whose presence, or by whose sanction the alleged confession was made, any authority? 2. Were the threats or promises of that character that should exclude the confession as one made involuntarily? Both these questions being answered in the affirmative, the evidence is excluded as a matter of law, the judge trying the facts as in other cases of mixed questions of law and fact; but either being answered in the negative, the evidence goes to the jury, and thereupon they try this as they do all the other facts of the case, giving such weight to the confession as they see fit. All evidence of confessions does not pass through this ordeal of trial by the judge, except to determine whether it belongs to the one class or the other; for if they have been made to persons not in authority, whether voluntarily or involuntarily, they go to the jury, to be by them discarded if they find that they have been extorted by threats or induced by promises of that kind that 'the prisoner would be likely to tell an untruth from fear of the threat or hope of profit from the promise.'" In applying this discretion he holds that, in the absence of any statute giving the complainant in a criminal case any authority as prosecutor, an admission to him or to his agent, even though to a private detective employed by him, is not to be deemed made to one in authority.

In *Com.* v. *Bond,* 170 Mass. 41, 48 N. E. 756, it is held that the admissibility in evidence of a confession of the commission of a crime rests in the discretion of the court, to be exercised in view of the circumstances under which it was made.

People v. *Barker,* 60 Mich. 277, 27 N. W. 539, holds that it is the province of the court to determine as to the competency of a confession, before admitting or rejecting it as evidence, when the question is free from doubt; but if the testimony is conflicting, the jury should decide.

113. Presence of jury.

Whether it is proper to allow the preliminary question to be tried in the hearing of the jury, see—[1]

[1]Affirmative: *Holsenbake* v. *State,* 45 Ga. 43.

Negative: *Ellis* v. *State,* 65 Miss. 44, 3 So. 188 (*dictum,* that the investigation should be conducted out of the presence and hearing of the jury, if requested by defendant); *Carter* v. *State,* 37 Tex. 362 (holding it error even to allow the confession to be stated in discussion before the jury, when the question of competency has not been decided). See also *ante,* Division XXXVIII., § 52.

114. Right to cross-examine.

When a confession of the accused is about to be proved by a witness, the counsel for the accused has a right to interpose and cross-examine the witness on the preliminary question whether it was voluntary.[1]

[1]In *Rufer* v. *State,* 25 Ohio St. 464, McIlvaine, Ch. J., says: "The question, where objection is made to the admissibility of the confession, must in the first instance be adjudged by the court; and the right

of the accused to inquire of the witness and prove that the confession was induced by improper threats or promises cannot be postponed until after the confession is introduced and the entire examination of the witness in chief has been concluded." Here it was held error to deny such right of the accused. But the error, being immaterial, was held not ground for reversal. See also *State* v. *Fidment*, 35 Iowa, 541. Arson; reversal for error in refusing to allow this. See also *Territory* v. *McClin*, 1 Mont. 394 (murder). And see *Brady* v. *United States*, 1 App. D. C. 246, where this was allowed, but no ruling made on this point.

115. Right to adduce other evidence.

When a confession of the accused is offered against him, his counsel has a right to interpose, and call another witness on the preliminary question as to whether it was voluntary.[1]

[1] *Com.* v. *Culver*, 126 Mass. 464 (here a confession was objected to on the ground that it was induced by favor by an officer. The government then called the officer to prove the voluntary character of the confession. The defendant then offered to call five witnesses to prove the contrary. Held error to admit the confession before hearing such other evidence); *Brown* v. *State*, 70 Ind. 576; *Lefevre* v. *State*, 50 Ohio St. 584, 35 N. E. 52.

Testimony may be introduced by one accused, on the hearing of the preliminary question as to the admissibility of a confession, in support of his contention that it was improperly obtained. *Roesel* v. *State*, 62 N. J. L. 216, 41 Atl. 408.

Brady v. *United States*, 1 App. D. C. 246, holds that confessions may properly be admitted in evidence without listening to counter proof offered by defendants to prove that they were involuntary, where upon the examination of the officers to whom the confessions were made the court finds no trace of any effort to influence the prisoners by inducements or threats,—Distinguishing *Com.* v. *Culver*, 126 Mass. 464, *supra*, on the ground that the refusal to hear the other evidence was, under the circumstances of that particular case, an abuse of the discretion vested in the trial court.

In *Irby* v. *State*, 95 Ga. 467, 20 S. E. 218, it was held that the court need not hear evidence that defendant's confession was freely and voluntarily made, before admitting it, where the witness who heard it testified that he held out no inducement, and did nothing to excite either hope or fear, and knew of nothing done by others to induce it; but such evidence might afterwards be introduced, and the question of whether or not the confession was free and voluntary left to the determination of the jury.

116. What involuntary; duress by unofficial captors.

The confession of an accused person made while in the hands of his captors, not officers, and threatened with violence, is inadmissible against him.[1]

[1]*State* v. *Revells,* 34 La. Ann. 381, 44 Am. Rep. 436. Murder; so held although he had been warned; conviction reversed for receiving it.

But mere threats, by one not in authority, do not render the consequent confession involuntary, unless in the presence and implied sanction of one in authority. *Smith* v. *Com.* 10 Gratt. 734, 740.

A confession made by one charged with stealing a hog, to the owner, is prima facie involuntary, and inadmissible in evidence, where, after having denied that he had an unmarked hog belonging to the prosecutor, the latter and another who was with him took him into custody without warrant, and accused him of stealing the hog, and stated that he would put him "where the dogs would not bother him," whereupon defendant confessed that a hog in his possession belonged to the prosecutor. *Beckham* v. *State,* 100 Ala. 15, 14 So. 859.

117. — consciousness of danger.

Fear, though induced by arrest and being confronted with evidence of guilt,[1] or by knowledge of public excitement against the accused,[2] does not alone render the confession incompetent.

[1]*People* v. *Thoms,* 3 Park. Crim. Rep. 256 (*dictum*); *Allen* v. *State,* 12 Tex. App. 190.

But an alleged confession which is shown to have been extorted from defendant by threats and menaces, and which does not connect him with the alleged crime, is inadmissible against him. *State* v. *Mason* (Idaho) 43 Pac. 63.

And a confession of crime, by one told that if he did not confess to the speaker he would have to confess to a justice of the peace, made in the presence of an accuser,—is not admissible. *Johnson* v. *State,* 76 Ga. 76.

A confession made to an officer before arrest, upon his charging the defendant with the crime of burglary, is admissible in evidence, although the officer at the time intended to make the arrest, where he had not informed the defendant of such intention. *Holmes* v. *State,* 32 Tex. Crim. Rep. 361, 23 S. W. 687.

[2]*Honeycutt* v. *State,* 8 Baxt. 371; *People* v. *Kurtz,* 42 Hun, 335, 338.

Voluntary statements of one accused of homicide, as to the killing, made to citizens, upon their riding up to him with a gun on the morning after the homicide, and speaking to him, are admissible in evidence against him as a confession, where, although they intended to take him, and would have prevented him from leaving them if he had attempted to do so, they said or did nothing to indicate their intention not to allow him to escape, or to cause him to believe that he was under arrest. *Craig* v. *State,* 30 Tex. App. 619, 18 S. W. 297.

But a confession by one accused of murder, made on his wife's informing him at the jail that she had been induced to come there and advise him to confess by a threat of a mob to hang them all if she did not do so,—is inadmissible as having been made under a threat of violence. *Wigginton* v. *Com.* 92 Ky. 282, 17 S. W. 634.

And a confession made to a sheriff by the defendant, charged with murder, while in jail being guarded against mob violence, is inadmissible in evidence, where, a short time before such confession, defendant made a similar confession to the deputy sheriff on a promise by the latter that if the defendant would tell him about the killing he would protect him from the mob from which he was in danger. *Taylor* v. *Com.* 19 Ky. L. Rep. 836, 42 S. W. 1125.

But in *Laughlin* v. *Com.* 18 Ky. L. Rep. 840, 37 S. W. 590, it was held that a confession by one charged with murder, after his arrest, and while confined in jail, made to the county attorney for whom the accused sent of his own accord, was not involuntary so as to be inadmissible in evidence, because the accused was in terror of a mob, or because confessions had been previously obtained from him by other persons by improper means.

No part of defendant's confession is admissible in evidence on a trial for murder, where at the time it was made he was carried into the woods by several persons who pretended to hang him, and told him that it would be best for him to own that he killed the man, if he did it. *Williams* v. *State,* 72 Miss. 117, 16 So. 296.

118. — confession to officer while in custody.

The fact that the confession was made to an officer having the accused in custody at the time does not alone render it inadmissible.[1]

[1] *Roesel* v. *State,* 62 N. J. L. 216, 41 Atl. 408; *People* v. *Rogers,* 18 N. Y. 9, 72 Am. Dec. 484 (reversing judgment of the supreme court in 3 Park. Crim. Rep. 632, which reversed a judgment of conviction of murder, and directing to sentence anew. Denio, J., says: "I have looked carefully into all the cases referred to by the defendant's counsel . . . and many others, and do not find that it has ever been held that the single fact of the prisoner being in custody was sufficient to exclude his declarations, whether made to the officer or to third persons"); *People* v. *Chapleau,* 121 N. Y. 266, 24 N. E. 469; *Murphy* v. *People,* 63 N. Y. 590, Affirming 4 Hun, 102, 6 Thomp. & C. 369; *People* v. *Druse,* 103 N. Y. 655, 8 N. E. 733, more fully, 5 N. Y. Crim. Rep. 10, Distinguishing *People* v. *Mondon,* 103 N. Y. 211, 57 Am. Rep. 709, 8 N. E. 496; *Com.* v. *Chance,* 174 Mass. 245, 54 N. E. 551; *State* v. *Berry,* 50 La. Ann. 1309, 24 So. 329; *Hopt* v. *Utah,* 110 U. S. 574, with note 28 L. ed. 262, 4 Sup. Ct. Rep. 202; *State* v. *Patterson,* 73 Mo. 695 (confession made while tied not necessarily incompetent); Stephen, Dig. Ev. (May's ed. 1887), 62 (approved by Hammond, J., in *United States* v. *Stone,* 8 Fed. 232; *Com.* v. *Knapp,* 9 Pick. 496, 20 Am. Dec. 491, 496. *Contra,* see *State* v. *Phelps,* 11 Vt. 116, 34 Am. Dec. 675.

Confessions by a convict to the officer in charge, who was investigating for purpose of inflicting discipline, held involuntary. *Wilson* v. *State,* 84 Ala. 426, 4 So. 383.

The facts that defendant, charged with murder, was under arrest, and that the officer having him in charge was armed, are not alone sufficient to exclude his voluntary statements to the officer in regard to the killing and how it occurred. There must have been some improper influence, proceeding from the person to whom the confessions were made, or from some other person, or arising from the surrounding circumstances, to exclude the statement of a defendant upon the ground that they were not freely and voluntarily made. The mere fact of arrest, and his being guarded by an officer who was armed, is not sufficient. The statements of the defendant, if true and believed, moreover, tended to exculpate and not to criminate him. *Hornsby* v. *State,* 94 Ala. 55, 10 So. 522.

So, the fact that a confession was made to the district attorney while the accused was confined in jail does not make it incompetent evidence, if voluntarily made, and not induced by promises, threats, or duress. *Com.* v. *Eagan,* 190 Pa. 10, 42 Atl. 374.

And the fact that a confession was made by one who was shackled and in custody, and when he had no counsel, is not sufficient to make it inadmissible. *State* v. *Gorham,* 67 Vt. 365, 31 Atl. 845.

The fact that the prisoner was tied during his examination before the committing magistrate will not affect the admissibility of his confession then made, unless he was tied in such a manner as to produce pain, or tend to induce or extort the confession from him. *State* v. *Rogers,* 112 N. C. 874, 17 S. E. 297.

And a confession made by a prisoner while under arrest, and secured to the buggy in which he was riding, by a chain attached to a handcuff on one hand to an officer having with him the warrant under which the prisoner had been committed to jail on a charge of larceny,—was not made under duress so as to render it inadmissible in evidence, unless some advantageous offer, threats, or actual force was used to induce it, by exciting hope or fear. *State* v. *Whitfield,* 109 N. C. 876, 13 S. E. 726.

A confession made by a prisoner while under arrest, and while kept in a dark cell for the purpose of obtaining a confession, is inadmissible against him, under 2 Hill's (Wash.) Anno. Statutes & Codes, § 1308, providing that a confession made under inducement may be given in evidence, except when made under "influence of fear produced by threats." *State* v. *McCullum,* 18 Wash. 394, 51 Pac. 1044.

119. —illegal custody.

The fact that the custody was held without process or under illegal process does not render the confession inadmissible.[1]

[1]*Balbo* v. *People,* 80 N. Y. 484.

Doubts on this point were expressed in *Hoober* v. *State,* 81 Ala. 51, 1 So. 574, where the question did not directly arise.

But in *Lancaster* v. *State* (Tex. Crim. App.) 31 S. W. 515, it was held that statements made by defendant before he had been warned, to officers who state that at the time such statements were made they would not have permitted defendant to go at large although they had no writ at the time,—are inadmissible against defendant.

120. — answering questions.

The fact that the confession was made in an answer to questions put, even by the officer having the accused in custody, does not render it incompetent.[1]

[1]*People* v. *Wentz,* 37 N. Y. 303 (arson; confession not incompetent because elicited by a question assuming the guilt of the prisoner); *Cox* v. *People,* 80 N. Y. 500, Affirming 19 Hun, 430 (Andrews, J.); *Murphy* v. *People,* 63 N. Y. 590, Affirming 4 Hun, 102, 6 Thomp. & C. 369 (here the prisoner made the statement in consequence of being asked by the officer who arrested him if he desired to make any statement of his whereabouts on the day of the murder, and being informed by the officer if he [the prisoner] desired to do so, he [the officer] would reduce the statement to writing for him); *People* v. *McGloin,* 12 Abb. N. C. 172, 91 N. Y. 241, Affirming 28 Hun, 150 (here it appeared that the officer stated to the prisoner he held in custody on a charge of murder, that he was aware of an attempt on the part of the prisoner the night before the arrest to steal a barrel of whisky. The court says: "It would be unreasonable to say that the defendant was moved to make this confession by fear of his exposure and punishment for the comparatively trivial crime of stealing, when he stood uninfluenced by the fact that he was in custody charged with the commission of a crime for which his life then stood in jeopardy."

In *People* v. *McCallam,* 103 N. Y. 587, 9 N. E. 502, it was held that an assertion of a constable that he had enough evidence to convict a person charged with crime; that she might consider herself under arrest therefor,—did not by itself constitute a threat which rendered inadmissible a statement subsequently made by the person arrested to the constable, as to facts relating to the offense charged.

A prisoner's confession to the officer arresting him or holding him in custody is not inadmissible merely because made in answer to a question which assumed his guilt. *State* v. *Berry,* 50 La. Ann. 1309, 24 So. 329.

121. — no warning.

The fact that a confession not made upon a judicial examination of the accused was made without warning him of the effect it might have does not render it incompetent.[1]

[1]*State* v. *Workman,* 15 S. C. 540, Citing 1 Greenl. Ev. § 229, to same effect; *State* v. *Howard,* 92 N. C. 772, mem. See also 7 Crim. L. Mag. 799. Cautioning necessary only upon the examination of the prisoner before a magistrate. Code, § 1146. Compare *Harris* v. *State,* 6 Tex. App. 97. *Dictum,* that if the accused, who had presented a written confession, had shown a desire to withdraw the document, it would not have been competent evidence.

In Texas a statement by defendant while under arrest, and without being cautioned as required by statute, is not admissible against him for any purpose. *White* v. *State* (Tex. Crim. App.) 38 S. W. 169.

And a warning to one about to make a confession, that any statement he makes "may be used for or against him," is not such a warning as the statute on that subject requires. *Pryor* v. *State,* 40 Tex. Crim. Rep. 643, 51 S. W. 375.

But declarations made by defendant shortly before his actual arrest are not inadmissible on the ground that he was not warned before making them. *McKenzie* v. *State* (Tex. Crim. App.) 32 S. W. 543.

And a confession by defendant while in jail is not inadmissible on the ground that he was not properly warned, where he was warned a day or two before. *Adams* v. *State,* 35 Tex. Crim. Rep. 285, 33 S. W. 354.

122. — previous advice.

A confession is not deemed induced by hope or fear because made after having obtained advice as to the legal consequences of the crime.[1]

[1]*State* v. *Crank,* 2 Bail. L. 66, 23 Am. Dec. 117, 127. Murder; here it appeared that the accused had asked the witness if those who concealed a murder were equally guilty with those who did it, and being told that the law so considered them, only they were not so rigorously dealt with, made the confession, and it was held admissible.

123. — collateral inducement.

The fact that the confession was made under hope or promise of a benefit of a collateral nature does not render it incompetent.[1]

[1]*State* v. *Tatro,* 50 Vt. 483, Redfield, J. (a case of a promise by a jailer to a prisoner chained in solitary confinement, to unchain him, and allow him to associate with other prisoners on making a full confession); Andrews, J., in *Cox* v. *People,* 80 N. Y. 500, Affirming 19 Hun, 430. And see *Stone* v. *State,* 105 Ala. 60, 17 So. 114, a trial for arson, where the court said that even if it was true that the confession was induced by there having been held out the promise of employment to commit other arsons to the persons who burned the property for which the defendant was on trial, yet this inducement involved only "a collateral benefit or boon," and not the holding out of any hope or promise of favor in respect of that crime, and hence could not have the effect of rendering the confession of that offense involuntary.

124. — artifice.

The fact that the confession was obtained by artifice practised upon the accused by the officer having him in charge will not render it inadmissible.[1]

[1]*Hardy* v. *United States,* 3 App. D. C. 35; *State* v. *Phelps,* 74 Mo. 135.

(murder), Citing *State* v. *Patterson*, 73 Mo. 695 (where authorities on confessions are fully reviewed); *State* v. *Jones*, 54 Mo. 478 (murder; a confession procured by telling the accused that an accomplice has divulged certain facts relating to the crime is admissible; and it makes no difference, apparently, whether the statement about the accomplice is true or not. Judgment affirmed); *People* v. *McMahon*, 15 N. Y. 384, 390 (*dictum*); *People* v. *Wentz*, 37 N. Y. 303 (*dictum*).

So, a confession obtained from a prisoner charged with a crime which he had previously denied, by means of a statement by the sheriff that they had a sure case against him, and a promise by the sheriff to use his influence in the prisoner's behalf, if he would admit his guilt,—is not admissible in evidence against him, nor are repetitions of such confession, made to other officers, though without further inducement. *People* v. *Castro*, 125 Cal. 521, 58 Pac. 133.

But a confession of one charged with theft, made to an officer after the latter had told him that another had given the whole thing away, and that it would be better for him to tell all about it, and that if he did he would do all he could to get defendant out of it,—is inadmissible on the trial for theft, as is also a later confession made in the belief that the sheriff was still friendly. *Gallagher* v. *State* (Tex. Crim. App.) 24 S. W. 288.

And a confession of guilt of larceny is not voluntary, and is inadmissible in evidence, where it was obtained by an untrue statement of the owner of the stolen property, that defendant had been seen to take the goods, and would be prosecuted if he did not settle at once. *Cook* v. *State*, 32 Tex. Crim. Rep. 27, 22 S. W. 23.

Confessions made by one accused of crime, to the officer arresting him, several hours after the arrest, and without solicitation, are not inadmissible because of false representations by the officer, made soon after the arrest, to a crowd, in the hearing of the accused, to the effect that the officer had come after him at the instance of his mother, and would befriend him if he was innocent. *Marable* v. *State*, 89 Ga. 425, 15 S. E. 453.

And a confession made by one charged with arson, while under no constraint, and before having been accused of any offense, in the presence of one not in authority as an officer, is not inadmissible because made in the proximity of concealed officers, and induced by the artifice and deception of the person to whom it was made in pretending that he was in sympathy with barn-burning, and wanted to have some burning done on his own account. *Stone* v. *State*, 105 Ala. 60, 17 So. 114.

A confession of murder by defendant to a detective not known to be such, upon his promise that if she would tell him "all about it" he would give her something so that she could not be "caught," is admissible in evidence. *State* v. *Harrison*, 115 N. C. 706, 20 S. E. 175.

And declarations made by defendant charged with murder, to detectives, for the purpose of qualifying himself for membership in a supposed band of criminals, that he committed the murder, are admissible against him; but the court should direct the jury to weigh it in the light of the circumstances under which it was made. *Com.* v. *Wilson*, 186 Pa. 1, 40 Atl. 283.

So, also, a conversation between the defendant and a third person, and a letter written by the former to the latter, are not inadmissible because they were procured by an artifice of the authorities, but without any threats or promises on their part. *Com.* v. *Goodwin*, 186 Pa. 218, 40 Atl. 412.

And a confession by a boy fifteen years old, in jail on a charge of murder in the first degree, is not incompetent merely because made to a detective assuming to be in jail on a similar charge, and to be planning an escape, in the absence of any persuasion, promise, or threats by the latter. *Burton* v. *State*, 107 Ala. 109, 18 So. 284.

125. — expectation of leniency.

A confession made under expectation of favor from the prosecution is inadmissible.[1]

And if it is uncertain whether the hope under which it was made originated with the accused, or was induced by those representing the prosecution, it is safer to exclude the confession.[2]

[1]*Bubster* v. *State*, 33 Neb. 663, 50 N. W. 953; *Harvey* v. *State* (Miss.) 20 So. 837.

In *State* v. *Phelps*, 11 Vt. 116, 34 Am. Dec. 672, it was so held, although the interview was of the prisoner's seeking, and no admissions were sought or expected by the person communicated with, and no direct assurances of favor were given to procure them. New trial granted for error in admitting such confession.

In *Com.* v. *Knapp*, 9 Pick. 496, 20 Am. Dec. 491, 496, a murder trial, it was held error to admit confessions made under hope of favor held out to the prisoner.

In *Newman* v. *State*, 49 Ala. 9, a prosecution for larceny, the person with whom the accused had been for two years said to him, "Tom, this is mighty bad; they have got the 'dead wood' on you, and you will be convicted," and at the same time said something about "owning up." The prosecutor said to the prisoner: "You are very young to be in such a difficulty as this; there must have been someone with you who was older, and I, if in your place, would tell who it was; it is not right for you to suffer the whole penalty and let someone who is guiltier go free; that it might go lighter with you." It was held that a confession made under the influence of such language was involuntary. New trial granted.

In *People* v. *Phillips*, 42 N. Y. 200, Affirming 57 Barb. 353, a confession made after the officer had told accused that "it would be better for him to own up" was held inadmissible. To the same effect, *People* v. *Ward*, 15 Wend. 231.

In *Com.* v. *Nott* (Mass.) 16 Rep. 493, a larceny trial, the words used to the accused, a police officer, before his arrest, in the police station and in the presence of a superior officer, were: "You had better own up. I was in the place when you took it. We have got you down fine. This is not the first you have taken. We have got other things against you nearly as good as this." Held to render the confession inadmissible. In New York the Code of Criminal Procedure excludes a confession only when made under the influence of fear produced by threats, or made upon a stipulation of the district attorney not to prosecute. *People* v. *McCallam,* 103 N. Y. 587, 9 N. E. 502, Affirming 3 N. Y. Crim. Rep. 189, holding it not error to admit a confession called out by a statement made by an officer to a prisoner that "they had found enough to convict her; she might as well own up;" and that she might consider herself under arrest.

A statement to defendant, accused of forgery, by a police officer by whom he was arrested, in substance that he had known defendant a long time, and would help him all he could, and if defendant said he did not forge the paper he would see the prosecutor and get him to compromise it, but if he did do it, it might be best for him to say so, but if not, to stick to it that he did not,—does not render the confession made by the defendant inadmissible. *Dotson* v. *State,* 88 Ala. 208, 7 So. 259.

Nor does a statement by an officer to one of several persons charged with murder, that if he was not the one who struck the blow, and would tell the truth, he would see what could be done for him, render incompetent a confession subsequently made by another prisoner, where the statement was not made to the latter at any time, and he attributes his confession solely to threats and fear of violence. *Hardy* v. *United States,* 3 App. D. C. 35.

The inducements to the making of confessions, which should exclude proof thereof, must come from one in authority, or be presented under circumstances likely to lead the defendant to suppose that they were sanctioned by one in authority. *State* v. *Holden,* 42 Minn. 350, 44 N. W. 123; *State* v. *Morgan,* 35 W. Va. 260, 13 S. E. 385. But a private detective is not a person in authority, whose promises or threats will make a confession inadmissible. *Early* v. *Com.* 86 Va. 921, 11 S. E. 795.

In Georgia a confession of guilt by an accused, made freely and voluntarily, is admissible in evidence against him, although made under the hope that his case might be settled without a prosecution, under Ga. Pen. Code, § 1006, where such hope was not induced by another, but existed entirely in his own mind. *Hecox* v. *State,* 105 Ga. 625, 31 S. E. 592.

In Texas the testimony of a witness indicted for arson, given on the preliminary trial of another person, on the persuasion of the city marshal, county attorney, and others, and the promise by the county attorney of immunity from prosecution, whether cautioned or not that it might be used against him,—is inadmissible in evidence against him, under Code Crim. Proc. arts. 749, 750, providing that a confession shall not be used unless freely made without compulsion or persuasion, or, if the party was under arrest or in jail, unless he was first cautioned that it might be used against him. *Lauderdale* v. *State,* 31 Tex. Crim. Rep. 46, 19 S. W. 679.

In Washington a confession is not incompetent because promises and inducements were held out to the defendant, if it was not made under the influence of fear produced by threats, under Wash. Code Proc. § 1308, providing that the confession of a defendant made under inducements, with all the circumstances, may be given against him, except when made under the influence of fear produced by threats. *State* v. *Coss,* 12 Wash. 673, 42 Pac. 127.

[3]*State* v. *Phelps,* 11 Vt. 116, 34 Am. Dec. 672. Compare *Com.* v. *Tuckerman,* 10 Gray, 190, and *Com.* v. *Knapp,* 9 Pick. 496, 20 Am. Dec. 491. Embezzlement; where the court, at p. 502, Am. Dec. 495, per Morton, J., says: "It is not because of any breach of good faith in admitting them, nor because they are extorted illegally (though there may be cases in which this would exclude them, as where a magistrate puts the accused upon his oath), but the reason is that in the agitation of mind in which the party charged is supposed to be, he is liable to be influenced by the hope of advantage or fear of injury to state things which are not true. . . . This influence which is to exclude the party's confessions must be external influence, and not the mere operations of his own mind."

126. Broken promise to turn state's evidence.

A confession, though formally made in writing upon the promise of the attorney general that the accused shall not be prosecuted if he turns state's evidence, becomes admissible against him in case of his refusal to testify at the trial of his accomplice.[1]

[1]*Com.* v. *Knapp,* 10 Pick. 477, 20 Am. Dec. 534, 540 (murder). Compare *Womack* v. *State,* 16 Tex. App. 178; *Lopez* v. *State,* 12 Tex. App. 27; *United States* v. *Hinz,* 35 Fed. 272.

127. Refusal of promise of immunity.

The fact that the district attorney, while inducing confession by arousing expectations of immunity, expressly refused to promise it, does not entitle the prosecution to use the confession.[1]

[1]*People* v. *Kurtz,* 42 Hun, 335, so holding under the provision of Code Crim. Proc. § 395, excluding confessions made under a stipulation of the district attorney not to prosecute.

And the hope of immunity where no promise has been made is not such inducement as to make inadmissible a confession by defendant charged with murder. *State* v. *Griffin,* 48 La. Ann. 1409, 20 So. 905.

128. Encouraging to tell the truth.

A simple encouragement to tell the truth, as distinguished from an encouragement to confess, does not, even at common law, render the confession consequently made inadmissible.[1]

[1]*Jackson* v. *State,* 29 Tex. App. 458, 16 S. W. 247; *State* v. *Meekins,* 41 La. Ann. 543, 6 So. 822; *Hardy* v. *United States,* 3 App. D. C. 35; *People* v. *Smith,* 3 How. Pr. 226 (a confession made after the constable who had arrested accused had said to him: "If you burnt the barn you had better tell me of it,"—held properly admitted, it appearing that the confession was made, not to the constable, but to another person who had held out no inducement. The court said: "In the present case there was no advice to the prisoner to make a general confession; certainly none to make a confession that was untrue." And the court distinguished *People* v. *Ward,* 15 Wend. 231, saying: "In that case there was an unqualified inducement held out by the committing magistrate that it would be better for the prisoner to make a full confession."

In *Reg.* v. *Reeve,* 12 Cox C. C. 179, two small boys were in custody on suspicion of obstructing a railway train, and the mothers and a policeman were present. One of the mothers said: "You had better, as good boys, tell the truth," whereupon the boys both confessed. It was held admissible. The inducement here was what a mother would say to her son. Conviction affirmed.

In *Matthews* v. *State,* 9 Lea, 128, 42 Am. Rep. 667, it was held that to say to the prisoner that "an honest confession is good for the soul" is not such a promise of temporal benefit or discharge from punishment for the crime charged as will render a confession inadmissible.

In *Com.* v. *Preece,* 140 Mass. 276, 5 N. E. 494 (arson), there was some conflict as to whether the officer to whom the confession was made said to the prisoner, "You had better tell about it," or merely asked him to tell the truth; and the court held that it could not say, as a matter of law, that the decision of the judge in admitting the evidence was erroneous, basing its conclusion on the presumption that he properly left it to the jury to determine whether the confession was voluntary,—Citing *Com.* v. *Nott,* 135 Mass. 269, and *Com.* v. *Smith,* 119 Mass. 305.

In *Reg.* v. *Hatts,* 49 L. T. N. S. 780, the prosecutor, before two policemen, said to two prisoners, his servants: "I know what has been going on between you; you had better speak the truth." One of the prisoners made a confession. It was held that it was not admissible. Compare *Kelly* v. *State,* 72 Ala. 244.

A statement made by the defendant to a person who had proposed to assist him in the concealment of the crime, and in answer to such offer, held admissible against him, because it appeared from the statement itself that he had no expectation of the proposed advantage. *Findley* v. *State,* 5 Blackf. 576, 36 Am. Dec. 557 558. Murder; new trial granted on another ground.

In the absence of statute the test is to inquire whether the accused was induced to believe that, whether true or false, it was to his interest to make a confession. *People* v. *Wolcott,* 51 Mich. 612, 17 N. W. 78, where persons acting apparently under authority obtained the confession by making accused believe that he would get off easily by making it.

That a fellow prisoner in jail with a defendant charged with murder told him that he had "better tell the truth; the white folks were going to break somebody's neck,"—does not, as matter of absolute law, render inadmissible confessions made then and there in the presence of fellow prisoners only. *Miller* v. *State*, 94 Ga. 1, 21 S. E. 128, Distinguishing *Green* v. *State*, 88 Ga. 516, 15 S. E. 10, on the ground that in the latter case it was held that the court below erred in not excluding a confession which the accused was led to make by the statement that it might be best for him to tell. In that case, however, this was said to the accused in the presence and apparently with the sanction of the sheriff, in whose custody he was at the time, by a person who had arrested him, and whose object evidently was not so much to ascertain the truth as to obtain a confession of guilt; and the accused, in view of the authority exercised by these persons, may have supposed that they were able to render him some aid in relation to the charge against him, and that it would be to his advantage to follow their advice and make such a statement as they desired him to make.

But *Ford* v. *State*, 75 Miss. 101, 21 So. 524, holds that a confession made to the marshal while defendant was in his custody, in response to his statement that it would be better for him to tell the facts about the matter, and a confession made the next day and under the influence of such statement, in the presence of such marshal and other persons,—are inadmissible.

A confession is not admissible when made by a defendant who sought the sheriff to find out if a confession would not be better for him, and was encouraged by the sheriff to think that it would be. *People* v. *Thompson*, 84 Cal. 598, 24 Pac. 384.

And where a prisoner sends for the sheriff, telling him that he wants to tell him all about the case, and the sheriff informs him that whatever he says will be used in evidence against him, but that if he will tell him all about it, so that he can get all the parties, he will do what he can for him, the confession is not admissible, under Tex. Crim. Code, arts. 749, 750. *Searcy* v. *State*, 28 Tex. App. 513, 13 S. W. 782.

But *Maull* v. *State*, 95 Ala. 1, 11 So. 218, held that a prisoner's confessions to the sheriff, for whom he sent, made upon his telling the sheriff that he sent for him to talk to him about his case, to which the latter answered that he would listen if he was going to tell the truth, but if not, he did not want to hear what he had to say, were voluntary and admissible in evidence.

129. Intoxication at the time of confession.

The fact that the accused was intoxicated at the time of confession does not render the confession incompetent, unless the intoxication was of such a degree as to incapacitate him from making a narration of past events or stating his own participation in a crime. Intoxication short of that goes to the credibility or weight, not to the competency, of the confession.[1]

[1]*State* v. *Berry*, 50 La. Ann. 1309, 24 So. 329; *White* v. *State*, 32 Tex. Crim. Rep. 625, 25 S. W. 784; *Lienpo* v. *State*, 28 Tex. App. 179, 12 S. W. 588; *Com.* v. *Howe*, 9 Gray, 110; *Eskridge* v. *State*, 25 Ala. 30 (holding that the confessions or admissions of a party are not necessarily inadmissible because by reason of intoxication he is unable to comprehend the effect of the admissions, or to give a true account of the occurrence to which they have reference); *State* v. *Grear*, 28 Minn. 426, 41 Am. Rep. 296, 10 N. W. 472 (holding that it was not error to refuse to allow accused to call other witnesses to prove intoxication, before the confession should be received,—Citing and relying on *Com.* v. *Howe*, 9 Gray, 110).

In *Finch* v. *State*, 81 Ala. 41, 1 So. 565, Somerville, J., says: "There is no rule of law which compels jurors to believe confessions made by a defendant when he is sober, in preference to those of a contradictory character made when drunk. The relative credibility of the statements is a question for the jury."

130. —liquor furnished by officer.

The fact that the accused was, at the time of the confession, under the influence of liquor supplied to him by the officer having him in custody, does not alone make the confession inadmissible.[1]

[1]*Jefferds* v. *People*, 5 Park. Crim. Rep. 522, 561 (not a ground for striking out confession that the officer to whom it was made had ingratiated himself into the friendship of the accused, and had freely supplied him with liquor for the purpose); *People* v. *Ramirez*, 56 Cal. 533, 38 Am. Rep. 73; *Balbo* v. *People*, 80 N. Y. 485.

131. Improper influence presumed to continue.

A confession, though apparently freely made, is prima facie incompetent if it be shown that the accused made a previous confession which was not voluntary.[1]

In such case, however, the second confession may be shown to be competent by evidence that the improper influence had meanwhile ceased to operate.[2]

[1]*Barnes* v. *State*, 36 Tex. 356; *Coffee* v. *State*, 25 Fla. 501, 6 So. 493; *State* v. *Drake*, 82 N. C. 592; *State* v. *Brown*, 73 Mo. 631. *Contra*, of confessions to different persons, *McAdory* v. *State*, 62 Ala. 154.

According to *Shrivers* v. *State*, 7 Tex. App. 450, a confession, incompetent because not voluntary when originally made, cannot be put in evidence against the accused by proving that it was repeated in his presence, while he was still in custody, and that he made no reply. But this was held on the ground that his condition as a prisoner protects him from such statements, even if made by himself—a rule not now generally in force.

A confession may be received in evidence, although promises or threats were used by persons in authority, if their influence was wholly done away with before the confession was made. *Early* v. *Com.* 86 Va. 921, 11 S. E. 795.

And a confession made in the presence of a sheriff, after the accused was duly warned, is not inadmissible on the ground that it was induced by promises of a detective who brought the prisoner from Columbus, Ohio, to New York, where he was placed in the hands of the sheriff. *State* v. *Willis,* 71 Conn. 293, 41 Atl. 820.

[3]*State* v. *Guild,* 10 N. J. L. 163, 18 Am. Dec. 404 (murder; although the first confession may have been made under improper influence, yet if the court thinks there has been a sufficient lapse of time to remove such influence between the first confession and the one offered against the prisoner and reduced to writing [as in this case five months], such confession subsequently made is admissible), Citing *Williams's Case,* 1 N. Y. City Hall Rec. 149; *Bowerhan's Case,* 4 N. Y. City Hall Rec. 138; *Stage's Case,* 5 N. Y. City Hall Rec. 178; *Milligan's Case,* 6 N. Y. City Hall Rec. 78 (confession admitted, and ruling sustained), Disapproving the rule laid down by Starkie, Ev. pt. 4, p. 49, which, however, agrees with the *dictum* in *Com.* v. *Knapp,* 9 Pick. 496, 20 Am. Dec. 491, 499; *United States* v. *Nardello,* 4 Mackey, 503 (holding that the fact that a confession by the prisoner, made early in the day, has been held involuntary, and therefore excluded, does not necessarily exclude a confession made in the afternoon).

132. Qualification of witness to prove confession.

A witness cannot testify to a confession if he could not understand[1] or does not remember[2] the substance of all that he heard the accused say in the confession and qualifying statements.

But it is not necessary that he should remember the precise words used,[3] nor that he should remember the entire conversation,[4] nor that he should be able to swear that he heard all that the accused may have said in the same conversation, that may have tended to qualify or explain the confession.[5]

[1]*People* v. *Gelabert,* 39 Cal. 663. Murder; holding that a witness who has a very imperfect knowledge of the language employed in the conversation, and who did not understand the whole of the conversation in which the supposed confession was made to him by the accused, is incompetent to testify as to such confession. Judgment reversed. To the same effect, *State* v. *Buster,* 23 Nev. 346, 47 Pac. 194, *Contra,* in a case perhaps distinguishable, *People* v. *Minisci,* 12 N. Y. S. R. 719.

But a witness is competent to testify to a confession which he swears was made by the accused to a third person in the dark, although he did not see the accused, but only knew him by his voice, as the sufficiency of the identification is for the jury. *Fussell* v. *State*, 93 Ga. 450, 21 S. E. 97.

[2]*Berry* v. *Com.* 10 Bush, 15. Homicide; held that a confession cannot be proved by a witness who does not remember the substance of all that was said in the same conversation. Judgment reversed for admitting what he did remember.

[3]*State* v. *Avery*, 31 La. Ann. 181; *State* v. *Desroches*, 48 La. Ann. 428, 19 So. 250.

[4]*Eskridge* v. *State*, 25 Ala. 30 (holding that evidence of a confession is not inadmissible because the witnesses were unable to detail everything that was said, where it does not appear that the account was garbled, tortured, or unfair); *Kendall* v. *State*, 65 Ala. 492 (holding that a witness may testify to confessions of the accused, though he does not recollect all the conversation at the time; the court says: "This in no manner militates against the principle that the whole of what the prisoner said on the subject should be taken together"); *State* v. *Madison*, 47 La. Ann. 30, 16 So. 566.

[5]*State* v. *Pratt*, 88 N. C. 639.

In *People* v. *Thoms*, 3 Park. Crim. Rep. 256, confessions made to a police officer at the time of arrest were held properly admitted against the objection that the prisoner spoke partly in English and partly in German, and that the witness did not understand German. Dean, J., said: "If the witness had said that a part of the same admission was in German and a part in English, I think the evidence would have been inadmissible. But it appears the admissions were at the police office, after the prisoner had been searched and the bills found; it does not appear that any portion of the admissions were in German." But the majority of the court, without passing on this point, reversed the judgment of conviction on another ground.

133. Confession of another offense.

If the accused, in the same conversation or communication, confessed not only the offense charged, but another offense also, the confession of the offense charged is not thereby rendered inadmissible; but if that part be competent the prosecution has a right to prove the whole.[1]

[1]*State* v. *Underwood*, 75 Mo. 230.

According to *Gore* v. *People*, 162 Ill. 259, 44 N. E. 500, a confession by the accused of a crime other than that charged, while not admissible as a substantive fact, may, when not separable from a competent confession, go to the jury under cautionary directions from the court.

134. Qualifying statements.

If a confession of the accused is received in evidence against him, he has a right to prove his own version of the conversation, which tends to qualify or explain the confession,[1] but not a subsequent conversation.[2]

[1]*People* v. *Penhollow*, 42 Hun, 103; *Mack* v. *State*, 48 Wis. 271, 4 N. W. 449; *State* v. *Brown*, 1 Mo. App. 86. The usual statement of the rule is all that was said on the same subject.

[2]*Real* v. *People*, 42 N. Y. 270, 279, Affirming 8 Abb. Pr. N. S. 314. Murder; although, when the confessions of the accused are given in evidence against him, all that he said in the same conversation, explanatory thereof and tending to discharge him from its effect, is competent in his behalf, yet such confessions cannot be explained by other statements in his own favor, made on a different occasion and at a subsequent time. Evidence properly rejected; judgment affirmed.

135. Testimony of accused to his own mental state.

The fact that a confession was made under excitement, and while in a state of great nervousness, does not deprive it of its character as a voluntary statement.[1]

But after the prosecution has introduced his confession, the accused testifying in his own behalf may explain his mental condition at the time of the confession.[2]

[1]*State* v. *Jones*, 47 La. Ann. 1524, 18 So. 515; *People* v. *Cokahnour*, 120 Cal. 253, 52 Pac. 505; *Carlisle* v. *State*, 37 Tex. Crim. Rep. 108, 38 S. W. 991; *Balls* v. *State* (Tex. Crim. App.) 40 S. W. 801.

[2]*Simmons* v. *State*, 61 Miss. 243, where it was held error to refuse to allow the accused to so testify.

136. Doubtful case.

If there is a reasonable doubt whether the confession was voluntary the evidence should be excluded.[1]

[1]The court should not admit in evidence a confession, if it entertains a reasonable doubt as to whether it was free and voluntary. *Hunter* v. *State*, 74 Miss. 515, 21 So. 305; *May* v. *State*, 38 Neb. 211, 56 N. W. 804.

In *People* v. *Barric*, 49 Cal. 342, a larceny trial, it was held that before confessions made to an officer can be received in evidence, it must appear affirmatively that they were made voluntarily. Here the defendant's counsel, by a preliminary examination of the witness, brought it out that it was doubtful whether the confession was voluntary. The court, however, admitted it, and for that error a new trial was granted. The court said: "We cannot too strongly urge on the district attorneys never to offer evidence of confessions except it has first been made to appear that they are made voluntarily." The rule in 1 Greenl. Ev. 219, was quoted with approval. And see *dictum* in *Ellis* v. *State*, 65 Miss. 44, 3 So. 188.

In *Hopt* v. *Utah,* 110 U. S. 574, 28 L. ed. 262, 4 Sup. Ct. Rep. 202, Harlan, J., well says: "The admissibility of such evidence [of confessions] so largely depends upon the special circumstances connected with the confession that it is difficult, if not impossible, to formulate a rule that will comprehend all cases. As the question is necessarily addressed in the first instance to the judge, and since his discretion must be controlled by all the attendant circumstances, the courts have wisely forborne to mark with absolute precision the limits of admission and exclusion."

According to *Burdge* v. *State,* 53 Ohio St. 512, 42 N. E. 594, confessions offered under conflicting proof as to whether they were or were not voluntary may be considered under instruction to disregard them if the jury are satisfied that they were involuntary.

137. Subsequent disclosure of nonvoluntariness.

Omission to object, and require the preliminary question to be investigated and determined before receiving the evidence of confession, does not preclude the defense from showing afterward that it was not voluntary, and thereupon requiring the evidence to be stricken out or excluded from the consideration of the jury by directing them to disregard it.[1]

[1]*Holland* v. *State,* 39 Fla. 178, 22 So. 298; *Metzger* v. *State,* 18 Fla. 481; *Bob* v. *State,* 32 Ala. 560. *Contra, State* v. *Rush,* 95 Mo. 199, 8 S. W. 221.

After a confession has been admitted by the court, either party has a right to produce before the jury the same evidence which was submitted to the court when it was called upon to decide the question of competency, and all other facts and circumstances relevant to the confession, or affecting its weight or credit as evidence; and if it should be thus made to appear at any time before the close of the evidence that the confession was made under such circumstances as to render it incompetent as evidence, it should be excluded by the court. *Ellis* v. *State,* 65 Miss. 44, 3 So. 188.

As to correcting its effect by instructions to the jury, see *post,* Division XLII.

138. Evidence of intoxication to impair effect of confession.

When a confession has been put in evidence the defense may show, on cross-examination or by other testimony, that the accused was under the influence of liquor when he made it;[1] but such evidence is not ground for striking out the confession,[2] unless the intoxication is clearly shown to have been of such a degree as to incapacitate him from making a narration of past events or to state his own participation in the crime.

[1]*State* v. *Feltes,* 51 Iowa, 495, 1 N. W. 755, holding that the time when the

jury is made acquainted with the condition of the accused, whether on cross-examination or otherwise, is immaterial.

[2]*Jefferds* v. *People,* 5 Park. Crim. Rep. 522, 561, where the court, sustaining a refusal to strike out, said: "It was a question of fact for the jury to determine what the condition of the prisoner was when he made the confessions, and how much reliance might be placed in them."

139. Cross-examining accused.

Although a confession has been excluded as not voluntary, if the accused thereafter testifies as a witness in his own behalf, he may be cross-examined as to anything in the conversation offered as a confession which is inconsistent with his testimony as a witness.[1]

[1]*Com.* v. *Tolliver,* 119 Mass. 312.

XIII. Consciousness of guilt.

See also, as to Admissions, §§ 41 *et seq.;* Confessions, §§ 103 *et seq.;* Demeanor, § 190; Intent, § 236; Motive, § 256; Silence, § 282; Tampering, § 295.

140. General rule.

The acts and conduct of a party at or about the time when he is charged to have committed a crime are always received as evidence of a guilty mind.[1]

[1]*Greenfield* v. *People,* 85 N. Y. 75, S. C., with note, 39 Am. Rep. 636, 640 (murder,—Citing Roscoe, Crim. Ev. 21, 22; *Linsday* v. *People,* 63 N. Y. 143); *Rains* v. *State,* 88 Ala. 91, 7 So. 315; *Com.* v. *Hurley,* 158 Mass. 159, 33 N. E. 342; *State* v. *Furr,* 121 N. C. 606, 28 S. E. 552. And in *State* v. *Baldwin,* 36 Kan. 1, 12 Pac. 318, it was held that the conduct and demeanor of a prisoner at the time of his arrest, or soon after the commission of the crime, is admissible to show a guilty mind, if the testimony is confined to a reasonable time after the discovery of the crime or his arrest. It seems that an inquiry to a jailer as to the conduct of the prisoner while in his charge (a period of four months after his arrest and discovery of the crime) is too general and irrelevant.

Thus, on a trial for rape, evidence is admissible that soon after the commission of the offense the defendant, on being hailed by an officer while approaching the state line, after a moment's conversation, fired his revolver at him. *State* v. *Taylor* (Mo.) 22 S. W. 806.

So, the refusal of a prisoner under arrest, and who had been injured in resisting arrest, to give his name, age, and residence, when a physician came to dress his wounds, is admissible as evidence of a purpose to conceal his identity, and as indicative of guilt. *State* v. *Taylor,* 70 Vt. 1, 42 L. R. A. 673, 39 Atl. 447.

And the conduct of defendant charged with illegally selling intoxicating liquors, in hiding a bottle of beer when the officers were searching the premises, is evidence against her, even though the officers had no warrant to search the premises, where she did not know of that fact. *Com.* v. *Acton,* 165 Mass. 11, 42 N. E. 329.

And the officer who made the arrest on a charge of larceny may testify that when he arrested defendant she had a basket containing packages and bundles, and thrust her hand into the basket and under the bundles; but he cannot add the words "as though she were trying to conceal something," since that is a mere inference, and inadmissible. *Bolling* v. *State,* 98 Ala. 80, 12 So. 782.

In *State* v. *Lucey,* 24 Mont. 295, 61 Pac. 994, it was held that testimony of the sheriff that, when arrested, defendant turned away, "as though he was about to be devoured," was admissible, in the absence of a specific objection that the expression was vague.

In *State* v. *Wisdom,* 119 Mo. 539, 24 S. W. 1047, a trial for murder, the admission of evidence that defendant, when requested with others to touch the body of the murdered man, refused to do so, was held not to be reversible error,—especially as the only objection to its admission was its immateriality.

141. Refusal to allow search.

The refusal to allow one's house to be searched without warrant,—and on the same principle refusal to submit to arrest when illegally attempted[1]—is not competent evidence against him as tending to show consciousness of guilt, for it is merely the exercise of a constitutional right.[2]

[1]The fact that defendant resisted arrest with knowledge of what he was being arrested for is not admissible as tending to show his guilt, where he knew that the arrest was illegal, and was resisting it solely on that ground; but such proof is admissible if, though he knew the arrest was illegal, he did not resist it because of that fact. *Russell* v. *State,* 37 Tex. Crim. Rep. 314, 39 S. W. 674.

Nor is it competent to show that defendant charged with murder resisted an arrest for another distinct and subsequent offense, which had no connection with, and could shed no light upon, the homicide. *State* v. *May,* 142 Mo. 135, 43 S. W. 637.

[2]*Murdock* v. *State,* 68 Ala. 567.

But evidence that defendant charged with stealing corn said to persons proposing to search his corncrib, that the key had been lost or mislaid, is admissible in connection with evidence that the stolen corn was found therein. *Hubbard* v. *State,* 107 Ala. 33, 18 So. 225.

142. Falsehood.

Evidence of falsehood on the part of the accused in giving an account of himself, or of the transaction or his relation to it, is competent as affording a legitimate presumption of guilt.[1]

For this purpose the prosecution may prove such declarations of the accused, and then prove their falsity.[2]

[1]It may be shown that an accused, when charged with the crime, denied the charge by asserting a falsehood. *State* v. *Bradley,* 64 Vt. 466, 24 Atl. 1053.

"The resort to falsehood and evasion by one accused of a crime affords of itself a presumption of evil intentions, and has always been considered proper evidence to present to a jury upon the question of the guilt or innocence of the person accused." Ruger, Ch. J., in *People* v. *Conroy,* 97 N. Y. 62, 80.

In *State* v. *Smith,* 5 Day, 175, 5 Am. Dec. 132, a prosecution for passing counterfeit money, it was held proper to admit evidence of the prisoner's conversation with a person who had passed other counterfeit money, the conversation consisting in the prisoner's denying that he knew such person, although he had entered the town where the money was passed in his company. The prisoner's *scienter* must be proved, and this is one of the best ways of doing it.

That the accused falsely represented himself to be the payee of a forged note is a circumstance tending to impeach the good faith of the transaction; and to justify the inference that he knew that one of the maker's names was forged, see *State* v. *Williams,* 66 Iowa, 573, 24 N. W. 52.

[2]*People* v. *Arnold,* 43 Mich. 303, 38 Am. Rep. 182, 5 N. W. 385 (opinion by Cooley, J., reviewing cases, and holding that a statement made by a defendant in his own behalf, on the first trial, may be put in evidence by the prosecution on the second trial, for the purpose of proving its falsity); *Coleman* v. *People,* 58 N. Y. 555. See also *infra,* §§ 297–301.

As to false theory of defense, see *post,* Division XLII., § 89.

143. Confronting with consequences of crime.

Evidence of the conduct, appearance, and bearing of the accused, when confronted with the scene or the results of the offense, is competent against him, although he may have been under arrest at the time.[1]

[1]*Handline* v. *State,* 6 Tex. App. 347; *State* v. *Broughton,* 29 N. C. (7 Ired. L.) 96, 45 Am. Dec. 507 (murder; held that the testimony of the prisoner on an examination before the grand jury who were investigating the offense generally, with a view to discover the perpetrator of the murder, and not to fix it upon the prisoner, his manner when being examined before them, his anxiety to fix the crime on someone else, are admissible against him).

144. Flight.

Evidence of the flight of the accused, or his concealment of himself, or evasion of arrest, is always competent,[1] at least on the question whether he was the one who committed the act.[2]

[1]*Clarke* v. *State*, 78 Ala. 474, 56 Am. Rep. 45 (homicide). See also 8 Crim. L. Mag. 19, where the headnote says: "Any conduct on the part of the accused indicating a consciousness of guilt, such as flight, concealment, etc., is competent against him"); *Ryan* v. *People*, 79 N. Y. 593, Affirming 19 Hun, 188 (assault and battery. "The evidence that the defendant made an effort to keep out of the way of the sheriff was very slight, if any, evidence of guilt. There are so many reasons for such conduct, consistent with innocence, that it scarcely comes up to the standard of evidence tending to establish guilt; but this and similar evidence has been allowed upon the theory that the jury will give it such weight as it deserves, depending upon the surrounding circumstances. It was not error to admit it"); *People* v. *Taylor*, 3 N. Y. Crim. Rep. 297 ("The conduct of a person charged with crime, immediately after the commission, is always the proper subject of inquiry. If he attempts to run away, or hide and evade the officer, it is a circumstance proper to go to the jury." Here the accused having on cross-examination denied that he was under a bed when arrested, it was held not error to allow the prosecution on the rebuttal to show that he was); *People* v. *Ogle*, 4 N. Y. Crim. Rep. 349 (not error to admit evidence designed to show flight on the part of the accused to avoid the consequences of the offense charged); *State* v. *Frederic*, 69 Me. 400 (evidence that the defendant, when about to be arrested by the officer, outran and for the time escaped him, is admissible without proof that he had been informed "that he was to be arrested on this identical charge." Its weight is for the jury. Exceptions overruled. A trivial case). And for other cases recognizing this rule, see *Allen* v. *United States*, 164 U. S. 492, 41 L. ed. 528, 17 Sup. Ct. Rep. 154; *State* v. *Van Winkle*, 80 Iowa, 15, 45 N. W. 388; *State* v. *Whitson*, 111 N. C. 695, 16 S. E. 322; *State* v. *Kent*, 5 N. D. 516, *sub nom. State* v. *Pancoast*, 35 L. R. A. 518, 67 N. W. 1052; *Buchanan* v. *State* (Tex. Crim. App.) 52 S. W. 769; *Henry* v. *State* (Tex. Crim. App.) 43 S. W. 340; *State* v. *Potter*, 108 Mo. 424, 22 S. W. 89. Compare *State* v. *Marshall*, 115 Mo. 383, 22 S. W. 452, holding that flight immediately after the occurrence is no evidence of guilt, unless the defendant fled to avoid arrest.

Property found on the line of flight competent. *McConkey* v. *Com.* 101 Pa. 416.

[2]*State* v. *Melton*, 37 La. Ann. 77; *People* v. *Winthrop*, 118 Cal. 85, 50 Pac. 390; *People* v. *Ah Choy*, 1 Idaho, 317 (holding that when there is no question as to who did the act, the only question being upon the degree of the offense, the accused is not entitled to give evidence tending to explain his flight).

So is evidence of his escape after his arrest. *Elmore* v. *State*, 98 Ala. 12, 13 So. 427; *State* v. *Hobgood*, 46 La. Ann. 855, 15 So. 406; *State* v. *Fitzgerald*, 63 Iowa, 268, 19 N. W. 202; *People* v. *Cleveland*, 107 Mich. 367, 65 N. W. 216. So also of his planning a flight or an escape.

People v. *Petmecky*, 2 N. Y. Crim. Rep. 450. Held not error to admit evidence that the accused, while in custody, awaiting trial, planned an escape. Or attempting it. *Clark* v. *Com.* 17 Ky. L. Rep. 540, 32 S. W. 131; *State* v. *Howell*, 117 Mo. 307, 23 S. W. 263; *State* v. *Palmer*, 65 N. H. 216, 20 Atl. 6; *Russell* v. *State*, 38 Tex. Crim. Rep. 590, 44 S. W 159; *Ryan* v. *State*, 83 Wis. 486, 53 N. W. 836.

This rule does not depend on the circumstances being part of the *res gestæ* of any fact in evidence, but on the tendency of such conduct to show a consciousness of guilt. *People* v. *Stanley*, 47 Cal. 113, 17 Am. Rep. 401 (robbery); *People* v. *Welsh*, 63 Cal. 167 (holding that the conduct of a party, both before and after the principal fact in issue, is admissible, not as part of the *res gestæ*, but as a circumstance connected with the act indicating the guilty intent).

145. Unsuccessful inquiry.

For the purpose of proving flight or concealment, it is competent to prove inquiries made for the accused at his reputed residence and his accustomed places of resort, and at places to which it was reasonably presumed he had gone; and that he could not be found there.[1]

[1]*People* v. *Ogle*, 104 N. Y. 511, 11 N. E. 53, Affirming 4 N. Y. Crim. Rep. 349 (murder; it being claimed by the prosecution that the defendant fled after the homicide; held not error to allow the prosecution to give evidence of such acts of the officers on seeking for him to arrest him); *Sylvester* v. *State*, 72 Ala. 201; *Koch* v. *State*, 115 Ala. 99, 22 So. 471; *State* v. *Lucey*, 24 Mont. 295, 61 Pac. 994. In *Clarke* v. *State*, 78 Ala. 474, 56 Am. Rep. 45, a homicide trial, it was held that the prosecution might prove a conversation between a wife and the officer inquiring for him with a view to his arrest, and his failure to disclose himself to the officer; but the jury should be instructed to disregard it as evidence, unless satisfied that he heard and understood the purport of the conversation. Reversed for failure to so instruct.

For the authorities on the same principle, as applicable in civil actions, see 1 Abbott, New Pr. & Forms, 649.

So, evidence that the sheriff had warrants for the arrest of defendant in his hands during three years, and had made diligent inquiry as to his whereabouts in the county, and failed to find him, is admissible to show defendant's flight. *Henry* v. *State* (Tex. Crim. App.) 43 S. W. 340.

But evidence on trial for larceny, by witness, that he looked for defendant three days when trying to arrest him for the theft, is inadmissible without further proof tending to show that he concealed himself from a consciousness of guilt. *McMunn* v. *State*, 113 Ala. 86, 21 So. 418.

Nor is it competent for a marshal to testify that he had been looking for defendant about two weeks before he learned of the theft of a horse, with which the defendant is charged, as tending to show the flight of defendant, it appearing that he was looking for him on account of another charge. *People* v. *Vidal*, 121 Cal. 221, 53 Pac. 558.

146. Means of flight.

Circumstantial evidence of the means apparently used in flight or escape is proper.[1]

[1]*State* v. *Fitzgerald,* 63 Iowa, 268, 19 N. W. 202, holding that evidence showing that a hole was made in the wall of the jail where the prisoner was confined, and that afterwards he was at liberty,—is sufficient to authorize an instruction that the jury might consider the escape as a fact in the case.

So, evidence is admissible on a trial for murder, that the prisoner had saws on his person in jail, with the intent to make his escape in case of his conviction. *State* v. *Duncan,* 116 Mo. 288, 22 S. W. 699.

And, to show flight after a homicide, it is competent to prove by witnesses living so near the accused, and accustomed to see him so often when at home that a failure to see him there would tend to show absence, that he was not seen there after the killing. *Gray* v. *State* (Fla.) 28 So. 53.

147. — occasion of flight.

When flight is competent as tending to show guilt, it is competent to show the circumstances of the occasion when the flight took place.[1]

[1]*People* v. *Lock Wing,* 61 Cal. 380. Assault; not error to admit evidence of a direction to arrest, which was immediately followed by the flight of defendant.

148. — rebuttal.

If evidence of flight or concealment has been given as tending to show guilt, the accused is entitled to give evidence in rebuttal, showing a motive consistent with innocence.[1]

[1]Thus *State* v. *Moncla,* 39 La. Ann. 868, 2 So. 814, holds that it is error to exclude evidence offered by the accused that he was very much excited at the time, and his mother and brother advised him to fly.

And *Batten* v. *State,* 80 Ind. 394, holds that it is error to exclude evidence that persons present followed and threatened him with violence.

And *Arnold* v. *State,* 9 Tex. App. 437, holds it error to exclude evidence that he was warned that his life was menaced by a mob. In *McKeon* v. *People,* 1 N. Y. Crim. Rep. 456, where the prosecution had given evidence tending to show that defendant had failed to appear for trial at the term for which he had given bail, though able to do so, it was held error to refuse to allow defendant, in order to rebut the inference of guilt or fear, to show the reasons for his nonattendance. In *State* v. *Mallon,* 75 Mo. 355, it was held error to exclude evidence that defendant was maltreated in jail.

And evidence that defendant was told that he had better run away if he wanted to save himself from a mob which was being formed to hang him if he was caught was held to be admissible in explanation of his flight, in *Lewallen* v. *State,* 33 Tex. Crim. Rep. 412, 26 S. W. 832.

But *Kennedy* v. *Com.* 14 Bush, 340, holds that "evidence of apprehended danger, in order to be admissible to rebut the inference of guilt which may be drawn from an escape and flight, should show such danger as could not have been readily, efficiently, and with entire safety provided against by the accused, either by his own act or through the instrumentality of the officers of the law." Here it appears that evidence that his escape was effected through fear of danger to his health from the odors of the jail was excluded. A new trial, however, was granted on other grounds. See also *State* v. *McDevitt,* 69 Iowa, 549, 29 N. W. 459.

And in *Taylor* v. *Com.* 90 Va. 109, 17 S. E. 812, a murder trial, general talk in the community, that if certain persons found defendant they would kill him without attempting to arrest him, was held inadmissible to rebut the fact of defendant's immediate flight and concealment and attempt to leave the state.

And *Howgate* v. *United States,* 7 App. D. C. 217, holds that evidence that an accused who fled from justice was aided in his escape by those charged with his safe-keeping, and that he subsequently conversed with officers of the government, is inadmissible to rebut the presumption of guilt arising from his flight.

So, testimony that defendant seemed afraid is inadmissible to rebut the inference of guilt afforded by the fact of flight, by showing that it was due to defendant's fears that the alleged killing would be summarily avenged, it being the witness's mere opinion. *Lewis* v. *State,* 96 Ala. 6, 11 So. 259.

And *People* v. *Clark,* 84 Cal. 573, 24 Pac. 313, holds that a defendant in a murder prosecution cannot give evidence to account for his flight, unless the prosecution prove the flight as tending to show his guilt.

In *Golin* v. *State,* 37 Tex. Crim. Rep. 90, 38 S. W. 794, it was held that evidence that defendant charged with murder of his wife told a witness that the neighborhood in which the crime was committed was a tough place, and that when he learned that he had been charged with the crime he fled from it because he was afraid he would be mobbed, was inadmissible unless some part of such conversation was brought out by the state.

149. —— refraining from flight, or returning.

The accused is not entitled to show, as tending to establish his innocence, that he had an opportunity to escape, but declined to avail himself of it.[1]

[1] *People* v. *Rathbun,* 21 Wend. 518, 519; *People* v. *Montgomery,* 53 Cal. 576; *Johnson* v. *State,* 94 Ala. 35, 10 So. 667; *Kennedy* v. *State,* 101 Ga. 559, 28 S. E. 979; *State* v. *Wilkins,* 66 Vt. 1, 28 Atl. 323.

Whether he is entitled to show that after flight he returned—query *State* v. *Moncla,* 39 La. Ann. 868, 2 So. 814; *People* v. *Gardiner,* 6 Park. Crim. Rep. 155, 208 (murder; held not error to exclude evidence offered by the accused that other prisoners broke out of the jail where the accused was confined, and tried to induce him to go out, but he refused).

150. Explaining absence from the trial.

The counsel for the accused has a right, when the accused is absent from the trial, and the trial is carried on notwithstanding, to give evidence explaining such absence, in order to preclude any inference that it arose from consciousness of guilt.[1]

[1] *State ex rel. Peacock* v. *Hudson County Quarter Sessions,* 46 N. J. L. 112, Reversing 50 N. J. L. 34, 12 Atl. 270, holding it error to exclude evidence that the departure of the accused was caused by his insanity; judgment therefore reversed.

XIV. Convicts as witnesses.

151. Common-law rule.

At common law neither mere verdict of guilty nor plea of guilty, unless followed by sentence, disqualifies one from testifying as a witness.[1]

[1] *People* v. *McGloin,* 12 Abb. N. C. 172, 91 N. Y. 241.

The rule was the same under the New York and Massachusetts statutes. *Ibid.; Fay* v. *Harlan,* 128 Mass. 244.

In Pennsylvania one is not incompetent as a witness under act of May 23, 1887, P. L. 158, because he has been convicted of murder, and is under sentence of death. *Com.* v. *Clemmer,* 190 Pa. 202, 42 Atl. 675.

In *State* v. *Sullivan,* 20 R. I. 114, 37 Atl. 673, it was held that a witness who had been convicted of the same crime as that for which defendant was on trial, and was serving a life sentence in the state prison therefor, was not incompetent by reason of such facts, but the weight of his testimony was for the jury.

In *Stanley* v. *State,* 39 Tex. Crim. Rep. 482, 46 S. W. 645, a witness was held not to be disqualified because of a conviction of a felony, until sentence had been passed upon and accepted by him, or, if he had appealed, until the affirmance of the judgment, under Tex. Pen. Code, art. 27, providing that an accused person is termed a convict after final condemnation by the highest court of resort which has jurisdiction of his case, and to which he may have thought proper to appeal.

Under Fla. Rev. Stat. § 1096, which provides that persons who may have been convicted in any court of the state of certain designated crimes shall not be competent witnesses prior to sentence, the person offered as a witness is competent, even though upon a trial previously had he was found guilty by the verdict of a jury. *Bishop* v. *State,* 41 Fla. 522, 26 So. 703.

Under 2 Ballinger's Anno. Codes & Statutes (Wash.) § 5992, providing that a person who has been convicted of perjury shall not be a competent witness unless the conviction shall have been reversed, or he shall have received a pardon, one who has been convicted of perjury is incompetent pending appeal on the ground that the judgment of conviction was absolutely void, as such judgment is conclusive against collateral attack. *State* v. *Harras,* 22 Wash. 57, 60 Pac. 58.

Under W. Va. Code, chap. 152, § 17, providing that a person convicted of felony shall not be a witness, unless he has been pardoned or punished therefor, but that a person convicted of felony and sentenced therefor, unless it be for perjury, may be examined as a witness in any criminal prosecution, by leave of court, though he has not been pardoned or served out his sentence, a person convicted of felony other than perjury, and sentenced therefor, may be examined as a witness in a prosecution for homicide, by leave of court, though he has not been pardoned or punished therefor. *State* v. *Hatfield* (W. Va.) 37 S. E. 626.

152. Conviction; how shown as affecting credibility.

Under modern statutes removing the common-law disqualification, the previous conviction for crime of one called as a witness may, for the purpose of affecting the credit due to his testimony, be shown, either by the record or by his cross-examination, upon which he must answer any question relevant to that inquiry; and the party cross-examining him is not concluded by his answer to such a question.[1]

[1] *People* v. *McGloin,* 12 Abb. N. C. 172, 91 N. Y. 241. So held under N. Y. Code Civ. Proc. § 832; *Com.* v. *Ford,* 146 Mass. 131, 15 N. E. 153. And see, generally, Civil Trial Brief, chap. VIII., pp. 176 *et seq.*, as to impeachment of witnesses.

153. Contradicting.

The record of a former conviction received in evidence cannot be contradicted by testimony that the convict was innocent.[1]

[1] *Com.* v. *Gallagher,* 126 Mass. 54. See also *Myers* v. *State,* 92 Ind. 390, holding that it cannot be attacked collaterally.

XV. Corpus delicti.

154. Corpus delicti, what is.

For the purposes of determining the order and competency of proof, the *corpus delicti* involves two elements: (1) Injury to a specific person, property, or right, or a violation of statute; and (2) criminal agency of some one in producing that injury or violation.[1]

[1] The cases of *State* v. *Dickson,* 78 Mo. 438, and *Lovelady* v. *State,* 14 Tex. App. 545, treating the agency of the accused as one element in the *corpus delicti,* are not in harmony with the general use of that phrase.

"The *corpus delicti* in murder is a compound fact, made up of death as a result, and criminal agency of another person as means." *Ruloff* v. *People,* 18 N. Y. 179, 192; *People* v. *Bennett,* 49 N. Y. 137, 143.

"A *corpus delicti* is always made up of two elements, in respect to which there is an important distinction which should never be overlooked in an investigation of this kind. In felonious homicides they consist, first, of the fact of death; and, secondly, of other facts and circumstances showing the criminal agency of another; and in all cases the former constitutes the basis of the latter inquiry, and in general ought to be first proved. And even supposing that a free and voluntary confession may, under some circumstances, be sufficient, as where the body has been destroyed by fire, or consumed by chemical means, or sunk in the sea after life was extinct, yet it could only be so where the particulars given in the confession itself furnish the most satisfactory proof that the party confessing had full knowledge that death had actually taken place through his own acts. No such question arises in this case, and therefore we forbear to pursue the inquiry. Where the fact of death is fully proved by other evidence, no reason is perceived why the free and voluntary confession of the party, if deliberately made, may not be sufficient to establish the other element of the *corpus delicti,* provided it satisfactorily appear that other evidence does not exist." *United States* v. *Williams,* 1 Cliff. 5, 26 Fed. Cas. No. 16,707, where, accordingly, the court did not pass on the question whether a free and voluntary confession, deliberately made, would be sufficient without corroboration, as many facts were proved independently of the confession, tending to show that a crime had been committed. This was a case of homicide on the high seas, and the body was thrown overboard.

155. Order of proof.

In homicide—and the same rule is, in the discretion of the court, applicable in other cases—no evidence against the accused is competent until proof of the *corpus delicti* has been given.[1]

[1] *People* v. *Hall,* 48 Mich. 482, 42 Am. Rep. 477, 12 N. W. 665, holding it error to disregard the rule requiring the *corpus delicti* to be shown before any other testimony is directed against the prisoner. The court says: "In many, and perhaps in most, cases, the order of proof is not very essential. But in cases of homicide, and in others, where justice demands it, the prosecution should not be allowed to proceed further until the death and its character shall have been shown, as far as the testimony can be separately given, and especially so far as can be shown from the post-mortem examination." Hence, held that in homicide evidence of malice on the part of the accused is improper before the fact of death by criminal means has been shown.

So, on a trial for wife murder, where evidence of the intimacy of accused with another woman was prematurely admitted. *People* v. *Millard,* 53 Mich. 67, 18 N. W. 562.

But evidence of pregnancy of the deceased by accused was held admissible, not as going to his motive, but as appertaining directly to the cause of death, in *People* v. *Aikin,* 66 Mich. 460, 33 N. W. 821.

Carl v. *State*, 125 Ala. 89, 28 So. 505, and *People* v. *Hess*, 85 Mich. 128, 48 N. W. 181, hold that error, if any, in admitting evidence of confessions before proof of the *corpus delicti*, is cured by the subsequent introduction of such evidence.

And *People* v. *Swetland*, 77 Mich. 53, 43 N. W. 779, and *People* v. *Whiteman*, 114 Cal. 338, 46 Pac. 99, hold that no prior proof of the *corpus delicti* is necessary in order to admit admissions of a person charged with forgery.

156. Evidence of corpus delicti not incompetent merely because relating to the accused.

To establish the *corpus delicti*, evidence of the condition of the person or object on which the alleged criminal act was done, preceding and leading up to the alleged act, is competent,[1] and the connected conduct of the accused, if part of such evidence, is not to be excluded merely on the ground that the *corpus delicti* must be proven before evidence connecting the accused can be received.[2]

[1] *People* v. *Aikin*, 66 Mich. 460, 33 N. W. 821.

[2] *People* v. *Aikin*, 66 Mich. 460, 33 N. W. 821; *People* v. *O'Neil*, 109 N. Y. 251, 16 N. E. 68 (bribery; where the court says: "Proof of the *corpus delicti* was in this case the same thing as proof of the defendant's connection with the crime. The one could not exist without the other").

And in *State* v. *Davis*, 48 Kan. 1, 28 Pac. 1092, it is held that evidence tending to prove both the *corpus delicti* and defendant's guilt may be introduced at the same time on a murder trial, where the *corpus delicti* cannot well be proved except by evidence tending also to show guilt.

157. Identification.

Identification of the person or property injured is an essential part of the requisite proof of the *corpus delicti*, within the rule as to order of proof, when the allegations of the indictment make such identity a part of the offense charged; otherwise not.[1]

[1] The reason is that it is as truly a crime, and as justly punishable, to kill an unknown person as one known, to steal the property of one unknown as that of one known. Ignorance of identity embarrasses the proof, and may cause fatal variance; but proof of *corpus delicti* may yet be complete, unless the offense charged is by the allegations of the indictment narrowed to an injury to a specified person or thing.

The authorities that appear to be to the contrary on this point are sound in so far as they hold that when the prosecution rests on allegation or proof of injury to a specified person or thing, evidence of identity is thereby made an essential part of the *corpus delicti*.

See, on this subject, *People* v. *Palmer*, 109 N. Y. 111, 16 N. E. 529; *Com.* v. *Webster*, 5 Cush. 295, 52 Am. Dec. 711.

158. Criminal intent.

Criminal intent is not an essential part of the *corpus delicti*, within the rule as to order of proof. It is commonly involved in the proof of *corpus delicti;* not, however, because it is a part thereof, but because the same evidence which proves the *corpus delicti* usually raises a presumption of criminal intent. But the proof of *corpus delicti* may be complete without it, and often is.[1]

[1]Thus, in homicide, evidence that the deceased, an unknown man, fell in the highway, mortally wounded by a bullet from an unknown source, and died, completes the proof of *corpus delicti* (subject to a question of variance if he is alleged in the indictment to be a person known); yet it raises no presumption as to whether the shooting was accidental or intentional, and does not point to the accused as the one who did it. Those elements of proof—identity of the injured, connection of the accused, and criminal intent—may then be shown in any way,—by confession or circumstantial evidence. For an illustration, see *People* v. *Woody*, 45 Cal. 289; *Campbell* v. *People*, 16 Ill. 17, 61 Am. Dec. 49.

159. Circumstantial evidence.

Circumstantial evidence of the *corpus delicti* is competent.[1]

[1]*Martin* v. *State*, 125 Ala. 64, 28 So. 92; *Holland* v. *State*, 39 Fla. 178, 22 So. 298; *Campbell* v. *People*, 159 Ill. 9, 42 N. E. 123; *Laughlin* v. *Com.* 18 Ky. L. Rep. 640, 37 S. W. 590.

But it is rarely if ever sufficient alone. See the following cases: *United States* v. *Williams*, 1 Cliff. 5, 21, Fed. Cas. No. 16,707 (where the homicide was on the high seas, and the body thrown overboard); *People* v. *Alviso*, 55 Cal. 230 (where the body had been consumed in a fire set by accused); *State* v. *Williams*, 52 N. C. (7 Jones L.) 446, 78 Am. Dec. 248 (where charred bones of a human being were found in the ashes of a wood pile); *McCulloch* v. *State*, 48 Ind. 109 (where a human skeleton was found, not quite entire, of the sex of the person charged to have been murdered, and corresponding to his size, and with the skull perforated and cut).

In *People* v. *Wilson*, 3 Park. Crim. Rep. 199, 207, Strong, J., said, charging the jury, that ordinarily there could be no conviction of murder until the body of deceased was discovered. That there were several exceptions to the rule, however, as where the murder had been on the high seas, at a great distance from the shore, and the body had been thrown overboard, or where the body had been entirely consumed by fire, or so far that it was impossible to identify it. But that in the case at bar the exception did not apply, as the scene of the supposed tragedy was near the shore, and there was strong reason to suppose that if a murder had been committed, the body of the deceased would be discovered. This case is cited with approval in *Ruloff* v. *People*, 18 N. Y. 179, 188.

And in *People* v. *Beckwith*, 45 Hun, 422, it was held, in a case of homicide committed prior to the enactment of Penal Code, § 181, that it was competent to establish the identity of the body by presumptive proof. The court said of *Ruloff's Case* that "the question of the identification of a dead body with the person named in the indictment did not arise in the case." And in *People* v. *Beckwith* the judgment of conviction was affirmed against the objection of want of direct proof. And the court of appeals holds the same under that statute. *People* v. *Beckwith*, 108 N. Y. 67, 15 N. E. 53, Affirming 45 Hun, 422. See also *People* v. *Palmer*, 46 Hun, 479.

In *United States* v. *Gibert*, 2 Sumn. 19, 27, Fed. Cas. No. 15,204, Story, J., said of the proposition that there ought to be no conviction of murder unless the murdered body was actually found: It "certainly cannot be admitted as correct in point of common reason or of law, unless courts of justice are to establish a positive rule to screen persons from punishment who may be guilty of the most flagitious crimes." See also *Com.* v. *Webster*, 5 Cush. 295, 52 Am. Dec. 711; *State* v. *Cardelli*, 19 Nev. 319, 10 Pac. 433 (grand larceny of chattel; held, discussing the principle and authorities at length, that direct evidence of the *corpus delicti* was not essential. In this case purchasers of a large ranch, with all the cattle upon it, received information some time after the purchase that cattle, supposed to have come from their ranch, had been sold to a butcher by one occupying a neighboring ranch; and on going to the butcher's they examined the hides which had been taken from five cattle, and identified them by the brands and earmarks as cattle taken from the ranch they had purchased. The main question upon the trial was whether this was sufficient to establish the *corpus delicti*, and it was held sufficient. It should be added that the cattle in this case had not been counted at the time of purchase, but there was some evidence tending to show that these five did not belong to the one who had sold them to the butcher, nor to other adjoining owners).

160. Rebuttal.

To disprove the *corpus delicti* the accused may contradict what is otherwise established against him by matter which in a civil case would amount to a conclusive admission or estoppel.[1]

[1]*State* v. *Hutchinson*, 60 Iowa, 478, 15 N. W. 298, and cases cited. County treasurer not estopped by his own account and vouchers.

161. Opinion evidence.

Testimony of a physician that from his examination it is his opinion that the miscarriage occurred from some foreign interference is admissible to prove the *corpus delicti* of a charge of abortion.[1]

[1]*Hauk* v. *State*, 148 Ind. 238, 46 N. E. 127, Rehearing denied in 148 Ind. 264, 47 N. E. 465.

XVI. Corroboration.

162. Order of proof.

Evidence competent only as corroborative should not be received before the fact which it is intended to corroborate has been shown.[1]

[1]It is essentially repugnant to the usages of courts, and to the declarations of the books by whose authority such testimony is received, that corroborating or confirmatory testimony should precede that which it is to corroborate or confirm. Until the introductory testimony be given, that which is merely corroborative is not relevant, and, in consequence, if objected to cannot be admitted without violating the best settled rules of evidence. *Burr's Trial* (Coomb's ed.) 149.

That hearsay testimony cannot be admitted as part of the affirmative evidence for a prosecution in a criminal case, on the ground that it is in supposed corroboration of the statement of another witness which may be the subject of attack or impeachment, see *State* v. *Guillory,* 45 La. Ann. 31, 12 So. 314.

163. Competency of evidence to corroborate accomplice.

Evidence offered for the purpose of corroborating an accomplice is inadmissible unless it be legally sufficient to corroborate him by showing such acts or admissions of the accused, or such participation with the accomplice at some stage of the transaction, as tend to prove the guilt of the accused.[1]

[1]*Com.* v. *Bosworth,* 22 Pick. 397; *Com.* v. *Holmes,* 127 Mass. 424, S. C., with note, 34 Am. Rep. 391, 400, 404.

So, the testimony of an accomplice may not be corroborated by proving statements that he made in the absence of the party against whom he is testifying. *Clay* v. *State,* 40 Tex. Crim. Rep. 556, 51 S. W. 212.

And on a prosecution for adultery previous statements made by the female in defendant's absence, that she was a married woman, are inadmissible as hearsay, in corroboration of her testimony as an accomplice. *Wiley* v. *State,* 33 Tex. Crim. Rep. 406, 26 S. W. 723.

In *Combs* v. *Com.* 15 Ky. L. Rep. 660, 25 S. W. 590, a prosecution for conspiring with others to commit murder, it was held that the testimony of one of such others, who had been previously convicted of the murder, as to facts and circumstances tending to connect the accused with the conspiracy, could not be corroborated by his own statements made to others in the absence of the accused.

XVII. Declarations of the accused.

See also *supra,* §§ 41, 103.

164. Declarations of the accused competent against him.

The rule that the declarations of a party to the record, in respect to matters within his knowledge, or of which he may be presumed to have knowledge, and relevant to the issue, are always competent against him,—is applicable in criminal proceedings.[1]

It allows such declarations of the accused to be proved against him for the purpose of following them up with evidence of their falsity.[2]

[1]On a trial for incest the acts and declarations of the defendant are competent evidence upon the question of consanguinity. *People* v. *Harriden*, 1 Park. Crim. Rep. 344.

On a trial for larceny it is not error to admit evidence of the acts and declarations of the accused prior to the commission of the act, such prior acts, etc., being the means by which the money was obtained. *Brulo* v. *People*, 16 Hun, 119.

And for other cases recognizing this rule, see *Fuller* v. *State*, 117 Ala. 36, 23 So. 688; *Davidson* v. *State*, 135 Ind. 254, 34 N. E. 972; *Bunckley* v. *State*, 77 Miss. 540, 27 So. 638; *State* v. *Mowry*, 21 R. I. 376, 43 Atl. 871; *Massey* v. *State*, 31 Tex. Crim. Rep. 371, 20 S. W. 758; *Weathersby* v. *State*, 29 Tex. App. 278, 15 S. W. 823; *Muscoe* v. *Com.* 87 Va. 460, 12 S. E. 790.

But that declarations made by defendant charged with murder, while attempting to qualify himself for membership in a supposed band of criminals, in regard to other crimes committed by him, are not admissible against him, see *Com.* v. *Wilson*, 186 Pa. 1, 40 Atl. 283.

[2]*Smith* v. *State*, 29 Fla. 408, 10 So. 894.

In *Coleman* v. *People*, 58 N. Y. 555, Affirming 1 Hun, 596, 4 Thomp. & C. 61, a trial for receiving stolen goods, evidence was held to have been properly admitted of declarations of the accused as to where he procured the goods, and the purpose for which they were intended, which declarations were afterwards proved to be untrue.

On a trial for forgery representations by defendant calculated to create an impression that he was a person of wealth and respectability, made partly to a person afterwards defrauded by the forgery and partly to his brother, who introduced defendant to the firm defrauded, are admissible in behalf of the state in connection with facts and circumstances tending to prove their falsity. *Lascelles* v. *State*, 90 Ga. 347, 16 S. E. 945.

For the incompetency of such declarations, when they amount to confessions of guilt, see *supra*, §§ 103 *et seq.*

For the competency of admissions of distinct facts, see *supra*, §§ 41 *et seq.*

165. Statements before the offense.

The statements of the accused, made prior to the offense, and with reference to its future commission, are not in the nature of confessions, and are admissible without the preliminary proof required for a confession.[1]

[1]*Banks* v. *State*, 13 Tex. App. 182. Here the statements were made in pursuance of a conspiracy with others.

So, on a trial for rape, evidence that about a month before the crime defendant said to another person "that he had a good thing, but it was not black," is admissible where, in connection with other facts, it tends to show the person to whom he referred. *Wood* v. *State*, 28 Tex. App. 61, 12 S. W. 405.

And that declarations of an accused, previous to the offense charged, are admissible in evidence against him, if they express a menace or ill-will towards the party injured, see *Wims* v. *State*, 90 Ala. 623, 8 So. 566.

166. Declarations of intent in act about to be done.

The question whether evidence of a declaration of the accused as to his intent in an act which he was about to do is competent in his favor depends upon whether it is sufficiently connected with the act to form a part of the *res gestæ*.[1]

[1]*Welch* v. *State*, 104 Ind. 347, 3 N. E. 850. Murder; here no evidence having been introduced by the state to show flight or evasion of arrest, held that evidence that the accused publicly stated his intention of going away to get work, and not to avoid prosecution, was inadmissible,—Citing *Hamilton* v. *State*, 36 Ind. 280, 10 Am. Rep. 22; *Austin* v. *Swank*, 9 Ind. 109.

In *United States* v. *Craig*, 4 Wash. C. C. 729, Fed. Cas. No. 14,883, a trial for conspiracy, Washington, J., charged the jury that the declaration of the accused of the purpose for which he was going to the house where he was apprehended among counterfeiters was proper evidence for their consideration, but the materiality of the evidence in relation to the innocence of his intention and acts depended upon the accordance of those declarations with his subsequent conduct; that if they believed his avowal of his purpose was insincere they should disregard his declaration.

167. One speaking on behalf of others.

The words of one assuming to speak for himself and others similarly situated, who are present and silent, may be taken as the declarations of all.[1]

[1]*Pawling* v. *United States*, 4 Cranch, 219, 2 L. ed. 601.

168. Declarations of accused in his own favor.

As a general rule, a statement made by the accused, even as to his own mental state, is not competent in his own favor.[1]

[1]For instances, see *People* v. *Dice*, 120 Cal. 189, 52 Pac. 477; *State* v. *Asbell*, 57 Kan. 398, 46 Pac. 770; *State* v. *Edwards*, 112 N. C. 901, 17 S. E. 521.

In *People* v. *Montgomery*, 13 Abb. Pr. N. S. 207, 251, Mullin, P. J., said:

"I am unable to understand why the declarations of the prisoner as to his want of memory of the occurrence, on the morning of the murder, can be received, so long as his declarations in his own favor are for almost all purposes properly excluded. The physicians testified that in the condition of his mind and body at the time, he would be likely to forget,—it was one of the effects of the disease under which he was laboring. This was all that was admissible. What he may have said as to the forgetfulness of the transactions of the morning was wholly incompetent."

But in *People* v. *Hawes*, 98 Cal. 648, 33 Pac. 791, a trial for murder, a voluntary statement by the defendant, made just after the commission of the crime, and consistent with the defense set up, that the deceased did it himself, was held to be admissible in evidence.

169. Except as part of the res gestae.

Declarations made by the accused as part of the *res gestæ* of an act which is already properly in evidence are competent in his own favor.[1]

[1]See *infra*, § 266. And see the following cases, where the declarations were held incompetent as not being *res gestæ*: *United States* v. *Cross*, 9 Mackey, 365 (acts and declarations of a person when he was arrested for murder, such as acts tending to show grief or mental distress, and declarations that he did not shoot deceased); *Stevenson* v. *United States*, 29 C. C. A. 600, 52 U. S. App. 647, 86 Fed. 106 (conversation and declarations of one accused of murder, after his arrest); *State* v. *Beard*, 126 Mo. 548, 29 S. W. 592 (self-serving statements made by defendant on trial for murder, two days after the commission of the crime); *Angus* v. *State*, 29 Tex. App. 52, 14 S. W. 443 (acts and declarations of defendant in the presence of third persons, but in the absence of deceased, with respect to antecedent acts and declarations of deceased evidencing his intention to kill defendant); *Gallaher* v. *State*, 28 Tex. App. 247, 12 S. W. 1087 (declarations made by an accused to his counsel, and advice given to him by the latter in a litigation with deceased, offered to show an absence of motive); *State* v. *Moore*, 104 N. C. 743, 10 S. E. 183 (what a prisoner says when arrested).

170. — the spontaneous expression of condition.

The natural and impulsive utterances of a person in apparent suffering, made to those who are in attendance or present in the performance of offices of kindness, for the purpose of giving relief or alleviation, are proper evidence of the actual pressure of the symptoms which the sufferer describes.[1]

[1]Woodruff, J., in *Teachout* v. *People*, 41 N. Y. 7 (on a trial for murder by poisoning, held it not error to prove complaints uttered by deceased. though not made to a physician during medical treatment); *State* v.

Mackey, 12 Or. 154, 6 Pac. 648 (holding declarations of one accused of murder, made at the time of the alleged killing, competent to prove his condition, ills, pains, and symptoms, whether arising from sickness or an injury by accident or violence at the time of the alleged killing); *Com.* v. *Jardine*, 143 Mass. 567, 10 N. E. 250 (assault; testimony tending to show that defendant was acting in self-defense, and that he was severely beaten, having been admitted without objection, held competent to show that, during his confinement, he made complaints of pain). And see note to *Travelers' Ins. Co.* v. *Mosley*, 19 L. ed. U. S. 437.

171. — explanation of possession.

Where the possession of property has been shown against the accused, as tending to prove guilt, his declarations made while in possession, and tending to explain his possession, are competent in his own favor.[1]

[1]*Bennett* v. *People*, 96 Ill. 602 (otherwise as to his statements respecting the source of his title); *Allen* v. *State*, 73 Ala. 23; *Bryant* v. *State*, 116 Ala. 445, 23 So. 40.

The declarations of a defendant who is found in possession of stolen property, explanatory of his possession, are for the consideration of the jury, together with all the other evidence, in determining the question of his guilt or innocence. *Bryant* v. *State*, 116 Ala. 445, 23 So. 40.

But upon a trial for theft of a cow, statements explanatory of his possession of the cow, made by the accused after he had sold it to another, are inadmissible. *Williams* v. *State*, 105 Ala. 96, 17 So. 86.

172. — completing statement already in evidence.

Where a statement of the accused has been put in evidence against him, any other declaration made by him at the same time, and tending to qualify or explain that which has been proved against him, is competent in his favor.[1]

[1]*Pharr* v. *State*, 10 Tex. App. 485; Wharton, Crim. Ev. § 691; *Crite* v. *Com.* (Va.) 12 Rep. 575 (murder); *Stevenson* v. *United States*, 29 C. C. A. 600, 52 U. S. App. 647, 86 Fed. 106.

XVIII. Declarations of confederates.

173. General rule—narrative of the past.

The general rule that when sufficient proof of a conspiracy has been given to establish the fact prima facie in the opinion of the judge, the acts and declarations of each conspirator in the furtherance of the common object are competent evidence against all, only applies to declarations made in the furtherance of the prosecution of the common object or constituting a part of the *res gestæ* of some act done for that purpose, and already properly in evidence.[1]

It does not admit a narrative of a past event, though made while acting in pursuance of the common purpose,[2] unless it was part of the preconcerted plan that such narrative should be given.

[1]*People* v. *Davis,* 56 N. Y. 95; *Hunter* v. *State,* 112 Ala. 77, 21 So. 65; *People* v. *Lane,* 101 Cal. 513, 36 Pac. 16; *Jenkins* v. *State,* 35 Fla. 737, 18 So. 182; *Baptist* v. *State,* 109 Ga. 546, 35 S. E. 658; *State* v. *Corcoran* (Idaho) 61 Pac. 1034; *State* v. *Grant,* 86 Iowa, 216, 53 N. W. 120; *State* v. *McGee,* 81 Iowa, 17, 46 N. W. 764; *State* v. *Rogers,* 54 Kan. 683, 39 Pac. 219; *Com.* v. *Smith,* 151 Mass. 491, 24 N. E. 677; *People* v. *Peckens,* 153 N. Y. 576, 47 N. E. 883; *State* v. *Turner,* 119 N. C. 841, 25 S. E. 810; *Seville* v. *State,* 49 Ohio St. 117, 15 L. R. A. 516, 30 N. E. 621; *Carpenter* v. *State* (Tex. Crim. App.) 51 S. W. 227; *McKenzie* v. *State,* 32 Tex. Crim. Rep. 568, 25 S. W. 426; *People* v. *Hampton,* 4 Utah, 258, 9 Pac. 508.

[2]*People* v. *Murphy,* 3 N. Y. Crim. Rep. 338.

So, a statement made by one of the persons engaged in a robbery, the day after the offense was committed, as to the location of the stolen property, is admissible against another party to the robbery, where such statement was made in pursuance of an agreement between the party against whom it is offered and the witness that the latter should accompany the person who made the statement, and that he would describe to him the location of the stolen property, the property having been found at the place indicated in the statement. *People* v. *Brady* (Cal.) 36 Pac. 949.

And on a conspiracy to defraud by forged notes, and divide the proceeds, statements by one of the conspirators, after the forged paper was issued, but before disposition or division of the property obtained for it, with reference to future contemplated acts to conceal the fraud so as to enable them to consummate the disposition of the fruits of the crime and division of the proceeds,—are admissible against the others, although they refer to a past act committed in execution of the conspiracy. *State* v. *Thaden,* 43 Minn. 253, 45 N. W. 447.

And where there is evidence tending to show a conspiracy to burn a house for the purpose of obtaining the insurance, evidence of acts and declarations of some of the conspirators, after the fire, in regard to the disposition of the property, is admissible as against all, as being in furtherance of the common design. *Com.* v. *Smith,* 151 Mass. 491, 24 N. E. 677.

So, also, acts and declarations of coconspirators to commit larceny, and divide the proceeds, are admissible against each other, although made after the larceny, when the objects of the conspiracy were not then fully accomplishd by the division of the stolen property. *Baker* v. *State,* 80 Wis. 416, 50 N. W. 518.

In *State* v. *Pratt,* 121 Mo. 566, 26 S. W. 556, a prosecution for forging a deed pursuant to a conspiracy between defendant and others to obtain a loan of money thereon, evidence of subsequent transactions regarding the land trade and letters between defendant's coconspirators was held admissible in evidence against defendant, where the criminal design was still pending and unaccomplished, although he was not shown to have been a participant in such subsequent transaction.

174. Limit of time.

The rule does not admit declarations made after the parties ceased to act together in furtherance of the common object.[1]

And the burden is on the prosecution to show when they were made.[2]

[1]*Stone* v. *People,* 13 Hun, 263 (deposition of one conspirator taken upon his examination before a magistrate, upon his being arrested, incompetent because made long after the accused and he had ceased to act together in furtherance of the conspiracy; conviction reversed); *United States* v. *Gunnell,* 5 Mackey, 196 (conspiracy to defraud; new trial granted because the declarations admitted were after the act); *Rowland* v. *State,* 45 Ark. 135 (holding, therefore, that the flight of the confederate could not be proved against the accused); *People* v. *Farrell,* 14 Utah, 414, 40 Pac. 703; *Brown* v. *United States,* 150 U. S. 93, 37 L. ed. 1010, 14 Sup. Ct. Rep. 37; *Everage* v. *State,* 113 Ala. 102, 21 So. 404; *People* v. *Opie,* 123 Cal. 294, 55 Pac. 989; *Dean* v. *State,* 130 Ind. 237, 29 N. E. 911; *State* v. *Grant,* 86 Iowa, 216, 53 N. W. 120; *State* v. *Young,* 55 Kan. 349, 40 Pac. 659; *Twyman* v. *Com.* 17 Ky. L. Rep. 1038, 33 S. W. 409; *State* v. *Palmer,* 79 Minn. 428, 82 N. W. 685; *State* v. *Harris,* 150 Mo. 56, 51 S. W. 481; *State* v. *English,* 14 Mont. 399, 36 Pac. 815; *State* v. *Hinkle,* 33 Or. 93, 54 Pac. 155; *State* v. *Rice,* 49 S. C. 418, 27 S. E. 452.

So, a statement by one of two persons charged with homicide, made after the killing, and while both were under arrest, is not admissible in evidence against the other, although made in his presence, and not denied by him. *Pryor* v. *State,* 40 Tex. Crim Rep. 643, 51 S. W. 375.

[2]*State* v. *Stair,* 87 Mo. 268, 56 Am. Rep. 449, 452. Murder; in order to render the declarations of one confederate admissible against the other, the state must show that such declarations were made while in the prosecution of their common purpose; and when the state fails to show when they were made, such declarations are inadmissible,—Citing *People* v. *Thoms,* 3 Park. Crim. Rep. 256; *State* v. *Duncan,* 64 Mo. 266. New trial granted.

175. Guilt of declarant, as principal.

The rule does not exclude admissions of the confederate when offered only to show his guilt, as a principal, in order to satisfy the common-law rule that the guilt of the principal must be shown on the trial of an accessory.[1]

[1]*United States* v. *Hartwell,* 3 Cliff. 221, Fed. Cas. No. 15,318. Here prin-

cipal and accessories had been jointly indicted, and, before the jury were impaneled, the principal pleaded *nolo contendere.* The court (Clifford, J.), said: "Confessions of the principal are certainly admissible to prove his own guilt, when the accessory is tried with him, and, if so, it cannot be admitted that the principal can acquit the accessory, in cases where there is no other sufficient evidence to prove his own guilt than his confessions, by pleading guilty, and retiring from the bar under his recognizance."

But that declarations of a codefendant, made after arrest, are inadmissible in behalf of the defense in a criminal prosecution, see *Crosby* v. *People,* 137 Ill. 325, 27 N. E. 49.

176. Antecedent declarations.

A declaration made before the formation of a combination is not made evidence against one afterward joining the combination, unless knowledge of the declaration is brought home to him.[1]

[1]*Cox* v. *State,* 8 Tex. App. 254, 34 Am. Rep. 746.

But evidence of what other conspirators had planned before defendant joined them is admissible against him, where he subsequently acted with them, and the same purpose was expressed and executed while he was with them. *Holtz* v. *State,* 76 Wis. 99, 44 N. W. 1107.

So, the acts and declarations of one of the members of a subsequently formed conspiracy to commit a crime are not admissible against a coconspirator, although one who joins a conspiracy already existent thereby ratifies any acts done or threats previously made by the conspirators in furtherance of a common design. *State* v. *May,* 142 Mo. 135, 43 S. W. 637.

177. Offense incidental to a continuing conspiracy.

On the trial of an indictment for an offense committed pursuant to a continuing conspiracy for the commission of successive offenses, evidence of such acts and declarations of a confederate, though made after the consummation of the particular offense on trial, is competent.[1]

[1]*Card* v. *State,* 109 Ind. 415, 9 N. E. 591. Forgery; evidence of subsequent forgeries by same combination competent.

So, in an action charging a conspiracy to rob and defraud from beginning to end of a transaction, any communications from one alleged conspirator to another, while the conspiracy was in progress, and relating to its subject-matter, are admissible in evidence as a part of the *res gestæ. Zellerbach* v. *Allenberg,* 99 Cal. 57, 33 Pac. 786.

178. General design enough.

It is not necessary that the common design should be shown to have specifically contemplated the details of the particular offense charged to have been committed in pursuance of it.

Proof of a general design, uniting both persons in a common criminal intent, in pursuance of which the act charged was committed, is enough.[1]

[1]In *State* v. *Morton*, 27 Vt. 310, 65 Am. Dec. 201, 202, an indictment of several for forgery upon a bank check, testimony of an agreement between the defendants to procure money by means of forged paper from banks, without reference to any particular one, is admissible for the purpose of implicating each defendant in the acts of the others in carrying forward the common design. Compare a somewhat similar question under *infra*, §§ 237–243.

Where there is sufficient evidence to justify the conclusion that several persons were acting with a common purpose and a common design to commit a crime, although there is no proof of a previous combination or confederacy to commit the offense in question, the conduct and actions of the several parties, and the parts they severally performed in the actual perpetration of the crime, are sufficient to make the acts and declarations of each, from the commencement to the consummation of the offense, evidence against the others. *Kelley* v. *People*, 55 N. Y. 565, 14 Am. Rep. 342, Affirming *Armsby* v. *People*, 2 Thomp. & C. 157; *People* v. *Van Tassel*, 156 N. Y. 561, 51 N. E. 274. See also *Hall* v. *State*, 3 Lea, 552.

179. Guilt of declarant as against himself—names of others.

Admissions are not to be excluded because made after the parties ceased to act together in furtherance of the common purpose, if offered as evidence only against the one who made them.[1]

If the admission or declaration mentions the other defendants it may be put in evidence, without omitting their names, the jury being instructed that they should only consider it against the defendant who made it.[2]

[1]*People* v. *Arnold*, 46 Mich. 268, 9 N. W. 406 (Cooley, J., said: "The fact that the offense is joint cannot exclude admissions. They are admissible against the party making them, and the court must protect the other by cautioning the jury not to permit the confession of his alleged associate to prejudice him"); *Lawson* v. *State*, 20 Ala. 64, 56 Am. Dec. 182.

[2]*State* v. *Dodson*, 16 S. C. 453, which followed *State* v. *Workman*, 15 S. C. 540, where this is shown to be the rules sanctioned by the English authorities and eminent text writers.

And it is error to admit such declarations over objection, without instructing the jury that they are competent only against the defendant who made them. *State* v. *Collins*, 121 N. C. 667, 28 S. E. 520.

180. Assent of one to confession by the other.

The assent of one of two accused that the other may confess is in itself a confession within this rule.[1]

[1]*Com.* v. *Knapp,* 9 Pick. 496, 20 Am. Dec. 491–496. This question was fully argued and decided, although the judgment did not turn upon it, because it arose on a misapprehension of the facts.

So, a statement by one of several persons concerned in a murder is admissible against another, where it is read over to the latter, and he expressly confirms the same, without compulsion or promise. *State* v. *Schmidt,* 136 Mo. 644, 38 S. W. 719.

181. Silence and conduct.

The rule applies as well to silence[1] and to conduct[2] as to express admissions.

[1]*People* v. *Murphy,* 3 N. Y. Crim. Rep. 338 (holding the silence of a confederate when spoken to on the subject, in the absence of the other, but while both were acting together in furtherance of the common purpose, competent against the other); *State* v. *Johnson,* 35 La. Ann. 842 (holding the statement of one in the presence of the other, and the silence of the latter, at a time after they had ceased to act together, competent against the latter). And see *infra,* §§ 282–291.

[2]*Reg.* v. *Blake,* 6 Q. B. 126, 137 (entries in books).

182. Degree of connection.

The least degree of collusion in the common purpose is sufficient to let in such declarations of one of the parties as evidence against the other.[1]

[1]*State* v. *Anderson,* 92 N. C. 737, 747.

183. Order of proof.

The court has power, in its discretion, to admit evidence of the declarations, before evidence of the combination has been received; and if the necessary evidence of combination is afterward supplied, the departure from regular order will not be reversible error, the accused not having been prejudiced in the end.[1]

[1]*State* v. *Ward,* 19 Nev. 297, 10 P. 133 (grand larceny). *People* v. *Compton,* 123 Cal. 403, 56 Pac. 44; *State* v. *True Nell,* 79 Mo. App. 243. And see *Avery* v. *State,* 10 Tex. App. 199; *State* v. *Anderson,* 92 N. C. 732; *State* v. *Walker,* 98 Mo. 95, 9 N. W. 646, 11 N. W. 1133; *Place* v. *Minster,* 65 N. Y. 89 (civil case).

People v. *Monnais,* 17 Abb. Pr. 345, holds that evidence of acts and declarations of an accomplice in the absence of the principal is properly received, if followed by evidence of complicity sufficient to be submitted to the jury. The court (Leonard, J.) said: "There was sufficient evidence, before the case was submitted to the jury, to warrant the conclusion that the two were acting in combination when the offense was committed. The objection related only to the order of proof."

The power was doubted by a *dictum* in *People* v. *Parish,* 4 Denio, 153. And see *Rowland* v. *State,* 45 Ark. 132. But it is now generally understood that it exists.

The court ought, however, to hold to the strict order of proof with a rigor proportioned to the gravity of the charge; and satisfactory reasons should appear before admitting damaging evidence apparently incompetent, upon the promise of the prosecution to render it competent by subsequent evidence.

And in *Murphy* v. *State,* 86 Wis. 626, 57 N. W. 361, it was expressly held that upon a trial of several persons for burglary, an existing conspiracy or confederacy between the defendants to commit crime must be proved before the fact that part of the stolen property was found on one of them was admissible as evidence against the others.

184. Preliminary proof.

The confederacy which renders the declaration admissible may be shown by circumstantial evidence,[1] or by the uncorroborated testimony of an accomplice.[2]

And it is enough to give evidence making a prima facie case of combination sufficient to go to the jury.[3]

[1]In *Kelley* v. *People,* 55 N. Y. 565, 14 Am. Rep. 342, which affirmed *Armsby* v. *People,* 2 Thomp. & C. 157, a case of larceny, the court said: "A conspiracy may be proved, as other facts are proved, by circumstantial evidence, and parties performing disconnected overt acts, all contributing to the same result and the consummation of the same offense, may, by the circumstances and their general connection or otherwise, be satisfactorily shown to be conspirators and confederates in the commission of the offense." And *Adams* v. *People,* 9 Hun, 89, holds that for this purpose evidence of intimate and confidential relations between them is competent.

In *United States* v. *Gooding,* 12 Wheat. 460, 6 L. ed. 693, an indictment for slave trading, Story, J., said: "In general, the rules of evidence in criminal and civil cases are the same. Whatever the agent does, within the scope of his authority, binds his principal, and is deemed his act. It must, indeed, be shown that the agent has the authority, and that the act is within its scope; but, these being conceded or proved, either by the course of business or by express authorization, the same conclusion arises, in point of law, in both cases. Nor is there any authority for confining the rule to civil cases. On the contrary, it is the known and familiar principle of criminal jurisprudence that he who commands, or procures, a crime to be done, if it be done, is guilty of the crime, and the act is his act. This is so true that even the agent may be innocent, when the procurer or principal may be convicted of guilt, as in the case of infants or idiots employed to administer poison. The proof of the command or procurement may be direct or indirect, positive or circumstantial; but this is matter for the consideration of the jury, and not of legal competency. So in cases of conspiracy and riot, when once the conspiracy or combination is established, the act of one conspirator in the prosecution of the enterprise is considered the act of all, and is evidence against all. Each is deemed to consent to, or command what is done by, any other, in furtherance of the common object." And see *Marler* v. *State*, 67 Ala. 55, 42 Am. Rep. 75; *Mussel Slough Case*, 5 Fed. 680; *Tarbox* v. *State*, 38 Ohio St. 581 (holding evidence that the same persons were, shortly prior to the time of the alleged crime, engaged in a conspiracy to commit crimes of a like character, competent).

So, acts of different persons who are shown to have known each other, or to have been in communication with each other, directed towards the accomplishment of the same object,—especially if by the same means and in the same manner,—may be satisfactory proof of a conspiracy. *Com.* v. *Smith*, 163 Mass. 411, 40 N. E. 189.

In *Murphy* v. *State*, 86 Wis. 626, 57 N. W. 361, it was held that proof that several persons accused of burglary were tramps and vagrants, and associated and confederated together in the commission of several crimes, down to within two hours of the burglary, and within 80 rods of the building within which it was committed; and that after the burglary they remained substantially together, wandering through the country until their arrest; and that when arrested they were sitting around a fire, and one of them was armed with a revolver; the carrying of such revolver by a tramp and the building of a fire being criminal offenses,—was sufficient evidence of a conspiracy and confederacy between them to render admissible against all the finding of a portion of the stolen property upon one of them.

•For this purpose the court is not at liberty to reject the uncorroborated testimony of self-confessed accomplices and members of the conspiracy. Nor can the court declare, as matter of law, that such testimony is not worthy of belief unless corroborated. The credibility of such testimony is a question for the jury, under the advice and direction of the court; and is not a question of law for the court. *United States* v. *McKee*, 3 Dill. 546, Fed. Cas. No. 15,685. This was on the trial, the court reserving till the close of the testimony the statement of the law to the jury on the point, in case of the accomplices not being corroborated.

In *Com.* v. *Crowninshield*, 10 Pick. 497, it is held that it is sufficient that the conspiracy is shown by the testimony of a competent witness. For this purpose the court will not inquire into the credibility of the testimony.

And *State* v. *Mushrush*, 97 Iowa, 444, 66 N. W. 746, holds that evidence of statements made within hearing of defendant, to effect that one of the party would make an assault upon a certain person, and that all the party would fight together if he needed help, is admissible as tending to show a conspiracy to which defendant was a party, although he did not make the statements or expressly assent to them.

Contra, Casey v. *State*, 37 Ark. 85, holding that declarations of an alleged accomplice, made in the absence of the accused, are inadmissible against him where the only evidence connecting the alleged accomplice with the crime charged is the testimony of another accomplice, because by statute the defendant could not be convicted upon the uncorroborated evidence of an accomplice. Judgment reversed. Compare *supra*, §§ 162, 163.

Ormsby v. *People*, 53 N. Y. 472, holding that to make the acts and declarations of an alleged confederate competent evidence against the accused, it must be proved prima facie, or such evidence given as to make the question one proper for the determination of the jury, that the accused has conspired with the confederates to commit the offense; conviction reversed for lack of such proof. To the same effect, see *Luttrell* v. *State*, 31 Tex. Crim. Rep. 493, 21 S. W. 248.

In *Farrell* v. *People*, 21 Hun, 485, Affirmed without opinion in 84 N. Y. 656, the court says: "There was sufficient evidence submitted to the jury to warrant the conclusion that these persons were thus acting in combination when the offense was committed."

Under the Oregon statute (1 Hill's (Or.) Anno. Laws, § 706) subd. 6, providing that after proof of a conspiracy the declaration or act of a conspirator against his coconspirator, and relating to the conspiracy, may be given in evidence, it is held that evidence which, reasonably and to the satisfaction of the trial judge, tends to create an inference of the existence of an unlawful agreement to commit a crime, is sufficient to permit the introduction of evidence of declarations and acts of alleged coconspirators with defendant. *State* v. *Moore*, 32 Or. 65, 48 Pac. 468. This case holds that a sufficient prima facie showing of a conspiracy to commit a larceny to render the acts and declarations of an alleged coconspirator admissible against defendant under this statute, making such evidence admissible after proof of a conspiracy, is made by evidence that the defendant and the alleged coconspirator arrived together in the city where the crime was committed, and leased a room for one week, which they jointly occupied; that the former, on the day of the larceny, called at the store where the crime was committed, and had a bill changed, and joined the defendant on the street; that the defendant later called at the store and assumed such a position as to obstruct the view of the attendant with whom he was conversing of the stolen money, which was lying upon the desk in the same place as when the bill was changed; and that shortly afterwards it was discovered that the money was missing.

People v. *Daniels*, 105 Cal. 262, 38 Pac. 720, holds that evidence of a conversation between alleged conspirators with defendant is admissible after evidence is introduced tending to prove a conspiracy, although a conspiracy is not shown to have actually been formed.

XIX. Decoys, detectives, informers, and spies as witnesses.

185. Competency.

A person who took part in the act constituting the offense, as a decoy, detective, informer, or spy, is not thereby rendered incompetent as a witness.[1]

Nor is he an accomplice within the rule requiring corroboration.[2]

[1]See authorities under *post*, Division XLII.

A decoy letter shown to have been delivered was held competent, as an act accompanying the transaction, equally as if it had been an oral message, in *McCarney* v. *People*, 83 N. Y. 408, 413, 414, 38 Am. Rep. 458. Letter with fictitious address not "mail matter." *United States* v. *Denicke*, 35 Fed. 407.

[2]*Com.* v. *Willard*, 22 Pick. 476; *People* v. *Smith*, 28 Hun, 626, and cases cited, Affirmed on this opinion in 92 N. Y. 665.

That the suspicions or beliefs of a person claiming to be a detective, of the guilt of defendant, whether expressed on or off the witness stand, are not admissible for the purpose of showing that he was not an accomplice although he pretended to conspire with the defendant, see *State* v. *Kilburn*, 16 Utah, 187, 52 Pac. 277.

186. Confession to decoy.

Where an officer, with the connivance of the public prosecutor, has himself arrested on a fictitious charge, and while in jail gains the confidence of the accused, and obtains from him a confession, such confession is not therefore incompetent to go to the jury.[1]

[1]*State* v. *Brooks*, 92 Mo. 542, 5 S. W. 257, 330. And see *supra*, § 124.

187. Right of explanation.

When the testimony of a decoy, detective, or other person who took part in the act constituting the offense, for the purpose of procuring evidence, has been received, the accused has a right to give full explanation.[1]

[1]In *Saunders* v. *People*, 38 Mich. 218, it appeared that the accused was arrested as a result of being decoyed into the commission of the offense. Cooley, J., said: " If he [the officer] testified truly, he was apparently conniving at and assisting in the crime charged; and though he may have done this, as he says, not by way of enticing defendant into crime, but only by allowing him the opportunity he sought and requested, yet it placed him in an equivocal position, and the jury ought to have had the benefit of all the light the former dealings of the parties would have thrown upon the transaction."

188. Participation, when a defense.

Participation in the act constituting the offense, by one who took part for the purpose of procuring evidence, is a defense, when any act which is an essential element in the offense itself was performed, not by the accused, but wholly by the detective,[1] or when the offense consisted in an entry or taking possession without consent of owner or occupant, and the participation of the detective manifested such consent.[2]

[1]In *State* v. *Jansen*, 22 Kan. 498, a detective having disclosed to the police the place of an intended burglary, the proprietor of the building, upon the direction of the police, left unfastened the rear door, which had usually been locked and barred in the night, and the defendant with the detective entered that door, the defendant lifting and opening it, and were arrested by the police and proprietor, who were lying in wait inside. It was held not error to refuse to charge that this was not burglary, and leave it to the jury whether the proprietor consented.

The court distinguished *Speiden* v. *State*, 3 Tex. App. 156, 30 Am. Rep. 126, saying: "In this case, the detectives did the breaking by the procurement of the bank officials, who not only consented thereto, but paid the detectives to do their bidding in working up the case—a portion of the programme in doing which was to break open and enter the building." The court also said: "Counsel have cited and commented upon several cases in which detectives figured, and in which the defendants were adjudged guiltless of the crime charged. But this feature distinguishes them,—that some act essential to the crime charged was in fact done by the detective, and not by the defendant, and this act not being imputable to the defendant, the latter's guilt was not made out."

[2]In *Speiden* v. *State*, 3 Tex. App. 156, S. C., 30 Am. Rep. 126, with note collecting other cases, a banker, suspecting defendant of an intention to rob his bank, employed detectives to act as decoys, and induce him to enter the bank with intent to rob it. It was held that the evidence was insufficient to warrant a conviction for burglary.

In *Johnson* v. *State*, 3 Tex. App. 590, the court distinguished *Speiden* v. *State*, 3 Tex. App. 156, 30 Am. Rep. 126, saying of it: "The facts . . . show that defendant had entered the bank at the solicitation of a detective rightfully in possession, with the consent of the owner;" and of the case at bar said: "That defendant had actually entered into an agreement . . . to burglariously enter the house . . . with intent to commit a theft, and the offense of conspiracy is complete, although the parties conspiring do not proceed to effect the object for which they have so unlawfully combined, The fact of such conspiracy once being established, the subsequent consent of the owner (or those acting for him) for the conspirators to enter the building will not affect their guilt in the least, unless the evidence shows that Higgins & Garwood, or the detective employed by them, suggested the offense, or in some way created the original intent or agreement to commit the offense as charged."

In *State* v. *Jansen*, 22 Kan. 498, the court thus explains *Reg.* v. *Johnson*, Car & M. 218: "All that the court pretends to decide is that where a door was opened by an employee of the owner of the house, acting under the orders of policemen in waiting, and thereafter the accused entered through the door so opened, no burglary was committed. Certainly not, because the opening of the door was legally done by an authorized person, without any illegal opening or breaking."

In the same case (*State* v. *Jansen*, 22 Kan. 498) the court thus distinguished *Allen* v. *State*, 40 Ala. 344, 91 Am. Dec. 476: "The detective unlocked and opened the door with the keys furnished by the owner, who was the detective's employer. Here there was no breaking. In this case (*Allen* v. *State*) the defendant [Allen] was assiduously persuaded to engage in the enterprise by the detective, who was acting under orders from his employer. The defendant was reluctant to undertake and timid in the execution of the alleged criminal act; so reticent and fearful was he, in fact, that about all he did was to accompany the detective to the building and witness what were unquestionably the authorized acts of the detective."

In *United States* v. *Whittier*, 7 Cent. L. J. 51, there is a *dictum* by Treat, J., that "a violation of law by one person, in order to detect an offender, will not excuse the latter, or be available to him as a defense."

189. Encouragement by complainant.

The mere fact that the complainant gave encouragement or opportunity for the commission of the offense is not a defense, if he did not induce the original intent.[1]

[1]In *Dodge* v. *Brittain*, Meigs, 84, an action for malicious prosecution, the court says, on the question whether plaintiff had committed a larceny: "No larceny can be committed of property the possession of which the owner parts from voluntarily. . . . They [the cases] none of them go further than to say that a man may direct a servant to appear to encourage the design of the thieves, and lead them on till the offense is complete, so long as he did not induce the original intent, but only provided for its discovery after it was formed. . . . In all these cases the possession of the property remains with the owner, and a trespass is committed in the taking by the thief. But such would not be the case if the master had directed the servant to deliver the property to the thief, instead of directing him to furnish facilities for his arriving at the place where it was kept."

In *Sanders* v. *State* (Tenn.) 30 Am. Rep. 130, note, the prosecutor was informed that the defendants were coming at a certain time to steal meat from his smokehouse. He left the door unfastened, and concealed himself with others near by, and so caught the defendants in the act of stealing; held not error to charge that if the stealing was the act of one E., and with the consent of the prosecutor, and the defendants only aided and abetted E., the defendants were not guilty; but otherwise if the plan was only to detect the crime, and not bring it about. The court held that a man may direct a servant to appear to encourage a design of the thieves, and to lead them on till the offense is complete, so long as he did not induce the original intent, but only provided for its discovery after it was formed. That if a man is suspected of an intent to steal, and another, to try him, leaves property in his way, which he takes, the taker is guilty of larceny. Otherwise if the master directs the servant to deliver the property to the thief, instead of directing him to furnish facilities for his arriving at the place where it is kept. See also *People* v. *Hanselman*, 76 Cal. 460, 18 Pac. 425. Of this case the editor in 2 Harvard Law Review says: "It is to be noticed in this case that probably the detective did not intend to pass the title to, nor yet to make the defendant a bailee of, the money taken. If that is so, the decision seems to be right."

In *Bell* v. *State* (Tex. Crim. App.) 56 S. W. 913, a prosecution for violating the local-option law, the complaining witness was asked on cross-examination if it was not a fact that when he purchased the whisky from defendant he intended to induce him to make the sale, and then prosecute him for it, to which he replied that "defendant had the reputation of constantly violating the local-option law." It was held that the answer should have been excluded as hearsay, and as tending to put in issue defendant's reputation, which issue had not been raised by him.

XX. Demeanor.

190. Competency.

Evidence of the demeanor of the accused, soon after the commission of the offense or at the time of his arrest, is competent as bearing upon the question of his consciousness of guilt;[1] but not in his own favor.[2]

[1]*Greenfield* v. *People*, 85 N. Y. 75, 39 Am. Rep. 636 (on trial for wife murder, held not error to show the prisoner's indifference and want of feeling immediately after the homicide); *State* v. *Brabham*, 108 N. C. 793, 13 S. E. 217. And see *supra*, § 140.

[2]The conduct or demeanor of accused at or about the time he was accused or arrested is not admissible in his favor. *Henry* v. *State*, 107 Ala. 22, 19 So. 23.

191. How proved.

An ordinary witness may state what he understood by expressions, gestures, and intonations, to which he has testified, and to whom they applied.[1]

[1]*Com.* v. *Sturtivant*, 117 Mass. 122, 19 Am. Rep. 401. See also *Leonard* v. *Allen*, 11 Cush. 241.

To the contrary as to intonations, *Messner* v. *People*, 45 N. Y. 1, holding that a witness, who heard cries proceeding from the house of the prisoner in the night, cannot testify whether the person was crying from joy or grief. The question should not call for the conjecture of the witness as to the cause of the cries, but for a description of them. See also *supra*, §§ 140–150.

XXI. Dying declarations.

192. Belief in impending death.

Declarations of one, to be admissible as dying declarations, must have been made under a sense or belief of his impending death.[1] But it is not necessary that the defendant should have expressly said in so many words that he was speaking under a belief of his impending death; it will be enough if it satisfactorily appears in any mode that the declarations were made under that sanction.[2] Nor, on the other hand, is the explicit statement of the declarant that he was going to die, alone, always enough to show that the declarations were really made under the belief of impending death.[3]

[1] *McQueen* v. *State*, 94 Ala. 50, 10 So. 433; *Evans* v. *State*, 58 Ark. 47, 22 S. W. 1026; *People* v. *Hawes*, 98 Cal. 648, 33 Pac. 791; *State* v. *Cronin*, 64 Conn. 293, 29 Atl. 536; *State* v. *Young*, 104 Iowa, 730, 74 N. W. 693; *Com.* v. *Thompson*, 159 Mass. 56, 33 N. E. 1111; *State* v. *Fletcher*, 24 Or. 295, 33 Pac. 575; *State* v. *Sullivan*, 20 R. I. 114, 37 Atl. 673; *State* v. *Baldwin*, 15 Wash. 15, 45 Pac. 650; *Sims* v. *State*, 36 Tex. Crim. Rep. 154, 36 S. W. 256; *Joslin* v. *State*, 75 Miss. 838, 23 So. 515.

[2] *State* v. *Sullivan*, 20 R. I. 114, 37 Atl. 673; *Justice* v. *State*, 99 Ala. 180, 13 So. 658; *Lester* v. *State*, 37 Fla. 382, 20 So. 232; *State* v. *Evans*, 124 Mo. 397, 28 S. W. 8; *Basye* v. *State*, 45 Neb. 261, 63 N. W. 811; *State* v. *Russell*, 13 Mont. 164, 32 Pac. 854; *Com.* v. *Matthews*, 89 Ky. 287, 12 S. W. 333.

The declarant's state of mind at the time of making a dying declaration need not be shown, to authorize the admission of such declaration in evidence. *State* v. *Reed*, 137 Mo. 125, 38 S. W. 574.

But whether or not such conditions existed may be determined, not only by what he said, but by his evident danger and all the surrounding circumstances. *Jones* v. *Com.* 20 Ky. L. Rep. 355, 46 S. W. 217.

So, evidence that a person whose dying declarations are offered in evidence had received extreme unction is admissible as showing the circumstances under which the declarations were made. *Carver* v. *United States*, 164 U. S. 694, 41 L. ed. 602, 17 Sup. Ct. Rep. 228.

[3] *Titus* v. *State*, 117 Ala. 16, 23 So. 77; *Starr* v. *Com.* 97 Ky. 193, 30 S. W. 397.

But that statements made by a man who was spitting large quantities of blood, that he was going to die, and repeated by him when others endeavored to encourage him, are sufficient to show that the declarations then made as to the cause of his death were made under a sense of impending death, see *People* v. *Samario*, 84 Cal. 484, 24 Pac. 283.

And in *Kirkham* v. *People*, 170 Ill. 9, 48 N. E. 465, evidence that deceased, who was a physician, declared, contrary to the view of other physicians who examined him, that the blow upon his head would cause a clot to form on his brain, and would result in his death, and stated on other occasions that death would inevitably result,—was held sufficient to lay the foundation for the introduction of his dying declarations.

193. Nearness of death.

It is not necessary that the declarant should have apprehended immediate death, in order to render his declarations admissible as dying declarations, but it is only necessary that he should have had no expectation of surviving the injury.[1]

[1]*State* v. *Sullivan*, 20 R. I. 114, 37 Atl. 673.

It is the impression of impending death, and not the rapid succession of it, which renders dying declarations admissible. *Pulliam* v. *State*, 88 Ala. 1, 6 So. 839.

So, the declarations are admissible although death did not immediately ensue, or a hope of recovery was subsequently entertained. *State* v. *Reed*, 53 Kan. 767, 37 Pac. 174.

And the competency of a dying declaration is not affected by the fact that death did not ensue for five days after it was made. *Moore* v. *State*, 96 Tenn. 209, 33 S. W. 1046.

194. Not generally competent.

A dying declaration is not admissible except where the death of the deceased is the subject of a charge of homicide, on trial, and the circumstances of the death are the subject of the declaration.[1]

[1]*People* v. *Davis*, 56 N. Y. 96; *Mora* v. *People*, 19 Colo. 255, 35 Pac. 179; *State* v. *Harper*, 35 Ohio St. 78; *Railing* v. *Com.* 110 Pa. 100, 1 Atl. 314, Overruling *Com.* v. *Bruce*, 41 Phila. Legal Int. 242. *Contra*, *Montgomery* v. *State*, 80 Ind. 338, 41 Am. Rep. 815, 3 Crim. L. Mag. 523, with note collecting recent authorities on their competency and mode of proof in homicide.

195. "Confronting accusers."

A dying declaration is not inadmissible in evidence on the ground that it violates the constitutional guaranty requiring an accused to be confronted with the witnesses against him.[1]

[1]*Taylor* v. *State*, 38 Tex. Crim. Rep. 552, 43 S. W. 1019; *State* v. *Baldwin*, 15 Wash. 15, 45 Pac. 650.

His rights are not infringed if he is confronted with the witness who testifies to the declaration. *People* v. *Corey*, 157 N. Y. 332, 51 N. E. 1024.

196. Declarations consisting of opinions, etc.

Declarations consisting of conclusions, opinions, and belief, which would not be received if the declarant were a witness, are inadmissible as dying declarations.[1]

[1] *State* v. *O'Shea,* 60 Kan. 772, 57 Pac. 970; *Jones* v. *Com.* 20 Ky. L. Rep. 355, 46 S. W. 217; *Williams* v. *State,* 40 Tex. Crim. Rep. 497, 51 S. W. 220; *State* v. *Elkins,* 101 Mo. 344, 14 S. W. 116; *People* v. *Lanagan,* 81 Cal. 142, 22 Pac. 482; *Jones* v. *State,* 52 Ark. 345, 12 S. W. 704.

197. Competency for accused.

Dying declarations are admissible on a trial for murder, as to the fact of the homicide and the person by whom it was committed, in favor of the defendant, as well as against him, if made by the party injured, under a sense of impending death.[1]

[1] *Mattox* v. *United States,* 146 U. S. 140, 36 L. ed. 917, 13 Sup. Ct. Rep. 50; *People* v. *Southern,* 120 Cal. 645, 53 Pac. 214.

So, a statement by one who had abandoned all hope of recovery, that he was wholly to blame for the difficulty, and brought on the trouble himself, is admissible, in favor of one accused of his murder, as a dying declaration. *Brock* v. *Com.* 92 Ky. 183, 17 S. W. 337.

But *State* v. *Nelson,* 101 Mo. 464, 14 S. W. 712, holds that evidence that deceased said he did not want defendant prosecuted, after he had given up all hope of recovery, and was conscious that he must die, is inadmissible for the defense on a murder trial; the prosecution of defendant being a matter for the state, and not for the deceased, to determine.

XXII. Entire conversation or document.

198. A part lets in all.

The introduction of a part of a conversation or writing renders admissible as much of the remainder as tends to explain or qualify what has been received;[1] and that is to be deemed a qualification which rebuts and destroys the inference to be derived from, or the use to be made of, the portion put in evidence.[2]

But distinct and independent statements, though in the same conversation, are not thereby rendered admissible.[3]

[1] The rule that all parts of a conversation, in substance at least, relating to a subject in controversy, must be produced in evidence, or all excluded, is not violated by permitting a person who can remember the particular language, or the substance of it, relating to the fact in issue, or the evidentiary fact sought to be established, to testify to such part, or by permitting part of the conversation to be testified to by one witness and part by another, if the portions together show with rea-

sonable distinctness the bearing of the conversation on the fact in controversy. *Fertig* v. *State*, 100 Wis. 301, 75 N. W. 960.

[1]*Rouse* v. *Whited*, 25 N. Y. 170, 82 Am. Dec. 337 (leading civil case); *Com.* v. *Goddard*, 14 Gray, 402 (favors a liberal rule allowing the whole of the conversation, as necessary to explain any part). To similar effect are *State* v. *Brown*, 21 Kan. 38; *Carver* v. *United States*, 164 U. S. 694, 41 L. ed. 602, 17 Sup. Ct. Rep. 228; *State* v. *Flowers*, 58 Kan. 702, 50 Pac. 938; *Terry* v. *State* (Tex. Crim. App.) 38 S. W. 986; *State* v. *Regan*, 8 Wash. 506, 36 Pac. 472; *Rounds* v. *State*, 57 Wis. 45, 14 N. W. 865.

This rule does not apply where a conversation with the accused was proved by his own witness, without objection by the state, and he seeks by means of the rule to get in evidence in his own favor of further statements forming part of the conversation. *State* v. *Elliott*, 15 Iowa, 72.

The fact that the accused, in a conversation with the witness, said something which the witness cannot remember, will not exclude his testimony of what he does remember. *Wright* v. *State*, 35 Ark. 639.

That the accused in a criminal trial was allowed, without objection, to prove a portion of a conversation which had taken place between himself and another, not within the *res gestæ*, did not entitle him, as matter of right, to introduce evidence of the entire conversation. *Horton* v. *State*, 110 Ga. 739, 35 S. E. 659.

And where, in a prosecution for having sexual intercourse with a female under sixteen years of age and not the wife of defendant, it appears that the complaining witness first stated to another several months after the act, that she had had sexual intercourse with the defendant, and the defendant, on cross-examination of the person to whom the prosecuting witness first confessed, endeavored to show that it was the former, and not the latter, who first suggested the defendant's name, and in so doing brought out a part of the conversation between the prosecuting witness and such other, it was not competent for the state, on redirect, to inquire of such witness as to whether or not prosecuting witness gave her any reason as to why she had intercourse with defendant, since such part of said conversation was not necessary to make the balance thereof intelligible; nor did such question call for the balance of such conversation. *People* v. *Flaherty*, 162 N. Y. 532, 57 N. E. 73, Reversing 27 App. Div. 535, 50 N. Y. Supp. 574.

[2]"When a statement forming part of a conversation is given in evidence by one party, whatever was said in the same conversation, tending to explain or qualify that statement, may be given in evidence by the other; but the latter cannot give in evidence distinct and independent statements in the same conversation, in no way connected with the statement proved by his adversary, on the ground that he had opened the subject by his examination." *People* v. *Beach*, 87 N. Y. 508, Reversing for error in admitting such evidence.

"The object of the rule," says Chief Justice Green, in *Cook* v. *State*, 24 N. J. L. 843, 849, "is not to permit the party to offer his acts and declarations in his own behalf, and thus to manufacture evidence for himself, but it is solely to show the full sense and meaning of the evidence offered against him, in order that it may be neither more nor less than the prisoner intended."

XXIII. Estoppel.

199. Not applicable in criminal cases.

Conclusive presumptions and estoppels have no place in criminal law, for the purpose of establishing the body of the crime charged. The defendant may prove the actual facts in dispute, notwithstanding any admission or confession he may have made to the contrary.[1]

[1]*State* v. *Hutchinson*, 60 Iowa, 478, 15 N. W. 298, holding, where a county treasurer was charged with embezzlement, that he might disprove his own settlement sheet, although by statute in civil case it would have been conclusive against him.

XXIV. Explaining omission of evidence.

200. Explanations competent.

When the good faith of the accused in refraining from testifying in his own behalf,[1] or that of either party in failing to call as a witness a person shown to be acquainted with the facts or a document called for, is questioned, the party has a right to give evidence explaining his course.[2]

[1]*Com.* v. *Costello*, 119 Mass. 214; *Woodruff* v. *Hurson*, 32 Barb. 557 (civil case).

So, in reference to a Chinese certificate, Greene, Ch. J., said: "Nonproduction of a certificate is a circumstance which, if alone and unexplained, may properly be regarded as proof that the person lacking it is one who is prohibited. But its nonproduction is open to explanation, and the presumption arising from its nonproduction to contradiction." *Re Lee Yip*, Cited and followed in *Re Ho King*, 14 Fed. 724.

In *People* v. *O'Hare*, 124 Mich. 515, 83 N. W. 279, defendant was convicted of stealing a harness, which he claimed he bought from a third party. During the progress of the trial, the court severely criticised defendant's counsel for his failure to subpœna this party, accused him of encouraging crime by picking up straw men, and stated that such a lawyer was not fit to practice. Defendant's attorney took exception to the remarks, stating that he was unable to subpœna the witness because he knew neither his first name nor his residence. In its instructions the court told the jury they might regard the absence of the witness as part of a plan to fabricate testimony. It was held that the court's remarks were unreasonable, beyond the court's province, and constituted reversible error.

Thus, testimony to show that certain conspirators had left the state is admissible to explain why they were not prosecuted, or present as witnesses. *Holtz* v. *State,* 76 Wis. 99, 44 N. W. 1107.

But evidence on a second trial for murder, that a witness for the state on a former trial is not called because parties interested in the prosecution found fault with his testimony after such trial, is inadmissible for defendant. *State* v. *Coella,* 8 Wash. 512, 36 Pac. 474.

201. —but not by imputations against the accused.

The prosecution is not entitled to show that a codefendant or a person implicated with the defendant has gone out of the jurisdiction, and refuses to return for the purpose of testifying,[1] unless it be shown that the accused is privy to the absence, or the object of such explanation is to lay a foundation for evidence otherwise inadmissible.

[1] *People* v. *Sharp,* 107 N. Y. 427, 463, 14 N. E. 319. Bribery; held error to allow the prosecution to prove by a detective that he had been employed by the district attorney to subpœna persons named in the indictment as codefendants, some of whom had already been proved to have been intermediaries; that they were now in Canada, and he had there served a subpœna upon one of them. It was not claimed by the prosecution that defendant was privy to their absence, or that the object of the testimony was to furnish a basis for evidence otherwise inadmissible. The court said: "The absence out of the jurisdiction of the court, of an associate, or one seemingly connected with the defendant in the act charged, is easily construed as evidence of guilt, and unless the occasion calls for such proof it should not be allowed."

Compare *Com.* v. *Costello,* 119 Mass. 214. Here, under indictment for forgery and uttering a forged bond to dissolve an attachment, the government proceeded on the ground that the two sureties thereto were accomplices, and that there were no persons of the name of the sureties to be found. The defendant, to explain their absence as witnesses in his behalf, offered to show that the prosecuting officer had openly threatened to prosecute them for perjury, and that they had thereupon fled the commonwealth, and had not returned, and that he had made efforts to procure their attendance as witnesses; held that excluding the testimony was error.

XXV. Experiments.

202. Experiments before the jury

It is in the discretion of the court whether to permit experiments relevant to the issue to be made before the jury during the trial,[1] or to refuse to permit them.[2] So it is discretionary whether to permit a witness explaining a tool or apparatus to experiment before the jury.[3]

[1]*State* v. *Smith*, 49 Conn. 383. And see, more fully, authorities reviewed in notes to *Leonard* v. *Southern Pac. Co.* (Or.) 15 L. R. A. 221, and *Chicago, St. L. & P. R. Co.* v. *Champion* (Ind.) 23 L. R. A. 861.

Thus, it is discretionary with the trial judge whether he will admit evidence as to the length of time it will take a candle to burn down to the point of one discovered where a fire occurred, or whether he will demonstrate that fact by experiment. *People* v. *Levine*, 85 Cal. 44, 22 Pac. 969, 24 Pac. 631.

And on a trial for burglary a mask, lantern, and other implements of burglary may be used by the prosecuting attorney to enable the witnesses to describe and illustrate the appearance of the burglar at the time of the commission of the offense, although they are not shown to be the property of defendant. *State* v. *Ellwood*, 17 R. I. 763, 24 Atl. 782.

An illustration by a police officer who arrested one accused of robbery, as to the manner in which he held a revolver when arrested, is admissible for the purpose of showing an attempt to conceal and pass it to a friend. *Goon Bow* v. *People*, 160 Ill. 438, 43 N. E. 593.

[3]*Polin* v. *State*, 14 Neb. 540, 16 N. W. 898. Refusal to direct sheriff to discharge pistol in order to show that it would go off at half cock, in support of theory that shooting was accidental.

So, refusal to permit a witness to illustrate on a wall or door in the courtroom the location of a bullet mark is not an abuse of discretion, where there is an offer to allow him to describe the bullet marks,—especially where the jury viewed the premises, and are particularly instructed to view such marks. *People* v. *Chin Hane*, 108 Cal. 597, 41 Pac. 697.

And the trial judge is not obliged to allow the power of vision of a witness under cross-examination to be tested by requiring him to go to a window and look at an object on the street invisible to the judge and jury from their positions. *Heath* v. *State*, 93 Ga. 446, 21 S. E. 77.

So, on a trial for the illegal sale of intoxicating liquors, it is proper to refuse to permit the person from whom defendant purchased the beverage which was sold to put together in the courtroom the ingredients from which it was made, and show the jury its composition, since such experiment could not enlighten the jury in regard to the question whether the beverage was intoxicating. *State* v. *Lindoen*, 87 Iowa, 702, 54 N. W. 1075.

So, also, an offer to show that liquor is not intoxicating, by permitting the jurors to taste and test the same, is properly refused, where the issue is not whether it is actually intoxicating, but whether or not it contains more than 1 per cent of alcohol. *Com.* v. *Brelsford*, 161 Mass. 61, 36 N. E. 677.

In *People* v. *Kinney*, 124 Mich. 486, 83 N. W. 147, where a bottle of cider was admitted in evidence in a prosecution for selling fermented liquor, it was held not error to permit the members of the jury to taste the contents, where the evidence tended to show that the cider was in the same condition as when purchased.

In *Galloway* v. *State* (Tex. Crim. App.) 57 S. W. 658, a prosecution for violating the local-option law, where the defense was that the liquor sold was not intoxicating, a juror, by consent of defendant, drank nearly a quart of the liquor which was offered in evidence. Affidavits of jurors stated that he made no statements as to the effect of it until after the verdict was rendered, when he said in the jury room that he believed that if a person drank enough of it, it would intoxicate him. It was held that it was not proper practice to permit the juror to drink the liquor, yet, in view of the facts that he made no statement to the other jurors as to the effect until after the verdict was rendered, and that the evidence was conclusive on the guilt of defendant, it was not cause for reversal.

[8]*People* v. *Hope*, 62 Cal. 291. No error to permit a witness with a burglar's tool to exhibit its parts, and make experiments with it in the presence of the jury. The object of the experiments not appearing in the record on appeal, the court will presume that it was legitimate.

It is discretionary with the trial court to admit proof as to mechanical or chemical experiments; and the court is not bound to stop proceedings in order to try such experiments in open court. *People* v. *Levine*, 85 Cal. 39, 24 Pac. 631, 22 Pac. 969.

203. Evidence of experiments out of court.

It is not error to receive evidence of experiments made out of the courtroom,[1] and to exhibit the apparatus used.[2] But, to be admissible in evidence, the experiments must be shown to have been made under the same conditions as those existing in the case on trial.[3] If the state is allowed to introduce evidence of experiments, the defendant is entitled to introduce the same kind of testimony in rebuttal.[4]

[1]Thus, evidence that it would be physically impossible to produce the conditions found on the person of the prosecutrix on a prosecution for rape, in the manner and under the circumstances described by her, is relevant and material. *People* v. *Baldwin*, 117 Cal. 244, 49 Pac. 186.

And where, on a prosecution for murder, there is a conflict in the evidence as to the distance from which the fatal shot was fired from a rifle, testimony as to the distance at which a rifle of that calibre would powder-mark clothing when discharged is material and competent, where the clothing of deceased was not so marked. *People* v. *Clark*, 84 Cal. 573, 24 Pac. 313.

It is competent for physicians who saw deceased lying on the ground at the place where the homicide occurred, and who located the pistol balls fired into his body, to testify with regard to an experiment made in the absence of defendant, in order to ascertain if possible the relative positions of the deceased and defendant when the fatal shot was fired. *Moore* v. *State*, 96 Tenn. 209, 33 S. W. 1046.

An experiment which, by the reproduction as nearly as possible of the conditions as to speed and distance, is designed to show the impossibility of the theory of the state, which depends upon the possibility of defendant's being able to commit the offense, to return to his wagon, and overtake a wagon which was preceding him within a given distance, is admissible, although it is not possible to determine whether the conditions attending the experiment were exactly similar to those attending the original transaction. *Clark* v. *State*, 38 Tex. Crim. Rep. 30, 40 S. W. 992.

But evidence that a witness had once shot a pistol hole through a dry plank as an experiment, to ascertain the size of the hole as compared with that of the ball, is inadmissible on a trial for a homicide committed with a pistol. *Evans* v. *State*, 109 Ala. 11, 19 So. 535.

[2]*Sullivan* v. *Com.* 93 Pa. 284, 13 Phila. 410.

[3]*State* v. *Justus*, 11 Or. 178, 8 Pac. 337; *Com.* v. *Piper*, 120 Mass. 185; *Petteway* v. *State*, 36 Tex. Crim. Rep. 97, 35 S. W. 646; *People* v. *Deitz*, 86 Mich. 419, 49 N. W. 296; *People* v. *Phelan*, 123 Cal. 551, 56 Pac. 424.

In *Clark* v. *State*, 38 Tex. Crim. Rep. 30, 40 S. W. 992, however, it is held that the fact that an experiment made under circumstances similar, or approximately similar to those surrounding the original transaction, may not have been under exactly similar conditions,—does not render it inadmissible if it serves to shed any light upon that transaction.

[4]*Smith* v. *State*, 2 Ohio St. 513.

XXVI. Flight.

204. Competency.

Evidence of the flight of one defendant is not competent for the purpose of showing the guilt of another, unless a connection of the latter with the attempt is shown.[1]

[1]*People* v. *Stanley*, 47 Cal. 113, 17 Am. Rep. 401 (robbery; the reason seems to be that acts and declarations of accomplices are admissible on the ground of *res gestæ*, while the flight of the accused is admissible as tending to show a guilty mind. New trial granted); *State* v. *Ruby*, 61 Iowa, 86, 15 N. W. 848 (attempt by other prisoners in same jail); *Whitaker* v. *State*, 106 Ala. 30, 17 So. 456. And see *supra*, §§ 140–150.

But *State* v. *Taylor*, 70 Vt. 1, 42 L. R. A. 673, 39 Atl. 447, holds that testimony that some of the persons arrested, and who made an assault in attempting to escape, ran off and hid in the bushes, and were afterwards brought in by the officer's assistants,—is admissible on trial for the assault.

Evidence of flight of defendant's brother is admissible on a trial for murder, to show the guilt of such brother, where the theory of the state is that defendant advised and agreed with his brother to commit the crime. *McIntyre* v. *State* (Tex. Crim. App.) 33 S. W. 347.

So, the flight of two of the persons who, the prosecution claims, were implicated in the larceny of property for receiving and concealing which the defendant is on trial is admissible to establish the fact of the theft, which is an essential step in the prosecution. *State* v. *Hanna*, 35 Or. 195, 57 Pac. 629.

XXVII. Former acquittal, conviction, or jeopardy.

See also *infra*, § 277; and *ante*, Division XVIII., §§ 15–46. As to Burden of Proof, see *post*, Division XLII., §§ 27 *et seq.*, 31.

205. Former acquittal or conviction of accomplice.

The former acquittal of an alleged accomplice is not competent in favor of the accused; nor is the former conviction of an accomplice competent against the accused.[1]

[1] *State* v. *Orr*, 64 Mo. 339; *Davis* v. *State*, 152 Ind. 145, 52 N. E. 754; *People* v. *Kief*, 58 Hun, 337, 343, 11 N. Y. Supp. 926, 12 N. Y. Supp. 896. Compare *Paul* v. *State*, 12 Tex. App. 346 (holding that upon the trial of an indictment charging a conspiracy, the record of acquittal of an alleged accomplice previously tried is admissible in behalf of the defendant; judgment reversed); and *Jackson* v. *State*, 33 Tex. Crim. Rep. 281, 26 S. W. 194, 622 (where it was held that the trial and acquittal of one jointly indicted with defendant for the crime of robbery, who testified as a witness for defendant, was admissible, when offered, where the state through the trial kept prominently before the jury his complicity in the robbery).

So, a record of the acquittal of a person charged with stealing property is not admissible in favor of defendant charged with receiving the property, knowing it to have been stolen. *State* v. *Sweeten*, 75 Mo. App. 127.

206. Record necessary.

In the absence of statute, a former acquittal or conviction can only be proved by the record,[1] or by secondary evidence after foundation laid.[2]

[1] *Walter* v. *State*, 105 Ind. 589, 5 N. E. 735; *State* v. *Rugan*, 68 Mo. 214. Compare *People* v. *Garcia*, 58 Cal. 102 (allowing "Register of Criminal Actions" to be competent); *Myers* v. *State*, 92 Ind. 390 (holding it not necessary that the record contain a copy of the appointment of the special judge before whom such judgment was rendered, or the reason for such appointment, or copy of the signature of the judge).

Modern statutes removing the disqualification of witnesses, which at common law resulted from conviction, allow the conviction to be proved, "for the purpose of affecting the weight of his testimony, either by the record or by his cross-examination, upon which he must answer any question relevant to that inquiry, and the party cross-examining him is not concluded by his answer to such a question." N. Y. Code Civ. Proc. § 832.

In *State* v. *Simpson*, 91 Me. 77, 39 Atl. 286, it was held that the docket entries in a case in which the record had not been fully extended might be read to the jury in support of an allegation of a former conviction.

And in *Territory* v. *Stocker*, 9 Mont. 6, 22 Pac. 496, on a plea of former jeopardy, the magistrate's docket of the former trial was held admissible, although the magistrate testified that another person than the one shown by the docket made the charge.

And *State* v. *Narcarm*, 69 N. H. 237, 45 Atl. 744, holds that where there was a misnomer in an indictment in a prosecution for a second offense, the original complaint and warrant, containing defendant's true name, with minutes indorsed thereon, were admissible as evidence of the former conviction.

[2]See *supra*, § 76.

207. Evidence of identity of offense necessary.

The identity of the offense charged in an indictment with that charged in the prior one must be shown.[1]

It may be shown by parol.[2]

[1]*Emerson* v. *State*, 43 Ark. 372.

[2]*Swalley* v. *People*, 116 Ill. 247, 4 N. E. 379; *Duncan* v. *Com.* 6 Dana, 295; *Marshall* v. *State*, 8 Ind. 498; *State* v. *Andrews*, 27 Mo. 267; *Porter* v. *State*, 17 Ind. 415 (error to reject parol testimony to establish identity).

For this purpose the magistrate before whom the former trial took place is a competent witness. *State* v. *Maxwell*, 51 Iowa, 314, 1 N. W. 666.

208. Former jeopardy; ground for discharge.

Proof of discharge of the jury without rendering a verdict is competent as negativing former jeopardy, although the record does not expressly show that the court was satisfied that the jury could not agree. This may be inferred from the fact of disagreement, and the direction of the court thereupon that they be discharged.[1]

[1]*People* v. *Harding*, 53 Mich. 481, 19 N. W. 155, Cooley, J. Compare *ante*, Division XVIII., §§ 15–41, as to what constitutes it.

That amendment may be made of the former record pending the present trial, see *Territory* v. *Christensen*, 4 Dak. 410, 31 N. W. 848, 851.

XXVIII. General issue.

209. Effect.

The plea of not guilty is a denial of every material allegation in the indictment,[1] and under it all matters of fact tending to establish a defense, which may not be presented under a special plea, may be given in evidence.[2]

But merely formal defects in abatement are deemed to be waived by this plea.[3]

[1] N. Y. Code Crim. Proc. § 338; *People* v. *Aleck*, 61 Cal. 137 (holding that this plea puts in issue all material averments, including the *locus delicti*); *Com.* v. *Briggs*, 5 Pick. 429.

[2] N. Y. Code Crim. Proc. § 339, providing that all matters of fact tending to establish a defense other than former conviction and acquittal may be given in evidence. And see *People* v. *Ah Lee*, 60 Cal. 85, holding to same effect under California statute.

The accused may avail himself of the statute of limitations under this plea. *State* v. *Ward*, 49 Conn. 429; *People* v. *Durrin*, 2 N. Y. Crim. Rep. 328 (holding that the defense of the statute of limitations must be given under a plea of not guilty, and in no other way); *United States* v. *Brown*, 2 Low. Dec. 267, Fed. Cas. No. 14,665.

The insanity of the accused may be shown under this plea. *Ostrander* v. *People*, 28 Hun, 38 (holding that the Statute Laws of 1874, chap. 446, providing for the examination of the sanity of the accused by commission, did not take away his right to have the question of his sanity passed upon by the jury under the plea of not guilty); *Bennett* v. *State*, 57 Wis. 69, 46 Am. Rep. 26, 14 N. W. 912 (holding that under the local statute, if insanity is specially pleaded, that issue must be first disposed of, but the trial of that issue and of the plea of not guilty may be treated as one for the purpose of moving for a new trial).

In Alabama a statute (act February 27, 1889 [Ala. Acts 1888–89, pp. 742–746] § 4) provides that in certain prosecutions, where the defense of insanity is set up, it shall be interposed by special plea at the time of the arraignment, which in substance shall be "Not guilty by reason of insanity;" and the defense of insanity cannot be introduced, as formerly, under a plea of "not guilty."

In *Green* v. *State*, 88 Tenn. 614, 14 S. W. 430, it is held that present insanity must be specially pleaded in a criminal case, and cannot be shown under a plea of not guilty.

N. Y. Code Crim. Proc. § 336, provides that whenever a person in confinement under indictment desires to offer the plea of insanity, he may present such plea at the time of his arraignment, as a specification, under the plea of not guilty. But the practice still is to prove the facts relied on as showing insanity at the time of the offense, under the plea of not guilty. The statute above cited is permissive, but not mandatory, for the burden is on the prosecution to satisfy the jury, on the whole evidence, that the act was that of a person criminally responsible. *O'Connell* v. *People*, 87 N. Y. 377, 41 Am. Rep. 379.

In *Jordan* v. *State*, 81 Ala. 20, 1 So. 577, it was held that evidence of former conviction was not admissible under plea of not guilty. To the same effect, under Ga. Pen. Code, § 950, *Hall* v. *State*, 103 Ga. 403, 29 S. E. 915. *Contra, Bryant* v. *State*, 72 Ind. 400.

[3]*United States* v. *Gale*, 109 U. S. 65, 27 L. ed. 857, 3 Sup. Ct. Rep. 1, holding that objections to the mode of selecting grand jurors, though under an unconstitutional statute, cannot be raised after plea of not guilty. And see *Abbott* v. *People*, 12 N. Y. Week. Dig. 282, Affirmed in 86 N. Y. 460; *State* v. *Drury*, 13 R. I. 540 (misnomer waived by plea); *State* v. *Day*, 58 Iowa, 678, 12 N. W. 733 (holding that under a plea of not guilty the court will not inquire whether the defendant was properly or improperly brought within its jurisdiction); *Mann* v. *State*, 37 Ark. 405.

XXIX. Good faith.

210. When competent.

Evidence that the accused acted in good faith, as, for instance, under advice of counsel, is not admissible as a defense, if the statute makes the act an offense irrespective of the motive or object of doing the act.[1]

But it is admissible in mitigation in those jurisdictions and cases where the jury are to fix the punishment by their verdict.[2]

[1]In *Gardner* v. *People*, 62 N. Y. 299, upon the trial of a misdemeanor (unlawful removal of an inspector of election), evidence that the accused acted under advice of counsel was held inadmissible as not amounting to a defense. Since the statute affixes the punishment to the intentional doing of the act, irrespective of motive or object, the good faith of the accused mitigates the character of the act, but does not negative the offense. See also *United States* v. *Buntin*, 10 Fed. 730.

So, evidence of defendant's good faith in making a promise of marriage is inadmissible on a prosecution under Cal. Pen. Code, §§ 268, 269, providing that every person who under promise of marriage seduces and has sexual intercourse with an unmarried female of chaste character is punishable, and that the intermarriage of the parties subsequent to the offense is a bar to a prosecution, provided the marriage takes place prior to the filing of an indictment or information. *People* v. *Samonset*, 97 Cal. 448, 32 Pac. 520.

[2]*Staples* v. *State*, 14 Tex. App. 136. Reversal for error in excluding evidence of good faith in making unlawful arrest.

XXX. Insanity.

As to Present Insanity, Precluding Trial, see *ante,* Division IX.

211. Insane witness.

An insane person may testify if the court is satisfied that he understands the nature of an oath, and is capable of testifying; it is for the jury to estimate the value of his testimony.[1]

[1] *Com.* v. *Reynolds,* cited in 92 Mass. 64. See also *People ex rel. Norton* v. *New York Hospital,* 3 Abb. N. C. 229, and note; *District of Columbia* v. *Armes,* 107 U. S. 519, 27 L. ed. 618, 2 Sup. Ct. Rep. 814.

212. Insanity; how proved, repute.

General reputation is not competent evidence of insanity.[1]

[1] *Brinkley* v. *State,* 58 Ga. 296 (murder; not error for the court to refuse to allow a witness to testify that defendant was generally regarded as a man of unsound mind, and that his reputation was that of a person of unsound mind before the commission of the alleged offense), Citing *Choice* v. *State,* 31 Ga. 424; *People* v. *Pico,* 62 Cal. 50 (holding it not error to refuse to allow the question, "What do you say as to his general reputation, whether sane or insane?"); *Cotrell* v. *Com.* 13 Ky. L. Rep. 305, 17 S. W. 149; *Cannon* v. *State* (Tex. Crim. App.) 56 S. W. 351; *State* v. *Coley,* 114 N. C. 879, 19 S. E. 705. And see *Walker* v. *State,* 102 Ind. 502, 1 N. E. 856, and cases cited.

213. Somnambulism.

Evidence that the accused had from infancy been afflicted with somnolentia, or somnambulism, is competent.[1]

[1] *Fain* v. *Com.* 78 Ky. 183, 39 Am. Rep. 213, reversing conviction for refusing to admit such evidence; also for other errors.

214. Declarations.

Declarations of a person whose mental condition is in question, whether made before or after the time at which the condition is to be established, are competent, so far as they tend to show his condition at the time in question.[1]

[1] *Cogswell* v. *Com.* 17 Ky. L. Rep. 822, 32 S. W. 935; *Peery* v. *Peery,* 94 Tenn. 328, 29 S. W. 1.

215. Conduct and circumstances.

Evidence of the acts and conduct, occurrences, and other circumstances, whether prior or subsequent to the time at which the mental condition of a person is to be established, which tend to shed light on the state of his mental faculties, is generally receivable for the purpose of showing what his mental condition was at the time in question.[1]

[1]Thus, evidence that defendant charged with murder seemed from the time of her arrest very unconcerned, and to think that she had done right, and to be unconscious of her condition, and have no apprehension or fear of punishment, and that she frequently laughed and sang, is admissible, in connection with evidence of her disordered mental condition before and at the time of committing the crime, to support the defense of insanity. *Green* v. *State*, 64 Ark. 523, 43 S. W. 973.

And evidence that, just prior to the alleged offense, accused was a witness at an important trial, and that his conduct there indicated that he was insane, is admissible. *Cannon* v. *State* (Tex. Crim. App.) 56 S. W. 351.

So, evidence as to defendant's conduct and apparent condition of mind while in jail is admissible to rebut evidence of a general and permanent state of dementia and diseased condition of mind. *People* v. *McCarthy*, 115 Cal. 255, 46 Pac. 1073.

French v. *State*, 93 Wis. 325, 67 N. W. 706, holds that evidence of the acts, conduct, and declarations of defendant charged with murder, offered on the question of his insanity, should not be limited to those occurring before the end of the fourth day after the homicide, where his condition at that time had not changed, although medicine had been administered to him to restore him to his normal condition.

But *State* v. *Lewis*, 20 Nev. 333, 22 Pac. 241, holds that, upon the question of sanity at the time of the homicide, acts or conversations of the accused at a subsequent time are not admissible as of course, but only when they tend to establish existence of insanity at the time of the homicide.

And *Dean* v. *State*, 105 Ala. 21, 17 So. 28, holds that evidence that when defendant, on trial for murder, became excited, he was very much excited and overbalanced, and to a considerable extent lost his reason, is properly excluded,—especially where the witness by whom such facts are sought to be proved testifies that defendant was not at all excited at the time of the killing.

216. Hereditary insanity.

Where there is evidence directly relating to the accused which tends to show insanity in him, it is competent to show the insanity of ancestors or progeny;[1] but it is in the discretion of the court to exclude it, unless evidence has first been given that the kind of insanity shown in the case has a hereditary tendency.[2]

[1]Abbott, Tr. Ev. 119 (65). See also *Cole's Trial*, 7 Abb. Pr. N. S. 321.

Thus, evidence that the grandmother, great uncle, and great aunt of defendant, charged with murder, had been insane, and that defendant's mother had been temporarily insane, is admissible in support of defendant's insanity, where the evidence has been adduced that defendant had shown signs of insanity. *Green* v. *State,* 64 Ark. 523, 43 S. W. 973.

So held in *Shaeffer* v. *State,* 61 Ark. 241, 32 S. W. 679, of evidence that defendant, charged with burglary, had a brother two years older who was an imbecile all his life, in connection with other evidence.

In *People* v. *Koerner,* 154 N. Y. 355, 48 N. E. 730, it is held that the declarations of the living members of a family as to the insanity of another living member are not admissible to prove such fact, under the rule applicable when the question of pedigree is involved, even if that rule extends to proof of insanity, as in any case it is limited to declarations by deceased persons, and is based upon the fact that they furnish the best evidence that can be obtained.

[2]*Walsh* v. *People,* 88 N. Y. 458.

So, evidence that an uncle of defendant, charged with murder, was insane, is inadmissible, in the absence of any affirmative evidence, or evidence derived from want of motive or other circumstances, that defendant himself was insane, or showed any symptoms of insanity at the time of the alleged crime. *State* v. *Van Tassel,* 103 Iowa, 6, 72 N. W. 497.

217. Evidence freely received.

In all inquiries relating to insanity, every reasonable latitude should be allowed in the examination of witnesses, however false or unfounded the court may consider the defense.[1]

[1]*Dejarnette* v. *Com.* 75 Va. 867.

218. Weak-mindedness.

Evidence as to whether defendant was a "strong or weak minded man" is incompetent on the question of his lack of responsibility for the criminal act.[1]

[1]*Dean* v. *State,* 105 Ala. 21, 17 So. 28.

So, evidence which merely tends to show that defendant charged with a crime is weak-minded and easily influenced, and liable to be led into wrongdoing by others, is inadmissible, where it is not claimed that he is either idiotic or insane, or incapable of understanding the nature of his action. *State* v. *Flowers,* 58 Kan. 702, 50 Pac. 938.

219. Eccentricity.

Evidence of eccentricity of character is not competent, even as bearing on the question of criminal intent, if insanity is not relied on as a defense.[1]

[1]*Sindram* v. *People,* 1 N. Y. Crim. Rep. 448, Affirmed in 88 N. Y. 196.

220. Opinion of expert as to mental soundness.

An expert[1] may testify directly as to mental capacity, in any of three ways:

1. If he has had adequate opportunity of personal examination of the accused, he may state his opinion positively, based upon his personal knowledge of the facts, but not an opinion based upon hearsay, nor an opinion based upon the testimony in the cause, unless such testimony as is relied on for the purpose is indicated hypothetically by the question, so that the opinion given shall be an hypothetical opinion.[2]

2. An expert who has heard all the testimony adduced upon the trial, bearing on the question, may, if it is not conflicting, be asked his opinion on the question of what the facts sworn to, if proved, would indicate as to the mental capacity.[3]

3. An expert may be asked what a supposed state of facts put to him hypothetically, but corresponding in detail to the facts already in evidence, on one side or the other, or on both sides, would indicate as to the mental capacity.[4]

[1]As to the effect on the opinions of medical experts, of the prohibition against divulging professional communications, and the reason of such privilege, see authorities reviewed in note to *Burt* v. *State* (Tex. Crim. App.) 39 L. R. A. 306.

And as to the right of a witness to give an opinion on the exact issue to be tried in respect to sanity, as applied to criminal prosecutions, see note to *Brown* v. *Mitchell* (Tex. Crim. App.) 36 L. R. A. 65.

That it is not essential to the admission of the opinion of an expert as to the sanity or insanity of defendant, based on his conduct in jail, that the defendant shall have been warned that his conduct will be observed for such purpose, see *Burt* v. *State,* 38 Tex. Crim. Rep. 397, 39 L. R. A. 305, 40 S. W. 1000, 43 S. W. 344.

[2]The authorities are in conflict upon this point. The true principle is, doubtless, that stated in the text; and it will usually be required that the testimony relied on shall be stated in substance in a hypothetical question,—a rule which many of the best-considered authorities lay down as absolute. It is only where the evidence is simple and harmonious that a question expressed to call for an opinion supposing the evidence to be true, without stating its substance, can be deemed sufficiently to indicate it hypothetically to the jury. Buswell, Insanity, § 263, Citing *Guetig* v. *State,* 66 Ind. 94, 32 Am. Rep. 99; *Webb* v. *State,* 9 Tex. App. 490; *Davis* v. *State,* 35 Ind. 496, 9 Am. Rep. 706; *People* v. *Thurston,* 2 Park. Crim. Rep. 49; *People* v. *Lake,* 12 N. Y. 358; *State* v. *Potts,* 100 N. C. 457, 6 S. E. 657; *People* v. *Wood,* 126 N. Y. 251, 27 N. E. 362. See also cases reviewed in note to *Burt* v. *State* (Tex. Crim. App.) 39 L. R. A. 306.

[3]*Sanchez* v. *People,* 22 N. Y. 147, 154; *People* v. *Lake,* 12 N. Y. 358; *Com.* v. *Rogers,* 7 Met. 500, 41 Am. Dec. 458; *State* v. *Hayden,* 51 Vt. 296. Compare *Bennett* v. *State,* 57 Wis. 69, 46 Am. Rep. 26, 14 N. W. 912, 918; Wharton, Crim. Ev. § 418; *Webb* v. *State,* 9 Tex. App. 490, 505; Chitty, Med. Jur. 356; Russell, Crimes, Sharswood's 9th ed. 27, note 1; 3 Greenl. Ev. § 5. For a full treatment of this branch of the subject, see note to *Burt* v. *State* (Tex. Crim. App.) 39 L. R. A. 310.

[4]*Cowley* v. *People,* 83 N. Y. 464, 470, 38 Am. Rep. 464, Citing *People* v. *Lake,* 12 N. Y. 358; *Guiterman* v. *Liverpool, N. Y. & P. S. S. Co.* 83 N. Y. 358; *People* v. *Augsbury,* 97 N. Y. 501 (holding question discretionary); *Dejarnette* v. *Com.* 75 Va. 867. And see further cases reviewed in note to *Burt* v. *State* (Tex. Crim. App.) 39 L. R. A. 315; Brief on the Facts, 2d ed. pp. 425 *et seq.*

221. — of ordinary witness.

A witness who is not an expert may testify to the facts and circumstances within his personal knowledge, bearing on the question of mental capacity; and after he has stated them, if they show reasonable means of forming an impression,[1] he may be asked, on either direct or cross-examination, the impression as to mental incapacity made on his mind at the time[2] by the acts and declarations to which he has testified; and may characterize them as rational or irrational.[3]

But a witness who is not an expert cannot state his opinion or impression unless he has first stated the facts and circumstances on which it was formed.[4]

Nor can he state his present opinion as evidence of insanity, as distinguished from the impression made upon his mind at the time of the circumstances to which he testifies.[5]

[1]Compare *Ford* v. *State,* 71 Ala. 385; *Re Carmichael,* 36 Ala. 514; *Powell* v. *State,* 25 Ala. 21; *People* v. *Pico,* 62 Cal. 50.

[2]*Com.* v. *Brayman,* 136 Mass. 438. Compare *State* v. *Pike,* 51 N. H. 105, S. C., with note to contrary, by L. F. Redfield, in 11 Am. L. Reg. N. S. 233; *Thomas* v. *State,* 40 Tex. 60; *Upstone* v. *People,* 109 Ill. 169.

In *State* v. *Buchler,* 103 Mo. 203, 15 S. W. 331, it is held that testimony of witnesses as to their impressions or opinions as to the appearance or expression of countenance of one accused of murder, just after the affray, is admissible.

[3]*People* v. *Conroy,* 97 N. Y. 62, Affirming 33 Hun, 119, Citing *Clapp* v. *Fullerton,* 34 N. Y. 190.

[4]*State* v. *Pennyman,* 68 Iowa, 216, 26 N. W. 82. And see cases cited in note to *Ryder* v. *State* (Ga.) 38 L. R. A. 723; Brief on the Facts, 2d ed. p. 428.

[5]*O'Brien* v. *People,* 36 N. Y. 276, 282; *Hickman* v. *State,* 38 Tex. 190.

222. Doubt of expert.

The testimony of an expert that he doubts whether the accused was sane is not competent as tending to show insanity. Hence, if the witness declines to express a positive opinion that insanity existed, it is not competent to ask him if he has doubts of the existence of mental capacity.[1]

[1]*Sanchez* v. *People,* 22 N. Y. 147, 154.

223. Rebutting.

Where insanity is made the defense to a criminal charge, and special acts are given in evidence, it is competent for the prosecution in rebuttal to prove other acts showing sanity.[1]

[1]*United States* v. *Holmes,* 1 Cliff. 98, Fed. Cas. No. 15,382, holding that the proof of such acts, being pertinent to the issue, are not open to the objection that it is an attempt to prove other crimes than the one charged; nor can it be considered an attack on the prisoner's character, which he himself has not put in issue.

That proof of partial insanity of defendant charged with murder renders admissible evidence on the part of the state that defendant was sane on all other subjects, see *People* v. *Hubert,* 119 Cal. 216, 51 Pac. 329.

And that witnesses examined by the state in rebuttal, on the question of insanity, who have had transactions with one accused of murder, and have known him for months immediately preceding the killing, may be asked by the state whether they ever observed anything about him, or in what he said or did, that indicated insanity, see *State* v. *Maier,* 36 W. Va. 757, 15 S. E. 991.

XXXI. Inspection.

See also *supra,* §§ 202, 203; and *infra,* §§ 322–324.

224. Exhibiting chattel.

When the nature, quality, and condition of an article are relevant to the issue, the court may allow the thing to be shown to the jury,[1] upon proper evidence as to the identity of the thing[2] and of its condition at the time in question.[3]

[1]*Ruloff's Case,* 11 Abb. Pr. N. S. 245, S. C., less fully reported, 45 N. Y. 213 (burglar's tools, piece of newspaper, and shoes fitting the accused); *Myers* v. *People,* 4 Thomp. & C. 292; *Foster* v. *People,* 63 N. Y. 619, Affirming 3 Hun, 6 (burglar's tools admissible, and held competent to prove their names and uses); *King* v. *State,* 13 Tex. App. 277 (clothing of the deceased admissible as tending to show position when killed, or direction of blow); *State* v. *Outerbridge,* 82 N. C. 617 (exhibition and comparison of bullets and molds in view of the jury; and proof that the bullet fitted the mold of the accused competent); *People* v. *Muller,*

32 Hun, 209 (photographs; on indictment for the sale of them, as deemed obscene); *Montrose* v. *State,* 72 Ga. 261, 53 Am. Rep. 840 (illustrations in indecent publication); *Com.* v. *Burke,* 12 Allen, 182 (holding that things stolen may be exhibited as evidence of their own value). And for some other cases illustrating the application of the rule, see *Bryant* v. *State,* 116 Ala. 445, 23 So. 40; *Starchman* v. *State,* 62 Ark. 538, 36 S. W. 940; *People* v. *Durrant,* 116 Cal. 179, 48 Pac. 75; *Painter* v. *People,* 147 Ill. 444, 35 N. E. 64; *Davidson* v. *State,* 135 Ind. 254, 34 N. E. 972; *State* v. *Peterson,* 110 Iowa, 647, 82 N. W. 329; *People* v. *Wright,* 89 Mich. 70, 50 N. W. 792; *State* v. *Murphy,* 118 Mo. 7, 25 S. W. 95; *State* v. *Porter,* 32 Or. 135, 49 Pac. 964; *Smith* v. *State* (Tex. Crim. App.) 58 S. W. 101; *State* v. *Roberts,* 63 Vt. 139, 21 Atl. 424.

The general rule that the accused cannot be compelled to criminate himself by words or acts is not applicable to a case where the police pulled off the shoes and socks from the prisoner's feet, and it was sought by the identification of such articles of clothing to connect the prisoner with the crime committed. What he wore in such a case witnessed against him, and not any act he did under coercion. *Franklin* v. *State,* 69 Ga. 36, 47 Am. Rep. 748, 749, Citing Greenl. Ev. 34, Bishop, Crim. Proc. 210, 211, and distinguishing *Day* v. *State,* 63 Ga. 667.

[a]As illustrating the necessity of proper identification of the article offered, see *Woolfolk* v. *State,* 85 Ga. 69, 11 S. E. 814; *State* v. *Porter,* 32 Or. 135, 49 Pac. 964; *Herman* v. *State,* 75 Miss. 340, 22 So. 873.

[b]Thus, in *State* v. *Goddard,* 146 Mo. 177, 48 S. W. 82, where the door of the room in which a homicide occurred was offered in evidence to show the location of the pistol balls therein, it was held that it should have been first shown, by preliminary questions, that it had remained in the same condition since the homicide.

225. Exhibiting person—identity.

On the trial of an issue involving the identity of a person, the court may allow him to be brought before the jury, in order that a witness may look upon him and testify.[1]

[1]*Atty. Gen.* v. *Fadden,* 1 Price, 403, where hab. corp. ad. test. was allowed, to bring him up. And see Civil Trial Brief, 2d ed. chap. XIX., p. 306.

226. — age.

The jury may, by inspection of a person in court, determine whether he is under age.[1]

[1]*People ex rel. Zeigler* v. *Special Sessions Ct. Justices,* 10 Hun, 224; *Com.* v. *Emmons,* 98 Mass. 6.

227. — of infant.

On the trial of an issue involving the age of a child, the court may allow the child to be shown to the jury.[1]

[1]N. Y. Pen. Code, § 19, embodying the act of 1882, and providing that "the

court or magistrate may direct an examination by one or more physicians, whose opinion shall also be competent evidence upon the question of age."

So, on a trial for rape of children under sixteen years of age, the jury may consider their appearance, in connection with their testimony, in determining their age. *Com.* v. *Phillips*, 162 Mass. 504, 39 N. E. 109.

228. Legitimacy—parentage.

As to whether it is competent on a question of race or parentage to exhibit an infant of tender years to the jury, the authorities are conflicting.[1]

[1]Affirmative: *Warlick* v. *White*, 76 N. C. 175 (legitimacy of a child alleged to be of mixed blood; error to refuse to allow it to be exhibited); *State* v. *Smith*, 54 Iowa, 104, 37 Am. Rep. 192, 6 N. W. 153 (bastardy; not error to exhibit a child over two years of age, the jury being charged that if they did not clearly see the resemblance between the child and the alleged putative father to disregard all the state's claims of resemblance); Disapproved in 22 Alb. L. J. 43; *Gaunt* v. *State*, 50 N. J. L. 490, 14 Atl. 600 (bastardy); *Finnegan* v. *Dugan*, 14 Allen, 197 (an action under a statute concerning maintenance of bastards; no error to instruct the jury that they might consider, with the other evidence, any resemblance between the child in court and the defendant, if they found such resemblance to exist. The age of the child does not appear). In *State* v. *Horton*, 100 N. C. 443, 6 S. E. 238, it was held not error to exhibit the child simply as corroborating by its existence testimony to seduction under promise of marriage. And in *Hutchinson* v. *State*, 19 Neb. 263, 27 N. W. 113 (bastardy), it was held not error merely to allow the child of seven months to be in the mother's arms while she was testifying.

Negative: In *People ex rel. Fuller* v. *Carney*, 29 Hun, 47, a bastardy trial, it was held reversible error to ask the mother of the child to "look at the child, and tell what the color of its eyes are." The court said: "This evidence enabled the court to compare the color of the child's eyes with those of the defendant, who was present in court. We do not regard this kind of evidence as safe or proper. . . . Common observation reminds us that in families of children different colors of hair and eyes are common, and that it would be dangerous doctrine to permit a child's paternity to be questioned or proved by the comparing of the color of its hair or eyes with that of the alleged parent,"—Citing with approval *Petrie* v. *Howe*, 4 Thomp. & C. 85, a civil case, holding that upon trial of action for criminal conversation with plaintiff's wife, it was reversible error to ask plaintiff the color of the hair of his four children, so that the jury could compare such color with that of the defendant and of the fifth child, in court with its mother, where the child was alleged to be the defendant's. So, in *State* v. *Danforth*, 48 Iowa, 43, 30 Am. Rep. 387, a trial for rape, it was held reversible error to exhibit a child three months old to the jury to corroborate the prosecution by reason of a supposed resemblance between the child and the defendant. And in *Hanawalt* v. *State*, 64 Wis. 84, 54 Am. Rep. 588, 24 N. W. 489, it was held reversible error to exhibit a child less than a year old to the jury for their inspection. The court said: "When applied to the immature child its worthlessness as evidence to establish the fact of parentage is greatly enhanced, and is of too vague, uncertain, and fanciful a nature to be submitted to the consideration of a jury." In *Risk* v. *State ex rel. Vestal*, 19 Ind. 153, it was held improper to admit an infant in evidence, and the court gave as a reason, among others, that "a child changes often and much in looks in the first three months of its existence."

In *Reitz* v. *State ex rel. Holden*, 33 Ind. 187, the trial judge ruled that it was improper to hold a child up before the jury for inspection, and told the jury to disregard it. And in *Clark* v. *Bradstreet*, 80 Me. 454, 15 Atl. 56, it was held reversible error at trial of a bastardy process to exhibit to the jury an infant six weeks old for the purpose of tracing a resemblance to the putative father. The court reviewed the cases, and said: "In a case like this, where the child was a mere infant, such evidence is too vague, uncertain, and fanciful, and, if allowed, would establish not only an unwise, but dangerous and uncertain, rule of evidence." See also *Ingram* v. *State ex rel. McIntosh*, 24 Neb. 33, 37 N. W. 943.

For an exhaustive review of the authorities on this question, see note to *State ex rel. Scott* v. *Harvey* (Iowa) 52 L. R. A. 500.

229. Inspection of defendant's person—compulsory.

It has been held error to compel the defendant to exhibit his person,[1] or any part thereof[2] to the jury as evidence against himself; and it has also been held error to admit evidence derived from a compulsory exhibition of the defendant's person, prior to the trial;[3] because such methods are deemed to compel him to be a witness against himself.

It is otherwise of incriminating articles found upon his person by searching, not by requiring him to produce them.[4]

[1]Upon the subject of the inspection of the person, I brief the following decisions, according to the number if not the weight of authority on this controverted question. But it has not been sufficiently considered that the power to bring one accused to the bar includes the power to see who he is and to prove his identity. A recognizance to appear would not be answered by coming in mask and domino. The constitutional right exempts the prisoner from criminating himself, but does not exempt his person from search, nor from inspection, nor from any examination which justice can make, notwithstanding his right to remain silent and passive. For articles on the question, see 22 Alb. L. J. 144, 6 Crim. L. Mag. 805, 15 Cent. L. J. 2, 207; and note to *Delaware, Lack. & W. R. Co.* (N. Y.) 14 L. R. A. 466.

So, in *State* v. *Jacobs*, 50 N. C. (5 Jones L.) 259, it was held reversible error to compel the defendant to exhibit himself to the inspection of the jury, upon his trial (as a free negro) for carrying arms, in order that the jury might determine his status as a free negro. The court said: "Admitting that the state has a right to compel his presence at the trial, it does not follow that he is bound to stand or sit within view of the jury. Indeed, if he were so bound, why call upon him to exhibit himself to them?"

But directing the accused on a prosecution to stand up so that he may be identified is not erroneous as compelling him to incriminate himself. *State* v. *Reasby*, 100 Iowa, 231, 69 N. W. 451.

Nor is it error to allow the state to make profert to the jury of the person of one charged to be the paramour of another charged with miscegenation, in order to determine by inspection whether he is a negro, as charged in the indictment. *Linton* v. *State*, 88 Ala. 216, 7 So. 261.

'In *Blackwell* v. *State*, 67 Ga. 76, it was held reversible error to compel defendant to stand up and enable a witness for the state to see and testify as to where the amputated leg of the prisoner was cut off, as corroborative of said witness's testimony as to the kind of tracks found near the place of the murder.

But in *State* v. *Ah Chuey*, 14 Neb. 79, 33 Am. Rep. 530, it was held no error and not unconstitutional, on a murder trial, for the court to compel the defendant, against his objection, to exhibit his arm, so as to show certain tattoo marks thereon to the jury, a witness having previously testified that such marks were upon defendant's arm.

And in *Johnson* v. *Com.* 115 Pa. 369, 9 Atl. 78, where the accused on trial for murder readily acceded to the request of the prosecution to stand up and open his mouth, and repeat the sentences used by the murderer at the time of the crime, for the purpose of enabling a witness on the stand to hear and see the prisoner with a view to identifying him, it was held no error, as the accused made no objection; and the court in a *dictum* expressed an opinion in support of such practice.

In *Thomas* v. *State*, 33 Tex. Crim. Rep. 607, 28 S. W. 534, the defendant, charged with murder, testified that deceased inflicted a certain wound upon him, and exhibited the wound to the court and jury to corroborate his testimony; and upon his further stating upon cross-examination that he had not exhibited that particular wound to others before the homicide, but had shown them another wound, it was held that the state might require that he exhibit both wounds.

'*People* v. *McCoy*, 45 How. Pr. 216, a trial for murder of a bastard child, ruled that the state should not be allowed to introduce evidence of the results of a forcible examination of defendant's person by two physicians appointed by the coroner, as it would be compelling defendant to testify against himself.

But *State* v. *Garrett*, 71 N. C. 85, 17 Am. Rep. 1, held it not error to admit upon a murder trial, evidence of the results of a compulsory unwrapping and examination of defendant's hand at the coroner's inquest, where such examination showed that defendant's hand was uninjured, although the defendant claimed that the deceased was burned to death and that defendant burned her hand in an attempt to extinguish the flames. The court attempted to distinguish *State* v. *Jacobs*, 50 N. C. (5 Jones L.) 259, on the ground that although these facts were obtained by methods not *per se* allowable, yet the results could be testified to by witnesses other than the defendant. In *Spicer* v. *State*, 69 Ala. 159, the court said: "The submission, by a female defendant, of her person to a private examination by physicians, is not a confession, although the result of the examination was a disclosure of facts of a criminative character; and such facts are competent evidence against her, although she was induced to submit to the examination through the assurance that it would be the best thing for her that she could do." Murder; judgment reversed on other grounds.

The evidence of the result of inspection of accused, in jail upon charge of rape which had infected a child, was held admissible in *People* v. *Glover*, 71 Mich. 303, 38 N. W. 874.

Chastang v. *State*, 83 Ala. 29, 3 So. 304, holding that it was competent to prove that a pistol was found on the person of the accused when arrested on a charge of carrying concealed weapons, he not having been required to produce it,—Distinguishing *Boyd* v. *United States*, 116 U. S. 616, 29 L. ed. 746, 6 Sup. Ct. Rep. 524, as applicable, where the accused was required to produce the incriminating evidence.

For a case of stripping a post-office employee suspected of embezzling letters, see *United States* v. *Denicke*, 35 Fed. 407.

Although the question does not seem to be passed upon by any appellate court, it seems that in those jurisdictions where the courts have regarded it as unconstitutional to compel submission to an inspection of the person, it would be deemed unconstitutional to compel the defendant to submit to scientific tests to determine the character of his mental operations.

In *People* v. *Ryan*, however (court of sessions, Watertown, N. Y., Oct. 1888, N. Y. Sun, Oct. 22, 1888), a defendant, indicted for a criminal assault upon a female, disclosed to his fellow prisoners his intention "to work the insanity dodge to get free." His conduct was so violent that a commission was appointed to ascertain his mental condition. The commission employed an expert who applied by force to the manacled prisoner the ether test, on the theory that one has no control over the voluntary action of the mind while passing into the resulting semi-comatose condition, and, therefore, the rational or irrational condition can thus be determined. Against objection, as a violation of the constitutional right, the court received the expert's testimony, founded on this test, that the accused was sane, and he was convicted and sentenced for nineteen years.

230. — comparison—compulsory.

For the same reason it has been held error to compel defendant at the trial to submit to the test of comparisons—for example, between his feet and tracks found near the scene of the crime.[1]

For the same reason it has been held error to admit evidence of such compulsory comparisons made out of court prior to the trial.[2]

[1]*Stokes* v. *State*, 5 Baxt. 619, 30 Am. Rep. 72. Murder; reversible error to permit the prosecuting attorney to bring a pan of mud into court and request the accused to put his foot therein, for the purpose of comparison with tracks near the scene of the murder and alleged to be the prisoner's, even though the court told the accused that he need not do so unless he wished, and told the jury that the refusal of the defendant to comply with the request was not to be taken as evidence against him. *Contra, Sprouse* v. *Com.* 81 Va. 374, requiring to write in court not error. But see *People* v. *DeKroyft*, 49 Hun, 71, 1 N. Y. Supp. 692, and cases cited.

In *Johnson* v. *State*, 59 N. J. L. 535, 38 L. R. A. 373, 37 Atl. 949, Affirming 59 N. J. L. 271, 35 Atl. 787, it was held that boots worn by defendant charged with murder, on the night the crime was committed, and impression in sand by such boots by way of illustration, might be exhibited to the jury in connection with evidence of footprints of a peculiar character in the dirt and soil near the body of the murdered person.

In *People* v. *Oliveria*, 127 Cal. 376, 59 Pac. 772, it was held that a defendant charged with robbery might be compelled to stand up for comparison in size by the prosecuting witness with the party who robbed him.

[2]In *Day* v. *State*, 63 Ga. 667 (burglary), it was held reversible error to admit evidence that the defendant had been forced to put his foot into tracks found near the scene of the crime, and that his shoe fitted the tracks, because this was being compelled to give testimony tending to criminate himself. *Contra, State* v. *Graham*, 74 N. C. 646 (stealing); *Walker* v. *State*, 7 Tex. App. 245, 32 Am. Rep. 595 (murder). In both these cases receiving such evidence was held not error.

231. — voluntary.

The accused may waive his right to refuse to submit to such personal tests before the jury.[1]

[1]In *People* v. *Mead*, 50 Mich. 228, 15 N. W. 95, where evidence had been given of tracks found near the scene of the burglary, it was held not reversible error to compel defendant, against objection by his counsel, to measure a shoe which he had already voluntarily tried on in the presence of the jury, because compelling such measurement was an error which did no legal injury to the defendant, as he had voluntarily submitted to the test of trying on the shoe. But the court in a *dictum* (per Cooley, J.) said: "Had there been any objection to the respondent's trying on the shoe, the court would have had no authority to require it, and even the simple matter of measurement the respondent might have declined had he seen fit."

232. — — rebuttal.

Where the accused voluntarily allows the jury to inspect his person as a part of his case in defense, it is proper to compel him to submit to an inspection by medical experts called by way of rebuttal on the part of the prosecution.[1]

[1]In *Gordon* v. *State*, 68 Ga. 814 (assault), it was held no error to compel the accused to allow a scar upon his head to be examined by a physician called by the prosecution, to show that it was the result of an old wound, and not of a recent blow, as had been claimed by the accused upon his voluntary exhibition of the scar to the jury.

233. Comparisons by witnesses other than the accused.

Although the accused cannot be compelled to make comparisons incriminating himself,[1] yet evidence may be given of such comparisons made by others,[2] subject to rebuttal by similar evidence on behalf of the accused;[3] for example, as to the correspondence in size and shape between the shoes of the accused and tracks found near the scene of the crime; and expert testimony will not be required.[4]

[1]See sections immediately preceding.

[2]In *State* v. *Morris*, 84 N. C. 756, it was held no error on a murder trial to admit evidence of persons who had measured footprints found near the scene of the homicide, and applied the measurements to the boots of the accused, and found a correspondence in size and shape, even though such measurement and comparison had taken place when the accused was neither present nor represented.

So, in *Meyers* v. *State*, 14 Tex. App. 35, it was held no error to admit testimony of witness for prosecution that under the direction of the sheriff, he had applied the boot taken from the foot of the accused to tracks near the place of the assault, and that they corresponded.

The constitutional prohibition against compelling a person accused of crime to give testimony incriminating himself is not violated by the officer to whose custody an accused is committed taking the latter's shoes and comparing them with certain tracks found near the scene of the alleged offense, and by his testifying to the result of the comparison. *Myers* v. *State*, 97 Ga. 76, 25 S. E. 252.

So, evidence is admissible that a witness measured tracks made by one accused of burglary, and also the tracks found in the yard after the burglary, and that the two corresponded. *Gilmore* v. *State*, 99 Ala. 154, 13 So. 536.

And evidence that some of the footprints leading to and from a burglarized house, which have been described, corresponded with shoes worn by defendant at the examining trial, is admissible. *Clark* v. *State* (Tex. Crim. App.) 26 S. W. 68.

And it is competent to prove that defendant's foot seemed to fit in tracks found at or near the place of the crime, when he voluntarily placed his foot in such tracks. *Potter* v. *State*, 92 Ala. 37, 9 So. 402.

And footprints found at or near the place where the crime was committed, corresponding to the tracks of the accused, may be shown to identify him as the guilty party on a prosecution for arson, but are insufficient to establish his guilt if they are not distinguished from ordinary footprints by any peculiar marks, and the correspondence between them and the tracks of the accused is merely in superficial shape, outline, and dimensions. *Whetston* v. *State,* 31 Fla. 240, 12 So. 661.

In *People* v. *Searcey,* 121 Cal. 1, 41 L. R. A. 157, 53 Pac. 359, it was held that a box of sand containing impressions of shoe tracks which a witness testifies that he made with the shoes of the accused person, and that they are identical with those he found in the sand upon a desert, is admissible in evidence for the purpose of accurately describing the appearance of the tracks on the desert, which are claimed to have been made by the accused.

But it was held incompetent to prove that the accused was excited when such comparison was being made, in *People* v. *Wolcott,* 51 Mich. 612, 17 N. W. 78, holding it reversible error to admit such evidence on trial for larceny of wheat, where evidence had been given that tracks were found and followed from where the wheat was taken, and that the boot of the accused was measured to see how it corresponded with the tracks.

In *State* v. *Melick,* 65 Iowa, 614, 22 N. W. 895, it was held reversible error to reject evidence offered by the accused to prove that his horse could not wear a shoe of the size of the tracks leading from the scene of the crime of burning property to the barn of the accused, where a witness for the prosecution had testified that such tracks corresponded in size with the shoes of defendant's horse. It was held also that evidence of such tracks so leading and so corresponding in size would not, in the absence of other incriminating evidence, be sufficient to warrant a conviction for burning property.

So, too, where evidence had been given that the defendant's shoe fitted a track found near the scene of the murder, and that fresh horse tracks led therefrom towards his house, it was held reversible error to reject evidence that at the time the tracks were being measured the defendant then offered to put his foot and shoe in the track, and also then requested that the horse tracks might be measured and compared with the feet and tracks of his horse. *Bouldin* v. *State,* 8 Tex. App. 332.

Com. v. *Pope,* 103 Mass. 440, holds that it is not error, but proper to admit the evidence of any person who has seen the boots and footprints, as the correspondence between them is a matter requiring no peculiar knowledge. And see *State* v. *Reitz,* 83 N. C. 634, to the same effect, where the witness had testified that it was his best opinion that certain tracks found near the place of the crime were those of the prisoner.

234. Photographs.

On the trial of an issue involving the condition, appearance, or identity of a person,[1] place,[2] or thing[3] at a previous time, a photograph taken at or reasonably near the time in question is competent, upon proper evidence of fidelity adequate for the purpose for which it is offered.[4]

[1]In *Ruloff's Case,* 11 Abb. Pr. N. S. 248, S. C., less fully, 45 N. Y. 213, it was held no error to admit photographs of deceased burglars, to aid in their identification, even where the bodies had been in the river for several days, and although the photographs were confessedly not so good as they would have been if taken at a more favorable angle. To similar effect, see *Cowley* v. *People,* 83 N. Y. 476, 38 Am. Rep. 464 (photograph of emaciated child); *Udderzook* v. *Com.* 76 Pa. 340; *State* v. *McCoy,* 15 Utah, 136, 49 Pac. 420; *State* v. *Kelley,* 46 S. C. 55, 24 S. E. 60; *State* v. *Ellwood,* 17 R. I. 763, 24 Atl. 782; *Com.* v. *Keller,* 191 Pa. 122, 43 Atl. 198; *People* v. *Webster,* 139 N. Y. 73, 34 N. E. 730; *Com.* v. *Morgan,* 159 Mass. 375, 34 N. E. 458; *State* v. *Windahl,* 95 Iowa, 470, 64 N. W. 420; *People* v. *Durrant,* 116 Cal. 179, 48 Pac. 75. And see, fully, on this question, authorities reviewed in note to *Dederichs* v. *Salt Lake City R. Co.* (Utah) 35 L. R. A. 802, 805.

[2]*Cozzens* v. *Higgins,* 1 Abb. App. Dec. 451; *People* v. *Buddensieck,* 103 N. Y. 487, 57 Am. Rep. 766, 9 N. E. 441; *People* v. *Fish,* 125 N. Y. 136, 26 N. E. 319; *Com.* v. *Robertson,* 162 Mass. 90, 38 N. E. 25; *Keyes* v. *State,* 122 Ind. 527, 23 N. E. 1097. And see note to *Dederichs* v. *Salt Lake City R. Co.* (Utah) 35 L. R. A. 802.

That photographs which are artistic reproductions of situations carefully planned by the chief witness for the state on a trial for murder, instead of being mere reproductions of the scene of the homicide, are inadmissible in evidence, see *Fore* v. *State,* 75 Miss. 727, 23 So. 710.

[3]*Chestnut Hill & S. H. Turnp. Co.* v. *Piper,* 15 W. N. C. 55 (civil case; holding that the fact that the photograph did not show every part of the ground did not require its exclusion); *Duffin* v. *People,* 107 Ill. 113, 47 Am. Rep. 431 (no error to admit a photograph of a promissory note, on trial for forgery thereof, where the note had been written in rapidly fading ink, and the photograph was offered merely to identify the words of the original, also offered in evidence. Held also that for such purpose it was not necessary to prove that the photograph had been taken by an expert).

But photographs are not admissible when offered merely to show that other persons have been guilty of like offenses. *People* v. *Muller,* 32 Hun, 209, holding it no error to reject photographs offered to show that other persons had sold pictures similar to those charged to be obscene.

[4]*Ruloff's Case,* 11 Abb. Pr. N. S. 248.

The court will not judicially notice the fidelity of a photograph offered in evidence; that fact must be established by proper evidence. See cases cited in note to *Dederichs* v. *Salt Lake City R. Co.* (Utah) 35 L. R. A. 803.

235. Diagrams.

A diagram of the scene of the crime, proved to be correct, is admissible in evidence.[1]

[1]In *Moon* v. *State,* 68 Ga. 687, it was held that the fact that part of the

diagram was drawn in red ink was not ground of objection, as immaterial, nor "as calculated to inflame the minds of the jury as suggestive of the bloody deed." The court also intimated that if witnesses for the defense did not agree with witnesses for the state as to its accuracy, it was the privilege of counsel for the accused to have a diagram prepared in accordance with the testimony of the defense, and to submit it to the jury in rebuttal. And in *People* v. *Jackson,* 111 N. Y. 362, 19 N. E. 54, it was held that the fact that the photograph included figures of men who had been stationed so as to show the positions occupied by the persons concerned at the time of the offense did not render it incompetent. And for some other cases see *Burton* v. *State,* 115 Ala. 1, 22 So. 585; *Adams* v. *State,* 28 Fla. 511, 10 So. 106; *People* v. *Johnson,* 140 N. Y. 350, 35 N. E. 604; *Rodriquez* v. *State,* 32 Tex. Crim. Rep. 259, 22 S. W. 978; *State* v. *Hunter,* 18 Wash. 670, 52 Pac. 247; *State* v. *Harr,* 38 W. Va. 58, 17 S. E. 794.

The correctness of a diagram of the scene of a homicide is sufficiently established to permit a witness to testify with reference to the position of the parties as shown by the diagram, where such witness and another witness who made the diagram testify that it is practically correct. *Fuller* v. *State,* 117 Ala. 36, 23 So. 688.

XXXII. Intent and knowledge.

236. Other offenses.

When criminal intent or guilty knowledge in respect of the act is an element in the offense charged,[1] evidence of other acts of the accused, manifesting that intent or knowledge, is competent, notwithstanding it may establish the commission of another offense not charged.[2]

[1]For a general discussion of intent as an element of crime, see note to *People* v. *Flack* (N. Y.) 11 L. R. A. 807.

[2]See, for instance, *State* v. *Phelps,* 5 S. D. 480, 59 N. W. 471; *Mason* v. *State,* 31 Tex. Crim. Rep. 306, 20 S. W. 564. But see cases cited in *ante,* §§ 60, 61, against admitting evidence of another offense.

For some special illustrations of this rule, see the following:

Abandoning child.—*Matthewson* v. *People,* 8 N. Y. Week. Dig. 278, holds that evidence that accused attempted to destroy the child immediately after birth is admissible to show intent to get rid of it.

Adultery.—*Com.* v. *Nichols,* 114 Mass. 285, 19 Am. Rep. 346, 348, held evidence of other acts of adultery committed between the same persons near the time charged, though in another country, admissible. The bill of exceptions did not state that any objection was made to the admissibility because of remoteness of time, nor that it did not corroborate the testimony of the woman. *State* v. *Williams,* 76 Me. 480, held evidence tending to prove illicit intercourse of the defendant with the same person charged in the indictment, both before and after the day on which an adultery was laid, competent to prove the relation and mutual disposition of the parties.

Arson.—*Com.* v. *McCarthy,* 119 Mass. 354; *Com.* v. *Bradford,* 126 Mass. 42 (holding that on the trial of an indictment for maliciously burning a building, the prosecution may show, on the question of intent, that the defendant previously set fire to the same building, or an adjoining shed). To the same effect, *People* v. *Lattimore,* 86 Cal. 403, 24 Pac. 1091. And *Meister* v. *People,* 31 Mich. 99, held evidence that a month before the fire the defendant wanted witness to burn the property admissible. The point was but slightly considered. New trial granted on other grounds. Otherwise of a like proposition made three or four years before. *Carncross* v. *People,* 17 N. Y. Week. Dig. 383.

Assault.—On a trial for assault with intent to murder, evidence of a previous difficulty between other persons, occurring a short time previous, and out of which the difficulty in which the assault was committed grew, is admissible. *Elmore* v. *State,* 110 Ala. 63, 20 So. 323. So held of evidence of a former or subsequent assault upon the same person to show intent. *State* v. *Pennington,* 124 Mo. 388, 27 S. W. 1106. To the same effect, see *Hamilton* v. *State* (Tex. Crim. App.) 56 S. W. 926; *Crass* v. *State,* 31 Tex. Crim. Rep. 312, 20 S. W. 579. "But this rule [admitting evidence of another offense] can have no application to two different assaults committed at different times and at different places and upon different persons, where the motive in one case could upon no sound principle be the same as in the other." Miller, J., in *People* v. *Gibbs,* 93 N. Y. 470. Accordingly, judgment was reversed for admitting such evidence. And that wrongs committed by defendant previous to the assault in question can be considered only with reference to the animus with which the act was committed, see *Beavers* v. *State,* 54 Ark. 336, 15 S. W. 1024.

Blackmail.—*People* v. *Haver,* 4 N. Y. Crim. Rep. 171 (blackmail and malicious annoyance. N. Y. Pen. Code, § 558). Evidence of letters of the same tenor sent by defendant to another person admitted on the question of intent only.

Bribery.—In *People* v. *Sharp,* 107 N. Y. 427, 14 N. E. 319 (an indictment for attempt to bribe member of common council of New York city in order to influence his action on application for consent to construct a street railway on Broadway in that city), it was held error to admit evidence of a corrupt proposal made by defendant about a year previous to the offense charged, to an engrossing clerk in the legislature, to pay said clerk a certain sum to alter a bill in reference to street railways, which the clerk then had in his possession, so that its terms might authorize the construction of a railroad on Broadway. The court said it was an act remote in point of time, different in purpose, and of an entirely separate and distinct matter forming no part of one main transaction,—Applying rule in *People* v. *Shulman,* 80 N. Y. 376, note.

Burglary.—In *People* v. *Mead,* 50 Mich. 228, 15 N. W. 95, the prosecution was allowed to show that the next day after the burglary accused picked up an article taken in the commission of a burglary on another house, that occurred in the vicinity on the same night, and claimed to have just found it there. The court held this proper on the ground that the several burglaries were substantially one transaction. In *State* v. *Weldon,* 39 S. C. 318, 24 L. R. A. 126, 17 S. E. 688, a trial for burglary, evidence of previous robberies was held admissible against a defendant who had been discharged from the service of the prosecutor on account of such robberies, and declared that he did not intend to work, and if he did not make his support out of the prosecutor he would out of somebody else. In *Hope* v. *People,* 83 N. Y. 418, 38 Am. Rep. 460, it was held not error to receive evidence of the previous concerting of a scheme to rob the same premises. In *Osborne* v. *People,* 2 Park. Crim. Rep. 583 (burglary of a store), it was held not error to admit evidence of facts tending to show larceny from an adjoining store, the entry of the two stores being regarded as a connected transaction. In *Stokes* v. *State,* 84 Ga. 258, 10 S. E. 740, evidence of the larceny of goods was held admissible to show the intent with which one accused of burglary broke and entered the building. *State* v. *Cowell,* 12 Nev. 337, held that on joint indictment for burglary of a dwelling house with intent to steal, it was proper to allow one of the defendants to testify for the prosecution as to an agreement made by him and the other defendants, a few days before the burglary, to commit a robbery on the person of the occupant of the dwelling house. This case was disapproved in an article in 6 Cent. L. J. 403, reviewing cases, as violating tha rule against admitting evidence of the commission of one offense on the trial for another. *Contra, People* v. *Greenwall,* 108 N. Y. 296, 15 N. E. 404, was a trial for murder, which, it appeared, had been committed by some one who had burglariously entered the house of deceased at night; the accused upon cross-examination by the prosecution as to his connection with another burglary at another house, he denied it, and also upon re-examination denied that he had ever entered any man's house in the nighttime with intent to steal. It was held error to permit the occupant of the other house, as a witness for the prosecution, to testify to facts showing that accused did burglariously enter his house at night. Conviction reversed. So, *People* v. *White,* 3 N. Y. Crim. Rep. 366, held it error to admit evidence of the accused taking other property from the same premises about a month previous to the alleged burglary. And *Hall* v. *People,* 6 Park. Crim. Rep. 671, held it error to admit evidence of a larceny committed previous to the burglary, the property stolen on both occasions being found on defendant's boat, but not in the same place thereon.

Counterfeiting.—*Dibble* v. *People,* 4 Park. Crim. Rep. 199, held it error to refuse to strike out evidence to show the subsequent uttering by the prisoner of other forged bills or notes, without its being shown that they were of the same manufacture as those charged in the indictment, or were in some way connected with the offense charged. See also *State* v. *Van Houten,* 3 N. J. L. 672, 4 Am. Dec. 407. Publishing counterfeit bill; holding evidence of passing other counterfeits on same day admissible. In *Bersch* v. *State,* 13 Ind. 434, 74 Am. Dec. 263 (passing counterfeit money), evidence that the defendant's wife had sold the witness other counterfeit money belonging to the defendant, in his absence, the defendant being subsequently advised thereof, and sanctioning it, was held properly admitted.

Crime committed to conceal a crime.—*Dunn* v. *State,* 2 Ark. 229, 35 Am. Dec. 54, where it appeared probable that the murder of which the prisoner was accused might have been committed to prevent his prosecution for a prior murder; evidence of the prior murder was admitted, but judgment superseded on other grounds.

Extortion.—In *State* v. *Lewis,* 96 Iowa, 286, 65 N. W. 295, evidence of other extortion and attempts to extort than those set forth in an indictment for extortion was held admissible to show the intent with which the threats charged in the indictment were made, but that it should be limited to that purpose.

False pretenses.—*Bielschofsky* v. *People,* 3 Hun, 40 (held not error to show that the prisoner, with one jointly indicted with him, practised the same fraud on another person a day or two prior to the commission of the offense charged in the indictment); *Shipply* v. *People,* 12 N. Y. Week. Dig. 239, Affirmed in 86 N. Y. 375, 40 Am. Rep. 551; (larceny; held not error to admit evidence that accused was engaged in similar frauds at about the same time, and accomplished by the same means). And for other cases holding competent evidence of other similar transactions, see *Housh* v. *People,* 24 Colo. 262, 50 Pac. 1036; *Farmer* v. *State,* 100 Ga. 41, 28 S. E. 26; *Com.* v. *Williamson,* 96 Ky. 1, 27 S. W. 812; *People* v. *Summers,* 115 Mich. 537, 73 N. W. 818; *State* v. *Wilson,* 143 Mo. 334, 44 S. W. 722; *People* v. *Peckens,* 153 N. Y. 576, 47 N. E. 883. See also *Weyman* v. *People,* 4 Hun, 511, Affirmed in 62 N. Y. 623; *State* v. *Myers,* 82 Mo. 558, 52 Am. Rep. 389 (obtaining money by trick and fraud; held not error to admit evidence of acts of the accused similar to that charged, and committed against other persons on the same day and in the same town), Citing many cases. To similar effect, *Trogdon* v. *Com.* 31 Gratt. 862 (evidence of similar acts of accused about same time admissible); *Rafferty* v. *State,* 91 Tenn. 655, 16 S. W. 728 (a trial for attempt to obtain money under a policy from a company, under false pretenses as to a loss at a fire; evidence that defendant had had many previous fires, at different places and under different names, upon which she collected insurance moneys, here admissible against her); *Mayer* v. *People,* 80 N. Y. 364 (obtaining goods by false representations as to solvency; held not error to admit evidence of similar contemporaneous representations to creditors from whom goods had previously been purchased, though no goods were obtained by means of such representations; held, however, that such evidence was admissible only on the question of intent, and that it would have been error to allow the jury to consider it on the question whether the defendant in fact made the representation charged. The jury were, however, properly cautioned); *People* v. *Henssler,* 48 Mich. 49, 11 N. W. 804 (obtaining indorsement on false pretense that proceeds were to be paid to a specified person, held allowable to show that respondent had previously obtained from the indorser sums which he claimed were to be paid, and afterwards said had been paid, to the same person, when in fact they had not been); *Reg.* v. *Francis,* L. R. 2 C. C. 128 (obtaining money from pawnbroker by false pretenses that a ring was a diamond ring; evidence that defendant had shortly before offered other false articles of jewelry to other pawnbrokers admissible); *Com.* v. *Coe,* 115 Mass. 481 (cheating by falsely pretending that a forged certificate of stock was genuine; evidence of the possession and use by the defendant of other forged certificates of stock about the same time admissible).

Falsification of accounts.—*United States* v. *Russell,* 19 Fed. 591. Other false accounts made by defendant at about the same time admissible.

Forgery.—In *People* v. *Everhardt,* 104 N. Y. 591, 11 N. E. 62, Affirming 5 N. Y. Crim. Rep. 91, a prosecution for uttering a forged check, where there was no direct or positive evidence that the accused personally forged it, it was held not error to admit evidence that he uttered forged checks on other occasions. In *Francis* v. *State,* 7 Tex. App. 501 (forgery of transfer from S. to B.), the prosecution was allowed to introduce conveyance to S. from one T., and prove that it and the certificate of acknowledgment were forgeries. In *Strang* v. *State,* 32 Tex. Crim. Rep. 219, 22 S. W. 680, an action for passing a forged instrument, to which the defense of good faith in indorsing another person's name on the check passed was set up, evidence that the accused had embezzled other funds, and had confessed the fact, was held admissible as throwing light on his intent in passing the instrument. In *Bishop* v. *State,* 55 Md. 138 (forging indorsement on bond, also uttering the same, knowing it to be forged), it was held competent for prosecution to show that on or about the time of the forgery charged the appellants held and uttered similar forged instruments. In *Garner* v. *State,* 5 Lea, 213, evidence of the passage of similar forged paper by defendant was held admissible to prove *scienter;* and there was *dictum* that proof of erasure on the paper thus passed, like the erasure on the instrument set out in the indictment, and the production of such paper, or tracing it back to the hands of the defendant, would make out a prima facie case of the forgery thereof. And *State* v. *Williams,* 2 Rich. L. 418, 45 Am. Dec. 741, held evidence that accused had uttered and passed other forged notes of the same character admissible. In *State* v. *Saunders,* 68 Iowa, 370, 27 N. W. 455, Seevers, J., says, without determining the question: "Undoubtedly, the crimes of forgery and uttering forged paper are within the exception. But the doubt seems to be whether the paper must not be of the same character or manufacture and precisely similar to that forged or uttered upon which the charge is based,"—Citing *Dibble* v. *People,* 4 Park. Crim. Rep. 199; *People* v. *Corbin,* 56 N. Y. 363, 15 Am. Rep. 427; *Morris* v. *State,* 8 Smedes & M. 762. In *Lindsey* v. *State,* 38 Ohio St. 507, on a charge of uttering and publishing forged deed with intent to defraud, other forged deeds, including deeds of trust to secure notes or bonds, found in possession of defendant, or proved to have been uttered and published by him, were held competent, notwithstanding objection that the deeds of trust were not of the "same description." The court approved, as abundantly supported by the weight of authority, a note byCowen & Hill to 1 Phillipps, Ev. 768, as follows: "On the whole, the decided balance of authority would seem to be in favor of receiving the evidence, whether the other bills, etc., be *ejusden generis* or not." And for other cases recognizing the rule, see *Com.* v. *White,* 145 Mass. 392, 14 N. E. 611; *Langford* v. *State,* 33 Fla. 233, 14 So. 815; *Anson* v. *People,* 148 Ill. 494, 35 N. E. 145; *Com.* v. *Russell,* 156 Mass. 196, 30 N. E. 763; *State* v. *Rose,* 70 Minn. 403, 73 N. W. 177; *State* v. *Hodges,* 144 Mo. 50, 45 S. W. 1093. But on a trial for forging a check, other checks passed by defendant, which were not paid on presentation, are inadmissible to show defendant's guilty knowledge, in the absence of proof that they were forged. *People* v. *Whiteman,* 114 Cal. 338, 46 Pac. 99.

Fraud.—In *People* v. *Dimick,* 107 N. Y. 13, 32, 14 N. E. 178 (larceny, with intent to deprive a marine insurance company of its property), the evidence showed that after loss of a cargo the accused changed the entries relating to the insurance so as to throw the loss on one company, for the purpose of shielding another company from loss. It was held not error to admit evidence of like instances, where he had changed insurance to shield the same company. See also *Taylor* v. *United States,* 3 How. 197, 11 L. ed. 559. Fraud on the revenue.

Homicide.—In *Reg.* v. *Cotton,* 12 Cox C. C. 400 (murder of child by poison, where the defense was that its death resulted from an accidental taking of such poison), evidence to prove that two other children of accused and a lodger in her house had died previous to the present charge from the same poison, was held admissible. In *State* v. *Shuford,* 69 N. C. 486 (murder of infant child), it was held error to admit a statement by the mother of the prisoner, and in her presence, that the prisoner "had a child this way before, and put it away," to show the prisoner made no reply, because there is no connection between the two crimes. In *Goersen* v. *Com.* 39 Phila. Legal Int. 148 (murder of wife by poison), it was held competent to show that defendant poisoned his wife's mother a few days before the death of his wife, and with the same description of poison; and this for the purpose of showing the design of the defendant to obtain their property, and rebutting the theory of accident or suicide, or the ignorant and negligent use of arsenic. In *Rucker* v. *State,* 7 Tex. App. 549 (murder), the prosecution was allowed to put in evidence indictment against defendant for assault upon one W. and also indictment against said W. and his bail-bond, on which the deceased was a surety. There was evidence of ill-will and threats of the defendant against the deceased on account of the latter's thus befriending W. In *Phillips* v. *State,* 62 Ark. 119, 34 S. W. 539 (wife murder), evidence that about two months before the killing defendant was seen whipping his wife, and that she had exhibited bruises on her arms and body, and that defendant had threatened to beat her to death if she would not stay at home, was held competent. And in *People* v. *Walters,* 98 Cal. 138, 32 Pac. 864, a trial for murder of a son, proof of the killing of his mother at the same time was held admissible to show malice, where the mother and son were representatives of one side of a family feud, and the defendant was upon the other side. In *West* v. *State* (Fla.) 28 So. 430, a murder trial, evidence of the killing of another person by the defendant contemporaneously with the murder for which he was on trial was held admissible, where it tended to prove the animus of the defendant in the commission of the murder for which he was on trial. So, in *People* v. *Seaman*, 107 Mich. 348, 65 N. W. 203, evidence that one charged with manslaughter in committing an abortion had committed abortions on other persons in the same house was held admissible, where he claimed that the case in question was one of childbirth. And in *Com.* v. *Birriolo*, 197 Pa. 371, 47 Atl. 355, a trial for murder of defendant's wife by burning, evidence of an assault of a similar character was held admissible to show the intent with which the burning for which defendant was on trial was committed, and to show that the act was wilful, and to prove motive. And in *People* v. *Coughlin*, 13 Utah, 58, 44 Pac. 94, evidence that defendant, charged with murder for killing a person while resisting arrest, four days before the homicide tried to kill the sheriff, who was attempting to arrest him, was held admissible as tending to show a deliberate intention to kill any person who might attempt his arrest.

Incest.—*State* v. *Markins*, 95 Ind. 464, 48 Am. Rep. 733, 735, holding that where the chief element of the offense charged consists in illicit intercourse between the sexes, evidence of previous lascivious conduct of the parties is admissible,—Citing *People* v. *Jenness*, 5 Mich. 305; *Lawson* v. *State*, 20 Ala. 65, 56 Am. Dec. 182; *Thayer* v. *Thayer*, 101 Mass. 111, 100 Am. Dec. 110; *State* v. *Bridgman*, 49 Vt. 202, 24 Am. Rep. 124; *State* v. *Pippin*, 88 N. C. 646; *State* v. *Kemp*, 87 N. C. 538. But it was conceded that acts of sexual intercourse subsequent to the offense charged would be inadmissible. *Lovell* v. *State*, 12 Ind. 18.

Indecent exposure of person.—In a prosecution for indecent exposure of person, evidence of like exposures before and after the commission of the offense charged is admissible to show that the act was designedly done. *State* v. *Stice*, 88 Iowa, 27, 55 N. W. 17.

Keeping gaming implements.—*Com.* v. *Certain Gaming Implements*, 141 Mass. 114, 5 N. E. 475. Evidence that the rooms where implements were found were resorted to for unlawful gaming at times previous to the day of seizure of such implements admissible.

Keeping intoxicating liquors.—*Com.* v. *Matthews*, 129 Mass. 487. Evidence being given that the defendant kept a saloon both before and after the date stated in the complaint, the prosecution was allowed to show that the defendant had liquor at his saloon a week or ten days after that date. So, in *Dobson* v. *State*, 5 Lea, 271 (sale of intoxicating liquors), where the defense was that the sale was made by a licensed druggist to fill the prescription of a physician, proof of other sales than the one for which the defendant was on trial was held admissible. And for other cases to similar effect, see *Sellers* v. *State*, 98 Ala. 72, 13 So. 530; *Hans* v. *State*, 50 Neb. 150, 69 N. W. 838; *Matkins* v. *State* (Tex. Crim. App.) 58 S. W. 108; *Pitner* v. *State*, 37 Tex. Crim. Rep. 268, 39 S. W. 662; *State* v. *White*, 70 Vt. 225, 39 Atl. 1085. Compare *Chipman* v. *People*, 24 Colo. 520, 52 Pac. 677, where it is held that evidence that defendant, charged with selling intoxicating liquors in quantities less than a gallon, without a license, in violation of 3 Mills's (Colo.) Anno.

Stat. § 1346, had made other sales to other persons at different times, is inadmissible to show defendant's intent in making the sale charged against him, although the prosecuting witness testifies that he bought the liquor for medicinal purposes, as a sale for such purpose is within the prohibition of the statute.

Larceny — connected theft.—*Phillips* v. *People,* 57 Barb. 353, Affirmed in 42 N. Y. 200 (held not error, on trial for stealing a horse, to admit evidence that accused stole a wagon from another person the same night, to use with it); *People* v. *Cunningham,* 66 Cal. 668, 6 Pac. 700, 846 (larceny of cattle belonging to T., where prosecution gave evidence tending to show that accused was captured driving away such cattle, and also a steer belonging to W., accused having given evidence tending to show that he came into possession of T.'s cattle innocently, by purchase; held not error to admit evidence tending to show that the steer belonging to W. was stolen, as being part of the same entire transaction. Compare previous decision in 4 West. Coast Rep. 506, 66 Cal. 673, 4 Pac. 1144 (the judge who rendered the prior decision dissented from the latter); *McCall* v. *State,* 14 Tex. App. 353 (theft of cow; prosecution permitted to prove that when the cow was taken she had a yearling with her, which the defendant penned with the cow, and which was branded by the defendant); *Moore* v. *State,* 28 Tex. App. 377, 13 S. W. 152 (a prosecution for the theft of a horse, evidence as to the theft of a saddle and slicker, which occurred about the same time and in the same neighborhood as the theft of the horse, held admissible, if at all, only as tending to show the intent of the defendant); *State* v. *Valwell,* 66 Vt. 558, 29 Atl. 1018 (evidence of defendant's participation in a larceny committed during the same night, and shortly before the larceny charged in the indictment was committed, held competent upon the question whether, in assisting his alleged accomplice in the acts charged, he knew that a crime was being committed). Compare *Snapp* v. *Com.* 82 Ky. 173, where the court says: "The rule has never been carried so far as to admit evidence against the accused of an independent larceny, although of the same character, for the purpose of convicting the party of the larceny for which he is being tried."

— committed by aid of same trick or device.—But see *People ex rel. Willis* v. *Special Sessions Justices' Ct.* 10 Hun, 158. Larceny committed while changing bill, held error to admit evidence of a former attempt to commit a like crime, to show intent, where the court said of *Weyman* v. *People,* 4 Hun, 511; *Bielschofsky* v. *People,* 3 Hun, 40, that there were "cases in which the other transactions admitted in evidence were connected more or less directly with the particular transaction charged against the accused." For cases on false pretenses and embezzlement, as made larceny by recent statute, see False Pretenses, *supra.*

Peculation.—*People* v. *Lyon,* 1 N. Y. Crim. Rep. 400, which was affirmed in 33 Hun, 623, which was reversed on other grounds in 99 N. Y. 210, 1 N. E. 763, Citing many cases (peculation of city moneys; the money was taken by defendant's partner in accordance with a previous agreement between them, held not error to allow, for the purpose of showing intent to defraud, proof of instances in which the partner had used money of the city for the business of the firm, after the time of the alleged agreements, up to and including the transaction charged); *People* v. *Cobler,* 108 Cal. 538, 41 Pac. 401 (evidence that defendant, on trial for embezzlement of taxes received from him as deputy assessor, collected similar taxes from other parties, and failed to pay over or account for the money so collected, held admissible to show guilty knowledge and intent); *People* v. *Hawkins,* 106 Mich. 479, 64 N. W. 736 (evidence of previous acts of embezzlement is admissible to prove intent in a prosecution for embezzlement). In *People* v. *DeGraff,* 5 N. Y. Crim. Rep. 561, 6 N. Y. S. R. 412, the two judges participating in the decision were divided on the question whether, under the peculation act for defrauding a county evidence of a similar transaction committed by the defendant in the following year was properly admitted as bearing on the question of guilty knowledge.

Perjury.—Evidence is admissible on a trial for perjury, to show that defendant endeavored to induce another person to give false testimony in the case in which he is alleged to have subsequently testified falsely. *Heflin* v. *State,* 88 Ga. 151, 14 S. E. 112.

Rape.—In cases of sexual crimes the admissibility of evidence of other similar crimes is based upon the ground that there was some logical connection between the crime proposed to be proved, other than merely the tendency to commit one crime as manifested by the tendency to commit another. *State* v. *Lapage,* 57 N. H. 245, 24 Am. Rep. 69, 83 (to show murder in an attempt to commit rape, held evidence of a previous rape on another person four years before the alleged offense inadmissible. Where a prisoner is tried for a particular crime, it is always competent to show, on the question of his guilt, that he has made an attempt at some prior time, not too distant, to commit the same offense); *People* v. *O'Sullivan,* 104 N. Y. 481, 58 Am. Rep. 530, 10 N. E. 880 (holding it not error in a trial for rape to receive such evidence of a prior attempt to commit rape upon the same female, conceding that it would not be admissible to prove an attempt to commit it upon another one). To the same effect, *State* v. *Patrick,* 107 Mo. 147, 17 S. W. 666, Distinguished in *People* v. *Sharp,* 107 N. Y. 427, 474, 14 N. E. 319.

Receiving stolen goods.—"If a person has frequently received articles of property of a particular kind from another, knowing that such other person stole them from a particular person or place, and he is offered on a subsequent occasion similar articles by the same person and under like circumstances, it does directly tend to establish that the articles thus offered were also known to be stolen. It is a natural and necessary inference, and one which every reasonable man would draw. It is an inference derived from the laws of human action." Church, Ch. J., in *Copperman* v. *People,* 56 N. Y. 591, where it was held not error to admit such evidence. But see *State* v. *Ward,* 49 Conn. 429 ("When it appears that a person is in the habit of buying different kinds of an article,—in this case iron,—some of it legitimately and honestly, the wrongful act in receiving one article is not competent to prove a criminal intent in receiving another, differing in time, kind of property, the person from whom stolen, and the person from whom received"); *Coleman* v.

People, 55 N. Y. 81 (conviction reversed). But after a second trial of same cause, held (58 N. Y. 555, 560) that evidence of stealing by the same persons from the same owners, of similar goods, and the buying by the accused, for inadequate price and apparently with knowledge, but a short time before the act charged, was competent.

"As a general rule, on the trial for one offense, proof is not admissible that the accused has committed another, though it be of the same kind. There are exceptions when guilty knowledge is a part of the crime, as where all the property made the subject of the proof has been stolen from the same person, and delivered to the receiver by the same thief, though at different times, and there is such a connection of circumstances as furnishes a natural inference that if he knew that one piece of it was stolen, he must have known that every piece was." Folger, Ch. J., in *People* v. *Dowling,* 84 N. Y. 478. Here, the prosecution having proved the finding of other goods, the offer of the prisoner to explain his possession of such goods was rejected. The court said if the proof on the part of the people was competent and relevant, the prisoner had not the right to give immaterial evidence because his adversary had done so before him. It was needed, then, to ask whether the people had the right to prove the finding of other goods. And then the above was laid down as the rule for the new trial. There were other sufficient grounds for the reversal. In *Shriedley* v. *State,* 23 Ohio St. 130, evidence that other goods, known to have been stolen, were previously received by the defendant from the same thief, was held admissible. To same effect, *Com.* v. *Johnson,* 133 Pa. 293, 19 Atl. 402. In *Kilrow* v. *Com.* 89 Pa. 480, evidence was admitted tending to show that defendant was personally implicated in three instances where larceny was attempted or committed; and that he took immediate steps to conceal certain goods upon information conveyed to him in relation to a fourth; that another person aided in the perpetration of each crime; and there was proof that between him and defendant the intercourse was constant and confidential. *State* v. *Ward,* 49 Conn. 429, holds that, to prove guilty knowledge on the part of the receiver, it may be proved that he had before received stolen goods from the same person from whom he received the goods in question; that it is not necessary that the goods should have been stolen from the same person nor be of the same character. The court explains *Copperman* v. *People,* 56 N. Y. 591; and *Coleman* v. *People,* 58 N. Y. 555, as not necessarily holding that it is.

Robbery.—*State* v. *Greenwade,* 72 Mo. 300, holding that if the evidence tends to prove the commission of the offense for which the prisoner stands indicted, it is no objection to it that it tends to prove another and distinct offense, as here, of another robbery, the two occurring within a few minutes of each other, in pursuance of the same conspiracy. To the same effect is *Davis* v. *State* (Tex. Crim. App.) 44 S. W. 1099.

237. — connection of the offenses.

To render evidence of another offense competent, as showing

criminal intent or guilty knowledge, the transactions must have such relation or connection with each other as to show a common motive or intent running through both, or the other offense sought to be proved must be of such nature as to show guilty knowledge at the time of the offense charged.[1]

[1]In *People* v. *Shulman*, 80 N. Y. 373, note, Earl, J., after a review of the cases, said: "It can make no difference whether the transaction sought to be proved to throw light upon the main issue occurred before or after the time of the alleged crime. They may be more significant in the one case than in the other, but in either case they reflect light upon the main transaction. Upon the trial of an indictment for passing counterfeit money, where the question to be determined is the guilty knowledge of the prisoner, it has some bearing upon that question that he continued to deal in the same kind of money; and the evidence of such dealing is of the same nature, and, so far as I can perceive, of the same value, as evidence of prior dealing. So, when a person is charged with procuring property by false pretenses, and the question is as to his knowledge, motive, or intent, evidence that soon after, and from time to time afterwards, he continued to obtain property from others, in the same way and for the same fraudulent purpose, obviously reflects light upon that question. Such evidence has a direct tendency to show the mind with which he obtained the goods at the prior date. . . . It is obviously impossible to lay down any general rule limiting the time within which such transactions must have taken place, in order to render proof of them competent. It is generally said in the cases that they must have occurred about the same time as the commission of the alleged crime, but that is quite indefinite, and in some of the reported cases proof of them has been received, although they occurred months before and after the time of the crime. Each case, as to the application of this rule, must depend largely upon its own circumstances, and not unfrequently the limit of them must rest entirely in the discretion of the judge presiding at the trial. . . . The longer the range of time the more conclusive would be the evidence; and yet, in such case the judge, in the exercise of his descretion, could restrain the investigation within reasonable limits. But there is one general rule which must apply to all such cases; there must be in the transactions thus sought to be proved some relation to or connection with the main transaction. That is, they must show a common motive or intent running through all the transactions, or they must be such as in their nature to show guilty knowledge at the time of the main transaction; and if they possess these characteristics, then it matters not whether they were before or after or near to or remote from the main transaction." The decision affirmed seems to be that in *Shulman* v. *People*, 14 Hun, 516 (see 76 N. Y. 624), —false pretenses,—where it was held that on the issue of falsity in a statement of pecuniary condition made in January, it was error to admit evidence of statements made by the prisoner in the following March,

for the purpose of showing knowledge of the falsity of the prior statement.

So, evidence on a murder trial that the accused had before killed a man is not competent to show the intent with which he shot deceased, or to attack his character for peace. *Kearney* v. *State*, 68 Miss. 233, 8 So. 292.

And evidence that defendant, charged with murder, tried to raise a difficulty with another person a short time before the first difficulty between deceased and defendant, is inadmissible. *Woodward* v. *State* (Tex. Crim. App.) 51 S. W. 1122.

And on a trial for larceny committed upon an expedition undertaken for the purpose of stealing a specific article, evidence that after such expedition was ended, the parties started on a new expedition in a different direction, with the end in view of accomplishing the original purpose of the first expedition,—is inadmissible. *State* v. *Kelley*, 65 Vt. 531, 27 Atl. 203.

But evidence that defendant, on trial for murder, knocked down another person two weeks before the commission of the crime, is admissible, where it was the beginning of the hostility between defendant and deceased. *State* v. *Dettner*, 124 Mo. 426, 27 S. W. 1117.

238. ——in point of time.

Evidence of another offense, adduced for the purpose of showing criminal intent or guilty knowledge, is competent, whether the other offense was committed before or after the offense now charged. But it must have been not too remote in point of time to afford reasonable ground of inferring intent or knowledge.[1]

[1] *People* v. *Shulman*, 80 N. Y. 373, note, Cited, *supra*, § 237; *State* v. *Williams*, 76 Me. 480 (before and after); *Bielschofsky* v. *People*, 3 Hun, 40 (before); *Reg.* v. *Cotton*, 12 Cox C. C. 406 (before).

So, evidence of murderous acts committed immediately after the murder charged in the indictment is competent as bearing upon the motive, intent, and other ingredients of the crime charged. *People* v. *Johnson*, 139 N. Y. 358, 34 N. E. 920.

And on a trial for robbery evidence of a subsequent robbery so recently committed, and in circumstances so similar to that for which defendant is on trial as to show that one was part of a system or series of criminal operations, is admissible to show defendant's guilty and common intent, and the manner of performing his acts. *State* v. *Balch*, 136 Mo. 103, 37 S. W. 808.

But evidence that defendant, charged with murder, made an assault with an open knife upon the deceased a year before the homicide, is incompetent to show intent or motive, or for any other purpose,—especially where defendant and deceased had been on friendly terms during the year preceding the killing. *Herman* v. *State*, 75 Miss. 340, 22 So. 872.

And evidence of an offer to sell a wagon embraced in a chattel mortgage is inadmissible to show an unlawful intent in pledging, five months earlier, a bicycle embraced in the same mortgage. *State* v. *Jeffries*, 117 N. C. 727, 23 S. E. 163.

239. Presumption of previous knowledge or intent.

Intent or knowledge shown to exist at a previous time, within reasonable limits, may be presumed to have continued to a subsequent time. Intent or knowledge shown to have existed at a subsequent time is not therefore presumed to have existed at a previous time, unless closely connected, either in point of time or by the nature of the transaction.[1]

[1] *Shulman* v. *People*, 14 Hun, 516, holding knowledge in March not to raise a presumption of knowledge in the previous January. See opinion on affirmance quoted *supra*, § 237.

The reason of the distinction in the text is that a fact of a continuous nature, shown once to have existed, is not presumed to have ended, unless its cessation is implied or shown. But it is not presumed to have preexisted indefinitely.

Compare *State* v. *Moriarty*, 50 Conn. 415 (charge of keeping intoxicating liquors for sale without license in May), where it was held not error to admit evidence for the purpose of showing intent that the accused had actually liquors on hand as for sale in June. The court said: "If the possession of the liquors, with an apparent intent to sell them, the next day after the main fact charged, would have been admissible against the defendant, it is difficult to see what difference it can make except in the weight of the evidence if the possession of the liquors had been a week later, or a month, or even three months, especially in connection with proof that the defendant had kept the place uninterruptedly during all the intervening months."

240. Evidence of character.

A distinct offense cannot be proved for the purpose of showing a criminal disposition or tendency on the part of the accused, unless the offenses are so connected in nature as to manifest a common motive or intent or a continuing guilty knowledge of the same subject.[1]

[1] *State* v. *Lapage*, 57 N. H. 245, 24 Am. Rep. 69–75. Cushing, Ch. J., says: "1. It is not permitted to the prosecution to attack the character of the prisoner unless he first puts that in issue by offering evidence of his good character. 2. It is not permitted to show the defendant's bad character by showing particular acts. 3. It is not permitted to show in the prisoner a tendency or disposition to commit the crime with which he is charged. 4. It is not permitted to give in evidence other crimes of the prisoner, unless they are so connected by circumstances with the particular crime in issue as that the proof of one fact with its circumstances has some bearing upon the issue on trial other than such as is expressed in the foregoing three propositions." See also *Shaffner* v.

Com. 72 Pa. 60 (murder of wife by poison; there being evidence of the criminal intimacy of accused with the wife of another man, on whose life was an insurance, the proceeds of which on his death accused endeavored to procure; held error to admit evidence that the husband died with the same symptoms as the defendant's wife, and that he was attended by accused); *Com.* v. *Jackson,* 132 Mass. 16 (obtaining property by false pretenses on sale of horse; evidence of similar pretenses made by defendant in sales to other persons, a short time previously to the sale in question, is inadmissible for the purpose of showing the intent with which the defendant made the sale of the horse. The court says: "The transaction formed no part of a single scheme or plan any more than the various robberies of a thief. They were entered upon as, from time to time, he might succeed in entrapping credulous or unwary persons").

241. Repelling presumption of mistake.

When it has been proved that the party charged did the act for which he is indicted, and the question still remains whether he committed it with guilty knowledge, or whether he acted under a mistake, evidence which tends to prove that he was pursuing a course of similar acts raises a presumption that he was not acting under a mistake, but with a guilty knowledge and intent, and is admissible for that purpose.[1]

[1]Such evidence is admissible notwithstanding the party may have been indicted for such other acts. An acquittal of forging, or uttering a particular forged paper, will not preclude the state from proving the fact of the possession or the uttering of such forged paper in another prosecution against the same party, for a crime of the same character. *Bell* v. *State,* 57 Md. 108, Citing Roscoe, Crim. Ev. 7th Am. ed. 93; *Reg.* v. *Francis,* 12 Cox C. C. 612; *King* v. *Whiley,* 2 Leach C. L. 985; *Bloomer* v. *State,* 48 Md. 529; 1 Wharton, Crim. L. 8th ed. § 715; *State* v. *Williams,* 2 Rich. L. 418, 45 Am. Dec. 741; *State* v. *McAllister,* 24 Me. 139; *Com.* v. *Percival,* Thacher C. C. 293; *Com.* v. *Price,* 10 Gray, 476, 71 Am. Dec. 668; *Kendrick* v. *Com.* 5 Leigh, 707; *Rex* v. *Smith,* 4 Car. & S. P. 411; *Smith & Dougherty's Case,* 4 N. Y. City Hall Rec. 167, 168; *State* v. *Houston,* 1 Bail. L. 300; *McCartney* v. *State,* 3 Ind. 354, 56 Am. Dec. 510; *State* v. *Jesse,* 20 N. C. (3 Dev. & B. L.) 103; *State* v. *Robinson,* 16 N. J. L. 508; *People* v. *Frank,* 28 Cal. 515; *King* v. *Vandercomb Case,* 2 Leach C. L. 720; *United States* v. *Randenbush,* 8 Pet. 288, 290, 8 L. ed. 948, 949.

So, on an indictment for embezzling fees, where the prosecution has elected to charge defendant with embezzling fees in certain cases, evidence of the embezzlement of other fees, which are to some extent parts of the same transaction, is admissible to rebut any inference of accident or mistake, and show defendant's knowledge and intent. *Stanley* v. *State,* 88 Ala. 154, 7 So. 273.

And on a trial for murder by drowning the deceased in a boat, evidence that defendant had previously tried to poison the deceased is admissible to show animus and intent, and to rebut the theory of accident. *Nicholas* v. *Com.* 91 Va. 741, 21 S. E. 364.

And on a trial for embezzlement of rents collected for defendant's employer, evidence of other acts of a similar nature is admissible to establish guilty knowledge, to exclude the possibility of accident or mistake in the accounting, and to show the felonious intent. *Edelhoff* v. *State,* 5 Wyo. 19, 36 Pac. 627.

242. Neglect deemed intentional.

Under a statute imposing an active duty, neglect or indifference may be equivalent to specific criminal intent.[1]

[1] *Cowley* v. *People,* 8 Abb. N. C. 1, 36, sustained on appeal, in 83 N. Y. 464, 38 Am. Rep. 464 (cruelty to children; a leading case); *United States* v. *Thompson,* 12 Fed. 245 (trial for carrying more passengers on a vessel than allowed by statute; held that the omission to take steps before leaving port to ascertain the number of passengers on board was evidence of intent to violate the statute). See also *United States* v. *Baldridge,* 11 Fed. 552, holding that under U. S. Rev. Stat. § 5515, as to elections, which does not specifically state that the misconduct or neglect of duty denounced must be with intent to affect the election, such act or omission is punishable, although no actual corrupt intent is shown.

243. Previous statements or preparations.

For the purpose of proving intent, it is competent to show statements and acts of the prisoner previous to the commission of the offense, tending to establish the existence of intent to do the act constituting the offense,[1] even though they be not part of the *res gestæ.*[2]

[1] *Walsh* v. *People,* 13 N. Y. Week. Dig. 570, Affirmed in 88 N. Y. 458 (murder; evidence of a conversation between the accused and a witness, on the day of the homicide, in which the prisoner inquired as to the effect of throwing pepper into a person's eyes, and as to the legal consequences, held competent); *Wilson* v. *State,* 33 Ark. 557, 34 Am. Rep. 52 (exhibiting pistol); *Ford* v. *State,* 71 Ala. 385 (homicide; it being shown that the homicide was committed in the afternoon, and that the defendant and deceased had had a difficulty in the morning of the same day, and that bad feelings existed between them during the intervening hours, held no error in admitting testimony, against defendant's objection, that after the first difficulty, and a short time prior to the fatal act, the defendant had proposed to exchange knives with the witness, showing him at the time a small knife, and assigning as a reason that his knife was too small); *People* v. *Minisci,* 12 N. Y. S. R. 719 (murder; holding that the fact of the accused carrying a loaded revolver upon his person was evidence of his intent to use it, when and as he should decide to do so; and as the evidence tended to show that he deliberately

aimed at a vital part, when within a few feet of his unoffending victim, the jury was authorized to find a murderous intent).

So, on a murder trial, statements of accused, showing his intention and hostile feeling towards deceased, are competent evidence against him. *McClernand* v. *Com.* 11 Ky. L. Rep. 301, 12 S. W. 148.

So held in *People* v. *Scott*, 153 N. Y. 40, 46 N. E. 1028, of evidence that defendant, charged with murder of his wife, redeemed from a pawnbroker the revolver with which the act was done, shortly before the killing.

And evidence for the state in a murder trial, that the defendant had weapons in his possession, is competent to show preparation for the crime. *State* v. *Kinsauls*, 126 N. C. 1095, 36 S. E. 31.

So, also, the declarations of deceased as he was leaving his home on the afternoon of the homicide, having a gun and pistol, that "he was going out to shoot some," are admissible as indicating a present purpose and intention. *Burton* v. *State*, 115 Ala. 1, 22 So. 585.

And evidence that defendant charged with murder said, two months before killing, that he would show deceased how to "throw slurs on him," and that he immediately afterwards got a pistol, and went with it down the street in the direction the deceased had gone,—is admissible to show malice, ill-will, or motive. *Linehan* v. *State*, 113 Ala. 70, 21 So. 497.

And evidence that a person made statements that he knew where there was a smokehouse full of meat that could be gotten at, and that he would live by work as long as he could, and when he could not, he would rustle for it, is admissible on his trial for the killing of another when burglarizing a smokehouse some time subsequent, as showing an intent to burglarize the particular house. *Hedrick* v. *State*, 40 Tex. Crim. Rep. 532, 51 S. W. 252.

A statement by defendant, charged with murder, about three hours before the homicide, that he would like to take witness with him, but he had "a dirty piece of business to do to-night," is admissible to show his animus towards deceased and the character and intent of his act in committing the homicide, though there is nothing in the words themselves to indicate that he referred to the deceased. *State* v. *Larkins* (Idaho) 47 Pac. 945.

And evidence that one accused of murder in killing an officer who was attempting to arrest him had previously stated that he expected arrest by another officer; and that he exhibited a deadly weapon, and indicated his intention to use it in case such officer attempted to arrest him,—is admissible to show his animus and a premeditated design to make resistance to the expected arrest. *Palmer* v. *People*, 138 Ill. 356, 28 N. E. 130.

[9]*State* v. *Edwards*, 34 La. Ann. 1012. Arson; evidence of prior declarations and threats of accused, though not part of the *res gestæ*, is admissible, when it legitimately tends to establish motive or intent in the accused to commit the crime with which he is charged, and for that purpose only.

244. Falsity of declarations of accused.

For the purpose of proving intent or knowledge, the prosecution, after showing in a proper case other similar offenses committed by the accused, may prove his declarations made in respect to such other acts, and then prove such declarations to have been untrue.[1]

[1]*Coleman* v. *People,* 58 N. Y. 555. Receiving stolen goods; previous connected transactions of the same kind having been proved, held competent to prove the statements of the accused as to the nature and extent of his business and the persons from whom and purposes for which he had received such goods, and then to prove that such statements were false.

245. Good faith and mistake of law.

If the accused did the act charged with knowledge of the facts, it is not competent to prove that he acted in good faith and under a mistake of the law.[1]

[1]Proper performance of a duty imposed by law is not dispensed with simply because the person thinks that in doing it in an authorized manner, or after his own fashion, he has done the best under the circumstances, in his judgment. The question is whether he has been guilty of wilful neglect, irrespective of motive or intent to commit the crime. *Cowley* v. *People,* 8 Abb. N. C. 1, 21 Hun, 415, Affirmed in 83 N. Y. 464, Affirming conviction under act to prevent wrong to children. So in *Com.* v. *Bradford,* 9 Met. 268 (illegal voting, not being a legal resident), it was held error to charge that the fact that accused had consulted counsel with reference to his right to vote, and had received an affirmative answer, could not be regarded as negativing a knowledge of his want of qualification,—Approved in *Hamilton* v. *People,* 57 Barb. 625, but distinguished on the ground that there was no proof (in *Hamilton* v. *People*) that he had made an honest statement of his case to counsel, and had believed their advice. In the latter case, a prosecution for illegal voting after being convicted of an infamous crime, and without being pardoned, it was held that, even though the indictment alleged the act to have been done knowingly (which is surplusage), accused could not prove absence of intent by evidence that he was advised by the governor, on an application for pardon, that it was unnecessary on account of his minority, and that he was advised by counsel that he had a right to vote,—at least in the absence of proof that he in good faith stated the case, and believed the advice.

In *State* v. *Goodenow,* 65 Me. 30 (adultery), it was held not error to refuse defendant's offer to prove that they acted in good faith under the advice of a justice of the peace, and honestly thought they were committing no offense.

And evidence that defendant, in a prosecution under N. C. Code, § 1120, for entry upon land after being forbidden, believed in good faith that he had the right to enter,—is immaterial where defendant's own evidence shows that the land on which he entered and which had formerly been a public road, had been blocked for ten or more years by wires put up for that purpose. *State* v. *Durham,* 121 N. C. 546, 28 S. E. 22.

But see *Weston* v. *Com.* 111 Pa. 251, 2 Atl. 191 (murder), where, it appearing that the homicide occurred in a conflict over the possession of a gas well, it was held not error to refuse to allow accused to prove that he had consulted counsel as to his title to the well, and had been advised of his right to prevent, by a show of arms, interference with his occupancy.

246. Good faith and mistake of fact.

Where criminal intent is material, and depends upon a knowledge of the facts, it is competent for the accused to show that he acted under mistake as to facts; and for this purpose to show information received by him from a third person in belief of which he acted.[1]

[1]*State* v. *Waltz,* 52 Iowa, 227, 2 N. W. 1102. Larceny of colts; held error to refuse offer of accused to show that he had been informed that the colts were not the property of the prosecuting witness, but the sale to him was a sham, and they in fact had been sold instead to the person with whom defendant was jointly indicted for their larceny.

247. Circumstantial evidence of intent.

When the illegality of the act or the degree of punishment depends upon the particular intent with which the act is done, every fact which will throw light upon the question of intent is competent.[1]

[1]The malicious intention is to be inferred from the situation of the parties, their acts and declarations, the nature and extent of the evidence, and the object to be accomplished. *Filkins* v. *People,* 69 N. Y. 101, 25 Am. Rep. 143 (statutory offense of assault with "intent to do bodily harm;" held error to exclude evidence tending to show that the alleged assault was committed while defending property against a trespasser; conviction reversed); *McNair* v. *State,* 14 Tex. App. 78 (theft; held error to charge, "The intent in all criminal cases is judged from the act," inasmuch as it confines the question of intent to the act; whereas intent is to be deduced from all the circumstances remotely or immediately attending the taking); *State* v. *Franks,* 64 Iowa, 39, 19 N. W. 832 (burglary; held not error to admit, against objection of accused, evidence of the possession by the prisoner, at the time of his arrest, shortly after the commission of the crime, of a set of burglar's tools, in order to show his intent in entering the house).

The manner, time, and place of an assault by a man upon a woman are all elements to be considered by the jury in arriving at a conclusion as to the intent with which the assault was made,—as to whether to commit a rape or a simple assault. *Fitzpatrick* v. *People,* 98 Ill. 269 (affirming conviction for rape against objection that offense was no more than a wanton assault); *Hunter* v. *State,* 29 Fla. 486, 10 So. 730.

And social customs founded on race differences, and the fact that there is difference of race between the accused and the woman alleged to have been assaulted, are competent in a prosecution for assault with intent to rape, upon the question whether the assault was committed with such intent, where the room in which such woman was sleeping was entered late at night, and there is nothing to indicate that the entry was by permission, or due to any encouragement held out by her. *Jackson* v. *State,* 91 Ga. 322, 18 S. E. 132.

So, recent possession of stolen property, unexplained, is a circumstance tending to show that the possessor was the thief. *Smith* v. *State,* 103 Ala. 40, 16 So. 12; *Porterfield* v. *Com.* 91 Va. 801, 22 S. E. 352; *Whitman* v. *State,* 42 Neb. 841, 60 N. W. 1025.

And that one accused of burglary has possession with others of a house in which stolen goods are found may be considered by the jury, in connection with all the other evidence, in passing upon the question of his guilt or innocence, see *Moncrief* v. *State,* 99 Ga. 295, 25 S. E. 735.

And it is proper for the jury to consider the quantity of liquors kept by a defendant in connection with the legitimate demands of his business, in determining whether or not such liquors were kept for a lawful purpose. *State* v. *Shank,* 79 Iowa, 47, 44 N. W. 241.

For illustration of evidence sufficient to sustain conviction for rape, see *Ware* v. *State,* 67 Ga. 349.

248. Circumstantial evidence in rebuttal.

On the question of criminal intent, it is competent to give evidence of any circumstances tending to show that the act was done with a different intent from that necessarily involved in the charge.[1]

[1]*Filkins* v. *People,* 69 N. Y. 101, 25 Am. Rep. 143 (where the court says: "It is only a presumption that a party intends the ordinary and probable consequences of his act, and such presumption may be rebutted by competent evidence"); *State* v. *Rivers,* 58 Iowa, 102, 43 Am. Rep. 112, 12 N. W. 117 (obtaining money by false pretenses; where the transactions were of a complicated nature; held competent for defendant to show the course of dealing between the parties, both before and after the date of the alleged crime, as reflecting the intent of the defendant, or throwing light upon the question whether the party was in fact deceived, or tending to show whether the creditor was using the criminal law to enforce the collection of a debt); *Taylor* v. *State,* 7 Tex. App. 659 (theft of one's own property in hands of bailee; *dictum,* that it would be error to refuse to allow accused to show the discharge of the debt, for which property had been pledged as security); *Sigler* v. *State,* 7 Tex. App. 283 (theft of horse; it appearing that the accused had sold the horse openly to one who testified that it was afterwards taken away by one claiming to be the owner, and that the accused had never indemnified him, held error to refuse to allow accused to show that he had indemnified such purchaser); *Robinson* v. *State,* 53 Md. 151, 36 Am. Rep. 399 (burglary of dwelling house in nighttime; held error to refuse to allow accused to show that the occupant of the house was a lewd

woman, and that the accused had had improper intimacy with her. Compare *People* v. *Soto,* 53 Cal. 415.

So, one on trial for embezzlement may show in his defense such facts and circumstances as tend to rebut the presumption that he intended to embezzle. *Spalding* v. *People,* 172 Ill. 40, 49 N. E. 993.

And evidence that the deceased, when he started to the interview in which he was killed by defendant, was unarmed, is admissible to show that his intention was peaceful, as bearing upon the defendant's claim of self-defense. *People* v. *Yokum,* 118 Cal. 437, 50 Pac. 686.

And evidence that the older sister of prosecutrix, on a trial for assault with intent to rape, was a lewd woman, is admissible to explain defendant's conduct, where there is evidence that he mistook the prosecutrix for such sister, and that under such circumstances he took her to a hotel intending to have carnal intercourse with her consent, and that he immediately desisted from his attempt to have intercourse on discovering his mistake. *Shell* v. *State* (Tex. Crim. App.) 38 S. W. 207.

But evidence on a prosecution for keeping intoxicating liquors with intent to sell, of defendant's acts after the seizure, is inadmissible in his favor, as he cannot make evidence for himself by showing his subsequent acts. *Com.* v. *Cleary,* 152 Mass. 491, 25 N. E. 834.

249. Testimony of the accused as to his intent.

Where the intent is a material question, the accused may testify in his own behalf as to what was his intent in doing the act.[1]

This rule is not confined to intent in the act charged, but allows such evidence in respect to intent in any other act shown by the evidence, if the intent therein reflects light upon the issue.[2]

[1]See, generally, in support of this rule: *State* v. *Ferguson,* 71 Conn. 227, 41 Atl. 769; *Wohlford* v. *People,* 148 Ill. 296, 36 N. E. 107; *Cummings* v. *State,* 50 Neb. 274, 69 N. W. 756; *Berry* v. *State,* 30 Tex. App. 423, 17 S. W. 1080; *Jackson* v. *Com.* 96 Va. 107, 30 S. E. 452; *Fischer* v. *State,* 101 Wis. 23, 76 N. W. 594 (absence of intent). See also *People* v. *Baker,* 96 N. Y. 340 (false pretenses; evidence of payments to defendant on the same account, before and after the one charged in the indictment, having been received,—held error to refuse to allow him to testify to the intent with which they were received); *Fenwick* v. *State,* 63 Md. 239 (assault with intent to kill; error to refuse to allow accused to testify what his intent was in getting the weapon with which he committed the assault); *People* v. *Moore,* 37 Hun, 84, 95, Appeal dismissed, it seems, but without opinion, in 103 N. Y. 682 (trial of banker for larceny by false representations in receiving draft and giving credit when insolvent; held error to refuse to allow him to testify in his own behalf to answer whether he had any intention of making an assignment, or intended and expected to go on with business, and pay his debts as they matured); *Babcock* v. *People,* 15 Hun, 347 (false pretenses; held error to refuse to allow accused to testify as to the absence of a fraudulent intent on his part); *People* v. *Hughes,* 11 Utah, 100, 39 Pac. 492

(holding it competent for one indicted for robbery to testify that at the time he took the money he honestly believed it was his own, and that he had a right to take it, as the existence of an intent to take property which does not belong to one is a necessary element of robbery); *White* v. *State,* 53 Ind. 595 (holding that where by statute a defendant in a criminal case may testify in his own behalf, it is competent for the accused to testify as to the intention with which he did the alleged criminal act. The fact that the intent is a fact which cannot, in the nature of things, be positively known to others, and about which other witnesses cannot directly testify, does not affect the competency of the testimony), Following *Greer* v. *State,* 53 Ind. 420). *Contra, Burke* v. *State,* 71 Ala. 377. And that defendant, accused of homicide, cannot testify to the uncommunicated intention with which he did the act, see *Lewis* v. *State,* 96 Ala. 6, 11 So. 259.

But defendant charged with libel cannot testify as to what he meant by the article in question, where the language of the article is not ambiguous. *State* v. *Heacock,* 106 Iowa, 191, 76 N. W. 654.

Nor is it error to refuse to let a witness state with what intent and purpose he fired a pistol at another, where he has already testified that he was shooting at him, and not shooting at random or for fun. *State* v. *Hultz,* 106 Mo. 41, 16 S. W. 940.

[3]*Kerrains* v. *People,* 60 N. Y. 221, 229, 19 Am. Rep. 158.

XXXIII. Intoxication.

250. As bearing on intent.

In cases of homicide,[1] and in other cases wherever a specific intent is to be proved against the accused,[2] evidence tending to show that he was so intoxicated that he could not have formed the intent is competent for the purpose of negativing intent.[3] In other cases not.

[1]*People* v. *Rogers,* 18 N. Y. 9, 17, 72 Am. Dec. 484; *State* v. *Mowry,* 37 Kan. 369, 10 Crim. L. Mag. 23, with note, 15 Pac. 282; *Hill* v. *State,* 42 Neb. 503, 60 N. W. 916; *State* v. *O'Neil,* 51 Kan. 651, 24 L. R. A. 555, 33 Pac. 287. And see fully on this question the authorities reviewed in note to *Harris* v. *United States* (D. C.) 36 L. R. A. 470.

In *Armor* v. *State,* 63 Ala. 173, it was held that the question whether the intoxication was of such a degree as to preclude forming a design or intent was a question, not for opinion of witnesses, but for the jury.

In *State* v. *Morgan,* 40 S. C. 345, 18 S. E. 937, it was held that the intoxication or drunkenness of the defendant on a trial for murder was not to be considered by the jury in determining the intent with which defendant acted.

[2]*People* v. *Burns,* 2 N. Y. Crim. Rep. 415. Burglary; held not error to charge that the jury might take into consideration the intoxication of the accused, in determining the intent with which he entered the building. See also numerous cases cited in article by John D. Lawson, in

23 Am. L. Reg. N. S. 236, and in note to *Harris* v. *United States* (D. C.) 36 L. R. A. 467.

But that evidence that one charged with assault with intent to rape was intoxicated five or six hours before the assault is properly excluded, as drunkenness at the time of the assault would be no defense, see *State* v. *Alcorn*, 137 Mo. 121, 38 S. W. 548.

[a] *People* v. *Marseiler*, 70 Cal. 98, 11 Pac. 503 (assault with deadly weapon; here, no specific intent being necessary, intoxication is not competent); *People* v. *Jones*, 2 Edm. Sel. Cas. 86 (Edmonds, J., in charging jury); *State* v. *Welch*, 21 Minn. 22 (illegal voting). *Contra*, compare the following: *People* v. *Harris*, 29 Cal. 678.

In *Driscoll* v. *People*, 47 Mich. 413, 11 N. W. 221, where one charged with robbery explained the taking as an attempt to get back his own property, it was held that the jury might consider his intoxication as bearing on the question of good faith.

In *Pigman* v. *State*, 14 Ohio, 555, 45 Am. Dec. 558, it was held that in that class of cases which depends upon guilty knowledge—as uttering counterfeits—evidence of the intoxication of accused is competent.

As to whether malice falls within this rule, compare, in the Affirmative: *Shannahan* v. *Com.* 8 Bush, 463, 8 Am. Rep. 465 (*dictum*); *Buckhannon* v. *Com.* 86 Ky. 110, 5 S. W. 358.

Negative: *Nichols* v. *State*, 8 Ohio St. 435, Approved in *State* v. *Robinson*, 20 W. Va. 713, 734, 43 Am. Rep. 799.

That it is competent on the question of fear or apprehension, in good faith, see 23 Am. L. Reg. N. S. 239, and cases cited.

That evidence of the intoxication of defendant at the time of a murder with which he is charged is immaterial, where the evidence shows that the crime was deliberate and premeditated, and was perpetrated in accomplishment of a pre-existing plot, see *People* v. *Miller*, 114 Cal. 10, 45 Pac. 986.

251. Susceptibility to intoxicants.

The defense, in endeavoring to negative intent by proof of intoxication, is not entitled to show that the accused was easily affected by intoxicating liquors.[1]

[1] *State* v. *Smith*, 49 Conn. 376. Murder; the court said: The question as to whether the accused was easily affected by intoxicating liquor, or had drunk much or little, was of no consequence. If he was in the condition of mind when he committed the fatal act which the jury were told they must find he was, he was capable of committing murder in the first degree; exclusion no error.

252. Intoxication in support of alibi.

Evidence of intoxication to a degree interfering with going about is competent, if offered in corroboration of evidence tending to prove an *alibi*, as distinguished from an offer to show intoxication in defense.[1]

[1]*Ingalls* v. *State*, 48 Wis. 647, 4 N. W. 785.

XXXIV. Letters.

253. Incriminating letters.

The fact that an unanswered letter or other paper was found in the custody of the accused, which had not been acknowledged by him, is not ground for the admission of the paper as evidence against him. The reason is that, were the rule otherwise, an innocent man, by the artifices of others, might be charged with a prima facie case of guilt which he might find it difficult to repel.[1]

[1]*Willett* v. *People*, 27 Hun, 469, Affirmed, without noticing the point in 92 N. Y. 29; *People* v. *Green*, 1 Denio, 614, 1 Park. Crim. Rep. 11, 33 (excluding a letter written to the defendant by his mother, after the commission of the murder, asking him to write her all about the occurrence).

A fortiori, letters intercepted in the post-office after the prisoner's arrest cannot be admitted against him. *King* v. *Hevey*, 1 Leach C. L. 229. See also *Com.* v. *Edgerly*, 10 Allen, 184.

A letter found upon the person of accused at the time of his capture, from which it is plainly inferable that the writer believed the accused guilty of the crime, and containing suggestions as to the advisability of care on the accused's part not to be apprehended, is inadmissible against the accused. *People* v. *Colburn*, 105 Cal. 648, 38 Pac. 1105.

But a letter shown to have been an answer to one by the defendant, or to have been invited by him, is admissible, although it never reached his possession. *Queen* v. *Cooper*, L. R. 1 Q. B. Div. 19. Here, indictment for obtaining money under false pretenses by publishing an advertisement in a public paper offering employment of a certain description to persons sending the publishers of the notice a specified sum, letters addressed as directed in the published notice were admitted.

Letters found in the office recently occupied, and in letter files kept by defendant charged with the embezzlement of money belonging to a corporation, which came into his hands as an agent, which letters are in the handwriting of the officers of such corporation, in regard to the nature of defendant's agency, and which appear to have been invited by letters from defendant, and to have been acted upon in the course of the agency,—are admissible against defendant. *Thalheim* v. *State*, 38 Fla. 169, 20 So. 938.

254. — by possession and handwriting of accused.

Press copies of letters purporting to be written by the accused, and found in his possession, are admissible against him, if they appear to be in his handwriting, and the originals cannot be found.[1]

[1]*Com.* v. *Jeffries*, 7 Allen, 548, 83 Am. Dec. 712.

XXXV. Mitigation.

255. Where jury fix punishment.

Where the statute authorizes the jury to fix the punishment in case the accused is found guilty, he is entitled to prove, on the trial, in mitigation of punishment, that he has already lain in prison on the charge contained in the indictment.[1]

If the punishment cannot be fixed by the jury, evidence in mitigation is not competent until after conviction.[2]

[1]*Kistler* v. *State*, 54 Ind. 400 (blackmail); *Fletcher* v. *People*, 117 Ill. 184, 7 N. E. 80.

So, evidence tending to show that the prosecuting witness in a criminal action is a person of bad character is competent as bearing upon his credibility as a witness, and in mitigation of punishment, but not as tending to show that defendant is innocent of the crime charged. *State* v. *Bush*, 122 Ind. 42, 23 N. E. 677.

And the jury may, on a prosecution for assault with intent to kill, consider the previous character of the accused in mitigation of his punishment, although, if he is guilty of the charge against him, such previous good character is not available to him as a defense, and will not entitle him to an acquittal. *Walker* v. *State*, 136 Ind. 663, 36 N. E. 356.

Evidence that the mother of a child requested the defendant, who acted as patriarch or priest of the religious community of which the mother was a member, to punish the child, is not admissible upon a trial for assault, for the purpose of justifying the punishment, but is admissible by way of mitigation, to reduce the offense from aggravated to simple assault. *Donnelley* v. *Territory* (Ariz.) 52 Pac. 368.

But a fact not known to defendant at the time of the commission of a homicide is inadmissible in mitigation of the offense. *Pitts* v. *State*, 29 Tex. App. 474, 16 S. W. 189.

[2]*Gardner* v. *People*, 62 N. Y. 299; *Rawlings* v. *Com.* 1 Leigh, 581, 19 Am. Dec. 757 (holding that upon a trial for assault and battery, evidence that the prosecutor on previous days had used provoking and abusive language to the defendant, is inadmissible in mitigation of the fine. The reason is that such language must be closely enough connected with the assault to become part of the *res gestæ*). And see *infra*, §§ 263, 264.

XXXVI. Motive.

[Motive is the inducement of intent. Hence evidence of motive is usually incompetent except where evidence of intent is competent. See also *supra*, §§ 236 *et seq.*]

256. Competency.

When intent is material, any fact is competent against the accused which tends to show the motive of the criminal act charged.[1]

The fact that the suggested motive is innocent in itself—as, for instance, the need of money, suggested as the motive for a robbery—does not make the evidence irrelevant.[2]

Nor is the evidence incompetent because it may tend to show the accused guilty of an offense other than that charged.[3]

[1]Direct evidence of the conduct of defendant before the commission of the crime charged, from which it is sought to infer motive for the crime, is not indispensable, but such conduct may be shown by circumstantial evidence. *State* v. *Smith*, 102 Iowa, 656, 72 N. W. 279.

For some illustrations, see the following cases:

Animosity.—In *State* v. *Dearborn*, 59 N. H. 348 (trial for obstructing railroad track), it was held not error to allow proof that accused had been twice arrested on criminal charges on the complaint of the railroad. So, evidence that a brother of one on trial for murder was killed by deceased is admissible as showing motive for the accused to kill deceased. *Pryor* v. *State*, 40 Tex. Crim. Rep. 643, 51 S. W. 375. And evidence of quarrels and disputes between defendant and the prosecuting witness on a trial for assault with intent to commit murder, at various times prior to the alleged assault, is admissible as tending to show ill-will on the part of defendant, and as evidence of a motive for assaulting the witness. *State* v. *Ackles*, 8 Wash. 462, 36 Pac. 597.

Desire for employment.—In *State* v. *McMahon*, 17 Nev. 365, 30 Pac. 1000 (maliciously burning lot of cord wood), evidence of prior statements of accused was held properly admitted as showing a motive on his part to obtain employment.

Domestic or sexual relations.—In *Pierson* v. *People*, 79 N. Y. 424, 35 Am. Rep. 524 (murder), it was held not error to admit evidence that the prisoner, who was a married man, was married to the wife of deceased shortly after the murder and at the marriage falsely swore that there was no legal objection to the marriage. So, in *Miller* v. *State*, 68 Miss. 221, 8 So. 273, evidence that a person accused of murder at once, and notoriously, appropriated the deceased's wife as his concubine, was held admissible as tending to show a motive for the crime. And in *People* v. *Stout*, 4 Park. Crim. Rep. 71 (murder), it was held not error to admit evidence that the prisoner had been guilty of incest with the wife of deceased, such evidence tending to show a motive for the murder,—*i. e.*, to avoid exposure and detection. So, in *Thomas* v. *State*, 117 Ala. 178, 23 So. 665, evidence that defendant, charged with assault and battery, soon after the assault married the prosecutor's sister, was held to be competent as tending to show motive for the assault, in connection with evidence that the prosecutor, immediately preceding the assault, had taken his sister away from a restaurant where the defendant was. And in *Shaw* v. *State,* 102 Ga. 660, 29 S. E. 477, evidence that the defendant, charged with wrecking a train upon which his wife, by his direction, was a passenger, was enamored of another woman, was held admissible for the purpose of showing motive, the question as to its weight being for the jury.

Disappointed expectations.—In *Hendrickson* v. *People,* 10 N. Y. 13, 31, 1 Park. Crim. Rep. 416, note (wife murder), it was held not error to admit the will of the father of the deceased, as tending to show that the prisoner had been disappointed in the pecuniary expectations he had entertained from his alliance with the family. And in *People* v. *Cuff,* 122 Cal. 589, 55 Pac. 407, it was held that to establish motive in a trial for an attempt to kill, the prosecution might show that the defendant had been a persistent and unsuccessful suitor for the hand of a young lady, and that the deceased was a successful suitor; but the details of the defendant's conduct during the courtship were inadmissible. So, also, in *State* v. *Lentz,* 45 Minn. 177, 47 N. W. 720, evidence for the state on a murder trial, that defendant was a suitor of deceased's sister, and that the only opposition to his suit was from the brother, which opposition, together with the declared intention of the sister not to act against the wishes of her brother, was known to defendant,—was held competent to prove a motive on defendant's part to commit the crime.

Money to be got.—In *Kennedy* v. *People,* 39 N. Y. 245, 253 (murder), it was held not error to admit evidence tending to show that the deceased had money. To the same effect, *State* v. *Donnelly,* 130 Mo. 642, 32 S. W. 1124. In *State* v. *Crowley,* 33 La. Ann. 782, an inventory of the succession of the deceased, which proved that he had in his house a certain amount of money, was admitted.

—and defendant's knowledge where it was.—In *Ettinger* v. *Com.* 98 Pa. 338, evidence that the accused knew of the money, and where it was kept, was held admissible.

—arson to defraud insurers.—In *Shepherd* v. *People,* 19 N. Y. 537 (arson), it was held not error to admit evidence tending to show that the building was insured for more than its value, and that the accused called for the insurance money; also evidence that the accused lived on bad terms with his wife, who was burned with the building, such evidence going to show a motive. In *Carncross* v. *People,* 1 N. Y. Crim. Rep. 518, evidence that the company, a foreign corporation, had complied with the law, and was authorized to transact business in the state, was held to be admissible as tending to show the validity of the insurance. In *Stitz* v. *State,* 104 Ind. 359, 4 N. E. 145, evidence of overvaluation was held admissible.

—need of money.—In *People* v. *Dewey,* 35 Hun, 308 (forgery), it was held not error to admit evidence tending to prove a deficiency in the accounts of the accused as a public officer. In *Fulmer* v. *Com.* 97 Pa. 503 (larceny), defendant, in order to prove lack of motive on his part, having produced a witness to testify that he had kept the defendant supplied with money at the time when the larceny was alleged to have occurred, it was held competent for the commonwealth on cross-examination to ask the witness whether defendant was not at the time of the alleged larceny in need of money and owing pressing debts. So, in *Perrin* v. *State*, 81 Wis. 135, 50 N. W. 516, evidence showing that one accused of larceny was financially embarrassed before the larceny, and had money to spend after it, and that he was a defaulter likely to be discovered at any time, was held admissible to show motive.

—immediate use of money.—In *Kennedy* v. *People*, 39 N. Y. 245, 255 (murder), it was held that evidence that the accused proposed, at about the time of the murder, to purchase land in the neighborhood, was properly admitted.

[a]"Motive is a minor or auxiliary fact, from which, when established in connection with other necessary facts, the main or primary fact of guilt may be inferred; and it may be established by circumstantial evidence, the same as any other fact. The proper inquiry, when the circumstance is offered, is, Does it fairly tend to raise an inference in favor of the existence of the fact proposed to be proved? If it does, it is admissible, whether such fact or circumstance be innocent or criminal in its character." Johnson, J., in *People* v. *Wood*, 3 Park. Crim. Rep. 681, holding it not error to admit evidence that the accused had been guilty of other acts of a felonious character.

That the concurrence of indifferent or good motives will not be a defense to an indictment for an intentional violation of the law, see article by Francis Wharton on "Comparative Criminal Jurisprudence," in 4 Crim. L. Mag. 1, 7.

[a]*People* v. *Wood*, 3 Park. Crim. Rep. 681; *Moore* v. *United States*, 150 U. S. 57, 37 L. ed. 996, 14 Sup. Ct. Rep. 26; *Schmitz* v. *People*, 178 Ill. 320, 52 N. E. 903; *Cross* v. *State*, 138 Ind. 254, 37 N. E. 790; *Territory* v. *McGinnis* (N. M.) 61 Pac. 208; *People* v. *Fitzgerald*, 156 N. Y. 253, 50 N. E. 846; *State* v. *Kent*, 5 N. D. 516, *sub nom. State* v. *Pancoast*, 35 L. R. A. 578, 67 N. W. 1052.

For some illustrations, see the following cases:

Arson.—*Jones* v. *State*, 63 Ga. 395, holding that where the creating of an opportunity to commit larceny from one building seems to have been the motive of setting fire to another on the same premises, evidence of the larceny is admissible against the prisoner on his trial for the arson.

Assault.—In *State* v. *Kline*, 54 Iowa, 183, 6 N. W. 184 (assault with intent to murder), evidence tending to show the seduction of the prosecuting witness by defendant, her pregnant condition, and the fact that he had procured medicine, soliciting her to take the same to procure an abortion, was held competent, but only to show motive for the crime charged in the indictment. In *Pontius* v. *People*, 21 Hun, 328, affirmed in 82 N. Y. 339 (assault with intent to kill), evidence that the accused had shortly before forged the name of the person on whom the assault was committed was held properly admitted. And in *People* v. *Kerrains*, 1 Thomp. & C. 333 (assault with intent to kill), it was held not error to admit evidence that defendant had maliciously injured the property of his employer, whom he had assaulted,—Reversed on other grounds in 60 N. Y. 221, 19 Am. Rep. 158. So, in *Horn* v. *State,* 102 Ala. 144, 15 So. 278 (assault with intent to murder), evidence of an assault upon other persons, disconnected in point of time and place from that in question, was held admissible, where the motive prompting each was the same. And in *People* v. *Wilson,* 117 Cal. 688, 49 Pac. 1054, evidence that defendant, charged with an assault with intent to murder an officer, had a short time before committed an assault on another person, for which offense an officer was attempting to arrest him without a warrant, was held admissible to show defendant's motive and intent, although it might tend to show that he had been guilty of another offense,—Citing *Moore* v. *United States,* 150 U. S. 61, 37 L. ed. 998, 14 Sup. Ct. Rep. 26.

Carrying concealed weapon.—*Shorter* v. *State,* 63 Ala. 129, where it was held that, to make out the defense of a threatened or apprehended attack, within the statutory exception, the motive or purpose of carrying the weapon must be defense against violence threatened or apprehended. If offense, instead of defense,—a meditated attack on another, and not an apprehended attack by him,—be the real motive, the party is guilty of violating the statute; and, as bearing on this question, the conduct and declarations of the accused and the prosecutor, during an altercation and subsequent rencontre between them, out of which the prosecution arose, are relevant and competent evidence.

Homicide.—In *Turner* v. *Com.* 86 Pa. 54, 27 Am. Rep. 683 (murder), evidence of adulterous intercourse between the accused and the deceased held properly admitted. So, in *People* v. *Sutherland,* 154 N. Y. 345, 48 N. E. 518, evidence that the defendant charged with murder enticed the deceased away from her husband, and was living in meretricious relations with her, was held to be competent, in connection with other evidence in the case, from which the jury might find that he suspected that she was also untrue to him, and the jealousy was the result of such suspicions. And in *Stephens* v. *People,* 19 N. Y. 549 (wife murder), the motive imputed to the accused being a desire to marry another woman, it was held not error to admit in evidence an anonymous letter written by the accused eleven months after the murder, addressed to a man about to marry such woman as tending in some degree to establish his previous affection for her, and disappointment in failing to obtain her. In *Reinhart* v. *People,* 82 N. Y. 607 (wife murder), it was held not error to allow the prosecution to show that a short time before the alleged murder the accused married another woman; also to show his prior and subsequent relations to her. In *State* v. *Chase,* 68 Vt. 405, 35 Atl. 336, evidence of adulterous intercourse between defendant charged with murder and the wife of the deceased was held admissible to show motive. To similar effect, see *Sullivan* v. *State,* 100 Wis. 283, 75 N. W. 956; *Johnson* v. *State,* 24 Fla. 162, 4 So. 535; *State* v. *Reed,* 53 Kan. 767, 37 Pac. 174; *Traverse* v. *State,* 61 Wis. 144, 20 N. W. 724 (murder; evidence of an act of adultery by the accused with the widow of the deceased, four or five days after the killing, was held not admissible as tending to show that the motive for the killing was not self-defense, as claimed by the accused, or to rebut any presumption of innocence arising from the circumstances under which the killing was done). See *Marler* v. *State*, 67 Ala. 55, 42 Am. Rep. 95, 68 Ala. 580 (murder; evidence of statements of the accused tending to show that he wished to get rid of deceased, who was an important witness against the accused in a suit for divorce that accused had commenced); *State* v. *Morris*, 84 N. C. 756 (murder; record of an indictment pending against the prisoner and others, charging them with larceny, and evidence that the deceased was implicated in the same, but, having turned state's witness was omitted from the indictment, held properly admitted); *State* v. *Grant*, 79 Mo. 113, 49 Am. Rep. 218 (murder of an officer attempting to arrest accused for larceny; evidence that the goods in question had been stolen shortly before the homicide held properly admitted).

Libel.—*Com.* v. *Damon*, 136 Mass. 441. Newspaper libel; held not error to admit similar articles in the paper within four months after the alleged libel, tending to show general and persistent ill-will. And articles published by defendant, charged with libel, subsequent to that on which the indictment is based, may be competent for the purpose of showing the motive prompting the article in question. *State* v. *Heacock*, 106 Iowa, 191, 76 N. W. 654. *Contra*, in a case of bribery, *People* v. *Sharp*, 107 N. Y. 427, 14 N. E. 319, Distinguishing *Pierson* v. *People*, 79 N. Y. 424, 35 Am. Rep. 524.

257. Order of proof.

Evidence of motive is not competent unless the *corpus delicti* has first been shown and evidence connecting the accused with it has also been given, or is included in the evidence of motive.[1]

[1] *People* v. *Hall*, 48 Mich. 482, 42 Am. Rep. 477, 12 N. W. 665. Murder of wife; held error to admit proof of motive before proof of fact of homicide. The proof of motive consisted of testimony showing that the accused had previously been intimate with another woman, this being the first testimony introduced by the prosecution. The court said: "When there is legal evidence leading to the belief that homicide has been committed, the motive of the criminal becomes important, and the relations of parties may therefore become relevant."

It is the better opinion also that before evidence tending to connect the *corpus delicti* with the accused has been given, evidence of motive is not competent unless it also has a distinct tendency to make such connection. In other words, there must be previous evidence pointing to the accused, or the motive attributed to the accused must point to the particular offense.

I find no reported decision squarely on the point. In *Overstreet* v. *State*, 46 Ala. 30 (arson), the prosecution, having proved the burning, the venue, and the ownership and value of the property, introduced one B., who testified that he was the owner of property burned in the building, that one of the defendants was unfriendly to him, and that another of the defendants had threatened the owner. It does not appear that, as preliminary to the evidence of malice and threats, any other evidence was offered tending to connect accused with the offense. Held properly admitted. The court said: "When it is shown that a crime has been committed, and the circumstances point to the accused as the guilty agent, proof of the motive . . . is nevertheless admissible."

258. Details of controversy.

When the existence of controversy is competent as tending to show motive, the question how far details of the controversy can be proved rests largely in the discretion of the court. Either party has a right to prove so much of the facts as is necessary to show the relation subsisting between the persons concerned, and the nature and force of the motives which it may be presumed to have engendered; but beyond that neither the merits nor the details of the controversy are necessarily competent.[1]

[1]*Commander* v. *State,* 60 Ala. 1 (murder; held that, though evidence of anticipated litigation between the prisoner and the deceased was admissible, yet it was not error to exclude evidence touching the merits of the litigation), Approved in *Gray* v. *State,* 63 Ala. 66; *State* v. *Hannett,* 54 Vt. 83 (arson; evidence admissible to show ill feeling of the accused towards one who had an interest in the building, but not the cause, merits, and consequences of the quarrel); *Pinckord* v. *State,* 13 Tex. App. 468 (where the wife of the accused was the injured person; held proper to prove that divorce suit had been commenced, and was pending, but error to permit the allegations of her petition in the divorce suit to be read to the jury as evidence, and especially so without explanation as to how far and for what purpose they were to be considered. More especially was it error to admit in evidence the judgment or decree of divorce, when it appeared to have been rendered subsequent to the alleged commission of the offense).

So, evidence as to the merits of a controversy between the defendant, charged with murder, and deceased, over a tract of land, in the course of which the homicide was committed, is immaterial. *People* v. *Yokum,* 118 Cal. 437, 50 Pac. 686.

To show motive for murder, it is competent to show that the accused had been indicted for robbery at the instance of deceased, but not to establish that offense by testimony of facts necessary to show guilt, or to permit the entire record, including the affidavit for a continuance, to be read to the jury. *Martin* v. *Com.* 14 Ky. L. Rep. 95, 19 S. W. 580.

259. Testimony of accused or witness.

When the motive of a party or witness in performing a particular act, or in making a particular declaration already in evidence, is material, he may himself testify in regard to it.[1]

[1]*Kerrains* v. *People,* 60 N. Y. 221, 19 Am. Rep. 159; *Cannon* v. *State,* 60 Ark. 564, 31 S. W. 150, 32 S. W. 128.

260. Cross-examination.

On cross-examination the accused may be interrogated as to his motive in doing an act already in evidence.[1]

[1]*Com.* v. *Damon*, 136 Mass. 441 (newspaper libel; held not error to allow accused, against his objection, to be asked on cross-examination his opinion of the articles complained of, for the purpose of showing a malicious intent on his part in publishing them); *Blake* v. *People*, 73 N. Y. 586.

261. Right of rebuttal.

When evidence tending to show motive on the part of the accused for the criminal act has been given, the accused has a right to give evidence tending to show a different motive, such as may repel the inference sought to be drawn from the motive imputed to him by the prosecution.[1]

[1]*Mack* v. *State*, 48 Wis. 271, 4 N. W. 449 (murder; evidence having been given tending to show that accused had criminal intimacy with the wife of the deceased, and that the deceased had discharged him from his employment, held error to exclude evidence offered by defendant to show the reason of leaving the employment); *People* v. *Odell*, 14 N. Y. Week. Dig. 403 (assault; the prosecution having proved the defendant's angry manner and words at the time of the assault, held error to refuse to allow defendant to testify that he had no such feelings towards the prosecutor until provoked by him).

XXXVII. Principal and accessory.

262. Conviction of principal.

The record of conviction of a principal is prima facie evidence of his guilt, against the accessory, where the two are included in one indictment, and separately tried;[1] but it is not conclusive.[2]

But evidence of conviction of one jointly indicted with defendant has no tendency to prove that defendant is innocent; and is inadmissible.[3]

[1]*Com.* v. *Knapp*, 10 Pick. 477, 20 Am. Dec. 534; *Levy* v. *People*, 80 N. Y. 327, Affirming 19 Hun, 383; doubted in 2 Phillipps, Ev. 49.

[2]*Levy* v. *People*, 80 N. Y. 327, Affirming 19 Hun, 383; *State* v. *Mosley*, 31 Kan. 355, 2 Pac. 782.

[3]*State* v. *Fertig*, 98 Iowa, 139, 67 N. W. 87.

XXXVIII. Punishment.

263. Evidence when jury fix punishment.

When the punishment is to be fixed by the jury in their verdict, either party may give in evidence facts relevant to the question of punishment.[1]

[1]In *State* v. *Kistler* (Ind.) 4 Rep. 87 (blackmail), evidence that the defendant had already undergone imprisonment for a definite period for the same offense (a new trial having been granted) was held admissible in mitigation,—it seems, because under the statute the punishment is to be recommended by the jury in their verdict.

In *People* v. *Hong Ah Duck*, 61 Cal. 387, a trial for murder, the statute giving discretion of imposing death or life imprisonment,—it was held competent for the prosecution to prove that the accused was already under sentence for life imprisonment.

In *Fields* v. *State*, 47 Ala. 603, 11 Am. Rep. 771, under the Alabama statute allowing the jury to fix the punishment on the trial of an indictment for murder, evidence of the general bad reputation of the deceased, as a turbulent, bloodthirsty, revengeful, dangerous man, was held admissible, although it might be sufficient to reduce the offense from murder to manslaughter. See also, as to circumstances of provocation which form a part of the *res gestæ*, and immediately inciting the action, *Simpson* v. *State*, 59 Ala. 1.

So, evidence that assault for which defendant is on trial was so severe as to cause the blood to flow is admissible to enable the jury to graduate the punishment,—especially where the defense is set up that defendant was a schoolteacher, and had the right to chastise the person assaulted, who was his pupil. *Kinnard* v. *State*, 35 Tex. Crim. Rep. 276, 33 S. W. 234.

And the facts as to a former conviction are properly introduced, before the verdict on the charge on which the defendant is being tried, under Ky. Stat. § 1130, providing that the punishment on a second conviction for felony shall be at least double the punishment imposed upon the first conviction, but that the judgment shall not be for increased penalty, unless the jury find from the record and other competent evidence the fact of a former conviction. *Sweeney* v. *Com.* 18 Ky. L. Rep. 1020, 39 S. W. 22.

264. Mitigation of punishment.

Where the punishment is fixed by the law, or is to be fixed by the court after conviction, evidence of facts not going to establish a defense are not rendered competent by their tendency to mitigate punishment.[1]

[1]See *supra*, § 255.

XXXIX. Reference to third person for information.

265. Limits of the rule.

The general rule that when a person refers to another for an answer on a particular subject, the answer is, in general, evidence against him,[1] does not let in the results of inquiries made by the third person in consequence of the reference,—such as what was entered in the books in his charge.[2]

[1]*Reg.* v. *Mallory,* 32 Week. Rep. 721, 50 L. T. N. S. 429, L. R. 13 Q. B. Div. 33. Receiving stolen goods. Evidence was given that the prisoner, being asked by the police what price he had given, said he did not know, but his wife would make out a list. Next day she, in his presence, produced a list. Held that the list was admissible against him. See also *Melville's Case,* 29 How. St. Tr. 750; *Duval* v. *Covenhoven,* 4 Wend. 564 (civil case).

[2]*Lambert* v. *People,* 76 N. Y. 220, 32 Am. Rep. 293. Nor does it let in statements on a different subject, such as information given to one who was sent for money (*Allen* v. *Killinger,* 8 Wall. 480, *sub nom. Murphy* v. *Killinger,* 19 L. ed. 470), or for instructions (*Duval* v. *Covenhoven,* 4 Wend. 564), and not for information.

XL. Res gestae.

266. Connection with the event.

The rule of the *res gestæ* admits declarations made under the impulse of the occasion, though somewhat separated in time and place, if so woven into it by the circumstances as to receive credit from it.[1]

[1]The admissibility of the declaration is the more clear in proportion as it is connected with the act by identity in the following respects: Time, place, persons present, and the subject of attention or motive. The lapse of time, the change of scene, the presence of other persons, all suggest, if they do not prove, the probability of the intervention of other motives between the impulse for the act and the impulse for the declaration. Hence, where the circumstances indicate that the act was done under great excitement, and the excitement or the engrossing sensations or emotions incidental to it were prolonged without other intervening distraction, the space of time within which declarations made may reasonably be regarded as admissible is proportionately extended. On the other hand, although the act be a disaster of an engrossing character, the intervention of some new subject or emotion, such as the arrest of the person even before any change of scene or presence, precludes the admission of subsequent declarations, for he may rightly be supposed to have been influenced in part by this intervening exigency, and not wholly by the original act and the motives which occasioned that act. For a comprehensive review of the authorities, see note to *Ohio & M. R. Co.* v. *Stein* (Ind.) 19 L. R. A. 733.

And for other cases sustaining the rule as stated in the text, see *Com.* v. *Hackett,* 2 Allen, 136; *Travelers' Ins. Co.* v. *Mosley,* 8 Wall. 397, 19 L. ed. 437 (a civil action; a leading case, but carrying the rule to the extreme of its usual limits, and not followed to that extent in all the states); *United States* v. *Snowden,* 2 App. D. C. 89; *Walker* v. *State,* 34 Fla. 167, 16 So. 80; *Keyes* v. *State,* 122 Ind. 527, 23 N. E. 1097; *People* v. *McArron,* 121 Mich. 1, 79 N. W. 944; *People* v. *Hughes,* 116 Mich. 80, 74 N. W. 309; *Sullivan* v. *State,* 58 Neb. 796, 79 N. W. 721; *State* v. *Davis,* 104 Tenn. 501, 58 S. W. 122; *People* v. *Callaghan,* 4 Utah, 49, 6 Pac. 49; *Ryan* v. *State,* 83 Wis. 486, 53 N. W. 836.

Bishop's statement of the rule.—"The doctrine of *res gestæ* is that when a part of a transaction has been given in evidence by one party, the other may call out on cross-examination, or show by witnesses of his own, the whole or any part of the rest. The *res gestæ* consists of two parts,—the accompanying acts and the declarations attending them. . . . It is impossible to deduce from the authorities an available rule as to what shall be deemed of the transaction, and what shall not. The subsidiary act need not transpire at the same instant with the main one, or always even on the same day; and, in reason, as well as in accordance with the current of the authorities, the time which divides the two is not the controlling consideration, though it may be taken into account. Is it presumable that distinctly and palpably it influenced or was influenced by the main act, or proceeded from the same motive? If so, it is admissible; otherwise not. Such is the doctrine in reason, and, it is submitted, the current of authority is, at least, not adverse. In general, subject to some apparent or real qualifications, what one said, in its nature explanatory, while performing an admissible act, whether he is a party or a third person, may be shown in evidence whenever the act is shown. In this way a defendant may even be entitled to introduce in his own behalf accompanying declarations not otherwise admissible. Statements, from whatever source, to be thus competent, must be contemporaneous with the act they would illustrate. Perhaps a few of the cases require them to be so in the strict sense. But it is, at least, the better doctrine that they are competent whenever near enough to the act, either before or after, to be prompted by the same motive, and apparently to constitute of it a part." 1 Bishop, Crim. Proc. §§ 1085, 1086.

Wharton's statement of the rule.—"*Res gestæ* are events speaking for themselves, through the instinctive words and acts of participants, not the words and acts of participants when narrating the events. What is said or done by participants, under the immediate spur of a transaction, becomes thus part of the transaction, because it is then the transaction that thus speaks. In such cases, it is not necessary to examine as witnesses the persons who, as participators in the transaction, thus instinctively spoke or acted. What they did or said is not hearsay; it is part of the transaction itself. And as long as the transaction continues, so long do acts and deeds emanating from it become part of it, so that, in describing it in a court of justice, they can be detailed. The question is, Is the evidence offered that of the event, speaking through participants, or that of observers speaking about the event? In the first case, what was thus said can be introduced without calling those who said it; in the second case they must be called. Nor are there any limits of time within which the *res gestæ* can be arbitrarily confined. They vary, in fact, with each particular case. . . . Declarations claimed to be part of the *res gestæ* may precede, accompany, or follow the transaction to which they relate. It is only when they accompany the transaction so as to be wrought up in it and to emanate from it that they can be rightfully regarded as excepted from the rule that excludes hearsay. It is agreed on all sides that narratives of a transaction after it has transpired are inadmissible unless as admissions by the party charged; and on the same principle declarations prior to the transaction are excluded. The conflicting cases are those in which, as a matter of fact, it was questioned whether the declarations offered were part of the transaction. . . . The distinguishing feature of declarations of this class is that they should be necessary incidents of the litigated act; necessary in this sense, that they are part of the immediate concomitants or conditions of such act, and are not produced by the calculated policy of the actors. In other words, they must stand in immediate causal relation to the act, and become part either of the action immediately producing it, or of the action which it immediately produces. Incidents that are thus immediately and unconsciously associated with an act, whether such incidents are doing or declarations, become in this way evidence of the character of the act." Wharton, Crim. Ev. §§ 262, 263.

The most important English case is *Reg.* v. *Bedingfield,* 14 Cox C. C. 341.

See also note to *Good* v. *State,* 20 Cent. L. J. 453, collecting cases on *res gestæ.*

Recent illustrations.—The victim of highway robbers at night immediately gave alarm, and returned to his house near by, and, a few minutes later, on the arrival of an officer, described to him the appearance of the assailants. Held that the statements thus made to the officer were admissible as sufficiently connected with the principal event to be its natural outgrowth and free from the suspicion of plan or afterthought. *State* v. *Horan,* 32 Minn. 394, 50 Am. Rep. 583, 20 N. W. 905. The court said: "Upon this subject the authorities are not uniform. Some courts are inclined to hold the rule with much strictness as to the time and circumstances under which the statements proposed to be shown are made, while others allow a wider range for its application, leaving it to be applied largely in the sound discretion of the trial court,"—Citing 15 Am. L. Rev. 85; *Com.* v. *Densmore,* 12 Allen, 537; *People* v. *Davis,* 56 N. Y. 102; *Com.* v. *McPike,* 3 Cush. 184, 50 Am. Dec. 727; *Travellers' Ins. Co.* v. *Mosley,* 8 Wall. 397, 19 L. ed. 437.

Our examination leads us to conclude that, especially in cases of tort involving personal injury, the weight of authority in this country is in favor of allowing evidence of the declarations or statements of the injured party touching the cause or circumstances of the injury, made so soon after the event, and under such circumstances as to warrant the trial court in presuming that they grew out of and were dependent upon it, and could not have been devised or contrived by the declarant for his own purposes. *Driscoll* v. *People,* 47 Mich. 413, 11 N. W. 221 (complaint to policeman); *People* v. *Dowling,* 84 N. Y. 478 (larceny; error to exclude what was said as to the mode of obtaining the property at the time of defendant's alleged purchase of it from third person. Folger, J., says: It was doubtless hearsay, and was not competent testimony to prove that the alleged vendors came by the property in the mode asserted. But as it was competent for the defendant to prove the acts by which the goods came into his possession, if he was able to, it was competent to prove all pertinent sayings and doings that then were made and done, as relevant upon the issue of guilty knowledge. It was competent. It was for the jury still to say whether it was of weight in showing the prisoner innocent in the transaction, if they found that the transaction took place as he testified), Citing *Rex* v. *Whitehead,* 1 Car. & P. 67; *Powell* v. *Harper,* 5 Car. & P. 590; *Hayslep* v. *Gymer,* 1 Ad. & El. 162. The cases to the contrary, cited from 3 Park. Crim. Rep. (*Wills* v. *People,* 473, and *People* v. *Rando,* 335), were doubtingly decided. On principle, such evidence must be competent.

Lovett v. *State,* 80 Ga. 255, 4 S. E. 912, holds it competent, in larceny, to show what defendant said to a neighbor soon after arriving home, and tending to show that he had brought the thing by mistake for his own.

In *State* v. *Walker,* 77 Me. 488, 1 Atl. 357, it was held error to exclude declaration made by the accused at the moment of shooting.

In *Monday* v. *State,* 32 Ga. 672, 79 Am. Dec. 314, a declaration immediately after being assaulted, showing impression as to the nature of the attack, was held admissible.

In *Com.* v. *M'Pike,* 3 Cush. 181, 50 Am. Dec. 727, a declaration of one escaping from an assault, as to who committed it, was held admissible.

In *Territory* v. *Davis* (Ariz.) 10 Pac. 359, a statement to eye-witnesses, made in a drug-store within three minutes after being shot, and within a few feet from the place, narrating the attack of the accused, was held admissible. See *contra, Kirby* v. *Com.* 77 Va. 681, 46 Am. Rep. 747.

In *Lander* v. *People,* 104 Ill. 248, witnesses to the identity of the accused as the perpetrator of the offense, were allowed to testify that on seeing him pass the next day, one exclaimed, "There goes the man!" and the other, "Yes, there he goes!"

Contra, People v. *Ah Lee,* 60 Cal. 85 (Sharpstein, J., says: "There are cases which hold that the declarations made by the party injured, as to the cause and manner of the injury, which terminated in his death, are admissible in evidence against the person charged with the homicide, although made after all action on the part of the wrongdoer, actual or constructive, had ceased. . . . It is perfectly obvious that there is a limit to the time within which such statements must be made, in order to be admissible in evidence as part of the *res gestæ.* But if made after the termination of the act to which they refer, they are merely narrative of a past transaction, whether made within a minute or an hour afterward. . . . The distinction between statements which constitute a part of the *res gestæ* and those which constitute 'dying declarations,' should be clearly defined or obliterated." In this case the crime was murder by stabbing. It not appearing that anything occurred between accused and deceased after the stabbing, held error to allow prosecution to ask a witness what he heard either of the parties say at the time of stabbing or immediately after); *State* v. *Davidson,* 30 Vt. 377, 73 Am.

Dec. 312 (subsequent declarations of a party injured when no one was present are not evidence to show the manner in which the injury occurred, however nearly contemporaneous with the occurrence).

For other cases involving the admissibility of declarations of the decedent on murder trial, see *Lambright* v. *State*, 34 Fla. 564, 16 So. 582 (declarations twelve hours after being shot inadmissible); *Gaines* v. *State*, 108 Ga. 772, 33 S. E. 632 (declaration immediately after the shooting admissible); *State* v. *Ellington* (Idaho) 43 Pac. 60 (statements made shortly after the infliction of the fatal hurt, and in a manner and under circumstances which preclude any presumption that they were the result of consideration or design); *Healy* v. *People*, 163 Ill. 372, 45 N. E. 230 (statements of a person mortally wounded by officers from whom he was escaping, that he did no wrong, are admissible against such officers, as part of the *res gestæ*, when made in their presence and hearing); *Green* v. *State*, 154 Ind. 655, 57 N. E. 637 (declaration of deceased that her husband had shot her, made after staggering back 5 feet from where she was standing when shot, placing her baby on the bed, and falling on her knees, admissible); *State* v. *McCarty*, 54 Kan. 52, 36 Pac. 338 (declarations of deceased, made prior to the fatal encounter, inadmissible where they do not properly constitute a part of the *res gestæ*); *Hughes* v. *Com.* 19 Ky. L. Rep. 497, 41 S. W. 294 (evidence that officer, for whose murder defendant is on trial, said, immediately after the shooting, that he had been shot, and that he directed the bystanders to catch defendant, admissible); *People* v. *O'Brien*, 92 Mich. 17, 52 N. W. 84 (statement by deceased to physician who was dressing his wound shortly after he received it, at a time when neither of them considered it dangerous, that defendant, accused of murder, inflicted the wound with a knife, incompetent); *State* v. *Thompson*, 141 Mo. 408, 42 S. W. 949 (statement by deceased, with whose murder by poison defendant is charged, to another person while eating the poisoned lunch, that it was brought to him by defendant, admissible); *Com.* v. *Van Horn*, 188 Pa. 143, 41 Atl. 469 (declarations by deceased immediately after defendant had cut her throat, and while she was in the act of fleeing from him, and he was in the act of fleeing from pursuit, admissible); *Freeman* v. *State* (Tex. Crim. App.) 51 S. W. 230 (statements by deceased as to how a difficulty occurred, made some thirty or sixty minutes after having been wounded by one accused of killing him, and, after having attended to several other matters, passed through a faint, and had his wounds dressed, admissible); *State* v. *Webster*, 21 Wash. 63, 57 Pac. 361 (conversation between husband and wife immediately after she received the fatal shot, in which she stated that she was shot fatally, and by whom the shot was fired, and implored her husband to take the children upstairs, or they would all be killed, and that the accused would shoot again, admissible).

267. The whole res gestae admissible.

Everything that happened in the immediate presence and hearing of the accused at the time of the offense is competent.[1]

[1] *M'Kee* v. *People*, 36 N. Y. 113, 3 Abb. Pr. N. S. 216, 34 How. Pr. 230,

holding it not error to permit the whole conversation which occurred at the time of the killing, in the presence and in the hearing of the prisoner, to be given in evidence.

In *People* v. *Potter*, 5 Mich. 1, 71 Am. Dec. 763, 764, every occurrence, every remark, and the whole conduct of the prisoner, from the time he and the deceased came together until the consummation of the crime, was held to be competent evidence, as part of the *res gestæ*, to enable the jury to determine whether any crime was committed, as well as to inform them as to its degree. See also *Liles* v. *State*, 30 Ala. 24, 68 Am. Dec. 108.

So, in *State* v. *Elvins*, 101 Mo. 243, 13 S. W. 937, a prosecution for an assault with intent to kill, testimony to show how the quarrel or altercation began, and all that was said and done about it by defendant up to the time when he fired the shot alleged to have constituted the assault, was held competent.

And in *Stitt* v. *State*, 91 Ala. 10, 8 So. 669, a murder trial, all that occurred between the parties, leading up to and culminating in the killing, and constituting one continuous transaction, was held admissible.

268. Previous declarations.

Conversation preceding an act may be admitted.[1]

[1]*Schnicker* v. *People*, 88 N. Y. 192; *Carpenter* v. *State*, 58 Ark. 233, 24 S. W. 247; *State* v. *Webster*, 21 Wash. 63, 57 Pac. 36; *Carr* v. *State*, 43 Ark. 99; *People* v. *Majone*, 91 N. Y. 211, Affirming 12 Abb. N. C. 187 (murder; held not error to admit evidence of conversation had by accused a few minutes before the killing, as throwing light on his state of mind and subsequent conduct, and explaining the language used by him at the time of the killing); *Cox* v. *State*, 64 Ga. 374, 37 Am. Rep. 76 (murder; where homicide occurred in fight with pistols, such fight being had in pursuance of agreement made an hour previously; held, all pertinent acts and declarations of the parties that took place between the agreement and the homicide were admissible as part of the *res gestæ*); *Com.* v. *Castles*, 9 Gray, 121, 69 Am. Dec. 278 (trial of an indictment for obtaining a signature to a mortgage by false pretenses; the fraud consisting in representing to the signer that the paper signed was a mortgage deed to his father; evidence held admissible, against the accused, of his previous conversations with the father as to procuring such signature, as showing the animus, and as part of the *res gestæ*. Evidence admitted and exception overruled.

But in *State* v. *Young*, 55 Kan. 349, 40 Pac. 659, a trial for abortion, statements made some time before the commission of the alleged offense, by the woman, who had died, that the defendant and her husband wanted her to have an abortion produced, but that she had determined to prevent them, and statements by her after the abortion had been produced, and which did not characterize or explain the act,—were held incompetent.

269. Declarations depending on the credit of the declarant.

A statement which depends entirely for its effect on the credit of the person making it is inadmissible.[1]

[1]*United States* v. *Angell,* 11 Fed. 34. Held not error to exclude.

The exclamations of a child at the time of a homicide are inadmissible as *res gestæ,* where, after the lapse of two years the child is not deemed to be possessed of sufficient comprehension and intelligence to be a competent witness as to the matters which called forth the exclamations. *Adams* v. *State,* 34 Fla. 185, 15 So. 905.

270. Res gestae involving another offense.

Circumstances otherwise competent as part of the *res gestæ* are not rendered incompetent by a tendency to prove another offense than that charged.[1]

[1]See, generally, *People* v. *Teixeira,* 123 Cal. 297, 55 Pac. 988; *State* v. *Taylor* (Mo.) 22 S. W. 806; *People* v. *Pallister,* 138 N. Y. 601, 33 N. E. 741; *State* v. *Wong Gee,* 35 Or. 276, 57 Pac. 914; *Hamilton* v. *State,* (Tex. Crim. App.) 56 S. W. 926.

In *Reyes* v. *State,* 10 Tex. App. 1 (attempt to commit robbery); it was held admissible to show that the killing was done in the perpetration, or in the attempt at the perpetration, of either arson, rape, robbery, or burglary.

So, in *Foster* v. *People,* 63 N. Y. 619, Affirming 3 Hun, 6 (trial for burglary), evidence that article not laid in indictment, a part of the stolen property, was taken with the articles specified; and evidence tending to identify it with a similar article seen thereafter in the possession of accused was held properly admitted as part of *res gestæ.*

But in *Berney* v. *State,* 69 Ala. 233, 44 Am. Rep. 513 (carrying concealed weapons), disorderly conduct of the defendant, which caused his arrest, and led to the discovery of the concealed weapon, was held irrelevant, and inadmissible against him. While such conduct may have been part of the *res gestæ,* and explanatory of the arrest, yet it had no tendency to prove or disprove the charge against the defendant, but did have a tendency to prejudice the jury unduly against him. The court said: "If the main fact in this cause, or if a material fact, was the arrest, that conduct would be so connected with it that evidence of it would be admissible. The main fact in controversy was the carrying of the pistol concealed." Conviction reversed.

And *Whilden* v. *State,* 25 Ga. 396, 71 Am. Dec. 181, a prosecution for stabbing, held that evidence of a prior fight between the prosecutor and prisoner was inadmissible, it appearing that the indictment was for the second fight, and that there was an interval of thirty minutes between the two. They were not closely enough connected to make the first fight part of the *res gestæ.*

271. Slight corroboration competent.

Evidence which tends to corroborate testimony as to the *res gestæ* is not incompetent merely because slight.[1]

[1]*Moyer* v. *Com.* 98 Pa. 338 (murder; accomplice having made statement as to *res gestæ,* held not error to admit proof of finding or articles where she had described them as located); *Linsday* v. *People,* 63 N. Y. 143, Affirming 5 Hun, 104, S. C., 67 Barb. 548 (on trial for murder, where an accomplice had testified that the prisoner and himself removed the body of deceased, on a certain night, to a spot specified; held not error to admit evidence that he was out until a late hour that night, as corroborating him in a material statement and as a part of the *res gestæ*).

So, upon a trial for assault with intent to murder, in which another assault upon the wife of the assaulted person is proved, the condition of the wife on the following day is admissible in evidence to corroborate the state's theory of what occurred, as developed by other evidence, and to discredit evidence on the part of the defendant. *Horn* v. *State,* 102 Ala. 144, 15 So. 278.

272. Acts and declarations of third persons.

The rule of the *res gestæ* admits the connected acts and declarations of third persons.[1]

Before the declarations of a third person can be received as part of the *res gestæ,* his actual presence at the occurrence must be shown.[2]

[1]*State* v. *Walker,* 78 Mo. 380, Citing *Newton* v. *Mutual Ben. L. Ins. Co.* 2 Dill. 154, Fed. Cas. No. 10,191; *Travellers' Ins. Co.* v. *Mosley,* 8 Wall. 397, 19 L. ed. 437; *People* v. *Lane,* 100 Cal. 379, 34 Pac. 856; *State* v. *Kaiser,* 124 Mo. 651, 28 S. W. 182; *Gerick* v. *State* (Tex. Crim. App.) 45 S. W. 717, 492; *Johnson* v. *State,* 88 Ga. 203, 14 S. E. 208.

In *State* v. *Walker,* the exclamation of a bystander, "Don't strike him, for you have shot him now," was held admissible as part of the *res gestæ.* being called out by, and illustrative of, the affray, while still in progress.

The *res gestæ* "may consist of sayings and doings of any one absorbed in the event, whether participant or bystander." 1 Wharton, Ev. § 259, Approved and applied in *State* v. *Walker,* 78 Mo. 380.

Compare *Ex parte Kennedy* (Tex. Crim. App.) 57 S. W. 648, where the remark, "Little Jack Kennedy (defendant) shot him, and there he goes," made by a bystander after the homicide, was held not to be *res gestæ,* but mere hearsay, and as such inadmissible against defendant.

So, in case of a homicide resulting from an affray which began in rough play, and in which several persons took part without concert or combination, acts of another person participating in the affray, showing a purpose to aid the defendant, who is on trial for the homicide, are not provable against him as part of the *res gestæ.* *Whitaker* v. *State,* 106 Ala. 30, 17 So. 456.

And on a prosecution for murder of one whose guilt depends solely upon his presence and encouragement of the killing, testimony that some one in an excited crowd, before the accused was present or knew of the cause of the excitement, cried out "Go for" the accused, calling him by name, is incompetent and prejudicial. *Omer* v. *Com.* 15 Ky. L. Rep. 694, 25 S. W. 594.

The declarations of a bystander upon seeing deceased starting back to the place where he had previously quarreled with the defendant, charged with his murder, to the effect that there was going to be trouble, is inadmissible upon the question as to which was the aggressor in the difficulty in which the homicide was committed. *Allen* v. *State,* 111 Ala. 80, 20 So. 490.

[a]*Flynn* v. *State,* 43 Ark. 289, holding that the exclamations of one appearing to have just left the place were not competent, without evidence that he had been a participant in the scene.

In *State* v. *Moore,* 38 La. Ann. 66, a witness testified that a child in his store called out, "You are being robbed," and thereupon he looked and saw the accused running out; and it was held admissible as a part of the *res gestæ.*

273. Declarations of another as to intent in contemplated act.

Whether the declarations of the defendant or deceased as to intent, when about to go to the place where the offense was committed, are competent, compare—[1]

[1]Affirmative: *State* v. *Dickinson,* 41 Wis. 299; *Harris* v. *State,* 96 Ala. 24, 11 So. 255; *State* v. *Lucey,* 24 Mont. 295, 61 Pac. 994.

Negative: *People* v. *Williams,* 3 Abb. App. Dec. 596. Denio, J., approved in 22 Alb. L. J. 4, where other cases on both sides are collected.

And that evidence that deceased stated to his wife, in the absence of defendant, that he intended to abandon a difficulty between him and defendant, is inadmissible, where it was not communicated to defendant, see *Com.* v. *Gray,* 17 Ky. L. Rep. 354, 30 S. W. 1015.

274. Evidence in favor of accused.

The rule of the *res gestæ* admits evidence in favor of the accused, as well as against him.[1]

[1]*State* v. *Rollins,* 113 N. C. 722, 18 S. E. 394; *Irvine* v. *State,* 104 Tenn. 132, 56 S. W. 845.

In *Dukes* v. *State,* 11 Ind. 557, 71 Am. Dec. 370–377, evidence as to the prisoner's appearance, manner, and condition of mind, as indicating alarm or otherwise, and the efforts made by him to sound an alarm to the public, was held admissible as part of the *res gestæ,* on behalf of the prisoner, who sought to justify a homicide as committed in self-defense, or in defense of personal property. It was excluded by the court below, and the judgment was reversed for this and other reasons.

In *Foster* v. *State,* 8 Tex. App. 248, it was held error to exclude evidence that the accused, within a minute after shooting, exclaimed, "I would shoot any man who was trying to cut my throat."

And in *Koller* v. *State,* 36 Tex. Crim. Rep. 496, 38 S. W. 44, evidence that defendant charged with murder told another, on going for his gun just before the homicide was committed, that he did not intend to kill the deceased, but that the latter could not insult him in the way he had done unless he would take it back, was held admissible for defendant, as part of the *res gestæ* as to his purpose in going for his gun and returning.

But the accused's self-serving statements, when he came into the police station to surrender himself, after committing a homicide, are not admissible as part of the *res gestæ.* *State* v. *Nocton,* 121 Mo. 537, 26 S. W. 551.

Nor, on a trial for murder, is a statement by deceased, a short time after he was shot by defendant, to the effect that the latter applied to him opprobrious epithets, and he struck him, admissible for defendant as part of the *res gestæ.* *State* v. *Pugh,* 16 Mont. 343, 40 Pac. 861.

275. Act admits conversation.

If the act is properly in evidence, the accused has a right to prove conversation constituting part of the *res gestæ* even though no part of the conversation has been proved against him.[1]

[1]*Mack* v. *State,* 48 Wis. 271, 4 N. W. 449. See also *State* v. *Daley,* 53 Vt. 442, 38 Am. Rep. 694; *Crite* v. *Com.* 12 Rep. 575, 5 Va. L. J. 568; *Morrow* v. *State,* 48 Ind. 432.

276. Tangible evidence.

Under the rule of the *res gestæ,* tangible evidence, such as the clothing worn by the deceased, showing the place and nature of the wound, may be received.[1]

[1]*People* v. *Knapp,* 71 Cal. 1, 11 Pac. 793, Citing *People* v. *Hong Ah Duck,* 61 Cal. 391. See also *supra,* §§ 224 et seq.

So held in *State* v. *Campbell,* 7 N. D. 58, 72 N. W. 935, of cartridges and chisel found in possession of defendant, charged with burglary, on his arrest within two hours after the commission of the burglary, and after being tracked over 3 miles through the snow, and a revolver and punch found within 2 or 3 feet of his place of concealment, which revolver he admits belongs to him.

And in *State* v. *Campbell,* 7 N. D. 58, 72 N. W. 935, of blacksmith's tools found in a building where the burglary for which defendant is on trial was committed, and which are shown to have been brought there without authority, and are such as might have been used in breaking the outside door, which was broken, or in endeavoring to open the safe, which had been battered.

XLI. Second offense.

[The fact that the accused had been guilty of a previous offense may be admissible, either as bearing on character when he has given evidence of good character (see *supra*, §§ 89–102), or as bearing on his credibility when he has testified in his own behalf (see *supra*, §§ 16–40), or, in some cases, as showing intent in the transactions charged on the present trial (see *supra*, §§ 236–249), or as subjecting him to greater punishment than if the present offense were his first. It is only in the latter aspect that it is here considered.]

277. Competency.

Evidence that the accused has been convicted of a previous offense, if offered for the purpose of bringing the present charge within a statute imposing severer punishment for a second offense,[1] is not admissible unless such previous conviction is alleged in the indictment.[2]

[1]In Missouri the record of a former conviction of defendant is admissible on the trial of an indictment drawn under Rev. Stat. 1889, § 3959, which provides in effect that the imprisonment of one convicted of a subsequent offense, committed after his discharge from imprisonment on a former conviction, shall be for the longest term prescribed for a conviction of such offense as the first offense, if the punishment therefor as a first offense is a limited term of years. *State* v. *Manicke,* 139 Mo. 545, 41 S. W. 223.

So, on a trial under Mo. Rev. Stat. 1889, § 3959, for a second offense by one discharged by pardon or by compliance with sentence, the certificate of discharge by the warden of the penitentiary, who is required to keep the record of discharge or pardon, is admissible, where defendant was discharged under the three-fourths rule, since in such case no pardon is necessary. *State* v. *Austin,* 113 Mo. 538, 21 S. W. 31.

And on a trial for petit larceny, second offense, an unauthorized amendment by the justice of the peace of his judgment of conviction of the former offense, so as to interline the date of its rendition, and to affix his name and official signature thereto, does not render it inadmissible in evidence, if it is otherwise admissible. *State* v. *Griffie,* 118 Mo. 188, 23 S. W. 878.

In New York a former conviction is to be proved before the verdict on the offense for which the defendant is being tried, under Pen. Code, § 688, providing in effect that a person who, after having been convicted in the state, commits any crime within the state, shall, upon conviction of such second offense, be subject to an enhanced penalty. *People* v. *Sickles,* 156 N. Y. 541, 51 N. E. 288, Affirming 26 App. Div. 470, 50 N. Y. Supp. 377.

In Texas the evidence of a previous conviction as the basis of a cumulative sentence under the Texas statute should not be submitted to the jury, as the jury has nothing to do with the matter. *Miller* v. *State* (Tex. Crim. App.) 44 S. W. 162.

In *Pryor* v. *Com.* (Va.) 26 S. E. 864, it was held that a record offered to prove previous conviction of defendant was admissible for that purpose, where it showed that defendant was convicted of the offense charged, and sentenced therefor by a justice to confinement for three months, and that he appealed therefrom to the court of the county, in which the justice's judgment was set aside by consent, and by further consent it was ordered that defendant be confined in jail two months from the date of committal by the justice.

[3]*Johnson* v. *People*, 55 N. Y. 512, Affirming 65 Barb. 342 (*dictum*); *State* v. *Ingersoll* (Wis. 1880) 2 Wis. Legal News, 208 (so holding in case of information; conviction reversed for error in compelling defendant to answer). See also *People* v. *King*, 64 Cal. 338, 30 Pac. 1028. And see cases cited in note to *Re Miller* (Mich.) 34 L. R. A. 406.

278. Limitations.

For this purpose the former conviction may be proved notwithstanding the period fixed by the statute of limitations has since intervened.[1]

[1]*State* v. *O'Neil*, 58 Vt. 140, 56 Am. Rep. 557, 2 Atl. 586.

279. Effect as bearing on character.

For the purpose of affecting the punishment, the former conviction is competent, notwithstanding it tends to prove bad character.[1]

[1]*Johnson* v. *People*, 55 N. Y. 512.

280. Identity of person.

A record of conviction of one of the same name as the present defendant is prima facie evidence that it was the same person.[1]

[1]*State* v. *Kelsoe*, 11 Mo. App. 91 (burglary). Otherwise if the name was very common. See note to *Spotten* v. *Keeler*, 22 Abb. N. C. 105.

281. Identity of offense.

It must affirmatively appear that the offense was the same as that charged in the present indictment.[1]

[1]*Jenkins* v. *State*, 78 Ind. 133. Compare cases under *supra*, §§ 205 *et seq.*

XLII. Silence as an admission.

282. General rule.

It is competent to prove against the accused any statement as to matters presumptively within his knowledge,[1] made in his hearing,[2] and tending directly or indirectly[3] to implicate him; and thereupon to show his demeanor,[4] his silence,[5] or his response,[6] as evidence of his acquiescence in the statement, unless it appears that such statement was made in the course of a judicial proceeding, or otherwise under circumstances in which a disclaimer would be inopportune or uncalled for.[7]

[1]This qualification—well noted in *Kelley* v. *People,* 55 N. Y. 565, 14 Am. Rep. 342—is not expressed in the cases generally, because nearly all the cases relate to statements directly referring to the conduct of the accused; but the principle is equally applicable to matters relevant as circumstantial evidence against him; and in this class of cases the qualification that the statements must be of matters presumptively within his knowledge is important.

An anonymous letter, no connection with or knowledge of which by prisoner was shown, received by one C., the owner of the premises for the burning of which prisoner was indicted, held not rendered admissible against the prisoner by the fact that at an interview between R., an alleged coconspirator with defendant, and C. R., making certain statements to C. about the letter, prisoner being present, remained silent; because the statement was not prompted by anything he said, and he was not called on to reply. *Wright* v. *People,* 1 N. Y. Crim. Rep. 462, where conviction was reversed for error in receiving such testimony.

[2]See authority under *infra,* § 290.

[3]*Franklin* v. *State,* 69 Ga. 36, 47 Am. Rep. 748. Murder; statements of the deceased touching his ownership of the shoes and socks the defendant had on, and which were pulled off his feet, made in the defendant's presence, and not denied by him, held admissible against him,—Citing *Moye* v. *State,* 66 Ga. 740.

[4]*Linsday* v. *People,* 63 N. Y. 143, Affirming 5 Hun, 104, S. C., more fully, 67 Barb. 548. Homicide; not error to admit evidence that the accused turned pale at the time of his arrest, charged with the murder, though such evidence was slight, if any, evidence of guilt.

The manner and conduct of an accused at different times when statements were made in his presence, tending to show guilt, in making explicit denials or equivocal expressions or remaining silent, are admissible in evidence against him. *Com.* v. *Trefethen,* 157 Mass. 180, 24 L. R. A. 235, 31 N. E. 961.

[5]*Kelley* v. *People,* 55 N. Y. 565, 574, 14 Am. Rep. 342. Grand larceny. The circumstances necessary to render the silence of the accused admissible as evidence of an admission are thus laid down by Allen, J.: 1. The declarations must be pertinent to the occasion. 2. In the presence and hearing of the parties interested, and under circumstances which rendered a contradiction or explanation reasonable, if not true. 3. They must be matters the truth of which was known to the accused. 4. A reply would have been natural and proper if the statements were false.

All the above circumstances concurring, the evidence was held properly admitted. Conviction affirmed. The court distinguished *Com.* v. *Kenney,* 12 Met. 235, 46 Am. Dec. 672, on the ground that in the latter case there was no independent evidence of *corpus delicti.*

1 Bishop, Crim. Proc. 3d ed. § 1254, states the rule thus: "Where one in the presence of the accused makes a declaration involving or implying his guilt, and there is opportunity for a reply, and the surroundings and persons are such as render it ordinarily expedient and proper, yet he remains silent, the entire fact may be shown with the other evidence to the jury."

Wharton, Crim. Ev. 8th ed. § 679, states it thus: "If A, when in B's presence and hearing, makes statements which B listens to in silence, interposing no objection, A's statements may be put in evidence against B whenever B's silence is of such a nature as to lead to the inference of assent."

In *State* v. *Suggs,* 89 N. C. 527 (robbery), it was held not error to admit evidence of a statement of a witness, tending to accuse the defendant, made in the latter's presence and hearing, when brought before the committing magistrate for identification merely, after a preliminary hearing had been had.

In *Ettinger* v. *Com.* 98 Pa. 338, it was held not error to admit testimony that on several occasions in the penitentiary the witness accused defendant of the murder, and he made no reply.

And for other cases instancing the application of this rule, see *State* v. *Belknap,* 39 W. Va. 427, 19 S. E. 507; *Kirby* v. *State,* 89 Ala. 63, 8 So. 110; *Williams* v. *State* (Ark.) 16 S. W. 816; *Miller* v. *State,* 68 Miss. 221, 8 So. 273; *State* v. *Plym,* 43 Minn. 385, 45 N. W. 848; *People* v. *Mallon,* 103 Cal. 513, 37 Pac. 512; *State* v. *Good,* 132 Mo. 114, 33 S. W. 790; *State* v. *Senn,* 32 S. C. 392, 11 S. E. 292; *Brown* v. *State,* 32 Tex. Crim. Rep. 119, 22 S. W. 596; *State* v. *Magoon,* 68 Vt. 289, 35 Atl. 310.

[6]See *infra,* § 291.

[7]See *infra,* § 285.

283. — although under arrest.

Such circumstances are not rendered incompetent by the mere fact that the accused was under arrest at the time.[1]

[1]In *Kelley* v. *People,* 55 N. Y. 565, 14 Am. Rep. 342, 346, the accused was arrested upon hot pursuit, and taken to a station house, and the prosecutor was there to identify him. He did identify him, and charged him with the robbery, stating the part he took in it. Although the statements were not addressed to him directly, he was the subject of the conversation and party to it, and could, without breach of propriety, have spoken. And it was held that the statements of the prosecutor were admissible against him,—Citing *Donnelly* v. *State,* 26 N. J. L. 601, and distinguishing *Com.* v. *Kenney,* 12 Met. 235, 46 Am. Dec. 672. See also *Murphy* v. *State,* 36 Ohio St. 628, holding that where two persons charged with a larceny, having the stolen property in their possession,

were taken into custody by a police officer, the declarations of one of them, assuming to speak for and implicating them both, made to the officer in the presence and hearing of the other person charged, who remained silent, are competent evidence for the state, on the separate trial of the latter. An express confession is not rendered incompetent by being made while under arrest; and the New York doctrine applies the same rule to the implied or tacit confession resulting from silence or peculiar demeanor or partial response. Compare, however, *People* v. *Koerner*, 154 N. Y. 355, 48 N. E. 730, where it is held that the statements by a physician to a police officer, in the presence of defendant, who was apparently unconscious that he was "shamming," are not admissible against defendant, upon the ground that by his silence he acquiesced therein, as silence, to have such effect, must be under circumstances which afford defendant an opportunity to act or speak, and properly or naturally call for some action or reply.

The cases in other jurisdictions are conflicting. See *Com.* v. *McDermott*, 123 Mass. 440, 25 Am. Rep. 120 (holding it error to admit the declaration of one arrested for same larceny, made in the defendant's presence, at the station house, while both were under arrest); *State* v. *Diskin*, 34 La. Ann. 919, 44 Am. Rep. 448 (where the accused was in the custody of an officer at the bedside of the dying man); *Com.* v. *Kenney*, 12 Met. 235, 46 Am. Dec. 672 (here the prosecuting witness at the watch house accused the defendant of stealing a bag of money from him, identifying the accused and the money which was found on him; held that the silence of the accused was an admission of neither the fact of stealing nor that the money belonged to the prosecuting witness. The reason given by the court is that the proceeding was in the nature of a preliminary examination [though not strictly so], and the defendant might well suppose that he had no right to say anything until regularly called upon to answer); *State* v. *Weaver*, 57 Iowa, 730, 11 N. W. 675; *People* v. *Young*, 108 Cal. 8, 41 Pac. 281 (evidence that defendant, on trial for murder, was taken after his arrest into the presence of the wounded man, and neither affirmed nor denied the statement of the latter to a third person to the effect that a certain purse found upon defendant at the time of arrest was the other's property, admissible); *Gardner* v. *State* (Tex. Crim. App.) 34 S. W. 945 (holding that silence of one under arrest, or his failure to deny statements made in his presence, cannot be used against him as a confession of the truth of the statements, in a prosecution for the crime for which he is under arrest, whether he had been cautioned as required by the Texas statute or not); *State* v. *Howard*, 102 Mo. 142, 14 S. W. 937 (holding that the rule that statements made in the presence and hearing of a person, uncontradicted by him, are implied admissions, has no operation when the party is under arrest at the time); *State* v. *Young*, 99 Mo. 666, 12 S. W. 879 (a prosecution for murder; testimony as to what a stranger said to the officer having the defndant in charge, in the latter's presence,—in substance that the officer had the right man,—incompetent); *State* v. *Murray*, 126 Mo. 611, 29 S. W. 700 (statement by an alleged conspirator that a certain conspirator fired the fatal shot, and afterwards robbed the deceased, made in the latter's presence, not admissible); *People* v. *Kessler,* 13 Utah, 69, 44 Pac. 97 (declaration by deceased, in the presence of defendant, that the latter was the person who assaulted him, to which the defendant made no reply, inadmissible where the police officer had previously told defendant to keep still).

In *State* v. *Sadler,* 51 La. Ann. 1397, 26 So. 390, it was held that statements made by a wounded man, that certain persons brought before him under arrest were the ones who wounded him, and that the true name of one was different from the name which he claimed, although those thus accused remained silent, and did not deny the charge,—might not be taken as a confession of guilt by them.

284. — statements made by one who is not a competent witness.

It makes no difference that the statements which call for a reply are made by a party who is incompetent to testify, because such statements are admitted, not as of themselves evidence of the truth of the facts stated, but simply to show what it is that calls for a reply, and the conduct of the defendant himself under the circumstances, as indicating an acquiescence in, or reputation of, the truth of the statement.[1]

[1]*Rex* v. *Smithies,* 5 Car. & P. 332. Statements made by a wife to the defendant, her husband, respecting his connection with the crime for which he was indicted—murder. See also *Rex* v. *Bartlett,* 7 Car. & P. 832 (statement of wife charging husband with murder); *People* v. *McCrea,* 32 Cal. 98 (statement of Chinaman who, by the California statute, was rendered incompetent to testify in cases where a white man was a party).

285. Silence at judicial hearing.

The rule that the silence of a person may be taken as an implied admission of the truth of statements made in his presence does not apply to silence at a judicial proceeding or hearing.[1]

[1]*People* v. *Willett,* 92 N. Y. 29, Affirming 27 Hun, 469, holding that where, during the proceedings before the coroner, a witness who had seen the accused on the night of the murder and identified him, identified him also before the coroner by means of his voice, among a number of others, all of whom passed in front of her, repeating the same expression as that used by the accused on the night in question, the silence of the defendant during this experiment before the coroner was not admissible against him. See also *United States* v. *Brown,* 4 Cranch, C. C. 508, Fed. Cas. No. 14,660; *Bell* v. *State,* 93 Ga. 557, 19 S. E. 244.

Mere silence while a party is held in custody under a criminal charge, and the charge is stated to him, affords no inference whatever of acquiescence in statements of others made in his presence; and such statements are not admissible against him, because he has a right to be silent, and therefore is not within the rule that the silence of one who is called upon to speak is an admission. *State* v. *Diskin,* 34 La. Ann. 919, 44 Am. Rep. 448, 449 (murder).

In *State* v. *Hale,* 156 Mo. 102, 56 S. W. 881, a trial for burglary, it was held error to admit testimony that at the preliminary trial the prosecuting witness, while testifying, exhibited to one of the defendants her pocketbook, and said: "Here is the pocketbook I had my money in. Don't you know that is the pocketbook?"—and that such defendant nodded his head, since no inference of guilt could be drawn from his silence when on trial, and not in a position to make a denial, and the nodding of his head was not an admission that the pocketbook was the one in which witness had her money.

So, in *State* v. *Dickey,* 46 W. Va. 319, 33 S. E. 231, it was held that a statement by the prosecuting attorney to the defendant's attorney, as to the manner in which the injury was inflicted upon deceased, was not admissible against defendant on a trial for homicide, although it was made in his presence, and he did not dissent therefrom, since, under the circumstances, he was not called upon to reply.

286. Unauthorized examination.

The fact that the supposed investigation was illegal and unauthorized does not render the silence of the accused competent, if the statements in the face of which he was silent were made during the pretended proceedings.[1]

[1]In *Donnelly* v. *State,* 26 N. J. L. 632, on this point, both the prevailing opinion and the dissenting opinion of Chancellor Williamson seem to concur. Compare, however, cases under *supra,* §§ 103 *et seq.*

287. Form of question.

In the absence of anything to raise doubt as to whether the accused heard or saw, it is competent for this purpose to ask a witness what was said or done "in the presence of the accused."[1]

[1]*Hochrieter* v. *People,* 2 Abb. App. Dec. 363; *Com.* v. *Brailey,* 134 Mass. 527, holding that, where it was shown that the statements were made in the accused's presence, it was for the jury under the circumstances to determine whether or not he heard them. *Contra, People* v. *Ah Yute,* 54 Cal. 89; *People* v. *Holfelder,* 5 N. Y. S. R. 488, 5 N. Y. Crim. Rep. 179 (both cases holding that defendant's silence cannot be taken to be an admission unless there is evidence that he heard the statement which he should have denied).

In *State* v. *Middleham,* 62 Iowa, 150, 17 N. W. 446, the question sustained was: "State what, if anything, was said by Mrs. Middleham, there in the presence and hearing of the defendant, concerning," etc.

Compare the following cases: *Long* v. *State,* 13 Tex. App. 211 (larceny of a cow. held error to admit evidence of a conversation between witness and another person separately indicted for larceny of the same cow, had in the defendant's presence, the witness testifying that he did not know whether the defendant overheard it or not, as the conversation was not addressed to him); *Jones* v. *State*, 65 Ga. 147 (holding it error to leave to the jury the question as to whether or not the defendant heard certain statements tending to accuse him of the crime, made by his wife to the witness in a cell adjoining that of her husband; the only evidence that the accused heard the statements being that the witness heard the defendant, as he, the witness, started out of the door, say to his wife, that she had better mind how she talked). See also *Ingle* v. *State*, 1 Tex. App. 307; *Lanergan* v. *People*, 39 N. Y. 39, 6 Park. Crim. Rep. 209 (holding it error to admit a declaration made in the presence of defendant, who was asleep). See *Moye* v. *State*, 66 Ga. 740 (holding that where inculpatory statements were made by a brother of the defendant in his presence, and under circumstances which would warrant the inference that he heard them, but did not deny them, they were admissible in evidence, the question whether they were so heard being left to the jury under proper instructions. The proof was that the defendant was near enough to the brother to hear the remark which tended to connect him with the crime, and that there was no noise to distract his attention); *Com.* v. *Sliney*, 126 Mass. 49 (where, evidence having been offered that the defendant could easily have heard the statements, it was held no error to leave it to the jury whether she in fact did hear them); *Com.* v. *Galavan*, 9 Allen, 271.

In *State* v. *Perkins*, 10 N. C. (3 Hawks) 377, it was held that it was properly left to the jury to determine whether, when the statements were made in the defendant's presence, he was so intoxicated as not to understand them.

288. Witness must have heard response if any.

The witness must be able to state what reply the defendant made, if he made any, or that no reply whatever was made.[1]

[1] *Williams* v. *State*, 42 Ark. 380, holding it error because it was not clear but that the accused denied the statement, as the witness left about that time. Compare *supra*, § 132.

289. Statement only implicating another than the accused not admissible.

If the statement, though made in the presence and hearing of the defendant, did not so implicate him as to call for a denial, it is inadmissible.[1]

[1] *Loggins* v. *State*, 8 Tex. App. 434 (holding it error to admit a statement made in the defendant's presence, by one jointly indicted for the same murder, but separately tried, to the effect that he, the speaker, had said that the accused would be killed for slaying his, the speaker's, son); *Wright* v. *People*, 1 N. Y. Crim. Rep. 462 (holding that an anonymous

letter threatening to burn the premises of the prosecutor, no connection with or knowledge of which by prisoner is shown, received by the owner of the premises for burning which the prisoner was indicted, is not rendered admissible in evidence against the defendant by the fact that at an interview between the defendant, the owner, and an alleged conspirator, the latter told the owner that these premises would be burned, the defendant remaining silent).

290. Explanation of silence consistent with innocence.

If the circumstances show a reasonable ground for silence, consistent with innocence, the evidence is incompetent.[1]

[1]*Slattery* v. *People,* 76 Ill. 217, with note (abortion; the defendant had promised to be on good behavior at a family interview, to which he had induced a friend, by means of such promise, to go with him, held that his silence at that interview under harsh accusations should not be construed as admitting them); *Com.* v. *Kenney,* 12 Met. 235, 46 Am. Dec. 672 (where the court, Shaw, Ch. J., used this language: "The circumstances were such that the court are of opinion that the declaration of the party robbed, to which the defendant made no reply, ought not to have been received as competent evidence of his admission, either of the fact of stealing, or that the bag and money were the property of the party alleged to be robbed. . . . If not strictly an official complaint to officers of the law, it was a proceeding very similar to it, and he might well suppose that he had no right to say anything until regularly called upon to answer"). Compare *supra,* § 285; and also cases under *supra,* §§ 103 *et seq.*

291. Response.

If the defendant responded, even impliedly or tacitly admitting the truth of the statement, both the statements and the response are competent.[1]

[1]*Com.* v. *Brown,* 121 Mass. 69, where a female having told an officer having the accused in charge that he had performed an abortion on her, the accused asked her, without denying the charge, if she had been previously operated upon by another person,—Citing *Com.* v. *Kenney,* 12 Met. 235, 46 Am. Dec. 672; and *Com.* v. *Galavan,* 9 Allen, 271.

XLIII. Stenographers' minutes.

292. Interpreted testimony.

Testimony given on a former trial of the same cause, through an interpreter, cannot be proved by the stenographer's minutes alone.[1]

[1]*People* v. *Ah Yute,* 56 Cal. 119.

293. Authentication.

The stenographer's minutes, though certified by him, are not competent without further authentication.[1]

Otherwise, where the statute makes them evidence.[2]

[1] *Rounds* v. *State*, 57 Wis. 45, 14 N. W. 865. See also *Golden Terra Min. Co.* v. *Smith*, 2 Dak. 377, 11 N. W. 98.

That unauthenticated minutes of the testimony of defendant in a criminal action, given on a former trial for the same offense, may by consent be read in evidence, see *Fertig* v. *State*, 100 Wis. 301, 75 N. W. 960.

[2] *State* v. *Frederic*, 69 Me. 400.

They may be admissible after his death as entries in the course of duty.

Where the stenographer who transcribed the minutes testified that his transcript was absolutely correct, but that he had not compared it; held not error to exclude it for want of comparison. *People* v. *McKinney*, 49 Mich. 334, 13 N. W. 619 (Cooley, J.). See also *infra*, §§ 297–310; and note to *Morehouse* v. *Morehouse*, 17 Abb. N. C. 421.

As to using to refresh memory, see *State* v. *Baldwin*, 36 Kan. 1, 12 Pac. 318; *Rounds* v. *State*, 57 Wis. 45, 14 N. W. 865; *Ellis* v. *State*, 25 Fla. 702, 6 So. 768.

A certificate that the transcript of a shorthand reporter's minutes, taken upon the examination of the accused before a committing magistrate, is a "true copy" of the testimony and the proceedings in the "within entitled action," but not showing the court or cause in which, nor the time at which, such testimony was taken, is not a compliance with Cal. Pen. Code, § 869, providing that such transcript, when certified as being a correct statement of the testimony and proceedings in the case, shall be prima facie a correct statement of such testimony and proceedings. *People* v. *Ward*, 105 Cal. 652, 39 Pac. 33.

XLIV. Surplusage.

294. The modern test.

Surplusage may be stricken out or disregarded, if the indictment remains sufficient without it; otherwise it cannot be.[1]

[1] "It is a general rule, irrespective of statute, that surplusage does not vitiate (an indictment), and to aid the sense it may be rejected. But by the introduction of such matter the prosecutor perils his case; for, if surplusage is so mixed up with essential allegations that one cannot be struck out without the other, the entire averment must be supported by the proof." Gillett, Crim. Law (1888) § 133.

XLV. Tampering with Witness or Juror.

295. Competency of evidence of.

It is competent to prove that the adverse party has tampered with a witness[1] or a juror.[2]

[1] *People* v. *Marion*, 29 Mich. 31; *Collins* v. *Com.* 12 Bush, 271 (holding that the prosecution could show that the accused participated in procuring the absence of a witness for the state on the trial). And that it is unnecessary to cross-examine the witness first, see *Martin* v. *Barnes*, 7 Wis. 239.

Letters written by the accused, threatening an anticipated witness, are, like attempts to escape from prison, admissible as some evidence of guilt, and, for the same reason, evidence of an attempt to shoot the witness is admissible, as the jury might find that it occurred in pursuance of the threat contained in the letters. *Adams* v. *People*, 9 Hun, 89; *Joseph* v. *Com.* 8 Ky. L. Rep. 53, 1 S. W. 4.

On the prosecution of a man and his paramour for murder of one upon whom she also bestowed favors, evidence is admissible that she attempted to bribe witnesses to leave the state, so as not to be present at her trial. *State* v. *Nocton*, 121 Mo. 537, 26 S. W. 551.

And it is competent to prove that accused stated to one of the witnesses for the state, in a threatening manner, that he did not want such witness to testify against him. *Gaines* v. *State* (Tex. Crim. App.) 37 S. W. 331. So held, in *State* v. *Baden*, 42 La. Ann. 295, 7 So. 582, of attempts by accused to intimidate a witness for the prosecution, as tending to establish a presumption of guilt. And such admissibility is not destroyed by the fact that, on a trial for the crime of intimidating the same witness, accused had been acquitted.

But a question of a witness on the trial of another for assaulting him, whether anyone spoke to him about a dismissal of the case, is not proper unless it is proposed to connect the defendant with it. *People* v. *Choy Ah Sing*, 84 Cal. 276, 24 Pac. 379.

And in *Gann* v. *State* (Tex. Crim. App.) 57 S. W. 668, a trial for the theft of a cow, it was held reversible error to permit a witness to testify, over defendant's objection, that such witness requested another witness not to testify against defendant as to facts within the latter's knowledge, in regard to the theft, where such request was made without authority of defendant.

So held in *Luttrell* v. *State*, 40 Tex. Crim. Rep. 651, 51 S. W. 930, of testimony that an attorney for defendant attempted to bribe a witness to leave the country, where there is no evidence tending to show that the attorney was authorized by defendant to bribe, or offer to bribe, the witness to leave, other than the fact that he was defendant's attorney.

And in *Foster* v. *State* (Tex. Crim. App.) 45 S. W. 803, it is held that evidence in a murder trial that one called upon the witness and demanded that she testify that the deceased at the time of the killing had no pistol, and that upon her refusal to promise to do so such person choked her,—is inadmissible.

In *Hanscom* v. *State,* 93 Wis. 273, 67 N. W. 419, it was held that evidence that an attorney for defendant, charged with perjury, said nothing to the latter about his receiving any money for testifying at the trial at which the alleged perjury was committed, was properly excluded, although some hearsay evidence that the district attorney had heard of a possible tampering with defendant had been introduced, where the trial judge expressly stated that there was no proof of any such tampering.

[2]*People* v. *Marion,* 29 Mich. 31.

So, on a criminal prosecution for libel in stating that the only hope of an attorney for the defense in a criminal prosecution lay in a packed jury, and that he relied upon bribing a juror, where evidence tending to prove these matters has been admitted, defendant should be allowed to prove that one of the jurors was bribed, and that he did in fact hang the jury in the case, and also to show the conduct of such juror in the jury room, and what he said and did, and how the jurors voted. *State* v. *Wait,* 44 Kan. 310, 24 Pac. 354.

296. Supplying testimony of witness kept away.

If a witness is wrongfully kept away by the accused, his testimony, taken on a former trial of the accused for the same offense, though under another indictment, may be given in evidence.[1]

[1]*Reynolds* v. *United States,* 98 U. S. 145, 25 L. ed. 244.

XLVI. Testimony given in Former Proceedings.

297. Testimony of accused at his preliminary examination, or as a suspect at inquest.

Testimony given by the accused on a judicial investigation, either when charged before the examining magistrate, or under arrest on suspicion at a coroner's inquest, is not competent against him at the trial, unless it appears that before it was given he was duly cautioned that it might be used against him, and that it was regularly taken according to law.[1] If these facts be shown, it is competent.[2]

[1]*People* v. *McMahon,* 15 N. Y. 384; *People* v. *Mondon,* 103 N. Y. 211, 57 Am. Rep. 709, 8 N. E. 496; *State* v. *Spier,* 86 N. C. 600 (excluding the testimony though not in the nature of a confession). Compare *People* v. *Herbert,* 61 Cal. 544; *Dickerson* v. *State,* 48 Wis. 288, 4 N. W. 321; *Farkas* v. *State,* 60 Miss. 847; *Rector* v. *Com.* 80 Ky. 468; *State* v. *Glass,* 50 Wis. 218, 36 Am. Rep. 845, 6 N. W. 500.

An examination of a prisoner taken before a committing magistrate, who testifies positively that he either read it to him, or that it was read to him by the clerk, that being the uniform custom of the court, is properly admitted in evidence. *Godfrey* v. *People,* 5 Hun, 369.

State v. *Glass,* 50 Wis. 218, 36 Am. Rep. 845, 6 N. W. 500 (manslaughter), holds that testimony given under oath on the preliminary examination of the prisoner may be given in evidence against him, as the statute, which allows a defendant in a criminal prosecution to testify in his own behalf at the preliminary examination, and which provides that his refusal or omission to do so shall create no presumption against him, removes from the testimony so given the element of compulsion.—Approves and follows *Dickerson* v. *State,* 48 Wis. 288, 4 N. W. 321; and *People* v. *Kelley,* 47 Cal. 125.

In *State* v. *O'Brien,* 18 Mont. 1, 43 Pac. 1091, 44 Pac. 399, testimony given by defendant charged with murder, upon being called before the coroner immediately after the homicide, was held inadmissible against him, where he testified without knowledge of his lawful rights, and without the aid of counsel, and under a belief that he had to answer the questions put to him.

Compare, for the rule where the magistrate had no authority, *People* v. *Gibbons,* 43 Cal. 557 (grand larceny, holding that the statement of a prisoner, voluntarily made under oath, in answer to interrogatories propounded by an examining magistrate, such magistrate having no authority to examine the prisoner under oath, is not admissible in evidence against him. New trial granted); and *People* v. *Sharp,* 107 N. Y. 427, 445, 14 N. E. 319.

In *People* v. *McGloin,* 91 N. Y. 241, affirming 28 Hun, 150, it was held not error to admit in evidence a written statement made by the accused after he was under arrest, and taken down in writing by a coroner, who was sent for for the purpose. The court (Ruger, Ch. J.) said: "The question . . . prior to the adoption of the Code of Criminal Procedure was the subject of some controversy and difference in the courts. . . . The difficulty, in brief, seemed to be in determining whether the reason for the objection rested upon the theory that the evidence was given in obedience to the requirements of a subpœna, and was therefore compulsory and objectionable as requiring a prisoner to give evidence which might criminate himself, or whether it was based upon the presumption that a prisoner giving evidence in relation to a crime, with the commission of which he is charged or suspected, gives it under such influences as produce an apprehension of danger and a mental disturbance, rendering it unjust to hold him responsible for what he says while subject to such influences. . . . It may be said that the following propositions were, prior to the adoption of the Criminal Code, well settled by law in this state: First, that all confessions material to the issue, voluntarily made by a party, whether oral or written, and however authenticated, were admissible as evidence against him on a trial for a criminal offense. . . . Second, it was no objection to the admissibility of such confessions that they had been taken under oath from a person attending before a coroner in obedience to a subpœna, upon an inquiry, conducted pursuant to law, into the causes of a homicide. . . . Third, that the confession or declaration sought to be given in evidence was in writing, and purported to be sworn to, was no objection to its admissibility, unless it also appeared that it was taken before a magistrate upon a judicial investigation against the person accused of the commission of the crime." Held, that Code Crim. Proc. §§ 188–200, did not apply to a statement sworn to before a coroner that the statement was admissible whether sworn to or not.

Of *People* v. *McGloin*, 91 N. Y. 241, the court says, in *People* v. *Mondon*, 103 N. Y. 211, 57 Am. Rep. 709, 8 N. E. 496: "The case . . . was not that of the examination of a prisoner on oath before a magistrate before whom he was taken involuntarily, . . . who, to all appearance, had power to require him to answer, but it was a clear case of a voluntary confession. The prisoner was not taken before any magistrate. . . . The coroner [acted] . . . not in any official capacity, but as a mere amanuensis to take down the confession and prove the contents. Whether sworn or unsworn is immaterial, as the confession was in no respect compulsory, but was voluntarily offered by the prisoner. It was not taken before a magistrate upon a judicial investigation against the person accused of the commission of the crime. It lacked this essential element of the *McMahon Case*, and is in no respect in conflict with it."

In Oregon the preliminary statement made by an accused before the magistrate is not admissible on the trial, unless signed and certified by the magistrate, as required by Hill's (Or.) Anno. Laws, § 1598, subd. 4, providing "that when the examination of the witnesses on the part of the state is closed, the magistrate must inform the defendant that it is his right to make a statement in relation to the charge against him; that the statement is designed to enable him, if he sees fit, to answer the charge, and explain the facts alleged against him; that he is at liberty to waive making a statement; and that his waiver cannot be used against him on the trial." *State* v. *Hatcher*, 29 Or. 309, 44 Pac. 584. To render admissible under this statute the preliminary statement made by him before the committing magistrate, it must affirmatively appear that before making such statement he was informed of his right to keep silent, and this is not shown by a recital of the magistrate thereon that "defendant was informed of his right to make a statement, and proceeded as follows." *Ibid.*

In West Virginia no statement made by one accused of murder, while testifying as a witness at the coroner's inquest, can be used against him on his trial, under W. Va. Code, chap. 152, § 20, providing that in a criminal prosecution, other than for perjury, evidence shall not be given against accused of any statement made by him as a witness upon a legal examination; but anything said by him before such examination is competent, if relevant. *State* v. *Hobbs*, 37 W. Va. 812, 17 S. E. 380.

But a statement made by a prisoner at the preliminary examination before the magistrate, when he was not sworn as a witness, is not excluded by this West Virginia statute. *State* v. *Welch*, 36 W. Va. 690, 15 S. E. 419.

As to whether the burden is on the prosecution to show that he was duly cautioned, compare, affirmative, *State* v. *Vincent*, Houst. Crim. Rep. (Del.) 11; negative, *People* v. *Stott*, 4 N. Y. S. R. 736, 5 N. Y. Crim. Rep.

61, holding that the presumption of due performance of official duty casts the burden of proving the contrary on the accused.

In my opinion the burden ought, in the absence of any controlling statute, to be on the prosecution. If on the accused, he may be unable to prove the fact without becoming a witness, which he should not be unnecessarily required to do upon a doubtful question of presumption.

[1]*Jackson* v. *State*, 39 Ohio St. 37. For other cases holding to similar effect, see *Oliver* v. *State*, 94 Ga. 83, 21 S. E. 125; *Davidson* v. *State*, 135 Ind. 254, 34 N. E. 972; *State* v. *Van Tassel*, 103 Iowa, 6, 72 N. W. 497; *State* v. *Mullins*, 101 Mo. 514, 14 S. W. 625; *People* v. *Wright*, 136 N. Y. 625, 32 N. E. 629, Citing *People* v. *Chapleau*, 121 N. Y. 266, 24 N. E. 469; *State* v. *Robinson*, 32 Or. 43, 48 Pac. 357; *United States* v. *Kirkwood*, 5 Utah, 123, 13 Pac. 234; *Lyons* v. *People*, 137 Ill. 602, 27 N. E. 677 (where the court says: "Where a man arrested by an officer, without a warrant, upon suspicion of having committed murder, is compelled to answer under oath as a witness at a coroner's inquest, statements which he thus makes are not admissible against him on his trial for the murder. The thing prohibited by the rule is 'the special interrogation of the accused,—the converting him, whether willing or not willing, into a witness against himself; assuming his guilt before proof, and subjecting him to an interrogation conducted on that hypothesis.' 2 Best, Ev. § 557. But it is otherwise where the statements made are voluntary, and where the oath taken is voluntary").

298. Testimony of accused as a witness at the inquest.

Testimony given by the accused as a mere witness, and not under arrest, though aware that he is suspected, is competent against him on trial of a subsequent indictment against him.[1]

[1]*Teachout* v. *People*, 41 N. Y. 7; *People* v. *Mondon*, 103 N. Y. 211, 8 N. E. 496, and cases cited; *Hendrickson* v. *People*, 10 N. Y. 13, 61 Am. Dec. 721; *Wilson* v. *State*, 110 Ala. 1, 20 So. 415; *People* v. *Burt*, 51 App. Div. 106, 64 N. Y. Supp. 417.

299. Testimony of accused on any previous judicial or official investigation.

Testimony compulsorily given by the accused on any former judicial or legislative investigation is not competent against him on his trial, for the purpose of tending to prove him guilty of the offense charged, because its use would be a violation of his constitutional privilege.

Testimony given under subpœna and oath, and in response to questions put by adverse counsel, is compulsorily given within this rule; although the accused neither denied the power of the investigating tribunal, nor claimed privilege before it.[1]

[1]*People* v. *Sharp*, 107 N. Y. 427, 444, 14 N. E. 319, Reversing 45 Hun, 460.

Testimony in legislative investigation. See also *United States* v. *Prescott*, 2 Dill. 405, Fed. Cas. No. 16,085. Testimony under examination under bankrupt act.

U. S. Rev. Stat. § 860, provides that "no pleading of a party, nor any discovery or evidence obtained from a party or witness by means of a judicial proceeding, in this or any foreign country, shall be given in evidence, or in any manner used against him or his property or estate, in any court of the United States, in any criminal proceeding, or for the enforcement of any penalty or forfeiture; provided that this section shall not exempt any party or witness from prosecution and punishment for perjury committed in discovering or testifying as aforesaid."

Since the enactment of the provisions of this section, witnesses in United States courts are no longer privileged from answering questions tending to criminate them. Roe, Crim. Proc. 44, Citing *United States* v. *Brown*, 1 Sawy. 531, Fed. Cas. No. 14,671; *United States* v. *McCarthy*, 18 Fed. 87. See *United States* v. *Distillery No. 26*, 6 Biss. 483, Fed. Cas. No. 14,966.

Questions that would render character of witness infamous, or which merely tend to degrade, and are not material to the issue, witness is not obliged to answer. Roe, Crim. Proc. Citing *United States* v. *Craig*, 4 Wash. C. C. 729, Fed. Cas. No. 14,883; *United States* v. *Dickinson*, 2 McLean, 325, Fed. Cas. No. 14,958; *Re Lewis*, 39 How. Pr. 155; *Re Graham*, 8 Ben. 419, Fed. Cas. No. 5,659; *United States* v. *Darnaud*, 3 Wall. Jr. 143, 178, Fed. Cas. No. 14,918. See 1 Burr's Trial, 215; *United States* v. *Miller*, 2 Cranch C. C. 247, Fed. Cas. No. 15,772; *Devaughn's Case*, 2 Cranch C. C. 501, Fed. Cas. No. 3,837; *Sanderson's Case*, 2 Cranch C. C. 638, Fed. Cas. No. 12,297.

Evidence of either of two defendants on a prosecution for conspiracy, given before an investigating committee, is admissible for the purpose of showing concerted action, though statements of one of such defendants cannot be regarded as proof of the guilt of the other. *Com.* v. *Hunton*, 168 Mass. 130, 46 N. E. 404.

300. Testimony on former trial of same cause.

Where a prisoner has testified in his own behalf, on a former trial of the same case, his answers given, even on cross-examination, will be deemed a voluntary confession, and admissible against him on his subsequent trial, even though he does not then testify. By volunteering his testimony he volunteers to answer all proper questions on cross-examination.[1]

[1] *State* v. *Eddings*, 71 Mo. 545, 36 Am. Rep. 496, Follows opinion of Judge Cooley in *People* v. *Arnold*, 43 Mich. 305, 38 Am. Rep. 182, 5 N. W. 385, pronouncing its reasons unanswerable. See also *State* v. *Jefferson*, 77 Mo. 136.

Otherwise, it is conceded, if he has been compelled to be a witness; but, even then, as to questions which he might have refused to answer as tending to criminate himself, his testimony may be deemed voluntary. *State* v. *Eddings*, 71 Mo. 545, 36 Am. Rep. 496. Compare, as to this latter point, *People* v. *Sharp*, 107 N. Y. 427, 444, 14 N. E. 319, holding subpœna and oath and examination by specific questions sufficient compulsion, without claim of privilege being made and overruled.

Portions of the testimony voluntarily given by a defendant in a criminal action, at the former trial, may be introduced and read against him on the final trial of the cause, without reading the entire testimony, if all that relates to the particular subject or fact is placed before the jury. *State* v. *Sorter*, 52 Kan. 531, 34 Pac. 1036.

But the transcript of the testimony of the accused at a former trial is not competent in his behalf, except to impeach or rebut the evidence of witnesses who have undertaken to detail his evidence at the former trial. *State* v. *Oliver*, 55 Kan. 711, 41 Pac. 954.

The testimony of defendant indicted for murder, given on the trial of another person charged with the same murder, is admissible against him, where it does not appear that he objected to testifying. *People* v. *Mitchell*, 94 Cal. 550, 29 Pac. 1106. *Contra* of the testimony given by defendant as a witness for the state, upon a trial of one jointly indicted with him. *Powell* v. *State* (Miss.) 23 So. 266.

301. Falsity of testimony on former trial.

The testimony given by the accused on a former trial, as a witness in his own behalf, as tending to exculpate him, whether given on direct or cross-examination, can be read in evidence against him on a subsequent trial for the same offense, for the purpose of proving its falsity, even though he has not testified as a witness on the subsequent trial.[1]

[1] *People* v. *Arnold*, 43 Mich. 303, 38 Am. Rep. 182, 5 N. W. 385, Approved in *State* v. *Eddings*, 71 Mo. 545, 36 Am. Rep. 496; *Lewis* v. *State*, 91 Ga. 168, 16 S. E. 986; *State* v. *Oliver*, 55 Kan. 711, 41 Pac. 954.

302. Testimony of absent witness on former trial.

The fact that a witness who testified on a former trial of the accused on the same charge is sick,[1] or beyond the jurisdiction,[2] or his residence or whereabouts is unknown,[3] is not ground for allowing his former testimony to be proved as evidence either for[4] or against[5] the accused.

The fact that he is dead,[6] or incapacitated by insanity,[7] is sufficient ground.

The fact that he is absent by the procurement of either party is sufficient ground for allowing it, as against such party.[8]

[1] *McLain* v. *Com.* 99 Pa. 86, holding the testimony not to have been rendered

admissible because the witness who gave it was too sick to attend the trial. To the same effect, *Com.* v. *McKenna,* 158 Mass. 207, 33 N. E. 389.

[5]*People* v. *Murphy,* 45 Cal. 137; *Sylvester* v. *State,* 71 Ala. 17; *Bergen* v. *People,* 17 Ill. 426, 65 Am. Dec. 672 (so holding even of a witness beyond the jurisdiction of the court by procurement of the defendant); *Collins* v. *Com.* 12 Bush, 271; *Hall* v. *State,* 6 Baxt. 522; *State* v. *Houser,* 26 Mo. 431 (*dictum,* that it would be otherwise if the absence of the witness was procured by the prisoner); *State* v. *Mc O'Blenis,* 24 Mo. 402,69 Am. Dec. 435; *Brogy* v. *Com.* 10 Gratt. 722; *Crite* v. *Com.* (Va.) 12 Rep. 575, 5 Va. L. J. 568; *United States* v. *Macomb,* 5 McLean, 286, Fed. Cas. No. 15,702; *United States* v. *Angell,* 11 Fed. 42. *Contra, Dolan* v. *State,* 40 Ark. 454; *Vaughan* v. *State,* 58 Ark. 353, 24 S. W. 885; *Davis* v. *State,* 9 Tex. App. 363; *Garcia* v. *State,* 12 Tex. App. 335. And see *Burton* v. *State,* 115 Ala. 1, 22 So. 585, to the effect that the substance of the evidence given by a witness in a criminal case before a tribunal of competent jurisdiction may be proved on a subsequent trial, in Alabama, where, after diligent search, he cannot be found within the jurisdiction of the court, or it is shown that his place of permanent residence is without the state.

Oral proof that a pardon was obtained, without showing that the original was lost, or that a certified copy could not be obtained from the secretary of state, is insufficient to render competent upon a trial for murder the reading of the testimony given at a former trial by a witness who had been convicted and sentenced for a felony. *Redd* v. *State,* 65 Ark. 475, 47 S. W. 119.

[6]*State* v. *King,* 86 N. C. 603 (disappearance not enough); *Harris* v. *State,* 73 Ala. 495 (to same effect).

So held in *People* v. *Gordon,* 99 Cal. 227, 33 Pac. 901, of evidence of a witness upon a former trial of a criminal prosecution under Cal. Pen. Code, § 686, providing that the defendant is entitled to be confronted with the witnesses against him, in the presence of the court, notwithstanding the witness cannot be found within the state.

[7]*United States* v. *Angell,* 11 Fed. 42.

[8]See cases in note 2, above.

[9]*State* v. *McNeil,* 33 La. Ann. 1332; *State* v. *Able,* 65 Mo. 357; *Hair* v. *State,* 16 Neb. 601, 21 N. W. 464, 4 Am. Crim. Rep. 127, with note; *State* v. *Johnson,* 12 Nev. 121; *Redd* v. *State,* 65 Ark. 475, 47 S. W. 119; *Waller* v. *State,* 102 Ga. 684, 28 S. E. 284.

The admission of the testimony given upon a former trial of a criminal case by a witness since deceased, who was then cross-examined, is not a violation of the provision of Wis. Const. art. 1, § 7, that in all criminal prosecutions the accused shall enjoy the right to meet the witnesses face to face. *Jackson* v. *State,* 81 Wis. 127, 51 N. W. 89.

So, where a witness who testified on a former trial is dead, his evidence may be reproduced on a subsequent trial in which his own testimony would be competent, if he were alive, although the prosecution in which the evidence was taken was discontinued. *Cox* v. *State,* 28 Tex. App. 92, 12 S. W. 493.

But depositions of witnesses, taken and used in a civil action or proceeding, are not made competent evidence in a criminal action by showing that the witnesses are dead, although the facts in controversy are the same in the two cases, under the Oklahoma statutes, which make no provision for showing by deposition the testimony of a witness since deceased, given in another action or proceeding. *Watkins* v. *United States,* 5 Okla. 729, 50 Pac. 88, Citing *People* v. *Restell,* 3 Hill, 289; *Kaelin* v. *Com.* 84 Ky. 354, 1 S. W. 594.

[7] *Marler* v. *State,* 67 Ala. 55, 42 Am. Rep. 95. But an insane person is not always disqualified to testify. See § 211.

A finding of insanity on the trial of the preliminary objection that the accused is insane at the time of trial, and therefore not to be put on his trial during the continuance of the disability, is not competent evidence of his insanity, for the purpose of letting in testimony previously given by him in another proceeding as that of a witness who has since become insane. *Marler* v. *State,* 67 Ala. 55, 42 Am. Rep. 95.

[8] *Reynolds* v. *United States,* 98 U. S. 145, 25 L. ed. 244. Bigamy; the provision of the Constitution, that the accused shall be confronted with the witnesses against him, the court holds, cannot be insisted on in order to protect the accused from the legitimate consequences of his own wrongful act. So held where the former trial, though for the same offense, was under a different indictment.

303. — on preliminary examination.

This rule applies to the testimony of a witness on a preliminary examination before a committing magistrate, provided the accused was there confronted with the witness, and had opportunity to cross-examine.[1] Otherwise of testimony taken in the absence of the accused.[2]

[1] *State* v. *McO'Blenis,* 24 Mo. 402, 69 Am. Dec. 435 (saying that it is admissible if taken in the presence of the accused); *State* v. *Fitzgerald,* 63 Iowa, 268, 19 N. W. 202 (to same effect); *Com.* v. *Keck,* 148 Pa. 639, 24 Atl. 161; *People* v. *Sierp,* 116 Cal. 249, 48 Pac. 88; *State* v. *George,* 63 Minn. 500, 63 N. W. 100; *Brown* v. *Com.* 73 Pa. 321, 13 Am. Rep. 740 (saying it is competent if the accused and his counsel were present). *Contra, McLain* v. *Com.* 99 Pa. 86 (intimating that it is inadmissible because there is no issue on such a hearing); *People* v. *Penhollow,* 42 Hun, 104, 106, and cases cited; *Sullivan* v. *State,* 6 Tex. App. 319, 32 Am. Rep. 580, 584; *United States* v. *Macomb,* 5 McLean, 286, Fed. Cas. No. 15,702. And see *Motes* v. *United States,* 178 U. S. 458, 44 L. ed. 1150, 20 Sup. Ct. Rep. 993, holding that the right of an accused under U. S. Const. Amend. 6, to be confronted with witnesses against him, is violated by permitting a deposition or statement of an absent witness, taken at an examining trial, to be read at the final trial, when it does not appear that the witness was absent by the suggestion, connivance,

or procurement of the accused, but it does appear that his absence was due to the negligence of the prosecution. So held in *State* v. *Lee,* 13 Mont. 248, 33 Pac. 690, of the admission in evidence of a magistrate's general recollection of the evidence of the prosecuting witness at the preliminary hearing.

But where defendant waives a preliminary examination required by statute, and the examining magistrate proceeds to examine the witness for the prosecution notwithstanding such waiver, the defendant cannot complain, and on his trial his waiver does not preclude the admissibility of the evidence so taken. *Percy* v. *State,* 125 Ala. 52, 27 So. 844. To the same effect is *State* v. *White* (Idaho) 61 Pac. 517. And see *State* v. *Potter* (Idaho) 57 Pac. 431, holding that depositions of witnesses taken upon the preliminary examination of a person charged with a criminal offense are not admissible as evidence against him upon his trial for that offense, in the absence of any statute permitting or authorizing the use of such depositions on the trial.

In Texas the testimony taken on an examining trial is not admissible for the state because of the death of the witness, under Code Crim. Proc. art. 774, providing that the "deposition" of a witness taken before an examining court, where defendant was present when such testimony was taken, and had the privilege of cross-examining the witness, may be read in evidence, as the mode of taking testimony and depositions before an examining court is entirely different. *Cline* v. *State,* 36 Tex. Crim. Rep. 320, 36 S. W. 1099, 37 S. W. 722.

So, evidence of witness at examining trial cannot be used on the trial against the accused, unless the latter has waived his right in the same manner, under the Texas Bill of Rights, § 10, providing that in all criminal prosecutions the accused shall have a speedy public "trial, by an impartial jury," and shall be "confronted with the witnesses against him." *Ibid.*

A habeas corpus proceeding is not an "examining trial," and the court in which it occurs is not an "examining court," within Tex. Code Crim. Proc. art. 774, making the deposition of a witness taken before an examining court admissible in evidence. *Childers* v. *State,* 30 Tex. App. 160, 16 S. W. 903.

[3] *State* v. *Hill,* 2 Hill L. 608, 27 Am. Dec. 407.

Evidence obtained at a post-mortem examination made after the commencement of a prosecution for murder, without notice to the accused, is not incompetent. *King* v. *State,* 55 Ark. 604, 19 S. W. 110.

304. What is former trial.

The fact that the jury on a previous trial disagreed does not take the case out of the rule. The trial is concluded when the case is closed, and submitted to the jury.[1]

[1] *Lawson* v. *Jones,* 61 How. Pr. 424 (civil case).

305. Omission of cross-examination.

A failure to cross-examine, when there was power and opportunity so to do, on the former trial or hearing, does not prevent the introduction of the witness's testimony on the subsequent trial.[1]

[1] *Bradley* v. *Mirick,* 25 Hun, 272, Affirmed in 91 N. Y. 293 (civil case); *McNamara* v. *State,* 60 Ark. 400, 30 S. W. 762.

306. Proof of death.

The death of the witness cannot be proved by mere hearsay.[1]

[1] *State* v. *Wright,* 70 Iowa, 152, 30 N. W. 388. Compare Abbott, Trial Ev. 64, 72.

307. Mode of proving testimony.

Testimony on a former trial, when competent, is to be proved by calling a witness who was present and heard it.[1]

Neither the minutes of the judge[2] nor the notes of a shorthand writer are (in the absence of statute)[3] competent, except when produced by him, and he testifies that they are a record of the substance of the testimony[4] made at the time, and correctly made;[5] and that he cannot repeat the testimony independently of them.

On such proof, he may read the testimony from his notes.[6]

His notes, though not so proved, may be used by him under the rule as to refreshing memory.

[1] *State* v. *DeWitt,* 2 Hill L. 282, 27 Am. Dec. 371 (denying a motion for new trial made because the evidence of one who heard the deceased witness testify was admitted to prove such testimony, instead of the judge's minutes); *Hutcherson* v. *State,* 33 Tex. Crim. Rep. 67, 24 S. W. 908.

And *State* v. *Mushrush,* 97 Iowa, 444, 66 N. W. 746, holds that the reporter's notes of testimony given at a trial are not the best evidence in the sense that the testimony as to what it was, of one who heard and remembered it, is secondary.

But *Powell* v. *State* (Miss.) 23 So. 266, holds oral testimony as to what defendant testified to before the magistrate inadmissible, where his written statement before the magistrate was taken down, and is introduced in evidence.

[2] *State* v. *DeWitt,* 2 Hill L. 282, 27 Am. Dec. 371, *supra.*

Under S. C. Stat. § 719, requiring the testimony of all witnesses examined upon a coroner's inquest, taken in writing and signed by the witnesses, to be filed with the clerk, the signed testimony is the best and highest evidence of what the witnesses testified to before the coroner. *State* v. *Prater,* 26 S. C. 198, 2 S. E. 108.

[3] See *supra,* §§ 292, 293.

The testimony of a witness at a preliminary examination, taken down by a shorthand reporter, and thereafter written out in longhand, and certified and filed, as required by Cal. Pen. Code, § 869, may be read in evidence upon the trial, under § 686, where it is admitted that such witness is dead. *People* v. *Douglass,* 100 Cal. 1, 34 Pac. 490.

People v. *Sligh,* 48 Mich. 54, 11 N. W. 782, holding it error to allow stenographer to read his minutes without swearing to their correctness.

It is no objection to the testimony of an attorney, as to the testimony of a witness given at a previous examination, that he says he can only state it upon referring to his minutes, which are not full, and that he may not be able to give the testimony with entire accuracy.

Com. v. *Goddard,* 14 Gray, 403. Compare *Huff* v. *Bennett,* 6 N. Y. 337, Affirming 4 Sandf. 120. Civil case; holding it error to allow minutes read by judge or referee, if he could not say they contained the testimony accurately, but may have omitted some things.

Hair v. *State,* 16 Neb. 601, 21 N. W. 464, 4 Am. Crim. Rep. 127, with note; *Horton* v. *State,* 53 Ala. 488; *State* v. *Camley,* 67 Vt. 322, 31 Atl. 840; *People* v. *Glassman,* 12 Utah, 238, 42 Pac. 956; *Roberts* v. *State,* 68 Ala. 515 (examination before magistrate may be thus read, though not signed.) See also *Lawson* v. *Jones,* 61 How. Pr. 424. *Contra,* where the statute provides for the filing of an authenticated record, thus implying that such record is the primary competent evidence. *People* v. *Cunningham,* 66 Cal. 668, 4 Pac. 1144, 6 Pac. 700, 846. And upon the rejection of the deposition of an absent witness taken at the preliminary examination in a criminal case, on the ground that the certificate is defective, the evidence given by him cannot be proved by the testimony of the stenographer who took it, since under Cal. Pen. Code, § 686, the only exception to the right of a defendant in a criminal action to be confronted with the witnesses is the deposition of a witness for the cross-examination of whom opportunity has been given, upon proof of his death, insanity, or absence from the state. *People* v. *Gardner,* 98 Cal. 127, 32 Pac. 880.

But testimony of witnesses in a former trial, read by the official stenographic reporter, from his notes, is admissible under Cal. Civ. Code Proc. § 2407, providing that a witness may refresh his memory respecting the fact by anything written by himself at the time such fact occurred, where the stenographer testifies that he took such notes, and that they are correct. *People* v. *Lem You,* 97 Cal. 224, 32 Pac. 11.

308. Bill of exceptions.

The testimony cannot be read from a bill of exceptions, without producing a witness who was present at the former trial, to show that the bill contains the substance of the testimony, within the rule.[1]

[1] *Kean* v. *Com.* 10 Bush, 190, 19 Am. Rep. 63 (reversed for error in allowing this); *State* v. *Able,* 65 Mo. 357; *Boner* v. *Com.* 19 Ky. L. Rep. 409, 40 S. W. 700.

309. Substance enough.

The rule that the witness must give such former testimony substantially and in all material particulars does not require him to produce the very language.[1]

[1] *Thompson* v. *State*, 106 Ala. 67, 17 So. 512; *Vaughan* v. *State*, 58 Ark. 353, 24 S. W. 885; *People* v. *Murphy*, 45 Cal. 137; *State* v. *O'Brien*, 81 Iowa, 88, 46 N. W. 752; *Smith* v. *Com.* 16 Ky. L. Rep. 169, 26 S. W. 1100; *Marler* v. *State*, 67 Ala. 55, 42 Am. Rep. 95; *Com.* v. *Goddard*, 14 Gray, 402; *Bennett* v. *State*, 32 Tex. Crim. Rep. 216, 22 S. W. 684, Overruling *Com.* v. *Richards*, 18 Pick. 434, 29 Am. Dec. 608.

In *Bush* v. *Com.* 80 Ky. 244, it is held that apparent or actual contradictions in the testimony of witnesses who purport to relate the substance of the evidence given by a deceased witness go, not to the admissibility of the testimony, but only to its weight with the jury. The court says: "Nor is it every incidental or immaterial matter in reference to which the memory of the witness appears to be at fault that will authorize the court to exclude the whole. If the statement appears on its face to cover the substance of what the deceased witness testified to, in reference to the material matters in issue, the evidence should be allowed to go to the jury for their consideration. When the witness states that he heard the whole of the testimony of the deceased witness, and that he remembers the substance thereof, the court will not be justified in taking it from the jury unless, from the statement of the witness himself it obviously appears that he does not remember the substance of what the deceased witness testified to, in reference to the material issues being considered."

To the same effect, *State* v. *Fitzgerald*, 63 Iowa, 268, 19 N. W. 202, and cases cited.

310. Preliminary question for the court.

The question whether the case is such as to make the testimony competent under the foregoing rules is for the court, and it is error for the court, without ruling on that question, to receive the testimony.[1]

[1] *People* v. *Willett*, 92 N. Y. 29, Affirming 27 Hun, 469. Held, that where the admissibility of evidence of the conduct of an accused person at a proceeding before a coroner is in question, it is error to submit to the jury the question whether it was a judicial proceeding; that the court should hold whether the proceeding was judicial or otherwise. Conviction reversed.

XLVII. Threats.

311. Threats by the accused.

Evidence of threats made by the accused is competent for the purpose of showing intent or motive.[1]

Threats that are sufficiently specific to point to the particular offense are also competent for the purpose of connecting the accused with the offense.[2]

[1]*Henderson* v. *State,* 70 Ala. 29 (assault with intent to murder; evidence of threats made by defendant against the person assaulted, "about two weeks before the difficulty between them," held admissible as showing malice, and as declaratory of his criminal intention); *Newton* v. *State,* 92 Ala. 33, 9 So. 404; *Babcock* v. *People,* 13 Colo. 515, 22 Pac. 817; *McCoy* v. *People,* 175 Ill. 224, 51 N. E. 777; *State* v. *Aughtry,* 49 S. C. 285, 26 S. E. 619, 27 S. E. 199; *Bolton* v. *State* (Tex. Crim. App.) 39 S. W. 672. And see note to *Wilson* v. *State* (Fla.) 17 L. R. A. 654.

Thus, in trespass for an assault and battery, evidence of threats to do the plaintiff bodily harm, made by the defendant before the alleged assault, or so immediately after it as to constitute a part of the transaction, is competent. *Caverno* v. *Jones,* 61 N. H. 623.

And threats of defendant to take the life of deceased if she left him are admissible upon proof given that she left him just before her death, although made six months before the homicide. *State* v. *Bradley,* 64 Vt. 466, 24 Atl. 1053.

So, evidence of threats, though ostensibly made in jest, by the accused on a prosecution for murder, to the deceased, is admissible, and may be construed by the jury, in the light of subsequent events, as bearing upon the question of malice. *People* v. *Holmes,* 111 Mich. 364, 69 N. W. 501.

[2]Such as threats to kill the deceased. *State* v. *Pollard,* 132 Mo. 288, 34 S. W. 29; *People* v. *Chaves,* 122 Cal. 134, 54 Pac. 596; *Painter* v. *People,* 147 Ill. 444, 35 N. E. 64.

This principle seems to have been overlooked in *State* v. *Norton,* 82 N. C. 628. Assault and battery; evidence of declarations of defendant, made two weeks before the assault (threatening the prosecutor), inadmissible. The court says: "If the defendant had been indicted for murder, for an assault with intent to kill, for a conspiracy or forgery, or any other offense, where the *scienter* or the *quo animo* constitutes a necessary part of the crime charged, such acts . . . are admissible. . . . But in our case neither malice nor intent, nor knowledge, nor motive forms any ingredient of the offense."

So held in *State* v. *Millmeier,* 102 Iowa, 692, 72 N. W. 275, of threats made by defendant charged with arson, against the person or property of one whose building was burned. To the same effect, see *State* v. *Lytle,* 117 N. C. 799, 23 S. E. 476.

312. — remoteness.

Evidence of threats as tending to show intent is not incompetent by reason of the remoteness of the time at which they were made, unless there has been some intervening change of relation. The reason is that animosity is often persistent and long-cherished, in proportion to its criminality. Lapse of time, therefore, while proper to be considered by the jury weighing the evidence, does not exclude it, if otherwise properly connected with the case.[1]

[1] *Territory* v. *Roberts*, 9 Mont. 12, 22 Pac. 132; *Babcock* v. *People*, 13 Colo. 515, 22 Pac. 817; *State* v. *Bradley*, 67 Vt. 465, 32 Atl. 238; *State* v. *Hoyt*, 46 Conn. 330 (murder; held not error to admit evidence of threats made thirteen years before); *Redd* v. *State*, 68 Ala. 492 (two years); *Everett* v. *State*, 62 Ga. 65 (three or four years); *Jefferds* v. *People*, 5 Park. Crim. Rep. 522 (murder; held not error to admit evidence of threats made by the accused two years prior to the murder. The court says: "It is no objection to such evidence that a period of years had expired since the threats were made. On the contrary, long-continued animosity and ill-will are better evidence of a state of mind which would ripen into deliberate murder than the hasty ebullition of passion"); *Pate* v. *State*, 94 Ala. 14, 10 So. 665 (threats four months previous to killing competent); *McDaniel* v. *State*, 100 Ga. 67, 27 S. E. 158; *State* v. *Helm*, 97 Iowa, 378, 66 N. W. 751; *Com.* v. *Crowe*, 165 Mass. 139, 42 N. E. 563; *Com.* v. *Quinn*, 150 Mass. 401, 23 N. E. 54; *People* v. *Eaton*, 59 Mich. 559, 26 N. W. 702; *State* v. *Wright*, 141 Mo. 333, 42 S. W. 934.

313. — ambiguousness.

The fact that a threat was couched in ambiguous language which does not necessarily point to the *corpus delicti*,[1] or which might bear an innocent meaning,[2] does not render the evidence of it incompetent.

[1] A threat, to be admissible on a murder trial, need not be directed against any particular person, nor need the threatened party be expressly named, if the facts and circumstances in evidence tend to point out the one against whom it is made, and make it clear that the deceased was the party intended. *Mathis* v. *State*, 34 Tex. Crim. Rep. 39, 28 S. W. 817.

So, evidence of threats by defendant charged with murder, an hour or so before the crime was committed, to kill someone, although no particular individual was alluded to, is admissible. *Brooks* v. *Com.* 100 Ky. 194, 37 S. W. 1043.

And statements of one accused of murder, the evening before the killing, to the effect that he intended to kill someone and then kill himself, are admissible, although indefinite as to the intended victim. *State* v. *Fitzgerald*, 130 Mo. 407, 32 S. W. 1113.

And *State* v. *Guy*, 69 Mo. 430, held it not error to admit evidence of a threat that did not contain the name of the deceased. Whether it referred to him or not the jury should determine. And in *Ford* v. *State*, 71 Ala. 385 (murder), it was held not error to admit evidence of threats by accused to injure someone not definitely designated, taken in connection with the explanatory circumstances, on proof of the *corpus delicti*. The weight or probable force of the threats is for the jury.

So, evidence that defendant, charged with murder, was heard to make threats "to kill a man before sundown," on the day of the murder, is admissible. *Hodge* v. *State,* 26 Fla. 11, 7 So. 593. To similar effect in *Snodgrass* v. *Com.* 89 Va. 679, 17 S. E. 238, of threats of the accused that he intended to kill somebody before sundown, in connection with evidence that he pointed to the deceased when in sight as the person he would kill, and made many demonstrations looking towards a difficulty with the deceased. Compare *Godwin* v. *State,* 38 Tex. Crim. Rep. 466, 43 S. W. 336, where it is held that evidence of general threats by defendant charged with murder, the night before the homicide, to kill some person, is inadmissible, in the absence of anything to show that the deceased was referred to thereby.

Evidence that defendant, charged with the murder of a policeman, stated about three weeks before the killing, in answer to a statement by a third person that such policeman was near, that the latter had "better not bother him,"—was held admissible as a threat, in *Wilson* v. *State,* 110 Ala. 1, 20 So. 415.

A remark of defendant charged with murder, upon displaying a pistol the forenoon preceding the shooting, "This means business some day," was held admissible against him, in *People* v. *Sutherland,* 154 N. Y. 345, 48 N. E. 518.

[3]*State* v. *Dieckman,* 11 Mo. App. 538. Murder; held not error to admit evidence of statement of accused that he was "going over to settle with deceased," such expression being part of a general chain of threats and hostile preparations. Evidence of threats susceptible of an innocent interpretation, but which, if taken in connection with other threats made directly against the deceased, may have a guilty meaning, may properly go to the jury.

314. Witness hearing only part.

A witness who heard or understood only a part of the threats or altercation relied on as showing motive or intent may nevertheless testify to what he did hear and understand.[1]

[1]*Redd* v. *State,* 68 Ala. 492; *State* v. *Moelchen,* 53 Iowa, 310, 5 N. W. 186 (witness allowed to testify to quarrel, though he did not understand the language, and knew only a single word spoken by the accused).

So, that a witness who overheard threats while passing the house of defendant, charged with murdering his wife, did not see the parties, and was not familiar with the voice of defendant, does not render her testimony as to such threats inadmissible, where other evidence tends to show that the threats overheard were made by defendant against his wife. *State* v. *Fiester,* 32 Or. 254, 50 Pac. 561.

On a trial for murder a witness may give his best recollection as to threats made by defendant. *State* v. *Henderson,* 24 Or. 100, 32 Pac. 1030.

315. Acts and gestures.

In support of an allegation of threats, evidence of threatening acts, gestures, etc., is admissible.[1]

[1] *Allen* v. *State*, 8 Tex. App. 361. Prosecution for false imprisonment by threats, where an allegation of improper detention by threats was held supported by proof of acts, gestures, etc.

So, evidence of threats and acts of violence on the part of defendant towards his wife, whom he is charged with having murdered, forming his course of conduct from shortly after their marriage nearly down to the time of the alleged homicide is admissible as tending to show malice and consequent motive for the crime. *Com.* v. *Holmes*, 157 Mass. 233, 32 N. E. 6.

316. Threats by deceased.

In cases of homicide evidence of threats by the deceased may be competent, though they were not communicated to the accused.[1]

[1] "Where the question is as to what was deceased's attitude at the time of the fatal encounter, recent threats may become relevant to show that this attitude was one hostile to the defendant, even though such threats were not communicated to the defendant. The evidence is not relevant to show the *quo animo* of the defendant; but it may be relevant to show that at the time of the meeting the deceased was seeking defendant's life." Wharton, Crim. Law, § 1027,—Approved in *Wiggins* v. *Utah*, 93 U. S. 465, 23 L. ed. 941, reversing conviction for error in rejecting such evidence. See also *Brown* v. *State*, 55 Ark. 593, 18 S. W. 1051; *Wilson* v. *State*, 30 Fla. 234, 11 So. 556, S. C., with note, 17 L. R. A. 654; *May* v. *State*, 90 Ga. 793, 17 S. E. 108; *State* v. *Helm*, 92 Iowa, 540, 61 N. W. 246; *Young* v. *Com.* 19 Ky. L. Rep. 929, 42 S. W. 1141; *State* v. *Hopper*, 142 Mo. 478, 44 S. W. 272; *State* v. *Tarter*, 26 Or. 38, 37 Pac. 53; *State* v. *Faile*, 43 S. C. 52, 20 S. E. 798; *State* v. *Cushing*, 14 Wash. 527, 45 Pac. 145; *State* v. *Evans*, 33 W. Va. 417, 10 S. E. 792.

But in *Turpin* v. *State*, 55 Md. 462, 538, the court, in reviewing the above authorities, added: "But the rule is correctly stated by Wharton in the same section, 'that such evidence is inadmissible, unless proof be first given that there was an overt act of attack, and that the defendant, at the time of the collision, was in apparent imminent danger.'"—Citing *People* v. *Alivtre*, 55 Cal. 263. To same effect, see *Jones* v. *State*, 116 Ala. 468, 23 So. 135; *Steele* v. *State*, 33 Fla. 348, 354, 14 So. 841, 842; *People* v. *Halliday*, 5 Utah, 467, 17 Pac. 118; *Hinson* v. *State*, 66 Miss. 532, 6 So. 463; *State* v. *Kenyon*, 18 R. I. 217, 26 Atl. 199; *State* v. *Cushing*, 17 Wash. 544, 50 Pac. 512.

In *Stokes* v. *People*, 53 N. Y. 164, 13 Am. Rep. 492 (murder), evidence having been given making it a question for the jury whether the act was perpetrated by the prisoner in defending himself against an attempt on the part of deceased to murder or inflict some great bodily harm upon him, it was held error to exclude evidence of violent threats made by the deceased against the prisoner shortly before the occurrence, though such threats were not communicated to the prisoner. The court said: "Threats to commit the crime for which a person is upon trial are constantly received as evidence against him, as circumstances proper to be considered in determining the question whether he has in fact committed the crime, for the reason that the threats indicate an intention to do it, and the existence of this intention creates a probability that he has in fact committed it."

Dupree v. *State*, 33 Ala. 380, 73 Am. Dec. 422, is an example of many cases, holding that threats proved to have been made and communicated to the prisoner but a short time before the commission of the homicide, which were indicative of an angry and revengeful spirit, are admissible in a prosecution for murder,—reversing judgment for exclusion of this evidence, and for other reasons.

And *Allison* v. *United States*, 160 U. S. 203, 40 L. ed. 395, 16 Sup. Ct. Rep. 252, holds that communicated recent threats are admissible in evidence in a murder case, on the question whether defendant had reasonable cause to apprehend an attack fatal to life or fraught with bodily injury, and was justified in acting on a slight hostile demonstration from the other.

But see *Carroll* v. *State*, 23 Ala. 28, 58 Am. Dec. 287, where it was held that unless it was shown that such threats were communicated to the defendant before the killing, they were inadmissible, because he would not have been influenced by them,—affirming conviction of murder, this evidence having been excluded.

But even though not communicated to the prisoner, such threats may be introduced to show the state of feeling entertained by the deceased towards the accused. *Keener* v. *State*, 18 Ga. 194, 63 Am. Dec. 269, 278. Indictment for murder; new trial granted because this evidence was excluded.

317. — anticipatory rebuttal.

It is only after evidence of threats by the deceased has been introduced that the prosecution can offer evidence that he did not intend to attack the accused.[1]

[1] *People* v. *Carlton*, 57 Cal. 83, 40 Am. Rep. 112, and cases cited.

XLVIII. Variance.

318. The modern test.

A variance is not now regarded as material unless it is such as might mislead the defense, or might expose the accused to the danger of being put twice in jeopardy for the same offense.[1]

[1] "The strictness of the ancient rule as to variance between the proof and the indictment has been much relaxed in modern times. Variances are

regarded as material, because they may mislead a prisoner in making his defense, and because they may expose him to the danger of being again put in jeopardy for the same offense." Earl, J., in *Harris* v. *People*, 64 N. Y. 148, holding that there was no fatal variance on a trial for perjury, where the indictment alleged that accused swore to there being 60,000 cigars in a building when burned, and it appeared that he swore there were 65,000.

In *People* v. *Dumar*, 106 N. Y. 502, 13 N. E. 325, which reversed 42 Hun, 80, a case of larceny, the variance between the indictment and the proof was held fatal to conviction, under the Code of Criminal Procedure. After specifying the four ways of committing larceny, as the offense is defined in § 528, the court pointed out that the indictment charged accused with grand larceny in the first degree, while the proof did no more than to show him guilty of obtaining possession of property by false pretenses, as that offense is defined in § 528. The court said: "The important difference between the former law and the present, so far as this case is concerned, is that the court is no longer called upon to decide whether an offense is larceny, embezzlement, or false pretenses; nor is justice liable to be defeated by too nice a discrimination. Each of these acts is larceny. But the general principle of pleading has not been substantially changed. Under either system an offense consists of certain acts done or omitted under certain circumstances, and under neither is any indictment sufficient which does not accurately and clearly allege all the ingredients of which the offense is composed, so as to bring the accused within the true meaning and intent of the statute defining the offense. Under the former this end was secured by rules formulated and applied by the courts through long series of decisions; under the latter it is made imperative by the provisions of the statute. In the case at bar, the defendant was left uninformed of the real act committed by him, and subjected to the charge of larceny for an act which he did not perform."

For some other recent cases holding the variance, if any at all, to be immaterial, see *Andrews* v. *State*, 123 Ala. 42, 26 So. 522 (evidence that defendant took money from the office of a railroad company, and that the office was in the same building and immediately adjoining the freight room of the company, no variance from the charge that the money was taken from the warehouse of the company); *Headley* v. *State*, 106 Ala. 109, 17 So. 714 (trial of an indictment for obtaining money under false pretenses, under 2 Ala. Code, § 4380, making it sufficient to allege an intent to injure or defraud generally, without naming the particular person intended to be defrauded; evidence of the particular person intended to be defrauded competent under a general allegation of intent to defraud); *Mason* v. *State*, 55 Ark. 529, 18 S. W. 827 (variance between an indictment for perjury alleged to have been committed in an inquiry concerning an election for presidential electors and a representative in Congress, and proof relating to an inquiry concerning an election for representative only, immaterial, where the court judicially knows that a representative and presidential electors were elected at the election charged in the indictment); *Sutton* v. *Com.* 17 Ky. L. Rep.

184, 30 S. W. 661 (difference between the number of a district in which a bonded warehouse is situated, as recited in a purported warehouse receipt copied in an indictment for forgery, and as shown by the receipt itself, not a legal variance); *Com.* v. *Warner,* 173 Mass. 541, 54 N. E. 353 (holding the specifications filed in a prosecution for embezzlement under the Massachusetts statutes, to be merely for the information and convenience of the defendant; and that it is within the discretion of the presiding judge to admit evidence which is entirely outside of the specifications if it is pertinent to the indictment, and the defendant is given sufficient opportunity to answer it); *State* v. *Brame,* 61 Minn. 101, 63 N. W. 250 (evidence that the defendant collected money as an attorney at law on accounts given him for that purpose, and misappropriated the money, not a variance from a complaint for larceny alleging that he received the money as agent); *Cunningham* v. *State,* 61 N. J. L. 67, 38 Atl. 847, Affirmed in 61 N. J. L. 666, 40 Atl. 690 (holding it competent, under an indictment charging defendant with procuring from another a large sum of money, to wit, $1,800, by falsely pretending that he had as her attorney commenced a suit for her, and expended that sum in its prosecution, to show that the defendant had procured several sums at different times under such false pretenses; and it is not necessary to prove that he had obtained as much as $1,800); *State* v. *Brown,* 6 Wash. 609, 34 Pac. 133 (warrant against several persons besides defendant in a prosecution for resisting an officer not a variance from an indictment alleging that the officer resisted was endeavoring to serve a warrant against such defendant); *Haines* v. *Territory,* 3 Wyo. 167, 13 Pac. 8 (evidence that one inducement for surrendering property was a partial payment of the purchase price not a variance from an indictment alleging that the property was obtained by false pretenses).

But that proof that the affidavit sworn to was made in a case in which a person named and others were plaintiffs is a fatal variance from an indictment charging perjury in swearing to an affidavit in a case in which but one person was plaintiff, see *Walker* v. *State,* 96 Ala. 53, 11 So. 401.

XLIX. Venue.

See also *ante,* Divisions XV., XVI., and *post,* Divison XLII.

319. Hearsay.

A boundary line being matter of common and public interest, hearsay testimony is competent for the purpose of showing it.[1]

[1] *People* v. *Velarde,* 59 Cal. 457; *Tidwell* v. *State,* 70 Ala. 33. And see *Boardman* v. *Reed,* 6 Pet. 328, 8 L. ed. 415.

As to declarations of ancient persons, see *Daggett* v. *Shaw,* 5 Met. 223, 226; *Hunnicutt* v. *Peyton,* 102 U. S. 333, 26 L. ed. 113.

320. Offense in or partly in another jurisdiction.

On the question of jurisdiction, where the offense is commenced in one locality, and completed in another, see the following cases.[1]

[1]*United States* v. *Comerford,* 25 Fed. 902 (sending obscene matter through the mail); *United States* v. *Guiteau,* 1 Mackey, 498 (murder; wound inflicted in one state, and death occurred in another); *State* v. *Kelly,* 76 Me. 331, 49 Am. Rep. 620. And see 13 Cinc. Wkly. L. Bul. 187; *United States* v. *Britton,* 2 Mason, 464, 470, Fed. Cas. No. 14,650 (forgery of check drawn in one state and presented in another); *Reg.* v. *Holmes,* 32 Week. Rep. 372 (fraudulently inducing another to send money through mails). See also *King* v. *Burdett,* 4 Barn. & Ald. 95; *Reg.* v. *Cooke,* 1 Fost. & F. 64; *People* v. *Mather,* 4 Wend. 229, 21 Am. Dec. 122 (leading American case on the locality of conspiracy). Compare *People* v. *Hall,* 57 How. Pr. 342; *Swan* v. *People,* 13 N. Y. Week. Dig. 519.

Where defendant was indicted for stealing four steers in one county, evidence that they ranged in that county, and were missed late in September, and were sold in another county on the 2d of October, was sufficient proof of the venue as laid in the indictment to support a conviction, since venue may be proven by circumstantial evidence. *Bloom* v. *State,* 68 Ark. 336, 58 S. W. 41.

321. Offense the place of which is unknown.

Without the aid of statute, the court cannot exercise jurisdiction if it be not practicable to ascertain whether or not the offense was committed within the territorial limits of jurisdiction.[1]

[1]*Ex parte Byers,* 32 Fed. 404. Offense committed on a vessel on the great lakes.

L. View.

322. General rule.

In the absence of statute,[1] the court cannot order a view except by consent.[2] With consent it may do so.[3]

[1]The practice of sending the jury out to have a view, although of common-law origin, is now generally regulated by statute in the various states; and cases applying these statutes, as well as cases involving the practice in the absence of statute, will be found exhaustively reviewed in note to *People* v. *Thorn* (N. Y.) 42 L. R. A. 368. See also Civil Trial Brief, 2d ed. chap. XIV., pp. 314 *et seq.*

On a trial for receiving stolen property, it is error, under Cal. Pen. Code, § 1119, to order the jury to view a portion of the property alleged to have been stolen; that section has reference solely to a view of the "place," and not of the property. *People* v. *Fitzpatrick,* 80 Cal. 538, 22 Pac. 215.

So, an order by the court in a criminal case, directing the jury to go to premises described by a witness, and that the witness be allowed to testify on the premises, is not justified under Fla. Rev. Stat. § 2918, providing that the court may order a view by the jury. *Garcia* v. *State*, 34 Fla. 311, 16 So. 223.

So, in *Hays* v. *Territory*, 7 Okla. 15, 54 Pac. 300, it is held that in Oklahoma the court cannot properly hear any evidence during a view of the scene of the homicide, although the jury is accompanied by the judge, the court stenographer, the county attorney, and the defendant and his attorneys.

[3] *Smith* v. *State*, 42 Tex. 444. Held reversible error to allow a view, even where the defendant consents thereto, in the absence of a statute authorizing a view in criminal cases. See also article by J. C. Thomson, in 26 Cent. L. J. 439.

[4] In *Com.* v. *Knapp*, 9 Pick. 496, 515, 20 Am. Dec. 491, upon the request of the jury to be allowed to view the place of the murder, and the consent of counsel for both sides, and the consent of the prisoner, "the court granted the request, but with hesitation, because they said this course was without precedent, and if it should turn out to be incorrect, they had doubts whether they could hold the prisoner to his consent."

The statutes of the various states usually make provision for ordering a view by the jury, in charge of proper officers, either of the scene of the crime or of the place where any material fact occurred.

The New York rule is found in Code Crim. Proc. §§ 411, 412.

Under a statute providing that "the court may order" a view by any jury impaneled to try a criminal case, it has been held that the order rested in the discretion of the court. *Chute* v. *State*, 19 Minn. 271, Gil. 230; *Com.* v. *Chance*, 174 Mass. 245, 54 N. E. 551.

323. Who may point out the place.

Usually an officer is sworn to point out the place to the jury, but a juror familiar with the locality may be directed by the court to perform this duty.[1]

[1] *State* v. *Adams*, 20 Kan. 311, holding it no error for the court to so direct. And see note to *People* v. *Thorn* (N. Y.) 42 L. R. A. 377, 381.

324. Presence of the accused.

In the absence of any controlling provision of statute,[1] the accused has a right to be present at the view in person or by counsel. But his presence is not essential within the rule that in felony the accused must be present at the trial. The court is not obliged to require him to go. He may waive his right to be present.[2]

[1] In *Foster* v. *State*, 70 Miss. 755, 12 So. 822, it was held that in so far as Miss. Code 1892, § 2391, providing for the view by the jury of the place in which an offense is charged to have been committed, by also provid-

ing that the officer in charge shall not speak to the jurors, or permit any other person so to do,—excludes the defendant from accompanying the jury and being present at the view, it is unconstitutional.

'In the conflict of authorities this appears to be the sound rule, supported by the reasoning of the best-considered cases.

A "view" is clearly the taking of evidence, if any person is permitted to point out the place. It can only be deemed not the taking of evidence when it involves nothing more than refreshing that common stock of knowledge which jurors possess, and which they may use in their duty in the cause. If it involves the examination of any detail, even such as distance, size, etc., as relevant to the facts in issue or to the testimony given, it is in so far a part of the trial. And in any case the opportunities for irregularity are so great that it seems indefensible to deny the right of the accused to be present.

If a person other than a juror is allowed to point out the place, the view necessarily involves evidence to the extent to which any statements are made or any information conveyed even by gesture; and although it may not be proper to instruct the jury to consider what they have seen as evidence, the statements made to them are a part of the trial, within the right of the accused to be present.

In the following cases the absence of the defendant from the view was held to be reversible error upon the general ground that the view is a part of the trial for taking evidence, and that he has a constitutional right to be present at the trial, and to confront the witnesses against him: *People* v. *Palmer*, 43 Hun, 397, Affirmed in 109 N. Y. 413, 17 N. E. 213, without discussing this point (held reversible error to refuse to permit the defendant and his counsel to be present at the view, under N. Y. Crim. Code Proc. §§ 411, 412, permitting view under charge of proper officers and prohibiting any communications with the jury on any subject connected with the trial, but silent as to the presence of defendant. The court held that the view was taking evidence in the absence of the defendant, and violated his constitutional rights); *People* v. *Bush*, 68 Cal. 623, 10 Pac. 169 (here it was so held, overruling *People* v. *Bonney*, 19 Cal. 426, and reversing judgment for absence of defendant. The court said there had already been a conflict of evidence submitted to the jury and that there was "little doubt that the order made for the view was for the reason that the court thought it necessary for the jury to determine, by looking at various physical objects extending along a road for some distance, which was the true and reliable testimony as to the matters where the conflict existed;" and as the principal witness for the people, in compliance with the order of the court, had pointed out and named to the jury the physical objects specified therein, the jury had viewed them "and therefrom must have determined which evidence upon certain points they deemed more worthy of belief. They thus received evidence in the absence of the judge, the defendant, and his counsel;" and that "it is impossible that a jury could go and view such a place without receiving some evidence through one of their senses, *viz.*, that of sight"); *Carroll* v. *State*, 5 Neb. 31 (under a statute permitting a view, but silent as to presence of defendant, held that the view should be in the presence of the prisoner, unless he declines the privilege, as he is entitled to have all the evidence received by the jury taken in his presence); *Benton* v. *State,* 30 Ark. 328 (under a statute allowing a view, and prohibiting any communications with the jury at the view, except the mere showing of the place, but silent as to defendant's presence, held that defendant's absence was reversible error in a case where the court directed the place to be pointed out by a juror familiar with the locality); *State* v. *Bertin,* 24 La. Ann. 46 (absence of defendant held reversible error, where on trial for burglary the court directed a witness for the state to point out at the view certain objects represented upon a diagram, but not to converse with the jury. Assuming that the instructions were strictly followed, the court said: "The witness gave testimony on the premises out of court, and in the absence of the accused, in the same way that a dumb person gives testimony; namely, by signs. . . . And it needs no argument to prove that the effect of such 'pointing out' in dumb show is as potent with a jury as if the verification of the diagram had been enforced with a multitude of words."

In *Sasse* v. *State,* 68 Wis. 530, 32 N. W. 849–853, the court, in a *dictum,* says it is "very questionable whether it [view] should have been taken in his [defendant's] absence, unless he expressly waived his right to be present," even though counsel for both sides were present; and the court were of the opinion that the object of the view "is not to obtain original testimony, in addition to, or contradiction of, the evidence given in court, or independent of it, but to obtain a perfect knowledge of the evidence, and to enable the jury better to understand it, and to consider it in the light and by the aid of the sensible objects and localities disclosed by the view." Judgment reversed on other grounds.

In *Rutherford* v. *Com.* 78 Ky. 639, the court, in a *dictum,* says that when, under § 236 of the Criminal Code, "the court directs a view of the place of the alleged crime by the jury, the accused, as well as the judge of the court, should be present. The presence of the prisoner and of the judge is as important as if evidence was being heard in court." But the court held that where, as here, the verdict must have been "guilty of murder," if all the evidence were excluded which the jury could have received on the view when acting within the directions of the court (as must be presumed in the absence of anything to the contrary), it followed that the record affirmatively showed that the defendant was not prejudiced by the error of his absence from the view, and such error was not ground for reversal. *Contra, State* v. *Adams,* 20 Kan. 311. Here a juror familiar with the locality pointed out the place to the jury, as directed by the court, and the absence of the defendant was held no error. *Shular* v. *State,* 105 Ind. 289, 55 Am. Rep. 211, 4 N. E. 870, held it no error to send a jury to view the place of a homicide, without directing that the accused should be present at the view. The statute provides that while the jury are absent to take the view, "no person, other than the officer and the person appointed to show them the place, shall speak to them on any subject connected with the trial;" and the court held that the "statute does not intend that the defendant or the judge shall accompany the jury; and it is equally clear that the view obtained by the jury is not to be deemed evidence," and that such statute is not unconstitutional.

For a full review of the authorities on this question, see *People* v. *Thorn* (N. Y.) 42 L. R. A. 381.

In *Hays* v. *Territory*, 7 Okla. 15, 54 Pac. 300, it is held that the court cannot compel defendant in a murder case to accompany the jury to view the premises where the homicide is alleged to have occurred, as the Oklahoma statutes permitting a view do not make it a part of the proceedings on the trial, and, by specifying the persons who shall be present thereat, impliedly exclude the presence of defendant.

XL.—TAKING THE CASE FROM THE JURY.

1. Withdrawing a juror.

The court has power to withdraw a juror at the request of the prosecution[1] or the accused,[2] and allow the cause to go over for the term.

[1]*People* v. *Olcott*, 2 Johns. Cas. 301, 1 Am. Dec. 168. Opinion by Kent, J., fully discussing the question, and sustaining a withdrawal at the request of the prosecutor.

[2]*McFall* v. *People*, 18 Hun, 382, holding it error to refuse the request of the accused solely on the ground of want of power. And see note to *Usborne* v. *Stephenson* (Or.) 48 L. R. A. 434, treating fully as to the practice of withdrawing a juror in a criminal case, and also as to the effect of such withdrawal upon a future trial.

2. Duty to direct acquittal.

If the evidence is not sufficient to sustain a verdict against a motion for a new trial, the accused is entitled to have the jury instructed to render a verdict of acquittal, without allowing them to retire to consider of a verdict.[1]

[1]*Howard* v. *State*, 108 Ala. 571, 18 So. 813; *State* v. *Hurley*, 58 Kan. 668, 50 Pac. 887; *Com.* v. *Hall*, 18 Ky. L. Rep. 783, 38 S. W. 498; *State* v. *Cady*, 82 Me. 426, 19 Atl. 908; *Howell* v. *People*, 5 Hun, 621, and cases cited, Affirmed in 69 N. Y. 607, on this opinion; *State* v. *Fiester*, 32 Or. 254, 50 Pac. 561; *People* v. *Bennett*, 49 N. Y. 147, Approved in *People*

v. *Dohring,* 59 N. Y. 374, 381, S. C. 17 Am. Rep. 349; *Com.* v. *Yost,* 197 Pa. 171, 46 Atl. 845; *State* v. *Wilson,* 10 Wash. 402, 39 Pac. 106; *State* v. *Myer,* 69 Iowa, 148, 28 N. W. 484; *State* v. *Flanagan* (W. Va.) 35 S. E. 862; *Com.* v. *Merrill,* 14 Gray, 415, 77 Am. Dec. 336 (error not to do so, even though not requested); *United States* v. *Fullerton,* 7 Blatchf. 177, Fed. Cas. No. 15,176. See also *State* v. *Bryson,* 82 N. C. 576. But *State* v. *Sanders,* 52 S. C. 580, 30 S. E. 616, holds that a verdict for defendant in a criminal case cannot be directed by a circuit judge.

For a statement of the rule requiring submission to the jury unless the facts are uncontroverted, and the inference certain, necessary, and undisputed, or unless there is no evidence of a necessary fact, see *United States* v. *Babcock,* 3 Dill. 577, Fed. Cas. No. 14,486.

If the evidence merely raises a suspicion or conjecture of guilt, it is not legal evidence, and the court should direct a verdict of not guilty; but if, considered as a whole, it is sufficient to warrant a verdict, it should be left to the jury. *State* v. *Eller,* 104 N. C. 853, 10 S. E. 313.

But the trial judge should withdraw the evidence from the jury in a criminal case, where there is only a mere scintilla of evidence of defendant's guilt, not sufficient to justify a verdict against him. *State* v. *Hairston,* 121 N. C. 579, 28 S. E. 492.

According to *People* v. *Eaton,* 59 Mich. 559, 26 N. W. 702, it is only where there is no evidence upon a material point that the court can take a case from the jury. To the same effect, *Wanzer* v. *State,* 41 Neb. 238, 59 N. W. 909.

A motion for a nonsuit, instead of asking the court to instruct the jury to find a verdict of not guilty, is not proper in criminal practice; and it is not error to deny it. *People* v. *Barnes* (Idaho) 9 Pac. 532; *State* v. *Jones,* 18 Or. 256, 22 Pac. 840; *State* v. *Hyde,* 22 Wash. 551, 61 Pac. 719. Compare *State ex rel. Thorndike* v. *Collins,* 68 N. H. 299, 44 Atl. 495.

And according to *State* v. *Keenan,* 7 Kan. App. 813, 55 Pac. 102, it is not proper practice in Kansas to demur to the evidence in a criminal prosecution.

To support a request for acquittal, defendant must state the ground therefor. The court is not obliged to guess it. *State* v. *Nulty,* 57 Vt. 543; *State* v. *Fiester,* 32 Or. 254, 50 Pac. 561.

In *State* v. *Welch,* 22 Mont. 92, 55 Pac. 927, the record presented, not a case of mere insufficiency of the evidence to warrant a conviction, but one of utter failure of proof. And it was held that the court should have granted the motion to instruct the jury to find the defendant not guilty. "There is a distinction," said the court, "between insufficiency of the evidence to justify a verdict and no evidence at all upon which to base it (*Louisiana & N. R. Co.* v. *Woodson,* 134 U. S. 614, 33 L. ed. 1032, 10 Sup. Ct. Rep. 628). In the one case the court may advise the jury to acquit the defendant, which advice the jury is not bound to follow (Pen. Code, § 2096), whereas, in the other case it is the duty of the court to direct a verdict of not guilty."

So, in California the court has no power peremptorily to order an acquittal under Pen. Code, § 1118, providing that if, at any time after the evidence on either side is closed, the court deems it insufficient to warrant a conviction, it may advise the jury to acquit, but the jury are not bound by the advice. *People* v. *Roberts*, 114 Cal. 67, 45 Pac. 1016. But this case holds that the error of the court in peremptorily directing an acquittal, instead of merely advising an acquittal and leaving the matter for the determination of the jury, does not demand a reversal upon an appeal by the People, as the proceedings below put the prisoner once in jeopardy, and he cannot be tried again.

The judge cannot, in the midst of a criminal trial, take the case from the jury, and peremptorily discharge one defendant from custody before verdict is rendered. *Boykin* v. *State*, 40 Fla. 484, 24 So. 141.

And a joint motion by two codefendants, praying that they both be discharged on the ground that the state has failed to introduce any evidence tending to connect them with the offense, is properly denied where there is some evidence tending to connect one of them with the commission thereof, although there is no evidence tending to connect the other defendant therewith. *Randolph* v. *State*, 100 Ala. 139, 14 So. 792.

3. —failure to support opening.

The mere fact that the prosecution has not proved all the facts stated in the opening is not ground for directing acquittal.[1]

[1] *State* v. *Meshek*, 61 Iowa, 316, 16 N. W. 143, holding conviction not error.

4. —to corroborate accomplice.

Where the testimony of an accomplice has been received against the accused, the court should not submit the case to the jury unless satisfied there is some corroborative evidence tending to connect the defendant with the commission of the crime.[1]

[1] *People* v. *Elliott*, 106 N. Y. 288, 12 N. E. 602, Reversing 5 N. Y. Crim. Rep. 204. And see *State* v. *Bruce*, 106 N. C. 792, 11 S. E. 475; and *Com.* v. *Parker*, 22 Ky. L. Rep. 368, 57 S. W. 484, involving this principle, but holding that there was sufficient corroborative evidence to take the case to the jury.

See also on this subject, *ante*, Division XXXIX., §§ 1 *et seq.*; and *post*, Division XLII., §§ 12–15.

5. Insufficient indictment or information.

When an information in a criminal cause fails to state a crime, on a trial had thereunder, it is not the proper practice, when the court discovers the defect, to direct a verdict of not guilty; but the jury should be discharged from further consideration of the case.[1]

[1] *State* v. *Dennison*, 60 Neb. 157, 82 N. W. 383. So held under Iowa Code 1873, § 4444. *State* v. *Kimble*, 104 Iowa, 19, 73 N. W. 348. To similar effect, see *State* v. *Brown*, 47 Ohio St. 102, 23 N. E. 747. Where the evi-

dence is excluded from the jury, upon a motion of the defendant in a criminal trial, on the ground that the indictment charges no offense against him, the jury should be discharged without rendering a verdict, there being no offense of which to acquit him, and no evidence for them to consider.

6. No power to direct conviction.

The court has no power to direct a conviction, however clear the evidence may be.[1]

[1] *United States* v. *Taylor*, 3 McCrary, 500; *Territory* v. *Kee*, 5 N. M. 510, 25 Pac. 924; *Howell* v. *People*, 5 Hun, 620 (*dictum*), Affirmed on this opinion in 69 N. Y. 607; *State* v. *Riley*, 113 N. C. 648, 18 S. E. 168; *Sims* v. *State*, 43 Ala. 33. *Contra*, *United States* v. *Anthony*, 11 Blatchf. 200, Fed. Cas. No. 14,459, which is disapproved in above cases.

Where all of the facts essential to a conviction are admitted, there is nothing for a jury to pass upon, and it is not error for the court to direct a verdict of guilty. *People* v. *Richmond*, 59 Mich. 570, 26 N. W. 770.

XLI.—COUNSEL'S ADDRESS TO THE JURY.

I. General rules.

1. Presence of the accused.

Defendant's absence during summing up, in cases less than capital, does not constitute error, unless he is shown to have been prejudiced thereby.[1]

[1]*State* v. *Paylor,* 89 N. C. 539; *Doyle* v. *Com.* 18 Ky. L. Rep. 518, 37 S. W. 153; *State* v. *Grate,* 68 Mo. 22. But see *Gladden* v. *State,* 12 Fla. 562. Trial for murder; defendant voluntarily absented himself during summing up; held error.

2. — of prosecuting attorney.

It is not error for the prosecuting attorney to absent himself while defendant's counsel is summing up.[1]

[1]*Wartena* v. *State,* 105 Ind. 445, 5 N. E. 20.

3. — of trial judge.

The trial judge must be present during counsel's argument to the jury.[1]

[1]*State* v. *Smith,* 49 Conn. 378 (holding it to be the duty of the trial judge to be present every moment during the actual progress of the trial); *Turbeville* v. *State,* 56 Miss. 793 (holding that if the record had disclosed even a temporary abandonment of the trial by the judge it would have been reversible error); *State* v. *Beuerman,* 59 Kan. 586, 53 Pac. 874 (holding that the presiding judge should not leave the courtroom, and go out of the sight and hearing of the jury and counsel during the argument), Citing *Meredeth* v. *People,* 84 Ill. 479; *Thompson* v. *People,* 144 Ill. 378, 32 N. E. 968; *State* v. *Smith,* 49 Conn. 376; *Turbeville* v. *State,* 56 Miss. 793; *Palin* v. *State,* 38 Neb. 862, 57 N. W. 743; *O'Brien* v. *People,* 17 Colo. 561, 31 Pac. 230. And see, more fully, cases reviewed in note to *Ellerbee* v. *State* (Miss.) 41 L. R. A. 569.

4. Nature of the right.

The presentation of his defense by argument to the jury, by himself or his counsel, is a constitutional right of the defendant (subject, however, to sufficient judicial control to prevent abuse), which may not be denied him, however clear the evidence may seem to the trial court.[1] He may, however, waive it.[2] If the argument is to be by counsel, he must be promptly on hand.[3]

[1]*Word* v. *Com.* 3 Leigh, 743; *Dille* v. *State,* 34 Ohio St. 617, 32 Am. Rep. 395 (where Gilmore, Ch. J., said: "The court has no discretionary power over the right itself, for it cannot be denied. And hence it has no right to prevent the accused from being heard by counsel, even if the evidence against him be clear, unimpeached, and conclusive, in the opinion of the court. But the exercise of the right is subject to judicial control, to the extent that it is necessary to prevent abuse of it").

Where the Constitution makes the jury in criminal cases the judges of the law and the facts, it is error for the court to refuse to permit counsel to argue the question of law to the jury. *Lynch* v. *State*, 9 Ind. 541.

Counsel for one of two jointly indicted and tried at the same time may be permitted to present to the jury such views as will tend to show his client's innocence, although such views may tend to implicate the other defendant. *State* v. *Mitchell*, 49 S. C. 410, 27 S. E. 424.

The trial judge may properly refuse permission to counsel for the accused to address his argument to the jury in the French language, on the ground that it is their mother tongue, where the jurors have been examined on their *voir dire* and cross-examined in the English language, without objection, and all witnesses for the state and defense have been interrogated and cross-interrogated in English. *State* v. *Cancienne*, 50 La. Ann. 1324, 24 So. 321.

In Montana a rule of court provides that if the attorney of either party offers himself as a witness in behalf of his client, and gives evidence on the merits of the case, he shall not argue the case or sum it up to the jury, unless on permission of the court; and in *State* v. *Gleim*, 17 Mont. 17, 31 L. R. A. 294, 41 Pac. 998, it is held that the enforcement of this rule is not error where it does not appear by the record that before the counsel testified he explained to the court his position, and asked permission to argue the case.

Palmer v. *People*, 4 Neb. 68.

And a refusal to submit the case to the jury without further argument is not an abuse of discretion, where, after the opening address for the state, defendant offers to waive further argument, and there are several counsel on both sides. *State* v. *Row*, 81 Iowa, 138, 46 N. W. 872.

And the defendant cannot, by waiving argument after the opening argument has been made, cut off the state's rights to be heard in a concluding address to the jury, under Tex. Code Crim. Proc. art. 667. *Vines* v. *State*, 31 Tex. Crim. Rep. 31, 19 S. W. 545.

In *Graves* v. *State*, 9 Tex. App. 559, it is held that neither defendant nor his counsel have the right, unnecessarily and without excuse, to delay the public business of the county. It is the duty of attorneys having business in court to attend its sessions; and the court when opened is not required either to have counsel called, or await their convenience.

The order of summing up varies somewhat in different jurisdictions. This is largely controlled by statute. The prevailing practice gives to the prosecution the closing argument to the jury.

By N. Y. Code Crim. Proc. § 388, unless the case is submitted without argument, the defendant or his counsel must commence, and the counsel for the People conclude, the argument.

In the United States courts the attorney of the government always has the right to close the argument before the jury on the general issue. *United States* v. *Bates*, 2 Cranch C. C. 405, Fed. Cas. No. 14,543.

State v. *Schnelle*, 24 W. Va. 767, holds that as the general burden of proving guilt is on the state, the defendant cannot demand the privilege of opening and closing where the defense is insanity.

For text-books on prevailing rule, see 1 Archbold, Crim. Pr. & Pl. 584–587; 1 Bishop, Crim. Proc. §§ 974, 975; 3 Wharton, Crim. Law, §§ 3007–3016; Robinson, Elementary Law, 330.

5. When made.

It is discretionary with the trial court to hear the summing up at the close of the evidence,[1] or to adjourn for the purpose of giving needed physical rest.[2]

[1]In *Wartena* v. *State*, 105 Ind. 445, 5 N. E. 20, immediate argument was compelled, requiring a night session, notwithstanding defendant's counsel objected on the ground that he was worn out by the labors of the case, and by attending a sick member of his family at night; and it was held that he having made his argument the prisoner was not prejudiced.

[2]*Hayes* v. *State*, 58 Ga. 35.

In *State* v. *Lewis*, 118 Mo. 79, 23 S. W. 1082, it was held that refusal of a court on a trial for murder to require the prosecuting attorney to close the argument before the jury immediately after the close of the argument for the defense, although there was ample time to do so, was not an abuse of discretion.

6. Number of counsel.

Unless limited by statute[1] or rule of court the number of counsel permitted to sum up is discretionary with the trial court.[2]

[1]In California the court is expressly authorized by Pen. Code, § 1095, to refuse to permit more than one counsel to argue the case for defendant, except in capital cases. *People* v. *Jones*, 123 Cal. 65, 55 Pac. 698.

In Texas a statute (art. 3051, Code Crim. Proc.) provides that the judge shall never restrict the argument in felony cases to a less number of attorneys than two on a side; but in *Morales* v. *State*, 1 Tex. App. 494, 28 Am. Rep. 419, it was held that this did not confer upon the prisoner or his counsel the right to have two speeches in his defense, where he had only one counsel; that if the prisoner wished to avail himself of the right to have two speeches on his side he must have two counsel to defend him, or if he had only one counsel, then he and his counsel must each make a speech.

[2]*People* v. *Ah Wee*, 48 Cal. 236.

7. Limiting time.

The allowance of time rests in the sound discretion of the court,[1] but its abuse is error.[2]

[1]*People* v. *Kelly*, 94 N. Y. 526 (assault with deadly weapon; no error to limit each side to half an hour); *Hart* v. *State*, 14 Neb. 572, 16 N. W. 905 (murder; argument limited to three hours, it not appearing that more time was needed, presumed to be sufficient); *Kizer* v. *State*, 12

Lea, 564 (each side limited to an hour and ten minutes). To same effect, see *Lee* v. *State*, 51 Miss. 566; *State* v. *Williams*, 69 Mo. 110; *State* v. *Hoyt*, 47 Conn. 518, 36 Am. Rep. 89; *Weaver* v. *State*, 24 Ohio St. 584; *State* v. *Riddle*, 20 Kan. 711; *State* v. *Collins*, 70 N. C. 241, 16 Am. Rep. 771 (murder; limitation to one hour and a half not error); *Vaughan* v. *State*, 58 Ark. 353, 24 S. W. 885 (so holding, but suggesting that it would be better to advise counsel of that fact previous to their argument, and of what the limit will be); *Yeldell* v. *State*, 100 Ala. 26, 14 So. 570; *Combs* v. *Com.* 97 Ky. 24, 29 S. W. 734; *Dixon* v. *State*, 46 Neb. 298, 64 N. W. 961; *Sullivan* v. *State*, 46 N. J. L. 446; *Stewart* v. *Com.* 117 Pa. 378, 11 Atl. 370; *Thompson* v. *Com.* 88 Va. 45, 13 S. E. 304.

In Connecticut a statute provides that "in no trial before the superior court shall counsel occupy more than one hour in argument, unless the court shall, on motion for special cause before the commencement of such argument, allow a longer time." Gen. Stat. § 9, p. 61. And in *State* v. *Nyman*, 55 Conn. 17, 10 Atl. 161, it is held that from time immemorial in that state each party to every cause in the superior court has had the privilege of being heard by two counsel, and that therefore the statute means that each party may occupy two hours in argument, without previous request. "Of course," said the court, "the sole purpose of the statute is to secure the more speedy dispatch of judicial business. Therefore it is quite immaterial whether the two hours shall be occupied by one counsel or by two; and if by two, whether in equal or unequal proportions. The practice has generally prevailed on the part of counsel to divide the time into unequal portions by agreement between themselves, and such division has been acquiesced in by the court, in the absence of previous formal request. When, therefore, in the case at bar, the senior counsel, after the commencement of his argument, asked the court for permission to occupy the fraction of an hour not used by his associate, he was without the letter of the statute, but he was within the reason and spirit of it, and within the interpretation sometimes put upon it by trial courts."

In Michigan a rule of the circuit court (rule 63), as amended in 1885, provides that not less than one hour on each side shall be allowed to counsel, if desired, in summing up the case, and not more than two, unless the court shall otherwise order. And in *People* v. *Smith*, 122 Mich. 284, 81 N. W. 107, it is held that under this rule the court has discretion to stop counsel after arguing thirty-five minutes.

In *State* v. *Collins*, 70 N. C. 241, 16 Am. Rep. 771, an indictment for murder, the court held that the trial judge had power to impose a reasonable time limit upon counsel's argument, although it said that the limitation imposed in that case (an hour and a half) was not one which it would recommend as a precedent worthy of general imitation. Mr. Justice Bynum dissented; contending that it was not within the power of the judge to impose any limitation whatever upon the argument, previous to its commencement; referring in his argument to *Re Spier*, 12 N. C. (1 Dev. L.) 491, as a case in which counsel confessedly spoke against time to save the life of accused by the expiration of the term of the court, insisting that the want of such authority to limit the argument, as exampled in that case, was sanctioned by the legislature of North Carolina, in that they shortly thereafter passed a statute enabling the judge in capital cases only to extend the time from day to day until the trial was finished.

Subsequent to the *Collins Case*, the legislature passed a statute "that any counsel appearing in any criminal case shall be entitled to address the court or jury for such a space of time as in his opinion may be necessary for the proper development and presentation of his case." And in *State* v. *Miller*, 75 N. C. 73, where the prisoner was represented by two attorneys, it was held that under this statute each one of the counsel appearing for the prisoner was entitled to address the jury, and that it was error for the presiding judge to refuse to hear but one of them.

But this applies only to the trial, and not to the argument of counsel on motions and questions arising during the trial,—such as the question of the admissibility of certain evidence. *State* v. *Jones*, 117 N. C. 768, 23 S. E. 247.

In South Carolina a statute (Gen. Stat. § 2166) expressly limits the time for argument to two hours for each counsel, "unless he shall first obtain the special permission of the court" to consume a longer time; and in *State* v. *Jones*, 29 S. C. 201, 7 S. E. 296, where there were two counsel on each side, it was held to be no error for the judge, previous to the argument, to limit the argument of counsel to the time allowed by the statute.

[a]*Dille* v. *State*, 34 Ohio St. 617, 32 Am. Rep. 395 (burglary; where testimony, lasting a day and a half, was circumstantial and conflicting, limitation to thirty minutes, defendant being represented by two counsel, held an abuse of discretion, and conviction reversed); *People* v. *Keenan*, 13 Cal. 581 (murder; defendant represented by two counsel, who were each restricted to an hour and a half, against their objection that they could not present all the points that might be urged within that time; held abuse of discretion; conviction reversed); *Wingo* v. *State*, 62 Miss. 311 (arson, where twelve witnesses were examined; limitation to an hour error); *White* v. *People*, 90 Ill. 117, 32 Am. Rep. 12 (larceny of a complicated character, presenting several issues of law and fact; five minutes' limit unreasonable, and substantially a denial of defendant's right to be heard. Conviction reversed); *Hunt* v. *State*, 49 Ga. 255, 15 Am. Rep. 677 (assault with intent to kill; limitation to forty minutes unreasonable); *State* v. *Nyman*, 55 Conn. 17, 10 Atl. 161 (murder; less than two hours allowed to defendant's two counsel; held error); *People* v. *Labadie*, 66 Mich. 702, 33 N. W. 806. To the same effect, see *People* v. *Green*, 99 Cal. 564, 34 Pac. 231; *Walker* v. *State*, 32 Tex. Crim. Rep. 175, 22 S. W. 685; *McLean* v. *State*, 32 Tex. Crim. Rep. 521, 24 S. W. 898.

A limitation of five minutes for argument was a virtual denial of the right of the accused to be heard by counsel, where there were four witnesses examined in chief by the prosecution, three on behalf of the accused, and two in rebuttal by the prosecution. *White* v. *People*, 90 Ill. 117, 32 Am. Rep. 12. The court said: "The plaintiffs in error had an undoubted right, under the very Bill of Rights itself, and by the law of the land, to defend by counsel, and to insist such counsel should have reasonable opportunity to discuss before the jury both the facts and the law of the case. This was a constitutional and substantial right of which no court could properly deprive them. It was not a mere empty and nominal right to have an argument made in their behalf, that would necessarily be but a brief and idle form,—to have a discussion of the law and the evidence that was confined within a space of time so short as to be wholly inadequate to afford any opportunity to examine or discuss either the law or the evidence involved. Surely, such was not the right deemed by the People of sufficient importance to be incorporated into the fundamental law of the land. . . . The fraction of time to which counsel was restricted was unreasonably short, and wholly insufficient to enable him, be he ever so terse, to discuss the case with a reasonable hope of any probable, if even possible, effect upon the determination of the issues."

8. Right to be heard on the whole case.

It is error to abridge the defendant's right to be heard on all the facts and circumstances which are in evidence.[1] But this does not give him the right to address the jury on questions of law which arose on the trial of the general issue.[2]

[1]*Beasley* v. *State,* 71 Ala. 328; *Com.* v. *Porter,* 10 Met. 265.

Counsel, in commenting upon evidence admitted without restriction as to its application to the issues involved, have the right to draw from it any inferences apparently reasonable and legitimate, and endeavor to convince the jury of the correctness of such inferences. *Smalls* v. *State,* 105 Ga. 669, 31 S. E. 571.

But stopping counsel for the accused from discussing facts not within the evidence is not error. *State* v. *Ussery,* 118 N. C. 1177, 24 S. E. 414; *Killins* v. *State,* 28 Fla. 313, 9 So. 711.

In *Ford* v. *State,* 34 Ark. 650, it was said that although the Arkansas Bill of Rights guaranteed to a person criminally accused the right to be heard by himself and counsel, the court might well deny counsel the right to make statements contradicting the evidence, although they might discuss the probable truth, consistency, or falsity of the evidence.

[2]*Stettinius* v. *United States,* 5 Cranch C. C. 573, Fed. Cas. No. 13,387.

9. Reading law books to the jury.

The trial court may in its discretion permit counsel, in summing up, to read the law to the jury,[1] or may refuse such permission.[2] It is for the court to say whether the law proposed to be read is appropriate to the case on trial;[3] and if read the court may comment on the same, and show wherein it is erroneous.[4]

[1]*People* v. *Treadwell,* 69 Cal. 226, 10 Pac. 502 (People's counsel was per-

mitted to read to the jury from law books); *Foster* v. *State,* 8 Tex. App. 248; *Wohlford* v. *People,* 148 Ill. 296, 36 N. E. 107.

On the trial of a criminal case, it is not the absolute right of counsel to read to the jury, as a part of his argument, extracts from law books which he claims state the law applicable to the case, since the jury is bound to receive and be governed by the law as declared by the court; and the court may allow or refuse such a mode of argument, in its discretion. *McGuire* v. *State,* 2 Ohio C. D. 318.

Upon a trial for keeping a saloon open on Sunday, the prosecuting attorney may read portions of the statute to the jury, and lay stress upon that portion providing that it shall not be necessary to prove that any liquor was sold. *People* v. *Ringsted,* 90 Mich. 371, 51 N. W. 519.

In Kansas, on a trial for libel, defendant's counsel has the right fairly to argue his theory of the law of the case to the jury, and in the course of his arguments may read from law books recognized as authorities bearing upon the case, under Kan. Code, § 309, providing that in all indictments for libel the jury, after receiving the direction of the court, shall have the right to determine at their discretion "the law and the fact." *State* v. *Whitmore,* 53 Kan. 343, 36 Pac. 748.

But permitting the counsel for the state, in his closing argument, to read to the jury, from an opinion published in the supreme court reports, statements with regard to certain matters in another criminal case, as evidence of certain facts in the libel case,—is error. *State* v. *Wait,* 44 Kan. 310, 24 Pac. 354.

[2]*Curtis* v. *State,* 36 Ark. 284. Prosecuting attorney not permitted to read the section of the statute defining murder in the first degree; held no error.

In *Bangs* v. *State,* 61 Miss. 363, defendant's counsel was not permitted to read the opinion of the appellate court reversing a former conviction; and it was held that refusal to permit reading of law books was not error in any case. *Dempsey* v. *State,* 3 Tex. App. 429, 30 Am. Rep. 148. To similar effect, see *Vernon* v. *State* (Tex. Crim. App.) 33 S. W. 364.

[3]*Hudson* v. *State,* 6 Tex. App. 565, 32 Am. Rep. 593 (the trial court would permit only so much of a reported case to be read as illustrated the case on trial, or discussed the weight of evidence); *State* v. *Smallwood,* 78 N. C. 560.

[4]*Powell* v. *State,* 65 Ga. 707. *Contra, State* v. *Hoyt,* 46 Conn. 330 (murder; defendant's counsel proposed to read the entire opinion of the appellate court in another case. He was permitted to read therefrom only such propositions of law as were pertinent to the case at bar; held error; he had the right to read the opinion in its entirety); *Hannah* v. *State,* 11 Lea, 201 (refusal to permit defendant's counsel to read law books to jury, error); *McMath* v. *State,* 55 Ga. 303.

10. Reading scientific books.

Reading scientific books is not permissible, because they are only expositions of theories, are not given under oath, and no opportunity is given to cross-examine the author.[1]

[1]*People* v. *Wheeler*, 60 Cal. 581, 44 Am. Rep. 70 (counsel was not permitted to read a work on insanity, it not having been shown to be a recognized authority. The appellate court, in a thorough review of the cases, sustained the ruling, and intimated that even if shown to be standard the book should not have been read); *Boyle* v. *State*, 57 Wis. 472, 15 N. W. 827 (error to permit prosecuting attorney to read from a scientific book. This case contains a full discussion of the subject); *Yoe* v. *People*, 49 Ill. 410 (the prosecuting attorney cannot read the testimony of a scientific expert in another case); *People* v. *Glover*, 71 Mich. 303, 38 N. W. 874; *State* v. *Rogers*, 112 N. C. 874, 17 S. E. 297; *State* v. *Soper*, 148 Mo. 217, 49 S. W. 1007. Compare *Scott* v. *People*, 141 Ill. 195, 30 N. E. 329, where it is held that it is not error to read to the jury on argument extracts from medical books which form a part of the evidence.

But in *State* v. *Hoyt*, 46 Conn. 330 (murder; defense insanity), defendant's counsel was not permitted to read from a standard work on insanity; and this was held error. In this jurisdiction the practice of reading from such book had so long prevailed that defendant had the right to rely on the custom.

In *State* v. *O'Neil*, 51 Kan. 651, 24 L. R. A. 555, 33 Pac. 287, it is held that while counsel in a criminal cause may be allowed, in the discretion of the court, to read from standard works on matters of science and art, by way of argument or illustration, they cannot make use of the privilege for the purpose of getting improper matter before the jury as evidence, or of presenting matters of law conflicting with the instructions of the court.

II. Improprieties by prosecution.

11. Objections, when and how taken.

The remedy for any improprieties on the part of the prosecuting attorney in summing up is to interpose by immediate objection; and the accused is entitled to a ruling on the objection, and to an exception if the objection be not sustained.[1]

[1]The reason is that unless both objection and exception are taken there is no means of review. *Com.* v. *Worcester*, 141 Mass. 58, 6 N. E. 700; *Mayes* v. *People*, 106 Ill. 306, 46 Am. Rep. 698; *Morrison* v. *State*, 76 Ind. 335; *State* v. *McMahon*, 17 Nev. 365, 30 Pac. 1000; *State* v. *McCool*, 34 Kan. 613, 9 Pac. 618, 745; *McLain* v. *State*, 18 Neb. 154, 24 N. W. 720; *People* v. *Ah Fook*, 64 Cal. 380, 1 Pac. 347; *People* v. *Haley*, 48 Mich. 495, 12 N. W. 671; *Gilmore* v. *State*, 37 Tex. Crim. Rep. 178, 39 S. W. 105; *Williams* v. *State*, 61 Wis. 281, 21 N. W. 56; *Rucker* v. *State*, 7 Tex. App. 549; *State* v. *Rivers*, 90 N. C. 738.

Even where such comments are forbidden by statute. *Price* v. *Com.* 77 Va. 393; *State* v. *Anderson*, 10 Or. 448.

But *Martin* v. *State*, 63 Miss. 505, 56 Am. Rep. 812, holds that the presiding judge should interfere, of his own motion, to prevent a breach of privilege by counsel; and if the comments were of such a character as to produce the conviction, it should be reversed.

12. Comments on defendant's failure to testify.

Under the statutes providing that the refusal or neglect of the accused to testify shall not be commented on nor act to his prejudice,[1] it is error to comment on such omission,[2] even in reply to comments previously made by defendant's counsel;[3] and this rule has sometimes been extended to the case of a codefendant.[4]

[1]See the statutes set out *ante*, Division XXXIX., § 16.

[2]*Showalter* v. *State*, 84 Ind. 562; *State* v. *Balch*, 31 Kan. 465, 2 Pac. 609; *Angelo* v. *People*, 96 Ill. 209, 36 Am. Rep. 132; *Austin* v. *People*, 102 Ill. 261 (held error unless the proofs of guilt were so clear that the court could say that defendant was not harmed thereby); *People* v. *Brown*, 53 Cal. 66; *State* v. *Banks*, 78 Me. 490, 7 Atl. 269; *Blackman* v. *State*, 78 Ga. 592, 3 S. E. 418; *State* v. *Ryan*, 70 Iowa, 154, 30 N. W. 397 (under statute forbidding such comment "during trial," a reference to the fact during argument to court, in presence of the jury, reversible error); *Reed* v. *State*, 29 Tex. App. 449, 16 S. W. 99; *State* v. *Garrington*, 11 S. D. 178, 76 N. W. 326; *State* v. *Hull*, 18 R. I. 207, 20 L. R. A. 609, 26 Atl. 191; *People* v. *Doyle*, 58 Hun, 535, 12 N. Y. Supp. 836; *Cunningham* v. *State*, 56 Neb. 691, 77 N. W. 60; *Yarbrough* v. *State*, 70 Miss. 593, 12 So. 551; *State* v. *Holmes*, 65 Minn. 230, 68 N. W. 11; *State* v. *Deves* (Kan. App.) 61 Pac. 511; *State* v. *Trauger* (Iowa) 77 N. W. 336; *Gilmore* v. *People*, 87 Ill. App. 128; *Gray* v. *State* (Fla.) 28 So. 53; *People* v. *Lemperle*, 94 Cal. 45, 29 Pac. 709; *Wilson* v. *United States*, 149 U. S. 60, 37 L. ed. 650, 13 Sup. Ct. Rep. 765; *State* v. *Howard*, 35 S. C. 197, 14 S. E. 481. And for other cases recognizing this doctrine, but holding that the argument in question did not violate the rule, see *State* v. *Griswold*, 73 Conn. 95, 46 Atl. 829; *Frazier* v. *State*, 135 Ind. 38, 34 N. E. 817; *State* v. *Ahern*, 54 Minn. 195, 55 N. W. 959; *McGuire* v. *State*, 2 Ohio C. D. 318; *Green* v. *State* (Tex. Crim. App.) 31 S. W. 386; *Sawyers* v. *Com.* 88 Va. 356, 13 S. E. 708.

A bastardy proceeding, though quasi-criminal and penal in its character, is not a criminal prosecution, within the Alabama statute providing that in all criminal prosecutions the failure of defendant to testify in his own behalf shall not be the subject of comment by counsel. *Miller* v. *State*, 110 Ala. 69, 20 So. 392.

In New Jersey the act of 1871, now § 8 of the evidence act (Gen. Stat. p. 1398), which permits an indicted person to become a witness in his own behalf by offering himself as such, does not provide that his failure to offer himself shall not raise any presumption against him, nor does it forbid allusion to such failure by counsel or court; and when facts have been testified to by witnesses for the prosecution, which concern the actions of defendant, and, if not true, may be disproved by him, his failure to offer himself as a witness may be considered and commented upon. *Parker* v. *State*, 62 N. J. L. 801, 45 Atl. 1092.

[3]*Com.* v. *Scott*, 123 Mass. 239, 25 Am. Rep. 87.

In *Ruloff* v. *People*, 45 N. Y. 213, 222, the court says that neither the prosecuting officer nor the judge has a right to allude to the fact that a person has not availed himself of the right to testify; and it would be the duty of the court promptly to interrupt a prosecuting counsel who should so far forget himself and the duties of his office as to make any such comment.

But *Parker* v. *State* (Tex. Crim. App.) 45 S. W. 812, holds that one convicted of crime cannot complain of a statement in the closing argument of the county attorney,—"Counsel for defendant says that the defendant is not compelled to open his mouth. That is true. The state cannot compel him to testify," where it was but a reiteration of the remark of the defendant's counsel, and upon the court's interference the county attorney stated that the state had nothing to rely upon for a conviction except the evidence in the record.

[4]*State* v. *Martin*, 74 Mo. 547; *State* v. *Graham*, 62 Iowa, 108, 17 N. W. 192; *Brock* v. *State*, 123 Ala. 24, 26 So. 329; *Coppin* v. *State*, 123 Ala. 58, 26 So. 333.

13. — on failure to prove good character.

It is reversible error to allow the prosecuting attorney to comment, in his argument, on defendant's omitting to prove good character.[1]

[1]*People* v. *Evans*, 72 Mich. 367, 40 N. W. 473.

Nor does improper argument by defendant's counsel, by making statements outside the evidence as to his client's good character, justify the state's counsel in arguing, against defendant's objection, that his failure to offer proof of good character raises an inference that his character is not good. *Bennett* v. *State*, 86 Ga. 401, 12 L. R. A. 449, 12 S. E. 806. But see *Barkman* v. *State* (Tex. Crim. App.) 52 S. W. 73, holding that arguments and statements of defendant's counsel, in which they discuss the character of defendant, may be answered by the state's attorney in his argument. See also *State* v. *Hyland*, 144 Mo. 302, 46 S. W. 195.

14. Comments on defendant's testimony.

If the defendant testifies on his own behalf, he places himself on the same footing as any other witness; and comments on the credibility of his testimony[1] or his omission to state all the facts relating to the transaction[2] are proper.

[1]*Boyle* v. *State*, 105 Ind. 469, 55 Am. Rep. 218, 5 N. E. 203; *Toops* v. *State*, 92 Ind. 13.

Thus, a comment of counsel in a criminal trial, that the testimony given by defendant in his own behalf "is the meanest and poorest kind," being merely a comment upon the weight and credibility of the evidence, is not error. *Pruitt* v. *State*, 92 Ala. 41, 9 So. 406.

So held in *People* v. *Louie Foo,* 112 Cal. 17, 44 Pac. 453, of a statement by the prosecuting attorney on the trial of a Chinaman, that the testimony of Chinese witnesses, unless corroborated by white witnesses, is insufficient to raise a reasonable doubt, but that the jury are the sole judges of the credibility of the witnesses.

And in *Maloy* v. *State,* 39 Fla. 432, 22 So. 719, of a statement by the prosecuting attorney in his closing argument, that the state's witness is entirely disinterested, but that is not the case with the defendant, who testified on the trial, but that he is charged with crime, and it is his interest to screen himself.

So, the state's attorney in his argument before the jury may comment on and allude to the admission of defendant on cross-examination, that he had been previously indicted for an offense, and should have turned state's evidence against his codefendant in that case. *Mirando* v. *State* (Tex. Crim. App.) 50 S. W. 714.

And the district attorney in a criminal case, which is not capital, in which the defendant employs counsel, may properly comment upon the weight to be given to an unsworn statement which the defendant is allowed to make, contrary to the practice in Massachusetts. *Com.* v. *McConnell,* 162 Mass. 499, 39 N. E. 107.

In *Siberry* v. *State,* 133 Ind. 677, 33 N. E. 681, it was held that harm from an improper comment in the presence of the jury, by the counsel for the state, as to the appearance and actions at the trial of a prisoner accused of murder, who had testified as a witness, was corrected by an admonition from the court that such remarks were improper, where he only intended to comment upon him as a witness.

[a]*State* v. *Tatman,* 59 Iowa, 471, 13 N. W. 632; *Solander* v. *People,* 2 Colo. 48; *State* v. *Harrington,* 12 Nev. 125; *Brashears* v. *State,* 58 Md. 563. Thus, defendant's failure, when a witness, to explain damaging facts peculiarly within his knowledge, is as much a subject of comment as though he were a party in a civil cause. *State* v. *Anderson,* 89 Mo. 312, 1 S. W. 135. To same effect, see *Cotton* v. *State,* 87 Ala. 103, 6 So. 372; *McFadden* v. *State,* 28 Tex. App. 241, 14 S. W. 128; *State* v. *Glave,* 51 Kan. 330, 33 Pac. 8; *Price* v. *United States,* 14 App. D. C. 391; *Lee* v. *State,* 56 Ark. 4, 19 S. W. 16; *Stover* v. *People,* 56 N. Y. 315, so holding, notwithstanding the New York Revised Statutes providing that the failure of the accused to testify should raise no presumption against him.

But *State* v. *Graves,* 95 Mo. 510, 8 S. W. 739, holds that where defendant testifies on one point only the prosecuting attorney may not comment on his failure to testify on other points. See also *State* v. *Fairlamb,* 121 Mo. 137, 25 S. W. 895, holding that it is improper for the prosecuting attorney, in a trial for murder, to comment in his argument upon defendant's failure to testify to any particular fact.

In *Gossett* v. *State,* 65 Ark. 389, 46 S. W. 537, it was held that an argument by the prosecuting attorney on a trial for theft of whisky, to the effect that defendant's refusal to answer a question as to where he got the whisky found in his possession was evidence of his guilt of the crime charged, was improper, where the defendant based his refusal on the ground that his answer would tend to convict him of unlawful distilling for which he was under indictment in the Federal court, there being nothing to indicate that that was not the real ground of his refusal.

A remark of the solicitor for the state, in his oral argument to the jury, that defendant did not deny certain testimony for the state, is improper where the defendant has not testified as a witness in the case. *Baker* v. *State,* 122 Ala. 1, 26 So. 194.

15. Personal belief or knowledge of prosecuting attorney.

It is improper for a prosecuting attorney in summing up to state his personal belief of defendant's guilt,[1] or to state facts as of his own knowledge.[2]

[1] *Raggio* v. *People,* 135 Ill. 533, 26 N. E. 377. *Contra, State* v. *Cater,* 100 Iowa, 501, 69 N. W. 880.

Thus, in *People* v. *Quick,* 58 Mich. 321, 25 N. W. 302, the prosecuting attorney said: "I stand here today under the solemnity of my official oath, and say to you as a man and a citizen, that I believe they [defendants] not only lied but I believe they committed wilful and deliberate perjury." Conviction was reversed on that account.

So, in *Martin* v. *State,* 63 Miss. 505, 56 Am. Rep. 812, the prosecuting attorney said: "Martin, the defendant, is a man of bad, dangerous, and desperate character, but I am not afraid to denounce the butcher boy, although I may, on returning to my home, find it in ashes over the heads of my defenseless wife and children." Conviction was reversed on that account.

Although it is not proper for the prosecuting attorney to tell the jury that he believes defendant guilty, he has the right to argue from the testimony that defendant is guilty, and to state what evidence convinces him, and should convince the jury, of such guilt. *People* v. *Hess,* 85 Mich. 128, 48 N. W. 181. To similar effect, see *Davis* v. *State* (Tex. Crim. App.) 44 S. W. 1099.

Nor is it error for the prosecuting attorney in a murder trial to make the remark in his argument to the jury: "They talk about defendant having his throat treated. In my opinion his throat needs one more application, and that is about 20 feet of rope," it being but a laconic way of saying defendant should be hanged, which would be a legitimate statement adduced from the evidence. *Morrison* v. *State,* 40 Tex. Crim. Rep. 473, 51 S. W. 358.

[2] *Hardtke* v. *State,* 67 Wis. 552, 30 N. W. 726 (reversing conviction because the prosecuting attorney said: "The defendant confessed this crime to me"); *Hamilton* v. *State,* 97 Tenn. 452, 37 S. W. 194; *People* v. *Dane,* 59 Mich. 550, 26 N. W. 781; *State* v. *Smith,* 75 N. C. 306 (prosecuting attorney stated: "The bold, brazen-faced rascal had the impudence to write me a note yesterday, begging me not to prosecute him, and threatening me that if I did he would get the legislature to impeach me." Held reversible error). But see *Heyl* v. *State,* 109 Ind. 589, 10 N. E.

916. Statement by prosecuting attorney that defendant was reputed to be a hotel thief, where proof of guilt of offense for which he was tried was perfectly clear under the circumstances, not reversible error.

An assertion by prosecuting counsel on a trial for burglary, that he and the jury know the defendants are robbers and burglars, is not such comment as the court is required to restrain, when the testimony for the People, if believed, establishes the guilt of the defendants. *Spahn* v. *People*, 137 Ill. 538, 27 N. E. 688.

16. Arguing from facts not in evidence.

It is error to allow the prosecuting attorney, against defendant's objections, to argue from facts not in evidence.[1]

But if defendant's counsel has in summing up commented on such facts, the court may permit a reply of like character.[2]

[1] *People* v. *Mitchell*, 62 Cal. 411; *Cross* v. *State*, 68 Ala. 476; *Ferguson* v. *State*, 49 Ind. 33; *Greene* v. *State*, 17 Tex. App. 395 (statement by prosecuting attorney that if a certain witness had been produced, she would have sworn to certain facts; held that unless adverse counsel had invited such remarks it was error).

So, when counsel, in addressing the jury, travel out of the record, and base an argument on facts not appearing in the record, it is the duty of the court, upon request of opposing counsel, to correct such abuse of privilege. *State* v. *Bokien*, 14 Wash. 403, 44 Pac. 889.

But the prosecuting attorney has a right, within reasonable limits, to draw his own deductions as to facts from other admitted or proved facts, and may declare that defendant made a certain statement, although he denies it, and it is not positively proved, if it may be inferred. *State* v. *Tippet*, 94 Iowa, 646, 63 N. W. 445.

[2] *Reeves* v. *State*, 84 Ind. 116; *People* v. *Bush*, 68 Cal. 623, 10 Pac. 169; *State* v. *Leabo*, 89 Mo. 247, 1 S. W. 289. But see *dictum, contra*, in *People* v. *Mitchell*, 62 Cal. 411. And *People* v. *Kramer*, 117 Cal. 647, 49 Pac. 842, expressly holds that improper arguments of counsel, not based upon the evidence, in an address to the jury, are not justified by the fact that opposing counsel had already committed a like impropriety.

17. Effect of rebuking counsel.

If the court promptly rebukes the prosecuting counsel for making improper statements, and the latter thereupon ceases to make them, the improper statements will not require a reversal,[1] unless forbidden by statute.[2] To make the error available, defendant must object,[3] and have a ruling by the court.[4]

[1] *Norton* v. *State*, 106 Ind. 163, 6 N. E. 126; *People* v. *Lee Ah Yute*, 60 Cal. 95; *State* v. *Degonia*, 69 Mo. 485; *United States* v. *Musser*, 4 Utah, 153, 7 Pac. 389; *State* v. *Rivers*, 90 N. C. 738; *Kellogg* v. *United States*, 43

C. C. A. 179, 103 Fed. 200; *People* v. *Sansome,* 98 Cal. 235, 33 Pac. 202; *Price* v. *United States,* 14 App. D. C. 391; *Shenkenberger* v. *State,* 154 Ind. 630, 57 N. E. 519; *State* v. *Davis,* 110 Iowa, 746, 82 N. W. 328; *State* v. *Kinsauls,* 126 N. C. 1095, 36 N. E. 31; *Barnes* v. *Com.* 101 Ky. 556, 41 S. W. 772; *People* v. *Swartz,* 118 Mich. 292, 76 N. W. 491; *Thurman* v. *State,* 2 Ohio C. D. 466.

Mere failure to stop the district attorney, when he was making an improper argument, is not a ground for new trial, where the jury were instructed to disregard his remarks, and he did not press the argument further after he was interrupted. *Com.* v. *Poisson,* 157 Mass. 510, 32 N. E. 906.

Conviction will not be reversed because the district attorney repeatedly traveled out of the record in his argument to the jury, unless the remarks under the circumstances were obviously of a character to impair the defendant's rights and prejudice his case, unless a charge to disregard such remarks was requested, and an exception reserved to the refusal to give it. *Lancaster* v. *State,* 36 Tex. Crim. Rep. 16, 35 S. W. 165.

[3]*Long* v. *State,* 56 Ind. 182, 26 Am. Rep. 19; *State* v. *Balch,* 31 Kan. 465, 2 Pac. 609; *Angelo* v. *State,* 96 Ill. 209, 36 Am. Rep. 132. But *contra,* *Petite* v. *People,* 8 Colo. 518, 9 Pac. 622; *United States* v. *Snyder,* 14 Fed. 554.

[4]*Price* v. *Com.* 77 Va. 393; *Herndon* v. *State,* 111 Ga. 178, 36 S. E. 634.

The verdict in a criminal case will not be disturbed for remarks of the prosecuting attorney, not objected to at the time, where no exceptions were taken thereto, and no brief is filed for the appellant, the indictment was sufficient, the instructions exceedingly fair to the defendant, and the evidence, though conflicting, sufficient to sustain the conviction. *State* v. *Green,* 117 Mo. 298, 22 S. W. 952.

[5]*State* v. *Anderson,* 10 Or. 448.

18. Alluding to defendant's failure to examine a witness.

If defendant calls a witness, and fails to examine him, it is not improper for the prosecuting attorney to comment on such omission.[1]

[1]*State* v. *Jones,* 77 N. C. 520; *State* v. *Kiger,* 115 N. C. 746, 20 S. E. 456. But see *Blackman* v. *State,* 78 Ga. 592, 3 S. E. 418, where the defendant asked for a continuance before trial because of absence of material witnesses. The witnesses were sent for, but were not called on the trial. Prosecuting attorney commented on the failure to call them, as evidence of guilt; held reversible error. To similar effect, *State* v. *Baker,* 23 Or. 441, 32 Pac. 161.

It is error in a criminal trial to allow the solicitor general to argue that the failure of the counsel for the accused to examine witnesses offered by the prosecution concerning a fact which had been ruled inadmissible as not proper rebutting evidence, or to offer them as his own, is an admission of the truth of the fact. *Johnson* v. *State,* 88 Ga. 606, 15 S. E. 667.

19. — to the presumption from possession of stolen goods.

Commenting upon the presumption of guilt arising from the possession of recently stolen property is legitimate.[1]

[1] *McLain* v. *State,* 18 Neb. 154, 24 N. W. 720.

20. — to resistance or flight of codefendant.

It is proper to comment on the fact that when defendant was arrested a codefendant resisted and escaped.[1]

[1] *Cummins* v. *People,* 42 Mich. 142.

21. Intemperance of language.

Intemperance of speech by the prosecuting attorney, to constitute error, must be shown to have prejudiced the defendant.[1]

[1] *Atkins* v. *State,* 11 Tex. App. 8; *State* v. *Banks,* 10 Mo. App. 111; *Brown* v. *State,* 121 Ala. 9, 25 So. 744; *People* v. *McMahon,* 124 Cal. 435, 57 Pac. 224; *Bishop* v. *Com.* 22 Ky. L. Rep. 760, 58 S. W. 817; *State* v. *Edie,* 147 Mo. 535, 49 S. W. 563; *Martinez* v. *State* (Tex. Crim. App.) 57 S. W. 838; *Ross* v. *State,* 8 Wyo. 351, 57 Pac. 924; *Scott* v. *State,* 7 Lea, 232; *Baysinger* v. *People,* 115 Ill. 419, 5 N. E. 375; *Price* v. *Com.* 77 Va. 393; *Epp* v. *State,* 102 Ind. 539, 1 N. E. 491. And see, fully on this question, note to *People* v. *Fielding* (N. Y.) 46 L. R. A. 641.

The impropriety must be gross to warrant reversal. *Wilson* v. *People,* 94 Ill. 299. On sustaining conviction for murder, held that, in no event, where the judgment is clearly right, under the evidence, will a conviction be reversed for intemperance of speech of prosecuting attorney.

But in *Bessette* v. *State,* 101 Ind. 85, conviction was reversed on account of the prosecuting attorney commenting on the personal appearance of the accused.

In *Berry* v. *State* (Miss.) 22 So. 826, it was held that a conviction of rape should be reversed on appeal for a remark by the district attorney in his closing argument, that a negro had been found guilty of the same offense at the previous term, although he put up a far better defense than defendant, and that defendant's counsel assisted in the prosecution, and thought such negro was guilty, and that the supreme court thought so, too, where the evidence of defendant's guilt was exceedingly unsatisfactory, and one of the jurors acted also as juror on the trial of such negro.

22. Erroneous statement of testimony.

Misstatements of the testimony in summing up do not of themselves constitute error,[1] especially if promptly corrected by the court;[2] nor do illogical inferences from the facts in evidence.[3]

[1] *People* v. *Barnhart,* 59 Cal. 402.

[2] *People* v. *Lee Ah Yute,* 60 Cal. 95.

Where the state's counsel in his argument misquotes the evidence, and, on being corrected, insists that, though the letter of the evidence be against him, its meaning by fair inference is equivalent to what he has insisted upon as its letter, it is proper to leave the legitimacy of the inference to the jury, and to refuse to determine the case, with a statement by the court that counsel can argue any conclusion drawn by him from the testimony, but that in representing the testimony he must not misquote the witnesses. *Ramsey* v. *State*, 92 Ga. 53, 17 S. E. 613.

Shular v. *State*, 105 Ind. 289, 55 Am. Rep. 211, 4 N. E. 870.

The prosecuting attorney may comment upon the testimony, and draw such inferences and conclusions therefrom as his reason may dictate that the facts warrant, but if he makes a wrong deduction the court will, on request therefore, correct it by giving a proper instruction. *State* v. *Moore*, 32 Or. 65, 48 Pac. 468.

But that a district attorney, or private counsel assisting him, should not press upon the jury any deductions from the evidence that are not strictly legitimate, but should act impartially, see *Com.* v. *Nicely*, 130 Pa. 261, 18 Atl. 737; *Nalley* v. *State*, 28 Tex. App. 387, 13 S. W. 670.

XLII.—INSTRUCTING THE JURY.

I. The right.
1. Right of the accused.
2. Necessity for request.
3. Time to request.
4. Ruling on requests; generally.
5. — complex request.
6. — modifying, limiting, and qualifying requests.
7. Requiring charge to be in writing.
8. Presence of jury at discussion.
9. Reading from books.
10. Withdrawing evidence.
11. Taking exception.

II. Accomplice as witness.
12. Necessity of corroboration.
13. Mutual corroboration.
14. Who are accomplices.
15. Requisite cogency of evidence.

III. Accused as witness.
16. Interest as bearing on credibility.
17. Right of the accused to an instruction.
18. Omission to testify for himself.

IV. Admissions and affidavits.
19. Admissions by counsel.
20. Admission of truth of affidavit.
21. Rebutting.
22. Use of part of affidavit.

V. Alibi.
23. Burden and measure of proof.
24. Cautioning the jury.
25. Evidence as to time and place.
26. To be considered in connection with other evidence.

I. The right.

1. Right of the accused.

Except in those jurisdictions where the jury are judges of the law, as well as of the facts, the accused has a right, unless there be a statute to the contrary, to have the jury instructed as to the law of the case.[1]

[1] *People* v. *Gray*, 5 Wend. 289 (but holding that omission was not error when to have given instructions would have kept the jury over Sunday); *State* v. *Heacock*, 106 Iowa, 191, 76 N. W. 654, and cases cited; *State* v. *Stonum*, 62 Mo. 596; N. Y. Code Crim. Proc. § 388; *Smith* v. *State*, 75 Miss. 542, 23 So. 260; *State* v. *Fulford*, 124 N. C. 798, 32 S. E. 577; *Mitchell* v. *State*, 36 Tex. Crim. Rep. 278, 33 S. W. 367, 36 S. W. 456; *People* v. *Hampton*, 4 Utah, 258, 9 Pac. 508; *Costigan* v. *Com.* 11 Ky. L. Rep. 617, 12 S. W. 629; *Sledge* v. *State*, 99 Ga. 684, 26 S. E. 756.

The trial court is bound to give instructions, properly drawn, correct in point of law, and applicable to the evidence, in all cases, when requested by a party, except when the matter of the instruction requested is sufficiently covered by instructions already or thereafter given, or when the request for the instruction comes too late, or when the state of the evidence is such that there is no case to be submitted to the jury. 2 Thomp. Trials, 1703, § 2374. And see succeeding sections of this division.

In *Goldman* v. *State*, 75 Md. 621, 23 Atl. 1097, it was held that the court might in its discretion advise the jury as to the law and legal effect of the evidence, under Md. Const. art. 15, § 5, making the jury judges both of the law and the facts, but was not bound to do so.

In *Com.* v. *McManus*, 143 Pa. 64, 14 L. R. A. 89, 21 Atl. 1018, 22 Atl. 761, it is held that to an instruction asked by an accused, that the jury are the judges of the law, as well as of the facts, and may upon the whole case determine the grade of the offense, it is proper to add that the statement of law by the court is the best evidence of the law, and that, viewing it as evidence only, the jury are to be guided by what the court has said with reference to the law.

There is no inhibition against a judge charging the jury before the evidence is introduced, but his preliminary charge must be construed with reference to the testimony thereafter introduced, and as forming a part of the general charge. *State* v. *McGee*, 55 S. C. 247, 33 S. E. 353.

2. Necessity for request.

It is a very general rule of practice in criminal and civil causes alike,[1] as to submitting to the jury a particular point, or particularizing or making more definite the points submitted, that partial nondirection, or omission to charge as to a particular issue, or mere generalization, indefiniteness, ambiguousness, and the like do not of themselves constitute reversible error in the absence of a specific request for more specific and comprehensive instructions.[2]

[1]For a general treatment of this question, see Civil Trial Brief, 2d ed. 408 *et seq.*

[2]For some instances, see *People* v. *White*, 116 Cal. 17, 47 Pac. 771; *People* v. *Arnold*, 116 Cal. 682, 48 Pac. 803; *Miller* v. *People*, 23 Colo. 95, 46 Pac. 111; *McGee* v. *State*, 117 Ala. 229, 23 So. 797; *Carroll* v. *State*, 99 Ga. 36, 25 S. E. 680; *Crum* v. *State*, 148 Ind. 401, 47 N. E. 833; *People* v. *Carter*, 117 Mich. 576, 76 N. W. 90; *State* v. *Broadbent*, 19 Mont. 467, 48 Pac. 775; *Trujillo* v. *Territory*, 7 N. M. 43, 32 Pac. 154; *State* v. *Adams*, 115 N. C. 775, 20 S. E. 722; *State* v. *Kendall*, 54 S. C. 192, 32 S. E. 300; *Whiting* v. *Dugan* (Tex. Civ. App.) 39 S. W. 148; *Marshall* v. *State*, 37 Tex. Crim. Rep. 450, 36 S. W. 86.

3. Time to request.

The general rule that requests to charge should be presented before the judge has charged the jury does not impair the right of the accused to present, after the charge, and before the jury retire, special requests occasioned by what has been charged; or to present, after they have once retired, special requests occasioned by their asking further instructions before verdict.[1]

[1]*People* v. *Garbutt*, 17 Mich. 9, 97 Am. Dec. 162, holding as above.

But *Venable* v. *State*, 1 Ohio C. D. 301, holds that a special charge applicable to the case on trial, and stating the law correctly, cannot be properly refused by the court because asked for by the defendants after the argument and general charge to the jury. See also *Chapman* v. *McCormick*, 86 N. Y. 479.

But *State* v. *Catlin*, 3 Vt. 530, 23 Am. Dec. 230, holds that if the judge is not reminded of his omission to charge upon a particular point before verdict returned, it is not error for him to refuse to charge on such point.

And *State* v. *Barbee*, 92 N. C. 820, holds that it is the defendant only, before the case is given to the jury, that has the right to ask for special instructions. See also 2 Thomp. Tr. 1715.

If the indictment contains several counts stating separate offenses, the court may, even at the close of the evidence, be asked to direct the jury to confine their verdict to one or the other. *People* v. *Dunn*, 90 N. Y. 104, 108, holding, however, that it was not error to refuse to charge that if they believed defendant guilty, and were in doubt as to which count, they should find him guilty of the lesser offense.

According to *Engeman* v. *State*, 54 N. J. L. 247, 23 Atl. 676, it is within the judicial discretion of the trial court to settle the time when requests to charge the jury shall be made.

4. Ruling on requests; generally.

The court may reject a requested instruction which does not find support in the evidence,[1] or which is not correct,[2] even though modification or explanation would remove the defects, and make it applicable to the case.[3]

So, too, as a general rule, the court is not obliged to give requested instructions in the language precisely as framed and submitted, however correct they may be; but he may, in lieu thereof, give instructions prepared by himself, covering, as he views the case, all the questions of law presented upon which it is necessary and advisable to instruct the jury,[4] unless it is otherwise expressly provided by statute.[5]

But it is error to reject instructions sound in law, and applicable to the evidence,[6] unless in lieu thereof other correct instructions so prepared by the court are given,[7] or unless the principles urged are substantially embodied in the court's charge already given.[8]

[1] *Rogers* v. *State*, 117 Ala. 9, 22 So. 666; *Bugg* v. *Com.* 18 Ky. L. Rep. 844, 38 S. W. 684; *Thalheim* v. *State*, 38 Fla. 169, 20 So. 938; *Smith* v. *State* (Tex. Crim. App.) 43 S. W. 794.

An instruction asked upon only a part of the evidence is properly refused. *Com.* v. *Cosseboom*, 155 Mass. 298, 29 N. E. 463.

[2] *Pool* v. *State*, 87 Ga. 526, 13 S. E. 556; *North Chicago Street R. Co.* v. *Williams*, 140 Ill. 275, 29 N. E. 672; *Carrall* v. *State*, 53 Neb. 431, 73 N. W. 939.

So, a requested instruction which ignores evidence is properly refused. *Compton* v. *State*, 110 Ala. 24, 20 So. 119.

So also is an unintelligible instruction. *People* v. *Vereneseneckockockhoff*, 129 Cal. 497, 58 Pac. 156, 62 Pac. 111.

And a requested instruction which omits a statutory qualification is properly refused. *Lyons* v. *People*, 137 Ill. 602, 27 N. E. 677.

Where one accused of a criminal offense requests an improper instruction upon his character, it is not error for the court to neglect to give any instruction upon that subject. *State* v. *McNamara*, 100 Mo. 100, 13 S. W. 938.

It is not error for the court to state that a request by defendant in a murder trial is involved, and that he does not understand it, and, upon the request being stated in different language, to charge as requested. *People* v. *Fitzthum*, 137 N. Y. 581, 33 N. E. 322.

[a]*Musgrove* v. *State*, 133 Ind. 297, 32 N. E. 885; *State* v. *Kelly*, 50 La. Ann. 597, 23 So. 543.

Requested instructions which need restriction, qualification, or modification should be refused; but, if they are given, the court should not subsequently lessen their force and effect by restrictions, qualifications, or modifications. *Burton* v. *State*, 115 Ala. 1, 22 So. 585. See also *State* v. *Caddle*, 35 W. Va. 73, 12 S. E. 1098, holding that the trial court is not bound to take each improper instruction asked, and remodel it so as to make it good law.

In *Com.* v. *Trimble*, 150 Mass. 89, 22 N. E. 439, a prosecution for keeping a liquor nuisance, it was held proper to refuse an instruction as to the meaning of the words "an intoxicated person," in Mass. Pub. Stat. chap. 100, § 9, cl. 4, by referring to similar language in chap. 207, § 25, providing for the punishment of persons "found in a state of intoxication," because the latter language needed interpretation equally with the former.

[b]*People* v. *Swartz*, 118 Mich. 292, 76 N. W. 491; *People* v. *Chadwick*, 7 Utah, 134, 25 Pac. 737; *Com.* v. *McManus*, 143 Pa. 64, 14 L. R. A. 89, 21 Atl. 1018, 22 Atl. 761. But see *State* v. *Allen*, 45 W. Va. 65, 30 S. E. 209, holding that a party has a right to have his instructions given in his own language, if there are facts in evidence to support them, and they contain a correct statement of the law, and are not vague, irrelevant, obscure, ambiguous, or calculated to mislead.

It is immaterial whether the instructions given in a criminal trial, if proper in themselves, are prepared and asked by the respective counsel, or prepared by the court, and given of its own motion. *State* v. *Rufus*, 149 Mo. 406, 51 S. W. 80.

And *State* v. *Beard*, 124 N. C. 811, 32 S. E. 804, holds that the manner in which the law of the case shall be stated to the jury and applied to the facts is left, to a very great extent, to the good sense and sound judgment of the judge who tries the case.

The giving of an instruction asked, in different language from that used in the request, is not error if the instruction given is substantially correct. *Com.* v. *Farrell*, 160 Mass. 525, 36 N. E. 475.

According to *State* v. *Luke*, 104 Mo. 563, 16 S. W. 242, it is the duty of the court, if it is dissatisfied with instructions asked, and believes them calculated to confuse the jury, to refuse them, and give an appropriate instruction upon the issue of fact involved. To same effect, see *State*

v. *Patrick*, 107 Mo. 147, 17 S. W. 666; *State* v. *Young* 99 Mo. 666, 12 S. W. 879.

Thus, in Alabama written requests to charge must be d spɔsed of in the exact form presented by counsel, under Code, § 2756. *Hooper* v. *State*, 106 Ala. 41, 17 So. 679.

And a request for a charge in a criminal case, preferred in writing, as provided by Ala. Code 1896, § 3328, cannot be properly refused on the ground that it has been given in the general written charge of the court, under § 3327, in view of the provision of § 3328, that requested charges which are given shall be taken by the jury upon retiring to consider their verdict. *Orr* v. *State*, 117 Ala. 69, 23 So. 696.

People v. *Strybe* (Cal.) 36 Pac. 3; *Crawford* v. *State* (Tex. Crim. App.) 34 S. W. 927; *Brooks* v. *State*, 96 Ga. 353, 23 S. E. 413; *State* v. *Thompson*, 45 La. Ann. 969, 13 So. 392; *People* v. *Seaman*, 107 Mich. 348, 65 N. W. 203.

The court cannot properly withhold instructions demanded by the evidence in a criminal case, because of the unreasonableness and inconsistency of the testimony on which the requests are based. *Hayes* v. *State* (Tex. Crim. App.) 39 S. W. 106.

Requested instructions which are pertinent and clear should be given, and others of a more general nature should not be substituted therefor. *State* v. *McCann*, 16 Wash, 249, 271, 47 Pac. 443, 49 Pac. 216.

People v. *Lemperle*, 94 Cal. 45, 29 Pac. 709; *State* v. *Stout*, 49 Ohio St. 270, 30 N. E. 437; *State* v. *Robinson*, 35 S. C. 340, 14 S. E. 766; *State* v. *Freidrich*, 4 Wash. 204, 29 Pac. 1055, 31 Pac. 332; *Lee* v. *State*, 56 Ark. 4, 19 S. W. 16; *Territory* v. *Lermo*, 8 N. M. 566, 46 Pac. 16.

Where the trial court throws aside all instructions requested, and prepares written instructions of its own, they must fairly instruct the jury on all legal questions involved in the case, and it must appear that no injury is done to the defeated party by the refusal of his requests. *Wacaser* v. *People*, 134 Ill. 438, 25 N. E. 564.

In *People* v. *Johnson*, 139 N. Y. 358, 34 N. E. 920, it is held that a request in a murder trial to charge that if the jury believe that after the defendant was struck upon the head with a club, by a person assaulted by him immediately before the commission of the crime charged, he was dazed, or his mind became in such a condition that he did not realize what he did after that, that he was not responsible for his acts, and that they must acquit him,—is substantially complied with by a charge to the effect that if the jury come to the conclusion that the blow affected the defendant's mind so that he did not know the nature of the act which he was doing, he is not guilty.

That refusal of the court to give a requested charge is not error where it has been substantially embodied in a preceding instruction already given, see *Ross* v. *State*, 8 Wyo. 351, 57 Pac. 924; *Miller* v. *State*, 29 Neb. 437, 45 N. W. 451; *Waters* v. *State*, 117 Ala. 108, 22 So. 490; *People* v. *Schmitt*, 106 Cal. 48, 39 Pac. 204; *State* v. *LaGrange*, 94 Iowa, 60, 62 N. W. 664; *State* v. *Booker*, 123 N. C. 713, 31 S. E. 376; *Battle* v. *State*, 105 Ga. 703, 32 S. E. 160; *Com.* v. *Magoon*, 172 Mass. 214, 51

N. E. 1082; *State* v. *Burlingame*, 146 Mo. 207, 48 S. W. 72; *State* v. *Bowser*, 21 Mont. 133, 53 Pac. 179; *Hite* v. *Com.* 96 Va. 489, 31 S. E. 895; *Jackson* v. *Com.* 17 Ky. L. Rep. 1197, 34 S. W. 14; *Brown* v. *State*, 62 N. J. L. 666, 42 Atl. 811; *People* v. *Hannigan*, 42 App. Div. 617, 58 N. Y. Supp. 703; *Johnson* v. *State*, 100 Tenn. 254, 45 S. W. 436; *State* v. *Bingham*, 42 W. Va. 234, 24 S. E. 883; *Fielder* v. *State* (Tex. Crim. App.) 49 S. W. 378.

But the refusal of an appropriate instruction is not justified in a close case, because covered by other instructions which were given, where it applies the correct legal doctrine directly and more clearly to the particular circumstances of the case. *Adams* v. *People*, 179 Ill. 633, 54 N. E. 296.

In *People* v. *Barthleman*, 120 Cal. 7, 52 Pac. 112, it was held that a statement that the court refused certain instructions asked by one of the parties because they had been given in other instructions was unnecessary in a criminal action, under Cal. Pen. Code, § 1137, providing that the jury can take into their room only the instructions which have been given.

As to marking requested instructions "given" or "refused," as required by statute, see Civil Trial Brief, 2d ed. 418 *et seq.*

5. — complex request.

When instructions are asked in the aggregate, or propositions are presented as one request, the whole may properly be rejected by the court, if there is anything objectionable in either of them.[1]

[1]*Pearce* v. *State*, 115 Ala. 115, 22 So. 502; *Oliver* v. *State*, 38 Fla. 46, 20 So. 803; *Kelly* v. *State*, 51 Neb. 572, 71 N. W. 299; *United States* v. *Musser*, 4 Utah, 153, 7 Pac. 389.

6. — modifying, limiting, and qualifying requests.

The court has power to modify, limit, and qualify a request to charge, so as to obviate objections raised, and conform the instruction to its own view of the law;[1] but it cannot be demanded, as matter of right, that the court do this, for the court may, if it is considered desirable, reject the requested instruction.[2] But the qualification of an instruction asked is error, if thereby the force of the instruction is essentially changed,[3] or if there is no evidence in the case upon which to base the qualification.[4]

[1]*People* v. *Sherman* (Cal.) 32 Pac. 879; *Benmengfield* v. *Com.* 15 Ky. L. Rep. 321, 22 S. W. 1020; *Smith* v. *State*, 75 Miss. 542, 23 So. 260; *Strother* v. *State*, 74 Miss. 447, 21 So. 147; *Lawhead* v. *State*, 46 Neb. 607, 65 N. W. 779; *State* v. *Rollins*, 113 N. C. 722, 18 S. E. 394; *State* v. *Workman*, 39 S. C. 151, 17 S. E. 694.

Where the force of an instruction which is requested and is proper in itself is not changed by an addition made to it by the court, there is no error in the mere fact of making the addition. *Wilson* v. *State,* 30 Fla. 234, 17 L. R. A. 654, 11 So. 556.

So, the court properly modifies a requested instruction that the verbal admissions of a party should be received with "great caution," by striking out the word "great," as Cal. Code Civ. Proc. § 2061, authorizing an instruction on that subject, does not use such word. *People* v. *Van Horn,* 119 Cal. 323, 51 Pac. 538.

And the court, in giving a requested instruction upon the necessity of the establishment beyond a reasonable doubt of each essential and independent fact in a series of facts relied upon to convict an accused, may omit a portion thereof which is calculated to confuse the minds of the jury, although not actually in conflict with the other portions, and not enunciating a wrong principle. *People* v. *Smith,* 106 Cal. 73, 39 Pac. 40.

A request for an instruction as to a rule of law should, if granted, be accompanied with such comments as will enable the jury to apply the rule to the facts which are claimed to be proved in the case. *State* v. *Duffy,* 66 Conn. 551, 34 Atl. 497.

And that a requested charge which is erroneous may be explained by the court after it is given, see *Williams* v. *State,* 113 Ala. 58, 21 So. 463.

That a court has as much right to limit requests for instructions to a proper number as to limit argument within proper limits, and should do so with proper caution to avoid injustice, see *Mabry* v. *State,* 71 Miss. 716, 14 So. 267.

[2]See *supra,* § 4, note 3.

[3]So held in *Young* v. *State*, 24 Fla. 147, 3 So. 881, unless the instruction is not pertinent, or unless the charge merely states the law to cover the case more fully.

According to *Owen* v. *State*, 89 Tenn. 704, 16 S. W. 115, where the charge given is incomplete or not sufficiently full, and accused is entitled to have added, as written, a proper, clear, and concise addition and explanation of the charge given, it is error to give to the jury what the court considers to be its meaning or substance when "boiled down."

[4]*Bennyfield* v. *Com.* 13 Ky. L. Rep. 446, 17 S. W. 271; *Castro* v. *State* (Tex. Crim. App.) 40 S. W. 985.

Thus, it is improper to add to an instruction for defendant, that he was justified in shooting to save his own life, the restriction "in case he was on the plantation road, and had a right to be there," where the evidence tends to show that the difficulty between defendant and deceased began on a plantation road on the place where they both resided, and that after they had left the road it became necessary for the defendant to shoot deceased in self-defense. *Maiden* v. *State* (Miss.) 11 So. 488.

And it is error for the court to eliminate from a requested instruction in a prosecution for seduction requiring an acquittal if the prosecutrix was prompted by lust or fear, the concluding portion that she must have relied on a promise of marriage, and on that alone, where there is evidence that she was influenced partly at least by fear or lust. *Barnes* v. *State,* 37 Tex. Crim. Rep. 320, 39 S. W. 684.

7. Requiring charge to be in writing.

In many of the states statutes or constitutional provisions make it the duty of the court to reduce to writing the charge or general instructions to the jury,[1] if requested by the prosecuting officer or the prisoner;[2] and when so required to be in writing, oral instructions are generally held to be fatal to a conviction,[3] unless the defendant consents to their being given orally.[4]

[1] Thus, in Wisconsin the judge must, before giving the same to the jury, reduce to writing and give as written his charge and instructions to the jury, unless a written charge be waived by counsel at the commencement of the trial, and except that the charge or instruction may be given orally if taken down by the official stenographer. Sanborn & Berryman, Anno. Stat. (Wis.) 1898, § 2853.

Under the Tennessee statute (Shannon's Code, § 7187) directing that the judge reduce his decision on tendered propositions to writing, he is not required to read to the jury any propositions to which he does not assent. *Foutch* v. *State,* 100 Tenn. 334, 45 S. W. 678.

[2] For instances, see Mills's (Colo.) Anno. Stat. § 1468, as applied in *Bradford* v. *People,* 22 Colo, 157, 43 Pac. 1013.

In Florida the judge may charge orally in trials for offenses not punishable capitally, if he is not requested by the state or the prisoner before the close of the evidence to charge in writing. *Luster* v. *State,* 23 Fla. 339, 2 So. 690.

[3] *People* v. *Max,* 45 Cal. 254; *Stewart* v. *State,* 50 Miss. 587; *Ehrlich* v. *State,* 44 Neb. 810, 63 N. W. 35; *Territory* v. *Lopez,* 3 N. M. 156, 2 Pac. 364; *Harkey* v. *State,* 33 Tex. Crim. Rep. 100, 25 S. W. 291; *Territory* v. *Kennedy,* 1 Ariz. 505, 25 Pac. 517; *Leonardo* v. *Territory,* 1 N. M. 291. And see Civil Trial Brief, 2d ed. 420 *et seq.*

[4] *People* v. *Kearney,* 43 Cal. 383.

For statements of the rules as to instructions with reference to the style, clearness, definiteness, and the like, which are applicable equally to civil and criminal causes, see Civil Trial Brief, 2d ed. 425–433.

8. Presence of jury at discussion.

The judge may in his discretion require the jury to retire during the argument of instructions.[1]

[1] *Casey* v. *State,* 37 Ark. 67.

9. Reading from books.

The reading of text-books and reports to the jury, and charging extracts therefrom as part of the law applicable to the case,[1] or the refusal[2] to do so, is discretionary.

What is read is subject to the same rules as any other part of the charge.

[1]*State* v. *Baldwin*, 36 Kan. 1, 12 Pac. 318; *People* v. *Niles*, 44 Mich. 606, 7 N. W. 192. Subject of course to such qualification as any statute requiring instructions to be drawn up in writing may add.

People v. *Minnaugh*, 131 N. Y. 563, 29 N. E. 750, holds that it is no ground for exception that the trial judge, in stating the law on a certain subject, did so by reading the doctrine to the jury from a reported case, if the doctrine as read was sound and applicable to the facts.

[2]*Houser* v. *State*, 58 Ga. 78.

But instructions taken from the reports of states having statutes dissimilar to those of the state where a criminal trial is had should not be given. *Ritchey* v. *People*, 23 Colo. 314, 47 Pac. 272, 384.

In *People* v. *Wessel*, 98 Cal. 352, 33 Pac. 216, a prosecution for rape, in which the principal testimony was that of the prosecutrix, who was an infant, it was held that defendant had no right under Cal. Const. art. 6, § 19, to have long statements from a text-book, as to the testimony of children, given as an instruction.

10. Withdrawing evidence.

It is not too late after argument is closed, for the party who has given improper evidence to call upon the judge to charge the jury that it was illegally admitted, and should be disregarded by them.[1]

The court may properly refuse an instruction withdrawing from the consideration of the jury evidence which tends to prove an irrelevant and immaterial fact, as well as one material and relevant; but it should not refuse an instruction, properly framed, limiting the consideration of such evidence by the jury to its legitimate purpose.[2]

[1]2 Thomp. Trials, 1711, § 2354, disapproving *Harrison* v. *Young*, 9 Ga. 359, 366. But whether such instruction will cure the error is another question.

[2]*Roberson* v. *State*, 40 Fla. 509, 24 So. 474.

11. Taking exception.

It is too late to except to the charge after the jury have retired.[1]

But it is within the discretion of the court to correct an error, and therefore to allow an exception to refusal, at any time when not too late to recall the jury for further instructions.[2]

[1]*Moett* v. *People*, 85 N. Y. 373, and cases cited; *People* v. *Bragle*, 88 N. Y.

585, 42 Am. Rep. 269, Overruling 10 Abb. N. C. 300; *Morrison* v. *State* (Fla.) 28 So. 97; *Magee* v. *State* (Tex. Crim. App.) 43 S. W. 98, 512. And see Civil Trial Brief, 2d ed. 272.

And exceptions to the refusal of instructions are too late under the New Hampshire court rule 54, when taken after the return of the verdict. *State* v. *Gale*, 69 N. H. 667, 39 Atl. 975.

But *State* v. *Pirlot*, 20 R. I. 273, 38 Atl. 656, holds that a defendant is entitled to except to an instruction allowed after the jury have retired, when he had no opportunity to except before their retirement.

[3]*People* v. *Hovey*, 92 N. Y. 554, Affirming 29 Hun, 382.

II. Accomplice as witness.

12. Necessity of corroboration.

The accused against whom the testimony of an accomplice has been received has a right to have the jury instructed that a conviction cannot be had[1] on the testimony of an accomplice alone,[2] but that there must be other evidence tending to connect the accused with the crime[3] so that his conviction will not rest entirely upon the testimony of the accomplice.[4]

[1]An instruction that the jury "ought not" to convict on the uncorroborated testimony of an accomplice is a sufficient direction to them "not to convict" on such testimony. *State* v. *Nelson*, 59 Kan. 776, 52 Pac. 868.

[2]The use of the words "only" and "alone" in charging a jury in a criminal case that a conviction cannot be had upon the testimony of an accomplice, unless corroborated by other evidence, as provided by Iowa Code 1893, § 4559, is not erroneous, since such words are implied in the statute itself. *State* v. *Smith*, 106 Iowa, 701, 77 N. W. 499.

[3]N. Y. Code Crim. Proc. § 399. See also 10 Crim. L. Mag. 172.

An instruction in the language of the Arkansas statute, that a conviction cannot be had in any case of felony on the testimony of an accomplice, unless corroborated by other evidence tending to connect defendant with the commission of the offense; and that the corroboration is not sufficient if it merely shows that the offense was committed and the circumstances thereof, although correct, is properly refused, where an instruction has been given that the testimony of the accomplice must be corroborated by other testimony tending to connect defendant with the commission of the crime, and that it is not necessary that such evidence be corroborated on "every point on which the accomplice has testified;" but that if the jury believe that he is corroborated as to the commission of the crime, and on any point tending to connect defendant with the crime, and the evidence with such corroboration is sufficient to satisfy their minds beyond a reasonable doubt that defendant is guilty, they will be authorized so to find. *Kent* v. *State*, 64 Ark. 247, 41 S. W. 849.

In *People* v. *Compton*, 123 Cal. 403, 56 Pac. 44, an instruction that a conviction may be had on the testimony of an accomplice, if the corroborative evidence tends "in any way" to connect defendant with the commission of the crime, is held erroneous, as the corroborative evidence, to be sufficient, must tend to show this connection when standing alone, without the aid of the testimony of the accomplice.

And in *People* v. *Lynch*, 122 Cal. 501, 55 Pac. 248, it was held that an instruction on a criminal trial that if the jury believe that an accomplice has testified, and believe beyond a reasonable doubt, from his testimony, that defendant is guilty as charged, and then, in connection therewith, believe from the evidence, outside of that which tends to connect defendant with the commission of the offense, other than shown in the commission itself and the circumstances thereof, they must find defendant guilty,—does not sufficiently point out the rule that a conviction cannot be had on the uncorroborated evidence of an accomplice, or show the degree of proof which is sufficient as corroborative of that of the accomplice.

In Iowa the statute (Code 1873, § 4559) is to the effect that a conviction cannot be had upon the testimony of an accomplice, unless he is corroborated by other evidence tending to connect defendant with the crime charged, and the "corroboration is not sufficient if it merely show the commission of the offense or the circumstances thereof;" and the omission of all reference to "the circumstances" in a charge embodying this statute renders it erroneous. *State* v. *Smith,* 102 Iowa, 656, 72 N. W. 279.

But the omission of the word "the," immediately before the words "circumstances thereof," is not bad on the ground that such omission implies that less than all the circumstances would not be sufficient corroboration. *State* v. *Russell,* 90 Iowa, 493, 58 N. W. 890.

And an instruction in a murder trial that a conviction cannot be had on the uncorroborated testimony of an accomplice is not erroneous in not specifying in what particular the evidence of such accomplice must be corroborated. *State* v. *Jackson,* 103 Iowa, 702, 73 N. W. 467.

A charge on accomplice's testimony need not state that corroborative testimony must tend directly and immediately to connect defendant with the commission of the crime, where the evidence outside the accomplice's testimony is sufficient of itself to sustain the conviction. *West* v. *State* (Tex. Crim. App.) 33 S. W. 227.

But an instruction that if the state relies for a conviction upon the testimony of a witness for defendant, the jury must require corroboration before they are authorized to convict, is misleading, where they are not told that the same rule does not apply to the witness where her testimony is in favor of defendant. *Josef* v. *State,* 34 Tex. Crim. Rep. 446, 30 S. W. 1067, Reversed on rehearing, 29 S. W. 774.

[4]*People* v. *Everhardt,* 104 N. Y. 591, 11 N. E. 62, Affirming 5 N. Y. Crim. Rep. 91; *Territory* v. *Neligh* (Ariz.) 10 Pac. 367; *Lumpkin* v. *State,* 68 Ala. 56. *Contra, State* v. *Jones,* 64 Mo. 391; *Bacon* v. *State,* 22 Fla. 51; *People* v. *O'Brien,* 60 Mich. 8, 26 N. W. 795. And see *State* v. *Donnelly,* 130 Mo. 642, 32 S. W. 1124; *State* v. *Sprague,* 149 Mo. 409, 50 S. W. 901.

According to *Com.* v. *Wilson,* 152 Mass. 12, 25 N. E. 16, it is a general rule of practice in Massachusetts to advise the jury not to convict upon the uncorroborated testimony of an accomplice, but it is not a rule of law; and it is not error in law for the judge to refuse so to advise the jury. See also *Com.* v. *Bishop,* 165 Mass. 148, 42 N. E. 560; *Com.* v. *Clune,* 162 Mass. 206, 38 N. E. 435.

13. Mutual corroboration.

Two or more accomplices cannot corroborate each other within the rule; but each requires the same corroboration as if there were but one.[1]

[1]*United States* v. *Hinz,* 35 Fed. 272, with note; *State* v. *Williamson,* 42 Conn. 261.

And it is error to charge that a certain witness is an accomplice, and that a conviction may be had on his testimony if properly corroborated by other evidence, without charging that one accomplice cannot corroborate another, where the only corroborative evidence upon which a conviction could properly be based in the testimony of one who, according to the accomplice's testimony, was also an accomplice. *McConnell* v. *State* (Tex. App.) 18 S. W. 645.

But a charge which states in effect, although not in distinct terms, that one accomplice cannot corroborate another, is correct. *Stevens* v. *State* (Tex. Crim. App.) 49 S. W. 105.

14. Who are accomplices.

To constitute one an accomplice he must have participated in the criminal intent.[1]

A person who co-operates with the accused in the commission of an offense, for the sole purpose of securing evidence against him, is not an accomplice.[2]

[1]*State* v. *McKean,* 36 Iowa, 343, 14 Am. Rep. 530.

Thus, where, in a prosecution for burglary, prosecutor testified that he took defendant to his place of business, and there stated to him that if he would bring back the goods, he would let him go, but if he did not, he would hand him over to the sheriff; that defendant was then told what had been stolen, and said he would go and bring back all he had, and did return the goods,—failure of the court to charge that the prosecutor was an accomplice, and as to the law relative to an accomplice's testimony, was error. *Campbell* v. *State* (Tex. Crim. App.) 57 S. W. 288.

So, in *Lattimore* v. *State* (Tex. Crim. App.) 57 S. W. 644, a trial for forgery, one of the witnesses for the state testified that at the instance of defendant he paid the note alleged to have been forged, cut off the alleged forged signatures and gave them to the parties whose signatures they purported to be, with the request that they say nothing about the matter, nor report it, and that he did not say anything to the grand jury because he did not want defendant disturbed while in his employ.

And it was held that the court should have instructed the jury either that the witness was an accomplice, or have defined "accomplices," and charged them that if they believed the witness an accomplice, then his uncorroborated evidence was not sufficient to convict.

But in *People* v. *Noelke*, 94 N. Y. 137, 46 Am. Rep. 128, a prosecution for the sale of lottery tickets, the principal witness for the People, a detective, having purchased tickets from defendant, it was held that he was not an accomplice, "since he purchased the tickets to detect and punish a crime, and not with intent to aid in committing one." See same case reported below, 29 Hun, 461, 466, for fuller discussion of same question.

In *Wright* v. *State*, 7 Tex. App. 575, 32 Am. Rep. 599, the witness had associated himself with a band of horse thieves for the purpose of convicting them. It was held that if he had co-operated with defendant with criminal intent he was an accomplice, but if for the sole purpose of detecting crime he was not.

Keith v. *State*, 38 Tex. Crim. Rep. 678, 44 S. W. 847, holds that an instruction on the law of accomplices is not required on a trial for giving away whisky on election day, because the party to whom the whisky was given testified, as he is not an accomplice.

And *Bolton* v. *State* (Tex. Crim. App.) 43 S. W. 984, holds that an instruction in regard to the distinction between an accomplice and a principal is not required, on a prosecution for selling intoxicating liquors, against the owner of the liquors sold, because the sale was made by an employee when defendant was not present, as all are principals in cases of misdemeanor.

In *Parker* v. *State*, 40 Tex. Crim. Rep. 119, 49 S. W. 80, it was held that a charge on accomplice testimony and the necessity of its corroboration need not be given in respect to the testimony of a fellow prisoner to whom the defendant confessed that he had committed the murder for the purpose of robbery, and told him where he had concealed the money taken, when he did not agree to do any act in reference to it, and no money was found at the place indicated.

[s]*St. Charles* v. *O'Mailey*, 18 Ill. 407, 412; *Reg.* v. *Mullins*, 3 Cox C. C. 526, 531. And in *State* v. *McAfee*, 148 Mo. 370, 50 S. W. 82, it is held that the precautionary instruction applicable to accomplice testimony is not necessary with reference to the testimony of a witness who testifies that he pretended simply to engage with defendant in a robbery, for the purpose of betraying him to the officers, and the defendant denies that the occurrence in question took place.

Thus one who buys stolen goods from the thief, under advice of an officer, for the purpose of detecting the thief, is not an accomplice. *People* v. *Barric*, 49 Cal. 342. And a detective who gains the confidence of defendant charged with having counterfeit coin, by professing himself one of the brotherhood and purchasing counterfeits from him, is at most but a feigned accomplice. *People* v. *Farrell*, 30 Cal. 316.

In *Campbell* v. *Com.* 84 Pa. 187, 197 (murder), defendant was a member of the so-called "Mollie Maguires." A detective entered the organization for the purpose of bringing criminals to justice, and aided and advised those who were about to commit crimes. And it was held that he was not an accomplice.

A woman who submits to a criminal abortion is not an accomplice; she is guilty of a distinctly different crime. *People* v. *Vedder,* 98 N. Y. 630; *Com.* v. *Boynton,* 116 Mass. 343; *Watson* v. *State,* 9 Tex. App. 237.

Nor is the receiver of stolen goods an accomplice, in a case of burglarious larceny. *State* v. *Hayden,* 45 Iowa, 11.

So, where the law forbids the sale of certain articles, a purchaser is not an accomplice. *Onondaga Excise Comrs.* v. *Backus,* 29 How. Pr. 33.

In *Com.* v. *Downing,* 4 Gray, 29, a prosecution for selling liquor in violation of law, the sole witness purchased of defendant; and it was held that he was not an accomplice. See also *Com.* v. *Willard,* 22 Pick. 476, holding that where the legislature forbids the selling, but is silent as to buying, the latter is not a crime, nor the buyer an accomplice.

And *Harrington* v. *State,* 36 Ala. 236, a prosecution for selling liquor to a slave, holds that neither the purchaser nor one participating in the purchase can be deemed the accomplice of the seller.

15. Requisite cogency of evidence.

In determining whether a witness is an accomplice, as needing corroboration, the jury may regard him as an accomplice without proof beyond a reasonable doubt.[1]

The corroborative evidence need not of itself be sufficient to show the commission of the crime, nor connect the defendant with it; nor need it be wholly inconsistent with the theory of the defendant's innocence. It is enough if it tends to connect the defendant with the commission of the crime.[2]

The sufficiency of the corroboration is a question for the jury.[3]

[1] *Com.* v. *Ford,* 111 Mass. 394, holding it reversible error to instruct the jury that a certain witness was not to be regarded as an accomplice unless he was "an admitted accomplice, or proved to be so beyond a reasonable doubt." The court said that it was a question for the jury, and also added that "whatever tends to show that he is in any way implicated may be considered by the jury in determining what credit they will give to his testimony, even if it does not show that he was strictly an accomplice."

[2] *People* v. *Elliott,* 106 N. Y. 288, 12 N. E. 602, Reversing 5 N. Y. Crim. Rep. 204; *Lumpkin* v. *State,* 68 Ala. 56; *State* v. *Hill,* 91 Mo. 423, 4 S. W. 121.

[3] *Com.* v. *Holmes,* 127 Mass. 424, 34 Am. Rep. 391; *People* v. *Everhardt,* 104 N. Y. 591, 11 N. E. 62, Affirming 5 N. Y. Crim. Rep. 91.

But whether the evidence is sufficient to go to the jury is a question for the court. See *ante,* Division XL.

III. Accused as witness.

16. Interest as bearing on credibility.

Where the accused has testified in his own behalf, it is proper to instruct the jury that, while the defendant's testimony is to be considered as that of any other witness, yet they should, in determining his credibility, consider the fact that he stands charged with a criminal offense, and is therefore an interested party.[1]

[1] *People* v. *Crowley*, 102 N. Y. 234, 6 N. E. 384; *Anderson* v. *State*, 104 Ind. 467, 4 N. E. 63; *Hamilton* v. *State*, 62 Ark. 543, 36 S. W. 1054; *People* v. *Herrick*, 59 Mich. 563, 26 N. W. 767; *Norris* v. *State*, 87 Ala. 85, 6 So. 371; *People* v. *Callaghan*, 4 Utah, 49, 6 Pac. 49; *People* v. *Hitchcock*, 104 Cal. 482, 38 Pac. 198; *State* v. *Fiske*, 63 Conn. 388, 28 Atl. 572; *Siebert* v. *People*, 143 Ill. 571, 32 N. E. 431; *State* v. *Young*, 104 Iowa, 730, 74 N. W. 693; *State* v. *Wiggins*, 50 La. Ann. 330, 23 So. 334, and cases cited; *People* v. *Resh*, 107 Mich. 251, 65 N. W. 99; *State* v. *Summar*, 143 Mo. 220, 45 S. W. 254; *Dixon* v. *State*, 46 Neb. 298, 64 N. W. 961; *Faulkner* v. *Territory*, 6 N. M. 464, 30 Pac. 905; *Gatliff* v. *Territory*, 2 Okla. 523, 37 Pac. 809; *State* v. *Nordstrom*, 7 Wash. 506, 35 Pac. 382; *Emery* v. *State*, 101 Wis. 627, 78 N. W. 145. To the same effect, see *People* v. *Cronin*, 34 Cal. 191; *People* v. *Rodundo*, 44 Cal. 538; *Minich* v. *People*, 8 Colo. 440, 9 Pac. 4; *Chambers* v. *People*, 105 Ill. 409; *Bressler* v. *People*, 117 Ill. 422, 8 N. E. 62; *State* v. *Moelchen*, 53 Iowa, 310, 5 N. W. 186; *People* v. *Calvin*, 60 Mich. 113, 26 N. W. 851; *State* v. *McGinnis*, 76 Mo. 326; *State* v. *Sanders*, 76 Mo. 35; *State* v. *Slingerland*, 19 Nev. 135, 7 Pac. 280; People v. Petmecky, 99 N. Y. 415, 2 N. E. 145 (holding it not error to charge that the interest he has in the issue is never to be excluded from the minds of the jury). For other cases, see 10 Crim. L. Mag. 193. They should not be given to understand that, as matter of law, they must weigh his interest against his credibility.

And according to *Com.* v. *Orr*, 138 Pa. 276, 20 Atl. 866, it is not only proper, but the duty of the court, to call the attention of the jury to the interest of defendant as affecting the question of his credibility as a witness.

There is no presumption on the subject, as matter of law, and the jury are properly instructed to allow the testimony of the accused such weight as in their judgment it ought to have. *Com.* v. *Wright*, 107 Mass. 403, holding it no error so to charge.

For a strong remonstrance against weighing the mere existence of motive to falsify against credibility, see *Wood* v. *State*, 48 Ga. 192, 292; *Berckmans* v. *Berckmans*, 17 N. J. Eq. 454, Affirming 16 N. J. Eq. 122. See also *State* v. *Johnson*, 16 Nev. 36; *Bird* v. *State*, 107 Ind. 154, 8 N. E. 14; *Veatch* v. *State*, 56 Ind. 586, 26 Am. Rep. 44; *Buckley* v. *State*, 62 Miss. 705.

In *Kirkham* v. *People*, 170 Ill. 9, 48 N. E. 465, it is held that an instruction that in weighing the evidence of defendant in a criminal case the jury has a right to consider his interest in the result, and should apply all the tests applicable to any witness, and, in addition, "consider the interest he has in the case, and the motive to swear falsely, in his own behalf," though not technically accurate in its phraseology, is not of a character to mislead the jury.

But in *People* v. *Lang,* 104 Cal. 363, 37 Pac. 1031, an instruction that the jury must remember that defendant's testimony is that of an accused man, and that while they are not to disbelieve him solely on that account, they must remember that he has a powerful motive to swear himself out of the charge,—is held erroneous.

And according to *State* v. *Webb* (Idaho) 55 Pac. 892, it is error to instruct the jury that it is proper for them to bear in mind the situation of defendant; how he may be affected by the verdict, and the interest he must feel in it; and to consider whether his position and interest may not affect his credibility, or color his evidence.

It is error to charge in bastardy proceedings prosecuted by the state, that so far as the pecuniary interest in the result of the suit is concerned the parties do not stand equal, the defendant having a direct pecuniary interest in it, and the complaining witness none, as under the Minnesota statutes a judgment against the defendant inures to the benefit of the complainant, although she is not technically a party to the proceedings. *State* v. *Nestaval,* 72 Minn. 415, 75 N. W. 725.

17. Right of the accused to an instruction.

The accused has the right to have an instruction based on his own testimony.[1]

[1]*State* v. *Partlow,* 90 Mo. 608, 59 Am. Rep. 31, 4 S. W. 14; *People* v. *Keefer,* 65 Cal. 232, 3 Pac. 818.

18. Omission to testify for himself.

Under the provision usual in statutes removing the disqualification of the accused, to the effect that his omission to testify shall not be used against him,[1] any allusion by the court in its instructions to the jury to the fact that the accused has not availed himself of the privilege is error.[2]

[1]For statutes forbidding omission to testify to be commented on; and as to the duty of the court in Indiana, Louisiana, Nevada, Oregon, Vermont, and Washington, to instruct the jury as to whether to be influenced by it, see *ante,* Division XXXIX. § 16.

[2]*Ruloff* v. *People,* 45 N. Y. 213, 11 Abb. Pr. N. S. 245; *Austin* v. *People,* 102 Ill. 261; *State* v. *Pearce,* 56 Minn. 226, 57 N. W. 652, 1065.

No inference either for or against the defendant in a criminal cause can be drawn from his omission to testify as a witness. *Com.* v. *Hanley,* 140 Mass. 457, 5 N. E. 468.

For similar rulings, see *People* v. *Hart,* 10 Utah, 204, 37 Pac. 330; *State* v.

Carnagy, 106 Iowa, 483, 76 N. W. 805; *State* v. *Landry*, 85 Me. 95, 26 Atl. 998; *People* v. *Rose*, 52 Hun, 33, 4 N. Y. Supp. 787; *State* v. *Myers*, 8 Wash. 177, 35 Pac. 580, 756; *Farrell* v. *People*, 133 Ill. 244, 24 N. E. 423.

The court should not qualify his instructions that the failure of defendant in a criminal case to take the stand should not raise any presumption against him, by stating that such rule does not incorporate into the evidence a denial which is not there, but that it simply requires the jury to consider the evidence as it is, not strengthened or weakened by the fact that the defendant does not take the stand; and that it does not say that the evidence shall be the same as if it contained a denial by him, or that the jury shall presume that the defendant would deny all incriminating facts if he took the stand. *People* v. *Fitzgerald*, 156 N. Y. 253, 50 N. E. 846.

But there is no covert insinuation against the accused in a charge to the jury that he is not bound to go on the stand, but can say: "Prove your case against me; it is my judgment that the situation is such that I am not bound to take the witness stand; and the law gives me that right, and the law gives me that privilege," where the judge also charges that no presumption can be taken against defendant for failure to take the witness stand. *People* v. *Hayes*, 140 N. Y. 484, 23 L. R. A. 830, 35 N. E. 951.

IV. Admissions and affidavits.

19. Admissions by counsel.

An admission by the prosecution of a distinct fact only incidentally involved, even though made in the course of summing up, is conclusive,[1] and the accused has a right to have the jury so instructed.[2]

Otherwise of a concession made hypothetically, for the sake of argument.[3]

[1]In *Com.* v. *Desmond*, 5 Gray, 80, it was assumed by the prosecuting attorney in summing up that one of his witnesses was an accomplice, as claimed by the defense in their argument; but the court nevertheless left it to the jury to say whether he was. And it was held that a new trial must therefore be granted. The court said "admissions made in the course of judicial proceedings are substitutes for and dispense with the actual proof of facts."

Contra, of an admission by defendant's counsel. *Clayton* v. *State*, 4 Tex. App. 515. And see *Sanderson* v. *State* (Tex. Crim. App.) 44 S. W. 1103, holding that a charge that the defendant, having admitted that he carried a pistol, and having failed to justify it, should be found guilty, where the admission was made by the defendant's counsel in his argument, was erroneous as being upon the weight of evidence, and authorizing a conviction upon admissions of counsel. But see *People* v. *Ross*, 115 Cal. 233, 46 Pac. 1059, where it is held that an instruction on a trial for robbery, referring to defendant as leading a dissolute life, is proper, where it is based on admissions or statements made by defendant's counsel in his address to the jury.

[2]*People* v. *Tyler*, 36 Cal. 522.

[3]*Com.* v. *Elliot*, 110 Mass. 104. Here both parties argued the case before the jury on the ground that the witness was an accomplice. The defendant's counsel argued that for that reason he was not entitled to credit. The court said: "The counsel for the prosecution may have argued that even if he were an accomplice, he was so corroborated as to be entitled to belief. It does not appear, and, in the case of an excepting party stating his own objection, we are not at liberty to presume, that the concession on the part of the prosecution went any farther than this."

20. Admission of truth of affidavit.

Where the admission received to meet an affidavit for continuance or postponement is an admission of the facts alleged, it is conclusive.[1]

If it is only an admission that the witnesses desired would, if present, testify as stated in the affidavit, it is not conclusive as to the facts to which such testimony would go.[2]

[1]*Mayfield* v. *State*, 110 Ind. 591, 11 N. E. 618, held it not error to charge that the facts stated in the affidavit for continuance must be taken as true, and that the weight and effect of such facts upon the merits were exclusively for the consideration of the jury.

[2]*State* v. *Underwood*, 76 Mo. 630. Error to refuse to charge that the testimony it was so admitted they would give was to be received by the jury as the testimony of such witnesses, and entitled to the same weight as if such absent witnesses had been sworn and given their evidence on trial.

21. Rebutting.

Testimony (even from one of such witnesses) that the facts were contrary to the testimony stated only makes a conflict of evidence. The accused is entitled to the benefit of the admission as to what the absent witness would have testified; and it is error, in the absence of the actual testimony of such witness, to instruct the jury that evidence to the contrary of the suggested facts may be considered in weighing the credit to be given to the supposed testimony which it is admitted would be given were the witness produced.[1]

[1]*Peterson* v. *State*, 63 Ala. 113.

22. Use of part of affidavit.

The prosecution, by reading as evidence against the accused part of the affidavit made and used by him on a motion for postponement or continuance of the trial, does not admit the truth of disconnected statements in other parts of it.[1]

[1] *State* v. *Hayes*, 78 Mo. 307.

V. Alibi.

23. Burden and measure of proof.

The question as to who is called upon to assume the burden of proof in a criminal prosecution in which an *alibi* is sought to be established, as well as with reference to the measure of proof by which it is to be established, has given rise to a great contrariety of opinion. But while it has been frequently claimed that the accused should be required to establish his defense of *alibi* by the same measure of proof as that by which the prosecution is required to show guilt, it has been uniformly held that he need not prove it beyond a reasonable doubt.[1] There are cases, however, which hold to the doctrine, to some extent, that a plea of *alibi* is an extrinsic evidence not arising out of the *res gestæ*,[2] and accordingly put upon the defendant the burden of proving his defense by a preponderance of the evidence.[3] On the other hand, there are cases which hold that the accused has the burden of proof after the state has made out a prima facie case, to the extent at least of raising a reasonable doubt.[4] And there are still other cases which hold that an allegation of an *alibi* is not an affirmative proposition made by the accused, with the burden of proof resting upon him.[5]

[1] *People* v. *Fong Ah Sing*, 64 Cal. 253, 28 Pac. 233; *Ackerson* v. *People*, 124 Ill. 563, 16 N. E. 847; *People* v. *Stone*, 117 N. Y. 480, 23 N. E. 13; *State* v. *Ward*, 61 Vt. 163, 17 Atl. 483; *Gallaher* v. *State*, 28 Tex. App. 247, 12 S. W. 1087.

[2] *People* v. *Lee Sare Bo*, 72 Cal. 623, 14 Pac. 310; *State* v. *Krewsen*, 57 Iowa, 588, 11 N. W. 7.

[3] *People* v. *Lee Sare Bo*, 72 Cal. 623, 14 Pac. 310; *Pate* v. *State*, 94 Ala. 14, 10 So. 665; *State* v. *Beasley*, 84 Iowa, 83, 50 N. W. 570; *State* v. *Ward*, 61 Vt. 163, 17 Atl. 483; *Trujillo* v. *Territory*, 7 N. M. 43, 32 Pac. 154. See cases cited in note to *State* v. *Thornton* (S. D.) 41 L. R. A. 530.

[4] *State* v. *Thornton*, 10 S. D. 349, 73 N. W. 196, and cases cited in note to same case, 41 L. R. A. 533.

[5] *Humphries* v. *State*, 18 Tex. App. 302; *Peyton* v. *State*, 54 Neb. 188, 74 N. W. 597; *Wright* v. *Territory*, 5 Okla. 78, 47 Pac. 1069; *Schultz* v. *Territory* (Ariz.) 52 Pac. 352. And for an exhaustive review of the authorities on this question generally, see note to *State* v. *Thornton* (S. D.) 41 L. R. A. 530.

24. Cautioning the jury.

It is error to charge the jury that an *alibi* is a suspicious defense.[1] But in those jurisdictions where the judge is not forbidden to express an opinion on the weight of evidence, the jury may properly be cautioned to subject the evidence of it to rigid scrutiny,[2] accompanying the caution with a statement that it is sufficient when properly made out by evidence, and of that they are the sole judges.[3]

[1] *People* v. *Kelly,* 35 Hun, 295, Approved in 10 Crim. L. Mag. 180.

And that instruction on a criminal trial that, though an *alibi* may be a "well-worn" defense, it is a legal one to the benefit of which defendant is entitled, is erroneous as disparaging such defense, see *State* v. *Crowell,* 149 Mo. 391, 50 S. W. 893.

[2] See charge of Chief Justice Shaw in *Com.* v. *Webster,* 5 Cush. 295, 318, 52 Am. Dec. 711.

That an instruction warning and cautioning the jury that an *alibi* is a defense easily proved, and hard to disprove, and that they should be careful and cautious in examining the evidence in respect thereto, is proper, see *People* v. *Tice,* 115 Mich. 219, 73 N. W. 108; *State* v. *Watson,* 102 Iowa, 651, 72 N. W. 283.

[3] *Nelms* v. *State,* 58 Miss. 362; *French* v. *State,* 12 Ind. 670, 74 Am. Dec. 229 (holds it error to charge that if the defendant seeks to prove an *alibi* he must do it by evidence which outweighs that given by the state tending to fix his presence at the place of the crime. The rule as to reasonable doubt is not different when the defendant sets up an *alibi* than it is when other affirmative matter is relied on.)

In Texas, unless requested to do so, the trial judge is not required to charge specially on the defense of *alibi* (*Davis* v. *State,* 14 Tex. App. 645); but where on the evidence it is relied upon as a defense, a refusal of the court to give a charge upon this subject is erroneous (*McGrew* v. *State,* 10 Tex. App. 539).

25. Evidence as to time and place.

To establish an *alibi* the range of evidence in respect to time and place must be such as reasonably to exclude the possibility of the presence of the accused.[1]

[1] *Wade* v. *State,* 65 Ga. 756; *Com.* v. *Seybert,* 4 Kulp, 4. And see cases reviewed in note to *State* v. *Thornton* (S. D.) 41 L. R. A. 541. But see *Ford* v. *State,* 101 Tenn. 454, 47 S. W. 703, where it is held that an instruction that proof of an *alibi* must cover the whole time in question, for, if it be possible that the prisoner could have been at both places, the proof of the *alibi* is of no value whatever, is too strong, as the evidence need not exclude the absolute possibility of presence at the time and place of the offense, to be of some value.

26. To be considered in connection with other evidence.

In passing upon the defense of an *alibi,* the jury have a right to consider all the evidence in the case tending to show guilt, as well as that relating to the alleged absence.[1]

Evidence tending to establish an *alibi,* even though not deemed by the jury sufficient for that purpose, may be considered by them, together with the other evidence in the cause, in determining whether guilt has been shown beyond a reasonable doubt.[2]

If upon the whole case there is a reasonable doubt whether defendant was present, he should be acquitted.[3]

[1] *McLain* v. *State,* 18 Neb. 154, 24 N. W. 720.

[2] *Watson* v. *Com.* 95 Pa. 418.

[3] *State* v. *Fry,* 67 Iowa, 475, 25 N. W. 738; *State* v. *Thornton,* 10 S. D. 349, 73 N. W. 196, S. C., with note, 41 L. R. A. 530 [Citing *Ackerson* v. *People,* 124 Ill. 563, 16 N. E. 847; *Hoge* v. *People,* 117 Ill. 44, 6 N. E. 796; *Hopps* v. *People,* 31 Ill. 392, 83 Am. Dec. 231; *State* v. *Howell,* 100 Mo. 628, 14 S. W. 4; *Howard* v. *State,* 50 Ind. 190; *State* v. *Hardin,* 46 Iowa, 623, 26 Am. Rep. 174; *Walker* v. *State,* 42 Tex. 360; *Harrison* v. *State,* 83 Ga. 129, 9 S. E. 542]; *State* v. *Spotted Hawk,* 22 Mont. 33, 55 Pac. 1026; *Hines* v. *State,* 40 Tex. Crim. Rep. 23, 48 S. W. 171; *People* v. *Kessler,* 13 Utah, 69, 44 Pac. 97. Compare *State* v. *Rivers,* 68 Iowa, 611, 27 N. W. 781, to the contrary.

And according to *Aneals* v. *People,* 134 Ill. 401, 25 N. E. 1022, a charge that if, after considering all the facts and circumstances, the jury have no reasonable doubt of the presence of defendant at the time of the alleged crime, the defense of *alibi* is not made out, is proper.

But an instruction to acquit if the jury have any reasonable doubt as to whether defendant was present at the time of the alleged offense is erroneous, as reasonable doubt is one arising from consideration by the jury of all the evidence. *Carlton* v. *People,* 150 Ill. 181, 37 N. E. 244.

People v. *Winters,* 125 Cal. 325, 57 Pac. 1067, holds that a requested instruction requiring an acquittal if the jury have a doubt upon the question of *alibi* is properly refused, where it omits the qualification that the doubt be a reasonable one.

In *State* v. *Price,* 55 Kan. 610, 40 Pac. 1001, it is held that the statement by the court in a criminal prosecution, that an *alibi* is a good defense if proved, is not erroneous or misleading, where the jury are directed in the same connection that if they have a reasonable doubt of the presence of the accused at the place of the commission of the crime, at the time thereof, they must acquit.

VI. Burden of proof.

27. General rule.

Except where the act charged against the accused is admitted to have been done by him, and he relies on some distinct substantial ground of defense,—such as insanity or a justification or former jeopardy, etc.,—the burden of proof is on the prosecution throughout; and the jury must be satisfied from the evidence beyond a reasonable doubt of the affirmative of the issue presented, that he is guilty as charged.[1]

[1]This is the rule as it seems now to be held by the highest authorities after much conflict of decision and opinion. *Lilienthal* v. *United States*, 97 U. S. 237, 266, 24 L. ed. 901, 905; *People* v. *Ribolsi*, 89 Cal. 492, 26 Pac. 1082; *Davis* v. *State*, 54 Neb. 177, 74 N. W. 599; *People* v. *McWhorter*, 93 Mich. 641, 53 N. W. 780; *Tiffany* v. *Com.* 19 Pittsb. L. J. N. S. 200, and cases cited; *Turner* v. *Com.* 86 Pa. 54, 74, 27 Am. Rep. 683. See *People* v. *Hill*, 49 Hun, 432, 3 N. Y. Supp. 564.

In *Herman* v. *State*, 75 Miss. 340, 22 So. 873, it is held that an instruction on a trial for murder that every homicide is presumed in law to be malicious, and therefore murder, and when the killing has been proved beyond a reasonable doubt, the law will presume the malice requisite to murder, shifting the burden of proof to defendant to show some circumstances of alleviation, justification, or excuse, unless the same arises out of evidence adduced against him by the state,—is bad in so far as it informs the jury that "the burden of proof is [then] shifted to the defendant;" that is, the burden of proof was shifted to the defendant after a killing had been proved to the satisfaction of the jury beyond every reasonable doubt, the legal presumption of malice being raised by the unexplained killing. "The burden of proof," said the court, "in such cases never shifts, as this court has before held; and the charge was erroneous to the extent indicated; but this inaccuracy of technical statement might or might not constitute reversible error. Whether reversible error or not would be dependent upon the character of the case and its peculiar circumstances. If clear that injury might have come to the accused by reason of the error, a reversal would follow, but otherwise not."

28. Negative.

The burden of proving the defendant's guilt may require the prosecution to prove a negative.[1]

[1]*Com.* v. *Samuel*, 2 Pick. 103; *State* v. *Morphy*, 33 Iowa, 270, 11 Am. Rep. 122 (holding that the state has the burden of proof to show beyond a reasonable doubt the guilt of the accused; hence, any negative matter, such as absence of self-defense, the want of sufficient provocation, etc., must be shown by the state; but whenever the matter of defense is wholly disconnected from the body of the offense, and is distinct affirmative matter, the burden is upon the defendant, *e. g.*, in case of homicide, that the deceased did not die of a wound inflicted by the accused, but from his own negligence, and want of care in attending to it), Followed in *State* v. *Shea*, 104 Iowa, 724, 74 N. W. 687; *State* v. *Hirsch*, 45 Mo. 429 (selling goods not the product of the state); *State* v. *Wilborne*, 87

N. C. 529 (false pretenses, falsity of representation by accused that he had certain securities must be proved by prosecution).

In *State* v. *Conahan*, 10 Wash. 268, 38 Pac. 996, a trial for mayhem, the burden of proving that the injury was not inflicted under justifiable circumstances was held to rest upon the state.

But in *Edwards* v. *State*, 39 Fla. 753, 23 So. 537, a trial for murder, it is held that where there is evidence that the wound inflicted was one from which death might ensue, that it was inflicted with murderous intent, and was followed by the death of the person wounded, the defendant has the burden of proving that the death did not result from such wound, but from some other cause.

So, in *State* v. *Lee*, 69 Conn. 186, 37 Atl. 75, a prosecution for abortion under Conn. Gen. Stat. § 1411, making abortion criminal unless necessary to save the life of the mother or that of the unborn child, it was held that the state need not in the first instance establish that the abortion was not so necessary.

29. Fact peculiarly within one's knowledge.

Where a fact is peculiarly within the knowledge of one party, rather than the other, the burden of proof may be imposed on the one having the means of proof.[1]

[1]*State* v. *Arnold*, 35 N. C. (13 Ired. L.) 184 (age); *Pounders* v. *State*, 37 Ark. 399 (consent of minor's parent that accused entertain him), *Contra*, *Conyers* v. *State*, 50 Ga. 103, 15 Am. Rep. 686; *State, Jackson, Prosecutor*, v. *Camden*, 48 N. J. L. 89, 2 Atl. 668 (liquor license; approving rule and reason as stated by Bishop, Statutory Crimes, § 1051); *Wheat* v. *State*, 6 Mo. 455, and cases cited; *Liggett* v. *People*, 26 Colo. 364, 58 Pac. 144; *State* v. *Ahern*, 54 Minn. 195, 55 N. W. 959; *Williams* v. *State*, 35 Ark. 430; *People* v. *Nyce*, 34 Hun, 298 (ferry license); *Flower* v. *State*, 39 Ark. 209 (physician's license). *S. P. State* v. *Higgins*, 13 R. I. 330; *State* v. *Keggon*, 55 N. H. 19 (in liquor case, prosecution not bound to prove that accused had not been appointed agent).

Compare *Com.* v. *Locke*, 114 Mass. 288, where it is held that the burden of proving affirmatively that a sale of liquor was in violation of law, by negativing the authority or license of the person by whom it was made, is placed on the government, yet it need not be proved by direct evidence, but may be inferred from circumstances. The authority of the defendant to sell being a fact within his knowledge, his failure to produce evidence thereof may be taken to aid the inference from other circumstancs. Exception overruled. See also *Mehan* v. *State*, 7 Wis. 670.

One charged with violating the Sabbath by operating a pump and fan in a coal mine, to prevent the accumulation of water and gas, has the burden of proving that such work is a work of "necessity," under the Arkansas statute making it a public offense to perform on that day any labor other than works of charity or necessity. *Shipley* v. *State*, 61 Ark. 216, 221, 32 S. W. 489, 33 S. W. 107. The court said that the necessity of the performance of the work proved was within the peculiar knowledge of the defendants, and the burden was on them to show it. To the same effect, see *Jackson* v. *State,* 88 Ga. 787, 15 S. E. 905.

30. Justification.

If the accused relies on a distinct affirmative fact in exoneration, the burden may be on him to show it.[1]

[1]*People* v. *Schryver,* 42 N. Y. 1, 1 Am. Rep. 480 (justifiable or excusable character of homicide); *Cook* v. *Territory,* 3 Wyo. 110, 4 Pac. 887. And see *Brown* v. *State,* 62 N. J. L. 666, 42 Atl. 811, where it is held that an instruction that one accused of murder is charged with the burden of proof of self-defense interposed as a justification is not erroneous where the court instructs the jury upon the fact of reasonable doubt in language comprehending every issue in the case,—Citing *People* v. *Schryver,* 42 N. Y. 1, 1 Am. Rep. 480, *supra,* and distinguishing *Stokes* v. *People,* 53 N. Y. 164, 13 Am. Rep. 492. Compare *People* v. *Downs,* 123 N. Y. 558, 25 N. E. 988 (where it is held error to charge that if a man takes human life he must be "able to excuse himself when called upon to answer;" and if not he must be found guilty of one or the other of the crimes "which are imputed to him by reason of the homicide," because it is casting the burden of proof on defendant. And that the error is not cured by charging that it is incumbent upon the People to prove beyond a doubt what grade of crime was committed, or that if there is a reasonable doubt that the prisoner intended to kill deceased, they must acquit of the crime of murder in both degrees); *People* v. *Coughlin,* 65 Mich. 704, 32 N. W. 905; *People* v. *McCarthy,* 110 N. Y. 309, 316, 18 N. E. 128 (explaining use of deadly weapon).

The burden of proving an affirmative defense such as a prior conviction, or where the charge is polygamy or divorce, is upon the defendant; and upon such a defense he has the entire burden throughout. Throop (Mass.) Digest, Citing *Com.* v. *Daley,* 4 Gray, 209; *Com.* v. *Boyer,* 7 Allen, 306.

So where, upon trial for murder, the defense is that the person supposed to have been murdered has since been seen alive. *Com.* v. *Webster,* 5 Cush. 295, 52 Am. Dec. 711.

And where, upon a trial for murder, the homicide is proved, all circumstances of accident, necessity, or infirmity must be established by the defendant, unless they arise out of the evidence against him. *Com.* v. *Webster,* 5 Cush. 295, 52 Am. Dec. 711. See also *Com.* v. *York,* 9 Met. 93, 43 Am. Dec. 373.

And according to *State* v. *Byrd,* 121 N. C. 684, 28 S. E. 353, the defendant who admits the killing with a deadly weapon, has the burden of showing such facts as would excuse the homicide, before he is entitled to an acquittal, although mitigating circumstances are shown which would reduce the crime to manslaughter.

Under Mont. Pen. Code, § 2081, regulating the burden of proof in murder trials, it is proper to charge that, upon proof of the commission of the homicide by the defendant, the burden of proving circumstances of mitigation or excuse devolves upon him, unless the proof on the part of the prosecution tends to show that the crime only amounts to manslaughter, or that he was excusable. *State* v. *Brooks*, 23 Mont. 146, 57 Pac. 1038.

So also under Utah Code Crim. Proc. § 268. *People* v. *Tidwell*, 4 Utah, 506, 12 Pac. 61.

But it is error to omit the qualification of Cal. Pen. Code, § 1105, "unless the proof on the part of the prosecution tends to show that the crime committed only amounts to manslaughter, or that the defendant was justifiable or excusable." *People* v. *Lemperle*, 94 Cal. 45, 29 Pac. 709.

31. Former jeopardy, etc.

Upon a plea of former acquittal, conviction, or jeopardy, the burden of proof to establish the identity of the two offenses rests upon the defendant.[1] But where a former acquittal or conviction is shown, it will be presumed, in the absence of evidence, to have been on the merits; and it is for the state to establish that the acquittal or conviction was produced by a variance,[2] or in consequence of a void indictment, or because of fraud,[3] or is otherwise unavailing to sustain the plea.[4]

[1] *Rocco* v. *State*, 37 Miss. 357, Followed in *Brown* v. *State*, 72 Miss. 95, 16 So. 202; *State* v. *Small*, 31 Mo. 197; *Com.* v. *Sutherland*, 109 Mass. 342; *Com.* v. *Hoffman*, 121 Mass. 369; *Cooper* v. *State*, 47 Ind. 61; *Hozier* v. *State*, 6 Tex. App. 542; *Morton* v. *State*, 37 Tex. Crim. Rep. 131, 38 S. W. 1019; *State* v. *Andrews*, 27 Mo. 267 (parol evidence may be given in addition to record).

Compare with *People* v. *M'Gowan*, 17 Wend. 386, holding that where it appears that the former indictment might have been sustained by proof which would be sufficient to sustain the second indictment, a prima facie case is made out for the prisoner by the production of the record; and it will then lie with the People to show that the offenses are substantially different.

[2] *Croft* v. *People*, 15 Hun, 484.

[3] *Ibid.*

[4] *State* v. *Maxwell*, 51 Iowa, 314, 1 N. W. 666; *Moore* v. *State*, 71 Ala. 307; *State* v. *Clenny*, 1 Head, 270.

VII. Character.

32. Good character to be considered irrespective of doubt.

If evidence of the good character of the accused has been given, the jury are to consider it with the other evidence in the case, whatever that may be. It is error to give them to understand that it is of no avail except in case of doubt,[1] or except against circumstantial evidence.[2]

If the accused has given such evidence, he is entitled to an instruction to the effect that evidence of good character may create a doubt.[3]

[1]In *Remsen* v. *People*, 43 N. Y. 6, Reversing 57 Barb. 324, Allen, J., says: "Evidence of good character is not only of value in doubtful cases and in prosecutions for minor offenses, but is entitled to be considered when the crime charged is atrocious, and also when the testimony tends very strongly to establish the guilt of the accused. It will sometimes of itself create a doubt when, without it, none would exist." This case is followed in *People* v. *Friedland*, 2 App. Div. 332, 37 N. Y. Supp. 974. And see, to the same effect, *People* v. *Clements*, 42 Hun, 353.

In *People* v. *Mead*, 50 Mich. 228, 15 N. W. 95, this rule was approved, but it was nevertheless held not error to instruct that if the evidence of his guilt is convincing beyond a reasonable doubt, the jury must convict notwithstanding the good reputation.

In *Com.* v. *Leonard*, 140 Mass. 473, 54 Am. Rep. 485, 4 N. E. 96, a well-considered case, it is held error to charge that evidence of the good character of the accused can only be considered where the other evidence is doubtful, and that it is not of the slightest consequence when that evidence is strong and the guilt of the defendant is impressed on the minds of the jury. The defendant had requested a charge that "good character, like all other facts in the case, should be considered by the jury, and if therefrom a reasonable doubt is generated in the minds of the jury as to the guilt of the accused, it is their duty to acquit." The court (Field, J.,) says that this request was a "correct statement of the law as it must now be held in this commonwealth. . . . It is not now the law, we think, that evidence of character can only be considered by the jury where the other evidence is doubtful, and that 'it is not of the slightest consequence' where the other 'evidence is strong' and the guilt of the defendant is impressed on the minds of the jury." The court questions the distinction taken in *Com.* v. *Webster*, 5 Cush. 295, 52 Am. Dec. 711, between atrocious and smaller offenses, and says: "The old rule that evidence of the good character of the defendant is not to be considered by the jury unless the other evidence leaves their minds in doubt has been much criticized, and the weight of authority is now against it,"—Citing numerous authorities.

And for some other cases recognizing the rule as stated *supra*, see *Hanney* v. *Com.* 116 Pa. 322, 9 Atl. 339 (to same effect); *State* v. *Northrup*, 48 Iowa, 583, 30 Am. Rep. 408; *State* v. *Sauer*, 38 Minn. 438, 38 N. W. 355 (held error to say it might determine in a case of doubt, implying, without expressly saying that it could not unless there was doubt); *State* v. *Henry*, 50 N. C. (5 Jones L.) 65; *State* v. *Keefe*, 54 Kan. 197, 38 Pac. 302; *People* v. *Van Dam*, 107 Mich. 425, 65 N. W. 277; *State* v. *Leppere*, 66 Wis. 355, 28 N. W. 376; *State* v. *Jones*, 52 Iowa, 150, 2 N. W. 1060; *State* v. *Lindley*, 51 Iowa, 343, 33 Am. Rep. 139, 1 N. W. 484; *State* v. *Holmes*, 65 Minn. 230, 68 N. W. 11; *Powers* v. *State*, 74 Miss. 777, 21 So. 657; *State* v. *Sloan*, 22 Mont. 293, 56 Pac. 364, and cases cited; *State* v. *Ormiston*, 66 Iowa, 143, 23 N. W. 370; *State* v. *Daley*,

53 Vt. 442, 38 Am. Rep. 694; *Wesley* v. *State*, 37 Miss. 327, 75 Am. Dec. 62; *People* v. *Hancock*, 7 Utah, 170, 25 Pac. 1093, and cases cited.

State v. *Sorter*, 52 Kan. 531, 34 Pac. 1036, holds that an instruction on a trial for murder, that evidence of the previous good character of defendant is competent in his favor, but that if the jury believe that defendant committed the crime as charged, it is their duty to find him guilty even though the evidence may satisfy their minds that he had previously sustained a good reputation and character as a peaceable, quiet, and law-abiding citizen,—is not erroneous.

In *People* v. *Sweeney*, 133 N. Y. 609, 30 N. E. 1005, it is held that a charge that good character will not avail as a defense if the crime charged has been conclusively proved beyond a reasonable doubt, is not erroneous as removing from the jury's consideration the evidence of good character, where it follows a charge that proof of good character raises the question whether a man having it is likely to commit the crime charged, and that it will likely outweigh evidence that might otherwise appear conclusive, and turn the scale in defendant's favor in a doubtful case,—Distinguishing *Remsen* v. *People*, 43 N. Y. 6, *supra*, note 1.

Com. v. *Eckerd*, 174 Pa. 137, 34 Atl. 305, holds that an instruction in a prosecution for murder, that previous good character is of great importance, but that evidence thereof is not to overcome the conclusion which properly follows, if the jury are satisfied beyond a reasonable doubt that the defendant is guilty,—is a correct statement of the law.

[3]*Stover* v. *People*, 56 N. Y. 315, holding it not error calling for reversal to charge that good character always is in favor of the prisoner against whom the proof is purely circumstantial. That when there is direct evidence of the commission of a crime by a prisoner, then good character goes for naught; when the proof is circumstantial, proof of good character is a matter to be taken into consideration, and is to have a very favorable influence upon the minds of the jury. Accused excepted to portion of charge as to good character going for naught where there is direct evidence of the crime; held that exception would have been well taken had there been such evidence in the case. See also *State* v. *Rodman*, 62 Iowa, 456, 17 N. W. 663.

[4]*People* v. *Bell*, 49 Cal. 486 (holding it error to refuse to instruct that evidence of good character may be sufficient to create a doubt where no doubt would have otherwise existed); *People* v. *Doggett*, 62 Cal. 27 (to same effect).

[5]"The question as to the weight of the testimony is entirely for the jury, and it is therefore error for the court to instruct them that it was [character is] entitled to little weight when the proof was strong." *Long* v. *State*, 23 Neb. 33, 36 N. W. 310.

There are, however, numerous minor cases to the contrary, this being a very common, though a questionable instruction. *Dabney* v. *State*, 113 Ala. 38, 21 So. 211, holds that a charge that the jury may look at the good character of defendant in connection with other evidence in the case, and that this good character may of itself be sufficient to generate a reasonable doubt of defendant's guilt, is properly refused. See also

Coppin v. *State,* 123 Ala. 58, 26 So. 333. And *McSwean* v. *State,* 113 Ala. 661, 21 So. 211, holds that a charge that if defendant charged with arson has proved a good character, the jury will consider such fact with all the evidence, and give him the benefit of "any doubt" such good character may generate, is properly refused, as defendant is entitled only to a "reasonable doubt."

In *Cancemi* v. *People,* 16 N. Y. 501, where a large number of witnesses had testified to good character of accused, it was held error to charge that such evidence was entitled to far inferior weight where the question was one of great and atrocious criminality than upon accusations of a lower grade,—Questioning *Com.* v. *Webster,* 5 Cush. 325, 52 Am. Dec. 711. Compare *McLain* v. *Com.* 99 Pa. 86. *Com.* v. *Webster,* is now regarded as overruled on this point. As to the proper instructions respecting evidence of character, see also article by Judge Seymour D. Thompson, 10 Crim. L. Mag. 192.

People v. *McArron,* 121 Mich. 1, 79 N. W. 944, holds that it is not error for the court to refuse to charge the jury in a trial for homicide, that evidence of defendant's good character prior to the alleged offense may be considered sufficient to raise a doubt of his guilt, when the charge given by the court is that under certain circumstances it may be considered sufficient to raise a reasonable doubt, and is to be taken with the other testimony, and given such weight as the jury think it entitled to.

In *Hammond* v. *State,* 74 Miss. 214, 21 So. 149, a charge that good character of a defendant is of itself a sufficient fact from which a reasonable doubt of guilt may arise is held to be properly refused where the court has itself charged that the good character of defendant is a fact to be considered in connection with all the evidence in determining his guilt or innocence. The court says, quoting from *Coleman* v. *State,* 59 Miss. 490: "Evidence of the good character of the accused should go to the jury as any other fact, and its influence in the determination of the case should be left to the jury, without any intimation from the court as to its value. The court should not tell the jury that satisfactory evidence of the good character of the accused is, or is not, sufficient to raise a reasonable doubt of his guilt."

And in *State* v. *Porter,* 32 Or. 135, 49 Pac. 964, it is held that a request by a defendant in a criminal cause to charge "that proof of good character may be sufficient of itself to create a reasonable doubt of defendant's guilt, although no such doubt would have existed but for such good character," although correct as an abstract proposition of law, is properly refused, since the form is vicious unless confined to a given case. "As an abstract proposition of law," said the court, "the instruction requested is no doubt correct, but the form is vicious unless confined to a given case. Under certain circumstances and conditions, such may be, and undoubtedly is, the effect of good character proven; but as a general rule applied to all cases it cannot be so treated. The rule of general application is that evidence of good character is always admissible in favor of the defendant in a criminal action, and it should be weighed and considered in connection with all other evidence in the cause in determining the guilt or innocence of the accused; and, when so considered, if there exists in the minds of the jury a reasonable doubt as to his guilt, he should be acquitted (*Com.* v. *Cleary,* 135 Pa. 64, 8 L. R. A. 302, 19 Atl. 1017; *Edgington* v. *United States,* 164 U. S. 361, 41 L. ed. 467, 17 Sup. Ct. Rep. 72; *State* v. *Henry,* 50 N. C. (5 Jones L.) 65; *People* v. *Ashe,* 44 Cal. 288; *People* v. *Raina,* 45 Cal. 292; *State* v. *Donovan,* 61 Iowa, 278, 16 N. W. 130; *State* v. *McMurphy,* 52 Mo. 251; *Jupitz* v. *People,* 34 Ill. 516); and this rule was practically adopted in *State* v. *Garrand,* 5 Or. 216. Under the rule, good character of the prisoner, when proven, becomes a fact in the case;—a circumstance tending in a greater or less degree to establish his innocence;—and it is not to be put aside by the jury in order to first determine whether the case is of doubtful sequence before laying into the scales such fact or circumstance. It may, when thus considered with other evidence in the case, leave the mind of the jury impressed with a reasonable doubt, or it may be sufficient within itself to engender such a doubt, while without it the other evidence may be convincing; and its value is matter for the determination of the jury under all the existing circumstances and conditions surrounding each particular case."

VIII. Confessions.

33. Jury not concluded as to voluntary character.

The ruling of the judge on the preliminary question whether a confession offered in evidence was voluntary is not conclusive on the jury.[1]

[1] *Woodford* v. *People,* 62 N. Y. 117, 20 Am. Rep. 464, Affirming 5 Thomp. & C. 539, 3 Hun, 310. *Contra, State* v. *Vann,* 82 N. C. 631 (well doubted in *People* v. *Kurtz,* 42 Hun, 335); *State* v. *Sanders,* 84 N. C. 728; *Wallace* v. *State,* 28 Ark. 531. And *Roesel* v. *State,* 62 N. J. L. 216, 41 Atl. 408, holds that after a decision by the court, based on conflicting evidence, that a confession was or was not voluntary, the question may be left to the jury, with the direction that they shall reject it if upon the whole evidence they are satisfied it was not voluntarily made,—Citing *Wilson* v. *United States,* 162 U. S. 613, 40 L. ed. 1090, 16 Sup. Ct. Rep. 895; *Hopt* v. *Utah,* 110 U. S. 574, 28 L. ed. 262, 4 Sup. Ct. Rep. 202.

In *Stallings* v. *State,* 47 Ga. 572, it was held not error to charge the jury: "If you do not believe that the confessions were freely and voluntarily made, . . . you will have to reject the confession entirely from your consideration."

This and the next two cases were approved in *People* v. *Kurtz,* 42 Hun, 335, as according with the weight of authority.

In *Earp* v. *State,* 55 Ga. 136, where a confession had gone to the jury without objection, it was held error to refuse to charge that, to make the confession evidence against the accused it must appear to the satisfaction of the jury that it was voluntary, etc.

In *People* v. *Barker,* 60 Mich. 277, 298, 27 N. W. 539 (conviction for murder affirmed), the court said: "Although we conceive it to be the province of the court to determine, in a case free from doubt, whether a confession is voluntary or not, before admitting or rejecting the same as evidence, yet in this case we think he properly submitted that question to the jury." The question was whether the confession was made under the influence of a prior confession to another person, which itself was inadmissible, being made to supposed counsel.

The proper instruction to the jury, in respect to the effect of evidence of a confession admitted by the court after contest as to the preliminary question whether it was voluntary, is that, if they believe from the evidence that the confession was untrue, they should disregard it; or if they believe from the evidence that it was made under the influence of hope or fear, they should take this into account in determining what weight or credit, if any, they would attach to it as evidence. *Ellis* v. *State*, 65 Miss. 44, 3 So. 188, reversing conviction for refusal of a request substantially to this effect, although it went so far as to add, inaccurately, that they might reject it if they believed it incompetent or produced by fear. Compare *Hunter* v. *State*, 74 Miss. 515, 21 So. 305; where it is held that a charge on a trial for murder that the jury should not consider a confession by defendant unless they believe that it was voluntarily made, and after he had been duly warned, is properly refused, as it is for the court to determine the competency of a confession. To similar effect, see *Holland* v. *State*, 39 Fla. 178, 22 So. 298.

The rule in Texas is that, after admitting a confession by defendant, which there is evidence to show was made while he was under duress, or, if he was in jail when he made it, was not preceded by a proper warning, the jury shall be instructed that if they believe the confession was made under duress, or when defendant was in jail, and not properly warned, and that it was not freely and voluntarily made, they shall exclude it altogether from their consideration, thus enabling the jury to pass upon the admissibliity of the confession. *Hamlin* v. *State*, 39 Tex. Crim. Rep. 579, 47 S. W. 656.

34. Cautioning the jury.

In those jurisdictions in which the judge is not allowed to express an opinion on the weight of evidence,[1] the accused has no right to have the jury cautioned against giving credit to a confession.[2]

[1]For some instances of instructions held improper as invading the province of the jury in this respect, see *Goodwin* v. *State*, 102 Ala. 87, 15 So. 571, a prosecution for murder, in which there is no evidence of threats made by the jailer to induce confessions by defendant; a charge to disregard such confessions in weighing the evidence, if the jury believe from the evidence that the jailer made any threats to defendant before they were made, held to have been properly refused. So held also of a charge to disregard defendant's confession if the jury believe from the evidence that the jailer told him that it would be worse for him if he did not confess.

Redd v. *State*, 63 Ark. 457, 40 S. W. 374 (where a charge that confessions, when deliberately and voluntarily made, are deemed to be among the most effectual proofs of defendant's guilt, is held improper); *Fincher* v. *People*, 26 Colo. 169, 56 Pac. 902 (where an instruction that if the jury find certain facts to exist with respect to the confession of defendant, it is entitled to great weight at their hands, is held improper), Citing *Com.* v. *Galligan*, 113 Mass. 202; *Blackburn* v. *Com.* 12 Bush. 181; *Com.* v. *Sanborn*, 116 Mass. 61; *State* v. *Gleim*, 17 Mont. 17, 31 L. R. A. 294, 41 Pac. 998; *Morrison* v. *State*, 41 Tex. 516; *Murphy* v. *People*, 63 N. Y. 590.

Hauk v. *State*, 148 Ind. 238, 46 N. E. 127, 47 N. E. 465, where a requested instruction that any admission or confession verbally made by defendant, and written down by another, is subject to mistake that may arise from misunderstanding the words used by defendant, or by using words not used by him, or substituting the language of the draftsman, is held to have been properly refused, although the court may properly call the attention of the jury to the question.

State v. *Cannon*, 52 S. C. 452, 30 S. E. 589, where a requested instruction was held to have been properly refused in a criminal cause, as invasive of the province of the jury, where it stated that if they found that a confession made by the defendant was made while he was suffering great pain and mental anguish, and while under the influence of narcotics, they should view it with great caution, give it no more weight than a feather, and that it was never safe to convict a defendant upon his uncorroborated statements.

'See article by Judge Seymour D. Thompson, in 10 Crim. L. Mag. 159, § 17, Citing authorities which condemn charge to effect of statement in 1 Greenl. Ev. § 200.

For cases on the danger of evidence of confessions, see those there cited, and *State* v. *Fields*, Peck. (Tenn.) 141 (agitation under which they are made). Verbal mistake or misrepresentation by witness. *Rex* v. *Simons*, 6 Car. & P. 541; Starkie, Ev. pt. 3, § 57, and note M; *State* v. *Long*, 2 N. C. (1 Hayw.) 455; *Rex* v. *Coleman*, Cited in Joy on Confessions, 108; *Cain* v. *State*, 18 Tex. 387; *Earle* v. *Picken*, 5 Car. & P. 542, note; *State* v. *Guild*, 10 N. J. L. 163, 185, 18 Am. Dec. 404.

Unsatisfactory character of the evidence. *Malin* v. *Malin*, 1 Wend. 625, 652; *Getman* v. *Getman*, 1 Barb. 499, 504; *Law* v. *Merrills*, 6 Wend. 268, Reversing 9 Cow. 65; *Stone* v. *Ramsey*, 4 T. B. Mon. 237; *Garrison* v. *Akin*, 2 Barb. 25, 27; *Myers* v. *Baker*, Hardin (Ky.) 544.

Danger of fabrication. *Lawless* v. *Queale*, 8 Ir. L. Rep. 382 (where the chief judge said: "I know by experience [meaning by observation] how easy it is to fabricate admissions);" *Lench* v. *Lench*, 10 Ves. Jr. 511; *Smith* v. *Burnham*, 3 Sumn. 435, Fed. Cas. No. 13,019.

For cases on the cogency of a well-proved confession. *Botts* v. *Williams*, 17 B. Mon. 687; *Ector* v. *Welsh*, 29 Ga. 443; *Higgs* v. *Wilson*, 3 Met. (Ky.) 337; *Mercer* v. *State*, 17 Ga. 146; *People* v. *Bennett*, 37 N. Y. 117.

35. Jury not bound to believe the whole.

Where the declarations of the accused are admitted against him, the jury are not bound to accept the whole because they believe a part.[1]

[1]*Hanrahan* v. *People*, 91 Ill. 142, where it was held not error to refuse to instruct that the jury had no right to reject any portion of the statement. See also *Hauk* v. *State*, 148 Ind. 238, 46 N. E. 127, 47 N. E. 465, where it is held proper for the court to refuse a requested instruction that if the jury believe that part of the defendant's confession which tends to incriminate another is false, they may disregard the confession entirely.

36. Necessity of corroboration.

The accused cannot be convicted upon evidence of his own confession, made out of court, without some other evidence of the criminal facts to which the confession relates.[1]

[1]*People* v. *Deacons*, 109 N. Y. 374, 16 N. E. 676, holding that proof of the finding of the body of the deceased, with unmistakable marks of the murder committed, is sufficient to sustain a conviction based upon a confession of murder.

According to *Wimberly* v. *State*, 105 Ga. 188, 31 S. E. 162, an instruction that a conviction may be lawfully had on a free and voluntary confession, though not otherwise corroborated than by proof of the *corpus delicti*, should not contain language from which the jury may infer that a confession so corroborated will require conviction; but the jury should be left free to pass on the question whether or not the corroborative evidence, together with that relating to the confession, is sufficient to satisfy them beyond a reasonable doubt of defendant's guilt.

And *Cargill* v. *Com.* 93 Ky. 578, 20 S. W. 782, holds that failure to instruct under Ky. Crim. Code, § 240, providing that a confession of a defendant, unless made in open court, will not warrant a conviction unless accompanied with other evidence that such an offense was committed,—is not erroneous where a witness testifies as to what accused swore upon a former trial, but it does not amount in the least degree to a confession.

An instruction that defendant cannot be convicted of rape on his uncorroborated confession need not be given where there is abundant corroboratory evidence. *Edens* v. *State* (Tex. Crim. App.) 43 S. W. 89.

IX. Consciousness of guilt.

37. Flight.

Flight of the accused may be considered by the jury as tending to show guilt,[1] but does not raise a presumption of law;[2] nor is he bound to explain beyond a reasonable doubt that it was consistent with his innocence.[3]

[1]*State* v. *Rodman*, 62 Iowa, 456, 17 N. W. 663 (larceny; holds it not error to charge that the attempt of the accused to escape should be considered as tending to establish guilt); *State* v. *King*, 78 Mo. 555 (holds it not error to charge that flight raises the presumption of guilt, and that the jury may take the flight into consideration in determining the guilt or innocence of the accused); *Sylvester* v. *State*, 71 Ala. 17 (holds it not error to charge that the flight may be considerd in connection with the other evidence as a circumstance of guilt); *Fox* v. *People*, 95 Ill. 71 (forgery; holds it error to instruct the jury that the flight of the accused was evidence of his guilt. It is only evidence tending to prove guilt).

In *State* v. *Thomas*, 58 Kan. 805, 51 Pac. 228, an instruction in a criminal action that if the jury find from the evidence that defendant, at or about the time the charge contained in the information was preferred against him, fled to a distant section of the country, and such flight was induced by the charge, they may consider such circumstances in determining the question of guilt or innocence,—is held correct.

In *State* v. *Hunt*, 141 Mo. 626, 43 S. W. 389, the court instructed the jury "that where there is evidence introduced as to an attempted escape by the defendant who has been charged with an offense, to avoid his arrest by the officers of the law and trial, such attempt to escape, in the absence of qualifying circumstances, raises a presumption of guilt; and if you find from the evidence in this case that the defendant did attempt to escape to avoid arrest and trial this is a circumstance to be considered by you, in connection with all the other evidence, to aid you in determining the question of the guilt or innocence of defendant;" and the instruction was approved, the question being whether the evidence in fact justified the instruction.

It is not every going away from the place of the homicide that raises the presumption of the guilt of the accused, and when the facts tend to show that the purpose of going away was not to avoid arrest, the instruction should be so framed as to include all the circumstances, that the defendant may have the benefit of such explanatory facts. *State* v. *Fairlamb*, 121 Mo. 137, 25 S. W. 895, Citing *State* v. *Mallon*, 75 Mo. 355; *State* v. *King*, 78 Mo. 555; *State* v. *Ma Foo*, 110 Mo. 7, 19 S. W. 222.

So, in *Com.* v. *Bezek*, 168 Pa. 603, 32 Atl. 109, an instruction on a trial for murder, that the jury may look upon the flight of defendant as evidence of guilt, and that they may also look upon it as evidence of the fear of summary punishment on his part at the hands of his pursuers, is held not to be objectionable.

An instruction on a trial for murder, that if defendant, on being informed that he was suspected of the homicide, "fled to avoid arrest," such fact is a circumstance prima facie indicative of guilt, is not objectionable as stating that if he fled to avoid arrest for larceny, which he is shown to have committed, it would be prima facie evidence of his guilt of the crime of murder. *State* v. *Seymour*, 94 Iowa, 699, 63 N. W. 661.

[2]*People* v. *Wong Ah Ngow*, 54 Cal. 151, 35 Am. Rep. 69 (homicide), held it error to charge that the flight of the defendant was strong presumptive evidence of his guilt, because no such presumption arose, as a matter of law, and the instruction was therefore "with respect to matters of fact," and was not cured by a correct statement of the law in another part of the charge.

So, in *Hickory* v. *United States*, 160 U. S. 408, 40 L. ed. 474, 16 Sup. Ct. Rep. 327, it is held that a charge that the law recognizes as true that the wicked flee when no man pursueth, but the innocent are as bold as a lion, and that this is a self-evidenced proposition which can be taken as an axiom, is erroneous when given on the trial of an accused person who fled after the crime. "This instruction was tantamount," said the court, "to saying to the jury that flight created a legal presumption of guilt so strong and so conclusive that it was the duty of the jury to act on it as an axiomatic truth. On this subject, also, it is true, the charge thus given was apparently afterwards qualified by the statement that the jury had a right to take the fact of flight into consideration, but these words did not correct the illegal charge already given. Indeed, taking the instruction that flight created a legal presumption of guilt with the qualifying words subsequently used, they were both equivalent to saying to the jury that they were, in considering the facts, to give them the weight which, as a matter of law, the court declared they were entitled to have; that is, as creating a legal presumption so well settled as to amount virtually to a conclusive proof of guilt."

[3]*Fox* v. *People*, 95 Ill. 71 (forgery), holds it error to charge that if flight is proved it must be satisfactorily explained as consistent with the innocence of the accused. This might be understood as requiring him to prove an innocent purpose beyond doubt.

X. Corpus delicti.

38. General rule as to sufficiency of evidence.

The jury should not convict without clear and distinct proof of the facts forming the basis of the offense or *corpus delicti.*[1]

But the proof need not be direct and positive.[2]

[1]*Ruloff* v. *People*, 18 N. Y. 179; *United States* v. *Searcey*, 26 Fed. 435; *State* v. *Keeler*, 28 Iowa, 551; *Taylor* v. *State*, 35 Tex. 97; *Smith* v. *Com.* 21 Gratt. 809 (where the judgment of conviction was reversed for insufficiency of evidence); *Stocking* v. *State*, 7 Ind. 326; *State* v. *Winner*, 17 Kan. 298; *Johnson* v. *Com.* 81 Ky. 325.

In *Ruloff* v. *People*, it is held error to refuse to direct an acquittal where the prosecution has no direct evidence that the person with whose murder the prisoner is charged is dead or has been murdered, or that her dead body has ever been found or seen by anyone. The fact of the death is the fundamental and material fact to be established in every case of murder. It should be shown either by witnesses who were present when the murderous act was done, or by proof of the body having been seen dead, or by proof of criminal violence adequate to produce death, and which accounts for the disappearance of the body.

In *People* v. *Parmelee*, 112 Mich. 291, 70 N. W. 577, it is held that the evidence of the *corpus delicti* is properly submitted to the jury in a murder trial, where it includes the opinion of two physicians that the deceased died from strangulation, and that the injury apparent on the body could not have been inflicted by herself, and testimony that a cry was heard from the vicinity where the body was afterwards found; that there was an indentation in the ground under the head; and that limbs requiring hard pressure to break were found broken under the head; that clots of blood and ruptured blood vessels were found in the throat near Adam's apple; that the upper end of the windpipe was crushed in nearly to the center; that the lungs were collapsed, the lower back part being filled with blood; that the membranes covering the brain were highly congested and bloody, and the nose pressed to one side; although it appears that she was unmarried, and was two months' pregnant, and a vial half filled with laudanum would have produced some of the symptoms discovered.

In *Gay* v. *State*, 40 Tex. Crim. Rep. 242, 49 S. W. 612, it was held that a requested charge on a trial for murder, that the death of deceased must be proved by identification of the portions of bones claimed by the state to be a portion of deceased's body, independent of the other evidence in the case, was properly refused as excluding from the consideration of the jury other evidence tending to identify the bones found as a part of the deceased's remains, save such identification as was given by witnesses, tending to prove that they recognized the fragments as portions of such remains, under Texas Pen. Code 1895, art. 654, providing that no person shall be convicted of homicide, unless the body of deceased, or portions of it, are found and sufficiently identified to establish the fact of the death of the person charged to have been killed,—Citing *State* v. *Davidson*, 30 Vt. 377, 73 Am. Dec. 312; *McCulloch* v. *State*, 48 Ind. 109; *State* v. *Williams*, 52 N. C. (7 Jones L.) 446, 78 Am. Dec. 248; *Campbell* v. *People*, 159 Ill. 9, 42 N. E. 123; *State* v. *Martin*, 47 S. C. 67, 25 S. E. 113; *Webster* v. *Com.* 5 Cush. 386.

[3] Direct proof in the statute (N. Y. Pen. Code, § 181) does not necessarily mean direct evidence exclusively. Circumstantial evidence of identity of the deceased, coupled with the confession of the accused, may amount to direct proof. *People* v. *Beckwith*, 108 N. Y. 67, 15 N. E. 53, Affirming 45 Hun, 422.

39. Confessions.

The *corpus delicti* cannot be established by the evidence of extra-judicial confessions or declarations of the accused;[1] but it may be by judicial confessions duly received.[2]

[1] *Hill* v. *State*, 11 Tex. App. 132; *South* v. *People*, 98 Ill. 261; *People* v.

Lane, 49 Mich. 340, 13 N. W. 622; *Priest* v. *State,* 10 Neb. 393, 6 N. W. 468; *Smith* v. *State,* 17 Neb. 358, 22 N. W. 780.

"Facts ascertained by reason of a prisoner's confession may be taken into consideration in establishing the *corpus delicti;* but the confession of a party, not made in open court or on examination before a magistrate, but to an individual, uncorroborated by circumstances, and without proof *aliunde* that a crime has been committed, will not justify a conviction. The *corpus delicti* must be proved beyond a reasonable doubt by evidence other than such extra-judicial confessions." *Pitts* v. *State,* 43 Miss. 472, 481, where the proof of the *corpus delicti* was held insufficient to sustain the conviction.

Although an extra-judicial confession uncorroborated is insufficient for a conviction, yet such a confession supported by extrinsic corroborative circumstances was held sufficient, though the *corpus delicti* was not established by direct and positive testimony. *State* v. *Patterson,* 73 Mo. 695.

The cases cited do not sustain the doctrine that the *corpus delicti* must be fully proved by the evidence independent of the confession. *United States* v. *Williams,* 1 Cliff. 5, 21, Fed. Cas. No. 16,707.

"Full proof of the body of the crime, the *corpus delicti,* independent of the confession, is not required by any of the cases, and in many of them slight corroborating facts were held sufficient." *People* v. *Badgley,* 16 Wend. 53, 59, where the corroborating facts were held sufficient.

In Kentucky, by express statute (Ky. Crim. Code, §§ 240, 241), it is provided that an extra-judicial confession will not warrant a conviction, unless accompanied with proof that the offense was committed; and that a conviction cannot be had on the testimony of an accomplice, unless corroborated by other evidence tending to connect defendant with the commission of the crime. But this statute neither requires nor authorizes an instruction that evidence of extra-judicial confession of guilt is not such evidence as the law makes necessary to corroborate the evidence of an avowed accomplice, and that the evidence of such accomplice cannot furnish the corroboration necessary to supprt the evidence of an extra-judicial confession. *Patterson* v. *Com.* 99 Ky. 610, 5 S. W. 765.

A judicial confession is sufficient on which to found a conviction. 1 Greenl. Ev. § 216.

In *State* v. *Cowan,* 29 N. C. (7 Ired. L.) 239, it was held that an explicit and full confession of a felony, duly made by a prisoner, upon examination on a charge before a magistrate, was sufficient to ground a conviction, though there be no other proof of the offense having been committed. The judgment of conviction was, however, reversed on other grounds.

"It seems that these [judicial] confessions, uncorroborated by any other proof of the *corpus delicti,* are sufficient to found a conviction, even if it be followed by a sentence of death, they being deliberately made under the deepest solemnities, with the advice of counsel and the protecting caution and oversight of the judge." *State* v. *Lamb,* 28 Mo. 218, 230.

40. Judicial confession competent.

A judicial confession, either upon the trial or in an examination duly made in court by the committing magistrate, is competent and sufficient evidence of the *corpus delicti*.[1]

[1]*Pitts* v. *State*, 43 Miss. 472, 481; *People* v. *Badgley*, 16 Wend. 53, 59. And see cases cited in note to *supra*, § 39.

41. Contributing cause.

Proof of the *corpus delicti* resulting from the inference that the wound inflicted caused the death is not impaired by testimony that disease contributed to produce or hasten the death.[1]

[1]*Powell* v. *State*, 13 Tex. App. 244.

In *People* v. *Lewis*, 124 Cal. 551, 45 L. R. A. 783, 57 Pac. 470, it is held that a requested instruction on a trial for homicide, that if the jury believe from the evidence that it is impossible to tell whether the deceasd died from a wound inflicted by himself or the one inflicted by the defendant, they must acquit, is properly refused as ignoring the proposition that both the wounds might have contributed to the death.

XI. Credibility.

42. Falsus in uno, etc.

Under the present rule as to the competency of convicts, the rule that if the jury believe that a witness has wilfully[1] testified falsely as to any fact[2] before them they are authorized to, but not bound to disbelieve his entire testimony,[3] applies to a witness shown to have been guilty of perjury.[4]

[1]The words "wilfully" and "material" should be expressed as qualifications of the rule given in Mont. Code Civ. Proc. § 3390, subd. 3, providing that the jury are to be instructed on all proper occasions "that a witness false in one part of his testimony is to be distrusted in others." *Cameron* v. *Wentworth*, 23 Mont. 70, 57 Pac. 648, Citing *People* v. *Hicks*, 53 Cal. 354.

The provision of Cal. Code Civ. Proc. § 2061, subd. 3, that a witness "false" in one part of his testimony is to be distrusted in others, may properly be modified in instructing the jury, by inserting the word "wilfully" before the word "false." *People* v. *Luchetti*, 119 Cal. 501, 51 Pac. 707.

An instruction that the jury may disregard the testimony of any witness who has given false testimony should not be given unless the testimony was given under oath, on a fact material to the issue, and was not only false, but wilfully false. *State* v. *Buchler*, 103 Mo. 203, 15 S. W. 331.

So, an instruction that if the jury believe any witness has sworn falsely regarding any material point, they must disregard his entire testimony, is properly refused. They must believe it was wilfully false. *State* v. *Freidrich*, 4 Wash, 204, 29 Pac. 1055, 30 Pac. 328, 31 Pac. 322; *Frazier* v. *State*, 56 Ark. 242, 19 S. W. 838; *Bonnie* v. *Earll*, 12 Mont. 239, 29 Pac. 882.

[2]It is error to substitute an instruction that a witness who has wilfully sworn falsely in one part of his testimony is to be distrusted in other parts, for a requested instruction that if a witness has wilfully sworn falsely to any "material" matter, it is the jury's duty to distrust his entire evidence. *People* v. *Plyler*, 121 Cal. 160, 53 Pac. 553.

[3]For some illustrations of the general rule, see *McClellan* v. *State*, 117 Ala. 140, 23 So. 653; *People* v. *Lon Yeck*, 123 Cal. 246, 55 Pac. 984; *State* v. *Martin*, 124 Mo. 514, 28 S. W. 12; *State* v. *Sexton*, 10 S. D. 127, 72 N. W. 84, 11 S. D. 105, 75 N. W. 895, and cases cited.

An instruction that if the accused has procured a witness to testify falsely in his behalf concerning a matter material to his defense, it is evidence tending to show that he is guilty of the crime charged, is not obnoxious to the rule forbidding the basing of an inference upon an inference, where the only testimony to which the charge applies was as to a transaction in which the witness and the accused were claimed to have been jointly engaged, affording inherent evidence of its intentional use. *State* v. *Magoon*, 68 Vt. 289, 35 Atl. 310.

And a requested instruction that when testimony is false in one part it is false in all, and that if the jury find that a certain witness testified falsely in one place they may disregard his testimony *in toto*, is properly modified by striking out the reference to a particular witness. *People* v. *Patterson*, 124 Cal. 102, 56 Pac. 882.

An instruction that the jury may disregard the entire evidence of a witness who has knowingly sworn falsely in relation to any material matter or statement may properly be modified by adding that they are not bound to do so if they still believe it worthy of credit. *State* v. *Baker*, 89 Iowa, 188, 56 N. W. 425.

But an instruction which does not leave the jury at liberty to give such credit to a corroborated witness who has sworn falsely as they think he deserves, but in effect requires them to give him credit, is erroneous. *State* v. *Patrick*, 107 Mo. 147, 17 S. W. 666.

So held in *People* v. *Oldham*, 111 Cal. 648, 44 Pac. 312, of an instruction that if the jury believe that any witness has wilfully and intentionally testified falsely to any material fact they may discard his evidence entirely; that it is a matter resting in their sound discretion, but that it is their "duty, as a matter of law, acting as jurors."

An instruction that if the jury believe that any witness for the "defense" has wilfully and knowingly sworn falsely to any material fact, they have a right to disregard his entire testimony except wherein it is corroborated by other credible evidence, is improper, where the witnesses for the prosecution are impeached by their own testimony. *Waters* v. *People*, 172 Ill. 367, 50 N. E. 148.

[4]*People* v. *Petmecky*, 99 N. Y. 415, 2 N. E. 145; *Moett* v. *People*, 85 N. Y. 373; *People* v. *Reavey*, 38 Hun, 418, 4 N. Y. Crim. Rep. 1; *Jordan* v.

State, 81 Ala. 20, 1 So. 577; *People* v. *O'Neil*, 109 N. Y. 251, 16 N. E. 68, Affirming 48 Hun, 36, and reaffirming rule in *Dunn* v. *People*, 29 N. Y. 529, 86 Am. Dec. 319. And see article by Judge Thompson, in 10 Crim. L. Mag. 167, 169, as to the maxim *falsus in uno*. He says: "It is, on the clearest principles, error for the judge to advise the jury that the testimony of a witness who has knowingly sworn falsely to a material fact is to be disregarded or disbelieved, unless corroborated by other testimony, or by circumstances. There is no rule which imperatively requires the jury to reject the testimony of such a witness, and such an instruction clearly invades their exclusive province of saying what witnesses they will believe and what they will disbelieve,"—Disapproving *Pierce* v. *State*, 53 Ga. 365.

43. Affirmative and negative testimony.

Neither party has a right to have the jury instructed that it is a rule of presumption that ordinarily a witness who testifies to an affirmative is to be preferred to one who testifies to a negative. This is a matter in the discretion of the court, and such an instruction, if given at all, should be given with caution.[1]

[1]This rule of presumption is doubtless sound. *State* v. *Chevallier*, 36 La. Ann. 81, 84; *Stitt* v. *Huikoper*, 17 Wall. 384, 394, 21 L. ed. 644, 647 (civil case).

"The propriety of giving the jury a caution upon this subject in any case is extremely doubtful, since it tends to disturb the operations of their minds in judging of the evidence, and to create impressions that their verdict is not to be returned according to their natural impressions of the truth derived from the evidence which they have heard, but from the application of artificial rules." Judge Seymour D. Thompson, in 10 Crim. L. Mag. 162.

It is not correct to charge that, as between witnesses, those who testify positively as to a fact are rather to be believed than those whose testimony is negative, since the credibility of a witness is a better test than the form in which his evidence is given. *Kimbrough* v. *State*, 101 Ga. 583, 29 S. E. 39.

A charge on the probative value of positive and negative testimony is not authorized by evidence of a witness that he heard a specified witness testify in another case, and that his recollection is that such witness did not identify defendant, but another person; that such witness said he recognized the latter by a scar on his face and by his coat; and that it is his recollection that such person was the only one the witness recognized, although he will not be positive as to all the witness testified to. *Humphries* v. *State*, 100 Ga. 260, 28 S. E. 25.

44. Testimony of experts.

It is error to tell the jury that the testimony of experts should be received with great caution.[1]

[1]The true rule is that "testimony of experts is to be considered like any

other testimony—is to be tried by the same tests, and is to receive just as much weight and credit as the jury deem it entitled to, when viewed in connection with all the circumstances." Judge Seymour D. Thompson, in 10 Crim. L. Mag. 174, citing, however, civil cases.

And the refusal of the court to instruct the jury in a criminal case that the testimony of a witness that blood found upon clothing of the accused was human blood, and detailing the method resorted to for determining the character of blood, mainly demonstrative of well-established scientific facts, should be received with great caution,—is not error, whatever the rule may be as to the necessity in a proper case of giving cautionary instructions as to expert testimony. *People* v. *Smith*, 106 Cal. 73, 39 Pac. 40.

Nor should the trial court on a trial for murder, in explaining the nature of expert and nonexpert testimony and the rules under which witnesses belonging to each class may give their opinions as to the sanity or insanity of defendant, charge that the testimony of expert witnesses is entitled to great weight, and add that it is the same with parties who associated with defendant, lived with him, and lived in the same community, as the probative value of the testimony of each witness should be determined by the jury. *Ryder* v. *State*, 100 Ga. 528, 38 L. R. A. 721, 28 S. E. 246.

According to *State* v. *Van Tassel*, 103 Iowa, 6, 72 N. W. 497, however, the court may properly instruct the jury that expert testimony as to handwriting is far from satisfactory, and should be received with great care and caution.

45. Hypothetical questions.

If expert testimony has been drawn out by a hypothetical question, the party affected has a right to have the jury cautioned not to take for granted the truth of the statements contained in such question, but to scrutinize the evidence, and determine from it whether the hypothesis be true.[1]

[1]Judge Seymour D. Thompson, in 10 Crim. L. Mag. 175, gives the following as an approved instruction: "You are not to take for granted that the statements contained in the hypothetical questions which have been propounded to the witnesses are true. Upon the contrary, you are to carefully scrutinize the evidence, and from that determine what, if any, of the averments are true, and what, if any, are not true. Should you find from the evidence that some of the material statements therein contained are not correct, and they are of such a character as to entirely destroy the reliability of opinions based upon the hypothesis stated, you may attach no weight whatever to the opinions based thereon. You are to determine from all the evidence what the real facts are, and whether they are correctly or not stated in the hypothetical question or questions. I need hardly remind you (for it will suggest itself to your minds) that an opinion based upon an hypothesis wholly incorrectly assumed or incorrect in its material facts, and to such an extent as to im-

pair the value of the opinion, is of little or no weight. Upon the matters stated in these hypothetical questions, and which are involved in this investigation, you are to give the defendant the benefit of all reasonable doubt, if any there should be, and where there is a reasonable doubt as to the truth of any one of the material facts stated, resolve it in the defendant's favor."

46. Witnesses who have been impeached.

The usual instruction, as stated by Judge Thompson, is as follows: "In determining the guilt or innocence of the defendants, the jury are to consider the entire evidence in the case; but they are at liberty to disregard the statements of such witnesses (if any there be) as have been successfully impeached, either by direct contradiction or by proof of general bad character, unless the statements of such witnesses have been corroborated by other evidence which has not been impeached."[1]

[1] 10 Crim. L. Mag. 171.

An instruction that, while testimony may be submitted for the purpose of impeaching a witness, it does not necessarily destroy his testimony, as it is a matter left with the jury to take into consideration, and give it the credit they think it entitled to, is proper. *Huff* v. *State*, 104 Ga. 521, 30 S. E. 808.

So, an instruction in a criminal case that the jury should consider the impeaching evidence in estimating the weight to be given the testimony of a witness, and also the fact, if they so find it, that the moral character of a witness has been successfully impeached, is proper. *Smith* v. *State*, 142 Ind. 288, 41 N. E. 595.

But an instruction that the jury are at liberty to disregard the statement of all such witnesses, if any, as have been successfully impeached, either by direct contradiction or by proof of having made different statements at other times, or by proof of bad reputation for truth and veracity, except in so far as they have been corroborated by other credible evidence or facts proved on the trial, without requiring the contradictory statements to be as to material facts, and ignoring explanatory evidence offered by witnesses as to the former different statements,—is properly refused. *Cobb* v. *State*, 115 Ala. 18, 22 So. 506.

So also is an instruction that the credibility of a witness may be impeached by statements out of court contrary to his testimony, and that if the jury believe that any witness has made such contradictory statements they would tend to impeach him, and the jury would be justified in rejecting his testimony if from all the evidence they believe it to be untrue. *Healy* v. *People*, 163 Ill. 372, 45 N. E. 230.

And refusal of an instruction that the jury will not be justified in believing a witness who has been impeached, or who has made different statements under oath, unless corroborated by other evidence, facts, and circumstances, is not error where the court instructs the jury to disbelieve such witness if not thoroughly satisfied that his evidence upon the trial is truthful. *State* v. *Patterson*, 52 Kan. 335, 34 Pac. 784.

An instruction leaving it to the jury to say whether or not a witness has been successfully impeached is erroneous, that being a question of law for the court. *State* v. *Patrick*, 107 Mo. 147, 17 S. W. 666.

XII. Decoys, detectives, informers, and spies.

[The propriety of the use of decoys and the question whether acting on the suggestion of a decoy is criminal depend in part on whether the offense is one of a nature to be recurrent or habitual, so that a decoy is merely putting before the suspect an additional occasion, such as every-day experience constantly presents, and only differing in the fact that it is so contrived as to preserve means of tracing the result; or whether it is a distinct temptation operating to induce the original intent of the accused.

Another distinction is that where the statute is expressly restricted to acts done with a particular intent or purpose, a decoy does not occasion an offense unless the detective acted with that intent or purpose in good faith, in setting the decoy in motion.]

47. Informers and spies; and decoys.

The mere fact that a witness acted as an informer or spy does not discredit his testimony.[1]

It is no objection to a conviction, when a prohibited act has been done, that it was discovered by decoy letters specially prepared for that purpose;[2] nor does the resort to such means discredit the testimony of an officer,[3] nor cast any imputation of crime upon him.[4]

[1] *St. Charles* v. *O'Mailey*, 18 Ill. 407 (action for penalty for illegal sale of liquors), where it was held that a witness was not to be discredited from the simple fact that he acted as an informer or spy. The court said: "Informers and spies may be abhorred and odious, not by reason of denouncing and giving information against crimes and criminals, but for their association and participation in lawless practices. We should not, therefore, mistake and denounce the only act through which society finds redress, instead of the crimes and criminals thus brought to light."

Compare *Com.* v. *Mason*, 135 Mass. 555, holding it not error to refuse a request to warn or caution against such testimony, if the judge simply ruled that such matters were to be considered by the jury. See also *Com.* v. *Downing*, 4 Gray, 29.

So, in *Hronek* v. *People*, 134 Ill. 139, 8 L. R. A. 837, 24 N. E. 861, an instruction that the evidence of private detectives and of the police should be received with a large degree of caution was held not to contain a correct proposition of law. "All the circumstances connected with a witness," said the court, "or that might tend to affect his credibility or bias his judgment, are competent to be shown to and considered by the jury in determining the weight and credit to be given to his testimony. In view of the facts and circumstances thus shown, it is for the jury to determine its weight as matter of fact."

And in *Copeland* v. *State*, 36 Tex. Crim. Rep. 576, 38 S. W. 210, it is held that a charge that the jury, in passing on the guilt or innocence of defendant, may consider the fact that the witnesses introduced by the state were paid and hired to catch defendant, if they believe that such witnesses were so paid and hired, is properly refused as charging on the weight of the testimony of particular witnesses.

In *People* v. *Everts*, 112 Mich. 194, 70 N. W. 430, an instruction on a trial for unlawfully selling liquor, that the claim of defendant that the liquor was purchased with a view to instituting a prosecution based on the evidence of the purchasers, was a circumstance affecting the credibility of such purchasers as witnesses, and their testimony should be more carefully scanned than it otherwise would be, was held sufficiently to present the claim that the testimony was furnished by detectives promised a reward for the detection and conviction of persons illegally selling liquor.

And *People* v. *Bennett*, 107 Mich. 430, 65 N. W. 280, holds that a charge informing the jury that if complainant in a prosecution under the Michigan local-option law was a hired witness and a spy, and asked the defendant to violate the law for the express purpose of instituting a criminal prosecution against him, such facts are to be considered in determining the credit due to his testimony,—is sufficiently favorable to the accused. To the same effect, see *People* v. *Rice*, 103 Mich. 350, 61 N. W. 540.

But in *State* v. *Shew*, 8 Kan. App. 679, 57 Pac. 137, it was held to be the duty of the trial court in a prosecution in which the state relied entirely upon the testimony of detectives, to instruct the jury to scrutinize their testimony closely,—Citing *Connor* v. *People*, 18 Colo. 373, 25 L. R. A. 341, 33 Pac. 159. Compare *State* v. *Keys*, 4 Kan. App. 14, 45 Pac. 727, where it is held that an instruction which characterizes a witness as a "spotter," and tells the jury to take his testimony with extreme care and suspicion, is properly refused where there is nothing in his conduct or demeanor to reflect unfavorably on his credibility, except his admission that he purchased intoxicating liquor from one reputed to be engaged in the illegal sale thereof, intending, if called upon, to testify thereto.

[3] *United States* v. *Moore*, 19 Fed. 39. The fact that the defendant was sending lottery tickets through the mails was ascertained by an officer sending in a letter the price of a lottery ticket, and receiving from the defendant through the mails such a ticket.

To same effect: *Bates* v. *United States*, 11 Biss. 70, 10 Fed. 92; *United States* v. *Whittier*, 5 Dill. 35, 39, Fed. Cas. No. 16,688; *United States* v. *Cottingham*, 2 Blatchf. 470, Fed. Cas. No. 14,872.

[4] *United States* v. *Slenker*, 32 Fed. 691. The court charged the jury to the effect that the detection of crime by means of test or decoy letters was

allowable; that witnesses resorting to this means to discover violations of the postal laws were justified, and were not to be discredited therefor; that this was often an indispensable mode of detecting crime; but conviction was reversed for defect in indictment.

[4]*Onondaga Excise Comrs.* v. *Backus,* 29 How. Pr. 33, 42. The court says the use of decoy letters has ever been employed, without bringing upon those who use these means the imputation either of crime or of participation therein. Conviction confirmed. See *ante,* Division XXXIX., §§ 185–189.

48. Detectives and decoys not accomplices.

A person who took part in the act constituting the offense, merely as a decoy or detective, for the purpose of securing evidence, is not an accomplice within the rule which requires the testimony of an accomplice to be corroborated.[1]

[1]*Copeland* v. *State,* 36 Tex. Crim. Rep. 575, 38 S. W. 210 (*dictum*); *People* v. *Noelke,* 94 N. Y. 137, 46 Am. Rep. 128 (holding that a detective who purchases a lottery ticket for the purpose of detecting and punishing the sale, in violation of law, is in no sense a party to the criminal act or intent, so as to become an accomplice); *People* v. *Farrell,* 30 Cal. 316 (having counterfeit coin in possession. The accused had a large amount of counterfeit coin for purposes of sale; and the only witness, acting in concert with the police, approached him, and represented to him that he was one of the "brotherhood," and, having gained his confidence, succeeded in purchasing. Conviction affirmed against objection that there must be corroboration); *Rex* v. *Despard,* 28 How. St. Tr. 346, 498 (high treason); *State* v. *McKean,* 36 Iowa, 343, 14 Am. Rep. 530 (horse stealing; a person having testified that he entered into an arrangement with the accused to steal the horse in question, and did assist in taking the horse; it was held not error to instruct the jury that if he acted, not with felonious intent, but as a detective, the prohibition against conviction on the uncorroborated testimony of an accomplice did not apply. Cole, J.: "The persons to whom the witness made the communications of his purpose to act the detective were not officers of law, or charged with any public duty to detect offenders. In this respect the case differs from *Rex* v. *Despard,* 28 How. St. Tr. 346. But this difference, perhaps, under our form of government and *régime,* would not be sufficient to defeat the application of the rule. The court left the credibility of the witness and the weight to be given to his testimony entirely to the consideration of the jury. Of these they were the proper judges." Conviction affirmed); *Com.* v. *Downing,* 4 Gray, 29 (the buyer of intoxicating liquor, for the express purpose of prosecuting for an unlawful sale, not an accomplice), Followed in *People* v. *Smith,* 28 Hun, 626 (holding that the provision of N. Y. Code Crim. Proc. § 399, against conviction on the uncorroborated testimony of an accomplice, did not apply to a conviction on the uncorroborated testimony of one so purchasing).

In *Com.* v. *Willard,* 22 Pick. 476 (a leading case), the court says: "It is difficult to draw any precise line of distinction between the cases in which the law holds it a misdemeanor to counsel, entice, or induce another to commit a crime, and where it does not. In general it has been considered as applying to cases of felony, though it has been held that it does not depend upon the mere legal and technical distinction between felony and misdemeanor. One consideration, however, is manifest in all the cases, and that is that the offense proposed to be committed by the counsel, advice, or enticement of another is of a high and aggravated character, tending to breaches of the peace or other great disorder and violence, being what are usually considered *mala in se* or criminal in themselves, in contradistinction to *mala prohibita* or acts otherwise indifferent than as they are restrained by positive law."

49. Question of intent for the jury.

Whether the intent of such a witness was merely to procure evidence, or was to commit a crime so that his testimony requires corroboration, is a question for the jury.[1]

[1]*People* v. *Bolanger*, 71 Cal. 17, 11 Pac. 799 (not error to charge that the rule requiring corroboration does not apply to a feigned accomplice); *Wright* v. *State*, 7 Tex. App. 574, 32 Am. Rep. 599 (theft; the principal witness for the prosecution having testified that he acquired his knowledge of the offense in the character of a detective and feigned accomplice, held not error to submit it to the jury whether he was an accomplice or not, and whether he had any such guilty participation as to require corroboration. Conviction affirmed).

XIII. Degree of the crime.

50. Duty to notice.

Where on the evidence the accused might be convicted in a lesser degree of the crime charged, it is the duty of the court in its instructions to embrace all the degrees of the crime to which the evidence is applicable.[1] But if it is clear from the evidence that a lesser degree of guilt is not involved, it is not error for the court to refuse such instructions.[2]

[1]*Territory* v. *Nichols*, 3 N. M. 103, 2 Pac. 78; *State* v. *Clemons*, 51 Iowa, 274, 1 N. W. 546; *Hudson* v. *State*, 40 Tex. 12; *Dennis* v. *State*, 112 Ala. 64, 20 So. 925; *Hicks* v. *State*, 25 Fla. 535, 6 So. 441; *State* v. *Adams*, 78 Iowa, 292, 43 N. W. 194; *Hudson* v. *State*, 101 Ga. 520, 28 S. E. 1010; *State* v. *Patterson*, 52 Kan. 335, 34 Pac. 784; *Petty* v. *Com.* 12 Ky. L. Rep. 919, 15 S. W. 1059; *People* v. *Palmer*, 96 Mich. 580, 55 N. W. 994; *State* v. *Miller*, 45 Minn. 521, 48 N. W. 401; *State* v. *Garrison*, 147 Mo. 548, 49 S. W. 508; *State* v. *Magers*, 35 Or. 520, 57 Pac. 197, and cases cited; *Augustine* v. *State* (Tex. Crim. App.) 52 S. W. 77; *State* v. *Dolan*, 17 Wash. 499, 50 Pac. 472; *Terrill* v. *State*, 95 Wis. 276, 70 N. W. 356; *Foster* v. *People*, 50 N. Y. 598 (holding that if the facts proved on a

trial of an indictment are capable of two constructions, or if in one view of the evidence a particular intent might be found, and yet the facts might justify the finding of an intent involving another degree of guilt, the court is bound, on request of the prisoner, to declare the rule of law applicable to the case in either aspect as the jury might determine the facts. But in the absence of a request, the court is not bound so to charge); *Buel* v. *People*, 78 N. Y. 492, 34 Am. Rep. 555; *Murphy* v. *People*, 3 Hun, 114; *Keener* v. *State*, 18 Ga. 194, 63 Am. Dec. 269; *Parrish* v. *State*, 18 Neb. 405, 25 N. W. 573.

According to *Territory* v. *Friday*, 8 N. M. 204, 42 Pac. 62, the introduction of any evidence whatever bringing homicide within the definition of any degree below murder in the first degree requires an instruction as to such degree, whether requested or not.

[a]*Compton* v. *State*, 110 Ala. 24, 20 So. 119; *Jones* v. *State*, 52 Ark. 345, 12 S. W. 704; *People* v. *Chaves*, 122 Cal. 134, 54 Pac. 596; *Kelly* v. *People*, 17 Colo. 130, 29 Pac. 805; *Hackett* v. *State*, 108 Ga. 40, 33 S. E. 842; *State* v. *Novak*, 109 Iowa, 717, 79 N. W. 465; *O'Brien* v. *Com.* 89 Ky. 354, 12 S. W. 471; *People* v. *Repke*, 103 Mich. 459, 61 N. W. 861; *State* v. *Lentz*, 45 Minn. 177, 47 N. W. 720; *State* v. *Sexton*, 147 Mo. 89, 48 S. W. 452; *Fager* v. *State*, 49 Neb. 439, 68 N. W. 611; *Sandoval* v. *Territory*, 8 N. M. 573, 45 Pac. 1125; *State* v. *Finley*, 118 N. C. 1161, 24 S. E. 495; *Gatliff* v. *Territory*, 2 Okla. 523, 37 Pac. 809; *Com.* v. *Crossmire*, 156 Pa. 304, 27 Atl. 40; *Fertig* v. *State*, 100 Wis. 301, 75 N. W. 960; *People* v. *Rogers*, 13 Abb. Pr. N. S. 370 (holding, on a trial for murder, that if no facts are proved to reduce it to manslaughter, a failure of the judge when requested to call the attention of the jury to the difference between the two crimes is not a ground for reversal); *State* v. *Rash*, 34 N. C. (12 Ired. L.) 382, 55 Am. Dec. 420; *Foster* v. *People*, 50 N. Y. 598 (holding that where there is no evidence tending to prove the accused guilty of murder in the second degree, it is not error to refuse to charge concerning such degree); *People* v. *Lee Gam*, 69 Cal. 552, 11 Pac. 183; *State* v. *Mahan*, 68 Iowa, 304, 20 N. W. 449, 27 N. W. 249 (holding that it was not error to instruct the jury, upon a trial for murder, that the defendant could not be convicted of a lesser offense than manslaughter, where there was no positive theory on the evidence that he was guilty of a lesser offense); *Davis* v. *State*, 14 Tex. App. 645; *Territory* v. *Thomason*, 4 N. M. 154, 13 Pac. 223. And see *State* v. *Dunn*, 80 Mo. 681 (holding that the defendant could not complain of an instruction as to a grade of manslaughter of which he was not convicted, though the instruction was erroneous).

People v. *McDonald*, 159 N. Y. 309, 54 N. E. 46, holds that upon the trial of an indictment for murder, the defendant is not entitled to an instruction that the jury may find the defendant guilty of assault in the first or second degree, if it is not satisfied that he is guilty of murder in any of its degrees.

According to *Territory* v. *Padilla*, 8 N. M. 510, 46 Pac. 346, the fact that proof shows deliberate and premeditated design on the part of defendant prior to the homicide unlawfully and maliciously to kill the deceased, and that the kind of weapon used and the way death was effected precludes the idea of an excusable or justifiable homicide as a defense, does not relieve the court of the duty of charging as to murder in the second degree, where there was no eyewitness to the homicide, and the circumstances under which it occurred do not appear.

XIV. Explaining omission to adduce evidence.

51. Omission justifies inference.

Where it has appeared that the accused, if innocent, had power to produce evidence other than by going upon the stand himself, controverting or explaining the testimony against him,[1] and he made no effort to procure it, although peculiarly within his knowledge and reach, it is proper to instruct the jury that they may take the fact into consideration in determining his guilt or innocence.[2]

If it has not so appeared, the accused is entitled to have the jury instructed that his omission to offer evidence is not to be considered by them.[3]

[1]This rule applies only where the accused is pressed by evidence calling for an explanation. *People* v. *McWhorter*, 4 Barb. 438, 440; *People* v. *Bodine*, 1 Denio, 281, 315.

[2]*State* v. *Grebe*, 17 Kan. 458. And see *Com.* v. *McCabe*, 163 Mass. 98, 39 N. E. 777 (holding that failure of defendant on trial for maintaining a liquor nuisance, to call as witnesses persons found by officers drinking beer in her kitchen, may be considered by the jury as tending to show defendant's guilt, where it does not appear that they cannot be procured by her); *Hinshaw* v. *State*, 147 Ind. 334, 47 N. E. 157 (holding that the failure of defendant charged with murder of his wife to produce as a witness a young woman who, the witnesses for the state testify, came to defendant's house at night, while he was alone, to testify to the truth of the matter, creates a presumption against him).

But this is not matter of right. *Brulo* v. *People*, 16 Hun, 119.

So also of failure of the prosecution. *Rice* v. *Com.* 102 Pa. 408. But it is not error to refuse to charge in a trial for murder, that a failure on the part of the commonwealth to produce a competent witness who was present at the time of the commission of the crime is a strong inference against the theory of the prosecution, and amounts to substantive evidence of the truth of the defendant's evidence denying the crime, where the witness was as available to the defense as to the prosecution. *Com.* v. *Schmous*, 162 Pa. 326, 29 Atl. 644.

But it is error to instruct them that failure to explain evidence makes it conclusive. *Gordon* v. *People*, 33 N. Y. 501.

[3]*Ormsby* v. *People*, 53 N. Y. 472.

52. Omission by accused as witness.

If the accused testified on his own behalf, the rule applies to his omission to make such an explanation by his own testimony.[1]

[1]*Stover* v. *People*, 56 N. Y. 315; *Brashears* v. *State*, 58 Md. 563.

53. Collateral circumstances.

This rule is not confined to direct evidence of the crime charged, but extends to material circumstances substantially strengthening the case of the prosecution.[1]

[1] *People* v. *Dyle*, 21 N. Y. 578. In this case the court held it a fair presumption that testimony as to the whereabouts of the prisoner and his confederates at a given time and place was within his power.

54. Evidence equally accessible, etc.

This rule does not apply where the evidence suggested to have been withheld appears to have been equally accessible to both parties,[1] and its materiality equally foreseen.[2]

[1] *State* v. *Rosier*, 55 Iowa, 517, 8 N. W. 345. And see *Com.* v. *Schmous*, 162 Pa. 326, 29 Atl. 644, *supra*.

[2] This is a necessary qualification. See, for instance, *Brulo* v. *People*, 16 Hun, 119.

55. Intent in suppressing.

Although it is proper to instruct the jury that the wilful suppression of evidence raises a presumption that the evidence if produced would be unfavorable, it is error to instruct the jury that intentional failure to produce that which might serve as evidence, or the intentional removal of it from the jurisdiction, raises a presumption of law to that effect, unless intention thereby to suppress evidence is shown.[1]

[1] *People* v. *Hurley*, 57 Cal. 145. Larceny; held error to charge that if the accused wilfully failed to produce certain property by wilfully sending it out of the country so that it could not be produced on the trial, this raised a presumption of law that the production of the property would be injurious to him. In the absence of a purpose to suppress the evidence, this circumstance would not raise the presumption. Compare *Tuttle* v. *People*, 36 N. Y. 431, 437, where evidence of the surreptitious removal of a document was held competent on the question of motive and intent. See more fully cases reviewed in note to *Hay* v. *Peterson* (Wyo.) 34 L. R. A. 581.

XV. Innocence.

56. Right to separate instruction.

Besides an instruction as to reasonable doubt the accused is also entitled to have the jury instructed that he is presumed to be innocent until the contrary is proved.[1]

This presumption accompanies him throughout the trial.[2]

[1] *People* v. *Van Houter*, 38 Hun, 168, and cases cited; *Cochran* v. *United*

States, 157 U. S. 286, 39 L. ed. 704, 15 Sup. Ct. Rep. 628; *Reeves* v. *State*, 29 Fla. 527, 10 So. 901; *State* v. *Harrison*, 23 Mont. 79, 57 Pac. 647. Compare *People* v. *Parsons*, 105 Mich. 177, 63 N. W. 69, where it is held that the omission of an instruction as to the presumption of innocence is not error where a full instruction as to reasonable doubt is given,—especially if the court instructs that nothing can be presumed against the defendant. And see *People* v. *Willett*, 105 Mich. 110, 62 N. W. 1115.

According to *State* v. *Smith*, 65 Conn. 283, 31 Atl. 206, the rule as to the presumption of innocence in favor of the accused is sufficiently expressed to the jury by an instruction requiring that guilt be established beyond a reasonable doubt; and an instruction that a presumption of innocence continues and is entitled to weight until the evidence offered by the state has overborne it and proved the accused guilty beyond a reasonable doubt puts too great a burden on the prosecution.

[1]*Barker* v. *State*, 48 Ind. 163; *Olive* v. *State*, 11 Neb. 1, 7 N. W. 444; *McMillan* v. *State*, 7 Tex. App. 142; *Haynes* v. *State*, 10 Tex. App. 480; *Campbell* v. *State*, 100 Ga. 267, 28 S. E. 71.

N. Y. Code Crim. Proc. § 389, provides that "a defendant in a criminal action is presumed to be innocent until the contrary be proved; and in case of a reasonable doubt whether his guilt is satisfactorily shown he is entitled to an acquittal." *People* v. *Van Houter*, 38 Hun, 168, holding that the refusal of the court to charge the presumption of the defendant's innocence as provided in this section of the Code, when requested by the defendant, constitutes error, notwithstanding the court charges that in case of reasonable doubt of the defendant's fault, he is entitled to an acquittal. The two propositions are not identical,—per Follett, J.

An instruction that the presumption of law is in favor of defendant's innocence, and such presumption continues through the trial until every material allegation in the information is established by the evidence to the exclusion of all reasonable doubt, is held in *Bartley* v. *State*, 53 Neb. 310, 73 N. W. 744, 55 Neb. 294, 75 N. W. 832, to be equivalent to the rule that the presumption of innocence is a matter of evidence, to the benefit of which the accused is entitled.

But an instruction that a presumption of guilt is met by a stronger presumption of innocence, and must give way to it, is confusing, and states an incorrect legal proposition in that the only presumption is one of innocence until the rendition of the verdict. *People* v. *Patterson*, 102 Cal. 239, 36 Pac. 436.

And an instruction in a criminal case, that the presumption of innocence goes with the prisoner until the case is submitted to the jury, is held erroneous in *People* v. *McNamara*, 94 Cal. 509, 29 Pac. 953, as suggesting that such presumption ceases upon the submission of the case to the jury.

But *People* v. *Winthrop*, 118 Cal. 85, 50 Pac. 390, holds that an instruction that the presumption of defendant's innocence accompanies him throughout the trial, and goes with the jury in their retirement, and that the evidence must be examined by the light of such presumption, and that it entitles the defendant to an acquittal unless it is overcome by such evidence as to satisfy the jury of the defendant's guilt beyond all reasonable doubt,—is not subject to the criticism that according to it the presumption ceases when the case is submitted to the jury.

Schintz v. *People,* 178 Ill. 320, 52 N. E. 903, holds that it is not error to strike out the words "beyond a reasonable doubt" from a requested instruction that the law presumes defendant innocent of the crime charged until he is proved guilty by competent evidence beyond a reasonable doubt, and that if the evidence leaves upon the minds of the jury any reasonable doubt of his guilt, it is their duty to acquit him.

That the substitution of the expression "attends the accused" for the word "prevails," in a requested instruction that "the presumption of innocence prevails throughout the trial," is proper, see *Emery* v. *State,* 101 Wis. 627, 78 N. W. 145.

XVI. Insanity.

[The rules here first stated as to what is insanity as a defense em- recognized as a defense. That additional ground, recognized in some body the results of the common-law test as now understood and ap- plied in those jurisdictions where moral or emotional insanity is not jurisdictions, is stated *infra,* § 63.]

57. The test—capacity.

The test of insanity at the time of the commission of the act, as a defense, is simply the capacity to distinguish between right and wrong in respect to the act.[1]

[1]It is true that it is not error to charge that if the accused knew the right and wrong of the act he is guilty, but it would be an error to say that if he did not know he is necessarily innocent. The reason is that ignorance is not a defense. Incapacity to know is. See § 58.

M'Naghten's Case, 10 Clark & F. 200. The leading English case, where what is known as the "right and wrong test" was established. The language of the judges does not make this distinction.

In an article in 7 Crim. L. Mag. 567, 595, being Everest's paper on the defense of insanity in criminal cases, with notes by John D. Lawson, the English cases are historically analyzed, and the "right and wrong" test is said to prevail in Alabama, California, Delaware, Georgia, Kansas, Maine, Massachusetts, Michigan, Minnesota, Mississippi, Missouri, Nebraska, New Jersey, New York, North Carolina, Ohio, Pennsylvania, Tennessee, Texas, and the Federal courts; but to have been abandoned in Illinois, Indiana, and New Hampshire.

Flanagan v. *People,* 52 N. Y. 467, 11 Am. Rep. 731, held it not error to charge in the language employed in *M'Naghten's Case,* that "to establish a defense on the ground of insanity it must be clearly proven that at the time of committing the act (the subject of the indictment) the party accused was laboring under such a defect of reason from disease of the mind as not to know the nature and quality of the act he was doing; and if he did know it, that he did not know he was doing wrong." The court by Andrews, J., said: "It must be regarded as the settled law of this state, that the test of responsibility for criminal acts, where unsoundness of mind is interposed as a defense, is the capacity of the defendant to distinguish between right and wrong at the time of, and with respect to, the act which is the subject of the inquiry. . . . The doctrine that a criminal act may be excused upon the notion of an irresistible impulse to commit it, where the offender has the ability to discover his legal and moral duty in respect to it, has no place in the law." To same effect, *Casey* v. *People*, 31 Hun, 158, Reversed on other grounds in 96 N. Y. 115; *Carr* v. *State*, 96 Ga. 284, 22 S. E. 570.

The distinction is well explained in Buswell on Insanity, § 437 (1885), where it is said by way of criticism of *M'Naghten's Case:* "The language of the rule as stated seems open to misconstruction. For, as it has often been construed, the rule appears to have a tendency to mislead juries, as inducing them to accept as the test of criminal responsibility the question whether the accused in fact believed his act to be wrong and criminal, whereas the question is whether he had mental power which ought to have enabled him to choose the right and avoid the wrong. The law on this subject seems to be more exactly expressed in the leading American case already cited [*Com.* v. *Rogers*, 7 Met. 500, 41 Am. Dec. 458], in which the rule was laid down that a party indicted is not entitled to an acquittal on the ground of insanity, if, at the time of the alleged offense, he had capacity and reason sufficient to enable him to distinguish between right and wrong, and understood the nature, character, and consequences of his act, and had mental power sufficient to apply that knowledge to his own act,"—Citing also *Flanagan* v. *People*, 52 N. Y. 467, 11 Am. Rep. 731; *Loeffner* v. *State*, 10 Ohio St. 598.

After instructing the jury that the capacity to distinguish between right and wrong in respect to the act is the test, it is not error to refuse to add that it must appear that he had capacity to know that the laws of God and man both forbid that act. *Moett* v. *People*, 85 N. Y. 373, 380. The court (Earl, J.) says: "The laws of God and the land are the measure of every man's act, and make it right or wrong, and it is right or wrong as it corresponds with such laws. When it is said that a prisoner must, at the time of the alleged criminal act, have sufficient capacity to distinguish between right and wrong with respect to such act, it is implied that he must have sufficient capacity to know whether such act is in violation of the law of God or of the land or both. It is not the duty of the trial judge to present the matter to the jury in every possible phase and in every form of language which the ingenuity of counsel can devise."

To the same effect are the comments on the *M'Naghten Case* in 1 Russell, Crimes, 9th Am. ed. 1877, 19, note; 7 Crim. L. Mag. 567, 581.

And in a recent work on Medical Jurisprudence of Insanity by Clevenger and Bowlby, in vol. 1, chaps. 6 and 7, this phase of the question of insanity, as well as those referred to in the succeeding sections of this division, is discussed at great length, and the authorities exhaustively collected and reviewed. And in vol. 2, chaps. 14, 16, and 25, of the same work, the authors review exhaustively the decisions as to alcoholism, morphinism, and epilepsy respectively.

58. Mere ignorance.

If the capacity to distinguish between right and wrong existed, it is immaterial whether actual knowledge existed.[1]

[1]The language of many of the cases fails to regard this distinction.

But ignorance, although it be ground for executive clemency, is not ground for finding that there has been no violation of the law.

See also *ante*, Division XXXIX., § 220, Citing Buswell, Insanity, § 437.

59. — ignorance of human law.

Neither knowledge of human law nor belief that it is binding need be shown. The reason is that to require this would excuse crime by reason of ignorance of the law or disrespect of it.

60. — ignorance of divine law.

Neither knowledge of nor belief in divine law need be shown, for to require this would make criminal responsibility depend on religious faith.

61. Belief in duty to violate law.

Belief that the divine law required the act to be done, though in violation of human law, does not excuse, unless amounting to an insane delusion, impairing the capacity to distinguish between right and wrong in respect to the act.[1]

[1]The reason is that such belief, although it may be ground for executive clemency, is not ground for finding that there has been no violation of law. Religious belief cannot be accepted as a justification of an overt act made criminal by the law of the land. *Reynolds* v. *United States*, 98 U. S. 145, 25 L. ed. 244, where a charge in accordance with the above rule was sustained. This was a case of polygamy. The court (Waite, Ch. J.) said: "A criminal intent is generally an element of crime, but every man is presumed to intend the necessary and legitimate consequence of what he knowingly does. Here the accused knew he had been once married, and that his first wife was living. He also knew that his second marriage was forbidden by law. When, therefore, he married the second time, he is presumed to have intended to break the law. And the breaking of the law is the crime. Every act necessary to constitute the crime was knowingly done, and the crime was therefore knowingly com-

mitted. Ignorance of a fact may sometimes be taken as evidence of a want of criminal intent, but not ignorance of the law."

Wharton & Stillé, Med. Jur. § 137, say: "The test . . . is, is the delusion pleaded as a defense the delusion of an insane person? If not, he has reason enough to dispel or correct it, and his refusal to do so does not invest him with irresponsibility."

Compare *United States* v. *Guiteau,* 10 Fed. 161, where Cox, J., in charging the jury, concluded by saying: "If you find from the whole evidence that at the time of the commission of the homicide the prisoner, in consequence of disease of mind, was laboring under such a defect of his reason that he was incapable of understanding what he was doing, or that it was wrong,—as, for example, if he was under an insane delusion that the Almighty had commanded him to do the act, and, in consequence of that, he was incapable of seeing that it was a wrong thing to do,—then he was not in a responsible condition of mind, and was an object of compassion, and not of justice, and ought to be now acquitted."

In *Com.* v. *Rogers,* 7 Met. 500, 41 Am. Dec. 458, Shaw, Ch. J., said: Monomania "may operate as an excuse for a criminal act. . . . A common instance is where he fully believes that the act he is doing is done by the immediate command of God, and he acts under the delusive but sincere belief that what he is doing is done by the command of a superior power which supersedes all human laws and the laws of nature." This is approved as sound in Wharton & Stillé, Med. Jur. § 134.

62. Lack of self-control.

If the capacity to distinguish between right and wrong in respect to the act existed, it is immaterial whether the accused had the power of self-control, unless the lack of such power raises a reasonable doubt whether he intended to do the act.[1]

[1] *People* v. *Carpenter,* 102 N. Y. 238, 250, 6 N. E. 584, Applying *Flanagan* v. *People,* 52 N. Y. 467, 11 Am. Rep. 731 (held that it is not error to refuse to charge on defendant's request, that "if some controlling disease was, in truth, the acting power within him [the prisoner], which he could not resist, or if he had not a sufficient use of his reason to control the passion which prompted the act complained of, he is not responsible"); *Walker* v. *People,* 88 N. Y. 81, Affirming 26 Hun, 67 (request to charge that "the test of criminal responsibility, where the defense of insanity is interposed to an indictment, is whether the accused had sufficient reason to know right from wrong, and whether or not he had sufficient power of control to govern his actions." Held not error to charge the first part of this proposition while refusing to charge the portion beginning with "whether or not").

In *Roberts* v. *State,* 3 Ga. 310, the court states that an exception to the general rule stated above exists where a man has sufficient reason to distinguish between right and wrong as to the particular act about to be committed, yet in consequence of some delusion the will is overmastered, and there is no criminal intent. But the qualification is added that the act itself must be connected with the peculiar delusion under which the person is laboring. See also *Danforth* v. *State*, 75 Ga. 614, 58 Am. Rep. 480; *Carr* v. *State*, 96 Ga. 284, 22 S. E. 570 (where this phase of the question was discussed, but held inapplicable to the case at bar).

63. Emotional or moral insanity.

In some jurisdictions the existence of insanity exonerating the accused is recognized, if the act charged was the result of disease irresistibly impelling him to do it, even though he knew that it was wrong.[1]

[1] *State* v. *Jones*, 50 N. H. 369, 9 Am. Rep. 242, note in 36 Am. Dec. 402; cases reviewed in *Leache* v. *State*, 22 Tex. App. 279, 58 Am. Rep. 638, 3 S. W. 539. And see *Parsons* v. *State*, 81 Ala. 577, 60 Am. Rep. 193, 2 So. 854, and cases there cited; *Dacey* v. *People*, 116 Ill. 555, 6 N. E. 165; *State* v. *Reidell*, 9 Houst. (Del.) 470, 14 Atl. 550.

64. Insanity induced by inebriety.

Insanity amounting to mental disease is none the less a defense because induced by inebriety, as distinguished from the immediate influence of present intoxication.[1]

Delirium tremens is a species of insanity.[2]

[1] *People* v. *Blake*, 65 Cal. 275, 4 Pac. 1; John D. Lawson in 23 Am. L. Reg. N. S. 227, Citing many cases as sustaining this position; 28 Moak Eng. Rep. 661 (note to *Reg.* v. *Davis*), Citing numerous authorities, both state and Federal; article on "The Medical Jurisprudence of Inebriety" (1887), 21 Am. L. Rev. 955; *People* v. *O'Connell*, 62 How. Pr. 436, which was affirmed, without noticing this point, in *O'Connell* v. *People*, 87 N. Y. 377, 41 Am. Rep. 379. And see 2 Clevenger, Med. Jur. chap. 14, where this question is treated at great length and the authorities reviewed.

[2] *Erwin* v. *State*, 10 Tex. App. 700; *Territory* v. *Davis* (Ariz.) 10 Pac. 359, with note collecting cases.

65. Burden on defense.

In the absence of evidence to the contrary, the legal presumption that a human being was sane is sufficient to sustain the burden of proof which is upon the prosecution to show sanity, and throw upon the accused the burden of proving insanity, if he relies on that defense.[1]

[1] *O'Connell* v. *People*, 87 N. Y. 377, 41 Am. Rep. 379, where it is held not error to charge that the defense of insanity is an affirmative defense, and the accused bound to satisfy the jury by proof that he is insane. The court says: "This result follows the general rule of evidence which re-

quires him who asserts a fact to prove it. That the first proposition was established is not denied. The legal presumption that every man is sane was sufficient to sustain the other until repelled, and the charge . . . goes no further. If the prisoner gave no evidence the fact stood; if he gave evidence tending to overthrow it, the prosecutor might produce answering testimony; but in any event he must satisfy the jury upon the whole evidence that the prisoner was mentally responsible, for the affirmative of the issue tendered by the indictment remained with the prosecutor to the end of the trial." See also *Walker* v. *People,* 8 N. Y. 81. And for other cases to similar effect, see *State* v. *Duestrow,* 137 Mo. 44, 91, 38 S. W. 554, 39 S. W. 266; *Kelch* v. *State,* 55 Ohio St. 146, 39 L. R. A. 737, 45 N. E. 6; *Com.* v. *Heidler,* 191 Pa. 375, 43 Atl. 211; *Burt* v. *State,* 38 Tex. Crim. Rep. 397, 39 L. R. A. 309, 330, 43 S. W. 1000, 43 S. W. 344; *Clawson* v. *State,* 59 N. J. L. 434, 36 Atl. 886. And for an exhaustive review of the authorities on this question, see note to *State* v. *Scott* (La.) 36 L. R. A. 721 *et seq.*

The maxim that applies to the order of proof is not always applicable as an instruction to the jury. See the distinction explained in Abbott's Civil Trial Brief, 2d ed. pp. 330–332.

As to the order of proof, the burden is on the defense according to the more generally received rule. It is an affirmative issue. If the defense gives no evidence, the legal presumption of sanity suffices (according even to the New York form of the rule, which is favorable to the accused) to sustain the burden which is upon the prosecution. It would not be correct to instruct the jury that the burden of proof is on the prosecution, in the absence of all evidence on the subject. If the defense assumes the burden and offers evidence, then it would be error, according to the New York decisions, to instruct the jury unqualifiedly that the burden is on him to prove insanity. But *Brotherton* v. *People,* 75 N. Y. 159, seems to be a clear authority for the doctrine that it is proper to instruct them, in substance, that in the absence of evidence on the subject from the prosecution, the burden is on the defense to give evidence raising at least a reasonable or well-founded doubt.

Judge Seymour D. Thompson says (10 Crim. L. Mag. 182): "The prevailing rule in regard to the defense of insanity seems to be that it is an affirmative defense, the burden to establish which is upon the accused, and that it must be shown by evidence which satisfies the minds of the jurors, which is quite a different thing from raising a reasonable doubt as to whether or not the accused was sane at the time when he committed the act."

66. — as to intoxication.

Whether, if intoxication be the cause of mental incapacity, the burden is on the accused or on the prosecution to show whether it was intoxication immediately previous, or merely habits of inebriety so long previous and so continued that the resulting unsoundness of mind is a defense—[1]

[1]Compare *People* v. *Bell,* 49 Cal. 485, 489; *United States* v. *McGlue,* 1 Curt. C. C. 1, 14, Fed. Cas. No. 15,679.

67. Proof beyond reasonable doubt not necessary.

It is not necessary to prove insanity beyond a reasonable doubt,[1] hence it is error to instruct the jury that it must be clearly proved,[2] or shown by clearly preponderating evidence.[3]

[1]In an article in 17 Am. L. Rev. 922, it is said: "The cases holding that burden of proving insanity is upon defendant usually follow that rule to its logical result, and hold that he must, to be entitled to acquittal, prove the fact by some degree of evidence, and that it is not sufficient for him to merely raise a reasonable doubt of sanity. But they do not agree as to the degree of proof required. A few cases are constantly cited in the text-books as requiring proof by defendant beyond a reasonable doubt, but they are local, and perhaps practically obsolete. The other cases are somewhat diverse in their expressions of the rule, some saying that the proof of insanity must be to the entire satisfaction of the jury, or to the reasonable satisfaction of the jury, or by satisfactory evidence; but an examination of them will show that these expressions mean no more than that the fact of insanity must be proved by a preponderance of the evidence, which is the expression more generally used."

In an article in 7 Crim. L. Mag. 431, on "the Defense of Insanity in Criminal Cases," it is stated in a note on page 438 that the doctrine that the prisoner must prove his insanity beyond a doubt, though maintained in a few early American cases, is now pretty well abandoned. The prevailing rule is said to be that the burden is on the accused, but that a preponderance of evidence in his favor is sufficient to overthrow the presumption. The rule is said to prevail in Alabama, Arkansas, California, Connecticut, Georgia, Iowa, Kentucky, Louisiana, Maine, Massachusetts, Ohio, Pennsylvania, Virginia, and West Virginia, while the rule that the burden rests on the prosecution to prove the prisoner sane is said to prevail in Illinois, Indiana, Kansas, Michigan, Mississippi, Nebraska, New Hampshire, New York, Tennessee, and Texas.

And for an exhaustive review of the authorities on this question, see note to *Scott* v. *State* (La.) 36 L. R. A. 726.

In an article in 8 Am. L. Rec. 193, is an elaborate argument in favor of the rule that where the defense is insanity the state must prove the prisoner's sanity beyond a reasonable doubt; and it is said that New York, New Hampshire, Indiana, Illinois, Kansas, Kentucky, Alabama, Georgia, and Michigan have adopted this rule after having for years strenuously maintained the contrary.

In an article in 14 Cent. L. J. 2, it is said that the cases that maintain the theory that the burden of proof of insanity rests upon the prosecution do so in the face of an overwhelming weight of authority. Cases from nineteen states are critically examined, and as a result it is stated that "while some few of them hold that the prisoner must establish his insanity beyond a doubt, and the others that a preponderance of the evidence is sufficient, they are all agreed that the burden rests with him, and not with the state." But it is also said that "the contrary theory has found favor with some of our ablest and most enlightened courts," as, for instance, those of Illinois, Indiana, Kansas, Michigan, Nebraska, and New Hampshire. And it is said that notwithstanding what is said in *People* v. *McCann,* 16 N. Y. 58, 69 Am. Dec. 642, it must be considered doubtful which of these theories is to be recognized in New York.

Walker v. *People,* 88 N. Y. 81, 26 Hun, 67, held it not error to charge that to establish a defense on the ground of insanity, it must be clearly proved that at the time of committing the act in question the accused was laboring under such a defect of reason from a disease of the mind as not to know the nature and quality of the act he was doing, and if he did know it, that he did not know that he was doing wrong. The court says: "If by this expression the jury were given to understand that the insanity must be proved beyond a reasonable doubt, it of course was at variance with the law of this state (*People* v. *McCann,* 16 N. Y. 58, 69 Am. Dec. 642). But if it meant that there should be clear and substantial evidence of insanity to justify an acquittal on that ground, it was unobjectionable (*People* v. *Schryver,* 42 N. Y. 1, 1 Am. Rep. 480)."

In *Coyle* v. *Com.* 100 Pa. 573, 4 Crim. L. Mag. 76, with note to 22 Am. L. Reg. N. S. 191, it is held error to charge that the presumption of sanity can only be overthrown by clearly preponderating evidence. The court said: "To require it to 'clearly preponderate' is practically saying it must be proved beyond all doubt and uncertainty. . . . Evidence fairly preponderating is sufficient." The court, however, concedes that the burden is on the accused to show insanity by evidence at least fairly preponderating.

In the note to *Coyle* v. *Com.* by H. W. Rogers, in 22 Am. L. Reg. N. S. 194, it is said that the theory announced in the principal case, that "inasmuch as every man is presumed to be sane, the presumption of sanity prevails necessarily until it is shown to be false by a preponderance of evidence. That the burden of proof rests on the prisoner to show his insanity to the satisfaction of the jury by a preponderance of the evidence" is the rule generally adhered to, and is maintained in Alabama, Arkansas, California, Iowa, Kentucky, Maine, Massachusetts, Missouri, North Carolina, Ohio, Pennsylvania, and Texas. See numerous authorities from those states cited.

68. Reasonable doubt of sanity enough.

If upon the whole evidence a reasonable doubt of sanity exists, the prisoner is entitled to acquittal.[1]

[1] *Brotherton* v. *People,* 75 N. Y. 159 (held that it was not error to charge that the "allegation of insanity is an affirmative issue which the defendant is bound to prove, and you must be satisfied from the testimony in-

troduced by him that he was insane,"—taking such expression in connection with another part of the charge, "that if 'there is a well-founded doubt whether this man was insane at the time he fired the pistol you will acquit him.'" Church, Ch. J., said: "Crimes can only be committed by human beings who are in a condition to be responsible for their acts; and upon this general proposition the prosecutor holds the affirmative, and the burden of proof is upon him. Sanity being the normal and usual condition of mankind, the law presumes that every individual is in that state. Hence a prosecutor may rest upon that presumption without other proof. The fact is deemed to be proved prima facie. Whoever denies this, or interposes a defense based upon its untruth, must prove it. The burden, not of the general issue of crime by a competent person, but the burden of overthrowing the presumption of sanity and of showing insanity, is upon the person who alleges it; and if evidence is given tending to establish insanity, then the general question is presented to the court and jury whether the crime, if committed, was committed by a person responsible for his acts; and upon this question the presumption of sanity and the evidence are all to be considered; and the prosecutor holds the affirmative, and if a reasonable doubt exists as to whether the prisoner is sane or not, he is entitled to the benefit of the doubt and to an acquittal." And of the particular charge the court said: "The prisoner was bound to prove that he was not sane; and whether insanity is called an affirmative issue, or it is stated that the burden of proof of insanity is upon the prisoner, in order to overcome the presumption of sanity, is not very material, if the jury are told, as they were in this case, that a reasonable doubt upon that question entitled the prisoner to an acquittal)," Followed in *O'Connell* v. *People*, 87 N. Y. 379, 41 Am. Rep. 379; *Casey* v. *People*, 31 Hun, 158, Reversed on other grounds in 96 N. Y. 115 (held that it was not error to refuse to charge that, on an interposition of the defense of insanity and testimony deduced in support of the plea, the presumption of sanity in the accused is prima facie overcome, and the prosecution, before there can be a conviction, must satisfy the jury, by affirmative proof of saneness, that the accused was not mentally diseased at the time of shooting. This case also held that it was not error to charge that every man is presumed to be sane, and that when a defendant avers the plea he must prove it; but if on the whole proof there is a reasonable doubt of sanity, the defendant must be given the benefit of the doubt); *Wagner* v. *People*, 4 Abb. App. Dec. 509, Affirming 54 Barb. 367 (held that it is not error to charge that, on the question of insanity, the accused is entitled to the benefit of any doubt that may arise; that is, the jury must be satisfied beyond all reasonable doubt that he was sane when he committed the act, but that if the jury are satisfied beyond reasonable doubt that the accused knew that the nature and quality of the act he was doing was wrong, the law holds him responsible).

In *People* v. *McCann*, 16 N. Y. 58, 69 Am. Dec. 642, where the only defense was insanity, it was held error to charge that unless the jury "were satisfied beyond a reasonable doubt that the prisoner was insane at the time of the homicide, he was not entitled to a verdict of acquittal on that ground." The court said: "The rule requiring the evidence to satisfy the jury beyond a reasonable doubt is one in favor of the individual on trial charged with crime, and is applicable only to the general conclusion, from the whole evidence, of guilty or not guilty;" and disapproved the rule in *State* v. *Spencer*, 21 N. J. L. 196, that, in order to acquit on the ground of insanity, the proof of insanity at the time of committing the act ought to be as clear and satisfactory as the proof of committing the act ought to be in order to find a sane man guilty.

Of *People* v. *McCann*, 16 N. Y. 58, 69 Am. Dec. 642, it was said in *Flanagan* v. *People*, 52 N. Y. 467, 471, 11 Am. Rep. 731: "The question was not in the case whether the prisoner would be entitled to the benefit of a doubt upon the evidence introduced by him to establish the defense. What is said by the learned judges upon the subject is entitled to such weight as their character and learning and their arguments entitle it to. . . . It is not necessary for us to consider the question in this case, but we prefer to leave it precisely where the cases cited leave it,—an open question, so far as judicial authority in this state is concerned."

Compare *Walker* v. *People*, 26 Hun, 67, 1 N. Y. Crim. Rep. 7, 14, where it was held not error to refuse to charge that the accused was not required to prove his insanity to avail himself of the defense, but merely to create a reasonable doubt upon that point, whereupon the burden of proving sanity fell upon the People. The jury were charged that if they found accused insane at the time of perpetrating the act in question, they should find him not guilty, on the ground of insanity; and also that if they found, beyond all reasonable doubt, that he committed the crime, and that he was not insane, they should convict; and also that if there was any reasonable doubt arising from the evidence, he was entitled to the benefit of the doubt, and they should acquit. Held, that the charge was not objectionable as failing to meet a request to charge that it was sufficient for the accused to create a reasonable doubt of his sanity. And in this case on appeal in 88 N. Y. 88, the court said: "The burden of establishing beyond a reasonable doubt, as one of the elements of guilt, that the prisoner was not insane, was by this charge cast upon the prosecution."

In *Walter* v. *People*, 32 N. Y. 147, Affirming 18 Abb. Pr. 147, the court says: "The prisoner's counsel requested the judge to charge as a proposition of law that in a case where the defense consists in the insanity of the prisoner, it becomes incumbent upon the prosecution to prove him sane. There was not a particle of evidence in this case showing the prisoner to have been insane when he committed the homicide. The defense of insanity failed utterly. Hence the legal proposition asked to be given to the jury was of the most abstract character, and for this reason the judge was not called upon to say anything about it. But as an abstract legal proposition it was manifestly unsound. Sanity is presumed to be the normal state of the human mind, and it is never incumbent upon the prosecution to give affirmative evidence that such state exists in a particular case."

And compare *State* v. *Hockett*, 70 Iowa, 442, 30 N. W. 742, 748, Distinguishing *State* v. *Jones*, 64 Iowa, 356, 17 N. W. 911, 20 N. W. 470, where it was held error to charge that "in order to establish insanity, it is not necessary that the proofs shall be direct and positive, but it may be shown by such facts and circumstances as convince the mind of its existence, the same as any other fact. But when the claim set up as a defense is unusual, unnatural, and out of the ordinary course of affairs, you are not required to take the same for granted, upon slight evidence, nor should you so find, except upon evidence of a reliable character, and which satisfies you that the defense has been made out."

Kearney v. *State*, 68 Miss. 233, 8 So. 292, holds that an instruction on a murder trial that if the jury have no reasonable doubt of the sanity of the accused at the time of the killing, they are to find him guilty, if they believe he shot and killed deceased, is erroneous, being in effect an instruction that if defendant was capable of malice the jury must convict upon proof only of the killing.

State v. *Brooks*, 23 Mont. 146, 57 Pac. 1038, holds that it is not error to refuse to instruct, in a capital case, that defendant should be acquitted if a fair preponderance of evidence shows his insanity, the correct rule being that he is entitled to an acquittal where the evidence raises a reasonable doubt of his sanity when the crime was committed.

In *People* v. *Barthleman*, 120 Cal. 7, 52 Pac. 112, an instruction that if the jury have a reasonable doubt of the sanity of the defendant at the time of the commission of the homicide charged they must acquit him is held to have been properly refused, the court stating that a reasonable doubt of the defendant's sanity is not enough to warrant an acquittal,—Citing *People* v. *Ward*, 105 Cal. 343, 38 Pac. 945.

69. Barbarity.

The barbarity of a crime should not alone be considered evidence of insanity.[1]

[1]*United States* v. *Lee*, 4 Mackey, 489, 54 Am. Rep. 293.

In *Kearney* v. *State*, 68 Miss. 233, 8 So. 292, an instruction on a murder trial, that an inference of insanity is not warranted from the mere commission of a crime, or from the enormity thereof, or from a mere apparent absence of adequate motive, since the law presumes a bad motive from a killing with a deadly weapon, and that it is prompted by malice, if nothing else appears in evidence, is held to violate Miss. Code, § 1714, prohibiting comment on the testimony or a charge as to the weight of evidence.

70. Grade of offense.

Insanity not amounting to a defense cannot reduce the grade of the offense.[1]

[1]*United States* v. *Lee*, 4 Mackey, 489, 54 Am. Rep. 293.

XVII. Intent.

71. Necessity of evidence.

To constitute criminal intent it is not necessary to show an intent to violate the law. The question is, Did the accused intend to do the thing he did do, and was that thing a violation of law? Where, however, the prohibition imposed by the law, or the punishment prescribed, depends upon the act being done with knowledge or with an evil intent, there must be evidence of such knowledge or evil intent, as well as of the intent to do the act.[1]

[[1]See also cases cited *ante*, Division XXXIX., §§ 236–249.

The principle above stated is now well settled, and constantly recognized in practice; and to this extent the tradition in the books, still insisted on by some text writers, that there is no crime without criminal intent, is unsound.

The application of the distinction has led to many conflicts in the cases. The question is in effect a question of statutory interpretation. A legislative intention to punish some acts which are declared unlawful except within certain limitations—such as receiving minors in liquor and gambling saloons—may well be deemed implied from a prohibition expressed without reference to knowledge or intent; although a legislative intention to punish, irrespective of such intent, some other offenses,—such as intrusion on lands,—could not be justly implied.]

"An offense punishable by indictment may be created by statute having in it no other circumstance of wrong beyond a mere breach of the law, in which case a criminal purpose or intent does not enter into the offense as an element of guilt." Bockes, J., in *People* v. *Grim*, 3 N. Y. Crim. Rep. 317, Approving rule in *Halsted* v. *State*, 41 N. J. L. 552, 32 Am. Rep. 247 In *People* v. *Grim* it was held necessary to show a criminal intent, under N. Y. Pen. Code, § 528.

Halsted v. *State*, 41 N. J. L. 552, 32 Am. Rep. 247. A leading case; indictment for violation of statute prohibiting board of county freeholders from incurring obligations in excess of appropriations. Conviction affirmed notwithstanding exclusion of evidence tending to show that accused acted under the advice of counsel, and in good faith, from pure and honest motives, and exercised due care and caution. The court said: None of the cases cited "can be said to sustain the proposition that, in cases where a statute in general terms prohibits the doing of a particular act, the court will interpolate into such statute the requirement of a corrupt motive as an ingredient of the offense, on the sole ground that otherwise it would be opposed to natural justice." Compare *People* v. *Stevens*, 109 N. Y. 159, 16 N. E. 53, below cited.

In *People* v. *Mahaney*, 41 Hun, 26, on trial for selling an article that was not butter, representing it to be butter, it was held unnecessary to give proof that defendant knowingly and intentionally represented the article sold to be butter. The court said: "Whether or not the seller knows his representations to be false, or intends to deceive, is immaterial. He subjects himself to the penalties of the statute by making the representation not knowing it to be true," and cited *Com.* v. *Farren*, 9 Allen, 489, as putting a like construction on a similar statute. Held, also, that under a provision of the same statute making the proof of sale and false representation presumptive evidence of guilt the presumption was not to be met by showing the absence of knowledge and intent to deceive. Compare *People* v. *Fulle*, 12 Abb. N. C. 196, holding criminal intent or negligence necessary to establish complaint for adulteration of food or drug.

People v. *Kibler*, 106 N. Y. 321, 12 N. E. 795. Selling adulterated milk contrary to statute; conviction affirmed notwithstanding absence of proof of criminal intent.

People v. *Roby*, 52 Mich. 577, 50 Am. Rep. 270, 18 N. W. 365. Conviction under Sunday liquor law sustained against objection that criminal intent was not shown. The court (Cooley, Ch. J.) said: "Many statutes which are in the nature of police regulations, as this is, impose criminal penalties irrespective of any intent to violate them, the purpose being to require a degree of diligence for the protection of the public which shall make violation impossible,"—Citing many cases.

"When an act forbidden by law is intentionally done, the intent to do the act is the criminal intent which imparts to it the character of an offense, and no one who violates the law, which he is conclusively presumed to know, can be heard to say that he had no criminal intent in doing the forbidden act. A party cannot excuse himself for an act intentionally done, and which is in violation of law, by saying he did not so intend. But where the acts are themselves equivocal, and become criminal only by reason of the intent with which they are done, both must unite to constitute the offense, and both facts must be proved in order to a conviction. In such case, unless the intent is proved, the offense is not proved. As the criminal intent may be and usually is inferred from the declarations and conduct of the accused, he is permitted to disavow the imputed purpose and repel the presumption. None of the cited cases go beyond this." Smith, Ch. J., in *State* v. *King*, 86 N. C. 603 (indictment for affray), where it was held not error to refuse to allow accused to show that he did not intend to bring about a breach of the peace.

Jones v. *State*, 67 Ala. 84. Bigamy; it being proved that accused married a second time while her first husband was living, held not error to exclude evidence tending to show that at the time of the second marriage she had reason to believe her first husband to be dead. The court said: "Every act was done by the appellant under all the circumstances expressed in the statute which is declared criminal, and from the act and the circumstances the criminal intent must be deduced. There was the intent to marry a second time, not knowing the husband to be dead, who had been absent for a period of about one year only; and this is the criminal intent, and the only intent which is of the essence of the offense."

That such is the settled law in England, see cases cited in *Farrell* v. *State* (Ohio) 30 Am. Rep. 617, note.

State v. *Probasco*, 62 Iowa, 400, 17 N. W. 607. Indictment under statute making it unlawful to permit minor to remain in billiard halls; conviction affirmed against objection that accused did not know that the person shown to be a minor was in his saloon. The court says: "The guilt of one charged with a crime does not depend upon his knowledge of the facts constituting the crime."

And in *Farrell* v. *State* (Ohio) 30 Am. Rep. 617, note, see numerous cases cited as sustaining the proposition that under a statute forbidding sale of liquor to minors ignorance that the vendee is a minor is no defense, though coupled with an honest belief that he is of full age.

Stern v. *State*, 53 Ga. 229, 21 Am. Rep. 266. Indictment under statute for allowing minor to play billiards without consent of parent or guardian. Conviction reversed, it appearing that accused honestly believed, from the appearance of the infant and from his answer to questions, that he was of full age. The court said: "To make a crime there must be the union of act and intent, or there must be criminal negligence." To same effect under Indiana statute, *Goetz* v. *State*, 41 Ind. 162.

Fox v. *State*, 3 Tex. App. 329, 30 Am. Rep. 144. Adultery under statute; conviction affirmed against objection of want of proof that accused at time of offense knew that the other party to the offense was a married woman. The court said: "It is the act of living together, and not the knowledge or intent, that constitutes the offense. When the statement of the act itself necessarily includes a knowledge of the illegality of the act, no averment of knowledge or bad intent is necessary. It is otherwise when guilty knowledge is a substantive ingredient of the offense."

Reg. v. *Prince*, L. R. 2 C. C. 154. Indictment for violation of statute against "unlawfully taking any unmarried girl, under the age of sixteen, out of the possession and against the will of her father, etc." Conviction affirmed, though accused in good faith believed the girl to be over sixteen. This on the ground that the word "unlawfully" meant without lawful warrant or authority, and that the act being wrong, irrespective of the girl's exact age, the ignorance of the accused formed no defense.

Fox v. *People*, 95 Ill. 71. Forgery; held error to charge in effect that if the accused falsely made the instrument in question, the law presumed the intent to defraud. The court said: "The merely falsely making the instrument, without the intention named, does not constitute the crime. . . . The instruction should have left it to the jury to find the intent. The mere making and possession does not necessarily prove an intent to defraud."

Gordon v. *State*, 52 Ala. 308, 23 Am. Rep. 575. Illegal voting, not being of full age; held error to refuse to charge that if the accused, in reliance on certain statements, honestly believed that he was of full age when he voted, he should not be convicted, if the evidence convinced the jury he was not of age. The court said: "The criminal intention being of the essence of crime, if the intent is dependent on a knowledge of particular facts, a want of such knowledge, not the result of carelessness or negligence, relieves the act of criminality."

Bosley v. *Davies*, L. R. 1 Q. B. Div. 84 (information for penalty for violating statute against "suffering any gaming or any unlawful game to be carried on" on the premises; conviction reversed, in the absence of evidence of actual or constructive knowledge on the part of the accused that gaming was carried on on his premises); *Felton* v. *United States*, 96 U. S. 699, 24 L. ed. 875 (action against distillers for penalty for "knowingly and wilfully" omitting, neglecting, and refusing to construct apparatus as required by statute. Judgment against defendants reversed on ground of absence of their knowledge of the defects in the apparatus. The court said: "Doing or omitting to do a thing knowingly and wilfully implies not only a knowledge of the thing, but a determination with a bad intent to do it or omit doing it"); *State* v. *Gillett*, 56 Iowa, 459, 9 N. W. 362 (assault with intent to do great bodily injury upon a child eight years of age, in whipping him; held not error to charge that a great bodily injury is an injury of a more grave and serious character than an ordinary battery; and the indictment charging that defendant intended to inflict such an injury on the boy, it was not only necessary for the state to prove that defendant committed an assault, but also to prove the intent with which he committed it, and that it was to inflict a grave and more serious injury than an ordinary battery or whipping; that if the proof should show an assault and battery, but fail to show the ulterior intent charged, the conviction could only be for an assault and battery); *People* v. *Utter*, 44 Barb. 170 (selling liquors on Sunday; held error to charge that if the jury believed that the defendant's bartender had sold liquor at his tavern on Sunday, then, inasmuch as there was no evidence that the defendant had given directions to the contrary, he was guilty of the offense charged, though he was ignorant of the sale, and did not assent to it, because in order to convict proof was needed of an intent to violate the statute).

Compare *Com.* v. *Briant*, 142 Mass. 463, 56 Am. Rep. 707, 8 N. E. 338; *People* v. *Stevens*, 109 N. Y. 159, 16 N. E. 53 (holding that the existence of a criminal intent is a necessary constituent of the offense of an unlawful intrusion on land, though not in terms made a part of the definition thereof by N. Y. Pen. Code, § 467; and that a charge to that effect was not error. The court said: "Section 467 . . . does not, it is true, in terms make the intent a material element of the offense; but it cannot be supposed that the legislature intended to subject a person to criminal punishment. . . . Looking at the reason of the thing, the ineffaceable distinction between innocence and crime, and the antecedent law, the existence of a criminal intent as a necessary constituent of the offense must be implied").

See *United States* v. *Stone*, 8 Fed. 232, as to intent in larceny by finder's concealment of thing.

For the rule where the statute prohibits the act positively, without reference to wilfulness, and the indictment unnecessarily alleges wilfulness, see *United States* v. *Smith*, 27 Fed. 854.

For some other recent cases of illustrative instructions on this question, see

Cobb v. *State,* 100 Ala. 19, 14 So. 362 (holding that a statute making it a felony to remove mortgaged chattels with intent to defraud the mortgagee, and making a violation thereof punishable as if the violator had stolen the property, does not constitute such violation the crime of larceny; and an instruction which would be proper in a larceny case, that a strong presumption that there was no intent to defraud arises if the transfer was open, and there was no subsequent attempt at concealment, is inappropriate in a prosecution under the statute); *Jones* v. *State,* 96 Ala. 102, 11 So. 399 (holding that instructions on a trial for assault with intent to commit murder, that there must have been the specific intent to murder the person assaulted, and that a specific felonious intent must be proved; that the doctrine of intent implied by law, different from the intent in fact, can have no application; and if there was not the intent to murder the person assaulted, although there may have been a general felonious intent, a conviction of the aggravated offense would be improper,—are erroneous); *Felker* v. *State,* 54 Ark. 489, 16 S. W. 663 (holding that an instruction on a trial for assault with intent to murder, charging that defendant will be guilty if, under certain circumstances, he shot at the prosecutor, is erroneous, when it does not make the intent to kill an essential element of the crime); *People* v. *Morino,* 85 Cal. 515, 24 Pac. 892 (holding that an instruction that if the jury believe that the defendant had no felonious intent to steal the property at the time he took it, they must acquit, even if they believe that he subsequently conceived the intent to appropriate it, is improperly refused when applicable to the evidence); *People* v. *Mize,* 80 Cal. 41, 22 Pac. 80 (holding that, in a prosecution for assault with intent to kill, the intent to kill is a question for the jury; and instructions which withdraw it from their consideration are erroneous); *State* v. *Hines* (Idaho) 51 Pac. 984 (holding that an instruction on a trial for grand larceny, that if the jury believe from the evidence that defendant had no felonious intent to steal the property described, at the time he took it, they must acquit, even if they believe that he subsequently conceived the intent of appropriating such property, sufficiently leaves the question of intent to the jury); *Friedrich* v. *People,* 147 Ill. 310, 35 N. E. 472 (holding that an instruction on a trial for assault with intent to commit murder, that every man is presumed to intend the natural and probable consequences of his act unless a different intent be proved; and the use of a deadly weapon in making an assault will be presumed to be with felonious and malicious intent unless a different intent be proved, is erroneous and misleading, as in effect stating that the case of the People is made out by proving the assault with a deadly weapon, and as making the use of a deadly weapon the basis of a presumption of felonious and malicious intent. Such intent must be proved); *State* v. *Grant,* 86 Iowa, 216, 53 N. W. 120 (holding that the element of intent to defraud is sufficiently included in a charge in a prosecution for conspiracy to defraud, that defendants are guilty if they were working and acting together with the purpose of obtaining certain notes by false and fraudulent pretenses); *Barnes* v. *State,* 40 Neb. 545, 59 N. W. 125 (holding that an instruction which authorizes a conviction for larceny, if the accused took away the property described, intending to deprive the owner thereof, and to convert it to his own use, provided that he intended to deprive the owner permanently of his property, is erroneous, as it omits the element of felonious intent); *Hughes* v. *Territory*, 8 Okla. 28, 56 Pac. 708 (holding that the word "steal" in Okla. Sess. Laws 1895, chap. 20, art. 1, § 1, making it a distinct and separate offense to "steal" any of the domestic animals therein enumerated, involves an intent to appropriate the animal; and it is error to charge that such intent may be inferred as a matter of law from the unlawful taking); *Shaw* v. *State*, 34 Tex. Crim. Rep. 435, 31 S. W. 361 (holding that where the law requires the intent to appear in order to find one guilty of murder, it is error to instruct the jury that the accused may be found guilty if the manner in which the weapon was used was reasonably calculated to produce death); *Boyd* v. *State*, 28 Tex. App. 137, 12 S. W. 737 (holding that on a prosecution for murder, in which the important issue is whether or not the mortal blow was inflicted with intent to kill, and the declarations of the defendant, made immediately after the blow was inflicted, are to the effect that he did not intend to kill deceased, the court should charge the law as declared in Tex. Pen. Code, arts. 612, 614, as to the nature of the instrument in determining intent, as well as upon the power to convict for assault and battery); *State* v. *Browne* (Idaho) 44 Pac. 552 (holding that intent feloniously and corruptly to wrong, cheat, or defraud the county of its money, or some part thereof, need not be proved in a prosecution under Idaho Rev. Stat. § 6975, subd. 4, against a county officer charged with having made an illegal deposit of public moneys); *State* v. *Johnson*, 6 Kan. App. 119, 50 Pac. 907 (holding that evidence of an intent to conceal a stolen body is not necessary on a trial under the Kansas statute for knowingly receiving a stolen body for purposes of dissection); *State* v. *McLean*, 121 N. C. 589, 42 L. R. A. 721, 28 S. E. 140 (holding that no specific intent, felonious or otherwise, on the part of defendants, need be proved on a prosecution under N. C. Acts 1885, chap. 90, providing that any person who, without due process of law or the consent of specified relatives, opens any grave to remove a dead body therefrom, shall be deemed guilty of a felony).

72. Burden of proof.

In cases where neither the prohibition of the law nor the punishment prescribed depends on a specific evil intent, it is proper to instruct the jury that if the accused is proved to have done the act charged, the burden is upon him to show that what he did was done lawfully and without criminal intent.[1]

[1] *Cowley* v. *People*, 21 Hun, 415, Affirmed in 83 N. Y. 464, 38 Am. Rep. 464.

According to *State* v. *Rollins*, 113 N. C. 722, 18 S. E. 394, there is no presumption that an officer who killed persons attempting to rescue a prisoner in his custody under lawful arrest acted without excess of force or malice and in good faith; but the burden remains upon him to show excuse or mitigation; and good faith and the absence of malice are matters of defense.

But *State* v. *Cross*, 42 W. Va. 253, 24 S. E. 996, holds that the defense of accidental killing on a prosecution for murder is a denial of criminal intent, and throws upon the state the burden of proving such intent beyond a reasonable doubt.

The burden of proof of intent is not shifted to defendant, as a matter of law, on a trial for assault with intent to kill, by proof of the use of a weapon calculated to produce death, although the jury may consider that fact in determining the intent. *Chrisman* v. *State*, 54 Ark. 283, 15 S. W. 889; *Beavers* v. *State*, 54 Ark. 336, 15 S. W. 1024; *State* v. *McKinzie*, 102 Mo. 620, 15 S. W. 149.

73. Circumstantial evidence.

Even when a specific criminal intent is necessary to be shown, direct evidence is not essential, but the intent may be inferred from the circumstances of the case.[1]

[1] *People* v. *Lilley*, 43 Mich. 521, 5 N. W. 982; *Allen* v. *United States*, 164 U. S. 492, 41 L. ed. 528, 17 Sup. Ct. Rep. 154; *Jackson* v. *State*, 94 Ala. 85, 10 So. 509; *Hicks* v. *State*, 25 Fla. 535, 6 So. 441; *Voght* v. *State*, 145 Ind. 12, 43 N. E. 1049; *People* v. *Resh*, 107 Mich. 251, 65 N. W. 99; *Ward* v. *State*, 58 Neb. 719, 79 N. W. 725; *McClain* v. *Com.* 110 Pa. 263, 1 Atl. 45; *Franklin* v. *State*, 37 Tex. Crim. Rep. 113, 38 S. W. 802, 1016; *State* v. *Anderson*, 5 Wash. 350, 31 Pac. 969.

In *State* v. *Teeter*, 69 Iowa, 717, 27 N. W. 485 (prosecution for burglary), it was held not error to charge that if the accused broke and entered the buildings, the jury should "look at all the facts and circumstances disclosed by the evidence to ascertain the intent with which he entered."

In *People* v. *Soto*, 53 Cal. 415 (burglary), it was held that if the building inhabited was entered through a window, clandestinely, at a late hour of night, after the lights had been extinguished, the jury would be justified in finding, from these circumstances, that the entry was with intent to commit larceny, affirming judgment against objection that verdict was not justified by the evidence.

In *State* v. *Ward*, 19 Nev. 297, 10 Pac. 133, it was held that although the defendant testified that he intended to return the property, the jury were at liberty to disregard such testimony, and decide, by the defendant's acts alone, as to his real intention at the time of taking; and that it was not error to instruct accordingly.

74. Presumption of criminal intent.

The presumption of criminal intent, even where it has been shown that the act charged was done with the knowledge of the facts, is not a presumption of law, but is a question for the jury. It is error to instruct them that the law presumes a criminal intent. They may be instructed that from such facts they may infer criminal intent.[1]

But where a specific intent is necessary to make the act criminal, the specific intent cannot be inferred from the act.[2]

[1] *People* v. *Baker*, 96 N. Y. 340, 2 N. Y. Crim. Rep. 218. False pretenses; it was held error to charge the jury that if they found that the defendant made the representations charged, and that they were false, and that he knew that they were false when he made them, then the law presumed the fraudulent intent. The court said: "The jury, from these facts, and from all the other facts, may infer a fraudulent intent, but the law does not presume a fraudulent intent."

People v. *Herrick*, 13 Wend. 87, holds it not error to charge that the proof of false representations knowingly made authorizes the jury to find a fraudulent intent.

Parrish v. *State*, 14 Neb. 60, 15 N. W. 357, holds the instruction that "one is presumed to do that which in fact he actually does do," although rather too broadly stated, yet not erroneous, no attendant circumstances being brought to light, and nothing but the naked result shown.

Compare *People* v. *Hunt*, 59 Cal. 430, holding it not error to charge, "When an unlawful act has been proved, the law presumes it to have been intended, and the proof of justification lies on the defendant." The instruction was objected to on the ground "that it required the defendant to prove his justification absolutely, whereas he is only obliged to prove his justification within, and not beyond, a reasonable doubt."

Some of the authorities at least which use the expression that the law presumes the intent mean no more than that the law enables the jury to presume the intent, and are not inconsistent with the principle that the presumption is one of fact, and not one of law. This is undoubtedly the true view. See Wharton, Crim. Ev. 764.

"In capital, as well as other cases, it must be held that a person intends that which is the natural and necessary consequence of an act done by him, and unless the act was done under circumstances which preclude the existence of such an intent, the jury had the right to find, from the result produced, an intention to effect it." Ruger, Ch. J., in *People* v. *Conroy*, 97 N. Y. 62, 77, on trial for murder, where it appeared that defendant, knowing the location of deceased, drew a pistol from his pocket with some difficulty, and turned around toward deceased and discharged it, the ball entering a vital part and causing death; held that the evidence was sufficient to establish premeditation.

Greenleaf says a sane man, voluntarily acting upon motives, must be presumed to contemplate and intend the necessary, natural, and probable consequences of his own acts. If, therefore, one voluntarily or wilfully does an act which has a natural tendency to destroy another's life, the natural and necessary conclusion from the act is that he intended so to destroy such person's life. 1 Greenl. Ev. § 18, which was followed in *People* v. *Majone*, 12 Abb. N. C. 187, Affirmed in 91 N. Y. 211, denying motion for new trial under statute, where it appeared that accused, at the time the crime was committed, said nothing, but came into the room where his wife's mother was, and placing a pistol to her head discharged it.

Bishop says: "Properly viewed, the question is a mixed one of law and fact, upon which, of necessity, the jury are to pass. It would be inaccurate to tell them that they are legally compelled to find murder" from the use of a deadly weapon. 2 Bishop, New Crim. Proc. § 601.

In *McDermott* v. *State*, 89 Ind. 187 (homicide), it is held not error to charge that where a homicide is caused by the intentional use of a deadly weapon in a manner likely to kill, the law presumes a malicious intention to kill, unless it occurred in self-defense or in a sudden heat caused by such provocation as by law reduces the killing to manslaughter.

According to *State* v. *Kortgaard*, 62 Minn. 7, 64 N. W. 51, the law will presume a criminal intent from the intentional commission of the act in itself unlawful. To similar effect, *People* v. *Boling*, 83 Cal. 380, 23 Pac. 421; *Norris* v. *State*, 87 Ala. 85, 6 So. 371.

And *State* v. *Doyle*, 107 Mo. 36, 17 S. W. 751, holds that a legal presumption of intent to kill is raised by the deliberate act of making an assault upon another with a deadly weapon.

But *People* v. *Landman*, 103 Cal. 577, 37 Pac. 518, holds that no presumption of law arises that one who assaulted another with a deadly weapon intended to kill him.

[2]*People* v. *Plath*, 100 N. Y. 590, 53 Am. Rep. 236, 3 N. E. 790. Intent in abduction cannot be presumed without evidence.

75. Sufficiency of presumption.

The presumption that every person intends the natural and probable consequences of his own acts is alone sufficient to justify the jury in inferring criminal intent, where specific intent is not required to be shown.[1]

[1]*Com.* v. *York*, 9 Met. 93, 43 Am. Dec. 373; *People* v. *Cadd*, 60 Cal. 640 holds it not error to charge that the presumption that an unlawful act was done with an unlawful intent, and that a person intends the ordinary consequences of his voluntary act, is by law satisfactory, if uncontradicted by other evidence; and that when the doing of an act is proven which, if coupled with guilty intent, would be a violation of law, the burden of showing the absence of guilty intent is usually upon the accused).

Contra, dictum in *People* v. *Sweeney*, 55 Mich. 586, 22 N. W. 50, that it is not alone sufficient to convict, but should be aided by evidence sufficient to avoid reasonable doubt. And see cases cited in notes to *supra*, § 74.

76. Intent merely to make a test case.

Intent is not deprived of criminal character by the fact that the purpose of the accused was simply to make a test case.[1]

[1]*Montross* v. *State*, 72 Ga. 261, 53 Am. Rep. 840, holding that where the

agent of a newspaper, knowing of the law against circulating obscene literature, violated it for the express purpose of making a test case, or of vindicating the character of his paper, and, to insure a prosecution, sought the chief of police, and gave him copies of the paper, he was properly convicted.

77. Miscarriage of intent.

Intent is not deprived of criminal character by the fact that the injury was inflicted on another person or other property than that which the accused intended to injure.[1]

[1]*Reg.* v. *Latimer*, 54 L. T. N. S. 768, holding, both on principle and authority, that where the accused had struck A. with a belt intending to injure him, and it bounded off and struck B., whom he did not mean to hit, he was properly convicted of an assault,—Citing and approving *Rex* v. *Hunt*, 1 Moody C. C. 93, and distinguishing *Reg.* v. *Pembliton*, 30 L. T. N. S. 405, L. R. 2 C. C. 119, 12 Cox C. C. 607.

See also *Burchett* v. *Com.* 8 Ky. L. Rep. 258, 1 S. W. 423, holding that the degree of the offense was not affected; and see cases collected in note.

Compare *Dillard* v. *State*, 65 Ark. 404, 46 S. W. 533, where it is held that the presumption that every person is supposed to contemplate the ordinary and natural consequences of his acts does not arise where the act fails of effect, or is attended by no consequences, and cannot be relied on to supply proof of an intent to kill, in a prosecution for an assault with intent to kill.

XVIII. Intoxication.

78. General rule.

Voluntary intoxication at the time of the act charged is neither a defense nor an excuse for crime; nor can it be considered by the jury upon the question of capacity to distinguish between right and wrong;[1] but it may be considered upon the question of physical capacity to do an act charged, or mental capacity to exercise a specific intent, or deliberation or premeditation necessary to be proved.[2]

Intoxication has sometimes been considered an aggravation.[3]

[1]*People* v. *Rogers*, 18 N. Y. 9, 17, 72 Am. Dec. 484, where it was held not error to refuse to charge to the effect that drunkenness might exist to such a degree that neither an intention to commit murder nor a motive for such an act could be imputed to the prisoner. Denio, J., said: "Modern cases . . . all agree . . . that mental alienation produced by drinking intoxicating liquors furnishes no immunity for crime," —Followed in *Kenny* v. *People*, 31 N. Y. 330; *People* v. *Blake*, 65 Cal. 275, 4 Pac. 1. See also *Flanigan* v. *People*, 86 N. Y. 554, 40 Am. Rep. 556; *State* v. *Keath*, 83 N. C. 626 (held not error to refuse to charge

that if accused committed the crime while under the influence of whisky, or upon sudden provocation, it was but manslaughter); *People* v. *Jones*, 63 Cal. 168 (murder; held not error to charge that insanity produced by intoxication would not destroy responsibility when the party, when sane and responsible, made himself voluntarily intoxicated; and that drunkenness was no excuse for crime, but was a circumstance for the consideration of the jury in determining the degree of the crime); *Smurr* v. *State*, 88 Ind. 504. And see cases collected in *Reg.* v. *Davis*, 28 Moak Eng. Rep. 657; and note to *Harris* v. *United States* (D. C.) 36 L. R. A. 465, where the question is treated exhaustively.

In *People* v. *Leonardi*, 143 N. Y. 360, 38 N. E. 372, an instruction requiring the jury to find that the accused was so completely intoxicated as to be incapable of realizing the wrongful nature of his acts, in order to relieve him of the charge of murder in the first degree, was held to require evidence of too great a degree of intoxication.

[a]See next section. And see cases reviewed in note to *Harris* v. *United States* (D. C.) 36 L. R. A. 470.

Voluntary intoxication is not a proper subject for inquiry in determining whether a homicide was murder in the second degree or manslaughter, as it is a subject for inquiry only in determining whether the person committing the crime was capable of deliberation and premeditation, which do not enter into either offense. *Wilson* v. *State*, 60 N. J. L. 171, 37 Atl. 954, 38 Atl. 428, Citing *Rex* v. *Carroll*, 7 Car. & P. 145; *Rex* v. *Meakin*, 7 Car. & P. 297; *People* v. *Rogers*, 18 N. Y. 9, 72 Am. Dec. 484; *State* v. *Tatro*, 50 Vt. 483; *State* v. *Johnson*, 40 Conn. 136; *State* v. *Mowry*, 37 Kan. 369, 15 Pac. 282.

So, defendant in a murder trial is entitled to an instruction embracing the declaration of Cal. Pen. Code, § 22, that whenever the actual existence of any particular purpose, motive, or intent is a necessary element to constitute any particular species or degree of crime, the jury may consider the fact that the accused was intoxicated at the time, where there is evidence making it applicable. *People* v. *Hill*, 123 Cal. 47, 55 Pac. 692.

And a charge that, to find defendant guilty of feloniously breaking into a store with intent to commit larceny, his intoxication at the time, if he was intoxicated, should be considered in determining his intent, sufficiently presents the defense that he was so intoxicated as to be incapable of forming such intent. *State* v. *Conners*, 95 Iowa, 485, 64 N. W. 295.

And according to *Ford* v. *State*, 46 Neb. 390, 64 N. W. 1082, an instruction that "drunkenness is no excuse for crime," and that defendant, charged with larceny, has the burden of showing that he was so under the influence of liquor at the time that he was mentally unable to form an intent in his mind to steal, or of raising a reasonable doubt whether he was thus under its influence,—correctly states the rule relating to the defense of intoxication.

In *State* v. *Hansen*, 25 Or. 391, 35 Pac. 976, 36 Pac. 296, a trial for murder in which the defense of intoxication was set up, an instruction under Hill's (Or.) Code, § 1358, providing that whenever the actual existence of any particular "motive, purpose, or intent" is a necessary element to constitute any particular degree of crime, the jury may take into consideration the fact that defendant was intoxicated, in determining his purpose, motive, or intent, which limits the inquiry to defendant's intent, and omits the words "purpose and motive," is held not to be erroneous, as the intent in such case is the test of criminal liability in determining the degree of guilt.

[a]*Cline* v. *State,* 43 Ohio St. 332, 1 N. E. 22 (*dictum*); *United States* v. *Claypool,* 14 Fed. 127 (charge to jury).

This doctrine was disapproved in 23 Am. L. Reg. N. S. 225, but citing as sustaining it *McIntyre* v. *People,* 38 Ill. 515; *Ferrell* v. *State,* 43 Tex. 503.

79. Intoxication as bearing on premeditation.

Wherever premeditation or deliberation is claimed to be proved against the accused, evidence tending to show that he was so much intoxicated at the time as to be incapable of such premeditation or deliberation may be considered by the jury.[1]

[1]*Hopt* v. *Utah,* 104 U. S. 631, 26 L. ed. 873, holding it error to refuse to charge accordingly, and following the decisions in Massachusetts and elsewhere. See also *State* v. *Robinson,* 20 W. Va. 713, 43 Am. Rep. 799; *State* v. *Mowry,* 37 Kan. 369, 15 Pac. 282; *People* v. *Batting,* 49 How. Pr. 392 (charge of Westbrook, J.). And see cases collected in note to *Harris* v. *United States* (D. C.) 36 L. R. A. 473.

This rule is said, in Buswell on Insanity, § 450, citing the above case, to be supported by the weight of modern authority, and by the weight of English authority.

Compare *People* v. *Mills,* 98 N. Y. 178, where, under N. Y. Pen. Code, § 22, it was held not error to refuse to charge that "if the defendant was, at the time of committing the act, intoxicated, the jury will consider that fact as an evidence tending to show an absence of premeditation and deliberation." The court said: "The most that could be claimed in regard to the intoxication would be that it was a question for the jury to determine, whether it did not tend to show an absence of premeditation and deliberation. The request went beyond this; it was too broad, and, as it stood, made any state of intoxication, however slight, evidence of an absence of premeditation and deliberation."

In *People* v. *Langton,* 67 Cal. 427, 7 Pac. 843, it was held not error to charge that, "as between murder in the second degree and manslaughter the drunkenness of the offender can form no legitimate matter of inquiry, for manslaughter is the unlawful killing of a human being without malice, express or implied, and without any mixture of deliberation, etc,"—Following *Pirtle* v. *State,* 9 Humph. 663.

In *State* v. *Fiske,* 63 Conn. 388, 28 Atl. 572, it is held proper to refuse a request to charge that the intoxication of defendant, charged with assault with intent to murder, is to be considered in determining the degree of the crime, and as tending to show whether the defendant was capable of premeditation; premeditation not being an element of the crime.

XIX. Limiting effect of evidence.

80. Limiting to special purpose.

If evidence has been received as proper for one purpose, although not for another,—for instance, evidence of another offense, received to show knowledge or intent,—the party affected has a right to an instruction that the jury must consider it only as bearing on the question in reference to which it was properly received.[1]

[1] *Therasson* v. *People*, 82 N. Y. 238 (error to refuse); *State* v. *Lewis*, 19 Or. 478, 24 Pac. 914; *Tidwell* v. *State*, 40 Tex. Crim. Rep. 38, 47 S. W. 466, 48 S. W. 184; *Coleman* v. *People*, 55 N. Y. 81 (first headnote); *People* v. *Gray*, 66 Cal. 271, 5 Pac. 240 (holding that the court should instruct the jury as to the purpose of evidence of similar acts to that charged offered to show intent, if so requested by the defense, but, in the absence of such a request, a failure to so instruct is not ground for a reversal); *Thornley* v. *State*, 36 Tex. Crim. Rep. 118, 34 S. W. 264, 35 S. W. 981 (holding that instructions with reference to the purpose and object of such testimony should be given whether such instructions are asked for or not); *Naverrete* v. *State* (Tex. Crim. App.) 40 S. W. 79 (holding that an instruction that evidence of an assault on another person by defendant charged with murder was admitted only to show motive on his part, as the deceased was a witness in the assault case, was not required where no request therefor was made).

As to effect on credibility, see *Boyle* v. *State*, 105 Ind. 469, 55 Am. Rep. 218, 5 N. E. 203.

According to *Thornley* v. *State*, 36 Tex. Crim. Rep. 118, 35 S. W. 981, 34 S. W. 264, instruction to limit effect of evidence of extraneous crimes is only necessary when there is danger of a conviction for an offense not charged, or of an unwarranted use of the testimony to the prejudice of the defendant.

As to limiting the effect of impeaching evidence, see *Holly* v. *Com.* 18 Ky. L. Rep. 441, 36 S. W. 532 (holding that no instruction, that evidence admitted to impeach the general moral character of defendant was only competent to discredit him as a witness, was necessary, where the jury could not have concluded that it was introduced for any other purpose); *People* v. *Foglesong*, 116 Mich. 556, 74 N. W. 730 (holding that testimony which is admitted for impeaching purposes only should be strictly limited to that purpose by instructions of the court,—especially where it would be strongly prejudicial to the person against whom it is offered unless so restricted); *State* v. *Taylor*, 121 N. C. 674, 28 S. E. 493; *Joy* v. *State* (Tex. Crim. App.) 51 S. W. 933; *Magee* v. *State* (Tex. Crim. App.) 43 S. W. 512, 98; *Owens* v. *State*, 35 Tex. Crim. Rep. 345, 33 S. W. 875.

That the court should instruct the jury in a criminal case that evidence which was inadmissible on the main issue, but was allowed for the purpose of showing a party to have acted as a detective, and not as an accomplice, was admitted for that purpose alone, see *Clay* v. *State,* 40 Tex. Crim. Rep. 556, 51 S. W. 212.

XX. Motive.

81. Need not usually be proved.

If the act charged and the criminal agency of the accused are shown beyond reasonable doubt, even if only by circumstantial evidence, it is not necessary that there be proof of motive.[1]

[1] *Hornsby* v. *State,* 94 Ala. 55, 10 So. 522; *McLain* v. *Com.* 99 Pa. 86 (holding it not error to so charge); *Clifton* v. *State,* 73 Ala. 473 (placing obstruction on railroad; held not error to refuse to charge that if the prosecution failed to show motive, the absence of motive might of itself generate that reasonable doubt which would require an acquittal); *Green* v. *State,* 38 Ark. 304 (murder; held not error to refuse to charge that proof of a motive is essential for conviction in a case depending upon circumstantial evidence); *Preston* v. *State,* 8 Tex. App. 30 (murder; conviction affirmed, notwithstanding lack of proof of motive).

Though proof of motive is of more or less importance in cases of purely circumstantial evidence, yet, where the defendant is indisputably the perpetrator of the alleged crime, there is no occasion for explaining the reason of his act. It is enough that the evidence does not absolutely exclude the existence of motive, as it may do, for instance, by showing the accused to have been insane. *People* v. *Minisci,* 46 Hun, 682, 12 N. Y. Supp. 719.

An instruction that in cases depending on circumstantial evidence an inquiry into the motives actuating the accused is important, because human experience shows that men do not commit crimes without a motive therefor, is properly refused, where the evidence in the case is not wholly circumstantial. *Dennis* v. *State,* 118 Ala. 72, 23 So. 1002.

But on a prosecution for murder, in which there is no evidence of any motive, but on the contrary the evidence establishes an entire absence of such motive, and that the accused and deceased were at all times the warmest of friends, and that for generations epilepsy had existed in the family of the accused, and that he had been subject to epileptic fits from childhood,—a refusal to charge that if no motive has been established for the crime it should be regarded as important on the question of epilepsy is error. *People* v. *Barber,* 115 N. Y. 475, 22 N. E. 182.

According to *Vaughan* v. *Com.* (Va.) 13 Va. L. J. 875, the absence of all evidence of an inducing cause or motive to commit a crime, when the fact is in reasonable doubt as to who committed it, affords a strong presumption of innocence.

And *State* v. *Foley,* 144 Mo. 600, 46 S. W. 733, holds that a defendant charged with murder is entitled to an instruction that the absence of any probable motive for the commission of the crime must be considered in his favor, where the evidence is circumstantial, and the jury have been instructed to find defendant guilty if they find that he committed the murder, although no motive for the deed is apparent.

82. Is not to be conjectured.

In cases of circumstantial evidence, motive may be material, or even may be regarded by the jury as controlling, but in such case it cannot be conjectured or imagined. If it be a necessary element in the case, it must appear by the evidence.[1]

[1]"Motive is an inducement, or that which leads or tempts the mind to indulge the criminal act. It is resorted to as a means of arriving at an ultimate fact, not for the purpose of explaining the reason of a criminal act which has been clearly proved, but from the important aid it may render in completing the proof of the commission of the act when it might otherwise remain in doubt. With motives, in any speculative sense, neither the law nor the tribunal which administers it has any concern. . . . It is in cases of proof by circumstantial evidence that the motive often becomes, not only material, but controlling; and in such cases the facts from which it may be inferred must be proved. It cannot be imagined any more than any other circumstance in the case." Church, Ch. J., in *People* v. *Bennett,* 49 N. Y. 137, 148. Murder; held error to suggest in the charge to the jury a motive not warranted by the evidence, which might have influenced their minds to the prejudice of the prisoner.

In *Eldridge* v. *State,* 27 Fla. 162, 9 So. 448, a charge that good motives in the publication of the alleged libel cannot be inferred, but must be proved, and, if defendant has failed to prove that it was published with good motives, all evidence going to prove its truth must be rejected and defendant convicted, is held to be erroneous as misleading the jury into the belief that they are never authorized to infer good motives from the facts and circumstances in evidence.

83. Sufficiency of the evidence.

Evidence of a motive not in itself criminal, for instance, the need of money, suggested as a motive for the commission of a robbery, should be weighed by the jury with extreme caution. Being in itself consistent with innocence, it cannot of itself warrant a conviction.[1]

[1]*Kennedy* v. *People,* 39 N. Y. 245.

XXI. Presumptions.

84. Distinction between legal presumption and jury's inference.

It is error to tell the jury, without qualification, that the evidence raises a presumption of a particular fact, or is sufficient to justify finding a particular fact, if it raises, not a presumption of law, but only a presumption of fact on which the jury might find either way.[1]

[1]Abbott's Civil Trial Brief, 2d ed. 450; *Stone* v. *Geyser Quicksilver Min. Co.* 52 Cal. 315; *Allison* v. *State,* 42 Ind. 354; *Read* v. *Hurd,* 7 Wend. 408.

XXII. Statutory prima facie evidence.

85. Validity of statute.

A statute making a fact prima facie evidence in a criminal case, which is not so at common law, is not necessarily unconstitutional.[1]

But under such a provision the jury should not be instructed that they must find according to the presumption.[2]

[1]*Auburn Excise Comrs.* v. *Merchant,* 103 N. Y. 143, 57 Am. Rep. 705, 8 N. E. 484; *Wooten* v. *State,* 24 Fla. 335, 1 L. R. A. 819, 5 So. 39, and cases cited; *Contra, State* v. *Beswick,* 13 R. I. 211, 43 Am. Rep. 26; *People* v. *Lyon,* 27 Hun, 180; *State* v. *Divine,* 98 N. C. 778, 4 S. E. 477; *Voght* v. *State,* 124 Ind. 358, 24 N. E. 680.

[2]*State* v. *Intoxicating Liquors,* 80 Me. 57, 12 Atl. 794, 39 Alb. L. J. 2, with notes of other cases.

The finding of implements, devices, or apparatus commonly used in games of chance in gambling houses or by gamblers does not constitute prima facie evidence that the implements found were used for gambling purposes, or that any person had procured, suffered, or permitted another to play for money or other valuable thing at any game in the place where they are found, under Fla. Rev. Stat. § 2648, providing that if such implements, etc., are found in any place, it shall be prima facie evidence that such place "is kept for gambling." *Richardson* v. *State,* 41 Fla. 303, 25 So. 880.

XXIII. Reasonable doubt.

86. Present rule.

The gist of the rule is that the law contemplates a doubt for which a good reason arising on the evidence can be given.[1]

If the requisite cogency of the reason require definition, it is proper to say that the question is whether the jury have such evidence as they would be willing to act upon in the more weighty and important matters relating to their own affairs.[2]

[1]*People* v. *Guidici,* 100 N. Y. 503, 3 N. E. 493; *Ellis* v. *State,* 120 Ala. 333, 25 So. 1; *Powell* v. *State,* 95 Ga. 502, 20 S. E. 483; *Butler* v. *State,* 102 Wis. 364, 78 N. W. 590; *Hopt* v. *Utah,* 120 U. S. 430, 439, 30 L. ed. 708,

711, 7 Sup. Ct. Rep. 614. *Contra, Carr* v. *State*, 23 Neb. 749, 37 N. W. 630; *State* v. *Cohen*, 108 Iowa, 208, 78 N. W. 857, and cases cited.

According to *State* v. *Morey*, 25 Or. 241, 35 Pac. 655, 36 Pac. 573, an instruction that "a reasonable doubt" is such a doubt as a juror can give a reason for is not reversible error, when given in connection with other instructions by which the court seeks so to define the term as to enable the jury to distinguish a reasonable doubt from some vague and imaginary one.

[2]See next section and note.

87. Terms of a proper charge defining reasonable doubt more fully.

It is proper to instruct the jury as follows: A reasonable doubt is a doubt based on reason, and which is reasonable in view of all the evidence. And if, after an impartial comparison and consideration of all the evidence, you can candidly say that you are not satisfied of the defendant's guilt, you have a reasonable doubt; but if after such impartial comparison and consideration of all the evidence, you can truthfully say that you have an abiding conviction of the defendant's guilt, such as you would be willing to act upon in the more weighty and important matters relating to your own affairs, you have no reasonable doubt. But if you can reconcile the evidence before you upon any reasonable hypothesis consistent with the defendant's innocence, you should do so, and in that case find him not guilty.[1]

[1]*Hopt* v. *Utah*, 120 U. S. 430, 439, 30 L. ed. 708, 711, 7 Sup. Ct. Rep. 614. The court (Field) here says: "The rule [as to reasonable doubt] may be, and often is, rendered obscure by attempts at definition which serve to create doubts instead of removing them. But an illustration like the one given in this case, by reference to the conviction upon which the jurors would act in the weighty and important concerns of life, would be likely to aid them to a right conclusion, when an attempted definition might fail. If the evidence produced be of such a convincing character that they would unhesitatingly be governed by it in such weighty and important matters, they might be said to have no reasonable doubt respecting the guilt or innocence of the accused, notwithstanding the uncertainty that attends all human evidence. The instruction in the case before us is as just a guide to practical men as can well be given; and if it were open to criticism it could not have misled the jury, when considered in connection with the further charge, that if they could reconcile the evidence with any reasonable hypothesis consistent with the defendant's innocence, they should do so, and in that case find him not guilty. The evidence must satisfy the judgment of the jurors as to the guilt of the defendant, so as to exclude any other reasonable conclusion."

See a full discussion of the subject in 2 Thompson, Trials, 1813–1854. See also article by same author in 10 Crim. L. Mag. 181, 187.

Below will be found a collection of some of the more recent cases.

United States.—*Hopt* v. *Utah,* 120 U. S. 430, 439, 30 L. ed. 708, 711, 7 Sup. Ct. Rep. 614, quoted *supra; United States* v. *Johnson,* 26 Fed. 682 (holding that a reasonable doubt is not a mere guess—a mere surmise—that one may not be guilty of what he is charged; it is a doubt that a jury may entertain as reasonable men, after a thorough review and consideration of the evidence—a doubt for which a good reason arising from the evidence can be given); *Dunbar* v. *United States,* 156 U. S. 185, 39 L. ed. 390, 15 Sup. Ct. Rep. 325 (holding the use of the words "probabilities" and "strong probabilities," in an instruction as to the weight of evidence in a criminal case, not to be prejudicial, where the court emphasizes the fact that the probabilities must be so strong as to exclude any reasonable doubt).

Alabama.—*Ray* v. *State,* 50 Ala. 104 (holding that it is incorrect to define a reasonable doubt as one for which a reason can be given. Every reason, whether based on substantial grounds or not, does not constitute a reasonable doubt in law; refusal of request no error); *Hale* v. *State,* 122 Ala. 85, 26 So. 236 (holding that a requested charge that if, after considering all the evidence, the jury have a reasonable doubt as to defendant's guilt, growing out of the evidence of a witness for the state, they must acquit him, should be given; holding also that a requested instruction that "if any individual juror is not convinced of defendant's guilt beyond all reasonable doubt and to a moral certainty, the jury cannot convict," should be given); *Lodge* v. *State,* 122 Ala. 107, 26 So. 200 (holding that a charge on reasonable doubt reciting that "it is not a mere doubt that authorizes an acquittal; the doubt which authorizes an acquittal must be a reasonable doubt,"—is correct). But a requested charge that if the jury have a reasonable doubt of defendant's guilt, growing out of the evidence or any part of it, he is entitled to the benefit of the doubt, and must be found not guilty, is properly refused as authorizing an acquittal, even though such doubt were dissipated by other evidence, or did not exist upon the whole evidence. And a request to charge the jury in a criminal trial to acquit if they "have a single doubt of guilt for which a reason can be found," should be refused. *Talbert* v. *State,* 121 Ala. 33, 25 So. 690. And an instruction that unless the evidence against an accused should be such as to exclude to a moral certainty "every hypothesis" but that of his guilt, instead of saying every "reasonable hypothesis," exacts too high a degree of proof. *King* v. *State,* 120 Ala. 329, 25 So. 178.

Arizona.—An instruction that if the jury have a doubt as to defendant's guilt, they must determine whether it is reasonable and sufficient in law to acquit him; and that a doubt, to authorize an acquittal, must be a reasonable one, and must arise from a careful and candid investigation of all the evidence, though not entirely free from criticism, is not incorrect. *Foster* v. *Territory* (Ariz.) 56 Pac. 738.

Arkansas.—An instruction on a trial for murder, that if the facts and circumstances proved "by the preponderance of evidence" are such as to satisfy the jury "beyond a reasonable doubt," such evidence is entitled to the same weight as direct testimony, is erroneous in allowing conviction upon a preponderance of the evidence. *Gill* v. *State,* 59 Ark. 422, 27 S. W. 598.

California.—*People* v. *Cheong Foon Ark,* 61 Cal. 527 (holding it error to refuse the following charge: "The evidence in a criminal case must satisfy the jury to a moral certainty, and beyond a reasonable doubt; that is, it must entirely satisfy the jury of the guilt of defendant before they can convict. If the jury are not entirely satisfied, they should acquit"); *People* v. *Kernaghan,* 72 Cal. 609, 14 Pac. 566 (holding the definition given by Chief Justice Shaw in *Com.* v. *Webster,* 5 Cush. 320, 52 Am. Dec. 711, to be correct and followed in California. But where the definition was correctly given, the defendant was not injured by the use of the following language: "Your mind should rest reasonably satisfied of the guilt of the defendant before a verdict of that character is given;" and "on the other hand, however, mere probabilities of innocence or doubts, however reasonable, which may beset your minds on all occasions, should not prevent such a verdict"); *People* v. *Winters,* 125 Cal. 325, 57 Pac. 1067 (holding that a full instruction upon the law of reasonable doubt is not rendered erroneous by a statement that the doubt which acquits must be a reasonable doubt in the sense mentioned, and no other); *People* v. *Dole,* 51 Pac. 945, 122 Cal. 486, 55 Pac. 581 (holding that an instruction that if, after consideration of the case, a juror entertains a reasonable doubt of the defendant's guilt, it is his duty not to vote for a verdict of guilty, or to be influenced in so voting, for the single reason that a majority of the jury are in favor of a verdict of guilty, should be given when requested); *People* v. *Hecker,* 109 Cal. 451, 30 L. R. A. 403, 42 Pac. 307 (holding that a requested instruction in a criminal action, which requires the jury to be convinced to "an absolute moral certainty" before conviction, is properly refused).

Colorado.—*Clare* v. *People,* 9 Colo. 122, 10 Pac. 799 (in this case the judge charged the jury that the rule requiring the jury to be satisfied of the defendant's guilt beyond a reasonable doubt, in order to warrant a conviction, does not require that the jury should be satisfied beyond a reasonable doubt of each link of the chain of circumstances relied on to establish the defendant's guilt; held error; the metaphor calculated to "mislead the jury"); *Graves* v. *People,* 18 Colo. 170, 32 Pac. 63 (holding that it is error on a murder trial, where the evidence is wholly circumstantial, to instruct the jury that they need not be satisfied beyond a reasonable doubt of each link in the chain of circumstances relied upon to establish guilt).

Connecticut.—It is not necessary for the court to attempt a definition of the expression "reasonable doubt." *State* v. *Smith,* 65 Conn. 283, 31 Atl. 206.

District of Columbia.—An instruction that the guilt of a prisoner must be established by "indisputable" evidence is properly refused. *United States* v. *Heath,* 9 Mackey, 272.

Florida.—A definition of reasonable doubt of guilt, in a charge, by stating that it must be a reasonable, sensible, and not a mere possible, doubt, and must be arrived at from considering all the evidence in the case,—is substantially correct. *Woodruff* v. *State,* 31 Fla. 320, 12 So. 653.

But it is error to qualify the rule requiring the guilt of accused to be proved beyond reasonable doubt, or to disparage it in the estimation of juries by giving, immediately after and in connection with a charge upon the subject, an instruction to the effect that the rule is designed to protect innocent persons who are wrongfully charged, and is not designed to enable persons to escape punishment who are shown to be guilty of the crime. *Gantling* v. *State*, 40 Fla. 237, 23 So. 857. And an instruction to acquit if any one of the jury entertains a reasonable doubt of guilt is properly refused, as it requires that if any one juror entertains such a doubt the other jurors, although satisfied of his guilt, should surrender their judgment to the one in doubt, and concur in an acquittal. *Boyd* v. *State*, 33 Fla. 316, 14 So. 836.

Georgia.—*Houser* v. *State*, 58 Ga. 78. Upon a burglary trial the court charged the jury "that the state must make out the case beyond a reasonable doubt; but that it is not necessary for the state to show that it is impossible for the crime to have been committed by anybody else, or that it might not, by bare possibility, have been done by someone else; but the state must show that it was the prisoner to a moral certainty." Upon appeal, sustaining the conviction, held a proper and correct charge.

A charge in a criminal case that defendant is entitled to any doubt the jury may have in their minds, but it must be a reasonable doubt; that if their minds are wavering, and they cannot decide, it is their duty to give the defendant the benefit of that doubt by a verdict of acquittal; and that such doubts extend to every material question and issue in the case, and may arise from a want of evidence, or spring out of the evidence,—is sufficiently full and accurate. *Burney* v. *State*, 100 Ga. 65, 25 S. E. 911. And after an instruction that the defendants cannot be found guilty until the evidence satisfies the jury of their guilt beyond a reasonable doubt, it is not erroneous to further charge that they must be satisfied of their guilt to a reasonable and moral certainty, which is explained to mean mental conviction excluding any reasonable doubt of guilt. *Bone* v. *State*, 102 Ga. 387, 30 S. E. 845.

Idaho.—*People* v. *Dewey*, 2 Idaho, 79, 6 Pac. 103. Upon a murder trial the following instruction was given: "A reasonable doubt is not a mere possible doubt, nor is it a captious or imaginary doubt, but is such a doubt as a prudent and reasonable man would be likely to act upon in determining important affairs of life." Held on appeal that while not the best definition which could be given, it was not erroneous. But an instruction that, however slight the "reasonable doubt" may be, if fairly based on the evidence, the jury must acquit defendant, should be refused as an attempt to define the degree to which a jury must be convinced to justify a verdict of guilty. *Anthony* v. *State* (Idaho) 55 Pac. 884.

Illinois.—*Bressler* v. *People*, 117 Ill. 422, 8 N. E. 62, holding the following charge to be correct: "The jury are instructed that the rule requiring the jury to be satisfied of a defendant's guilt beyond a reasonable doubt, in order to warrant a conviction, does not require that the jury should be satisfied beyond a reasonable doubt of each link in the chain of circumstances relied upon to establish the defendant's guilt. It is sufficient if, taking the testimony all together, the jury are satisfied beyond a reasonable doubt that the defendant is guilty."

Contra, Clare v. *People,* 9 Colo. 122, 10 Pac. 799; *Marion* v. *State,* 16 Neb. 349, 20 N. W. 289 (disapproving a similar instruction).

An instruction that every fact necessary to constitute the crime charged against defendant must be proved beyond a reasonable doubt is properly refused, as the reasonable doubt which the jury is permitted to entertain must be in regard to defendant's guilt on the whole evidence, and not on any particular fact in the case. *Williams* v. *People,* 166 Ill. 132, 46 N. E. 749. An instruction that the degree of evidence required to convict a defendant in a criminal case must be such as to remove all doubt from the mind of a reasonable man is properly refused, since it is not every doubt that may exist in the mind of a reasonable man that arises to the dignity of a reasonable doubt. *Padfield* v. *People,* 146 Ill. 660, 35 N. E. 469.

Indiana.—*Bradley* v. *State,* 31 Ind. 492, holding that the test of certainty beyond all reasonable doubt should be such certainty as would justify the mind to action, not only in matters of importance, but those of the very highest importance, involving the dearest interest; charge erroneous. See also *Brown* v. *State,* 105 Ind. 385, 5 N. E. 900; *Densmore* v. *State,* 67 Ind. 306, 33 Am. Rep. 96 (in this case the judge charged that "a reasonable doubt is one suggested by or arising out of the proof made, and after a full and fair consideration of all the evidence, pro and con, remains in the mind, causing some degree of uncertainty as to the alleged crime." Held error in not allowing for a reasonable doubt, which may arise from the lack or want of evidence); *Stitz* v. *State,* 104 Ind. 359, 4 N. E. 145 (holding it error to charge the jury to the effect that an acquittal is not warranted unless a reasonable doubt is entertained by all the jurors); *Colee* v. *State,* 75 Ind. 511 (holding that an omission to define a reasonable doubt does not constitute error where the defendant's counsel has failed to ask for an instruction); *Reynolds* v. *State,* 147 Ind. 3, 46 N. E. 31 (holding that an instruction that it is necessary for the state to prove defendant guilty as charged beyond a reasonable doubt, but that if the proof is such that it would control or decide the conduct of reasonably prudent and conscientious men in the most important affairs of life, under circumstances where they were not compelled to act, then, as matter of law, the facts so established are deemed to be established beyond a reasonable doubt, and the jury should convict with such proof before them,—is not objectionable as invading the province of the jury); *Sutherlin* v. *State,* 148 Ind. 695, 48 N. E. 246 (holding that instructions given upon "reasonable doubt," in a murder trial, which do not include a statement of the rule that in circumstantial evidence it must, before conviction, exclude every reasonable hypothesis of innocence, and that merely to coincide with guilt is not the degree of proof required,—are not erroneous, where such instruction is fully and clearly given in charges subsequent to those complained of); *Rains* v. *State,* 152 Ind. 69, 52 N. E. 450 (holding that an instruction that the rule as to reasonable doubt does not require the jury to be satisfied beyond a reasonable doubt of "each link in the chain of evidence relied upon to establish his [defendant's] guilt" is not erroneous, where from the entire charge on the question of reasonable doubt it must be apparent to the jury that the court only intends to negative the necessity of establishing beyond a reasonable doubt each subsidiary or minor fact or circumstance, as distinguished from the material or elementary facts).

Iowa.—*State* v. *Sloan,* 55 Iowa, 217, 7 N. W. 516 (holding that it is improper to charge a jury that a reasonable doubt "is such a doubt as fairly and naturally arises in the minds of the whole jury"); *State* v. *Van Tassel,* 103 Iowa, 6, 72 N. W. 497 (holding that an instruction that, to authorize a conviction, the minds of the jury must be brought to an abiding conviction, beyond a reasonable doubt, of the defendant's guilt, after a full consideration of the whole case, is not erroneous because it fails to use the words "to a moral certainty," as a binding conviction beyond a reasonable doubt is equivalent to that); *State* v. *Judiesch,* 96 Iowa, 249, 65 N. W. 157 (holding that an instruction on trial for seduction, that if there is any one material fact proved to the satisfaction of the jury "by a preponderance of the evidence," which is inconsistent with defendant's guilt, it is sufficient to raise a reasonable doubt,—is misleading, as authorizing the jury to believe that defendant has the burden of proving by a preponderance of the evidence that he did not have sexual intercourse with the prosecutrix).

Kansas.—*State* v. *Witt,* 34 Kan. 488, 8 Pac. 769 (holding it error to refuse to charge to the effect that if any one of the jury should, after consideration of all the evidence and consultation with his fellow jurors, entertain a reasonable doubt of the defendant's guilt, the jury could not find the defendant guilty. The defendant was entitled to a charge reminding each juror of his individual duty, notwithstanding that a general charge on the subject had been given); *State* v. *Rogers,* 56 Kan. 362, 43 Pac. 256 (holding that an instruction that, before the jury are warranted in finding defendant guilty, they must be able truthfully and conscientiously to say that his guilt has been established by the evidence beyond reasonable doubt; and that if any of the jurors entertain a reasonable doubt as to whether defendant's guilt has been established, they cannot convict, but that they cannot acquit unless all the jurors entertain a reasonable doubt,—is not erroneous.)

Kentucky.—An instruction in reference to reasonable doubt is not erroneous because it requires the doubt to grow out of the whole evidence. *Baker* v. *Com.* 13 Ky. L. Rep. 571, 17 S. W. 625.

Maine.—*State* v. *Rounds,* 76 Me. 123 (on a forgery trial the court charged the jury that "the law only requires that degree of certainty in the minds of the jurors, before rendering a verdict of guilty, as would exist in their minds in coming to a conclusion on matters of grave interest and importance to themselves,"—held on appeal that while this definition was too vague, yet the giving of the following instruction in addition thereto cured the error: "A reasonable doubt is a doubt arising in the mind, for which some fair, just reason can be given"); *State* v. *Richards,* 85 Me. 252, 27 Atl. 122 (holding that an instruction in a criminal case in which the question is whether the accused was a criminal agent, that circumstances to justify conviction, should all be consistent with each other, point to the guilt of the accused, and be at variance with any rational presumption of innocence, is not erroneous).

Massachusetts.—*Com.* v. *Costley,* 118 Mass. 1, holding that proof beyond a "reasonable doubt" and proof to a "moral certainty" are equivalent expressions. Each signifies such proof as satisfies the judgment and conscience of the jury as reasonable men, and applying their reason to the evidence before them, that the crime charged has been committed by the defendant, and so satisfies them as to leave no other reasonable conclusion possible.

Michigan.—*Semon* v. *People,* 42 Mich. 141, 3 N. W. 304 (holding that it was not error for the trial court to deny defendant's request to charge the jury that they should not find against defendant unless the evidence satisfied them of his guilt beyond a reasonable doubt; nor was it error to charge them that they might be satisfied by a clear preponderance of evidence); *People* v. *Stubenvoll,* 62 Mich. 329, 28 N. W. 883 (holding that the phrase "reasonable doubt" is not of such unknown or uncommon signification that an exposition by a trial judge is called for; and where the judge charges that the term implies a doubt arising out of the facts and circumstances of the case, or maintaining which you can give some good reason, while not accurate, is not of sufficient consequence to be assigned as error); *People* v. *Swartz,* 118 Mich. 292, 76 N. W. 491 (holding that an instruction on reasonable doubt is not improper which states that it must be a fair doubt, based on reason and common sense, and not an imaginary, captious, or possible one; and that "it is such a doubt as may leave your minds, after a careful examination of all the evidence in the case, in that condition that you cannot say that you have an abiding conviction, to a moral certainty, from the evidence of the case, of the truth of the charge); *People* v. *Pichette,* 111 Mich. 461, 69 N. W. 739 (holding that an instruction on a trial for burning a sawmill, that it is claimed that defendant was in his own house from a specified time until after the fire broke out, with the exception of a few moments when he went out, during all of which time he was in sight of his wife; and that if that is true, defendant is "not guilty, and you should so say, or if you have a reasonable doubt about it you should so say,"—sufficiently states that the jury should acquit if they have a reasonable doubt on the subject); *People* v. *Wells,* 112 Mich. 648, 71 N. W. 176 (holding that an instruction upon the trial of a criminal case, that if a reasonable doubt of any of the facts necessary to convict is raised in the minds of the jury by the "ingenuity of counsel," the doubt is decisive in favor of defendant's acquittal, is properly refused).

Minnesota.—An instruction in a criminal action, that it is the duty of the jurors carefully to examine all the evidence, and honestly endeavor to reach a verdict; but that if any juror, after duly weighing and considering all the evidence and instructions, is not satisfied beyond all reasonable doubt that defendant is guilty, it will be his duty to vote for defendant's acquittal, and refuse to agree to a verdict of guilty, although all the other jurors may be satisfied beyond a reasonable doubt of defendant's guilt, is properly refused, as inviting the jury to disagree if possible. *State* v. *Rue,* 72 Minn. 296, 75 N. W. 235.

Mississippi.—*Nelms* v. *State,* 58 Miss. 362 (holding it error to refuse to charge that if there is a probability of the innocence of the defendant, then a reasonable doubt of his guilt exists, and the jury must find a verdict of not guilty. Conviction reversed); *Hammond* v. *State,* 74 Miss. 214, 21 So. 149 (holding that a charge that all that is required, for the jury to convict defendant, is to consider all the facts and circumstances in evidence, and from them "to conscientiously believe, beyond a reasonable doubt," that he committed the crime, is not objectionable because the word "conscientiously" is used); *Powers* v. *State,* 74 Miss. 777, 21 So. 657 (holding that a charge is erroneous which, after stating that the term "reasonable doubt" is indefinable, declares that it is the duty of the jury to convict when the evidence satisfies them as fair, reasonable, and conscientious men, of the guilt of the accused); *Williams* v. *State,* 73 Miss. 820, 19 So. 826 (holding that an instruction that "abiding conviction of guilt," or "full satisfaction of guilt," is the equivalent of a belief beyond a reasonable doubt, is erroneous).

Missouri.—*State* v. *Gonce,* 79 Mo. 600 (upon a bigamy trial defendant requested, but the court refused, the following instruction: "The burden of proof to establish the guilt of defendant devolves upon the state, and the law clothes him with a presumption of innocence which attends and protects him until it is overcome by testimony which proves his guilt beyond a reasonable doubt. By a reasonable doubt is meant a substantial doubt based upon the evidence, or want of evidence, in the case, and not a bare possibility of defendant's innocence,"—held on appeal that the failure to give this instruction was reversible error, and that in every criminal case the defendant is entitled to an instruction as to reasonable doubt; and it is error for the court to refuse it, no matter how clear the evidence may seem against him); *State* v. *Shaeffer,* 89 Mo. 271, 1 S. W. 293 (holding that a charge that if all the facts and circumstances proved can be as reasonably reconciled with the theory that defendant is innocent as with the theory that he is guilty, the defendant should be acquitted, is contrary to the meaning of the term "reasonable doubt"); *State* v. *Payton,* 90 Mo. 220, 2 S. W. 394 (holding that where the court told the jury that "reasonable doubt," as used in the instructions, meant a real reasonable doubt based upon the testimony or want of testimony in the case, and not a mere possibility of the defendant's innocence, the use of the word "real" could not be regarded as reversible error); *State* v. *David,* 131 Mo. 380, 33 S. W. 28 (holding that an instruction that a reasonable doubt of defendant's guilt which will authorize an acquittal must be a substantial doubt based on the evidence and all the facts and circumstances proved, and not a mere possibility of innocence; but that if the whole evidence leaves the minds of the jurors in such condition that they are morally certain of neither defendant's guilt nor his innocence, a reasonable doubt exists, and they must acquit,—is correct); *State* v. *Duncan,* 142 Mo. 456, 44 S. W. 263 (holding that an instruction that a reasonable doubt is a substantial doubt of defendant's guilt, with a view to all the evidence in the case, and not a mere possibility of defendant's innocence, is not subject to the criticism that it entirely ignores that element of doubt that may arise from the insufficiency of the evidence, and casts upon defendant the burden of proving his innocence). An instruction in a criminal case, that if the jury entertain a reasonable doubt as to defendant's guilt or innocence, they shall acquit, but that a doubt which will authorize an acquittal must be a substantial doubt arising out of a due consideration of all the testimony, and not a mere possibility of defendant's innocence, is not misleading on the subject of reasonable doubt, where the jury are also instructed that the indictment is not of itself any evidence of defendant's guilt, and that defendant is not required to prove his innocence, but the law requires the prosecution to prove defendant's guilt, as charged in the indictment, beyond a reasonable doubt. *State* v. *Sacre,* 141 Mo. 64, 41 S. W. 905, Distinguishing *State* v. *Blue,* 136 Mo. 41, 37 S. W. 796, which holds that an instruction defining reasonable doubt to be a "substantial doubt growing out of and consistent with the evidence" is misleading in excluding all reasonable doubt arising from want of evidence.

Montana.—An instruction that a reasonable doubt is a real substantial doubt of defendant's guilt, upon the whole evidence and not a mere possibility of his innocence; and that such a doubt is said to exist when the jury do not feel an abiding conviction, to a moral certainty, of the truth of the charge, or where the evidence does not satisfy the judgment of the truth of the charge with such certainty that a prudent man would feel safe in acting upon it in his own most important affairs and dearest personal interests,—is not erroneous, although it is better to adhere to the definitions which have received the approval of the supreme court. *State* v. *Clancy,* 20 Mont. 498, 52 Pac. 267.

Nebraska.—*Parrish* v. *State,* 14 Neb. 60, 15 N. W. 357, holding that an instruction on a murder trial that although the proof might not be unequivocally and absolutely certain, yet that if it were morally satisfactory and convincing, it was all that the law required, was not erroneous. And an instruction upon a murder trial that a doubt, to justify an acquittal, must be a reasonable one; that one produced by undue sensibility in the juror's mind, in view of the consequences of the verdict, is not a reasonable doubt; that a juror cannot create sources or materials of doubt by resorting to trivial or fanciful suppositions and remote conjectures as to possible states of facts differing from that established by the evidence, nor disbelieve, if from the evidence he believes as a man; and that if, after a careful and impartial consideration of all the evidence in the case, the jury can say they feel an abiding conviction of the guilt of the defendant, and are fully satisfied to a moral certainty of the truth of the charge against him, they are satisfied beyond a reasonable doubt,—is correct. *Willis* v. *State,* 43 Neb. 102, 61 N. W. 254. So, a charge on reasonable doubt is not erroneous because it states that a doubt produced by undue sensibility in the mind of any juror in view of the consequences of his verdict, is not a reasonable doubt; and that a juror is not allowed to create sources or materials of doubt by resorting to trivial or fanciful suppositions and remote conjectures as to possible states of facts different from those established by the evidence; and that they are not at liberty to disbelieve as jurors if from the evidence they believe as men; and that their oath imposes no obligation to doubt where no doubt would exist if no oath were administered. *Davis* v. *State,* 51 Neb. 301, 70 N. W. 984. And an instruction that a reasonable doubt to justify an acquittal must arise from a candid and impartial investigation of all the evidence in the case is not subject to the criticism that it deprives the defendant of the right to the benefit of any doubt arising from the want of evidence in the case. *Bartley* v. *State,* 53 Neb. 310, 73 N. W. 744, 55 Neb. 294, 75 N. W. 832. It is not error to instruct the jury that "by reasonable doubt" is meant an actual, substantial doubt of guilt arising from evidence, or want of evidence, in the case. *Ferguson* v. *State,* 52 Neb. 432, 72 N. W. 590.

New Jersey.—The law of reasonable doubt is sufficiently given in a trial for larceny, by a charge that defendant is entitled to the benefit of a reasonable doubt; that the duty is on the state to prove to the satisfaction of the jury, beyond a reasonable doubt, that defendant has committed the specified crime with which she is charged in the indictment, and if it fails to do so defendant is entitled to an acquittal; and that the jury are to decide the question simply upon the evidence produced before them, and, in consideration of that evidence, to give the defendant the benefit of every reasonable doubt that arises in their minds as to the commission of the crime, and say on their oaths, from the evidence, whether she is guilty or not. *Gardner* v. *State,* 55 N. J. L. 17, 26 Atl. 30. And it is not error to refuse a charge that defendant is entitled to "a reasonable doubt upon every and any question of fact in the case." *Acker* v. *State,* 52 N. J. L. 259, 19 Atl. 258.

New Mexico.—An instruction that the jury need not be satisfied beyond a reasonable doubt of each link in the chain of circumstances relied on to establish guilt; and that it is sufficient if, taking the testimony altogether, they are satisfied beyond a reasonable doubt that the defendant is guilty, though likely to cause the jury to misunderstand "link" for "material fact," is not erroneous, when they have been fully instructed as to the necessity of believing beyond a reasonable doubt that every material fact has been proved. *Faulkner* v. *Territory,* 6 N. M. 464, 30 Pac. 905. An instruction that "a reasonable doubt is not a mere possibility of a doubt, but it must be a reasonable doubt growing out of all the evidence and circumstances in evidence in the case,"—sufficiently defines reasonable doubt. *Chavez* v. *Territory,* 6 N. M. 455, 30 Pac. 903.

New York.—*People* v. *Guidici,* 100 N. Y. 503, 3 N. E. 493 (where, upon a trial for murder, the judge charged the jury as follows: "You must understand what a reasonable doubt is. It is not a mere guess or surmise that the man may not be guilty; it is such a doubt as a reasonable man may entertain after a fair review and consideration of the evidence; a doubt for which some good reason arising from the evidence can be given." It was objected on appeal that the charge was erroneous in so far as it charged that it must be a doubt for which some good reason arising from the evidence can be given. Held no error; that, taken in connection with the rest of the charge, it simply distinguishes a reasonable doubt from such as was merely vague and imaginary. An indefinable doubt which cannot be stated with the reason upon which it rests, so that it may be examined and discussed, can hardly be considered reasonable, as such a one would render the administration of justice impracticable,—Citing and approving 3 Greenl. Ev. 4th ed. § 29, note); *Walker* v. *People*, 88 N. Y. 81 (holding that where the court has charged the true rule as to reasonable doubt upon the whole case it cannot be required to subdivide it and charge separately as to each of the elements necessary to constitute the crime). See also *Walker* v. *People*, 1 N. Y. Crim. Rep. 7, 22; *People* v. *Cruger*, 38 Hun, 500, Reversed on another point in 102 N. Y. 510, 55 Am. Rep. 830, 7 N. E. 555 (in this case Davis, P. J., says: "The true rule in respect of 'reasonable doubt' relates to the effect which the whole evidence of a case, as presented on both sides, with all its surrounding circumstances, produces upon the minds of a jury; and it entitles the defendant to the benefit of a reasonable doubt which still exists upon the question of guilt after the jury have fully and fairly considered such evidence and circumstances, and find that they fail to produce satisfactory conclusions of the guiltiness of the accused"); *People* v. *Willett*, 36 Hun, 500, (where the accused sets up an affirmative defense, such as great provocation, sudden passion, etc., the burden does not rest upon the prisoner to establish, even to a reasonable probability, the truth of such defense. If upon the whole evidence of both sides a reasonable doubt is created as to the guilt of the prisoner, he is entitled to the benefit of it. A refusal to charge this in substance held error, reversing conviction of murder); N. Y. Crim. Code, § 389, provides that in case of reasonable doubt whether defendant's guilt is satisfactorily shown, he is entitled to an acquittal; and by § 390 it is provided that where there is a reasonable ground of doubt in which of two or more degrees of a crime the defendant is guilty, he can be convicted of the lowest of those grades only. An instruction on a trial for murder, that a reasonable doubt is not a mere whim, guess, or surmise, or a mere subterfuge to which resort may be had in order to avoid doing a disagreeable thing, but that it is such a doubt as reasonable men may entertain after a careful and honest review and consideration of the evidence, and is founded in reason and comes from reason and survives reason, is sufficient. *People* v. *Barker*, 153 N. Y. 111, 47 N. E. 31.

North Carolina.—A charge that "reasonable doubt" means wholly satisfied, or satisfied to a moral certainty, is substantially correct, and sufficient without defining such doubt in the words asked, no set formula being required. *State* v. *Whitson*, 111 N. C. 695, 16 S. E. 332. And *State* v. *Rogers*, 119 N. C. 793, 26 S. E. 142, hold that an instruction in a bastardy prosecution, that the jury may convict upon testimony that "satisfies" them of defendant's guilt, is erroneous, as it exacts too low a degree of proof.

Ohio.—An instruction that the jury must be satisfied from a preponderance of the evidence that defendant used no more force than was necessary to repel the assailant is erroneous upon a prosecution for shooting with intent to kill, as in determining the questions upon a preponderance of the evidence the jury are not required to be "satisfied." *Jordan* v. *State*, 13 Ohio C. C. 471.

Oklahoma.—An instruction that when the jury are "reasonably" convinced that the evidence is sufficient to overcome the presumption of defendant's innocence, it should cease thereafter to influence their minds, is erroneous. *Horn* v. *Territory*, 8 Okla. 52, 56 Pac. 846.

Pennsylvania.—It is error in an instruction to define a reasonable doubt as "such a doubt as would influence or control you in your actions in any of the important transactions of life." *Com.* v. *Miller*, 139 Pa. 77, 21 Atl. 138.

South Carolina.—An instruction on a trial for murder that a reasonable doubt is a strong doubt based on the testimony is not objectionable. *State* v. *Summer*, 55 S. C. 32, 32 S. E. 771.

South Dakota.—An instruction on a trial for murder that if any one of the jury, after having considered all the evidence in the case and consulted with his fellow jurymen, shall entertain a reasonable doubt of defendant's guilt, the jury cannot find defendant guilty, is properly refused where the individual responsibility of each juror is sufficiently covered by the general charge to enable each juror to understand that in order to convict defendant he must be satisfied from the evidence beyond a reasonable doubt that defendant committed the crime as charged in the indictment. *State* v. *Phelps*, 5 S. D. 480, 59 N. W. 471.

Texas.—*Pharr* v. *State*, 10 Tex. App. 485 (holding upon a trial for murder the following charge to be no error: "All the circumstances when taken together must lead to a satisfactory conclusion and produce an effect—a reasonable and moral certainty that the defendant, and no other person, committed the offense charged"); *May* v. *State*, 6 Tex. App. 191 (upon a trial for misdemeanor, held no error to omit to charge concerning a reasonable doubt). The jury in a prosecution for rape should be instructed on defendant's behalf that to convict they must find beyond a reasonable doubt that the prosecutrix was compelled to submit, and if they have a reasonable doubt whether or not she consented they must acquit. *Owens* v. *State*, 39 Tex. Crim. Rep. 391, 46 S. W. 240. But a requested instruction that to authorize a conviction it must appear from the evidence beyond a reasonable doubt, not only that the crime as charged has been committed, but there must be proof, established beyond a reasonable doubt, pertinently identifying defendant with the crime beyond a mere probability or strong suspicion,—is properly refused. *Hamblin* v. *State* (Tex. Crim. App.) 50 S. W. 1019, 51 S. W. 1111. An instruction that if the jury have a reasonable doubt, "from the evidence," of defendant's guilt, they will acquit, is not objectionable on the ground that it prevents an acquittal for want of evidence. *Tomlinson* v. *State* (Tex. Crim. App.) 43 S. W. 332.

Virginia.—The words "to doubt is to acquit" are properly eliminated from an instruction in a trial for murder, when not followed by the qualification that the doubt must be a reasonable one of the sufficiency or certainty of the evidence of guilt,—especially where the law of reasonable doubt is given in a favorable form for the prisoner. *Taylor* v. *Com.* 90 Va. 109, 17 S. E. 812.

Washington.—An instruction that reasonable doubt should grow out of the evidence in the case, and not be merely conjectural, speculative, or imaginary, is not subject to the objection that it assumes that any doubt in the minds of the jury would be a speculative, conjectural, or imaginary one. *State* v. *Krug,* 12 Wash. 288, 41 Pac. 126. But it is not error to refuse a requested instruction that if any one of the jury, after having considered all the evidence, and after having consulted with his fellow jurymen, entertains a reasonable doubt of the guilt of defendant, the jury cannot find defendant guilty. *State* v. *Williams,* 13 Wash. 335, 43 Pac. 15.

Washington Territory—*Leonard* v. *Territory,* 2 Wash. Terr. 381, 7 Pac. 872.

West Virginia.—A requested instruction that if there is a conflict of the evidence or circumstances as to whether the killing was done in self-defense, and the circumstances or other evidence preponderate in favor of self-defense, or if it is equally balanced, the jury ought not to convict of murder or manslaughter,—is properly refused. *State* v. *Staley,* 45 W. Va. 792, 32 S. E. 198, Citing *Com.* v. *York,* 9 Met. 93, 43 Am. Dec. 373, Overruling *State* v. *Zeigler,* 40 W. Va. 594, 21 S. E. 763.

Wisconsin.—An instruction that if there is one single material fact in the case proved to the satisfaction of the jury by a preponderance of the evidence, it is sufficient to raise a reasonable doubt, and justify an acquittal, is not misleading, as tending to imply that, unless some substantive fact is proved by the preponderance of the evidence, it will not raise a reasonable doubt, where full and accurate instructions are given as to the presumption of innocence, the propriety of the most charitable construction of the facts, and the necessity that every reasonable doubt should be removed before conviction. *Butler* v. *State,* 102 Wis. 364, 78 N. W. 590. An instruction that reasonable doubt is, as its name implies, a doubt resting in reason, and must arise out of the whole evidence fairly and rationally considered, is proper in connection with an instruction that the legal presumption is that the accused is innocent. *Emery* v. *State,* 101 Wis. 627, 78 N. W. 145. This case also holds that an instruction that the expression "beyond a reasonable doubt" does not mean beyond a mere doubt or possibility of innocence; and that if guilt is established by evidence beyond any doubt, founded on reason and common sense as applied thereto, a conviction should follow though the jury may believe there is doubt on the question, not arising, however, to the certainty of a reasonable doubt, or though they yet believe in the possibility of innocence,—is proper. And this case further holds that it is proper to instruct the jury that "guilty beyond a reasonable doubt arising out of or based on the evidence," and "guilty beyond a reasonable doubt arising out of or for want of evidence," means the same thing in that the presumption of innocence must be overcome and guilt be established by the evidence beyond a reasonable doubt.

XXIV. Special verdict.

88. Common-law power.

In the absence of statute restriction, the judge may direct a special verdict,[1] or a finding upon a special question of fact.[2]

[1] 1 Chitty, Crim. Law, 642; article in 10 Crim. L. Mag. 11, stating the practice.

In South Carolina the court is not required to charge that the jury, upon finding defendant guilty of murder, may find a special verdict recommending him to the mercy of the court, whereupon punishment shall be reduced to imprisonment for life. *State* v. *Owens,* 44 S. C. 324, 22 S. E. 244.

[2] This practice, though rare, is generally allowable, as it is in civil cases. See Civil Trial Brief, p. 161. And see N. Y. Code Crim. Proc. §§ 436 *et seq.*, which allows it except in libel.

But *Smith* v. *State,* 59 Ohio St. 350, 52 N. E. 826, holds that criminal actions are not within the purview of Ohio Rev. Stat. §§ 5200, 5201; and the court is not required to direct the jury to return special findings upon the issue raised by the plea of not guilty.

And *People* v. *Roat,* 117 Mich. 578, 76 N. W. 91, holds that defendant in a criminal trial is not entitled to have any special question submitted to the jury, as any limitation upon the right of the jury to find a verdict in criminal cases is against the policy of the law.

XXV. Theory of defense.

89. False theory.

A false theory of defense, shown to have been originated by the accused or by his friends, and with his privity, is evidence tending to show guilt. In such a case it is proper to instruct the jury that if the attempted explanation is not true, it places the defendant in the position of making an attempted explanation which fails of convincing, and leads to the opposite result, of pointing rather to his guilt.[1]

[1] *Pilger* v. *Com.* 112 Pa. 220, 5 Atl. 309 (arson).

XXVI. Venue.

90. Judicial notice.

The court should take judical notice of the territorial boundary lines of its own jurisdiction,[1] and whether a city,[2] town,[3] or incorporated village,[4] referred to by the evidence is within the county where the trial is had.

The court has power to take judicial notice that a street or wharf or other public place referred to in the evidence is within a municipality within the county.[5]

[1] *United States* v. *Brave Bear,* 3 Dak. 34, 13 N. W. 565, holding that consequently it will take judicial notice that a crime committed at a place on an Indian reservation within such boundary lines is within the jurisdiction of the court. See also *Hoyt* v. *Russell,* 117 U. S. 401, 29 L. ed. 914, 6 Sup. Ct. Rep. 881. Compare *United States* v. *Anderson,* 17 Blatchf. 238, Fed. Cas. No. 14,448.

[2] *Sullivan* v. *People,* 122 Ill. 385, 13 N. E. 248 (proof that a crime was committed in Chicago is proof that it was committed in Cook county, as the court will take judicial notice that Chicago is in Cook county); *State* v. *Burns,* 48 Mo. 438 (homicide; holding that public statutes enable the court to recognize the city of St. Louis as in the county of St. Louis).

[3] *People* v. *Breese,* 7 Cow. 429. *Contra, Moye* v. *State,* 65 Ga. 754; *State* v. *Quaite,* 20 Mo. App. 405.

[4] *People* v. *Telford,* 56 Mich. 541, 23 N. W. 213. Blank in name of county in complaint for selling liquor in a specified village not ground for dismissal at trial, because courts take judicial notice of municipalities within their jurisdiction. And see more fully on this question cases reviewed in note to *Olive* v. *State* (Ala.) 4 L. R. A. 33.

[5] The authorities are at variance on this subject, but I deem it clear that the court has power to take such notice, although not bound to do so. Proof may be required by the trial court; and in the absence of such proof, the appellate court may reverse; yet, on the other hand, if the court exercises the power, conviction should not be reversed merely because they exercise it, but, if at all, only in case they are mistaken as to the fact. Compare the following cases: *State* v. *Burns,* 48 Mo. 438 (here the evidence showed that the homicide was committed in Mullanphy street, but did not show that such street was in the city of St. Louis; held that it was properly submitted to the jury to find whether the crime was committed in the county of St. Louis, because if they found that it was committed in the city of St. Louis, it would follow that it must have been in the county, inasmuch as the public statutes recognize the city of St. Louis as being in the county of St. Louis); *Dougherty* v. *People,* 118 Ill. 160, 8 N. E. 673 (holding that the court will not take judicial notice that certain streets referred to by the witnesses are in the city of Chicago, or elsewhere in Cook county, although there are streets of the same names in that city); *Com.* v. *Ackland,* 107 Mass. 211 (holding that on an indictment for illegally maintaining a tenement in Boston, it will be presumed that witnesses who testified that the tenement was on India wharf meant India wharf, in Boston); *Evans* v. *State,* 17 Fla. 192 (keeping house of ill fame; the only evidence disclosed by the record as to the venue was that the defendant lived at the wharf known as Commendencia wharf; no proof that such

wharf was in the county of the trial; held insufficient, and judgment reversed).

91. Circumstantial evidence or inference enough.

It is not necessary that witnesses be produced to testify that the offense was committed in the place charged; it is enough if the proof be circumstantial or inferential.[1]

[1]Wharton, Crim. Ev. § 108; *State* v. *West*, 69 Mo. 401, 33 Am. Rep. 506 (murder). See also *State* v. *Jones*, 1 McMull, L. 236, 36 Am. Dec. 257.

In *Com.* v. *Costley*, 118 Mass. 2 (homicide), the body was found, with marks of injuries upon it sufficient to cause death, in a river in the heart of a county, in such a condition as to show that it must have been thrown there by the force of the tide or current; and it was held not error to instruct the jury that this was sufficient to warrant them in concluding that the homicide was committed in that county.

In *Hoffman* v. *State*, 12 Tex. App. 406 (disorderly house), there was evidence that the keeper had in the house a license to sell beer from the proper officer of the county; and it was held sufficient to go to the jury.

United States v. *Britton*, 2 Mason, 464, 470, Fed. Cas. No. 14,650, holds that a check drawn in Philadelphia, in favor of a person then in Philadelphia, but presented in an altered and forged state in Massachusetts, should be presumed, in the absence of all proof to the contrary, to have been altered and forged in Massachusetts. The court, Story, J., in instructing the jury, laid down this rule: "If its existence in a forged state is not proved in any other place, it must, from the necessity of the case, be presumed to have been forged where its existence in such state is first made known. . . . If the law were otherwise, it would be almost impossible to convict any person of a forgery, for such acts are done in retirement and concealment, far from the sight of all persons but confederates in guilt."

Spencer v. *Com.* 2 Leigh, 751 (forging bank notes) held the fact that the notes, together with plates, implements, and materials for forging such notes, were found in the defendant's possession in the county of B., to be prima facie proof sufficient to warrant the court in instructing the jury that they ought to find that the forging was done in the county of B.

In *State* v. *Poindexter*, 23 W. Va. 805, it was held that from proof that the writing was found in the possession of the prisoner, in the county where he had uttered or attempted to utter it, there being no evidence that the forgery was committed in any other county, the jury might infer that the forgery was committed in that county.

In *Johnson* v. *State*, 62 Ga. 299 (forgery), evidence that defendant lived in the county, and within it admitted the forgery, there being no evidence that he had ever been out of the county, was held sufficient proof of venue to support a verdict of guilty.

In *Carter* v. *State*, 40 Tex. Crim. Rep. 225, 47 S. W. 979, 49 S. W. 74, 619, it was held that a requested instruction on venue in a criminal trial was properly refused when the body of the deceased was found in the county under circumstances indicating that he was killed there, and in the absence of testimony that he was killed elsewhere.

And in *Rollins* v. *State*, 32 Tex. Crim. Rep. 566, 25 S. W. 125, it was held that charges asked on a prosecution for theft, in reference to the venue, were properly refused where the venue was not a disputed question, the property a few hours after the theft having been taken from defendant in the same county as that in which it was stolen and where the indictment was found.

Compare, for cases where venue was held not proved, *Parkes Case*, 2 East P. C. 963, 992, 2 Leach C. L. 775 (where the date of instrument was in another county than that where the prisoner was indicted, and there was no proof that he had ever had it in his possession in the latter county); *Rex* v. *Crocker*, 5 Bos. & P. 87 (where the forged bill was found on the prisoner in the county where he was indicted, but bore date two years before, at a time when he was a resident of another county, and where he resided for more than a year after that date); *Reg.* v. *Treadgold*, 39 L. T. N. S. 291 (embezzlement. It was the duty of the accused, a commercial traveler, to remit daily to his employers, who resided in London, the moneys which he collected, without reduction. The prisoner on the 1st and 2d of March, 1878, collected at Newark two sums which he did not remit or account for till the 1st week in April, when one of his employers went to Grantham, where the prisoner resided, saw him, and taxed him with receiving moneys and not accounting for them. The defendant then and there handed to his employer a list of moneys he had collected and not accounted for, including the above two sums. There was no evidence that the prisoner returned to Grantham on either of the days, or at what time of the respective days he received the two sums of money; held no evidence of any embezzlement within the borough of Grantham; conviction quashed).

92. Approximate evidence sufficient.

Evidence showing the commission of the offense to have taken place in near proximity to a place shown to be within the county is sufficient to go to the jury, if no question on the point has been raised.[1]

[1]In *Binfield* v. *State*, 15 Neb. 484, 19 N. W. 607 (homicide), evidence that the deceased was shot in H. county, taken to a house half a mile away, and thence, after a few days, to a house across one channel of Platte river, so as to be more convenient to his attending physician, at which latter place he died, was held sufficient to sustain a verdict assuming that the death actually occurred in H. county, because when a certain status is proved to exist as to a person or thing, such status will be presumed to continue until the contrary be shown.

In *State* v. *Benson*, 22 Kan. 471 (assault with intent to kill), testimony of a witness that he resided in P. county, and that the offense charged was committed on his premises and near his residence, is held sufficient to show that the offense was committed in P. county. And see *Maples* v. *State*, 3 Heisk, 408 (holding that the venue was sufficiently proved by evidence that the crime was committed in a cabin in the yard of a witness who testified that he lived in the county where the indictment was found); *Pike* v. *State*, 8 Lea, 577 (to same effect, on testimony that the building was his property and within 50 yards of his dwelling), Distinguishing *Franklin* v. *State*, 5 Baxt. 613, where the act was within 75 yards, but not shown to be on the same property.

93. **Evidence on part of defense.**

Proof of venue afforded by the evidence on behalf of the defense will supply the omission of such proof on the part of the prosecution.[1]

[1] *Scott* v. *State*, 42 Ark. 73. Here, the state having proved that the property stolen was in defendant's residence, it was held that an omission to show what county he resided in was cured by the defendant's testimony that he lived in the county in which the trial was had.

94. **Requisite cogency; reasonable doubt.**

The prosecution is not required to establish the venue of the offense beyond reasonable doubt; but evidence from which it may be reasonably inferred is sufficient.[1]

[1] *Achterberg* v. *State*, 8 Tex. App. 463. Maiming cattle; offense shown to have been committed within sight of witness's premises, which premises were shown to have been within the county. *Contra, dictum* in *Moye* v. *State*, 65 Ga. 754 (larceny; evidence showed act to have been committed in a specified town, but no evidence that the town was within the county); *Rooks* v. *State*, 65 Ga. 330 (malicious mischief).

XLIII.—DOCUMENTS FOR THE JURY.

1. **General rule as to documents in evidence.**

In the absence of a statute to the contrary, the judge may, in his discretion, allow documents (except, in most of the states, depositions)[1] which have been admitted in evidence to be taken by the jury when retiring to deliberate upon their verdict, unless objected to because written upon or underscored to call attention to special portions of them.[2]

[1]It is improper in criminal cases to permit the jury to take depositions in behalf of the accused to their room on retiring; but the court on request should have any portion of such deposition reread to them. *State* v. *Lowry,* 42 W. Va. 205, 24 S. E. 561.

And according to *Com.* v. *Ware,* 137 Pa. 465, 20 Atl. 806, it is proper to refuse to send out, at the request of the jury, the testimony of a witness to settle a dispute as to his testimony; it being the duty of the jury, when desiring information as to any matter of fact or question of law, to come into court and state their difficulty to the judge.

Baker v. *Com.* 13 Ky. L. Rep. 571, 17 S. W. 625, however, holds it to be discretionary with the trial court whether it will refuse to allow the jury to take a deposition to the jury room.

[2]A jury, upon retiring to consider their verdict, may carry with them, by leave of the court, anything introduced before them as evidence. *Grayson* v. *State,* 40 Tex. Crim. Rep. 573, 51 S. W. 246.

So held in *Davis* v. *State,* 91 Ga. 167, 17 S. E. 292, of a book admitted in evidence.

And in *Burton* v. *State,* 115 Ala. 1, 22 So. 585 (a murder trial), of a diagram introduced in evidence for the purpose of showing the *locus in quo,* and of explaining and elucidating the testimony of witnesses in respect thereto. Compare *English* v. *State,* 31 Fla. 340, 356, 12 So. 689, holding that the court may properly refuse to permit a plan of a building introduced in evidence to be sent to the jury room, unless all the evidence in the case goes with it.

So, in *State* v. *Webster,* 21 Wash. 63, 57 Pac. 361, it is held that exhibits properly introduced in evidence, and explanatory of the evidence of witnesses, may be taken to the jury room, under 2 Ballinger's Anno. Codes & Statutes (Wash.) § 5004, directing that the jury may take with them the pleadings and all papers received as evidence, except depositions or such documents as ought not, in the opinion of the court, to be taken from the person having them in possession,—Citing *People* v. *Cochran,* 61 Cal. 548. But see *State* v. *Raymond,* 53 N. J. L. 260, 21 Atl. 328, where it is held that the jury should not be allowed to take with them from the bar the exhibits read in evidence at the trial.

According to *State* v. *Moody,* 18 Wash. 165, 51 Pac. 356, permitting the jury on a trial for murder, to take to the jury room for investigation the dying declarations of the deceased, is reversible error.

State v. *Webster,* 21 Wash. 63, 57 Pac. 361, however, holds that the accidental taking into the jury room, in a trial for murder, of a memorandum of a dying declaration made by a stenographer, but not read to deceased, and unsigned, which was read to the jury by defendant's counsel, and received and marked an exhibit in the cause, after being offered in evidence by him,—is not reversible error, where it could not in any event injure the defendant.

For other authorities collected, see Abbott's Civil Trial Brief, 2d ed., Division XXII.; and 2 Thompson, Trials, 1935, etc. That the contrary rule seems to prevail in Indiana, see Abbott's Civil Trial Brief, 2d ed., Division XXII.; and in North Carolina, 2 Thompson, Trials, 1927, note 5, Citing civil cases.

The present New York statute allows documentary evidence to go out "only upon the consent of the defendant and the counsel for the People." N. Y. Code Crim. Proc. § 425.

2. — used, but not in evidence.

The judge may also allow documents forming part of the record of the trial, or properly used before the jury on the trial, such as the indictment[1] and the plea, and bills of particulars, and the judge's written instructions,[2] to be taken out, provided the jury understand that they are not evidence.

Other documents must not be taken out.[3]

[1] *State* v. *Delong*, 12 Iowa, 453; *Herrold* v. *Com.* 10 Ky. L. Rep. 70, 8 S. W. 194 (indictment allowed to be taken out though indorsed with a previous conviction); *Masterson* v. *State*, 144 Ind. 240, 43 N. E. 138. And for other authorities on this rule generally, see Abbott's Civil Trial Brief, 2d ed. Division XXII.

So held in *Howard* v. *People*, 27 Colo. 396, 61 Pac. 595, as to allowing the jury to take the information and affidavit on which it was based, on retiring, where the prisoner's counsel, knowing of it, interposed no objection. To the same effect, see *Cargill* v. *Com.* 93 Ky. 578, 20 S. W. 782.

A transcript of the docket of the committing magistrate is not evidence which can be admitted and given to the jury in a criminal case, to take with them to their room, under Dak. Code Crim. Proc. § 383, as papers in the cause. *Territory* v. *Jones*, 6 Dak. 85, 50 N. W. 528.

[2] *State* v. *Tompkins*, 71 Mo. 613; *Benton* v. *State*, 30 Ark. 328.

So, under Alabama Code, §§ 3327, 3328, requiring that the judge's charge must be reduced to writing on the motion of either party to either a criminal or a civil action, and that such written instructions shall be taken by the jury to the jury room when they retire, a defendant in a criminal case cannot complain of the jury's taking with them to the jury room the general charge of the court, which was reduced to writing on his motion. *Ragland* v. *State*, 125 Ala. 12, 27 So. 983.

The writing upon an instruction given to the jury in a criminal case, taken with them to their room, of the word "guilty" through inadvertence of the judge, is reversible error, unless it clearly appears that no injury resulted to the defendant therefrom. *Hawkins* v. *State*, 32 Fla. 248, 13 So. 353.

Jones v. *State*, 89 Ind. 82 (law reports containing a former reversal in the cause); *People* v. *Dowdigan*, 67 Mich. 92, 34 N. W. 411 (testimony of complainant and a witness before the justice and the warrant of arrest); *Johnson* v. *State*, 27 Fla. 245, 9 So. 208. *Contra*, *Edwards* v. *Territory*, 1 Wash. Terr. 196 (allowing copy of statutes to go out).

According to *Bernhardt* v. *State*, 82 Wis. 23, 51 N. W. 1009, possession by the jury of the statute, and reading its provisions as to the crime charged and its penalties, and discussing their verdict in connection therewith, without the knowledge or consent of the court, is not such error as requires a reversal.

And *State Bank* v. *Brewer*, 100 Iowa, 576, 69 N. W. 1011, holds that permitting the jury to take to their room the original notes sued on is not prejudicial, where copies thereof were contained in the pleadings, as the jury may take the pleadings with them.

3. Irrelevant matter in relevant document.

It is not necessarily an objection to allowing a document containing relevant matter to go out, that it contains also irrelevant matter.[1]

[1]2 Thompson, Trials, 1941.

According to *Dunn* v. *People*, 172 Ill. 582, 50 N. E. 137, however, it is not the exercise of a sound discretion to deliver to the jury in a murder trial, for use in the jury room, written dying declarations introduced in evidence, where the court rules that certain portions of the written statement indicated by marks are not admissible, notwithstanding that it orally directs the jury not to consider such marked phrases.

4. Document put in evidence, but withdrawn.

A document which the court, after receiving it as evidence, has instructed the jury not to consider as such, cannot be sent out, even though such instruction be reiterated on sending it out.[1]

[1]*Com.* v. *Edgerly*, 10 Allen, 184, 187. Letter inclosing counterfeit bill; reversal for error in this.

5. Standards of comparison.

Papers not otherwise in evidence, but properly used as standards of comparison to aid the jury in determining a question of handwriting, may, in the discretion of the judge, be allowed to go out.[1]

[1]This seems implied in the statute (*contra*, *People* v. *Page*, 1 Idaho, 102); but the leave should not be given if the contents of the writing so used could be prejudicial to the accused, otherwise illegal evidence might be got before the jury in the guise of a test paper. In New York consent is necessary. See *supra*, § 1, notes.

And *Bailey* v. *State* (Tex. Crim. App.) 38 S. W. 992, expressly holds that the court may allow the jury to take into the jury room the several genuine signatures of defendant introduced by him and the state for comparison with the signature in question.

So held in *State* v. *Wetherell*, 70 Vt. 274, 40 Atl. 728, of criminatory letters alleged to have been written by the defendant on trial for a crime, together with papers admitted for the purpose of a comparison of the handwriting.

But *Phillips* v. *State*, 62 Ark. 119, 34 S. W. 539, holds that a request by the jury to permit them to take a writing claimed to have been written by defendant, while they improperly have a motion for a continuance by defendant, that they may compare the signatures on the two papers, is properly refused.

6. Tangible evidence.

Objects put in evidence on the trial cannot go to the jury room without leave of court.[1]

[1]*McCoy* v. *State*, 78 Ga. 490, 3 S. E. 768.

And, in New York, consent. See *supra*, § 1.

McCoy v. *People*, 175 Ill. 224, 51 N. E. 777, holds that the jury in a murder trial may be allowed to take a revolver with which the homicide is claimed to have been committed, and which has been introduced in evidence.

So held in *Chalk* v. *State*, 35 Tex. Crim. Rep. 116, 32 S. W. 534, of a coat used in evidence on a trial for murder.

To similar effect in *State* v. *Cushing*, 14 Wash. 527, 45 Pac. 145, of the clothing worn by the deceased at the time of the shooting, and the gun with which the shooting was done, introduced in evidence.

And in *Taylor* v. *Com.* 90 Va. 109, 17 S. E. 812, a trial for murder in which cartridge hulls found at the scene of the killing had been introduced by the prosecution, and the defendant's Winchester rifle, with shells fired from it during the trial, had been introduced by the defendant to show that the plunger struck the shell differently from those introduced by the prosecution, it was held that the jury, who were permitted to take the gun and shells to their room without objection, might take it apart and examine the plunger, and ascertain that they had been recently tampered with, and fixed so as to explode the cartridge differently from those used by the murderers and put in evidence.

And in *Adams* v. *State*, 93 Ga. 166, 18 S. E. 553, a trial for perjury in swearing, upon a prosecution for burglary, that pantaloons alleged to have been stolen were found by defendant and given to the mother of the alleged burglar, it was held proper for the sheriff to hand such pantaloons, which were admitted in evidence, to the jury after they had retired, with directions to be sure not to lose them.

But *Hansing* v. *Territory*, 4 Okla. 443, 46 Pac. 509, holds that it is error for the court in a murder trial to permit the jury to take to the jury room, and have in their possession while deliberating, the weapons used by the defendants, and the hat worn by the deceased, showing the bullet holes, as the only statutory provision on the subject is that in Okla. Stat. 1893, § 5237, authorizing the jury to take into the jury room all papers received in evidence, or copies of such parts of public records or private documents given in evidence as ought not, in the opinion of the court, to be taken from the person having them in possession.

7. Several documents.

If there are several documents, and counsel do not agree which are to be sent out, it is proper practice, on sending out any one or more, to send all that have been put in evidence relating to the same subject.[1]

[1]According to *Rainforth* v. *State*, 61 Ill. 365, all that have been put in evidence must, if the counsel for the accused requests it, be sent out, or none.

8. Jurors' notes.

Notes taken by a juror during the trial may be taken out.[1]

[1]*Long* v. *State*, 95 Ind. 481; N. Y. Code Crim. Proc. § 426. For other states, see Abbott's Civil Trial Brief, 2d ed. p. 483.

XLIV.—FURTHER INSTRUCTIONS AFTER THE JURY RETIRE.

1. In what cases given.

After the jury have retired to deliberate upon their verdict, the court, in the absence of statute, has power, in its discretion and of its own motion, to recall them, and give further instructions,[1] or to withdraw or correct erroneous instructions;[2] but neither party can of right demand this.

A request by the jury for further instructions may be refused if they have already been fully instructed.[3]

When the jury make a reasonable request for further instructions, it may be error to refuse;[4] but after the jury have retired the judge is not bound to comply with the request of either party to give additional instructions upon a point not covered by a request from the jury, even if only to explain or modify those already given, for this rests in the discretion of the court.

Neither party has a right to discuss by counsel the law or the evidence afresh, in the presence of the jury.

Further instructions, if given, are subject to exception for error, like those given before the jury retire.[5]

[1] *Gwatkin* v. *Com.* 9 Leigh, 678, 33 Am. Dec. 264; *Benavides* v. *State,* 31 Tex. Crim. Rep. 173, 20 S. W. 369; *People* v. *Perry,* 65 Cal. 568; *State* v. *Chandler,* 31 Kan. 201, 1 Pac. 787. [*Contra, Hannahan* v. *State,* 7 Tex. App. 610 (statutory)]; *People* v. *Perry,* 65 Cal. 568; *Buntin* v. *State,* 68 Ind. 38. For additional authorities, see Abbott's Civil Trial Brief, 2d ed. Division XXIII., pp. 484 *et seq.* See also *Com.* v. *Snelling,* 15 Pick. 321.

[2] *Greenfield* v. *People,* 85 N. Y. 75, 39 Am. Rep. 636, 23 Hun, 454; *State* v. *Lightsey,* 43 S. C. 114, 20 S. E. 975.

According to *State* v. *Raven,* 115 Mo. 419, 22 S. W. 376, it is proper for the trial court, upon the jury's making a written request, in the presence of defendant and her counsel, for information as to whether there is a degree between murder in the second degree and manslaughter in the third degree, thereupon to prepare an instruction omitted from the court's former charge, correctly defining manslaughter in the second degree, and, upon objection made to giving it at such time, to offer to reopen the case for argument upon all the instructions.

[3] *Jackson* v. *State,* 49 N. J. L. 252, 9 Atl. 740. *Contra,* perhaps, under N. Y. Code Crim. Proc. § 427.

[4] N. Y. Code Crim. Proc. § 427; *People* v. *Cassiano,* 30 Hun, 388, holding it error to refuse the request of the jury for instructions as to the extent of punishment. And see *Caston* v. *State,* 31 Tex. Crim. Rep. 304, 20 S. W. 585 (holding that the court upon a criminal prosecution may, at the request of the jury, recall them and charge them again); *Harper* v. *State,* 109 Ala. 66, 19 So. 901 (holding likewise; and also that if an attorney offers further instructions in such case the court must pass upon them).

The court, when asked by the jury for further instructions, need not confine itself to the points upon which information is asked. *People* v. *M'Kay,* 122 Cal. 628, 55 Pac. 594. See also *Powell* v. *State,* 95 Ga. 502, 20 S. E. 483 (holding a recharge in a murder trial, on the subject of malice, as well as voluntary manslaughter, in response to a request by the jury to recharge on the latter, not erroneous); *State* v. *Kessler,* 15 Utah, 142, 49 Pac. 293 (to the effect that the court in a trial on an indictment for murder may, at the request of the jury upon their return into court after retiring to consider their verdict, read the law as to the punishment of voluntary and involuntary manslaughter).

[5]Parties may reserve exceptions to the additional instructions given to the jury upon their return into court after having retired to consider their verdict. *Orr* v. *State,* 107 Ala. 35, 18 So. 142.

The failure of the court to reduce to writing additional instructions given at the request of the jury after they have deliberated on the case, and the giving of such instructions orally, is reversible error, where the court had been duly requested to give its entire charge in writing, under Ga. Code, § 244, as that section was not repealed by the act providing for the appointment of official court reporters. *Bowden* v. *Achor,* 95 Ga. 243, 22 S. E. 254.

2. Manner of giving.

Further instructions after the jury have retired should be given only in open court,[1] and when counsel on both sides and the accused are present, or have had notice and an opportunity of being present.[2] In felony the accused must always be present.[3]

[1]*State* v. *Patterson,* 45 Vt. 308, 12 Am. Rep. 200.

Written instructions should not be sent in, even by consent. *Hoberg* v. *State,* 3 Minn. 262, Gil. 181. Compare *People* v. *Kelly,* 2 N. Y. Crim. Rep. 15, 94 N. Y. 526.

[2]*Martin* v. *State,* 51 Ga. 567; *State* v. *Davenport,* 33 La. Ann. 231; *People* v. *Cassiano,* 30 Hun, 388; *Dixon* v. *State,* 13 Fla. 636; *Doyle* v. *United States,* 10 Fed. 269; *State* v. *Meagher,* 49 Mo. App. 579; *People* v. *Trim,* 37 Cal. 274 (statutory); N. Y. Code Crim. Proc. § 427. See comments on this rule in *Cornish* v. *Graff,* 36 Hun, 160. For other authorities, see Abbott's Civil Trial Brief, 2d ed. Division XXIII., p. 486. *Contra, State* v. *Pike,* 65 Me. 111, holding that the court is not bound to send for counsel who choose to absent themselves.

In *Martin* v. *State,* 51 Ga. 567, *supra,* the court said: "It is said that under the rule we hold in this case courts might be embarrassed in the administration of justice; that cases could not be conducted with certainty to a conclusion, if counsel for a prisoner could stop the trial by wilfully absenting himself from the courthouse. To this objection it may be replied that courts are armed with plenary authority to enforce the discharge of duty on the part of all their officers. And, besides,—a fitting and proper penalty on derelict counsel in the case supposed,—they could, in cases when the necessity arose, require the defendant to procure other counsel, or make the appointment for him. If the absence of counsel resulted from a cause which would be a good ground for continuance, and it would not be proper to substitute other counsel, it were better that there should be a continuance, or at least a temporary postponement, than that one not skilled in the law, and who was largely ignorant of his legal rights, and perhaps totally ignorant of the practice on which those rights rested, should lose a privilege the value of which cannot be estimated, and which the organic law says shall not be taken from him. So, in this case, it would not probably have taken much time—possibly a few minutes—to have secured the attendance of defendant's counsel, or, had that been impossible, other counsel might have been chosen by the defendant or appointed by the court. An effort in that direction would have been proper. As this important privilege was lost to the defendant in this case, and at a critical stage of the trial, through a mistake of the state's counsel,—at least it is positively so stated by defendant's counsel, and doubtless the court was misled by it,—we think that there should be a new trial."

But the absence of the counsel of the accused, if it is impossible to procure him, will not make it improper for the court to give additional instructions to the jury, where they are taken down by the reporter. *People* v. *Robinson*, 86 Mich. 415, 49 N. W. 260.

In *State* v. *Hale*, 91 Iowa, 367, 59 N. W. 281, after the jury had been out a short time, the court brought them in, interrogated them as to the cause of their failure to agree, and gave them additional instructions. The defendant was absent during all of these proceedings, and his counsel came in during the course thereof, but made no objection until after the instructions were given; and it was held that the court committed no error to the defendant's prejudice.

According to *People* v. *Mayes*, 113 Cal. 618, 45 Pac. 860, recalling the jury, and giving an additional instruction in the absence of the attorney for the accused on a criminal prosecution, but in the presence of the accused himself, is not error, where the court directs that an exception on behalf of the accused be entered thereto.

Sufficient notice, under N. Y. Code Crim. Proc. § 427, that further instructions would be given if asked by the jury, during the counsel's absence, was given when, before the jury agreed, on counsel's stating he was about to go home, the judge told him that he would attend during the evening to receive the verdict and answer the jury, and that the counsel could make any motion he desired in the morning. *People* v. *Kennedy*, 57 Hun, 532, 11 N. Y. Supp. 244.

And refusal of the court to give the jury further instructions was held not to be a communication in the absence of defendant or his counsel, within § 427 of the Code, in *People* v. *Parker*, 137 N. Y. 535, 32 N. E. 1013.

Maurer v. *People*, 43 N. Y. 1 (holding the absence of the accused to be error, notwithstanding his counsel was present, and failed to object); *Linbeck* v. *State*, 1 Wash. 336, 25 Pac. 452; *Kinnemer* v. *State*, 66 Ark. 206, 49 S. W. 815; *Jones* v. *State*, 26 Ohio St. 208; *Waller* v. *State*, 40 Ala. 325; *Bonner* v. *State*, 67 Ga. 510; *Com.* v. *House*, 6 Pa. Super. Ct. 92, and cases cited; *State* v. *Alexander*, 66 Mo. 148; *State* v. *Blackwelder*, 61 N. C. (Phil. L.) 38; *Territory* v. *Lopez*, 3 N. M. 156, 2 Pac. 364; *Roberts* v. *State*, 111 Ind. 340, 12 N. E. 500, and cases cited (holding that an instruction which was erroneous and prejudicial to the accused could not be withdrawn in his absence; *Shipp* v. *State*, 11 Tex. App. 46 (holding that the right to be present cannot be waived by the defendant's counsel); N. Y. Code Crim. Proc. § 427 (providing as above). Compare with *Meece* v. *Com.* 78 Ky. 586, holding that whether it will be error to give further instructions in the absence of the accused depends upon the fact whether he is prejudiced thereby, which is to be inferred from the whole case. See also *Doyle* v. *United States,* 10 Fed. 269.

The rule should not be applied when he is out on bail. *Jackson* v. *State,* 49 N. J. L. 252, 9 Atl. 740; *People* v. *Soto,* 65 Cal. 621, 4 Pac. 664.

3. Further evidence.

The court has power in its discretion to recall a witness, that he may repeat testimony as to which the jury are in doubt, or to allow new evidence to be taken on a question of fact on which they are in doubt.[1]

[1]*Com.* v. *Ricketson,* 5 Met. 412, *dictum,* sanctioning course of judge in allowing a witness to be called to testify on a point as to which the jury inquired. And see Abbott's Civil Trial Brief, 2d ed. Division VIII.; *Tarver* v. *State,* 43 Tex. 564.

So, the jury may, if they so desire, have a deposition taken upon the examining trial reread to them, when they have disagreed about it. *Clark* v. *State,* 28 Tex. App. 189, 12 S. W. 729.

But the jury cannot, after retiring to consider their verdict, hear testimony which has not already been placed before them. *Lorance* v. *State,* 37 Tex. Crim. Rep. 453, 36 S. W. 93.

That the reading of evidence to the jury by the court reporter from his notes on a trial for felony, after they have been sent out to consider their verdict, in the absence of defendant's counsel, and without notice to him, is reversible error, although defendant is present in court in charge of the sheriff, see *Bartell* v. *State,* 40 Neb. 232, 58 N. W. 716.

But the absence of a prisoner from the courtroom when the jury came in and heard, at their own request, a certain portion of the evidence read, did not violate the rights of the accused, where he was absent at his own request to be taken to the jail, and not be brought back until after the verdict. *State* v. *Haines,* 36 S. C. 504, 15 S. E. 555.

4. Effect of adequate further instructions.

An error in instructing or refusing to instruct the jury may be cured by a full and complete withdrawal of the objectionable matter, or compliance with the request in further instructions properly given under these rules.[1]

[1]*Greenfield* v. *People,* 85 N. Y. 75, 39 Am. Rep. 636.

In *Gray* v. *State* (Fla.) 28 So. 53, after the retirement of the jury under the charge of the court, they returned into court, and requested to know whether, under the law, they must find a verdict of murder in the first degree or acquit, or whether they could find the deceased guilty of some lesser offense, and the court reread to them portions of the charge given bearing on the matter inquired about. Thereupon defendant objected to a word in the charge on the ground that it was indefinite, and the court added in writing, and read to the jury, the explanation of the word as insisted on by the defendant. It was held that the objection made was removed by the explanation given by the court.

5. Inducing agreement.

The court must not coerce the jury into agreement by intimidation or threats to subject them to any unreasonable inconvenience;[1] nor should it suggest as a reason for agreeing that failure to agree is "almost to confess incompetency."[2] And it is error, in lecturing the jury upon the necessity of agreeing upon a verdict, to use language reflecting upon the intelligence of some of the jurors.[3] But when satisfied that there is no reasonable prospect of an agreement, the court may discharge them.[4]

[1] See authorities in Abbott's Civil Trial Brief, 2d ed. 489.

For some illustrative cases recognizing the impropriety of the judge's coercing the jury into agreement, but holding that the facts of the case at bar did not come within the rule, see *Dow* v. *State,* 31 Tex. Crim. Rep. 278, 20 S. W. 583 (where the court, upon the jury's returning to the courtroom and reporting that they could not agree, directed them to return to the jury room, and urged them to reconcile their differences and agree upon a verdict); *Odette* v. *State,* 90 Wis. 258, 62 N. W. 1054 (to the effect that a statement, on urging the jury to be reasonable, and not obstinate, that they may return to their room and continue to deliberate until they arrive at a verdict, cannot be fairly regarded as a threat that they cannot be discharged until they agree); *State* v. *Olds,* 106 Iowa, 110, 76 N. W. 644 (where the court stated to the jury after they had been out for some time, and had reported that they could not agree, that it was very important that a verdict should be arrived at, and that they should retire again and make an earnest effort to reach a verdict, and that in the meantime the court would consider the matter, and see if there were any additional instructions he could give them); *Johnson* v. *State,* 60 Ark. 45, 28 S. W. 792 (where the court, upon the jury's stating that they had not agreed, after considering the case for ninety-four hours, told them that the case had been a great expense to the county, and ought to be decided, and, while the court did not ask them to yield any question of conscience, they must not be obstinate or too tenacious of their views); *Territory* v. *McGinnis* (N. M.) 61 Pac. 208 (to the effect that a remark by the court, at the close of its charge on Saturday, that if they should not find a verdict by 8 o'clock Sunday morning they would have to remain in the jury room until Monday morning, was insufficient to show coercion of the jury prejudicial to defendant, where all the evidence in the case was heard on Friday, and the arguments of counsel and charge of the court on Saturday, and the jury returned their verdict on Saturday night); *Territory* v. *King,* 6 Dak. 131, 30 N. W. 623 (where the court said to the jury, when before it for further instructions, after having been out twenty-eight hours:

"I think you will be able to arrive at a verdict in this case; the case has been twice tried, at a great deal of expense to this county, and it seems to me, gentlemen, that you ought to agree on a verdict").

In Florida a statute (Rev. Stat. § 1093) provides that a jury which returns into court a second time without having agreed on a verdict shall not be sent out again without their own consent, unless they ask further explanation of the law. And this statute applies to criminal as well as civil cases. *Adams* v. *State,* 34 Fla. 185, 15 So. 905. They should not be sent out a third time without their consent, unless they ask further explanation of the law. *Tuberson* v. *State,* 26 Fla. 472, 7 So. 858. And see *Lambright* v. *State,* 34 Fla. 564, 16 So. 582, where the jury, after retiring, returned a second time, and stated that they did not believe that they could agree on a verdict, but requested certain portions of the charge to be redelivered; and it was held that they were properly sent back after recharging.

A verdict will not be reversed on the ground that the jury were kept together too long after they reported their failure to agree, where they were kept together less than thirty hours, and the record shows nothing which indicates that they were coerced into rendering a verdict not in accordance with their convictions. *Gilbert* v. *Com.* 21 Ky. L. Rep. 415, 51 S. W. 590.

[2]*People* v. *Sheldon,* 156 N. Y. 268, 41 L. R. A. 644, 50 N. E. 840.

[3]*State* v. *Tulip,* 9 Kan. App. 454, 60 Pac. 659.

In *People* v. *Kindleberger,* 100 Cal. 367, 34 Pac. 852, a remark to the jury on a criminal trial, upon returning to court after being out thirteen hours without agreeing, that the court was utterly at a loss to know why twelve honest men could not agree upon a verdict, was held to be reversible error; and that the error was not cured by a subsequent statement that the jury were sole judges of all questions of fact and of the credibility of witnesses, and that the court had no right to trench upon their province in this respect.

[4]*People* v. *Green,* 13 Wend. 55; *Queen* v. *Charlesworth,* 1 Best & S. 523.

But saying to the jury that if they do not agree before adjournment, they will have to remain in their room over night, is not a threat of imprisonment or punishment, within this rule. *Berry* v. *People,* 19 Alb. L. J. 336, 77 N. Y. 588.

XLV.—DISCHARGE ON DISAGREEMENT.

1. Power of the court. 2. Authorizing officer to discharge.

1. Power of the court.

The court has discretionary power to discharge the jury from giving a verdict, in case of disagreement, whenever in its opinion there is a manifest necessity for such an act, or the ends of public justice will otherwise be defeated.[1]

[1]*United States* v. *Perez*, 9 Wheat. 579, 6 L. ed. 165; *State* v. *Gamble*, 2 Penn. (Del.) 368, 45 Atl. 716; *Lovett* v. *State*, 80 Ga. 255, 4 S. E. 912; *State* v. *Crump* (Idaho) 47 Pac. 814 (Idaho Rev. Stat. § 7905); *State* v. *Rudy*, 9 Kan. App. 69, 57 Pac. 263 (Kan. Gen. Stat. 1897, chap. 95, § 291); *State* v. *Billings*, 140 Mo. 193, 41 S. W. 778; *Com.* v. *Townsend*, 5 Allen, 216 (saying it may be done whenever they have deliberated so long without coming to any agreement as to satisfy the court that further attempts to agree will be unavailing). The reason of the rule is that a discharge without reasonable necessity is equivalent to acquittal, by enabling the accused to plead former jeopardy if brought to trial again. See *ante*, Divison XVIII., § 16.

According to 5 Crim. L. Mag. 771, 772, there must be unavoidable necessity.

According to *Lovett* v. *State*, 80 Ga. 255, 4 S. E. 912, it is enough that the judge is satisfied that they cannot agree. Discharge after only an hour and a half's deliberation sanctioned.

State v. *Fuselier*, 51 La. Ann. 1317, 26 So. 264, however, holds that the necessity *vel non* of discharging a jury in a criminal case rests in the discretion of the trial court.

The provisions of the Florida statute (Rev. Stat. §§ 1093, 2925) that if the jury, after due deliberation, return into court a second time without having agreed upon a verdict, they shall not be sent out again without their own consent, unless they ask from the court some further explanation of the law, are not intended to furnish an exclusive rule by which the discharge of the jury for disagreement may be effected, and in no way affect the discretion vested in the court to order such discharge upon proper occasion. *Smith* v. *State*, 40 Fla. 203, 23 So. 854.

So, under the South Carolina statute (Rev. Stat. § 2409) providing that where a jury, after due and thorough deliberation, return into court without having agreed on a verdict, the court may state anew the evidence, and send them out for further deliberation, but if they return a second time without having agreed on a verdict they shall not be sent out again without their own consent, unless they ask some further explanation of the law, the discharge of a jury on returning to the courtroom for the third time, after deliberating for about sixteen hours, with the announcement that they had not agreed, and without asking for further instructions, was held not an abuse of discretion, in *State* v. *Stephenson*, 54 S. C. 234, 32 S. E. 305, Citing *Com.* v. *Purchase*, 2 Pick. 521, 13 Am. Dec. 452.

But it is reversible error for the court to discharge the jury in a criminal case, and direct a verdict of guilty to be entered, as such procedure is not a trial by the jury, where the latter does not acquiesce in the direction of the court. *People* v. *Collinson*, 85 Mich. 105, 48 N. W. 292.

In *Thomas* v. *State*, 124 Ala. 48, 27 So. 315, the jury returned to the courtroom, and stated that they were unable to agree, whereupon the court stated that he would discharge them, but that he could not do so unless defendant would consent, and that defendant had so far refused such consent. He then asked defendant's attorney, in the presence of the jury, if he refused to consent to the discharge. This was held error.

2. Authorizing officer to discharge.

The court may direct the officer to discharge the jury if they do not agree by a specified time, or to ask them then if they are likely to agree, and to discharge them if they answer that they are not.[1]

[1] *Com.* v. *Townsend,* 5 Allen, 216.

XLVI.—VERDICT.

I. HOW RECEIVED.

1. Time; Sunday.

The court may be opened on Sunday to receive a verdict in a cause submitted to the jury on a previous day, and then may be adjourned over.[1]

[1] *State* v. *Ricketts,* 74 N. C. 187; *Com.* v. *Marrow,* 3 Brewst. (Pa.) 402; *Walker* v. *State,* 13 Tex. App. 618 (statutory); *Territory* v. *Nichols,* 3

N. M. 103, 2 Pac. 78; *Meece* v. *Com.* 78 Ky. 586; N. Y. Code Civ. Proc. § 6; *State* v. *Canty,* 41 La. Ann. 587, 6 So. 338; *Huffman* v. *State,* 28 Tex. App. 174, 12 S. W. 588; *State* v. *Crisp,* 126 Mo. 605, 29 S. W. 699 (Mo. Rev. Stat. 1889, § 3260); *Milligan* v. *Territory,* 2 Okla. 164, 37 Pac. 1059 (Okla. Code Crim. Proc. chap. 68, art. 11, § 8). And see *State* v. *Straub,* 16 Wash. 111, 47 Pac. 227, where it is held that the reception of a verdict in a criminal action on a nonjudicial day is not prohibited by Wash. Const. art. 4, § 6, providing that the courts shall always be open "except on nonjudicial days."

2. Presence of the accused.

In felony the accused must be present when the verdict is rendered,[1] and his counsel cannot waive the right.[2]

In misdemeanor the accused need not be present.[3]

[1] *People* v. *Beauchamp,* 49 Cal. 41; *Price* v. *State,* 36 Miss. 531, 72 Am. Dec. 195; N. Y. Code Crim. Proc. § 434; *People* v. *Perkins,* 1 Wend. 91; *Rose* v. *State,* 20 Ohio, 31; *Finch* v. *State,* 53 Miss. 363; *State* v. *Jenkins,* 84 N. C. 812, 37 Am. Rep. 643; *Temple* v. *Com.* 14 Bush, 769, 29 Am. Rep. 442; *Cook* v. *State,* 60 Ala. 39, 31 Am. Rep. 31.

State v. *Kelly,* 97 N. C. 410, 2 S. E. 185, holds, however, that his flight is a waiver of the right. See also *United States* v. *Loughery,* 13 Blatchf. 267, Fed. Cas. No. 15,631; *State* v. *Perkins,* 40 La. Ann. 210, 3 So. 647; *Falk* v. *United States,* 15 App. D. C. 446; *Tight* v. *State,* 7 Ohio, pt. 1, p. 180, 28 Am. Dec. 626; *Hill* v. *State,* 17 Wis. 675, 86 Am. Dec. 736; *Barton* v. *State,* 67 Ga. 653, 44 Am. Rep. 743; *Lynch* v. *Com.* 88 Pa. 189, 32 Am. Rep. 445; *Com.* v. *McCarthy,* 163 Mass. 458, 40 N. E. 766. *Contra,* holding it error to proceed though accused had fled, *State* v. *Buckner,* 25 Mo. 167; *State ex rel. Battle,* 7 Ala. 259; *Summeralls* v. *State,* 37 Fla. 162, 20 So. 242. See also where he was out on bail, *Sneed* v. *State,* 5 Ark. 431, 41 Am. Dec. 102; *State* v. *Spores,* 4 Or. 198; *Clark* v. *State,* 4 Humph. 254.

Error, if any, in returning a verdict, in the absence of defendant in a criminal action, was held to be cured by having defendant brought into court and the verdict again announced and recorded, in *State* v. *Hutchinson,* 95 Iowa, 566, 64 N. W. 610.

In *State* v. *Hope,* 100 Mo. 347, 8 L. R. A. 608, 13 S. W. 490, a statute permitting a verdict when defendant is voluntarily or wilfully absent was held not to violate his constitutional right to be present at the trial.

Correction of the record at the same term at which a verdict was rendered, by naming the degree of murder, is not such a substantive step in the trial as requires the presence of the accused. *McNamara* v. *State,* 60 Ark. 400, 30 S. W. 762.

[2] *State* v. *Jenkins,* 84 N. C. 812, 37 Am. Rep. 643; *Waller* v. *State,* 40 Ala. 325; *Prine* v. *Com.* 18 Pa. 103.

[3] *Sawyer* v. *Joiner,* 16 Vt. 497; *State* v. *Shepard,* 10 Iowa, 126; *Warren* v. *State,* 19 Ark. 214, 68 Am. Dec. 214; N. Y. Code Crim. Proc. § 434.

3. — of his counsel.

If the counsel for the accused has notice and an opportunity to be present,[1] it is not error to receive the verdict in the counsel's absence, if the accused is present, and suffers no prejudice.[2]

[1]*Smith* v. *State,* 51 Wis. 615, 37 Am. Rep. 845, 8 N. W. 410, holding notice necessary under a constitutional right "to be heard by himself and counsel" at the trial. See also *Temple* v. *Com.* 14 Bush, 769, 29 Am. Rep. 442. Compare *Barnard* v. *State,* 88 Wis. 656, 60 N. W. 1058, holding that the attorney of defendant on a criminal trial need not be notified so that he can be present at the reception of the verdict when received in regular session. And see cases in next note.

Where a public announcement was made by the judge in open court, in the hearing of the accused and his counsel, that if the jury should agree upon a verdict during the recess then about to be taken, the courthouse bell would be rung, whereupon court would convene and receive the verdict, and the court did so convene, inquired for prisoner's counsel, and waited for them over twenty minutes, it was not error to receive the verdict in the absence of the prisoner's counsel, the prisoner himself being present. *Crusen* v. *State,* 10 Ohio St. 258. To similar effect, *Davis* v. *State,* 14 Ind. 358.

So, where the judge, in the presence of accused and counsel, notified the jury that he would receive their verdict if they found it the next day, which was Thanksgiving, accused was without cause to complain, though his counsel was not present when the verdict was rendered. *State* v. *Atkinson,* 104 La. 570, 29 So. 279.

In *Weaver* v. *State,* 24 Ohio St. 584, the case was given to the jury about 10 o'clock at night; the court notified counsel that the verdict would be received promptly upon the agreement of the jury, and that when the jury agreed the courthouse bell would be rung as notice. The jury agreed about half past six o'clock the next morning, and the bell was then rung; after an interval of twenty minutes the bell was rung a second time, and after another interval of ten minutes the jury were brought into court, and the prisoner's counsel not appearing, the sheriff by direction of the court called them at the courthouse door, and they still not appearing, the verdict was received in their absence, but in the presence of the prisoner. It was held that all that could be required of the judge was to afford counsel a reasonable opportunity to be present, and that in that case that was certainly done.

Baker v. *State,* 58 Ark. 513, 25 S. W. 603, holds that the fact that the verdict in a felony case was returned in the absence of counsel for the accused does not constitute ground for reversal, where it sufficiently appears that the accused could not have been prejudiced because of such absence.

[2]*Beaumont* v. *State,* 1 Tex. App. 533, 28 Am. Rep. 424; *O'Bannon* v. *State,* 76 Ga. 29; *Richardson* v. *State,* 7 Tex. App. 486; *State* v. *Lee Ping Bow,* 10 Or. 27; *State* v. *Jones,* 91 N. C. 654; *People* v. *Bennett,* 65 Cal. 267, 3 Pac. 868; *Martin* v. *State,* 79 Wis. 165, 48 N. W. 119; *Huffman* v.

State, 28 Tex. App. 174, 12 S. W. 588; *Sutcliffe* v. *State*, 18 Ohio, 469, 51 Am. Dec. 459. These cases do not hold notice to the counsel necessary.

The reception of the verdict in the absence of defendant's counsel is not error requiring a reversal, where there is nothing indicating that the defendant is prejudiced thereby. *People* v. *Willson*, 109 N. Y. 345, 16 N. E. 540. In this case it appeared that there was a misunderstanding between counsel and the judge, the former understanding that he was to be sent for when the jury came in, and the latter understanding that the counsel desired to be sent for only in case the jury came in for further instructions. The defendant's counsel was not therefore sent for. But when the jury rendered their verdict the judge caused them to be polled, and the court said it could not perceive how the absence of counsel in any way prejudiced the defendant's rights.

4. — of court or a judge.

The verdict can only be received in open court.[1] The judge[2] or several judges[3] holding the court must be present.

[1]*Nomaque* v. *People*, 1 Ill. 109, 12 Am. Dec. 157; *State* v. *Bray*, 67 N. C. 283; *Longfellow* v. *State*, 10 Neb. 105, 10 N. W. 420; *Hayes* v. *State*, 107 Ala. 1, 18 So. 172.

And according to *Jackson* v. *State*, 102 Ala. 76, 15 So. 351, a verdict in a criminal case, received by the judge at his hotel, in the presence of the defendant, upon which the jury are discharged, is illegal under Ala. Code, § 749, requiring the courts to be held at the courthouses.

[2]*McClure* v. *State*, 77 Ind. 287, holding that he cannot delegate the power. And *Quinn* v. *State*, 130 Ind. 340, 30 N. E. 300, holds that it is error to direct an attorney to receive a verdict in a criminal trial, unless he has been appointed a special judge. Compare *State* v. *Austin*, 108 N. C. 780, 13 S. E. 219, where it is held competent, except in capital cases, for the verdict to be received by the clerk in the absence of the trial judge from the courtroom, if no objection is made, and opportunity is given defendant to object.

And a defendant in a prosecution for a felony was entitled to be discharged where a writing delivered to the clerk during a recess of the court by the jury, who then dispersed, was received as a verdict by the court, and the jury, which had been reassembled, discharged. *Hayes* v. *State*, 107 Ala. 1, 18 So. 172.

But a conviction of murder will not be reversed because the verdict was received by a special judge during the temporary absence of the regular judge who presided at the trial, where there is no claim that any question affecting defendant's rights was decided by him, and defendant and his counsel announced that they were ready to have the verdict read, and at their request the jury was polled. *Rainey* v. *Com.* 19 Ky. L. Rep. 390, 40 S. W. 682.

According to *State* v. *Finder*, 10 S. D. 103, 72 N. W. 97, the regular circuit judge may receive the verdict in a criminal case, where another judge has been called in upon an affidavit of prejudice, and the latter judge is absent when the verdict is rendered.

A special verdict, although not completely responsive, is properly received and entered by the local resident judge, where the judge who presided at the trial by interchange was called away before it was returned. *State* v. *Allen*, 69 Miss. 508, 10 So. 473.

[3]*Hinman* v. *People*, 13 Hun, 266, holding the absence of an associate or side judge fatal.

5. Verdict on plea of former acquittal, etc.

Upon a plea of former acquittal or conviction the verdict should be "for the People," or "for the defendant."[1]

[1]*People* v. *Burch*, 1 N. Y. S. R. 751; N. Y. Code Crim. Proc. § 437.

6. Calling the jury.

Upon the return of the jury into court the accused has the right to have the names of the jurors called before their verdict is received,[1] and the verdict cannot be received unless they are all present.[2]

[1]Common Practice, N. Y. Code Crim. Proc. § 433.

And *Givens* v. *State*, 76 Md. 485, 25 Atl. 689, holds that failure of the clerk to call the jury in a criminal case to hearken to their verdict as the court has recorded it, and require their assent to it, is reversible error.

In *Milligan* v. *Territory*, 2 Okla. 164, 37 Pac. 1059, it is held that the reception of the written verdict of a jury by the trial court, reading of it to them by the clerk, and inquiry by the judge if that is their verdict, to which an affirmative answer is given, and a poll of the jury by the judge, to which each juror answers that the verdict so read is his verdict,—is a substantial compliance with Okla. Laws, § 5254, providing that the clerk must immediately record the verdict in full, read it to the jury, and inquire of them whether it is their verdict, and, if no disagreement is expressed, the verdict is complete.

[2]*State* v. *Meyers*, 68 Mo. 266 (embezzlement); *Com.* v. *Gibson*, 2 Va. Cas. 70 (murder).

II. Form and substance.

7. Oral.

In the absence of statute to the contrary,[1] the jury must declare their verdict, if general, orally.[2]

[1]In Texas a statute (Tex. Code Crim. Proc. art. 705) provides that the verdict must be in writing, but does not expressly require that it shall be

written with pen and ink; and it is not a valid objection to a verdict otherwise good that it was written with a lead pencil. *Ellis* v. *State*, 30 Tex. App. 601, 18 S. W. 139.

[2] *Com.* v. *Tobin*, 125 Mass. 203, 28 Am. Rep. 220 (holding it error to receive a written verdict, because utterance is a safeguard against mistake); *United States* v. *Vigol*, 2 Dall. 346, note, 1 L. ed. 409, Fed. Cas. No. 16,-621; *Lord* v. *State*, 16 N. H. 325, 41 Am. Dec. 729 (holding it proper to reject a written verdict); N. Y. Code Crim. Proc. § 435.

Contra, *State* v. *Glass*, 50 Wis. 218, 36 Am. Rep. 845, 6 N. W. 500, holding a written general verdict not irregular; and, moreover, objection to it waived by polling the jury by consent.

Compare *State* v. *Webber*, 90 Me. 108, 37 Atl. 877, holding that the jury is not required to give oral verdict in a criminal case not punishable by imprisonment for life, where they have rendered a sealed verdict,—Citing *Com.* v. *Tobin*, 125 Mass. 203, 28 Am. Rep. 220. This case also holds that an indorsement on indictment on a trial for maintaining a liquor nuisance, of "guilty as charged in the indictment," inclosed in a sealed wrapper, followed by an oral verdict of guilty in open court, is sufficient, —Citing *Com.* v. *Carrington*, 116 Mass. 37.

State v. *Reed*, 49 La. Ann. 704, 21 So. 732, holds that while a written verdict is unnecessary in a criminal case, where such a one is returned, and, on the jury being polled, each juror answers that the verdict as read is his verdict, it is substantially an oral verdict.

8. Orthography, etc.

Neither incorrect orthography nor ungrammatical language will vitiate a verdict, where the sense is clear. It should be reasonably construed, and in such manner as to give to it the meaning intended by the jury.[1]

[1] *Birdwell* v. *State* (Tex. Crim. App.) 20 S. W. 556; *Harris* v. *State* (Tex. Crim. App.) 34 S. W. 922; *McGee* v. *State*, 39 Tex. Crim. Rep. 190, 45 S. W. 709.

So held of a verdict spelling the word "guilty" "guity." *Whitley* v. *State* (Tex. Crim. App.) 56 S. W. 69; *Pace* v. *State* (Tex. Crim. App.) 20 S. W. 762. See also *Price* v. *State*, 36 Tex. Crim. Rep. 403, 37 S. W. 743, where the letters intended for "l" and "t" had a loop at the top, and the cross was over the former only.

So also in *Hamilton* v. *State* (Tex. Crim. App.) 34 S. W. 280, of a verdict containig the expression "apess" instead of "assess," with regard to the punishment.

And in *Augustine* v. *State* (Tex. Crim. App.) 52 S. W. 77, of a verdict where the word "penitentiary" was spelled "peintentiary."

And in *State* v. *McNamara*, 100 Mo. 100, 13 S. W. 938, of a verdict spelling it "pertentiary."

And a verdict of "guilty of murder in the second decree," instead of "degree," is not void, as being for an offense unknown to the statutes, since, the meaning being apparent, the mistake is immaterial. *Wilson* v. *Territory* (Ariz.) 60 Pac. 697.

9. General verdict.

A general verdict of "guilty" is sufficient without the addition of other words.[1] And if the offense admits of degrees, such a verdict is a conviction of the highest degree which the indictment warrants.[2]

[1]*Blount* v. *State,* 49 Ala. 381; *Rollings* v. *State,* 62 Ind. 46; *Preuit* v. *People,* 5 Neb. 377; N. Y. Code Crim. Proc. § 437; *Evans* v. *State,* 58 Ark. 47, 22 S. W. 1026; *Barton* v. *Com.* 17 Ky. L. Rep. 580, 32 S. W. 171, 396 (holding that a verdict is not defective because it merely finds the defendant guilty, without adding the words "as charged in the indictment," under Ky. Crim. Code Prac. § 257, requiring the jury simply to find the accused guilty or not guilty, and to fix the degree, in case there are different degrees of the offense charged); *State* v. *Maloney,* 7 N. D. 119, 72 N. W. 927 (holding that a verdict that the jury find defendant guilty of an assault and battery with a sharp and dangerous weapon, with intent to do bodily harm, is sufficient, without the addition of the words "without justifiable cause or excuse," under N. D. Rev. Codes, § 7145, defining an aggravated assault and battery,—Distinguishing *State* v. *Johnson,* 3 N. D. 150, 54 N. W. 547; *Ackerman* v. *State,* 7 Wyo. 504, 54 Pac. 228, and citing *People* v. *McCarty,* 48 Cal. 557; *Armstrong* v. *People,* 37 Ill. 459; *Blount* v. *State,* 49 Ala. 381, *supra*).

So, a verdict on a trial for murder, of "guilty of the felony of murder in the first degree," is substantially proper, and the addition afterwards, by order of the court, of the words "in manner and form as charged in the bill of indictment," is a mere formality, which does not prejudice the prisoner. *State* v. *Kinsauls,* 126 N. C. 1095, 36 S. E. 31.

And a verdict finding the defendant guilty under the first and third counts of an indictment containing three counts, followed by the words, "We disagree as to the second count," is valid, since such additional words do not qualify the previous meaning, and may be regarded as surplusage. *State* v. *McGee,* 55 S. C. 247, 33 S. E. 353.

[2]*Kennedy* v. *People,* 39 N. Y. 245; *Fitzgerrold* v. *People,* 37 N. Y. 413; *Welch* v. *State,* 50 Ga. 128, 15 Am. Rep. 690; *Yarborough* v. *State,* 86 Ga. 396, 12 S. E. 650; *St. Clair* v. *United States,* 154 U. S. 134, 38 L. ed. 936, 14 Sup. Ct. Rep. 1002; *People* v. *Perez,* 87 Cal. 122, 25 Pac. 262; *Siple* v. *State,* 154 Ind. 647, 57 N. E. 544; *Timmerman* v. *Territory,* 3 Wash. Terr. 445, 17 Pac. 624; *Cook* v. *Territory,* 3 Wyo. 110, 4 Pac. 887. *Contra, Hogan* v. *State,* 30 Wis. 428, 11 Am. Rep. 575, disapproving this rule.

10. Special verdict.

A special verdict is that by which the jury find the facts only, leaving the judgment to the court. It must present the conclusions of fact, as established by the evidence, and not the evidence to prove them; and these conclusions of fact must be so presented that nothing remains to the court but to draw from them conclusions of law.[1] It need not be in any particular form, but is sufficient if it present the facts found by the jury.[2]

[1]This is the language of N. Y. Code Crim. Proc. § 438.

And *State* v. *Savage*, 36 Or. 191, 60 Pac. 610, 61 Pac. 1128, holds a verdict that a jury finds Otis Savage guilty of larceny only, and assessed the value of the coin stolen at $14,000, to be a valid special verdict, under Hill's (Or.) Anno. Laws, § 1379, defining a special verdict.

In *Com.* v. *Zacharias*, 181 Pa. 126, 37 Atl. 185, Affirming 5 Pa. Dist. R. 475, a special verdict which found that defendant was the part owner of drug-stores, and received part of the profits made by them, employed registered pharmacists to sell drugs and put up prescriptions, was not a registered pharmacist himself, and personally sold no drugs and compounded no prescriptions,—was held to be insufficient to justify a conviction under Pa. act June 16, 1891, forbidding any person to "open or carry on as manager" any "retail" drug or chemical store, or to be engaged in the business of compounding or dispensing medicines, without having obtained a certificate from the state pharmaceutical examining board and having been duly registered.

In *State* v. *Finlayson*, 113 N. C. 628, 18 S. E. 200, a special verdict in a prosecution for refusing and neglecting to pay a license tax required by a city ordinance was held to be fatally defective in failing clearly to state the trade or occupation carried on by the defendant, and to set forth the specific provisions of the ordinance alleged to have been violated.

And in *State* v. *Yount*, 110 N. C. 597, 15 S. E. 231, a special verdict is held to be fatally defective on an indictment for selling meat without a license, if it fail to find as a fact that the defendant had or had not paid the tax and obtained license.

So, a special verdict that does not find that the defendant practised "for fee or reward" does not justify an adjudication that the defendant is guilty under an indictment based on N. C. Acts 1885, chap. 117, § 2, making it an indictable offense to practise medicine under the conditions therein named, without an examination and license. *State* v. *Call*, 121 N. C. 643, 28 S. E. 517.

The rule requiring a special verdict to state all the circumstances constituting the offense does not apply to either a general verdict or a special verdict, as, for instance, a verdict for an offense of an inferior degree included in the accusation of a higher crime. *Rookey* v. *State*, 70 Conn. 104, 38 Atl. 911.

[2]N. Y. Code Crim. Proc. § 440.

In *State* v. *Hay*, 126 N. C. 999, 49 L. R. A. 588, 35 S. E. 459, a special verdict, in a prosecution for the violation of an ordinance for compulsory vaccination, that defendant had been examined by S., a reputable physician, who told him that he did not need vaccination, and that P., another physician, told him that he had rheumatism, and could not submit to vaccination,—was held too ambiguous and defective to determine whether the jury found either that defendant did not need vaccination, or that his condition of health made it dangerous for him to submit thereto.

11. Less offense; or attempt.

The jury may find defendant guilty of any offense the commission of which is necessarily included in that with which he is charged in the indictment, or of an attempt to commit such an offense.[1]

[1]*United States* v. *Leonard,* 2 Fed. 669; *People* v. *Jackson,* 3 Hill, 92; *Re Alcorn* (Idaho) 60 Pac. 561; *Dedieu* v. *People,* 22 N. Y. 178 (holding under an indictment charging the first degree of arson that the prisoner might be convicted in the third degree). See also *People* v. *Taylor,* 3 N. Y. Crim. Rep. 297, Affirmed on opinion below, it seems, but no opinion reported, in 101 N. Y. 608; *State* v. *Throckmorton,* 53 Ind. 354, 16 Am. L. Reg. N. S. 234.

U. S. Rev. Stat. § 1035, provides that "in all criminal causes the defendant may be found guilty of any offense the commission of which is necessarily included in that with which he is charged in the indictment, or may be found guilty of an attempt to commit the offense so charged; provided that such attempt be itself a separate offense."

N. Y. Code Crim. Proc. § 444, provides that "upon an indictment for a crime consisting of different degrees, the jury may find the defendant not guilty of the degree charged in the indictment, and guilty of any degree inferior thereto, or of an attempt to commit the crime."

§ 445. "In all other cases the defendant may be found guilty of any crime the commission of which is necessarily included in that with which he is charged in the indictment."

In Texas a statute (Code Crim. Proc. art. 751) provides that, in prosecution of crimes of different degrees, defendant may be found not guilty of the higher, but guilty of the lower, degree; but in a prosecution for aggravated assault, with the issue of simple assault submitted, a general verdict of guilty, with a fine assessed at the minimum for aggravated, and the maximum for simple, assault, is uncertain, and cannot stand. *Lee* v. *State* (Tex. Crim. App.) 55 S. W. 814. Nor does art. 751 apply except in case a lesser degree is affirmatively charged; and a verdict in a trial for rape which finds the defendant guilty as charged in the indictment, and assesses his punishment at fifty years' imprisonment, where the court charged both upon rape and an assault with intent to rape, sufficiently indicates the crime of which the defendant is convicted, although the punishment might have been inflicted in either case, when rape only is charged in the indictment. *McGee* v. *State,* 39 Tex. Crim. Rep. 190, 45 S. W. 709, Overruling *Guest* v. *State,* 24 Tex. App. 530, 7 S. W. 242.

12. Stating degree.

Where a statute[1] requires that a verdict of guilty must specify the degree, a verdict which does not do so is a nullity,[2] unless the indictment charges only one degree, in which case, notwithstanding the statute, a general verdict of guilty is a conviction of the degree charged.[3]

[1] Such as N. Y. Pen. Code, § 10. And see other statutes referred to in cases cited in succeeding note.

[2] *Buster* v. *State*, 42 Tex. 315; *People* v. *Coch*, 53 Cal. 627; *State* v. *Rover*, 10 Nev. 388, 21 Am. Rep. 745; *Fuller* v. *State*, 110 Ala. 655, 20 So. 1020; *Hembree* v. *State* (Ark.) 58 S. W. 350 (Sandels & H. Dig. § 2255); *Porter* v. *State*, 57 Ark. 267, 21 S. W. 467 (holding, however, that the Arkansas statute applies only to a trial of an indictment for murder in the first degree, and not to one charging murder in the second degree); *People* v. *Lee Yune Chong*, 94 Cal. 379, 29 Pac. 776 (Cal. Pen. Code, § 1157; holding also that such defect does not entitle the prisoner to discharge, but only to a new trial); *Nelson* v. *State*, 32 Fla. 244, 13 So. 361 (Fla. Rev. Stat. § 2383); *State* v. *Pettys*, 61 Kan. 860, 60 Pac. 735 (Kan. Crim. Act, § 38); *State* v. *Jackson*, 99 Mo. 60, 12 S. W. 367; *Harbolt* v. *State* (Tex. Crim. App.) 40 S. W. 983 (Tex. Pen. Code 1895, art. 712); *Allen* v. *State*, 85 Wis. 22, 54 N. W. 999. And *Brooks* v. *State* (Tex. Crim. App.) 60 S. W. 53, holds that under the Texas statute a verdict finding defendant guilty of poisoning, as charged in the indictment, is not sufficient, though the statute makes murder by poisoning murder of the first degree.

According to *State* v. *Staley*, 45 W. Va. 792, 32 S. E. 198, a verdict finding defendant not guilty of murder in the first or second degree, as charged in an indictment, and finding him guilty of voluntary manslaughter, is sufficient in form.

[3] *People* v. *Rugg*, 98 N. Y. 537; *State* v. *Adams*, 20 Kan. 311; *State* v. *Steptoe*, 1 Mo. App. 19; *People* v. *Manners*, 70 Cal. 428, 11 Pac. 643.

A verdict on a trial for aggravated assault, that the jury find defendant guilty as charged in the indictment, is not bad for failure sufficiently to specify the grade of assault, where the offense of aggravated assault was alone submitted by the charge, and the issue of simple assault was not before the jury. *Styles* v. *State*, 37 Tex. Crim. Rep. 599, 40 S. W. 498.

It is not essential, to a conviction of assault with intent to murder, that the verdict should specify the degree of murder that it finds the defendant guilty of having intended to commit, as under Fla. Rev. Stat. § 2403, there is no distinction, as to such assaults, between those committed with an intent to commit murder in the first and those with intent to commit murder in the second degree, and the offense cannot be predicated of an assault with an intent to commit murder in the third degree. *Davis* v. *State*, 35 Fla. 614, 17 So. 565.

13. Grounds or recommendation to mercy.

A statement of the grounds of the verdict[1] or a recommendation to mercy[2] may be disregarded as surplusage.

[1]*Opinion of the Justices*, 120 Mass. 600.

[2]*Ibid.; Stephens* v. *State*, 51 Ga. 236; *People* v. *Long*, 44 Mich. 296, 6 N. W. 673; *State* v. *O'Brien*, 22 La. Ann. 27.

So, also, it seems, of a recommendation of the full penalty of the law. *State* v. *Hutchinson*, 7 Nev. 53.

14. Several defendants.

On a joint trial the verdict must enable the court to say with certainty how it is to affect the several defendants respectively.[1]

But it may find one or more guilty, and disregard the others.[2]

[1]*Favor* v. *State*, 54 Ga. 249.

While defendants jointly indicted may be jointly tried, the verdict and judgment must be several; and therefore a verdict finding "the defendants" (naming them) guilty of voluntary manslaughter, and fixing "their punishment at confinement in the penitentiary for a period of twenty-one years," followed by a joint judgment, cannot be sustained. *Arnold* v. *Com.* 21 Ky. L. Rep. 1566, 55 S. W. 894.

If the law leaves it to the jury to assess a fine, they must assess a separate one against each, not a lump sum against all. *Flynn* v. *State*, 8 Tex. App. 398; *Lawrence* v. *State* (Tex. Crim. App.) 30 S. W. 668; *State* v. *Nichols*, 12 Rich. L. 672. Compare *Mootry* v. *State*, 35 Tex. Crim. Rep. 450, 33 S. W. 877, 34 S. W. 126, where a verdict that the jury find the defendants (naming them) "guilty of murder in the first degree, as charged in the indictment, and assess their punishment at death," is held not to be defective on the ground that it fails to assess the punishment of each defendant, as it is clear therefrom that the assessment of the punishment is directed against both.

[2]*Bloomhuff* v. *State*, 8 Blackf. 205; U. S. Rev. Stat. § 1036; *Com.* v. *Wood*, 12 Mass. 313; *Fife* v. *Com.* 29 Pa. 429; N. Y. Code Crim. Proc. § 446.

15. Assessing punishment.

Where the law requires the jury to assess the punishment, the judge cannot supply their omission to do so;[1] but assessing the punishment is not enough without a finding of guilty.[2]

When the law does not require them to assess the punishment, the judge may disregard as surplusage so much of their verdict as attempts to do so.[3]

[1]*State* v. *Warne*, 27 Mo. 418.

And *O'Connor* v. *State*, 37 Tex. Crim. Rep. 267, 39 S. W. 368, holds that a verdict of guilty on a trial for having possession of a forged instrument with intent to pass the same, which does not fix the punishment, is absolutely void under Tex. Pen. Code 1895, art. 544, prescribing the punishment for such offense at not less than two or more than five years, and Tex. Code Crim. Proc. 1895, art. 750, requiring the verdict to assess the punishment in all cases where it is not absolutely fixed by law at some particular penalty.

But *Behler* v. *State*, 22 Ind. 345, holds that the right to have the jury assess the fine is waived if the accused does not object to the court's doing so.

So, in *Bealer* v. *State*, 150 Ind. 390, 50 N. E. 302, a trial for receiving stolen property, it is held that a verdict is not defective for failure to fix the punishment, since it will be presumed when the record is silent that the jury were properly instructed that the offense was one which might in their discretion be brought within the provisions of the indeterminate sentence law, and that the verdict was returned under its provisions.

And in *Skelton* v. *State*, 149 Ind. 641, 49 N. E. 901, a verdict stating that defendant is guilty of petit larceny, and that his age is twenty-two years, is held sufficient, although the amount of fine and punishment to be inflicted is not stated therein as required by Ind. Rev. Stat. 1894, § 1906, as Ind. Acts 1897, § 8, p. 69, provides that in all cases of felony, if the defendant is found to be between sixteen and thirty years of age, and is not guilty of treason or murder in the first or second degree, it shall only be stated in the verdict that defendant is guilty of the crime charged, naming it, and that his age is that found by the jury to be his true age.

That there is no impropriety in adding together the length of punishment each juror thinks the defendant should suffer, and dividing the sum by twelve, after determining upon defendant's guilt, for the sole purpose of ascertaining the average sense of the jury, where there is no agreement to be bound by the result, see *Ulrich* v. *State*, 30 Tex. App. 61, 16 S. W. 769; *McAnally* v. *State* (Tex. Crim. App.) 57 S. W. 832. Otherwise if there is an agreement to be so bound. *Williams* v. *State*, 66 Ark. 264, 50 S. W. 517, holding, however, that the error is cured by remitting so much of the punishment as exceeds the minimum punishment allowed by law.

[7]*Wynn* v. *State*, 1 Blackf. 28.

[8]*Harvey* v. *Com.* 23 Gratt. 941; *Wickham* v. *State*, 7 Coldw. 525.

As to finding amount involved, see *People* v. *Bork*, 96 N. Y. 188; *Thalheim* v. *State*, 38 Fla. 169, 20 So. 938 (holding that the jury on a trial for embezzlement of property alleged to exceed $100 in value should ascertain and fix the value of the property sufficiently to show whether it was $100 or more, under the Florida statute subjecting one who embezzles property of the value of $100 or more to a greater punishment than that of one who embezzles less than that amount); *Bartley* v. *State*, 53 Neb. 310, 73 N. W. 744, 55 Neb. 294, 75 N. W. 832 (holding the requirement of Neb. Code Crim. Proc. § 488, that a verdict of conviction for embezzlement shall declare the value of the property embezzled, to be substantially complied with by a declaration that the "amount" embezzled was a specified number of dollars,—Citing *Grant* v. *State*, 55 Ala. 201; *Duvall* v. *State*, 63 Ala. 12; *State* v. *Barr*, 61 N. J. L. 131, 38 Atl. 817; *Hildreth* v. *People*, 32 Ill. 36); *Holmes* v. *State*, 58 Neb. 297, 78 N. W. 641 (holding that a general verdict of guilty of the crime of larceny from the person, which omits a statement of the value of the property alleged to have been stolen, as required by Neb. Comp. Stat. 1897, p. 1434, is insufficient to support a sentence and judgment based thereupon), Citing *Armstrong* v. *State*, 21 Ohio St. 357; *Harris* v. *State*, 57 Ohio St. 92, 48 N. E. 284.

16. Sealed verdict.

Where a sealed verdict is allowed,[1] the jury[2] and the verdict,[3] still unsealed, must both be in court, in order that the verdict may be received; and it is the assent of the jury in open court to the verdict so produced which gives it legal effect.[4]

[1]In some states they are allowed in felonies less than capital by an order of the court. *Com.* v. *Carrington*, 116 Mass. 37; *Com.* v. *Costello*, 128 Mass. 88; *United States* v. *Bennett*, 16 Blatchf. 338, Fed. Cas. No. 14,-571 (misdemeanor).

Compare with *People* v. *Kelly*, 46 Cal. 355, holding upon a trial for rape, that a sealed verdict could not be allowed unless the defendant consented.

In other jurisdictions a sealed verdict is permitted even in capital cases. *State* v. *Engle*, 13 Ohio, 490; *Reins* v. *People*, 30 Ill. 256 (held proper on defendant's consent, and even without it, if it is not shown that the jury was improperly influenced during their separation).

[2]*Doyle* v. *United States*, 10 Fed. 269, 11 Biss. 100; *Wright* v. *State*, 11 Ind. 569.

[3]*Com.* v. *Dorus*, 108 Mass. 488. See also *Com.* v. *Durfee*, 100 Mass. 146.

[4]*Com.* v. *Tobin*, 125 Mass. 203, 28 Am. Rep. 220.

17. Amending.

If the verdict returned by the jury finds the accused guilty of a crime for which he cannot be convicted,[1] or it appears that the verdict is not in fact the verdict which the jury intended to return,[2] or that it is irresponsive,[3] or unintelligible,[4] or legally absurd,[5] the court may, before the verdict is recorded, direct the jury to amend it.

By the New York statute, if it appears to the court that the jury have mistaken the law, the judge may explain the reason for that opinion, and direct them to reconsider their verdict, but if, after doing so, they return the same verdict, it must be entered; and the court cannot require them to reconsider a verdict of acquittal.[6]

[1]*People* v. *Bush*, 3 Park. Crim. Rep. 552.

[2]*State* v. *Gilkie*, 35 La. Ann. 53.

The court may allow the jury to put in proper form a verdict which they have returned in improper form, or, at their request, have the solicitor general do so for them, they unanimously stating that the verdict as formulated by him is their real finding. *Brantley* v. *State*, 87 Ga. 149, 13 S. E. 257.

[3]*State* v. *Bishop*, 73 N. C. 44; *State* v. *Keasley*, 50 La. Ann. 761, 23 So. 900; *Grant* v. *State*, 33 Fla. 291, 14 So. 757, S. C., 23 L. R. A. 723, with note containing an exhaustive review of the authorities on this question generally.

[4]*Turbaville* v. *State*, 58 Ga. 545; *Cook* v. *State*, 26 Ga. 593; *State* v. *Steptoe*, 1 Mo. App. 19; *People* v. *Biles*, 2 Idaho, 103, 6 Pac. 120; *Com.* v. *Thompson*, 116 Mass. 346; *Com.* v. *Lang*, 10 Gray, 11.

[5]*People* v. *Ah Gow*, 53 Cal. 627 ("verdict that the accused is guilty of the indictment").

[6]N. Y. Code Crim. Proc. §§ 447, 448.

In *Burk* v. *Com.* 5 J. J. Marsh. 675, it was held, on an indictment for unlawful gaming, where the judge saw, from the reason stated in the verdict of acquittal, that the jury were under a mistake of fact, that he might recall a witness, and, after hearing him, the jury might amend their verdict.

18. — after separation.

After the verdict has been recorded, and the jury, after being discharged, have separated, they cannot be recalled to amend their verdict.[1]

But the mere announcement of their discharge does not, before they have dispersed and mingled with the bystanders, preclude recalling them.[2]

[1]*Sargent* v. *State*, 11 Ohio, 472; *Mills* v. *Com.* 7 Leigh, 751; *People* v. *Lee Yune Chong*, 94 Cal. 379, 29 Pac. 776; *State* v. *Dawkins*, 32 S. C. 17, 10 S. E. 772; *Allen* v. *State*, 85 Wis. 22, 54 N. W. 999. And see civil authorities in Abbott's Civil Trial Brief, 2d ed. Division VIII.

And that it is reversible error to send out for further deliberation upon their verdict a jury in a criminal case who have rendered an incomplete sealed verdict during the night, and have been allowed to separate, see *Farley* v. *People*, 138 Ill. 97, 27 N. E. 927.

[2]*Levells* v. *State*, 32 Ark. 585; *State* v. *Whittier*, 21 Me. 341, 38 Am. Dec. 272 (holding that after the jurors have separated on rendering a general verdict, it is irregular to make new inquiries of the jurors concerning the verdict. Where there is material error in the verdict, a new trial should be granted, but where, however, such inquiries have not injured the accused, the verdict should not be set aside).

In *Com.* v. *Breyessee*, 160 Pa. 451, 28 Atl. 824, it was held that a verdict of conviction was not invalidated by the fact that after the jury were discharged a form for a verdict in pencil was discovered on the back of the indictment, in which the defendant's name was different from that in the recorded verdict, whereupon the jurors were recalled, and, upon being interrogated, stated that the verdict as recorded was the one actually rendered by them.

III. Polling the Jury.

19. The right.

Either party has a right[1] to have the jury polled, on the rendering of their verdict, whether oral[2] or sealed,[3] at any time before it is recorded.

And the judge in his discretion may, of his own motion, direct that the jury be polled.[4]

[1]In some jurisdictions it is not matter of right, but discretionary with the court. *Com.* v. *Costley,* 118 Mass. 1; *State* v. *Whitman,* 14 Rich. (L.) 113; *State* v. *Hoyt,* 47 Conn. 518, 36 Am. Rep. 89; *Fellows's Case,* 5 Me. 333.

[2]*State* v. *Young,* 77 N. C. 498; *Williams* v. *State,* 63 Ga. 306; *Williams* v. *State,* 60 Md. 402; N. Y. Code Crim. Proc. § 450; *Blankinship* v. *State,* 112 Ga. 402, 37 S. E. 732; *State* v. *Reppetto,* 66 Mo. App. 251.

According to *Bell* v. *Hutchings,* 86 Ga. 562, 12 S. E. 974, the refusal of the trial judge to poll the jury upon their answer to a specific question is not ground for reversal.

[3]*State* v. *Callahan,* 55 Iowa, 364, 7 N. W. 603; *Stewart* v. *People,* 23 Mich. 63, 9 Am. Rep. 78. Compare *United States* v. *Bridges,* 10 Cent. L. J. 7.

A sealed verdict is a mere nullity, where, at the time it was delivered to and opened by the court, one of the jurors who signed it was ill and unable to appear, and the unsuccessful party was consequently deprived of his right to poll the jury, in the absence of a waiver of such right. *District of Columbia* v. *Humphries,* 11 App. D. C. 68.

[4]*Harris* v. *State,* 31 Ark. 196.

But *State* v. *Burns,* 148 Mo. 167, 49 S. W. 1005, holds that it is not necessary, in a criminal trial, that the court poll the jury of its own motion, without a demand therefor by defendant or his counsel.

20. Time to poll.

The proper time to ask for the polling is after the verdict is announced,[1] but before it is recorded.[2]

[1]*Tilton* v. *State,* 52 Ga. 478; *State* v. *Sheets,* 89 N. C. 543; N. Y. Code Crim. Proc. § 450.

[2]*Blankinship* v. *State,* 112 Ga. 402, 37 S. E. 732.

Entry in rough minutes is not necessarily such a recording as to render it too late. *Warner* v. *New York C. R. Co.* 52 N. Y. 437, 11 Am. Rep. 724.

A request to poll the jury comes too late, where the verdict in due form has been announced and recorded and affirmatively responded to by the entire jury. After this is done, the separate answers of the jurors, if not in harmony with the previously recorded verdict, may be treated as surplusage. *Com.* v. *Schmous,* 162 Pa. 326, 29 Atl. 644.

21. Waiver of the right.

The right to poll the jury is waived by consenting to their discharge[1] or by failing to claim it seasonably.[2] But mere consent that they may return a sealed verdict does not waive the right to poll the jury when they return to the courtroom to affirm the verdict.[3]

[1]*Brown* v. *State,* 63 Ala. 97; *Smith* v. *State,* 59 Ga. 513, 27 Am. Rep. 393; *United States* v. *Bridges,* 10 Cent. L. J. 7.

[2]*Joy* v. *State,* 14 Ind. 139; *People* v. *Nichols,* 62 Cal. 518; *State* v. *Atkinson,* 104 La. 570, 29 So. 279.

[3]*Stewart* v. *People,* 23 Mich. 63, 9 Am. Rep. 78. See *supra,* § 16.

22. The question.

The question put to a juror on polling must be simply, "Is this your verdict?"[1]

[1]*Leighton* v. *People,* 10 Abb. N. C. 261, Affirmed without discussing this point in 88 N. Y. 117 (here it was held no error to decline to inform the jury that the answer given should be the conscientious, individual opinion of each man); N. Y. Code Crim. Proc. § 450; *Bean* v. *State,* 17 Tex. App. 60. For other authorities, see Abbott's Civil Trial Brief, 2d ed. Division VIII.

When such demand is made, each juror should be questioned individually and separately as to his agreement to the verdict, and it is not sufficient to question the jurors collectively and in concert, although each and all express their assent to the verdict. *Blankinship* v. *State,* 112 Ga. 402, 37 S. E. 732.

23. Directing answer.

If the answer is evasive or qualified, the judge may direct the jury to answer yes or no.[1]

[1]*State* v. *Sheets,* 89 N. C. 543; *Gose* v. *State,* 6 Tex. App. 121.

In *Williams* v. *State,* 60 Md. 402, where the verdict under the statute fixed the punishment, but the jurors, when polled, answered "guilty," and said nothing as to punishment, it was held that the verdict, although thereupon recorded in full and read in full, was a nullity.

The trial court may properly refuse to allow a juror, when being polled, to make an explanation, and require him to give a correct answer to the question, "Is this your verdict?" *State* v. *Tomlinson*, 7 N. D. 294, 74 N. W. 995, Citing *Bean* v. *State*, 17 Tex. App. 60; *Winslow* v. *State*, 76 Ala. 42, and Distinguishing *State* v. *Austin*, 6 Wis. 205; *Rothbauer* v. *State*, 22 Wis. 468.

But the exact words used by a juror upon a poll of the jury in a murder trial are not material, if they indicate clearly his assent individually to the verdict. *Com.* v. *Buccieri*, 153 Pa. 535, 570, 26 Atl. 228, 245.

24. Further interrogation.

If the answer is in the affirmative, further inquiry is inadmissible.[1]

[1]*Bean* v. *State*, 17 Tex. App. 60, holding that it was proper to refuse to allow the question whether the accused was found guilty as principal or as accessory.

IV. Recording and final assent.

25. Time for recording.

When the verdict is given, and is such as the court may receive, the clerk must immediately record it in full upon the minutes.[1]

[1]N. Y. Code Crim. Proc. § 451.

Compare *People* v. *Gilbert*, 57 Cal. 96, where, under a similar statute, it was held that failure to record till after the jury were discharged, since it did not prejudice, might be disregarded.

26. Assent to the verdict as recorded.

The verdict as recorded must be read to the jury, and the jury asked whether it is their verdict. If any of the jury disagree, the fact must be entered on the minutes, and the jury again sent out. But if no disagreement is expressed, the verdict is complete, and the jury must be discharged.[1]

[1]N. Y. Code Crim. Proc. § 451.

A verdict does not become complete and final until recorded and affirmed by the jury. *Grant* v. *State*, 33 Fla. 291, 23 L. R. A. 723, 14 So. 757.

But filing a verdict and reading therefrom to the jury, and asking each of the jurors if that is his verdict, instead of recording it at length in the minutes, does not affect its validity. *State* v. *Depoister*, 21 Nev. 107, 25 Pac. 1000.

In *Com.* v. *Price*, 10 Kulp, 41, the jury agreed, separated, and, on coming into court, one juror dissented, whereupon the jury was sent out again, without objection from defendant, and agreed on the same verdict; and it was held that a motion for a new trial could not be sustained, as defendant's objection was too late.

XLVII.—MOTION IN ARREST OF JUDGMENT.

1. When motion to be made.
2. Power of court.
3. Grounds.
4. One or more good counts.

1. When motion to be made.

In the absence of statute, motion in arrest should be made, if at all, before the expiration of the term at which the trial is had,[1] and before sentence.[2]

[1] *Palatka & I. River R. Co.* v. *State*, 23 Fla. 546, 3 So. 158 (after the term).

According to *State* v. *Feamster*, 12 Wash. 461, 41 Pac. 52, however, a motion in arrest of judgment is seasonably made after conviction on a second trial, where the jury disagreed on the first trial.

[2] 1 Chitty, Crim. Law, 664. This is the generally prevalent rule. *Territory* v. *Corbett*, 3 Mont. 50.

N. Y. Code Crim. Proc. § 469, provides that "the motion must be made before or at the time when the defendant is called for judgment. If made before, it must be on notice to the district attorney or in his presence."

A motion in arrest of judgment, made after default, but before the entry of judgment, is within the meaning of Mass. Pub. Stat. chap. 214, § 27, providing that "no motion in arrest of judgment shall be allowed for a cause existing before verdict, unless the same affects the jurisdiction of the court," as that statute does not require a verdict to have been rendered in order to make it applicable. *Com.* v. *Swain*, 160 Mass. 354, 35 N. E. 862; *Com.* v. *Melville*, 160 Mass. 307, 35 N. E. 863.

A motion in arrest of judgment cannot be filed in a criminal case in the supreme court of Vermont. *State* v. *O'Neil*, 66 Vt. 356, 29 Atl. 376.

2. Power of court.

The court may arrest judgment on its own motion and without application therefor.[1]

[1] *Younger* v. *State*, 37 Ark. 116 (holding that the court ought to do so where conviction is founded on a defective indictment); N. Y. Code Crim. Proc. § 468.

3. Grounds.

A motion to arrest judgment must be founded on some fundamental defect in the indictment.[1] The defect must appear from the record itself.[2] Evidence extrinsic to the record cannot be received[3] even though such evidence was given on the trial.[4]

[1]*State* v. *Godfrey,* 24 Me. 232, 41 Am. Dec. 382 (holding that the indictment is not aided by verdict, where all the facts alleged, if true, constitute no offense); *State* v. *Smith,* 12 Mont. 378, 30 Pac. 679 (holding that lack of legal authority in the prosecuting attorney to make and file an information is not ground for arrest of judgment, under Mont. Comp. Stat. div. 3, § 357, limiting such grounds to lack of legal authority in a grand jury to find an indictment and failure of the facts stated to constitute a public offense); *United States* v. *Goggin,* 9 Biss. 269, 1 Fed. 49 (so far as this case seems to sanction the rule that any objection good on demurrer is fatal in arrest, it is too broad, for some defects are cured by verdict); *Com.* v. *Swinney,* 1 Va. Cas. 146, 5 Am. Dec. 512 (holding failure of indictment sufficiently to charge statutory crime sufficiently good ground); *Hogan* v. *State* (Fla.) 28 So. 763 (holding that judgment should be arrested when the verdict finds the accused guilty of an offense not charged or included in the charge made in the indictment); *Hall* v. *State* (Tex. Crim. App.) 38 S. W. 996 (holding that judgment should be arrested where the indictment shows that the offense was committed subsequent to its presentment); *State* v. *Morey,* 2 Wis. 494, 60 Am. Dec. 439 (uncertainty of indictment held sufficient ground). And see *State* v. *Halder,* 2 McCord L. 377, 13 Am. Dec. 738, to same effect.

But mere defects or uncertainties in a criminal pleading, or the imperfect statement of an essential element of a public offense in an indictment therefor, will not sustain a motion in arrest of judgment. *State* v. *Arnold,* 146 Ind. 651, 660, 42 N. E. 1095, 43 N. E. 871. To the same effect, see *Jones* v. *State,* 32 Tex. Crim. Rep. 108, 22 S. W. 149 (where the indictment failed to allege that it was presented in court); *People* v. *Taylor,* 119 Cal. 113, 51 Pac. 37, 638 (where the information failed to allege that the acts alleged to constitute the burglary were done "contrary to the force and effect of the statute in such case made and provided"); *State* v. *Bildstein,* 44 La. Ann. 778, 11 So. 37 (where the indictment was not wholly written).

And *State* v. *Dunn,* 109 N. C. 839, 13 S. E. 881, holds that a motion in arrest of judgment upon an indictment, for a defect therein, must be denied where the indictment charges any offense, although not the one intended.

U. S. Rev. Stat. § 1025, provides that no "defect or imperfection in matter of form only which shall not tend to the prejudice of the defendant is available." Applied in *United States* v. *Chase,* 27 Fed. 807.

Under N. Y. Code Crim. Proc. §§ 331, 467, only two objections are available: (1) To the jurisdiction of the court over the subject of the indictment; (2) that the facts stated do not constitute a crime. *People*

v. *Kelly*, 94 N. Y. 526; *People* v. *Budlensieck*, 103 N. Y. 487, 57 Am. Rep. 766, 9 N. E. 44. And see *People* v. *Knatt*, 156 N. Y. 302, 50 N. E. 835, Reversing 19 App. Div. 628, 46 N. Y. Supp. 1098, holding that the objection that the court in which an indictment was found, and the court in which it was tried, had no jurisdiction of the offense charged, may be properly raised under § 331, at the trial, or by motion in arrest of judgment after the trial.

United States v. *Gale*, 109 U. S. 65, 27 L. ed. 857, 3 Sup. Ct. Rep. 1, holds that the objection that persons have been improperly excluded from serving on the grand jury under an unconstitutional law is not available.

And *Teal* v. *State*, 22 Ga. 75, 68 Am. Dec. 482, holds that failure to read the indictment at the trial does not affect the "real merits" within the Georgia statute. And in *Ratteree* v. *State*, 77 Ga. 774, it is held that under the liberal system of pleading in Georgia, a motion in arrest of judgment may be overruled although the accusation does not set forth the offense in the terms and language of the Code, if it states it so distinctly that the jury may understand it.

United States v. *McKee*, 4 Dill. 1, Fed. Cas. No. 15,688, holds that the objection that trial was had on copy of indictment instead of original, without objection at trial, is not available.

Com. v. *Fagan*, 15 Gray, 194, holds erasures and interlineations in indictment, though not noted, and the use of the abbreviation "sd" for "said," not available.

Com. v. *Butler*, 1 Allen, 4, holds a misnomer not available.

Case v. *People*, 6 Abb. N. C. 151, and *Conner* v. *State*, 25 Ga. 515, 71 Am. Dec. 184, hold that variance between indictment and evidence is not available.

State v. *Bledsoe*, 47 Ark. 233, 1 S. W. 149, holds that defect of proof on trial is not available.

Alexander v. *Com.* 105 Pa. 1, holds that the objection that jury separated at adjournment is not available.

In Indiana a motion in arrest of judgment cannot be granted under the statute authorizing such a motion to be made only for want of jurisdiction and want of sufficient facts, because a count for murder is joined in the indictment with a count for voluntary manslaughter. *Siberry* v. *State*, 149 Ind. 684, 39 N. E. 936, 47 N. E. 458.

And in South Dakota, where defendant appears generally to a complaint charging a violation on divers days of a city ordinance with respect to nuisance, after a verdict of guilty, a motion in arrest of judgment on the ground that several offenses are charged in the complaint, treating the prosecution as a criminal action, comes too late, as the defect is demurrable under Dak. Comp. Laws, § 7292, providing that the joinder of offenses in an indictment is ground of demurrer, and under § 7452 such a defect is not ground for motion in arrest after the right to take advantage of it by demurrer has been waived. *Lead* v. *Klatt*, 13 S. D. 140, 82 N. W. 391.

In Washington a statute (2 Ballinger's Anno. Codes & Statutes, § 6967) provides that arrest of judgment in a criminal case may be had on the ground that the grand jury had no authority to inquire into the offense charged, by reason of its not being within the jurisdiction of the court, or that the facts stated did not constitute a crime or misdemeanor; but judgment will not be arrested on the ground that defendant was examined before the grand jury, and not informed that his evidence would be used against him, where the court had jurisdiction, and the indictment sufficiently stated a crime. *State* v. *Hyde,* 22 Wash. 551, 61 Pac. 719.

In North Dakota a motion in arrest of judgment in a criminal action, made on grounds not mentioned in Rev. Codes 1899, § 8275, is properly overruled. *State* v. *Montgomery,* 9 N. D. 405, 83 N. W. 873.

[1]Where a judgment rendered has been reversed, and a new trial is had upon the same indictment in the same court, the entire proceedings constitute one record, and a motion in arrest of judgment on the ground of a former acquittal of a higher offense charged in the indictment is good, where such defect appears on the record so considered. *Golding* v. *State,* 31 Fla. 262, 12 So. 525; *People* v. *Chaves,* 122 Cal. 134, 54 Pac. 596; *Smith* v. *State,* 29 Fla. 408, 10 So. 894; *Herron* v. *State,* 93 Ga. 554, 19 S. E. 243; *State* v. *Davis,* 126 N. C. 1007, 35 S. E. 464; *State* v. *Warner,* 69 Vt. 30, 37 Atl. 246; *Gray* v. *Com.* 92 Va. 772, 22 S. E. 858; *State* v. *Martin,* 38 W. Va. 568, 18 S. E. 748; *Barnard* v. *State,* 88 Wis. 656, 60 N. W. 1058.

According to *Henning* v. *State,* 106 Ind. 386, 55 Am. Rep. 756, 6 N. E. 803, the clerk's minutes of the manner in which the members of the grand jury were selected is not part of the record within this rule; but the recitals of the indictment, the indorsement on it, and the copies of the record entries are.

[2]*Busey* v. *State,* 85 Md. 115, 36 Atl. 257; *State* v. *Eaves,* 106 N. C. 752, 8 L. R. A. 259, 11 S. E. 370; *Com.* v. *Brown,* 150 Mass. 334, 23 N. E. 98; *Cooper* v. *State,* 88 Ala. 107, 7 So. 47; *King* v. *State,* 91 Tenn. 617, 20 S. W. 169; *State* v. *Carver,* 49 Me. 588, 77 Am. Dec. 275 (objection that the grand jury were not legally drawn not available because requiring extrinsic proof); *People* v. *Johnson,* 71 Cal. 384, 12 Pac. 261 (holding that under Cal. Pen. Code, §§ 1004, 1185, the defects must appear on the face of the indictment); *People* v. *Kelly,* 94 N. Y. 526 (holding that before and since the adoption of the New York Criminal Code a motion to arrest could not be made save for defects appearing upon the record); *State* v. *Crawford,* 32 La. Ann. 526; *State* v. *Creight,* 1 Brev. 169, 2 Am. Dec. 656 (hence an objection that the indictment was amended after the bill was found is not available because it requires extrinsic proof); *State* v. *Bledsoe,* 47 Ark. 233, 1 S. W. 149.

That one of the grand jurors by whom an indictment was found under Fla. act June 8, 1891, was not a competent grand juror, is waived by not pleading the fact in abatement. It is insufficient to take the objection by motion in arrest of judgment supported by affidavit. *Reynolds* v. *State,* 33 Fla. 301, 14 So. 723.

[3]*Jacobowsky* v. *People,* 6 Hun, 524, Affirmed in 64 N. Y. 659.

An order denying the motion is appealable within § 517 of the New York Code of Criminal Procedure. *People* v. *Bork,* 1 N. Y. Crim. Rep. 393. The decision in the same case, 96 N. Y. 188, Reversing 31 Hun, 360, does not involve this question.

4. One or more good counts.

If there is a good count which will sustain the judgment, judgment cannot be arrested because others may be bad.[1]

[1]*United States* v. *Patterson,* 6 McLean, 466, Fed. Cas. No. 16,011.

A motion in arrest of judgment upon a special verdict of "guilty of assault with intent to kill," under an indictment charging in the first count an assault with intent to murder, maim, and kill, and in the second count an assault and battery, should be sustained as to the second count, where a *nolle prosequi* of the intent to kill has not been entered; but the verdict cures the duplicity in the first count, and judgment may be entered thereon. *State* v. *Leavitt,* 87 Me. 72, 32 Atl. 787.

XLVIII.—MOTION FOR NEW TRIAL.

1. Right of the accused.
2. Power of the court.
3. Several defendants.
4. When to move.
5. Presence of the accused.
6. Cross-examining an affiant.

1. Right of the accused.

The accused has a right before sentence to be heard by the court by way of motion for a new trial.[1]

[1]*Ohms* v. *State,* 49 Wis. 415, 5 N. W. 834. The reason assigned is that he has a right to the judgment of the court, as well as that of the jury.

2. Power of the court.

A court of general jurisdiction has inherent power, in the absence of statute, to grant a new trial on motion, in cases of misdemeanor, if satisfied that justice has not been done.[1]

The power of a court of inferior or limited jurisdiction, and of any court in case of felony, depends upon statute.[2]

[1]*Appo* v. *People,* 20 N. Y. 531, 550; 2 Thompson, Trials, p. 2060.

[2]The New York statute is N. Y. Code Crim. Proc. § 465. See also *United States* v. *Macomb,* 5 McLean, 286, Fed. Cas. No. 15,702; *United States* v. *Williams,* 1 Cliff. 5 Fed. Cas. No. 16,707.

3. Several defendants.

One of several defendants may move for a new trial, irrespective of the others.[1]

A motion on behalf of several, granted as to one, may be denied as to the others,[2] except in cases of conspiracy.[3]

[1]*Dutcher* v. *State*, 16 Neb. 30, 19 N. W. 612. So far as this case holds that an application on behalf of several must be granted as to all or none, it is not consistent with the weight of authority.

[2]*Kemp* v. *Com.* 18 Gratt. 969; *Seborn* v. *State*, 51 Ga. 164.

[3]*Queen* v. *Gompertz*, 9 Q. B. 824.

4. When to move.

In the absence of statute,[1] a motion for new trial must be made before the expiration of the term at which the trial is had;[2] and it is too late after judgment[3] or after making motion in arrest of judgment.[4]

But the court in its discretion may, before the expiration of the term, open judgment to allow the motion to be made, or may give leave to argue a motion for new trial before the decision of a motion in arrest simultaneously made.[5]

[1]In Missouri a statute (Rev. Stat. 1889, § 4270) requires such motions to be made within four days after verdict; and a motion filed more than four days after verdict is a nullity. *State* v. *Maddox*, 153 Mo. 471, 55 S. W. 72.

And in Wyoming a statute (Rev. Stat. § 5416) provides that application for a new trial shall be by motion, which shall be filed within three days after verdict is rendered, unless additional time be granted by the court. And where defendant has failed to file his motion for a new trial within three days after the rendition of the verdict, an assignment of error based on the court's refusal to grant a new trial will not be considered on appeal. *Casteel* v. *State* (Wyo.) 62 Pac. 348.

[2]*Cobb* v. *State*, 78 Ga. 801, 3 S. E. 628; *State* v. *Kinsauls*, 126 N. C. 1095, 36 S. E. 31.

[3]*People* v. *Bradner*, 107 N. Y. 1, 13 N. E. 87 (under Code Crim. Proc. § 466). *People* v. *Hovey*, 30 Hun, 354; *Ex parte Holmes*, 21 Neb. 324, 32 N. W. 69 (under Neb. Crim. Code, § 490).

[4]*United States* v. *Simmons*, 14 Blatchf. 473, Fed. Cas. No. 16,289. If made before judgment, it can be heard after judgment. *Territory* v. *Corbett*, 3 Mont. 50. See also *State* v. *Hoyt*, 46 Conn. 330.

[5]*United States* v. *Simmons*, 14 Blatchf. 473, Fed. Cas. No. 16,289. For conflicting decisions in civil cases on the relations between motion in arrest and motion for new trial, see 2 Thompson, Trials, p. 2063.

5. Presence of the accused.

In felony the accused has a right to be present on the argument of a motion for a new trial, when made as matter of right.[1]

[1]The authorities are conflicting, some holding that the right does not extend to motions after verdict, others holding that it continues until final judgment. See, for the general principle, *ante*, Division V. Compare *Bond* v. *Com.* 83 Va. 581, 3 S. E. 149; *Bonardo* v. *People*, 182 Ill. 411, 55 N. E. 519; *Williams* v. *State* (Fla.) 27 So. 869; *Territory* v. *Chenowith*, 3 N. M. 318, 5 Pac. 532; *Com.* v. *Costello*, 121 Mass. 371, 23 Am. Rep. 277; *Lillard* v. *State*, 151 Ind. 322, 50 N. E. 383; *State* v. *Clark*, 32 La. Ann. 558; *Simpson* v. *State*, 56 Miss. 297; *Davis* v. *State*, 51 Neb. 301, 70 N. W. 984; *People* v. *Ormsby*, 48 Mich. 494, 12 N. W. 671; *State* v. *Hoffman*, 78 Mo. 256.

Where the motion was denied on the ground that the accused had fled, his subsequent recapture was ground for mandamus to compel the allowance of exceptions. *Monyhan* v. *State* (Ohio) 5 Week. L. Bull. 395.

6. Cross-examining an affiant.

The court may send for and personally examine a witness who has made an affidavit in support of the motion.[1]

[1]*Glidewell* v. *State*, 15 Lea, 133. Compare *United States* v. *Angney*, 6 Mackey, 66.

But the New York statute (Code Crim. Proc. § 465) providing that on applications for new trial on the ground of newly discovered evidence, the court can compel the personal appearance of parties for the purpose of personal examination and cross-examination under oath "upon the contents of the affidavits which they subscribed," does not empower a court to compel the appearance of persons for examination who have not sworn to affidavits presented on the motion for new trial. *People* v. *Moore*, 29 Misc. 574, 62 N. Y. Supp. 252.

XLIX.—SENTENCE.

1. By whom pronounced.
2. Time when.
3. Presence of the accused.
4. Presence of the indictment.
5. Pendency of motion for new trial.
6. Asking accused why not.
7. Clerk may put the question.
8. Suggestion of present mental incapacity.
9. Suspending sentence.
10. Irresponsive or insufficient verdict.
11. Effect of several counts.
12. — same transaction charged in different ways.

1. By whom pronounced.

Sentence may be pronounced by one of the several judges before whom the trial was had,[1] or by the successor in office of the trial judge, in case of the omission of the trial judge to pronounce it.[2] But a sentence imposed after the court pronouncing the same has been abolished by an act of the legislature cannot be allowed to stand.[3]

[1] *United States* v. *Gordon,* 5 Blatchf. 18, Fed. Cas. No. 15,231.

[2] *Pegalow* v. *State,* 20 Wis. 61, holding that a successor in office had such power at common law. Compare *Weaver* v. *People,* 33 Mich. 296, holding that where the law fixes a maximum but not a minimum punishment, and judgment has been suspended because the trial judge thinks that punishment ought not to be imposed, the accused cannot be subsequently sentenced by another judge, although another judge may sentence in case of mere omission.

As to constitutional power to change the judge, see *People* v. *Bork,* 96 N. Y. 188.

[3] *Gorman* v. *People,* 17 Colo. 596, 31 Pac. 335.

2. Time when.

A statutory provision requiring sentence to be passed within a specified time after verdict,[1] or requiring a specified time to elapse before sentence,[2] may be waived by the prisoner.

[1] *People* v. *Everhardt,* 104 N. Y. 591, 11 N. E. 62, Affirming 5 N. Y. Crim. Rep. 91.

[2] *People* v. *Robinson,* 46 Cal. 94.

3. Presence of the accused.

It is error in felonies to pronounce sentence in the absence of the accused.[1] It is discretionary to do so in misdemeanors involving a fine or pecuniary penalty.[2]

[1] *Dunn* v. *Com.* 6 Pa. 384 (holding it error where the record on appeal did not affirmatively show that the defendant was personally present when sentence was pronounced); *Safford* v. *People,* 1 Park. Crim. Rep. 474

(to same effect); *State* v. *McClain*, 156 Mo. 99, 56 S. W. 731; *Kelly* v. *State*, 3 Smedes & M. 518; *Hamilton* v. *Com.* 16 Pa. 129; *Gibson* v. *State*, 39 Ala. 693; *Graham* v. *State*, 40 Ala. 659; *People* v. *Winchell*, 7 Cow. 525 (where, upon a conviction for perjury, the defendant was not personally present before the court to be sentenced, being out on bail, the court refused to render judgment).

It seems that it is not error to sentence in the absence of the accused, if such absence is voluntary. *Lynch* v. *Com.* 88 Pa. 189, 32 Am. Rep. 445 (misdemeanor); *Middlebrook* v. *State*, 43 Conn. 257, 21 Am. Rep. 650 (contempt of court); *Harris* v. *People*, 138 Ill. 63, 27 N. E. 706.

[2]*Son* v. *People*, 12 Wend. 344; *Ex parte Tracy*, 25 Vt. 93; *Com.* v. *Crump*, 1 Va. Cas. 172.

N. Y. Code Crim. Proc. § 473, provides that "for the purpose of judgment, if the conviction be for a felony, the defendant must be personally present; if it be for a misdemeanor, judgment may be pronounced in his absence."

In Virginia the rule of the common law, that judgment for corporal punishment can be pronounced only when the defendant is personally present, is displaced by Va. Code, § 4076, providing that no *capias* to hear judgment shall be necessary in any prosecution for a misdemeanor, but the court may proceed to judgment in the absence of the accused, and if such judgment requires confinement in jail the court may make such order as may be necessary for the arrest of the person against whom such judgment is, and for the execution thereof. *Shiflett* v. *Com.* 90 Va. 386, 18 S. E. 838.

State v. *Campbell*, 42 W. Va. 246, 24 S. E. 875, holds that although a defendant charged with a misdemeanor punishable by imprisonment may appear by counsel, judgment of imprisonment cannot be rendered unless the defendant is present at its rendition.

4. Presence of the indictment.

It is not indispensable that the original indictment should be before the court. If lost or destroyed without fault of the prosecution, its place may be supplied by a copy.[1]

[1]*Mount* v. *State*, 14 Ohio, 295, 45 Am. Dec. 542.

5. Pendency of motion for new trial.

The pendency of a motion for new trial does not suspend the power of the court to pass sentence.[1]

[1]*State* v. *Hoyt*, 47 Conn. 518, 36 Am. Rep. 89.

And a sentence pronounced after overruling a motion for a new trial is not invalidated by subsequently entertaining and denying another motion for a new trial. *Fletcher* v. *State*, 37 Tex. Crim. Rep. 193, 39 S. W. 116.

In *Com.* v. *Brown*, 167 Mass. 144, 45 N. E. 1, it is held that Mass. Stat.

1885, chap. 469, authorizing the court to impose sentence notwithstanding defendant's exceptions, is constitutional.

6. Asking accused why not.

When sentence is about to be pronounced the accused must be given opportunity to say why it should not be pronounced.[1]

[1]The reason is that he must have opportunity to move for a new trial, or in arrest of judgment, or both, or suggest his present mental incapacity; and that even if he does not wish to do so, he is entitled to notice of what is about to be done.

There is much conflict of authority as to whether the omission of the question is necessarily error. That it is essential in all felonies, see *Croker* v. *State*, 47 Ala. 53; *Mullen* v. *State*, 45 Ala. 43, 6 Am. Rep. 691; *Safford* v. *People*, 1 Park. Crim. Rep. 474; *Dent* v. *People*, 46 How. Pr. 264; *McCue* v. *Com.* 78 Pa. 185, 21 Am. Rep. 7; *Graham* v. *People*, 63 Barb. 469.

That it is essential in capital cases only, see *Jones* v. *State*, 51 Miss. 718, 24 Am. Rep. 658; *Bressler* v. *People*, 117 Ill. 422, 8 N. E. 62 (holding it not to be necessary in minor felonies; refusing to rule as to capital cases); *State* v. *Taylor*, 27 La. Ann. 393, 21 Am. Rep. 561; *Turner* v. *United States*, 13 C. C. A. 443, 30 U. S. App. 108, 66 Fed. 287 (not necessary in misdemeancr cases).

That this omission, even in capital cases, is not error, see *State* v. *Smith*, 33 La. Ann. 1414; *Warner* v. *State*, 56 N. J. L. 686, 29 Atl. 505; *State* v. *Hoyt*, 47 Conn. 518, 36 Am. Rep. 89 (where actual motion in arrest was made). Especially if it appears from the record (*Territory* v. *Webb*, 2 N. M. 147), or by his having moved in arrest or for new trial (*State* v. *Johnson*, 67 N. C. 55; *Lillard* v. *State*, 151 Ind. 322, 50 N. E. 383; *State* v. *Hoyt*, 47 Conn. 518, 36 Am. Rep. 89), that he knew what his rights were. And that the omission to do so is not ground for reversal in any case, see *Gillespie* v. *People*, 176 Ill. 238, 52 N. E. 250.

But the better opinion is that omission will not necessitate new trial, but only resentence. See *infra*, § 26.

7. Clerk may put the question.

It is not necessary for the judge personally to ask the accused why sentence should not be pronounced. The clerk of the court may, and generally does, put the question.[1]

[1]*State* v. *Ross*, 32 La. Ann. 854.

8. Suggestion of present mental incapacity.

In the absence of statute,[1] a suggestion or plea of present insanity interposed after verdict as a reason why sentence should not be pronounced does not require trial by jury, but may be determined by the court.[2]

But the court may in its discretion call in a jury to determine the question.[3]

[1]In Georgia a statute (Code, §§ 4666, 4666*a*) provides that "if, after any convict shall have been sentenced to the punishment of death, he shall become insane, the sheriff of the county, with concurrence and assistance of the ordinary thereof, shall summon a jury of twelve men to inquire into such insanity; and if it be found, by the inquisition of such jury, that such convict is insane, the sheriff shall suspend the execution of the sentence directing the death of such convict, and make report of the said inquisition and suspension of execution to the presiding judge of the district, who shall cause the same to be entered on the minutes of the superior court of the county where the conviction was had;" and that "when any person shall, after conviction of a capital crime, become insane, and shall be so declared in accordance with the provisions of § 4666 of the Code, it shall be the duty of the judge to certify the fact, and the said convict shall be received into the lunatic asylum, there to be safely and securely kept, and treated as other adjudged insane persons." The words "after conviction" in § 4666*a* are not to be construed as limited to persons who have been sentenced by the preceding section on the subject, which prescribes an investigation after a convict has been sentenced. *Nobles* v. *Georgia*, 168 U. S. 398, 42 L. ed. 515, 18 Sup. Ct. Rep. 87, 100 Ga. 554, 38 L. R. A. 577, 28 S. E. 68.

[2]*Laros* v. *Com.* 84 Pa. 200, 211; *Bonds* v. *State*, Mart. & Y. 143, 17 Am. Dec. 795. And for a full review of the authorities on this question, see note to *Baughn* v. *State* (Ga.) 38 L. R. A. 577 *et seq.*

In *Com.* v. *Buccieri*, 153 Pa. 535, 570, 26 Atl. 228, 245, it is held that a plea of present insanity interposed by one convicted of murder, when called for sentence, not corroborated in any manner by affidavit or statement of any specific fact, is properly disregarded, in the absence of anything to raise a doubt in the mind of the court as to the sanity of the prisoner.

[3]*Bonds* v. *State*, Mart. & Y. 143, 17 Am. Dec. 795, above cited (*dictum* citing common-law authorities).

Compare *ante*, Division IX., as to present mental incapacity.

9. Suspending sentence.

The court has power to suspend sentence in its discretion, when the interests of justice appear to demand it.[1]

[1]*People* v. *Mueller*, 4 Crim. L. Mag. 725; *People* v. *Graves*, 2 N. Y. Crim. Rep. 123; *People* v. *Harrington*, 15 Abb. N. C. 161; *Ex parte Williams*, 26 Fla. 310, 8 So. 425; *People ex rel. Forsyth* v. *Monroe County Court of Sessions*, 141 N. Y. 288, 36 N. E. 386, 23 L. R. A. 856, with note reviewing authorities (holding that a statute authorizing a court to sus-

pend sentence in a criminal case after conviction does not encroach upon the constitutional powers of the executive to grant reprieves and pardons). *Contra*, *People* v. *Morrisette*, 20 How. Pr. 118; *Neal* v. *State*, 104 Ga. 509, 42 L. R. A. 190, 30 S. E. 858; *Re Markuson*, 5 N. D. 180, 64 N. W. 939; *Re Webb*, 89 Wis. 354, 27 L. R. A. 356, 62 N. W. 177. And *Crane* v. *State*, 94 Tenn. 86, 98, 28 S. W. 317, holds that the sentence of one convicted of bigamy will not be suspended until he can apply for a pardon, under the permissive provisions of Mill. & V. (Tenn.) Code, § 6096, where his guilt is clearly shown, although he has been a quiet, orderly, respectable citizen and valuable member of society for several years.

As to whether, and how long, after suspending sentence, the court may pass sentence, compare *People* v. *Reilly*, 53 Mich. 260, 18 N. W. 849; *Weaver* v. *People*, 33 Mich. 296; *Ex parte Williams*, 26 Fla. 310, 8 So. 425; *State* v. *Addy*, 43 N. J. L. 113, 39 Am. Rep. 547; *People ex rel. Smith* v. *Allen*, 155 Ill. 61, 41 L. R. A. 473, 39 N. E. 568; *Gibson* v. *State*, 68 Miss. 241, 8 So. 329; *People ex rel. Forsyth* v. *Monroe County Court of Sessions*, 141 N. Y. 288, 23 L. R. A. 856, 36 N. E. 386; *Weber* v. *State*, 58 Ohio St. 616, 41 L. R. A. 472, 51 N. E. 116.

10. Irresponsive or insufficient verdict.

A verdict which finds the accused guilty of an act for which he cannot be punished under the indictment, or which omits from its findings any essential legal element necessary to constitute the offense charged, will not sustain sentence.[1]

[1]Thus, under an indictment for assault with intent to murder, a verdict of guilty of an assault with intent to commit manslaughter is a nullity because the statute does not provide for such an offense. *State* v. *White*, 41 Iowa, 325, 20 Am. Rep. 602.

So is a verdict of guilty of misdemeanor in whipping his wife. *Manigault* v. *State*, 53 Ga. 113.

So is a verdict of guilty of an intent to maim. *Allen* v. *State*, 52 Ala. 391.

For other illustrations, see *Wright* v. *People*, 33 Mich. 300; *Gibbs* v. *State*, 34 Tex. 134; *Rhoads* v. *Com.* (Pa.) 4 Cent. Rep. 725, 6 Atl. 245; *Stephens* v. *State*, 56 Ga. 604; *Riflemaker* v. *State*, 25 Ohio St. 395; *O'Connell* v. *State*, 55 Ga. 191; *State* v. *Davis*, 20 La. Ann. 354; *Com.* v. *Call*, 21 Pick. 509, 32 Am. Dec. 284; *Reg.* v. *York*, 1 Den. C. C. 335; *State* v. *Stewart*, 91 N. C. 566; *State* v. *Brown*, 2 N. C. (1 Hayw.) 100, 1 Am. Dec. 548; *Dyer* v. *Com.* 23 Pick. 402; *State* v. *Rollins*, 8 N. H. 550; *Com.* v. *Adams*, 127 Mass. 15.

11. Effect of several counts.

If, upon an indictment containing several counts, a general verdict be rendered,[1] or a plea of guilty put in,[2] the accused may be sentenced appropriately to either count which is good, notwithstanding the other counts may be bad.[3]

[1]*People* v. *Dunn,* 90 N. Y. 104, Reversing 27 Hun, 272; *Claassen* v. *United States,* 142 U. S. 140, 35 L. ed. 966, 12 Sup. Ct. Rep. 169.

[2]*Polinsky* v. *People,* 73 N. Y. 65.

[3]*United States* v. *Patterson,* 6 McLean, 466, Fed. Cas. No. 16,011; *People* v. *Willett,* 102 N. Y. 251, 6 N. E. 301; *Haynes* v. *United States,* 42 C. C. A. 34, 101 Fed. 817; *Evans* v. *United States,* 153 U. S. 584, 38 L. ed. 830, 839, 14 Sup. Ct. Rep. 934, 939.

In *Re Tutt,* 55 Kan. 705, 41 Pac. 957, it was held that a sentence of a defendant charged with burglary in a freight car, under Kan. Laws 1871, chap. 121, § 1, and with larceny under § 3, to confinement in the penitentiary at hard labor for five years, was supported by a verdict finding him guilty of burglary and larceny as charged, and fixing the value of the stolen property at $6, although the conviction for burglary was a nullity, as the conviction of larceny under § 3 was alone sufficient to support a sentence not exceeding seven years.

12. — same transaction charged in different ways.

If an indictment charges in different ways, in several counts, an offense relating to the same transaction, a general verdict of guilty will sustain a sentence of the highest crime charged.[1]

[1]*Hawker* v. *People,* 75 N. Y. 487.

In *Griffen* v. *State,* 46 Neb. 282, 64 N. W. 966, a separate sentence upon a conviction under each of two counts of an information charging in one count forgery of a note, and in the other uttering it, was held to be erroneous, as the two acts constitute but one crime.

So, in *Re Walsh,* 37 Neb. 454, 55 N. W. 1075, it was held that but one penalty could be inflicted under an indictment charging the forgery of a bank check and the fraudulent utterance of the same, on a general plea of guilty, as the two counts charged but a single offense.

Compare *Com.* v. *Fitchburg R. Co.* 120 Mass. 372 (holding that if the same offense is charged as committed by different means or in different modes, in various distinct counts, a general verdict of guilty upon the indictment is a conviction of only one offense, and is deemed to be on that count to which the evidence is applicable); *State* v. *Crank,* 2 Bail. L. 66, 23 Am. Dec. 117 (holding that under a general verdict judgment may be given on any or all counts, according as they may be supported by proof). See also *State* v. *Smith,* 5 Day, 175, 5 Am. Dec. 132.

13. — inconsistent counts.

A general verdict of guilty upon an indictment containing inconsistent counts will not sustain sentence.[1]

[1]*Com.* v. *Haskins,* 128 Mass. 60, holding that a general verdict of guilty

upon an indictment charging the defendant in one count with larceny of a chattel and in another with receiving the chattel knowing it to have been stolen, was bad as inconsistent, and could not be cured by the entry of a *nolle presequi* as to the second count. And *James* v. *State*, 104 Ala. 20, 16 So. 94, holds that a motion in arrest of judgment on a general verdict of guilty should be sustained where the indictment in different counts charges arson in the second and third degrees. See also *State* v. *Johnson*, 75 N. C. 123, 22 Am. Rep. 666.

In *State* v. *Basserman*, 54 Conn. 88, 6 Atl. 185, it is held that no objection can be made to a general verdict on several counts, if a separate verdict is not asked for.

But *State* v. *Dugan* (N. J. L.) 46 Atl. 566, holds that when counts in an indictment are joined for offenses different, but not positively repugnant, and a general verdict of guilty is rendered, the correct practice is to sentence on the count containing the charge of the highest crime.

14. Separate verdict.

Where an indictment sets forth several counts, the jury may convict as to some and acquit as to others;[1] and where the accused is convicted as to one, and the verdict is silent as to the other counts, he will be deemed to have been acquitted of such counts.[2]

[1] *Com.* v. *Edds*, 14 Gray, 406.

[2] *State* v. *Gannon*, 11 Mo. App. 502; *State* v. *Whitton*, 68 Mo. 91; *Richards* v. *Com.* 81 Va. 110. See, as to several counts charging the same offense, *supra*, §§ 11–13.

15. Evidence in mitigation.

Where the court has a discretion as to the punishment to be inflicted, evidence of circumstances material to its exercise may be received.[1]

[1] N. Y. Code Crim. Proc. § 483. And see *People* v. *M'Kay*, 122 Cal. 628, 55 Pac. 594, where it is held to be discretionary with the court whether it will hear evidence in mitigation of the punishment, under Cal. Pen. Code, § 1203.

The practice allows the offer of evidence in mitigation of sentence after plea of *nolo contendere*, as well as after plea of guilty. *Com.* v. *Horton*, 9 Pick. 206.

16. Sentence must be complete.

The court cannot, on imposing a partial sentence, reserve the power to impose the remainder of the full sentence at a future time.[1]

[1] *People* v. *Felker*, 61 Mich. 110, 27 N. W. 869.

17. Less than full penalty.

The accused has no right to object that the court, in sentencing, imposes a punishment less than the full penalty allowed by law, if not of a different kind.[1]

[1] *People* v. *Bauer,* 37 Hun, 407; *McQuoid* v. *People,* 8 Ill. 76; *People* v. *Rouse,* 72 Mich. 59, 40 N. W. 57. And see *State* v. *Arnold,* 144 Ind. 651, 42 N. E. 1095, 43 N. E. 871, holding that the fact that a verdict assesses less than the minimum of imprisonment authorized by statute does not render it void, and the defendant waives the irregularity by failing to object at the proper time. Compare with *Dillon* v. *State,* 38 Ohio St. 586, holding that a sentence imposing a greater or less fine or imprisonment than a statute prescribes is error, but omitting either when the statute prescribes both is not ground for reversal. See also *King* v. *Bourne,* 7 Ad. & El. 58. Error to sentence to transportation for seven years when the statute punishment was death.

18. Hard labor.

The court cannot add hard labor when the statute simply prescribes imprisonment.[1] Otherwise if the law allows imprisonment in a prison where the requirement of labor is lawful.[2]

[1] *Haynes* v. *United States,* 42 C. C. A. 34, 101 Fed. 817; *Ex parte Reynolds,* 87 Ala. 138, 6 So. 335.

[2] *Ex parte Karstendick,* 93 U. S. 396, 23 L. ed. 889; *United States* v. *Pridgeon,* 153 U. S. 48, 38 L. ed. 631, 14 Sup. Ct. Rep. 746; *Ex parte Maher,* 25 Nev. 422, 62 Pac. 1. And see cases on both sides of this question in *Hodge* v. *Queen,* 5 Crim. L. Mag. 391, 404; and note to *Topeka* v. *Boutwell* (Kan.) 27 L. R. A. 593.

A sentence to state prison necessarily involves imprisonment at hard labor if the statute prescribes that mode of punishment. The sentence need not express that the prisoner is to be put at hard labor. *Done* v. *People,* 5 Park. Crim. Rep. 364.

And a sentence which directs merely that the convict "be confined and restrained in the state prison, conformable to the rules and regulations thereof," for a certain time, while it is defective in form under Minn. Gen. Stat. 1894, § 7402, requiring sentences in such cases to be for confinement at hard labor, it is not so in substance, since § 7492 provides that every person sentenced to confinement in the state prison shall be compelled to perform a reasonable amount of hard labor. *State ex rel. Hull* v. *Wolfer,* 68 Minn. 465, 71 N. W. 681.

In Kentucky a statute (Gen. Stat. chap. 29, § 2) allows the jury to direct imprisonment at hard labor in case a fine is not paid; but this statute applies only to misdemeanors, and not to bribery, where as part of the punishment defendant is excluded from office and suffrage. *Eldridge* v. *Com.* 87 Ky. 365, 8 S. W. 892.

And for a full treatment of the question of cruel and unusual punishments, see note to *State ex rel. Garvey* v. *Whitaker* (La.) 35 L. R. A. 561.

19. Accused already under previous sentence.

The fact that defendant is already under conviction and imprisonment for an unexpired term for the commission of another crime is no objection to passing sentence for the offense of which he is now convicted.[1]

[1]*Thomas* v. *People*, 67 N. Y. 218; *Re Edwards*, 43 N. J. L. 555, 38 Am. Rep. 652, with note by J. H. Stewart.

So, a prisoner may be convicted of murder, and sentenced to be hanged for a crime committed while he was under sentence to prison for life for a former murder. *Singleton* v. *State*, 71 Miss. 782, 16 So. 295.

And a statement by the court in passing sentence upon one convicted of a crime, that the sentence will begin at the expiration of the sentence the defendant is serving out at the time, is harmless, although there is no evidence that defendant has been convicted of another crime. *King* v. *State*, 32 Tex. Crim. Rep. 463, 24 S. W. 514.

And the term of imprisonment for the escape during the first term of an accused convicted of two offenses and sentenced for two terms, the second to commence at the expiration of the first, the additional term to commence from the time he would otherwise have been discharged,—does not commence to run until he has served out the full term imposed by the two former judgments. *Ex parte Irwin*, 88 Cal. 169, 25 Pac. 1118.

20. Recapture after escape.

Where prisoners escape after verdict, but before sentence, they may, on recapture and proof of identity, be afterwards sentenced.[1]

[1]*Thurman* v. *State*, 54 Ark. 120, 15 S. W. 84. And see note to *Re Edwards*, 43 N. J. L. 555, 38 Am. Rep. 652, citing many cases.

And that one sentenced to imprisonment in jail has been allowed by the sheriff to go at large for more than the term for which he was sentenced does not, under the Texas Code, entitle him to a discharge because the term has expired, but he may be treated as an escaped prisoner. *Ex parte Wyatt*, 29 Tex. App. 398, 16 S. W. 301.

And according to *Henderson* v. *Jones*, 52 Ohio St. 242, 27 L. R. A. 290, 39 N. E. 805, an escaped convict who, under another name, is convicted and sentenced to the same penitentiary for another crime, may, at the expiration of the latter sentence, be held to serve out the remainder of his first sentence.

The provisions of Kan. Laws 1891, chap. 152, § 28, that an escaped or mutinous convict shall be resentenced for the full term for which he was originally sentenced, without counting the time he has been imprisoned, is unconstitutional as not only placing him twice in jeopardy, but punishing him twice for the same offense; and also as making the punishment depend, not on the offense committed, but on the date of the original sentence. *State* v. *Lewin*, 53 Kan. 679, 37 Pac. 168.

21. Date for commencing imprisonment.

Sentence to imprisonment must either be for a specified term, or must specify the date at which it is to commence.[1]

[1]See *State* v. *Smith,* 10 Nev. 106; *Clifford* v. *State,* 30 Md. 575.

One calendar month's imprisonment, when commencing on a day other than the first of the month, dates from the day of imprisonment to the corresponding numerical day, less one, in the next month in the calendar. If, owing to the shortness of the next month, there is no such corresponding day, the imprisonment will termiate on the last day of such next month. *Migotti* v. *Colville,* 27 Week. Rep. 744.

The court has no power, in pronouncing sentence on one convicted of an offense, to provide that the imprisonment shall begin at some future indefinite time pending on the happening of a contingency; and a commitment on such sentence, after the expiration of the term of imprisonment named therein, is illegal. *Re Strickler,* 51 Kan. 700, 33 Pac. 620.

In *People* v. *Huntley,* 112 Mich. 569, 71 N. W. 178, a sentence of a convict, in state prison for an assault committed therein, to take effect from the day it was pronounced, was held not to be invalid for uncertainty as to when such sentence would begin, although the time when the former sentence would expire was uncertain.

But *Jones* v. *Territory,* 4 Okla. 45, 43 Pac. 1072, holds that a judgment in a criminal cause is not bad for failure to name a date at which the imprisonment will commence, as such judgment takes effect from the date of its entry, unless a different time is fixed therein.

22. — after subsisting sentence.

A sentence to imprisonment may be awarded to take effect upon the expiration of another term of imprisonment imposed upon conviction under another indictment.[1]

[1]*Re White,* 50 Kan. 299, 32 Pac. 36; *Blitz* v. *United States,* 153 U. S. 308, 38 L. ed. 725, 14 Sup. Ct. Rep. 924; *Fitzpatrick* v. *People,* 98 Ill. 269; *Kite* v. *Com.* 11 Met. 581; *People* v. *Forbes,* 22 Cal. 135; *Re Packer,* 18 Colo. 525, 33 Pac. 578; *State* v. *Smith,* 5 Day, 175, 5 Am. Dec. 132; *Brown* v. *Com.* 4 Rawle, 259, 26 Am. Dec. 130; N. Y. Pen. Code, § 694. And according to *Re Walsh,* 37 Neb. 454, 55 N. W. 1075, although a person convicted of several distinct offenses, each punishable by imprisonment in the penitentiary, charged in separate counts of the same indictment, may be separately sentenced for each offense of which he is found guilty, the judgment should not fix the day on which each successive term should begin, but should direct it to commence at the expiration of the preceding one.

And in *People* v. *Huntley,* 112 Mich. 569, 71 N. W. 178, it is held that a convict imprisoned in state prison, convicted of a crime committed therein, may be sentenced to imprisonment to begin at the expiration of the term which he was serving at the time such offense was committed, although the date of the expiration of such term is uncertain, under Mich. Pub. Acts 1887, act No. 132, § 3, authorizing the term of sentence in such case to commence forthwith, or at the expiration of the term of sentence the convict may be serving at the time.

Contra,—in some jurisdictions it has been held that such sentences, in the absence of statute authorizing them, are void for uncertainty. *Bloom's Petition*, 53 Mich. 597, 19 N. W. 200; *Picket* v. *State*, 22 Ohio St. 405; *United States* v. *Patterson*, 29 Fed. 775; *Ex parte Roberts*, 9 Nev. 44, 16 Am. Rep. 1; *Miller* v. *Allen*, 11 Ind. 389.

23. Excessive sentences.

In cases wherein the court has full jurisdiction of the person and subject-matter of the offense, that a sentence exceeds in extent or time that which is authorized by law does not render the legal or authorized portion of the sentence void, but only leaves the portion of the sentence in excess open to question and attack.[1]

[1]*People ex rel. Trainor* v. *Baker*, 89 N. Y. 460; *Ex parte Mooney*, 26 W. Va. 36, 53 Am. Rep. 59; *Ex parte Shaw*, 7 Ohio St. 81, 70 Am. Dec. 55; *Sennott's Case*, 146 Mass. 489, 16 N. E. 448. *Contra, Ex parte Cox* (Idaho) 32 Pac. 197; *Ex parte Page*, 49 Mo. 291. For a full review of the authorities on this question, see note to *Re Taylor* (S. D.) 45 L. R. A. 136.

24. Fine against joint defendants.

A sentence to pay a fine awarded against defendants jointly indicted must be several against each defendant.[1]

[1]*Waltzer* v. *State*, 3 Wis. 785; *State* v. *Hopkins*, 7 Blackf. 494; *Caldwell* v. *Com.* 7 Dana, 229; *State* v. *Gay*, 10 Mo. 440.

25. Cumulative sentences.

Whether cumulative sentences can be imposed for several offenses under the same indictment, compare—[1]

[1]Affirmative: *Castro* v. *Queen*, 44 L. T. N. S. 350, L. R. 9 Q. B. 350; *Fletcher* v. *People*, 81 Ill. 116 (holding that there should be a separate sentence for each count); *United States* v. *Groesbeck*, 4 Utah, 487, 11 Pac. 542; Wharton, Crim. Pl. & Pr. § 910; 3 So. Law Rev. N. S. 50 (J. P. Bishop); *Re Esmond*, 42 Fed. 827; *Re Wilson*, 11 Utah, 114, 39 Pac. 498; *Com.* v. *Birdsall*, 69 Pa. 482, 8 Am. Rep. 283; *United States* v. *Patterson*, 29 Fed. 775 (*dictum*). And see *Re McLaughlin*, 58 Vt. 136; *Ex parte Hibbs*, 26 Fed. 421. In Texas the Code of Criminal Procedure of 1895, art. 840, provides that where one is convicted in two or more cases, and the punishment assessed in each case is confinement in the penitentiary or county jail, "the judgment and sentence" shall be rendered in each case in the same manner as if there had been but one con-

viction, except that "judgment" in the second and subsequent convictions shall be that the punishment shall begin when the judgment and sentence in the preceding conviction shall have ceased to operate; and a final sentence of one convicted of felony in several cases may provide for cumulative punishment, although the first judgments in the second and subsequent convictions do not recite the cumulations. *Ex parte Crawford,* 36 Tex. Crim. Rep. 180, 36 S. W. 92. And *Stewart* v. *State,* 37 Tex. Crim. Rep. 135, 38 S. W. 1143, holds that this statute applies to misdemeanor cases, as well as felony cases, as felonies are not punishable by confinement in the county jail.

Negative: *People ex rel. Tweed* v. *Liscomb,* 60 N. Y. 559, 19 Am. Rep. 21, holding, upon an indictment for several misdemeanors, that even where several distinct crimes may be united in the same indictment, cumulative punishment may not be imposed unless a statute expressly authorizes it; and that the provision of the Revised Statutes [re-enacted, N. Y. Pen. Code, §§ 694, 695] had application to convictions and punishment under different indictments. *Harper Case,* approved in 10 Crim. L. Mag. 293.

If sentences are cumulative and for different offenses, they must all be pronounced on the same day. *Com.* v. *Foster,* 122 Mass. 317, 23 Am. Rep. 326; note to *Re Edwards* (N. J. L.) 38 Am. Rep. 652.

26. Amending sentence.

The court has power during the term to expunge an irregular sentence[1] or one imposed without asking what the prisoner has to say,[2] and pass sentence anew, or to amend or correct a sentence;[3] but the power ceases when the sentence has been put into operation,[4]—especially if the term has expired.[5]

[1] *Miller* v. *Finkle,* 1 Park. Crim. Rep. 374 (sentence not adjusted to expire in summer season); *People* v. *Davis,* 46 N. Y. S. R. 213, 19 N. Y. Supp. 781 (to same effect).

[2] *State* v. *Trezevant,* 20 S. C. 363, 47 Am. Rep. 840. See also *Kinsler* v. *Territory,* 1 Wyo. 112; *McCue* v. *Com.* 78 Pa. 185, 21 Am. Rep. 7; *Keech* v. *State,* 15 Fla. 591. *Contra, Messner* v. *People,* 45 N. Y. 1, holding that for such error a new trial must be directed.

[3] *Ex parte Casey,* 18 Fed. 86; *State* v. *Hughes,* 35 Kan. 626, 57 Am. Rep. 195, 12 Pac. 58; *Com.* v. *Weymouth,* 2 Allen, 144, 79 Am. Dec. 776; *Price* v. *Com.* 77 Va. 393; *Com.* v. *Mayloy,* 57 Pa. 291. Compare with *People* v. *Felker,* 61 Mich. 110, 27 N. W. 869.

And an error in a sentence in a criminal prosecution, consisting in adding "at hard labor" to the "imprisonment in the penitentiary" provided by statute, and which renders the judgment voidable only, and not void, may be corrected by amendment by the United States circuit court of appeals before which the case is brought on writ of error, without the reversal of the judgment and the granting of a new trial. *Jackson* v. *United States,* 102 Fed. 473, 42 C. C. A. 452.

The power of the court to correct a judgment sentencing a person to death and to solitary confinement until execution is not lost by the fact of imprisonment after sentence, on the ground that this is the suffering of a part of the sentence. *McGinn* v. *State*, 46 Neb. 427, 30 L. R. A. 450, 65 N. W. 46.

[4] *Ex parte Lange*, 18 Wall. 163, 21 L. ed. 872; *State* v. *Cannon*, 11 Or. 312, 2 Pac. 191 (holding that, after the sentence has been executed, judgment may not be reversed even at the same term); *State* v. *Warren*, 92 N. C. 825.

So, a journal entry of judgment in a criminal case cannot be amended after the sentence, as stated in such journal entry, has been fully served, and the fine and costs paid, by adding thereto that defendant be committed to jail until he give the good behavior bond provided for in the judgment. *State* v. *McBee* (Kan. App.) 61 Pac. 1093.

And the court, after passing sentence in a criminal case, and reducing it to writing, should not change it, and make the penalty more severe, simply because defendant's counsel gives notice of his intention to move for a new trial. *Meaders* v. *State*, 96 Ga. 299, 22 S. E. 527.

But changing the mittimus after sentence of a prisoner, to conform to a change in the location of the state penitentiary, does not change or modify the judgment of conviction, but may be done at a subsequent term of court. *Kingen* v. *Kelley*, 3 Wyo. 566, 15 L. R. A. 177, 28 Pac. 36.

[5] *People* v. *Whitson*, 74 Ill. 20; *Pifer* v. *Com.* 14 Gratt. 710; *Com.* v. *Foster*, 122 Mass. 317, 23 Am. Rep. 326 (holding that where defendant has been found guilty generally, upon an indictment alleging several distinct offenses, and sentenced thereunder upon some of the counts and imprisoned, he cannot thereafter, no continuation having been granted for such purpose, be sentenced on the other counts, though the first sentence was erroneous); *United States* v. *Patterson*, 29 Fed. 775.

L.—RESTORATION OF PROPERTY.

1. At common law.
2. Under modern statutes.
3. Application by prosecutor.
4. Application by the accused.
5. — restoration of possession without trial of title.
6. Right of third person to oppose.
7. Application by third person.

1. At common law.

In the absence of statute, the court before which the accused is found guilty has power to award a writ of restitution of the stolen property[1] to the person from whom the property was taken, or to the owner, if the accused was found guilty by reason of the evidence given or procured by such person or owner.[2]

[1]Or the proceeds thereof. 1 Hale P. C. 542.

[2]2 Bishop, Crim. Proc. §§ 756, 757; 1 Hale P. C. 541.

2. Under modern statutes.

By the New York statute and similar statutes in some other jurisdictions, if the property stolen or embezzled has not already been delivered to the owner prior to the trial, "the court before which the trial is had for stealing or embezzling it may, on proof of his title, order it to be restored to the owner;"[1] and as such statutes are remedial and are to be liberally construed, the proceeds of, or substitute for, the stolen property, may be restored thereunder.[2] And upon conviction[3] or plea of guilty, the trial court may, it seems, proceed to determine the question of ownership in a summary way.[4]

[1]N. Y. Code Crim. Proc. § 688. For the provisions of statute as to the custody and disposition of stolen property before and pending trial, and the disposal thereof, if unclaimed, see N. Y. Code Crim. Proc. §§ 685–691 (superseding similar provisions of the Revised Statutes). For further provisions applying to New York city, see N. Y. city consolidation act of 1882, §§ 288–293, as amended by Laws 1884, chap. 180.

In *Simpson* v. *St. John*, 93 N. Y. 363, it is held that replevin cannot be maintained against the officers having charge of stolen property pending the trial. In affirming the order denying an application for arrest of the officer refusing to surrender the property to the sheriff in such action, the court says: "Such a temporary retention of property . . . in no manner denies or affects the title of the true owner, but postpones his right of possession until the exigencies of the prosecution are satisfied. . . . The property . . . is therefore in the custody of the law, and cannot be taken away until that custody is ended by conviction or acquittal, or by an order of the magistrate permitting its surrender to the owner (*Houghton* v. *Bachman*, 47 Barb. 388). The provisions of the Revised Statutes upon the subject are superseded by those of the Code of Criminal Procedure (§§ 685, 686 *et seq.*). . . . Under these provisions it is apparent that, pending a prosecution of the criminal, the stolen property in the custody of an officer is in the custody of the court,"—Distinguishing *Lynch* v. *St. John*, 8 Daly, 143, as deciding "nothing to the contrary," for the court in that case recognized the doctrine here laid down, but said that "after his [the accused's] conviction or acquittal, the property clerk can have no claim to it as against the rightful owner."

In *Weller* v. *Ely*, 45 Conn. 547, it was held (affirming judgment for defendant) that the purchaser of stolen goods could not maintain replevin for them against the local authorities, to whom he had delivered such goods for use upon the trial of the accused, even under a stipulation to return them if not identified at the trial to his satisfaction, because the provisions of the statute placed them in the custody of the law, and in order to sustain such replevin the plaintiff must show a general or special property, with the right to immediate possession and a wrongful detention.

In *Lance* v. *Cowan*, 1 Dana, 195, it was held that where a district attorney, as custodian of the stolen property pending trial, has delivered the property or its proceeds to the rightful owner upon the conviction of the accused, no action will lie against him therefor at the suit of third persons.

In *Fitzgerald* v. *Jordan*, 11 Allen, 128, it is held that the officer arresting a person accused of larceny ought, upon the discharge of the complaint, to return to him the goods taken from him, and trover will lie against the officer for failure to do so upon demand, even though the prosecutor has already taken them in execution against the officer for a conversion thereof. Judgment reversed on other grounds.

[2] 2 Bishop, Crim. Proc. § 758, and cases cited.

In *Lance* v. *Cowan*, 1 Dana, 195, the court said that the owner "had a legal right to restitution. When the thief shall have converted the thing stolen into any other thing, 'the owner may have the produce, instead of the specific chattel.'"

Contra, *Com.* v. *Boudrie*, 4 Gray, 418, holding that under the Massachusetts statute to the effect that upon conviction of the offender, the stolen property shall be restored to the owner, the right of the owner to a summary restitution is confined to the identical articles alleged to have been stolen, and cannot be extended so as to include other property found in possession of the thief or to money arising from the sale of the property stolen.

Hence an order restoring money to the prosecutor was held erroneous and illegal, and exceptions thereto sustained, because the evidence at the trial only tended "to show that it was the money stolen or the proceeds of the money stolen."

[3] As to acquittal of the accused, see *infra*, § 5.

[4] Because such summary determination could not bind third persons who would be left free to try the question of title in a civil action. *State* v. *Williams*, 61 Iowa, 517, 16 N. W. 587. *Dictum*, that under a statute substantially like that of New York, a "conviction would be sufficient evidence that the [stolen] money did not belong to the defendant. The only question for the [trial] court would be as to whether it belonged to the person from whom it was alleged to have been stolen. The court, we presume, might properly enough proceed to determine such question in a summary way. No third person would be affected by the finding."

In *Reg.* v. *Macklin*, 5 Cox C. C. 216, upon a plea of larceny of the goods, and upon an application by the prosecutor for an order of restitution (under an English statute), which application was opposed by certain pledgees of the goods, the court suggested that the accused should be brought into court, and that affidavits should be made by both sides of any matters they deemed necessary to state, so that the court could come to a conclusion upon the facts; but intimating that the plea of guilty and its consequent effect upon the disposition of the goods by the court could not be binding upon third persons.

In *Lance* v. *Cowan*, 1 Dana, 195, the court in a *dictum* says that a Kentucky statute of 1805, providing that the court rendering judgment of conviction "shall not order restitution after the term at which conviction was had," did not affect the owner's right of recaption or his right of action.

3. Application by prosecutor.

Both at common law[1] and under modern statutes, the complainant may apply to the trial court for an order of restitution of the goods to him as owner thereof, when the accused is convicted or pleads guilty.[2] The conviction or plea is sufficient evidence that the accused has no title to the property.[3]

[1] 2 Bishop, Crim. Proc. §§ 756, 757.

[2] N. Y. Code Crim. Proc. § 688.

[3] *State* v. *Williams*, 61 Iowa, 517, 16 N. W. 587 (*dictum*).

4. Application by the accused.

Upon acquittal the court must presume that the property was not stolen.[1]

[1] *State* v. *Williams*, 61 Iowa, 517, 16 N. W. 587 (*dictum*).

5.—restoration of possession without trial of title.

In the absence of statute, the accused, upon acquittal, is entitled to an order from the trial court that property taken from his possession and in custody of the court or its officer be restored to his possession.

The acquittal is not conclusive on the question of title, which may be tried elsewhere; but it is error for the trial court, without statute authority, to proceed to try the question of title before restoring possession when asked.[1]

[1] *State* v. *Williams*, 61 Iowa, 517, 16 N. W. 587, *supra*. Here the title of the accused to property taken from his person by search warrant was contested after acquittal; held error to refuse to restore and to hold the property and summon a jury to try title; for the Iowa statute only applied to conviction, and the state ought not to be a party to nor bear the expense of trial of the title.

Whether N. Y. Code Crim. Proc. § 688, is sufficiently broad to require the court to try adverse claims in case of acquittal may well be doubted, although there seems to be no authority on the point.

6. Right of third person to oppose.

Upon the conviction of the accused or his pleading guilty, the trial court may hear counsel in behalf of third persons in opposition to any application for an order of restitution.[1]

[1]As to acquittal, see *supra*, § 5; *Reg.* v. *Macklin*, 5 Cox C. C. 216. Ruled, against objection of the prosecutor, that the court should hear counsel in behalf of third persons claiming as pledgees.

7. Application by third person.

At common law restitution was granted only to the prosecutor or person who caused, by evidence which he gave or procured, the conviction and attainder of the accused;[1] but the modern statutes seem to allow third persons to claim ownership, and apply for an order of restitution, even though not acting as complainants nor furnishing evidence leading to a conviction.[2]

[1]2 Bishop, Crim. Proc. § 756, 757.

[2]N. Y. Code Crim. Proc. § 688, and cases under *supra*, § 2. Mr. Bishop (2 Crim. Proc. § 762) states that "neither at common law nor under the statutes can the court order restitution to a third person of goods belonging to him not the prosecutor's, found in the possession of a convicted felon,"—citing an English case as authority. But the general language of the New York statute (Code Crim. Proc. § 688), and that of several other jurisdictions, would seem to allow this.

INDEX.

C.

K.

L.

V.